UNIVERSITY CASEBOOK SERIES

Intellectual Property and Unfair Competition

Fifth Edition

by

Edmund W. Kitch
Joseph M. Hartfield and Sullivan and Cromwell Research
Professor of Law
The University of Virginia

Harvey S. Perlman
Professor of Law
University of Nebraska

Formerly:
Legal Regulation of the Competitive Process
Cases, Materials and Notes on Unfair Business Practices,
Trademarks, Copyrights and Patents

First Edition, 1972; Second Edition, 1979; Third Edition, 1986; Fourth Edition, 1989;
Fourth Edition Revised, 1991

NEW YORK, NEW YORK
Foundation Press

1998

PRINTED ON 10% POST
CONSUMER RECYCLED PAPER

Intellectual Property and Unfair Competition

Fifth Edition

SUMMARY OF CONTENTS

TABLE OF CONTENTS

TABLE OF CASES

Principal cases are in bold type. Non-principal cases are in roman type. References are to Pages.

CHAPTER 1

THE PROBLEM OF ENTRY

A. The Common Law

Tuttle v. Buck

Supreme Court of Minnesota, 1909.
107 Minn. 145, 119 N.W. 946.

This appeal is from an order overruling a general demurrer to a complaint in which the plaintiff alleged: That for more than ten years last past he has been and still is a barber by trade, and engaged in business as such in the village of Howard Lake, Minn., in said county, where he resides, owning and operating a shop for the purpose of his said trade. That until the injury hereinafter complained of his said business was prosperous, and plaintiff was enabled thereby to comfortably maintain himself and family out of the income and profits thereof, and also to save a considerable sum per annum, to wit, about $800. That the defendant, during the period of about 12 months last past, has wrongfully, unlawfully, and maliciously endeavored to destroy plaintiff's said business and compel plaintiff to abandon the same. That to that end he has persistently and systematically sought, by false and malicious reports and accusations of and concerning the plaintiff, by personally soliciting and urging plaintiff's patrons no longer to employ plaintiff, by threats of his personal displeasure, and by various other unlawful means and devices, to induce, and has thereby induced, many of said patrons to withhold from plaintiff the employment by them formerly given. That defendant is possessed of large means, and is engaged in the business of a banker in said village of Howard Lake, at Dassel, Minn., and at divers other places, and is nowise interested in the occupation of a barber; yet in the pursuance of the wicked, malicious, and unlawful purpose aforesaid, and for the sole and only purpose of injuring the trade of the plaintiff, and of accomplishing his purpose and threats of ruining the plaintiff's said business and driving him out of said village, the defendant fitted up and furnished a barber shop in said village for conducting the trade of barbering. That failing to induce any barber to occupy said shop on his own account, though offered at nominal rental, said defendant, with the wrongful and malicious purpose aforesaid, and not otherwise, has during the time herein stated hired two barbers in succession for a stated salary, paid by him, to occupy said shop, and to serve so many of plaintiff's patrons as said defendant has been or may be able by the means aforesaid to direct from plaintiff's shop. That at the present time a barber so

1

employed and paid by the defendant is occupying and nominally conducting the shop thus fitted and furnished by the defendant, without paying any rent therefor, and under an agreement with defendant whereby the income of said shop is required to be paid to defendant, and is so paid in partial return for his wages. That all of said things were and are done by defendant with the sole design of injuring the plaintiff, and of destroying his said business, and not for the purpose of serving any legitimate interest of his own. That by reason of the great wealth and prominence of the defendant, and the personal and financial influence consequent thereon, he has by the means aforesaid, and through other unlawful means and devices by him employed, materially injured the business of the plaintiff, has largely reduced the income and profits thereof, and intends and threatens to destroy the same altogether, to plaintiff's damage in the sum of $10,000.

■ ELLIOTT, J. (after stating the facts as above). It has been said that the law deals only with externals, and that a lawful act cannot be made the foundation of an action because it was done with an evil motive. * * *

We do not intend to enter upon an elaborate discussion of the subject, or become entangled in the subtleties connected with the words "malice" and "malicious." We are not able to accept without limitations the doctrine above referred to, but at this time content ourselves with a brief reference to some general principles. It must be remembered that the common law is the result of growth, and that its development has been determined by the social needs of the community which it governs. Necessarily its form and substance has been greatly affected by prevalent economic theories. For generations there has been a practical agreement upon the proposition that competition in trade and business is desirable, and this idea has found expression in the decisions of the courts as well as in statutes. But it has led to grievous and manifold wrongs to individuals, and many courts have manifested an earnest desire to protect the individuals from the evils which result from unrestrained business competition. The problem has been to so adjust matters as to preserve the principle of competition and yet guard against its abuse to the unnecessary injury to the individual. So the principle that a man may use his own property according to his own needs and desires, while true in the abstract, is subject to many limitations in the concrete. Men cannot always, in civilized society, be allowed to use their own property as their interests or desires may dictate without reference to the fact that they have neighbors whose rights are as sacred as their own. The existence and well-being of society requires that each and every person shall conduct himself consistently with the fact that he is a social and reasonable person. The purpose for which a man is using his own property may thus sometimes determine his rights. * * *

Many of the restrictions which should be recognized and enforced result from a tacit recognition of principles which are not often stated in the decisions in express terms. Sir Frederick Pollock notes that not many years ago it was difficult to find any definite authority for stating as a general proposition of English law that it is wrong to do a willful wrong to one's neighbor without lawful justification or excuse. But neither is there any express authority for the general proposition that men must perform their contracts. Both principles, in this generality of form and conception, are modern and there was a time when neither was true. After developing the idea that law begins, not with authentic general principles, but with the enumeration of particular remedies, the learned writer continues: "If there exists, then, a positive duty to avoid harm, much more, then, exists the negative duty of not doing willful harm, subject, as all general duties must be subject, to the necessary exceptions. The three main heads of duty with which the law of torts is concerned, namely, to abstain from willful injury, to respect the property of others, and to use due diligence to avoid causing harm to others, are all alike of a comprehensive nature." Pollock, Torts, (8th Ed.) p. 21. He then quotes with approval the statement of Lord Bowen that "at common law there was a cause of action whenever one person did damage to another, willfully and intentionally, without just cause and excuse." In Plant v. Woods, 176 Mass. 492, 57 N.E. 1011, 51 L.R.A. 339, 79 Am.St.Rep. 330, Mr. Justice Hammond said: "It is said, also, that, where one has the lawful right to do a thing, the motive by which he is actuated is immaterial. One form of this statement appears in the first headnote in Allen v. Flood, as reported in [1898] A.C. 1, as follows: 'An act lawful in itself is not converted by a malicious or bad motive into an unlawful act, so as to make the doer of the act liable to a civil action.' If the meaning of this and similar expressions is that, where a person has the lawful right to do a thing irrespective of his motive, his motive is immaterial, the proposition is a mere truism. If, however, the meaning is that where a person, if actuated by one kind of a motive, has a lawful right to do a thing, the act is lawful when done under any conceivable motive, or that an act lawful under one set of circumstances is therefore lawful under every conceivable set of circumstances, the proposition does not commend itself to us as either logically or legally accurate."

* * *

It is freely conceded that there are many decisions contrary to this view; but, when carried to the extent contended for by the appellant, we think they are unsafe, unsound, and illy adapted to modern conditions. To divert to one's self the customers of a business rival by the offer of goods at lower prices is in general a legitimate mode of serving one's own interest, and justifiable as fair competition. But when a man starts an opposition place of business, not for the sake of profit to himself, but regardless of loss to himself, and for the sole purpose of driving his competitor out of business, and with the intention of himself retiring upon the accomplishment of his malevolent purpose, he is guilty of a wanton wrong and an actionable tort. In such a case he would not be exercising his legal right, or doing an act which can be judged separately from the motive which actuated him. To call such conduct competition is a perversion of terms. It is simply the application of force without legal justification, which in its moral quality may be no better than highway robbery.

Nevertheless, in the opinion of the writer this complaint is insufficient. It is not claimed that it states a cause of action for slander. No question of conspiracy or combination is involved. Stripped of the adjectives and the statement that what was done was for the sole purpose of injuring the plaintiff, and not for the purpose of serving a legitimate purpose of the defendant, the complaint states facts which in themselves amount only to an ordinary everyday business transaction. There is no allegation that the defendant was intentionally running the business at a financial loss to himself, or that after driving the plaintiff out of business the defendant closed up or intended to close up his shop. From all that appears from the complaint he may have opened the barber shop, energetically sought business from his acquaintances and the customers of the plaintiff, and as a result of his enterprise and command of capital obtained it, with the result that the plaintiff, from want of capital, acquaintance, or enterprise, was unable to stand the competition and was thus driven out of business. The facts thus alleged do not, in my opinion, in themselves, without reference to the way in which they are characterized by the pleader, tend to show a malicious and wanton wrong to the plaintiff.

A majority of the Justices, however, are of the opinion that, on the principle declared in the foregoing opinion, the complaint states a cause of action, and the order is therefore affirmed.

Affirmed.

JAGGARD, J., dissents.

Sorenson v. Chevrolet Motor Co.

Supreme Court of Minnesota (1927)
171 Minn. 260, 214 N.W. 754.

[The plaintiff had an agency contract with the defendant, Chevrolet, terminable by either party after adequate notice. Plaintiff had a successful business and advertised extensively. Defendant Sander was plaintiff's competitor. The complaint charging a conspiracy to destroy plaintiff's business alleged that "Sander knew of plaintiff's contract with the corporation and defendants agreed to acquire plaintiff's business for Sander. Pursuant to this plan and the agreement between defendants, the corporation wrongfully repudiated its contract with plaintiff without giving the notice therein required for cancellation. Plaintiff's business was thereby destroyed by the wrongful acts of defendants. This was done with actual malice toward plaintiff and such malice of the two defendants was well known to each and adopted by both of them." In reversing the lower court which sustained demurrers, the court noted:]

Every act done by a businessman in diverting trade from a competitor to himself is an act intentionally done, and when successful is an injury to the competitor because to that extent it lessens his profits. But it is not wrongful. Trade must be free and unrestricted but the competitor should operate within the zone of fair dealing. Competition justifies the use of all lawful and fair means to gain the trade that would otherwise go to a competitor in business.

* * *

Under his contract with the corporation, plaintiff had built up a valuable business. His relations with the company were mutually satisfactory. Sander, a stranger to the contract, wished to put an end to the business relations between plaintiff and the company and induced the company to repudiate the contract. If he had done this for no other purpose than to deprive plaintiff of the benefits of the contract and of his established business, under all the cases Sander would be liable for his wrongful interference in the contract relations between plaintiff and the company. But, according to the complaint, Sander had another motive. Not only did he wish to deprive plaintiff of his business, but he also desired to appropriate the business to himself. It cannot be said that this desire furnishes an excuse or justification for an act which would otherwise be unlawful. On the contrary, it accentuates the inherent wrongfulness of Sander's conduct. Under these circumstances, it would be contrary to the decided weight of authority to hold that Sander was serving his legitimate interests, or that his conduct was free from wrong, or that, since plaintiff has a cause of action against the company for breach of contract, Sander should go scot-free. It seems clear that elementary principles of business ethics demonstrate the unlawfulness of Sander's conduct, and the law ought to insist on as high a standard of business morality as prevails among reputable business men.

* * *

When one has knowledge of the contract rights of another, his wrongful inducement of a breach thereof is a willful destruction of the property of another and cannot be justified on the theory that it enhances and advances the business interests of the wrongdoer. * * *

Witte Transportation Co. v. Murphy Motor Freight Lines, Inc.

Supreme Court of Minnesota (1971).
291 Minn. 461, 193 N.W.2D 148.

[Plaintiff and defendant were competing motor common carriers who both used "routing letters" as an integral and important part of their business. A "routing letter" is a letter from a consignee requesting a shipper to ship goods only by a specified carrier. Salesmen for each carrier sought to obtain "routing letters" from its customers, oftentimes preparing the letters in advance for their signatures. The defendant had several letters prepared in the process of soliciting new business, but they were never signed by the consignees. However, copies of the unsigned letters were delivered to the consignors. The Minnesota Supreme Court framed the issue: "Does the evidence sustain the trial court's finding in substance that defendant intentionally, maliciously, and wrongfully interfered with the business relationship between plaintiff and its customers?"]

This court has long recognized that there lies an action for the wrongful interference with noncontractual as well as contractual business relationships.

Tuttle v. Buck, 107 Minn. 145, 119 N.W. 946 (1909). Other courts that have considered this question have likewise held, almost universally, that the tort of interference with contractual rights should be extended to include noncontractual business relationships.

Defendant argues that, even if there was an interference with the business relationship of the plaintiff and its customers, there was not sufficient malice or intent to bring the present case within the scope of tortious interference with a business relationship. Although it is true that the basis of liability in Tuttle v. Buck, supra, was predicated upon an intentional, malicious attack upon the business of another, in subsequent cases we have explained that malicious intent of the kind found in Tuttle is not a prerequisite to a finding of liability. The scope of the tort encompasses a broader legal area than the narrow limits of the facts in Tuttle. For example, we later held that an action could be based on "the intentional doing of a wrongful act without legal justification or excuse, or, otherwise stated the wilful violation of a known right * * *, malice in the sense of ill-will or spite not being essential." Carnes v. St. Paul Union Stockyards Co., 164 Minn. 457, 462, 205 N.W. 630, 631 (1925).

However, we have never allowed a recovery for negligent wrongful interference with a business relationship. The wrongful act of interference must have been intentionally done. The courts generally have not recognized a negligent wrongful interference with a business relationship as an actionable tort.

[The court concluded that an administrative failure resulted in the delivery of the letters and that there was no evidence to support a finding that the letters were prepared or delivered with intent to deceive. A judgment for the plaintiff was reversed.]

NOTES

1. The New York Secretary of State denied a license to a woman barber who planned to wear a see-through uniform and serve cocktails. N.Y. Times, July 10, 1969. What result if Buck had resorted to such devices to destroy plaintiff's business?

2. The Minnesota Supreme Court observed in *Sorenson* that the nature of competition requires a firm to attempt to inflict injury on its competitors by appropriating their customers and thereby their profits. This is the competitive process resulting in better products and services at lower prices. Which of the opinions, *Tuttle, Sorenson,* or *Witte* best adjusts common law doctrines to take this observation into account? In *Witte* do you suspect that the competitive relationship between the parties will be considered in determining "legal justification or excuse"? Can *Tuttle* and *Sorenson* be distinguished? Does the court lose sight of the distinction in *Witte*? Consider Justice Traynor's dictum in Imperial Ice Co. v. Rossier, 18 Cal.2d 33, 36, 112 P.2d 631, 633 (1941):

Whatever interest society has in encouraging free and open competition by means not in themselves unlawful, contractual stability is generally accepted as of greater importance than competitive freedom. Competitive freedom, however, is of sufficient importance to justify one competitor in inducing a third party to forsake another competitor if no contractual relationship exists between the latter two.

3. If you were a Minnesota consumer which of the competing rules announced by the court in the three cases would you prefer?

4. Should it make any difference if the banker in *Tuttle,* solely for the purpose of injuring plaintiff, had subsidized the losses of a competing barber by making an unsecured loan at a low interest rate? If the banker promised such loans to customers of the banker's barber shop?

5. *The English Cases.* Tuttle v. Buck has its historical antecedents in the English common law. The famous House of Lords Trilogy and its progeny provide useful counterpoints to the development of the American doctrines. The Trilogy consists of three cases: Mogul Steamship Co. v. McGregor, Gow & Co., 23 Q.B.Div. 598 (1889); aff'd [1892] A.C. 25 (1891); Allen v. Flood, [1898] A.C. 1; and Quinn v. Leatham, [1901] A.C. 495.

In *Mogul,* shipowners formed an association to regulate the number of ships sent by members to loading ports, the division of cargoes, and the freight charges. A rebate of 5 per cent was allowed to all shippers who exclusively used association members. Plaintiffs were shipowners excluded from the association. The association underbid plaintiffs and reduced freights so low that plaintiffs were unable to show a profit. Plaintiffs brought an action for damages against the associated owners alleging a conspiracy to injure plaintiffs. Held, for defendants.

The opinion of Bowen, L.J. contains the statement of the correlative rights of competitors:

> What, then, are the limitations which the law imposes on a trader in the conduct of his business as between himself and other traders? * * * No man, whether trader or not, can, * * * justify damaging another in his commercial business by fraud or misrepresentation. Intimidation, obstruction, and molestation are forbidden; so is the intentional procurement of a violation of individual rights, contractual or other, assuming always that there is no just cause for it. The intentional driving away of customers by shew of violence; * * * the obstruction of actors on the stage by preconcerted hissing; * * * the disturbance of wild fowl in decoys by the firing of guns; * * * the impeding or threatening servants or workmen; * * * the inducing persons under personal contracts to break their contracts; * * * all are instances of such forbidden acts. But the defendants have been guilty of none of these acts. They have done nothing more against the plaintiffs than pursue to the bitter end a war of competition waged in the interest of their own trade. To the argument that a competition so pursued ceases to have a just cause or excuse when there is ill-will or a personal intention to harm, it is sufficient to reply * * * that there was here no personal intention to do any other or greater harm to the plaintiffs than such as was necessarily involved in the desire to attract to the defendants' ships the entire tea

freights of the ports, a portion of which would otherwise have fallen to the plaintiffs' share. I can find no authority for the doctrine that such a commercial motive deprives of "just cause or excuse" acts done in the course of trade which would but for such a motive be justifiable. So to hold would be to convert into an illegal motive the instinct of self-advancement and self-protection, which is the very incentive to all trade.

Lord Justice Bowen decided also that to impose a standard of reasonableness on commercial conduct would be to "impose a novel fetter upon trade * * *. A man is bound not to use his property so as to infringe upon another's right * * *. If engaged in actions which may involve danger to others, he ought, speaking generally, to take reasonable care to avoid endangering them. But there is surely no doctrine of law which compels him to use his property in a way that judges and juries may consider reasonable * * *. If there is no such fetter upon the use of property known to the English law, why should there be any such fetter upon trade?"

6. The Restatement, Third, of Unfair Competition § 1 (1995) provides that a person causing harm to another's commercial relations by competitive acts is not liable unless the acts constitute deceptive marketing, trademark infringement, appropriation of trade values, or are "determined to be actionable as an unfair method of competition, taking into account the nature of the conduct and its likely effect on both the person seeking relief and the public". The Restatement places the burden of proof on the person alleging injury to "establish facts sufficient to subject the actor to liability." Comment *a*. Do you think a general catch-all provision that permits courts to determine which methods of competition are "unfair" is a wise policy? Consider Article 10*bis* of the Paris Convention for the Protection of Industrial Property which requires all signatory countries to offer effective protection against unfair competition and defines "unfair competition" as "[a]ny act of competition contrary to honest practices in industrial or commercial matters . . . ."

7. An alternative to giving courts wide latitude to define unfair competition is to delegate that authority to an administrative agency with sufficient expertise in commercial practices. The Federal Trade Commission is authorized to prevent "unfair or deceptive acts or practices in or affecting commerce." 15 U.S.C.A. §45. The Commission has established its own process for determining when an act is "unfair":

> The Commission requires that a preponderance of the evidence support the factual propositions underlying a determination that an existing act or practice is legally unfair. Before promulgating an unfairness rule the Commission requires answers to the following questions: (1) Is the act or practice prevalent (2) Does the act or practice injure consumers (3) Is the proposed rule likely to reduce that injury (4) Is the injury to consumers outweighed by countervailing benefits that flow from the act or practice at issue and (5) Can consumers reasonably avoid the injury.

Ophthalmic Practice Rules, 16 C.F.R. Part 456, 57 Fed. Reg. 10286, at 10287 (1989). The test was approved in Pennsylvania Funeral Directors Ass'n v. FTC, 41 F.3d 81 (3d Cir. 1994) (affirming rule preventing funeral directors from charging a casket handling fee when customers purchased a casket from third parties) and American Financial Services Ass'n v. FTC, 767 F.2d 957 (D.C. Cir. 1985) (affirming rules that prevented wage assignments for default in consumer loans and nonpossessory security interests in household goods other than purchase money securities).

8. *Anti-trust Laws.* The federal anti-trust laws are designed to preserve and foster a competitive economy. Section 1 of the Sherman Act makes illegal contracts, combinations, or conspiracies in restraint of trade and § 2 prohibits a person or combination of persons from securing or attempting to secure a monopoly. Section 4 of the Clayton Act authorizes a private action by any person "injured in his business or property by reason of anything forbidden in the anti-trust laws * * *." The anti-trust laws serve as background context for the material considered in this course. In the development of the laws of unfair competition and in fashioning administrative regulations, it may be well to remember that the anti-trust laws provide protection and relief from the most egregious "market imperfections".

B. The Regulation of Public Goods

International News Service v. Associated Press

Supreme Court of the United States, 1918.
248 U.S. 215

■ MR. JUSTICE PITNEY delivered the opinion of the Court.

[Associated Press is a news gathering organization. Local newspapers become members and are thus entitled to purchase access to news collected from around the world. Member newspapers agree not to use AP supplied news in any way other than in their newspaper. Each member is also obligated to gather local news and supply it to AP. International News Service is a competing organization with similar operating methods. AP brings this action to enjoin INS from taking published AP news stories and distributing them to INS member papers for publication.]

The only matter that has been argued before us is whether defendant may lawfully be restrained from appropriating news taken from bulletins issued by complainant or any of its members, or from newspapers published by them, for the purpose of selling it to defendant's clients. Complainant asserts that defendant's admitted course of conduct in this regard both violates complainant's property right in the news and constitutes unfair competition in business. And notwithstanding the case has proceeded only to the stage of a preliminary injunction, we have deemed it proper to consider the underlying questions, since they go to the very merits of the action and are presented upon facts that are not in dispute. As presented in argument, these questions are: (1) Whether there is any property in news; (2) whether, if there be property in news collected for the purpose of being published, it survives the instant of its publication in the first newspaper to which it is communicated by the news-gatherer; and (3) whether defendant's admitted course of conduct in appropriating for commercial use matter taken from bulletins or early editions of Associated Press publications constitutes unfair competition in trade.

The federal jurisdiction was invoked because of diversity of citizenship, not upon the ground that the suit arose under the copyright or other laws of the United States. Complainant's news matter is not copyrighted. It is said that it could not, in practice, be copyrighted, because of the large number of dispatches that are sent daily; and, according to complainant's contention, news is not within the operation of the copyright act. Defendant, while apparently conceding this, nevertheless invokes the analogies of the law of literary property and copyright, insisting as its principal contention that, assuming complainant has a right of property in its news, it can be maintained (unless the copyright act be complied with) only by being kept secret and confidential, and that upon the publication with complainant's consent of uncopyrighted news of any of complainant's members in a newspaper or upon a bulletin board, the right of property is lost, and the subsequent use of the news by the public or by defendant for any purpose whatever becomes lawful.

* * *

In considering the general question of property in news matter, it is necessary to recognize its dual character, distinguishing between the substance of the information and the particular form or collocation of words in which the writer has communicated it.

No doubt news articles often possess a literary quality, and are the subject of literary property at the common law; nor do we question that such an article, as a literary production, is the subject of copyright by the terms of the act as it now stands. * * *

But the news element—the information respecting current events contained in the literary production—is not the creation of the writer, but is a report of matters that ordinarily are publici juris; it is the history of the day. It is not to be supposed that the framers of the Constitution, when they empowered Congress "to promote the progress of science and useful arts by securing for limited times to authors and inventors the exclusive right to their respective writings and discoveries" (Const. art. 1, § 8, par. 8), intended to confer upon one who might happen to be the first to report a historic event the exclusive right for any period to spread the knowledge of it.

We need spend no time, however, upon the general question of property in news matter at common law, or the application of the copyright act, since it seems to us the case must turn upon the question of unfair competition in business. And, in our opinion, this does not depend upon any general right of property analogous to the common-law right of the proprietor of an unpublished work to prevent its publication without his consent; nor is it foreclosed by showing that the benefits of the copyright act have been waived. We are dealing here not with restrictions upon publication but with the very facilities and processes of publication. The peculiar value of news is in the spreading of it while it is fresh; and it is evident that a valuable property interest in the news, as news, cannot be maintained by keeping it secret. Besides, except for matters improperly disclosed, or published in breach of trust or confidence, or in violation of law, none of which is involved in this branch of the case, the news of current events may be regarded as common property. What we are concerned with is the business of making it known to the world, in which both parties to the present suit are engaged. That business consists in maintaining a prompt, sure, steady, and reliable service designed to place the daily events of the world at the breakfast table of the millions at a price that, while of trifling moment to each reader, is sufficient in the aggregate to afford compensation for the cost of gathering and distributing it, with the added profit so necessary as an incentive to effective action in the commercial world. The service thus performed for newspaper readers is not only innocent but extremely useful in itself, and indubitably constitutes a legitimate business. The parties are competitors in this field; and, on fundamental principles, applicable here as elsewhere, when the rights or privileges of the one are liable to conflict with those of the other, each party is under a duty so to conduct its own business as not unnecessarily or unfairly to injure that of the other. * * *

Obviously, the question of what is unfair competition in business must be determined with particular reference to the character and circumstances of the business. The question here is not so much the rights of either party as against the public but their rights as between themselves. See Morison v. Moat, 9 Hare, 241, 258. And, although we may and do assume that neither party has any remaining property interest as against the public in uncopyrighted news matter after the moment of its first publication, it by no means follows that there is no remaining property interest in it as between themselves. For, to both of them alike, news matter, however little susceptible of ownership or dominion in the absolute sense, is stock in trade, to be gathered at the cost of enterprise, organization, skill, labor, and money, and to be distributed and sold to those who will pay money for it, as for any other merchandise. Regarding the news, therefore, as but the material out of which both parties are seeking to make profits at the same time and in the same field, we hardly can fail to recognize that for this purpose, and as between them, it must be regarded as quasi property, irrespective of the rights of either as against the public.

* * *

The question, whether one who has gathered general information or news at pains and expense for the purpose of subsequent publication through the press has such an interest in its publication as may be protected from interference, has been raised many times, although never, perhaps, in the precise form in which it is now presented.

Board of Trade v. Christie Grain & Stock Co., 198 U.S. 236, related to the distribution of quotations of prices on dealings upon a board of trade, which were collected by plaintiff and communicated on confidential terms to numerous persons under a contract not to make them public. This court held that, apart from certain special objections that were overruled, plaintiff's collection of quotations was entitled to the protection of the law; that, like a trade secret, plaintiff might keep to itself the work done at its expense, and did not lose its right by communicating the result to persons, even if many, in confidential relations to itself, under a contract not to make it public; and that strangers should be restrained from getting at the knowledge by inducing a breach of trust.

In National Tel. News Co. v. Western Union Tel. Co., 119 Fed. 294, 56 C.C.A. 198, 60 L.R.A. 805, the Circuit Court of Appeals for the Seventh Circuit dealt with news matter gathered and transmitted by a telegraph company, and consisting merely of a notation of current events having but a transient value due to quick transmission and distribution; and, while declaring that this was not copyrightable although printed on a tape by tickers in the offices of the recipients, and that it was a commercial not a literary product, nevertheless held that the business of gathering and communicating the news—the service of purveying it—was a legitimate business, meeting a distinctive commercial want and adding to the facilities of the business world, and partaking of the nature of property in a sense that entitled it to the protection of a court of equity against piracy.

Other cases are cited, but none that we deem it necessary to mention.

Not only do the acquisition and transmission of news require elaborate organization and a large expenditure of money, skill, and effort; not only has it an exchange value to the gatherer, dependent chiefly upon its novelty and freshness, the regularity of the service, its reputed reliability and thoroughness, and its adaptability to the public needs; but also, as is evident, the news has an exchange value to one who can misappropriate it.

The peculiar features of the case arise from the fact that, while novelty and freshness form so important an element in the success of the business, the very processes of distribution and publication necessarily occupy a good deal of time. Complainant's service, as well as defendant's, is a daily service to daily newspapers; most of the foreign news reaches this country at the Atlantic seaboard, principally at the city of New York, and because of this, and of time differentials, due to the earth's rotation, the distribution of news matter throughout the country is principally from east to west; and, since in speed the telegraph and telephone easily outstrip the rotation of the earth, it is a simple matter for defendant to take complainant's news from bulletins or early editions of complainant's members in the eastern cities and at the mere cost of telegraphic transmission cause it to be published in western papers issued at least as early as those served by complainant. Besides this, and irrespective of time differentials, irregularities in telegraphic transmission on different lines, and the normal consumption of time in printing and distributing the newspaper, result in permitting printed news to be placed in the hands of defendant's readers sometimes simultaneously with the service of competing Associated Press papers, occasionally even earlier.

Defendant insists that when, with the sanction and approval of complainant, and as the result of the use of its news for the very purpose for which it is distributed, a portion of complainant's members communicate it to the general public by posting it upon bulletin boards so that all may read, or by issuing it to newspapers and distributing it indiscriminately, complainant no longer has the right to control the use to be made of it; that when it thus reaches the light of day it becomes the common possession of all to whom it is accessible; and that any purchaser of a newspaper has the right to communicate the intelligence which it contains to anybody and for any purpose, even for the purpose of selling it for profit to newspapers published for profit in competition with complainant's members.

The fault in the reasoning lies in applying as a test the right of the complainant as against the public, instead of considering the rights of complainant and defendant, competitors in business, as between themselves. The right of the purchaser of a single newspaper to spread knowledge of its contents gratuitously, for any legitimate purpose not unreasonably interfering with complainant's right to make merchandise of it, may be admitted; but to transmit that news for commercial use, in competition with complainant—which is what defendant has done and seeks to justify—is a very different matter. In doing this defendant, by its very act, admits that it is taking material that has been acquired by complainant as the result of organization and the expenditure of labor, skill and money, and which is salable by complainant for money, and that defendant in appropriating it and selling it as its own is endeavoring to reap where it has not sown, and by disposing of it to newspapers that are competitors of complainant's members is appropriating to itself the harvest of those who have sown. Stripped of all disguises, the process amounts to an unauthorized interference with the normal operation of complainant's legitimate business precisely at the point where the profit is to be reaped, in order to divert a material portion of the profit from those who have earned it to those who have not; with special advantage to defendant in the competition because of the fact that it is not burdened with any part of the expense of gathering the news. The transaction speaks for itself, and a court of equity ought not to hesitate long in characterizing it as unfair competition in business.

The underlying principle is much the same as that which lies at the base of the equitable theory of consideration in the law of trusts—that he who has fairly paid the price should have the beneficial use of the property. Pom.Eq.Jur. § 981. It is no answer to say that complainant spends its money for that which is too fugitive or evanescent to be the subject of property. That might, and for the purposes of the discussion we are assuming that it would, furnish an answer in a common-law controversy. But in a court of equity, where the question is one of unfair competition, if that which complainant has acquired fairly at substantial cost may be sold fairly at substantial profit, a competitor who is misappropriating it for the purpose of disposing of it to his own profit and to the disadvantage of the complainant cannot be heard to say that it is too fugitive or evanescent to be regarded as property. It has all the attributes of property necessary for determining that a misappropriation of it by a competitor is unfair competition because contrary to good conscience.

The contention that the news is abandoned to the public for all purposes when published in the first newspaper is untenable. Abandonment is a question of intent, and the entire organization of the Associated Press negatives such a purpose. The cost of the service would be prohibitive if the reward were to be so limited. No single newspaper, no small group of newspapers, could sustain the expenditure. Indeed, it is one of the most obvious results of defendant's theory that, by permitting indiscriminate publication by anybody and everybody for purposes of profit in competition with the newsgatherer, it would render publication profitless, or so little profitable as in effect to cut off the service by rendering the cost prohibitive in comparison with the return. The practical needs and requirements of the business are reflected in complainant's by-laws which have been referred to. Their effect is that publication by each member must be deemed not by any means an abandonment of the news to the world for any and all purposes, but a publication for limited purposes; for the benefit of the readers of the bulletin or the newspaper as such; not for the purpose of making merchandise of it as news, with the result of depriving complainant's other members of their reasonable opportunity to obtain just returns for their expenditures.

It is to be observed that the view we adopt does not result in giving to complainant the right to monopolize either the gathering or the distribution of the news, or, without complying with the copyright act, to prevent the reproduction of its news articles, but only postpones participation by complainant's competitor in the processes of distribution and reproduction of news that it has not gathered, and only to the extent necessary to prevent that competitor from reaping the fruits of complainant's efforts and expenditure, to the partial exclusion of complainant, and in violation of the principle that underlies the maxim "sic utere tuo," etc.

It is said that the elements of unfair competition are lacking because there is no attempt by defendant to palm off its goods as those of the complainant, characteristic of the most familiar, if not the most typical, cases of unfair competition. Howe Scale Co. v. Wyckoff, Seamans, etc., 198 U.S. 118. But we cannot concede that the right to equitable relief is confined to that class of cases. In the present case the fraud upon complainant's rights is more direct and obvious. Regarding news matter as the mere material from which these two competing parties are endeavoring to make money, and treating it, therefore, as quasi property for the purposes of their business because they are both selling it as such, defendant's conduct differs from the ordinary case of unfair competition in trade principally in this that, instead of selling its own goods as those of complainant, it substitutes misappropriation in the place of misrepresentation, and sells complainant's goods as its own.

Besides the misappropriation, there are elements of imitation, of false pretense, in defendant's practices. The device of rewriting complainant's news articles, frequently resorted to, carries its own comment. The habitual failure to give credit to complainant for that which is taken is significant.

Indeed, the entire system of appropriating complainant's news and transmitting it as a commercial product to defendant's clients and patrons amounts to a false representation to them and to their newspaper readers that the news transmitted is the result of defendant's own investigation in the field. But these elements, although accentuating the wrong, are not the essence of it. It is something more than the advantage of celebrity of which complainant is being deprived.

The doctrine of unclean hands is invoked as a bar to relief; it being insisted that defendant's practices against which complainant seeks an injunction are not different from the practice attributed to complainant, of utilizing defendant's news published by its subscribers. At this point it becomes necessary to consider a distinction * * * between two kinds of use that may be made by one news agency of news taken from the bulletin and newspapers of the other. The first is the bodily appropriation of a statement of fact or a news article, with or without rewriting, but without independent investigation or other expense. * * * This practice complainant denies having pursued and the denial was sustained by the finding of the District Court. It is not contended by defendant that the finding can be set aside, upon the proofs as they now stand. The other use is to take the news of a rival agency as a "tip" to be investigated, and if verified by independent investigation the news thus gathered is sold. This practice complainant admits that it has pursued and still is willing that defendant shall employ.

* * *

As to securing "tips" from a competing news agency, the District Court (240 Fed. 991, 995), while not sanctioning the practice, found that both parties had adopted it in accordance with common business usage, in the belief that their conduct was technically lawful, and hence did not find in it any sufficient ground for attributing unclean hands to complainant. The Circuit Court of Appeals (245 Fed. 247) found that the tip habit, though discouraged by complainant, was "incurably journalistic," and that there was "no difficulty in discriminating between the utilization of tips and the bodily appropriation of another's labor in accumulating and stating information."

We are inclined to think a distinction may be drawn between the utilization of tips and the bodily appropriation of news matter, either in its original form or after rewriting and without independent investigation and verification: whatever may appear at the final hearing, the proofs as they now stand recognize such a distinction; both parties avowedly recognize the practice of taking tips, and neither party alleges it to be unlawful or to amount to unfair competition in business. In a line of English cases a somewhat analogous practice has been held not to amount to an infringement of the copyright of a directory or other book containing compiled information. * * *

There is some criticism of the injunction that was directed by the District Court upon the going down of the mandate from the Circuit Court of Appeals. In brief, it restrains any taking or gainfully using of the complainant's news, either bodily or in substance from bulletins issued by the complainant or any of its members, or from editions of their newspapers, *"until its commercial value as news to the complainant and all of its members has passed away."* The part complained of is the clause we have italicized; but if this be indefinite, it is no more so than the criticism. Perhaps it would be better that the terms of the injunction be made specific, and so framed as to confine the restraint to an extent consistent with the reasonable protection of complainant's newspapers, each in its own area and for a specified time after its publication, against the competitive use of pirated news by defendant's customers. But the case presents practical difficulties; and we have not the materials, either in the way of a definite suggestion of amendment, or in the way of proofs, upon which to frame a specific injunction; hence, while not expressing approval of the form adopted by the District Court, we decline to modify it at this preliminary stage of the case, and will leave that court to deal with the matter upon appropriate application made to it for the purpose.

The decree of the Circuit Court of Appeals will be affirmed.

MR. JUSTICE CLARKE took no part in the consideration or decision of this case.

MR. JUSTICE HOLMES, dissenting.

When an uncopyrighted combination of words is published there is no general right to forbid other people repeating them—in other words there is no property in the combination or in the thoughts or facts that the words express. Property, a creation of law, does not arise from value, although exchangeable—a matter of fact. Many exchangeable values may be destroyed intentionally without compensation. Property depends upon exclusion by law from interference, and a person is not excluded from using any combination of words merely because some one has used it before, even if it took labor and genius to make it. If a given person is to be prohibited from making the use of words that his neighbors are free to make some other ground must be found. One such ground is vaguely expressed in the phrase unfair trade. This means that the words are repeated by a competitor in business in such a way as to convey a misrepresentation that materially injures the person who first used them, by appropriating credit of some kind which the first user has earned. The ordinary case is a representation by device, appearance, or other indirection that the defendant's goods come from the plaintiff. But the only reason why it is actionable to make such a representation is that it tends to give the defendant an advantage in his competition with the plaintiff and that it is thought undesirable that an advantage should be gained in that way. Apart from that the defendant may use such unpatented devices and uncopyrighted combinations of words as he likes. The ordinary case, I say, is palming off the defendant's product as the plaintiff's, but the same evil may follow from the opposite falsehood—from saying whether in words or by implication that the plaintiff's product is the defendant's, and that, it seems to me, is what has happened here.

Fresh news is got only by enterprise and expense. To produce such news as it is produced by the defendant represents by implication that it has been acquired by the defendant's enterprise and at its expense. When it comes from one of the great news collecting agencies like the Associated Press, the source generally is indicated, plainly importing that credit; and that such a representation is implied may be inferred with some confidence from the unwillingness of the defendant to give the credit and tell the truth. If the plaintiff produces the news at the same time that the defendant does, the defendant's presentation impliedly denies to the plaintiff the credit of collecting the facts and assumes that credit to the defendant. If the plaintiff is later in Western cities it naturally will be supposed to have obtained its information from the defendant. The falsehood is a little more subtle, the injury a little more indirect, than in ordinary cases of unfair trade, but I think that the principle that condemns the one condemns the other. It is a question of how strong an infusion of fraud is necessary to turn a flavor into a poison. The dose seems to me strong enough here to need a remedy from the law. But as, in my view, the only ground of complaint that can be recognized without legislation is the implied misstatement, it can be corrected by stating the truth; and a suitable acknowledgment of the source is all that the plaintiff can require. I think that within the limits recognized by the decision of the Court the defendant should be enjoined from publishing news obtained from the Associated Press for ___ hours after publication by the plaintiff unless it gives express credit to the Associated Press; the number of hours and the form of acknowledgment to be settled by the District Court.

MR. JUSTICE MCKENNA concurs in this opinion.

MR. JUSTICE BRANDEIS, dissenting.

* * *

No question of statutory copyright is involved. The sole question for our consideration is this: Was the International News Service properly enjoined from using, or causing to be used gainfully, news of which it acquired knowledge by lawful means (namely, by reading publicly posted bulletins or papers purchased by it in the open market) merely because the news had been originally gathered by the Associated Press and continued to be of value to some of its members, or because it did not reveal the source from which it was acquired?

* * *

News is a report of recent occurrences. The business of the news agency is to gather systematically knowledge of such occurrences of interest and to distribute reports thereof. The Associated Press contended that knowledge so acquired is property, because it costs money and labor to produce and because it has value for which those who have it not are ready to pay; that it remains property and is entitled to protection as long as it has commercial value as news; and that to protect it effectively the defendant must be enjoined from making, or causing to be made, any gainful use of it while it retains such value. An essential element of individual property is the legal right to exclude others from enjoying it. If the property is private, the right of exclusion may be absolute; if the property is affected with a public interest, the right of exclusion is qualified. But the fact that a product of the mind has cost its producer money and labor, and has a value for which others are willing to pay, is not sufficient to ensure to it this legal attribute of property. The general rule of law is, that the noblest of human productions—knowledge, truths ascertained, conceptions, and ideas—become, after voluntary communication to others, free as the air to common use. Upon these incorporeal productions the attribute of property is continued after such communication only in certain classes of cases where public policy has seemed to demand it. These exceptions are confined to productions which, in some degree, involve creation, invention, or discovery. But by no means all such are endowed with this attribute of property. The creations which are recognized as property by the common law are literary, dramatic, musical, and other artistic creations; and these have also protection under the copyright statutes. The inventions and discoveries upon which this attribute of property is conferred only by statute, are the few comprised within the patent law. There are also many other cases in which courts interfere to prevent curtailment of plaintiff's enjoyment of incorporeal productions; and in which the right to relief is often called a property right, but is such only in a special sense. In those cases, the plaintiff has no absolute right to the protection of his production; he has merely the qualified right to be protected as against the defendant's acts, because of the special relation in which the latter stands or the wrongful method or means employed in acquiring the knowledge or the manner in which it is used. Protection of this character is afforded where the suit is based upon breach of contract or of trust or upon unfair competition.

The knowledge for which protection is sought in the case at bar is not of a kind upon which the law has heretofore conferred the attributes of property; nor is the manner of its acquisition or use nor the purpose to which it is applied, such as has heretofore been recognized as entitling a plaintiff to relief.

First. Plaintiff's principal reliance was upon the "ticker" cases; but they do not support its contention. The leading cases on this subject rest the grant of relief, not upon the existence of a general property right in news, but upon the breach of a contract or trust concerning the use of news communicated; and that element is lacking here. * * *

Second. Plaintiff also relied upon the cases which hold that the common law right of the producer to prohibit copying is not lost by the private circulation of a literary composition, the delivery of a lecture, the exhibition of a painting, or the performance of a dramatic or musical composition. These cases rest upon the ground that the common law recognizes such productions as property which, despite restricted communication, continues until there is a dedication to the public under the copyright statutes or otherwise. But they are inapplicable for two reasons: (1) At common law, as under the copyright acts, intellectual productions are entitled to such protection only if there is underneath something evincing the mind of a creator or originator, however modest the requirements. The mere record of isolated happenings, whether in words or by photographs not involving artistic skill, are denied such protection. (2) At common law, as under the copyright acts, the element in intellectual productions which secures such protection, is not the knowledge, truths, ideas, or emotions which the composition expresses, but the form or sequence in which they are expressed; that is, "some new collocation of visible or audible points—of lines, colors, sounds, or words." * * *

Third. If news be treated as possessing the characteristics not of a trade secret, but of literary property, then the earliest issue of a paper of general circulation or the earliest public posting of a bulletin which embodies such news would, under the established rules governing literary property, operate as a publication, and all property in the news would then cease. * * *

Fourth. Plaintiff further contended that defendant's practice constitutes unfair competition, because there is "appropriation without cost to itself of values created by" the plaintiff; and it is upon this ground that the decision of this court appears to be based. To appropriate and use for profit, knowledge and ideas produced by other men, without making compensation or even acknowledgement, may be inconsistent with a finer sense of propriety; but, with the exceptions indicated above, the law has heretofore sanctioned the practice. Thus it was held that one may ordinarily make and sell anything in any form, may copy with exactness that which another has produced, or may otherwise use his ideas without his consent and without the payment of compensation, and yet not inflict a legal injury; and that ordinarily one is at perfect liberty to find out, if he can by lawful means, trade secrets of another, however valuable, and then use the knowledge so acquired gainfully, although it cost the original owner much in effort and in money to collect or produce. * * *

It is also suggested that the fact that defendant does not refer to the Associated Press as the source of the news may furnish a basis for the relief. But the defendant and its subscribers, unlike members of the Associated Press, were under no contractual obligation to disclose the source of the news; and there is no rule of law requiring acknowledgement to be made where uncopyrighted matter is reproduced. * * *

Fifth. * * *

The rule for which the plaintiff contends would effect an important extension of property rights and a corresponding curtailment of the free use of knowledge and of ideas; and the facts of this case admonish us of the danger involved in recognizing such a property right in news, without imposing upon news-gatherers corresponding obligations. * * *

A Legislature, urged to enact a law by which one news agency or newspaper may prevent appropriation of the fruits of its labors by another, would consider such facts and possibilities and others which appropriate inquiry might disclose. Legislators might conclude that it was impossible to put an end to the obvious injustice involved in such appropriation of news, without opening the door to other evils, greater than that sought to be remedied. * * *

Or legislators dealing with the subject might conclude, that the right to news values should be protected to the extent of permitting recovery of damages for any unauthorized use, but that protection by injunction should be denied, just as courts of equity ordinarily refuse (perhaps in the interest of free speech) to restrain actionable libels, and for other reasons decline to protect by injunction mere political rights; and as Congress has prohibited courts from enjoining the illegal assessment or collection of federal taxes. If a Legislature concluded to recognize property in published news to the extent of permitting recovery at law, it might, with a view to making the remedy more certain and adequate, provide a fixed measure of damages, as in the case of copyright infringement.

Or again, a Legislature might conclude that it was unwise to recognize even so limited a property right in published news as that above indicated; but that a news agency should, on some conditions, be given full protection of its business; and to that end a remedy by injunction as well as one for damages should be granted, where news collected by it is gainfully used without permission. If a Legislature concluded (as at least one court has held, New York and Chicago Grain and Stock Exchange v. Board of Trade, 127 Ill. 153, 19 N.E. 855) that under certain circumstances news-gathering is a business affected with a public interest; it might declare that, in such cases, news should be protected against appropriation, only if the gatherer assumed the obligation of supplying it at reasonable rates and without discrimination, to all papers which applied therefor. If legislators reached that conclusion, they would probably go further, and prescribe the conditions under which and the extent to which the protection should be afforded; and they might also provide the administrative machinery necessary for insuring to the public, the press, and the news agencies, full enjoyment of the rights so conferred.

Courts are ill-equipped to make the investigations which should precede a determination of the limitations which should be set upon any property right in news or of the circumstances under which news gathered by a private agency should be deemed affected with a public interest. Courts would be powerless to prescribe the detailed regulations essential to full enjoyment of the rights conferred or to introduce the machinery required for enforcement of such regulations. Considerations such as these should lead us to decline to establish a new rule of law in the effort to redress a newly disclosed wrong, although the propriety of some remedy appears to be clear.

NOTES

1. *Historical Note.* International News Service's troubles began in 1916 when the British government banned the Hearst owned INS from using the Official Press Bureau and all other facilities for the transmission of news from Great Britain. The ban arose from stories published in American newspapers and attributed to an INS correspondent in London, about the battle of Jutland and air raids over London. The dispatches indicated that the British navy had admitted an "overwhelming defeat" by the German navy. Since news transmission at the time was officially censored by the British government, the Home Secretary was asked in the House of Commons whether the censor had passed such news accounts. He replied that no such dispatches were sent from Britain and that they must have been composed in the New York offices of INS. This "garbling" of news accounts was cited as the reason for the ban. The New York American, a Hearst newspaper, published the reply of the manager of INS which read in part: "The English censors have been threatening for many months to deny the International News Service the privilege of the mails and cables because the International News Service did not print the kind of news that the English desired to have printed in this country. * * * It is the intention of the International News Service to continue printing the news, all the news, and nothing but the news." N.Y. Times, October 11, 1916, at 11, col. 4.

The following story was carried by the New York Times on Jan. 25, 1918, at 3, col. 7:

> The United Press Association announced yesterday that the International News Service, against which The Associated Press recently secured an injunction to prevent the pirating of news, had walked straight into a trap set by The United Press to show that the International News was pirating the news of that organization. The International News incidentally brought into newspaper fame a hitherto unknown official, "Under Foreign Secretary Nelotsky," whose name, spelled backwards, reads "stolen" with the "ky" thrown in for "Russian camouflage."

> Early in the day The United Press inserted "Nelotsky" in a dispatch from Petrograd, but soon "killed" this name for all its papers. Within a short time, The United Press says, papers receiving the International News Service appeared with "M. Nelotsky" figuring prominently in an alleged dispatch from London recounting in a general way the same facts set forth in The United Press cable from Petrograd. The United Press says it made sure that the Nelotsky story was sent over the wires of the International News.

> The story was printed in papers receiving the International News Service in Boston, New York, Pittsburgh, Detroit, Chicago, Kansas City, San Francisco, and elsewhere.

The New York Times commented editorially that "[t]raps of this sort are rather cruel, but of their efficiency there is no doubt, and when one really wants a hide to nail up on one's barn door—well, one uses the trap that will supply the hide, as in this instance." N.Y. Times, Jan. 26, 1918, at 12, col. 5.

2. *Acceptance of the INS Doctrine.* The majority opinion in *INS* stands as the foundation for development of the "misappropriation" doctrine of unfair competition. Its checkered career will be repeatedly explored throughout much of this material. The case, read in its broadest sense, was a dramatic departure from the existing tort concepts regulating business practices. The opinions of Holmes and Brandeis reveal the more traditional analyses.

The *INS* decision was not widely utilized by the lower courts. To be sure several courts referred approvingly to it in dictum but most often in cases where more traditional causes of action dictated the same result. Some early decisions read the majority opinion narrowly. In Harvey Hubbell, Inc. v. General Elec. Co., 262 Fed. 155 (S.D.N.Y.1919) various manufacturers including plaintiff and defendant were marketing different types of electric plugs and wall receptacles for electric appliances making interchangeability impossible. Standardization was sought by many manufacturers but resisted by General Electric. Unable to reach an agreement, the other manufacturers standardized using General Electric's system as the standard. GE brought an action for unfair competition. The court denied relief. "No court has ever gone to the extent of permitting the establishment of a monopoly of proportions or measurements, in the absence of some patent protection. To do so would be practically to engross the particular business. * * * To do so would be to stifle competition." The court limited *INS* to cases of fraud and bribery.

Other courts applied the principle without referencing *INS*. In Meyer v. Hurwitz, 5 F.2d 370 (D.Pa.1925) the plaintiff designed and manufactured a post card vending machine. He sold the machine at cost and made his profit by selling cards. Defendant produced cards designed to be sold through plaintiff's machine and priced the cards below what plaintiff charged. There was some evidence defendant's cards caused the machines to jam. The court, without citing *INS*, held for the plaintiff because defendant "appropriated to himself the plaintiff's system and organization for the purpose of underselling him * * *." For an early case granting an injunction based on *INS*, see National Telephone Directory Co. v. Dawson Mfg. Co., 214 Mo.App. 683, 263 S.W. 483 (St. Louis Ct.App.1924). The defendant distributed covers with advertising to fit over the plaintiff's telephone book, thus covering up advertising sold by plaintiff. The court issued an injunction. "A more flagrant case of unfair competition is nowhere disclosed by the books. In fact, the scheme is more than unfair competition; it amounts to an actual appropriation of the plaintiff's property by the defendants to their own business purposes."

Such an inauspicious beginning did not promise a lively career for the misappropriation doctrine. And in 1929, Judge Learned Hand attempted to seal the grave. In Cheney Bros. v. Doris Silk Corp., 35 F.2d 279 (2d Cir.1929) he wrote of *INS*:

> While it is of course true that law ordinarily speaks in general terms, there are cases where the occasion is at once the justification for, and the limit of, what is decided. This appears to us such an instance; we think that no more was covered than situations substantially similar to those then at bar. The difficulties of understanding it otherwise are insuperable. We are to suppose that the court meant to create a sort of common-law patent or copyright for reasons of justice. Either would flagrantly conflict with the scheme which Congress has for more than a century devised to cover the subject-matter.

Whatever binding effect *INS* might have had was removed by Erie R.R. Co. v. Tompkins, 304 U.S. 64 (1938) since *INS* was a diversity case decided on the basis of federal common law no longer applicable to such actions after *Erie*. However, subsequent decisions involving a variety of factual situations breathed new life into the doctrine. These are considered throughout the remainder of this material.

3. Would your view of the principal case differ if Associated Press had by-laws which in addition to prohibiting members from selling AP dispatches to non-members also gave member publishers veto power over the application of competing newspapers for membership in the organization? Such by-laws were in existence in various forms from 1900 until 1943 when they were struck down as violative of the Sherman Act. United States v. Associated Press, 52 F.Supp. 362 (S.D.N.Y.1943), affirmed 326 U.S. 1 (1945).

4. What was "misappropriated" in *INS?* How would the various judges in *INS* have ruled in Tuttle v. Buck? Is the issue the same in both cases? Trade practice cases can involve the interest of consumers as well as those of the two competitors. How did the consumer's interest fare in *INS?* What about the interest of the advertisers in Associated Press affiliated newspapers who bear a large part of the cost of newspaper production through the price of advertising? Was their interest considered by any of the Justices? Assume you were interested in establishing a competing news gathering agency. Which opinion would most encourage you to make a large investment in such an operation?

5. Consider Brandeis' discussion of the copyright and patent statutes. Why are they relevant to the factual situation? Likewise, what is Hand's concern in the quote from *Cheney?* Would Meyer v. Hurwitz be a different case if the post card vending machine was patented?

6. The Restatement, Third, of Unfair Competition § 38, Comment *b* takes a very restrictive view of the *INS* decision: "Although courts have occasionally invoked the *INS* decision on an ad hoc basis to grant relief against commercial appropriations, they have not articulated coherent principles for its application. It is clear that no general rule of law prohibits the appropriation of a competitor's ideas, innovations, or other intangible assets once they become publicly known." Id. at 411. See, Gary Myers, The Restatement's Rejection of the Misappropriation Tort: a Victory for the Public Domain, 47 S. Car. L. Rev. 673 (1996). See also, Gordon, On Owning Information: Intellectual Property and the Restitutionary Impulse, 78 Va. L. Rev. 149 (1992); Raskind, The Misappropriation Doctrine as a Competitive Norm of Intellectual Property, 75 Minn. L. Rev. 875 (1991); Baird, Common Law Intellectual Property and the Legacy of International News Service v. Associated Press, 50 U.Chi.L.Rev. 411 (1983).

PROBLEMS

1. (a). Microsoft Corporation establishes a series of Websites on the Internet, one for each major city in the United States. On each "city site"

Microsoft provides information on restaurants and events. Microsoft profits from this venture by selling advertising which appears on the city site and is viewed by any computer user visiting the site. Microsoft also includes on the site hyperlinks to other sites related to the particular city. A hyperlink is text or graphics describing another site which is set off in a different color or underlined. By clicking on the hyperlink the user is immediately transported to the other site. One hyperlink on each of Microsoft's city sites is to Ticketmaster's Website where users can purchase tickets to live entertainment in various cities. Microsoft does not obtain Ticketmaster's permission to hyperlink to its site. Does Ticketmaster have an *INS* claim against Microsoft?

(b). New software permits Websites to engage in "framing". The site, as viewed by a computer user, appears to be divided into separate frames with the content of each frame being independent of the content of the other frame. Microsoft adopts framing software for its city sites and creates one frame in which the Microsoft logo and advertising appears and a larger frame with hyperlinks to other sites. A user linking to the Ticketmaster site would see the Ticketmaster site in one frame and simultaneously see the Microsoft logo and advertising in the other frame. Does use of the framing software in this way enhance Ticketmaster's *INS* claim?

(c). What result if the framing software results in a clear view of Microsoft's advertisers but cuts off advertising Ticketmaster sold for its own site?

2. Sports Team Analysis and Tracking Systems (Inc) ("STATS") sells subscriptions to a pager service through which customers can receive real time scores and other data on National Basketball Association ("NBA") games. Motorola hires reporters to watch the games on TV or listen to them on the radio and feed information into a personal computer for receipt by subscribers on handheld pagers. Scores are updated every two to three minutes. STATS also maintains a website that provides more comprehensive and detailed real-time game information. The website is updated every 15 seconds. Does the NBA have an *INS* claim against STATS?

3. A computer user interested in finding Internet websites on a particular subject must use a search engine—a program which can search a large number of sites for a particular word or phrase. For example, if a user wanted to find the Microsoft website a search engine could be directed to look for the term "Microsoft". All websites with the word "Microsoft" would be listed for the searcher. A "metatag" is a word included on a website which is not visible to the user but is used by a search engine to identify the contents of the site. Happy Clams, a restaurant in New York, inserts the word "Microsoft" in a metatag on its home page. Is this actionable under *INS*? What if a competing software company used the "Microsoft" metatag on its homepage? What if a site devoted to pornographic pictures included the metatag?

4. Rural Telephone is a small telephone exchange with 7000 customers. It uses its subscriber information to compile a telephone book which is distributed free. Rural receives substantial revenue from the sale of advertising in the yellow pages of its directory. Feist Publications obtains a free copy of Rural's phone book and combines its listings with 10 other small exchanges into one larger phone book. Feist also distributes its book free and competes with Rural for yellow page advertising. Does Rural have an *INS* claim against Feist? Suppose the rule was that compilations of names in telephone books were not capable of protection under the copyright laws.

5. A commodity exchange, unconnected with Dow Jones, wishes to develop a futures contract based on the "Dow Jones Average of 30 Industrials." Can the Dow Jones Company object on the basis of *INS?*

6. Could the Estate of Elvis Presley assert an *INS* claim against an Elvis Presley imitator who travels the country performing under the banner "The Big El Show"?

Sears, Roebuck & Co. v. Stiffel Co.

Supreme Court of the United States, 1964.
376 U.S. 225, 84 S.Ct. 784, 11 L.Ed.2d 661,
rehearing denied 376 U.S. 973,84 S.Ct. 1131,
12 L.Ed.2d 87.

■ MR. JUSTICE BLACK delivered the opinion of the Court.

The question in this case is whether a State's unfair competition law can, consistently with the federal patent laws, impose liability for or prohibit the copying of an article which is protected by neither a federal patent nor a copyright. The respondent, Stiffel Company, secured design and mechanical patents on a "pole lamp"—a vertical tube having lamp fixtures along the outside, the tube being made so that it will stand upright between the floor and ceiling of a room. Pole lamps proved a decided commercial success, and soon after Stiffel brought them on the market Sears, Roebuck & Company put on the market a substantially identical lamp, which it sold more cheaply, Sears' retail price being about the same as Stiffel's wholesale price. Stiffel then brought this action against Sears in the United States District Court for the Northern District of Illinois, claiming in its first count that by copying its design Sears had infringed Stiffel's patents and in its second count that by selling copies of Stiffel's lamp Sears had caused confusion in the trade as to the source of the lamps and had thereby engaged in unfair competition under Illinois law. There was evidence that identifying tags were not attached to the Sears lamps although labels appeared on the cartons in which they were delivered to customers, that customers had asked Stiffel whether its lamps differed from Sears', and that in two cases customers who had bought Stiffel lamps had complained to Stiffel on learning that Sears was selling substantially identical lamps at a much lower price.

The District Court, after holding the patents invalid for want of invention, went on to find as a fact that Sears' lamp was "a substantially exact copy" of Stiffel's and that the two lamps were so much alike, both in appearance and in functional details, "that confusion between them is likely, and some confusion has already occurred." On these findings the court held Sears guilty of unfair competition, enjoined Sears "from unfairly competing with [Stiffel] by selling or attempting to sell pole lamps identical to or confusingly similar to" Stiffel's lamp and ordered an accounting to fix profits and damages resulting from Sears' "unfair competition."

The Court of Appeals affirmed.[1] That court held that, to make out a case of unfair competition under Illinois law, there was no need to show that Sears had been "palming off" its lamps as Stiffel lamps; Stiffel had only to prove that there was a "likelihood of confusion as to the source of the products"— that the two articles were sufficiently identical that customers could not tell who had made a particular one. Impressed by the "remarkable sameness of appearance" of the lamps, the Court of Appeals upheld the trial court's findings of likelihood of confusion and some actual confusion, findings which the appellate court construed to mean confusion "as to the source of the lamps." The Court of Appeals thought this enough under Illinois law to sustain the trial court's holding of unfair competition and thus held Sears liable under Illinois law for doing no more than copying and marketing an unpatented article.[2] We granted certiorari to consider whether this use of a State's law of unfair competition is compatible with the federal patent law.

Before the Constitution was adopted, some States had granted patents either by special act or by general statute,[3] but when the Constitution was adopted provision for a federal patent law was made one of the enumerated powers of Congress because, as Madison put it in The Federalist No. 43, the States "cannot separately make effectual provision" for either patents or copyrights.[4] That constitutional provision is Art. I, § 8, cl. 8, which empowers Congress "To promote the Progress of Science and useful Arts, by securing for limited Times to Authors and Inventors the exclusive Right to their respective Writings and Discoveries." Pursuant to this constitutional authority, Congress in 1790 enacted the first federal patent and copyright law and ever since that time has fixed the conditions upon which patents and copyrights shall be granted. These laws, like other laws of the United States enacted pursuant to constitutional authority, are the supreme law of the land. When state law touches upon the area of these federal statutes, it is "familiar doctrine" that the federal policy "may not be set at naught, or its benefits denied" by the state law. Sola Elec. Co. v. Jefferson Elec. Co., 317 U.S. 172, 173, 176 (1942). This is true, of course, even if the state law is enacted in the exercise of otherwise undoubted state power.

---

1. No review is sought here of the ruling affirming the District Court's holding that the patent is invalid.

2. 313 F.2d, at 118 and nn. 6, 7. * * * The Court of Appeals, by holding that because Illinois forbids misleading use of trade names it also forbids as unfair competition the mere copying of an article of trade without any palming off, thus appears to have extended greatly the scope of the Illinois law of unfair competition beyond the limits indicated in the Illinois cases and beyond any previous decisions of the Seventh Circuit itself. Because of our disposition of these cases we need not decide whether it was correct in doing so.

3. See I Walker, Patents (Deller ed. 1937), § 7.

4. The Federalist (Cooke ed. 1961) 288.

The grant of a patent is the grant of a statutory monopoly;[5] indeed, the grant of patents in England was an explicit exception to the statute of James I prohibiting monopolies. Patents are not given as favors, as was the case of monopolies given by the Tudor monarchs but are meant to encourage invention by rewarding the inventor with the right, limited to a term of years fixed by the patent, to exclude others from the use of his invention. During that period of time no one may make, use, or sell the patented product without the patentee's authority. But in rewarding useful invention, the "rights and welfare of the community must be fairly dealt with and effectually guarded." Kendall v. Winsor, 21 How. 322, 329 (1859). To that end the prerequisites to obtaining a patent are strictly observed, and when the patent has issued the limitations on its exercise are equally strictly enforced. To begin with, a genuine "invention" or "discovery" must be demonstrated "lest in the constant demand for new appliances the heavy hand of tribute be laid on each slight technological advance in an art." Cuno Engineering Corp. v. Automatic Devices Corp., 314 U.S. 84, 92 (1941). Once the patent issues, it is strictly construed. It cannot be used to secure any monopoly beyond that contained in the patent, the patentee's control over the product when it leaves his hands is sharply limited, and the patent monopoly may not be used in disregard of the antitrust laws. Finally, and especially relevant here, when the patent expires the monopoly created by it expires, too, and the right to make the article—including the right to make it in precisely the shape it carried when patented—passes to the public.

Thus the patent system is one in which uniform federal standards are carefully used to promote invention while at the same time preserving free competition.[6] Obviously a State could not, consistently with the Supremacy Clause of the Constitution, extend the life of a patent beyond its expiration date or give a patent on an article which lacked the level of invention required for federal patents. To do either would run counter to the policy of Congress of granting patents only to true inventions, and then only for a limited time. Just as a State cannot encroach upon the federal patent laws directly, it cannot, under some other law, such as that forbidding unfair competition, give protection of a kind that clashes with the objectives of the federal patent laws.

In the present case the "pole lamp" sold by Stiffel has been held not to be entitled to the protection of either a mechanical or a design patent. An unpatentable article, like an article on which the patent has expired, is in the public domain and may be made and sold by whoever chooses to do so. What Sears did was to copy Stiffel's design and to sell lamps almost identical to those sold by Stiffel. This it had every right to do under the federal patent

---

5. Patent rights exist only by virtue of statute. Wheaton v. Peters, 8 Pet. 591, 658 (1834).

6. The purpose of Congress to have national uniformity in patent and copyright laws can be inferred from such statutes as that which vests exclusive jurisdiction to hear patent and copyright cases in federal courts, 28 U.S.C. § 1338(a), and that section of the Copyright Act which expressly saves state protection of unpublished writings but does not include published writings, 17 U.S.C. § 2. 17 U.S.C. § 2 [of the 1909 Copyright Act, no longer in effect].

laws. That Stiffel originated the pole lamp and made it popular is immaterial. "Sharing in the goodwill of an article unprotected by patent or trade-mark is the exercise of a right possessed by all—and in the free exercise of which the consuming public is deeply interested." Kellogg Co. v. National Biscuit Co., supra, 305 U.S. at 122. To allow a State by use of its law of unfair competition to prevent the copying of an article which represents too slight an advance to be patented would be to permit the State to block off from the public something which federal law has said belongs to the public. The result would be that while federal law grants only 14 or 17 years' protection to genuine inventions, States could allow perpetual protection to articles too lacking in novelty to merit any patent at all under federal constitutional standards. This would be too great an encroachment on the federal patent system to be tolerated.

Sears has been held liable here for unfair competition because of a finding of likelihood of confusion based only on the fact that Sears' lamp was copied from Stiffel's unpatented lamp and that consequently the two looked exactly alike. Of course there could be "confusion" as to who had manufactured these nearly identical articles. But mere inability of the public to tell two identical articles apart is not enough to support an injunction against copying or an award of damages for copying that which the federal patent laws permit to be copied. Doubtless a State may, in appropriate circumstances, require that goods, whether patented or unpatented, be labeled or that other precautionary steps be taken to prevent customers from being misled as to the source just as it may protect businesses in the use of their trademarks, labels, or distinctive dress in the packaging of goods so as to prevent others, by imitating such markings, from misleading purchasers as to the source of the goods. But because of the federal patent laws a State may not, when the article is unpatented and uncopyrighted, prohibit the copying of the article itself or award damages for such copying. The judgment below did both and in so doing gave Stiffel the equivalent of a patent monopoly on its unpatented lamp. That was error, and Sears is entitled to a judgment in its favor.

Reversed.

Compco Corp. v. Day-Brite Lighting, Inc.

Supreme Court of the United States, 1964.
376 U.S. 234, 84 S.Ct. 779, 11 L.Ed.2d 669, rehearing denied 377 U.S. 913,
84 S.Ct. 1162, 12 L.Ed.2d 183.

■ MR. JUSTICE BLACK delivered the opinion of the Court.

As in Sears, Roebuck & Co. v. Stiffel Co., 376 U.S. 225, the question here is whether the use of a state unfair competition law to give relief against the copying of an unpatented industrial design conflicts with the federal patent laws. Both Compco and Day-Brite are manufacturers of fluorescent lighting fixtures of a kind widely used in offices and stores. Day-Brite in 1955 secured from the Patent Office a design patent on a reflector having cross-ribs claimed to give both strength and attractiveness to the fixture. Day-Brite also sought, but was refused, a mechanical patent on the same device. After Day-Brite had begun selling its fixture, Compco's predecessor began making and selling fixtures very similar to Day-Brite's. This action was then brought by Day-Brite. One count alleged that Compco had infringed Day-Brite's design patent; a second count charged that the public and the trade had come to associate this particular design with Day-Brite, that Compco had copied Day-Brite's distinctive design so as to confuse and deceive purchasers into thinking Compco's fixtures were actually Day-Brite's, and that by doing this Compco had unfairly competed with Day-Brite. The complaint prayed for both an accounting and an injunction.

The District Court held the design patent invalid; but as to the second count, while the court did not find that Compco had engaged in any deceptive or fraudulent practices, it did hold that Compco had been guilty of unfair competition under Illinois law. The court found that the overall appearance of Compco's fixture was "the same, to the eye of the ordinary observer, as the overall appearance" of Day-Brite's reflector, which embodied the design of the invalidated patent; that the appearance of Day-Brite's design had "the capacity to identify [Day-Brite] in the trade and does in fact so identify [it] to the trade"; that the concurrent sale of the two products was "likely to cause confusion in the trade"; and that "[a]ctual confusion has occurred." On these findings the court adjudged Compco guilty of unfair competition in the sale of its fixtures, ordered Compco to account to Day-Brite for damages, and enjoined Compco "from unfairly competing with plaintiff by the sale or attempted sale of reflectors identical to, or confusingly similar to" those made by Day-Brite. The Court of Appeals held there was substantial evidence in the record to support the District Court's finding of likely confusion and that this finding was sufficient to support a holding of unfair competition under Illinois law.[1] Although the District Court had not made such a finding, the appellate court observed that "several choices of ribbing were apparently available to meet the functional needs of the product," yet Compco "chose precisely the same design used by the plaintiff and followed it so closely as to make confusion likely." A design which identifies its maker to the trade, the Court of Appeals held, is a "protectable" right under Illinois law, even though the design is unpatentable.[2] We granted certiorari.

* * *

Notwithstanding the thinness of the evidence to support findings of likely and actual confusion among purchasers, we do not find it necessary in this case to determine whether there is "clear error" in these findings. They, like those in Sears, Roebuck & Co. v. Stiffel Co., 376 U.S. 225, were based wholly on the fact that selling an article which is an exact copy of another

---

1. The Court of Appeals also affirmed the holding that the design patent was invalid. No review of this ruling is sought here.

2. As stated in Sears, Roebuck & Co. v. Stiffel Co., 376 U.S., at p. 228, n. 2, we do not here decide whether the Court of Appeals was correct in its statement of Illinois law.

unpatented article is likely to produce and did in this case produce confusion as to the source of the article. Even accepting the findings, we hold that the order for an accounting for damages and the injunction are in conflict with the federal patent laws. Today we have held in Sears, Roebuck & Co. v. Stiffel Co., 376 U.S. 225, that when an article is unprotected by a patent or a copyright, state law may not forbid others to copy that article. To forbid copying would interfere with the federal policy, found in Art. I, § 8, cl. 8, of the Constitution and in the implementing federal statutes, of allowing free access to copy whatever the federal patent and copyright laws leave in the public domain. Here Day-Brite's fixture has been held not to be entitled to a design or mechanical patent. Under the federal patent laws it is, therefore, in the public domain and can be copied in every detail by whoever pleases. It is true that the trial court found that the configuration of Day-Brite's fixture identified Day-Brite to the trade because the arrangement of the ribbing had, like a trademark, acquired a "secondary meaning" by which that particular design was associated with Day-Brite. But if the design is not entitled to a design patent or other federal statutory protection, then it can be copied at will.

As we have said in *Sears*, while the federal patent laws prevent a State from prohibiting the copying and selling of unpatented articles, they do not stand in the way of state law, statutory or decisional, which requires those who make and sell copies to take precautions to identify their products as their own. A state of course has power to impose liability upon those who, knowing that the public is relying upon an original manufacturer's reputation for quality and integrity, deceive the public by palming off their copies as the original. That an article copied from an unpatented article could be made in some other way, that the design is "nonfunctional" and not essential to the use of either article, that the configuration of the article copied may have a "secondary meaning" which identifies the maker to the trade, or that there may be "confusion" among purchasers as to which article is which or as to who is the maker, may be relevant evidence in applying a State's law requiring such precautions as labeling; however, and regardless of the copier's motives, neither these facts nor any others can furnish a basis for imposing liability for or prohibiting the actual acts of copying and selling. And of course a State cannot hold a copier accountable in damages for failure to label or otherwise to identify his goods unless his failure is in violation of valid state statutory or decisional law requiring the copier to label or take other precautions to prevent confusion of customers as to the source of the goods.

Since the judgment below forbids the sale of a copy of an unpatented article and orders an accounting for damages for such copying, it cannot stand.

Reversed.

MR. JUSTICE HARLAN, concurring in the result.*

In one respect I would give the States more leeway in unfair competition "copying" cases than the Court's opinions would allow. If copying is

---

* This opinion also applies to Sears, Roebuck & Co. v. Stiffel Co., 376 U.S. 225.

found, other than by an inference arising from the mere act of copying, to have been undertaken with the dominant purpose and effect of palming off one's goods as those of another or of confusing customers as to the source of such goods, I see no reason why the State may not impose reasonable restrictions on the future "copying" itself. Vindication of the paramount federal interest at stake does not require a State to tolerate such specifically oriented predatory business practices. Apart from this, I am in accord with the opinions of the Court, and concur in both judgments since neither case presents the point on which I find myself in disagreement.

NOTES

1. The sweep of the language in *Sears* and *Compco* seemed for awhile to auger revolutionary change in the American law of unfair competition. See, e.g., Callmann § 60.4(a): "These startlingly disappointing companion decisions so revolutionized our thinking with respect to the law of unfair competition that almost every one of its previously accepted premises must now be re-examined." See also Derenberg, Product Simulation: A Right or a Wrong?, 64 Colum.L.Rev. 1192 (1964): "The roof had seemingly fallen in on a vast structure of federal and state precedents laboriously built up since the days of the Court's famous decision in the *International News* case."

2. *Sears* and *Compco* must be viewed in the context of Erie R.R. v. Tompkins, 304 U.S. 64 (1938). Prior to *Erie* unfair competition was an area in which the power of the federal courts to announce common law rules played an important role. The last of those cases was Kellogg Co. v. National Biscuit Co., 305 U.S. 111 (1938), infra, Chapter 3. Although the federal unfair competition cases did not rely on a preemption doctrine, the opinions showed an awareness of the need to announce unfair competition law compatible with the patent and copyright statutes. As long as the federal courts were in a position to make the accommodation themselves, it was unnecessary to develop a preemption theory. But *Erie* ended the power of the federal courts to declare rules of federal common law in diversity cases and in the 1950's state unfair competition law particularly in the important states of New York and California began to depart significantly from the earlier federal law.

3. Is unfair competition law an area where there is a need for substantial uniformity? Is product simulation an area where there is a need for substantial uniformity?

4. The Court in *Sears* and *Compco* could have relied on a narrower version of the preemption theory to reach the same result. In Singer Mfg. Co. v. June Mfg. Co., 163 U.S. 169, 185 (1896), the Court said:

It is self evident that on the expiration of a patent the monopoly created by it ceases to exist, and the right to make the thing formerly covered by the patent becomes public property. It is upon this condition that the patent is granted. It follows, as a matter of course, that on the termination of the patent there passes to the public the right to make the machine in the form in which it was constructed during the patent.

The Court could have simply extended the principle to designs covered by invalid as well as expired patents on the theory that the act of obtaining a patent constituted a dedication by disclosure of the patent to public use. But the Court in its discussion put no weight on the fact that there was an invalid patent covering the pole lamp. Rather the Court relied on the existence of the patent system itself without regard to whether the particular design had been patented. This broad use of the preemption doctrine is the radical element of the opinions—although it is not altogether clear that Mr. Justice Black was aware of the implications of this approach.

Further complications are created by the fact that the Court did not make any distinction in its discussion between the mechanical and design patent statutes and the fact that it simultaneously relied on the copyright statute. The Court did not specify whether its preemption theory was based on an interpretation of the legislation, or was a constitutional doctrine interpreting the constitutional copyright and patent power as exclusive.

Bonito Boats, Inc. v. Thunder Craft Boats

United States Supreme Court, 1989.
489 U.S. 141, 109 S.Ct. 971, 103 L.Ed.2d 118.

■ JUSTICE O'CONNOR delivered the opinion of the Court.

[Florida enacted legislation that prohibited use of the direct molding process to duplicate boat hulls. The statute made it unlawful to use the process or to knowingly sell boat hulls duplicated by that process. Direct molding involves using an original hull as a "plug" and spraying it with fiberglass to create a mold from which additional hulls can be made. Bonito claimed that Thunder Craft used the process to copy Bonito's successful Model 5VBR hull. The 5VBR was unpatented and had been on the market five years before the statute was enacted. The Florida Supreme Court denied relief on the basis that the statute was preempted under *Sears* and *Compco*. In an earlier case the Federal Circuit had upheld a similar California law. Interpart Corp. v. Italia, 777 F.2d 678 (1985).]

* * *

The attractiveness of [the patent system's grant of monopoly in return for disclosure] and its effectiveness in inducing creative effort and disclosure of the results of that effort, depend almost entirely on a backdrop of free competition in the exploitation of unpatented designs and innovations. The novelty and nonobviousness requirements of patentability embody a congressional understanding, implicit in the Patent Clause itself, that free exploitation of ideas will be the rule, to which the protection of a federal patent is the exception. Moreover, the ultimate goal of the patent system is to bring new designs and technologies into the public domain through disclosure. State law protection for techniques and designs whose disclosure has already been induced by market rewards may conflict with the very purpose of the patent laws by decreasing the range of ideas available as the building blocks of further innovation. The offer of federal protection from competitive exploitation of intellectual property would be rendered meaningless in a world where substantially similar state law protections were readily available. To a limited extent, the federal patent laws must determine not only what is protected, but also what is free for all to use.

* * *

The pre-emptive sweep of our decisions in *Sears* and *Compco* has been the subject of heated scholarly and judicial debate. Read at their highest level of generality, the two decisions could be taken to stand for the proposition that the States are completely disabled from offering any form of protection to articles or processes which fall within the broad scope of patentable subject matter. Since the potentially patentable includes "anything under the sun that is made by man," Diamond v. Chakrabarty, 447 U.S. 303, 309 (1980) (citation omitted), the broadest reading of *Sears* would prohibit the States from regulating the deceptive simulation of trade dress or the tortious appropriation of private information.

That the extrapolation of such a broad pre-emptive principle from *Sears* is inappropriate is clear from the balance struck in *Sears* itself. The *Sears* Court made it plain that the States "may protect businesses in the use of their trademarks, labels, or distinctive dress in the packaging of goods so as to prevent others, by imitating such markings, from misleading purchasers as to the source of the goods." *Sears*, supra, 376 U.S., at 232 (footnote omitted). Trade dress is, of course, potentially the subject matter of design patents. Yet our decision in *Sears* clearly indicates that the States may place limited regulations on the circumstances in which such designs are used in order to prevent consumer confusion as to source. Thus, while *Sears* speaks in absolutist terms, its conclusion that the States may place some conditions on the use of trade dress indicates an implicit recognition that all state regulation of potentially patentable but unpatented subject matter is not *ipso facto* pre-empted by the federal patent laws.

* * *

At the heart of *Sears* and *Compco* is the conclusion that the efficient operation of the federal patent system depends upon substantially free trade in publicly known, unpatented design and utilitarian conceptions. In *Sears,* the state law offered "the equivalent of a patent monopoly," 376 U.S., at 233 in the functional aspects of a product which had been placed in public commerce absent the protection of a valid patent. While, as noted above, our decisions since *Sears* have taken a decidedly less rigid view of the scope of federal preemption under the patent laws, we believe that the *Sears* Court correctly concluded that the States may not offer patent-like protection to intellectual creations which would otherwise remain unprotected as a matter of federal law. Both the novelty and the nonobviousness requirements of federal patent law are grounded in the notion that concepts within the public grasp, or those so obvious that they readily could be, are the tools of creation available to all. They provide the baseline of free competition upon which the patent system's incentive to creative effort depends. A state law that substantially interferes with the enjoyment of an unpatented utilitarian or design conception which has been freely disclosed by its author to the public at large impermissibly contravenes the ultimate goal of public disclosure and use which is the centerpiece of federal patent policy. Moreover, through the creation of patent-like rights, the States could essentially redirect inventive efforts away from the careful criteria of patentability developed by Congress over the last 200 years. We understand this to be the reasoning at the core of our decisions in *Sears* and *Compco* and we reaffirm that reasoning today.

III

We believe that the Florida statute at issue in this case so substantially impedes the public use of the otherwise unprotected design and utilitarian ideas embodied in unpatented boat hulls as to run afoul of the teaching of our decisions in *Sears* and *Compco*. It is readily apparent that the Florida statute does not operate to prohibit "unfair competition" in the usual sense that the term is understood. The law of unfair competition has its roots in the common-law tort of deceit: its general concern is with protecting consumers from confusion as to source. While that concern may result in the creation of "quasi-property rights" in communicative symbols, the focus is on the protection of consumers, not the protection of producers as an incentive to product innovation. * * *

With some notable exceptions, including the interpretation of the Illinois law of unfair competition at issue in *Sears* and *Compco*, the common-law tort of unfair competition has been limited to protection against copying of nonfunctional aspects of consumer products which have acquired secondary meaning such that they operate as a designation of source. The "protection" granted a particular design under the law of unfair competition is thus limited to one context where consumer confusion is likely to result; the design "idea" itself may be freely exploited in all other contexts.

In contrast to the operation of unfair competition law, the Florida statute is aimed directly at preventing the exploitation of the design and utilitarian conceptions embodied in the product itself. * * * To accomplish this goal, the Florida statute endows the original boat hull manufacturer with rights against the world, similar in scope and operation to the rights accorded a federal patentee. Like the patentee, the beneficiary of the Florida statute may prevent a competitor from "making" the product in what is evidently the most efficient manner available and from "selling" the product when it is produced in that fashion. The Florida scheme offers this protection for an unlimited number of years to all boat hulls and their component parts, without regard to their ornamental or technological merit. Protection is available for subject matter for which patent protection has been denied or has expired, as well as for designs which have been freely revealed to the consuming public by their creators.

* * *

That the Florida statute does not remove all means of reproduction and sale does not eliminate the conflict with the federal scheme. In essence, the Florida law prohibits the entire public from engaging in a form of reverse engineering of a product in the public domain. This is clearly one of the rights vested in the federal patent holder, but has never been a part of state protection under the law of unfair competition or trade secrets. * * *

Moreover, * * * the competitive reality of reverse engineering may act as a spur to the inventor, creating an incentive to develop inventions which meet the rigorous requirements of patentability. The Florida statute substantially reduces this competitive incentive, thus eroding the general rule of free competition upon which the attractiveness of the federal patent bargain depends. The protections of state trade secret law are most effective at the developmental stage, before a product has been marketed and threat of reverse engineering becomes real. During this period, patentability will often be an uncertain prospect, and to a certain extent, the protection offered by trade secret law may "dovetail" with the incentives created by the federal patent monopoly. See Goldstein, Kewanee Oil Co. v. Bicron Corp.: Notes on a Closing Circle, 1974 Sup.Ct.Rev. 81, 92. In contrast, under the Florida scheme, the would-be inventor is aware from the outset of his efforts that rights against the public are available regardless of his ability to satisfy the rigorous standards of patentability. Indeed, it appears that even the most mundane and obvious changes in the design of a boat hull will trigger the protections of the statute. Given the substantial protection offered by the Florida scheme, we cannot dismiss as hypothetical the possibility that it will become a significant competitor to the federal patent laws, offering investors similar protection without the quid pro quo of substantial creative effort required by the federal statute. The prospect of all 50 States establishing similar protections for preferred industries without the rigorous requirements of patentability prescribed by Congress could pose a substantial threat to the patent system's ability to accomplish its mission of promoting progress in the useful arts.

Finally, allowing the States to create patent-like rights in various products in public circulation would lead to administrative problems of no small dimension. The federal patent scheme provides a basis for the public to ascertain the status of the intellectual property embodied in any article in general circulation. * * *

The Florida scheme blurs this clear federal demarcation between public and private property. One of the fundamental purposes behind the Patent and Copyright Clauses of the Constitution was to promote national uniformity in the realm of intellectual property. * * * This purpose is frustrated by the Florida scheme, which renders the status of the design and utilitarian "ideas" embodied in the boat hulls it protects uncertain. Given the inherently ephemeral nature of property in ideas, and the great power such property has to cause harm to the competitive policies which underlay the federal patent laws, the demarcation of broad zones of public and private right is "the type of regulation that demands a uniform national rule." Ray v. Atlantic Richfield

Co., 435 U.S. 151, 179 (1978). Absent such a federal rule, each State could afford patent-like protection to particularly favored home industries, effectively insulating them from competition from outside the State.

* * *

Nor does the fact that a particular item lies within the subject matter of the federal patent laws necessarily preclude the States from offering limited protection which does not impermissibly interfere with the federal patent scheme. As *Sears* itself makes clear, States may place limited regulations on the use of unpatented designs in order to prevent consumer confusion as to source. In *Kewanee* [reproduced in Chapter 4 of this casebook], we found that state protection of trade secrets, as applied to both patentable and unpatentable subject matter, did not conflict with the federal patent laws. In both situations, state protection was not aimed exclusively at the promotion of invention itself, and the state restrictions on the use of unpatented ideas were limited to those necessary to promote goals outside the contemplation of the federal patent scheme. * * *

The Florida statute is aimed directly at the promotion of intellectual creation by substantially restricting the public's ability to exploit ideas which the patent system mandates shall be free for all to use. Like the interpretation of Illinois unfair competition law in *Sears* and *Compco,* the Florida statute represents a break with the tradition of peaceful co-existence between state market regulation and federal patent policy. The Florida law substantially restricts the public's ability to exploit an unpatented design in general circulation, raising the specter of state-created monopolies in a host of useful shapes and processes for which patent protection has been denied or is otherwise unobtainable. It thus enters a field of regulation which the patent laws have reserved to Congress. The patent statute's careful balance between public right and private monopoly to promote certain creative activity is a "scheme of federal regulation . . . so pervasive as to make reasonable the inference that Congress left no room for the States to supplement it." Rice v. Sante Fe Elevator Corp., 331 U.S. 218, 230 (1947).

Congress has considered extending various forms of limited protection to industrial design either through the copyright laws or by relaxing the restrictions on the availability of design patents. See generally Brown, Design Protection: An Overview, 34 U.C.L.A.L.Rev. 1341 (1987). Congress explicitly refused to take this step in the copyright laws, see 17 U.S.C. § 101; H.R.Rep. No. 94–1476, p. 55 (1976), U.S.Code Cong. & Admin.News 1976, pp. 5659, 5668, and despite sustained criticism for a number of years, it has declined to alter the patent protections presently available for industrial design. See Report of the President's Commission on the Patent System, S.Doc. No. 5, 90th Cong., 1st Sess., 20–21 (1967); Lindgren, The Sanctity of the Design Patent: Illusion or Reality?, 10 Okla.City L.Rev. 195 (1985). It is for Congress to determine if the present system of design and utility patents is ineffectual in promoting the useful arts in the context of industrial design. By offering patent-like protection for ideas deemed unprotected under the present federal scheme, the Florida statute conflicts with the "strong federal policy favoring free competition in ideas which do not merit patent protection." *Lear, Inc.*, 395 U.S., at 656. We therefore agree with the majority of the Florida Supreme Court that the Florida statute is preempted by the Supremacy Clause and the judgment of that court is hereby affirmed.

NOTES

1. *Bonito Boats* strongly reaffirmed *Sears* and *Compco*. The moral underpinnings of the misappropriation doctrine are strong and in the 25 years between *Sears* and *Bonito* (as the student will soon discover) doubts were cast on the scope or continued viability of preemption. A unanimous court and a broadly worded opinion renewed the vigor of the preemptive force of the patent and copyright laws.

2. The preemption issue faced by the Supreme Court in *Sears, Compco,* and *Bonito Boats* involves the allocation of authority between federal and state governments and surfaces in a wide-variety of contexts. A lawyer dealing with unfair competition and intellectual property issues must obviously be aware of the limits of state power. But these cases raise more fundamental concerns about the nature of intellectual property itself. The federal patent and copyright systems create substantial national rights for authors and inventors in their writings and discoveries. Why does the Supreme Court think that additional rights of more limited scope granted by state courts would interfere with federal policies? What are the federal policies at stake here? What policy arguments would lead to the conclusion that if a design is not protected by a patent or copyright it should not be protected at all? Wouldn't society be better off by a rule that accorded broad property rights to those who innovate, regardless of the limitations in the patent and copyright statutes? Do innovators necessarily lose by these decisions?

3. Isn't *Bonito Boats* the most radical of the decisions? Nothing in the Florida law prohibited a competitor from copying the design of the boat hull. The Florida statute only prohibited one method of doing so, a method that directly appropriates the plaintiff's own product. At least in *Sears* and *Compco* the defendants designed their own products using the plaintiff's as a model — they imitated the design but did not directly appropriate it. If the law generally should reward creativity, then the defendant in *Sears* at least displayed the amount of talent necessary to make a good copy. Is there a difference in moral standing between the person who paints an acceptable rendition of a Warhol painting and the person who uses computers to scan and reproduce the painting? Between a singing group that sells recordings of their imitation of The Grateful Dead and the off shore company that buys a single Grateful Dead CD and transfers it to a master CD from which it produces and sells CDs? Would a policy favoring competitive markets distinguish between immitation and appropriation?

4. Can you justify on moral or economic grounds a decision that allows the defendant to copy the plaintiff's design? Is it appropriate to characterize the defendant's actions as "stealing"?

A. Alchian & W. Allen, Exchange and Production Theory in Use

251–53 (1969).*

There is a class of goods known as "public goods," wherein the amount of use of the good or service by one person does not reduce the amount available to others *if* the good has been produced. Classic examples are melodies, poems, ideas, and theories. Anyone can use them without in any way reducing someone else's supply. If I hum a new tune, you can hum it too. *Once the good is produced,* any restriction on its use by some person, say by charging a price for each use, would be "inefficient"—in the sense that the restriction reduces the total utility of the members of the community. Someone has less utility and *no one* else thereby gets more. (It is not a *free* good once it is produced, for even more of it might be desired; but, it is a public good in the sense that no actual or potential user supplants some other possible user.)

Exclusion of any potential user would be undesirable if we accept the simplest ethical criterion that more for some people, if it does not mean less for anyone else, is certainly desirable. However, accepting this criterion creates a conflict of goals. We want to encourage the invention of new ideas, melodies, and literature, and we want them fully used. But to charge for their use in order to provide incentive for development and invention will restrict their use. How can we induce people to create public goods if we prohibit charging for their use?

* * *

The problem of public goods is a relatively new one in economic analysis. Perhaps in a few more decades, more definitive analyses can be accomplished and rigorous implications perceived. The problem is covered here to warn against blind carryover of principles from private goods to public goods as if there were no difference.

Millar v. Taylor

4 Burrows 2302 (K.B. 1769)

■ MANSFIELD, J.

[B]ecause it is just, that an author should reap the pecuniary profits of his own ingenuity and labour. It is just, that another should not use his name, without his consent. It is fit, that he should judge when to publish, or whether he ever will publish. It is fit, he should not only choose the time, but the manner of publication; how many; what volume; what print. It is fit, he should choose to whose care he will trust the accuracy and correctness of the impression; to whose honesty he will confide, not to foist in additions: with the other reasonings of the same effect.

James Boyle, Shamans, Software, and Spleens: Law and the Construction of the Information Society *

The Bellagio Declaration
Appendix B, Pgs. 195–196 (1996)

Contemporary intellectual property law is constructed around the notion of the author, the individual, solitary and original creator, and it is for this figure that its protections are reserved. The "author" in the modern sense is the sole creator of unique works of art, the originality of which warrants their protection under the laws of intellectual property—particularly those of "copyright" and "authors' rights." The notion, however, is neither natural nor inevitable. Rather, it arose at a specific time and place—eighteenth-century Europe—in connection with a particular information technology—print. Nevertheless, it remains the dominant paradigm in our global, multicultural, post-colonial electronic age, a paradigm that stretches beyond copyright to influence all types of intellectual property rights. We must recognize that there is a politics to "authorship"; as presently understood, it is a gate through which one must pass in order to be given property rights, a gate that shuts out a disproportionate number of non-Western, traditional, collaborative, or folkloric modes of production.

* * *

In general, systems built around the author paradigm tend to obscure the importance of "the public domain," the intellectual and cultural commons from which future works will be constructed. The assumption of these systems is that one must reward creators in order to ensure new production. Yet the "reward" has its costs. Each intellectual property right, in effect, fences off some portion of the public domain, making it unavailable to future creators. If one is concerned about promoting future production of books, ideas, inventions, and works of art, then one must be just as careful in one's protection of a vigorous and diverse public domain, a "commons" of scientific literary, and artistic raw material, as one is in one's protection of the author's right sand incentives. Recently, there has been a dangerous international tendency to suppress the former concern and to concentrate only on the latter.

Mark A. Lemley, Romantic Authorship and the Rhetoric of Property

Reviewing, James Boyle, Shamans, Software, And Spleens: Law and the Construction of the Information Society. Cambridge: Harvard University Press, 1996.
75 Tex. L. Rev. 873 (1997)[†]

III. Propertization

In this Part, I want to suggest in very general terms an alternate explanation for certain trends in intellectual property law—and perhaps in information law more generally. The explanation is that the rhetoric and economic theory of real property are increasingly dominating the discourse and conclusions of the very different world of intellectual property. * * *

The idea of propertization begins with a fundamental shift in the rhetoric of intellectual property law. In part, one might see this as an issue of terminology. Patent and copyright law have been around in the United States since its origin, but only recently has the term "intellectual property" come into vogue. Those who pay attention to that sort of thing may find this shift in terminology important, or at least symbolic; certainly the rise of the "property rights" view of intellectual property seems to coincide with the widespread use of the new phrase. * * *

The rise of property rhetoric in intellectual property cases is closely identified not with common-law property rules in general, but with a particular economic view of property rights. This view, which emerges from the Chicago School law-and-economics movement, emphasizes the importance of private ownership as the solution to the economic problem known as the "tragedy of the commons." The central idea is that joint or public ownership of a piece of property is inefficient because nonowners who use the property have no incentive to take care of it. Thus, common land shared by cattle owners is overgrazed because in the private calculus of each cattle owner the benefit from grazing exceeds the benefit from holding off. The Chicago argument is that dividing the commons into private property solves this problem by making each property owner liable for the consequences of her own actions. Further, if one assumes that efficient transactions will always occur, it does not particularly matter who gets the property entitlement, as the owner will simply sell or rent the property to the most productive user.

If one concludes that this logic applies to intellectual property as well, as some (but not all) Chicago economists apparently have, the implications are obvious. The way to get private parties to invest efficiently in innovation is to give them exclusive ownership rights in what they produce. Thus, the efficient thing to do on this view is to confer strong property rights on intellectual property creators, encouraging them to invest enough (but not too much) in identifying, developing, and commercializing new inventions. Further, if one postulates that transactions involving intellectual property are costless, society as a whole should benefit, since the owners of intellectual property rights will license those rights to others whenever it is economically efficient to do so.

I think the influence of this approach can be seen in two general trends in recent intellectual property cases. First, there is currently a strong tendency to "propertize" everything in the realm of information. Intellectual property law is expanding on an almost daily basis as new rights are created or existing rights are applied to give intellectual property owners rights that they never would have had in an earlier time. * * *

Second, even within the realm of existing intellectual property rights, the power the intellectual property owner has over those rights is increasing. Copying is less likely to be excused as a fair use of the copyright than ever before, particularly if the licensor can show that some money could have been squeezed out of the user. * * *

In short, what is going on here is not the product of some eighteenth-century vision of authorship with unfortunate consequences. Rather, it is a wholesale attack on the public domain in intellectual property law. The attack does not simply consist of multiple efforts to whittle away the scope of that domain for the benefit of those who get to own pieces of it, though that is certainly part of it. Rather, the attack is more fundamental—a challenge to the very idea of the public domain as an intrinsic part of intellectual property law.

Now, I happen to think that the "propertization" of intellectual property is a very bad idea. It is not at all clear to me that commons are always a bad thing, even in real property law. I am further unconvinced that the Chicago approach to real property, even if valid in that context, maps well onto intellectual property. We do not, after all, propertize other public goods (such as national defense or lighthouses), attempting to give their creators a legal right to exclude others. If anything, the public nature of a good seems to suggest that propertization is a uniquely bad idea, precisely because the consumption of that good is "nonrivalrous"—it does not take away from the creator of that good. Rather, intellectual property is in some sense a necessary evil—a restriction on the free flow of information to the minimum extent necessary to encourage needed investment in innovation. As such, we should be sensitive to the problem of giving intellectual property owners too much protection. Finally, even if the property-rights approach to intellectual property is theoretically sound, it depends critically on the demonstrably false assumption that transactions in intellectual property are costless, and on the premise that efficient licensing will always occur. * * *

Prof. doesn't agree

NOTES

1. The preceding cases from *INS* to *Bonito Boats* illustrate the tensions imbedded in intellectual property doctrines. Is protection owed to those who innovate because of some natural law principle associated with rewarding labor or ingenuity or recognizing innovation as an embodiment of its creator's personality? Or, are rights accorded to creators as economic incentives for innovation? Does *INS* represent the former ("reap where it has not sown")? Do *Sears, Compco,* and *Bonito Boats* represent the latter by assuming that federal copyright and patent systems are carefully calibrated to provide the proper incentives with which any other system of protection would interfere?

2. A good overview of the competing philosophies applicable to protecting creative activities is Justin Hughes, The Philosophy of Intellectual Property, 77 Geo. L. J. 287 (1988) (observing that even the labor and personality theories attributable respectively to John Stuart Mill and Hegel have limitations on the extent of the rights recognized). See also Wendy J. Gordon, On Owning Information: Intellectual Property and the Restitutionary

Impulse, 78 Va. L. Rev. 149 (1992); Alfred C. Yen, Restoring the Natural Law: Copyright as Labor and Possession, 51 Ohio. St. L.J. 517 (1990).

3. The "public goods" problem outlined in the excerpt from Alchian and Allen explains the difficulty of fashioning economic incentives for creativity. If the efficient *distribution* of public goods requires they be given away free, any property right allowing the owner to charge a price for distribution is inefficient. On the other hand, if an incentive to create is thought necessary, some property right (or some other subsidy) is required. If an incentive is thought necessary, how can the right amount of incentive (the scope of the property right) be determined? Can we have too much creativity? Can creativity be premature? Can a regime of broad property rights actually reduce the level of creativity?

The first assumption of an economic justification for property rights in creativity is that creators are animated by economic incentives. One popular view may be that "inventive or artistic genius" is largely immune from economic incentives or that real innovation occurs primarily as a flash of insight or by pure accidental discovery. The image of Newton or Franklin is more romantic, but probably not as prevalent, as the calculated investment of governments, universities, and business firms in research and development. A study based on data derived from the patent system concluded that "invention is largely an economic activity which, like other economic activities, is pursued for gain. " J. Schmookler, Invention and Economic Growth 206 (1966).

4. Even if innovation is driven by economic incentives, some incentives may exist naturally without legally enforceable rights. See, Schmookler, id. at 37–38:

Since many results of corporate research today are apparently unpatented, it seems probable that this period of initial advantage is both a necessary and, usually, a sufficient condition for a large part of present-day corporate research. In its absence, any one firm would be better off to engage in no research at all. It would need merely to copy its competitors' inventions. Its own research would presumably help its rivals as much as itself, and under these conditions, little or no industrial research would occur. Since the magnitude of industrial research today is enormous, it is clear that this situation does not obtain. One may surmise that it is either the advantage of being first or the necessity for catching up which motivates corporate invention. Once one firm in an industry engages in research, its rivals are perforce obligated to follow suit to maintain their own relative standing.

The lead time monopoly alone, without copyright protection, has been suggested to be a sufficient incentive for the production of written material. Breyer, The Uneasy Case for Copyright: A Study of Copyright in Books, Photocopies, and Computer Programs, 84 Harv.L.Rev. 281 (1970).

There are, of course, limits on the extent of a lead time monopoly. See W. Nordhaus, Invention, Growth, and Welfare 61 (1969):

There are two powerful forces that tend to reduce any technological lead. First, other firms tend to catch up by performing parallel or

identical research and narrowing the difference in the stock of technological information. A second and perhaps more important force comes
from the inappropriability of scarce knowledge. The mobility of labor,
industrial spying, disclosure in patents, and the inability to seal off the
research and productive processes tend to erode the differential level of
knowledge among firms.

See also, Plant, The Economic Theory Concerning Patents for Inventions, 1
Economica 30 (N.S.1934).

It should not be assumed that reverse engineering of a competitor's
innovation is a costless or low cost activity. If an innovation can be commercially exploited in secrecy, the lead time monopoly may be extensive and
the costs of piercing the secrecy (including overcoming any legal barriers to
doing so) may be high. Even where the cost of acquiring the knowledge is
low, the ability to absorb and utilize what is acquired is in many instances
conditioned on having developed a base of basic knowledge, skilled employees, and capital equipment. If you or I acquired information about a new
pollution-free electric engine developed by Ford Motor Company it would be
very costly for us to establish production of the engine in competition with
Ford. On the other hand, a company already in the automobile business
conducting research on its own engine might be able to exploit the Ford
innovation at relatively little cost.

Does the lead time advantage depend itself on the legal rules that permit the enforcement of secrecy surrounding innovations? Does the lead time
advantage depend on employee loyalty? On the nature of the innovation?
Should the availability of a lead time advantage affect other legal rules
relating to protection of innovation? Did Associated Press have a lead time
advantage? Did Stiffle?

5. The economic analysis of public goods is greatly complicated once
one considers that utilization of the public good itself has costs (or to put it
another way, requires the use of additional resources) and attention is
shifted to the problem of creating incentives for the efficient timing of the
utilization of these additional resources. See Barzel, The Optimal Timing of
Innovations, 50 Rev.Econ. & Stat. 348 (1968). These problems are discussed
in connection with the patent system in Kitch, The Nature and Function of
the Patent System, 20 J.L. & Econ. 265 (1977).

6. Can we rely on private property rights to provide the "right" (efficient) amount of innovation? See the following excerpt from *Shamans,
Software, and Spleens, supra* at 41-42:

> * * * A person reading the confident sounding statements of legal schol-
> ars about the superior efficiency of the patent regime over the copyright
> regime, or the economic efficiency of the regulation of insider trading, or
> the law of fraud, would be surprised to find that economists cannot even
> agree over the absolutely basic question of whether, in the absence of
> commodification [awarding of property rights] there will be underinvest-
> ment or overinvestment in the production of information. Kenneth Arrow
> takes a position that seems to support the Court's result in the INS case,

arguing that, without property rights, too little information will be produced because producers of information will not be able to capture its true value. Eugene Fama and Arthur Laffer, by contrast, argue that too much information will be generated, because some information will be produced only in order to gain some temporary advantage in trading, thus redistributing wealth but not achieving greater allocative efficiency. In other words, in the absence of information property rights, there may be inefficient investment of social resources in activities that merely slice the pie up differently, rather than making it bigger. Jack Hirschleifer gives a similar analysis of patent law, ending up with the conclusion that patent law may be either a necessary incentive for the production of inventions or an unnecessary legal monopoly in information that overcompensates an inventor who has already had the opportunity to trade on the information implied by his or her discovery. It is hard to think of a more fundamental disagreement. (Footnotes omitted)*

Lemley in the excerpt above mentions the lighthouse as a classic "public good" — once it is constructed everyone can use it without diminishing its use by others but how do you get it constructed? It was always thought since it would be difficult to confer a property right on the owner (how would the owner enforce a charge on boats which used the light to avoid the shoals) the only solution was publicly financed lighthouses. But see, Coase, The Lighthouse in Economics, 17 J.L. & Econ. 357 (1974).

C. The Regulation of Advertising

Friedman v. Rogers

Supreme Court of the United States, 1979.
440 U.S. 1

■ MR. JUSTICE POWELL delivered the opinion of the Court.

Texas law prohibits the practice of optometry under a trade name. It also requires that four of the six members of the State's regulatory board, the Texas Optometry Board, be members of the Texas Optometric Association, a professional organization of optometrists. A three-judge District Court sustained the constitutionality of the statute governing the composition of the Texas Optometry Board against a challenge based on the First and Fourteenth Amendments. But it held that the prohibition of the practice of optometry under a trade name ran afoul of First Amendment protection of commercial speech. 438 F.Supp. 428 (E.D. Tex.1977). These appeals and cross-appeal bring both of the District Court's holdings before the Court.

I

The Texas Legislature approved the Texas Optometry Act (the Act) in 1969, repealing an earlier law governing the practice of optometry in the

* From Shamans, Software and Splees by James Boyle. Copyright © 1996 by the President and Fellows of Harvard College.   Reprinted by permission of Harvard University Press.

State. Section 2.01 of the Act establishes the Texas Optometry Board (the Board) and § 2.02 prescribes the qualifications for Board members. The Board is responsible for the administration of the Act, and has the authority to grant, renew, suspend, and revoke licenses to practice optometry in the State. The Act imposes numerous regulations on the practice of optometry, and on several aspects of the business of optometry. Many of the Act's business regulations are contained in § 5.13, which restricts fee splitting by optometrists and forbids an optometrist to allow his name to be associated with any optometrical office unless he is present and practicing there at least half of the hours that the office is open or half of the hours that he practices, whichever is less. Section 5.13(d), at issue here, prohibits the practice of optometry under an assumed name, trade name, or corporate name.[6]

The dispute in this case grows out of the schism between "professional" and "commercial" optometrists in Texas. Although all optometrists in the State must meet the same licensing requirements, and are subject to the same laws regulating their practices, they have divided themselves informally into two groups according to their divergent approaches to the practice of optometry. Rogers, an advocate of the commercial practice of optometry and a member of the Board, commenced this action by filing a suit against the other five members of the Board. He sought declaratory and injunctive relief from the enforcement of § 2.02 of the Act, prescribing the composition of the Board, and § 5.13(d) of the Act, prohibiting the practice of optometry under a trade name. [Rogers used the trade name "Texas State Optical" or "TSO".]

[Section 2.02 of the Act required four of the six members to be affiliated with the Texas Optometric Association (TOA). Commercial optometrists were ineligible for membership. Rogers claimed this statutory scheme deprived him of equal protection and due process. The TOA intervened to support the statute; the Texas Senior Citizens Association intervened on behalf of Rogers claiming their membership was deprived of Fourteenth Amendment rights by the restrictions on commercial optometrists. In part of the opinion omitted below, a unanimous Supreme Court affirmed the District Court's ruling sustaining the constitutionality of § 2.02 as reasonably related to a valid state interest in regulating optometrists.]

---

6. Section 5.13(d) provides in part:
"No optometrist shall practice or continue to practice optometry under, or use in connection with his practice of optometry, any assumed name, corporate name, trade name, or any name other than the name under which he is licensed to practice optometry in Texas * * * " The scope of the prohibition in § 5.13(d) is limited by various provisions in § 5.13 that make it clear that the Act does not proscribe partnerships for the practice of optometry, or the employment of optometrists by other optometrists. Regarding partner-ships, counsel for the defendant Board members indicated at oral argument that § 5.13(d) does not require that the names of all partners be included in the name used to identify the office of an optometrical partnership. Tr. of Oral Arg., at 28. With respect to employees, § 5.13 provides that "[o]ptometrists who are employed by other optometrists shall practice in their own names, but may practice in an office listed under the name of the individual optometrist or partnership of optometrists by whom they are employed."

II

In holding that § 5.13(d) infringes First Amendment rights, the District Court relied primarily on this Court's decisions in Bates v. State Bar of Arizona, 433 U.S. 350 (1977), and Virginia State Board of Pharmacy v. Virginia Citizens Consumer Council, 425 U.S. 748 (1976). A trade name is a form of advertising, it concluded, because after the name has been used for some time, people "identify the name with a certain quality of service and goods." It found specifically "that the Texas State Optical [TSO] name has come to communicate to the consuming public information as to certain standards of price and quality, and availability of routine services," and rejected the argument that the TSO name misleads the public as to the identity of the optometrists with whom it deals. Balancing the constitutional interests in the commercial speech in question against the State's interest in regulating it, the District Court held that the prohibition of the use of trade names by § 5.13(d) is an unconstitutional restriction of the "free flow of commercial information." 438 F.Supp., at 430–431.

A

A review of *Virginia Pharmacy* and *Bates* shows that the reliance on them by the court below, a reliance reasserted here by Rogers and the TSCA (the plaintiffs), was misplaced. At issue in *Virginia Pharmacy* was the validity of Virginia's law preventing advertising by pharmacists of the prices of prescription drugs. After establishing that the economic nature of the pharmacists' interest in the speech did not preclude First Amendment protection for their advertisements, the Court discussed the other interests in the advertisements that warranted First Amendment protection. To individual consumers, information about prices of prescription drugs at competing pharmacies "could mean the alleviation of physical pain or the enjoyment of basic necessities." Id., at 764. Society also has a strong interest in the free flow of commercial information, both because the efficient allocation of resources depends upon informed consumer choices and because "even an individual advertisement, though entirely 'commercial,' may be of general public interest." Ibid. The Court acknowledged the important interest of the State in maintaining high standards among pharmacists, but concluded that this interest could not justify the ban on truthful price advertising when weighed against the First Amendment interests in the information conveyed.

In the next Term, the Court applied the rationale of *Virginia Pharmacy* to the advertising of certain information by lawyers. After weighing the First Amendment interests identified in *Virginia Pharmacy* against the State's interests in regulating the speech in question, the Court concluded that the truthful advertising of the prices at which routine legal services will be performed also is protected by the First Amendment. Bates v. State Bar of Arizona, supra.

In both *Virginia Pharmacy* and *Bates*, we were careful to emphasize that "[s]ome forms of commercial speech regulation are surely permissible." Virginia Pharmacy, supra, at 770, Bates, supra, 433 U.S., at 383. For example, restrictions on the time, place, or manner of expression are permissible provided that "they are [imposed] without reference to the content of the regulated speech, that they serve a significant governmental interest, and that in so doing they leave open ample alternative channels for communication of the information." Virginia Pharmacy, supra, 425 U.S., at 771. Equally permissible are restrictions on false, deceptive, and misleading commercial speech.

> "Untruthful speech, commercial or otherwise, has never been protected for its own sake. Gertz v. Robert Welch, Inc., 418 U.S. 323, 340 (1974); Konisberg v. State Bar, 366 U.S. 36, 49, and n. 10 (1961). Obviously, much commercial speech is not provably false, or even wholly false, but only deceptive or misleading. We foresee no obstacle to a State's dealing effectively with this problem. The First Amendment, as we construe it today, does not prohibit the State from insuring that the stream of commercial information flows cleanly as well as freely." *Virginia Pharmacy,* supra, at 771–772; accord, *Bates,* supra, 433 U.S., at 383.

Regarding the permissible extent of commercial speech regulation, the Court observed in *Virginia Pharmacy* that certain features of commercial speech differentiate it from other varieties of speech in ways that suggest that "a different degree of protection is necessary to insure that the flow of truthful and legitimate commercial information is unimpaired." 425 U.S., at 771–772 n. 24. Because it relates to a particular product or service, commercial speech is more objective, hence more verifiable, than other varieties of speech. Commercial speech, because of its importance to business profits, and because it is carefully calculated, is also less likely than other forms of speech to be inhibited by proper regulation. These attributes, the Court concluded, indicate that it is "appropriate to require that a commercial message appear in such a form * * * as [is] necessary to prevent its being deceptive. * * * They may also make inapplicable the prohibition against prior restraints." Ibid. (citations omitted); see id., at 775–781, 96 S.Ct., at 1832–1835 (concurring opinion of Mr. Justice Stewart).[9]

---

9. The application of First Amendment protection to speech that does "no more than propose a commercial transaction," Pittsburgh Press Co. v. Human Relations Comm'n, 413 U.S. 376, 385 (1973), has been recognized generally as a substantial extension of traditional free-speech doctrine which poses special problems not presented by other forms of protected speech. Jackson & Jeffries, Commercial Speech: Economic Due Process and the First Amendment, 65 Va.L.Rev. 1 (1979); Note First Amendment and Misleading Advertising, 57 B.U.L.Rev. 833 (1977). Cf. Note, First Amendment Protection for Commercial Advertising: The New Constitutional Doctrine, 44 U.Chi.L.Rev. 205 (1976). By definition, commercial speech is linked inextricably to commercial activity: while the First Amendment affords such speech "a limited measure of protection," it is also true that "the State does not lose its power to regulate commercial activity deemed harmful to the public whenever speech is a component of that activity." Ohralik v. Ohio State Bar Assn., 436 U.S. 447, 456 (1978). Because of the special character of commercial speech and the relative novelty of First Amendment protection for such speech, we act with caution in confronting First Amendment challenges to economic legislation that serves legitimate regulatory interests. Our decisions dealing with more traditional First Amendment problems do not extend automatically to this as yet uncharted area. See, e.g., id., at 462 n. 20 (overbreadth analysis not applicable to commercial speech). When dealing with restrictions on commercial speech we frame our decisions narrowly, "allowing modes of regulation [of commercial speech] that might be impermissible in the realm of noncommercial expression." Id., at 456.

B

Once a trade name has been in use for some time, it may serve to identify an optometrical practice and also to convey information about the type, price, and quality of services offered for sale in that practice. In each role, the trade name is used as part of a proposal of a commercial transaction. Like the pharmacist who desired to advertise his prices in *Virginia Pharmacy,* supra, the optometrist who uses a trade name "does not wish to editorialize on any subject, cultural, philosophical, or political. He does not wish to report any particularly newsworthy fact, or to make generalized observations even about commercial matters." 425 U.S., at 761. His purpose is strictly business. The use of trade names in connection with optometrical practice, then, is a form of commercial speech and nothing more.

A trade name is, however, a significantly different form of commercial speech from that considered in *Virginia Pharmacy* and *Bates.* In those cases, the State had proscribed advertising by pharmacists and lawyers that contained statements about the products or services offered and their prices. These statements were self-contained and self-explanatory. Here, we are concerned with a form of commercial speech that has no intrinsic meaning. A trade name conveys no information about the price and nature of the services offered by an optometrist until it acquires meaning over a period of time by associations formed in the minds of the public between the name and some standard of price or quality. Because these ill-defined associations of trade names with price and quality information can be manipulated by the users of trade names, there is a significant possibility that trade names will be used to mislead the public.

The possibilities for deception are numerous. The trade name of an optometrical practice can remain unchanged despite changes in the staff of optometrists upon whose skill and care the public depends when it patronizes the practice. Thus, the public may be attracted by a trade name that reflects the reputation of an optometrist no longer associated with the practice. A trade name frees an optometrist from dependence on his personal reputation to attract clients, and even allows him to assume a new trade name if negligence or misconduct casts a shadow over the old one. By using different trade names at shops under his common ownership, an optometrist can give the public the false impression of competition among the shops. The use of a trade name also facilitates the advertising essential to large-scale commercial practices with numerous branch offices, conduct the State rationally may wish to discourage while not prohibiting commercial optometrical practice altogether.

The concerns of the Texas Legislature about the deceptive and misleading uses of optometrical trade names were not speculative or hypothetical, but were based on experience in Texas with which the legislature was familiar when in 1969 it enacted § 5.13(d). The forerunner of § 5.13(d) was adopted as part of a "Professional Responsibility Rule" by the Texas State Board of Examiners in Optometry in 1959. In a decision upholding the validity of the Rule, the Texas Supreme Court reviewed some of the practices that had prompted its adoption. Texas State Bd. of Examiners in Optometry v. Carp, 412 S.W.2d 307, appeal dismissed and cert. denied, 389

U.S. 52 (1967). One of the plaintiffs in that case, Carp, operated 71 optometrical offices in Texas under at least 10 different trade names. From time
to time, he changed the trade names of various shops, though the licensed
optometrists practicing in each shop remained the same. He purchased the
practices of other optometrists and continued to practice under their names,
even though they were no longer associated with the practice. In several
instances, Carp used different trade names on offices located in close proximity to one another and selling the same optical goods and services. The
offices were under common management, and had a common staff of
optometrists, but the use of different trade names facilitated advertising
that gave the impression of competition among the offices.

The Texas court found that Carp used trade names to give a misleading
impression of competitive ownership and management of his shops. It also
found that Rogers, a party to this suit and a plaintiff in *Carp,* had used a trade
name to convey the impression of standardized optometrical care. All 82 of his
shops went under the trade name "Texas State Optical" or "TSO," and he
advertised "scientific TSO eye examination[s]" available in every shop. 412
S.W.2d, at 312. The TSO advertising was calculated as well, the court found,
to give "the impression that [Rogers or one of his brothers] is present at a particular office. Actually they have neither been inside nor seen some of their
eighty-two offices distributed generally over Texas." Id., at 313. Even if Rogers'
use and advertising of the trade name were not in fact misleading, they were
an example of the use of a trade name to facilitate the large-scale commercialization which enhances the opportunity for misleading practices.[13]

It is clear that the State's interest in protecting the public from the
deceptive and misleading use of optometrical trade names is substantial and
well-demonstrated.[14] We are convinced that § 5.13(d) is a constitutionally
permissible state regulation in furtherance of this interest. We emphasize, in

13. Although the individual defendants
and the TOA (collectively, the defendants) rely
primarily on *Carp* to establish the history of
false and misleading uses of optometrical
trade names, some evidence of such practices
also was included in the deposition testimony
presented to the District Court. A former associate of Carp's testified to some of the trade
name abuses that had occurred in their business. Shannon Deposition, at 8. Rogers' testimony showed that the "Texas State Optical"
name was used by offices wholly owned by
him, partly owned by him, and by offices in
which he had no ownership interest. The dissenting opinion states that the "Rogers organization is able to offer and enforce a degree of
uniformity in care at all of its offices * * *."
Post, at 900. This was not Rogers' testimony.
He stated that he exercised "no control whatsoever" over "office policy routines" in those
TSO offices in which he owned no interest.

Rogers' Deposition, at 16. It appears from
Rogers' testimony that his primary business
relationship with such offices was their participation in the TSO advertising and their
purchase of materials and equipment from his
supply house. Id., at 16–18, 22–23.

14. The plaintiffs argue that the fact that
the public might be subject to similar deception
by optometrists who do not use trade names
but practice in partnerships or with numerous
employees shows that the State actually was
not concerned with misleading and deceptive
practices when it enacted § 5.13(d). The plaintiffs have not attempted to show, however, that
any of the demonstrated abuses associated
with the use of trade names also has occurred
apart from their use. Tr. of Oral Arg., at 29.
There is no requirement that the State legislate more broadly than required by the problem
it seeks to remedy. See Williamson v. Lee
Optical Co., 348 U.S. 483, 489 (1955).

so holding, that the restriction on the use of trade names has only the most incidental effect on the content of the commercial speech of Texas optometrists. As noted above, a trade name conveys information only because of the associations that grow up over time between the name and a certain level of price and quality of service. Moreover, the information associated with a trade name is largely factual, concerning the kind and price of the services offered for sale. Since the Act does not prohibit or limit the type of informational advertising held to be protected in *Virginia Pharmacy* and *Bates*, the factual information associated with trade names may be communicated freely and explicitly to the public. An optometrist may advertise the type of service he offers, the prices he charges, and whether he practices as a partner, associate, or employee with other optometrists. Rather than stifling commercial speech, § 5.13(d) ensures that information regarding optometrical services will be communicated more fully and accurately to consumers than it had been in the past when optometrists were allowed to convey the information through unstated and ambiguous associations with a trade name. In sum, Texas has done no more than require that commercial information about optometrical services "appear in such a form ... as [is] necessary to prevent its being deceptive." *Virginia Pharmacy,* supra, 425 U.S., at 771–772 n. 24.

* * *

IV

* * * The case is remanded with instructions to dissolve the injunction against the enforcement of § 5.13(d).

So ordered.

MR. JUSTICE BLACKMUN, with whom MR. JUSTICE MARSHALL joins, concurring in part and dissenting in part.

* * *

I do not agree with the Court's holding that the Texas Optometry Act's § 5.13(d), which bans the use of a trade name "in connection with" the practice of optometry in the State, is constitutional. In my view, the Court's restricted analysis of the nature of a trade name overestimates the potential for deception, and underestimates the harmful impact of the broad sweep of § 5.13(d). The Court also ignores the fact that in Texas the practice of "commercial" optometry is *legal.* It has never been outlawed or made illegal. This inescapable conclusion is one of profound importance in the measure of the First Amendment rights that are asserted here. It follows, it seems to me, that Texas has abridged the First Amendment rights not only of Doctor Rogers but of the members of the intervenor-plaintiff Texas Senior Citizens Association by absolutely prohibiting, without reasonable justification, the dissemination of truthful information about wholly legal commercial conduct.

I

* * *

In 1976, Texas had 934 resident licensed optometrists divided almost evenly between "professional" and "commercial" factions. Rogers is the leader of the commercial forces. He and his associates operate more than 100 optometry offices. Before the enactment of § 5.13(d) in 1969, and where still allowed by a grandfather provision, § 5.13(k) (which, but for the decision of the District Court, would have expired on January 1, 1979), their offices use the name Texas State Optical, or TSO. An optometrist who agrees to participate with Rogers in his organization must obey an elaborate set of restrictions on pain of termination. He must purchase all inventory and supplies from Rogers Brothers; do all laboratory work at their laboratory; abide by their policies concerning the examination of patients; take patients on a first-come-first-served basis rather than by appointment; and retain Rogers Brothers at 4% of net cash to do all accounting and advertising. App. A71–A98. As a result of these and other rules, the Rogers organization is able to offer and enforce a degree of uniformity in care at all its offices along with other consumer benefits, namely, sales on credit, adjustment of frames and lenses without cost, one-stop care, and transferability of patient records among Texas State Optical offices.[2] The TSO chain typifies commercial optometry, with its emphasis on advertising, volume, and speed of service.

The Court today glosses over the important private and public interests that support Rogers' use of his trade name. For those who need them, eyeglasses are one of the "basic necessities" of life in which a consumer's interest "may be as keen, if not keener by far, than his interest in the day's most urgent political debate." Virginia Pharmacy Board, 425 U.S., at 763–764. For the mobile consumer, the Rogers trade name provides a valuable service.[3] Lee Kenneth Benham, a professor and economist whose studies in this area have been relied upon by the Federal Trade Commission,[4] testified in a deposition which is part of the record here:

2. Rogers owns some Texas State Optical offices; in others he is merely a partner; and in still others he has no financial interest other than licensing the TSO trade name and selling optical supplies and services to the "associated" optometrist. The Court, ante, at 13 n. 13, relies on Rogers' deposition testimony to suggest that he exerts no control at all over associated offices. The representative contract introduced into evidence, however, requires that, as a condition of using the TSO trade name, the licensee must operate the office in accord with TSO policy and purchase all optical material from Rogers Brothers Laboratory. App. A82–A83. See Brief for Appellee *Texas Optometric Association, Inc.*, in No. 77–1164, pp. 16–18. The parties do not question the District Court's factual finding that the TSO trade name is associated with certain standards of quality. See infra, at 900–901 [Casebook page 61].

3. Trade names are a vital form of commercial speech. It has even been suggested that commercial speech can be defined as "speech referring to a brand name product or service that is not itself protected by the first amendment, issued by a speaker with a financial interest in the sale of the product or service or in the distribution of the speech." Note, First Amendment Protection for Commercial Advertising: The New Constitutional Doctrine, 44 U.Chi.L.Rev. 205, 254 (1976).

4. The Federal Trade Commission has promulgated a rule pre-empting certain state laws that restrict advertising of ophthalmic goods and services. 43 Fed.Reg. 24006 (1978). The Commission's statement of basis and purpose characterize the Benham studies as "reliable." Id., at 23995. See Benham, The Effect of Advertising on the Price of Eyeglasses, 15 J.Law & Econ. 337 (1972); Benham & Benham, Regulating Through the Professions: A Perspective on Information Control, 18 J.Law & Econ. 421 (1975).

"One of the most valuable assets which individuals have in this large mobile country is their knowledge about trade names. Consumers develop a sophisticated understanding of the goods and services provided and the prices associated with different trade names. This permits them to locate the goods, services, and prices they prefer on a continuing basis with substantially lower search costs than would otherwise be the case. This can perhaps be illustrated by pointing out the information provided by such names as Sears, Neiman Marcus or Volkswagen. This also means that firms have an enormous incentive to develop and maintain the integrity of the products and services provided under their trade name: the entire package they offer is being judged continuously by consumers on the basis of the samples they purchase." App. A–336.

And the District Court found in this case that "the Texas State Optical name [TSO] has come to communicate to the consuming public information as to certain standards of price and quality, and availability of particular routine services." 438 F.Supp. 428, 431 (ED Tex.1977).

The Rogers trade name also serves a distinctly public interest. To that part of the general public that is not then in the market for eye care, a trade name is the distinguishing characteristic of the commercial optometrist. The professional faction does not use trade names. Without trade names, an entirely legal but regulated mode of organizing optometrical practice would be banished from that public's view. * * *

II

The Court characterizes as "substantial and well-demonstrated" the state interests offered to support suppression of this valuable information. Ante, at 897. It first contends that because a trade name has no intrinsic meaning, it can cause deception. The name may remain unchanged, it is pointed out, despite a change in the identities of the optometrists who employ it. Secondly, the Court says that the State may ban trade names to discourage commercial optometry while stopping short of prohibiting it altogether. Neither of these interests justifies a statute so sweeping as § 5.13(d).

A

Because a trade name has no intrinsic meaning, it cannot by itself be deceptive. A trade name will deceive only if it is used in a misleading context. The hypotheticals posed by the Court, and the facts of Texas State Bd. of Examiners in Optometry v. Carp, 412 S.W.2d 307 (Tex.Sup.Ct.), appeal dis'd and cert. denied, 389 U.S. 52 (1967), concern the use of optometric trade names in situations where the name of the practicing optometrist is kept concealed. The deception lies not in the use of the trade name, but in the failure simultaneously to disclose the name of the optometrist. In the present case, counsel for the State conceded at oral argument that § 5.13(d) prohibits the use of a trade name even when the optometrist's name is also prominently displayed. Tr. of Oral Arg. 39. It thus prohibits wholly truthful speech that is entirely removed from the justification on which the Court most heavily relies to support the statute.

The Court suggests that a State may prohibit "misleading commercial speech" even though it is "offset" by the publication of clarifying information. Ante, at 895 n. 11. Corrected falsehood, however, is truth, and, absent some other regulatory justification, a State may not prohibit the dissemination of truthful commercial information. By disclosing his individual name along with his trade name, the commercial optometrist acts in the spirit of our First Amendment jurisprudence, where traditionally "the remedy to be applied is more speech, not enforced silence." Linmark Associates, Inc. v. Willingboro, 431 U.S., at 97, quoting Whitney v. California, 274 U.S. 357, 377 (1927) (Brandeis, J., concurring). The ultimate irony of the Court's analysis is that § 5.13(d), because of its broad sweep, actually encourages deception. That statute, in conjunction with § 5.13(e), prevents the consumer from ever discovering that Rogers controls and in some cases employs the optometrist upon whom the patient has relied for care. In effect, the statute conceals the fact that a particular practitioner is engaged in commercial rather than professional optometry, and so deprives consumers of information that may well be thought relevant to the selection of an optometrist.

B

The second justification proffered by the Court is that a State, while not prohibiting commercial optometry practice altogether, could ban the use of trade names in order to discourage commercial optometry. Just last Term, however, the Court rejected the argument that the States' power to create, regulate, or wind-up a corporation by itself could justify a restriction on that corporation's speech. See First National Bank v. Bellotti, 435 U.S. 765, 780 n. 16 (1978). Moreover, this justification ignores the substantial First Amendment interest in the dissemination of truthful information about legally available professional services. See Bigelow v. Virginia, 421 U.S. 809, 822–825 (1975). It is not without significance that most of the persons influenced by a trade name are those who, by experience or by reputation, know the quality of service for which the trade name stands. The determination that banning trade names would discourage commercial optometry, therefore, necessarily relies on an assumption that persons previously served thought that the trade name practitioner had performed an acceptable service. If the prior experience had been bad, the consumer would want to know the trade name in order to avoid those who practice under it. The first and second stated purposes of § 5.13 are "to protect the public in the practice of optometry," and to "better enable members of the public to fix professional responsibility." These purposes are ill-served by a statute that hinders consumers from enlisting the services of an organization they have found helpful, and so, in effect, prevents consumers from protecting themselves.

The Court repeatedly has rejected the "highly paternalistic" approach implicit in this justification. See First National Bank v. Bellotti, 435 U.S., at 791, n. 31. There is nothing about the nature of an optometrist's services that justifies adopting an approach of this kind here. An optometrist's duties are confined by the statute, § 1.02(1), to measuring the powers of vision of the eye and fitting corrective lenses. See Williamson v. Lee Optical Co., 348 U.S. 483, 486 (1955) (defining terms). The optometrist does not treat disease. His service is highly standardized. Each step is controlled by statute. § 5.12. Many of his functions are so mechanical that they can be duplicated by machines that would enable a patient to measure his own vision. Patients participate in the refraction process, and they frequently can easily assess the quality of service rendered. The cost per visit is low enough—$15 to $35—that comparison shopping is sometimes possible. See App. A420. Because more than half the Nation's population uses eyeglasses, 43 Fed.Reg. 23992 (1978), reputation information is readily available. In this context, the First Amendment forbids the choice which Texas has made to shut off entirely the flow of commercial information to consumers who, we have assumed, "will perceive their own best interest if only they are well enough informed." Virginia Pharmacy Board, 425 U.S., at 770.

NOTES

1. *Virginia Pharmacy*, cited in the principal case, was the first case to apply First Amendment protections to commercial speech. The reaction among commentators was mixed. BeVier, The First Amendment and Political Speech: An Inquiry into the Substance and Limits of Principle, 30 Stan.L.Rev. 299 (1978); Bork, Neutral Principles and Some First Amendment Problems, 47 Ind.L.J. 1 (1971). These authors generally would limit the protections of the First Amendment to political speech—speech essential to representative democracy—and to speech necessary for individual self-fulfillment, i.e., educational speech, artistic expression. *Virginia Pharmacy,* in their view, unnecessarily withdraws from the political process and majoritarian control the power to regulate one element of the economic marketplace when it is generally conceded that other elements are subject to regulation. Presumably Virginia could have set the price at which prescription drugs were sold so why shouldn't it be allowed to take the less drastic step of prohibiting price advertising?

First Amendment protection for commercial speech is defended in Coase, Advertising and Free Speech, 6 J. of Leg.Stud. 1 (1977), printed in Advertising and Free Speech 1 (Hyman & Johnson ed. 1977). Professor Coase supports *Virginia Pharmacy* on economic grounds because it reduces governmental regulation of the marketplace. He argues that the first amendment is not limited to political expression since "Nude dancing is now covered, or uncovered, by the first amendment and it would be difficult to argue that this activity . . . is vital to the working of a democratic system." 6 J.Leg.Stud. at 13. If "self-fulfillment" is the appropriate value, in Coase's view, individual consumer choices in the marketplace are, for most people "more important than much of what is protected by the First Amendment." Id. at 14. For the simple view that commercial speech is "speech" and thus protected see Countryman, Advertising Is Speech, in Advertising and Free Speech 35 (Hyman & Johnson ed. 1977).

2. The fact that the First Amendment is applicable to commercial speech is now well established. More controversial is whether commercial speech should enjoy the same level of protection as other speech. *Virginia Pharmacy* suggested that commercial speech was different and thus governmental regulations directed at commercial speech were subject to different rules. In Central Hudson Gas & Elec. Corp. v. Public Service Comm'n of New York, 447 U.S. 557, 566 (1980) the Court invalidated a Commission rule that prohibited a regulated electric utility from engaging in promotional advertising. In doing so the court adopted a four-part analysis for commercial speech cases:

> At the outset, we must determine whether the expression is protected by the First Amendment. For commercial speech to come within that provision, it at least must concern lawful activity and not be misleading. Next, we ask whether the asserted governmental interest is substantial. If both inquires yield positive answers, we must determine whether the regulation directly advances the governmental interest asserted, and whether it is not more extensive than is necessary to serve that interest.

The *Central Hudson* test has sparked considerable controversy in the Supreme Court. In Posadas de Puerto Rico Associates v. Tourism Company of Puerto Rico, 478 U.S. 328 (1986), the Court upheld a Puerto Rico regulation which prohibited legal gambling casinos in Puerto Rico from advertising in media directed at Puerto Rican residents. Only advertisements directed at tourists were permitted. Justice Rehnquist, writing for a 5 member majority, found that the interest in reducing demand for casino gambling among residents was substantial, the advertising ban "directly advanced" that interest, and the regulation was not more extensive than necessary. The Court suggested that the "greater power to completely ban casino gambling necessarily includes the lesser power to ban advertising of casino gambling . . . ." However, in Rubin v. Coors Brewing Co., 514 U.S. 476 (1995) the Court declared unconstitutional a federal regulation prohibiting disclosure of the alcoholic content of beer on labels, dismissing the government's claimed justification that the regulation was needed to prevent beer manufacturers from competing by increasing alcoholic content. The Court reaffirmed *Central Hudson* but Justice Stevens concurred separately arguing that regulations of accurate and complete commercial speech should be subject to the same scrutiny as non-commercial speech.

In 44 Liquormart, Inc. v. Rhode Island, 517 U.S. 484 (1996) Rhode Island prohibited the advertising of liquor prices asserting the measure was designed to discourage consumption by preventing sales and other methods of price competition. Justice Stevens writing for Justices Kennedy and Ginsburg, held that where a state prohibits truthful speech about a lawful activity, the justification for the regulation must be evaluated in accordance with a stricter standard of review noting that:

> [B]ans that target truthful, nonmisleading commercial messages rarely protect consumers from such harms. Instead, such bans often serve

only to obscure an "underlying governmental policy" that could be implemented without regulating speech. In this way, these commercial speech bans not only hinder consumer choice, but also impede debate over central issues of public policy.

Justice O'Connor writing for the Chief Justice and Justices Breyer and Souter found the Rhode Island statute unconstitutional under *Central Hudson*. Justice Thomas argued that any attempt to prohibit truthful speech about a lawful activity is invalid. Justice Scalia concurred in the judgment.

3. [3]In Glickman v. Wileman Brothers & Elliott, Inc., 117 S.Ct. 2130 (1997) the Court in a 5-4 vote upheld an agricultural marketing order that required all California fruit growers to pay an assessment for generic advertising promoting California fruit. One producer argued this forced payment for speech violated the First Amendment. The majority found that the regulation did not prohibit a producer from communicating any message, did not compel persons to engage in actual or symbolic speech, and did not compel the producers to endorse political or ideological viewpoints. An assessment for speech is valid as long as it is for speech germane to the lawful objectives of the collective and is not ideological. *Glickman* was distinguished from cases such as Keller v. State Bar of Cal., 496 U.S. 1(1990) holding that an integrated bar association could not require an assessment of members for ideological activities not "germane" to the purpose for which compelled association is justified. Justices Souter and the Chief Justice found the regulation in *Glickman* failed the *Central Hudson* test while Justice Thomas, now joined by Justice Scalia, argued that truthful commercial speech should receive the same degree of protection as any other speech.

4. Presumably, the First Amendment prohibits governmental regulation of "false or deceptive" political speech. How does the First Amendment affect the regulation of false or deceptive commercial advertising? Is the *Friedman* case still good law? Does Justice Powell convince you that a trade name is "a significantly different form of commercial speech" from advertised prices? Do either convey information unless attached to underlying goods or services? Can advertised prices be used deceptively? Consider bait and switch schemes or the relevance of the automobile sticker price to the price likely to be paid by a consumer.

5. [3]Federal preemption of state regulations has played an increasingly important role in the regulation of commercial activity including speech. In Morales v. Trans World Airlines, Inc., 504 U.S. 374 (1992) the Court held that the Federal Airline Deregulation Act which prohibited states from enforcing any law "relating to rates, routes, or services" invalidated state regulations of the content and format of airline advertising because it would have a significant affect on rates. In Wolens v. American Airlines, Inc., 513 U.S. 219 (1995), the plaintiff sued American Airlines seeking money damages for breach of contract and violation of the Illinois Consumer Fraud Act based on American's retroactive change in the criteria for use of its frequent flier miles. The Court found the claim under the Consumer Fraud Act preempted but allowed the breach of contract claim to proceed.

We do not read the ADA's preemption clause, however, to shelter airlines from suits alleging no violation of state-imposed obligations, but seeking recovery solely for the airline's alleged breach of its own, self-imposed undertakings. * * * A remedy confined to a contract's terms simply holds parties to their agreements—in this instance, to business judgments an airline made public about its rates and services.

6. The preemptive effect of Federal advertising regulation can become a significant issue in personal injury litigation. In Cipollone v. Liggett Group, Inc., 505 U.S. 504 (1992) the plaintiff sought recovery for personal injuries allegedly caused by cigarette smoking. The claims involved failure to warn, breach of express warranty, and fraudulent misrepresentation. The defendant cigarette manufacturers argued these causes of action were preempted by (1) the 1965 federal statute mandating warnings on cigarette packages which preempted the imposition of any other statement relating to smoking and health, and (2) the 1969 federal statute which prohibited any other "requirement or prohibition based on smoking and health . . . with respect to the advertising or promotion of cigarettes . . . ." A majority of the Court held the 1965 statute did not preempt tort claims for personal injury but merely prohibited state imposition of a different "statement" on cigarette packages.   Justice Stevens in an opinion for four Justices held the 1969 statute preempted claims based on failure to warn and fraudulent misrepresentations based on advertising but not express warranty claims. Two other Justices argued the 1969 statute preempted all claims. See also Shaw v. Dow Brands, Inc., 994 F.2d 364 (7th Cir. 1993) holding the preemption clause of the Federal Insecticide, Fungicide and Rodenticide Act which prohibited any state "requirements for labeling or packaging in addition to or different from those required [by the Act]" preempted a personal injury claim based on strict liability and negligence for injuries caused by inhalation of a regulated substance.

The Economics of Advertising

The debate on the impact of advertising stems primarily from disagreement on its role in the economy. One view asserts that advertising simply provides the consuming public with information necessary to make market decisions. Under this view consumers retain control of the kind and quality of goods produced by exercising an informed choice in purchasing decisions. Viewed as information commercial speech takes on an emotionally neutral mask, and, if one of the values of the First Amendment is to reduce ignorance and to seek truth then this type of information is both worthy and entitled to dissemination. From an economic perspective, the informational content of advertising promotes efficiency and should be encouraged.

The critics of advertising, on the other hand, minimize the informational value of commercial advertising, arguing that its major role is not to inform but to persuade. Under this view, the advertiser acquires power—the psychological power to dictate the tastes and wants of consumers and the economic power to escape the rigors of a competitive market. Resources expended to acquire this power are thought to represent waste. Henry Simon, an avowed libertarian economist, wrote:

It is a commonplace that our vaunted efficiency in production is dissipated extravagantly in the wastes of merchandising. This economic system is one which offers rewards, both to those who direct resources into industries where the indirect pecuniary demand is greatest and to those who divert pecuniary demand to commodities which they happened to be producing. Profits may be obtained either by producing what consumers want or by making consumers want what one is actually producing. The possibility of profitably utilizing resources to manipulate demand is, perhaps, the greatest source of diseconomy under the existing system. If present tendencies continue, we may soon reach a situation where most of our resources are utilized in persuading people to buy one thing rather than another, and only a minor fraction is actually employed in creating things to be bought. Simons, Economic Policy for a Free Society, (1948) p. 71.

If one thinks that advertising is largely a waste of resources, one is encouraged, or at least not restrained, to make the legal requirements for its use complex and demanding. These requirements will raise the costs of advertising and reduce the amount accordingly. Viewed as a manipulative technique, it is easier to construct a societal interest in regulating the scope and content of commercial messages. Conversely if one thinks that advertising provides information and promotes efficiency one is likely to approach regulation of commercial speech with the same skepticism as one approaches regulation of political speech.

One of the difficulties in reviewing the economic impact of advertising is that the subject matter encompasses widely disparate phenomena. Commercial speech includes a range of media from the classified section of a newspaper to the commercial message on television to the front yard "for sale" sign. Presumably the promotional activities of the showroom salesman and the label on the product are also included. And advertising impacts on a variety of different purchasing decisions—from an impulsive purchase of a candy bar to the deliberate acquisition of a new automobile.

The economic case against advertising emanates primarily from Chamberlain, The Theory of Monopolistic Competition (5th ed. 1946); Bain, Barriers to New Competition (1956); Bain, Industrial Organization (1968). Advertising allows a merchant to differentiate his product from those of other producers. To the extent that consumer preference values this differentiation, the advertiser can raise his price above competing producers. This gives the advertiser some control over price, as distinguished from the producer in a purely competitive market who cannot raise his price above the market. This differentiation has monopoly characteristics—to the extent a consumer wants a "George's Pizza" as distinguished from any other pizza, he has only a single source of supply.

Professor Bain argues in addition that product differentiation also serves as a barrier to the entry of new firms into a market and to that extent detracts from a competitive model. As he states it:

The established firms in an industry may enjoy a product-differentiation advantage over potential entrants because of the preference of buyers for the products of established firms over new ones. If so, any potential entrant may be unable to secure a selling price as high (relative to average costs) as established firms can when selling their products in competition with the entrant.

The resulting disadvantage to the entrant can be reflected in three alternative ways. First, it may be that established firms can charge prices above minimal average costs and the competing entrant would be able to charge only a lower price that does not cover his average costs. Second, it is possible that to secure a comparably favorable price, the entrant would have to incur sales-promotion costs per unit of output greater than those of established firms, again having average costs greater than his price. Finally, even if neither of these disadvantages is incurred so long as the entrant supplies a limited fraction of the market, he might be unable, at comparable prices and selling costs, to secure a sufficiently large market share to enable him to support an economically large production and distribution organization. Excluded from realizing available economies of large scale production and distribution, he might again find his average costs above his selling price, even though established firms were receiving prices in excess of minimal average costs. Bain, Industrial Organization, 255–56 (1968).

Proponents of limited trademark protection have used Chamberlain's and Bain's theories. See Brown, Advertising and the Public Interest: Legal Protection of Trade Symbols, 57 Yale L.J. 1165 (1948); Muellen, Sources of Monopoly Powers: A Phenomenon Called "Product Differentiation", 18 Amer.U.L.Rev. 1 (1968); Alexander, Honesty and Competition (1965). Comanor and Wilson, Advertising and Market Power (1974), is an ambitious statistical study that finds evidence that industries with high rates of advertising enjoy higher profitability, among other things. The authors read the evidence as supportive of the barrier to entry hypothesis.

The opponents of advertising also deplore the "waste" of resources devoted to changing the tastes and wants of consumers. This assumes, of course, that changing tastes is bad, per se, or that the change resulting from advertising is in the wrong direction. See Galbraith, The New Industrial State (1967). But see, Nelson, The Economic Consequences of Advertising, 48 J.Bus. 213 (1975) ("We economists have no theory of taste changes, so this approach leads to no behavioral predictions.") and Coase, Advertising and Free Speech, 6 J.Leg. Studies 1, 11 (1977) ("It is not easy to gauge the effect of advertising on taste, in part because it is obviously not great, but judging by the emphasis in advertisements on convenience, cleanliness, and beauty, such effect as it has is presumably generally in the right direction."). See also J. Simon, Issues in the Economics of Advertising 205–206 (1970) discounting the extent to which advertising affects a consumer's propensity to consume rather than to save.

A second line of analysis, first developed in George J. Stigler, The Economics of Information, 69 J. of Pol.Econ. 213 (1961), reprinted in George J. Stigler, The Organization of Industry (1968), has argued that advertising is primarily informative and contributes to efficiency. Stigler's analysis is built around a simple and admittedly atypical case: a market of undifferentiated products emanating from numerous sellers with different prices. The problem for the buyer is to find the correct price at which to buy. You might think that the answer is obvious: the lowest. But it is not. Assume that a buyer finds a seller and, inquiring of his price, is told it is twenty-five dollars. What does the buyer do? He must weigh the expected gain from finding a seller with a lower price against the costs to him in time and travel of further search. His decision whether to accept or engage in further search will be determined by his estimate of the likely dispersion of prices, the relation of the price asked to his estimate of the averages and ranges of that dispersion, and of his own costs of further search. If he thinks the price dispersion small (and hence any gain from further search small) and the price quoted in the lower part of the range, he will tend to accept. If his costs of further search are high (requiring, for instance, a long car ride) he will tend to accept. If he thinks them low (requiring perhaps, only a few more phone calls) he will tend to search further.

The advertising of prices lowers the buyer's cost of search. The advertising communicates to him information about the market that he would otherwise have to acquire through his own search costs. The seller is providing a service to the buyer, which reduces the real cost of the purchase to him because the real cost of the purchase is the cost of the product plus the cost of the search for the right price. The buyer may be willing to pay a higher price for an advertised product because the advertised product may in real terms, when search costs are considered, be cheaper. It is this consumer willingness to pay more that makes advertising profitable for the seller.

Stigler's approach views the consumer as needing not one, but two, products—the thing he wants to buy and information about the price at which he can purchase. More generally, the consumer has a demand for utility satisfying products and services and a demand for information about what may satisfy those utilities. Every transaction can be viewed as the sale of a product or service and the provision of information about that product. The resources necessary to produce that information will be provided by both the seller and the buyer. The seller will have to hold himself out for business, offer descriptions or samples of the product, and perhaps, depending on the product, provide additional information. The buyer will have to take the time to identify sellers in the market and learn something about the relative quality of their goods and prices. The extent to which the seller provides the resources as compared to the buyer will be determined by their relative efficiency in providing the information. The seller has many advantages—he is constantly in the market, he knows the product intimately, and he will know much about the previous (and hence about likely future) buyers of his product. The seller who reaches his prospect in his living room easy chair with a brief interruption of an entertainment program reduces the costs the prospect must incur to learn about the products.

A notable trend during the period of the trademark cases in this book—approximately 1850 to the present—has been the emergence of goods marketed with national trademarks and advertising and a reduction in the expenses and hence price markups of retail merchants. The modern supermarket with its branded and advertised products is able to function with a relatively low labor cost (as a percentage of sales) because consumers arrive at the store themselves equipped to pick out what they will buy. In this process, expenditures for advertising have reduced both the costs of buyers in obtaining comparative product information and the costs of retailers in acquiring and distributing the information. This has produced a less costly distribution system. The emergence of a strong national law of trademarks has paralleled this development. It will be interesting to see whether the last preserves of the non-branded supermarket product—the produce and meat departments—will survive. Already there are incursions.

One might argue, however, that much of advertising contains little perceptible information. What is the informational content of a television commercial depicting the magical appearance of a crown on the head of a taster of margarine, or the evaluations of the relative merits of automatic coffee makers by a former sports figure, or the demonstration that a particular brand of shaving cream can shave sandpaper? The most extensive analysis of advertising's informational role has been by Phillip Nelson: The Economic Consequences of Advertising, 48 J.Bus. 213 (1975); Advertising as Information, 82 J.Pol.Econ. 729 (1974); The Economic Value of Advertising in Advertising and Society (Brozen ed. 1974); Information and Consumer Behavior, 78 J.Pol.Econ. 311 (1970).

Nelson divides goods into "search" goods and "experience" goods. Search goods are those in which most of the information relevant to the purchasing decision can be acquired by examining the product itself prior to purchase. Experience goods are those for which the relevant qualities are not observable—the life expectancy of a television set, the taste of a can of tuna, or the skills of a lawyer. It would be expected that regarding search goods, advertising would be objective and readily informative since the consumer can determine the accuracy of the advertisement prior to purchase. No amount of advertisement will persuade a consumer that a two wheel bicycle is really a tricycle. With regard to experience goods, Nelson contends that the basic information a consumer gains from advertising is the fact that a given seller advertises: "Their [advertisements for experience goods] total informational role—beyond the relation of brand to function—is simply contained in their existence. The consumer believes that the more a brand advertises the more likely it is to be a better buy. In consequence, the more advertisements of a brand the consumer encounters and remembers, the more likely he is to try the brand." Nelson, The Economic Value of Advertising, supra at 50. Nelson suggests that this

reaction to advertising is not irrational since "advertised brands are better
* * *. Simply put, it pays to advertise winners rather than losers." The
seller who has the incentive to advertise the most is the seller who satisfies
the highest percentage of the consumers who examine or try the product.

Consider the situation of a customer who wishes to select a product and
a price from the array of products and prices confronting him. How should
he proceed? The consumer must have a strategy for sampling the available
goods. His strategy must give him guidance on two questions: what to search
or sample first, second, and so on; and how to know when to stop. The heart
of Nelson's approach is the assumption that consumer tastes tend to cluster
around a mean, and that therefore the best search strategy (assuming no
other information) is to start at the mean. In other words, the best working
rule (until disproved by experience) is that the consumer will want what
most other consumers want. Advertising makes the use of this rule cheaper
for the consumer because the consumer's rough sense of the relative frequency of advertising is his cheapest guide to where that mean lies.

Why is advertising a good guide to the mean? Advertising pays only to
the extent that it results in sales. The advertiser of a product whose qualities are not satisfactory will experience a rapid drop off in repeat customers.
You may buy that supposedly great tasting mouthwash once, but not twice.
The advertiser of the product that satisfies a high percentage of customers
will obtain a string of repeat purchases from a single ad, but the advertiser
of the unsatisfactory product will not. The advertiser of the satisfactory
product will obtain a higher return from each dollar expenditure of advertising than the seller of the unsatisfactory product, and will, therefore,
advertise more. This force will, over time, make the frequency of advertising a reliable guide to the mean, and hence a reliable guide to an efficient
search process.

Thus viewed, much that has bothered economists and others about
advertising becomes explicable. Sellers are clamoring for our attention so
that we might perceive their relative importance in the market. The super-
star testimonial, the slogans, and the demonstrations are not really
designed to persuade us of anything. Rather, they are designed to capture
our attention and a bit of our memory, much as we might find it easier to
remember Mr. Perlman's name if, upon introduction, we paused to think of
an oyster.

The real life consumer, of course, does not start the search without any
information. He may know much about his own preferences—and indeed
that in many product areas he prefers to purchase goods with characteristics
quite different from the mean—think for instance of clothing, jewelry, furniture, and art. But how does he find a seller who purveys to his special tastes?
Why not start with the seller whose advertising he likes? The analysis does
not mean that because Sears advertises hardware supplies extensively
everyone will start the search at Sears. A buyer may prefer a neighborhood
store, or a seller aiming at the professional, not the do-it-yourself market,
and start his search elsewhere. And of course there are many other consumer

strategies that do not rely on advertising—the observation of the behavior of others, inquiries of friends who have already searched, and so on.

Nelson uses his analysis to explore a number of interesting questions about advertising. He predicts that the amount of advertising space dedicated to goods whose qualities are principally experience would exceed that dedicated to goods whose qualities are principally search. He makes the prediction on the ground that search information can be communicated in words while superior experience qualities can only be effectively communicated by leaving the consumer with an impression of a higher advertising intensity. The first takes words, the second space. An analysis of advertising in *New Yorker* magazine in 1965 led him to the finding that as the volume of advertising by brand increased, the physical size of the advertisements increased more for experience than for search goods. 82 J.Pol.Econ. at 740–43, supra.

Nelson used his analysis to explore other interesting questions. Why are advertising expenditures per sales dollar higher for small, repeat purchase non-durables than for large durables? Id. at 747–49. Will *Consumer Reports* report more on experience goods or search goods? 78 J.Pol.Econ. at 321–323, supra. Will sellers of search goods tend to cluster more than sellers of experience goods? Id. at 323–325. And what is the impact of advertising on industry structure. 48 J.Bus. at 213, supra.

Neither Stigler nor Nelson provide direct quantitative estimates of the relative importance of advertising for consumer welfare. Are the effects trivial or significant? That question was illuminated in Lee Benham, The Effect of Advertising on the Price of Eyeglasses, 15 J. of Law & Econ. 337 (1972). As its use by the United States Supreme Court in *Bates* and *Virginia Pharmacy* attests, the article has had an unusual impact on public policy, partly because its results were replicated in a series of studies undertaken by the Federal Trade Commission. Benham's study made use of the fact that some states— as part of the regulation of the "profession" of eyeglass dispensing— prohibited advertising of the service. He was able to obtain data providing the actual purchase price of eyeglasses in all states—both those that permitted advertising and those that did not. He found that the mean price paid for a pair of eyeglasses in states with complete restrictions was $33.04 and in states with no advertising restrictions was $26.34. Table I. 15 J. of Law & Econ. 342. In other words, consumers saved $6.70 (or 25%) a pair from advertising.

Neither the direction nor magnitude of this difference is predicted by the Stigler-Nelson analysis. That theory only predicted that the consumer would be better off with advertising net of price and search costs. Even if the price were higher, the consumer would be better off because his search cost would be less by more than the higher price. But the Benham results suggest that advertising has a second effect. Because search costs are lower, consumers search more, and this added search (in terms of useful information obtained) makes competition more effective. For instance, if it is cheaper for the consumer to search, he will search more firms, and thus more firms will effectively be in the market. This increased competition will put more pressure on firms to be efficient, and the overall cost structure of the industry will be affected. Thus Benham found that in states that permitted advertising, commercial sellers had a relatively larger, and eye doctors a relatively smaller, share of the eyeglass market. Table 4, Id. at 351.

Two works conclude that advertising tends to stimulate rather than inhibit competition. J. Simon, Issues in the Economics of Advertising (1970) and J. Lambing, Advertising, Competition and Market Conduct in Oligopoly Over Time (1976). The latter is an econometric analysis of advertising in nine Western European countries using 16 product classes, 170 brands, and a 10-year observation period. Both works contain extensive and useful bibliographies. A more recent review of the economic literature concludes that advertising "has both pro-and anti-competitive influences and there is much left to understand about its role within the competitive process." Andy Bearne, The Economics of Advertising: A Reappraisal, 1 Econ. Issues 23 (Mar. 1996).

CHAPTER 2

DECEPTIVE PRACTICES

A. Competitors' Remedies
(1) False Advertising at Common Law

Ely-Norris Safe Co. v. Mosler Safe Co.

United States Circuit Court of Appeals, Second Circuit, 1925.
7 F.2d 603.

Suit in equity by the Ely-Norris Safe Company against the Mosler Safe Company. From decree of dismissal, plaintiff appeals. Reversed.

The jurisdiction of the District Court depended upon diverse citizenship, and the suit was for unfair competition. The bill alleged that the plaintiff manufactured and sold safes under certain letters patent, which had as their distinctive feature an explosion chamber, designed for protection against burglars. Before the acts complained of, no one but the plaintiff had ever made or sold safes with such chambers, and, except for the defendant's infringement, the plaintiff has remained the only manufacturer and seller of such safes. By reason of the plaintiff's efforts the public has come to recognize the value of the explosion chamber and to wish to purchase safes containing them. Besides infringing the patent, the defendant has manufactured and sold safes without a chamber, but with a metal band around the door, in the same place where the plaintiff put the chamber, and has falsely told its customers that this band was employed to cover and close an explosion chamber. Customers have been thus led to buy safes upon the faith of the representation, who in fact wished to buy safes with explosion chambers, and would have done so, but for the deceit.

The bill prayed an injunction against selling safes with such metal bands, and against representing that any of its safes contained an explosion chamber. From the plaintiff's answers to interrogatories it appeared that all the defendant's safes bore the defendant's name and address, and were sold as its own. Furthermore, that the defendant never gave a customer reason to suppose that any safe sold by it was made by the plaintiff.

Before HOUGH, MANTON, and HAND, CIRCUIT JUDGES.

■ HAND, CIRCUIT JUDGE (after stating the facts as above). This case is not the same as that before Mr. Justice Bradley in New York & Rosendale Co. v. Coplay Cement Co. (C.C.) 44 F. 277, 10 L.R.A. 833. The plaintiffs there manufactured cement at Rosendale, N.Y., but it did not appear that they were the only persons making cement at that place. There was no reason,

65

therefore, to assume that a customer of the defendant, deceived as to the place of origin of the defendant's cement, and desiring to buy only such cement, would have bought of the plaintiffs. It resulted that the plaintiffs did not show any necessary loss of trade through the defendant's fraud upon its own customers. We agree that some of the language of the opinion goes further, but it was not necessary for the disposition of the case.

American Washboard Co. v. Saginaw Mfg. Co., 103 F. 281 (C.C.A.6), 43 C.C.A. 233, 50 L.R.A. 609, was, however, a case in substance like that at bar, because there the plaintiff alleged that it had acquired the entire output of sheet aluminum suitable for washboards. It necessarily followed that the plaintiff had a practical monopoly of this metal for the articles in question, and from this it was a fair inference that any customer of the defendant, who was deceived into buying as an aluminum washboard one which was not such, was a presumptive customer of the plaintiff, who had therefore lost a bargain. This was held, however, not to constitute a private wrong, and so the bill was dismissed.

* * *

We must concede, therefore, that on the cases as they stand the law is with the defendant, and the especially high authority of the court which decided American Washboard Co. v. Saginaw Mfg. Co., supra, makes us hesitate to differ from their conclusion. Yet there is no part of the law which is more plastic than unfair competition, and what was not reckoned an actionable wrong 25 years ago may have become such today. We find it impossible to deny the strength of the plaintiff's case on the allegations of its bill. As we view it, the question is, as it always is in such cases, one of fact. While a competitor may, generally speaking, take away all the customers of another that he can, there are means which he must not use. One of these is deceit. The false use of another's name as maker or source of his own goods is deceit, of which the false use of geographical or descriptive terms is only one example. But we conceive that in the end the questions which arise are always two: Has the plaintiff in fact lost customers? And has he lost them by means which the law forbids? The false use of the plaintiff's name is only an instance in which each element is clearly shown.

In the case at bar the means are as plainly unlawful as in the usual case of palming off. It is as unlawful to lie about the quality of one's wares as about their maker; it equally subjects the seller to action by the buyer. * * * The reason, as we think, why such deceits have not been regarded as actionable by a competitor, depends only upon his inability to show any injury for which there is a known remedy. In an open market it is generally impossible to prove that a customer, whom the defendant has secured by falsely describing his goods, would have bought of the plaintiff, if the defendant had been truthful. Without that, the plaintiff, though aggrieved in company with other honest traders, cannot show any ascertainable loss. He may not recover at law, and the equitable remedy is concurrent. The law does not allow him to sue as a vicarious avenger of the defendant's customers.

But, if it be true that the plaintiff has a monopoly of the kind of wares concerned, and if to secure a customer the defendant must represent his own as of that kind, it is a fair inference that the customer wants those and those only. Had he not supposed that the defendant could supply him, presumably he would have gone to the plaintiff, who alone could. At least, if the plaintiff can prove that in fact he would, he shows a direct loss, measured by his profits on the putative sale. If a tradesman falsely foists on a customer a substitute for what the plaintiff alone can supply, it can scarcely be that the plaintiff is without remedy, if he can show that the customer would certainly have come to him, had the truth been told.

Yet that is in substance the situation which this bill presents. It says that the plaintiff alone could lawfully make such safes, and that the defendant has sold others to customers who asked for the patented kind. It can make no difference that the defendant sold them as its own. The sale by hypothesis depended upon the structure of the safes, not on their maker. To be satisfied, the customer must in fact have gone to the plaintiff, or the defendant must have infringed. Had he infringed, the plaintiff could have recovered his profit on the sale; had the customer gone to him, he would have made that profit. Any possibilities that the customers might not have gone to the plaintiff, had they been told the truth, are foreclosed by the allegation that the plaintiff in fact lost the sales. It seems to us * * * that if this can be proved, a private suit will lie.

Decree reversed.

Mosler Safe Co. v. Ely-Norris Safe Co.

Supreme Court of the United States, 1927.
273 U.S. 132, 47 S.Ct. 314, 71 L.Ed. 578.

■ MR. JUSTICE HOLMES delivered the opinion of the Court.

* * *

At the hearing below all attention seems to have been concentrated on the question passed upon and the forcibly stated reasons that induced this Court of Appeals to differ from that for the Sixth Circuit. But, upon a closer scrutiny of the bill than seems to have been invited before, it does not present that broad and interesting issue. The bill alleges that the plaintiff has a patent for an explosion chamber as described and claimed in said Letters Patent; that it has the exclusive right to make and sell safes containing such an explosion chamber; that no other safes containing such an explosion chamber could be got in the United States before the defendant, as it is alleged, infringed the plaintiff's patent, for which alleged infringement a suit is pending. It then is alleged that the defendant is making and selling safes with a metal band around the door at substantially the same location as the explosion chamber of plaintiff's safes, and has represented to the public that the said metal band was employed to cover or close an explosion chamber by reason of which the public has been led to purchase defendant's said safes as and for safes containing an explosion chamber, such as is manufactured and sold by the plaintiff herein. It is alleged further that sometimes the defendant's safes have no explosion chamber under the band but are bought by those who want safes with a chamber and so the defendant has deprived the plaintiff of sales, competed unfairly and damaged the plaintiff's reputation. The plaintiff relies upon its patent suit for relief in respect of the sales of safes alleged to infringe its rights. It complains here only of false representations as to safes that do not infringe but that are sold as having explosion chambers although in fact they do not.

It is consistent with every allegation in the bill and the defendant in argument asserted it to be a fact, that there are other safes with explosion chambers beside that for which the plaintiff has a patent. The defendant is charged only with representing that its safes had an explosion chamber, which, so far as appears, it had a perfect right to do if the representation was true. If on the other hand the representation was false as it is alleged sometimes to have been, there is nothing to show that customers had they known the facts would have gone to the plaintiff rather than to other competitors in the market, or to lay a foundation for the claim for a loss of sales. The bill is so framed as to seem to invite the decision that was obtained from the Circuit Court of Appeals, but when scrutinized is seen to have so limited its statements as to exclude the right to complain.

Decree reversed.

NOTES

1. In American Washboard Co. v. Saginaw Mfg. Co., 103 Fed. 281 (6th Cir.1900) the defendant sold a washboard purporting to have a rubbing face of aluminum but which in fact was made of zinc. Plaintiff was the only manufacturer of a genuine aluminum washboard. The Sixth Circuit upheld a lower court demurrer. It held that the complaint did not allege "passing off" of the defendant's washboard as that of the plaintiff and was therefore deficient.

> It [the complaint in analogizing to the passing off cases] loses sight of the thoroughly established principle that the private right of action in such cases is not based upon fraud or imposition upon the public, but is maintained solely for the protection of the property rights of complainant. It is true that in these cases it is an important factor that the public are deceived, but it is only where this deception induces the public to buy the goods as those of complainant that a private right of action arises * * *. It is doubtless morally wrong and improper to impose upon the public by the sale of spurious goods, but this does not give rise to a private right of action unless the property rights of the plaintiff are thereby invaded. There are many wrongs which can only be righted through public prosecution, and for which the legislature, and not the courts, must provide a remedy.

If plaintiff has a monopoly on aluminum washboards, should the court presume an infringement of its property rights? Must there be a showing that consumers prefer aluminum washboards?

2. The defendant produces flour in Chicago but falsely advertises its flour as coming from Minneapolis. Could various flour mills actually located in Minneapolis sue the defendant for false advertising? Must the plaintiffs demonstrate that flour from Minneapolis had a reputation for quality valued by consumers? Would the plaintiffs be aided if they could get all of the flour producers in Minneapolis to join as plaintiffs? Could one Minneapolis flour mill bring a class action on behalf of all other similarly situated flour mills? See Pillsbury-Washburn Flour Mills Co. v. Eagle, 86 Fed. 608 (7th Cir.1898), cert. denied 173 U.S. 703 (1899) (action permitted by some flour mills on showing that Minneapolis flour had a reputation of high quality); Grand Rapids Furniture Co. v. Grand Rapids Furniture Co., 127 F.2d 245 (7th Cir.1942)(action permitted under similar circumstances as a class action). But see, California Apparel Creators v. Wieder of California, 162 F.2d 893 (2d Cir.1947) (action not allowed where 75 of 4500 California swimwear producers sued New York producer of "California swimwear" in a class action and no evidence demonstrated consumers attached any significance to "California" when associated with swimwear."

3. Could a company with the name "California Sportswear Co." obtain an injunction against a New York swimwear producer calling itself "California Sportswear Incorporated"?

4. *The Position of the American Law Institute.* The efforts of the American Law Institute to restate the law of false advertising are instructive. The first edition of the Restatement of Torts published in 1939 contained the following provision:

§ 761. False Advertising—Liability to Competitor

One who diverts trade from a competitor by fraudulently representing that the goods which he markets have ingredients or qualities which in fact they do not have but which the goods of the competitor do have is liable to the competitor for the harm so caused, if,

(a) when making the representation he intends that it should, or knows or should know that it is likely to, divert trade from the competitor, and

(b) the competitor is not marketing his goods with material fraudulent misrepresentations about them.

When the proposed section was before the Institute, opponents argued that the section extended *Mosler* to allow any competitor to sue regardless of whether it was a monopolist. Judge Hand, in defending the proposal, reminded the Institute that the language "One who diverts trade" imposes on the plaintiff in the case "what is ordinarily an insuperable objection, how can he prove that the goods which sold by the defendant diverted trade from him if there are a number of people who are engaged in that particular business." Noting that "under modern procedure * * * you can gather into one suit all the persons who would be affected whose trade collectively could be damaged and, therefore, has been damaged," Hand argued that the section required plaintiffs "show, as the text reads, that they have lost the bargain and it is difficult for me to see how that differs from any other case when by improper means a customer has been diverted." A motion to strike the entire section was defeated 37 to 51. The following day a motion to reconsider that action was defeated 55 to 70. 16 ALI Proceedings 130 (1938–39).

In 1963, the Institute reviewed a proposed revision which, read: "One falsely markets goods or services * * * if, in the marketing process, he makes any material false representation which is likely to induce persons to purchase, to the commercial detriment of another, the goods or services which he markets." Restatement, Second, Torts § 712 (Tent.Draft No. 8, 1963). The tentative draft was approved on condition the commentary reflect that the section may go slightly beyond the reported decisions. 40 ALI Proceedings 152 (1963). Causing particular difficulty in the debate was the meaning of "commercial detriment" and the appropriateness of an illustration which read: "A manufactures solid walnut furniture. B, a competitor, manufacturers veneer furniture which he falsely represents to be solid walnut. B is subject to liability to A." Illus. No. 9.

A similar hypothetical bothered the Institute during debate on the 1939 provision:

> Mr. Shulman: . . . when a merchant falsely advertises that furniture, for example, is solid mahogany and it turns out to be mahogany veneer, the reputation of solid mahogany furniture is destroyed in the market and dealers who sell solid mahogany furniture are injured in exactly the same way under these circumstances as in the other case [passing off].

> Judge Tuttle: I cannot agree with that argument because the reason they are going to be dissatisfied is that they have found out that what they bought from that chap was not solid mahogany and he is the one who risks his reputation and it is not injuring the reputation of solid mahogany at all.

16 ALI Proceedings 135 (1938–1939).

If Illustration No. 9 is the law, would there be a different result in the following case: A manufactures veneer walnut furniture. B, a competitor, manufactures veneer furniture which he falsely represents to be solid walnut. A sues B?

The debate in 1963, however informative, proved futile. The American Law Institute removed all sections relating to unfair competition from the final version of the Restatement, Second, Torts.

In 1995 the ALI published the Restatement, Third, of Unfair Competition, § 2 of which provides: "One who, in connection with the marketing of goods or services, makes a representation relating to the actor's own goods, services, or commercial activities, that is likely to deceive or mislead prospective purchasers to the likely commercial detriment of another is subject to liability to the other. . . ." There is a "likely commercial detriment" when a representation is "material" and there is a "reasonable basis for believing that the representation has caused or is likely to cause a diversion of trade from the other or harm to the other's reputation or good will." Id. at § 3. Does this draft go beyond the common law?

5. Why does the common law appear to be reluctant to give competitors a remedy for false advertising? If the advertisement is false and capable of misleading consumers, why should it matter that the competitor cannot show direct injury? Isn't the public better off if competitors were able to at least obtain an injunction against the false statements?

6. Consider 35 U.S.C. § 292. The statute prohibits false indications that a product is patented and provides a fine of $500 for each offense. Subsection (b) allows "any person" to sue for the penalty, half of which is retained by the person bringing the action.

7. What action, short of further litigation, should Ely-Norris now take? Should it advertise to inform potential customers that Mosler's safes do not have explosion chambers? What are the incentives and disincentives operating on that decision? Does it make a difference if Ely-Norris is the only producer of genuine explosion chamber safes? What if an explosion chamber is not worth what it costs? What if only a very few consumers base their decision between competing safes on the presence of an explosion chamber? Are you convinced by the argument that competition alone will produce truth in advertising without legal intervention?

(2) Disparagement

Early in its history, the common law provided a remedy for false statements attacking the personal integrity and reputation of the plaintiff. The action for personal defamation grew to involve a number of technical distinctions, one of which divided the offending statements into per se defamations and those statements requiring proof of special damages. The question in all of these cases was essentially whether the statements of the defendant had injured the reputation of the plaintiff. Those statements which would obviously cause that result were classified as libel per se or slander per se. In such cases, the plaintiff was entitled to recover damages for the dignitary harm without the necessity of showing actual economic loss. However, in those cases where the statements were such that their injurious effect was in doubt, the plaintiff was required to prove "special damages" as an element of the cause of action. The special damage rule required the plaintiff to show some specific economic harm resulting from the defendant's statement. A further distinction between statements made in writing (libel) and those made orally (slander) was also considered crucial and resulted in differing rules and results.

The developing doctrinal content of personal defamation had an impact on other cases confronting early common law courts. In these cases the statements of the defendant were directed at the property of the plaintiff rather than at the plaintiff's reputation or integrity. For example, the defendant would spread the false rumor that the plaintiff did not have valid title to the property plaintiff was then attempting to sell. Plaintiff would contend that the false statement of the defendant made it difficult to sell the property and required a reduction in the price. It is also easily seen that by implication the defendant's statement also attacked the integrity of the plaintiff by alleging that plaintiff was fraudulently attempting to sell property to which the plaintiff did not have title. The analogy to personal defamation was compelling and around 1600 the common law devised a cause of action for "slander of title" to compensate plaintiff. This action was subsequently extended to protect against statements calling into question the title to personalty and eventually to statements denouncing the quality rather than the title of the plaintiff's property. As the following material will demonstrate, the cause of action for false statements directed against property remains in search of a comfortable name. It has been variously denominated as "slander of title", "trade libel", "disparagement", and "injurious falsehood". The last reference was apparently coined by Sir John Salmond in his treatise on torts and was adopted by the American Law Institute to refer to any false statement harmful to the interests of another. See Restatement, Second, Torts § 623A (1977). "Disparagement" will be utilized in this material as a narrower term used generally to describe injurious falsehoods in a commercial context.

Hurlbut v. Gulf Atlantic Life Insurance Co.

Supreme Court of Texas, 1987
749 S.W.2d 762

■ CAMPBELL, JUSTICE.

[Gulf Atlantic proposed to Hurlbut and Hovater that the latter form a partnership to sell and service group health insurance policies which would be underwritten by Gulf Atlantic. In reliance on Gulf Atlantic's assurances, Hurlbut and Hovater formed "Agency Associates" with start up funds from Gulf Atlantic. To sell group insurance state approval of a master policy was required, but at Gulf's urging, Hurlbut and Hovater began sales without such approval. One purchaser, who was concerned about the inability of Agency Associates to produce a master policy, called William Barnes, the president of Gulf Atlantic, who denied that Gulf Atlantic was underwriting the insurance program. This purchaser called the Attorney General. Hurlbut, however, was again reassured by Barnes that Gulf Atlantic was still underwriting the program and a meeting was held between Hurlbut and Barnes to "straighten out the matter." However, at the meeting in the presence of a representative of the Attorney General's Office, Barnes again said that Hurlbut and Hovater did not have authority to sell group insurance for Gulf Atlantic. Although Hurlbut and Hovater cooperated with the Attorney General, the assets of Agency Associates were placed in receivership, their insurance licenses were revoked, and both were arrested and jailed. Hurlbut and Hovater filed suit against Gulf Atlantic, alleging among other causes, that Barnes made false statements disparaging their business.]

The plaintiffs also obtained favorable jury findings on their claims of business disparagement and tortious interference with contract. In analyzing these claims and the evidence supporting them, the court of appeals concluded that they were in essence a claim for slander and barred by the one year statute of limitations. TEX.REV.CIV.STAT.ANN. Art. 5524(1) (Vernon 1958). We find no reversible error in the judgment of the court of appeals as it pertains to these two claims.

The general elements of a claim for business disparagement are publication by the defendant of the disparaging words, falsity, malice, lack of privilege, and special damages. The tort is part of the body of law concerned with the subject of interference with commercial or economic relations. The Restatement identifies the tort by the name "injurious falsehood" and notes its application "in cases of the disparagement of property in land, chattels, or intangible things or of their quality." Restatement (Second) of Torts § 623A, comment a (1977).

The court of appeals recognizes that an action for injurious falsehood or business disparagement is similar in many respects to an action for defamation. Both involve the imposition of liability for injury sustained through publications to third parties of a false statement affecting the plaintiff. The two torts, however, protect different interests. The action for defamation is to protect the personal reputation of the injured party, whereas the action for injurious falsehood or business disparagement is to protect the economic interests of the injured party against pecuniary loss.

More stringent requirements have always been imposed on the "plaintiff seeking to recover for injurious falsehood in three important respects— falsity of the statement, fault of the defendant and proof of damage." Restatement (Second) of Torts § 623A, comment g (1977). Regarding falsity, the common law presumed the defamatory statement to be false and truth was a defensive matter. The plaintiff in a business disparagement claim, however, must plead and prove the falsity of the statement as part of his cause of action. Regarding fault, the defendant in a defamation action was held strictly liable for his false statement whereas the defendant in an action for business disparagement or injurious falsehood is subject to liability "only if he knew of the falsity or acted with reckless disregard concerning it, or if he acted with ill will or intended to interfere in the economic interest of the plaintiff in an unprivileged fashion." Id. Finally regarding damages, the common law required plaintiff in a defamation action to prove special damages in only a limited number of situations, whereas pecuniary loss to the plaintiff must always be proved to establish a cause of action for business disparagement.

In the present case there is evidence to support findings that the statements of Gulf Atlantic were false and malicious in the sense that Gulf Atlantic knew them to be false. It is, however, with the element of special damages that the plaintiffs have some difficulty.

Proof of special damages is an essential part of the plaintiffs' cause of action for business disparagement. The requirement goes to the cause of action itself and requires that plaintiff "establish pecuniary loss that has been realized or liquidated as in the case of specific lost sales." W. Keeton, Prosser and Keeton on the Law of Torts, § 128 at 971 (5th Ed.1984). Furthermore, the communication must play a substantial part in inducing others not to deal with the plaintiff with the result that special damage, in the form of the loss of trade or other dealings, is established.

Our examination of the record reveals no evidence of the direct, pecuniary loss necessary to satisfy the special damage element of a claim for business disparagement. The court of appeals found no evidence of special injury to the business, writing:

No evidence was offered of damages resulting from loss of business expected from any particular customer or prospective customer to whom disparaging statements were made by defendants. The damages alleged and proved resulted only indirectly from the disparaging statements alleged, and more immediately from the receivership, the orders revoking their licenses, and their prosecution for misappropriation of insurance premiums.

696 S.W.2d at 98–9. In this regard we agree with the Court of Appeals that the damages proven were personal to the plaintiffs.

[The Court also examined the defendant's claim that the false statements made to the Attorney General were absolutely privileged. However, the court found that statements made to public officials outside the context of formal proceedings are only conditionally privileged—that is, privileged unless not made in good faith. The court then held:]

In the context of a tort such as business disparagement or injurious falsehood, only absolute privileges have relevance to the defendant. This is because the tort itself incorporates malice as an element of recovery; hence, if the plaintiff carries his burden, he likewise defeats any conditional privilege.

NOTES

1. A cause of action for product disparagement must be distinguished from personal defamation. The leading case defining the different categories of disparaging speech in this context is National Refining Co. v. Benzo Gas Motor Fuel Co., 20 F.2d 763 (8th Cir.1927), cert. denied 275 U.S. 570 (1927):

(1) Those where, though the alleged libelous statement is made in reference to goods or product, there are also included libelous words in reference to the vendor or producer, which impute to him, in connection with the goods or product, fraud, deceit, dishonesty, or reprehensible business methods. * * * No SPECIAL D REQ'D

(2) Those where the alleged libelous statement is made merely as to the quality of the goods or product of another. In those cases special damage must be alleged and proved, or no recovery can be had. * * *

(3) Those where the alleged libelous statements amount to no more than assertions by one tradesman that his goods are superior to those of his rival. Here no recovery can be had, though the statements are false and malicious, and though special damage is alleged. * * *

In this case, the owner of the only service stations selling Benzo gasoline, a gasoline containing a coal derivative, complained of statements in a pamphlet distributed by the defendant, a seller of White Rose gasoline products. The pamphlet in addition to promoting the benefits of White Rose gasoline, proclaimed that gas with benzo was affirmatively harmful to automobiles, and urged consumers to purchase White Rose, "an honestly made gasoline." The court found the statements to be in category 2 requiring proof of special damages. But see, Tex Smith, The Harmonica Man, Inc. v. Godfrey, 198 Misc. 1006, 102 N.Y.S.2d 251 (1951) where Arthur Godfrey's comment about plaintiff's $2.98 ukulele that "to sell the instrument as a ukulele might not be contrary to law but that people who did it should be jailed" was held to be actionable as a personal defamation.

2. *Puffing.* The Restatement, Second, of Torts § 647 (1977) provides a competitor a conditional privilege to make unfavorable comparisons "if the comparison does not contain false assertions of specific unfavorable facts regarding the rival competitor's things." The puffing rule was applied in Smith-Victor Corp. v. Sylvania Electric Products, Inc., 242 F.Supp. 302, 308 (N.D.Ill.1965) as follows:

> Both parties agree that advertising which merely states in general terms that one product is superior is not actionable. Statements such as "far brighter than any lamp ever before offered for home movies," and "the beam floods an area greater than the coverage of the widest wide angle lens," fall in this category. * * *

> Nevertheless, statements which ascribe absolute qualities to the defendant's product, such as 35,000 candlepower and 10-hour life, could give rise to a legal liability if they were not true. These exceed the traditional bounds of puffing.

Putting aside any potential constitutional issues, why should the seller of goods or services be free to falsely tout his wares with false opinions? Should a seller's opinions about the goods be considered an express warranty to purchasers? Is the marketplace well served by a puffing privilege? See, Preston, The Great American Blow-up: Puffery in Advertising and Selling (1975) arguing that if puffing were prohibited advertisers would provide more information in their advertising. Do you agree?

3. *Intent, Malice and Knowledge of Falsity.* It is widely accepted that a cause of action for product disparagement requires that the defendant intend the statement to result in harm to the interests of another and that the defendant know the disparaging statement is false or act in reckless disregard of its truth. This was not however always the case. An early leading article, Smith, Disparagement of Property, 13 Colum.L.Rev. 13, 121 (1913), concluded that in the absence of privilege, liability would result from innocent and negligent misstatements as well as those which were intentionally uttered to cause harm. Smith's position dramatically influenced the drafters of the first Restatement of Torts which announced liability for unprivileged disparagement regardless of the intent or knowledge of the defendant.

The Restatement, Second, of Torts was heavily influenced by Supreme Court decisions imposing First Amendment limitations on personal defamation actions. The version ultimately adopted reads as follows:

§ 623A. Liability for Publication of Injurious Falsehood—General Principle

One who publishes a false statement harmful to the interests of another is subject to liability for pecuniary loss resulting to the other if

(a) he intends for publication of the statement to result in harm to interests of the other having a pecuniary value, or either recognizes or should recognize that it is likely to do so, and

(b) he knows that the statement is false or acts in reckless disregard of its truth or falsity.

Caveats:

The Institute takes no position on the questions of:

(1) Whether, instead of showing the publisher's knowledge or reckless disregard of the falsity of the statement, as indicated in Clause (b), the other may recover by showing that the publisher had either

(a) a motive of ill will toward him, or

(b) an intent to interfere in an unprivileged manner with his interests; or

(2) Whether either of these alternate bases, if not alone sufficient, would be made sufficient by being combined with a showing of negligence regarding the truth or falsity of the statement.

4. *Special Damages.* In most common law disparagement cases, the plaintiff wins or loses depending on the ability to demonstrate special damages. What is the role of special damages in these cases, particularly considering that we normally do not require such proof for personal defamation? If my competitor says something disparaging about my goods, shouldn't some damage be presumed? How am I to discover those consumers who, on the basis of hearing the disparagement, purchased my competitor's goods instead of mine?

Some modern cases have relaxed the proof necessary to show special damages. In Porous Media Corp. v. Pall Corp., 110 F.3d 1329 (8th Cir. 1997) the court, applying Minnesota law, found the following evidence sufficient:

Porous's claim for special damages was based on lost growth opportunities and specific lost sales. Porous demonstrated that it initially achieved sales growth in the paper/power markets but that its sales plateaued or declined after the disparagement by Pall. In fact, the paper/power markets were the only markets in which Porous failed to achieve significant growth in sales. Porous introduced marketing reports from Pall which claimed that Pall's sales literature, which included false or misleading information about Porous's products, was helpful in competing against companies like Porous and had resulted in regaining some lost sales for Pall. One of Pall's distributors, Bill Brown, testified that his use of Pall's negative literature regarding Porous was helpful in retaining business. Steven Edwards, a salesman for one of Pall's distributors, testified that his use of Pall's comparative literature influenced customers and that a specific customer had switched back to Pall's products from Porous's after reviewing the negative literature. Porous introduced the "Will-Fit Alert," a memo prepared by an employee of Pall, which Porous argued contained false and deceptive comparisons between Porous's and Pall's filters. The memo states that Pall's comparison to Porous's filters caused Consolidated Paper to abandon Porous and use only Pall's filters. Patrick Spearman, a vice president of Porous in charge of marketing, testified that Porous lost a number of specific customers because of Pall's disparaging statements, and that Porous was also unable to approach numerous other potential customers. Spearman and his brother, Michael Spearman, another principal for Porous, were both qualified as experts in the filter industry. They testified that Pall's disparagement was the cause of the harm to Porous and excluded other potential causes for Porous's failure to grow in the paper/power markets. Finally, Porous's expert economist, Dr. Michael Brookshire, testified as to Porous's lost growth opportunity by comparing Porous's sales in the paper/power markets with the geometric average growth rate of Porous's sales in all of its markets, and in the pneumatics and instrumentation markets, which Porous argues are the markets most similar to the paper/power markets.

There are some limitations on the Minnesota rule, however. See Advanced Training Systems, Inc. v. Caswell Equipment Co., Inc., 352 N.W.2d 1 (Minn. 1984):

> It has long been the law that plaintiff may not recover for product disparagement unless plaintiff is able to prove special damages in the form of pecuniary loss directly attributable to defendant's false statements. Where plaintiff cannot show loss of specific sales, the modern view allows plaintiff to prove a general decline of business, so long as this is shown to be the result of defendant's disparaging statements and other possible causes are eliminated. * * *

Plaintiffs make two arguments in support of their contention that they nevertheless proved special damages at trial. First, they argue that ATS suffered pecuniary loss because defendants' disparaging statements prevented the company from growing as fast as it otherwise would have. The company has done quite well despite defendant's campaign, and in fact has captured about 97 percent of the market for portable firearms training equipment. Plaintiffs nevertheless contend that their business would probably have been more successful in its early years had defendant not disparaged their products. This allegation of damage is clearly "too speculative" to meet the requirement that special pecuniary loss in a disparagement case be proved with particularity.

Plaintiffs also argue that Edwin Taylor suffered special pecuniary loss when he expended time and money attempting to counteract defendant's propaganda. Plaintiffs contend that these expenses were reasonably incurred in an effort to mitigate their losses and should have been considered an item of special damage. Taylor may not collect his expenses from defendant, however, unless defendant's conduct was tortious. Efforts to mitigate damages in tort are not compensable unless plaintiff proves a tort, and where special damages are an essential element of plaintiff's action, they must be proved before mitigation expenses may be considered. Plaintiff cannot create a cause of action in disparagement through his own conduct where defendant has otherwise failed to provide him with one.

5. An early New York case, Marlin Firearms co. v. Shields, 171 N.Y. 384, 64 N.E.163 (1902), relying on free speech values and the right to a jury trial, declared that a product disparagement plaintiff, although free to sue for damages, could not enjoin the disparaging statements. This rule was rejected in Black & Yates, Inc. v. Mahogany Ass'n, Inc., 129 F.2d 227 (3d Cir. 1942), the court commenting that the "irrelevance of 'free speech' and of 'a libel is for a jury' are patent. Freedom of discussion of public issues does not demand lack of 'previous restraint' for injury to private individuals. Disparagement of goods presents no confusing or complicated matter of personality requiring the sympathetic attention of one's peers." 129 F.2d at 231. Are you confident that under modern constitutional doctrine, injunctive relief should be available? In *Marlin* the plaintiff manufactured and sold rifles and the defendant published a gun magazine. In *Black & Yates*, the parties were direct competitors. Does it matter whether the defendant is a competitor or a newspaper?

Consider, Organization for a Better Austin v. Keefe, 402 U.S. 415 (1971) (invalidating as a prior restraint a lower court injunction enjoining the defendants, OBA, a racially integrated community association, from distributing leaflets accusing Keefe, a real estate broker, of "panic peddling" and "blockbusting". See also Matter of National Service Corp., 742 F.2d 859 (5th Cir.1984) (invalidating on First Amendment grounds an injunction to prohibit a creditor from superimposing on defendant's billboard advertising plaintiff's company the phrase "Beware, This Company Does Not Pay Its Bills.")

6. Many courts and litigants frustrated by the restricted relief available in disparagement have searched for different rhetoric with some success. In Royer v. Stoody Co., 192 F.Supp. 949 (W.D.Okl.1961), affirmed 374 F.2d 672 (10th Cir.1967), the court held that for an unfair competition claim, the plaintiff must allege and prove the publication complained of was false and was intended to deceive, but that the special damage rule would be inapplicable. ("Even in trade libel cases, the trend is toward doing away with the necessity of alleging special damages.") See also H.E. Allen Mfg. Co., Inc. v. Smith, 224 App.Div. 187, 229 N.Y.S. 692 (1928) which avoided the *Marlin* result by awarding injunctive relief on a claim of unfair competition.

7. *Disparagement by consumers.* Should different rules govern a suit by the seller of a product against a consumer for disparagement? In Menard v. Houle, 298 Mass. 546, 11 N.E.2d 436 (1937) the defendant, unhappy with the automobile he purchased from plaintiff, outfitted the vehicle with signs reading in part "Don't believe what they say, this car is no good; I tried to have it fixed but they can't fix it and they will do nothing about it . . . this car was no good when I got it; don't be a sucker, this car is no good but it looks all right." Apparently, the defendant also tied lemons to the automobile, drove it around the city and left it parked on the public streets. The court granted an injunction though noting that injunctive relief was not normally available in disparagement cases. Compare Willing v. Mazzocone, 482 Pa. 377, 393 A.2d 1155 (1978) where a client of a law firm wearing a "sandwich-board" sign around her neck reading "LAW—FIRM of QUINN— MAZZOCONE *Stole money from me*—and Sold-me-out-to-the INSURANCE

COMPANY", marched back and forth in front of plaintiff's office and periodically rang a cow bell or blew a whistle to attract attention. The Pennsylvania Supreme Court overturned the lower court's injunction as violative of free speech.

8. *Disparagement by independent testing agencies.* Should different rules govern a suit for disparagement by the seller of a product against an independent testing company? An important early case is Advance Music Corp. v. American Tobacco Co., 296 N.Y. 79, 70 N.E.2d 401 (1946). The plaintiff, a music publisher, claimed that the radio program "Hit Parade" which purported to play the top ten songs of the week based on extensive and accurate national surveys, intentionally excluded plaintiff's songs. The first complaint filed by plaintiff based on slander of property was dismissed because it did not allege special damages. The amended complaint alleged and the New York Court of Appeals approved a "prima facie tort" cause of action which makes actionable any "intentional infliction of temporal damages" unless justified by the defendant. *Advance Music* is often cited as the leading case adopting a generalized intentional tort to fill in the gaps between the specialized intentional torts, i.e. libel, assault, etc. What about other independent testing and rating services? Should a lawyer have a claim against Martindale Hubbell for a poor rating in its directory? See Ellsworth v. Martindale-Hubbell Law Directory, Inc., 68 N.D. 425, 280 N.W. 879 (1938); Ellsworth v. Martindale-Hubbell Law Directory, Inc., 69 N.D. 610, 289 N.W. 101 (1939). (plaintiff proved special damages by showing diminution of business but subsequently failed to show that the rating caused the harm).

Kemart Corp. v. Printing Arts Research Lab., Inc.

United States Court of Appeals, Ninth Circuit, 1959.
269 F.2d 375, cert. denied 361 U.S. 893, 80 S.Ct. 197, 4 L.Ed.2d 151.

[Printing Arts held the Marx patent No. 2,191,939 on a photoengraving process. The patentee was the "actual operating head" of Printing Arts. On October 6, 1948, Albert McCaleb, President and Director of Printing Arts, and also their patent attorney, rendered a written opinion to Printing Arts that the process employed and licensed by Kemart was infringing the Marx patent. The written opinion advised that "all users of the Kemart process, insofar as you are able to identify them, be notified of the existence of your aforesaid patent * * * its nature and coverage, and their infringement thereof." On October 7, 1948, Marx displayed the letter to the President of Kemart and other individuals attending the national convention of photoengravers. On November 10, McCaleb sent a letter to Kemart which read in part: "I have now been instructed to institute suit for infringement of the above identified patent against a representative user of the Kemart process, and intend so to do just as soon as certain prerequisite information can be obtained." On November 23, 1948, Kemart instituted a declaratory judgment action to declare its right to use and license the Kemart process without interference from Printing Arts, to declare the Marx patent void, for an injunction precluding Printing Arts from threatening Kemart's licensees with infringement suits, and for damages resulting from Printing Arts' "wrongful acts and doings". On the same day, Kemart sent a letter to its licensees advising them of the litigation and that it had been instituted "for the purpose of protecting you and ourselves against a series of threats by * * * Printing Arts * * * ." The letter also indicated that Printing Arts' threats were false and contrary to fair competition. This letter was subsequently printed in a photoengraving trade journal at the request of Kemart. On March 28, 1949, the lower court denied Kemart a temporary injunction precluding Printing Arts from bringing a patent infringement suit against Kemart's licensees. This fact was subsequently printed in the trade journal at the request of Printing Arts and in addition, that Printing Arts would "when it is legally advisable" bring an action against a licensee.

Kemart received several letters from its licensees during 1949, some canceling their license agreement and others demanding that Kemart take steps to protect them against infringement suits by posting bonds.

In opinions preceding the one reproduced below, the court held that Kemart did not infringe the Printing Arts patents. The remaining issue concerned Kemart's suit for damages against Printing Arts for "unfair competition and trade libel". The lower court found that prior to the litigation Printing Arts reasonably believed its patent valid and infringed, that this belief was based on advice of experienced although interested counsel and not upon careless ascertainment of their rights. The lower court concluded that Ohio law granted a privilege in this situation as a defense to trade libel. Kemart appealed.]

■ BONE, SENIOR JUDGE.

Regardless of the applicable state law, the problem presented by the facts shown here must be handled in essentially the same manner. It is clear from the record (and is not challenged by the parties) that all the publications attributable to Printing Arts were disparaging either to the "person" or the property of Kemart. The lower court found that, with regard to each of these publications, Printing Arts acted without malice in an effort to protect what it reasonably believed to be its valid and existing property rights. These efforts were reasonably calculated to adequately protect its claimed rights without *unnecessary* damage to the parties concerned. In this manner the elements of the defense of privilege were brought into the record. * * *

It is the general rule in the United States that a qualified privilege is recognized in cases where the publisher and the recipient of the publication have a common interest which might be reasonably believed to be protected or furthered by the publication and the publication is made reasonably and in good faith. Though these cases involve disparagements made by an employer concerning an employee, the *privilege* involved is the same as that involved in the instant case. Both Printing Arts (the publisher) and the recipient members of the photoengraving industry attending the convention had an interest (in this case a pecuniary interest) in the subject matter of the publication.

* * *

[The court held that California law applied to one of the publications at issue.] The law of California is clear in respect to privileged publications of claimed defamatory material. Section 47 of the California Civil Code provides:

"A privileged publication or broadcast is one made—

* * *

"3. In a communication, without malice, to a person interested therein, (1) by one who is also interested * * * "

In the instant case, the publisher of the claimed defamation (Printing Arts) is the holder of a competing patent. The recipients of the claimed defamatory publications were the present and the prospective licensees of the here competing patent owners. Both are financially interested in the subject matter of the claimed defamation and thus clearly come within the terms of the stated privilege. It is unnecessary to determine whether the tort involved in the instant case is one for unfair competition or one for libel since the California courts have applied the above statutory privilege to both types of wrongs.

Since the claimed defamations appearing in the Bulletin and the other "trade" journals were privileged, it was necessary for Kemart, in order to prevail, to show "actual malice" as distinguished from malice inferred from the false communication in and of itself. The "actual malice" required to overcome the statutory privilege is to be distinguished from that sometimes inferred from the intentional doing of a wrongful act without justification. In the instant case, the trial court made a specific finding that no such malice existed on the part of Printing Arts and that the said Printing Arts had reasonable cause to believe that its charge of patent infringement by the Kemart process was true. The only conclusion which this court can reach is that Printing Arts was qualifiedly privileged in making the complained-of publications and that this privilege was not overcome by an adequate showing of malice. Printing Arts cannot, therefore, be held liable for the damage flowing from those publications.

* * *

Flotech, Inc. v. E. I. Du Pont de Nemours & Company,

United States Court of Appeals, First Circuit, 1987.
814 F.2d 775.

[DuPont, makers of "Teflon", issued a press release that after its "review of data available within the Company and from outside sources" it was of the opinion that adding "Teflon" to motor oil was "not useful". Plaintiff sold a product called "Tufoil," a motor oil with Teflon purchased from DuPont. Plaintiff sued DuPont for defamation and product disparagement.]

Under Restatement (Second) of Torts § 594 (1977), an otherwise defamatory publication is conditionally privileged if it is reasonable to believe that the information to be published affects a sufficiently important interest of the publisher and publication will serve to protect that interest. Massachusetts courts have recognized a conditional privilege if the publication is reasonably necessary to the protection or furtherance of a legitimate business interest. A publication is similarly protected if the publisher reasonably believes that the information to be published will affect a sufficiently important interest of the recipient and the recipient is a person whom the publisher has an obligation to inform. Restatement (Second) of Torts § 595 (1977). Conditional privileges such as these represent a balance between "the interest of the defamed person in the protection of his reputation [and] the interests of the publisher, of third persons and of the public in having the publication take place." Id. § 595 Comment (b). The "condition" on the privilege is that the publication not be abused. Restatement (Second) of Torts § 595 Comment (a) (privilege abused if statement published despite knowledge of or reckless disregard for the falsity of the statement, if published for an improper purpose (such as competition for prospective pecuniary advantage), or if repeated excessively); Restatement (Second) of Torts § 599 (1977).

It seems clear to us that a company's statement in good faith that it views its own product as ineffective for a particular purpose may fall within both the "business interest" and "public protection" privileges—even if the statement by implication can be understood to comment on the effectiveness of a third-party's product. A company must have the freedom to protect its image and that of its products by deciding not to sell a particular item for a purpose that the company has come to believe is inappropriate. This right is even more compelling if the company fears possible product liability resulting from the suspect use of its product. Moreover, it is reasonable for a company whose reputation is based on the high quality performance of its goods to believe it necessary to announce this decision to the public in order to erase the tarnish and alleviate the possible economic harm from the inappropriate use.

NOTES

1. For a case similar to *Kemart* in which the defendant was unsuccessful in establishing a privilege see International Industries & Developments, Inc. v. Farbach Chemical Co., 241 F.2d 246 (6th Cir.1957). Here it was shown that the defendant did not subject the plaintiff's product to a readily available chemical analysis prior to sending out 8000 letters to the trade alleging plaintiff's product infringed defendant's patent. The Sixth Circuit found the "record supports the conclusion of the trial court that the issuance of the notice of infringement was done in implied malice in law, if not in actual malice, and in bad faith constituting unfair competition."

2. Should the conditional privilege apply to any case in which a business disparages its competitor's goods? Are consumers and competing businesses interested in the quality of goods in the marketplace? Or does the *Kemart* case depend on the fact that licensees of an infringing patent are also liable for patent infringement? Would consumers have a similar privilege to make disparaging statements about goods? What about third parties such as the press or a consumer advocacy organization like Consumers Union? Does the privilege in *Kemart* blend with privileges that might be constructed under the First Amendment?

NOTES ON PRODUCT DISPARAGEMENT BY GOVERNMENTAL AGENCIES

1. Should the government have a privilege to comment on the quality of goods in the marketplace? Consider the following description from Ernest Gellhorn, Adverse Publicity by Administrative Agencies, 86 Harv. L. Rev. 1380, 1408 (1973):

> The controversy can be traced to the 1959 cranberry episode, a public announcement which was in effect an involuntary recall. In the cranberry episode, the FDA issued a national public warning for the first time, with consequences so devastating to the industry that henceforth the mere threat of a public announcement functioned to help enforce a voluntary recall procedure. On November 9, 1959, a day still known as "Black Monday" in the industry, Secretary of Health, Education, and Welfare Arthur Flemming held a news conference at which he urged the public not to buy cranberries grown in Washington and Oregon, saying they might be contaminated with a chemical weed killer, aminotriazole, that had been found to cause cancer in laboratory rats. Although the Secretary admitted he had no information suggesting that cranberries from other states were dangerous, he would not say they were safe. Answering a reporter's question, the Secretary stated he would not be eating cranberries that Thanksgiving. Not surprisingly, most of the nation followed suit. Since cranberries are purchased primarily for the holiday season, virtually the entire crop remained unsold, even though 99 percent of it was subsequently "cleared" and marketed as government "approved."

2. Plaintiffs have generally been unsuccessful in obtaining injunctions to prohibit governmental agencies from issuing press releases based on agency complaints prior to hearings. In FTC v. Cinderella Career & Finishing Schools, Inc., 404 F.2d 1308 (D.C.Cir.1968) the court reversed a lower court injunction which would have prohibited the Federal Trade Commission from issuing a press release notifying the public of the Commission's complaint charging respondent with deceptive practices. The court recognized that the respondent would likely suffer injury to his business because of the release but noted the Commission's "broad delegation of power . . . to eliminate unfair or deceptive business practices in the public interest" and the specific statutory authority to "alert the public to suspected violations of the law by factual press releases . . . ." The court did not decide whether a false release would be subject to injunctive relief. In B. C. Morton International Corp. v. FDIC, 305 F.2d 692 (1st Cir.1962) the court found that plaintiff had stated a cause of action for injunctive relief prohibiting publication of a press release where the plaintiff alleged the agency deliberately misrepresented the application of federal law for the specific purpose of destroying plaintiff's business.

Congress has made some effort to control agency discretion. In the Consumer Product Safety Act, 15 U.S.C.A. §2055(b)(1) the Consumer Product Safety Commission is required to give 30 days notice prior to public disclosure of information about product safety unless public health or safety require a shorter period. The provision also gives the manufacturer an opportunity to submit comments and requires a retraction if the Commission finds that its public disclosure was inaccurate or misleading. See GTE Sylvania Inc. v. Consumer Product Safety Comm., 404 F.Supp. 352 (D.Del.1975) where the court found the Commission's collection and verification of information relating to the safety of television sets so unreliable that threatened public disclosure would not be "fair in the circumstances" nor "reasonably related to effectuating the purposes of this chapter" and enjoined the agency from releasing the information. In GTE Sylvania Inc. v. Consumers Union of the United States, 445 U.S. 375 (1980) the Supreme Court held that the information enjoined from disclosure by the district Court in GTE Sylvania, supra, could not be obtained by interested parties under the Freedom of Information Act.

3. A producer injured by disparaging governmental publicity is unable generally to recover damages. In Hall v. United States, 274 F.2d 69 (10th Cir.1959) inspectors for the U.S. Department of Agriculture as a result of a negligently conducted inspection declared plaintiff's cattle diseased, forcing plaintiff to sell his cattle at a substantial reduction in price. In fact the cattle were not diseased. Plaintiff brought this suit under the Federal Tort Claims Act, 28 U.S.C. § 2674, for damages resulting from the inspectors' negligence. Although the federal government has waived sovereign immunity for negligence actions, 28 U.S.C. § 2680(h) exempts the government from liability for claims arising out of "libel, slander, misrepresentation, deceit, or interference with contract rights." The court denied plaintiff recovery holding that § 2680(h) applied because loss resulted from the "misrepresentation" that the cattle were diseased and not from the "negligence" in conducting the tests. For a similar result under a state tort claims act patterned after the federal law see Hubbard v. State, 163 N.W.2d 904 (Iowa 1969). The United States Supreme Court relied heavily on the *Hall* case in United States v. Neustadt, 366 U.S. 696 (1961) when it held that "misrepresentation" in § 2680(h) included negligent as well as willful misrepresentation.

Government officials acting within the scope of their duties have an "absolute privilege" which precludes civil suits for damages for "defamation and kindred torts". Barr v. Matteo, 360 U.S. 564 (1959).

Congress eventually provided $9 million dollars in relief to cranberry growers injured by the adverse publicity in the 1959 episode.

Bose Corporation v. Consumers Union of United States, Inc.

United States Court of Appeals, First Circuit, 1982.
692 F.2d 189.

[The Bose Corporation sued the publisher of Consumer Reports, a monthly consumer magazine, for product disparagement arising out of an article evaluating various stereo speakers including those of the plaintiff and containing the following paragraph:

> But after listening to a number of recordings, it became clear that the panelists could pinpoint the location of various instruments much more easily with a standard speaker than with the Bose system. Worse, individual instruments heard through the Bose system seemed to grow to gigantic proportions and tended to wander about the room. For instance, a violin appeared to be 10 feet wide and a piano stretched from wall to wall. With orchestral music, such effects seemed inconsequential. But we think they might become annoying when listening to soloists. On an impulse, we also played some monophonic records through the Bose. To our surprise, they too acquired the same spacial openness and size distortions as the stereo records.

The district court found one statement false and disparaging and published with reckless disregard of its falsity and in a subsequent trial assessed damages of $115,296 plus interest and costs of $95,609.64. CU appeals both on liability and damages.]

The court determined that under the applicable law of product disparagement, it was the plaintiff's burden to prove that the statements made by CU were of a disparaging or defamatory nature and that the statements were false. After concluding that "the Article, when read as a whole is disparaging," the court proceeded to analyze in detail each alleged factual error in the article to determine if it was false and if it was disparaging. * * *

The district court's finding of liability was based on part of one sentence in the article which reads: "Worse, individual instruments heard through the Bose system seemed to grow to gigantic proportions and tended to wander about the room." The court, in its analysis, divided the sentence into two parts. It found that the description "seemed to grow to gigantic proportions" had not been proven false but found the statement that the instruments "tended to wander about the room" was both false and disparaging. The evidence on which this finding was based is summarized as follows. CU's two employees who conducted the listening test "testified that the wandering sounds they heard were confined to an area within a few feet of the wall near which the Bose 901 loudspeakers were placed." CU conceded that the words "about the room" might not have described the wandering with precise accuracy, but argued that the *wandering* of sound was important to consumers, not *where* it wandered. CU maintained that the statement was substantially true because it accurately described the important observation. The district court referred to testimony that an amount of movement is expected with all stereo speakers and concluded that the location of the sounds' movement was as important to a consumer as the fact of movement. Thus, the court found the statement not to be substantially true. After rejecting CU's argument that the statements in the article about "a violin appear[ing] to be 10 feet wide and a piano stretch[ing] from wall to wall" modified the statements about wandering sounds to imply that the wandering occurred along the wall between the speakers, the court stated that the ordinary meaning of "about" the room was "around" the room. The court found the statement to be disparaging: "A statement that attributes such grotesque qualities as instruments wandering about the room to the plaintiff's product could have no effect other than to harm the reputation of the product." The use of the word "worse" to introduce the statement in the article showed that CU intended it to have a harmful effect.

Having determined that Bose had proved by a preponderance of the evidence that the statement about individual instruments tending to wander about the room was false and disparaging, the district court proceeded to analyze the impact of the first amendment on the standard of care required of CU. It cited several lower court decisions and discussed the first amendment balance between the need for an uninhibited press and the legitimate state interest in compensating victims of defamation in concluding that the actual malice standard of New York Times v. Sullivan, 376 U.S. 254, (1964), applies to product disparagement cases. It then applied the analysis of Bruno & Stillman, Inc. v. Globe Newspaper Co., 633 F.2d 583 (1st Cir.1980), to conclude that "Bose is a public figure, at least with respect to the limited issues of the characteristics and quality of the Bose," and was required to show by clear and convincing proof that CU's false statement was published with knowledge that it was false or with reckless disregard of its truth of falsity. CU's project engineer, Arnold Seligson, conducted the listening test and wrote the words upon which the statements in the article were based. Due in part to his demeanor at trial, the court found that Seligson's testimony as to what the words "about the room" meant was not credible. Seligson maintained that he perceived that the wandering sounds were confined to an area near the wall behind the loudspeakers. The court found that Seligson was too intelligent to not be aware of the ordinary meaning of "about" and thus concluded that Seligson knew at the time of publication that the article did not accurately describe the effects he had perceived during the test. In the court's view, this was clear and convincing proof that CU "published a false statement of material fact with the knowledge that it was false or with reckless disregard of its truth or falsity."

Our Review

As the parties acknowledge, the first amendment permeates our review. The question of the truth or falsity of the statement that individual instruments tended to wander about the room is intertwined with the question of whether that statement is one of opinion or fact; both questions are difficult to answer. CU argues that if the statement is considered in its full context it becomes clear that the statement is merely the opinion of the panelists who conducted the listening test. This full context includes the tentative language that "instruments * * * *seemed* to grow" and "*tended* to wander," that "[w]ith orchestral music, such effects *seemed* inconsequential [although] we *think they might* become annoying when listening to soloists," and finally that "the Bose system is so unusual that a prospective buyer must listen to it and judge for himself." CU cites numerous cases to support the proposition that a reviewer's published description of what he or she observed in a public performance, book, or restaurant is protected by the first amendment. Also, the Supreme Court has stated that "[u]nder the First Amendment there is no such thing as a false idea. However pernicious an opinion may seem, we depend for its correction not on the conscience of judges and juries but on the competition of other ideas." Gertz v. Robert Welch, Inc., 418 U.S. 323, 339–40 (1974) (dictum) (footnote omitted). This statement of the Court implies that an opinion can be neither true nor false as a matter of constitutional law. The proposition that an opinion can be neither true nor false also is reasonable as a matter of common sense. The determination of whether a statement is one of opinion or fact, however, is difficult to make and perhaps unreliable as a basis for decision. Although CU's argument that the statement is an opinion is plausible, the seeming scientific nature of the article—indicated by quantitative ratings, a description in the beginning of the article of the laboratory testing performed, and the use of such terms as "panelists" and "engineers" to describe the CU employees who performed the tests—would support the position that the statements are factual. * * *

Due to our ultimate conclusion that Bose has failed to meet its burden of proof with respect to actual malice, however, we will assume that the statement was both factual and false and not explore further the intricacies of these concepts. * * *. There can be little question that the statement was disparaging.

At oral argument Bose acknowledged that it does not dispute the finding of the district court that the corporation is a public figure with respect to the subject matter of the CU article. Bose also conceded that the rule of *New York Times v. Sullivan* applies in this case, and thus accepted the district court's conclusion that the actual malice standard applies to product disparagement cases. As we have indicated earlier, the district court analyzed both of these issues at length and we accept its conclusions for the purposes of this case.

We focus, therefore, on the district court's holding that Bose proved by clear and convincing evidence that CU published the words "individual instruments * * * tended to wander about the room" with knowledge that they were false or with reckless disregard of their truth or falsity. In performing this review we are not limited to the clearly erroneous standard of Fed.R.Civ.P. 52(a); instead, we must perform a de novo review, independently examining the record to ensure that the district court has applied properly the governing constitutional law and that the plaintiff has indeed satisfied its burden of proof.

* * *

[The court reviewed the proof of actual malice required of a plaintiff under *New York Times v. Sullivan* and its progeny noting that actual malice requires a showing that the defendant had serious doubts as to the truth of the publication which must be shown by "clear and convincing proof".]

* * *

It is helpful to compare the research and editing procedures followed by CU in publishing its article on loudspeakers with publishers' procedures that have been examined in other cases. One court, in finding that the plaintiff—a public figure—had failed to show actual malice, reviewed CU's work in publishing a series of articles in 1978 attacking the claims of certain organizations and individuals that fluoridization causes, among other things, cancer and birth defects. Yiamouyiannis v. Consumers Union of the United States, Inc., 619 F.2d 932. It stated:

> It is clear that appellee, through its agents, made a thorough investigation of the facts. Scientific writings and authorities in the field were consulted; authoritative scientific bodies speaking for substantial segments of the medical and scientific community were investigated. The unquestioned methodology of the preparation of the article exemplifies the very highest order of responsible journalism: the entire article was checked and rechecked across a spectrum of knowledge and, where necessary, changes were made in the interests of accuracy.

Id. at 940. Although we would refrain from describing CU's loudspeaker article as exemplifying the very highest order of responsible journalism, CU does not have to meet such high standards to prevail. In addition, these two CU projects are distinguishable. In the fluoridization article there existed an abundance of scientific research and writing which CU merely cited in drawing its conclusions. In the instant case, CU had the much more difficult task of performing the original research.

It is important to point out that in conducting the listening test CU used experts, Seligson and Lefkow, who brought their expertise and experience to bear in evaluating the Bose speakers. * * * The Second Circuit found lack of expertise to be evidence of malice in Goldwater v. Ginzburg, 414 F.2d 324 (2d Cir.1969). The court affirmed a jury finding of actual malice in an article stating that Senator Goldwater suffered from the mental disease of paranoia. The court noted that this conclusion "was reached only upon his [the author's] own non-expert evaluation of Senator Goldwater's life and political career." Id. at 331.

Some evidence of actual malice may be found "if there is a complete departure from the standards of investigation and reporting ordinarily adhered to by responsible publishers." CU's editorial procedures reveal no evidence of actual malice. [T]he testimony in this case indicated that normal editorial procedures were followed; there was no evidence of CU knowingly departing from these procedures in order to publish the article regardless of its truth or falsity. After testing the loudspeakers, Seligson prepared a rough draft of the manuscript, commonly referred to as a "report to editorial," which was reviewed by an associate technical director. The Editorial Department then reviewed this report and drafted the manuscript for publication. Among other editorial alterations, the Department changed Seligson's words that instruments "suffered [from] a tendency to wander around the room" to the statement ultimately published that instruments "tended to wander about the room." This manuscript was sent back to Seligson for "line by line checking" and then forwarded to the associate technical director for his review. It was then returned to the Editorial Department. These same procedures were applied to galley proofs, second galley proofs, page proofs, and second page proofs. The associate technical director testified that when he performed his reviews the words "tended to wander about the room" conjured up "the mental image * * * of the sound moving about in front of the listener." He also testified that when he approved the article for publication he never really pondered the meaning of the word "about" in the statement. The most we can conclude from this is that in reviewing the manuscript CU employees could have inquired more painstakingly into the precise language being used.

Even though we accord relatively little weight to CU's claims of good faith and lack of any motivation to disparage the Bose 901, we are unable to find clear and convincing evidence that CU published the statement that individual instruments tended to wander about the room with knowledge that it was false or with reckless disregard of whether it was false or not. The evidence presented merely shows that the words in the article may not have described precisely what the two panelists heard during the listening test. CU was guilty of using imprecise language in the article—perhaps resulting from an attempt to produce a readable article for its mass audience. Certainly this does not support an inference of actual malice. * * * To find actual malice in this case would be to interpret that concept to require little more than proof of falsity * * *.

Due to our holding on the issue of liability, there is no need for us to review the district court's findings on damages.

Reversed.

LEVIN H. CAMPBELL, CIRCUIT JUDGE (concurring).

In joining as I do in the court's opinion, I wish merely to emphasize my understanding that this court is in no way passing upon the actual merits of the district court's finding that Bose Corporation was a public figure.

Bose Corporation v. Consumers Union of United States, Inc.

Supreme Court of the United States, 1984.
466 U.S. 485, 104 S.Ct. 1949, 80 L.Ed.2d 502.

[The United States Supreme Court granted certiorari to consider solely the question whether the Court of Appeals properly rejected the "clearly erroneous" standard of review of Rule 52(a) for the lower court's finding of actual malice. The Court held that Rule 52(a) did not apply. The concluding paragraphs of the opinion read:]

The Court of Appeals entertained some doubt concerning the ruling that the *New York Times* rule should be applied to a claim of product disparagement based on a critical review of a loudspeaker system. We express no view on that ruling, but having accepted it for purposes of deciding this case, we agree with the Court of Appeals that the difference between hearing violin sounds move around the room and hearing them wander back and forth fits easily within the breathing space that gives life to the First Amendment. We may accept all of the purely factual findings of the District Court and nevertheless hold as a matter of law that the record does not contain clear and convincing evidence that Seligson or his employer prepared the loudspeaker article with knowledge that it contained a false statement, or with reckless disregard of the truth.

It may well be that in this case, the "finding" of the District Court on the actual malice question could have been set aside under the clearly erroneous standard of review, and we share the concern of the Court of Appeals that the statements at issue tread the line between fact and opinion. Moreover, the analysis of the central legal question before us may seem out of place in a case involving a dispute about the sound quality of a loudspeaker. But though the question presented reaches us on a somewhat peculiar wavelength, we reaffirm the principle of independent appellate review that we have applied uncounted times before. We hold that the clearly erroneous standard of Rule 52(a) of the Federal Rules of Civil Procedure does not prescribe the standard of review to be applied in reviewing a determination of actual malice in a case governed by New York Times v. Sullivan. Appellate judges in such a case must exercise independent judgment and determine whether the record establishes actual malice with convincing clarity.

The judgment of the Court of Appeals is affirmed.

It is so ordered.

U. S. Healthcare Inc. v. Blue Cross of Greater Philadelphia

United States Court of Appeals, Third Circuit, 1990.
898 F.2d 914.

■ SCIRICA, CIRCUIT JUDGE.

[U.S. Healthcare operates a Health Maintenance Organization and Blue Cross/Blue Shield, in order to compete, began offering a preferred provider organization program entitled "Personal Choice". The respective programs differ as to their operation but are designed to deliver health care while permitting some control by the insurer over costs. Both parties engaged in aggressive comparative advertising campaigns attacking features of the other's program. Among the more provocative claims, Blue Cross asserted that HMO doctors have a financial incentive not to refer patients to needed specialists while U.S. Healthcare claimed that many Personal Choice doctors did not have admitting privileges at area hospitals. Suit initially was brought by U.S. Healthcare claiming defamation, commercial disparagement, and unfair competition under § 43(a) of the Lanham Act. Blue Cross filed similar counterclaims. After initially deadlocking on all claims, the jury finally returned a verdict against Blue Cross on its counterclaims. The trial court scheduled a new trial on U.S. Healthcare's claims.]

The case was never retried. Instead, Blue Cross/Blue Shield filed a motion under Fed.R.Civ.P. 50(b) requesting the court to direct entry of judgment in its favor, on the grounds that the advertisements were entitled to heightened constitutional protection under the First Amendment, and that U.S. Healthcare had not met the applicable standard of proof, set forth in New York Times Co. v. Sullivan, 376 U.S. 254 (1964), et seq. The district court granted the motion. The court held that because the objects of the advertisements are "public figures," and because the matters in the advertisements are "community health issues of public concern," heightened constitutional protections attach to this speech. The court reasoned that the First Amendment limited the power of the state and of Congress to award damages resulting from the allegedly false and misleading advertisements. Accordingly, the district court held that in order to prevail on their respective claims of Lanham Act violation, commercial disparagement, defamation and tortious interference with contract, both parties were required to prove each claim by clear and convincing evidence: (1) that the other side published the advertisements with knowledge or with reckless disregard of their falsity, and (2) that the advertisements were false. Applying this standard of proof, the court concluded that "[a]lthough the jury could reasonably have concluded that both sides had proven falsity and actual malice by a preponderance of the evidence, neither side has presented clear and convincing evidence [of this]."

This appeal followed.

[The court reviewed the substantive elements of the various legal claims and concluded that aspects of the advertisements appeared actionable under § 43(a), defamation, and commercial disparagement. It then examined applicability of the First Amendment holding first that the advertisements fit clearly within the category of "commercial speech" because they were disseminated as part of a promotional campaign, they tout one specific product over another, they were motivated by the desire for revenue, and they are not the type of speech that is likely to be chilled by the threat of legal liability.]

At the outset, we note that it is of no consequence that the defendants (and counterclaim defendants) here are not members of the broadcast and print media. * * * In addition, we do not limit our consideration of the applicability of the *New York Times* standard to the parties' claims for defamation alone. The Supreme Court has already applied a similar analysis to other torts[.]

* * *

Therefore, while the speech here is protected by the First Amendment, we hold that the First Amendment requires no higher standard of liability than that mandated by the substantive law for each claim. The heightened protection of the actual malice standard is not "necessary to give adequate 'breathing space' to the freedoms protected by the First Amendment." Hustler Magazine, Inc. v. Falwell, 485 U.S. 46, 56, (1988).

Having concluded that the speech here is commercial speech that does not warrant heightened constitutional protection, we nonetheless proceed to consideration of the nature and weight of the state's interest in compensating individuals for injuries resulting from each of the distinct torts alleged. We have previously discussed the state and federal interests implicated. As we shall see in this case, however, traditional defamation analysis is not well suited to strike the proper balance between the state and federal interests and First Amendment values in the context of commercial speech.

In weighing the state interest, we must look to the status of the claimants. See [Gertz v. Robert Welch, Inc., 418 U.S. 323, at 342–45 (1974).] As we have noted, the Court has determined that the state has only a "limited" interest in compensating public persons for injury to reputation but has a "strong and legitimate" interest in compensating private persons for the same injury. See Gertz, 418 U.S. at 343 & 348–49. Contending that the actual malice standard applies because a public figure is implicated, Blue Cross/Blue Shield argues that the following factors render U.S. Healthcare a "public figure": it has voluntarily exposed itself to public comment on the issues involved in this dispute; it is a contributor to the ongoing debate concerning health care insurance; it is among the nation's largest providers of HMO-type insurance coverage; it markets its products extensively and aggressively, and has a substantial annual advertising budget; and it frequently and consistently asserts the advantages of its method of health care financing and delivery, and has done so in advertisements, press releases, professional journals, newspapers, magazines and speeches before public assemblies. These activities, Blue Cross/Blue Shield submits, "constitute a voluntary effort to influence the consuming public." Similar statements can be made regarding Blue Cross/Blue Shield.

* * *

Under traditional defamation analysis, the parties' considerable access to the media and their voluntary entry into a controversy are strong indicia that they are limited purpose public figures. Indeed, inflexible application of these factors would warrant a finding of public figure status and facilitate a finding of heightened constitutional protection. Nonetheless, we hold that these corporations are not public figures for the limited purpose of commenting on health care in this case.

As noted, Gertz defines the limited purpose public figure as one who has "thrust [himself] to the forefront of particular public controversies in order to influence the resolution of the issues involved." 418 U.S. at 345. Although some of the advertisements touch on matters of public concern, their central thrust is commercial. Thus, the parties have acted primarily to generate revenue by influencing customers, not to resolve "the issues involved."

While discerning motivations of the speaker is often difficult, we have a more fundamental reason for declining to find limited purpose public figure status in this case. The express analysis in Gertz is not helpful in the context of a comparative advertising war. Most products can be linked to a public issue. See [Central Hudson Gas & Elec. Corp. v. Public Serv. Comm'n, 447 U.S. 557 (1980)] at 563 n. 5. And most advertisers—including both claimants here—seek out the media. Thus, it will always be true that such advertisers have voluntarily placed themselves in the public eye. It will be equally true that such advertisers have access to the media. Therefore, under the *Gertz* rationale, speech of public concern that implicates corporate advertisers—i.e., typical comparative advertising—will always be insulated behind the actual malice standard. We believe a corporation must do more than the claimants have done here to become a limited purpose public figure under *Gertz*.

In summary, we conclude that the speech at issue does not receive heightened protection under the First Amendment. Because this speech is chill-resistant, the *New York Times* standard is not, as we have noted, "necessary to give adequate 'breathing space' to the freedoms protected by the First Amendment." Hustler Magazine, Inc. v. Falwell, 485 U.S. 46, 56 (1988). Therefore, the standard of proof needed to establish the substantive claims is that applicable under federal and state law.

For these reasons, we hold that the district court erred in applying the *New York Times* standard to the claims in this case and in directing entry of judgment under Fed.R.Civ.P. 50(b). Accordingly, we will reverse the judgment of the district court and remand for proceedings consistent with this opinion.

Dairy Stores, Inc. v. Sentinel Pub. Co.

Supreme Court of New Jersey, 1986.

104 N.J. 125, 516 A.2d 220.

[During a drought in 1981 sales of bottled spring water increased dramatically. The defendant Sentinel Publishing Co. published in its newspaper an article by defendant Kathleen Dzielak casting doubt on whether "Covered Bridge Crystal Clear Spring Water" sold by the plaintiff (Krauszer's Food Stores) was in fact pure spring water. The presence of chlorine in water is strong evidence that it is not spring water. Dzielak took a container of the water to an independent state-certified laboratory for testing. The laboratory supervisor recognized the label and told her Krauszer was a client of the lab. The supervisor nonetheless reported to Dzielak that the water contained no chlorine. Skeptical, Dzielak took the sample to two additional laboratories. One (Patterson Clinic Lab) reported the presence of chlorine. The other's report could not be understood. With this information, a story was published under a banner headline reading "Spring water/Independent lab analysis casts doubt on content" reporting the results of the Patterson lab and its director's comments that "I can't see how it could possibly be spring water unless the spring source was contaminated and chlorine was added at the source."

Both the trial court and the appellate division held the media defendant was protected by the First Amendment in the absence of proof of actual malice and that Paterson Lab, as an outside consultant to a media defendant, was also protected.]

■ POLLOCK, J.

* * *

[F]or the purposes of this appeal, we assume that the articles were not only disparaging, but also false and defamatory. As a result, the distinction between defamation and product disparagement disappears, and our attention shifts to whether the publications were privileged and whether the defendants abused any such privilege.

–III–

The evolution of the law of defamation reflects the tension between society's competing interests in encouraging the free flow of information about matters of public concern and in protecting an individual's reputation. At one time, the common law placed so high a premium on the protection of a person's reputation that it imposed strict liability for the publication of a defamatory statement. More recently, the United States Supreme Court has declared that publishers may not be held liable for certain defamatory statements without showing that they were at least negligent. That declaration is consistent with the increasing awareness of the need for public information on a wide variety of issues.

Traditionally, the common law has accommodated that need by recognizing that some otherwise defamatory statements should be "privileged," i.e., that their publication does not impose liability on the publisher. Privileges may be "absolute," which means that the statements are completely immune, or "qualified." A qualified privilege may be overcome, with the result that the publisher will be liable, if publication of a defamatory statement was made with "malice." Common-law malice, or malice-in-fact, has meant variously that the statement was published with an improper purpose or ill will, or without belief or reasonable grounds to believe in its truth.

Certain statements, such as those made in judicial, legislative, or administrative proceedings, are absolutely privileged because the need for unfettered expression is crucial to the public weal. Other statements, such as those made outside those forums but for the public welfare, enjoy a qualified privilege. * * *

Insofar as defenses to product disparagement are concerned, a qualified privilege should exist wherever it would exist in a defamation action. Because the common law historically has held the interest in one's reputation as more worthy of protection than the interest of a business in the products that it makes, it follows that the right to make a statement about a product should exist whenever it is permissible to make such a statement about the reputation of another.

One illustration of a qualified privilege is fair comment, which is sometimes described as rendering a statement non-libelous. No matter how described, the defense is lost upon a showing that the statement was made with malice. The roots of fair comment are imbedded in the common law, but in recent years, those roots have intertwined with others arising from constitutional law. * * *

The constitutional considerations begin with New York Times Co. v. Sullivan, 376 U.S. 254 (1964), in which the United States Supreme Court first declared that the first amendment protected certain otherwise defamatory statements. * * *

Three years after declaring that the actual malice test applied to public officials, the Court extended the test to public figures. Curtis Publishing Co. v. Butts; Associated Press v. Walker, 388 U.S. 130 (1967). Then, in what has come to be regarded as the high-water mark of constitutionally-protected speech, a plurality of the Court declared the actual malice standard applicable to statements about private individuals who became involved in matters of public or general interest. Rosenbloom v. Metromedia, Inc., 403 U.S. 29, 43 (1971). Since then, however, the Court has retrenched and declared that the actual malice test applies only to public figures or those private figures who become so involved in a particular public controversy that they become public figures for a limited range of issues. Gertz v. Robert Welch, Inc., supra, 418 U.S. at 351–52.

Notwithstanding withdrawal of constitutional protection from matters of general or public interest, the Court recognized that states might want to grant broader speech protection in setting the appropriate standard of care in defamation actions concerning private individuals. Gertz v. Robert Welch, Inc., supra, 418 U.S. at 348–49. Even before the United States Supreme Court accorded constitutional protection to statements about "public officials" and "public figures," the common law recognized that statements about matters of public concern should be protected. Through the principle of fair comment, courts have allowed commentary on public officials, private institutions that spend public funds, creative and scientific works presented to the public, and economic and social welfare events such as strikes and demonstrations. Although constitutional considerations have dominated defamation law in recent years, the common law provides an alternative, and potentially more stable, framework for analyzing statements about matters of public interest.

Another reason for turning to the common law is that the constitutional concepts do not comfortably fit the activities or products of a corporation. * * * The term "public figure" includes individuals who engage in a public controversy and ill fits a corporation, which ordinarily is interested not in thrusting itself into such a controversy, but in selling its products.

Lower federal courts, although differing on the nature and amount of activity needed to support the characterization of a corporation as a public figure, have concluded that corporations and their products can be viewed as public figures. * * * Other courts have noted, however, that the sale of a product "cannot easily be deemed a public controversy." * * * Nonetheless, the Supreme Court has yet to address whether corporations or their products can be classified as public figures.

* * *

A

Generally speaking, the doctrine of fair comment extends to virtually all matters of legitimate public interest. * * *

We recognize that not everything that is newsworthy is a matter of legitimate public concern, and that sorting such matters from those of a more private nature may be difficult. * * *

Some courts have developed criteria for determining whether the activities and products of corporations constitute matters of public interest. As previously indicated, matters of public interest include such essentials of life as food and water. Widespread effects of a product are yet another indicator that statements about the product are in the public interest. Still another criterion is substantial government regulation of business activities and products. * * *

Because the present case involves a product that is unquestionably a matter of legitimate public concern, we believe it is more prudent to extend that standard for the time being only to such products, leaving to another day the determination whether the standard should apply to statements about all products no matter how prosaic or innocuous. To this extent, we disagree with our concurring colleague, who would extend the actual malice standard to a disparaging statement about any product.

B

Throughout the country, courts have divided on the issue whether fair comment should be restricted to statements of opinion or should extend to factual statements. Underlying the distinction is the premise that the widest possible latitude should extend to expressions of opinion on matters of public concern, but that factual misstatements should be more narrowly confined.

The majority view is that fair comment extends to opinion only, but a respected minority view holds that statements of fact should also be protected. * * *

The need for the free flow of information and commentary on matters of legitimate public concern leads us to conclude that fair comment should extend beyond opinion to statements of fact. When confronting such a matter, a publisher should not be unduly inhibited in analyzing whether a statement is an immune opinion or a potentially culpable statement of fact. We believe we come close to fulfilling the policy considerations that underlie fair comment if we evaluate factual statements as the subject of a qualified privilege. * * *

C

* * *

The fair comment defense, the purpose of which is to foster the discussion of matters of legitimate public concern, is closely related to the constitutional protection accorded to statements about public officials and public figures. Although the adoption of the actual malice test is not constitutionally compelled, we conclude that the defense of fair comment, like the constitutional protection, should be overcome only by proof of actual malice.

* * *

As society in general, and the sale of goods in particular, becomes more complex, the general welfare requires the dissemination of more and more information to the consuming public. Consumers, who are often separated from those in the early stages of a chain of distribution, have a legitimate need to learn about the reputation of the business entities in that chain and of the goods that are being distributed. From that need emanates the right to publish information concerning the nature and quality of goods intended for human consumption, and the reputations of those who make, distribute, and sell those goods.

D

[W]e conclude that the actual malice standard should apply to non-media as well as to media defendants.

–IV–

Turning to Sentinel's articles, three statements are critical. The lead sentence in the article published under Dzielak's by-line states: "A sample bottle of 'Covered Bridge Crystal Clear Spring Water,' sold at Krauszer's convenient food stores, does not contain pure spring water, according to a laboratory analysis obtained by the Sentinel Newspapers." The next sentence states that the director of Paterson's laboratory said that "pure spring water should not contain any chlorine." The director continued by stating: " 'I can't see how it could possibly be spring water unless the spring source was contaminated and chlorine was added at the source.' "

We conclude that the statement that the Covered Bridge bottle "does not contain spring water" and that "pure spring water should not contain any chlorine" may fairly be viewed as statements of fact. Although testing for the presence of chlorine is a scientific procedure that results in the formulation of an opinion, the statement is more a factual assertion than an expression of an opinion.

We find, however, that the statement of the director that he "can't see how it could possibly be spring water unless the spring source was contaminated and chlorine was added at the source" is an expression of pure opinion. It states the director's opinion, and the factual basis for it. For instance, the article recites that chlorine dissipates at a "high rate" on exposure to "air or other substances," and that tests were repeated several times to rule out testing error. It also states countervailing facts, such as that the seal had already been broken on the bottle containing the tested water. We conclude that the director's opinion was made on the basis of stated facts, and is a statement of "pure opinion," entitled to absolute immunity.

[The court found no evidence to support a finding of actual malice.]

The judgment of the Appellate Division is affirmed.

GARIBALDI, J., concurring.

The plaintiff in this case has pursued a cause of action for defamation. The majority recognizes, however, that the cause of action could also be for product disparagement. I find that plaintiff's cause of action is solely one for product disparagement. I join in the Court's judgment because I am satisfied that the requirement of actual malice should be applied in a product disparagement case.

TURF LAWNMOWER REPAIR, INC. V. BERGIN RECORD CORP., 139 N.J. 392, 655 A.2d 417 (1995). cert. denied, 116 S.Ct. 752 (1996). The New Jersey Supreme Court returned to the question of establishing the appropriate standard for defamation of a business. The defendant newspaper ran an investigative series which concluded that the plaintiff, a lawnmower repair shop, engaged in a systematic fraud on the consuming public by performing unnecessary or shoddy repairs on lawn mowers. The court posed the issue to be: "whether actual malice is the appropriate standard for all businesses, or whether negligence is the more appropriate standard of proof in defamation actions that involve businesses whose activities do not concern matters of public health or safety, do not constitute consumer fraud, or whose businesses are not subject to substantial government regulations." Adopting the latter view, the court reasoned:

Many businesses are sole proprietorships or small individually-owned stores, like a local "mom and pop" stationery store, shoemaker, tailor, cleaner, or barber. Although those stores are important in the daily life of their communities, their owners are not "public figures." Nor do their activities involve "matters of public concern" that the United States Supreme Court and the vast majority of federal and state courts have made subject to the heightened actual-malice standard of proof. Neither the public nor the owners of those ordinary businesses see the owners in the vortex of a public controversy by selling their product or service to the public. Nor does our opinion change because those businesses do limited advertising. Most businesses do advertise if only in a local shopping flyer, to attract customers and to succeed. Such advertising is insufficient to thrust the business or its owner into the public spotlight.

Moreover, most of those businesses and their owners have neither the financial resources nor "access to the channels of effective communication . . . to counteract false statements" to protect their business and their livelihood from a defamatory newspaper report. They are neither traditional 'public figures' nor do they engage in activities that constitute traditional matters of public concern. Therefore, in respect of such prosaic and innocuous everyday businesses, we conclude that the negligence standard best balances the interests of the public in preserving an uninhibited, robust, and free press and the interests of a private individual and a business in preserving their reputation and good name.

The public does, however, have a legitimate interest in any business charged with criminal fraud, a substantial regulatory violation, or consumer fraud that raises a matter of legitimate public concern. When the media addresses those issues of legitimate and compelling public concern, the actual-malice standard of proof will apply, regardless of the type of business involved. In so ruling, we seek a balance between a private person's right of privacy and the public's right to know of various dangers in our society.

The court ultimately found that the Bergen Record's article raised sufficient evidence of consumer fraud to require plaintiff to prove actual malice, a burden unmet in this case.

Judge Pollock concurred:

> * * * I would temper the majority's concern for the vulnerability of repair people, with some concern for the vulnerability of consumers. For me, the analogy of repair people to the "local 'mom and pop' stationery store, shoemaker, tailor, cleaner, or barber" does not work. Anyone who needs a repair person, unlike someone buying a newspaper or leaving a suit at the dry cleaners, is generally vulnerable. The motorist whose car breaks down on the highway is vulnerable to the demands of the tow truck operator and the service station. The individual with a broken washing machine does not enjoy equal bargaining power with the appliance repair person. And the homeowner with a broken lawn mower is open to exploitation.

> Unlike the majority, I would characterize as in the public interest articles about businesses that exploit vulnerable consumers.

NOTES

1. Which of the approaches in the principal cases seems to effectuate the best balance between the public's interest in free speech and the producer's interest in being free of unfair product disparagement? Is the "public interest" test a better approach in product cases than the "public figure" test? Is this an area where the courts should draw a distinction between the liability of competitors and the liability of non-market participants (newspapers)? Can cases against competitors be viewed as "commercial speech" cases and subjected to less careful First Amendment *and* common law scrutiny? Is there any reason to encourage statements by one competitor about the goods of another? On the other hand, given the discount that most consumers presumably give to the credibility of competitor generated comparisons, is there much risk in allowing these statements considerable "breathing room"?

2. Are disparaging statements about services more likely to also involve personal defamation than disparaging statements about goods?

3. Is a court an effective forum for resolving the truth or falsity of commercial comparisons? Should the rules favor independent testing agencies by granting them a significantly broader privilege to error in making product comparisons? Consider how the rules of product disparagement should apply to disparagement by consumers or publications such as Consumers Reports?

PROBLEM

In Auvil v. CBS "60 Minutes", 67 F.3d 816 (9th Cir. 1995) Plaintiffs sued CBS on behalf of themselves and other Washington State apple growers claiming that a CBS broadcast entitled "'A' is for Apple" disparaged apples in general causing the plaintiffs harm. The broadcast was an exposé on the use of the pesticide Alar which was sprayed on apples and, according to a report by the Natural Resources Defense Council, was carcinogenic. Following the broadcast, consumer demand for apples fell, and the industry suffered damage. The Ninth Circuit granted a summary judgment motion in favor of CBS on the grounds that the plaintiffs had not raised a genuine issue of material fact as to the falsity of the broadcast. Thereafter, many states adopted statutes directed at disparagement of perishable food products. The Alabama statute is reproduced below. Is it enforceable? Would the statute be more defensible if it required the statement to be knowingly false?

Ala. Code § 6–5–621 Definitions.

As used in this article, the following terms have the following meanings:

(1) Disparagement. The dissemination to the public in any manner of false information that a perishable food product or commodity is not safe for human consumption. The information shall be deemed to be false if it is not based upon reasonable and reliable scientific inquiry, facts, or data.

(2) Perishable food product or commodity. Any agricultural or aquacultural food product which is sold or distributed in a form that will perish or decay beyond marketability within a short period of time.

Ala Code § 6–5–622 Cause of action.

Any person who produces, markets, or sells a perishable food product or commodity, and suffers damage as a result of another person's disparagement of perishable food products or commodities has a cause of action for damages and for any other relief a court of competent jurisdiction deems appropriate, including but not limited to, compensatory and punitive damages.

(3) Interlude: Federal-State Tensions: The search for Uniformity

The purpose here is to explore again the tension between state and federal authority regarding the general law of unfair competition with emphasis on the regulation of market-place deception. In this area, claims of state authority conflict with the interest in uniform regulation. The concern for uniformity intensified with the advent of national televised advertising. The development of the internet as a commercial marketplace will raise issues of not only national but international uniformity.

(a) Common Law Application

The major cases studied thus far have been federal cases, i.e., *INS, Mosler,* and *American Washboard.* All were decided prior to Erie R.R. Co. v. Tompkins, 304 U.S. 64 (1938). During the reign of Swift v. Tyson, 41 U.S. (16 Pet.) 1 (1842), which authorized a federal common law in diversity cases, much of the law of unfair competition was developed by federal courts because diversity of citizenship and a large amount in controversy were more likely to coexist in suits between business enterprises. It should be noted that neither *Swift* nor *Erie* were trade practice cases, *Swift* involving the issue of whether a preexisting debt constituted valuable consideration in the law of negotiable instruments and *Erie* involving the question of whether a person on a commonly used footpath which ran for a short distance alongside the tracks of the defendant's railroad was a licensee or trespasser. In *Erie* Justice Brandeis recognized the dilemma of federalism: "In attempting to promote uniformity of law throughout the United States, the doctrine [of Swift] had prevented uniformity in the administration of the law of the state."

Is there any reason why *Erie* should not be equally applicable to a case involving unfair competition? Or trademark infringement? Or the type of deception in *Mosler?* Consider the applicability of *Erie* to the factual situation of the *INS* case. What problems would Associated Press and International News face if their dispute were subject to varying laws of 50 states?

It has been assumed by the Supreme Court that *Erie* applies to cases of unfair competition and common law trademark infringement. Kellogg Co. v. National Biscuit Co., 305 U.S. 111 (1938). In Hurn v. Oursler, 289 U.S. 238 (1933) which has been codified in 28 U.S.C. § 1338(b) federal courts were given original jurisdiction over state unfair competition claims "when joined with a substantial and related claim under the copyright, patent . . . or trademark laws". Some argued that federal law should govern these appended state claims but there is little support in the cases.

(b) Model and Uniform State Legislation

States have developed informal mechanisms designed to promote uniform laws, one of which is the National Conference of Commissioners on Uniform State Laws. The Uniform Commercial Code is one of its major achievements. The wide acceptance of the UCC illustrates the potential for uniformity through state legislation. In the trade regulation area the Commissioners have promulgated the Uniform Deceptive Trade Practices Act, 7A Uniform L.Ann. 35 (1997), and the Uniform Consumer Sales Practices Act, 7A Uniform L.Ann. 1 (1997).

With the assistance of the Federal Trade Commission, the Council of State Governments has recommended for adoption by the states the Unfair Trade Practices and Consumer Protection Act. Council of State Governments, 1970 Suggested State Legislation 141. The act provides both public enforcement and private remedies and is often referred to as a "little FTC Act." See Lovett, State Deceptive Trade Practice Legislation, 46 Tul.L.Rev. 724 (1972) (reporting that 36 states have adopted legislation similar to the Act). These enactments are considered in a subsequent section of this Chapter.

(c) Federal Legislation

Congress has authority to directly regulate interstate commerce. In 1914 Congress established the Federal Trade Commission to enforce the anti-trust laws. The Commission also attempted to deal with market-place deception and was given express authority to do so in 1938.

In addition Congress has legislated against deception in particular industries. For example, the Automobile Information Disclosure Act, 15 U.S.C. § 1231 et seq. requires a label to be affixed to new automobiles disclosing identifying information such as the make, model, and serial number of the vehicle and other items such as the suggested retail price and other costs. Willful failure to comply is a criminal offense subject to a $1,000 fine. In 1972, Congress enacted the Motor Vehicle Information and Cost Savings Act, 15 U.S.C. § 1901 et seq., subchapter IV of which provides liability of 3 times the amount of damage or $1,500, whichever is greater, in addition to attorneys fees and costs for falsifying odometer readings on automobiles. In the Interstate Land Sales Full Disclosure Act, 15 U.S.C. § 1701 et seq. Congress required land developers in interstate commerce to furnish prospective purchasers with a statement containing the description of the land, conditions affecting access to the property, availability of sewage disposal and utility service, and any encumbrances on the property. False statements or omissions constituting a material misrepresentation subjects the developer to a private cause of action by the injured purchaser. And in 1977 Congress passed the Fair Debt Collection Practices Act, 15 U.S.C. § 1692 et seq. which provides a civil remedy for persons injured by false, deceptive or misleading representations in connection with the collection of debts. Some industries are subjected to even more pervasive regulation. For example, the sale of securities is heavily regulated to assure full and accurate disclosure of information. Securities Act of 1933, 15 U.S.C.A. § 77(a) et. seq.

Congress has responded to the need for a law of general applicability governing private causes of action for unfair competition although in each instance, the provision was incorporated into a bill designed to accomplish other more publicized purposes and for long periods of time went unnoticed. In 1920, Congress amended the federal trade mark registration act of 1905 in order to implement certain international conventions. Section 3 of the Act of 1920 contained a provision for a limited private cause of action for false advertising applicable to false designations of origin as applied to goods but not services. The provision also required a showing of intent to deceive. Act of March 19, 1920, ch. 104, § 3, 41 Stat. 534.

In 1946 Congress replaced both the acts of 1905 and 1920 with the Lanham Act, a complete revision of the federal trademark statutes. Sections 43(a) and 44 of that enactment became the foundation upon which some sought to build a national law of false advertising and other forms of unfair competition.

(4) The Lanham Act—Section 43 (a)

Lanham Act § 43(a) (1946–1989)

§ 1125. False designations of origin and false descriptions forbidden

(a) Any person who shall affix, apply, or annex, or use in connection with any goods or services, or any container or containers for goods, a false designation of origin, or any false description or representation, including words or other symbols tending falsely to describe or represent the same, and shall cause such goods or services to enter into commerce, and any person who shall with knowledge of the falsity of such designation of origin or description or representation cause or procure the same to be transported or used in commerce or deliver the same to any carrier to be transported or used, shall be liable to a civil action by any person doing business in the locality falsely indicated as that of origin or in the region in which said locality is situated, or by any person who believes that he is or is likely to be damaged by the use of any such false description or representation.

Lanham Act § 43(a) as amended by the Trademark Revision Act of 1988

15 U.S.C. § 1125 (a)
Effective November 16, 1989

SEC. 132. Unregistered marks, descriptions, and representations.

(a) Any person who, on or in connection with any goods or services, or any container for goods, uses in commerce any word, term, name, symbol, or device, or any combination thereof, or any false designation of origin, false or misleading description of fact, or false or misleading representation of fact, which—

(1) is likely to cause confusion, or to cause mistake, or to deceive as to the affiliation, connection, or association of such person with another person, or as to the origin, sponsorship, or approval of his or her goods, services, or commercial activities by another person, or

(2) in commercial advertising or promotion, misrepresents the nature, characteristics, qualities, or geographic origin of his or her or another person's goods, services, or commercial activities,

shall be liable in a civil action by any person who believes that he or she is or is likely to be damaged by such act.

NOTES

1. *History of § 43(a).* Although § 43(a) became effective in 1947 with passage of the Lanham Act, early decisions narrowed its impact. In California Apparel Creators v. Wieder of California, 162 F.2d 893 (2d Cir.1947) the Second Circuit in dictum suggested and in Chamberlain v. Columbia Pictures Corp., 186 F.2d 923 (9th Cir.1951) the Ninth Circuit specifically held that the *Mosler* doctrine applied to § 43(a) cases. See also Samson Crane Co. v. Union Nat. Sales, Inc., 87 F.Supp. 218, 222 (D.Mass.1949), affirmed mem. 180 F.2d 896 (1st Cir.1950) (§ 43(a) applies only to activities akin to trademark infringement and does not "bring within its scope any kind of undesirable business practice * * *."). These decisions sparked great disappointment in several commentators. See Callmann, False Advertising as a Competitive Tort, 48 Colum. L.Rev. 876, 885 (1948): "Instead of welcoming the new law and using its language and sweep as a basis for bypassing an unhappy precedent, the court's dictum [in California Apparel] apparently accepts the devitalizing interpretation that the new provision merely codifies the doctrine of *Grand Rapids * * *."*

The first broad interpretation of § 43(a) came in L'Aiglon Apparel v. Lana Lobell, Inc., 214 F.2d 649 (3d Cir.1954) (defendant advertised its $6.95

dress by using a picture of plaintiff's $17.95 dress). The Third Circuit rejected the claim that § 43(a) was merely declarative of existing law (*Mosler*) and held that the section created a new statutory tort of broad scope. Most courts quickly accepted the Third Circuit's view, and the section became widely used in false advertising, unfair competition and trademark cases. Although a number of issues of interpretation arose in the implementation of the section significant amendments to the section did not occur until the Trademark Revision Act of 1988.

2. *The Trademark Revision Act of 1988—§ 43(a)*. Students should make a careful comparison of the old and amended § 43(a).

The amended version applies to four categories of statements: (1) a word, name, symbol, or device, or any combination thereof; (2) a false designation of origin; (3) a false or misleading description of fact; and (4) a false or misleading representation of fact. The first category mirrors the definition of "trademark" in § 45 of the Lanham Act. By incorporating a second category, "false designation of origin" did Congress confer a meaning to "origin" different from its use to describe the "source" of goods or services in the trademark sense? Under the old section "origin" was interpreted to mean both geographic origin and origin of manufacture. See Federal–Mogul–Bower Bearings, Inc. v. Azoff, 313 F.2d 405 (6th Cir.1963). What does the phrase add to categories (3) and (4)? And what is the difference between a "description" of fact (category (3)) and a "representation" of fact (category (4))?

There are two substantive prohibitions in the amended version. The statement to be actionable must either (1) likely cause confusion as to the relationship between the speaker and another or their goods, or (2) misrepresent the "nature, characteristics, qualities, or geographic origin" of goods or services. Presumably statements in categories (1) and (2) would primarily fit prohibition (1) and statements in categories (3) and (4) would primarily fit prohibition (2). In this view the section appears to provide for a cause of action analogous to trademark infringement and separately for a cause of action for false advertising.

The last phrase of the amended version is a standing provision that permits any person who "is or is likely to be damaged" to bring a civil action.

Under the first prohibition, who must likely be confused? Consumers? Potential consumers? Reasonable persons? Competitors? Is there a connection between these persons and the persons authorized to bring suit? The second prohibition requires that the statement "misrepresents" the listed features of the goods or services. Because the second prohibition does not require confusion, mistake, or deception, does it mean Congress intended to prohibit any false statement regardless of whether consumers take it seriously? Does the misrepresentation have to be "material" or reasonably relied upon?

Does the amended version attach penalties to innocent misrepresentations? If it does, is it vulnerable to a First Amendment challenge?

The original section provided that the goods or services about which the statements were made must be placed in interstate commerce by the person making the statements. The amended version requires that the statements themselves be used "in commerce". Section 45 of the Lanham Act defines "commerce" broadly. What is the consequence of the amendment to § 43(a)? See Burger King of Florida, Inc. v. Brewer, 244 F.Supp. 293 (W.D.Tenn.1965) which held that a "purely intrastate business is in interstate commerce for purposes of § 43(a) of the Lanham Act if it has a substantial economic effect on interstate commerce." Under the amended version, are statements made by the salesclerk of an interstate department store actionable? Is a misrepresentation in a classified advertisement actionable under the amended version if copies of the newspaper are in interstate commerce?

The original section applied to statements regarding goods or services. The amended version uses the phrase "goods, services, or *commercial activities*" in describing the prohibited acts but not in describing the categories of statements covered by the Act? What might be included in "commercial activities"? What is the consequence of omitting the phrase in the first part of the section?

In the amended version the false advertising prohibition, but not the trademark prohibition, is limited to "commercial advertising or promotion". Is there a First Amendment justification for this distinction? Do either of the prohibitions protect a non-profit association? A governmental entity? Do they both apply to a classified advertisement by a non-merchant seller?

3. Why should the law prohibit false advertising only if someone is likely to be injured?

4. The scope of § 43(a) and the patience of a federal judge were both tested in Rare Earth, Inc. v. Hoorelbeke, Inc., 401 F.Supp. 26 (S.D.N.Y.1975). The case involved an incorporated rock group who performed under the trademark "Rare Earth." When the group split into two factions, a controversy arose over which group had the controlling shares in the corporation and thus the right to perform as the "Rare Earth." The action was brought in federal court under § 43(a) to prevent deception and palming off by unauthorized use or interference with the "Rare Earth" mark, but the resolution of the controversy depended almost exclusively on the validity of the title to corporate shares asserted by the competing members and this in turn depended on construction of the Michigan Business Corporation Act and Article 8 of the Michigan Uniform Commercial Code. The court recognized federal subject jurisdiction under the Lanham Act

> despite gnawing reservations. . . . However, in this age of congested court calendars—"a time when our dockets are burgeoning with matters peculiar to federal courts"—litigants who seek to advance primarily state law claims are well advised to proceed in the state courts and, thereby, permit other litigants, who have no other forum available to them, an opportunity to advance exclusively federal controversies before federal courts. The present, somewhat discursive endeavor is well concluded with the following words of the modern poet and popular singer Bob Dylan:
>
> . . . goodbye's too good a word, gal
>
> So I'll just say fare thee well

I ain't sayin' you treated me unkind

You could have done better but I don't mind

You just kinda wasted my precious time

But don't think twice, it's all right.

Johnson & Johnson v. Carter-Wallace, Inc.

United States Court of Appeals, Second Circuit, 1980.
631 F.2d 186.

■ MANSFIELD, CIRCUIT JUDGE.

* * *

Johnson's claim arises out of Carter's use of baby oil in NAIR and its advertising campaign regarding that inclusion. In 1977, Carter added baby oil to its NAIR lotion and initiated a successful advertising campaign emphasizing this fact. NAIR is sold in a pink plastic bottle with the word "NAIR" written in large, pink letters. A bright turquoise-blue banner, open at both ends, contains the words "with baby oil." In addition to its packaging of NAIR, Carter's television advertisements emphasize that NAIR contains baby oil.[2]

Alleging (1) that Carter is making false claims for NAIR with baby oil and (2) that it is packaging and advertising NAIR so as to give consumers the false impression that NAIR is a Johnson & Johnson product, plaintiff filed the instant suit for injunctive relief under § 43(a) of the Lanham Act, 15 U.S.C. § 1125(a), and under New York's common law of unfair competition. Section 43(a) of the Lanham Act provides for two separate causes of action: one is for "false designation of origin," the other for a "false description or representation, including words or symbols tending falsely to describe or represent" the product. Johnson's false representation claim alleges that Carter's "NAIR with baby oil" campaign falsely represents to consumers that the baby oil in NAIR has moisturizing and softening effect on the skin of the user. While recognizing that Carter's advertising makes no explicit claims for its product, Johnson alleges that this claim is implicit in the manner in which NAIR has been marketed. It contends that these false claims have unfairly dissuaded consumers from using its products in favor of NAIR with baby oil.

---

2. The court has viewed samples of Carter's television advertisements. Carter's commercials all featured several young women dancing and singing while dressed in clothing that revealed their legs. A typical audio portion of these commercials is as follows:

"Who's got Baby Oil?

Nair's got Baby Oil.

If you're a baby goil, Nair with Baby Oil.

Nair with Baby Oil.

It takes off the hair * * * so your legs feel baby smooth.

And Nair's baby-soft scent * * * smells terrific, baby.

Who's got Baby Oil?

Nair's got Baby Oil.

Soft-smelling Nair with Baby Oil.

Nair, for baby-smooth legs."

* * *

At the close of plaintiff's case, the trial court granted defendant's motion to dismiss the action. Plaintiff appeals from the dismissal of its false advertising claim under § 43(a). The propriety of the dismissal of its false designation of origin claim is not raised on appeal.

In dismissing Johnson's false advertising claim, the trial court did not reach either the question of whether Carter advertises or implies in its advertising that baby oil as an ingredient in NAIR has a moisturizing and softening effect, or the issue of whether such a claim is false. Instead, its dismissal was "granted on the ground that [Johnson] failed to carry its burden of proving damage or the likelihood of damage." Just what that burden is and what evidence will satisfy it, are the central issues in this appeal.

DISCUSSION

Prior to the enactment of § 43(a) of the Lanham Act, false advertising claims were governed by the common law of trade disparagement. Under the common law, liability was generally confined to "palming-off" cases where the deceit related to the origin of the product. Ely-Norris Safe Co. v. Mosler Safe Co., 7 F.2d 603 (2d Cir.1925), revd. on other grounds, 273 U.S. 132 (1926). In these cases the offending product was foisted upon an unwary consumer by deceiving him into the belief that he was buying the plaintiff's product (normally an item with a reputation for quality). Other instances of false advertising were safe from actions by competitors due to the difficulty of satisfying the requirement of proof of actual damage caused by the false claims. In an open market it is normally impossible to prove that a customer, who was induced by the defendant through the use of false claims to purchase the product, would have bought from the plaintiff if the defendant had been truthful.

The passage of § 43(a) represented a departure from the common law action for trade disparagement and from the need to prove actual damages as a prerequisite for injunctive relief. This departure marked the creation of a "new statutory tort" intended to secure a market-place free from deceitful marketing practices. The new tort, as subsequently interpreted by the courts, differs from the common law action for trade disparagement in two important respects: (1) it does not require proof of intent to deceive, and (2) it entitles a broad range of commercial parties to relief.

The broadening of the scope of liability results from a provision in § 43(a) allowing suit to be brought "by any person who believes that he is or is likely to be damaged by the use of any false description or representation." 15 U.S.C. § 1125(a). Whether this clause is viewed as a matter of standing to sue or as an element of the substantive claim for relief, certain bounds are well established. On the one hand, despite the use of the word "believes," something more than a plaintiff's mere subjective belief that he is injured or likely to be damaged is required before he will be entitled even to injunctive relief. On the other hand, as the district court in this case recognized, a plaintiff seeking an injunction, as opposed to money damages, need not quantify the losses actually borne. What showing of damage in between those two extremes will satisfy the statute is the subject of the instant dispute.

Johnson claims, in effect, that once it is shown that the plaintiff's and the defendant's products compete in a relevant market and that the defendant's ads are false, a likelihood of damage sufficient to satisfy the statute should be *presumed* and an injunction should issue "as a matter of course." The district court, in contrast, drew the line as follows: "Of course, J&J [Johnson] need not quantify its injury in order to obtain injunctive relief. But J&J must at least prove the existence of some injury caused by Carter." The court had said that "J&J has failed to prove that its loss of sales was in any way *caused* by NAIR's allegedly false advertising."

Both the case law and the policy behind § 43(a) indicate that the district court's construction of the statute placed too high a burden on the plaintiff in this case. To require a plaintiff to "prove the existence of some injury caused by" the defendant, is to demand proof of actual loss and specific evidence of causation. Perhaps a competitor in an open market could meet this standard with proof short of quantified sales loss, but it is not required to do so. The statute demands only proof providing a reasonable basis for the belief that the plaintiff is likely to be damaged as a result of the false advertising. The correct standard is whether it is *likely* that Carter's advertising has caused or will cause a loss of Johnson sales, not whether Johnson has come forward with specific evidence that Carter's ads actually resulted in some definite loss of sales. * * * Contrary to Johnson's argument, however, the likelihood of injury and causation will not be presumed, but must be demonstrated. If such a showing is made, the plaintiff will have established a reasonable belief that he is likely to be damaged within the meaning of § 43(a) and will be entitled to injunctive relief, as distinguished from damages, which would require more proof. We believe that the evidence offered by Johnson, though not overwhelming, is sufficient to prove a likelihood of damage from loss of sales.

Initially, we find that Johnson has shown that it and Carter are competitors in a relevant market. Although Johnson's Baby Oil and Lotion do not compete with NAIR in the narrower depilatory market, they do compete in the broader hair removal market. NAIR is used for hair removal by depilation. Johnson's Baby Lotion has been promoted as a substitute for shaving cream and is used for removal of hair by shaving. Also, both of Johnson's products are used as skin moisturizers after shaving or after the use of depilatories. Such indirect competitors may avail themselves of the protection of § 43(a); the competition need not be direct. Moreover, Carter's advertising campaign itself, by its emphasis on baby oil, directly links the depilation and the moisturizer markets. Johnson's stake in the shaving market gives it a "reasonable interest to be protected against the alleged false advertising." 1 R. Callman, Unfair Competition, Trademarks and Monopolies, § 18.2(b) at 625 (3d ed. 1967).

To prove a likelihood of injury Johnson must also show a logical causal connection between the alleged false advertising and its own sales position. This it has done with specific evidence. It has shown that large numbers of consumers in fact use its baby lotion for shaving and its baby oil as an after-shave and after-depilation moisturizer. Carter's "NAIR with baby oil" campaign affects both markets. First, NAIR's share of the hair removal market has increased since its baby oil advertising began. For each new depilatory user, a corresponding decline in the use of shaving products such as oils and lotions appears probable. Second, the use of baby oil after depilation is likely to be reduced if, as Johnson contends, Carter's advertising conveys to consumers the idea that NAIR's baby oil has a moisturizing and softening effect and leads the consumer to believe that use of a second, post-depilation, moisturizer is unnecessary. Of course, if Carter's ads are truthful, then its gains at Johnson's expense are well earned. If false, however, the damage to Johnson is unfair.

Johnson's case is supported by more than just the above logic. First, sales of its baby oil have in fact declined. Second, a consumer witness testified at trial that she switched from use of baby oil by shaving to NAIR because it was advertised as containing baby oil. Third, Johnson introduced surveys indicating that some people, after viewing NAIR ads, thought they would not have to use baby oil if they used NAIR. Together, Johnson's evidence was enough to prove a likelihood of competitive injury resulting from the NAIR advertising.

That much of the decline in Johnson's Baby Oil sales may be due to competition from lower priced baby oils, does not save Carter. * * * Further, the possibility that the total pecuniary harm to Johnson might be relatively slight does not bar injunctive relief.

Finally, Johnson's inability to point to a definite amount of sales lost *to Carter* (a failure which would bar monetary relief) does not preclude injunctive relief. Likelihood of competitive injury sufficient to warrant a § 43(a) injunction has been found in the absence of proof of actual sales diversion in numerous cases. * * *

Sound policy reasons exist for not requiring proof of actual loss as a prerequisite to § 43(a) injunctive relief. Failure to prove actual damages in an injunction suit, as distinguished from an action for damages, poses no likelihood of a windfall for the plaintiff. The complaining competitor gains no more than that to which it is already entitled—a market free of false advertising.

While proof of actual diversion of sales is not required for a § 43(a) injunction to issue, proof that the advertising complained of is in fact false is essential. This issue, though briefed by parties in this case, is not before the court at this time. The district court did not reach the question for purposes of determining whether permanent relief should issue. Since the action was dismissed at the close of the plaintiff's case, Carter was afforded no opportunity to introduce additional evidence answering the plaintiff on this point. Johnson, having shown that it is likely to be damaged by Carter's advertising, must prove that the NAIR advertising was false before being entitled to injunctive relief under the Lanham Act. Should the district court find that the defendant's advertising conveys a false message, irreparable injury for the purpose of injunctive relief would be present for the very reason that in an open market it is impossible to measure the exact amount of Johnson's damages. * * *

Accordingly, this cause is reversed and remanded for further proceedings in conformity with this opinion. We retain jurisdiction.

Ortho Pharmaceutical Corporation v. Cosprophar, Inc.

United States Court of Appeals, Second Circuit,
1994 32 F.3d 690

[Ortho manufacturers a drug called RETIN-A containing tretinoin, a retinoid of Vitamin A that the FDA classifies as a drug. The drug is obtainable by prescription and is approved only for the treatment of acne. Ortho may not promote the drug for other uses although physicians may lawfully prescribe the drug for "off-label" uses. After a 1988 article in the Journal of the American Medical Association advocating use of RETIN-A for treatment of photo damaged skin, "off-label" uses of RETIN-A increased significantly. Ortho developed a product called RENOVA, a cream identical to RETIN-A, and is seeking FDA approval to market RENOVA for treatment of photo damaged skin. Cosprophar, in 1988, introduced a line of cosmetics using the family name "ANTI-AGE" specifically advertised as beneficial for photo damaged or wrinkled skin. The advertisements claimed the products are associated with "retinol" and indicated that products based on tretinoin are less safe. Cosprophar's products were non-prescription but were marketed exclusively through pharmacies to give them credibility. Ortho brought this § 43(a) claim alleging that Cosprophar's advertisements were false. Cosprophar argued that Ortho had no standing under § 43(a).]

* * * This appeal requires us to decide what evidence a plaintiff suing under § 43(a) of the Lanham Act must submit to demonstrate that its interests were or will likely be damaged by another business's allegedly false or misleading advertising. We hold that since Ortho's products are not obviously in competition with Cosprophar's, Ortho was required to submit proof demonstrating that consumers view Cosprophar's cosmetics as a comparable substitute for Ortho's drugs. Because Ortho failed to do so, and because Ortho failed to submit sufficient proof on its state law claims, we affirm the judgment of the district court.

* * *

* * * In order to establish standing to sue under [§ 43 (a)] a plaintiff must demonstrate a "reasonable interest to be protected" against the advertiser's false or misleading claims and a "reasonable basis" for believing that this interest is likely to be damaged by the false or misleading advertising, Coca-Cola Co. v. Tropicana Prods., Inc., 690 F.2d 312, 316 (2d Cir.1982). The "reasonable basis" prong embodies a requirement that the plaintiff show both likely injury and a causal nexus to the false advertising.

Although Judge Tenney ruled that Ortho had not satisfied its burden on either ground, we turn first to his decision that Ortho failed to demonstrate a "reasonable basis" to believe that it is likely to be injured by Cosprophar's advertising since we find this issue to be dispositive. We will assume for the purposes of our discussion that Ortho has a protectable interest in its off- label sales of RETIN-A and in its future sales of RENOVA.

This circuit has adopted a flexible approach toward the showing a Lanham Act plaintiff must make on the injury and causation component of its claim. We have held that, while a plaintiff must show more than a "subjective belief" that it will be damaged, it need not demonstrate that it is in direct competition with the defendant or that it has definitely lost sales because of the defendant's advertisements. However, we have also maintained that "[t]he likelihood of injury and causation will not be presumed, but must be demonstrated in some manner." The type and quantity of proof required to show injury and causation has varied from one case to another depending on the particular circumstances. On the whole, we have tended to require a more substantial showing where the plaintiff's products are not obviously in competition with defendant's products, or the defendant's advertisements do not draw direct comparisons between the two. * * *

Here, the district court found that "Ortho and Cosprophar are not in direct competition given the nature of their products: one is a drug requiring a doctor's prescription, the other is a cosmetic available in a pharmacy." Without disputing this finding, Ortho claims that it will be harmed by Cosprophar's advertising in three ways. First, it asserts that consumers who currently buy Cosprophar's cosmetics consequently will not buy RETIN-A. Second, it claims that consumers who are dissatisfied with Cosprophar's cosmetics will be discouraged from buying Ortho's products in the future. Third, it claims that consumers who like Cosprophar's cosmetics will continue to purchase them and will thus have no occasion to try either RETIN-A or RENOVA. As proof of this injury, Ortho relies solely on (a) Cosprophar's advertisements, and (b) statements made by a Cosprophar employee that its cosmetics were introduced to take advantage of the publicity surrounding transretinoic acid. The able district judge determined that this evidence was insufficient to establish that Ortho would likely be injured by Cosprophar's conduct. We agree.

The missing link in Ortho's proof is evidence that Cosprophar's advertising will have the effect on consumers that Ortho says it will—in other words, that consumers will see Cosprophar's cosmetics as substitutes for Ortho's drugs. In other cases, this link has been supplied by consumer surveys or consumer witnesses. For example, in *Johnson & Johnson,* a case upon which Ortho places much reliance, the plaintiff introduced market surveys indicating that some consumers thought they would not have to use the plaintiff's product (baby oil) if they used defendant's product (a depilatory which claimed to contain baby oil) and testimony from a consumer witness who stated that she switched from using plaintiff's baby oil to using defendant's depilatory because of defendant's advertisement.

* * *

At trial, and again as part of its post-trial submissions, Ortho unsuccessfully attempted to introduce three market research surveys into evidence. Judge Tenney rejected this proffer because Ortho failed to show that the surveys were properly conducted and that they were business records within the meaning of Fed.R.Evid. 803(6). Judge Tenney further noted that even if admissible, the surveys did not establish a causal link between Cosprophar's advertisements and any damage claimed by Ortho because they merely corroborated the undisputed fact that consumers were aware of the alleged benefits of RETIN- A and did not address "alternative skin-care treatments, alternative products, or specifically, defendant's products."

Ortho does not challenge the district court's ruling excluding its surveys. Instead, it argues that it was not required to submit evidence of consumer perceptions because Cosprophar's advertisements draw comparisons to Ortho's drugs and therefore supply the necessary link between the two companies' products. Ortho points to excerpts from Cosprophar's advertisements which discuss the publicity regarding trans-retinoic acid and indicate that Cosprophar's retinol-based cosmetics are superior for the treatment of photoaged skin because they have no side effects. Specifically, Cosprophar's advertisements state that "interest in retinol in Europe reached very high levels after the discovery at a prominent University of the anti-wrinkle potential of transretinoic acid" with a citation to the 1988 JAMA article; that interest in anti-wrinkle products "is only partially met by two other products available on the market," one of which is "the dermatologist-prescribed anti-acne treatments based on retinoic acid"; and that "[u]sers of transretinoic acid . . . complained of reddening and irritation while these effects have never been noted with the use of retinol in anti-wrinkle treatment." Ortho acknowledges that Cosprophar's advertisements refer to transretinoic acid, not specifically to RETIN-A or RENOVA, but argues that it is unnecessary to submit proof that consumers identify the ingredient in their products by its scientific name. Ortho also argues that a witness for Cosprophar admitted that the company tried to link its products to Ortho's drugs because she conceded that the ANTI-AGE RETARD line of cosmetics was introduced in 1988 in part "to tap into . . . consumer interest in anti-aging products" and that Cosprophar took "advantage of the publicity, of the transretinoic acid."

For support of its advertisement-linkage analysis, Ortho relies on the decisions in Johnson & Johnson and Upjohn Co. v. Riahom Corp., 641 F.Supp. 1209 (D.Del.1986). However, both cases are distinguishable. In *Johnson & Johnson,* this court relied on the linkage in defendant's advertising between its product and plaintiff's product as proof that plaintiff had a "reasonable interest to be protected against the alleged false advertising." 631 F.2d at 190. In order to find that plaintiff had established a likelihood of injury, the court looked not only at the advertisements but also at plaintiff's market research indicating that the advertisements led consumers to believe that they would no longer need plaintiff's product. Thus, *Johnson & Johnson* does not establish that advertising-linkage alone is sufficient proof of injury.

The *Upjohn* case is no more helpful. In that case, the defendant's advertisements did not simply compare its products to plaintiff's products; they expressly incorporated materials relating to plaintiff and its research in such a manner as to suggest that defendant's product was associated with plaintiff. The court determined that this use of plaintiff's publicity was adequate proof of an injury because of the possibility of false attribution. Such a danger does not exist in this case. Ortho argues, however, that the Upjohn court also found injury based solely on the false claims in defendant's advertising without any reference to consumer research. To the extent this is true, the Upjohn court appeared to supply the missing link by presuming that defendant's false claims would adversely affect plaintiff's sales. See 641 F.Supp. at 1225 (stating that defendant's false claims "definitely tend to induce consumers to purchase their product, thereby depriving [plaintiff] of potential customers and sales"). While there may be room for such a presumption in cases where there is a question of false designation of goods, our circuit has expressly disfavored presumptions of harm in cases where the products are not obviously in competition or where the defendant's advertisements make no direct reference to any competitor's products.

Under the standards of this Circuit, Ortho has failed to present sufficient evidence to establish that it will likely be damaged by Cosprophar's conduct.

NOTES

1. In *Johnson & Johnson*, why isn't proof of competition between the plaintiff and the defendant sufficient to satisfy the standing requirement of § 43(a)? Does the additional evidence relied upon by the court to prove the "logical connection" between the false advertisement and potential injury to the plaintiff add anything to the fact that the parties were in competition? Or is the problem that here they only indirectly compete in that the plaintiff does not make a depilatory with baby oil but only baby oil alone? If McDonalds made a false statement about its hamburgers, what evidence would Burger King have to introduce to obtain standing?

2. In the District Court, Judge Tenney held that Ortho failed to show a reasonable interest to be protected because it could not, even if it wanted, market its product for photo-damaged skin due to FDA regulations. Why isn't it sufficient that physicians were able to, and did, prescribe RETIN-A for photo damaged skin and thus put Ortho in direct competition with Cosprophar? Actually, Johnson & Johnson, Ortho's parent corporation, was accused by the Federal Drug Administration of improperly promoting Retin A for an unapproved use. Johnson & Johnson in 1988 held a series of news conferences and talk show appearances highlighting studies and doctor testimonials that Retin A worked as a wrinkle cream. FDA asked the Justice Department to investigate. In 1996 the FDA approved the marketing of Retin A for this purpose. See, Robert Langreth, J & J's Assault on Wrinkles Is Finally Won, Wall Street Journal, at B4 (Jan. 3, 1996).

3. In the *Coca-Cola* case referred to in *Ortho*, Tropicana used an advertisement that claimed its orange juice was "fresh squeezed". Coca-Cola claimed the advertisement was false and injured its sales of its own orange juice made from concentrate. Coca-Cola introduced market studies showing that consumers were likely to be misled into thinking "fresh squeezed" meant the orange juice was unprocessed. There were, however, no studies indicating that consumers, if not deceived, would have purchased Coca-Cola's product. How does this factual situation differ from that in *Ortho*?

4. Under what circumstances, if any, can a plaintiff assert standing under § 43(a) without introducing a consumer survey?

5. The 1988 amendments to § 43(a) limit the applicability of the false advertising provisions to statements made "in commercial advertising or promotion". The limitation was applied in Gordon & Breach Science Publishers v. American Institute of Physics, 859 F. Supp. 152 (S.D.N.Y. 1994). G & B was a commercial publisher of a scientific academic journal; AIP and APS were non-profit publishers of competing journals. Henry Barschall, a physics professor at the University of Wisconsin and an APS officer, conducted a survey to show that non-profit publisher's journals were more cost effective. The survey showed G & B to be among the least cost effective publishers and AIP to be among the best. Both AIP and APS published articles by Barschall containing the results of his survey along with his commentary suggesting that librarians should purchase more non-profit publications. Reprints of the Barschall article were distributed at a librarians' conference. G & B, claiming the surveys misrepresented the facts, brought suit under § 43(a) of the Lanham Act.

After reviewing the legislative history and case law, the court concluded:

> The principles from the cases and legislative history may be summed up as follows: In order for representations to constitute "commercial advertising or promotion" under Section 43(a)(1)(B), they must be: (1) commercial speech; (2) by a defendant who is in commercial competition with plaintiff; (3) for the purpose of influencing consumers to buy defendant's goods or services. While the representations need not be made in a "classic advertising campaign," but may consist instead of more informal types of "promotion," the representations (4) must be disseminated sufficiently to the relevant purchasing public to constitute "advertising" or "promotion" within that industry.

The court held that publication of the articles themselves was not "commercial advertising or promotion" and "[t]o hold otherwise would be to squelch the expression of facts and opinions which might not otherwise find ready expression through commercial media." However, the court held that secondary uses of the surveys such as distribution of reprints of the articles at librarians' conferences and other disseminations of the survey results to librarians were actionable. On this latter point see the court's subsequent opinion at 905 F. Supp. 169, 180 (1995): "Defendants' use of the surveys directly to target relevant consumers is precisely the type of promotional activity that the Lanham Act seeks to regulate. . . . This element of consumer-orientation — of directly targeting relevant purchasers — pervades virtually all of defendant's secondary uses. We find it dispositive."

See also, Semco, Inc. v. Amcast, Inc., 52 F.3d 108 (6th Cir. 1995). The editor of a trade journal requested the president of a company to submit for publication an article describing a manufacturing process. He complied but included self-serving statements about his company's own products. The court held the article was "commercial advertising or promotion" and could be constitutionally sanctioned if false.

Alpo Petfoods, Inc. v. Ralston Purina Co.

United States Court of Appeals, District of Columbia Circuit, 1990.
913 F.2d 958.

■ CLARENCE THOMAS, CIRCUIT JUDGE:

In this case, Ralston Purina Co. and ALPO Petfoods, Inc. two of the leading dog food producers in the United States, have sued each other under § 43(a) of the Lanham Act alleging false advertising. ALPO asserts that Ralston has violated § 43(a) by claiming that its Puppy Chow products can lessen the severity of canine hip dysplasia (CHD), a crippling joint condition. Ralston, for its part, attacks ALPO's claims that ALPO Puppy Food contains "the formula preferred by responding vets two to one over the leading puppy food."

[The trial court found that Ralston's CHD related claims were false because they lacked sufficient empirical support and that the claims materially increased Ralston's sales at the expense of ALPO and other competitors. The court also found that ALPO had no basis for its veterinarian preference claims. These findings were affirmed but the Court of Appeals reversed a finding that Ralston's violation was wilful and in bad faith.]

B. Monetary Award in Favor of ALPO

Besides challenging the district court's conclusion that its CHD-related advertising violated section 43(a), Ralston attacks the monetary remedy for that violation: a $10.4 million judgment in favor of ALPO under section 35(a) of the Lanham Act. Ralston concentrates its attack on the court's decision to use Ralston's advertising costs as a measure of monetary relief, a method derived from U-Haul, Int'l, Inc. v. Jartran, Inc., 793 F.2d 1034, 1042 (9th Cir.1986). Ralston argues that the court made an error of law in adopting *U-Haul*, and that the court incorporated clearly erroneous findings of fact into its *U-Haul* analysis. Reviewing the court's decision on monetary relief for abuse of discretion we agree that the award against Ralston must be vacated.

The district court's opinion states that Ralston's false advertising caused ALPO financial harm, and describes the $10.4 million award to ALPO as damages. * * * The two-part analysis supporting the amount of the monetary relief, however, shows that the court actually awarded Ralston's profits to ALPO. In deciding the amount of relief, the district court first adopted the reasoning in *U-Haul*, 793 F.2d at 1042. In that case, the Ninth Circuit affirmed an unprecedented $40 million award to a competitor injured by a section 43(a) violation. * * * The district court here, after using the *U-Haul* approach to calculate Ralston's profits at $10.4 million [assuming that a firm's profits are at least equal to its advertising expenditures], confirmed that figure by comparing it with "the 11 million dollar adjusted net profits Ralston earned from the sales of its Puppy Chow products during the period of its CHD advertising program." *ALPO*, 720 F.Supp. at 215; see id. at 212, 215 ("adjusted net profits" figure equals Ralston's nationwide pre-tax profits, multiplied by ALPO's percentage share of non-Ralston puppy food market).

Leaving aside whether the *U-Haul* standard[9] or the district court's alternative calculation[10] accurately measures the profits that Ralston derived from its false advertising, we hold that this case does not justify an award of profits. Section 35(a) authorizes courts to award to an aggrieved plaintiff both plaintiff's damages and defendant's profits, but, as this court noted in [Foxtrap, Inc. v. Foxtrap, Inc., 671 F.2d 636, at 641 (D.C.Cir.1982)] courts' discretion to award these remedies has limits. Just as "any award based on plaintiff's damages requires some showing of actual loss," id. at 642; an award based on a defendant's profits requires proof that the defendant acted willfully or in bad faith. Proof of this sort is lacking. Ralston's decision to run CHD-related advertising that lacked solid empirical support does not, without more, reflect willfulness or bad faith. * * *

In [Reader's Digest Ass'n v. Conservative Digest, Inc., 821 F.2d 800 (D.C.Cir.1987)] we "left open the possibility that a court could properly award damages to a plaintiff when the defendant has been unjustly enriched." 821 F.2d at 807–08 (citing *Foxtrap*, 671 F.2d at 641 & n. 9). The unjust-enrichment theory, which emerged in trademark cases in which the infringer and the infringed were not competitors, holds that courts should divest an infringer of his profits, regardless of whether the infringer's actions have harmed the owner of the infringed trademark. Awards of profits are justified under the theory because they deter infringement in general and thereby vindicate consumers' interests. * * * As we state below, however, we doubt the wisdom of an approach to damages that permits courts to award profits for their sheer deterrent effect.

* * * Based on *Foxtrap*, as well as our concern that deterrence is too weak and too easily invoked a justification for the severe and often cumbersome remedy of a profits award, see Koelemay, *Monetary Relief for Trademark Infringement Under the Lanham Act*, 72 Trademark Rep. 458, 493–94, 536–37 (1982), we hold that deterrence alone cannot justify such an award.

Since this case lacks the elements required to support the court's award of Ralston's profits, we vacate the $10.4 million judgment in favor of ALPO.

---

9. The Ninth Circuit has already noted the limitations of the *U-Haul* rule. See Harper House, 889 F.2d at 209 n. 8 (justification for *U-Haul* rule weakens in cases that do not involve passing off or direct comparative advertising). Commentators, too, have criticized the decision. See, e.g., Comment, *Money Damages and Corrective Advertising: An Economic Analysis*, 55 U.Chi.L.Rev. 629, 638–42 (1988) (refuting premise that defendants' advertising costs reflect value of plaintiffs' lost reputation and good will); Comment, *Monetary Relief for False Advertising Claims Arising Under Section 43(a) of the Lanham Act*, 34 UCLA L.Rev. 953, 955 n. 6, 973–74 (1987) (large awards under *U-Haul* give firms

incentives to attack rivals, particularly new entrants, with false-advertising suits). But cf. Best, *Monetary Damages for False Advertising*, 49 U.Pitt.L.Rev. 1, 18–22 (1987) (praising U-Haul for easing plaintiffs' burden of proving actual damages, but noting that the U-Haul surrogate measure itself can lead to overcompensation). * * *

10. As Ralston points out, the alternative calculation "assumes that (1) all of Ralston's Puppy Chow profits were attributable solely to its advertising and (2) all the profits attributable to advertising were due to the CHD claims." Brief of Appellant at 47 (emphasis deleted).

We do not mean, however, to deny ALPO all monetary relief for Ralston's false advertising. Because the district court has so far focused on awarding Ralston's profits it has not yet decided what actual damages ALPO has proved. On remand, the court should award ALPO its actual damages, bearing in mind the requirement that any amount awarded have support in the record, as well as the following points about the governing law.

In a false-advertising case such as this one, actual damages under section 35(a) can include:—profits lost by the plaintiff on sales actually diverted to the false advertiser;—profits lost by the plaintiff on sales made at prices reduced as a demonstrated result of the false advertising;—the costs of any completed advertising that actually and reasonably responds to the defendant's offending ads;[11] and—quantifiable harm to the plaintiff's good will, to the extent that completed corrective advertising has not repaired that harm.[12]

When assessing these actual damages, the district court may take into account the difficulty of proving an exact amount of damages from false advertising, as well as the maxim that " 'the wrongdoer shall bear the risk of the uncertainty which his own wrong has created.' " Otis Clapp & Son v. Filmore Vitamin Co., 754 F.2d 738, 745 (7th Cir.1985). At the same time, the court must ensure that the record adequately supports all items of damages claimed and establishes a causal link between the damages and the defendant's conduct, lest the award become speculative or violate section 35(a)'s prohibition against punishment. * * *

Section 35(a) also authorizes the court to "enter judgment according to the circumstances of the case, for any sum above the amount found as actual damages, not exceeding three times such amount." Lanham Act 35(a). This provision gives the court discretion to enhance damages, as long as the ultimate award qualifies as "compensation and not [as] a penalty." Id.; see Koelemay, 72 Trademark Rep. at 516–19, 521–25 (discussing interplay of damages enhancement provision and antipenalty clause); see also Getty Petroleum Corp. v. Bartco Petroleum Corp., 858 F.2d 103, 112–13 (2d Cir.1988) (in trademark infringement case, interpreting section 35(a) to ban any awards of punitive damages), cert. denied, 109 S.Ct. 1642 (1989). Given this express statutory restriction, if the district court decides to enhance damages under section 35(a), it should explain why the enhanced award is compensatory and not punitive.

---

11. See also Best, 49 U.Pitt.L.Rev. at 23 ("For this approach to be effective, the plaintiff's responsive marketing campaign must be found to have been a reasonable response to the defendant's conduct."); Comment, 55 U.Chi.L.Rev. at 633 ("Although courts should make available the defense that the counter-advertising performed was unreasonable or wasteful, most courts are willing to accept counter-advertising costs as recoverable business losses.").

12. The thin body of case law on actual damages for successful false-advertising claims reflects the fact that litigants, who best understand their real losses, almost always settle these cases once a court has given its view of the merits. See Comment, 55 U.Chi.L.Rev. at 631.

C. Denial of Monetary Relief in Favor of Ralston

[The trial court had denied Ralston relief even though it found ALPO's advertising false because "[t]he magnitude of the wrongdoing by Ralston in comparison to that of ALPO is so much greater that a damage award would not be justified," because ALPO, but not Ralston, had shown remorse, and because the court considered Ralston's counterclaim "an afterthought." The Court of Appeals held that a denial of damages was not proper on this basis. "Since section 35(a) expressly provides for compensation, rather than punishment, courts dealing with offsetting meritorious claims must let the degree of injury that each party proves, rather than the degree of opprobrium that the court attaches to each party's conduct, determine the monetary relief."

The Court of Appeals also reversed the lower court's award of attorneys fees to ALPO because Ralston's behavior was not wilful or in bad faith.]

Alpo Petfoods, Inc. v. Ralston Purina Company

United States Court of Appeals, District of Columbia, 1993.
997 F.2d. 949.

■ D. H. GINSBURG, CIRCUIT JUDGE:

[On remand from the Court of Appeals [ALPO Petfoods Inc. v. Ralston Purina Co., 778 F. Supp. 555 (D.D.C. 1991)], the district court awarded ALPO $12,140,356.50 and Ralston $53,434.86 in damages and awarded Ralston an additional $797,560 in attorneys fees. The court concluded that neither party could show lost profits caused by the respective false claims. However, the court awarded ALPO $3,585,610 to reimburse it for advertising and promotional expenses incurred in response to Ralston's false CHD campaign. The court also found that Ralston's false advertising delayed ALPO's plans to expand its puppy food market nationwide and awarded ALPO $4,507,961 representing the present value of the foregone income stream caused by this delay. The district court then enhanced the award by 50%.

The Court of Appeals upheld the award for responsive advertising even though ALPO's advertising did not refer specifically to Ralston's false claim. The Court observed that requiring a direct reference would give broader circulation to the false claims. To arrive at an award for the responsive advertising the district court had evidence of what ALPO had planned to spend on advertising before Ralston's false claims and subtracted this figure from what it actually spent. The difference was assumed to be the amount necessary to respond to Ralston's false claims. The Court of Appeals approved the methodology, rejected Ralston's claim that ALPO should not be allowed to recover more in responsive advertising than Ralston spent on the false advertising, but remanded to the district court to reduce the award by a pro rata amount attributable to ALPO's own false advertising.]

B. Delay of ALPO's Income Stream

Although the district court declined to speculate about the profits that either party lost on sales diverted to the other, the court did award

ALPO the profits it lost due to the need, in view of Ralston's CHD campaign, to defer its national expansion. The court calculated ALPO's losses from the profits that ALPO had projected it would earn when it first decided to enter the national puppy food market. Early year losses and later year profits (projected into the indefinite future) were reduced to present value; the court then computed the present value of that same income stream assuming a five year delay in getting it started and awarded ALPO the difference, some $4.5 million.

Ralston argues that the delay in ALPO's receipt of income from a national rollout of ALPO Puppy Food is not a permissible category of damages, and is purely speculative. We disagree on both counts.

When we remanded this case earlier for the district court to recompute the damage award we noted that:

> [A]ctual damages under section 35(a) can include: profits lost by the plaintiff on sales actually diverted to the false advertiser, profits lost by the plaintiff on sales made at prices reduced as a demonstrated result of the false advertising, the costs of any completed advertising that actually and reasonably responds to the defendant's offending ads, and quantifiable harm to the plaintiff's good will, to the extent that completed corrective advertising has not repaired that harm.

ALPO II, 913 F.2d at 969. While we did not specifically itemize a delay in the receipt of a stream of income as a compensable category of damages, the district court correctly understood that our list of such categories was illustrative, not exhaustive. The statute itself suggests as much, for it specifically authorizes the court, if it finds that a recovery based upon profits would be inadequate, "in its discretion [to] enter judgment for such sum as the court should find to be just," and to award the plaintiff what is in effect the time value of its deferred profits is hardly an abuse of discretion.

Nor do we view the award as unduly uncertain. The district court found that ALPO would have expanded nationally but was stymied by Ralston's false advertisements. The court therefore looked at ALPO's projections, prepared in the ordinary course of business and on the basis of which it was prepared to risk its own capital, in order to estimate the profits that ALPO would have reaped from that expansion. ALPO was not certain to succeed, of course, but the question is who is to bear the now-hypothetical risk that it would fail? We answered that question when we remanded this case to the district court: When assessing actual damages, the court may take into account the difficulty of proving an exact amount of damages from false advertising, as well as the maxim that "the wrongdoer shall bear the risk of uncertainty which his own wrong has created." That is what the district court has done—to Ralston's chagrin.

The district court erred, however, in refusing to reduce the award to reflect ALPO's alternative use of the funds it did not have to expend on a national rollout. In order to reflect economic reality, damages awarded in order to compensate for loss of a business opportunity should equal the plaintiff's " 'opportunity cost,' or the return it could have made on an alternative investment" of the funds not spent on the foregone opportunity.

ALPO retained the use of the funds it would have spent on a national rollout; presumably it did not put the money under a mattress but obtained some (albeit a second best) return on that capital. That ALPO may in fact have spent some or all of the money on a responsive advertising campaign, as the district court found, is beside the point. The responsive campaign itself constituted, in effect, an alternative investment, the return on which is the prejudgment interest to which ALPO is entitled.

To award ALPO prejudgment interest without reducing the award made in compensation for the loss of the future income stream would be double counting. The district court should therefore reduce the award for deferral of ALPO's future income stream in order to reflect the return on capital it presumably received from alternative investments, using the prejudgment interest rate as a measure of that return.

* * *

Section 35(a) of the Lanham Act authorizes the court to award up to three times a plaintiff's actual and proven damages so long as the result is compensatory, not punitive. The district court enhanced the award to ALPO by 50% in order to cover its lost profits (i.e., on sales diverted from ALPO to Ralston), compensate ALPO for a permanent distortion in the market for puppy food, and for interest and inflation. Ralston says the enhancement is speculative, punitive, and an indirect attempt to award attorneys' fees to ALPO notwithstanding our earlier reversal of such an award.

The last allegation is as unworthy of counsel as it is unnecessary to Ralston's cause. An enhancement is appropriate to compensate a Lanham Act plaintiff only for such adverse effects as can neither be dismissed as speculative nor precisely calculated. Interest and inflation are not such elusive quanta. Lost profits and market distortion are, however, appropriate bases for the catch-all enhancement contemplated by § 35(a). We thus remand this aspect of the award to the district court to compute the precise amounts to be awarded for interest and the effect of inflation, and to reconsider such enhancement as may be appropriate solely in order to compensate ALPO for its lost profits on sales diverted to Ralston and the continuing distortion of the market owing to Ralston's false advertising.

NOTES

1. Under the original version of § 43(a) it was uncertain whether the remedies provided in other provisions of the Lanham Act for trademark infringement were applicable to false advertising cases. The 1988 amendments make it clear that the remedies provided in § 34(a) (injunctions), § 35(a) (profits which may be a sum the court determines to be "just", damages including the possibility of treble damages, costs, and in "exceptional cases" reasonable attorneys fees), and § 36 (destruction of infringing articles) apply to § 43(a) violations. The more onerous penalties in § 34(d) and § 35(b) are reserved for registered marks. The Restatement, Third, of

Unfair Competition, § 36 and §37 apply the same rules for damages and profits to both trademark infringement and false advertising claims.

2. Can the monetary remedies fashioned for trademark infringement be easily applied to a false advertising case? Consider whether the following situations present different problems of proving money damages:

A. The defendant makes generalized false claims about its own product. (ALPO)

B. The defendant falsely claims that its product has been proven to be better than the plaintiff's. (U-Haul).

C. The defendant uses a trademark that is confusingly similar to the trademark of the plaintiff.

3. In which of the situations in Note 2 would you award the plaintiff the profits earned by the defendant as a result of the false claims? In *Alpo,* the court, after observing that profits are awarded in trademark cases where there is a purposeful attempt to trade on the good-will of the trademark owner, held that in broader false advertising cases " 'willfulness' and 'bad faith' require a connection between a defendant's awareness of its competitors and its actions at those competitors' expense." Do you see why something like this is required? If *A* makes an intentionally false statement about its own goods, how many of *A's* competitors could recover its profits?

4. Why did Congress in section 35(a) of the Lanham Act provide authority for judges to treble an actual damage award as long as it was "compensatory" and not punitive? What categories of damages fit into Judge Ginsburg's category of "adverse effects as can neither be dismissed as speculative nor precisely calculated?"

Johnson & Johnson * Merck Consumer Pharmaceuticals Company v. Smithkline Beecham Corporation

United States Court of Appeals, Second Circuit, 1992.
960 F.2d 294

■ WALKER, CIRCUIT JUDGE.

[The parties are manufacturers of nonprescription antacids. The plaintiff, J & J * Merck, makes MYLANTA which contains aluminum and magnesium hydroxide. The defendant makes TUMS which uses calcium carbonate. Defendant produced two comparative commercials. In the first ("Ingredients") competing products including MYLANTA, ROLAIDS, and MAALOX appear on the screen with their ingredients, i.e., aluminum and magnesium. TUMS then appears with the voice-over stating it is "aluminum free" and that "only TUMS helps wipe out heartburn and gives you calcium you need every day." After complaints to the television networks, defendant withdrew "Ingredients" and began using "Ingredients-Revised". This second commercial listed the ingredients of the competing products but deleted all references to TUMS as "aluminum free". It continued to emphasized that TUMS contained calcium, which was good for users, and the others did not. A shorter version of this commercial compared TUMS only to MYLANTA. Plaintiff brought suit under § 43(a) of the Lanham Act alleging "Ingredients-Revised" was false and misleading in that it falsely represented that (1) TUMS had nutritional benefits, and (2) aluminum and magnesium were unsafe for human consumption. The district court found that plaintiff had failed to show that the assertion of nutritional benefits for TUMS was false. She also found that the commercials did not "communicate the message that aluminum or magnesium are harmful or unsafe." On appeal, plaintiff abandoned its attack on the calcium claim.]

J & J * Merck contends that, even though the content of the challenged commercials is literally true, Ingredients-Revised preys upon a publicly held misperception that the ingestion of aluminum causes Alzheimer's disease. According to J & J * Merck, the commercials accomplish this by repeatedly juxtaposing the absence of aluminum in TUMS with its presence in MYLANTA. In turn, this repetition supposedly links MYLANTA with an allegedly popularly held, yet unsubstantiated concern that aluminum is associated with Alzheimer's. Since the aluminum/Alzheimer's connection has not been scientifically established, J & J * Merck argues that Ingredients-Revised purposefully taps into a preexisting body of public misinformation in order to communicate the false and misleading message that aluminum-based antacids are harmful.

The gravamen of J & J * Merck's claim is that advertisers may be held liable for the knowing exploitation of public misperception. While this argument presents a novel theory of Lanham Act liability—one which we neither reject nor embrace—we note that, in any event, it would be unavailing in this case. Because J & J * Merck has failed to show that it has suffered any injury as a result of the challenged TUMS commercials, it cannot obtain relief under any theory of Lanham Act liability that is premised upon an implied falsehood.

I. *Liability for Implied Falsehoods*

* * *

The law governing false advertising claims under the Lanham Act is well settled in this circuit. In order to recover damages or obtain equitable relief, a plaintiff must show that either: 1) the challenged advertisement is literally false, or 2) while the advertisement is literally true it is nevertheless likely to mislead or confuse consumers.

Where, as here, a plaintiff's theory of recovery is premised upon a claim of implied falsehood, a plaintiff must demonstrate, by extrinsic evidence, that the challenged commercials tend to mislead or confuse consumers. It is not for the judge to determine, based solely upon his or her own intuitive reaction, whether the advertisement is deceptive. Rather, as we have reiterated in the past, "[t]he question in such cases is—what does the person to whom the advertisement is addressed find to be the message?" That is, what does the public perceive the message to be?

The answer to this question is pivotal because, where the advertisement is literally true, it is often the only measure by which a court can determine whether a commercial's net communicative effect is misleading. Thus, the success of a plaintiff's implied falsity claim usually turns on the persuasiveness of a consumer survey. * * *

[I]n attempting to show that the district court's findings on this point were clearly erroneous, J & J * Merck argues that Judge Cedarbaum failed sufficiently to consider factors other than consumer survey evidence, such as: 1) the general "commercial context" or sea of information in which consumers are immersed; 2) the defendant's intent to harness public misperception; 3) the defendant's prior advertising history; and 4) the sophistication of the advertising audience. This argument causes us some discomfort.

Appellant's criticism of the district court's findings misconstrues the proper role of consumer survey evidence in the analysis of implied falsehood claims. Generally, before a court can determine the truth or falsity of an advertisement's message, it must first determine what message was actually conveyed to the viewing audience. Consumer surveys supply such information.

Three of the factors listed by J & J * Merck, i.e., commercial context, defendant's prior advertising history, and sophistication of the advertising audience, only come into play, if at all, during the latter part of the court's analysis. In a particular case, these factors may shed some light on whether the challenged advertisement contributed to the meaning that was ultimately gleaned by the target audience. In other words, in determining whether an advertisement is likely to mislead or confuse, the district court may consider these factors after a plaintiff has established "that a not insubstantial number of consumers," *Coca-Cola Co.* [Coca-Cola Co. v. Tropicana Products Inc., 690 F.2d 312 (2d Cir. 1982)], 690 F.2d at 317, hold the false belief allegedly communicated in the ad.

Absent such a threshold showing, an implied falsehood claim must fail. This follows from the obvious fact that the injuries redressed in false advertising cases are the result of public deception. Thus, where the plaintiff cannot demonstrate that a statistically significant part of the commercial audience holds the false belief allegedly communicated by the challenged advertisement, the plaintiff cannot establish that it suffered any injury as a result of the advertisement's message. Without injury there can be no claim, regardless of commercial context, prior advertising history, or audience sophistication.

[The court acknowledged its rule that shifts the burden to the defendant to show an absence of consumer confusion "where a plaintiff adequately demonstrates that a defendant has intentionally set out to deceive the public," and the defendant's "deliberate conduct" in this regard is of an "egregious nature * * * ." Resource Developers, Inc. v. Statue of Liberty-Ellis Island Foundation, Inc., 926 F.2d 134, 140 (2d Cir.1991). However, the court held there was insufficient evidence of defendant's intent in this case.]

II. *The Bruno and Ridgway Survey*

At trial, J & J * Merck introduced the results of a consumer survey that it had conducted in conjunction with Bruno and Ridgway Research Associates, a marketing firm that conducts between 200–300 such surveys each year. According to Mr. Joseph Ridgway, the firm's president and J & J * Merck's expert witness, the survey was designed to assess what messages are communicated to consumers by Ingredients-Revised. In order to gain this information, 150 male and 150 female adult nonprescription antacid users were shown the commercial and interviewed in eight different shopping malls.

The aspects of the survey that are relevant to this appeal are those which concern the commercial's message regarding aluminum. Questions 8a and 8b asked: "Aside from trying to get you to buy the product, what are the main ideas the commercial communicates to you?" and "What other ideas does the commercial communicate to you?" Out of the 300 people surveyed, 18 people generally responded that "other antacids contain ingredients that are bad/harmful to you," only six of which specifically commented that "aluminum is not good for you." Two other responses were listed in the survey's tally as "aluminum is bad for brain/causes alzheimer's," and lastly, one additional response was recorded under the heading "miscellaneous negative aluminum comments." Questions 14a-c were asked of the 220 respondents who recalled Ingredients-Revised stating that MAALOX and MYLANTA contained aluminum and magnesium. They respectively inquired:

14a—What, if anything, does the commercial communicate to you about the aluminum and magnesium in Maalox and Mylanta?

14b—What else, if anything, does the commercial communicate to you about the aluminum and magnesium in Maalox and Mylanta?

14c—Based on the commercial you just saw, how do you feel about taking a product for heartburn that contains aluminum and magnesium?

Of the 220 people who responded to these questions, 83 answered with a comment classified as "not good for you/harmful/detrimental to your health." Three answered that aluminum causes Alzheimer's disease and, in addition, 38 responded that these ingredients are not needed by the body.

By adding up all negative comments made about either aluminum or magnesium in response to any of the survey questions, Mr. Ridgway concluded that Ingredients-Revised communicated to 45% of those surveyed that aluminum is either unhealthful or not good for you.

Smithkline and Jordan called Dr. Yoram Wind, a professor of marketing, as their expert witness to testify on nature of the messages communicated by Ingredients-Revised. Dr. Wind strongly criticized the Bruno and Ridgway study primarily on two grounds. First, he testified that, in his opinion, the survey was almost wholly comprised of leading questions. Second, he faulted the study for not taking into account the fact that respondents may have brought with them previously acquired information regarding calcium and aluminum, and for failing to adjust the survey accordingly. In his opinion, the study should have contained a control group—people who were asked similar questions that sought to elicit their beliefs regarding the safety of antacid ingredients, but who were not shown the challenged commercials beforehand.

The evidentiary value of a survey's results rests upon the underlying objectivity of the survey itself. This objectivity, in turn, "depends upon many factors, such as whether [the survey] is properly 'filtered' to screen out those who got no message from the advertisement, whether the questions are directed to the real issues, and whether the questions are leading or suggestive." American Home Products Corp. v. Johnson & Johnson, 654 F.Supp. 568, 590 (S.D.N.Y.1987).

Judge Cedarbaum's analysis of the Bruno and Ridgway survey was wholly in keeping with these principles. After hearing testimony from the parties' experts, and reviewing the results of the study itself, she specifically found that the study "did not show that 'Ingredients-Revised' communicates that the aluminum ... in Mylanta is harmful or unsafe." In her view, the responses to questions 8a and 8b, which elicited only nine anti-aluminum reactions from the 300 people surveyed, were "the most persuasive evidence of the message communicated by 'Ingredients-Revised.'" She attributed this to the fact that questions 8a and 8b were "open-ended," and, therefore, more objective.

On the other hand, Judge Cedarbaum discounted the value of the 86 anti-aluminum/magnesium responses obtained from the 220 people who answered questions 14a-c on the grounds that those questions ranged from being "somewhat leading" to "very leading." Accordingly, she rejected Mr. Ridgway's calculation that Ingredients-Revised communicated an anti-aluminum message to 45% of those surveyed—a figure largely based upon answers received to questions 14a-c.

* * *

The probative value of any given survey is a fact specific question that is uniquely contextual. While certain types of survey questions may be appropriate to discern the message of one advertisement, they may be completely inapposite with regard to another. * * * After reviewing the record in this case, we conclude that Judge Cedarbaum's evaluation of the survey questions is not clearly erroneous.

J & J * Merck also argues that the district court erroneously adopted Dr. Wind's opinion regarding the necessity of a controlled study. It contends that, "[t]he object of Mr. Ridgway's survey, like any advertising communication test, was to measure the impact of an ad upon consumers *in the real world*—not in some artificial or 'control[led]' environment." This contention lacks merit for two reasons. First, Judge Cedarbaum drew no conclusion from the fact that the survey lacked a control; indeed, her legal discussion makes no mention of it whatsoever. Second, we find J & J * Merck's opposition to a control study at odds with its own proposed theory of Lanham Act liability, i.e., that liability exists for exploiting publicly held misperceptions even where the challenged advertising is literally truthful. In these types of cases, the purpose of a control study is to identify the portion of the survey population that held extrinsic beliefs prior to viewing an advertisement—for example, the unsubstantiated belief that aluminum causes Alzheimer's disease. Thus, a control would likely be indispensable proof in an action premised on J & J * Merck's theory. After all, without such evidence it would be hard to imagine how a plaintiff could ever convincingly establish that there was, in the first instance, a public misperception for the defendant to exploit.

Since J & J * Merck did not submit persuasive extrinsic evidence that the challenged TUMS' commercials communicated a false message to consumers by implication or otherwise, we cannot say the district court was clearly erroneous in rejecting it. Accordingly, its false advertising claims must fail.

* * *

CASTROL, INC. V. QUAKER STATE CORP., 977 F.2d 57 (2nd Cir. 1992). Quaker State's 10W–30 motor oil commercial stated: "Up to half of all engine wear can happen when you start your car. At this critical time, tests prove Quaker State 10W–30 protects better than any other leading 10W–30 motor oil." Castrol alleged the claim was false. The Second Circuit held:

> A plaintiff's burden in proving literal falsity thus varies depending on the nature of the challenged advertisement. Where the defendant's advertisement claims that its product is superior, plaintiff must affirmatively prove defendant's product equal or inferior. Where, as in the current case, defendant's ad explicitly or implicitly represents that tests or studies prove its product superior, plaintiff satisfies its burden by showing that the tests did not establish the proposition for which they were cited. We have held that a plaintiff can meet this burden by demonstrating that the tests were not sufficiently reliable to permit a conclusion that the product is superior. The Procter "sufficiently reliable" standard of course assumes that the tests in question, if reliable, would prove the proposition for which they are cited. If the plaintiff can show that the tests, even if reliable, do not establish the proposition asserted by the defendant, the plaintiff has obviously met its burden. In such a case, tests which may or may not be "sufficiently reliable," are simply irrelevant.

Quaker State had tests conducted by Rohm and Haas showing that its oil flowed faster to engine parts on engine start-up than other oil. However, the district court judge credited the testimony of experts for Castrol that in any engine there is enough residual oil on start-up to provide protection and thus the tests could not prove Quaker State oil protected better against start-up engine wear. The advertised claim was thus literally false and a preliminary injunction was granted.

BASF CORP. V. OLD WORLD TRADING CO., INC., 41 F.3d 1081 (7th Cir. 1994). Old World advertised that its antifreeze met all auto manufacturer's specifications. BASF challenged the claim under § 43(a) primarily by proving that Old World did not have adequate tests of its antifreeze to establish the claim. Old World argued that under *Castrol*, BASF had the burden of proving that in fact the antifreeze did not meet the specifications. BASF argued that a claim that a product "meets specifications" implies that it has been subjected to tests. If experts testify that a "meets specifications" claim is not truthful unless required tests have been passed, would that be sufficient proof of falsity or would BASF need a survey to show that consumers believed that a "meets specifications" claim means that tests have been passed? While adopting the *Castrol* logic, the Seventh Circuit held:

> The meaning of a given advertisement is a question of fact and the district court rejected Old World's interpretation. * * * Old World has not shown that this finding was clearly erroneous. * * * The district court found that meeting specifications means that all requisite tests were performed and passed. Since Old World did not perform the tests, its claim was literally false, and the district court did not err in finding Old World liable under the Lanham Act or state law.

GRODEN V. RANDOM HOUSE, INC., 61 F.3d 1045 (2nd Cir. 1995). Gerald Posner wrote a book entitled "Case Closed" which refuted numerous conspiracy theories surrounding the Kennedy assassination, including that contained in Robert Groden's "High Treason". Random House placed an advertisement for Posner's book containing the names and photographs of the conspiracy theorists, including Groden, with a headline reading: "GUILTY OF MISLEADING THE AMERICAN PUBLIC". The ad concluded with a brief summary of Posner's thesis: "ONE MAN. ONE GUN. ONE INESCAPABLE CONCLUSION." Groden filed a Lanham Act § 43(a) claim arguing the "guilty of misleading" and the "one man-one gun" statements were false. The Second Circuit rejected the claims:

> In order to be actionable under the Lanham Act, a challenged advertisement must be literally false or, though literally true, likely to mislead or confuse consumers. However, statements of opinion are generally not the basis for Lanham Act liability. See Restatement (Third) of Unfair Competition § 3 cmt. d (1993). . . .

> Moreover, the statements "GUILTY OF MISLEADING THE AMERICAN PUBLIC" and "ONE MAN. ONE GUN. ONE INESCAPABLE CONCLUSION." are not literally false with respect to the work being advertised, because they accurately describe the thesis of Case Closed. The Lanham Act does not prohibit false statements generally. It prohibits only false or misleading descriptions or false or misleading representations of fact made about one's own or another's goods or services. No matter what the true facts might be concerning the

Kennedy assassination, the ad's statements said nothing false about Posner's book.

Although the District Court did not reach the argument, we also note . . . that any attempt to apply the Lanham Act to appellees' ad would raise substantial free speech issues. . . . In the context of expressive works, we have been careful not to permit overextension of the Lanham Act to intrude on First Amendment values. . . . With a subject of such manifest public interest as the Kennedy assassination, ample leeway must be accorded to statements that advertise books by expressing opinions, no matter how extravagantly worded, about the merits of opposing viewpoints. Id. at 1552–53.

PROBLEM

Pennzoil in a commercial advertisement claimed that its motor oil "outperforms any leading motor oil against viscosity breakdown" and provides "longer engine life and better engine protection." Castrol, a competitor, brings suit under the Lanham Act with evidence that industry-recognized tests for viscosity breakdown of motor oils relied upon by automobile manufacturers showed that Pennzoil does not outperform Castrol motor oils. Pennzoil relies on a different test promulgated by the American Society of Testing and Materials which shows Pennzoil experiences a smaller percent viscosity loss under test conditions than Castrol oils. Pennzoil also introduces a consumer survey and expert testimony that purport to show that consumers interpret the advertisement as nothing more than a "dangling comparative" claim which they ignore.

1. Is the advertisement "literally false"? What does the advertisement mean? Pennzoil does not claim expressly that it conducted tests. Does the advertisement imply some testing? Can you be certain unless you have a consumer survey on whether consumers think the advertisement implies testing?

2. Consider Pennzoil's argument that it had a "reasonable basis" for believing the truth of its claims and thus is not liable under § 43(a)?

3. Consider Castrol's argument that the advertisement implies that Pennzoil's advantage in viscosity breakdown leads to greater protection against engine wear. Does Castrol need consumer survey evidence to sustain this argument?

4. Should Castrol have the burden of showing that consumers regard the advertised claims as material in their purchase of motor oil?

NOTES ON DISPARAGEMENT UNDER § 43(a)

1. The original version of § 43(a) was interpreted not to permit a cause of action for disparagement. Bernard Food Industries v. Dietene Co., 415 F.2d 1279 (7th Cir.1969). At the same time false comparative advertisements which *both* disparaged the plaintiff's goods and made explicit claims about the defendant's goods were actionable. Skil Corp. v. Rockwell International Corp., 375 F.Supp. 777 (N.D.Ill.1974). Is any claim made by a producer about a competitor's goods an implicit claim about the producer's goods?

2. The 1988 amendment to § 43(a) clearly provides a cause of action for disparagement. Subparagraph (a)(2) applies to misrepresentations by a person relating to "his or her or *another person's* goods * * *." However, the provision applies only where the statement is made "in commercial advertising or promotion". Is a salesclerk's disparagement of a competitor's product included? Does the section apply to disparaging statements made by consumers? Does it apply to an unflattering review of a product in a magazine like Consumers Reports? If the claims made in the book involved in Groden v. Random House are protected by the First Amendment, should the advertisement of the book be similarly protected?

3. How much of a common law disparagement action is carried over into § 43(a)? Must the plaintiff show special damages or any particular intent on the part of the defendant? Does a First Amendment analysis require some recasting of the elements of a disparagement case under § 43(a)?

4. Are the remedial provisions in §§ 34–36 of the Lanham Act appropriate for a disparagement claim? Should an accounting for profits ever be awarded for disparagement?

NOTES ON DECEPTION UNDER § 43(a)

1. Section 43(a) of the Lanham Act authorizes a cause of action by anyone "likely to be injured" by a false or misleading advertisement. Even if an advertised claim is literally false, can anyone claim a likelihood of injury without proof that consumers understand the claim and regard it material to their purchasing decisions? Or would it be proper to presume materiality and injury on the basis that the defendant has invested advertising dollars in making a literally false claim?

2. *Puffing*. The courts have recognized that the common law doctrine of "puffing" is applicable in § 43(a) cases. See Cook, Perkiss and Liehe, Inc. v. Northern California Collection Service Inc., 911 F.2d 242 (9th Cir.1990): "The common theme that seems to run through cases considering puffery in a variety of contexts is that consumer reliance will be induced by specific rather that general assertions. . . . Here, the alleged misrepresentations in NCC's advertisement are merely general in nature. . . . The advertisement does not contain the kind of detailed or specific factual assertions that are necessary to state a false advertising cause of action under the Act." Can a claim advertised as supported by tests ever be considered puffing?

3. If consumer surveys are required to demonstrate how consumers interpret an impliedly false claim, what result if 51% of those surveyed interpret the claim to say what is in fact true but the other 49% interpret the claim to make a statement that is in fact false? Should the claim be actionable if only 10% of those surveyed give it its false meaning?

4. What about consumer preference claims, i.e., "consumers prefer brand 'X' over brand 'Y' 2 to 1"? In Vidal Sassoon, Inc. v. Bristol–Myers Co., 661 F.2d 272 (2d Cir.1981) the challenge was to the reports and methodology of the tests that purported to show that consumers preferred defendant's shampoo. The court held:

> where depictions of consumer test results or methodology are so significantly misleading that the reasonably intelligent consumer would be deceived about the product's inherent quality or characteristics, an action under § 43(a) may lie.

On the other hand in The Proctor & Gamble Co. v. Chesebrough–Pond's Inc., 588 F.Supp. 1082 (S.D.N.Y.1984), affirmed 747 F.2d 114 (2d Cir.1984), Judge Goettel refused to establish standards for the validity of consumer testing under § 43(a). The parties used different testing methodologies in arriving at their inconsistent conclusions that their respective hand lotion was the most effective. After finding seven days of expert testimony "incomprehensible", the court refused to enjoin either advertisement:

> Here, we are confronted with somewhat inconsistent product claims based on tests that were conducted in apparent good faith but with somewhat differing results. The difference in the results, in turn, was partially caused by the different test protocols that the parties chose. As a consequence, neither of the parties has successfully proven that the other has chosen tests and conducted them in such a manner as to mislead the public. Courts are not always able to determine whether an advertising claim is true or false ... and where this occurs, the only possible conclusion is that the moving party has failed to prove by a preponderance of the evidence that the advertising claim is false.

5. For a critical examination of the proof requirements in false advertising cases see Lillian R. BeVier, Competitor Suits for False Advertising Under Section 43(a) of the Lanham Act: A Puzzle in the Law of Deception, 78 Va. L. Rev. 1 (1992).

NOTES ON COMPARATIVE ADVERTISING

1. The over-the-counter analgesic industry has waged a comparative advertising war in both the marketplace and the courts. These cases seem to have tested the patience of several judges: American Home Products Corp. v. Johnson & Johnson, 654 F.Supp. 568 (S.D.N.Y.1987) (Advil I) ("Small nations have fought for their very survival with less resources and resourcefulness than these antagonists have brought to their epic struggle for commercial primacy in the OTC analgesic field."); American Home Products Corp. v. Johnson & Johnson, 671 F.Supp. 316 (S.D.N.Y.1987) (Advil II); American Home Products Corp. v. Johnson & Johnson, 672 F.Supp. 135 (S.D.N.Y.1987); McNeilab, Inc. v. American Home Products Corp., 848 F.2d 34 (2d Cir.1988) ("[This controversy] has brought anything but relief to the federal courts. Instead, repeated and protracted litigation has created a substantial headache. The competitive battlefield has shifted from the shelves of supermarkets and drugstores to the courtroom."). The fascinating history of the competition and litigation in this industry and the customary use of what Mark Twain called "stretchers"—"stories which, while not being untrue, do not tell the whole truth" is described in Charles C. Mann and Mark L. Plummer, The Aspirin Wars: Money, Medicine, and 100 Years of Rampant Competition (1991).

In "Advil I" the competition between aspirin and acetaminophen was complicated by the advent of ibuprofen, a new pain killer that works like aspirin but is said to cause less gastrointestinal irritation. At issue were multiple claims in advertisements by Johnson & Johnson attempting to link ibuprofen ("Advil") to aspirin in its side effects and to claim a superiority for Tylenol. The claims, for the most part, were literally true but capable of creating false impressions. The court described its fact finding process as follows:

> The trial lasted four weeks, and involved the in-court testimony of 22 witnesses, many of them world-renowned physicians and medical researchers specializing in pharmacology, nephrology, hepatology, gastroenterology, hematology, epidemiology, and more particularly in the systemic effects of analgesics. The testimony of 37 additional witnesses was presented by deposition.

> Many hundreds of exhibits, filling eight file drawers, were received in evidence, most of them copies of technical articles, couched in the arcane language of medical science, packed with numerical data and embellished with graphs and tables. * * *

> Almost a thousand pages of post-trial briefs and proposed findings were filed. But before the reply briefs had even been received by the Court, the attorneys for one of the parties sent a letter to the Court urging a prompt decision because the opposing party had recently resumed the broadcasting of certain challenged television commercials which it had voluntarily suspended in order to obtain a continuance of the trial.

In the end, the court issued an injunction prohibiting continuation or resumption of advertising practices by both parties based on its evaluation of the scientific evidence and its relation to its interpretation of the advertisements.

Are these issues the kind that judges should resolve? Can consumers police this type of deception? Is a governmental agency in a better position to develop the complex factual background necessary to measure the relative safety and effectiveness of non-prescription drugs?

2. Must a comparative advertisement fully disclose all relevant comparisons between the two products even if some are not as favorable as others or may the advertiser pick the comparison that sets off its product best? In "Advil I", supra note 1, the defendant advertised a checklist of side effects comparing those associated with the plaintiff's product and those associated only with its own product. It omitted some side effects associated only with its own product. Is this a violation of § 43(a)? The court held it was. See also American Home Products Corp. v. Johnson & Johnson, 672 F.Supp. 135 (S.D.N.Y.1987) where Johnson & Johnson counterclaimed for damages under § 43(a) on the basis that AHP failed to warn consumers of the risk of Reyes Syndrome associated with its aspirin based "Anacin" even though AHP fully complied with labeling requirements imposed by the Food and Drug Administration. The court found compliance with FDA requirements to be a defense to any § 43(a) action.

3. It has been suggested that truthful disparagement in comparative advertisements should also be prohibited. Wolff, Unfair Competition by Truthful Disparagement, 47 Yale L.J. 1304 (1938). Would an analysis based on *INS* reach that result? Could you argue that use of your competitor's name constitutes trademark infringement?

4. If you were looking for the best value in laundry detergent, which of the following advertisements would be most helpful? (1) SAFE detergent is the cheapest detergent on the market. (2) SAFE detergent gives more washes per box than any other detergent. (3) SAFE detergent gives 5 more washings per box than SANE detergent. (4) Sarah Anne, otherwise unidentified, prefers SAFE detergent. (5) Independent tests by a consumer organization confirm SAFE detergent is the best value in laundry detergent. If all of the above advertisements were in advertising paid for by the manufacturer of SAFE detergent, on which would you most readily rely?

5. Is there an economic disincentive to engage in comparative advertising? Assume the case of two competing producers of disposable razors. If Producer *A* extolls the benefits of *A*'s disposable razor demonstrating its ease of operation and low cost, *A* stands the chance of attracting new sales from customers of Producer *B* and from those persons using electric or nondisposable razors. If Producer *B* retaliates with an affirmative campaign showing only the good qualities of its razor, *B* may retain its customers, get new customers formerly buying *A*'s razor, and may also convince some electric or nondisposable razor users to try *B*'s razor. The result may be that *A* and *B* will be sharing a larger market for disposable razors than before and may both be better off. On the other hand, if *A* initiates a campaign attacking the safety characteristics and shaving ability of *B*'s razor in comparison to its own, *A* may succeed in causing some of *B*'s customers to switch to nondisposable razors, and if *B* retaliates with an attack on *A*'s product, both *A* and *B* may end up with the same relative shares of a smaller market. If we now assume a five producer market in which *A* is the leading producer, *B* may decide not to expend funds to attack *A*'s razor for *B* may not capture all of the customers convinced by the attack. Those who cease buying from *A* may now begin buying from *C, D,* or *E. B* is, however, more likely to capture a higher percentage of the returns from advertising if *B* exclusively extolls the benefits of its own product.

Of course comparative advertising may have a mixture of self-adulation and competitor disparagement in various intensities, and this may enhance or reduce the force of the analysis.

Does the analysis lead you to any particular policy position regarding the legal rules that ought to govern comparative advertising?

---

(5) The Lanham Act—Section 44

General Motors v. Ignacio Lopez De Arriortua

United States District Court, E.D. Michigan (1996)
948 F. Supp. 684

■ EDMUNDS, DISTRICT JUDGE.

[General Motors Corp. ("GM"), an American Corporation, and Adam Opel AG ("Opel"), a German Corporation, brought suit against Volkswagen AG ("VW"), a German Corporation, Volkswagen of America, Inc.("VWOA"), VW's American subsidiary, the "Lopez Group" consisting of various individuals including Jose Ignacio Lopez, who were previously employed by GM and are now employed by VW, and the "VW Group" consisting of officers of VW.]

Plaintiffs allege that while Lopez was a high level GM executive, he secretly communicated with VW representatives and agreed to leave GM and join VW. He agreed to bring confidential business plans and trade secret information with him. Lopez worked with the other Lopez Group Defendants to secretly collect confidential information. In March of 1993, the Lopez Group Defendants left GM and Opel to join VW where they were paid significantly higher salaries. They allegedly took over 20 cartons of stolen documents with them. Plaintiffs allege that Defendants copied the documents and entered them into VW computers, and then proceeded to shred the documents and cover up the theft.

On March 7, 1996, Plaintiffs filed this suit. Counts 3 and 4 of their complaint allege that Defendants violated the Lanham Act, 15 U.S.C. § 1126 [§ 44], and that Defendants violated the Copyright Act, 17 U.S.C. § 101 et seq. The complaint further alleges that VW has used and continues to use the trade secret information to reduce its costs and to increase its market share. Defendants moved to dismiss count 3 (Lanham Act) and count 4 (Copyright Act). For the reasons set forth below, Defendants' motions are denied. [The Court's consideration of the copyright claim is omitted—Ed.]

All Defendants (except Alvarez, Piazza, and Versteeg who have not been served) have moved to dismiss count 3 of the complaint. Count 3 alleges that Defendants violated the substantive terms of the Paris Convention, an international agreement incorporated into section 44 of the Lanham Act, 15 U.S.C. § 1126. Defendants contend that the Lanham Act does not incorporate any substantive provisions of the Paris Convention, and thus that Plaintiffs have failed to state a viable claim for relief. They argue that the Paris Convention only required that signatory nations provide the same trademark protection to foreign citizens that they provide to their own citizens. Courts are split on the issue of whether section 44(b) of the Lanham Act incorporates substantive rights set forth in the Paris Convention.

Generally, the Lanham Act prohibits two types of unfair competition: trademark infringement (15 U.S.C. § 1114) and false designation of origin or "passing off" (15 U.S.C. § 1125). In addition, the Lanham Act provides rights stipulated by international conventions respecting unfair competition. 15 U.S.C. § 1127. * * * This purpose is implemented in sections 44(b), (h), and (i). * * * Under section 44(h), foreign citizens are entitled to protection against unfair competition * * * The Act specifically provides under section 44(i) that United States citizens shall have the same rights as foreigners. * * *

One treaty incorporated by this section is the International Convention for the Protection of Industrial Property, the Paris Convention. 24 U.S.T. 2140 (July 14, 1967). The Paris Convention requires signatory nations to prohibit unfair competition:

> (1) The countries of the Union are bound to assure to nationals of such countries effective protection against unfair competition.
>
> (2) Any act of competition contrary to honest practices in industrial or commercial matters constitutes an act of unfair competition.

Paris Convention, article 10bis. The broad concept of unfair competition set forth in the Paris Convention has been described as follows:

> Article 10bis is not premised upon the narrow meaning of "unfair competition" as it was understood in American common law, but adopts the more liberal construction of the European countries such as France, Germany and Switzerland * * *. The statement that unfair competition is competition "contrary to honest practice" is not a definition; it merely expresses the concept that a particular act of competition is to be condemned as unfair because it is inconsistent with currently accepted standards of honest practice. It impliedly affirms that unfair competition is too broad a concept to be limited to any narrow definition such as for instance, passing off.

4A Rudolf Callmann, The Law of Unfair Competition, Trademarks and Monopolies, § 2610 (4th ed.1994). The United States and Germany are both signatories to the Paris Convention.

Defendants concede that the Lanham Act incorporates the Paris Convention. However, they contend that the Paris Convention does not provide substantive rights, and that it only requires "national treatment." One authority on trademark law explained this interpretation of the Convention:

> The Paris Convention is essentially a compact between the various member countries to accord in their own countries to citizens of the other contracting parties' trademark and other rights comparable to those accorded their own citizens by their domestic law. The underlying principle is that foreign nationals should be given the same treatment in each of the member countries as that country makes available to its own citizens ["national treatment"]. The Convention is not premised upon the idea that the trademark laws of each member nation shall be given extraterritorial application, but on exactly the converse principle that each nation's law shall have only territorial application.

In re Compagnie Generale Maritime, 993 F.2d 841, 850 (Fed.Cir.1993) (Nies, J., dissenting) (quoting 1 McCarthy, Trademarks and Unfair Competition, § 19:24, at 927 (2d Ed.1984) (emphasis added)).

Agreeing with the "national treatment" analysis, in Vanity Fair Mills, Inc. v. T. Eaton Co., 234 F.2d 633, 644 (2d Cir.), cert. denied, 352 U.S. 871 (1956), the Second Circuit interpreted the Paris Convention and the Lanham Act as providing only limited protection from acts of unfair competition. In that case, plaintiff was an American company who brought suit against a Canadian company, alleging that the defendant violated plaintiff's trademark when it sold goods in Canada using plaintiff's "Vanity Fair" label. The court held that the Paris Convention was premised on the concept of national treatment and that the laws of the signatory nations should not have extraterritorial application. Thus, plaintiff could not hold the defendant Canadian corporation liable under American law for a trademark violation that occurred in Canada.

Contrary to *Vanity Fair*, other courts have held that the Lanham Act incorporates international agreements. In Toho Co. v. Sears, Roebuck & Co., 645 F.2d 788, 792 (9th Cir.1981), a Japanese company brought suit against Sears, an American company, alleging unfair competition. The court explained that sections 44(b) and (h) incorporated the provisions of a treaty between the United States and Japan. "The federal right created by subsection 44(h) is coextensive with the substantive provisions of the treaty involved.... [S]ubsections (b) and (h) work together to provide federal rights and remedies implementing federal unfair competition treaties." *Toho*, 645 F.2d at 792. The U.S.-Japan treaty only required national treatment. Thus, the court reasoned that the Japanese company was entitled to bring the same claims as an American company would be entitled to bring: both claims for trademark infringement and false designation of origin under the Lanham Act as well as a claim for unfair competition under state law. * * *

Still other courts have taken *Toho* one step further and have held that the Lanham Act incorporates the substantive provisions of the Paris Convention and thus creates a federal law of unfair competition applicable in international disputes. In Maison Lazard et Compagnie v. Manfra, Tordella & Brooks, Inc., 585 F.Supp. 1286, 1289 (S.D.N.Y.1984), a French company brought suit against an American company, alleging that the American company sold commemorative Olympic coins overseas in violation of the plaintiff's exclusive right to make such sales. In essence, the French company claimed that the defendant misappropriated an exclusive right and that this constituted unfair competition under the Paris Convention. The court followed *Toho*, holding that the Lanham Act incorporated the Convention. Because the Paris Convention provides broad protection from unfair competition, the court held that the plaintiff had a valid federal claim for misappropriation of an exclusive right.

The court is persuaded that *Toho* and *Maison Lazard* properly interpret the Lanham Act as incorporating the substantive provisions of the Paris Convention. The express purpose of the Lanham Act dictates this result. "The intent of this chapter is ... to provide rights and remedies stipulated by treaties and conventions...." 15 U.S.C. § 1127. The Paris Convention provides that signatory countries must protect individuals from unfair competition. Article 10bis. Subsection (b) of the Lanham Act implements this concept by providing that foreigners are entitled to benefits "to the extent necessary to give effect to any provision" of a convention. Subsection (h) specifies that foreigners are entitled "to protection against unfair competition."

The intent of Congress to incorporate substantive rights is further manifested in subsection (i), which provides that United States citizens shall be entitled to the same rights as foreign citizens. It was necessary to enact subsection (i) to make it clear that United States citizens were entitled to additional rights provided by the treaties incorporated. If the incorporation of the treaty did not incorporate additional rights, it would have been unnecessary to enact section 44(i). Interpreting section 44(b) as merely requiring "national treatment" renders section 44(i) superfluous. Courts must interpret statutes so as to give effect to every word and to avoid rendering certain language superfluous.

The legislative history also reveals Congressional intent to incorporate additional rights and to provide such rights both to foreigners and to citizens. Congress expressed its concern that Americans be given the same protection from unfair competition as foreigners.

> We have the curious anomaly of this Government giving by treaty and by law with respect to trade-marks and unfair competition to nationals of foreign governments greater rights than it gives its own citizens. . . .This [subsection 44(i) in the final draft] is an attempt to put the citizen on an equality with the foreigner. . . .

Hearings on H.R. 4744 Before the Subcomm. on Trademarks of the House Comm. on Patents, 76th Cong., 1st Sess. (1939), p. 164. Congress also explained that the Paris Convention prohibited unfair competition more broadly than did the Lanham Act. "The European Convention [meaning the Paris Convention] however, goes much farther than that and prohibits commercial bribery among other things. . . ." Id. at 168.[4]

Opel seeks the right to sue for unfair competition pursuant to 44(h), and GM seeks to enforce the same rights pursuant to section 44(i). Because the Lanham Act incorporates the Paris Convention's broad prohibition against unfair competition, Plaintiffs have stated a claim.[5]

Defendants also claim that the Lanham Act does not reach extraterritorial acts. This is incorrect. Congress has the power to regulate even

---

4. Defendants also contend that if the Paris Convention provides substantive rights it is not clear what those rights are. While the precise nature of these rights is not clear at this juncture, it is clear that the rights provided by the Paris Convention include protection from commercial bribery. It also should be noted that because Plaintiffs seek the enforcement of foreign law, it is their obligation to inform the court of the content of that law.

5. Defendants also argue that interpreting section 44 as incorporating the Paris Convention would eliminate diversity jurisdiction in all actions involving unfair competition. This is overstated. The court's holding is limited to the circumstances of this case. The Lanham Act incorporates the substantive provisions of the Paris Convention and thus creates a federal law of unfair competition applicable in international disputes. Diversity jurisdiction would still apply in a domestic dispute. It should also be noted that this issue is not before the court. The court has proper federal question jurisdiction in this case.

entirely foreign commerce where it has a substantial effect on commerce between the states or between the United States and foreign countries. *Vanity Fair*, 234 F.2d at 641. "Particularly is this true when a conspiracy is alleged with acts in furtherance of that conspiracy taking place in both the United State and Foreign Countries." *Id.*

* * *

Being fully advised in the premises, having read the pleadings, and for the reasons explained above the court hereby orders as follows:

Defendants' joint motion to dismiss counts 3 and 4 is DENIED * * *

NOTES

1. The interpretation of § 44 in the *Lopez* case has the potential to significantly alter the law of unfair competition as it applies to American companies. Trade is increasingly international in scope. Two general issues arise with § 44. The first is whether the federal courts have subject matter jurisdiction over a claim of unfair competition, and the second is what substantive law applies. As the court's discussion suggests, international norms of unfair competition may be significantly different than those of domestic law. Article 10bis of the Paris Convention is a broadly worded prohibition whereas American law tends to define acts of unfair competition with more specificity. Could Article 10bis be fairly read to include a claim of "misappropriation" even broader than that adopted in INS v. AP? Could the Article be read to incorporate the European view that using a competitor's trademark in comparative advertising is an infringement? To eliminate the requirement of "special damages" in disparagement actions?

2. The American laws of agency and trade secrets (see Chapter 4) deal directly with the claims by General Motors against Lopez, although the rules that govern the conduct of employees who change employment are very fact specific and give substantial weight to the policy of preserving employee mobility. How will General Motors meet its burden of showing the substantive legal principles of Article 10bis applicable to its claim? As judge would you admit into evidence the expert testimony of lawyers familiar with international legal norms? Would you admit expert testimony of CEO's of international firms?

3. Is § 44 limited to cases in which at least one of the parties is a foreign national or could the section be applicable to a controversy between two American companies regardless of diversity of citizenship? The argument derives from subsections (b), (h) and (i) which grant American citizens the same rights as foreign nationals. Stauffer v. Exley, 184 F.2d 962 (9th Cir.1950) was the first decision to apply § 44 to a suit between two American citizens. The controversy involved use in interstate commerce of the unregistered trade name "Stauffer System" by a California resident and use of the name "Stauffer" by another California resident in its business. The cause of action was for unfair competition; diversity of citizenship was not present nor was there a specific claim under federal statutory law because the trade name was unregistered. The leading case rejecting this interpretation was L'Aiglon Apparel v. Lana Lobell, Inc., 214 F.2d 649 (3d Cir.1954). The Third Circuit relied heavily on the legislative history of the Lanham Act to conclude that the section was applicable only when a foreign national was involved. Most other Circuits follow the *L'Aiglon* decision and the Ninth Circuit has limited *Stauffer* so that § 44 has been "rendered . . . nugatory in suits between United States citizens." Toho Co. Ltd. v. Sears, Roebuck & Co., 645 F.2d 788 (9th Cir.1981).

4. The interpretation of § 44 of the Lanham Act does not exhaust the issue of the potential applicability of the provisions of international conventions to purely domestic lawsuits involving unfair competitive practices. An international convention may apply even in a lawsuit between two American citizens, in an American court, involving questions unrelated to foreign commerce if the treaty or convention is self-executing. Article VI of the United States Constitution reads in part as follows: "This Constitution, and the Laws of the United States which shall be made in Pursuance thereof; and all Treaties made, or which shall be made, under the Authority of the United States, shall be the Supreme Law of the Land; and the Judges in every State shall be bound thereby, any Thing in the Constitution or Laws of any State to the Contrary notwithstanding . . . ."

If an international agreement is self-executing, it does not depend on implementing legislation by Congress in order to be effective between private parties. The provisions become part of the domestic law of the United States through operation of the Supremacy Clause. According to American Law, a treaty is self-executing if its language indicates that the drafters intended it to be self-executing. Restatement, Second, of Foreign Relations Law § 141 (1965). The final determination rests with the courts. Id. § 154. If the convention is part of the domestic law, the federal district courts would have subject matter jurisdiction over actions thereunder. 28 U.S.C.A. § 1331. Diversity of citizenship would be unnecessary. It should be noted that a federal statute enacted after ratification of an international convention and inconsistent with the convention's provisions supersedes the convention as domestic law if Congress intended such a result. Restatement, Second, of Foreign Relations Law § 145 (1965).

The Supreme Court has suggested without a direct holding that the Convention of Paris is not self-executing. Cameron Septic Tank Co. v. City of Knoxville, 227 U.S. 39 (1913). On the other hand the Court assumed that the General Inter-American Convention for Trade Mark and Commercial Protection, an agreement similar in content and scope to the Paris Convention, was self-executing. Bacardi Corp. v. Domenech, 311 U.S. 150 (1940). In early cases the First Circuit and Third Circuit split on the nature of the Paris Convention. United Shoe Mach. Co. v. Duplessis Shoe Mach. Co., 155 Fed. 842 (1st Cir.1907) (not self-executing); Hennebique Const. Co. v. Myers, 172 Fed. 869 (3d Cir.1909) (self-executing although not necessary for decision). More contemporary courts likewise disagree. Master, Wardens, etc. v. Cribben & Sexton Co., 202 F.2d 779 (C.C.P.A.1953) ("That treaty [Paris Convention] is part of our law and no special legislation in the

United States was necessary to make it effective here [citing Bacardi Corp. v. Domenech]. However, terms of the treaty applicable to the situation in the case at bar were embodied in [§ 44 of the Lanham Act]."); Vanity Fair Mills v. The T. Eaton Co., 234 F.2d 633 (2d Cir.1956), cert. denied 352 U.S. 871 (1957) (holding that the plaintiff "would appear to be correct" in arguing the convention is self-executing); Ortman v. Stanray Corp., 371 F.2d 154 (7th Cir.1967) (not self-executing). None of the cases involved a purely domestic controversy between two American citizens.

5. What effect should be given Congressional intent as expressed in the last paragraph of § 27 of the Lanham Act, a portion of which reads: "The intent of this chapter is to . . . provide rights and remedies stipulated by treaties and conventions respecting trade-marks, trade names, and unfair competition entered into between the United States and foreign nations"?

6. If § 44 applies only where a foreign national is a party to the action, whether as plaintiff or defendant, consider the result where an American citizen engages in business conduct which is prohibited by a convention but not by American domestic law. The conduct results in damage to two competitors, one of whom is an American citizen and one of whom is a foreign national. Could Congress have intended to grant the foreign competitor greater rights than the American competitor?

B. Consumers' Remedies

Consumers play an important role in policing the marketplace for deceptive practices. Through their purchasing decisions they can penalize sellers who have deceived them in the past or who have developed a general reputation for dishonesty. By taking precautions consumers can reduce the risk of being victimized by deceptive practices. In addition, the law provides an array of substantive legal remedies for consumers who are injured when products or services do not meet their expectations—expectations often formulated on the basis of what is said by the seller about the seller's goods or services. Legal claims by consumers are largely beyond the scope of this book. The *Colligan* case raises the issue of whether consumers have standing to sue under the Lanham Act. The notes that follow are designed merely to remind students of some of the many consumer remedies available.

Colligan v. Activities Club of New York, Ltd.

United States Court of Appeals, Second Circuit, 1971.
442 F.2d 686.

[The plaintiffs, parents of two parochial school children, brought an action on behalf of their own children and on behalf of all high school students in the New York metropolitan area claiming that the defendants had used false descriptions and representations regarding a ski tour service offered to high school students. The plaintiffs' children had experienced one of defendant's tours which fell far short of what was advertised.]

In seeking redress of this apparently misfortune-strewn ski weekend brought about by the Club's misrepresentations, appellants have sought to invoke the jurisdiction of a federal court, rather than turning to traditionally available state court forums and remedies and have appended their state common law claims by way of invoking the doctrine of pendent jurisdiction. Seemingly unable to bring themselves within other federal statutes specially conferring federal court jurisdiction, and additionally unable to meet the minimum monetary requirements of 28 U.S.C. § 1331 or 28 U.S.C. § 1332, appellants imaginatively have brought this action pursuant to §§ 39 and 43(a) of the Lanham Act.

The issue of consumer standing to sue under § 43(a) is one of first impression for this and apparently any federal court. * * *

Appellants' principal contention is that the language of § 43(a), specifically the term "any person," is so unambiguous as to admit of no other construction than that of permitting consumers the right to sue under its aegis. On the face of the complaint all the prerequisites of § 43(a) seem to be met: (1) defendants are persons (2) who used false descriptions and misrepresentations (3) in connection with goods and services, (4) which defendants caused to enter commerce; (5) appellants are also persons (6) who believe themselves to have been in fact damaged by defendants' misdescriptions and misrepresentations.

Viewing the terms of § 43(a) in isolation there do not appear to be any vague words or inconsistent phrases which might permit any other inference than that which appellants would have us draw—i.e., that "any person" means exactly what it says. It is further suggested that if Congress had desired, it could and would have limited or narrowed the class of protected plaintiffs to commercial parties merely by saying so. We reject this line of maxims of statutory construction in favor of Judge Learned Hand's more practical instruction that "[w]ords are not pebbles in alien juxtaposition," and therefore turn first to § 43(a)'s legislative history.

We agree with appellants that "[t]he Lanham Act of 1946 has a very long and convoluted legislative history," which with respect to § 43(a) we find to be inconclusive and therefore of little or no help in resolving the issue decided today. * * *

The congressional statement of purpose of the Act is contained in § 45, which in pertinent part states: "The intent of this chapter * * * is to protect persons engaged in such commerce against unfair competition." In this, the only phrase referring to the class of persons to be protected by the Act, as defined by their conduct and the source of the injuries sought to be protected against, no mention at all is made of the "public" or of "consumers." The legislative history of the Act, such as it is, adds nothing. We do know to a reasonable certainty, however, that the consumer protection explosion and the wholesale displacement (though not preemption) of traditional state statutory and common law remedies—matters pregnant with manifold consequences of great importance—were never considered or foreseen by Congress prior to the enactment of § 43(a). We conclude, therefore, that Congress' purpose in enacting § 43(a) was to create a special and limited unfair competition remedy, virtually without regard for the interests of consumers generally and almost certainly without any consideration of consumer rights of action in particular. The Act's purpose, as defined in § 45, is exclusively to protect the interests of a purely commercial class against unscrupulous commercial conduct.

* * * Since Congress deliberately excluded from coverage virtually all categories of unfair competition but for false advertising, it could not have intended to create a whole new body of substantive law completely outside the substantive scope of unfair competition. Yet this is what appellants would have us find, under the guise of granting them standing, for the question of consumer standing and that of the creation of wholly new federal common law of consumer protection under § 43(a) cannot be disentwined.

Moreover, consumers' use of § 39 of the Act, which requires the allegation of neither a minimum monetary amount in controversy nor diverse citizenship, in combination with the expansive jurisdictional delineation given the phrase "in commerce," and the procedural advantages of bringing suit in federal court, would lead to a veritable flood of claims brought in already overtaxed federal district courts, while adequate private remedies for consumer protection, which to date have been left almost exclusively to the States, are readily at hand. Great strides are now being made in this area to expand the already numerous remedies available in state courts, and this court has no desire to interfere with that process by an unprecedented interpretation of longstanding federal law.

Affirmed.

NOTES

1. *Consumer Standing Under Section 43(a).* The issue of consumer standing under § 43(a) was reviewed in an exhaustive opinion by Judge Pollak in Serbin v. Ziebart International Corp., 11 F.3d 1163 (3rd Cir. 1993). *Serbin* consolidated two classic consumer law suits: purchasers of a defendant's rust protection policy for automobiles claimed that the advertisements they relied upon were false and consumers of gasoline alleged advertising claims that defendant's gasoline provided more power and quicker acceleration were false. Acknowledging that the plain meaning of the statute would lead to incorporating consumer standing, the court concluded:

> The question of policy that underlies these appeals is not whether false advertising is a bad thing. It is, and consumers are victimized by it. The question of policy is what institution, or set of institutions, should be charged with identifying false advertising, ameliorating its malign consequences, and, in the long run, shrinking its dominion. State courts have substantial authority in this field by virtue of judge-made misrepresentation law, and some state legislatures have, through such legislation as the Uniform Deceptive Trade Practices Act, undertaken to widen that authority. Congress conferred a measure of public enforcement authority on the Federal Trade Commission and, through

section 43(a) of the Lanham Act, has vested in the federal courts jurisdiction to entertain certain categories of private law suits predicated on claims of false advertising. Given this commitment of institutional resources to the cause of consumers injured by false advertising, if Congress had intended to make the additional commitment involved in recognizing a federal tort of misrepresentation and in bestowing access to federal fora without regard to the amount in issue, we are confident that the legislative history of the Lanham Act would have borne clear witness to that commitment. Because we find no clear indication of such an unusual commitment and because we are satisfied that section 43(a) had an important, though narrower and quite distinct purpose, we join the Second Circuit in holding that Congress, when authorizing federal courts to deal with claims of false advertising, did not contemplate that federal courts should entertain claims brought by consumers. Id. at 1178–79.

In Arnesen v. The Raymond Lee Organization, Inc., 333 F.Supp. 116 (C.D.Cal.1971) the court held that consumers had standing to sue under § 43(a) of the Lanham Act.

2. Although it is clear in most courts that consumers may not sue under § 43(a), the outer reaches of standing under the section are far from clear. Persons with some commercial interest other than as a competitor may have standing, particularly if the claim is one of passing off rather than merely false advertising. See Halicki v. United Artists Communications Inc., 812 F.2d 1213 (9th Cir.1987) (a movie producer denied standing to sue under § 43(a) to recover against movie theaters who falsely advertised its movie as "R" rated when in fact it was rated "PG"). The court held § 43(a) inapplicable because the injury did not arise out of competition. In Smith v. Montoro, 648 F.2d 602 (9th Cir.1981) an actor was allowed to bring suit under § 43(a) against a film distributor who was not giving the actor proper credit for his appearance in a film. Compare, Waits v. Frito-Lay, Inc., 978 F.2d 1093, 1109 (9th Cir. 1992) (singer permitted standing to sue under § 43(a) for unauthorized use of an imitation of the singer's voice in a radio commercial):

> We have recognized that simple claims of false representations in advertising are actionable under section 43(a) when brought by competitors of the wrongdoer, even though they do not involve misuse of a trademark. The plaintiff's claim in *Halicki* was exclusively such a "false advertising" claim, for it sought redress for a simple misrepresentation as to a product's quality, the content of a movie. We were at pains to point out that the plaintiff's injury was not related to the Lanham Act's purpose of preventing the "deceptive and misleading use of marks," declaring that the statute's purposes with regard to the use of trademarks were irrelevant to his claim. Rather, where the misrepresentation simply concerns a product's qualities, it is actionable under section 43(a) only insofar the Lanham Act's other purpose of preventing "unfair competition" is served. * * *

> The plaintiff's claim in *Smith*, on the other hand, was a type of false association claim stemming from the misuse of a mark, for it

alleged the wrongful removal of the plaintiff's name and the wrongful substitution of another's name. *Smith* teaches that where such a claim is presented, the plaintiff need not be a competitor, for the Lanham Act also grants a cause of action to certain noncompetitors who have been injured commercially by the "deceptive and misleading use of marks." Those with standing to bring such a claim include parties with a commercial interest in the product wrongfully identified with another's mark, as in *Smith*, or with a commercial interest in the misused mark.

3. Consumers have been successful in a few instances in arguing that Congress intended to create an implied cause of action under a federal regulatory statute. See, Kipperman v. Academy Life Insurance Co., 554 F.2d 377 (9th Cir. 1977) (consumer cause of action implied under the federal law prohibiting mailing of unsolicited merchandise).

4. State law provides consumers with a number of traditional remedies for disappointment in the marketplace. The Uniform Commercial Code enforces express and implied warranties against sellers of goods and the law of torts provides a remedy for misrepresentation. For product-caused personal injury, consumers of goods often may recover in strict liability in tort. Beginning with the "consumer revolution" in the 1970's, many states adopted specific consumer protection legislation regulating the enforcement of consumer contracts. Consumer injury often goes unredressed not because of the absence of a substantive cause of action but because the costs associated with pursuing legal remedies exceed the injury. A seller may misrepresent the quantity of vegetables in its vegetable soup and may reap significant profits from the deception over the many cans of soup sold. However, the difference between the value of the soup as misrepresented and the value of the soup as sold (often the measure of damages in consumer claims)may be only a few cents. One procedural response is the consumer class action, allowing one consumer to aggregate the claims of all consumers. However class actions create their own problems, including the perception that only the lawyers for the plaintiff class benefit. The debate surrounding consumer class actions and consumer remedies, although beyond the scope of this book, give context to the law of unfair competition where suits by competitors may be seen as a more efficient method of policing the marketplace.

5. Government regulation might serve as an alternative to private remedies. Does the interest in compensating injured parties and deterring prohibited conduct always merge to give a strong push in favor of private remedies? What possible motivation would Congress have to deny private relief? Is the answer dependent on whether all deceptive practices involve social costs? Or whether deception can be adequately defined? Or on the nature of the remedy—damages, injunction, penalty—that is available? Or on the size of the budget given the public agency for enforcement purposes? For an analysis of these questions see Becker & Stigler, Law Enforcement, Malfeasance and Compensation of Enforcers, 3 J.Leg.Studies 1 (1974) and Landes & Posner, The Private Enforcement of Law, 4 J.Leg.Studies 1 (1975).

C. State Unfair Competition Statutes

During the 1960's and 1970's when national attention was focused on consumer protection, most states adopted unfair competition or consumer protection legislation. These enactments were modeled after the Uniform Deceptive Trade Practices Act (UDTPA), proposed by the National Conference of Commissioners on Uniform State Laws, or the Unfair Trade Practices and Consumer Protection Law (UTPCPL), proposed by the Federal Trade Commission for enactment by the states. These model laws are reproduced in the statutory supplement.

The major thrust of the UDTPA appears to codify the law of false advertising as applied between competitors. Section 2 provides a laundry list of "deceptive trade practices" all of which contain some element of misrepresentation. The remedial provision (§ 3) permits a "person likely to be damaged" to obtain injunctive relief, the costs of the action, and attorneys fees where the defendant "willfully" engaged in the deceptive practice. It is unlikely that the drafters envisioned consumer lawsuits because an individual consumer's interest is seldom satisfied by injunctive relief alone.

The UTPCPL, on the other hand, is a much broader assault on unwanted trade practices and currently dominates the field in the state courts. Most versions of the statute prohibit acts that are "unfair" as well as acts that are "deceptive". The state attorney general is given broad powers to adopt rules and regulations and to seek civil penalties for violations. But private actions are authorized and, in some versions, substantial private remedies are available.

The states did not adopt and have not maintained a uniform approach to this consumer protection legislation. The model proposed by the FTC itself contained alternative provisions and some state legislatures adopted their own alternatives which generally broadened the statute's applicability. The process of judicial interpretation followed by legislative clarification or adjustment has further eroded the uniformity of the original proposal. The notes below outline the major areas of diversity.

NOTES: VARIATIONS IN THE UTPCPL

1. *Substantive prohibitions.* The FTC's original proposal contained three alternative formulations of the substantive prohibitions. These alternatives are reproduced in the statutory supplement. Alternative 3 incorporates the list of deceptive practices in the UDTPA with the addition of the catchall provision in subparagraph (13) to include "unfair" as well as "deceptive" acts. Some states made alterations in the formulation of the specific prohibitions by, for example, adding a "knowingly" requirement to some of the prohibited acts.

One of the most significant features of the Consumer Protection Act was adopted by most states. It directs state courts when construing the substantive prohibitions of the act to give "great weight" to opinions by the federal courts and Federal Trade Commission defining unfair and deceptive acts under the Federal Trade Commission Act. Combined with the private remedial provisions of the state statutes, the effect of this provision is to incorporate FTC jurisprudence into the substantive law of each state.

Most state formulations also permit the state attorney general to adopt rules and regulations defining unfair or deceptive acts or practices which in turn can be enforced through the private remedies afforded by the act. Some state attorneys general have actively promulgated consumer protection regulations.

2. *Standing for private remedies.* The original FTC proposal contained a very limited standing provision defining who could seek private remedies under the act. Section 8 provided private actions to

> "[a]ny person who *purchases or leases goods or services primarily for personal, family or household purposes and thereby* suffers any ascertainable loss of money or property, real or personal, as a result of the use or employment by another of a method, act or practice declared unlawful by Section 2 of this Act . . . ."

This provision limits private relief to consumers purchasing for personal use. However, many jurisdictions adopted a modified form omitting the emphasized language. The revised form permits any injured person to bring suit. Massachusetts adopted a separate section providing a private remedy to "any person who engages in the conduct of any trade or commerce and who suffers any loss" from a prescribed act. Mass.Gen.Laws.Ann. 93A § 11.

3. *Private remedies.* The FTC proposal permits recovery of actual damages or $200 whichever is greater. States adopted different statutory damage amounts.

The act also authorizes punitive damages and equitable relief as well as "reasonable attorney's fees and costs". Many states have expanded on these remedies. In Massachusetts a "wilful or knowing" violation requires the court to provide "up to three but not less than two times [the actual damages]." Mass.Gen.Laws.Ann. 93A § 9. In North Carolina if damages are awarded for any violation of the act the court is *required* to treble them. N.Car.G.S. § 75–16. See also, Fargo Women's Health Organization, Inc. v. FM Women's Help and Caring Connection, 444 N.W.2d 683 (N.D.1989) where the court implied an action for damages including punitive damages for false advertising from a state variation that provided only for criminal penalties and injunctive relief.

4. In some jurisdictions the statutory causes of action have begun to take on increasing importance in regulating business practices. In others, the potential of these statutes has not yet been fully perceived. In part this can be explained by the differences in standing and remedial provisions. Massachusetts, North Carolina, Washington, and Texas particularly have experienced a burgeoning number of cases explained in part by the availability of multiple damages and attorneys fees and the courts' willingness to give a broad interpretation to what acts are encompassed within the statute.

5. *Bibliography.* See, G. Richard Snell, Substituting Ethical Standards for Common Law Rules in Commercial Cases: An Emerging Statutory Trend, 82 Nw. U. L. Rev. 1198 (1988); Leaffer & Lipson, Consumer Actions Against Unfair or Deceptive Acts or Practices: The Private Uses of Federal Trade Commission Jurisprudence, 48 Geo.Wash.L.Rev. 521 (1980). A treatise-like treatment of the cases can be found in National Consumer Law Center, Unfair and Deceptive Acts and Practices (1997).

Jays Foods, Inc. v. Frito–Lay, Inc.

United States Dist. Ct., N.D. Illinois, 1987.
664 F.Supp. 364, affirmed, 860 F.2d 1082 (7th Cir. 1988)

■ MORAN, DISTRICT JUDGE.

* * *

Jays intended to show at trial that Frito–Lay attempted to influence the allocation of retail shelf space by engaging in several unfair and deceptive practices. First, Jays would show that Frito–Lay urged retailers to allocate shelf space based on total snack food sales but it failed to use the shelf space it gained that way in a profit maximizing manner. For example, Frito–Lay devoted all newly gained space to its comparatively slow-selling regular potato chips. Second, Jays would show that Frito–Lay gained additional shelf space by presenting retailers with misleading and incomplete shelf space studies. For example, one such study, Frito–Lays' "mini-analysis," examined only total sales of snack foods, ignoring other variables such as profits, inventory turnover, location and service. Jays also would show that Frito–Lay stacked its products at the front of retail shelves, leaving unused space behind ("dummying up"), and left more of its products in certain stores than sales justified, moving them to stores with higher inventory turnover only just in time to prevent them from going stale ("rolling stock"). Jays contends that these practices enabled Frito–Lay to occupy excessive shelf space at the expense of Frito–Lay's competitors, such as Jays.

Third, Jays would show that Frito–Lay engaged in promotional programs directly tied to the allocation of additional shelf space, a practice that Jays characterizes as "buying space." Finally, Jays would show that Frito–Lay took steps to skew sales when retailers were conducting shelf space tests to protect its shelf space allocations.

DISCUSSION

After the summary judgments on the antitrust claims [in favor of defendant] this court determined that the two state law claims remained, a very small tail on what had been a large and now dead dog. * * *

[Jays' first state law claim, under the Illinois version of the Uniform Deceptive Trade Practices Act, was dismissed because Jays sought damages and the act provides only injunctive relief.]

If Jays is to recover damages it must proceed under the Consumer Fraud Act, which provides:

> Unfair methods of competition and unfair or deceptive acts or practices, including but not limited to the use or employment of any deception, fraud, false pretense, false promise, misrepresentation or the conceal- ment, suppression or omission of any material fact, with the intent that others rely upon the concealment, suppression or omission of such mate- rial fact, or the use or employment of any practice described in Section 2 of the "Uniform Deceptive Trade Practices Act" ... are hereby declared unlawful whether any person has in fact been misled, deceived or dam- aged thereby. In construing this section consideration shall be given to the interpretations of the Federal Trade Commission and the federal courts relating to Section 5(a) of the Federal Trade Commission Act.

Ill.Rev.Stat. ch. 121, ¶ 262; see Ill.Rev.Stat. ch. 121 ¶ 270a (providing for a private damage action).

The Consumer Fraud Act incorporates Section 2 of the Deceptive Trade Practices Act by reference, but it is considerably broader. Like the Federal Trade Commission Act, 15 U.S.C. § 41 et seq., the Consumer Fraud Act applies to "unfair methods of competition." Unfair methods of competition include violations of the federal antitrust laws. However, Jays cannot pro- ceed on an antitrust theory because of Frito–Lay's earlier successful sum- mary judgment motions. Except for the possible violations of the Deceptive Trade Practices Act, Jays must show that Frito–Lay's shelf space practices were unfair even though they did not violate the antitrust laws. The Consumer Fraud Act is, by its terms, wide-ranging. In interpreting it, con- sideration shall be given to interpretations of the Federal Trade Commission Act, but the decision as to what is "unfair" is left to juries and the courts rather than to an administrative agency having experience and expertise. Perhaps for this reason the Illinois courts have moved cautiously in fleshing out the contours of the Act. * * *

In this action Jays has failed to develop any evidence showing that con- sumers are injured by Frito–Lay's conduct. The Illinois courts have limited liability under the Consumer Fraud Act to conduct that implicates con- sumer protection concerns. * * *

Several federal courts in this district, including this court, have fol- lowed that limitation. The Illinois Supreme Court has not squarely faced the issue, but its decisions also support limiting liability under the Consumer Fraud Act to conduct that deceives or exploits consumers. * * *

The Illinois courts have not uniformly formulated this consumer injury limitation and some courts have stated that it does not apply. See e.g., M & W Gear, 97 Ill.App.3d at 913–14, 53 Ill.Dec. at 730, 424 N.E.2d at 365. However, those cases have either involved consumer plaintiffs or conduct from which injury to consumers could be readily inferred. In *M & W Gear* the plaintiff successfully sued a competitor for false advertising. On appeal, the defendant argued that the plaintiff had failed to plead or prove any adverse effect on the public. The court rejected any public injury requirement and affirmed judgment for the plaintiff. [T]he *M & W Gear* court could easily have held that false advertising gives rise to a conclusive presumption of public injury to consumers. In Tague v. Molitor Motor Co., 139 Ill.App.3d 313, 316, 93 Ill.Dec. 769, 770–71, 487 N.E.2d 436, 437–38 (5th Dist.1985), the court rejected a public injury requirement, but there the plaintiff was a consumer complaining of odometer tampering and other misconduct in connection with the sale of a used car. In Duncavage v. Allen, 147 Ill.App.3d 88, 102, 100 Ill.Dec. 455, 463, 497 N.E.2d 433, 441 (1st Dist.1986), the court concluded that a tenant was a consumer under the Consumer Fraud Act, and relied on *Tague* in allowing a suit on behalf of a deceased tenant against a landlord.

This court concludes * * * that some consumer injury is an essential element of any claim under the Consumer Fraud Act. Perhaps where the plaintiff is a consumer, no further public injury need be shown. But where a suit is between competitors, as it is here, a plaintiff must show that the defendant's misconduct injured consumers generally.

Although the consumer injury requirement is an independent element of any Consumer Fraud Act claim, including claims based on the incorporated Deceptive Trade Practices Act violations, it is similar in some respects to the issue of unfairness. The consumer injury requirement developed in part from concepts applied in determining whether a trade practice is unfair under section 5 of the Federal Trade Commission Act, 15 U.S.C. § 45. A practice that is neither a violation of the antitrust laws nor deceptive may still be unfair under section 5 if it offends some established public policy, if it is immoral, unethical, oppressive or unscrupulous, or if it is substantially injurious to consumers. * * * The Federal Trade Commission has further refined the concept of unfairness under the FTC Act, clarifying that its primary focus is consumer injury; the public policy theory is used mainly to cross-check and confirm a finding of consumer injury, and the theory of immoral or unscrupulous conduct was abandoned altogether as an independent basis of liability. [C]onsumer injury under the Consumer Fraud Act can take two forms. Violations may affect consumers directly or indirectly by affecting competition. The plaintiff here has not attempted to set forth any evidence of a direct injury to consumers. Frito–Lay's alleged misconduct was directed to retailers, not to consumers. Further, although plaintiff contends that consumer's purchasing decisions were affected by changes in shelf space allocation, this court does not believe that such an effect can be characterized as an injury.

Rather, Jays' case depends on showing that consumers are injured because Frito–Lay's conduct was anti-competitive. [The court reviewed the evidence and prior precedent and concluded that while Frito–Lay was arguably an "over-zealous competitor" its activities were not anticompetitive or exclusionary.] * * *

Without evidence that Frito–Lay's shelf space activities were anticompetitive, Jays cannot establish the consumer injury element of its claim under the Consumer Fraud Act. For the same reason Jays cannot establish that Frito–Lay's non-deceptive shelf space practices were unfair. If Jays were seeking injunctive relief, perhaps plaintiff nevertheless could proceed to trial under the Illinois Deceptive Trade Practices Act, Ill.Rev.Stat. ch. 121, ¶ 311 et seq., on its claim that Frito–Lay deceived retailers by using incomplete data in its shelf allocation "mini-analysis" or by sabotaging retailers' own shelf-space studies. However, it cannot recover damages under the Deceptive Trade Practices Act. Under the circumstances, Frito–Lay is entitled to summary judgment.

NOTES

1. In 1990 the Illinois legislature amended the consumer protection act to provide that "proof of a public injury, a pattern, or an effect on consumers generally shall not be required" when a party seeks damages. However, subsequently a new amendment required proof of public injury only when the defendant was a car dealer. Andy Norman, Consumer Fraud Act Suits Against Car Dealers After the Public Injury Amendment, 84 Ill. B.J. 84 (1996). If the plaintiff need not prove some public injury or injury beyond damage to the plaintiff, does the act include a broad range of cases that would normally fall under the common law? In Lake County Grading Co. v. Advance Mechanical Contractors, Inc., 275 Ill. App. 3d 452, 654 N.E.2d 1109 (1995) the court held that the act should not apply to all breaches of contract but only those that "implicate consumer protection concerns."

2. Consideration of the full potential of the consumer protection acts in regulating market behavior is beyond the scope of these materials. In states such as Illinois which permit suits between competitors, these acts may become a significant part of the law of unfair competition. As the *Jays Foods* case illustrates, most of the acts incorporate rules and decisions of the Federal Trade Commission into a state's unfair competition law. As will be demonstrated in the next section of this chapter, the FTC has broadly interpreted its jurisdiction to prohibit "unfair and deceptive acts and practices".

3. In a consumer suit under its version of the consumer protection Act, the Vermont Supreme Court acknowledged that the legislature intended to provide a cause of action for deception much broader than common law fraud by eliminating any requirement of a showing of intentional conduct by the defendant. Poulin v. Ford Motor Co., 147 Vt. 120, 513 A.2d 1168 (1986). And see, Nei v. Boston Survey Consultants, Inc., 388 Mass. 320, 446 N.E.2d 681 (1983) where the Massachusetts Supreme Judicial Court suggests that the common law limitations on liability for nondisclosure might not be applicable under the statute.

4. One implication of the consumer protection acts is that they may supersede the Uniform Commercial Code and provide broader consumer remedies for breach of contracts for the sale of goods. A leading case in Massachusetts is Slaney v. Westwood Auto, Inc., 366 Mass. 688, 322 N.E.2d 768 (1975) where a consumer sued a used car dealer for breach of his promise made as part of a sales transaction to repair defects in the used car purchased by the consumer. The consumer alleged breach of express and implied warranty under the Uniform Commercial Code as well as a violation of the

Consumer Protection Act. The plaintiff also sought rescission and reimbursement for expenses. The trial court sustained the defendant's demurrer to the CPA claim holding (1) the statute provided no cause of action for a "classic breach of express or implied warranty under the Commercial Code", and (2) a purchaser's right of rescission is governed exclusively by the Commercial Code. The Supreme Judicial Court reversed holding the CPA created a new, separate cause of action for any act or practice defined as unfair or deceptive under the statute. In an important passage the court held:

> The [CPA] claim for relief is the creation of that statute. It is, therefore, sui generis. It is neither wholly tortious nor wholly contractual in nature, and is not subject to the traditional limitations of preexisting causes of action such as tort for fraud and deceit. 322 N.E.2d at 779.

The court observed that while the common law of deceit requires reliance by the buyer and knowledge of the falsity by the seller, neither are required under the act. Similarly, a breach of warranty is actionable under the act even though it may duplicate or conflict with provisions of the Uniform Commercial Code.

See also, V.S.H. Realty, Inc. v. Texaco, Inc., 757 F.2d 411 (1st Cir. 1985) where the court refused to enforce an "as is" provision of a real estate contract against a sophisticated purchaser who brought a claim under a consumer protection act.

5. Do the consumer protection acts pose a threat to the law of contracts generally? Consider Martin v. Lou Poliquin Enterprises, Inc., 696 S.W.2d 180 (Tex.App.1985). The defendant agreed to place an advertisement in the telephone directory for the plaintiff's business and subsequently assured plaintiff the advertisement would appear. When the advertisement failed to appear the plaintiff brought an action under the state's CPA. The court affirmed an award of damages and attorney's fees to the plaintiff. The court held that a consumer need not prove the passing of consideration but only that the consumer initiated the purchasing process in good faith.

> An individual initiates the purchasing process when he (1) presents himself to the seller as a willing buyer with the subjective intent or specific 'objective' of purchasing, and (2) possesses at least some credible indicia of the capacity to consummate the transaction. 696 S.W.2d at 184–85.

The court also held that a provision in the "contract" which limited the defendant's liability to refunding the cost of the advertisement did not prevent the plaintiff from recovering under the act. Although the waiver would probably have been effective in a suit for breach of contract, "[the CPA] states . . . that a consumer's waiver of any ... provision [thereunder] is contrary to public policy and is unenforceable and void." 696 S.W.2d at 186.

See also Smith v. Baldwin, 611 S.W.2d 611 (Tex.1980) where the court held the doctrine of substantial performance applies only to contract claims and not to claims under the consumer protection act.

6. The scope of the transactions covered by the consumer protection acts varies from state to state. Some statutes provide specific exemptions for some industries such as banking or insurance. Where free of express statutory exemptions, courts continue to explore the reach of the statutes with some expanding the scope to include industries already regulated by other enactments. Thus some courts have provided private remedies for unfair insurance practices even though insurance companies are closely regulated by state insurance departments. Credit transactions including debt collections are subject to both state and federal regulation but it has been held that a violation of the Federal Fair Debt Collections Practices Act is automatically a violation of the Federal Trade Commission Act and thus becomes also a violation of the consumer protection act providing the consumer with private remedies. See In re Scrimpsher, 17 B.R. 999 (Bkrtcy.N.Y.1982). Courts have applied the state statutes to the franchise industry, another industry heavily regulated by other enactments.

Doliner v. Brown

Appeals Court of Massachusetts, Norfolk, 1986.
21 Mass.App.Ct. 692, 489 N.E.2d 1036.

■ KAPLAN, JUSTICE.

[Doliner began negotiations to acquire an apartment house suitable for conversion to condominiums. He met with Green and Bendetsen to secure financing. These discussions were not confidential. Green and Bendetsen in turn met with Brown and described the potential transaction in order to get Brown to participate in the financing. Doliner reached an agreement on the purchase price for the property with the owners but the sales contract was not completed because Doliner's financing was uncertain. At this point Brown intervened and purchased the property from the owners.]

1. As one of the actors in this story put it, Brown "scooped" Doliner. That, however, was far from encompassing the tort of interference with prospective contractual relations. A competitor may "interfere" with another's contractual expectancy by picking the deal off for himself, if, in advancing his own interest, he refrains from employing wrongful means.* * *

[The court found Brown and Doliner to be "competitors" and held that Brown committed no independent tort such as fraud in obtaining the contract for himself.]

2. The remedy of businessman against businessman of G.L. c. 93A, § 11, may be invoked against an "unfair method of competition" or an "unfair or deceptive act or practice declared unlawful by [§ 2] or by any rule or regulation issued under [§ 2(c)]" by the Attorney General. These references point to Federal Trade Commission lore as a source of interpretation. As to the first-quoted phrase, Brown was not engaged in any practice considered abusive of, or injurious to competition such as may be discerned in the theft of trade secrets, or in passing off, or in adjacent business torts. Embraced in the other quoted phrase have been examples of extortion or similar oppression, breach of warranty, misrepresentation, betrayal of fiduciary duty, violation of specific regulations of the Attorney General. It is recognized that the language is broad enough to take in some reprehensible

acts committed in business contexts that elude conventional definitions and categories. The courts are not invited by the statute to punish every departure from "the punctilio of an honor the most sensitive" (Meinhard v. Salmon, 249 N.Y. 458, 464, 164 N.E. 545 [1928]), but they may enforce standards of behavior measurably higher than perfidy. They need not necessarily endorse a pattern of behavior because it happens to be current in the market place. We tried to suggest a mood, although we could not prescribe a rule, when we said in Levings v. Forbes & Wallace, Inc., 8 Mass.App.Ct. 498, 504, 396 N.E.2d 149 (1979), that a new tort may be recognized under § 11 when the questioned conduct "attain[s] a level of rascality that would raise an eyebrow of someone inured to the rough and tumble of the world of commerce." The situations have to be sized up one by one. In our view the present case is outside § 11 unless we are prepared to say that the statute enacts a rule of noblesse oblige by which a party is to be barred from competing for a business advantage because he is made aware that another has been exerting himself to the same end. That would be an extravagant rule of law.

Judgment affirmed.

BROWN, JUSTICE (concurring in part and dissenting in part).

It is with utmost reluctance that I concur, even in part. I only wish that the law would aid the needy as assiduously as it does the greedy. Brown did more than sabotage Doliner's contractual expectancy; he "pick[ed] the deal off for himself." The judge found that were it not for Brown's closing with the owners, they would have signed a purchase and sale agreement with Doliner, assuming the latter had been able to achieve satisfactory financing.

In the real estate game, one never commits fully until the "numbers" have been canvassed fully. Here, the numbers were very clearly set out by Green and Bendetson during their visit to Brown. Brown told them that he would consider seriously taking a fifty percent position in the *secondary financing* of the deal. No sooner had the two messengers departed than the defendant rushed to the phone, putting in motion his plan to "scoop" the entire deal. If that is not wrong—and the majority opinion concludes that it is not wrong under principles of common and statutory law—then perhaps there is something amiss in the common law and in our statutory scheme.

It is not enough for me that the common law be viewed as simply a mirror of the manner and mores of the marketplace. Fundamental principles of decency and fairness, resplendent in other areas of common law, ought to be recognized here. I disapprove of a view which condones conduct as reprehensible as that exhibited by the defendant in this case. Ethics and morality do have a place in our economic system, the greatest example of capitalism in the history of the world. In this regard, see the instructive discussion in Meinhard v. Salmon, 249 N.Y. 458, 464, 164 N.E. 545 (1928). Nevertheless, having reviewed the authorities cited in the majority opinion, and mindful of the role of an intermediate appellate court not "to alter established rules of law governing principles of substantive liability" (Burke v. Toothaker, 1 Mass.App.Ct. 234, 239, 295 N.E.2d 184 [1973]), I am constrained to join in part 1 of the majority opinion.

Should have secured non-compete Agrmt. or similar...

Turning from the common law to our own statutory law, I respectfully dissent from the majority's view that the defendant's conduct was not actionable under G.L. c. 93A, § 11. In formulating applicable standards of conduct under chapter 93A, we are advised "to discover and make explicit those unexpressed standards of fair dealing which the conscience of the community may progressively develop." Commonwealth v. DeCotis, 366 Mass. 234, 242, 316 N.E.2d 748 (1974), quoting Judge Learned Hand in Federal Trade Commn. v. Standard Educ. Soc., 86 F.2d 692, 696 (2d Cir.1936), rev'd in part, 302 U.S. 112, 58 S.Ct. 113, 82 L.Ed. 141 (1937). In this case, I would characterize the totality of the defendant's conduct as having been infused with a high enough "level of rascality" (Levings v. Forbes & Wallace, Inc., 8 Mass.App.Ct. 498, 504, 396 N.E.2d 149 [1979]) not only to have raised the plaintiff's eyebrow, but also to have permitted him to recover under § 11.

Chapter 93A has established in general, for businesses as well as for consumers, a path of conduct higher than that trod by the crowd in the past. It troubles me to see such a substantial deviation from that path.

NOTES

1. The formulation of a standard for "unfairness" under the Federal Trade Commission Act takes on new significance for state courts under the consumer protection acts. When the FTC "unfairness" standard was first formulated the only sanction available to the Commission was to seek a cease and desist order against the prohibited conduct. Can that standard be comfortably transported to a regime of treble and punitive damages and attorneys fees?

2. In Quaker State Oil Refining Corp. v. Garrity Oil Co, Inc., 884 F.2d 1510 (1st Cir. 1989) the court reformulated the Massachusetts "rascality" standard to mean that a "claimant must show that the defendant's actions fell 'within at least the penumbra of some common-law, statutory, or other established concept of unfairness,' or were 'immoral, unethical, oppressive or unscrupulous,' and resulted in 'substantial injury . . . to competitors or other businessmen." Should a standard of "unfairness" be built on the immorality of the defendant's conduct or on a requirement of consumer injury or both? Do you agree with Justice Kaplan or Justice Brown in *Doliner?*

3. There appears to be a growing number of competitor suits under the state statutes. Passing off and trademark infringement cases are quite common under the UDTPA and claims under the state act are often added to federal trademark actions. See, e.g., Brunswick Corp. v. Spinit Reel Co., 832 F.2d 513 (10th Cir.1987) (standards of proof under Oklahoma Act similar to that required under the Lanham Act). These claims can also be brought under the consumer protection acts with some advantages. In Polo Fashions, Inc. v. Craftex, Inc., 816 F.2d 145 (4th Cir.1987) the owner of the "Polo" and "Ralph Lauren" trademarks brought suit under the Lanham Act and the North Carolina Unfair Trade Practices Act. The court held that while damages could not be awarded under the Lanham Act because 15 U.S.C. § 1111 requires the statutory notice of registration before damages are permitted, damages were available (and trebled) under the state statute. But see, Sideshow, Inc. v. Mammoth Records, Inc., 751 F.Supp. 78 (E.D.N.C.1990) limiting *Polo Fashions* to intentional infringement and holding the North Carolina automatic trebling statute does not apply to innocent and unintentional infringement of unregistered trademarks because the plaintiff is "not an injured consumer and has several other adequate remedies."

In Unique Concepts, Inc. v. Manuel, 669 F.Supp. 185 (N.D.Ill.1987) the defendant filed counterclaims under common law disparagement and the Illinois Consumer Fraud and Deceptive Practices Act. The common law claim was rejected for failure to assert and prove special damages. "The statutory actions offer far more flexibility than do claims for common law commercial disparagement. Any conduct in a business which creates a likelihood of consumer confusion or misunderstanding is potentially actionable. * * * The apparatus of defamation does not apply; indeed, the statements made need not actually have been false, but only misleading. * * * Most importantly for the case at bar, in an action for disparagement brought under the Deceptive Practices statutes there is no need to plead or prove special damages. * * * In *M & W Gear* [97 Ill.App.3d at 909–911, 424 N.E.2d at 362–363], damages were proven through expert testimony, extrapolating lost profits from sales figures before and after the disparaging communication." But see, Dulgarian v. Stone, 420 Mass. 843, 652 N.E.2d 603(1995)(statements that do not constitute defamation at common law are not actionable under the CPA).

4. Those courts that have freed claims under the consumer protection acts from the limitations of analogous common law claims have also displayed a willingness to abandon some of the common law strictures on damages. See, e.g., Bernard v. Central Carolina Truck Sales, 68 N.C.App. 228, 314 S.E.2d 582 (1984) where the seller misrepresented the character and quality of a used tractor. The court refused to apply the common law rule of damages for fraudulent inducement which requires a plaintiff to choose between rescission with recovery of the purchase price or affirmation of the contract with recovery of the difference in market value between the goods as sold and the goods as represented. The court awarded the plaintiff full restitution including the monthly payments plus interest he had paid on the loan with no subtraction for the use by plaintiff of the tractor. The amount thus calculated was trebled under the North Carolina mandatory trebling statute.

5. The consumer protection acts may be a useful alternative to or additional claim in tort cases. In a landlord-tenant dispute in Brown v. LeClair, 20 Mass. App. Ct. 976, 482 N.E.2d 870 (1985) the plaintiff was able to treble normal tort damages for a variety of torts including assault and battery by using the CPA. In Pope v. Rollins Protective Services Co., 703 F.2d 197 (5th Cir.1983) the plaintiff purchased a burglar alarm system from defendant. The system was represented to be far more effective than it was and burglars were able to enter plaintiff's house by disabling the system. Plaintiff was assaulted in the process. She sued defendant for the misrepresentations under the Texas Deceptive Trade Practices Act claiming physical injuries and mental anguish. The Fifth Circuit held that Texas tort law would permit recovery for mental anguish in this circumstance and affirmed an award of $150,000 which was trebled under the Texas CPA. See also Ellis v. Northern Star Company, 326 N.C. 219, 388 S.E.2d 127 (1990) where the court held a libel per se in a business setting is a violation of the CPA but the plaintiff must elect between punitive damages under common law libel or treble damages under the act.

treble = 3x's

6. In a few jurisdictions courts have engrafted additional limitations on the applicability of the consumer protection acts in private lawsuits. In Washington the plaintiff must prove the defendant's acts affect the "public interest". Hangman Ridge Training Stables, Inc. v. Safeco Title Ins. Co., 105 Wash.2d 778, 719 P.2d 531 (1986). "[I]t is the likelihood that additional plaintiffs have been or will be injured in exactly the same fashion that changes a factual pattern from a private dispute to one that affects the public interest." It is reported that of the 42 states that allow a private cause of action under similar statutes, only six have imposed a showing of a "public interest" by a private plaintiff. Leaffer & Lipson, Consumer Actions Against Unfair or Deceptive Acts or Practices: The Private Uses of Federal Trade Commission Jurisprudence, 48 Geo.Wash.L.Rev. 521 (1980).

7. Almost all of the state acts authorize successful plaintiffs to recover attorneys fees. To the extent that the acts now encompass a good share of what otherwise would be common law tort and contract actions, the statutes have reversed the long standing American rule against the award of attorneys fees.

D. The Federal Trade Commission

The Federal Trade Commission was initially established in 1914 for the primary purpose of enforcing the anti-trust laws. Its charter gave it authority to "prevent * * * unfair methods of competition in commerce." In addition to anti-competitive behavior, the Commission also pursued deceptive activities but a series of Supreme Court decisions narrowed the Commission's jurisdiction by requiring proof that any deceptive practice also be shown to inflict injury on competition. Federal Trade Commission v. Raladam Co., 283 U.S. 643 (1931). Congress responded in 1938 by enacting the Wheeler-Lea Amendments clarifying that the Commission had authority over "unfair *and deceptive* practices in commerce." 52 Stat. 111 (1938). Since 1938 the Commission has been given regulatory authority far beyond anti-trust enforcement. For example, the Magnuson-Moss Warranty-Federal Trade Commission Improvement Act of 1975, Pub. L. No. 93–637, 88 Stat. 2183 (1974) codified Commission regulation of product warranties and gave the Commission broad enforcement powers.

In many states the unfair competition acts incorporate by reference the body of jurisprudence on unfair and deceptive practices created by the

Federal Trade Commission. Although the federal courts have consistently denied a private plaintiff standing to enforce a rule or decision of the FTC directly, the state acts indirectly may achieve that result. An in-depth study of the FTC is beyond the scope of this book. The following material is designed to provide a glimpse of the FTC in order to suggest the richness of what is now incorporated into state law. We focus primarily on FTC jurisprudence relating to deceptive activities which is central to the state acts and to the scope of this book. The Commission regulates in a much broader arena including business practices, commonly referred to as acts of unfair competition, that raise antitrust concerns such as predatory pricing, exclusive dealing, monopolization and vertical integration. We omit these matters, most of which are included in courses in Antitrust.

The Commission throughout its history has been controversial because it has authority to regulate or sanction a broad range of business practices. Some critics argue that competitive forces and private lawsuits adequately discourage most inappropriate competitive behavior. See, Posner, Regulation of Advertising by the FTC (Amer. Ent. Inst. 1973). Others emphasize that the proper role of the Commission is to correct for market defects. Robert Pitofsky, Beyond Nadar: Consumer Protection and the Regulation of Advertising, 90 Harv. L. Rev. 661 (1977). Commissioners are appointed by the President so that the Commission has tended to reflect the political mood of the times. Thus in the 1970's during the era of consumer protection, the Commission creatively expanded its activities. However, during the 1980's in more conservative times and with new appointees, the Commission acted with considerably more restraint.

The general authority of the Commission remains to prevent "unfair and deceptive" acts and practices. To determine whether a particular activity is subject to Commission enforcement it must be assessed under both the Commission standards for "deception" and for "unfairness".

(1) Deceptive Acts or Practices

In many instances the Commission has issued cease and desist orders against market conduct that is clearly deceptive and designed to defraud consumers. The following cases are more controversial but suggest some of the inherent difficulties in deception as a concept and the range of discretion courts are prepared to grant the Commission in defining deceptive conduct.

CHARLES OF THE RITZ DISTRIB. CORP. V. FTC, 143 F.2d 676 (2d Cir. 1944). Charles of the Ritz marketed a cosmetic preparation named "Rejuvenescence Cream" and advertised that it was capable of restoring "natural moisture necessary for a live, healthy skin." The Commission found the trademark and advertisement deceptive because it falsely represented "that Rejuvenescence Cream will rejuvenate and restore youth or the appearance of youth to the skin, regardless of the condition of the skin . . . ." Charles of the Ritz defended with the argument that there was no deception because no "straight-thinking person could believe that its cream would actually rejuvenate" and that there was no evidence before the Commission that any actual consumers were deceived. The Second Circuit upheld the Commission:

> [The Federal Trade Commission Act] was not "made for the protection of experts, but for the public—that vast multitude which includes the ignorant, the unthinking and the credulous," * * * and the "fact that a false statement may be obviously false to those who are trained and experienced does not change its character, nor take away its power to deceive others less experienced." Federal Trade Commission v. Standard Education Soc., 302 U.S. 112, 116. * * * The important criterion is the net impression which the advertisement is likely to make upon the general populace. * * * And, while the wise and the worldly may well realize the falsity of any representations that the present product can roll back the years, there remains "that vast multitude" of others who, like Ponce de Leon, still seek a perpetual fountain of youth. As the Commission's expert further testified, the average woman, conditioned by talk in magazines and over the radio of "vitamins, hormones, and God knows what," might take "rejuvenescence" to mean that this "is one of the modern miracles" and is "something which would actually cause her youth to be restored." It is for this reason that the Commission may "insist upon the most literal truthfulness" in advertisements, Moretrench Corp. v. Federal Trade Commission, 2 Cir., 127 F.2d 792, 795, and should have the discretion, undisturbed by the courts, to insist if it chooses "upon a form of advertising clear enough so that, in the words of the prophet Isaiah, 'wayfaring men, though fools, shall not err therein.'" General Motors Corp. v. Federal Trade Commission, 2 Cir., 114 F.2d 33, 36, certiorari denied 312 U.S. 682.

> That the Commission did not produce consumers to testify to their deception does not make the order improper, since actual deception of the public need not be shown in Federal Trade Commission proceedings. * * * Representations merely having a "capacity to deceive" are unlawful, and, as we have seen, the facts here more than warrant a conclusion of such capacity. Likewise it is not material that there was no consumer testimony as to the meaning of petitioner's representations. The testimony of the dermatologist, a person whose occupation took him among the buyers of Rejuvenescence Cream, is a qualified source of information "as to the buyers' understanding of the words they hear and use." * * *

FEDERAL TRADE COMMISSION V. ALGOMA LUMBER CO., 291 U.S. 67 (1934). A species of pine tree known as "white pine" was sought after for its superior qualities as a building material. This "white pine" grew predominantly in northeastern states and around the Great Lakes. In 1880 the pinus ponderosa, classified botanically as a yellow pine, was sold in local markets in California as "California white pine" or "white pine." It took ten years for California white pine to appear in markets in the midwest where it came into conflict with the indigenous white pine. In 1924 based on complaints and local investigations the FTC filed a complaint against the sellers of California white pine on the grounds that consumers were deceived. The respondents defended on the grounds that (1) the two woods were equivalent so no consumer was injured, and (2) the respondents had no intent to deceive. The Supreme Court, through Justice Cardozo, held that even if the woods were equivalent, the practice of using the term "white pine" was deceptive and then observed:

> The evidence here falls short of establishing two meanings with equal titles to legitimacy by force of common acceptation. On the contrary, revolt against the pretender, far from diminishing, has become increasingly acute. With the spread of business eastward, the lumber dealers who sold pines from the states of the Pacific Coast were involved in keen competition with dealers in lumber from the pines of the east and middle west. In the wake of competition came confusion and deception, the volume mounting to its peak in the four or five years before the Commission resolved to act. Then, if not before, misbranding of the pines was something more than a venial wrong. The respondents, though at fault from the beginning, had been allowed to go their way without obstruction while the mischief was not a crying one. They were not at liberty to enlarge the area of their business without adjusting their methods to the needs of new conditions. * * * More than half the members of the industry have disowned the misleading name by voluntary action and are trading under a new one. The respondents who hold out are not relieved by innocence of motive from a duty to conform. Competition may be unfair within the meaning of this statute and within the scope of the discretionary powers conferred on the Commission, though the practice condemned does not amount to fraud as understood in courts of law. Indeed there is a kind of fraud, as courts of equity have long perceived, in clinging to a benefit which is the product of misrepresentation, however innocently made. That is the respondents' plight today, no matter what their motives may have been when they began. They must extricate themselves from it by purging their business methods of a capacity to deceive.

FEDERAL TRADE COMMISSION V. COLGATE-PALMOLIVE CO., 380 U.S. 374 (1965). At issue was a Commission order attacking a television commercial purporting to show that "Rapid Shave", a shaving cream, could shave sandpaper. The television viewer saw Rapid Shave applied to what appeared to be sandpaper and then "shaved" by a razor. In fact, the Rapid Shave was applied to a piece of plexiglas to which sand had been applied. The examiner found (1) Rapid Shave could in fact shave real sandpaper although not in the short time represented by the commercial, and (2) if real sandpaper had been used for the commercials, the inadequacies of television transmission would have made it appear to viewers to be nothing more than plain colored paper. The Court formulated the issue to be whether it was deceptive to represent the "truth" through undisclosed use of mock-ups on television. The Court upheld the Commission's order arguing that the misrepresentation was that viewers had "objective proof of a seller's product claim over and above the seller's word" and that they had seen the proof with their own eyes:

> In commercials where the emphasis is on the seller's word, and not on the viewer's own perception, the respondents need not fear that an undisclosed use of props is prohibited by the present order. On the other hand, when the commercial not only makes a claim, but also invites the viewer to rely on his own perception, for demonstrative proof of the claim, the respondents will be aware that the use of undisclosed props in strategic places might be a material deception.

Justices Harlan and Stewart dissented believing that "the proper legal test in cases of this kind concerns not what goes on in the broadcasting studio, but whether what is shown on the television screen is an accurate representation of the advertised product and of the claims made for it."

FEDERAL TRADE COMMISSION V. MARY CARTER PAINT CO., 382 U.S. 46 (1965). Mary Carter Paint distributed paint under the "Mary Carter" label in more than 27 states through over 500 retail outlets. Its share of the national paint market was under one percent although the company did increase its sales from one million dollars in 1955 to 12 million in 1960. The basic business policy of Mary Carter consistently followed for ten years was to sell one gallon of "Mary Carter" paint at a price comparable to the leading national brands and to give the purchaser a second can "free". The policy arose when leading paint manufacturers succeeded in creating a public psychology equating quality paint with price. Paint priced below the "quality price" was not deemed by the consuming public to be quality paint. The Commission counsel conceded that the quality of Mary Carter paint was not at issue, and that Mary Carter paint was as good as or superior to paints marketed at the "quality price". The advertised price was the only price at which the purchaser could buy Mary Carter paint. Generally the purchaser accepted the second can but it was optional. One could not buy a single can for half the price by rejecting the "free" can. There was no evidence at the hearing of consumer complaints or of any deception of Mary Carter customers. The Supreme Court, through Justice Brennan, upheld the Commission:

> In sum, the Commission found that Mary Carter had no history of selling single cans of paint; it was marketing twins, and in allocating what is in fact the price of two cans to one can, yet calling one "free," Mary Carter misrepresented. It is true that respondent was not permitted to show that the quality of its paint matched those paints which usually and customarily sell in the $6.98 range, or that purchasers of paint estimate quality by the price they are charged. If both claims were established, it is arguable that any deception was limited to a representation that Mary Carter has a usual and customary price for single cans of paint, when it has no such price. However, it is not for courts to say whether this violates the Act. "[T]he Commission is often in a better position than are courts to determine when a practice is 'deceptive'

within the meaning of the Act." Federal Trade Comm'n v. Colgate-Palmolive Co., 380 U.S. 374, 385. There was substantial evidence in the record to support the Commission's finding; its determination that the practice here was deceptive was neither arbitrary nor clearly wrong. The Court of Appeals should have sustained it. * * *

Federal Trade Commission Policy Statement on Deception

Issued, October 14, 1983.

[The policy statement on deception was issued in a letter sent to the chairmen of the Senate Commerce, Science and Transportation Committee and House Energy and Commerce Committee by the Chairman of the Commission. The Commission applied its new policy for the first time in In re Cliffdale Associates, Inc., 103 F.T.C. 110 (1984) a case that hardly tested the limits of the policy. Cliffdale had marketed the "Ball–Matic Gas Save Valve" promoted as a gas saving device. The claims were found to be untrue. The central thrust of the policy statement follows:]

Certain elements undergird all deception cases. First, there must be a representation, omission or practice that is likely to mislead the consumer. Practices that have been found misleading or deceptive in specific cases include false oral or written representations, misleading price claims, sales of hazardous or systematically defective products or services without adequate disclosures, failure to disclose information regarding pyramid sales, use of bait and switch techniques, failure to perform promised services and failure to meet warranty obligations.

Second, we examine the practice from the perspective of a consumer acting reasonably in the circumstances. If the representation or practice affects or is directed primarily to a particular group, the Commission examines reasonableness from the perspective of that group.

Third, the representation, omission, or practice must be a "material" one. The basic question is whether the act or practice is likely to affect the consumer's conduct or decision with regard to a product or service. If so, the practice is material, and consumer injury is likely, because consumers are likely to have chosen differently but for the deception. In many instances, materiality, and hence injury, can be presumed from the nature of the practice. In other instances, evidence of materiality may be necessary.

Thus, the Commission will find deception if there is a representation, omission or practice that is likely to mislead the consumer acting reasonably in the circumstances, to the consumer's detriment.

NOTES

1. The "fools test" for deception announced in *Charles of the Ritz* was the articulated standard of the Commission until adoption of the policy statement in 1983. Application of the "fools test" can be quite amusing. See,

Gelb v. FTC, 144 F.2d 580 (2d Cir.1944) (upholding Commission order that claim that Clairol colored hair "permanently" was deceptive because it had no effect on new hair even though the court thought it unlikely that "any user . . . could be so credulous."); Allen B. Wrisley Co. v. FTC, 113 F.2d 437 (7th Cir.1940) (rejecting a Commission finding that some consumers might believe "Palm and Olive Soap" was made of 100% olive oil and observing "we suppose that by the same process of mental reaction, such witness would believe that the words 'goose grease and lard' meant 100% lard and no goose grease, or that if shown a picture of a cow and a horse, would be led to believe he had seen a picture of two horses."]. Notwithstanding the "fools test", the Commission has always recognized the doctrine of "puffing" which reflects the fact that all statements in advertisements are not to be taken with the same seriousness. One commentator has argued that the "fools test" most directly relates to appellate review, that is it reflects the courts' willingness to give the Commission broad leeway in policing the market-place. See Gellhorn, Proof of Consumer Deception Before the Federal Trade commission, 17 U. Kan. L. Rev. 559 (1969). To what extent should this apply in a state unfair competition act suit attempting to incorporate Commission jurisprudence? Should the policy statement be incorporated as well?

2. One argument for deference to the Commission's viewpoint in deception cases is that the Commission has an accumulated expertise. How does this relate to incorporating Commission decisions under the state unfair competition acts? Should the rule of *Colgate Palmolive* apply in private litigation?

3. In *Algoma*, the Commission faced the need to essentially arbitrate the conflict between two "white pines". At that point in time, the only remedy available to the Commission was to issue a cease and desist order. In such a setting it is easy to defend a rule that makes the intent of the parties irrelevant. Should the same rule apply to private suits under the state unfair competition acts?

4. *Mary Carter* suggests at least the possibility that some deceptive behavior may have pro-competitive effects. If consumers actually believe that you have to pay $15.00/gallon for paint and Mary Carter discovers a way to make equal quality paint for $7.50, aren't consumers better off being "deceived" by the "second can free" policy? Do consumers really think the second can is free?

(2) Unfair Acts or Practices

The Commission has considerable discretion in defining what acts or practices are "unfair." See Notes after Tuttle v. Buck in Chapter 1, supra. In addition the Commission has applied an unfairness test to advertisements to buttress its authority over deceptive practices.

PFIZER, INC., 81 F.T.C. 23 (1972). The complaint filed before the Commission attacked an advertisement for "Un-Burn", an over the counter product for minor burns, which proclaimed that "Un-Burn actually anesthetizes nerves in sensitive sunburned skin." The complaint charged the advertisement to be both deceptive and unfair. It claimed the advertisement was deceptive in that it impliedly represented that Pfizer had substantiated the claim but the Commission found no such implied representation. The complaint also charged it was unfair for an advertiser to make affirmative product claims without having a reasonable basis for making those claims. The Commission upheld this theory of unfairness and remanded the case to determine whether Pfizer had a reasonable basis for making the claim:]

Given the imbalance of knowledge and resources between a business enterprise and each of its customers, economically it is more rational, and imposes far less cost on society, to require a manufacturer to confirm his affirmative product claims rather than impose a burden upon each individual consumer to test, investigate, or experiment for himself. The manufacturer has the ability, the knowhow, the equipment, the time and the resources to undertake such information by testing or otherwise—the consumer usually does not.

Turning to that part of the complaint which challenges respondent's marketing practices as unfair, the Commission is of the view that it is an unfair practice in violation of the Federal Trade Commission Act to make an affirmative product claim without a reasonable basis for making that claim. Fairness to the consumer, as well as fairness to competitors, dictates this conclusion. Absent a reasonable basis for a vendor's affirmative product claims, a consumer's ability to make an economically rational product choice, and a competitor's ability to compete on the basis of price, quality, service or convenience, are materially impaired and impeded. * * *

The question of what constitutes a reasonable basis is essentially a factual issue which will be affected by the interplay of overlapping considerations such as (1) the type and specificity of the claim made—e.g., safety, efficacy, dietary, health, medical; (2) the type of product—e.g., food, drug, potentially hazardous consumer product, other consumer product; (3) the possible consequences of a false claim—e.g., personal injury, property damage; (4) the degree of reliance by consumers on the claims; (5) the type, and accessibility, of evidence adequate to form a reasonable basis for making the particular claims. More specifically, there may be some types of claims for some types of products for which the only reasonable basis, in fairness and in the expectations of consumers, would be a valid scientific or medical basis. The precise formulation of the "reasonable basis" standard, however, is an issue to be determined at this time on a case-by-case basis. This standard is determined by the circumstances at the time the claim was made and further depends on both those facts known to the advertiser, and those which a reasonably prudent advertiser should have discovered. Such facts should be possessed *before* the claim is made.

NOTES

1. Commission orders requiring two scientifically controlled studies for comparative effectiveness and freedom from side effects claims for nonprescription analgesics were upheld. Bristol-Myers Co. v. Federal Trade Commission, 738 F.2d 554 (2d Cir.1984); Sterling Drug, Inc. v. Federal Trade Commission, 741 F.2d 1146 (9th Cir.1984). In both cases, the Commission imposed the "two controlled studies" standard only for advertising that claimed superiority over other similar products. Statements in the advertisements that merely claimed an abstract not a comparative level of effectiveness or safety were subjected to the "reasonable basis" standard. "A reasonable basis for such a claim shall consist of competent and reliable scientific evidence supporting that claim." However, in Thompson Medical Co., Inc. v. Federal Trade Commission, 791 F.2d 189 (D.C.Cir.1986) a Commission order required two "well-controlled, double-blinded clinical studies" prior to any advertisement claiming effectiveness for Aspercreme, a topical over the counter analgesic. The court upheld the Commission noting that although the requirement had not formerly been imposed on a non-comparative efficacy claim, the Commission reserved in *Pfizer* the option of selecting the appropriate level of substantiation for all claims.

2. Should any of these tests for deception or unfairness be applicable in a private suit by a competitor under the state unfair competition acts?

3. *Commission Rule-making.* In addition to its adjudicatory role, the Commission has also promulgated numerous rules and guidelines related to unfair or deceptive practices in particular industries. The Federal Trade Commission did not have explicit authority to adopt rules until 1975 although it had previously adopted rules. For example in 1964 the Commission promulgated a rule requiring health warnings on cigarettes but was preempted by Congress which established a statutory scheme for the regulation of cigarette advertising. In 1969 the Commission adopted a rule requiring octane ratings to be posted on gas pumps. The Commission successfully defended its authority to adopt the rule after losing initially in the district court. National Petroleum Refiners Ass'n v. FTC, 482 F.2d 672 (D.C.Cir.1973), cert. denied 415 U.S. 951 (1974).

In 1975 Congress gave the Commission specific authority to promulgate "rules which define with specificity acts or practices which are unfair or deceptive acts or practices in or affecting commerce. . . ." 15 U.S.C.A. § 57(a) This new authority resulted from or coincided with strong consumer protection sentiments and the Commission used its power to take some bold and innovative steps. Some of these efforts are still in force, such as a rule that abolished the common law "holder in due course" rule for purchasers of consumer credit contracts and permitted a debtor to assert against the purchaser of the credit contract, all claims and defenses which the debtor could assert against the seller of the goods. Preservation of Consumers' Claims and Defenses, 16 C.F.R. § 433.1 et seq. (1998). See also, for example, Used Motor Vehicle Trade Regulation Rule, 16 C.F.R. § 455.1 et.seq. (1998) prohibiting misrepresentations by dealers of used automobiles.

The rapid expansion of Commission rulemaking activity and a shift in public sentiment toward deregulation collided in 1980 with enactment of the Federal Trade Commission Improvements Act of 1980, Pub. Law 96–252 (1980). Some of its significant provisions are: (1) a prohibition on promulgation of a rule relating to standards and certification except pursuant to the

Commission's power to enforce the antitrust laws (§ 7); (2) a limitation on Commission rulemaking relating to television advertising directed at children (§ 11); (3) a restriction on the Commission's power to regulate the funeral industry (§ 19); and (4) most significantly, a provision subjecting any Commission rule to a review and potential veto by Congress prior to its enforcement (§ 21). The legislative veto was subsequently declared unconstitutional. United States House of Representatives v. FTC, 463 U.S. 1216 (1983).

Does a competitor (or a consumer) now have a private cause of action to enforce any of these rules under the state unfair competition acts?

CHAPTER 3

TRADEMARKS

A. The Fundamentals
Kellogg Co. v. National Biscuit Co.

Supreme Court of the United States, 1938.

305 U.S. 111, 59 S.Ct. 109, 83 L.Ed. 73, rehearing denied 305 U.S. 674, 59 S.Ct. 246, 83 L.Ed. 437.

■ MR. JUSTICE BRANDEIS delivered the opinion of the Court.

This suit was brought in the federal court for Delaware[1] by National Biscuit Company against Kellogg Company to enjoin alleged unfair competition by the manufacture and sale of the breakfast food commonly known as shredded wheat. The competition was alleged to be unfair mainly because Kellogg Company uses, like the plaintiff, the name shredded wheat and, like the plaintiff, produces its biscuit in pillow-shaped form.

Shredded wheat is a product composed of whole wheat which has been boiled, partially dried, then drawn or pressed out into thin shreds and baked. The shredded wheat biscuit generally known is pillow-shaped in form. It was introduced in 1893 by Henry D. Perky, of Colorado; and he was connected until his death in 1908 with companies formed to make and market the article. Commercial success was not attained until the Natural Food Company built, in 1901, a large factory at Niagara Falls, New York. In 1908, its corporate name was changed to "The Shredded Wheat Company"; and in 1930 its business and goodwill were acquired by National Biscuit Company.

[Kellogg Company began making breakfast cereals in 1905, experimented with a product somewhat like Shredded wheat from 1912 to 1919, and in 1928 began manufacturing Kellogg's Shredded Wheat.

The district court first held against Nabisco finding that on the expiration of a patent the name of the article passes into the public domain. The Circuit Court of Appeals first affirmed and then on rehearing granted

---

1. The federal jurisdiction rests on diversity of citizenship—National Biscuit Company being a New Jersey corporation and Kellogg Company a Delaware corporation. Most of the issues in the case involve questions of common law and hence are within the scope of Erie R. Co. v. Tompkins, 1938, 304 U.S. 64. But no claim has been made that the local law is any different from the general law on the subject, and both parties have relied almost entirely on federal precedents.

Nabisco relief, describing the trademark as "consisting of a dish, containing two biscuits submerged in milk." Nabisco sought clarification when Kellogg argued it was only prohibited from using the term "Shredded Wheat" when displayed in combination with the biscuits submerged in milk. The court clarified its decree and enjoined Kellogg:

> "(1) from the use of the name 'Shredded Wheat' as its trade name, (2) from advertising or offering for sale its product in the form and shape of plaintiff's biscuit, and (3) from doing either."

The Supreme Court granted certiorari.]

The plaintiff concedes that it does not possess the exclusive right to make shredded wheat. But it claims the exclusive right to the trade name "Shredded Wheat" and the exclusive right to make shredded wheat biscuits pillow-shaped. It charges that the defendant, by using the name and shape, and otherwise, is passing off, or enabling others to pass off, Kellogg goods for those of the plaintiff. Kellogg Company denies that the plaintiff is entitled to the exclusive use of the name or of the pillow-shape; denies any passing off; asserts that it has used every reasonable effort to distinguish its product from that of the plaintiff; and contends that in honestly competing for a part of the market for shredded wheat it is exercising the common right freely to manufacture and sell an article of commerce unprotected by patent.

First. The plaintiff has no exclusive right to the use of the term "Shredded Wheat" as a trade name. For that is the generic term of the article, which describes it with a fair degree of accuracy; and is the term by which the biscuit in pillow-shaped form is generally known by the public. Since the term is generic, the original maker of the product acquired no exclusive right to use it. As Kellogg Company had the right to make the article, it had, also the right to use the term by which the public knows it. Compare Saxlehner v. Wagner, 216 U.S. 375; Holzapfel's Compositions Co. v. Rahtjen's American Composition Co., 183 U.S. 1. Ever since 1894 the article has been known to the public as shredded wheat. For many years, there was no attempt to use the term "Shredded Wheat" as a trade-mark. When in 1905 plaintiff's predecessor, Natural Food Company, applied for registration of the words "Shredded Whole Wheat" as a trade-mark under the so-called "ten year clause" of the Act of February 20, 1905, c. 592, sec. 5, 33 Stat. 725, 15 U.S.C. § 85, William E. Williams gave notice of opposition. Upon the hearing it appeared that Williams had, as early as 1894, built a machine for making shredded wheat, and that he made and sold its product as "Shredded Whole Wheat". The Commissioner of Patents refused registration. The Court of Appeals of the District of Columbia affirmed his decision, holding that "these words accurately and aptly describe an article of food which * * * has been produced for more than ten years * * *." Natural Food Co. v. Williams, 30 App.D.C. 348.[3]

---

3. The trade-marks are registered under the Act of 1920. 41 Stat. 533, 15 U.S.C. §§ 121–128 (1934), 15 U.S.C. §§ 121–128. But it is well settled that registration under it has no effect on the domestic common-law rights of the person whose trade-mark is registered. Charles Broadway Rouss, Inc., v. Winchester Co., 2 Cir., 300 F. 706, 713, 714; Kellogg Co. v. National Biscuit Co., 2 Cir., 71 F.2d 662, 666.

Moreover, the name "Shredded Wheat", as well as the product, the process and the machinery employed in making it, has been dedicated to the public. The basic patent for the product and for the process of making it, and many other patents for special machinery to be used in making the article, issued to Perky. In those patents the term "shredded" is repeatedly used as descriptive of the product. The basic patent expired October 15, 1912; the others soon after. Since during the life of the patents "Shredded Wheat" was the general designation of the patented product, there passed to the public upon the expiration of the patent, not only the right to make the article as it was made during the patent period, but also the right to apply thereto the name by which it had become known. As was said in Singer Mfg. Co. v. June Mfg. Co., 163 U.S. 169, 185:

"It equally follows from the cessation of the monopoly and the falling of the patented device into the domain of things public that along with the public ownership of the device there must also necessarily pass to the public the generic designation of the thing which has arisen during the monopoly. * * *

"To say otherwise would be to hold that, although the public had acquired the device covered by the patent, yet the owner of the patent or the manufacturer of the patented thing had retained the designated name which was essentially necessary to vest the public with the full enjoyment of that which had become theirs by the disappearance of the monopoly."

It is contended that the plaintiff has the exclusive right to the name "Shredded Wheat", because those words acquired the "secondary meaning" of shredded wheat made at Niagara Falls by the plaintiff's predecessor. There is no basis here for applying the doctrine of secondary meaning. The evidence shows only that due to the long period in which the plaintiff or its predecessor was the only manufacturer of the product, many people have come to associate the product, and as a consequence the name by which the product is generally known, with the plaintiff's factory at Niagara Falls. But to establish a trade name in the term "shredded wheat" the plaintiff must show more than a subordinate meaning which applies to it. It must show that the primary significance of the term in the minds of the consuming public is not the product but the producer. This it has not done. The showing which it has made does not entitle it to the exclusive use of the term shredded wheat but merely entitles it to require that the defendant use reasonable care to inform the public of the source of its product.

The plaintiff seems to contend that even if Kellogg Company acquired upon the expiration of the patents the right to use the name shredded wheat, the right was lost by delay. The argument is that Kellogg Company, although the largest producer of breakfast cereals in the country, did not seriously attempt to make shredded wheat, or to challenge plaintiff's right to that name until 1927, and that meanwhile plaintiff's predecessor had expended more than $17,000,000 in making the name a household word and identifying the product with its manufacture. Those facts are without legal significance. Kellogg Company's right was not one dependent upon diligent exercise. Like every other member of the public, it was, and remained, free to make shredded wheat when it chose to do so; and to call the product by its generic name. The only obligation resting upon Kellogg Company was to identify its own product lest it be mistaken for that of the plaintiff.

Second. The plaintiff has not the exclusive right to sell shredded wheat in the form of a pillow-shaped biscuit—the form in which the article became known to the public. That is the form in which shredded wheat was made under the basic patent. The patented machines used were designed to produce only the pillow-shaped biscuits. And a design patent was taken out to cover the pillow-shaped form.[4] Hence, upon expiration of the patents the form, as well as the name, was dedicated to the public. As was said in Singer Mfg. Co. v. June Mfg. Co., supra, page 185: "It is self-evident that on the expiration of a patent the monopoly granted by it ceases to exist, and the right to make the thing formerly covered by the patent becomes public property. It is upon this condition that the patent is granted. It follows, as a matter of course, that on the termination of the patent there passes to the public the right to make the machine in the form in which it was constructed during the patent. We may therefore dismiss without further comment the complaint as to the form in which the defendant made his machines."

Where an article may be manufactured by all, a particular manufacturer can no more assert exclusive rights in a form in which the public has become accustomed to see the article and which, in the minds of the public, is primarily associated with the article rather than a particular producer, than it can in the case of a name with similar connections in the public mind. Kellogg Company was free to use the pillow-shaped form, subject only to the obligation to identify its product lest it be mistaken for that of the plaintiff.

Third. The question remains whether Kellogg Company in exercising its right to use the name "Shredded Wheat" and the pillow-shaped biscuit, is doing so fairly. Fairness requires that it be done in a manner which reasonably distinguishes its product from that of plaintiff.

Each company sells its biscuits only in cartons. The standard Kellogg carton contains fifteen biscuits; the plaintiff's twelve. The Kellogg cartons are distinctive. They do not resemble those used by the plaintiff either in size, form, or color. And the difference in the labels is striking. The Kellogg cartons bear in bold script the names "Kellogg's Whole Wheat Biscuit" or "Kellogg's Shredded Whole Wheat Biscuit" so sized and spaced as to strike the eye as being a Kellogg product. It is true that on some of its cartons it had a picture of two shredded wheat biscuits in a bowl of milk which was quite similar to one of the plaintiff's registered trade-marks. But the name Kellogg was so prominent on all of the defendant's cartons as to minimize the possibility of confusion.

Some hotels, restaurants, and lunchrooms serve biscuits not in cartons, and guests so served may conceivably suppose that a Kellogg biscuit served

---

4. The design patent would have expired by limitations in 1909. In 1908 it was declared invalid by a district judge on the ground that the design had been in public use for more than two years prior to the application for the patent and theretofore had already been dedicated to the public. Natural Foods Co. v. Bulkley, No. 28,530, U.S.Dist.Ct., N.Dist.Ill., East.Div. (1908).

is one of the plaintiff's make. But no person familiar with plaintiff's product would be misled. The Kellogg biscuit is about two-thirds the size of plaintiff's; and differs from it in appearance. Moreover, the field in which deception could be practiced is negligibly small. Only 2½ per cent of the Kellogg biscuits are sold to hotels, restaurants and lunchrooms. Of those so sold 98 per cent are sold in individual cartons containing two biscuits. These cartons are distinctive and bear prominently the Kellogg name. To put upon the individual biscuit some mark which would identify it as the Kellogg product is not commercially possible. Relatively few biscuits will be removed from the individual cartons before they reach the consumer. The obligation resting upon Kellogg Company is not to insure that every purchaser will know it to be the maker but to use every reasonable means to prevent confusion.

It is urged that all possibility of deception or confusion would be removed if Kellogg Company should refrain from using the name "Shredded Wheat" and adopt some form other than the pillow-shape. But the name and form are integral parts of the goodwill of the article. To share fully in the goodwill, it must use the name and the pillow-shape. And in the goodwill Kellogg Company is as free to share as the plaintiff. Compare William R. Warner & Co. v. Eli Lilly & Co., 265 U.S. 526, 528, 530. Moreover, the pillow-shape must be used for another reason. The evidence is persuasive that this form is functional—that the cost of the biscuit would be increased and its high quality lessened if some other form were substituted for the pillow-shape.

Kellogg Company is undoubtedly sharing in the goodwill of the article known as "Shredded Wheat"; and thus is sharing in a market which was created by the skill and judgment of plaintiff's predecessor and has been widely extended by vast expenditures in advertising persistently made. But that is not unfair. Sharing in the goodwill of an article unprotected by patent or trade-mark is the exercise of a right possessed by all—and in the free exercise of which the consuming public is deeply interested. There is no evidence of passing off or deception on the part of the Kellogg Company; and it has taken every reasonable precaution to prevent confusion or the practice of deception in the sale of its product.

Fourth. By its "clarifying" decree, the Circuit Court of Appeals enjoined Kellogg Company from using the picture of the two shredded wheat biscuits in the bowl only in connection with an injunction against manufacturing the pillow-shaped biscuits and the use of the term shredded wheat, on the grounds of unfair competition. The use of this picture was not enjoined on the independent ground of trade-mark infringement. Since the National Biscuit Company did not petition for certiorari, the question whether use of the picture is a violation of that trade-mark although Kellogg Company is free to use the name and the pillow-shaped biscuit is not here for review.

Decrees reversed with direction to dismiss the bill.

MR. JUSTICE MCREYNOLDS and MR. JUSTICE BUTLER are of opinion that the decree of the Circuit Court of Appeals is correct and should be affirmed. To them it seems sufficiently clear that the Kellogg Company is fraudulently seeking to appropriate to itself the benefits of a goodwill built up at great cost by the respondent and its predecessors.

NOTES

1. This chapter considers how and to what extent a firm may establish and protect the identity of the goods or services it provides. The most common device used for this purpose is the brand name which most often is a word or combination of words, prominently displayed on the goods or in association with the services. The firm is not limited, however, to word marks. The *Kellogg* case, for example, involves three different allegedly identifying devices, the word mark "Shredded-Wheat", the product packaging including the picture of two biscuits in a bowl of milk, and the pillow-shaped form of the product itself. The law of trademarks is applicable to all of these identifying devices.

Trademark law is primarily concerned with a firms's need to identify its goods or services among its customers or potential customers. In this market context the proper identification of goods or services with a prominent trademark may serve multiple purposes. First, the trademark may help to identify the firm responsible for the goods or services. A purchaser with a question or complaint about the goods may be aided by the trademark in finding the responsible firm. It should be recognized, however, that trademarks alone seldom provide much information. To actually locate the name and address of the manufacturer of "Crest" toothpaste, a purchaser would either need to look elsewhere on the product or do further investigation. Second, a trademark may be used by the purchaser to identify the particular goods he or she intends to buy. Thus, a purchaser who wants only "Crest" toothpaste rather than any toothpaste uses the trademark to find the proper goods. Here, the purchaser may not know or care who actually makes "Crest" toothpaste. Sometimes this role of trademarks is described as guaranteeing the quality of goods or services but what is meant is that the mark guarantees a consistent level of quality—that is, the purchaser is likely to get the same quality of product each time a purchase is made. It is this role of trademarks that is referred to when courts observe that the purpose of trademark law is to protect consumers from being confused as to the "source" of goods or services.

One of the most influential law review articles in trademark law is Schechter, The Rational Basis of Trademark Protection, 40 Harv.L.Rev. 813 (1927). The author is interpreted as suggesting that trademarks play a much broader role in the marketplace by actually creating demand for goods or services. The consumers' interest in identifying "Crest" toothpaste can be protected by prohibiting any other manufacturer of toothpaste from using the word "Crest". But should other manufacturers be prohibited from using the word "Crest" on toothbrushes, or cosmetics generally, or wrist watches, or automobiles? To what extent do you think that a consumer, thrilled with the quality of "Crest" toothpaste, will be driven to purchase a "Crest" automobile? Moreover, how should trademark law adjust to a marketplace where trademarks, rather than identifying the goods consumers demand, are demanded in their own right? A fan of the Chicago Bears or the Nebraska Cornhuskers or a patron of Hard Rock Cafe or Planet Hollywood may purchase a T-shirt or hat or other item not because the trademark identifies the quality of the underlying good but to obtain the trademark itself as an emblem.

2. Legal protection for trademarks is intimately associated with a firm's willingness to invest in advertising. For a firm to capture the returns from advertising, it must be able to distinguish its goods from those of others. A single farmer has little incentive to advertise the benefits of corn because the gain from this investment will be shared by all corn growers. While protection of trademarks per se is free from controversy, the *scope* of protection may be impacted by a lawmaker's or fact-finder's view of the benefits and costs of advertising.

Proponents of limited trademark protection utilize the economic analysis advanced by Chamberlin, The Theory of Monopolistic Competition (5th ed. 1946). See Brown, Advertising and the Public Interest: Legal Protection of Trade Symbols, 57 Yale L.J. 1165 (1948); Alexander, Honesty and Competition (1965); Galbraith, The New Industrial State (1967); Mueller, Sources of Monopoly Power: A Phenomenon Called "Product Differentiation" 18 Amer.U.L.Rev. 1 (1968). Under this view, the protection of trademarks permits firms to differentiate its products from others resulting in a degree of monopoly power over price. Thus, to the extent consumers prefer "Crest" brand toothpaste to other brands, the producer of "Crest" can charge a higher price being the only source of "Crest" toothpaste. At some point this higher monopoly price is thought to be disadvantageous to the consumer.

Advocates of stronger and more expansive trademark protection believe consumers are advantaged by both advertising and the identification of the source of products. This view builds upon the theories advanced in Stigler, The Economics of Information, 69 J. Political Econ. 213 (1961). In Stigler's view the consumer faces two separate costs in purchasing a product: the nominal cost of the product and the information costs associated with searching for the right product to purchase. Sellers can generally reduce consumer search costs through advertising but will do so only if they can identify their products. Similarly, if trademarks signal a constant quality, consumers, once they find their preferred product, can forego repeated costs of research and experimentation by relying on a favored brand name. In this view, trademarks (and advertising) benefit consumers by reducing the search cost component of the price they pay for their purchases. See W. Landes & R. Posner, Trademark Law: An Economic Perspective, 30 J. Law & Econ. 265 (1987). For earlier classic defenses of stronger trademark protection see Pattishall, Trade–Marks and The Monopoly Phobia, 50 Mich.L.Rev. 967 (1952); Rogers, The Lanham Act and The Social Functions of Trade–Marks, 14 Law & Contemp.Prob. 173 (1949).

3. A trademark represents the investment of the trademark owner in developing the mark so that consumers will use it to identify the owner's goods or services. Oftentimes this investment is referred to as the "good-will" of the business. As illustrated by *INS v. AP*, there are strong themes in the law to protect investment by conferring property rights. Are there counter-vailing interests here? What interests do the competitors of the trademark owner have? Do consumers have a strong interest in broad protection of trademarks? Does Justice Brandeis in the *Kellogg* case protect the investment of the National Biscuit Co.? What interest does Kellogg have in the use of the term "Shredded-Wheat"? Or in selling the produce in pillow-shape? Or in having a picture of two biscuits in a bowl of milk on its package? Does the consumer care whether Kellogg uses the designation "Shredded-Wheat" if both cereals are of the same quality? If Kellogg's is of higher quality? Lesser quality? Would a price differential in the products alter any of your answers?

4. *Bibliography.* The following is a sampling of works that may be helpful in understanding the law of trademarks:

a. McCarthy, Trademarks and Unfair Competition (loose-leaf service with periodic updates).

b. Callmann, The Law of Unfair Competition, Trademarks and Monopolies (loose-leaf service with periodic updates).

c. Gilson, Trademark Protection and Practice (loose-leaf service with periodic updates).

d. W.R. Cornish, Intellectual Property: Patents, Copyright, Trademarks and Allied Rights (London, Sweet & Maxwell), discusses the English unfair competition and trademark law with attention to the practices of other members of the European Common Market.

e. American Law Institute, Restatement, Third, of Unfair Competition (1995).

Shaw v. Time-Life Records

Court of Appeals of New York, 1975.
38 N.Y.2d 201, 379 N.Y.S.2d 390, 341 N.E.2d 817.

[Artie Shaw, a famous band leader and musician in the 1920s, 30s, and 40s, brought causes of action against Time-Life Records for invasion of his privacy, unauthorized use of his name, damage to his reputation, and unfair competition. Shaw had originally recorded several songs for RCA. RCA arranged with Reader's Digest Record Album Service to issue a four record set entitled "Swing with Artie Shaw" which were the original performances electronically enhanced for stereo. Time-Life, in competition with the RCA release and without Shaw's permission, produced a series of recordings of music of the "Swing Era" containing 25 of Shaw's arrangements. The songs were played by modern musicians and promoted as "Artie Shaw versions". Shaw received royalties from RCA but not from Time-Life. Shaw did not have copyrights to the musical compositions and the copyright law did not protect arrangements or performances.]

■ JASEN, JUDGE.

The plaintiff's claim for damages based on unfair competition, the fourth cause of action in the amended complaint, stands on a different footing. While Time-Life was entitled to copy Shaw's arrangements and to compete with Shaw's own records, Time-Life was under an obligation to "use reasonable care to inform the public of the source of its product" and to identify its own merchandise "lest it be mistaken for that of the plaintiff." (Kellogg Co. v. National Biscuit Co., 305 U.S. 111, 119, hearing den., 305 U.S. 674.) While the use of Shaw's name is permissible, dishonesty in the use of the name is condemned. * * * Time-Life could not "palm off" its records as being the personal work of Shaw * * *.

The essence of an unfair competition claim is that the defendant assembled a product which bears so striking a resemblance to the plaintiff's product that the public will be confused as to the identity of the products. * * * The test is whether persons exercising "reasonable intelligence and discrimination" would be taken in by the similarity. * * * The defendant's promotional materials offered consumers an opportunity to purchase "Artie Shaw versions" of Swing Era classics. It is impossible to say as a matter of law, that reasonably discriminating consumers would discern that these "versions" were not authentic Shaw performances, but were instead attempted re-creations by modern day musicians. We believe that the plaintiff has made a sufficient factual showing to entitle him to present his case to the jury. A triable issue of fact exists as to whether reasonably discriminating members of the public would be confused or misled by defendant's advertising. Thus, in this limited respect, the defendant's motion for summary judgment was properly denied. * * *

NOTES

1. At common law trademark law is a specialized part of the more general tort of unfair competition. Both involve the same species of deception, passing off one's goods as those of another. The *Shaw* case illustrates the rule outside the trademark context. Does this also explain why Justice Brandeis in *Kellogg* could conclude that even though there was no protectible interest in the term "Shredded Wheat", Kellogg was still obliged to use the mark "fairly"?

2. There is much confusion in the cases on what constitutes "palming off" or "passing off," and the extent to which it is an essential element of a claim for unfair competition. Some cases have emphasized the intent of the defendant to "palm off" his goods as those of someone else. Others, like *Shaw,* have emphasized likelihood of confusion. And it has been suggested that for the broader tort of unfair competition *either* a likelihood of confusion *or* an unsuccessful attempt to fool the public might be sufficient. Whose interest is being protected in *Shaw?* In those cases requiring intent? Is there a first amendment objection if intent or at least negligence is not required? Can you distinguish the facts in *Shaw* from a case in which a defendant publishes a report that Shaw's music is inferior? What remedy would you authorize in a case where the defendant intended to pass off his goods as another's but was unsuccessful?

3. In which of the following circumstances would you impose liability on *X*?

a. *X* makes widgets and sells them using *Y's* trademark.

b. *X* makes widgets and sells them using a sample of *Y's* widgets.

c. *X* purchases *Y's* widgets and sells them as his own without *Y's* permission.

d. *X* purchases *Y's* widgets, removes *Y's* trademark, and sells them unbranded.

See, Borchard, Reverse Passing-Off-Commercial Robbery or Permissible Competition, 67 Trademark Rep. 1 (1977).

Legal Sources of Trademark Protection

Unlike patents and copyrights, trademark protection derived from the common law rather than from legislation or constitutional provision. In England, and subsequently in the United States, a firm obtained rights in a mark through adoption and use. No prior registration was required; the firm merely designed the mark and applied it to its goods. In contrast, in most foreign countries trademarks are protected when registered with a governmental agency. The first merchant to register a given mark is entitled to its exclusive use.

The common law remains today as a basic source of protection for trademarks in the United States. Adoption and use remain acceptable first steps in obtaining protection. In 1988 Congress adopted a limited intent-to-use system of registration which moderates the adoption and use requirements of the common law. Even where registration statutes have been enacted, common law principles determine to a large extent when a firm has acquired a sufficient interest in a trademark to be worthy of registration and what protection is provided for registered marks. Thus, where trademark problems arise there is often a complex interplay between common law rules and statutory provisions. The federal registration statute is popularly known as the Lanham Act. Most states have state trademark registration acts, the language often being patterned after the Lanham Act. And both § 43(a) of the Lanham Act and the Uniform Deceptive Trade Practices Act are broad enough to include claims for trademark infringement.

NOTE: A BRIEF HISTORY OF FEDERAL TRADEMARK LEGISLATION

Apparently trademarks were not of great importance during colonial times or early in the history of the United States. Although the founding fathers enshrined the patent and copyright systems into the constitution, trademarks were not mentioned. There was little public interest in trademark protection, although as early as 1791 Thomas Jefferson, as Secretary of State received a petition from one Samuel Breck and other "proprietors of a sailcloth manufactory in Boston, praying that they may have the exclusive privilege of using particular marks for designating the sailcloth of their manufactory." Jefferson transmitted the petition to the Second Congress along with his report which recognized that manufacturers should have an exclusive right to some mark on their goods and that "this should be done by general laws, extending equal right to every case to which the authority of the Legislature should be competent." 14 Amer. State Papers 48 reprinted in Report of The Commissioners Appointed to Revise the Statutes Relating to Patents, Trade and Other Marks, and Trade and Commercial Names, S.Doc. No. 20, 56th Cong., 2d Sess. 92 (1902). Congress did not act on the federal level. The first trademark statute enacted in the United States was in New York in 1845 and was designed to prevent fraud in the use of common law marks. In fact, the first reported case involving a trademark was in 1837 in Massachusetts. Thompson v. Winchester, 19 Pick. 214 (Mass.1837).

International demands rather than American public opinion led to the first federal attempt at trademark legislation. In 1868 treaties were concluded with Russia and Belgium granting reciprocal rights in trademarks for the citizens of each country trading in the other. However, a Russian or Belgian citizen, to obtain rights under the treaty, had to register the mark in the United States Patent Office. The Patent Office had no authority to receive such registrations.

In 1870 Congress enacted the first federal trademark registration act, primarily to implement the treaties agreed upon two years earlier, and secondarily, to provide American citizens with the same rights that foreign merchants had in the United States. Act of July 8, 1870, ch. 230, 16 Stat. 198. This enactment was part of a substantial revision of the patent and copyright laws. Perhaps since the attention of Congress regarding trademark legislation was directed to continental Europe because of the treaties, the first statute created substantive trademark rights as well as recognizing those rights created by common law. It allowed registration by persons "who are entitled to the exclusive use of any lawful trade-mark or *who intend to adopt and use* any trademark for exclusive use within the United States." (Emphasis added). Only citizens of countries not granting reciprocal rights to citizens of the United States were precluded from registering under the act. The act provided remedies for infringement, jurisdiction in federal courts, and a thirty-year period of protection with the option to renew the registration for an additional thirty years.

Six years later finding that "The public generally, the honest manufacturers and honest dealers throughout the country are being constantly swindled by counterfeit trade-marks" and that "worthless parties engaged in such dishonest practices are not prevented by civil actions" Congress passed the Act of August 14, 1876, ch. 274, 19 Stat. 141 providing criminal penalties of up to two years imprisonment and one thousand dollars fine for infringing, counterfeiting, making, or using a registered mark with "intent to defraud."

Shortly thereafter, the United States Supreme Court held both statutes unconstitutional. In re Trade-Mark Cases, 100 U.S. 82 (1879). The Court, in an opinion by Justice Miller, noted that trademarks had always been protected by state law, and thus for Congress to act required specific authority in the Constitution. With regard to the patent and copyright clause, the Court held that a trademark could not be considered a discovery of an inventor or a writing of an author because unlike patents and copyrights, protection under the trademark acts did not "depend upon novelty, upon invention, upon discovery, or upon any work of the brain. It requires no fancy or imagination, no genius, no laborious thought. It is simply founded on priority of appropriation." The Court also refused to uphold the legislation under the commerce clause because the scope of neither statute was limited to interstate commerce.

The Court left open two important questions: (1) whether "the trademark bears such a relation to commerce in general terms as to bring it within congressional control, when used or applied to the classes of commerce which fall within that control" and (2) whether Congress has authority to enact trademark legislation from its treaty-making power and its authority to pass laws necessary to carry such treaties into effect.

Apparently the country was pleased with its short sampling of federal trademark registration for it is reported that many petitions were sent to Congress and "great publicity was given to the subject by the press of the country." See Report, supra, at 103. The New York Times on November 19, 1879, noted that the "value put upon the statute by the mercantile community is shown by the fact that, notwithstanding the large fee for registration, about 8,000 trade-marks have been registered since the law was passed in 1879. * * * State laws for this purpose cannot prove otherwise than unsatisfactory and objectionable." And a constitutional amendment to authorize Congress to regulate the "exclusive right to adopt and use trademarks" was introduced in the House.

In 1881, the act of 1870 was substantially reenacted but applied only to "owners of trade-marks used in commerce with foreign nations, or with the Indian tribes." This implemented the treaties with Russia and Belgium but did not extend federal registration to marks used in interstate commerce. Act of March 3, 1881, ch. 138, 21 Stat. 502.

Concern over the precise interpretation of the Supreme Court's view of Congressional power to enact trademark legislation explains to a large extent the omission of interstate commerce from the act of 1881. Likewise, it took Congress almost twenty-five years before it passed another registration act for interstate commerce—the Act of February 20, 1905, ch. 592, 33 Stat. 724, which has been described as "a slovenly piece of legislation, characterized by awkward phraseology, bad grammar and involved sentences. Its draftsmen had a talent for obscurity amounting to genius." Rogers, The Expensive Futility of the United States Trade-Mark Statute, 12 Mich.L.Rev. 660 (1914).

The act allowed registration of marks used in interstate commerce for a period of twenty years with an unlimited right of renewal. Registration constituted prima facie evidence of ownership of the mark, entitled the federal courts to jurisdiction, and provided remedies for infringement. In addition, the act allowed anyone injured by the registration of a mark at any time to petition the Commissioner of Patents for cancellation of the registration.

Interpretations of the Act of 1905 were influenced by the Trade-Mark Cases. In American Steel Foundries v. Robertson, 269 U.S. 372 (1926) the

Supreme Court gratuitously noted that Congress "has been given no power to legislate upon the substantive law of trade-marks" and therefore the 1905 act entitled only the registration of "such marks as that law [common law of trade-marks] and the general law of unfair competition of which it is a part, recognized as legitimate." And in American Trading Co. v. H.E. Heacock Co., 285 U.S. 247 (1932) the Court, in deciding a conflict between a mark registered under a local act in the Philippine Islands authorized by an act of Congress and a mark registered under the act of 1905, both being applied to commerce solely within the Philippine Islands, held the Philippine mark had superior rights because although Congress had the right to authorize the Philippine Commission to enact a substantive trademark statute for the Philippines, the Act of 1905 did not create substantive rights because "Congress, by virtue of the commerce clause, has no power to legislate upon the substantive law of trademarks." For a time, lower federal courts assumed no Congressional power over substantive trademark rights.

In 1943, the Seventh Circuit in a widely cited opinion directly held that not only did congress have authority to create substantive trademark rights but it had done so in the Act of 1905. Philco Corp. v. Phillips Mfg. Co., 133 F.2d 663, 668 (7th Cir.1943).

The Act of 1905 did not satisfy those who wanted a national law of trademarks. Various successful attempts at "tinkering" with the Act of 1905 were paralleled by attempts at total revision beginning as early as 1924. Finally Representative Fritz G. Lanham introduced a trademark bill in 1938 which eventually after modification was enacted in 1946 and became effective in 1947. The Lanham Act embodied the labors of several interest groups including the National Association of Manufacturers, the United States Trademark Association and the American Bar Association. See Hearings on H.R. 102 Before the Subcomm. on Trade-Marks of the House Comm. on Patents, 77th Cong., 1st Sess., at 134 (1941). A fuller treatment of the background to eventual passage of the Lanham Act can be found in McCarthy, Trademarks and Unfair Competition § 5.4 (1997). For an extensive contemporaneous interpretation of the act see Robert, The New Trade-Mark Manual (1947) which also provides a valuable comparison between the Lanham Act and the Act of 1905.

The Trademark Revision Act of 1988, with an effective date of November 16, 1989, was the first major revision of the Lanham Act after its enactment.

An Overview of National and International Protection

National Protection under the Lanham Act

The Lanham Act, 15 U.S.C. § 1051 et seq., enacts the federal regime of trademark registration. Administered by the Patent and Trademark Office (PTO) the Act creates two separate registers, the "Principal Register" (§ 1) and the "Supplemental Register" (§ 23).

The Principal Register is designed to affect trademark rights and controversies within the United States. Since 1947 the Act has provided that a "trademark owner" who has adopted and used a mark can apply for federal registration on the Principal Register. An application for registration is extensively examined by the PTO to determine if it qualifies for registration. This can delay registration for months or even years. If the PTO determines the application sets forth a mark entitled to be registered, the mark is published in the Official Gazette of the Patent and Trademark Office. Interested persons have 30 days after publication to file an opposition to registration (§ 13). If no opposition is filed, a registration is issued. A registration remains in force for 10 years provided the owner files an affidavit in the fifth year showing the mark is still in use (§ 8). The registration can be renewed for an unlimited number of additional 10 year terms by filing an affidavit within 6 months of expiration indicating the mark is still in use (§ 9).

The Lanham Act as originally enacted required that a trademark owner first use the mark in commerce before applying for a registration. In 1988 amendments were adopted to permit trademark owners to apply for protection under the Lanham Act prior to actual use if they could demonstrate a bona fide intention to use the mark in the future (§ 1(b)). Within six months after an intent to use application is filed, the trademark owner must file a statement that the mark has been actually used. The PTO can give an applicant additional time to demonstrate use, not to exceed 24 months after filing (§ 1(d)). No registration issues until the mark is actually used but once use and registration occur, the owner's priority of use reverts back to the date of filing the application based on intent to use.

Controversies involving the validity of the application or registration of a mark may arise in a number of different contexts. An applicant may contest the denial of an application by the examiner (§ 20). Persons who might be injured by the registration may seek to oppose the registration prior to its issuance (§ 13) or may seek to cancel the registration after it is issued (§ 14). If the Commissioner believes the mark in an application resembles a registered mark or a mark in another pending application, the Commissioner can declare an interference proceeding which allows the owners of the two competing marks to litigate their respective rights (§ 16).

Proceedings for all of the above disputes are heard by the PTO's Trademark Trial and Appeal Board (§ 17). Until 1982, appeals from the Board's decisions were to the Court of Customs and Patent Appeals. In 1982 Congress created the United States Court of Appeals for the Federal Circuit (§ 21(a)) which hears direct appeals from the Board. A party may forego a direct appeal to the Federal Circuit and file a civil action in an appropriate federal district court (§ 21(b)).

International Protection of Trademarks

The Principal Register of the Lanham Act affects trademark rights within the United States. However, trademarked goods and services flow increasingly in a global economy. For more than a century, the countries of the world have struggled to provide an efficient mechanism for trademark owners to secure international protection of their trademarks. Although some international agreements have been negotiated, the United States has not participated. Thus, it remains largely true today that an American trademark owner interested in protecting a mark throughout the world must seek registration of the mark in each individual country. There have been renewed efforts at an agreement the United States could accept.

The protection of intellectual property, including trademarks, has become a major issue in efforts to implement freer trade policies among the nations of the world. Businesses in developed countries, such as the United States, have a comparative advantage in research and development activity that produces patented and copyrighted goods and also a significantly greater interest in the protection of famous brand names. In some developing countries, pirating of intellectual property has become an important industry, resulting in weak substantive laws or little actual enforcement of intellectual property rights.

The pressure for seeking international agreement on the proper scope of trademark protection and for establishing an efficient mechanism for international registration will play a significant role in the development of American domestic trademark law. Several past attempts at more sensible international trademark systems have been frustrated because the United States has been unwilling to change certain features of its domestic trademark law which are inconsistent with that of most other countries. For example, most countries do not require the trademark owner to actually use the mark prior to registration. Similarly most countries do not have an elaborate, time-consuming examination procedure prior to registration of a trademark. In the past few years, some changes in the Lanham Act have been adopted to bring it into conformity with the views of the international community. More such efforts are likely to occur in the near future.

The following is a very general outline of past and current developments in this area:

1. International Registration Systems

a. International Convention for the Protection of Industrial Property (1883). The earliest international agreement aimed at multinational registration and protection of trademarks was the International Convention for the Protection of Industrial Property, signed in Paris in 1883. The principle underlying the Convention of Paris is that member states agree to confer on nationals of other member states the same entitlement relating to the protection of marks as are extended to their own citizens.

The Paris Convention provides that once a citizen obtains a trademark registration in the citizen's home country, every other signatory country must accept that registration for filing in its domestic system and to accord the owner the same rights it accords its own citizens. The scheme still requires the trademark owner to pursue registration in each country. The Supplemental Register of the Lanham Act is designed to allow an American company to satisfy the domestic registration requirement without the extended time period required for examination of the application under the Principal Register. The Supplemental Register, however, has little impact on domestic rights and, accordingly has few restrictions as to the marks that can be registered. Section 44 of the Lanham Act implements the Paris

Convention by extending the benefits of Lanham Act registration to citizens of countries that provide reciprocal rights to American citizens.

A major feature of the Paris Convention, implemented by § 44 of the Lanham Act, is that upon compliance with certain conditions the date of filing an application for registration in the applicant's home country becomes the date of filing in a foreign country for purposes of determining priority between competing marks in the foreign country. This constructive priority date applies as long as the foreign application is filed within 6 months of the filing of the domestic application. This feature causes some difficulty in the United States because the Lanham Act, unlike the law in most other countries, required, until the 1988 revisions, adoption and use of a mark prior to registration. Thus it was possible for a foreign national to register in its home country prior to using the mark, then register under the Lanham Act and claim priority in the United States over an American company who was the prior user of the mark in the United States.

b. Trademark Registration Treaty (1973). In Vienna in 1973 fourteen countries, including the United States, signed the Trademark Registration Treaty ("TRT"). This agreement provides for an international filing system administered by the World Intellectual Property Organization ("WIPO"). A trademark owner could file a single registration for a trademark with WIPO and designate the signatory countries in which actual registration is sought. The filing would then be automatically forwarded to those countries and reviewed under their respective domestic laws as though it were a domestic trademark application. Registration would follow in accordance with the domestic law of each country but the priority in each country would be the date of the international filing. The treaty provides that no member state can refuse trademark registration on grounds of nonuse of the mark within three years of filing of the international application. Implementation in the United States would have required change in the Lanham Act. The treaty has not been ratified by the United States Senate.

c. The Madrid Registration of Marks Treaty (Madrid Agreement) (1890). The Madrid Agreement established a system for international registration of marks. Under the Agreement once a company obtained a registration under its own domestic law, it could register the mark with WIPO and designate those countries within the agreement in which protection was sought. The filing with WIPO automatically constituted an application for domestic registration in these designated foreign countries. Each country had 12 months to reject the application. If the application was not rejected, the company automatically obtained a registration in the foreign country, subject to that country's laws. This system facilitated foreign registrations for it required that a company only do two things: obtain a registration in its home country and file an application with WIPO. The agreement was signed by about thirty nations.

The United States did not join the Madrid Agreement because some of its components would place American companies at a disadvantage. First, the international registration was based on *registration* in the trademark owner's home country. Because of the delay caused by the examination procedures under the Lanham Act, American companies would run the risk that someone would obtain priority by obtaining an earlier registration under the laws of another country. Moreover, the PTO would have difficulty complying with the 12 month period for rejection of an international registration, given its workload. American companies also objected to the requirement that trademark applications under the Madrid Agreement were to be in the French language and to the doctrine of "central attack". Under this doctrine, if the trademark owner's domestic registration were canceled within five years, it had the effect of also canceling all of the other registrations obtained through the Agreement.

(d) *The Madrid Protocol.* The Madrid Protocol is a separate international agreement designed to respond to the concerns of the United States with the Madrid Agreement. Under the Protocol, the international filing could be based on a domestic *application* rather than an actual registration. A domestic application would support an international filing that would be automatically transmitted to each designated country for examination. Other countries would have up to 25 months to reject the international registration. The doctrine of "central attack" was abandoned so that if a domestic registration is canceled, the international registrations are transformed into national applications with the same priority date. The Protocol also allowed applications to be in English. Legislation to permit the United States to join the Madrid Protocol has been introduced in Congress. See generally, Schechter, Facilitating Trademark Registration Abroad: The Implications of U.S. Ratification of the Madrid Protocol, 25 Geo. Wash. J. Int'l L & Econ. 419 (1991).

2. Intellectual Property and International Trade.

With the increased globalization of the economy, the countries of the world have undertaken considerable efforts to reduce tariffs and other barriers to world trade. The United States, Canada, and Mexico concluded the North American Free Trade Agreement ("NAFTA") designed to encourage unencumbered trade among the three countries. More broadly, the United States participates in the General Agreement on Tariffs and Trade ("GATT") which for many years has been the forum for trade discussions. In the most recent round of GATT negotiations, the Uruguay Round, the United States succeeded in placing the protection of intellectual property on the agenda. This was a recognition that failure of countries to protect intellectual property can have an inhibiting effect on trade.

The NAFTA agreement contains extensive provisions relating to intellectual property including trademarks in Part Six. The NAFTA provisions are similar to those contained in the GATT agreement, which in the GATT are called the Trade Related Aspects of Intellectual Property Rights, Including Trade in Counterfeit Goods ("TRIPS"). The United States Congress approved the NAFTA accord and the GATT agreement both of which required amendments to the Lanham Act.

The thrust of these agreements is to assure minimal standards of protection of intellectual property rights in the signatory countries. With regard to trademarks, the agreements address both the substantive rights to be accorded trademark owners as well as the procedural mechanisms required to enforce trademark rights. For example, Article 1708 of the NAFTA provides the minimum substantive law standards which, for the most part, are consistent with current United States law. Of particular significance is paragraph 6 which adopts Article 6bis of the Paris Convention relating to "well-known" marks. In most countries other than the United States, trademark rights are acquired by registration not by use. It was not uncommon for a local resident of a foreign country to register a well-known mark, i.e., FORD for automobiles, and thus demand payment before the mark owner could do business in that country. Article 6bis and now the NAFTA agreement require the signatory countries to refuse registration or to allow cancellation of registration of "well-known" marks. The GATT TRIPS contains similar provisions. See, Section 2, Article 16.

Other provisions of the agreements set out the minimum requirements for civil judicial procedures for enforcement of intellectual property rights and also provide for adoption of provisional remedies to prevent infringements, criminal penalties for "willful trademark counterfeiting", and enforcement of intellectual property rights at the border. The effect of these agreements will be to exert pressure to harmonize the domestic law of the affected nations.

"Trademark," "Trade Name," And "Secondary Meaning"

Trademark and trade name. The common law historically distinguished between "trademarks" and "trade names." The former came to signify those marks or devices which were arbitrary and were distinctive enough to identify the user's goods; "trade names" referred to those marks or devices which had a primary meaning other than identifying the user's goods, such as a surname or a descriptive word. To be protected, the "trade name" owner had to show that his mark had come to distinguish his goods in the minds of the consuming public, i.e. that it had attained a secondary meaning or significance. The Restatement of Torts § 715 (1938) outlined the requirements for a trademark: (a) it was adopted and used to denominate goods, (b) it was affixed to the goods, and (c) it was not a "common or generic name for the goods or a picture of them, or a geographical, personal, or corporate or other associate name, or a designation descriptive of the goods or of their quality, ingredients, properties or functions * * *." Section 716 defined trade name as any designation which is adopted and used to denominate goods or services or a business and has "acquired a special significance as the name thereof * * *".

At common law there were distinctions in the scope of protection accorded the designation depending on whether it was a "trademark" or "trade name."

The enactment of the Lanham Act in 1946 redefined these terms. Section 45 of the Lanham Act, 15 U.S.C. § 1127, defines "mark" "trademark" and "trade name." The Lanham Act definition of "trademark" includes any mark used to identify goods regardless of whether it is an arbitrary or descriptive term. Thus common law "trade names" are included within the definition of "trademark" under the Act.

A "trade name" under the Lanham Act identifies a person's "business or vocation". Under the Lanham Act, the distinction between trademark and trade name becomes whether the mark identifies the goods or services of the producer or the producer's business. The trademark "Pepsi" identifies the soft drink and the trade name "Pepsico, Inc." identifies the business. Of course, in some situations a mark may function *both* as a trademark and a trade name.

Section 2, 15 U.S.C. § 1052, sets out the requirements a trademark owner must meet to obtain a registration. The beginning clause of this section uses the term "trademark" and prohibits the Patent Office from refusing to register any "trademark" unless it fits the specifically listed prohibitions. Thus, the Act assumes there is a pre-existing "trademark" prior to registration.

Subsection 2(e) codifies the descriptive, geographical, or surname distinctions of the common law. By reading the introductory clause of § 2 with subsection (e) it can be seen that a trademark which is descriptive is still a trademark and yet it cannot be registered under § 2(e). However, § 2(f) allows marks which are "merely descriptive," "primarily geographically descriptive," or "primarily merely a surname" to be registered notwithstanding § 2(e) if the mark is "distinctive of the applicant's goods in commerce." What is the difference between "distinctive" in 2(f) and "distinguish" as used in the introductory clause? If a "mark" is *merely* descriptive" how could it be "distinctive" of the applicant's goods?

The only reference to "trade name" in section 2 is in subsection (d) which precludes registration of a "mark" which so resembles a "mark or trade name previously used in the United States." "Trade names" as defined in § 45 are not registrable on the Principal Register. On the other hand, § 44(g) provides protection to foreign nationals for trade names or commercial names "without the obligation of filing or registration whether or not they form parts of marks."

The Lanham Act specifically recognizes three other types of marks: service marks (§ 3), certification marks (§ 4), and collective marks (§ 4). They are each defined in § 45 and considered later in this Chapter.

The Lanham Act definitions have been adopted by courts even in common law trademark and unfair competition cases.

Secondary meaning. Under the traditional common law, a trade name (descriptive, geographic, or surname term) included any designation which had acquired "special significance." Under the Lanham Act, descriptive, geographical and surname marks can be registered if they become "distinctive of the applicant's goods." The common law referred to this "special significance" as "secondary meaning" and many of the Lanham Act cases use the term also. The classical definition of secondary meaning is by Judge Denison in G. & C. Merriam Co. v. Saalfield, 198 F. 369, 373 (6th Cir.1912):

> [Secondary meaning] contemplates that a word or phrase originally, and in that sense primarily, incapable of exclusive appropriation with reference to an article on the market, because geographically or otherwise descriptive, might nevertheless have been used so long and so exclusively by one producer with reference to his article

that, in that trade and to that branch of the purchasing public, the word or phrase had come to mean that the article was his product; in other words, had come to be, to them, his trademark. So it was said that the word had come to have a secondary meaning, although this phrase, "secondary meaning," seems not happily chosen, because, in the limited field, this new meaning is primary rather than secondary: that is to say, it is, in that field, the natural meaning.

Proof of secondary meaning is the critical issue in many trademark cases. The consumer association of the mark with the producer may be proved by direct or circumstantial evidence. Direct evidence may consist of the testimony of actual consumers or scientific surveys of actual consumers. A number of courts have noted that the direct testimony of consumers should not be given great weight, particularly where their selection was not in accord with recognized techniques to assure randomness and reliability. Scientific surveys have been increasingly utilized, and their probative value obviously depends on the objectivity of the sampling technique. However, as the direct evidence becomes more scientific, the Court must confront the difficult question of what percentage of the appropriate class of consumers must have formed the association in order to support a finding of secondary meaning. Would 100% be required? A majority? Would 25% be sufficient? What if 55% of the consumers associated a descriptive term with producer X but 25% continued to believe it was merely descriptive and did not refer to any producer? In this later situation who has an interest in using the term?

Proof of "distinctiveness" for purposes of Lanham Act registrations is similar to proof of secondary meaning at common law. Both direct and circumstantial evidence are used. Section 2(f) of the Act provides that exclusive and continuous use of a mark for 5 years "before the date on which the claim of distinctiveness is made" may be considered to be prima facie evidence of distinctiveness. The Commissioner is not required to accept the presumption in all cases.

B. Problems of Validity
(1) Distinctiveness
(a) Descriptive Marks

Zatarains, Inc. v. Oak Grove Smokehouse, Inc.

United States Court of Appeals, Fifth Circuit, 1983.
698 F.2d 786.

■ GOLDBERG, CIRCUIT JUDGE:

* * *

I. FACTS AND PROCEEDINGS BELOW

A. THE TALE OF THE TOWN FRIER

Zatarain's is the manufacturer and distributor of a line of over one hundred food products. Two of these products, "Fish-Fri" and "Chick-Fri," are coatings or batter mixes used to fry foods. These marks serve as the entreè in the present litigation.

Zatarain's "Fish-Fri" consists of 100% corn flour and is used to fry fish and other seafood. "Fish-Fri" is packaged in rectangular cardboard boxes containing twelve or twenty-four ounces of coating mix. The legend "Wonderful FISH–FRI ®" is displayed prominently on the front panel, along with the block Z used to identify all Zatarain's products. The term "Fish-Fri" has been used by Zatarain's or its predecessor since 1950 and has been registered as a trademark since 1962.

Zatarain's "Chick-Fri" is a seasoned corn flour batter mix used for frying chicken and other foods. The "Chick-Fri" package, which is very similar to that used for "Fish-Fri," is a rectangular cardboard container labeled "Wonderful CHICK–FRI." Zatarain's began to use the term "Chick-Fri" in 1968 and registered the term as a trademark in 1976.

Zatarain's products are not alone in the marketplace. At least four other companies market coatings for fried foods that are denominated "fish fry" or "chicken fry." Two of these competing companies are the appellees here, and therein hangs this fish tale.

Appellee Oak Grove Smokehouse, Inc. ("Oak Grove") began marketing a "fish fry" and a "chicken fry" in March 1979. Both products are packaged in clear glassine packets that contain a quantity of coating mix sufficient to fry enough food for one meal. The packets are labelled with Oak Grove's name and emblem, along with the words "FISH FRY" OR "CHICKEN FRY." Oak Grove's "FISH FRY" has a corn flour base seasoned with various spices; Oak Grove's "CHICKEN FRY" is a seasoned coating with a wheat flour base.

Appellee Visko's Fish Fry, Inc. ("Visko's") entered the batter mix market in March 1980 with its "fish fry." Visko's product is packed in a cylindrical eighteen-ounce container with a resealable plastic lid. The words "Visko's FISH FRY" appear on the label along with a photograph of a platter of fried fish. Visko's coating mix contains corn flour and added spices.

Other food manufacturing concerns also market coating mixes. * * *

III. THE TRADEMARK CLAIMS

A. *BASIC PRINCIPLES*

1. *Classifications of Marks*

The threshold issue in any action for trademark infringement is whether the word or phrase is initially registerable or protectable.

* * *

Courts and commentators have traditionally divided potential trademarks into four categories. A potential trademark may be classified as (1) generic, (2) descriptive, (3) suggestive, or (4) arbitrary or fanciful. These categories, like the tones in a spectrum, tend to blur at the edges and merge together. The labels are more advisory than definitional, more like guidelines than pigeonholes. Not surprisingly, they are somewhat difficult to articulate and to apply.

A *generic* term is "the name of a particular genus or class of which an individual article or service is but a member." [Vision Center v. Opticks, Inc., 596 F.2d 111, 115 (5th Cir.1980)] A generic term connotes the "basic nature of articles or services" rather than the more individualized characteristics of a particular product.

* * *

A *descriptive* term "identifies a characteristic or quality of an article or service," Vision Center, 596 F.2d at 115, such as its color, odor, function, dimensions, or ingredients. Descriptive terms ordinarily are not protectable as trademarks, Lanham Act § 2(e)(1), 15 U.S.C. § 1052(e)(1) (1976); they may become valid marks, however, by acquiring a secondary meaning in the minds of the consuming public. See id. § 2(f), 15 U.S.C. § 1052(f). Examples of descriptive marks would include "Alo" with reference to products containing gel of the aloe vera plant and "Vision Center" in reference to a business offering optical goods and services. As this court has often noted, the distinction between descriptive and generic terms is one of degree. The distinction has important practical consequences, however; while a descriptive term may be elevated to trademark status with proof of secondary meaning, a generic term may never achieve trademark protection.

A *suggestive* term suggests, rather than describes, some particular characteristic of the goods or services to which it applies and requires the consumer to exercise the imagination in order to draw a conclusion as to the nature of the goods and services. A suggestive mark is protected without the necessity for proof of secondary meaning. The term "Coppertone" has been held suggestive in regard to sun tanning products.

Arbitrary or *fanciful* terms bear no relationship to the products or services to which they are applied. Like suggestive terms, arbitrary and fanciful marks are protectable without proof of secondary meaning. The term "Kodak" is properly classified as a fanciful term for photographic supplies; "Ivory" is an arbitrary term as applied to soap.

2. Secondary Meaning

As noted earlier, descriptive terms are ordinarily not protectable as trademarks. They may be protected, however, if they have acquired a secondary meaning for the consuming public.

* * * Proof of secondary meaning is an issue only with respect to descriptive marks; suggestive and arbitrary or fanciful marks are automatically protected upon registration, and generic terms are unprotectible even if they have acquired secondary meaning.

3. The "Fair Use" Defense

Even when a descriptive term has acquired a secondary meaning sufficient to warrant trademark protection, others may be entitled to use the mark without incurring liability for trademark infringement. When the allegedly infringing term is "used fairly and in good faith only to describe to users the goods or services of [a] party, or their geographic origin," Lanham Act § 33(b)(4), 15 U.S.C. § 1115(b)(4) (1976), a defendant in a trademark infringement action may assert the "fair use" defense. The defense is available only in actions involving descriptive terms and only when the term is used in its descriptive sense rather than its trademark sense. In essence, the fair use defense prevents a trademark registrant from appropriating a descriptive term for its own use to the exclusion of others, who may be prevented thereby from accurately describing their own goods. The holder of a protectable descriptive mark has no legal claim to an exclusive right in the primary, descriptive meaning of the term; consequently, anyone is free to use the term in its primary, descriptive sense so long as such use does not lead to customer confusion as to the source of the goods or services.

* * *

B. "FISH–FRI"

1. Classification

* * * Courts and commentators have formulated a number of tests to be used in classifying a mark as descriptive.

A suitable starting place is the dictionary, for "[t]he dictionary definition of the word is an appropriate and relevant indication 'of the ordinary significance and meaning of words' to the public." American Heritage, 494 F.2d at 11 n. 5; see also Vision Center, 596 F.2d at 116. Webster's Third New International Dictionary 858 (1966) lists the following definitions for the term "fish fry": "1. a picnic at which fish are caught, fried, and eaten; * * *. 2. fried fish." Thus, the basic dictionary definitions of the term refer to the preparation and consumption of fried fish. This is at least preliminary evidence that the term "Fish-Fri" is descriptive of Zatarain's product in the sense that the words naturally direct attention to the purpose or function of the product.

The "imagination test" is a second standard used by the courts to identify descriptive terms. This test seeks to measure the relationship between the actual words of the mark and the product to which they are applied. If a term "requires imagination, thought and perception to reach a conclusion as to the nature of goods," Stix Products, 295 F.Supp. at 488, it is considered a suggestive term. Alternatively, a term is descriptive if standing alone it conveys information as to the characteristics of the product. In this case, mere observation compels the conclusion that a product branded "Fish-Fri" is a prepackaged coating or batter mix applied to fish prior to cooking. The connection between this merchandise and its identifying terminology is so close and direct that even a consumer unfamiliar with the product would doubtless have an idea of its purpose or function. It simply does not require an exercise of the imagination to deduce that "Fish-Fri" is used to fry fish. Accordingly, the term "Fish-Fri" must be considered descriptive when examined under the "imagination test."

A third test used by courts and commentators to classify descriptive marks is "whether competitors would be likely to need the terms used in the trademark in describing their products." Union Carbide Corp. v. Ever-Ready, Inc., 531 F.2d 366, 379 (7th Cir.1976). A descriptive term generally relates so closely and directly to a product or service that other merchants marketing similar goods would find the term useful in identifying their own goods. Common sense indicates that in this case merchants other than Zatarain's might find the term "fish fry" useful in describing their own particular batter mixes. While Zatarain's has argued strenuously that Visko's and Oak Grove could have chosen from dozens of other possible terms in naming their coating mix, we find this position to be without merit. As this court has held, the fact that a term is not the only or even the most common name for a product is not determinative, for there is no legal foundation that a product can be described in only one fashion. There are many edible fish in the sea, and as many ways to prepare them as there are varieties to be prepared. Even piscatorial gastronomes would agree, however, that frying is a form of preparation accepted virtually around the world, at restaurants starred and unstarred. The paucity of synonyms for the words "fish" and "fry" suggests that a merchant whose batter mix is specially spiced for frying fish is likely to find "fish fry" a useful term for describing his product.

A final barometer of the descriptiveness of a particular term examines the extent to which a term actually has been used by others marketing a similar service or product. This final test is closely related to the question whether competitors are likely to find a mark useful in describing their products. As noted above, a number of companies other than Zatarain's have chosen the word combination "fish fry" to identify their batter mixes. Arnaud's product, "Oyster Shrimp and Fish Fry," has been in competition with Zatarain's "Fish-Fri" for some ten to twenty years. When companies from A to Z, from Arnaud to Zatarain's, select the same term to describe their similar products, the term in question is most likely a descriptive one.

* * * The district court in this case found that Zatarain's trademark "Fish-Fri" was descriptive of the function of the product being sold. Having applied the four prevailing tests of descriptiveness to the term "Fish-Fri," we are convinced that the district court's judgment in this matter is not only not clearly erroneous, but clearly correct.

2. Secondary Meaning

Descriptive terms are not protectable by trademark absent a showing of secondary meaning in the minds of the consuming public. To prevail in its trademark infringement action, therefore, Zatarain's must prove that its mark "Fish-Fri" has acquired a secondary meaning and thus warrants trademark protection. The district court found that Zatarain's evidence established a secondary meaning for the term "Fish-Fri" in the New Orleans area. We affirm.

* * *

In assessing a claim of secondary meaning, the major inquiry is the consumer's attitude toward the mark. The mark must denote to the consumer "a single thing coming from a single source" to support a finding of secondary meaning. Both direct and circumstantial evidence may be relevant and persuasive on the issue.

Factors such as amount and manner of advertising, volume of sales, and length and manner of use may serve as circumstantial evidence relevant to the issue of secondary meaning. While none of these factors alone will prove secondary meaning, in combination they may establish the necessary link in the minds of consumers between a product and its source. It must be remembered, however, that "the question is not the *extent* of the promotional efforts, but their *effectiveness* in altering the meaning of [the term] to the consuming public." Aloe Creme Laboratories, 423 F.2d at 850.

Since 1950, Zatarain's and its predecessor have continuously used the term "Fish-Fri" to identify this particular batter mix. Through the expenditure of over $400,000 for advertising during the period from 1976 through 1981, Zatarain's has promoted its name and its product to the buying public. Sales of twelve-ounce boxes of "Fish-Fri" increased from 37,265 cases in 1969 to 59,439 cases in 1979. From 1964 through 1979, Zatarain's sold a total of 916,385 cases of "Fish-Fri." The district court considered this circumstantial evidence of secondary meaning to weigh heavily in Zatarain's favor.

In addition to these circumstantial factors, Zatarain's introduced at trial two surveys conducted by its expert witness, Allen Rosenzweig. In one survey, telephone interviewers questioned 100 women in the New Orleans area who fry fish or other seafood three or more times per month. Of the women surveyed, twenty-three percent specified *Zatarain's* "Fish-Fri" as a product they "would buy at the grocery to use as a coating" or a "product on the market that is especially made for frying fish." In a similar survey conducted in person at a New Orleans area mall, twenty-eight of the 100 respondents answered *"Zatarain's* 'Fish-Fri' " to the same questions.

The authorities are in agreement that survey evidence is the most direct and persuasive way of establishing secondary meaning. The district court believed that the survey evidence produced by Zatarain's, when coupled with the circumstantial evidence of advertising and usage, tipped the scales in favor of a finding of secondary meaning. Were we considering the question of secondary meaning *de novo,* we might reach a different conclusion than did the district court, for the issue is close. Mindful, however, that there is evidence in the record to support the finding below, we cannot say that the district court's conclusion was clearly erroneous. Accordingly, the finding of secondary meaning in the New Orleans area for Zatarain's descriptive term "Fish-Fri" must be affirmed.

3. The "Fair Use" Defense

* * * The district court determined that Oak Grove and Visko's were entitled to fair use of the term "fish fry" to describe a characteristic of their goods; we affirm that conclusion.

Zatarain's term "Fish-Fri" is a descriptive term that has acquired a secondary meaning in the New Orleans area. Although the trademark is valid by virtue of having acquired a secondary meaning, only that penumbra or fringe of secondary meaning is given legal protection. Zatarain's has no legal claim to an exclusive right in the original, descriptive sense of the term; therefore, Oak Grove and Visko's are still free to use the words "fish fry" in their ordinary, descriptive sense, so long as such use will not tend to confuse customers as to the source of the goods.

The record contains ample evidence to support the district court's determination that Oak Grove's and Visko's use of the words "fish fry" was fair and in good faith. Testimony at trial indicated that the appellees did not intend to use the term in a trademark sense and had never attempted to register the words as a trademark. * * * In addition, Oak Grove and Visko's consciously packaged and labeled their products in such a way as to minimize any potential confusion in the minds of consumers.

Car-Freshner Corp. v. S.C. Johnson & Son, Inc.

United States Court of Appeals, Second Circuit, 1995
70 F.3d 267

[Car-Freshner sells flat scented cardboard air fresheners for cars. These air fresheners are in the shape of a pine tree and come in a variety of colors and odors including a green, pine-scented version. Johnson & Johnson sells a line of plug-in air fresheners for homes under the trademark "Glade". The plug-ins have a plastic case that holds a replaceable fragrance cartridge which is activated when plugged into an electrical socket. At Christmas time Johnson makes a pine-tree-shaped plug-in with a pine scent called "Holiday Pine Potpourri". Car-Freshener claims the pine-tree shape plug-in infringes its exclusive right to the pine-tree shape for air fresheners. The court assumes that Car-Freshener has established trademark rights in the pine-tree shape.]

It is a fundamental principle marking an outer boundary of the trademark monopoly that, although trademark rights may be acquired in a word or image with descriptive qualities, the acquisition of such rights will not prevent others from using the word or image in good faith in its descriptive sense, and not as a trademark. The principle is of great importance because it protects the right of society at large to use words or images in their primary descriptive sense, as against the claims of a trademark owner to exclusivity. This common-law principle is codified in the Lanham Act * * * 15 U.S.C. § 1115(b)(4).

The district court rejected Johnson's claim of fair use because it believed such a defense could be mounted only against a mark classed as "descriptive" in the four-tiered hierarchy of trademark law—generic, descriptive, suggestive, and arbitrary or fanciful. Although there is authority for that proposition, we believe that notion is misguided. It is true that the doctrine can apply only to marks consisting of terms or images with descriptive qualities. That is because only such terms or images are capable of being used by others in their primary descriptive sense. But it should make no difference whether the plaintiff's mark is to be classed on the descriptive tier of the trademark ladder (where protection is unavailable except on a showing of secondary meaning). What matters is whether the defendant is using the protected word or image descriptively, and not as a mark.

Whether the mark is classed as descriptive (and thus ineligible for protection without secondary meaning) depends on the relationship between the mark and the product described. Thus words like SWEET or CHEWY would be descriptive for a candy, but would be suggestive, or even arbitrary or fanciful, if used in connection with bed sheets, a computer, or an automobile. Regardless whether the protected mark is descriptive, suggestive, arbitrary, or fanciful as used in connection with the product or service covered by the mark, the public's right to use descriptive words or images in good faith in their ordinary descriptive sense must prevail over the exclusivity claims of the trademark owner. * * * If any confusion results to the detriment of the markholder, that was a risk entailed in the selection of a mark with descriptive attributes.

In short, fair use permits others to use a protected mark to describe aspects of their own goods, provided the use is in good faith and not as a mark. That is precisely the case here. Johnson's use of the pine-tree shape describes two aspects of its product. The pine tree refers to the pine scent of its air freshening agent. Furthermore, as a Christmas tree is traditionally a pine tree, the use of the pine-tree shape refers to the Christmas season, during which Johnson sells this item. Johnson's use of the pine-tree shape is clearly descriptive. There is no indication that Johnson uses its tree shape as a mark. Its pine-tree-shaped air fresheners come in boxes prominently bearing the "Glade Plug-Ins" trademark as well as Johnson's corporate logo. Each unit has "Glade" imprinted across the front of the product itself.

Car-Freshner contends that Johnson adopted the mark in bad faith and therefore cannot claim fair use. Car-Freshner bases its argument primarily on the fact that Johnson adopted its tree shape with knowledge of Car-Freshener's use of the tree shape and without consulting counsel. There is no merit to this argument. As Johnson was fully entitled to use a pine-tree shape descriptively notwithstanding Car-Freshener's use of a tree shape as a mark, the fact that it did so without consulting counsel has no tendency to show bad faith. * * *

We thus affirm the dismissal of Car-Freshner's complaint.

NOTES

1. Courts have had great difficulty drawing the line between suggestive and descriptive marks.   In Union National Bank of Texas, Laredo v. Union National Bank of Texas, 909 F.2d 839 (5th Cir.1990) the Fifth Circuit, following *Zatarains,* reversed the lower court's decision that "Union National Bank" was descriptive as a matter of law. The court suggested the richness of the proper analysis:

> The English language, more than most, is in a constant state of flux. A word which is today fanciful may tomorrow become descriptive or generic. * * * Thus, the trier of fact must be aware of, or informed of, common, up-to-date usage of the word or phrase. Furthermore, even were usage not constantly changing, the context in which a word or phrase appears is relevant to determining the proper category for purposes of trademark protection eligibility. The word or phrase must be compared to the product or service to which it is applied. For example, the word "fish,"

previously discussed, was said to be generic as it describes a category of aquatic life. Yet "fish" as used in "fish market" turns "fish" into a descriptive term if it describes a type of "market." Used in the phrase "FishWear" for dive clothing, "fish" may be suggestive if the intent is to suggest that divers who wear this clothing will be able to "swim like a fish." On the other hand, with respect to clothing worn while fishing, "FishWear" might be descriptive. Finally, "fish," used in the name of a product totally unrelated to anything having to do with fish, or suggestive thereof, such as "Fish National Bank," would appear to be arbitrary.

2. For an illustrative list of marks held to be either descriptive or suggestive see J. Thomas McCarthy, Trademarks and Unfair Competition §§ 11.24 (descriptive) & 11.72 (suggestive) (1997). Some examples of marks held descriptive are: "Beef & Brew" restaurant; "Beer Nuts" salted nuts; "Fashionknit" sweaters; "Holiday Inn" motel; "Joy" detergent; "Raisin Bran" cereal; "World Book" encyclopedia. Examples of marks held suggestive are: "Action Slacks" pants; "Chicken of the Sea" tuna; "Citibank"; "Gobble Gobble" processed turkey meat; "Orange Crush" orange drink; "Q-Tips"; "Rapid-Shave" shaving cream.

3. Is the distinction between descriptive and suggestive marks a workable tool for deciding which marks will be granted legal protection? Are you satisfied that the court reached the correct decision in *Zatarains?* What evidence did the court rely on? The court regards consumer perceptions as significant on whether the descriptive term has acquired secondary meaning. If the ultimate issue in the case is how consumers perceive these terms, shouldn't the court be looking to see whether consumers think the term is descriptive? Could the difficult distinction between descriptive and suggestive marks be avoided by requiring proof of consumer understanding in both circumstances?

4. How does the analysis in *Car-Freshner* differ from that in *Zatarains?* Is a focus on the interests of the parties rather than on the abstract consideration of the characteristics of the marks a better way of resolving these disputes? Should the second-in-time user be required to show that its use is, in fact, descriptive? If its use is not descriptive, should the use be enjoined?

5. The issue of descriptiveness arises in two different contexts. When an applicant applies for a registration in the Patent and Trademark Office, the trademark examiner must make a decision whether the term qualifies for registration or is excluded as descriptive under § 2(e). In many instances this will be an abstract decision without the existence of competing claimants asserting a right to use the term, either in a descriptive or a trademark sense. However, in the litigated cases there is always a defendant who has used the term in some way permitting consideration of competing interests.

6. The courts may hesitate to protect some marks that, although not descriptive, may be of such a nature that, like descriptive marks they ought not to be withdrawn from common usage. See The Different Drummer, Ltd. v. Textron, Inc., 306 F.Supp. 672 (S.D.N.Y.1969) refusing to protect Thoreau's phrase: "The man who hears a different drummer drumming" for cologne. Although the words may even be fanciful, "their true source, Thoreau's Walden, is the property of all English-speaking peoples." But see, Roux Laboratories, Inc. v. Clairol, Inc., 427 F.2d 823 (CCPA 1970) where the slogan "Hair Color So Natural Only Her Hairdresser Knows For Sure" was permitted to be registered for hair coloring products on proof of secondary meaning.

7. *Deceptive and Misdescriptive Marks.* Section 2(e)(1) of the Lanham Act precludes registration of "deceptively misdescriptive" marks as well as "merely descriptive" marks. In addition section 2(a) denies registration to "deceptive" trademarks and such mark may not be protected even if they become "distinctive" under section 2(f). Should "Old Crow Whiskey" be denied registration under either or both provisions unless it is made from old crows?

The Federal Circuit established the test for "deceptive" marks in In re Budge Mfg. Co., Inc., 857 F.2d 773 (1988). To be deceptive a court must answer the following questions: "(1) Is the term misdescriptive of the character, quality, function, composition or use of the goods? (2) If so, are prospective purchasers likely to believe that the misdescription actually describes the goods? (3) If so, is the misdescription likely to affect the decision to purchase?" The applicant sought registration of the mark "Lovee Lamb" for synthetic automobile seat covers. The court found the mark misdescriptive because the covers were not made from lamb and since others make covers from sheepskin which were more expensive it was possible to infer purchasers were likely to believe the misdescription and act upon it. The burden thus shifted to the applicant to prove otherwise. The court also noted that the deception could not be discounted by truthful statements in associated advertising and labeling. See also, Germain, Trademark Registration Under Sections 2(a) and 2(e) of the Lanham Act: the Deception Decision, 44 Fordham L.Rev. 249 (1975).

Section 43(a) of the Lanham Act, 15 U.S.C. § 1125(a), may also be applicable to misdescriptive trademarks.

8. There seems to be growing interest in the § 2(a) provision that prohibits registration of "scandalous matter". See In re McGinley, 660 F.2d 481 (CCPA 1981) where a mark comprising an embracing nude couple "appearing to show the male genitalia" was denied registration against claims that "scandalous" was vague and in violation of the First Amendment. The court suggested that the term applied to material that is offensive to a sense of propriety or morality from the standpoint of a "substantial composite of the general public." See also In re Tinseltown, Inc., 212 U.S.P.Q. 863 (TTAB 1981) (the mark "Bullshit" denied registration as scandalous). But see, In re Mavety Media Group Ltd., 33 F.3d 1367 (Fed. Cir. 1994) (vacating denial of registration of "Black Tail" for adult entertainment magazine featuring naked African-American women). The court held that, since under prior decisions members of the general public would have standing to challenge the registration of a mark alleged to be "scandalous," the best approach in unclear cases was to give the applicant the benefit of the doubt and publish the mark for registration.

(b) Generic Marks

Elizabeth Brayer, George Eastman: A Biography *

John Hopkins Univ.Press, 1996, pg. 72

There was a downside to the wide use of the term "Kodak." The public was so smitten with Eastman's little camera that manufacturers saw their chance for a free publicity ride. Candy makers turned out "Kodak Bon-Bons" until they were stopped by injunction. The letter "K" turned up everywhere—in King Kodak, Kodak Komics, the Kodak Kid (Eastman), new Kodaks for Kristmas, or even Kolumbus Day. Some of these were Eastman advertising gimmicks, but they were so emulated that Eastman's attorneys were kept busy. Book titles and characters exploited the craze. *Captain Kodak: A Camera Story* by Alexander Black was a popular novel for young adults published in 1898. By 1912 banks were distributing "Kodisks" or "snapshots in sound," and stores and photo finishers were displaying the Kodak name in such a way that it appeared they were branches of the company. By 1915 there was a phony Kodak Company in Florida. At first Eastman was pleased that he had "made a new word to express the whole thing" and that he could "eliminate the word camera." But he had seen the Celluloid Company lose its trademark as the word "celluloid" passed into generic use and came to mean at first any thermoplastic, then to stand for the film used in shooting motion pictures, and finally to evolve into a sobriquet for motion pictures themselves. Even within Eastman's lifetime, efforts were made to protect that valuable asset, the word "Kodak" as a trademark. The Eastman Kodak Company of the late twentieth century carefully insists upon the usage "Kodak camera" or "Kodak film" and never "the Kodak" or "kodak as you go." However "kodak" as a verb—as Strong and other early aficionados used it is still listed in *Webster's Third New International Dictionary*.

Kellogg Co. v. National Biscuit Co.

Supra page 165.

Genesee Brewing Company, Inc. v. Stroh Brewing Co.

United States Court of Appeals, Second Circuit, 1997
124 F.3d 137

■ CALABRESI, CIRCUIT JUDGE:

This trademark case concerns the right of a brewer to identify its beer with the words "Honey Brown." Beer can be either lager or ale, and in this case, the plaintiff uses the words "Honey Brown" (and others) on its lager product, while the defendant uses the same words (and others) on its ale product. In resolving the appeal, we explicitly endorse the rule that, when a producer creates a new product that differs from an established product class in a particular characteristic, the law of trademark will not grant the producer the exclusive right to label its product with words that are necessary to describe that new characteristic. Applying that rule, we find that the phrase "Honey Brown" is generic as applied to ales—such as the beer produced by the defendant—since those words are needed to describe a beer in the traditional category of "brown ale" that is brewed with the addition of honey. Because the plaintiff's beer is a lager, and not an ale, and "brown lager" is not a traditional category of beer, it is perhaps possible that the phrase "Honey Brown" may not be generic as applied to the plaintiff's own product. But that is a question we need not decide today. It is enough for us to hold that since the words "Honey Brown" are generic as applied to the defendant's product, the defendant has a right to use them and the plaintiff cannot recover for trademark infringement. The plaintiff may be able to recover for unfair competition, but the particular preliminary relief sought is inappropriate given the generic nature of the words "Honey Brown" as used by the defendant on its product. We therefore affirm the district court's denial of a preliminary injunction.

BACKGROUND

In this era of renewed interest in quality beers, sometimes dubbed the "Renaissance of Beer," MICHAEL JACKSON, MICHAEL JACKSON'S BEER COMPANION 8 (1993) [hereinafter, JACKSON, BEER COMPANION] many large brewing companies have attempted to cash in on the growing consumer demand for unique, well-made beers, by brewing specialty beers of their own. In order to conceal the identity of the producer—beer connoisseurs are typically wary of mass-produced beers—these companies market specialty beers under small-town names. See Bill McDowell, In Craft Beer, It's "Style" over Brand Substance, ADVERTISING AGE, Mar. 10, 1997, at 20 (noting that "major breweries have been . . . criticized for building marketing cachet by hiding their own specialty beer efforts behind subsidiaries with faux-microbrand names"). And so it is with this case, a dispute between two of America's largest brewing companies— the Genesee Brewing Company ("Genesee") and the Stroh Brewing Company ("Stroh")— doing business as Highfalls Brewing Company and Northern Plains Brewing Company, respectively.

Despite extensive efforts, many large brewers have had little success in the craft-brewing business. Occasionally, however, a large brewer develops a specialty beer that becomes a popular favorite. A recent example is plaintiff Genesee's "JW Dundee's Honey Brown Lager." Sales of that brew, which was introduced in January 1994, have climbed to over 2.5 million cases a year, making it one of the four best-selling specialty beers in the country.

Genesee refers to this beer simply as "Honey Brown." Apparently, prior to Genesee's product, no beer had been marketed with a brand name that included those words. Genesee's labeling and advertising emphasize "Honey

Brown," and Genesee chose that title as the beer's "bar call." Consumers have followed suit. The record is flooded with menus, fliers, and unsolicited letters that confirm 1) that a large number of beer drinkers refer to Genesee's product using only the words "Honey Brown," and 2) that many menus list "Honey Brown" among brands of beer, like "Budweiser" and "Coors."

[At the time of this decision Genesee had not been successful in obtaining a registration of the mark.]

In early 1996, defendant Stroh began to market "Red River Valley Honey Brown Ale," with the conceded purpose of competing with Genesee. Stroh's label and advertising, like Genesee's, place emphasis on the words "Honey Brown." * * *

Once Stroh began to produce its "Honey Brown," other brewers introduced products with these words in their names. There are now numerous beers in the marketplace with brand names that contain the words "Honey Brown," including "J.J. Wainwright's Evil Eye Honey Brown," "Bank Draft Honey Brown Ale," "Tivoli Honey Brown Lager," and "Algonquin Honey Brown Lager."

[This suit was filed under § 43(a) of the Lanham Act seeking to enjoin Stroh from using the term "Honey Brown". The district court denied a preliminary injunction finding the term to be generic.]

DISCUSSION
* * *

The district court found that "Honey Brown" is generic, and hence automatically ineligible for protection. That classification is a fact-bound determination, and so long as the district court utilized the correct legal standard it will be upheld unless clearly erroneous.

Genesee argues that the district court, by basing its conclusion that "Honey Brown" is generic solely on the framework laid out in the Third Circuit's opinion in A.J. Canfield Co. v. Honickman, 808 F.2d 291 (3d Cir.1986) (Becker, J.), rather than on the "primary significance test" used in this circuit, employed the wrong legal standard. We reject this contention.

The "primary significance test" is the law of the land; it was adopted by the Supreme Court in Kellogg Co. v. National Biscuit Co., 305 U.S. 111, 118, 59 S.Ct. 109, 113, 83 L.Ed. 73 (1938), and subsequently codified by Congress in the Trademark Clarification Act of 1984, Pub.L. No. 98–620, § 102, 98 Stat. 3335 (codified at 15 U.S.C. § 1064). Under this familiar test, a plaintiff seeking to establish a valid trademark "must show that the primary significance of the term in the minds of the consuming public is not the product but the producer." Kellogg, 305 U.S. at 118, 59 S.Ct. at 113. To satisfy this requirement, a trademark need not only and exclusively indicate the producer (the "source"), but may, instead, serve a " 'dual function—that of identifying a product while at the same time indicating its source,' " Canfield, 808 F.2d at 300 (quoting S.Rep. No. 98–627, 98th Cong. 5 (1984)). "[A] mark is not generic merely because it has some significance to the public as an indication of the nature or class of an article. In order to become generic the principal significance of the word must be its indication of the nature or class of an article, rather than an indication of its origin." King-Seeley Thermos Co. v. Aladdin Indus., Inc., 321 F.2d 577, 580 (2d Cir.1963).

The Third Circuit did not disregard the primary significance test in *Canfield*. Rather, it explained that the test—of itself—is of limited usefulness when the operative question is whether a new product name, even if it does tend to indicate the producer or source of the product, must nonetheless be considered a product genus or type, rather than merely a product brand. See Canfield, 808 F.2d at 299–301. For, as Judge Becker noted in Canfield, the "primary significance" test suffers from a potential weakness: it does not tell us how to deal with situations in which, while "a term signifies a product that emanates from a single source," that term is needed also to designate "not only a product brand but . . . also a product genus." Id. at 301.

In confronting these situations, courts must remember that

> [t]he genericness doctrine prevents trademarks from serving as the substitutes for patents, and protects the public right to copy any non-patented, functional characteristic of a competitor's product. Trademark law seeks to provide a producer neither with a monopoly over a functional characteristic it has originated nor with a monopoly over a particularly effective marketing phrase. Instead the law grants a monopoly over a phrase only if and to the extent it is necessary to enable consumers to distinguish one producer's goods from others and even then only if the grant of such a monopoly will not substantially disadvantage competitors by preventing them from describing the nature of their goods. Accordingly, if a term is necessary to describe a product characteristic that a competitor has a right to copy, a producer may not effectively preempt competition by claiming that term as its own.

Id. at 305 (citations omitted). Thus, explained Judge Becker,

> to be consistent with the primary significance test, whether a product brand with a name used by one producer constitutes its own genus must turn on the extent to which the brand name communicates functional characteristics that differentiate the brand from the products of other producers. In making these calculations, consumer understanding will determine the extent to which a term communicates functional characteristics and the significance of a term's role in doing so because of a dearth or abundance of alternative terms that effectively communicate the same functional information.

Id.

With these principles in mind, the Canfield court, * * * promulgated a test to determine if a new product name must be deemed also to refer to a product genus or type, rather than simply to an individual product brand:

> If a producer introduces a product that differs from an established product class in a particular characteristic, and uses a common descriptive term of that characteristic as the name of the product, then the product should be considered its own genus. Whether the term that

identifies the product is generic then depends on the competitors' need to use it. At the least, if no commonly used alternative effectively communicates the same functional information, the term that denotes the product is generic. If we held otherwise, a grant of trademark status could effectively prevent a competitor from marketing a product with the same characteristic despite its right to do so under the patent laws.

Canfield, 808 F.2d at 305–06. We adopt that test today, and conclude that Canfield is based on long-standing and integral principles of trademark law. As such, it is a useful complement to, rather than a rejection of, the primary significance test.

The case before us is appropriate for analysis under *Canfield*. Like *Canfield* (which concerned "Diet Chocolate Fudge Soda"), the case involves, in Judge Telesca's words, "a relatively new product that . . . differs from an established product class in a significant, functional characteristic," and "uses the common descriptive term for that characteristic as its name." As such, although "Honey Brown" is clearly descriptive of Genesee's product—the beer is sweet, flavored with honey, and deep brown in color—it still might, of necessity, signify a generic category (or subcategory) of beer. * * *

Employing the Canfield analysis, the district court had little trouble concluding that Genesee's mark is generic as applied to Stroh's product. We find the issue somewhat more complicated than did the district court, but we reach the same result.

The district court accepted Stroh's assertion that "brown beer" is a category of beer, and found that "Honey Brown" differs from this category by the addition of the descriptive word "honey"—which is not an ordinary ingredient of brown beers—and that "[t]he word 'honey' is a commonly used descriptive term for which there is no effective equivalent." Accordingly, the district court concluded that "Honey Brown" is a generic mark not entitled to protection.

The problem with the district court's analysis is that, as Genesee correctly argues, there is no such category of beer as "brown beer." Beers have traditionally been divided into two general categories: 1) ales, which are fermented at high temperatures for short periods of time; and 2) lagers, which are fermented at low temperatures for longer periods of time. See JACKSON, BEER COMPANION, at 66 ("In modern usage, ale indicates a brew that has a warm fermentation, traditionally with strains of yeast that rise to the top of the vessel. These 'top-fermenting' yeasts distinguish ales from lagers, where the yeasts work at cool temperatures, at the bottom of the vessel.").[9] Until the development of lagering techniques in the 19th century, all beers were made with ale yeasts. See MICHAEL JACKSON, THE NEW WORLD GUIDE TO BEER 9–10 (1988) [hereinafter, JACKSON, WORLD GUIDE]. Today, most English, Irish, Scottish, and Belgian beers are ales,

---

9. An ale "is likely to have a fruity aroma and palate, and often a complex flavor," JACKSON, BEER COMPANION, at 66, whereas "[l]ager yeasts produce beers that are characteristically clean and rounded, though not always complex," id. at 196.

while most German, Czech, Austrian, and Dutch beers are lagers. See JACKSON, BEER COMPANION, at 66–67, 196–97.

The category of ales is further divided into numerous subcategories (e.g., pale ale, porter, stout), as is the category of lagers (e.g., pilsner, bock, Oktoberfest). Thus, "ale" and "lager" are to zymurgy what "plant" and "animal" are to biology—the primary taxonomic divisions, each of which is further subdivided into numerous more specific but still generic classifications.

One traditional subcategory of ale is brown ale. * * * There is no comparable subcategory of "brown lager." Nor is there a general category of "brown beer" that somehow encompasses both lagers and ales. Such a category would be antithetical to the fundamental notion that, absent a handful of hybrid and miscellaneous styles, all barley-based beer styles represent subcategories of the general categories of lager and ale.[10]

Stroh asserts first that "brown ale" is a category of beer, and then that any beer that is brown and includes honey can be placed in a "honey brown" subcategory of "brown ales." The problem with this analysis is that many beers that are using the name "Honey Brown"—including Genesee's—are not brown ales at all. They are not even ales; they are lagers. As such, it is simply not the case that Genesee's and Stroh's products both fall into the same subcategory of beer: brown ales brewed with honey. It follows that the district court's conclusion "that there is a category of 'brown' beers in the market place, and both plaintiff's and defendant's beers are distinct from that category in that they contain honey," was clearly erroneous.

This does not solve the problem, however. It merely complicates it. It is well-established that "[a] word may be generic of some things and not of others." Soweco, Inc. v. Shell Oil Co., 617 F.2d 1178, 1183 (5th Cir.1980). "To take a familiar example, 'Ivory' would be generic when used to describe a product made from the tusks of elephants but arbitrary as applied to soap." Abercrombie & Fitch, 537 F.2d at 9 n. 6. * * *

This same principle applies to the Canfield analysis. A mark that is descriptive, suggestive, arbitrary, or fanciful when applied to some products may nonetheless be generic when applied to certain other products, namely those products that require the use of the mark in order to convey their nature to the consumer. * * *

So it is with this case. It is conceivable—though we certainly do not suggest, let alone decide—that Genesee's mark—"Honey Brown"—when applied to a lager (like its own beer) might be deemed descriptive, rather than generic. For this to be so, a court would have to find that there were ways to convey the fact that a lager is brown in color and flavored with honey without using the words "Honey Brown" (at least in the order or way

---

10. It is arguable that a category of "red beer"—largely the creation of marketing and advertising, rather than brewmasters—which includes both lagers and ales has developed in the marketplace, in defiance of traditional beer taxonomy. See, e.g., Jon Morgan, Tops in Hops, BALT. SUN, May 7, 1995, Sun. Mag. at 35. The record provides no support for the notion that there is a comparable category of brown beer.

that Genesee has used them to identify its lager), and that consumers at large (as opposed to the beer cognoscenti) did not understand "brown beer" (or "brown lager") to be a generic category of beer.

But when applied to an ale, the mark is generic. There are numerous styles of beer in the marketplace, the names of which consist of a time-honored beer category modified by a new, creative ingredient or flavor. Examples include maple porter, pumpkin ale, nut brown ale, raspberry wheat, cranberry lambic, and oatmeal stout. In some of these new beer styles, the innovative ingredient is honey. As a result, there are honey wheats, honey porters, and honey cream ales on the market. Under the Canfield reasoning, which we have adopted, none of these names may be trademarked. Someone is always the first to sell these products, and if that brewer were granted a monopoly on the name, subsequent producers would lose the right to "describe [their] goods as what they are." CES Publishing Corp., 531 F.2d at 13.

That principle controls this case. There is a recognized category of beers in the marketplace known as "brown ales." And Stroh's product, Red River Valley Honey Brown Ale (but not Genesee's product, JW Dundee's Honey Brown Lager) can be placed within that category,[14] or more precisely, within a new subcategory of that category—brown ales made with honey: "honey brown ales." Indeed, Stroh developed Red River Valley Honey Brown Ale by altering its "brown ale recipe to include honey and brown sugar which created a smoother and sweeter brown ale." Because the addition of the word "honey" is necessary to indicate a brown ale that is brewed with honey, Stroh has the right to call its beer a "Honey Brown Ale."

We therefore affirm the district court's conclusion that Genesee is not likely to succeed on the merits of its trademark infringement claim.

* * *

The district court was correct that Genesee's state law claim of unfair competition is not viable without a showing of bad faith. But a plaintiff may recover for unfair competition in violation of federal law without a showing of bad faith. See Johnson & Johnson v. Carter-Wallace, Inc., 631 F.2d 186, 189 (2d Cir.1980) (noting that § 43(a) of the Lanham Act "does not require proof of intent to deceive" in order to sustain a claim of unfair competition). * * *

The fact that Genesee's mark is generic as applied to Stroh's product also does not preclude a finding that Stroh has violated the Lanham Act by engaging in unfair competition. * * *

Thus, to recover for unfair competition, Genesee must show: 1) * * * secondary meaning; and 2) [likelihood of confusion]. And Stroh will, nonetheless, escape liability if it has "use[d] every reasonable means to prevent confusion" as to the source of the products, Kellogg, 305 U.S. at 121, 59

---

14. In fact, Red River Valley Honey Brown Ale competed in the "English Brown Ale" category at the 1997 World Beer Championships. See Buyer's Guide for Beer Lovers, ALL ABOUT BEER, July 1997, at 41.

S.Ct. at 115. The district court did not consider whether these factors had been shown.

Genesee has, in fact, proffered evidence that might, if believed and not sufficiently countered by Stroh's evidence, support a finding at trial of both secondary meaning and a likelihood of confusion that Stroh has not taken all reasonable steps to prevent. Specifically, Genesee has attempted to show that, intentionally or not, Stroh is marketing its beer in such a way as to lead consumers to believe that they are getting Genesee's product.

Genesee's beer has become the fourth best selling specialty brew in the country, and consumers and bartenders refer to it simply as "Honey Brown"—a phrase that had apparently never been used to describe a beer before Genesee introduced its product. The words "Honey Brown" dominate Genesee's labeling and advertising materials, and according to Genesee, consumers expect to get Genesee's product when they order a "Honey Brown."

Stroh has also chosen to emphasize the words "Honey Brown" on its label, rather than the words "Red River Valley" or "Honey Brown Ale." Stroh's marketing memoranda to distributors emphasize the need to compete with Genesee's product, and to beat Genesee into certain untapped markets, even though the two products are not, in fact, examples of the same subcategory of beer. And Stroh has arranged to have Safeway Food Stores counter-coupon Genesee's product. (This means that Safeway gives coupons for Red River Valley Honey Brown Ale to any person who purchases JW Dundee's Honey Brown Lager.) Moreover, according to Genesee, many of the restaurants and bars that list Genesee's product simply as "Honey Brown" on their menus and tap lists—which list brands of beer, not kinds of beer—have switched from Genesee's product to Stroh's less-expensive product without changing their menus.

All of this evidence could potentially support a finding that there is a likelihood of confusion and that Stroh has not "taken every reasonable precaution to prevent confusion or the practice of deception in the sale of its product." Kellogg, 305 U.S. at 122, 59 S.Ct. at 115. If Genesee can establish this at trial, along with secondary meaning, it may be granted an injunctive remedy that, while allowing Stroh to continue to market its beer and sell it as a "honey brown ale," would require Stroh to make more of an effort to ensure that its product is not confused with Genesee's.

Nevertheless, the district court did not err in denying the preliminary injunction. For the preliminary relief that Genesee requested—an injunction forbidding Stroh from using the words "Honey Brown" on its product—is inappropriate in a claim of unfair competition with respect to a generic mark. * * *

CONCLUSION

Stroh has the right to add honey to its brown ale, and it has the right to call its beer what it is: a honey brown ale. Accordingly, Genesee may not recover for trademark infringement, and the district court properly refused to enjoin Stroh from using those words to label its beer. While Genesee has stated a claim for unfair competition, the specific preliminary injunctive relief that Genesee has sought is not available to it. We therefore affirm the district court's order without considering whether at trial Genesee is likely to succeed on the merits of its unfair competition claim.

NOTES

1. *The Lanham Act.* The original language of the Lanham Act did not expressly prohibit the registration of "generic" marks nor did it use the term "generic" mark. Section 2(e) precludes registration of "merely descriptive" marks which arguably could include generic descriptiveness. However § 2(e) marks can be registered under § 2(f) if distinctive and by definition generic marks cannot be distinctive. Section 14(c) of the original Lanham Act authorized cancellation of a registration at any time if it "becomes the common descriptive name of an article or substance" and section 15(4) prohibited a "common descriptive name" from becoming incontestible. Even with these ambiguities courts denied registration to generic marks. See, e.g., Application of G.D. Searle & Co., 360 F.2d 650 (CCPA 1966) ("the pill" for an oral contraceptive denied registration).

In the Trademark Revision Act of 1988 these provisions were amended so that the words "common descriptive name of an article or substance" became "the generic name for the goods or services".

2. A significant episode in the development of the generic mark doctrine involved the famous "Monopoly" board game. The game was invented and sold by Parker Brothers beginning in 1935 under the registered mark "Monopoly". General Mills purchased Parker Brothers. In 1973 Anti–Monopoly Inc. began selling a board game called "Anti–Monopoly". General Mills claimed trademark infringement. Twice the trial judge upheld the "Monopoly" mark and found an infringement. Twice the trial court was reversed. Anti–Monopoly, Inc. v. General Mills Fun Group, 684 F.2d 1316 (9th Cir.1982), cert. denied 459 U.S. 1227 (1983) (citing earlier decisions). The Ninth Circuit struggled with whether "Monopoly" was a source indicator or whether it was the generic name of the product. As in *Kellogg,* the product, here the board game, was unique in that it differed from other similar products. The question was whether "Monopoly" was its own genus or whether it was part of the genus "board games" or "real estate trading games". Finding the game its own genus and purporting to apply the "primary significance test" announced in *Kellogg,* the court held that the issue was whether purchasers were motivated to purchase the product because of the product or the producer—did consumers want a board game named "Monopoly" or did they want a Parker Brothers board game? Relying on a survey that disclosed 65% of those surveyed wanted the game regardless of who made it, the court held the mark generic.

The reaction to the *Anti–Monopoly* decision was largely negative. See Greenbaum, Ginsburg, and Weinberg, A Proposal for Evaluating Genericism After "Anti–Monopoly", 73 Trademark Rep. 101 (1983): "[T]he relegation of MONOPOLY to a 'unique' product category presents an extreme exercise in 'sophistry', and a substantial misconception of the way goods are promoted and marketed * * *. Furthermore, if the product is its own 'genus', its trademark is virtually, by definition, generic." *Id.* at 109. See also, Zeisel, The Surveys That Broke Monopoly, 50 U.Chi.L.Rev. 896 (1983) which suggests that the surveys relied upon by the majority were flawed and also argues that Monopoly should not be a 'genus': "It would seem that before anyone can demand that a trade name be canceled because it had become generic, a genus must have come into existence, that is a real genus of at least two members." *Id.* at 908–909.

Congress reversed the *Anti–Monopoly* decision for Lanham Act purposes by adding the last two sentences in section 14(3) and the last sentence in the definition of "abandonment" in section 45. The legislative history describes the purposes of these amendments as follows:

> (a) Clarify that a mark may have a "dual purpose" of identifying goods and services and indicating the source of the goods and services; (b) Clarify that a mark may serve to identify a unique product or service so long as the mark serves also to identify a single source of the product or service; (c) Clarify that identification of a mark with a source does not require that the identity of a producer or producers be known by the consumer; and (d) Prohibit the use of the "motivation test" in determining genericism, and reaffirm the use of the "primary significance" test. U.S.Cong. & Admin.News, 98th Cong., Second Sess. 5718, 5725 (1984).

3. Does the *Genesee* decision successfully resolve the problem of trademarks used on unique products? For the test in *Genesee* to apply the product must first differ from the established product class and second, the product name must be descriptive of the differentiating characteristic. Should the test for whether a product is its own genus depend on what the producer calls it? Do you think the following marks may be generic: "cellophane", "dos" for a computer operating system, "metalock" as a method of metal repair, "trampoline"?

4. Consider the relevance of the following evidence as to whether a mark is generic: the capitalization of the term by the party claiming the mark, whether the mark is used as a noun or an adjective, the results of a search of an on-line database of newspapers showing that the term is predominantly used without capitalization to refer to the product. Do you think the terms "sticky-note" or "post-it notes" are generic for the ubiquitous yellow removable notes. Run an on-line search of these terms and see what you think.

5. Two forms of surveys are commonly employed to test consumer understanding of whether a term is generic. The first was accepted in American Thermos Products Co. v. Aladdin Industries, Inc., 207 F. Supp. 9 (D. Conn. 1962), aff'd, 321 F.2d 577 (2d Cir. 1963) to show that "Thermos" was a generic term. Consumers were essentially asked: "If you were going to buy the type of container that is used to keep liquids, like soup, coffee, tea and lemonade, hot or cold for a period of time, what would you ask for—that is, what would you tell the clerk you wanted?" Seventy-five percent of a 3000 person sample said "Thermos". However, 12 percent later said they thought "Thermos" had some trademark significance. If "Thermos" was the dominant brand of these products how do you determine the significance of the majority response? The other survey is the "Teflon" survey. Participants are first instructed that there are brand names and common names and given an example, such as Chevrolet and automobile. They are then asked to categorize a list of other names as either brand names or common names. Surveyors include on the list some clear brand names, some clear common names, and the target term. The results of the survey in the Teflon case were:

Name	Brand/%	Common/%	D/Know/%
STP	90	5	5
Thermos	51	46	3
Margarine	9	91	1
Teflon	68	31	2
Jello	75	25	1
Refrigerator	6	94	—
Aspirin	13	86	—
Coke	76	24	—

Does the survey provide strong evidence on the genericness of "Teflon"? How would you interpret the survey if the contested term was "Thermos"? If consumers attach *both* a generic and a source meaning to a term what result should follow as to protection of the mark?

In *Canfield,* cited in *Genesee,* Judge Becker attacked surveys as follows:

In contrast to the advocates of this survey technique, we do not believe that a direct survey of public views can truly measure consumer understanding if a term identifies a product that arguably constitutes its own genus. As we have discussed above, generic marks signifying goods produced by only one manufacturer may function both as generic terms, signifying the product genus, and as brand names, indicating continuity of source. Faced with a mark like shredded wheat, the consumer has no reason to define it either as the name of a brand or as the name of a genus because the term functions most efficiently as both. Accordingly, a survey inquiring whether a designation like shredded wheat is a brand name or a product name forces respondents to make a false dichotomy. Because consumers will never have had a reason to consider the question before, such a survey might not elicit real attitudes but merely answers developed on the spot that would be highly susceptible to the influences of survey phraseology.

Perhaps more significantly, directly surveying the public without first differentiating the product brand from the product genus-or at least without first offering a definition for the distinction-would not, in the context of this case, test the meaning of words to the public but would rather request a legal conclusion. A conscientious survey respondent, when asked whether a term is a brand name or product name, might ask, "Exactly what do you mean by product name and what do you mean by brand name?" Using the primary significance test and taking account of the anonymous source rule, we would be compelled to answer: "A brand name primarily signifies a product brand while a product name primarily signifies a product genus." The respondent then asks: "How do I distinguish a product brand from a product genus?" If we seek to answer this question with the results of this survey, we can only answer in a circular fashion: "That question depends on the answers we obtain from you and other respondents." We simply cannot circumvent the requirement of defining the distinction between product brand and product genus by asking the public to tell us if a name is a brand name or the name of a product genus; we can only ignore it.

Some commentators have suggested that, instead of providing a definition of product brand and product genus, a survey may simply provide examples of brand names and product names. See Greenbaum, Ginsburg & Weinberg, *supra,* at 118. We do not agree. Such a technique would presumably rest on the assumption that even though we, as courts, cannot define the distinction between brand and genus names without first distinguishing between brand and genus categories, the public can. We can think of no reason to support this assumption. Such a technique might also rest on the assumption that a list of examples might convey the distinction between brand and genus categories. But examples would only do so where the distinction is obvious, a situation we do not face. Finally, such a technique would not eliminate the fact that members of the public have no reason to distinguish between brand and genus name when they contemplate a genus with only one brand.

6. If you were counsel to a firm about to market a game or a soft drink that had the potential for becoming as popular as "Monopoly" or "Honey Brown", what advice would you give regarding the naming and promotion of the product?

7. What must a company do to protect itself from a claim that its mark has become generic? It has been reported that the Coca-Cola Company maintains a "Trade Research Department" consisting of 25 investigators who order "Coke" in restaurants and send the drink served back to headquarters for chemical analysis. The company also has an aggressive litigation policy against restaurants serving Coke substitutes. Coca-Cola has sued 800 retailers since 1945. The company asserts the policy is necessary to prevent its mark from becoming generic. Some retailers assert that the policy actually is designed to force restaurant owners into serving Coke since liability for infringement arises even in the absence of intent to infringe and as one owner was quoted: "There's just no way we can guarantee on a busy night—when as many as 2,000 people cram into our bar—that one of our waitresses or waiters won't forget to warn a customer who asks for a rum and Coke that we serve rum and Pepsi." Wall St.J., March 9, 1978, at 1, col. 4. The Coca-Cola

Company survived an antitrust attack against its trademark enforcement policies in Coca-Cola Co. v. Overland, Inc., 692 F.2d 1250 (9th Cir.1982). Summary judgment was awarded to Coca-Cola because Overland failed to provide evidence of attempted monopolization or of specific retailers who were influenced by the enforcement policy to switch to "Coke".

8. *Generic Marks and the Constitution.* In San Francisco Arts & Athletics Inc. v. United States Olympic Committee, 483 U.S. 522 (1987), the Supreme Court upheld the right of the Olympic Committee to prohibit the use of the term "Olympic" in association with the "Gay Olympic Games". The petitioner argued the word "Olympic" was generic and not protectible, that the petitioner's use did not result in consumer confusion, and that protection in this context violated the first amendment. The Court held that even though the Congressional act giving the Committee exclusive rights in the term did not require a showing of confusion, the "limited property right in the word 'Olympic' falls within the scope of trademark law protections, and thus certainly within constitutional bounds" particularly since this was commercial speech. In dissent, Justice Brennan argued the absence of traditional elements of trademark law gave the Committee control over the word in a broad range of noncommercial contexts which infringed upon first amendment values.

PROBLEMS

1. In 1961 Eastern Air Lines initiated the "Eastern Shuttle" air service between Boston, New York, and Washington, D.C. Extensively advertised and marketed, the "shuttle" offered hourly flights, on-board ticketing, no reservation requirement, and a separate terminal. Eastern guaranteed seat availability on each "shuttle" by maintaining back-up aircraft for unexpected demand. Eastern obtained a Lanham Act registration for the mark "Air-Shuttle". Until 1980 the airlines were heavily regulated and no other airline offered a similar service. However, after deregulation New York Air began competing with Eastern and offered a "shuttle" service between the three cities. New York Air advertised its service as the "shuttle and more" with free food and reserved seating. In fact, New York Air did not have back-up aircraft so could not guarantee seat availability although this was not stated in the advertisement. What claims can Eastern successfully make against New York Air? Is "shuttle" a generic term? Assume that a survey of consumers shows that 10% of those surveyed connected the word "Air-Shuttle" with Eastern Air Lines.

2. Ed Entrepreneur contracts with AT&T for exclusive rights to the telephone number 1–800–356–9377 and pays an annual fee. The mnemonic for this number can be 1–800-FLOWERS. Ed operates a nation-wide floral delivery service and heavily advertises the 1–800-FLOWERS telephone number, in such advertisements as "if you know someone down and out, dial 1–800-FLOWERS and brighten their day." Charlie Clever, a small florist in Lincoln, Nebraska, contracts with his local telephone company for the number 402–356–9377 (FLOWERS) and uses the mnemonic in his local advertising. Can Ed successfully stop Charlie from using the phone number? Could Charlie establish a website with the address \\www.flowers.com?

In re Seats

United States Court of Appeals for the Federal Circuit, 1985.
757 F.2d 274.

■ MARKEY, CHIEF JUDGE.

[The applicant sought to register the mark "Seats" as a service mark for a ticket reservation service arguing that the mark had become distinctive under 2(f). The Trademark Trial and Appeal Board made two findings. It first found the mark so inherently descriptive as to be incapable of functioning as a trademark and denied registration without regard to the evidence of distinctiveness. However the Board also found that if it had considered the evidence it would have found the mark "distinctive". Registration was denied.]

The Board did not find that SEATS was generic. Nor could it have so found. The term "seats" may be generic in relation to chairs or couches or bleachers. It is clearly not generic to reservation services. Contrary to the Board's statement, Seats is not selling seats, as would for example a furniture merchant, but is selling a reservation service, and consideration of whether generic terms are *per se* unregistrable, * * * is not here involved.

It is equally clear that SEATS is not "the common descriptive name" of reservation services (assuming the quoted phrase has a meaning different from "generic"). That is true when purchasers of the services will be seated and when "standing room" is involved. Nor did the Board find that SEATS was the common descriptive name of the services involved (as stated above, it did find the mark merely descriptive of the product and function under § 2(e)(1)). On the contrary, the Board recognized that issuance of the registration here sought would not deprive others of the use of "seats" in connection with such services. Competitors would remain free to advertise "seats are available", "balcony seats—$12.00", "reserve your seats through us", etc, and theaters may employ "SEATS" in advertisements and on box offices and ticket windows.

In this application, Seats seeks registration under § 2(f) and has filed what the Board described as extensive evidence of acquired distinctiveness. The Board has found that evidence sufficient to establish "acquired distinctiveness." We cannot say on the record before us that that finding is clearly erroneous. The Board was at liberty to have found that evidence insufficient to have established an acquired distinctiveness, in light of what it considered an over-balancing descriptiveness content in the mark sought to be registered. It appeared to reach its ultimate conclusion, however, on the ground that other terms, which it considered synonymous, could not by any evidence have been shown to have acquired distinctiveness. Whether terms not sought to be registered could or could not acquire distinctiveness is irrelevant where, as here, the claim is that the mark sought to be registered has acquired distinctiveness and the Board has found that the evidence establishes the truth of that claim.

NOTES

1. *Generic Marks and Secondary Meaning.* The line between generic and descriptive terms is important because descriptive terms can be protected as marks if they become distinctive. In generic mark cases, some courts have recognized a "de facto" secondary meaning—that is there is evidence that some consumers recognize the term as source-identifying—but nonetheless the mark cannot be protected because it is generic and cannot acquire "de jure secondary meaning". See Miller Brewing Co. v. Falstaff Brewing Corp., 655 F.2d 5 (1st Cir.1981) ("Lite" for beer). As *In re Seats* and the case in the note below suggest, there is a temptation to recategorize terms in order to avoid the bright-line rule.

2. In American Aloe Corp. v. Aloe Creme Laboratories, Inc., 420 F.2d 1248 (7th Cir.), cert. denied 400 U.S. 820 (1970), the issue was whether the mark "Aloe Essence" infringed the mark "Alo–Hands" when both were used on cosmetics and the main ingredient of each was aloe, a gel of the aloe vera plant. The Seventh Circuit in denying protection became categorical:

> The case is unlike Coca–Cola Co. v. Koke Co. of America, 254 U.S. 143 (1920) where the term Coke or Coca was originally descriptive of the extract of Coca leaves, or cocaine contained in the plant, but which lost this generic sense when the plaintiff was compelled to remove any effective cocaine from the product, after which Coca or Coke acquired a purely secondary meaning. Neither is this case controlled by those decisions which have found that exact copies or phonetic equivalents infringe purely suggestive names which have acquired trade name significance, such as Douglas Laboratories Corp. v. Copper Tan, Inc., 210 F.2d 453 (2nd Cir.1954) which said "Coppertone" for sun tan lotion was suggestive rather than descriptive, and Orange Crush Co. v. California Crushed Fruit Co., 297 F. 892 (D.C.Cir.1924) which said "Crush" was not descriptive of a soft drink and was not used in its generic sense; nor is it in the same class with those which hold that terms having a general descriptive but not denominative sense acquired secondary meaning. Keller Products, Inc. v. Rubber Linings Corp., 213 F.2d 382, 47 A.L.R.2d 1108 (7th Cir.1954) (Tub Cove v. Tub Kove); Speaker v. Shaler Co., 87 F.2d 985 (7th Cir.1937) (Hot Patches v. Hot Patches—for vulcanizing products); Barton v. Rex–Oil Co., Inc., 29 F.2d 474 (3rd Cir.1928) (Dynashine v. Dye & Shine—for shoe polish). It must also be distinguished from the Supreme Court's decision in Armstrong Paint & Varnish Works v. Nu–Enamel Corp., 305 U.S. 315 (1939) where the essentially descriptive and denominative term "nu-enamel" had acquired a secondary meaning at least partially through its widespread application to products other than enamel—such as paint brushes.
>
> This case is properly classified with those where the term in question was the common name for the article sold and hence denominative of that article regardless of source. Kellogg Co. v. National Biscuit Co.,

305 U.S. 111 (1938) (shredded wheat); Henry Heide, Inc. v. George Ziegler Co., 354 F.2d 574 (7th Cir.1965) (ju-jubes); Donald F. Duncan, Inc. v. Royal Tops Manufacturing Co., 343 F.2d 655 (7th Cir.1965) (yo-yos) and particularly with those cases where the term was denominative of the prime or distinguishing ingredient in the product. Compare LeBlume Import Co. v. Coty, 293 F. 344 (2nd Cir.1923) (Lorigan v. L'Origan de Coty—for perfume); Pinaud, Inc. v. Huebschman, 27 F.2d 531 (E.D.N.Y.1928) (Lilas De France v. Lilas De France—for perfume); Wells & Richardson Co. v. Siegel, Cooper & Co., 106 F. 77 (N.D.Ill.1900) (Celery Compound v. Celery Compound) with Dixi–Cola Laboratories, Inc. v. Coca–Cola Co., 117 F.2d 352 (4th Cir.1941) (cola v. cola—for soft drink containing extract of cola nut). It is clear from an examination of the cases that while the test may be stated in the same language in both types of cases, it is much more difficult to establish secondary meaning in a denominative term (as used herein) than in a purely descriptive one.

In Aloe Creme Laboratories, Inc. v. Milsan, Inc., 423 F.2d 845 (5th Cir.1970), cert. denied 398 U.S. 928 (1970), the Fifth Circuit also refused to protect the "Alo" mark but rejected the Seventh Circuit's enhanced burden of proof for secondary meaning: "By placing 'Alo' in [the denominative] category, the [Seventh Circuit] denied secondary meaning without the necessity of discussing any evidence relevant to the claim. . . . A claim of secondary meaning presents a question of fact. . . . We agree with [the Seventh Circuit] insofar as it holds that the evidentiary burden, necessary to establish secondary meaning, is substantial where the mark applied to an article designates a principal ingredient desired by the public."

3. Some cases seemed to suggest that there is an automatic loss of trademark rights for any name applied to a patented article once the patent expires. An important case was Singer Mfg. Co. v. June Mfg. Co., 163 U.S. 169 (1896), relied on in *Kellogg*. The Court in *Singer* held the mark "Singer" as applied to sewing machines was generic because the patents expired.

4. For literature on the economic foundation of the generic doctrine see Folsom & Teply, Trademarked Generic Words, 89 Yale Law J. 1323 (1980); Swann, The Economic Approach to Genericism: A Reply to Folsom and Teply, 70 Trademark Reporter 243 (1980); Folsom and Tepley, A Comparative View of the Law of Trademarked Generic Words, 6 Hastings Int'l and Comparative L.Rev. 1 (1982).

———

(c) Geographic Marks

In re Nantucket, Inc.

United States Court of Customs and Patent Appeals, 1982.
677 F.2d 95.

■ MARKEY, CHIEF JUDGE.

Nantucket, Inc. (Nantucket) appeals from a decision of the Trademark Trial and Appeal Board (board) affirming a refusal to register the mark

NANTUCKET for men's shirts on the ground that it is "primarily geographically deceptively misdescriptive." In re Nantucket, Inc., 209 USPQ 868 (TTAB 1981). We reverse.

On March 13, 1978, Nantucket, based in North Carolina, filed application serial number 162,716 for registration of NANTUCKET for men's shirts on the principal register in the Patent and Trademark Office (PTO), alleging a date of first use of February 2, 1978.

Refusal to register was based on § 2(e)(2) of the Lanham Act, 15 U.S.C. § 1052(e)(2) * * *.

[Trademark Manual of Examining Procedure] § 1208.02 indicates that a mark is *primarily geographical,* inter alia, if it "is the name of a place which has general renown to the public at large and which is a place from which goods and services are known to emanate as a result of commercial activity."

The examiner, citing a dictionary definition of "Nantucket" as an island in the Atlantic Ocean south of Massachusetts, concluded that the mark NANTUCKET was either primarily geographically descriptive or primarily geographically deceptively misdescriptive, depending upon whether Nantucket's shirts did or did not come from Nantucket Island.

* * *

The board correctly notes that its test for registrability of geographic terms is "easy to administer" and "*minimizes* subjective determinations by eliminating any need to make unnecessary inquiry into the nebulous question of whether the public associates particular goods with a particular geographical area in applying Section 2(e)(2)." [Emphasis in original.] Ease-of-administration considerations aside, the board's approach does raise the question of whether public association of goods with an area must be considered in applying § 2(e)(2). That question is one of first impression in this court. We answer in the affirmative.

The board's test rests mechanistically on the one question of whether the mark is recognizable, at least to some large segment of the public, as the name of a geographical area. NANTUCKET is such. That ends the board's test. Once it is found that the mark is the name of a known place, i.e., that it has "a readily recognizable geographic meaning," the next question, whether applicant's goods do or do not come from that place, becomes irrelevant under the board's test, for if they do, the mark is "primarily geographically descriptive"; if they don't, the mark is "primarily geographically deceptively misdescriptive." Either way, the result is the same, for the mark must be denied registration on the principal register unless resort can be had to § 2(f).

One flaw in the board's test resides in its factoring out the nature of applicant's goods, in contravention of § 2(e)(2)'s requirement that the mark be evaluated "when applied to the goods of the applicant," and that registration be denied only when the mark is geographically descriptive or deceptively misdescriptive "of them" (the goods).

Another flaw in the board's test lies in its failure to give appropriate weight to the presence of "deceptively" in § 2(e)(2). If the goods do not originate in the geographic area denoted by the mark, the mark might in a vacuum be characterized as geographically misdescriptive, but the statutory characterization required for denial of registration is "geographically *deceptively* misdescriptive." [Emphasis supplied.] Before that statutory characterization may be properly applied, there must be a reasonable basis for believing that purchasers are likely to be deceived.

* * *

Section 2(e)(2) provides that registration shall not be refused *unless* the mark is primarily geographically deceptively misdescriptive of the goods. The only indication of record that NANTUCKET is primarily a geographical term resides in dictionary listings referring to Nantucket Island as a summer resort and former whaling center. There is no evidence of record to support a holding that the mark NANTUCKET as applied to men's shirts is "deceptively misdescriptive." There is no indication that the purchasing public would expect men's shirts to have their origin in Nantucket when seen in the market place with NANTUCKET on them. Hence buyers are not likely to be deceived, and registration cannot be refused on the ground that the mark is "primarily geographically deceptively misdescriptive."

Accordingly, the decision of the board is reversed.

Reversed.

NIES, JUDGE, concurring.

I join the court's holding that there must be an indication that "the purchasing public would expect men's shirts to have their origin in Nantucket when seen in the marketplace with NANTUCKET on them." Moreover, I agree that on the present record the board's decision holding that NANTUCKET for men's shirts is "primarily geographically deceptively misdescriptive" must be reversed. I choose to concur, however, because I reach the same conclusion from a different direction, and because the court leaves open what the PTO must show to make a prima facie case under § 2(e)(2) with respect to this application.

Appellant had urged that the court adopt the rule that a goods/place association can be established under § 2(e)(2) only if the place identified by the geographic name claimed as a mark was "noted for" the goods, like IDAHO for potatoes or PARIS for perfume. The standard of registrability enunciated by the court has not been restricted to such a stringent test. To have done so would have created as rigid a rule in favor of registration as the board had used to deny registration. If a geographic name were arbitrary in the absence of a reputation for the goods, any trader who is the *first* to use any geographic name for particular goods would, thereby, appropriate it to his exclusive use. Moreover, the rationale advanced by appellant is not limited to geographic names of places where the likelihood of future commercial exploitation by others is small but would be equally applicable if the claimed mark for shirts were CHICAGO. The answer to the basic question of public association of goods with a place, i.e., geographic descriptiveness, cannot be decided on this simplistic basis.

* * *

A geographic term may be used in a manner which is (1) inherently distinctive, which includes arbitrary and suggestive usage, (2) generic, (3) descriptive, (4) deceptively misdescriptive, or, (5) deceptive. Different consequences flow from the finding of what is the appropriate category or categories for the mark, which to some extent overlap. In any event, such a determination can only be made by consideration of the specific goods on which the name or term is used. In every case the issue which must be resolved is: What meaning, if any, does the term convey to the public with respect to the goods on which the name is used?

In resolving the question of registrability of geographic names, the development of the law with respect to protection of such terms provides guidance. * * * Thus, we must start with the concept that a geographic name of a place of business is a descriptive term when used on the goods of that business. There is a public goods/place association, in effect, presumed.

However, as with other terms which are descriptive when first used, it came to be recognized that through substantially exclusive and extensive use, a merchant might develop a protectible goodwill in such a geographically descriptive name upon proof that the name ceased being informational to the public and came to indicate a source of goods. Thus, if a manufacturer located in Chicago were to display the name CHICAGO on his shirts, for example, it has been the law for over a century that he could prevent another's subsequent use only if he could establish "secondary meaning" in the term. Until secondary meaning has been developed in a descriptive term, the public cannot be confused that the term indicates source in a particular user and others are free to make comparable use of the term. While a merchant in Chicago will not be deprived of his right to use the name in a non-trademark display if another acquires trademark rights in CHICAGO, he does become limited in the choice of marks for related goods or services and must operate, thereafter, under the constraints of avoiding likelihood of confusion with CHICAGO per se for shirts. * * *

Since the mark CHICAGO is, thus, unregistrable even to a Chicago manufacturer who is the first to use that name for shirts without a showing of distinctiveness, one cannot accept, as urged by appellant, that the law recognizes better rights, ipso facto, in a company not located there which happens to be the first to use that name for shirts. It is simply illogical to say that CHICAGO is descriptive of shirts if the manufacturer is located in Chicago, but arbitrary, if he is not located there. The public is not aware of the actual locations of most businesses. The public is aware of trade practice and makes, or is presumed likely to make, a goods/place association in either instance. Nor is it any less objectionable to a Chicago merchant if the term is used by a non-local rather than another local merchant. * * *

Arguably any nondescriptive use, even if arbitrary, is, in a sense, misdescriptive. Accordingly, the word "deceptively" was inserted before "misdescriptive" in both § 2(e)(1) and § 2(e)(2), again, to avoid technical rejections of applications to register marks such as IVORY for soap, or ALASKA for bananas.

Thus, where usage would be understood by the public as arbitrary, i.e., misdescriptive but not "deceptively" so, the term or name claimed as a mark is registrable without a showing of distinctiveness. On the other hand, if the public would perceive a misdescriptive use of a geographic name as a descriptive use, the claimed mark is deceptively misdescriptive and unregistrable without secondary meaning. That a place is "noted for" goods is only one circumstance under which a geographic name would be barred by § 2(e)(2). "Noted for" and "public association" thus, are not equivalent tests for determining public goods/place association.

* * *

Concerning the authority cited by the appellant, it is apparent that the issue of whether the public is likely to believe a particular geographic name is informational when it appears on a product has been lost sight of in some decisions, which have applied mechanical rules wholly inappropriate to trademark cases. A geographic name is not unprotectible or unregistrable because it can be labeled a geographic name, but because it tells the public something about the product or the producer about which his competitor also has a right to inform the public. Thus, the names of places devoid of commercial activity are arbitrary usage.

* * *

It is also apparent that some opinions fail to grasp that the defense of geographic descriptiveness, put forth by an alleged infringer, should be available only to one with a legitimate personal interest in use of the name. * * *

* * *

NOTES

1. The common law also denied protection to geographic marks unless they acquired secondary meaning. In American Waltham Watch Co. v. United States Watch Co., 173 Mass. 85, 53 N.E. 141 (1899) the plaintiff, the first producer of "Waltham Watches" in Waltham, Massachusetts, proved secondary meaning in a suit against another Waltham manufacturer and obtained an injunction prohibiting the defendant from any use of the terms "Waltham Watches" in its advertising or from any indication that it was located in Waltham without an accompanying statement clearly distinguishing its watches from those of the plaintiff. The Supreme Judicial Court of Massachusetts affirmed. In 1963 the Seventh Circuit upheld a Federal Trade Commission order against the successor to the plaintiff who had purchased the good-will of the plaintiff but now sold imported watches under the name "Waltham". The Commission order required that consumers be given notice that watches were no longer made by the original company in Waltham. Waltham Watch Co. v. FTC, 318 F.2d 28 (7th Cir.1963).

2. *Deceptive Geographic Marks.* In addition to § 2(e), the "deceptive" mark provision of § 2(a) has been applied to geographically misdescriptive marks. For application of a "materiality" test to distinguish between marks that are "geographically deceptively misdescriptive" under § 2(e) and those that are "deceptive" under § 2(a) see In re House of Windsor, 221 U.S.P.Q. 53 (TTAB 1983) (denying registration to the mark "Bahia" for cigars under § 2(a) because the registrant had no connection with the Bahia province of Brazil which is known for its tobacco.):

> If the evidence shows that the geographical area named in the mark is an area sufficiently renowned to lead purchasers to make a goods-place association but the record does not show that goods like applicant's or goods related to applicant's are a principal product of that geographical area, then the deception will most likely be found not to be material and the mark, therefore, not deceptive. On the other hand, if there is evidence that goods like applicant's or goods related to applicant's are a principal product of the geographical area named by the mark, then the deception will most likely be found material and the mark, therefore, deceptive.

3. *Lanham Act Provisions and International Agreements.* Article 1712 of the NAFTA agreement provides that "[e]ach party shall . . . refuse to register, or invalidate the registration of, a trademark containing or consisting of a geographical indication with respect to goods that do not originate in the indicated territory, region or locality, if use of the indication in the trademark for such goods is of such a nature as to mislead the public as to the geographical origin of the good." Marks that have been used continuously for 10 years or in good faith before the signature of the Agreement are exempt from the provision.

This provision required an amendment to § 1052 of the Lanham Act. Under the earlier version and under the common law a geographic term that misdescribed the origin of goods could be protected as a trademark if it acquired secondary meaning. Thus, the mark "Mexico City Tacos" could be protected even though the tacos were made in Texas if consumers came to associate the mark with a common source. Under Article 1712 if some consumers are likely to believe that the mark suggests the tacos were made in Mexico, the mark would be invalid. Section 1052 was amended to provide that while geographically descriptive marks may be protected if distinctive, geographically *misdescriptive* marks may not be protected unless they had become distinctive prior to December 8, 1993.

Article 22 of the GATT TRIPS also addresses geographic designations in a similar fashion. However, Article 23 is a specific provision designed to protect geographical indications identifying wines and spirits. Article 23 requires a signatory to prevent use of a geographical indication for wines not originating in that location even if accompanied by the true origin. Thus if all burgundy wines are thought to come from a specific region in France, the United States would be required to prevent California vintners from selling "California Burgundy". Again, an exception is provided for names used continuously for ten years or in good faith preceding the agreement.

   4. *Certification Marks.* Section 45, 15 U.S.C. § 1127, defines, and section 4, 15 U.S.C. § 1054, permits to be registered certification marks "including indications of regional origins." Section 14(e), 15 U.S.C. § 1064(e), provides specific grounds for cancellation of certification marks. A certification mark, as its name suggests, is used to certify that goods produced by someone other than the mark's owner meets certain standards or comes from some particular geographic region. And § 2(e) of the Act which prevents registration of geographic marks specifically exempts from its provisions marks of regional origin registered as certification marks.

   In Community of Roquefort v. William Faehndrich, Inc., 303 F.2d 494 (2d Cir.1962) the plaintiff, a municipality, owned the registered certification mark "Roquefort" for a sheep's milk blue-mold cheese cured in caves in Roquefort, France. The defendant sold cheese not made in Roquefort as "Imported Roquefort Cheese". The decision analyzes the interplay between § 2(e) and the certification mark provisions. The mark "Roquefort" could have at least three separate connotations: (1) it could refer to the city of Roquefort in which it has geographic significance; (2) it could refer to cheese made in Roquefort, France by a variety of producers in which it could be used to certify such fact; or (3) it could refer to any sheep's milk blue mold cheese wherever produced. As the court observes, a geographic term "does not require a secondary meaning in order to qualify for registration as a certification mark. * * * On the other hand, a geographical name registered as a certification mark must continue to indicate the regional origin, mode of manufacture, etc. of the goods upon which it is used, just as a trade-mark must continue to identify a producer. . . . Therefore, if a geographical name which has been registered as a certification mark, identifying certain goods, acquires principal significance as a description of those goods, the rights cease to be incontestable * * * and the mark is subject to cancellation * * *." The court found no evidence that the "Roquefort" had become descriptive of all sheep milk blue-mold cheese wherever produced and found for the plaintiff.

   See also Black Hills Jewelry Mfg. Co. v. Gold Rush, Inc., 633 F.2d 746 (8th Cir.1980) where three independent producers of "Black Hills Gold Jewelry" each located in the Black Hills area of South Dakota sued to enjoin the defendant from selling jewelry as "Black Hills Gold Jewelry" when it was made outside the region. The court affirmed the district court's holding that the plaintiffs were not entitled to exclusive use of the mark because there was no showing of secondary meaning, i.e., that the term referred to these three producers. Similarly the court refused to consider a common law certification mark because certification marks are owned by someone *other than the producers of the goods.* However, the court did affirm an injunction against the defendant finding (1) that the mark was not generic as to the particular design of the jewelry but did retain geographical significance, and (2) the defendant's use of the term for jewelry not made in the region violated section 43(a) of the Lanham Act.

Section 14(5), 15 U.S.C. § 1064, which lists the grounds upon which a certification mark may be canceled, provides greater insight into the nature of a certification mark. Owners of certification marks may not themselves produce goods under the mark and may also not "discriminately refuse" to certify goods meeting the standards represented by the mark.

5. *Collective Marks.* Certification marks should be distinguished from collective marks, the latter being marks that are adopted by organizations to identify their members or the goods and services of their members. See 15 U.S.C. § 1127. Collective marks, like certification marks, are owned by the organization but used by others. Collective marks may signify that the particular seller of goods is a member of a cooperative or other organization. In non-commercial settings, fraternal names or symbols indicating membership in an organization would be a collective mark. In theory certification marks specify that the goods or services meet particular standards or have particular characteristics while collective marks identify only membership. However, to the extent membership in an organization requires certain attributes, the line between the two becomes uncertain. Does it make a difference whether something is classified as a certification or collective mark? See, Opticians Association of America v. Independent Opticians of America, Inc., 920 F.2d 187 (3rd Cir. 1990).

PROBLEMS

1. How would you advise a client who wishes to use the mark "Rodeo Drive" as the mark for its perfume made in New York? Would you give the same advice if instead of perfume the product was wine?

2. Beef producers in the Midwest decided to promote the sale of corn-fed beef by forming the "Midwest Corn-Fed Beef Cooperative" (MCBC). They develop a seal with the words "Midwest, Corn-Fed" for use by grocery stores on meat purchased from any MCBC member. In addition to its promotional activities for corn-fed beef produced in the Midwest, MCBC also contracts with manufacturers of farm and ranch supplies to produce tools, feed supplements, and other items which are sold in MCBC stores under the "Midwest, Corn-Fed" label. To join MCBC, a rancher has to have his beef operation inspected by MCBC personnel and meet criteria designed to assure that the beef produced is largely corn-fed and that other sanitary conditions are met. Only ranchers in Nebraska, South Dakota, Wyoming, and Colorado are eligible for membership. Members share in the profit of MCBC. Non-members can purchase goods in MCBC stores. MCBC distributes membership cards, bumper stickers, and sweatshirts bearing the MCBC logo, "Midwest, Corn-Fed" to its members. What would you advise MCBC regarding possible registration of their trademarks under the Lanham Act? What kind of claim could MCBC make against: (1) an association of ranchers in Iowa which used the slogan: "Corn-fed in the Midwest"; (2) a non-member of MCBC who wears an MCBC sweat shirt to a state fair.

(d) Personal Names

Taylor Wine Co., Inc. v. Bully Hill Vineyards, Inc.

United States Court of Appeals, Second Circuit, 1978.
569 F.2d 731.

■ GURFEIN, CIRCUIT JUDGE:

[The grandfather of defendant Walter S. Taylor began a winery on an estate called Bully Hill in 1878 and with others formed a partnership engaging in the wine business. The assets, other than Bully Hill, were sold during the grandfather's lifetime to the plaintiff, the Taylor Wine Company, which has marketed wine under the Taylor label since 1880 and has registered 13 Taylor trademarks. The Taylor trademarks came to identify the plaintiff company.

Walter S. Taylor purchased the Bully Hill estate in 1958 from strangers and in 1970 established the defendant company which produced wine under the name of Bully Hill. In 1977 defendant began marketing a new line of "Walter S. Taylor" wine. The name was prominently displayed on the labels with the statement "Owner of the Estate" or "Owner of the Taylor Family Estate." Plaintiff sued for trademark infringement; the lower court enjoined Bully Hill from use of the word "Taylor" on any of its labeling, packaging, advertising or promotional materials.]

Appellant contends that its use of "Taylor" as a trademark does not infringe the appellee's trademarks because the appellant's wines are better and are not in actual competition with appellee's wines. It also urges us to say that the injunction is too broad, in any case, and that it would be enough if we made Bully Hill add some distinguishing words if it chooses to use Walter S. Taylor's own surname as a trademark.

This is not a case where a first comer seeks to save himself a place in a new market he has not yet entered by denying to a man the use of his own name in exploiting that market. The wines of defendant and plaintiff compete in the same general market. It is a truism that every product has its own separate threshold for confusion of origin. Wine is a product whose quality is accepted by many simply on faith in the maker. They can perhaps identify the vintner better than the wine.

It is doubtless true that some wartime soldiers did bring back from Europe an inchoate taste for wine and for some of its nuances, and that other Americans have acquired a similar taste. Yet, the average American who drinks wine on occasion can hardly pass for a connoisseur of wines. He remains an easy mark for an infringer. Whether appellant's or appellee's wines are better is not the issue. Trespass upon the secondary meaning of the Taylor brand name, developed at great cost over the years, cannot be forgiven on the ground that subtlety of taste will avoid the confusion inherent in the overlapping labels and representations of origin.

We do not doubt that Walter S. Taylor, a former employee of the plaintiff, knew well the customer appeal of the Taylor name, nor that he chose to capitalize on the name as if his grandfather had left it to him as an inheritance. The only serious question we must meet is whether the injunction is too broad.

The conflict between a first comer who has given a secondary meaning (as well as trademark registration) to a family name, and a later comer who wishes to use his own true family name as a trademark in the same industry has been one of the more interesting issues in the law of trademark infringement. The problem is made more difficult when the second comer has his own background of experience in the particular industry, and is not simply a newcomer.

In the nineteenth and earlier twentieth centuries, both the state and federal courts tended to be highly solicitous of an individual's personal right to use his name in trade.

With the passage of the Federal Trade-Mark Act of 1905, 33 Stat. 724, and an increasing commercial reliance on marketing techniques to create name recognition and goodwill, the courts adopted a more flexible approach to the conflicting property interests involved in surname trademark infringement cases. By 1908, the Supreme Court was willing to enjoin the use of a surname unless accompanied by a disclaimer. Shortly thereafter, in Thaddeus Davids Co. v. Davids, 233 U.S. 461 (1914) and L.E. Waterman Co. v. Modern Pen Co., 235 U.S. 88 (1914), the Supreme Court established what has since become a guiding principle in trademark surname cases. Once an individual's name has acquired a secondary meaning in the marketplace, a later competitor who seeks to use the same or similar name must take "reasonable precautions to prevent the mistake." L.E. Waterman Co., supra, at 94.

It is, however, difficult to distill general principles as to what are "reasonable precautions" from the Supreme Court's decisions in *Thaddeus Davids* and *Waterman*. In *Davids*, supra, the Court affirmed without modification a lower court decree enjoining entirely the use of the words "Davids" or "Davids Mfg. Co." in connection with the manufacturing and sale of inks. 233 U.S. at 472. In Waterman, supra, on the other hand, the Supreme Court affirmed without modification a lower court's injunction which simply prescribed the use of a full first name instead of an initial, and required a notice of disclaimer.

Since the field is one that does not lend itself to strict application of the rule of *stare decisis* because the fact patterns are so varied, we must try to identify the elements that have influenced decisions on the adequacy of the remedy.

For example, the fact that an alleged infringer has previously sold his business with its goodwill to the plaintiff makes a sweeping injunction more tolerable. So, too, if an individual enters a particular line of trade for no apparent reason other than to use a conveniently confusing surname to his advantage, the injunction is likely to be unlimited.

If, however, the second comer owns the company himself and evinces a genuine interest in establishing an enterprise in which his own skill or knowledge can be made known to the public, that argues in favor of allowing him to use his own name in some restricted fashion. * * *

When confusion is likely, however, there must obviously be some limitation on an individual's unrestricted use of his own name. * * * Yet, he may retain a limited use of the family name even though goodwill has been conveyed to the plaintiff.

* * *

We do not doubt the necessity for an injunction in this case, but we think that its provisions were too broad. Walter S. Taylor is apparently a scholar of enology and a commentator on wines. He runs a wine museum in the Finger Lakes District, and seems to be a person sincerely concerned with the art of wine-growing. Yet, in granting him the right to let people know that he is personally a grower and distributor of regional wines, the public must be assured that he does not by his "estate bottled" nomenclature and his claims to being the "original" Taylor, confuse the public into believing that his product originates from the Taylor Wine Company which is so well-known.

We have concluded that neither Bully Hill nor Walter S. Taylor should use the "Taylor" name as a trademark, but that the defendant may show Walter's personal connection with Bully Hill. He may use his signature on a Bully Hill label or advertisement if he chooses, but only with appropriate disclaimer that he is not connected with, or a successor to, the Taylor Wine Company. He must also be restrained from using such words as "Original" or "Owner of the Taylor Family Estate." He must, in short, not pretend that his grandfather or his father passed anything on to him as a vintner. To the extent that Walter S. Taylor can exploit his *own* knowledge and techniques as a person, he may do so with the limitations noted, if he refrains from trading on the goodwill of the plaintiff company by competing unfairly.

The order is affirmed in part, modified in part, and remanded for further proceedings in accordance with this opinion.

Levitt Corp. v. Levitt

United States Court of Appeals, Second Circuit, 1979.
593 F.2d 463.

[William J. Levitt founded Levitt and Sons in 1929 and rose to national prominence in the housing industry. He constructed several "Levittowns" in the Northeast. In 1968 he sold the company and its good will including the "Levitt" marks. In 1975 he entered a covenant with the new Levitt Corporation (successor to the purchaser) agreeing not to enter the residential housing industry until 1977 and after that date not to use the name "Levitt" as a corporate title, trademark, or trade name in the construction business, although he reserved the right to use his own name publicly as a corporate officer as long as it was not likely to create confusion. Levitt Corporation began seven residential developments in Florida, seeking to capitalize on the value of the Levitt name among residents of the Northeast who were approaching retirement age. In 1978, William Levitt publicly announced that he and the International Construction Corporation would build a "new Levittown" in Orlando, Florida. He purchased advertisements in Northeast newspapers bearing the names "Levittown, Florida," and referring to "Levitt and Sons" to "Levitt's Engineering and Planning Department." The advertisements also identified William Levitt as the founder of the company responsible for the successful Levittowns in the Northeast. Levitt Corporation sued William Levitt for trademark infringement.

In addition to enjoining William Levitt's use of the "Levitt" mark and requiring him to issue corrective advertisements, the district court enjoined any publicity concerning William Levitt's connection in any way with the Orlando project for two years and in addition permanently forbid William Levitt from publicizing his former connection with Levitt and Sons in any future residential development. William Levitt argued these latter two restrictions were too broad.]

■ IRVING R. KAUFMAN, CHIEF JUDGE.

We believe that several persistent themes may be distilled from the judicial attempts to resolve conflicting interests in the use of trade names by imposing appropriate injunctive relief. If the infringing party has had some experience of his own in an industry, and wishes to establish a business under his own name, it is considered unfair to preclude him from using his name under all circumstances and for all times, although the first-comer has established a reputation and goodwill under the same appellation.

Where, as here, however, the infringing party has previously sold his business, including use of his name and its goodwill, to the plaintiff, sweeping injunctive relief is more tolerable. * * * Goodwill is a valuable property right derived from a business's reputation for quality and service. * * * To protect the property interest of the purchaser, then, the courts will be especially alert to foreclose attempts by the seller to "keep for himself the essential thing he sold, and also keep the price he got for it," Guth v. Guth Chocolate Co., supra, 224 F. at 934. And if the district court finds that the seller has attempted to arrogate to himself the trade reputation for which he received valuable consideration, broad remedies may be effected to restore to the plaintiff the value of his purchase.

* * *

The record makes it plain that the promotion of William J. Levitt's name and the manner in which it has been repeatedly linked to Levitt Corporation's marks has created substantial confusion with the plaintiff's venture. We think that the remedy fashioned by Judge Pratt is a reasonable means of dispelling some of the confusion caused by the defendants' advertising campaign. It will also allow Levitt Corporation to make up some of the ground it lost in Florida due to the dissipation of its goodwill.

* * *

Based on the evidence before him, Judge Pratt concluded that any attempt to call public attention to Mr. Levitt's achievements as President of Levitt and Sons would inevitably connect his name to the "spectacular success" of that firm. Moreover, publicity associating Mr. Levitt with the corporate history would create confusion with the marks of Levitt Corporation, resulting in the dilution of the goodwill purchased by the plaintiffs. Accordingly, the district judge permanently enjoined the defendants, in connection with future residential developments, from issuing press releases, brochures, advertising, or publicity concerning Mr. Levitt's prior association with the projects of Levitt and Sons.

The findings on which Judge Pratt predicated this portion of the decree are not clearly erroneous, and justify the relief granted. Mr. Levitt's 1975 contract explicitly forbade confusing uses of his name, and Levitt Corporation's trade reputation is symbolized by the marks "Levittown," "Levitt and Sons," and "Strathmore." To permit Mr. Levitt to proclaim his "track record" by recounting his stewardship of Levitt and Sons would, perforce, free him to link his name to those marks and profit from the ensuing confusion.[12] Accordingly, since we believe that Judge Pratt reasonably determined that an injunction of this scope was necessary to prevent confusion and to protect the value of plaintiff's goodwill, we affirm.

PROBLEM

Mark Levinson is a famous designer of "high-end" audio equipment. Consumers attach great value to a "Levinson designed" system. He was employed by Madrigal, a manufacturer of audio components. During his employment he assigned the "permanent and exclusive right, title and interest to the trade name 'Mark Levinson' " for use with audio equipment. Madrigal marketed the "Mark Levinson Line" of audio components. Levinson subsequently left Madrigal and formed Cello, his own audio manufacturing company. Through advertising and other means Levinson let consumers know that he was designing systems for this new company. Madrigal seeks an injunction prohibiting Levinson from generating any publicity, written or oral, regarding his association with Cello. What result? Does Levinson have a claim against Madrigal if it applies the "Mark Levinson Line" to audio components designed by someone else?

NOTES

1. The terms of the preliminary injunction in *Taylor* were approved with some modifications in Taylor Wine Co. Inc. v. Bully Hill Vineyards Inc., 590 F.2d 701 (2d Cir.1978). Subsequent developments are described in The Taylor Wine Co., Inc. v. Bully Hill Vineyards, Inc., 208 U.S.P.Q. 80 (W.D.N.Y.1979) in which Bully Hill was held in contempt for repeated and intentional violations of both the preliminary and permanent injunctions.

12. Under these circumstances, a disclaimer of any *current* relationship between Mr. Levitt and the corporation will not protect the plaintiff's rights, for the effect of such a statement would be to inform the public that the achievements to which Levitt Corporation justly lays claim really are attributable to the efforts of someone else, now in business for himself.

From the record it appeared Walter Taylor did not think kindly of the court's decision. One example was an advertising brochure showing a portrait of Walter Taylor with the caption "Unknown But Not Unloved" and a textual paragraph which read: "Due to complex factors beyond human control, history regarding Walter S. _____ will have to be kept secret until the Federal Courts decide how much the public should know about him . . . . Where he came from and how he suddenly arrived on this planet involved with grape growing and wine making without ancestors, heritage or a father. Usually Walter S. _____ will without notice appear at his winery next to you, and as you meet him personally, he will request that you agree with the Federal Court's position on his unique status. You will be requested to concentrate only on the unobvious, in order to satisfy his insecure competition 'down in the valley' because of his stand against 'the proliferation of Evil.' " Id. at 85.

2. See David B. Findlay, Inc. v. Findlay, 18 N.Y.2d 12, 271 N.Y.S.2d 652, 218 N.E.2d 531 (1966), cert. denied 385 U.S. 930 (1967), where the Court of Appeals split 4–3 in affirming an injunction prohibiting Wally Findlay from using the name "Findlay" in connection with his new art gallery at 17 East 57th St. in competition with his brother's art gallery located at 13–15 East 57th St. and known in the trade as "Findlay's on 57th St." The dissenting opinion declared that "proof of confusion—understandably inevitable when there is a similarity of name—is irrelevant since confusion resulting from the honest use of one's own name is not actionable."

3. *Lanham Act Provisions.* Section 2(e) of the Lanham Act precludes registration of a mark which "is primarily merely a surname" unless it has become "distinctive" under subsection 2(f). The most thorough analysis of the language is contained in Ex Parte Rivera Watch Corp., 106 U.S.P.Q. 145 (Com. of Pat.1955):

A trademark is a trademark only if it is used in trade. When it is used in trade it must have some impact upon the purchasing public, and it is that impact or impression which should be evaluated in determining whether or not the primary significance of a word when applied to a product is a surname significance. If it is, and it is only that, then it is primarily merely a surname. Reeves, Higgins, and Wayne are thus primarily merely surnames. If the mark has well known meanings as a word in the language and the purchasing public, upon seeing it on the goods, may not attribute surname significance to it, it is not primarily merely a surname. "King," "Cotton," and "Boatman" fall in this category.

There are some names which by their very nature have only a surname significance even though they are rare surnames. Seidenberg, if rare, would be in this class. And there are others which have no meaning—well known or otherwise—and are in fact surnames which do not, when applied to goods as trademarks, create the impression of being surnames.

It seems to me that the test to be applied in the administration of this provision in the Act is not the rarity of the name, nor whether it is the applicant's name, nor whether it appears in one or more telephone directories, nor whether it is coupled with a baptismal name or initials. The test should be: What is its primary significance to the purchasing public?

Section 2(c) prohibits registration of a mark which consists of a "name * * * identifying a particular living individual except by his written consent" and § 2(a) prohibits registration of a mark which may "falsely suggest a connection with persons, living or dead * * * ." In Lucien Piccard Watch Corp. v. 1868 Crescent Corp., 314 F.Supp. 329 (S.D.N.Y.1970) the registered mark "Da Vinci" was upheld as not violating § 2(a) because it was "scarcely likely to mislead any substantial number of purchasers into believing that Leonardo DaVinci was in any way responsible for the design or production of the goods" and was held not to be "primarily merely a surname" because it "comes very near having as its exclusive connotation" the historical figure and thus is not regarded as a current surname.

4. *Corporate Names and Service Marks.* The Lanham Act does not provide registration for "trade names", i.e., names of businesses. Section 3 authorizes registration of "service marks" and provides them with the same protection as trademarks. In theory the distinction between trademarks and trade names is clear. "Pepsico, Inc" is the trade name, i.e., the name under which the company does business, and "Pepsi" is the trademark, i.e., the identifier of the goods. However, particularly with businesses that provide services rather than goods the same mark may function as both. Thus "AAA Auto Repair" may be both the name of the company (trade name) and may also be the mark that identifies the services the company provides (service mark). See In re Amex Holding Corp., 163 U.S.P.Q. 558 (TTAB 1969) (Whether or not a term used as a trade name also performs the function of a service mark is one of fact to be determined from the manner in which it is used and the possible impact thereof upon purchasers.) See also Communications Satellite Corp. v. Comcet, Inc., 429 F.2d 1245 (4th Cir.1970), cert. denied 400 U.S. 942 (1971) where the mark "Comsat" was held to be both a trade name and a service mark.

If a mark is held to be a "trade name" identifying the business itself rather than its goods or services, there is no protection under the Lanham Act (except under § 44 for international trade purposes). However, a business or corporate name is protected by the common law against confusion created by uses of similar names. One of the leading cases is Lawyers Title Ins. Co. v. Lawyers Title Ins. Corp., 109 F.2d 35 (D.C.Cir.1939), cert. denied 309 U.S. 684 (1940):

> Some of the opinions speak in terms of "property" as the basis for [enjoining second users of a trade name], others in the language of unfair competition with a conclusive presumption of public confusion and of injury to the prior appropriator's business in cases of nominal identity. The larger number frankly assimilate corporate names to trade-marks or to trade names, with results varying somewhat according to the classification adopted but in respects not material here.

> Whether one or another approach is taken * * * relief is granted under circumstances, upon considerations and subject to limitations equally applicable either to trade-marks or to trade names. Either confusion of the public or injury to the plaintiff's business, actual or probable, generally both, will be found implicit in the facts.

5. The selection of a corporate name is often dictated by a regulatory environment. See, e.g., Massachusetts Mutual Life Insurance Co. v.

Massachusetts Life Insurance Co., 356 Mass. 287, 249 N.E.2d 586 (1969) where the state corporation and insurance laws required the plaintiff to have the words "mutual", "life", and "insurance" in its name.

6. The corporation laws of most states prohibit incorporation under a name which is similar to that of a corporation already registered. See, e.g. Revised Model Business Corp. Act, §§ 4.01–4.03 (prohibits registration of name that cannot be distinguished from the name of another domestic or registered foreign corporation.) In addition, many states have statutes derived from the Model State Trademark Act promulgated by the United States Trademark Association which provide for the protection of "trade names" which are defined as "a word, or a name, or any combination of the foregoing in any form or arrangement used by a person to identify his business, vocation, or occupation and distinguish it from the business, vocation, or occupation of others."

(2) Subject Matter

The standard trademark case involves a conflict over the right to use a word or symbol in connection with goods and services. However, trademark or unfair competition doctrines may protect other forms of identification such as the shape of the product or the product's image as created by its packaging. Whether there are generic limits to the type of items that can be protected is not generally of concern. There are, however, some cases that press the borders of trademark law and in doing so raise interesting questions at the interface between trademark law and the copyright and patent systems.

In re Morton-Norwich Products, Inc.

United States Court of Customs and Patent Appeals, 1982.
671 F.2d 1332.

■ RICH, JUDGE.

* * *

BACKGROUND

Appellant's application seeks to register the following container configuration as a trademark for spray starch, soil and stain removers, spray cleaners for household use, liquid household cleaners and general grease removers, and insecticides:

Appellant owns U.S. Design Patent 238,655, issued Feb. 3, 1976, on the above configuration, and U.S. Patent 3,749,290, issued July 31, 1973, directed to the mechanism in the spray top.

The above-named goods constitute a family of products which appellant sells under the word-marks FANTASTIK, GLASS PLUS, SPRAY 'N WASH, GREASE RELIEF, WOOD PLUS, and MIRAKILL. Each of these items is marketed in a container of the same configuration but appellant varies the color of the body of the container according to the product.

[The trademark examiner refused to register the design in the face of the appellant's evidence that consumers spontaneously associate the design with appellant's products, that by 1978 over 132 million containers had been sold, that competing products use differently designed sprayers, and a consumer survey. The examiner held that the design "is no more than a non-distinctive purely functional container for the goods plus a purely functional spray trigger controlled closure * * * essentially utilitarian and non-arbitrary * * *." The appeal board within the patent office affirmed holding: " * * * the configuration of which it seeks to register, is dictated primarily by functional (utilitarian) considerations, and is therefore unregistrable despite any de facto secondary meaning * * *."]

In our view, it would be useful to review the development of the principles which we must apply in order to better understand them. In doing so, it should be borne in mind that this is not a "configuration of *goods*" case but a "configuration of the *container for* the goods" case. One question is whether the law permits, on the facts before us, exclusive appropriation of the precise configuration described in the application to register. Another facet of the case is whether that configuration in fact functions as a trademark so as to be entitled to registration. We turn first to a consideration of the development of the law on "functionality."

A trademark is defined as "any word, name, symbol, or device or any combination thereof adopted and used by a manufacturer or merchant *to identify his goods* and distinguish them from those manufactured or sold by others" (emphasis ours). 15 U.S.C. § 1127 (1976). Thus, it was long the rule that a trademark must be something other than, and separate from, the merchandise to which it is applied.

Aside from the trademark/product "separateness" rationale for not recognizing the bare design of an article or its container as a trademark, it was theorized that all such designs would soon be appropriated, leaving nothing for use by would-be competitors.

* * *

This limitation of permissible trademark subject matter later gave way to assertions that one or more *features* of a product or package design could legally function as a trademark. It was eventually held that the *entire* design of an article (or its container) could, without other means of identification, function to identify the source of the article and be protected as a trademark.

That protection was limited, however, to those designs of articles and containers, or features thereof, which were "nonfunctional." This requirement of "nonfunctionality" is not mandated by statute, but "is deduced entirely from court decisions." In re Mogen David Wine Corp., 328 F.2d 925, 932 (CCPA 1964) (Rich, J., concurring). It has as its genesis the judicial theory that there exists a fundamental right to compete through imitation of a competitor's product, which right can only be *temporarily* denied by the patent or copyright laws:

> If one manufacturer should make an advance in effectiveness of operation, or in simplicity of form, or in utility of color; and if that advance did not entitle him to a monopoly by means of a machine or process or a product or a design patent; and if by means of unfair trade suits he could shut out other manufacturers who plainly intended to share in the benefits of unpatented utilities * * * he would be given gratuitously a monopoly more effective than that of the unobtainable patent in the ratio of eternity to seventeen years. [Pope Automatic Merchandising Co. v. McCrum-Howell Co., 191 F. 979, 981–82 (7th Cir.1911).]

An exception to the right to copy exists, however, where the product or package design under consideration is "nonfunctional" and serves to identify its manufacturer or seller, and the exception exists even though the design is *not* temporarily protectible through acquisition of patent or copyright. Thus, when a design is "nonfunctional," the right to compete through imitation gives way, presumably upon balance of that right with the originator's right to prevent others from infringing upon an established symbol of trade identification.

This preliminary discussion leads to the heart of the matter—how do we define the concept of "functionality," and what role does the above balancing of interests play in that definitional process?

I. Functionality Defined

* * *

[I]t has been noted that one of the "distinct questions" involved in "functionality" reasoning is, "In what *way* is [the] subject matter functional or utilitarian, factually or legally?" In re Honeywell, Inc., 497 F.2d 1344, 1350, (CCPA 1974) (Rich, J., concurring). This definitional division, * * * leads to the resolution that if the designation "functional" is to be utilized to denote the *legal* consequence, we must speak in terms of de facto functionality and de jure functionality, the former being the use of "functional" in the lay sense, indicating that although the design of a product, a container, or a feature of either is directed to performance of a function, it *may* be legally recognized as an indication of source. De jure functionality, of course, would be used to indicate the opposite—such a design may not be protected as a trademark.

This is only the beginning, however, for further definition is required to explain *how* a determination of whether a design is de jure functional is to be approached. We start with an inquiry into "utility."

A. "Functional" means "utilitarian"

From the earliest cases, "functionality" has been expressed in terms of "utility." * * * This broad statement of the "law", that the design of an article "having utility" cannot be a trademark, is incorrect and inconsistent with later pronouncements.

We wish to make it clear * * * that a discussion of "functionality" is *always* in reference to the *design* of the thing under consideration (in the sense of its *appearance*) and *not* the thing itself. No doubt, by definition, a dish always functions as a dish and has its utility, but it is the appearance of the dish which is important in a case such as this, as will become clear.

* * *

Thus, it is the "utilitarian" *design* of a "utilitarian" *object* with which we are concerned, and the manner of use of the term "utilitarian" must be examined at each occurrence. The latter occurrence is, of course, consistent with the lay meaning of the term. But the former is being used to denote a *legal consequence* (it being synonymous with "functional"), and it therefore requires further explication.

B. *"Utilitarian" means "superior in function (de facto) or economy of manu-facture," which "superiority" is determined in light of competitive necessity to copy*

* * *

Thus, it is clear that courts in the past have considered the public policy involved in this area of the law as, not the *right* to slavishly copy articles which are not protected by patent or copyright, but the *need* to copy those arti-cles, which is more properly termed the right to compete *effectively*. * * *

[handwritten margin note: Functional copying is allowed because it is needed in order to compete effectively]

More recent cases also discuss "functionality" in light of competition. One court noted that the "question in each case is whether protection against imitation will hinder the competitor in competition." Truck Equipment Service Co. v. Fruehauf Corp., 536 F.2d 1210, 1218, (8th Cir.1976). Another court, upon suit for trademark infringement (the alleged trademark being plaintiff's building design), stated that "enjoining others from using the building design [would not] inhibit competition in any way." Fotomat Corp. v. Cochran, 437 F.Supp. 1231, 1235, (D.Kan.1977). This court has also referenced "hindrance of competition" in a number of the "func-tionality" cases which have been argued before it. * * *

Given, then, that we must strike a balance between the "right to copy" and the right to protect one's method of trade identification, * * * what weights do we set upon each side of the scale? That is, given that "func-tionality" is a question of fact, * * * what facts do we look to in determin-ing whether the "consuming public has an interest in making use of [one's design], superior to [one's] interest in being [its] sole vendor"? Vaughan Novelty Mfg. Co. v. G.G. Greene Mfg. Corp., 202 F.2d 172, 176, (3d Cir.), cert. denied 346 U.S. 820 (1953).

II. Determining "Functionality"

A. In general

Keeping in mind, as shown by the foregoing review, that "functionality" is determined in light of "utility," which is determined in light of "superior-ity of design," and rests upon the foundation "essential to effective competi-tion," there exist a number of factors, both positive and negative, which aid in that determination.

Previous opinions of this court have discussed what evidence is useful to demonstrate that a particular design is "superior." In In re Shenango Ceramics, Inc., 362 F.2d 287, 291 (1966), the court noted that the existence of an expired utility patent which disclosed the *utilitarian advantage of the design* sought to be registered as a trademark was *evidence* that it was "functional." It may also be significant that the originator of the design touts its utilitarian advantages through advertising.

Since the effect upon competition "is really the crux of the matter," it is, of course, significant that there are other alternatives available.

* * *

It is also significant that a particular design results from a comparatively simple or cheap method of manufacturing the article. * * *

B. *The case at bar*

1. *The evidence of functionality*

We come now to the task of applying to the facts of this case the distilled essence of the body of law on "functionality" above discussed. The question is whether appellant's plastic spray bottle is de jure functional; is it the best or one of a few superior designs available? We hold on the basis of the evidence before the board, that it is not. * * * Of course, the spray bottle is highly useful and performs its intended functions in an admirable way, but that is not enough to render the *design* of the spray bottle—which is all that matters here—functional.

[The court examined both the spray bottle and the spray top and held that their shapes were not dictated by de facto functional concerns. Evidence of other spray bottles and tops with different designs suggested the design here was not a design that competitors required in order to compete.]

What is sought to be registered, however, is no single design feature or component but the overall composite design comprising both bottle and spray top. While that design must be *accommodated* to the functions performed, we see no evidence that it was *dictated* by them and resulted in a functionally or economically superior design of such a container.

Applying the legal principles discussed above, we do not see that allowing appellant to exclude others (upon proof of distinctiveness) from using this trade dress will hinder competition or impinge upon the rights of others to compete effectively in the sale of the goods named in the application, even to the extent of marketing them in *functionally* identical spray containers. The fact is that many others are doing so. Competitors have apparently had no need to simulate appellant's trade dress, in whole or in part, in order to enjoy all of the *functional* aspects of a spray top container. Upon expiration of any patent protection appellant may now be enjoying on its spray and pump mechanism, competitors may even copy and enjoy all of its functions without copying the external appearance of appellant's spray top.

* * *

2. *The relationship between "functionality" and distinctiveness*

One who seeks to register (or protect) a product or container configuration as a trademark must demonstrate that its design is "nonfunctional," as discussed above, and that the design functions as an indication of source, whether inherently so, because of its distinctive nature, or through acquisition of secondary meaning. These two requirements must, however, be kept separate from one another.

* * *

While it is certainly arguable that lack of distinctiveness may, where appropriate, permit an inference that a design was created primarily with an eye toward the utility of the *article,* that fact is by no means conclusive as to the "functionality" of the *design* of that article. Whether in fact the design is "functional" requires closer and more careful scrutiny. We cannot say that there exists an inverse proportional relationship in all cases between distinctiveness of design and functionality (de facto or de jure).

* * *

[The court remanded to the patent office for consideration of the issue of distinctiveness of the mark.]

NOTES

1. Most designs have some elements that are functional. Some designs consist of a combination of functional elements. How are such designs to be characterized? See, Restatement, Third, of Unfair Competition, § 17, Comment *b* at 174 (1995):

> When the matter claimed as a trademark consists of the overall design of a product or its packaging, or the design of a combination or arrangement of features, eligibility for trademark protection is determined by the functionality of the claimed design as a whole. The fact that the overall design or combination contains individual features that are themselves functional does not preclude protection for the composite. The issue is whether trademark protection should be recognized in the particular combination or arrangement of features, and the functionality of the combination or arrangement as a whole is determinative. If the overall shape of a bottle is distinctive and nonfunctional, for example, the shape may be protected as a trademark despite the inclusion of a top that is functionally configured to accept a standard bottle cap. Protection of the overall design, however, will not preclude others from adopting the functional constituents. If the overall design of a product or package is otherwise functional, however, the addition of minor nonfunctional elements will not render the overall design protectable; trademark rights will be limited to only the nonfunctional elements.

2. Can a building be protected as a trademark? See Fotomat Corp. v. Photo Drive-Thru, Inc., 425 F.Supp. 693 (D.N.J.1977) (kiosks well-suited for drive-in sales not protectible but unique or arbitrary elements of design protected if secondary meaning established). Could famous buildings be trademarks? The Sears Tower in Chicago? The Transamerica building in San

Francisco? Could the companies that own these buildings prevent others from using a picture of the buildings in advertisements? Could they prevent others from building similar buildings? Could someone other than the owner trademark the building?

3. Are there some design elements that are in such limited supply that allowing someone to appropriate them as trademarks would hinder competition? Whether color alone can be protected as a trademark has divided the courts. See, NutraSweet Co. v. Stadt Corp., 917 F.2d 1024 (7th Cir. 1990) (absolute bar to protecting color alone); In re Owens-Corning Fiberglas Corp., 774 F.2d 1116 (Fed. Cir. 1985) (registration of color pink for insulation approved); Master Distributors, Inc. v. Pako Corp., 986 F.2d 219 (8th Cir. 1993) (upheld protection for blue splicing tape known as "the blue tape." The issue was resolved in **Qualitex Co. v. Jacobson Products Co., Inc.**, 514 U.S. 159 (1995), where the Supreme Court in a unanimous opinion, protected the green-gold shade of Qualitex's press pads against use by a competitor of similarly colored pads and gave an encompassing interpretation to the Lanham Act's definition of a trademark:

> * * * Both the language of the Act and the basic underlying principles of trademark law would seem to include color within the universe of things that can qualify as a trademark. The language of the Lanham Act describes that universe in the broadest of terms. It says that trademarks "includ[e] any word, name, symbol, or device, or any combination thereof." § 1127. Since human beings might use as a "symbol" or "device" almost anything at all that is capable of carrying meaning, this language, read literally, is not restrictive. The courts and the Patent and Trademark Office have authorized for use as a mark a particular shape (of a Coca-Cola bottle), a particular sound (of NBC's three chimes), and even a particular scent (of plumeria blossoms on sewing thread). If a shape, a sound, and a fragrance can act as symbols why, one might ask, can a color not do the same?
>
> A color is also capable of satisfying the more important part of the statutory definition of a trademark, which requires that a person "us[e]" or "inten[d] to use" the mark "to identify and distinguish his or her goods, including a unique product, from those manufactured or sold by others and to indicate the source of the goods, even if that source is unknown." 15 U.S.C. § 1127. True, a product's color is unlike "fanciful," "arbitrary," or "suggestive" words or designs, which almost automatically tell a customer that they refer to a brand. But, over time, customers may come to treat a particular color on a product or its packaging (say, a color that in context seems unusual, such as pink on a firm's insulating material or red on the head of a large industrial bolt) as signifying a brand. And, if so, that color would have come to identify and distinguish the goods—i.e. "to "indicate" their "source"—much in the way that descriptive words on a product (say, "Trim" on nail clippers or "Car-Freshner" on deodorizer) can come to indicate a product's origin. Again, one might ask, if trademark law permits a descriptive word with secondary meaning to act as a mark, why would it not permit a color, under similar circumstances, to do the same?

To the defendant's argument that colors were in limited supply and thus protection might give one competitor an unfair advantage, the Court observed:

> This argument is unpersuasive, however, largely because it relies on an occasional problem to justify a blanket prohibition. When a color serves as a mark, normally alternative colors will likely be available for similar use by others. Moreover, if that is not so—if a "color depletion" or "color scarcity" problem does arise—the trademark doctrine of "functionality" normally would seem available to prevent the anticompetitive consequences that Jacobson's argument posits, thereby minimizing that argument's practical force.

* * *

The upshot is that, where a color serves a significant nontrademark function—whether to distinguish a heart pill from a digestive medicine or to satisfy the "noble instinct for giving the right touch of beauty to common and necessary things," G.K. Chesterton, Simplicity and Tolstoy 61 (1912)—courts will examine whether its use as a mark would permit one competitor (or a group) to interfere with legitimate (nontrademark-related) competition through actual or potential exclusive use of an important product ingredient. That examination should not discourage firms from creating aesthetically pleasing mark designs, for it is open to their competitors to do the same. But, ordinarily, it should prevent the anticompetitive consequences of Jacobson's hypothetical "color depletion" argument, when, and if, the circumstances of a particular case threaten "color depletion."

Wallace International Silversmiths, Inc. v. Godinger Silver Art Co., Inc.

United States Court of Appeals, Second Circuit, 1990.
916 F.2d 76.

■ WINTER, CIRCUIT JUDGE:

Wallace International Silversmiths ("Wallace") appeals from Judge Haight's denial of its motion for a preliminary injunction under Section 43(a) of the Lanham Act, 15 U.S.C. § 1125(a) (1988), prohibiting Godinger Silver Art Co., Inc. ("Godinger") from marketing a line of silverware with ornamentation that is substantially similar to Wallace's GRANDE BAROQUE line. Judge Haight held that the GRANDE BAROQUE design is "a functional feature of 'Baroque' style silverwear" and thus not subject to protection as a trademark. We affirm.

[Wallace's GRANDE BAROQUE pattern, made of fine sterling silver, was a popular silverware line selling for several thousand dollars per place setting. The pattern is described as "ornate, massive and flowery [with] indented, flowery roots and scrolls and curls along the side of the shaft, and flower arrangements along the front of the shaft." Godinger's silverware, selling for $20 per place setting, contained "typical baroque elements including an indented root, scrolls, curls, and flowers" in a similar arrangement but with different dimensions.]

* * * Judge Haight found that the similarities between the Godinger and Wallace designs involved elements common to all baroque-style designs used in the silverware market. He noted that many manufacturers compete in that market with such designs and found that "[t]he 'Baroque' curls, roots and flowers are not 'mere indicia of source.' Instead, they are requirements to compete in the silverware market." Judge Haight concluded that "the 'Grande Baroque' design is a functional feature of 'Baroque' style silverware," relying on Pagliero v. Wallace China Co., 198 F.2d 339 (9th Cir.1952).

Although we agree with Judge Haight's decision, we do not endorse his reliance upon *Pagliero*. That decision allowed a competitor to sell exact copies of china bearing a particular pattern without finding that comparably attractive patterns were not available to the competitor. It based its holding solely on the ground that the particular pattern was an important ingredient in the commercial success of the china. We rejected *Pagliero* in *LeSportsac* [LeSportsac, Inc. v. K Mart Corp., 754 F.2d 71 (2nd Cir.1985)], and reiterate that rejection here. Under *Pagliero*, the commercial success of an aesthetic feature automatically destroys all of the originator's trademark interest in it, notwithstanding the feature's secondary meaning and the lack of any evidence that competitors cannot develop non-infringing, attractive patterns. By allowing the copying of an exact design without any evidence of market foreclosure, the *Pagliero* test discourages both originators and later competitors from developing pleasing designs.

Our rejection of *Pagliero*, however, does not call for reversal. Quite unlike *Pagliero*, Judge Haight found in the instant matter that there is a substantial market for baroque silverware and that effective competition in that market requires "use [of] essentially the same scrolls and flowers" as is found on Wallace's silverware. Based on the record at the hearing, that finding is not clearly erroneous and satisfies the requirement of *Stormy Clime* that a design feature not be given trade dress protection where use of that feature is necessary for effective competition.

Stormy Clime is arguably distinguishable, however, because it involved a design that had both aesthetic and utilitarian features. If read narrowly, *Stormy Clime* might be limited to cases in which trademark protection of a design would foreclose competitors from incorporating utilitarian features necessary to compete in the market for the particular product. In the instant case, the features at issue are strictly ornamental because they neither affect the use of the silverware nor contribute to its efficient manufacture. The question, therefore, is whether the doctrine of functionality applies to features of a product that are purely ornamental but that are essential to effective competition.

Our only hesitation in holding that the functionality doctrine applies is based on nomenclature. "Functionality" seems to us to imply only utilitarian considerations and, as a legal doctrine, to be intended only to prevent competitors from obtaining trademark protection for design features that are necessary to the use or efficient production of the product. Even when the doctrine is referred to as "aesthetic" functionality, it still seems an apt description only of pleasing designs of utilitarian features. Nevertheless, there is no lack of language in case law endorsing use of the defense of aesthetic functionality where trademark protection for purely ornamental features would exclude competitors from a market. * * *

We put aside our quibble over doctrinal nomenclature, however, because we are confident that whatever secondary meaning Wallace's baroque silverware pattern may have acquired, Wallace may not exclude competitors from using those baroque design elements necessary to compete in the market for baroque silverware. It is a first principle of trademark law that an owner may not use the mark as a means of excluding competitors from a substantial market. Where a mark becomes the generic term to describe an article, for example, trademark protection ceases. Where granting trademark protection to the use of certain colors would tend to exclude competitors, such protection is also limited. Finally, as discussed supra, design features of products that are necessary to the product's utility may be copied by competitors under the functionality doctrine.

In the instant matter, Wallace seeks trademark protection, not for a precise expression of a decorative style, but for basic elements of a style that is part of the public domain. As found by the district court, these elements are important to competition in the silverware market. We perceive no distinction between a claim to exclude all others from use on silverware of basic elements of a decorative style and claims to generic names, basic colors or designs important to a product's utility. In each case, trademark protection is sought, not just to protect an owner of a mark in informing the public of the source of its products, but also to exclude competitors from producing similar products. We therefore abandon our quibble with the aesthetic functionality doctrine's nomenclature and adopt the Restatement's view that, where an ornamental feature is claimed as a trademark and trademark protection would significantly hinder competition by limiting the range of adequate alternative designs, the aesthetic functionality doctrine denies such protection. See Third Restatement of the Law, Unfair Competition, Ch. 3, § 17(c) at 213–14. This rule avoids the overbreadth of *Pagliero* by requiring a finding of foreclosure of alternatives while still ensuring that trademark protection does not exclude competitors from substantial markets.

Of course, if Wallace were able to show secondary meaning in a precise expression of baroque style, competitors might be excluded from using an identical or virtually identical design. In such a case, numerous alternative baroque designs would still be available to competitors. Although the Godinger design at issue here was found by Judge Haight to be "substantially similar," it is not identical or virtually identical, and the similarity involves design elements necessary to compete in the market for baroque silverware. Because according trademark protection to those elements would significantly hinder competitors by limiting the range of adequate alternative designs, we agree with Judge Haight's denial of a preliminary injunction.

Affirmed.

ROMM ART CREATIONS LTD. V. SIMCHA INTERNATIONAL, INC., 786
F. SUPP. 1126 (E.D.N.Y. 1992). Romm Art obtained the exclusive right to distribute posters of the original art works of Itzchak Tarkay whose collection
known as "Women and Cafes" had a distinctive style. The defendant, Asher
Wainer ("Wainer") is president and sole owner of Simcha, which is the distributor of limited editions and posters of the art work of Patricia Govezensky—
the "Patricia" line which simulates the Tarkay style. Romm sued Wainer
under § 43(a) of the Lanham Act for trade dress infringement. The court
observed that "this suit falls within a rarely-tread area of the law, namely, the
application of trade dress protection to works of art." However, the court
applied traditional trade dress analysis finding that Tarkay had priority, that
the style of the works had obtained secondary meaning, and that the Patricia
works created a likelihood of confusion:

> Having examined the color patterns and shading of the Tarkay works,
> the placement of figures in each of the pictures examined, the physical
> attributes of his women, the depiction of women sitting and reclining,
> their characteristic clothing vis-a-vis those portrayed by Patricia, the
> Court concludes that there is "sufficient similarity between the products
> to scrutinize the evidence for proof of confusion." The test for determining
> similarity is whether the labels create the "same overall impression" when
> viewed separately. In light of the fact that the Tarkay and Patricia pat-
> terns are not dictated by function, and that a variety of patterns is possi-
> ble, the similarity of the patterns is striking. When this striking similar-
> ity is factored into the likelihood of confusion analysis, in light of the
> strength of the Tarkay trade dress, consumer confusion is a likely result.

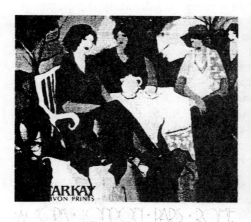

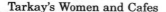

Tarkay's Women and Cafes   The "Patricia" line

NOTES

1. What exactly does the plaintiff in *Wallace* claim as its protectable
trade dress? In *Romm*? Can the defendant in either case know what is being

claimed? Does it matter? Are *Wallace* and *Romm* consistent with each other? Consider the following from Landscape forms, Inc. v. Columbia Cascade Co., 113 F. 3d 373 (2d Cir. 1997):

> . . . we still recognize that there is no question that trade dress may protect the "overall look" of a product. . . . Nonetheless, focus on the overall look of a product does not permit a plaintiff to dispense with an articulation of the specific elements which comprise its distinct dress. Without such a precise expression of the character and scope of the claimed trade dress, litigation will be difficult, as courts will be unable to evaluate how unique and unexpected the design elements are in the relevant market. Courts will also be unable to shape narrowly-tailored relief if they do not know what distinctive combination of ingredients deserves protection. Moreover, a plaintiff's inability to explain to a court exactly which aspects of its product design(s) merit protection may indicate that its claim is pitched at an improper level of generality, i.e., the claimant seeks protection for an unprotectable style, theme or idea.

2. Does *Romm* mean that all art works with an identifiable style are protected by trademark law? If Patricia Govezensky's name had been prominently displayed on the defendant's prints, would the result have been different? If ordinary consumers could not tell the difference between some of the cubist works of George Braques and those of Pablo Picasso, would a court have to decide which artist had perfected the style first?

3. See Judge Newman's attempt to resolve these issues in Jeffrey Milstein, Inc. v. Greger, Lawlor, Roth, Inc. 58 F.3d 27 (2d Cir. 1995) where the plaintiff asserted trade dress protection in greeting cards consisting of photographs die cut to the shape of the object in the photograph:

> Second, just as copyright law does not protect ideas but only their concrete expression, neither does trade dress law protect an idea, a concept, or a generalized type of appearance. See, e.g., Hartford House Ltd. v. Hallmark Cards, Inc. * * *. Examples of ideas or concepts too general to warrant protection are the "theme" of skeletons engaging in sexual activities, which plaintiff used in its t-shirt design, see Fashion Victim [v. Sunrise Turquoise, Inc., 785 F. Supp. 1302 (N.D. Ill. 1992)] and the "generalized concept" of grotesque figures in toys * * *. By contrast, the concrete expression of an idea in a trade dress has received protection. See, Hartford House * * *.

> Drawing the line between "ideas" or "concepts" on the one hand and "concrete expressions" on the other may sometimes present close questions. Often a helpful consideration will be the purpose of trade dress law: to protect an owner of a dress in informing the public of the source of its products, without permitting the owner to exclude competition from functionally similar products * * *. The level of generality at which a trade dress is described, as well as the fact that a similar trade dress is already being used by manufacturers of other kinds of products, may indicate that that dress is no more than a concept or idea to be applied to particular products.

4. How does copyright law relate to this decision? Could another author write a cold war spy thriller in the style of Tom Clancy without infringing Clancy's trademark? If the copyright law does not protect the style or theme of a copyrighted work, could Congress have intended to grant protection under the trademark laws?

5. Can a trademark itself ever be functional? Automobile manufacturers do not provide interior floor mats as standard equipment but they do offer optional floor mats with the manufacturer's logo in colors and shapes designed for their automobiles. There is a consumer demand for accessories that display the logo of the automobile manufacturer. Is there any way that independent companies can compete with the automobile manufacturers in providing floor mats with logos without infringing the trademark rights in the logo? Does it matter what consumers think when they see the logo on the floor mats? See Plasticolor Molded Products v. Ford Motor Co., 713 F.Supp. 1329 (C.D.Cal.1989): "Where a copied product feature is partially functional but partially source-identifying, we are presented with three alternatives. First, we could find that the source-identifying aspects of the feature trump the functional aspects, and simply apply the standard law of trademark infringement. Second, we could find the opposite, and hold that the feature is unprotected from copying. Third, we could attempt to find an appropriate middle ground." Is there an appropriate middle ground?

Two Pesos, Inc. v. Taco Cabana, Inc.

Supreme Court of the United States, 1992
505 U.S. 763, 112 S. Ct. 2753, 120 L. Ed.2d 615,
rehearing denied, 505 U.S. 1244, 113 S. Ct. 20, 120 L. Ed.2d 947

■ JUSTICE WHITE delivered the opinion of the Court.

The issue in this case is whether the trade dress[2] of a restaurant may be protected under § 43(a) of the Trademark Act of 1946 (Lanham Act), 15 U.S.C. § 1125(a), based on a finding of inherent distinctiveness, without proof that the trade dress has secondary meaning.

I

Respondent Taco Cabana, Inc., operates a chain of fast-food restaurants in Texas. The restaurants serve Mexican food. The first Taco Cabana restaurant was opened in San Antonio in September 1978, and five more restaurants had been opened in San Antonio by 1985. Taco Cabana describes its Mexican trade dress as

---

2. The District Court instructed the jury: "'[T]rade dress' is the total image of the business. Taco Cabana's trade dress may include the shape and general appearance of the exterior of the restaurant, the identifying sign, the interior kitchen floor plan, the decor, the menu, the equipment used to serve food, the servers' uniforms and other features reflecting on the total image of the restaurant." 1 App. 83–84. The Court of Appeals accepted this definition * * *.

"a festive eating atmosphere having interior dining and patio areas decorated with artifacts, bright colors, paintings and murals. The patio includes interior and exterior areas with the interior patio capable of being sealed off from the outside patio by overhead garage doors. The stepped exterior of the building is a festive and vivid color scheme using top border paint and neon stripes. Bright awnings and umbrellas continue the theme." 932 F.2d 1113, 1117 (CA5 1991).

In December 1985, a Two Pesos, Inc., restaurant was opened in Houston. Two Pesos adopted a motif very similar to the foregoing description of Taco Cabana's trade dress. Two Pesos restaurants expanded rapidly in Houston and other markets, but did not enter San Antonio. In 1986, Taco Cabana entered the Houston and Austin markets and expanded into other Texas cities, including Dallas and El Paso where Two Pesos was also doing business.

In 1987, Taco Cabana sued Two Pesos in the United States District Court for the Southern District of Texas for trade dress infringement under § 43(a) of the Lanham Act, 15 U.S.C. § 1125(a), and for theft of trade secrets under Texas common law. The case was tried to a jury, which was instructed to return its verdict in the form of answers to five questions propounded by the trial judge. The jury's answers were: Taco Cabana has a trade dress; taken as a whole, the trade dress is nonfunctional; the trade dress is inherently distinctive; the trade dress has not acquired a secondary meaning in the Texas market; and the alleged infringement creates a likelihood of confusion on the part of ordinary customers as to the source or association of the restaurant's goods or services. Because, as the jury was told, Taco Cabana's trade dress was protected if it either was inherently distinctive or had acquired a secondary meaning, judgment was entered awarding damages to Taco Cabana. In the course of calculating damages, the trial court held that Two Pesos had intentionally and deliberately infringed Taco Cabana's trade dress.

The Court of Appeals ruled that the instructions adequately stated the applicable law and that the evidence supported the jury's findings. In particular, the Court of Appeals rejected petitioner's argument that a finding of no secondary meaning contradicted a finding of inherent distinctiveness.

In so holding, the court below followed precedent in the Fifth Circuit. In Chevron Chemical Co. v. Voluntary Purchasing Groups, Inc., 659 F.2d 695, 702 (CA5 1981), the court noted that trademark law requires a demonstration of secondary meaning only when the claimed trademark is not sufficiently distinctive of itself to identify the producer; the court held that the same principles should apply to protection of trade dresses. The Court of Appeals noted that this approach conflicts with decisions of other courts, particularly the holding of the Court of Appeals for the Second Circuit in Vibrant Sales, Inc. v. New Body Boutique, Inc., 652 F.2d 299 (1981), cert. denied, 455 U.S. 909 (1982), that § 43(a) protects unregistered trademarks or designs only where secondary meaning is shown. Chevron, supra, at 702. We granted certiorari to resolve the conflict among the Courts of Appeals on the question whether trade dress which is inherently distinctive is protectable under § 43(a) without a showing that it has acquired secondary meaning. We find that it is, and we therefore affirm.

II

* * * [I]t is common ground that § 43(a) protects qualifying unregistered trademarks and that the general principles qualifying a mark for registration under § 2 of the Lanham Act are for the most part applicable in determining whether an unregistered mark is entitled to protection under § 43(a).

A trademark is defined in 15 U.S.C. § 1127 as including "any word, name, symbol, or device or any combination thereof" used by any person "to identify and distinguish his or her goods, including a unique product, from those manufactured or sold by others and to indicate the source of the goods, even if that source is unknown." In order to be registered, a mark must be capable of distinguishing the applicant's goods from those of others. § 1052. Marks are often classified in categories of generally increasing distinctiveness; following the classic formulation set out by Judge Friendly, they may be (1) generic; (2) descriptive; (3) suggestive; (4) arbitrary; or (5) fanciful. The Court of Appeals followed this classification and petitioner accepts it. The latter three categories of marks, because their intrinsic nature serves to identify a particular source of a product, are deemed inherently distinctive and are entitled to protection. In contrast, generic marks—those that "refe[r] to the genus of which the particular product is a species," Park' N Fly, Inc. v. Dollar Park and Fly, Inc., 469 U.S. 189, 194 (1985), * * * are not registrable as trademarks.

Marks which are merely descriptive of a product are not inherently distinctive. When used to describe a product, they do not inherently identify a particular source, and hence cannot be protected. However, descriptive marks may acquire the distinctiveness which will allow them to be protected under the Act. * * *

The general rule regarding distinctiveness is clear: an identifying mark is distinctive and capable of being protected if it either (1) is inherently distinctive or (2) has acquired distinctiveness through secondary meaning. Restatement (Third) of Unfair Competition, § 13, pp. 37–38, and Comment a (Tent. Draft No. 2, Mar. 23, 1990). It is also clear that eligibility for protection under § 43(a) depends on nonfunctionality. It is, of course, also undisputed that liability under § 43(a) requires proof of the likelihood of confusion.

The Court of Appeals determined that the District Court's instructions were consistent with the foregoing principles and that the evidence supported the jury's verdict. Both courts thus ruled that Taco Cabana's trade dress was not descriptive but rather inherently distinctive, and that it was not functional. None of these rulings is before us in this case, and for present purposes we assume, without deciding, that each of them is correct. In going on to affirm the judgment for respondent, the Court of Appeals, following its prior decision in *Chevron*, held that Taco Cabana's inherently distinctive trade dress was entitled to protection despite the lack of proof of secondary meaning. It is this issue that is before us for decision, and we agree with its resolution by the Court of Appeals. There is no persuasive reason to apply to trade dress a general requirement of secondary meaning which is at odds with the principles generally applicable to infringement suits under § 43(a).

* * * Petitioner argues that the jury's finding that the trade dress has not acquired a secondary meaning shows conclusively that the trade dress is not inherently distinctive. The Court of Appeals' disposition of this issue was sound:

> "Two Pesos' argument—that the jury finding of inherent distinctiveness contradicts its finding of no secondary meaning in the Texas market—ignores the law in this circuit. While the necessarily imperfect (and often prohibitively difficult) methods for assessing secondary meaning address the empirical question of current consumer association, the legal recognition of an inherently distinctive trademark or trade dress acknowledges the owner's legitimate proprietary interest in its unique and valuable informational device, regardless of whether substantial consumer association yet bestows the additional empirical protection of secondary meaning." 932 F.2d, at 1120, n. 7.

Although petitioner makes the above argument, it appears to concede elsewhere in its briefing that it is possible for a trade dress, even a restaurant trade dress, to be inherently distinctive and thus eligible for protection under § 43(a). Recognizing that a general requirement of secondary meaning imposes "an unfair prospect of theft [or] financial loss" on the developer of fanciful or arbitrary trade dress at the outset of its use, petitioner suggests that such trade dress should receive limited protection without proof of secondary meaning. Petitioner argues that such protection should be only temporary and subject to defeasance when over time the dress has failed to acquire a secondary meaning. This approach is also vulnerable for the reasons given by the Court of Appeals. If temporary protection is available from the earliest use of the trade dress, it must be because it is neither functional nor descriptive but an inherently distinctive dress that is capable of identifying a particular source of the product. Such a trade dress, or mark, is not subject to copying by concerns that have an equal opportunity to choose their own inherently distinctive trade dress. To terminate protection for failure to gain secondary meaning over some unspecified time could not be based on the failure of the dress to retain its fanciful, arbitrary, or suggestive nature, but on the failure of the user of the dress to be successful enough in the marketplace. This is not a valid basis to find a dress or mark ineligible for protection. The user of such a trade dress should be able to maintain what competitive position it has and continue to seek wider identification among potential customers.

This brings us to the line of decisions by the Court of Appeals for the Second Circuit that would find protection for trade dress unavailable absent proof of secondary meaning, a position that petitioner concedes would have to be modified if the temporary protection that it suggests is to be recognized. * * * The Second Circuit has nevertheless continued to deny protection for trade dress under § 43(a) absent proof of secondary meaning, despite the fact that § 43(a) provides no basis for distinguishing between trademark and trade dress.

The Fifth Circuit was quite right in *Chevron*, and in this case, to follow the *Abercrombie* [Abercrombie & Fitch Co., 537 F.2d 4 (2d Cir. 1976)] classifications consistently and to inquire whether trade dress for which protection is claimed under § 43(a) is inherently distinctive. If it is, it is capable of identifying products or services as coming from a specific source and secondary meaning is not required. This is the rule generally applicable to trademark, and the protection of trademarks and trade dress under § 43(a) serves the same statutory purpose of preventing deception and unfair competition. There is no persuasive reason to apply different analysis to the two. * * *

It would be a different matter if there were textual basis in § 43(a) for treating inherently distinctive verbal or symbolic trademarks differently from inherently distinctive trade dress. But there is none. The section does not mention trademarks or trade dress, whether they be called generic, descriptive, suggestive, arbitrary, fanciful, or functional. Nor does the concept of secondary meaning appear in the text of § 43(a). Where secondary meaning does appear in the statute, 15 U.S.C. § 1052 (1982 ed.), it is a requirement that applies only to merely descriptive marks and not to inherently distinctive ones. We see no basis for requiring secondary meaning for inherently distinctive trade dress protection under § 43(a) but not for other distinctive words, symbols, or devices capable of identifying a producer's product.

Engrafting onto § 43(a) a requirement of secondary meaning for inherently distinctive trade dress also would undermine the purposes of the Lanham Act. Protection of trade dress, no less than of trademarks, serves the Act's purpose to "secure to the owner of the mark the goodwill of his business and to protect the ability of consumers to distinguish among competing producers. National protection of trademarks is desirable, Congress concluded, because trademarks foster competition and the maintenance of quality by securing to the producer the benefits of good reputation." *Park' N Fly*, 469 U.S., at 198, 105 S.Ct., at 663, citing S.Rep. No. 1333, 79th Cong., 2d Sess., 3–5 (1946) (citations omitted). By making more difficult the identification of a producer with its product, a secondary meaning requirement for a nondescriptive trade dress would hinder improving or maintaining the producer's competitive position.

Suggestions that under the Fifth Circuit's law, the initial user of any shape or design would cut off competition from products of like design and shape are not persuasive. Only nonfunctional, distinctive trade dress is protected under § 43(a). The Fifth Circuit holds that a design is legally functional, and thus unprotectable, if it is one of a limited number of equally efficient options available to competitors and free competition would be unduly hindered by according the design trademark protection. This serves to assure that competition will not be stifled by the exhaustion of a limited number of trade dresses.

On the other hand, adding a secondary meaning requirement could have anticompetitive effects, creating particular burdens on the start-up of small companies. It would present special difficulties for a business, such as respondent, that seeks to start a new product in a limited area and then expand into new markets. Denying protection for inherently distinctive nonfunctional trade dress until after secondary meaning has been established would allow a competitor, which has not adopted a distinctive trade dress of its own, to appropriate the originator's dress in other markets and to deter the originator from expanding into and competing in these areas.

As noted above, petitioner concedes that protecting an inherently distinctive trade dress from its inception may be critical to new entrants to the market and that withholding protection until secondary meaning has been established would be contrary to the goals of the Lanham Act. Petitioner specifically suggests, however, that the solution is to dispense with the requirement of secondary meaning for a reasonable, but brief period at the outset of the use of a trade dress. Reply Brief for Petitioner 11–12. If § 43(a) does not require secondary meaning at the outset of a business' adoption of trade dress, there is no basis in the statute to support the suggestion that such a requirement comes into being after some unspecified time.

III

We agree with the Court of Appeals that proof of secondary meaning is not required to prevail on a claim under § 43(a) of the Lanham Act where the trade dress at issue is inherently distinctive, and accordingly the judgment of that court is affirmed. It is so ordered.

[Justice Stevens concurred observing that while it was not clear that the text of § 43(a) included a federal cause of action for infringement of an unregistered trademark or trade dress, the federal courts had "transformed" the language over the years and he agreed with the transformation. Justice Thomas concurred on the basis that the text of § 43(a) clearly encompassed trade dress claims without reference to provisions relating to registration.]

NOTES

1. The original jury verdict against Two Pesos was for $3.7 million. After the Supreme Court's ruling, Taco Cabana filed a second suit seeking an additional $5 million. Subsequently Two Pesos signed a letter of intent to sell its 34 unit chain of restaurants to Taco Cabana. The Wall Street Journal, Pg. B8, Col. 1, January 14, 1993.

2. Is there a practical difference between trademarks and trade dress that affects the application of the concept of inherent distinctiveness? Envision a box of Kodak brand film. Is there any ambiguity in the purpose for which the word "Kodak" appears on the box? Can it serve any other function besides identifying the producer of the film? Now consider the familiar yellow color of the box. Is the color "inherently distinctive" and thus protectable? Or, is it just another pretty color? Would you want to have some evidence that consumers recognized the color yellow as identifying Kodak brand film before you prohibited another manufacturer from using the color on its film? Would you want to know the manufacturer's intention as to the selection of the yellow color?

In this same context, consider the design of a product itself. How would you assess whether a park bench was inherently distinctive? Or the shape of a stacking chair? If a client comes to you with a design of a park bench or stacking chair, what will you look at to determine whether there is a risk of infringing someone else's trade dress? If the defendant in Compco Corp. v. Day-Bright Lighting (Chapter 1) came to you with the idea of copying the plaintiff's fluorescent lighting fixture reflector, what would you advise?

Krueger International, Inc. v. Nightingale Inc.

United States District Court, S.D. New York, 1996.
915 F. Supp. 595.

Krueger's chair design   Nightingale's chair design

[The above graphics are not part of the court's opinion.]

■ SOTOMAYOR, DISTRICT JUDGE.

Plaintiff, a manufacturer of metal-frame stacking chairs, alleges tha' defendant, a competitor, has "slavishly copied" its chair design and thereby infringed its trade dress under § 43(a) of the Lanham Act, 15 U.S.C. § 1125(a). The plaintiff, Krueger International, Inc. ("KI"), moves for a preliminary injunction against the defendant, Nightingale Inc. ("NI"), on the grounds that the KI design is distinctive and that NI's design is confusingly similar. KI seeks to enjoin NI from advertising, manufacturing or selling copies of the KI chair. For the reasons discussed below, KI's motion is DENIED.

* * *

This case presents one of the most difficult analytical issues in all of trade dress law: how to determine whether a product design is "inherently distinctive." The issue is particularly pressing and unresolved in this circuit, whose rule for trade dress protection was upended three and a half years ago by the Supreme Court in Two Pesos, Inc. v. Taco Cabana, Inc., 505 U.S. 763 (1992). Prior to *Two Pesos*, a plaintiff seeking trade dress protection in this circuit had to prove that the dress had acquired secondary meaning. *Two Pesos*, which unified the standard for trademark and trade dress law, held that protection for trade dress requires either inherent distinctiveness or secondary meaning, but not both.

* * *

The classic test for determining the distinctiveness of a trademark was outlined in *Abercrombie & Fitch* [Abercrombie & Fitch Co. v. Hunting World, Inc., 537 F.2d 4 (2d Cir. 1976)] and the test has since been extended to trade dress as well. Under the *Abercrombie* test, marks are classified as either (1) generic, (2) descriptive, (3) suggestive, or (4) arbitrary or fanciful. Suggestive, arbitrary and fanciful marks and dresses are always considered inherently distinctive, in that their "intrinsic nature serves to identify a particular source of a product" or they are "capable of identifying a particular source of the product," whether or not the trade dress has acquired secondary meaning or a wide public association with the source. * * *

But as many courts have observed in varying degrees of frustration, the *Abercrombie* classifications do not translate easily to the trade dress context. The problem is not severe when the trade dress involves product packages and labels, which, like trademarks, at least have the advantage of using words and symbols independent of the product to convey information to consumers. The problem is often daunting, however, when it comes to product designs. Does the shape of a chair seat "suggest" a chair seat? Does it "describe" a chair seat? Or is it just a chair seat? No matter how beautifully designed, an industrial product is what it is. This conundrum recently led the Second Circuit in Knitwaves, Inc. v. Lollytogs Ltd., 71 F.3d 996 (2d Cir.1995), to abandon the *Abercrombie* test for product design and announce a new test. I believe, however, that this new test is not particularly helpful because it does not clearly address the standards in this area as set by the Supreme Court.

In *Knitwaves*, this circuit announced a departure from its earlier approach to trade dress law. *Knitwaves* involved the design of children's sweaters, particularly the use of "leaf" and "squirrel" designs placed on the sweaters. The court stated (1) that the Abercrombie classifications "make little sense when applied to product features" and were therefore "inapplicable" to product designs, and (2) that henceforth the new test for inherent distinctiveness is whether the manufacturer "used" or "intended to use" the design "to identify the source and distinguish his or her goods." In adopting this approach, the court cited approvingly to the Third Circuit decision in Duraco

Prods., Inc. v. Joy Plastic Enterprises, Ltd., 40 F.3d 1431, 1440–41 (3d Cir.1994). The *Duraco* approach, however, leaves much to be desired. The Eighth Circuit instead has recently made a forceful and persuasive argument that the Supreme Court has not authorized us to abandon *Abercrombie*, no matter how much difficulty it causes. Stuart Hall Co. v. Ampad Corp., 51 F.3d 780, 788 (8th Cir.1995). As the Eighth Circuit reasoned, *Two Pesos* was clearly a case of product design and it expressly approved the application of the *Abercrombie* classifications to the design of a Mexican restaurant chain. Moreover, the entire thrust of *Two Pesos* was to unify the standards for trademark and trade dress, not to balkanize this complex field into yet more subcategories. I agree with the Eighth Circuit's conclusion that the Supreme Court envisions trade dress as a "single concept" with trademark law requiring a single test for inherent distinctiveness.

Further, I believe that *Knitwaves's* new test for inherent distinctiveness confuses the analytical requirements for inherent distinctiveness with those of secondary meaning. Inherent distinctiveness cannot hinge on how a producer intends to promote a design. If such were the case, the evidentiary requirements for inherent distinctiveness would be almost identical to those for secondary meaning, and there would be no point in having two categories. A producer could only prove "intent" by producing evidence of how he or she has advertised (or positioned) the product, and by producing consumer surveys showing how well the advertising worked. This is precisely the kind of evidence required for a showing of secondary meaning. * * *

Knitwaves, however, does provide some guidance for a workable approach to inherent distinctiveness, particularly when read in conjunction with efforts by other courts. The Fifth and Eighth Circuits offer particularly useful instruction. The Fifth Circuit's *Chevron* test, first developed for product packaging, states that "[i]f the features of the trade dress sought to be protected are arbitrary and serve no function either to describe the product or assist in its effective packaging," the dress is inherently distinctive. Chevron Chemical Co. v. Voluntary Purchasing Groups, Inc., 659 F.2d 695, 702 (5th Cir.1981) (packaging of lawn and garden products), cert. denied, 457 U.S. 1126 (1982). This is essentially a test of functionality. The Supreme Court explicitly approved the application of the *Chevron* test to product designs in its decision in *Two Pesos*.

The Eighth Circuit also emphasizes the issue of functionality, asking:

> whether, and how much, the trade dress is dictated by the nature of the product. . . . If the specific design of the trade dress is only tenuously connected with the nature of the product, then it is inherently distinctive. . . . If the design of the trade dress is dictated by the nature of the product, then secondary meaning must be proven.

A third test based on the *Abercrombie* classifications was developed 19 years ago by the Court of Customs and Patent Appeals:

> In determining whether a design is arbitrary or distinctive this court has looked to whether it was a 'common' basic shape or design, whether it was unique or unusual in a particular field, [or] whether it was a mere refinement of a commonly-adopted and well-known form of orna-

mentation for a particular class of goods view by the public as a dress or ornamentation for the goods.

Seabrook Foods, Inc. v. Bar-Well Foods Ltd., 568 F.2d 1342, 1344 (C.C.P.A.1977). The *Seabrook* test is the most useful of the three tests, in my view, because it clarifies the importance of market context. The *Seabrook* test asks "whether the design, shape or combination of elements is so unique, unusual or unexpected in this market that one can assume without proof that it will automatically be perceived by customers as an indici[um] of origin." * * * Any test of inherent distinctiveness must ask, "Inherently distinctive as compared to what?" The various tests of functionality, discussed in greater detail infra, serve much the same purpose; they ask whether a given design is functionally necessary in a given market (and therefore common) or whether it is more akin to a hood ornament. * * *

The *Seabrook* approach is fully consistent with the case law in the Second Circuit. Before *Two Pesos*, the question of market context generally arose in light of the so-called functionality defense. In the wake of *Two Pesos*, this circuit has continued to apply a *Seabrook*-type analysis to the puzzle of inherent distinctiveness. In *Knitwaves*, the court examined the clothing market and concluded that when people buy clothing, they do not tend to use overall design as an indicator of source. *Knitwaves* also quoted approvingly from the Restatement (Third) of Unfair Competition, which asks whether "because of the nature of the [design] and the context in which it is used, prospective purchasers are likely to perceive it" as a source-identifier. When considered in this light, *Knitwaves*'s emphasis on the producer's "intent" may be analogous to asking, "What is the custom in this industry?" Or: "How does this industry, including this claimant, use designs?"

Before applying these principles to the instant case, it is appropriate to address some common misconceptions about the interplay of patent law and trade dress law. The plaintiff in this case contends that because the Matrix chair has received a design patent, this patent constitutes proof of inherent distinctiveness. The defendant argues just the opposite: that KI is unlawfully seeking to extend its expired patent monopoly, and that patented designs can never claim the protection of trade dress law. Both arguments are incorrect. A design patent is analytically distinct from a protectable trade dress, and industrial products may qualify for both kinds of protection without violating the policy goals of either patent or trade dress law. * * * When a design patent expires, the design becomes copyable. It may not, however, be copied in such a way that customers are deceived about what they are buying.

The existence of a design patent, however, is relevant to the functionality defense. Because a design patent is granted only for non- functional designs, it can serve as evidence that a plaintiff's trade dress is not functional. This is not tantamount to saying, however, that a design patent always serves as a trademark. At best, a design patent can only help rebut the functionality defense; it cannot do the whole job of proving inherent distinctiveness. The plaintiff still needs to show that, in its market at the time of the alleged infringement, the design is both ornamental and deserving of trade dress protection.

The problem [of functionality], of course, is that a design feature may be both functional and pleasing. (Indeed, many industrial designs combine these two elements.) This has led the courts into a hopeless tangle about the difference between aesthetics and functionality. Some courts developed a doctrine of "aesthetic functionality" that was both unnecessary and illogical. If a pleasing design helped to sell a product, so the theory went, its aesthetic appeal became an "essential" competitive quality that could not in fairness be denied to others. Thus the doctrine of "aesthetic functionality" denied trade dress protection to design features whose only sin was to delight the senses. * * *

* * * *Knitwaves* seems to instruct that a design can serve only one primary purpose: either aesthetic or source-identifying, but not both. This approach is neither helpful nor logical. In the instant case, it would force me to determine whether the plaintiff chose its chair design because it was attractive or because it was meant to serve as a trademark (i.e., a source identifier). The likely answer is, both. Moreover, this plaintiff never had to choose between the two objectives because the design was patented and could not be copied. In more general terms, every producer hopes to create a design that is more pleasing than not and that that design will be associated with it. Every producer hopes that it and its trade dress will be remembered because its design is pleasing, not because it is ugly. * * *

Applying these principles to the facts before me, I conclude that plaintiff KI has a protectable trade dress in the overall look of its Matrix chair. Although each of the individual design elements serves both functional and aesthetic purposes, it is the overall look that I must consider. I base my following conclusions on the photographs of competing chairs submitted by the parties and the accompanying affidavits describing the high density stacking chair market. On this evidence, I find that the seat, the back and the Z- shaped connecting rods of the KI chair give the Matrix chair a distinctive overall look. Applying *Seabrook*, I find that this particular look is unique among high density stacking chairs and that manufacturers of these chairs generally seek unique designs as an important source identifier. Unlike the clothing industry, in which labels are prominent because designs change frequently, the chair industry does not rely heavily on labels to communicate with customers and its designs remain stable over time. Although the chair manufacturers' names appear prominently on shipping containers and hang tags, customers generally throw these away. The sole permanent label is molded into the plastic underneath the seat, where a sophisticated buyer would find it but a less sophisticated one might not. No consumer would see the label without looking for it.

* * *

To determine whether the design features at issue are functional, I must ask whether their shape is "dictated by the functions to be performed." The answer is clearly no. The function of a chair is to provide a place to sit. A stacking chair, in addition, must stack. On the evidence before me, many other designs serve these functions equally well. Therefore I find that the design features at issue are ornamental, not functional. Next I must address whether there are sufficient alternative arrangements to permit competition. I find that defendant has not met its burden of showing that the supply of alternative designs would be unduly limited if defendant could not replicate the Matrix chair.

NOTES

1. *Knitwaves* and *Duraco*, both cited in Krueger are important examples of the courts efforts to apply inherent distinctiveness to trade dress. Below are the trade dresses involved in those cases. Do they help cast light on the difficulties in this area?

Leaf and Squirrel Sweaters: Plaintiff's (left) and Defendant's (right)

Duraco's Grecian Urn

Joy Plastic's Grecian Urn

2. Which of the various tests for inherent distinctiveness makes the most sense? Does it make a difference whether the case involves product packaging as distinct from the configuration of the product itself? Do you agree with Judge Sotomayor in *Krueger* that *Two Pesos* involved a case of "product design"?

3. Judge Sotomayor seems to suggest that a product design is either functional or inherently distinctive. If this were true there would be no room for application of the secondary meaning doctrine because a functional design cannot be protected even if it has acquired some distinctiveness. Can you think of a product design feature that would be descriptive but not functional?

4. *Product Configurations.* Both before and after *Two Pesos*, courts have suggested that product configurations could not be subjected to the same test as product packaging. The Second Circuit applied the *Abercrombie* classifications to packaging in The Paddington Corp. v. Attiki Importers & Distributors, 996 F.2d 577 (2d Cir. 1993) (competing bottles of Ouzo, a Greek alcoholic beverage).

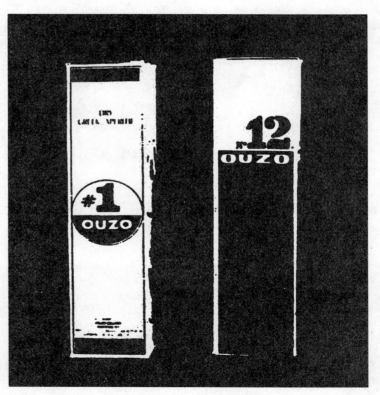

Defendants packaging (left); plaintiff's packaging (right)

The court found that a custom of an industry to package products in a particular way made the packaging "generic". As an example of a descriptive trade dress the court suggested an illustration of a shining car on a bottle of car wax. However, in *Knitwaves*, cited in *Krueger*, the court held that *Paddington* was not applicable to product features as oppose to product packaging:

> Not only does the classification of marks into "generic," "descriptive," "suggestive," or "arbitrary or fanciful" make little sense when applied to product features, but it would have the unwelcome, and likely unintended, result of treating a class of product features as "inherently distinctive," and thus eligible for trade dress protection, even though they were never intended to serve a source-identifying function.

The Second Circuit continued to recognize the distinction between configurations and packaging in Fun-Damental Too, Ltd. v. Gemmy industries Corp, 111 F.3d 993 (2d Cir. 1997) (the *Abercrombie* classification applies to packaging but not to configurations).

Duraco Products, Inc. v. Joy Plastic Enterprises, LTD., 40 F.3d 1431 (3rd Cir. 1994), also cited in *Krueger,* involved Duraco's "Grecian Classics" plastic planters which were plastic planters made to look like marble. The district court denied protection on the grounds that the trade dress was at best "descriptive", was without secondary meaning, and was functional. Judge Becker affirmed but took a separate path. Rejecting the traditional *Abercrombie* classification, he suggested a new approach:

> Synthesizing the principles explored in the preceding sections, we think that there is a proper set of circumstances for treating a product configuration as inherently distinctive. These circumstances are characterized by a high probability that a product configuration serves a virtually exclusively identifying function for consumers — where the concerns over "theft" of an identifying feature or combination or arrangement of features and the cost to an enterprise of gaining and proving secondary meaning outweigh concerns over inhibiting competition, and where consumers are especially likely to perceive a connection between the product's configuration and its source. In particular, we think that, to be inherently distinctive, a product configuration — comprising a product feature or some particular combination or arrangement of product features — for which Lanham Act protection is sought must be (i) unusual and memorable; (ii) conceptually separable from the product; and (iii) likely to serve primarily as a designator of origin of the product.

For a case rejecting the *Abercrombie* analysis and applying the test of determining whether the configuration is "unique, unusual or unexpected" see Publications International, LTD v. Landoll, Inc., 1997 WL 769349 (N.D. Ill. 1997)

5. The Restatement, Third, of Unfair Competition § 16, Comment *b* (1995) acknowledges that "unique and prominent" trade dress may be inherently distinctive. However, the Restatement goes on to provide:

> As a practical matter, however, it is less common for consumers to recognize the design of a product or product feature as an indication of

source. Product features are more likely to be seen merely as utilitarian or ornamental aspects of the goods. In addition, the competitive interest in copying product designs is more substantial than in the case of packaging, containers, labels, and related subject matter. Product designs are therefore not ordinarily considered inherently distinctive and are thus normally protected only upon proof of secondary meaning.

Vornado Air Circulation Systems, Inc. v. Duracraft Corporation

United States Court of Appeals for the Tenth Circuit, 1995
58 F.3d 1498, cert. denied 516 U.S. 1067 (1996)

■ STEPHEN H. ANDERSON, CIRCUIT JUDGE.

This case presents an issue of first impression in our circuit concerning the intersection of the Patent Act and the Lanham Trade-Mark Act. We must decide whether a product configuration is entitled to trade dress protection when it is or has been a significant inventive component of an invention covered by a utility patent.

After expiration of any patents or copyrights on an invention, that invention normally passes into the public domain and can be freely copied by anyone. The district court found, however, that because the spiral structure of the household fan grill in question is "nonfunctional," a status largely determined by the availability of enough alternative grill designs so that other fan manufacturers can effectively compete without it, the grill can serve as trade dress. The court held that the grill could be protected under Lanham Act section 43(a) against copying by competitors, because that copying was likely to confuse consumers.

The court's injunction effectively prevents defendant Duracraft Corp. from ever practicing the full invention embodied in the patented fans of plaintiff Vornado Air Circulation Systems, Inc., after Vornado's utility patents expire. For the reasons discussed below, we find this result to be untenable. We hold that although a product configuration must be nonfunctional in order to be protected as trade dress under section 43(a), not every nonfunctional configuration is eligible for that protection. Where a product configuration is a significant inventive component of an invention covered by a utility patent, so that without it the invention cannot fairly be said to be the same invention, patent policy dictates that it enter into the public domain when the utility patents on the fans expire. To ensure that result, it cannot receive trade dress protection under section 43(a). The district court's order is reversed.

* * *

The idea of using a spiral grill on a fan is not new. * * * Vornado began selling its fans with spiral grills in November 1988, at a time when it was the only fan company using that type of grill. On January 9, 1989,

If no patent would they have had trade dress protection?

Vornado's founders, Donald J. Moore and Michael C. Coup, applied for a utility patent on their ducted fan with a spiral grill. They asserted, among other things, that their spiral grill produced an optimum air flow, although their own tests had shown that it performed about the same as the more common straight radial grill, and later tests suggested that some other grills worked better in some respects.

Their patent application claimed a fan with multiple features, including the spiral grill. The inventive aspect of Vornado's spiral grill was that the point of maximum lateral spacing between the curved vanes was moved inboard from the grill's outer radius, so that it was at the impeller blade's point of maximum power. Vornado emphasizes that its fan grill was not patentable by itself because a spiral grill per se was already in the public domain as "prior art," a patent law term for what was already known from previous patents or other sources.

On May 22, 1990, Messrs. Moore and Coup were issued a utility patent. They subsequently applied for and on February 22, 1994, were granted a reissue patent expanding their claims, including those that involved the arcuate-shaped grill vane structure.

Vornado advertised its grill as the "Patented AirTensity TM Grill," although the company had no separate patent on the grill. Between January 1989 and August 1990, Vornado sold about 135,000 fans. In its advertising, the company touted the grill as a "true achievement in aerodynamic efficiency," "the result of determinant ergonomic design," with "[u]nique AirTensity TM vortex action," accomplishing "a high degree of safety and functionality."

In August 1990, Duracraft began offering an inexpensive electric household fan called the Model DT-7 "Turbo Fan." The grill on Duracraft's Turbo Fan incorporated a spiral vane structure that was copied from Vornado's considerably more expensive fan models but was purposely designed not to infringe Vornado's patent. Apart from its look-alike grill and some aspects of the fan blade design, the Turbo Fan differed significantly from Vornado's fans in its overall configuration, its base and duct structure, its center knob, neon colors, packaging, labeling, and price. The box in which the Turbo Fan came had a circle cut out of the front so that the grill design showed through and was emphasized when the fan was displayed in its box.

By November 1992, Duracraft had sold nearly one million Turbo Fans in the United States. The Turbo Fan was the company's second-largest-selling household fan product.

Vornado sued, alleging that Duracraft had intentionally copied Vornado's grill design, but both sides agreed that the Turbo Fan did not infringe Vornado's patents. Vornado argued during the bench trial that the curved vanes in the "Patented AirTensity Grill" were legally nonfunctional, which they had to be in order to be protected as trade dress under section 43(a).

The district court found that the spiral grill was functional in a lay sense but not in a legal sense, based on our definition of trade dress functionality in terms of the competitive need to use a feature. The district court found that Vornado's grill did in fact perform a unique function in the way that it shaped the flow of air coming from the fan, but the difference in air flow produced by it as compared with other grill designs was not great enough for a customer to perceive, so it made no competitive difference. The court also noted that other feasible grill structures could easily do as well on other relevant performance tests, and the spiral grill was not shown to be cheaper to manufacture.

The district court did not find enough evidence to support a finding of aesthetic functionality, a type of functionality based on decorativeness or attractiveness, which we have previously recognized. Nor did the district court find that Duracraft would suffer a marketing disadvantage if it could not use the spiral grill. The court found that the grill's value lay not in its operational attributes but primarily in its appearance, which the court said suggests something about the fan's performance and creatively suggests Vornado's identity.

The court found that the grill design was nonfunctional and held that trade dress protection of nonfunctional product configurations under the Lanham Act was not incompatible with patent law. The court further found that the grill design was a suggestive symbol combined with a device, and thus inherently distinctive, so that no showing of secondary meaning was required. The court found that consumers were likely to be confused by Duracraft's use of a similar grill, and granted Vornado an injunction but no damages on the section 43(a) claim.

* * *

* * * Duracraft argues that *Bonito Boats* means that useful product features, which comprise utility patent subject matter, may not be protected as trademarks or trade dress and thereby be permanently monopolized by a single producer.

Vornado replies that there is no problem or inconsistency in its ability to obtain both patent protection for its fan in toto and trade dress protection for its spiral grill. Vornado argues 1) that of the main Supreme Court cases on which Duracraft relies, *Sears, Compco,* and *Bonito Boats* are all distinguishable, and *Kellogg* predates the Lanham Act; 2) that the Supreme Court and Congress both have said section 43(a) applies to product shapes; and 3) that the functionality doctrine properly reconciles the Patent Act with the Lanham Act, for if a product feature is not necessary to competition, no patent law purpose is served by allowing it to be copied.

We find each of these arguments wanting. At the same time, we need not rule as broadly as Duracraft would have us do either. We need not deal with whether every useful or potentially patentable product configuration is excluded from trade dress protection. Vornado does not argue that its grill was not a significant inventive component of its patented fans. Without that particular grill, the Vornado fan would not be the same invention that it is. We focus, therefore, on the law with regard to product configurations that are patented inventions or significant components thereof, and whether these product configurations can serve as trade dress.

[The court discussed the major Supreme Court preemption cases but held that notwithstanding some distinctions "we find it impossible to ignore the clear and continuing trend they collectively manifest in favor of the public's right to copy." The court also found nothing in the legislative history of § 43(a) or the patent act to help resolve the issue.]

Despite what appears to be a widespread perception that product configurations covered by utility patents are automatically functional for Lanham Act purposes, the district court in our case ably demonstrated that this is not so. Configurations can simultaneously be patentably useful, novel, and nonobvious and also nonfunctional, in trade dress parlance.

patents can also be TM.

This is the case because to meet patent law's usefulness requirement, a product need not be better than other alternatives or essential to competition. To obtain a utility patent, an inventor need only show that an invention is 1) useful in the sense of serving some identified, beneficial purpose, and then—much more difficult to prove—that it is 2) novel, i.e., not previously known, and 3) nonobvious, or sufficiently inventive, in light of prior art.

Functionality, by contrast, has been defined both by our circuit, and more recently by the Supreme Court, in terms of competitive need. If competitors need to be able to use a particular configuration in order to make an equally competitive product, it is functional, but if they do not, it may be nonfunctional. The availability of equally satisfactory alternatives for a particular feature, and not its inherent usefulness, is often the fulcrum on which Lanham Act functionality analysis turns.

As some courts have explained the competitive need test, it conceivably could allow one producer to permanently appropriate any distinctive patented invention for exclusive trademark or trade dress use as soon as its patent expired and sufficient alternatives became available to make the invention no longer one of a few superior designs.

Given that the functionality doctrine does not eliminate overlap between the Patent Act and the Lanham Act, we must decide whether Vornado is right that this doctrine nevertheless should be used to limit patent law's public domain.

Except to the extent that Congress has clearly indicated which of two statutes it wishes to prevail in the event of a conflict, we must interpret and apply them in a way that preserves the purposes of both and fosters harmony between them. Where, as here, both cannot apply, we look to their fundamental purposes to choose which one must give way.

First, patent law seeks to foster and reward invention; second, it promotes disclosure of inventions to stimulate further innovation and to permit the public to practice the invention once the patent expires; third, the stringent requirements for patent protection seek to assure that ideas in the public domain remain there for the free use of the public.

* * *

In this respect, it is significant that the framers of the patent system did not require an inventor to demonstrate an invention's superiority to existing products in order to qualify for a patent. That they did not do so tells us that the patent system seeks not only superior inventions but also a multiplicity of inventions. A variety of choices is more likely to satisfy the desires of a greater number of consumers than is a single set of products deemed "optimal" in some average sense by patent examiners and/or judges. And the ability to intermingle and extrapolate from many inventors' solutions to the same problem is more likely to lead to further technological advances than is a single, linear approach seeking to advance one "superior" line of research and development. We conclude that patent law seeks the invention and the passing into the public domain of even what trade dress law would consider nonfunctional inventions.

Allowing an inventor both patent and trade dress protection in a configuration would not necessarily inhibit invention directly. Quite the opposite, this double benefit would probably increase an inventor's direct incentives to pursue an idea. But the inventor's supply of ideas itself and freedom to experiment with them might diminish if the inventor had to do a competitive market analysis before adopting useful features from others' inventions once their patents expired.

As to the second patent law objective, encouraging public disclosure of inventions, it is not immediately apparent what effect, if any, the trade dress protection in question would have. But this case clearly shows that trade dress protection can directly interfere with the public's ability to practice patented inventions after the patents have expired, and that it undermines the principle that ideas in the public domain should stay there. We conclude that the inability freely to copy significant features of patented products after the patents expire impinges seriously upon the patent system's core goals, even when those features are not necessary to competition.

* * *

The degree to which a producer's goodwill will be harmed by the copying of product configurations correlates with the degree of consumer confusion as to source or sponsorship that is likely to result from the copying. We do not doubt that at least some consumers are likely to ignore product labels, names, and packaging and look only to the design of product features to tell one brand from another. These consumers are likely to be confused by similar product designs, and to the degree that this confusion is tolerated, the goals of the Lanham Act will be undermined.

But the Lanham Act, like common-law unfair competition law and most state unfair competition statutes, has never provided absolute protection against all consumer confusion as to source or sponsorship.

* * *

We recognize also that consumer confusion resulting from the copying of product features is, in some measure, a self-fulfilling prophecy. To the degree that useful product configurations are protected as identifiers, consumers will come to rely on them for that purpose, but if copying is allowed, they will depend less on product shapes and more on labels and packaging.

We conclude that protecting against that degree of consumer confusion that may arise from the copying of configurations that are significant parts of patented inventions is, at best, a peripheral concern of section 43(a) of the Lanham Act.

Given, then, that core patent principles will be significantly undermined if we do not allow the copying in question, and peripheral Lanham Act protections will be denied if we do, our answer seems clear. Much has been said in this and other section 43(a) cases about whether a second competitor needs to use a particular product design to compete effectively. But where Lanham Act goals are not the only ones at stake, we must also examine the degree to which a first competitor needs to use a useful product feature instead of something else—a name, a label, a package—to establish its brand identity in the first place.

It would defy logic to assume that there are not almost always many more ways to identify a product than there are ways to make it.

We hold that where a disputed product configuration is part of a claim in a utility patent, and the configuration is a described, significant inventive aspect of the invention, so that without it the invention could not fairly be said to be the same invention, patent law prevents its protection as trade dress, even if the configuration is nonfunctional.

In future cases, the contribution of a particular configuration to the inventiveness of a patented product may not always be clear, and we do not wish to rule out the possibility that a court may appropriately conduct a factual inquiry to supplement its reading of the patent's claims and descriptions.

But in this case, we do not find it necessary to remand for such an inquiry. Vornado included the arcuate grill vane structure as an element of its patent claims and described the configuration as providing "an optimum air flow." Then, after the first patent issued and Vornado subsequently found evidence that other grill structures worked as well as or better than the spiral grill, Vornado did not repudiate or disclaim in any way the grill element of its patent. Instead, Vornado sought and received a reissue patent that expanded its claims with respect to the grill.

Even if we discount entirely Vornado's extensive advertising campaign emphasizing the importance of the "AirTensity Grill," this patent history on its face obviates any need for a remand on the question of inventive significance. We simply take Vornado at its word. Because the "Patented AirTensity Grill" is a significant inventive element of Vornado's patented fans, it cannot be protected as trade dress.

The district court's order is REVERSED.

NOTES

1. It would be possible to formulate an argument that trade dress protection for product configurations is preempted by the patent laws regardless of whether the configuration at issue was or had been patented. In Kohler Co. v. Moen Inc., 12 F.3d 632 (7th Cir. 1993) the Seventh Circuit considered whether in general trade dress protection for product configurations conflicted with the patent system and concluded it did not. Judge Cudahy dissented arguing that the Lanham Act federalized common law and thus was subject to the preemption arguments of *Sears, Compco,* and *Bonito Boats* and that the existence of both design and utility patent systems prevented common law (or Lanham Act) protection for product design.

2. If the plaintiff asserts trade dress protection under § 43(a), a federal statute, on what basis can the defendant claim the protection is "preempted" by another federal statute, i.e., the patent laws?

3. *Vornado* highlights the possible conflicts between the utility patent law and trade dress protection. One might suppose that since a utility patent must be "useful" and a "functional" design cannot be protected as trade dress, the conflict disappears. However, the term "useful" in the patent system requires some utility whereas "functionality" in trade dress doctrine requires a showing that competitors need the design in order to compete. The critical section of the patent statute is § 112 which imposes the rules for the specification and claims of a patent application. Consider that under this section the patent owner must set forth three separate things: (1) a written description of the invention so as to allow a person skilled in the art to practice the invention; (2) the "best mode contemplated by the inventor of carrying out his invention"; and (3) the precise elements of the specification the inventor claims as his or her invention. A product design disclosed in a patent can thus either be: (1) one of many designs useful in practicing the invention; (2) the "best mode" design for practicing the invention, or (3) a design specifically claimed by the inventor as the invention. Should designs in any or all of these categories be foreclosed from trade dress protection?

4. The interaction between trade dress protection and the utility patent system evolves around concepts of functionality since a utility patent must be a "useful" device. On the other hand, a design to be eligible for a design patent can not be useful but rather must be "ornamental". How do you think the court should evaluate the interaction between trade dress protection and the design patent law? A design infringes a patented design if it is "substantially similar". The test for "substantial similarity" for purposes of design patent infringement is whether the patented and the infringing designs resemble each other enough to cause the ordinary observer to be deceived into purchasing "one supposing it to be the other." If this duplicates the likelihood of confusion test for trademark infringement, should any trade dress protection be permitted? Is the substantial similarity test the same as the test for trademark infringement?

5. Does the same problem of preemption arise under the copyright statute? Suppose a company develops a comic book character who appears in copyrighted comic books. The company then makes a doll of the character and copyrights the doll. If another company starts to manufacturer a competing doll of the character is there both a copyright and a trade dress infringement claim? The test for copyright infringement involves consideration of whether the second doll is "substantially similar". See Campbell v. Osmond, 917 F. Supp. 1574 (M.D.Fla. 1996).

(3) Incontestability: Sections 14, 15 & 33 of the Lanham Act

The Lanham Act introduced the concept of "incontestability" to trademark law. The incontestability of a trademark is determined by the interaction of §§ 14, 15, and 33 of the Act.

Section 14 provides the grounds upon which the registration of a mark on the Principal Register can be cancelled. The section does not use the term "incontestable". It authorizes any person "who believes that he is or will be damaged" by the registration to petition to cancel the registration. Subsection (1) allows cancellation within 5 years of the initial registration of the mark if the petitioner can demonstrate any defect in the registration. After the five year period, cancellation is only available on the grounds listed in subsections (3)–(5).

Section 15 provides that once a mark is used for five consecutive years subsequent to the date of its registration, "the right of the registrant *to use* such registered mark in commerce shall be incontestable." (emphasis added). Section 15 speaks to use; section 14 speaks to cancellation. However, section 15 incorporates as exceptions to the incontestable right the grounds in section 14 for which marks can be cancelled at any time.

Section 33 describes the effect of any registration under the Act. Subsection (a) makes the registration alone "prima facie evidence" of the registrants ownership and rights in the mark but preserves "any legal or equitable defense or defect" that could be asserted against an unregistered mark. In contrast, subsection (b) governs if the registration of the mark has become "incontestable". An incontestable registration becomes "conclusive" evidence of the registrant's "exclusive" right to use the mark subject only to those defenses specified in the subsection. Note, however, that the provisions in § 14 authorizing cancellation "at any time" are exceptions to incontestability under § 15 and thus limit the reach of § 33(b).

Park 'n Fly, Inc. v. Dollar Park and Fly, Inc.

Supreme Court of the United States, 1985.
469 U.S. 189, 105 S.Ct. 658, 83 L.Ed.2d 582.

[The petitioner operates long-term parking lots near airports in a variety of cities including San Francisco and in 1971 secured a Lanham Act registration for its mark "Park 'N Fly". In 1977 it filed an affidavit required by § 15, 15 U.S.C. § 1065, stating the mark had been registered and in continuous use for five consecutive years. Respondent also provides long-term airport parking services under its trademark "Dollar Park and Fly" in Portland, Oregon. Petitioner filed an infringement action against the respondent and respondent counterclaimed seeking cancellation of the registration. Respondent argued the petitioner's mark was unenforceable because it was merely descriptive. The District Court found for petitioner holding that an incontestable mark cannot be challenged on the grounds that it is merely descriptive. The Ninth Circuit reversed holding that incontestability provides a defense against cancellation but may not be used offensively to enjoin another's use. The United States Supreme Court granted certiorari to resolve a dispute between the circuits on the scope of the incontestability provisions.]

■ JUSTICE O'CONNOR delivered the opinion of the Court.

* * *

This case requires us to consider the effect of the incontestability provisions of the Lanham Act in the context of an infringement action defended on the grounds that the mark is merely descriptive. Statutory construction must begin with the language employed by Congress and the assumption that the ordinary meaning of that language accurately expresses the legislative purpose.

* * *

One searches the language of the Lanham Act in vain to find any support for the offensive/defensive distinction applied by the Court of Appeals. The statute nowhere distinguishes between a registrant's offensive and defensive use of an incontestable mark. On the contrary, § 33(b)'s declaration that the registrant has an "exclusive right" to use the mark indicates that incontestable status may be used to enjoin infringement by others. A conclusion that such infringement cannot be enjoined renders meaningless the "exclusive right" recognized by the statute. Moreover, the language in three of the defenses enumerated in § 33(b) clearly contemplates the use of incontestability in infringement actions by plaintiffs. See §§ 33(b)(4)–(6), 15 U.S.C. §§ 1115(b)(4)–(6).

The language of the Lanham Act also refutes any conclusion that an incontestable mark may be challenged as merely descriptive. A mark that is merely descriptive of an applicant's goods or services is not registrable unless the mark has secondary meaning. Before a mark achieves incontestable status, registration provides prima facie evidence of the registrant's exclusive right to use the mark in commerce. § 33(a), 15 U.S.C. § 1115(a). The Lanham Act expressly provides that before a mark becomes incontestable an opposing party may prove any legal or equitable defense which might have been asserted if the mark had not been registered. Ibid. Thus, § 33(a) would have allowed respondent to challenge petitioner's mark as merely descriptive if the mark had not become incontestable. With respect to incontestable marks, however, § 33(b) provides that registration is *conclusive* evidence of the registrant's exclusive right to use the mark, subject to the conditions of § 15 and the seven defenses enumerated in § 33(b) itself. Mere descriptiveness is not recognized by either § 15 or § 33(b) as a basis for challenging an incontestable mark.

* * *

III

Nothing in the legislative history of the Lanham Act supports a departure from the plain language of the statutory provisions concerning incontestability. * * * The incontestability provisions, as the proponents of the Lanham Act emphasized, provide a means for the registrant to quiet title in the ownership of his mark. The opportunity to obtain incontestable status by satisfying the requirements of § 15 thus encourages producers to cultivate the good will associated with a particular mark. This function of the incontestability provisions would be utterly frustrated if the holder of an incontestable mark could not enjoin infringement by others so long as they established that the mark would not be registrable but for its incontestable status.

Respondent argues, however, that enforcing petitioner's mark would conflict with the goals of the Lanham Act because the mark is merely descriptive and should never have been registered in the first place.

* * *

Respondent's argument that enforcing petitioner's mark will not promote the goals of the Lanham Act is misdirected. Arguments similar to those now urged by respondent were in fact considered by Congress in hearings on the Lanham Act. * * * These concerns were answered by proponents of the Lanham Act, who noted that a merely descriptive mark cannot be registered unless the Commissioner finds that it has secondary meaning. Id., at 108, 113 (testimony of Karl Pohl, U.S. Trade Mark Assn.). Moreover, a mark can be challenged for five years prior to its attaining incontestable status. Id., at 114 (remarks of Rep. Lanham).

* * *

VI

We conclude that the holder of a registered mark may rely on incontestability to enjoin infringement and that such an action may not be defended on the grounds that the mark is merely descriptive. The judgment of the Court of Appeals is reversed and the case is remanded for further proceedings consistent with this opinion.

It is so ordered.

JUSTICE STEVENS, dissenting.

* * *

The mark "Park 'N Fly" is at best merely descriptive in the context of airport parking. * * * Petitioner never submitted any such proof to the Commissioner, or indeed to the District Court in this case. Thus, the registration plainly violated the Act.

* * *

If the registrant of a merely descriptive mark complies with the statutory requirement that prima-facie evidence of secondary meaning must be submitted to the Patent and Trademark Office, it is entirely consistent with the policy of the Act to accord the mark incontestable status after an additional five years of continued use. For if no rival contests the registration in that period, it is reasonable to presume that the initial prima-facie showing of distinctiveness could not be rebutted. But if no proof of secondary meaning is ever presented, either to the Patent and Trademark Office or to a court, there is simply no rational basis for leaping to the conclusion that the passage of time has transformed an inherently defective mark into an incontestable mark.

* * *

Congress enacted the Lanham Act "to secure trade-mark owners in the goodwill which they have built up." But without a showing of secondary meaning, there is no basis upon which to conclude that petitioner has built up any good will that is secured by the mark "Park 'N-Fly." In fact, without a showing of secondary meaning, we should presume that petitioner's business appears to the consuming public to be just another anonymous, indistinguishable parking lot. When enacting the Lanham Act, Congress also wanted to "protect the public from imposition by the use of counterfeit and imitated marks and false trade descriptions." Upon this record there appears no danger of this occurrence, and as a practical matter, without any showing that the public can specifically identify petitioner's service, it seems difficult to believe that anyone would imitate petitioner's marks, or that such imitation, even if it occurred, would be likely to confuse anybody.

On the basis of the record in this case, it is reasonable to infer that the operators of parking lots in the vicinity of airports may make use of the words "park and fly" simply because those words provide a ready description of their businesses, rather than because of any desire to exploit petitioner's good will. There is a well-recognized public interest in prohibiting the commercial monopolization of phrases such as "park and fly." * * *

* * *

In exercising its broad power to do equity, the federal courts certainly can take into account the tension between the apparent meaning of § 33(b) and the plain command in § 2(e), (f) of the Act prohibiting the registration of a merely descriptive mark without any proof of secondary meaning. Because it would be "demonstrably at odds with the intent of Congress" to grant incontestable status to a mark that was not eligible for registration in the first place, the Court is surely authorized to require compliance with § 2(f) before granting relief on the basis of § 33(b).

The Legislative History

The language of § 2(e), (f) expressly demonstrates Congress' concern over granting monopoly privileges in merely descriptive marks. However, its failure to include mere descriptiveness in its laundry list of grounds on which incontestability could be challenged is interpreted by the Court today as evidence of congressional approval of incontestable status for all merely descriptive marks.

This history is unpersuasive because it is perfectly clear that the failure to include mere descriptiveness among the grounds for challenging incontestability was based on the understanding that such a mark would not be registered without a showing of secondary meaning. To read Congress' failure as equivalent to an endorsement of incontestable status for merely descriptive marks without secondary meaning can only be described as perverse.

The Practical Argument

The Court suggests that my reading of the Act "effectively emasculates § 33(b) under the circumstances of this case." But my reading would simply require the owner of a merely descriptive mark to prove secondary meaning before obtaining any benefit from incontestability. If a mark is in fact "distinctive of the applicant's goods in commerce" as § 2(f) requires, that burden should not be onerous. If the mark does not have any such secondary meaning, the burden of course could not be met. But if that be the case, the purposes of the Act are served, not frustrated, by requiring adherence to the statutory procedure mandated by Congress.

* * *

NOTES

1. Do the incontestability provisions of the Lanham Act upset the balance trademark law attempts to achieve between protecting competition and prohibiting consumer confusion? Are there other policies that support the provisions?

2. Section 33(b) (as well as § 14(3)) makes "abandonment by the registrant" a defense. Can you construct an argument that a mark that is "merely descriptive" has in fact lost "its significance as a mark" under the definition of abandonment in § 45 and accordingly has been "abandoned"? For an argument that the economic function of trademarks would best be enhanced by permitting persons to challenge an incontestable mark on the basis of lack of current distinctiveness, see Naresh, Incontestability and Rights in Descriptive Marks, 53 U.Chi.L.Rev. 953 (1986).

3. The Lanham Act does not expressly provide for the defense of functionality. Can the owner of a functional product configuration obtain a monopoly if it achieves an incontestable registration before competitors seek to enter the market? In Shakespeare Co. v. Silstar Corp. Of America, Inc., 9 F.3d 1091 (4th Cir. 1993) cert. denied, 511 U.S. 1127 (1994), the court held that since functionality is not a listed defense it could not be asserted in a case where the defendant incorporated a clear, fiberglass tip on a fishing rod that was similar to the tip first used by the plaintiff. On remand, however, the district court held that the defendant's use of the functional fiberglass tip established a "fair use" defense. Section 33(b)(4) provides for a fair use defense against an incontestable mark. The Fourth Circuit affirmed. Shakespeare Co. v. Siltar Corp. Of America, Inc., 110 F.3d 234(4th Cir. 1997), cert. denied, 118 S.Ct. 688 (1998).

Does a functional element fit comfortably into the language of 33(b)(4)? Is it descriptive? Was the fiberglass tip "a use, other than as a mark"? If there was evidence that the defendant in *Shakespeare* intentionally copied the tip (which there was), could its actions have been "in good faith only to describe the goods . . ."?

4. A mark may be refused registration under § 2(d) if it is likely to cause confusion with a preexisting mark. However, after five years a registration may not be canceled for this reason under § 14. However § 14(3) permits cancellation "at any time" if the registration was obtained contrary to § 2(a). This section provides a mark may not be registered if it falsely suggests "a connection with persons, living or dead . . . ." Aren't § 2(a) and § 2(d) really the same in that a mark that creates a likelihood of confusion at the same time suggests a connection between the goods and another "person" (§ 45 defines "person" to include corporations)? The courts have been troubled by this apparent method of escaping the 5 year limit for cancellation and accordingly destroying the incontestable nature of a mark. See University of Notre Dame Du Lac v. J.C. Gourmet Food Imports Co., Inc., 703 F.2d 1372 (Fed.Cir.1983) where the University objected to the defendant's sale of "Notre Dame" cheese. The court approved of earlier rulings by the Trademark Trial and Appeal Board that in a trademark action under § 2(a) intent to deceive as well as likelihood of confusion must be shown. Even though the University had not sold cheese or related products it could also rely on § 2(a) if it could show an injury similar to violation of its right of privacy. However, that required that the use of the term "Notre Dame" "point uniquely" to the University. Noting that the term is used for churches as well as the University, the court denied relief.

C. Problems of Priority and Infringement
(1) Adoption, Affixation and Use

Blue Bell, Inc. v. Farah Mfg. Co., Inc.

United States Court of Appeals, Fifth Circuit, 1975.
508 F.2d 1260.

■ GEWIN, CIRCUIT JUDGE:

In the spring and summer of 1973 two prominent manufacturers of men's clothing created identical trademarks for goods substantially identical in appearance. Though the record offers no indication of bad faith in the design and adoption of the labels, both Farah Manufacturing Company (Farah) and Blue Bell, Inc. (Blue Bell) devised the mark "Time Out" for new lines of men's slacks and shirts. Both parties market their goods on a national scale, so they agree that joint utilization of the same trademark would confuse the buying public. Thus, the only question presented for our review is which party established prior use of the mark in trade. A response to that seemingly innocuous inquiry, however, requires us to define the chameleonic term "use" as it has developed in trademark law.

* * *

Farah conceived of the Time Out mark on May 16, after screening several possible titles for its new stretch menswear. Two days later the firm adopted an hourglass logo and authorized an extensive advertising campaign bearing the new insignia. Farah presented its fall line of clothing, including Time Out slacks, to sales personnel on June 5. In the meantime, patent counsel had given clearance for use of the mark after scrutiny of current federal registrations then on file. One of Farah's top executives demonstrated samples of the Time Out garments to large customers in Washington, D.C. and New York, though labels were not attached to the slacks at that time. Tags containing the new design were completed June 27. With favorable evaluations of marketing potential from all sides, Farah sent one pair of slacks bearing the Time Out mark to each of its twelve regional sales managers on July 3. Sales personnel paid for the pants, and the garments became their property in case of loss.

Following the July 3 shipment, regional managers showed the goods to customers the following week. Farah received several orders and production began. Further shipments of sample garments were mailed to the rest of the sales force on July 11 and 14. Merchandising efforts were fully operative by the end of the month. The first shipments to customers, however, occurred in September.

Blue Bell, on the other hand, was concerned with creating an entire new division of men's clothing, as an avenue to reaching the "upstairs" market. Though initially to be housed at the Hicks-Ponder plant in El Paso, the new division would eventually enjoy separate headquarters. On June 18 Blue Bell management arrived at the name Time Out to identify both its new division and its new line of men's sportswear. Like Farah, it received clearance for use of the mark from counsel. Like Farah, it inaugurated an advertising campaign. Unlike Farah, however, Blue Bell did not ship a dozen marked articles of the new line to its sales personnel. Instead, Blue Bell authorized the manufacture of several hundred labels bearing the words Time Out and its logo shaped like a referee's hands forming a T. When the labels were completed on June 29, the head of the embryonic division flew them to El Paso. He instructed shipping personnel to affix the new Time Out labels to slacks that already bore the "Mr. Hicks" trademark. The new tags, of varying sizes and colors, were randomly attached to the left hip pocket button of slacks and the left hip pocket of jeans. Thus, although no change occurred in the design or manufacture of the pants, on July 5 several hundred pair left El Paso with two tags.

Blue Bell made intermittent shipments of the doubly-labeled slacks thereafter, though the out-of-state customers who received the goods had ordered clothing of the Mr. Hicks variety. Production of the new Time Out merchandise began in the latter part of August, and Blue Bell held a sales meeting to present its fall designs from September 4–6. Sales personnel solicited numerous orders, though shipments of the garments were not scheduled until October.

By the end of October Farah had received orders for 204,403 items of Time Out sportswear, representing a retail sales value of over $2,750,000. Blue Bell had received orders for 154,200 garments valued at over $900,000. Both parties had commenced extensive advertising campaigns for their respective Time Out sportswear.

Soon after discovering the similarity of their marks, Blue Bell sued Farah for common law trademark infringement and unfair competition, seeking to enjoin use of the Time Out trademark on men's clothing. Farah counter-claimed for similar injunctive relief. The district court found that Farah's July 3 shipment and sale constituted a valid use in trade, while Blue Bell's July 5 shipment was a mere "token" use insufficient at law to create trademark rights. While we affirm the result reached by the trial court as to Farah's priority of use, the legal grounds upon which we base our decision are somewhat different from those undergirding the district court's judgment.

Federal jurisdiction is predicated upon diversity of citizenship, since neither party has registered the mark pursuant to the Lanham Act. Given the operative facts surrounding manufacture and shipment from El Paso, the parties agree the Texas law of trademarks controls. In 1967 the state legislature enacted a Trademark Statute. Section 16.02 of the Act explains that a mark is "used" when it is affixed to the goods and "the goods are sold, displayed for sale, or otherwise publicly distributed." Thus the question whether Blue Bell or Farah established priority of trademark use depends upon interpretation of the cited provision. Unfortunately, there are no Texas cases construing § 16.02. This court must therefore determine what principles the highest state court would utilize in deciding such a question. In view of the statute's stated purpose to preserve common law rights, we conclude the Texas Supreme Court would apply the statutory provision in light of general principles of trademark law.

A trademark is a symbol (word, name, device or combination thereof) adopted and used by a merchant to identify his goods and distinguish them from articles produced by others. * * * Ownership of a mark requires a combination of both appropriation and use in trade. * * * Thus, neither conception of the mark * * * nor advertising alone establishes trademark rights at common law. * * * Rather, ownership of a trademark accrues when goods bearing the mark are placed on the market. * * *

The exclusive right to a trademark belongs to one who first uses it in connection with specified goods. * * * Such use need not have gained wide public recognition, * * * and even a single use in trade may sustain trademark rights if followed by continuous commercial utilization. * * *

The initial question presented for review is whether Farah's sale and shipment of slacks to twelve regional managers constitutes a valid first use of the Time Out mark. Blue Bell claims the July 3 sale was merely an internal transaction insufficiently public to secure trademark ownership. After consideration of pertinent authorities, we agree.

Secret, undisclosed internal shipments are generally inadequate to support the denomination "use." Trademark claims based upon shipments from a producer's plant to its sales office, and vice versa, have often been disallowed. * * * Though none of the cited cases dealt with *sales* to intra-corporate personnel, we perceive that fact to be a distinction without a difference. The sales were not made to customers, but served as an accounting device to charge the salesmen with their cost in case of loss. The fact that some sales managers actively solicited accounts bolsters the good faith of Farah's intended use, but does not meet our essential objection: that the "sales" were not made to the public.

The primary, perhaps singular purpose of a trademark is to provide a means for the consumer to separate or distinguish one manufacturer's goods from those of another. Personnel within a corporation can identify an item by style number or other unique code. A trademark aids the public in selecting particular goods. As stated by the First Circuit:

> It seems to us that although evidence of sales is highly persuasive, the question of use adequate to establish appropriation remains one to be decided on the facts of each case, and that evidence showing, first, adoption, and second, *use in a way sufficiently public to identify or distinguish the marked goods in an appropriate segment of the public mind as those of the adopter of the mark,* is competent to establish ownership.

New England Duplicating Co. v. Mendes, 190 F.2d 415, 418 (1st Cir.1951) (Emphasis added).

Farah nonetheless contends that a recent decision of the Board so undermines all prior cases relating to internal use that they should be ignored. In Standard Pressed Steel Co. v. Midwest Chrome Process Co., 183 U.S.P.Q. 758 (TTAB 1974) the agency held that internal shipment of marked goods from a producer's manufacturing plant to its sales office constitutes a valid "use in commerce" for registration purposes.

An axiom of trademark law has been that the right to register a mark is conditioned upon its actual use in trade. * * * Theoretically, then, common law use in trade should precede the use in commerce upon which Lanham Act registration is predicated. Arguably, since only a trademark owner can apply for registration, any activity adequate to create registrable rights must perforce also create trademark rights. A close examination of the Board's decision, however, dispels so mechanical a view. The tribunal took meticulous care to point out that its conclusion related solely to registration use rather than ownership use.

Priority of use and ownership of the Time Out mark are the only issues before this court. The language fashioned by the Board clearly indicates a desire to leave the common law of trademark ownership intact. The decision may demonstrate a reversal of the presumption that ownership rights precede registration rights, but it does not affect our analysis of common law use in trade. Farah had undertaken substantial preliminary steps toward marketing the Time Out garments, but it did not establish ownership of the mark by means of the July 3 shipment to its sales managers. The gist of trademark rights is actual use in trade. Though technically a "sale", the July 3 shipment was not "publicly distributed" within the purview of the Texas statute.

Blue Bell's July 5 shipment similarly failed to satisfy the prerequisites of a bona fide use in trade. Elementary tenets of trademark law require that labels or designs be affixed to the merchandise actually intended to bear the mark in commercial transactions. Furthermore, courts have recognized that the usefulness of a mark derives not only from its capacity to identify a certain manufacturer, but also from its ability to differentiate between different classes of goods produced by a single manufacturer. * * * Here customers had ordered slacks of the Mr. Hicks species, and Mr. Hicks was the fanciful mark distinguishing these slacks from all others. Blue Bell intended to use the Time Out mark on an entirely new line of men's sportswear, unique in style and cut, though none of the garments had yet been produced.

While goods may be identified by more than one trademark, the use of each mark must be bona fide. Mere adoption of a mark without bona fide use, in an attempt to reserve it for the future, will not create trademark rights. * * * In the instant case Blue Bell's attachment of a secondary label to an older line of goods manifests a bad faith attempt to reserve a mark. We cannot countenance such activities as a valid use in trade. Blue Bell therefore did not acquire trademark rights by virtue of its July 5 shipment.

We thus hold that neither Farah's July 3 shipment nor Blue Bell's July 5 shipment sufficed to create rights in the Time Out mark. Based on a desire to secure ownership of the mark and superiority over a competitor, both claims of alleged use were chronologically premature. Essentially, they took a time out to litigate their differences too early in the game. The question thus becomes whether we should continue to stop the clock for a remand or make a final call from the appellate bench. * * *

Careful examination of the record discloses that Farah shipped its first order of Time Out clothing to customers in September of 1973. Blue Bell, approximately one month behind its competitor at other relevant stages of development, did not mail its Time Out garments until at least October. Though sales to customers are not the *sine qua non* of trademark use, * * * they are determinative in the instant case. These sales constituted the first point at which the public had a chance to associate Time Out with a particular line of sportswear. Therefore, Farah established priority of trademark use; it is entitled to a decree permanently enjoining Blue Bell from utilization of the Time Out trademark on men's garments.

The judgment of the trial court is affirmed.

Warnervision Entertainment Inc. v. Empire of Carolina, Inc.

United States Court of Appeals, Second Circuit, 1996.
101 F.3d 259.

■ VAN GRAAFEILAND, CIRCUIT JUDGE:

Prior to 1988, an applicant for trademark registration had to have used the mark in commerce before making the application. Following the enactment of the ITU [intent-to-use] provisions in that year, a person could seek registration of a mark not already in commercial use by alleging a bona fide intent to use it. Registration may be granted only if, absent a grant of extension, the applicant files a statement of commercial use within six months of the date on which the Commissioner's notice of allowance pursuant to 15 U.S.C. § 1063(b) is issued. The ITU applicant is entitled to an extension of another six months, and may receive further extensions from the Commissioner for an additional twenty four months. If, but only if, the mark completes the registration process and is registered, the ITU applicant is granted a constructive use date retroactive to the ITU filing date. 15 U.S.C. § 1057(c). This retroactive dating of constructive use permits a more orderly development of the mark without the risk that priority will be lost. The issue we now address is whether the creator of a mark who files an ITU application pursuant to 15 U.S.C. § 1051(b) can be preliminarily enjoined from engaging in the commercial use required for full registration by 15 U.S.C. § 1051(d) on motion of the holder of a similar mark who commenced commercial use of its mark subsequent to the creator's ITU application but prior to the ITU applicant's commercial use. A brief statement of the pertinent facts follows.

On September 9, 1994, TLV sent the Patent and Trademark Office ("PTO") an ITU application for the mark "REAL WHEELS," stating an intent-to-use the mark in commerce on or in connection with [miniature scale toy vehicles]. The application was filed on September 23, 1994. Around the same time, two other companies, apparently acting in innocence and good faith, decided that the "REAL WHEELS" mark would fit the products they were preparing to market. One of them, Buddy L, a North Carolina manufacturer that had been marketing toy replicas of vehicles for many years, selected the name for its 1995 line of vehicle replicas. The other, WarnerVision Entertainment Inc., found the name suitable for certain of its home videos which featured motorized vehicles. The videos and vehicles were shrink-wrapped together in a single package. Both companies ordered trademark searches for conflicts in the name, but, because TLV's application had not yet reached the PTO database, no conflict was found.

Both companies then filed for registration of their mark. However, because WarnerVision's application was filed on January 3, 1995, three days before Buddy L's, it was approved, and Buddy L's was rejected. Buddy L nonetheless continued with its marketing efforts and entered into negotiations with TLV for a possible license based on TLV's ITU application.

Unfortunately, Buddy L encountered financial problems, and on March 3, 1995, it filed for relief under Chapter 11 of the Bankruptcy Law as a debtor in possession. Thereafter, in an auction sale approved by the Bankruptcy Court, Buddy L sold substantially all of its assets to Empire. On October 20, 1995, Empire purchased from TLV all of TLV's title and interest in and to the REAL WHEELS product line, trademarks and good will associated therewith, including the September 23, 1994 ITU application. At the same time, Empire licensed TLV to use the REAL WHEELS mark for toy automobiles. On November 13, 1995, WarnerVision brought the instant action.

In granting the preliminary injunction at issue, the district court quoted the Supreme Court's admonition in Connecticut Nat'l Bank v. Germain, 503 U.S. 249, 253–54(1992), to the effect that when the words of a statute are unambiguous, judicial inquiry as to its meaning is complete. We do not quarrel with this statement as a general proposition; however, we question its application in the instant case. Section 1057(c) of Title 15, the statute at issue, provides that, "[c]ontingent on the registration of a mark . . . the filing of the application to register such mark shall constitute constructive use of the mark, conferring a right of priority, nationwide in effect. . . ." Empire is not claiming constructive use based on registration. Registration will not take place until after the section 1051(d) statement of use is filed and further examination is had of the application for registration. Empire contends that the district court erred in granting the preliminary injunction which bars it from completing the ITU process by filing a factually supported statement of use.

We agree. Empire does not contend that the filing of its ITU application empowered it to seek affirmative or offensive relief precluding WarnerVision's use of the REAL WHEELS mark. It seeks instead to assert the ITU filing as a defense to WarnerVision's efforts to prevent it from completing the ITU registration process. In substance, Empire requests that the normal principles of preliminary injunction law be applied in the instant case. This accords with the stated intent of Congress that the Lanham Act would be governed by equitable principles, which Congress described as "the core of U.S. trademark jurisprudence." See S.Rep. No. 515, 100th Cong., 2d Sess. 30 (1988), reprinted in 1988 U.S.C.C.A.N. 5577, 5592.

As the International Trademark Association ("ITA") correctly notes at page 9 of its amicus brief, if Empire's ITU application cannot be used to defend against WarnerVision's application for a preliminary injunction, Empire will effectively be prevented from undertaking the use required to obtain registration. In short, granting a preliminary injunction to WarnerVision would prevent Empire from ever achieving use, registration and priority and would thus effectively and permanently terminate its rights as the holder of the ITU application. Quoting 2 McCarthy on Trademarks and Unfair Competition § 19.08[1][d] at 19–59 (3d ed. 1992), the ITA said "this result 'would encourage unscrupulous entrepreneurs to look in the record for new [intent-to-use] applications by large companies, rush in to make a few sales under the same mark and sue the large company, asking for a large settlement to permit the [intent-to-use] applicant to proceed on its plans for use of the mark.' " This vulnerability to pirates is precisely what the ITU enactments were designed to eliminate.

The ITU provisions permit the holder of an ITU application to use the mark in commerce, obtain registration, and thereby secure priority retroactive to the date of filing of the ITU application. Of course, this right or privilege is not indefinite; it endures only for the time allotted by the statute. But as long as an ITU applicant's privilege has not expired, a court may not enjoin it from making the use necessary for registration on the grounds that another party has used the mark subsequent to the filing of the ITU application. To permit such an injunction would eviscerate the ITU provisions and defeat their very purpose.

This is not to say that a holder of a "live" ITU application may never be enjoined from using its mark. If another party can demonstrate that it used the mark before the holder filed its ITU application or that the filing was for some reason invalid, then it may be entitled to an injunction. WarnerVision says that it made analogous use of the REAL WHEELS mark before TLV filed its ITU application and also that the assignment to Empire of TLV's ITU application was invalid. But the district court did not pass on these contentions, and we will not consider them in the first instance.

* * * We vacate that portion of the district court's orders that grants WarnerVision preliminary injunctive relief and remand to the district court for further proceedings not inconsistent with this opinion.

We affirm the district court's denial of Empire's application for a preliminary injunction enjoining WarnerVision from using the REAL WHEELS mark for toys outside the video cassette market. Empire does not claim that it may use TLV's ITU application offensively to obtain this injunction, and we express no opinion on this subject. Empire says only that Buddy L, a company it acquired in a bankruptcy sale, made analogous use of the mark prior to WarnerVision's first use of the mark. On the record before us, we cannot say that the district court abused its discretion in denying a preliminary injunction on this ground.

NOTES

1. The acquisition of trademark rights at common law requires adoption and use of the mark. The common law, as did the Trademark Act of 1905, also requires the mark be "affixed" (physically attached) to the goods or their container. Although the common law of unfair competition protects an unaffixed mark with secondary meaning, the date of affixation is important in establishing priority of use of the mark where there are competing claims. The *Blue Bell* case illustrates part of the problem associated with the "affixation" requirement given that Blue Bell's use of Time Out was not affixed to the actual goods to be marketed identified by the mark.

Passage of the Lanham Act relaxed but did not abandon the affixation requirement. Prior to 1989 § 45 of the Act defined "use in commerce" as use "on the goods or their containers or the displays associated therewith or on the tags or labels affixed thereto". This was broadened in the 1988 revisions to provide that "if the nature of the goods makes such placement impracticable, then on documents associated with the goods or their sale". The amendment was directed toward trademarking goods sold in bulk. Section 45 also defines "use" of service marks.

The affixation requirement and the Lanham Act prevent the establishment of trademark priority by advertising use alone. The use must be in connection with goods. Thus a manufacturer cannot preserve his rights to a mark prior to the availability and sale of the goods. See, In re Sanger Telecasters Inc., 1 U.S.P.Q.2d 1589 (TTAB 1986) (for service marks extensive advertising does not support registration prior to the actual rendition of services.)

2. A priority of use system creates a risk that pre-marketing investments in development of a trademark may be lost by an intervening use. Understandably courts are reluctant to cause a forfeit of this investment unless absolutely necessary. In Manhattan Industries, Inc. v. Sweater Bee by Banff, Ltd., 627 F.2d 628 (2d Cir. 1980) three separate companies began using the mark "Kimberly" for clothing on May 9, May 10, and May 11 respectively. The mark became available on May 7th when General Mills formally abandoned the mark. The Second Circuit essentially held that all of the uses were close enough in time to make selection of one winner inequitable and required each company to "differentiate its product from that of the other company * * *."

3. A descriptive mark is not "used" for purposes of priority until it has acquired secondary meaning. This means there is a possibility that a second-in-time user could acquire priority by massive advertising designed to more quickly achieve secondary meaning. This caused some courts to adopt the "secondary meaning in the making" doctrine to protect the first users of a non-distinctive mark from intentional infringement. Metro Kane Imports, Ltd. v. Federated Department Stores Inc., 625 F. Supp. 313 (S.D.N.Y. 1985). However, most courts have rejected the doctrine. Laureyssens v. Idea Group, Inc., 964 F.2d 131 (2d Cir. 1992).

4. *Intent-to-Use.* The intent-to-use provisions, added to the Lanham Act in 1989 and at issue in the *WarnerVision* case, were designed to provide more security to pre-marketing investments in trademarks. How do these provisions relate to the common law? What result in *Blue Bell* if Blue Bell had filed an intent-to-use application on July 5? If Farah's September shipment to customers had been limited to stores in the Eastern United States, what effect would be given to an intent-to-use application by Blue Bell on October 1? Can a manufacturer who intends to use a descriptive term or a surname mark acquire some breathing room in order to obtain secondary meaning by filing an intent-to-use application?

5. Article 6^{quinquies} of the Paris Convention provides that a trademark duly registered in its country of origin "shall be accepted for filing and protected" by other signatories. In most countries of the world a trademark may be registered prior to actual use. Does adoption of the Paris Convention require the U.S. to accept for registration trademarks prior to their actual use in the United States? Can the U.S. require that the trademarks be in actual use somewhere in the world?

Section 44 of the Lanham Act implements the Paris Convention. Section 44(c) suggests that use in the United States is not required if the mark has been registered in its country of origin. Moreover, § 44(d) provides that if the applicant files the U.S. application within 6 months of filing the foreign application, the applicant's priority is determined on the basis of the dates of its foreign application. This provision allows a foreign national who had not used a mark in the United States to nonetheless obtain priority in the United States against a domestic company who was the first to actually use the mark. The 1988 revisions amended § 44(e) to require the foreign applicant as part of its application for registration in this country to state a bona fide intention to use the mark in the United States.

Under the rule of Crocker Nat'l Bank v. Canadian Imperial Bank of Commerce, 223 U.S.P.Q. 909 (T.T.A.B. 1984) a foreign applicant under § 44 may obtain a registration even though it has never used the mark anywhere in the world! If a foreign national registered under § 44 without using the mark could it enjoin a domestic company who subsequently began using the mark? How would the foreign registrant show a likelihood of confusion?

6. For a description of a systematic program designed to attempt to preserve marks for future use see The Proctor & Gamble Co. v. Johnson & Johnson Inc., 485 F.Supp. 1185 (S.D.N.Y.1979).

7. After Blue Bell does a manufacturer's priority date of first use change every time changes are made in the underlying goods?

---

(2) Geographic Limitations

Hanover Star Milling Co. v. Metcalf

Supreme Court of the United States, 1916.
240 U.S. 403.

[In 1872 the plaintiff, Allen & Wheeler Company, an Ohio firm, adopted and used the mark, "Tea Rose" on flour and sold flour under that mark between 1872 and 1904 in Ohio, Pennsylvania, and Massachusetts, but not in Alabama. In 1885 Hanover Star Milling Co., an Illinois company, adopted the same mark for flour in good faith and without notice of plaintiff's prior use, and in 1904 began using the mark on flour in Alabama and other south-eastern states. Allen & Wheeler sued Hanover for trademark infringement seeking to prohibit Hanover's use of the mark anywhere in the United States. The Supreme Court, Justice Pitney, held for the defendant:]

Expressions are found in many of the cases to the effect that the exclusive right to the use of a trade-mark is founded on priority of appropriation. * * * In the ordinary case of parties competing under the same mark in the same market, it is correct to say that prior appropriation settles the question. But where two parties independently are employing the same mark upon goods of the same class, but in separate markets wholly remote the one from the other, the question of prior appropriation is legally insignificant, unless at least it appear that the second adopter has selected the mark with some design inimical to the interests of the first user, such as to take the benefit of the reputation of his goods, to forestall the extension of his trade, or the like.

That property in a trade-mark is not limited in its enjoyment by territorial bounds, but may be asserted and protected wherever the law affords a remedy for wrongs, is true in a limited sense. Into whatever markets the use of a trade-mark has extended, or its meaning has become known, there will the manufacturer or trader whose trade is pirated by an infringing use be entitled to protection and redress. But this is not to say that the proprietor of a trade-mark, good in the markets where it has been employed, can monopolize markets that his trade has never reached and where the mark signifies not his goods but those of another. We agree with the court below that "since it is the trade and not the mark, that is to be protected, a trade-mark acknowledges no territorial boundaries of municipalities or states or nations, but extends to every market where the trader's goods have become known and identified by his use of the mark. But the mark, of itself, cannot travel to markets where there is no article to wear the badge and no trader to offer the article."

* * *

■ MR. JUSTICE HOLMES concurring.

* * *

I think state lines, speaking always of matters outside the authority of Congress, are important in another way. I do not believe that a trade-mark established in Chicago could be used by a competitor in some other part of Illinois on the ground that it was not known there. I think that if it is good in one part of the State it is good in all. But when it seeks to pass state lines it may find itself limited by what has been done under the sanction of a power coordinate with that of Illinois and paramount over the territory concerned. If this view be adopted we get rid of all questions of penumbra, of shadowy marches where it is difficult to decide whether the business extends to them. We have sharp lines drawn upon the fundamental consideration of the jurisdiction originating the right. In most cases the change of jurisdiction will not be important because the new law will take up and apply the same principles as the old, but when, as here, justice to its own people requires a State to set a limit, it may do so, and this court cannot pronounce its action wrong.

Burger King of Florida, Inc. v. Hoots

United States Court of Appeals, Seventh Circuit, 1968.
403 F.2d 904.

■ KILEY, CIRCUIT JUDGE.

Defendants' appeal presents a conflict between plaintiffs' right to use the trade mark "Burger King," which plaintiffs have registered under the Federal Trade Mark Act, and defendants' right to use the same trade mark which defendants have registered under the Illinois Trade Mark Act. The district court resolved the conflict in favor of plaintiffs in this case of first impression in this Circuit. We affirm the judgment restraining the defendants from using the name "Burger King" in any part of Illinois except in their Mattoon, Illinois, market, and restraining plaintiffs from using their trade mark in the market area of Mattoon, Illinois.[3]

* * *

Plaintiff Burger King of Florida, Inc. opened the first "Burger King" restaurant in Jacksonville, Florida, in 1953. By 1955, fifteen of these restaurants were in operation in Florida, Georgia and Tennessee; in 1956

---

3. The district court defined the Mattoon market area as a circle having a radius of twenty miles, and a center located at the defendants' place of business in Mattoon, Illinois.

the number operating in Alabama, Kentucky and Virginia was twenty-nine; by 1957, in these states, thirty-eight restaurants were in operation.

In July, 1961, plaintiffs opened their first Illinois "Burger King" restaurant in Skokie, and at that time had notice of the defendants' prior registration of the same mark under the Illinois Trade Mark Act. Thereafter, on October 3, 1961, plaintiffs' certificate of federal registration of the mark was issued. Subsequently, plaintiffs opened a restaurant in Champaign, Illinois, and at the time of the trial in November, 1967, were operating more than fifty "Burger King" restaurants in the state of Illinois.

In 1957 the defendants, who had been operating an ice cream business in Mattoon, Illinois, opened a "Burger King" restaurant there. In July, 1959, they registered that name under Illinois law as their trade mark, without notice of plaintiffs' prior use of the same mark. On September 26, 1962, the defendants, with constructive knowledge of plaintiffs' federal trade mark, opened a second similar restaurant, in Charleston, Illinois.

Both parties have used the trade mark prominently, and in 1962 they exchanged charges of infringement in Illinois. After plaintiffs opened a restaurant in Champaign, Illinois, defendants sued in the state court to restrain plaintiffs' use of the mark in Illinois. Plaintiffs then brought the federal suit, now before us, and the defendants counter-claimed for an injunction, charging plaintiffs with infringement of their Illinois trade mark.

We hold that the district court properly decided that plaintiffs' federal registration of the trade mark "Burger King" gave them the exclusive right to use the mark in Illinois except in the Mattoon market area in Illinois where the defendants, without knowledge of plaintiffs' prior use, actually used the mark before plaintiffs' federal registration. The defendants did not acquire the exclusive right they would have acquired by their Illinois registration had they actually used the mark throughout Illinois prior to the plaintiffs' federal registration.

We think our holding is clear from the terms of the Federal Trade Mark Act. Under 15 U.S.C. § 1065 of the Act, plaintiffs, owners of the federally registered trade mark "Burger King," have the "incontestable" right to use the mark in commerce, except to the extent that such use infringes what valid right the defendants have acquired by their continuous use of the same mark prior to plaintiffs' federal registration.

Under 15 U.S.C. § 1115(b), the federal certificate of registration is "conclusive evidence" of plaintiffs' "exclusive right" to use the mark. This Section, however, also provides a defense to an exclusive right to use a trade mark: If a trade mark was adopted without knowledge of the federal registrant's prior use, and has been continuously used, then such use "shall" constitute a defense to infringement, provided that this defense applies only for the area in which such continuous prior use is proved. Since the defendants have established that they had adopted the mark "Burger King" without knowledge of plaintiffs' prior use and that they had continuously used the mark from a date prior to plaintiffs' federal registration of the mark, they are entitled to protection in the area which that use appropriated to them.

Plaintiffs agree that the defendants as prior good faith users are to be protected in the area that they had appropriated. Thus, the question narrows to what area in Illinois the defendants have appropriated by virtue of their Illinois registration.

At common law, defendants were entitled to protection in the Mattoon market area because of the innocent use of the mark prior to plaintiffs' federal registration. They argue that the Illinois Trade Mark Act was designed to give more protection than they already had at common law, and that various provisions of the Illinois Act indicate an intention to afford Illinois registrants exclusive rights to use trade marks throughout the state, regardless of whether they actually used the marks throughout the state or not. However, the Act itself does not express any such intention. And no case has been cited to us, nor has our research disclosed any case in the Illinois courts deciding whether a registrant is entitled to statewide protection even if he has used the mark only in a small geographical area.

* * *

* * * Under 15 U.S.C. § 1115(b) of the Lanham Act, the federal certificate can be "conclusive evidence" of registrant's "exclusive right." And 15 U.S.C. § 1127 of the Act provides that "The intent of this chapter is * * * to protect registered marks used in such commerce from interference by State * * * legislation." The Illinois Act, however, provides only that a certificate of registration "shall be admissible * * * evidence as competent and sufficient proof of the registration * * *." Ill.Rev.Stat. Ch. 140, § 11 (1967).

Moreover, we think that whether or not Illinois intended to enlarge the common law with respect to a right of exclusivity in that state, the Illinois Act does not enlarge its right in the area where the federal mark has priority. * * * Congress expanded the common law, however, by granting an exclusive right in commerce to federal registrants in areas where there has been no offsetting use of the mark. Congress intended the Lanham Act to afford nationwide protection to federally-registered marks, and that once the certificate has issued, no person can acquire any additional rights superior to those obtained by the federal registrant.

* * *

We conclude that if we were to accept the defendants' argument we would be fostering, in clear opposition to the express terms of the Lanham Act, an interference with plaintiffs' exclusive right in interstate commerce to use its federal mark.

The undisputed continuous market for the defendants' "Burger King" products was confined to a twenty mile radius of Mattoon. There is no evidence before us of any intention or hope for their use of their Illinois mark beyond that market. Yet they seek to exclude plaintiffs from expanding the scope of their national exclusive right, and from operating fifty enterprises already begun in Illinois. This result would clearly burden interstate commerce.

The defendants argue also that unless they are given the right to exclusive use throughout Illinois, many persons from all parts of Illinois in our current mobile society will come in contact with the defendants' business and will become confused as to whether they are getting the defendants' product, as they intended.

We are not persuaded by this argument. Defendants have not shown that the Illinois public is likely to confuse the products furnished by plaintiffs and by defendants. We are asked to infer that confusion will exist from the mere fact that both trade marks co-exist in the state of Illinois. However, the district court found that the defendants' market area was limited to within twenty miles of their place of business. The court's decision restricted the use of the mark by plaintiffs and defendants to sufficiently distinct and geographically separate markets so that public confusion would be reduced to a minimum. The mere fact that some people will travel from one market area to the other does not, of itself, establish that confusion will result. Since the defendants have failed to establish on the record any likelihood of confusion or any actual confusion, they are not entitled to an inference that confusion will result.

For the reasons given, the judgment of the district court is affirmed.

Dawn Donut Co. v. Hart's Food Stores, Inc.

United States Court of Appeals, Second Circuit, 1959.
267 F.2d 358.

[Plaintiff, Dawn Donut Co., has since 1922 continuously used the trademark "Dawn" upon various bulk packages of dough mixes for doughnuts, cakes, and other baked goods. It distributes the mixes and licenses the use of the marks "Dawn" and "Dawn Donut" principally to individuals who agree to establish retail bakeries under the name "Dawn Donut Shops." Defendant, Hart Food Stores, owns and operates a retail grocery chain within several New York counties. The products of defendant's baker are distributed through its grocery stores and since August 30, 1951 have carried the mark "Dawn". The distribution of defendant's products is limited to an area within a 45 mile radius of Rochester, New York. Plaintiff has not licensed the use of its mark at the retail level within 60 miles of defendant's trading area except for one "Dawn Donut Shop" operated in Rochester during 1926–27.

[Plaintiff's mark was registered federally in 1927 and the registration was renewed in 1947 under the Lanham Act. Defendant's mark is unregistered. The district court found that defendant's use of the mark "Dawn" was without any actual notice of plaintiff's use or registration and was adopted in good faith from the slogan "Baked at midnight, delivered at Dawn" which had been used by the defendant from 1929 to 1935.]

■ LUMBARD, CIRCUIT JUDGE. The principal question is whether the plaintiff, a wholesale distributor of doughnuts and other baked goods under its federally registered trademarks "Dawn" and "Dawn Donut," is entitled under the provisions of the Lanham Trade-Mark Act to enjoin the defendant from using the mark "Dawn" in connection with the retail sale of doughnuts and baked goods entirely within a six county area of New York State surrounding the city of Rochester. The primary difficulty arises from the fact that although plaintiff licenses purchasers of its mixes to use its trademarks in connection with the retail sales of food products made from the mixes, it has not licensed or otherwise exploited the mark at the retail level in defendant's market area for some thirty years.

* * *

Defendant's principal contention is that because plaintiff has failed to exploit the mark "Dawn" for some thirty years at the retail level in the Rochester trading area, plaintiff should not be accorded the exclusive right to use the mark in this area.

We reject this contention as inconsistent with the scope of protection afforded a federal registrant by the Lanham Act.

Prior to the passage of the Lanham Act courts generally held that the owner of a registered trademark could not sustain an action for infringement against another who, without knowledge of the registration, used the mark in a different trading area from that exploited by the registrant so that public confusion was unlikely. Hanover Star Milling Co. v. Metcalf, 1916, 240 U.S. 403; * * *

But the Lanham Act, 15 U.S.C. § 1072, provides that registration of a trademark on the principal register is constructive notice of the registrant's claim of ownership. Thus, by eliminating the defense of good faith and lack of knowledge, § 1072 affords nationwide protection to registered marks, regardless of the areas in which the registrant actually uses the mark.

That such is the purpose of Congress is further evidenced by 15 U.S.C. § 1115(a) and (b) which make the certificate of registration evidence of the registrant's "exclusive right to use the * * * mark in commerce." "Commerce" is defined in 15 U.S.C. § 1127 to include all the commerce which may lawfully be regulated by Congress. These two provisions of the Lanham Act make it plain that the fact that the defendant employed the mark "Dawn," without actual knowledge of plaintiff's registration, at the retail level in a limited geographical area of New York state before the plaintiff used the mark in that market, does not entitle it either to exclude the plaintiff from using the mark in that area or to use the mark concurrently once the plaintiff licenses the mark or otherwise exploits it in connection with retail sales in the area.

Plaintiff's failure to license its trademarks in defendant's trading area during the thirty odd years that have elapsed since it licensed them to a Rochester baker does not work an abandonment of the rights in that area. We hold that 15 U.S.C. § 1127, which provides for abandonment in certain cases of non-use, applies only when the registrant fails to use his mark, within the meaning of § 1127, anywhere in the nation. Since the Lanham Act affords a registrant nationwide protection, a contrary holding would create an insoluble problem of measuring the geographical extent of the abandonment. * * *

Accordingly, we turn to the question of whether on this record plaintiff has made a sufficient showing to warrant the issuance of an injunction against defendant's use of the mark "Dawn" in a trading area in which the plaintiff has for thirty years failed to employ its registered mark.

The Lanham Act, 15 U.S.C. § 1114, sets out the standard for awarding a registrant relief against the unauthorized use of his mark by another. It provides that the registrant may enjoin only that concurrent use which creates a likelihood of public confusion as to the origin of the products in connection with which the marks are used. Therefore if the use of the marks by the registrant and the unauthorized user are confined to two sufficiently distinct and geographically separate markets, with no likelihood that the registrant will expand his use into defendant's market, so that no public confusion is possible, then the registrant is not entitled to enjoin the junior user's use of the mark. * * *

As long as plaintiff and defendant confine their use of the mark "Dawn" in connection with the retail sale of baked goods to their present separate trading areas it is clear that no public confusion is likely.

* * *

The decisive question then is whether plaintiff's use of the mark "Dawn" at the retail level is likely to be confined to its current area of use or whether in the normal course of its business, it is likely to expand the retail use of the mark into defendant's trading area. If such expansion were probable, then the concurrent use of the marks would give rise to the conclusion that there was a likelihood of confusion.

* * *

Accordingly, because plaintiff and defendant use the mark in connection with retail sales in distinct and separate markets and because there is no present prospect that plaintiff will expand its use of the mark at the retail level into defendant's trading area, we conclude that there is no likelihood of public confusion arising from the concurrent use of the marks and therefore the issuance of an injunction is not warranted. *A fortiori* plaintiff is not entitled to any accounting or damages. However, because of the effect we have attributed to the constructive notice provision of the Lanham Act, the plaintiff may later, upon a proper showing of an intent to use the mark at the retail level in defendant's market area, be entitled to enjoin defendant's use of the mark.

* * *

Application of Beatrice Foods Co.

United States Court of Customs and Patent Appeals, 1970.
429 F.2d 466.

[Beatrice Foods Co.(prior user) adopted the mark "Homestead" for margarine in 1953. Fairway Foods (prior applicant) adopted the same mark for dairy products in 1956. In 1962, Fairway filed an application for registration on the Principal Register. Beatrice Foods, alleging prior use, filed an opposition to Fairway's application. Fairway had used the mark only in Wisconsin, Minnesota, Iowa, South Dakota, North Dakota, eastern Montana and the upper peninsula of Michigan. Fairway amended its application to restrict it to those areas. Beatrice then filed its own application for registration of the mark requesting rights throughout the United States except in those areas listed by Fairway. A concurrent use proceeding under § 2(d) was instituted. The parties filed a stipulation setting out their agreement to the allocation of geographic areas for use of the mark.

The Trademark Trial and Appeal Board held that (1) in concurrent use proceedings the applicants were only entitled to registrations in their respective areas of actual use and neither would receive registrations covering areas of non-use, and (2) the actual use must have occurred prior to the time of filing the application for registration.]

■ BALDWIN, JUDGE. This represents the first occasion on which this Court has been asked to review a decision of the Trademark Trial and Appeal Board in a Concurrent Use Proceeding instituted under § 2(d) of the Lanham Trademark Act, 15 U.S.C. § 1052(d). * * *

Beatrice Foods Co., the prior user, has appealed from the decisions of the board refusing to permit its registration to cover that portion of the United States lying outside both the territory of Fairway and the area where Beatrice had made actual use of the mark prior to filing its application. * * *

The position taken by the board in this case is obviously inconsistent with the practice of granting unrestricted registrations in cases where there is only a single applicant, and must therefore find support and justification, if at all, in the language of the proviso to § 2(d) or in some policy surrounding the proviso which differs from that behind the rest of the Lanham Act upon which the practice of granting unrestricted registrations in all other cases is based.

Looking first at the language of the proviso, we find that it sets out two requirements for the issuance of concurrent registrations for the same or similar marks to more than one person: first, such persons must "have become *entitled to use* such marks as a result of their concurrent lawful *use* in commerce *prior to* (i) the earliest of the filing dates of the applications pending," (emphasis added); and, second, it must be determined "that confusion, mistake, or deception is not likely to result from the continued use" of the marks by such persons. When it is determined that the likelihood of confusion, mistake or deception will be avoided only "under conditions and limitations as to the mode or place of use of the marks or the goods in connection with which such marks are used", the Commissioner is empowered to prescribe such conditions and limitations "with which such mark is registered to the respective persons." We find nothing in the language of the proviso, which, per se, *requires* the result reached by the board in this case.

Considering now the policy behind this provision of the act, it is our view that the proviso reflects a recognition, by the framers of that statute, that occasions do and will arise where two or more persons will independently adopt the same or a similar trademark and use it under the same or similar circumstances, and indicates their concern that a mechanism be provided for an equitable resolution of the problems which such concurrent use creates. As we see it, this is nothing more than an application of the basic policies underlying the Lanham Act as a whole.

It should be emphasized that what the parties here are seeking, and what the statute, in the proviso to § 2(d), authorizes, are concurrent federal *registrations*. Much confusion can be avoided by recognizing that such registrations would not, in and of themselves, create any new right to *use* the trademark or to assert rights based on ownership of the trademark itself. Rights of trademark ownership, for example, the right to enjoin another from use of the mark, must be based upon actual use and can be enforced only in areas of existing business influence (i.e., current use or probability of expansion). * * *

Rights appurtenant to the ownership of a federal trademark registration, on the other hand, may be considered supplemental to those recognized at common law, stemming from ownership of a trademark. A federal registration gives certain procedural rights, such as the right to invoke jurisdiction of the federal courts (15 U.S.C. § 1121), and the right to rely on certain evidentiary presumptions (15 U.S.C. § 1115), but more importantly, the constructive notice provision of § 22 of the Lanham Act (15 U.S.C. § 1072), takes away from future users of the mark registered the defense of innocent appropriation. The owner of a federal registration now has the security of knowing that no one else may, henceforth legitimately adopt his trademark and create rights in another area of the country superior to his own. In this respect, this provision of § 22 is, perhaps, the best example of the intent of Congress to provide for a thriving business environment by granting nationwide protection to expanding businesses. It is the right to have this protection which the party Beatrice is, in effect, seeking through this appeal. As urged by Beatrice, it would be illogical and inconsistent with the objectives of the Lanham Act, not to provide for nationwide coverage where there is more than one registration—provided there will be no public confusion created thereby. The constructive notice provision of § 22 of the act was promulgated with the hope of cutting down on the number of instances of concurrent use and the uncertainty and confusion attached thereto. Leaving territory open, as does the requirement by the board in this case, would frustrate this policy and increase rather than reduce the possibility of confusion and litigation.

The foregoing is not intended to imply that the Patent Office is required to issue registrations covering the whole of the United States in all circumstances. Certainly the applicant or applicants may always request territorially restricted registrations. In addition, in carrying out the Commissioner's duty under the proviso of § 2(d) of determining whether confusion, mistake or deception is likely to result from the continued concurrent use of a mark by two or more parties, it may be held that such likelihood will be prevented only when each party is granted a very limited territory with parts of the United States granted to no one.

* * *

We have concluded that in concurrent use proceedings in which neither party owns a registration for the mark, the starting point for any determination as to the extent to which the registrations are to be territorially restricted should be the conclusion that the prior user is prima facie entitled to a registration covering the entire United States. Such a prior user, who applies for a registration before registration is granted to another party, is entitled to a registration having nationwide effect no less than if there were no concurrent user having registrable rights.[13] His rights and, therefore, his registration, should be limited only to the extent that any other subsequent user, who can establish the existence of rights earlier than the prior user's application for registration, can also prove a likelihood of confusion, mistake or deception.

Having decided that, once jurisdiction is settled by way of the parties' establishing prior concurrent use, the primary concern of the Patent Office, in determining whether and to what extent registrations are to be granted, is to be the avoidance of any likelihood of confusion, we see no reason why agreements such as that worked out by the parties here should not be considered. Unquestionably, such stipulations are never binding on the board. Nevertheless, if it can be determined that they are in good faith, there can be no better assurance of the absence of any likelihood of confusion, mistake or deception than the parties' promises to avoid any activity which might lead to such likelihood.

* * *

Appellant, Fairway Foods, Inc., the prior applicant, appeals from the board's refusal to permit its registration to cover the Upper Peninsula of Michigan and the eastern counties of Montana. For the reasons fully set forth in our opinion in No. 8294, the board's decision with regard to Fairway must also be reversed and the case remanded.

Because of the importance of the issues, however, and the fact that this case is one of first impression in this court, we will comment on the questions as to what circumstances, if any, short of actual use of the trademark, may create rights in a territory sufficient to warrant inclusion of that territory in a geographically restricted registration, and up to what time prior to registration any proof regarding the territorial extent of trademark rights be submitted. It will be remembered that Fairway asserted, on behalf of its rights to the contested areas, previous business activity, dominance of contiguous areas, a history of expansion, presently planned expansion into the two areas, and possible present penetration into Montana by way of goods bought in the Dakotas. It should also be noted that some of the activity relied on by Fairway occurred subsequent to its filing date. The board, in its decision, stated the requirements to be no less than *actual* use *prior* to the earliest filing date. We think both requirements are wrong.

The Commissioner of Patents has the statutory responsibility to make sure that concurrent registrations are limited so as to prevent the likelihood

---

13. On the other hand, where the prior user does not apply for a registration before registration is granted to another, there may be valid grounds, based on a policy of rewarding those who first seek federal registration, and a consideration of the rights created by the existing registration, for limiting his registration to the area of actual use and permitting the prior registrant to retain the nationwide protection of the act restricted only by the territory of the prior user.

of confusion, mistake or deception from occurring. Where a party has submitted evidence sufficient to prove a strong probability of future expansion of his trade into an area, that area would then become an area of likelihood of confusion if a registration covering it was granted to the other party. For example, many forms of evidence which would ordinarily be proffered to show a likelihood of *expansion* would be the same kind submitted to argue a likelihood of *confusion* if another party began use of the mark in that area. Thus, based on the premise that territorially restricted registrations must issue and, further, that said registrations combined will encompass the entire United States, if a likelihood of confusion is to be avoided, the territories of the parties must be limited in such a way as to exclude from each the area of probable expansion of the other party. Considering the Commissioner's indicated responsibility, which, of course, is based on a desire to protect the public, submission of evidence such as that submitted by Fairway in this case should be encouraged. And reiterating what was said earlier, any attempt, by the parties themselves, to solve the problem of public confusion, should be given serious consideration by the Patent Office.

With regard to the question as to the time prior to which evidence of trademark usage must be established, we have already indicated that the board was in error. * * *

* * * The extent to which concurrent registrations must be territorially restricted has an effect on the rights of both parties. In addition, there is the paramount interest of the public to be considered. We feel, therefore, that it is both necessary and proper for the Patent Office to determine the "conditions and limitations" with which the marks are to be registered "on the basis of facts as they exist at the time when the issue of registrability is under consideration." * * * In the present type of proceeding this would apparently mean up to the close of the testimony period. We have considered the possible problems which might result from such practice, but find they are outweighed by the interests involved.

Reversed and remanded.

NOTES

1. The "good faith" of a party adopting a trademark is relevant under *Hanover Star Milling* at common law and may be relevant to the opening paragraph of § 15 of the Lanham Act which preserves trademarks "acquired under the law of any State." What does "good faith" mean? Does proof that the junior user knew about the remote use of the senior user prior to the junior user's adoption of the mark bar a showing of good faith? Suppose your client comes across a small, family operated diner in a small town in Montana named "Mel's Diner". Your client, whose name is Mel, wants to open a "Mel's Diner" in Tampa, Florida. Can he do so? Can a competitor in Tampa obtain an assignment of the trademark from the family in Montana and then sue Mel for infringement arguing he adopted the mark in bad faith?

2. Both the common law and the Lanham Act assume that the same mark can be used in different territories and that the courts will find it necessary to define the scope of each use. Justice Holmes suggestion that state lines be used did not receive wide acceptance. Does a common law trademark extend beyond the territory of actual use? What is the territory of actual use? For a trademark on goods, is it the geographic area where the goods can be purchased? Or does it include additional areas where the goods are advertised? What is the territory of actual use of the trademark "Disney World" as applied to a theme park in Orlando, Florida? The "New York Yankees" as applied to a baseball team?

A leading common law case defining the prior user's rights is Sweetarts v. Sunline, Inc., 380 F.2d 923 (8th Cir.1967) (prior user protected in area of significant market penetration and not where transactions have been "so small, sporadic, and inconsequential that present or anticipated market penetration is *di minimus.*") Is there a principle to help decide this issue?

Would you permit a party to argue that it should have priority in the zone of its natural expansion, that is, that its mark is not used or known in a territory but it is most likely to expand there? See, Restatement, Third, Unfair Competition § 19, Comment *c* (1995) (rejecting the doctrine and observing it has rarely been decisive in the cases).

3. The Lanham Act contains a number of provisions relevant to determining priority of use and the extent of geographic protection. Section 22 makes the issuance of a registration "constructive notice of the registrant's claim of ownership." Section 7(c) makes the filing of an application "constructive use of the mark". What is the difference between constructive notice and constructive use? How do either relate to the good faith defense?

The other two provisions of importance are § 15 and §33. The first paragraph of § 15 preserves valid common law rights as an exception to an incontestable mark. Section 33(a), while making the registration prima facie evidence of ownership, preserves all legal defenses which would include prior use in remote territories under *Hanover Star Milling.* Section 33(b)(5) provides a separate defense to incontestability. Before the defense is available, the defendant must show its mark was adopted "without knowledge of the registrant's prior use". This provision speaks of knowledge and not good faith and assumes that a registrant's use is prior to the defendant's. Section 22 would provide constructive knowledge for purposes of § 33(b). Section 33(b)(5) also provides that the defendant must have "continuously used" the mark from a date prior to the constructive use date in § 7(c). And, the defense created applies only in the area of the continuous prior use. How do §§ 15 and 33(b)(5) relate to each other?

4. Consider footnote 13 in the *Beatrice* opinion. What should the rule be after *Beatrice* if the junior user is the first to register the mark and is an expanding business? See Weiner King, Inc. v. Wiener King Corp., 615 F.2d 512 (CCPA 1980)(junior user under the facts obtained nation-wide rights subject to the senior users prior use). See also, Noah's Inc. v. Nark, Inc., 560 F.Supp 1253 (E.D.Mo.1983), affirmed 728 F.2d 410 (8th Cir.1984), where the senior user, who could show little expansion activity, was the first to file for registration but was opposed by the junior user who had made plans to expand but was prevented from doing so by lawsuits threatened by senior user. The court awarded the national registration to the junior user subject to the senior user's prior use.

5. How should an intent-to-use application affect issues arising between conflicting uses of the same mark? Section 7(c), providing constructive use, is applicable to applications based on intent-to-use.

6. Should the Lanham Act be extended to provide relief against acts of infringement that take place outside the territorial borders of the United States? Courts have consistently held that the copyright and patent statutes have no extraterritorial effect. However, in Steele v. Bulova Watch Co., 344 U.S. 280 (1952) the Court applied the Lanham Act to the manufacture and sale of counterfeit "Bulova" watches in Mexico by a United States citizen suggesting that the counterfeit watches could impact on Bulova's reputation in the United States. See also, Levi Strauss & Co. v. Sunrise International Trading Inc., 51 F.3d 982 (11th Cir. 1995) where the Lanham Act was applied to the manufacture of counterfeit "501" jeans in China for sale in Europe. The court noted that some of the jeans passed through the United States on the way to Europe and that two pairs of the jeans were found in a United States warehouse. Is such an extension of the Lanham Act justified? See generally, Curtis A. Bradley, Territorial Intellectual Property Rights in an Age of Globalism, 37 Va. J. Int'l L. 505 (1997). Could application of the Act be based on post-sale confusion, i.e., consumers who purchase counterfeit jeans in Europe are likely to visit the United States or United States citizens visiting Europe are likely to buy counterfeit jeans?

7. *Internationally well-known marks.* Should a trademark owner be entitled to injunctive relief against an infringing use in a country in which the owner has not used the mark? In other words, does the *Dawn Donut* analysis apply in international conflicts? Article 6bis of the Paris Convention contains a provision for the protection of "well-known" marks. And Article 16 of the GATT Trips agreement makes the "well-known" mark provisions applicable in signatory countries. Article 16(2) suggests that a mark may become well-known by promotion of the mark rather than by sale of the goods to which the mark is used. In McDonald's Corp. v. Joburgers Drive-Inn Restaurant (Pty) Ltd., 4 All S.A. 1 (1996) the South African appellate division dealt with a South African fast food restaurant which used "McDonalds", "Big Mac" and the golden arches, all trademarks owned by McDonalds. McDonalds had no outlet in South Africa and thus no technical good-will in the marks although the court recognized that the McDonald marks were widely known in South Africa. The court interpreting South African trademark legislation against the background of Article 6bis of the Paris Convention, granted McDonalds an injunction prohibiting the defendant from using the marks. Does § 43(c) of the Lanham Act respond to the well-known marks problem?

PROBLEMS

1. (a). ABC Co. begins using the mark "Good and Chewy" on its cinnamon rolls in 1985. XYZ begins using the mark on its cinnamon rolls in

1988. Neither party registers the mark. What are the rights of the parties in 1989 if they are both selling in the same territory? In remote territories?

(b). Same facts as (a) except that ABC registers its mark on the principal register in 1987. What are XYZ's rights in 1989 if they are selling in the same territory? In remote territories? In 1996 if ABC's registration has become incontestable?

(c). Same facts as (a) except that XYZ is the first to register its mark on the principal register in 1985. ABC does not register its mark. What are ABC's rights in 1989 if they are selling in the same territory? In remote territories? In 1996 if XYZ's mark has become incontestable?

2. In 1988 Steaks, Inc., begins operating a chain of restaurants under the mark "The Steak Factory" in Ohio. Customers of the restaurant can also purchase raw steaks at a counter inside the restaurant, packaged with the "Steak Factory" mark. Steaks registers the mark in 1990 for "restaurant services" and receives an incontestable registration in 1995. In 1980, Bob's, a small neighborhood grocery store in Albuquerque had begun using the mark "The Steak Factory" on steaks and other meat products sold to customers of its grocery store. It did not register its mark and does not know about the Ohio restaurants. In 1989 Bob's begins selling its "Steak Factory" steaks in Texas through a few local grocery stores in Houston. In 1996 Steaks decides to market frozen steaks by mail and obtains a new registration in 1997 for "The Steak Factory" for "steaks, hamburgers, and other specialty meats". In 1998, Steaks announces the opening of its "Steak Factory" restaurant in Houston, Texas, and is promptly sued by Bob's. Does Steaks' incontestable mark come into play?

3. Could the Mattoon, Illinois, Burger King, the plaintiff in the *Burger King* case, *supra,* establish a home page on the Internet using its Burger King mark? Could it register www.burgerking.com as the domain name for its home page?

––––––

(3) Test for Infringement

Libman Company v. Vining Industries, Inc.

United States Court of Appeals, Seventh Circuit, 1995
69 F.3d 1360, cert.denied, 116 S. Ct. 1878 (1996)

■ POSNER, CHIEF JUDGE.

The Libman Company brought suit against Vining Industries for infringement of a federally registered trademark on a broom. After a bench trial, the district judge enjoined Vining from selling the infringing line of brooms and in addition awarded Libman almost $1.2 million in monetary relief, representing Vining's profits from that sale. The main ground of the appeal, and the only one we need discuss, is that the district judge committed clear error in finding that consumers were likely to mistake Vining's broom for Libman's.

A broom has, of course, a head of bristles. In 1993, after being twice turned down, Libman succeeded in registering with the U.S. Patent and Trademark Office a trademark that consists of a color scheme in which one vertical band or segment of bristles is a different color (a "contrasting" color, in the language of the trademark registration) from the remaining bristles. The particular choice of contrasting colors is not part of the trademark, however. The contrasting-color band was sometimes red and sometimes green or black, the rest of the bristles being either a very dark gray, verging on black, with the red band, or a lighter gray with the green or black band. Libman had begun marketing these brooms in 1990. They sold well. In 1993 Vining began marketing its own contrasting-color broom, the contrasting colors being light and medium gray.

The parties agree that Libman cannot prove infringement of its trademark without proving that consumers of brooms are likely to be confused about the source of Vining's brooms—and to think that they are Libman's. A trademark is not a property right, but an identifier; so, provided no one is likely to be confused by the alleged infringer, there is no impairment of the interest that the trademark statute protects. The evidence of likelihood of confusion in this case is vanishingly thin. Vining sold several hundred thousand of the allegedly infringing brooms, yet there is no evidence that any consumer ever made such an error; if confusion were likely, one would expect at least one person out of this vast multitude to be confused, or more precisely one would expect Libman to have been able to find one such confused person. Nor was any survey conducted in an effort to determine the likelihood of confusion. The district court pointed out, moreover, that "from a distance, with the cardboard cover in place, the [Vining] broom doesn't have the appearance of a Libman broom." The head of each broom is sold with a plastic wrapper around it, but the opaque label affixed to Vining's wrapper, unlike the label on Libman's wrapper, is so large that it hides the contrasting colors of the bristles. It does not hide them completely, but, especially since they are merely different shades of gray, you have to peer pretty closely to notice this feature of the broom. The labels are not similar and of course the brand names are different. Consistent with the different style of packaging, Libman's advertising (at least the advertising that is in the record, but that is all we have to go on) shows the undressed broom, its contrasting colors boldly displayed. Vining's does not.

But "with their covers removed," the judge went on to say, "the two brooms are quite similar in appearance." The photographs in the record do not support this characterization, as the only thing the brooms have in common, besides being brooms, is that their bristles are in contrasting color bands rather than being all of one color. But this is an element of similarity and we shall not quibble over the district judge's use of the word "quite." The brooms, however, are sold in their wrappers. There is no evidence that the wrapper is ever removed before a sale to the consumer. (There is evidence that at trade shows the wrapper is sometimes removed, but those are promotions to the trade, not to consumers.) A consumer who is curious about the strength or stiffness or other tactile properties of the bristles can feel them through the plastic wrapper, which is very thin; she would have no occasion to ask the salesman to remove the wrapper.

So why is the undressed state of the broom relevant? Because the consumer might, upon removing the opaque wrapper from the Vining broom when she brought the broom home, think that she had bought a Libman rather than a Vining. Here is how her confusion might hurt Libman: The two brands of broom, though sold through the same type of outlet (supermarkets and mass-market retailers), are rarely sold by the same outlet, the reason being that retailers prefer to stock only one brand of broom. It's a cheap but bulky item; they don't want to fill up the store with different brands of it. Because a broom is so cheap (under $10), consumers don't spend a lot of time mulling over their decision whether to buy. If their old broom is wearing out, which usually happens after a year or so, they'll look for a new one the next time they find themselves in a store that sells brooms. Suppose that in 1993 you buy a Libman broom. You like it; you think it's a great broom; and you associate the contrasting color bands with the name "Libman." Eventually the broom wears out and you have to buy a new one. You find yourself in a store that does not stock the Libman broom (you don't know this), but only the Vining broom. If you saw them side to side you would know that the Libman, and not the Vining, broom was the one you had had a good experience with. But you don't see them side to side. All you see is a broom that has contrasting color bands. You think it's a Libman broom, and buy it. Had you known it was not a Libman broom you would have waited to replace your old broom until you found yourself in a store that stocked the Libman broom.

This is a plausible narrative, one consistent not only with the objectives of trademark law but also with a large number of cases which hold that where, as in this case, the public does not encounter the parties' trademarks together, the existence of minor differences that would clearly distinguish them in a side-by-side comparison does not refute an inference of likely confusion.

It would have been nice had the district judge mentioned this theory of confusion rather than just moving without transition or explanation from the fact that the parties' brooms are not confusingly similar when seen side by side to the conclusion that one infringed the trademark of the other. Libman did not object when at argument we judges looked at the brooms side by side and remarked their dissimilar appearance. It further muddied the waters at the argument by describing this case, as its brief had done as well, as a case of "reverse confusion." The term refers in trademark law to an entirely different practice, that of the alleged infringer's so saturating the market with advertising for his trademark that the public comes to believe that he, rather than the plaintiff, is the source of the plaintiff's trademarked product.

In view of the conceptual confusion it comes as no great surprise that Libman neglected to present evidence to support its misnamed theory that satisfied consumers of its broom might be fooled when they shopped for a replacement in a store that sold only Vining's broom. To insist on evidence might seem to be to commit the error of thinking that proof of actual confusion is required in a trademark-infringement case, and of course it is not unless damages are sought. Libman sought injunctive relief and Vining's profits, not damages. But our point is only that a finding of likely confusion can no more be based on pure conjecture or a fetching narrative alone than any other finding on an issue on which the proponent bears the burden of proof.

To this Libman might reply that deliberate copying ("bad faith") is one of the factors that courts rely on in determining the likelihood of confusion. It is. But in context, "bad faith" in the district judge's opinion does not appear to mean that Vining was trying to confuse consumers. So far as appears—and it is all that the record supports—Vining noticed that Libman's brooms were selling briskly, inferred that consumers like brooms with contrasting color bands, and decided to climb on the bandwagon. We call that competition, not bad faith, provided there is no intention to confuse, and, so far as appears, there was none. * * *

The two brooms are not packaged alike and do not have similar names; while the "undressed" brooms are similar, they are not identical; the appearance of the brooms in advertising was dissimilar; and the trademark is a thin one, since adding a colored stripe is hardly a distinctive way of marking a product. We now know, of course, that a color can be a trademark. And we do not hold that Libman's contrasting-color trademark was insufficiently distinctive to be registrable. Still, we're in the gray area (pardon the pun) where a rather commonplace design used for a trademark may be taken by consumers as a form of decoration—a way, here, of jazzing up the humblest of utilitarian products. We pointed out that Vining may have taken it so in deciding to produce a similar broom.

We do not want to make a fetish of testimony, expert or otherwise. Sometimes it is obvious just from comparing the products that consumers are likely to be confused as to their source. But this is not such a case. If the record were limited to the brooms themselves and the advertising for them, no reasonable person would think that there was a substantial danger of confusion. We take the district judge to have acknowledged this in the passage we quoted earlier from his opinion. Libman's narrative of possible confusion cannot be regarded as better than a hypothesis, and a hypothesis that has not been tested. It should not have been very hard for Libman to find some satisfied owners of its brooms and confront them with the Vining broom and see whether they thought it was the same brand of broom. Without such evidence it would be pure speculation to conclude that anyone, let alone a significant fraction of the broom-buying public, could have been misled into believing that the Vining broom and the Libman broom were one and the same brand. Restatement (Third) of Unfair Competition § 20, comment g (1995).

Either consumers are confused at the point of sale, or they become confused later and this carries over to the next time they are in the market for the product. The district court rightly disparaged the first theory and failed to discuss the second. The evidence supports neither, and the judgment for the plaintiff must therefore be reversed with instructions to enter judgment for the defendant.

REVERSED.

COFFEY, Circuit Judge, dissenting.

I am unable to join in the majority opinion because I believe it is contrary to the law of this circuit regarding "likelihood of confusion" and because I am concerned that my colleagues have disregarded the "clearly erroneous" standard of review that governs a district court's findings in this area. Given the centrality of the "likelihood of confusion" concept in the law of trademark infringement, I must respectfully dissent.

* * *

[The majority's] analysis, in my view, departs from well-established precedent in this circuit, which holds that "[a] variety of factors may be material in assessing the likelihood of confusion" and that "[n]one of these factors by itself is dispositive of the likelihood of confusion question." The relevant factors, as they have been delineated by this court, are:

(1) similarity between the marks in appearance and suggestion;
(2) similarity of the products;
(3) area and manner of concurrent use;
(4) degree of care likely to be exercised by consumers;
(5) strength of complainant's mark;
(6) actual confusion; and,
(7) intent of defendant to 'palm-off his product as that of another.'

The majority's approach to the likelihood-of-confusion issue "sweeps under the rug" our well-established seven-factor test, and instead dwells on Libman's failure to produce evidence of actual confusion * * * This fetishizing of actual confusion evidence flatly contradicts this court's oft-stated holding that "the plaintiff need not show actual confusion in order to establish likelihood of confusion." Sands, Taylor & Wood Co. v. Quaker Oats Co., 978 F.2d 947, 960 (7th Cir.1992), cert. denied 507 U.S. 1042 (1993).

Obviously, evidence of actual confusion can be highly probative of the likelihood of confusion. For this reason, our cases recognize that such evidence, when available, is "entitled to substantial weight." Nevertheless, the nature of a particular product can make it unlikely that this kind of evidence will ever surface. Under such circumstances * * * the absence of actual confusion evidence is not particularly significant[.] * * *

As discussed in more detail below, it is the trial court, as trier of fact, and not the court of appeals, that evaluates and weighs the factors. * * *

I am satisfied, as my colleagues apparently are not, that the district court engaged in a careful and reasoned weighing of the evidence. The court analyzed the factors as follows:

The two brooms are similarly designed [factor # 1], are similar products [factor # 2], and have the same sale outlets and purchasers [factor # 3]. The two products are advertised through the same media [factor # 3]. Libman has no evidence of actual confusion [factor # 6]. But as the witness Robert Libman pointed out, the purchase of a broom is not a large expense item and is not an event that is likely to cause a buyer to call up and complain about being confused about which product he or she bought [factor # 4]. There is some evidence in the record that purchasers recognize the Libman mark and occasionally call . . . asking where they may purchase the broom they saw advertised [factor # 5]. . . . While a market study of likelihood of confusion would have been helpful evidence to the court, the elements of a prima facie showing of likelihood of confusion are present and Vining has not rebutted that showing. The court finds, therefore, that it is more probably true than not that [Vining's] use of a contrast color band on its brooms is likely to cause confusion among ordinary purchasers as to the source of the brooms.

With respect to the question of Vining's bad faith (i.e., its intent to "palm- off"), the court found that "while the evidence is not strong . . . there was certainly no effort on its part to avoid infringement. In fact, at best it appears that [Vining] just didn't care." [factor # 7].

The trial judge (as the trier of fact) thus considered each and every one of the required factors and concluded that a likelihood of confusion existed, notwithstanding the absence of actual confusion evidence. I am unable to join in the majority opinion because I believe that it elevates one of these factors—actual confusion—to a status that is clearly inconsistent with our precedent in this area. If the court wishes to embark on a new course and give actual confusion a more prominent role than the other analytical elements, it should do so explicitly.

* * *

It seems to me that the majority, contrary to our own precedent, has evaluated the likelihood of confusion afresh and substituted its own judgement for that of the district court. My colleagues are too willing to revisit factual issues: not just the ultimate factual issue in this case (likelihood of confusion), but subsidiary findings on issues such as the strength of Libman's mark and the similarity of the broom designs. * * *

* * * It is not as though the trial judge concluded that Lake Michigan and the Sahara Desert are confusingly similar because they are both large. In other words, although I happen to agree with the trial court's finding, my agreement or disagreement is beside the point. The court's clearly-stated finding of similarity is not so tenuous that it should leave any of the members of this panel with "a definite and firm conviction" that a mistake has been committed. The same is true of the district judge's ultimate determination that ordinary purchasers were likely to be confused as to the source of Vining's brooms.

Lang v. Retirement Living Publishing Co., Inc.

United States Court of Appeals, Second Circuit, 1991
949 F.2d 576

■ OAKES, CHIEF JUDGE:

* * *

I

This dispute turns on who holds the right to use the words "New Choices" in a trade name as that term is used in the Lanham Act, 15 U.S.C. § 1127 (1988). In 1985, author and educator Doe Lang formed New Choices Press, which to date has published one book entitled The Secret of Charisma: What It Is and How To Get It, and has issued cassettes similarly dealing with the development of charisma. In 1988, Retirement Living (a subsidiary of Reader's Digest Association) purchased 50 Plus, a magazine designed, not surprisingly, for readers over fifty. As part of an effort to revamp the publication, Retirement Living decided to change the magazine's name and ultimately selected New Choices For The Best Years.

Lang runs New Choices Press out of her apartment in New York City. Her apartment is also home to her image consulting firm, Charismedia, of which she is the president. Lang has advertised her charisma-building products and services and has also received considerable media attention. Only a few of the advertisements and articles, however, mention New Choices Press. Despite this advertising and publicity, New Choices Press remains a modest-sized business. Through late 1989, New Choices Press's sales have totaled approximately $85,000. One-half of these sales were made through a distributor. The remainder, direct sales, have consistently amounted to less than $2,000 a year. New Choices Press has never published a magazine, nor does it have any plans to do so. Lang has considered publishing several self-help guides but at present these plans have not crystallized. The name "New Choices Press" appears in small block letters, above a sun and pedestal design, on the spine of the charisma book.

The name of Retirement Living's magazine, New Choices For The Best Years, figures prominently at the top of the cover, with "New Choices" in larger hollow slanted letters on top, and "For The Best Years" in smaller block letters below. The magazine has over 580,000 subscribers. Like its predecessor, the magazine focuses primarily on the interests of readers between the ages of 45 and 65.

Retirement Living selected the name New Choices For The Best Years after considering other similar names and directing its outside trademark counsel to conduct a trademark search. The search did reveal New Choices Press and, in response, the law firm sent an associate to the premises to investigate. The associate determined, of course, that the address was that of an apartment house. The associate also determined that New Choices Press published one book and several tapes, but furnished no product or services entitled "New Choices."

Beginning in late 1988, Lang's office received a number of phone calls from persons trying to reach New Choices For The Best Years, whose number was not yet in the telephone directory. The calls ceased from September 1989 to May 1990 after both the Manhattan Yellow and White Pages listed New Choices For The Best Years in the summer of 1989. In late May 1990, however, the magazine changed its phone number and once more Lang received misdirected calls. Retirement Living claims that this new series of calls resulted from the phone company's failure to give out the correct number, and the remedying of this error caused the misdirected calls to cease. Lang, on the other hand, maintains that the calls persisted at least up to December 1990.

Meanwhile, the first set of phone calls prompted Lang, in May 1989, to bring suit in state court to enjoin Retirement Living from using the name "New Choices", under New York General Business Law, N.Y. Gen.Bus.Law

§ 133 (McKinney 1988). Retirement Living removed the suit to federal district court, where Lang's motions for preliminary injunctive relief were denied. No. 89 Civ. 3868 (S.D.N.Y. Nov. 6, 1989), aff'd, 898 F.2d 137 (2d Cir.1990) (unpublished summary order). Upon completion of discovery, the district court granted Retirement Living's motion for summary judgment, Lang v. Retirement Living Publishing Co., Inc., 759 F.Supp. 134 (S.D.N.Y.1991), thus giving rise to this appeal.

II

The central issue in trade name infringement cases such as this one is the same as it is in trademark cases, namely, whether there is a likelihood of confusion. See Restatement (Third) of Unfair Competition § 20 (Tent. Draft No. 2, 1990). Whether a trademark owner receives judicial protection depends on "whether there is any likelihood that an appreciable number of ordinarily prudent purchasers are likely to be misled, or indeed simply confused, as to the source of the goods in question." McGregor-Doniger Inc. v. Drizzle Inc., 599 F.2d 1126, 1130 (2d Cir.1979) (quoting Mushroom Makers, Inc. v. R.G. Barry Corp., 580 F.2d 44, 47 (2d Cir.1978) (per curiam), cert. denied, 439 U.S. 1116, 99 S.Ct. 1022, 59 L.Ed.2d 75 (1979)). Appellant argues that the resolution of this issue on a motion for summary judgment is inappropriate in general, and especially inappropriate given the factual complexity of this case.

Although appellant does not dispute [the general standards applicable to summary judgment actions] she asserts that they require greater justification for a grant of summary judgment in a trademark case, since the existence of a likelihood of confusion may involve a series of inferences. Our cases, however, show that summary judgment may be appropriate in certain trademark actions. * * * Thus, our task in this appeal is to determine whether Lang has raised a genuine issue of fact on the issue of the likelihood of confusion. For this, we turn to the eight-factor test first set forth in Polaroid Corp. v. Polarad Electronics Corp., 287 F.2d 492 (2d Cir.), cert. denied, 368 U.S. 820, 82 S.Ct. 36, 7 L.Ed.2d 25 (1961) as supplemented by the Restatement, supra, §§ 20–23.

The Polaroid test looks to the following factors: the strength of the prior owner's mark, the similarity between the two marks, the competitive proximity of the products, the likelihood that the prior user will bridge the gap, actual confusion, the defendant's good faith, the quality of defendant's product, and the sophistication of the buyers. In applying this test, the list of factors "does not exhaust the possibilities," and "[n]o single Polaroid factor is determinative." Instead, each factor must be considered in the context of the others, and balanced to determine whether a likelihood of confusion exists. Additionally, we note that in reviewing the district court's determinations, its "findings on each of the Polaroid factors are entitled to considerable deference."

1. Strength of the Mark

Here, the inquiry focuses on "the distinctiveness of the mark, or more precisely, its tendency to identify the goods" as coming from a particular source. The district court found that "the indisputable evidence shows that Dr. Lang's mark is weak." The court explained that 1) there was extensive third party use of the words "Choice" or "Choices" in the titles of publications; 2) the layout of Lang's mark was prosaic; 3) Lang's business was limited; and 4) media coverage and marketing was limited and did not emphasize the name "New Choices Press."

The parties agree, although the court is not so confident, that Lang's trade name is suggestive. Lang argues that as a suggestive name, her name is entitled to protection and is strong without evidence of secondary meaning. Although a suggestive mark is entitled to registration without evidence of secondary meaning, suggestiveness is not necessarily dispositive of the issue of the strength of the mark. Ultimately, the strength of the mark turns on its " 'origin- indicating' quality, in the eyes of the purchasing public," so that in a given case whether the mark has acquired "secondary meaning" is a matter which may be relevant and probative and hence useful in determining the likelihood of confusion. Accordingly, we next evaluate the strength of Lang's name by examining the degree to which the words "New Choices" tend to identify Doe Lang's business in the public's eye.

As we have suggested, extensive third party use of the words "Choice" and "Choices" weighs against a finding that Lang's trade name is strong. Similarly, the ordinary layout of the words "New Choices" tends to undermine the claim that it is recognizable to, or distinctive in the minds of, consumers. New Choices Press's total sales of only $85,000 since 1985, spread throughout the nation and in several foreign countries, and largely in reference to the one book on charisma, further negates the inference that New Choices Press is associated in the public's mind with Lang's book and tapes. Finally, most of the articles and advertisements referring to Lang's book and tapes do not refer to New Choices Press at all, thus making it doubtful that this publicity has led consumers to associate the book with its publishing source. These factors, taken together, indicate that the district court determined correctly that Lang's trade name is weak.

2. Similarity of the Marks

This factor looks to whether the similarity of the marks is likely to provoke confusion among prospective purchasers. In making this determination, a court should look at the general impression created by the marks, taking into account all factors that potential purchasers will likely perceive and remember. The district court found that despite similarities, there seemed to be little chance that consumers will confuse Lang's publishing company with Retirement Living's magazine.

Both designations include as their focal point the words "New Choices." However, Lang's name always includes the word "Press," whereas Retirement Living's mark always includes the words "For The Best Years." The typeface also serves to distinguish the two designations, as does the location of the designations on the products. As such, the general impression conveyed to the public by these designations differs significantly, and therefore we agree with the district court that the similarities do not create an issue of fact on the likelihood of consumer confusion.

3. Proximity of the Products

This factor focuses on whether the two products compete with each other. To the extent goods (or trade names) serve the same purpose, fall within the same general class, or are used together, the use of similar designations is more likely to cause confusion. The district court found that the products were not proximate.

Because Retirement Living's magazine caters to the interests of older adults generally, whereas Lang's publishing house markets her book and tapes to all people who seek specifically to enhance their charisma, the products neither compete nor serve the same purpose. Lang's book and tapes are best classified as image-building products; Retirement Living's magazine addresses diverse topics of interest to mature consumers, including travel, finance, health, and nutrition. The two companies' products are not used together. Although both Lang's publishing house and Retirement Living's magazine are in the field of publishing, this does not render them proximate. Because of these differences, we agree with the district court that the products are not proximate, and thus this factor also fails to give rise to a question of fact regarding the likelihood of consumer confusion.

4. Bridging the Gap

This factor turns on the likelihood that Lang will enter Retirement Living's market. The district court correctly found that Lang's expansion plans remained "wholly speculative."

The district court did not draw a favorable inference from Lang's evidence regarding her expansion plans, and it is argued that as the non-movant, the court should have drawn all inferences in her favor and thus should not have dismissed her plans so summarily. Even if there were such an error, however, there is no genuine issue of fact as to the likelihood of confusion for two reasons. First, even if Lang does effectuate her expansion plans, she will not have "bridged the gap" because the plans do not include the publication of either a magazine or any other publication directed specifically to the interests of older adults. Second, "the intent of the prior user to expand or its activities in preparation to do so, unless known by prospective purchasers, does not affect the likelihood of confusion." Restatement, supra, § 21 reporter's note at 210 (emphasis added). Lang has provided no evidence that prospective purchasers would assume that New Choices Press would publish a magazine or other publication aimed at older adults.

5. Actual Confusion

The approximately four hundred phone calls and several letters received by Lang from people attempting to reach Retirement Living's magazine obviously reflect some sort of confusion. At issue is whether this is the type of confusion against which the Lanham Act was designed to protect.

The Lanham Act seeks to prevent consumer confusion that enables a seller to pass "off his goods as the goods of another." Programmed Tax Systems, Inc. v. Raytheon Co., 439 F.Supp. 1128, 1132 (S.D.N.Y.1977) (quoting Jean Patou, Inc. v. Jacqueline Cochran, Inc., 201 F.Supp. 861, 863 (S.D.N.Y.1962), aff'd, 312 F.2d 125 (2d Cir.1963). In *Programmed Tax*

Systems, the court explained that the relevant confusion is that which affects "the purchasing and selling of the goods or services in question." The Restatement concurs * * * for the proposition that "trademark infringement protects only against mistaken purchasing decisions and not against confusion generally." Restatement, supra, § 20 reporter's note at 179.

It is not clear what prompted the error on the part of each caller. The evidence shows that the calls ceased following the listing of New Choices For The Best Years in local phone books, likely indicating that the confusion resulted from the absence of any listing for New Choices For The Best Years. The evidence also shows, however, that several callers did have some question about whether the two entities were affiliated. At any rate, no evidence links the confusion evinced by the calls to any potential or actual effect on consumers' purchasing decisions.

Moreover, a closer look at Lang's claim shows that her reliance on the phone calls as evidence of actual confusion is misplaced. Appellant emphasizes that because this case involves reverse confusion, the commercial injury she has suffered is an erosion of goodwill and a loss of control over her reputation, and as such is a more subtle injury than the customary diversion of trade engendered by direct confusion. Reverse confusion exists when a subsequent user selects a trademark that is likely to cause consumers to believe, erroneously, that the goods marketed by the prior user are produced by the subsequent user. The misdirected phone calls are not relevant because, even if we infer in Lang's favor that they reflect consumer confusion, those consumers erroneously believed that the senior user (Lang) was the source of the junior user's (Retirement Living) magazine. Evidence of actual reverse confusion that might support Lang's claim would involve purchasers or prospective purchasers of Lang's products who believed that they were produced by or affiliated with Retirement Living's magazine. Appellant, however, has failed to proffer any such evidence. Similarly, Lang has not shown that these misdirected callers were prospective purchasers of Lang's products. In sum, there is no reason to believe that confusion represented by the phone calls could inflict commercial injury in the form of either a diversion of sales, damage to goodwill, or loss of control over reputation. Accordingly, this evidence failed to demonstrate a genuine issue as to any material actual confusion.

6. Good Faith

This factor "looks to whether the defendant adopted its mark with the intention of capitalizing on plaintiff's reputation and goodwill and any confusion between his and the senior user's product." Although the district court correctly acknowledged that "[i]ssues of good faith are generally ill-suited for disposition on summary judgment" we agree with its determination that Retirement Living acted in good faith.

Selection of a mark that reflects the product's characteristics, request for a trademark search and reliance on the advice of counsel are factors that support a finding of good faith. Here, the name New Choices For The Best Years reflects the image that its new owners sought to convey, and Retirement Living requested a trademark search and relied on the advice of its counsel in choosing the name. Further, Retirement Living's prior knowledge of Lang's trade name does not give rise to a necessary inference of bad faith, because adoption of a trademark with actual knowledge of another's prior registration of a very similar mark may be consistent with good faith.

At bottom, Lang relies, as evidence of bad faith, on Retirement Living's attorneys' inability to recall conversations leading up to Retirement Living's selection of the magazine's name. However, in light of the facts leading up to Retirement Living's choice of the mark and the improbability that Retirement Living would choose this mark in the hope of capitalizing on New Choices Press' reputation, the attorneys' forgetfulness fails to raise a genuine issue of fact.

In sum, our consideration of the relevant Polaroid factors compels the legal conclusion that Lang failed to raise a genuine issue of material fact on the existence of a likelihood that Retirement Living's use of its mark will confuse reasonably prudent purchasers. Accordingly, the district court properly granted summary judgment for Retirement Living on Lang's Lanham Act claim.

NOTES

1. Do you agree with Judge Posner or Judge Coffey? Assume that the brooms of Libman and Vining were of similar quality. Is it likely that any consumer would complain of being confused? Is it likely that any consumer would know that the wrong broom had been purchased? Should the defendant be liable for infringement even though consumers are not injured and do not complain of the confusion? Does Judge Posner suggest that a consumer survey should be conducted in such cases? What questions would you ask in such a survey?

Consider that the test of "likelihood of confusion" requires proof of a hypothesis (likelihood) about the state of mind (confusion) of a hypothetical set of consumers. This is not proof of a past fact or occurrence but rather an inference about what is likely to happen in the marketplace. What consequence does this have for the proof that is likely to be available? For the role of the fact finder in the trial of these matters?

2. What kind of consumer confusion is prohibited by trademark law? When the same mark is used on directly competing goods, the nature of the confusion is relatively clear. However, consider the following situations:

a. Drug A is produced by a number of different companies in red and blue capsules. NewCo begins producing drug B in a red and blue capsule. Evidence suggests that there is a likelihood that consumers will confuse the two capsules. Is NewCo liable for trademark infringement?

b. A consumer purchases a watch purporting to be a "Rolex" watch for $10 from a man on a street corner in New York. Is the seller liable for trademark infringement? Do you think a reasonable consumer would think that a real Rolex watch can be purchased for $10? What is the "narrative" leading to confusion in this case?

c. First Co sells jeans, T-shirts, jackets, and shorts under the trademark "Bongo". Bongo clothing is sold exclusively in department stores. Second Co decides to open a restaurant called "Bongo's Cafe". Is there a narrative leading to confusion in this case? Would it make any difference if Second Co's restaurant was modeled after such restaurants as Hard Rock Cafe and Planet Hollywood in which there is a separate gift shop where patrons can purchase T-shirts, caps, and jackets with the "Bongo Cafe" logo?

d. Small Co begins using the mark "Big-Foot" on tires and sells them from a single location. Large Co subsequently adopts the "Big Foot" mark for its tires and launches a massive nation-wide advertising campaign. The vast majority of consumers come to identify the "Big Foot" mark with Large Co. Is there a "narrative" leading to confusion in this case?

3. Judge Oakes' opinion in *Lang* represents the predominant method of analyzing the issue of likelihood of confusion. While each federal circuit and many state supreme courts have their own formulation of the list of factors to be considered, they all include essentially three separate inquiries. The first set of factors looks at the realities of the marketplace in which consumers are likely to confront the competing trademarks in order to draw an inference of a likelihood of confusion. These factors include the similarity of the trademarks, the strength of the plaintiff's mark, the way in which the goods are marketed and distributed, the care and sophistication that consumers are likely to bring to the purchase of the goods in question, and the degree to which the goods compete. The second inquiry is whether there is evidence of actual confusion. Certainly proof that consumers are actually confused makes a stronger case than the effort to draw inferences from the market context. The third inquiry focuses on the intent of the defendant.

4. *Marketplace factors.*

a. *Strength of the plaintiff's mark.* Judge Oakes suggests this factor relates to the distinctiveness of the plaintiff's mark. This means that the categorization of the mark, i.e., descriptive, suggestive, arbitrary, will be relevant again to the issue of likelihood of confusion. Does this suggest that the trademark owner who is able to convince a fact-finder the mark is "suggestive" and thus protectable without proof of secondary meaning may still need to present proof of secondary meaning to establish the mark's strength? How does the use of the mark by third parties relate to its strength? Is Judge Posner really saying that the decoration on Libman's broom was a very weak mark, particularly since it was not visible when packaged? Should evidence of extensive use and large advertising expenditures be relevant to a mark's strength?

Should the registration of a mark on the Principal Register create a presumption that the mark is a strong one? What if the registration is incontestable?

b. *Similarity of the marks.* This factor requires the fact finder to compare the two competing marks. In comparing two marks courts apply comparisons of the appearance, sound and meaning of the two terms. What evidence is available to prove that two marks are similar in appearance?

Does this require only that the plaintiff introduce the two marks and that the court make a subjective assessment of their similarity? Two marks that are not similar in appearance may nonetheless sound alike. Could you use the mark "Ikon" to compete with the famous "Nikon" cameras? Could you make an "Air-O" shirt to compete with an "Arrow" shirt? Courts also consider the meaning of the terms. If Mobil Oil used a picture of a flying horse as its trademark, could you adopt the word mark "Pegasus" for your gasoline products? Could you compete with the maker of "Cyclone" fences by marketing your fence as a "Tornado" fence?

Courts generally apply the anti-dissection rule which requires that the similarity of the two marks be judged on their overall appearance rather than through a comparison of individual components. At the same time it is clear that there are marks that have a dominant component that may overcome similarities in other aspects of the mark. Consider Bristol-Myers Squibb Co., v. McNeil-P.P.C., Inc, 973 F.2d 1033 (2d Cir. 1992). McNeil began selling "Tylenol PM" in a package that was colored and arranged in a fashion similar to Bristol-Myers' "Excedrin PM". The district court found the two trade dresses "strongly similar", but the Second Circuit held that "although they share many similar elements, the prominence of the trade names on the two packages weighs heavily against a finding of consumer confusion resulting from the overall look of the packaging." However, in Fun-Damental Too, Ltd. v. Gemmy industries Corp., 111 F.3d 993 (2d Cir. 1997) the Second Circuit held that unlike *Bristol-Myers* where the trade names were easily recognizable, less well-known trade names may not be sufficient to distinguish two similar packages.

The fact-finder must also assess the similarity of the marks in as close a context as possible to the context in which consumers will confront the marks. Consumers may distinguish between similar marks if they see them side-by-side on a grocer's shelf but not if they are in different aisles or different stores.

c. *Similarity of marketing and distribution.* The manner in which goods are marketed and the channels in which they are distributed may impact on the likelihood of confusion between competing marks. If the plaintiff's goods are sold only in department and specialty stores and the defendant's goods were sold only through mail order, would the likelihood of confusion be reduced? What if plaintiff sold only to lawyers and defendant sold only to doctors? What if plaintiff sold only to lawyers and defendant sold to the general public?

d. *Care and sophistication of purchasers.* Are the differences in two relatively similar marks more likely to be noticed by consumers on inexpensive or expensive goods? On cereal purchased in a grocery store or on appliances purchased at a discount electronic store? Are purchasing agents for large corporations more or less likely to be confused then consumers generally?

e. *Competitive proximity of the goods.* What is the likelihood of confusion if an identical trademark is used by one company for lipstick and another company for bulldozers? What about use of the same mark on the following goods: (1) vitamin pills and vegetable juice, (2) a magazine directed at teenage girls and clothing for teenage girls, (3)beer and cigarettes, (4) soft-drinks and toilet bowl cleaner, (5) candy and dolls, and (6)fresh citrus fruit and hair shampoo. What does the consumer have to believe in these situations before confusion can occur. In a contest between the lipstick company and the bulldozer company, would evidence that the bulldozer company used the mark first and was, in fact, planning to produce a lipstick using the trademark be relevant?

5. *Actual Confusion.* The rule in trademark cases is that while evidence of actual confusion is always significant, it is never necessary. This is a recognition that in dispersed markets, evidence of actual consumers who were confused is difficult to obtain. Nonetheless, the testimony of consumers who were confused, if credible, is strong evidence. Misdirected mail or telephone calls are often asserted as evidence of actual confusion. Consider, however, Judge Oakes' assessment of the misdirected telephone calls in *Lang*. In an infringement action by the Duluth News-Tribune against the Saturday Daily News & Tribune a reporter for plaintiff testifies that he called a potential interview subject introducing himself as from the "News-Tribune" and the person asked "which News-Tribune". Is this good evidence of actual confusion?

The power of evidence of actual confusion leads some trademark owners to desperation. See Reed-Union Corp. v. Turtle Wax, Inc., 77 F.3d 909 (7th Cir. 1996) where Judge Easterbrook quoted a district court's finding regarding one witness's testimony of actual confusion:

> [One witness related] the story of an elderly gentleman in Massachusetts who approached a Reed Union sales representative at a gas station to compliment him in the shine of his car. The Reed Union representative said, "Why I use NU FINISH," to which the old gentleman responded, "I do too, but I don't get the same shine." The old gentleman then went to the trunk of his car where he produced FINISH 2001. This story might be a fine commercial, but it is inherently unbelievable to this Court.

6. *Consumer Surveys.* Judge Posner suggests that the plaintiff might have introduced surveys of consumers to prove a likelihood of confusion. Expensive survey evidence is increasingly used in an attempt to prove a likelihood of confusion. See, Symposium, The Structure and Uses of Survey Evidence in Trademark Cases, 67 Trademark Rep. 97 (1977). The availability of surveys has brought the appearance of a mathematical rigor to the likelihood of confusion inquiry. What percentage of consumers must be confused to constitute a trademark infringement? Courts have recognized that in any marketplace there is some base line of confused consumers. Even with efforts to control for this background confusion, should a survey showing 25% of respondents confused be sufficient? 12%? 7%?

How would you go about conducting a survey to show that consumers of cereal were confused by a new cereal called "Tall Brand" if you represented the makers of "All Bran"? Would you stop consumers at random in a shopping mall, show them the two boxes, and ask them if they were produced by the same company? Would you show individual consumers either one box or the other and ask them "Do you know if the company that produces this product produces any other cereal product?" Would you hand consumers entering a grocery store a $3.00 off coupon for "All Bran" and see how many asked to redeem the coupon for "Tall Brand"? Consider the following:

> Most surveys do not measure actual confusion. Surveys only give us information about a controlled and artificial world from which we are asked to draw inferences about the real world. One might be able to draw helpful inferences from a survey of randomly selected pedestrians in a shopping mall who are interrogated about pictures of two products, but to claim their responses are direct proof of the responses of actual consumers as they make their purchasing decisions is going too far.

Harvey S. Perlman, The Restatement of the Law of Unfair Competition: A Work in Progress, 80 Trademark Rep. 461, 472 (1990).

7. If the question is whether consumers are likely to be confused, why is the intention of the defendant relevant since the consumer will never know what that intention is? If the plaintiff is able to prove intent, many courts hold that an inference arises that (a) the plaintiff's mark has secondary meaning and (b) the defendant's use created a likelihood of confusion. The assumption behind the inference is that if a firm intentionally tried to create confusion it probably succeeded (or at least should not be able to defend on the basis that it tried but failed). Courts must be careful in permitting the inference in those cases where there may be an intent to copy but not an intent to confuse. For example, competitors have the right to intentionally copy generic or functional devices. See Blau Plumbing, Inc. v. S.O.S. Fix–It, Inc., 781 F.2d 604 (7th Cir.1986) ("The problem is that evidence of intent is often ambiguous. Maybe therefore a court should insist on other evidence of distinctiveness and not allow a trademark infringement case to get to a jury merely on proof that the defendant may have been trying to confuse consumers about whose brand they were buying * * *."). See, Restatement, Third, of Unfair Competition § 22 (1995).

International Order of Job's Daughters v. Lindburg & Co.

United States Court of Appeals, Ninth Circuit, 1980.
633 F.2d 912.

■ FLETCHER, CIRCUIT JUDGE.

[Job's Daughters, a young woman's fraternal organization, sued Lindeburg for making jewelry displaying the fraternal emblem of the organization without their permission. Job's Daughters licenses the use of its emblem by several "official jewelers" and it sells some jewelry directly to its members. Lindeburg requested a license and was refused.]

Resolution of this issue turns on a close analysis of the way in which Lindeburg is using the Job's Daughters insignia. In general, trademark law is concerned only with identification of the maker, sponsor, or endorser of the product so as to avoid confusing consumers. Trademark law does not prevent a person from copying so-called "functional" features of a product which constitute the actual benefit that the consumer wishes to purchase, as distinguished from an assurance that a particular entity made, sponsored, or endorsed a product.

* * *

Application of the [functionality doctrine] to this case has a special twist because the name "Job's Daughters" and the Job's Daughters insignia are indisputably used to identify the organization, and members of Job's Daughters wear the jewelry to identify themselves as members. In that context, the insignia are trademarks of Job's Daughters. But in the context of this case, the name and emblem are functional aesthetic components of the jewelry, in that they are being merchandised on the basis of their intrinsic value, not as a designation of origin or sponsorship.

It is not uncommon for a name or emblem that serves in one context as a collective mark or trademark also to be merchandised for its own intrinsic utility to consumers. We commonly identify ourselves by displaying emblems expressing allegiances. Our jewelry, clothing, and cars are emblazoned with inscriptions showing the organizations we belong to, the schools we attend, the landmarks we have visited, the sports teams we support, the beverages we imbibe. Although these inscriptions frequently include names and emblems that are also used as collective marks or trademarks, it would be naive to conclude that the name or emblem is desired because consumers believe that the product somehow originated with or was sponsored by the organization the name or emblem signifies.

Job's Daughters relies on Boston Professional Hockey Ass'n, Inc. v. Dallas Cap & Emblem Mfg., Inc., 510 F.2d 1004 (5th Cir.), cert. denied, 423 U.S. 868 (1975), in which the Boston Bruins and other National Hockey League clubs brought a trademark infringement suit against a company that sold replicas of the NHL team emblems. The Fifth Circuit, applying the Lanham Act infringement test and focusing on the "likelihood of confusion," found infringement:

> The confusion or deceit requirement is met by the fact that the defendant duplicated the protected trademarks and sold them to the public knowing that the public would identify them as being the teams' trademarks. The certain knowledge of the buyer that the source and origin of the trademark symbols were the plaintiffs satisfies the requirement of the act. The argument that confusion must be as to the source of the manufacture of the emblem itself is unpersuasive, where the trademark, originated by the team, is the triggering mechanism for the sale of the emblem.

510 F.2d at 1012. Job's Daughters asserts that *Boston Hockey* supports its contention that even purely functional use of a trademark violates the Lanham Act. We reject the reasoning of *Boston Hockey*. Interpreted expansively, *Boston Hockey* holds that a trademark's owner has a complete

monopoly over its use, including its functional use, in commercial merchandising.[10] But our reading of the Lanham Act and its legislative history reveals no congressional design to bestow such broad property rights on trademark owners. Its scope is much narrower: to protect consumers against deceptive designations of the origin of goods and, conversely, to enable producers to differentiate their products from those of others. * * * The *Boston Hockey* decision transmogrifies this narrow protection into a broad monopoly. It does so by injecting its evaluation of the equities between the parties and of the desirability of bestowing broad property rights on trademark owners. A trademark is, of course, a form of business property. See J. McCarthy, Trademarks and Unfair Competition §§ 2:6–2:7 (1973). But the "property right" or protection accorded a trademark owner can only be understood in the context of trademark law and its purposes. A trademark owner has a property right only insofar as is necessary to prevent consumer confusion as to who produced the goods and to facilitate differentiation of the trademark owner's goods. See id. The *Boston Hockey* court decided that broader protection was desirable. In our view, this extends the protection beyond that intended by Congress and beyond that accorded by any other court.

* * *

Our holding does not mean that a name or emblem could not serve simultaneously as a functional component of a product and a trademark. See Dallas Cowboys Cheerleaders, Inc. v. Pussycat Cinema, Ltd., 604 F.2d 200, 204 (2d Cir.1979). That is, even if the Job's Daughters' name and emblem, when inscribed on Lindeburg's jewelry, served primarily a functional purpose, it is possible that they could serve secondarily as trademarks if the typical customer not only purchased the jewelry for its intrinsic functional use and aesthetic appeal but also inferred from the insignia that the jewelry was produced, sponsored, or endorsed by Job's Daughters. We recognize that there is some danger that the consumer may be more likely to infer endorsement or sponsorship when the consumer is a member of the group whose collective mark or trademark is being marketed. Accordingly, a court must closely examine the articles themselves, the defendant's merchandising practices, and any evidence that consumers have actually inferred a connection between the defendant's product and the trademark owner.

We conclude from our examination of the trial judge's findings and of the underlying evidence that Lindeburg was not using the Job's Daughters name and emblem as trademarks. The insignia were a prominent feature of each item so as to be visible to others when worn, allowing the wearer to

---

10. The Fifth Circuit itself has apparently retreated from a broad interpretation of *Boston Hockey*. In Kentucky Fried Chicken Corp. v. Diversified Packaging Corp., 549 F.2d 368 (5th Cir.1977), the court began its analysis of Kentucky Fried Chicken's infringement claim by noting that it "reject[ed] any notion that a trademark is an owner's 'property' to be protected irrespective of its role in the protection of our markets," and described the *Boston Hockey* holding as premised on a finding that consumers were likely to believe that the emblems somehow originated from the hockey clubs. 549 F.2d at 389.

publicly express her allegiance to the organization. Lindeburg never designated the merchandise as "official" Job's Daughters' merchandise or otherwise affirmatively indicated sponsorship. Job's Daughters did not show a single instance in which a customer was misled about the origin, sponsorship, or endorsement of Lindeburg's jewelry, nor that it received any complaints about Lindeburg's wares. Finally, there was evidence that many other jewelers sold unlicensed Job's Daughters jewelry, implying that consumers did not ordinarily purchase their fraternal jewelry from only "official" sources. We conclude that Job's Daughters did not meet its burden of proving that a typical buyer of Lindeburg's merchandise would think that the jewelry was produced, sponsored, or endorsed by the organization. The name and emblem were functional aesthetic components of the product, not trademarks. There could be, therefore, no infringement.

The judgment of the district court is reversed and the case is remanded for the entry of judgment in favor of appellant Lindeburg.

NOTES

1. The emblem cases, represented by *Job's Daughters* and *Boston Hockey,* depend upon a showing of confusion of sponsorship, that is, that consumers will believe that the trademark owner sponsors or in some way approves of the defendant's use of the mark. At the heart of the issue is the assumption one makes about the market for licensed trademarks and the extent to which trademark owners do in fact license and control their marks. The Eleventh Circuit had the occasion to reaffirm *Boston Hockey* in University of Georgia Athletic Association v. Laite, 756 F.2d 1535 (11th Cir.1985) where the defendant began marketing "Battlin Bulldog Beer" in cans featuring the University's colors and a picture of the "Georgia Bulldog"—the emblem of the University's athletic program. A disclaimer— "not associated with the University of Georgia"—appeared in small lettering on the cans. The Court of Appeals affirmed the lower court's holding of likelihood of confusion and took issue with *Job's Daughters:*

> The record in the instant case reveals that, in one week, at least ten to fifteen members of the public contacted UGAA to inquire about the connection between [the beer and the University]. * * * This evidence indicates that, contrary to the unsupported assertion of the Ninth Circuit in *Job's Daughters,* at least some members of the public do assume that products bearing the mark of a school or a sports team are sponsored or licensed by the school or team [citing survey showing almost half of all persons shown football jerseys of the NFL believed manufacturers were required to obtain license from the team]. 756 F.2d at 1546, n. 28.

2. In Boston Athletic Ass'n v. Sullivan, 867 F.2d 22 (1st Cir.1989) the court extended the emblem cases to their logical (?) conclusion. The BAA held registered marks for "Boston Marathon" and a unicorn logo used in association with the annual Boston Marathon. The defendants imprinted T-shirts as follows: "1987 Marathon [picture of runners] Hopkinton–Boston" and "Boston [picture of runners] 1988". The court awarded summary judgment to the plaintiff finding both confusion of goods ("public are likely to confuse defendant's shirts with those of plaintiff") and confusion of sponsorship (if "(1) defendants intentionally referred to the Boston Marathon on its shirts, and (2) purchasers were likely to buy the shirts precisely because of that reference, we think it fair to presume that purchasers are likely to be confused about the shirt's source or sponsorship."). Does this give the sponsor a monopoly on the event itself? Note the defendants did not use the plaintiff's trademark; they only referred to the event. Can the National Football League prevent others from producing any souvenirs that refer to the Super Bowl? Could a television station cover the Boston Marathon as a news event without permission from the race organizers and announce in advance they were going to show "The Boston Marathon"? See WCVB-TV v. Boston Athletic Association, 926 F.2d 42 (1st Cir. 1991) where the First Circuit moved away from its holding in *Sullivan.*

3. What is the precise injury in confusion of sponsorship cases? Is there an element of misappropriation theory? Is there a public policy justification for permitting others to profit from the fame associated with these emblems? If it is adopted as a test for trademark infringement, are there any principles that can be developed to limit its application or does the test presage protection of marks without regard to the goods or services upon which they are used? To what extent should consumer understanding (or misunderstanding) about the law of trademarks dictate the result. If consumers believed that the law prohibits use of another's mark without the mark owner's permission, doesn't this fact alone then create the predicate for a finding of confusion? In *Job's Daughters* what weight would you give the results of a consumer survey that asked the question: "Do you think the maker of this ring [holding up the defendant's ring] needed the permission of Jobs Daughters to use its emblem?"

4. How does the *Jobs Daughters* decision relate to the following information from the marketplace. It is reported that Universities are earning approximately $2.5 billion dollars a year from licensing their logos for use on merchandise. See Roger Thurow, "Go Team Go: Win One For the Logo!" Wall Street Journal, pg. B12 (Nov. 22, 1996):

> This year, though, the mighty M looks vulnerable. Michigan's royalties settled down at $4 million last year, and with weaker-than-usual football and basketball teams of late, another slide looms. Nebraska, with back-to-back national football crowns, has seen Herbie the Husker royalties rise past $3 million. Kentucky, fresh off a national basketball title, has pushed its blue Wildcat close to $3 million. Florida, which has national-football-championship aspirations and a spiffy new Gator-head logo, is nearing $2 million. And then there's the pent-up logo mania at Ohio State, one of the nation's largest schools, which hasn't been to the New Year's Day Rose Bowl game since 1985

At the professional level, the National Football League and the National Basketball Association are reported to have $3 billion in licensing revenues. The NFL confiscates over $1 million in counterfeit goods during the

Super Bowl alone. Roger Thurow, "Busting Bogus Merchandise Peddlers With the Logo Cops", Wall Street Journal, pg. B1 (Oct. 24, 1997). And consider how trademark rules will apply to the announcement that the NBA has licensed the names and logos of its 29 teams to the company that operates Hard Rock Cafes to develop NBA theme restaurants. Stefan Fatsis, NBA to Join Hard Rock Cafe in Packed Arena, Wall Street Journal, pg. B1 (Feb. 2, 1998).

5. The Restatement, Third, of Unfair Competition § 20, Comment *e*, at 214 (1995) provides: "If purchasers believe that the organization has authorized or approved the sale of merchandise bearing the mark, the mark serves a trademark function and the unauthorized use is an infringement. On the other hand, if the appearance of the mark on the merchandise is perceived by prospective purchasers merely as a means for them to use the goods to indicate membership or support for the organization, the use of the mark creates no likelihood of confusion and is not an infringement." Is this consistent with *Jobs Daughters*?

PROBLEM

You are retained by the Order of the Sleeping Cow, a non-profit fraternal organization. The organization has developed an organizational symbol—"the sleeping cow design"—which it wants to use on its organizational jewelry as well as on t-shirts and other wearing apparel. Heartened by the large licensing fees generated by athletic teams and the enthusiastic response of its members to the sleeping cow design, it asks you to advise the organization on how best to protect the design and to reap the benefits of the design's use in the marketplace. You, of course, are familiar with *Job's Daughters*. What do you advise the Order to do? Were there clear mistakes made by Job's Daughters? Will the Order have more protection if it markets the sleeping cow design only to its members rather than to the general public?

Mead Data Central, Inc. v. Toyota Motor Sales, U.S.A. Inc.

United States Court of Appeals, Second Circuit, 1989.
875 F.2d 1026.

■ VAN GRAAFEILAND, D., CIRCUIT JUDGE:

Toyota Motor Sales, U.S.A., Inc. and its parent, Toyota Motor Corporation, appeal from a judgment of the United States District Court for the Southern District of New York (Edelstein, J.), enjoining them from using LEXUS as the name of their new luxury automobile and the division that manufactures it. The district court held that, under New York's antidilution statute, N.Y.Gen.Bus.Law § 368–d, Toyota's use of LEXUS is likely to dilute the distinctive quality of LEXIS, the mark used by Mead Data Central, Inc. for its computerized legal research service. On March 8, 1989, we entered an order of reversal, stating that an opinion would follow. This is the opinion.

THE STATUTE

Section 368–d of New York's General Business Law, which has counterparts in at least twenty other states, reads as follows:

> Likelihood of injury to business reputation or of dilution of the distinctive quality of a mark or trade name shall be a ground for injunctive relief in cases of infringement of a mark registered or not registered or in cases of unfair competition, notwithstanding the absence of competition between the parties or the absence or confusion as to the source of goods or services.

[The court reviewed the evidence of the respective uses of the marks involved. The district court found that 76% of attorneys and accountants associated LEXIS with Mead's service but only 1% of the general adult population did so (and half of this one percent were attorneys). Toyota had plans for an $18 million advertising campaign during the first nine months for its new LEXUS cars. Toyota knew of Mead's mark prior to adopting LEXUS but its lawyers advised them there was no conflict.]

THE LAW

The brief legislative history accompanying section 368–d describes the purpose of the statute as preventing "the whittling away of an established trade-mark's selling power and value through its unauthorized use by others upon dissimilar products." 1954 N.Y. Legis.Ann. 49 (emphasis supplied). * * *

[S]ome courts have gone so far as to hold that, although violation of an antidilution statute does not require confusion of product or source, the marks in question must be sufficiently similar that confusion may be created as between the marks themselves. We need not go that far. We hold only that the marks must be "very" or "substantially" similar and that, absent such similarity, there can be no viable claim of dilution.

[The court disputed the district court's observation that the two marks were pronounced the same in "everyday spoken English"—"we liken LEXUS to such words as 'census', 'focus' and 'locus' and differentiate it from such words as 'axis', 'aegis' and 'iris' "—and concluded that "everyday spoken English" was not the proper test:

> We take it as a given that television and radio announcers usually are more careful and precise in their diction than is the man on the street. Moreover, it is the rare television commercial that does not contain a visual reference to the mark and product, which in the instant case would be the LEXUS automobile. We conclude that in the field of commercial advertising, which is the field subject to regulation, there is no substantial similarity between Mead's mark and Toyota's.]

There are additional factors that militate against a finding of dilution in the instant case. Such a finding must be based on two elements. First, plaintiff's mark must possess a distinctive quality capable of dilution. Second, plaintiff must show a likelihood of dilution[.] As section 368–d expressly states, a plaintiff need not show either competition between its product or service and that of the defendant or a likelihood of confusion as to the source of the goods or services.

Distinctiveness for dilution purposes often has been equated with the strength of a mark for infringement purposes. It also has been defined as uniqueness or as having acquired a secondary meaning. * * * In sum, the statute protects a trademark's "selling power." However, the fact that a mark has selling power in a limited geographical or commercial area does not endow it with a secondary meaning for the public generally.

The strength and distinctiveness of LEXIS is limited to the market for its services—attorneys and accountants. Outside that market, LEXIS has very little selling power. Because only one percent of the general population associates LEXIS with the attributes of Mead's service, it cannot be said that LEXIS identifies that service to the general public and distinguishes it from others. Moreover, the bulk of Mead's advertising budget is devoted to reaching attorneys through professional journals.

This Court has defined dilution as either the blurring of a mark's product identification or the tarnishment of the affirmative associations a mark has come to convey. Mead does not claim that Toyota's use of LEXUS would tarnish affirmative associations engendered by LEXIS. The question that remains, therefore, is whether LEXIS is likely to be blurred by LEXUS.

Very little attention has been given to date to the distinction between the confusion necessary for a claim of infringement and the blurring necessary for a claim of dilution. * * * Although the antidilution statute dispenses with the requirements of competition and confusion, it does not follow that every junior use of a similar mark will dilute the senior mark in the manner contemplated by the New York Legislature.

As already stated, the brief legislative history accompanying section 368–d described the purpose of the statute as preventing "the whittling away of an established trademark's selling power and value through its unauthorized use by others upon dissimilar products." The history disclosed a need for legislation to prevent such "hypothetical anomalies" as "Dupont shoes, Buick aspirin tablets, Schlitz varnish, Kodak pianos, Bulova gowns, and so forth", and cited cases involving similarly famous marks, e.g., Tiffany & Co. v. Tiffany Productions, Inc., 147 Misc. 679 (1932), aff'd, 237 A.D. 801, aff'd, 262 N.Y. 482 (1933); Philadelphia Storage Battery Co. v. Mindlin, 163 Misc. 52 (1937). 1954 N.Y.Legis.Ann. 49–50.

It is apparent from these references that there must be some mental association between plaintiff's and defendant's marks.

> [I]f a reasonable buyer is not at all likely to link the two uses of the trademark in his or her own mind, even subtly or subliminally, then there can be no dilution. . . . [D]ilution theory presumes some kind of mental association in the reasonable buyer's mind between the two party's [sic] uses of the mark.

2 J. McCarthy [Trademarks and Unfair Competition] § 24.13 at 213–14.

This mental association may be created where the plaintiff's mark is very famous and therefore has a distinctive quality for a significant percentage of the defendant's market. However, if a mark circulates only in a limited market, it is unlikely to be associated generally with the mark for a dissimilar product circulating elsewhere. As discussed above, such distinctiveness as LEXIS possesses is limited to the narrow market of attorneys and accountants. Moreover, the process which LEXIS represents is widely disparate from the product represented by LEXUS. For the general public, LEXIS has no distinctive quality that LEXUS will dilute.

The possibility that someday LEXUS may become a famous mark in the mind of the general public has little relevance in the instant dilution analysis since it is quite apparent that the general public associates nothing with LEXIS. On the other hand, the recognized sophistication of attorneys, the principal users of the service, has substantial relevance. Because of this knowledgeable sophistication, it is unlikely that, even in the market where Mead principally operates, there will be any significant amount of blurring between the LEXIS and LEXUS marks.

For all the foregoing reasons, we hold that Toyota did not violate section 368–d. We see no need therefore to discuss Toyota's remaining arguments for reversal.

SWEET, District Judge, concurring:

I concur, but write separately because I disagree with the majority's conclusion that LEXIS is not a strong mark capable of dilution and that LEXIS and LEXUS differ significantly in pronunciation, and I have a different view of the factors that are necessary to a finding of dilution.

* * *

By treating similarity of the marks as a separate element of a dilution cause of action and by evaluating the dilution claim without developing an analytical framework, the majority threatens to muddy the already murky waters of antidilution analysis. * * *

Defining likelihood of dilution as "tarnishing" is helpful because that principle can be applied in practice. See, e.g., Dallas Cowboys Cheerleaders, Inc. v. Pussycat Cinema, Ltd., 604 F.2d 200 (2d Cir.1979) (plaintiff's distinctive uniform diluted by defendant's use of a similar uniform in an X-rated movie); Coca-Cola Co. v. Gemini Rising, Inc., 346 F.Supp. 1183 (E.D.N.Y.1972) (plaintiff's "Coca-Cola" mark diluted by defendant's use of similar lettering in printing "Cocaine" on poster). "Blurring," however, offers practitioners and courts only marginally more guidance than "likelihood of dilution."

There is much to be gained by defining a general concept like "blurring" more specifically. As in this instance, confusion in the doctrine has created problems for trademark attorneys advising their clients about adopting trademarks, for potential litigants assessing their chances of pursuing or defending against dilution claims, and for courts attempting to apply the statute. See Shire, 77 Trademark Rep. at 288. In the trademark infringement context, Judge Friendly defined a similarly broad standard—likelihood of confusion—by articulating a multi-factor balancing test * * *. Polaroid Corp. v. Polaroid Elecs. Corp., 287 F.2d 492,

495 (2d Cir.), cert. denied, 368 U.S. 820 (1961). This test has provided practitioners and district courts a helpful framework for assessing likelihood of confusion.

Like likelihood of confusion, blurring sufficient to constitute dilution requires a case-by-case factual inquiry. A review of the anti-dilution cases in this Circuit indicates that courts have articulated the following factors in considering the likelihood of dilution caused by blurring:

(1) similarity of the marks

(2) similarity of the products covered by the marks

(3) sophistication of consumers

(4) predatory intent

(5) renown of the senior mark

(6) renown of the junior mark

The application of these factors here requires reversal of the decision below, although on a basis that I believe differs from that stated by the majority.

[Judge Sweet reviewed each factor. He thought the district court's findings were for the most part correct: that the marks were similar, the products were dissimilar, the consumers of Mead's service were sophisticated, Toyota did not have predatory intent, and the LEXIS mark was strong within its narrow market only.]

The only finding that supports a likelihood of dilution is the district court's conclusion that LEXUS eventually may become so famous that members of the general public who now associate LEXIS or LEXUS with nothing at all may associate the terms with Toyota's automobiles and that Mead's customers may think first of Toyota's car when they hear LEXIS. This analysis is problematic. First, section 368–d protects a mark's selling power among the consuming public. Because the LEXIS mark possesses selling power only among lawyers and accountants, it is irrelevant for dilution analysis that the general public may come to associate LEXIS or LEXUS with Toyota's automobile rather than nothing at all. Second, the district court offered no evidence for its speculation that LEXUS's fame may cause Mead customers to associate "LEXIS" with Toyota's cars. It seems equally plausible that no blurring will occur—because many lawyers and accountants use Mead's services regularly, their frequent association of LEXIS with those services will enable LEXIS's mark to withstand Toyota's advertising campaign.

Therefore, even if we accept the district court's finding regarding the renown of the LEXUS mark, however, reversal still is required. The differences in the marks and in the products covered by the marks, the sophistication of Mead's consumers, the absence of predatory intent, and the limited renown of the LEXIS mark all indicate that blurring is unlikely.

Panavision International, L. P. v. Toeppen

United States Court of Appeals, Ninth Circuit, 1998
1998 WL 178553

■ DAVID R. THOMPSON, CIRCUIT JUDGE:

This case presents two novel issues. We are asked to apply existing rules of personal jurisdiction to conduct that occurred, in part, in "cyberspace." In addition, we are asked to interpret the Federal Trademark Dilution Act as it applies to the Internet.

* * *

The Internet is a worldwide network of computers that enables various individuals and organizations to share information. The Internet allows computer users to access millions of web sites and web pages. A web page is a computer data file that can include names, words, messages, pictures, sounds, and links to other information.

Every web page has its own web site, which is its address, similar to a telephone number or street address. Every web site on the Internet has an identifier called a "domain name." The domain name often consists of a person's name or a company's name or trademark. For example, Pepsi has a web page with a web site domain name consisting of the company name, Pepsi, and . com, the "top level" domain designation: Pepsi.com.

The Internet is divided into several "top level" domains: .edu for education; .org for organizations; .gov for government entities; .net for networks; and .com for "commercial" which functions as the catchall domain for Internet users.

Domain names with the .com designation must be registered on the Internet with Network Solutions, Inc. ("NSI"). NSI registers names on a first-come, first- served basis for a $100 registration fee. NSI does not make a determination about a registrant's right to use a domain name. However, NSI does require an applicant to represent and warrant as an express condition of registering a domain name that (1) the applicant's statements are true and the applicant has the right to use the requested domain name; (2) the "use or registration of the domain name ... does not interfere with or infringe the rights of any third party in any jurisdiction with respect to trademark, service mark, trade name, company name or any other intellectual property right"; and (3) the applicant is not seeking to use the domain name for any unlawful purpose, including unfair competition.

A domain name is the simplest way of locating a web site. If a computer user does not know a domain name, she can use an Internet "search engine." To do this, the user types in a key word search, and the search will locate all of the web sites containing the key word. Such key word searches can yield hundreds of web sites. To make it easier to find their web sites, individuals and companies prefer to have a recognizable domain name.

Panavision holds registered trademarks to the names "Panavision" and "Panaflex" in connection with motion picture camera equipment.

Panavision promotes its trademarks through motion picture and television credits and other media advertising.

In December 1995, Panavision attempted to register a web site on the Internet with the domain name Panavision.com. It could not do that, however, because Toeppen had already established a web site using Panavision's trademark as his domain name. Toeppen's web page for this site displayed photographs of the City of Pana, Illinois.

On December 20, 1995, Panavision's counsel sent a letter from California to Toeppen in Illinois informing him that Panavision held a trademark in the name Panavision and telling him to stop using that trademark and the domain name Panavision.com. Toeppen responded by mail to Panavision in California, stating he had the right to use the name Panavision.com on the Internet as his domain name. Toeppen stated:

> If your attorney has advised you otherwise, he is trying to screw you. He wants to blaze new trails in the legal frontier at your expense. Why do you want to fund your attorney's purchase of a new boat (or whatever) when you can facilitate the acquisition of 'PanaVision.com' cheaply and simply instead?

Toeppen then offered to "settle the matter" if Panavision would pay him $13,000 in exchange for the domain name. Additionally, Toeppen stated that if Panavision agreed to his offer, he would not "acquire any other Internet addresses which are alleged by Panavision Corporation to be its property."

After Panavision refused Toeppen's demand, he registered Panavision's other trademark with NSI as the domain name Panaflex.com. Toeppen's web page for Panaflex.com simply displays the word "Hello."

Toeppen has registered domain names for various other companies including Delta Airlines, Neiman Marcus, Eddie Bauer, Lufthansa, and over 100 other marks. Toeppen has attempted to "sell" domain names for other trademarks such as intermatic.com to Intermatic, Inc. for $10,000 and americanstandard.com to American Standard, Inc. for $15,000.

Panavision filed this action against Toeppen in the District Court for the Central District of California. Panavision alleged claims for dilution of its trademark under the Federal Trademark Dilution Act of 1995, 15 U.S.C. § 1125(c), and under the California Anti-dilution statute, California Business and Professions Code § 14330. Panavision alleged that Toeppen was in the business of stealing trademarks, registering them as domain names on the Internet and then selling the domain names to the rightful trademark owners. The district court determined it had personal jurisdiction over Toeppen, and granted summary judgment in favor of Panavision on both its federal and state dilution claims. This appeal followed.

[The Ninth Circuit held that the simple registration of someone else's trademark as a domain name was not sufficient to subject the party domiciled in one state to jurisdiction in another; here the defendant engaged in a scheme which would have the effect of injuring the plaintiff in California, its principle place of business. This was sufficient to support jurisdiction over the defendant.]

In order to prove a violation of the Federal Trademark Dilution Act, a plaintiff must show that (1) the mark is famous; (2) the defendant is making a commercial use of the mark in commerce; (3) the defendant's use began after the mark became famous; and (4) the defendant's use of the mark dilutes the quality of the mark by diminishing the capacity of the mark to identify and distinguish goods and services. 15 U.S.C. § 1125(c).

Toeppen does not challenge the district court's determination that Panavision's trademark is famous, that his alleged use began after the mark became famous, or that the use was in commerce. Toeppen challenges the district court's determination that he made "commercial use" of the mark and that this use caused "dilution" in the quality of the mark.

1. Commercial Use

Toeppen argues that his use of Panavision's trademarks simply as his domain names cannot constitute a commercial use under the Act. Case law supports this argument. See Panavision International, L.P. v. Toeppen, 945 F.Supp. 1296, 1303 (C.D.Cal.1996) ("Registration of a trade[mark] as a domain name, without more, is not a commercial use of the trademark and therefore is not within the prohibitions of the Act."); Academy of Motion Picture Arts & Sciences v. Network Solutions, Inc., — F.Supp. —, 1997 WL 810472 (C.D.Cal. Dec.22, 1997) (the mere registration of a domain name does not constitute a commercial use); Lockheed Martin Corp. v. Network Solutions, Inc., 985 F.Supp. 949 (C.D.Cal.1997) (NSI's acceptance of a domain name for registration is not a commercial use within the meaning of the Trademark Dilution Act).

Developing this argument, Toeppen contends that a domain name is simply an address used to locate a web page. He asserts that entering a domain name on a computer allows a user to access a web page, but a domain name is not associated with information on a web page. If a user were to type Panavision.com as a domain name, the computer screen would display Toeppen's web page with aerial views of Pana, Illinois. The screen would not provide any information about "Panavision," other than a "location window" which displays the domain name. Toeppen argues that a user who types in Panavision.com, but who sees no reference to the plaintiff Panavision on Toeppen's web page, is not likely to conclude the web page is related in any way to the plaintiff, Panavision.

Toeppen's argument misstates his use of the Panavision mark. His use is not as benign as he suggests. Toeppen's "business" is to register trademarks as domain names and then sell them to the rightful trademark owners. He "act[s] as a 'spoiler,' preventing Panavision and others from doing business on the Internet under their trademarked names unless they pay his fee." Panavision, 938 F.Supp. at 621. This is a commercial use. See Intermatic Inc. v. Toeppen, 947 F.Supp. 1227, 1230 (N.D.Ill.1996) (stating that "[o]ne of Toeppen's business objectives is to profit by the resale or licensing of these domain names, presumably to the entities who conduct business under these names.").

As the district court found, Toeppen traded on the value of Panavision's marks. So long as he held the Internet registrations, he curtailed

Panavision's exploitation of the value of its trademarks on the Internet, a value which Toeppen then used when he attempted to sell the Panavision.com domain name to Panavision.

* * *

Toeppen made a commercial use of Panavision's trademarks. It does not matter that he did not attach the marks to a product. Toeppen's commercial use was his attempt to sell the trademarks themselves. Under the Federal Trademark Dilution Act and the California Anti-dilution statute, this was sufficient commercial use.

2. Dilution

"Dilution" is defined as "the lessening of the capacity of a famous mark to identify and distinguish goods or services, regardless of the presence or absence of (1) competition between the owner of the famous mark and other parties, or (2) likelihood of confusion, mistake or deception." 15 U.S.C. § 1127. [FN6]

Trademark dilution on the Internet was a matter of Congressional concern. Senator Patrick Leahy (D-Vt.) stated:

[I]t is my hope that this anti-dilution statute can help stem the use of deceptive Internet addresses taken by those who are choosing marks that are associated with the products and reputations of others.

141 Cong. Rec. § 19312–01 (daily ed. Dec. 29, 1995) (statement of Sen. Leahy).

To find dilution, a court need not rely on the traditional definitions such as "blurring" and "tarnishment." Indeed, in concluding that Toeppen's use of Panavision's trademarks diluted the marks, the district court noted that Toeppen's conduct varied from the two standard dilution theories of blurring and tarnishment. The court found that Toeppen's conduct diminished "the capacity of the Panavision marks to identify and distinguish Panavision's goods and services on the Internet." Id.

* * *

Toeppen argues he is not diluting the capacity of the Panavision marks to identify goods or services. He contends that even though Panavision cannot use Panavision.com and Panaflex.com as its domain name addresses, it can still promote its goods and services on the Internet simply by using some other "address" and then creating its own web page using its trademarks.

We reject Toeppen's premise that a domain name is nothing more than an address. A significant purpose of a domain name is to identify the entity that owns the web site. "A customer who is unsure about a company's domain name will often guess that the domain name is also the company's name." Cardservice Int'l v. McGee, 950 F.Supp. 737, 741 (E.D.Va.1997).

Using a company's name or trademark as a domain name is also the easiest way to locate that company's web site. Use of a "search engine" can turn up hundreds of web sites, and there is nothing equivalent to a phone book or directory assistance for the Internet.

Moreover, potential customers of Panavision will be discouraged if they cannot find its web page by typing in "Panavision.com," but instead are forced to wade through hundreds of web sites. This dilutes the value of Panavision's trademark.* * *

Toeppen's use of Panavision.com also puts Panavision's name and reputation at his mercy. See Intermatic, 947 F.Supp. at 1240 ("If Toeppen were allowed to use 'intermatic.com,' Intermatic's name and reputation would be at Toeppen's mercy and could be associated with an unimaginable amount of messages on Toeppen's web page.").

We conclude that Toeppen's registration of Panavision's trademarks as his domain names on the Internet diluted those marks within the meaning of the Federal Trademark Dilution Act, 15 U.S.C. § 1125(c), and the California Anti-dilution statute, Cal.Bus. & Prof.Code § 14330.

NOTES

1. The dilution doctrine had its birth in a law review article: Frank Schechter, The Rational Basis of Trademark Protection, 40 Harv. L. Rev. 813 (1927). Early trademark cases took a narrow view of confusion of sponsorship or association so that infringement was largely limited to use of another's mark on goods that directly competed with the other's goods. Schechter advanced the theory that in addition to identifying source, trademarks had the power to generate sales and thus should be more broadly protected. Over time approximately 25 states adopted dilution statutes of the kind considered in *Mead Data*. However, state courts largely ignored them or interpreted them narrowly. The first major case to give a state statute a broad interpretation was Allied Maintenance Corp. v. Allied Mechanical Trades, Inc., 42 N.Y.2d 538, 399 N.Y.S.2d 628, 369 N.E.2d 1162 (1977). The plaintiff at a well-established building maintenance firm, sought to prevent an installer of ventilating equipment from using its trade name "Allied Maintenance". The New York Court of Appeals, thought the statute extended infringement doctrines beyond a likelihood of confusion to a likelihood of dilution, but nonetheless held that it applied only to truly distinctive marks of which "Allied Maintenance" was not one.

2. The adoption of the Federal Dilution Act, 15 U.S.C. §1125(c), in 1996, significantly changed the prosecution and defense of federal trademark infringement actions. Although factually intensive, the analysis of likelihood of confusion has a significant body of precedent and trademark owners, old and new, can make educated guesses about the likelihood of infringement. Dilution has no such body of precedent.   In Ringling Bros.—Barnum & Bailey Combined Shows, Inc. v. Utah Division of Travel Dev., 955 F. Supp. 605 (E.D.Va. 1997) the Utah agency used the phrase "The Greatest Snow on Earth" in promoting skiing in Utah and the circus brought a dilution action under the new federal statute. The court defined dilution as follows:

> The Act's causation requirement confirms the validity of the insight that dilution by blurring occurs when consumers mistakenly associate (or confuse) the two marks. It is not open to serious dispute

that the Act requires a causal nexus between the use of the junior mark and the dilution of the famous mark. It is precisely this causal nexus that is reflected in the mistaken or confused association of the marks in the minds of consumers and which, of course, results in the proscribed dilution of the famous mark. Put another way, famous marks can lose their distinctiveness or power to identify and distinguish goods and services for various reasons other than the use of a junior mark. Absent a demonstration or reasonable inference of the causal nexus between the actionable dilution and a junior mark, a court cannot attribute the dilution to the junior mark's use. This nexus is demonstrated where consumers mistakenly link or associate the two marks

Does the *Ringling* case help bring reasonable certainty to the issue? Can you fashion a survey that would detect dilution? In *Ringling* the plaintiff asked residents of Utah and other states to indicate an association for the phrase "THE GREATEST _____ ON EARTH" and then to complete the phrase. What result if a significant percentage of respondents indicate the phrase refers to skiing in Utah and then completes the phrase inserting the word "SNOW"? How would you use survey evidence to establish the casual link between the defendant's use of the mark and any dilution of the plaintiff's mark? Should a company with a famous mark take a survey immediately before any diluting marks appear in order to establish a baseline against which to measure any future dilution?

3. Is the concept of dilution as applied in *Panavision* any clearer? Is the problem here one of bad faith. We know that if another user in good faith adopts a trademark in a remote area prior to registration by another, the remote use is protected even though it forecloses the registrant from fully exploiting the mark. If someone adopts a domain name in good faith that happens to be anothers trademark, could that be dilution as well?

4. Section 1125(c) introduces the concept of a "famous" mark. Many state statutes have been interpreted to apply only to marks that are "highly distinctive." How does one know if a mark is "famous" or "highly distinctive." Do the factors listed in § 1125(c)provide any real help? See, Restatement, Third, of Unfair Competition § 25, Comment *e, at 268* (1995): "As a general matter, a trademark is sufficiently distinctive to be diluted by a nonconfusing use if the mark retains its source significance when encountered outside the context of the goods or services with which the mark is used by the trademark owner. For example, the trademark KODAK evokes an association with the cameras sold under that mark whether the word is displayed with cameras or simply appears alone." Does this definition help?

5. How would you describe the concept of blurring? Does the psychological phenomenon of "conditioned response" illustrated by Pavlov's salivating dogs provide a clue? If every time consumers hear the word "McDonalds" they begin salivating for a hamburger, will use of "McDonalds" on pencils, bulldozers, lipstick, and computers tend to diminish that response? Is that something the law should protect?

6. Does the concept of dilution provide more or less security for users of trademarks? If your client wants to adopt a mark for lipstick and you find a prior use on bulldozers, what advice do you now give? Consider Ringling Bros.-Barnum Bailey Combined Shows, Inc. v. B.E. Windows Corp., 937 F. Supp. 204 (S.D.N.Y. 1996) where the court refused to enjoin on a dilution theory the defendant from using the phrase "The Greatest Bar on Earth" for a restaurant at the top of the New York World Trade Center. The court acknowledged that the phrase was a famous mark but decided that Ringling was only entitled to broad protection in the amusement or circus context and that Ringling failed to demonstrate a likelihood of dilution outside that context.

7. Does dilution raise problems of reconciling trademark law with the copyright and patent statutes? Should dilution be applied to trade dress consisting of a product configuration? In Sunbeam Products, Inc. v. The West Bend Company, 39 U.S.P.Q.2d 1545 (S.D.Miss. 1996, aff'd, 123 F.3d 246 (5th Cir. 1997) the trial court was prepared to grant a preliminary injunction against West Bend for copying the shape of Sunbeam's famous Mixmaster stand food mixer. The Fifth Circuit avoided the issue by indicating that the preliminary injunction could be affirmed on likelihood of confusion grounds.

8. What relief should be accorded in a dilution case. Should profits ever be awarded? Damages? If damages are awarded, how should they be measured? Section 1125(c)(2) permits only injunctive relief absent a showing of willfulness.

PROBLEMS: INTERNET DOMAIN NAMES AND 1–800 NUMBERS

1. How should the courts resolve the following cases:

a. Ernie uses his ford.com website to advertised used cars. What claims can you make on behalf of Ford Motor Company?

b. Assume Ford Motor Company obtained the ford.com address first. Ernie registers for "ford.org". Does Ford Motor Company have any complaint? If Ernie uses the site to sell used cars?

c. Dan Toyota, a farmer in Iowa, registers a website under the address "toyota.com" to advertise his Toyota Brand Salsa. Does the Toyota Motor Company have a cause of action?

The extraordinary expansion of commercial activity on the Internet has caused the United States Government to propose adding additional generic top-level domain names. Will this solve the trademark problem? It is possible that there are throughout the world several companies entitled to use the word "Ford" as a trademark for products and services far removed from the automobile industry. It would be possible on the Internet to establish a single website under the "ford.com" address. The viewer reaching this address could be presented with a menu of companies with the name "Ford" and hyperlinks to each one. Would this solve the problem?

2. The national motel chain Holiday Inns uses the number 1–800-HOLIDAY as its national reservation number. Call Management is a telephone answering service that makes reservations for a number of different hotel chains including Holiday Inns. Call Management knows that one of the most common mistakes made in dialing telephone numbers is to substitute a zero for the letter "O". Accordingly, it reserves the 1–800 number that corresponds to the 1–800-HOLIDAY number but that has a zero in place of the "O" in "Holiday". A customer dialing the number using a zero would hear the following message:

> Hello. You have misdialed and have not reached Holiday Inns or any of its affiliates. You've called 800 Reservations, America' fastest growing independent computerized hotel reservation service. One of our highly trained hotel reservation specialists will he with you momentarily to provide the Holiday Inns number or to assist you in finding the lowest rate at over 19,000 properties worldwide, including such hotel chains as Holiday Inns, Guest Quarters, Hampton Inn, Sheraton, Comfort Inn, and many more. If you are a member of a hotel's frequent guest program, have that number ready. Please stay on the line, assistance is just a moment away.

Does Holiday Inns have a claim against Call Management?

Deere & Company v. MTD Products, Inc.

United States Court of Appeals, Second Circuit, 1994
41 F.3d 39

■ JON O. NEWMAN, CHIEF JUDGE.

[The parties are competing manufacturers of lawn tractors. Deere has used a deer design (Deere Logo) as a trademark for over 100 years on agricultural and lawn equipment and has registered different versions of the Deere Logo, all of which "depict a static, two-dimensional silhouette of a leaping male deer in profile." MTD developed an advertisement comparing its Yard-Man lawn tractor to that of Deere. As part of the advertisement MTD used an altered, animated form of the Deere Logo. "Specifically, the MTD deer looks over its shoulder, jumps through the logo frame (which breaks into pieces and tumbles to the ground), hops to a pinging noise, and, as a two-dimensional cartoon, runs, in apparent fear, as it is pursued by the Yard-Man lawn tractor and a barking dog." Deere filed a complaint under the Lanham Act for trademark infringement and under Section 368-d of the New York statutes for trademark dilution. The district court found no likelihood of confusion but did award a preliminary injunction on the dilution claim.]

Although a number of dilution cases in this Circuit have involved use of a trademark by a competitor to identify a competitor's products in comparative advertising, as well as use by a noncompetitor in a humorous variation of a trademark, we have not yet considered whether the use of an altered version of a distinctive trademark to identify a competitor's product and achieve a humorous effect can constitute trademark dilution. Though we find MTD's animated version of Deere's deer amusing, we agree with Judge McKenna that the television commercial is a likely violation of the anti-dilution statute. We therefore affirm the preliminary injunction.

[The court first described the two traditional categories of dilution, "blurring" and "tarnishment" articulated in Mead Data Central, Inc. v. Toyota Motor Sales (see, casebook, supra).]

The District Court's analysis endeavored to fit the MTD commercial into one of the two categories we have recognized for a section 368-d claim. However, the MTD commercial is not really a typical instance of blurring, because it poses slight if any risk of impairing the identification of Deere's mark with its products. Nor is there tarnishment, which is usually found where a distinctive mark is depicted in a context of sexual activity, obscenity, or illegal activity. But the blurring/tarnishment dichotomy does not necessarily represent the full range of uses that can dilute a mark under New York law.

In giving content to dilution beyond the categories of blurring or tarnishment, however, we must be careful not to broaden section 368-d to prohibit all uses of a distinctive mark that the owner prefers not be made. Several different contexts may conveniently be identified. Sellers of commercial products may wish to use a competitor's mark to identify the competitor's product in comparative advertisements. As long as the mark is not altered, such use serves the beneficial purpose of imparting factual information about the relative merits of competing products and poses no risk of diluting the selling power of the competitor's mark. Satirists, selling no product other than the publication that contains their expression, may wish to parody a mark to make a point of social commentary, to entertain, or perhaps both to comment and entertain. Such uses risk some dilution of the identifying or selling power of the mark, but that risk is generally tolerated in the interest of maintaining broad opportunities for expression.

Sellers of commercial products who wish to attract attention to their commercials or products and thereby increase sales by poking fun at widely recognized marks of noncompeting products, risk diluting the selling power of the mark that is made fun of. When this occurs, not for worthy purposes of expression, but simply to sell their own products, that purpose can easily be achieved in other ways. The potentially diluting effect is even less deserving of protection when the object of the joke is the mark of a directly competing product. The line-drawing in this area becomes especially difficult when a mark is parodied for the dual purposes of making a satiric comment and selling a somewhat competing product.

Whether the use of the mark is to identify a competing product in an informative comparative ad, to make a comment, or to spoof the mark to enliven the advertisement for a noncompeting or a competing product, the scope of protection under a dilution statute must take into account the degree to which the mark is altered and the nature of the alteration. Not every alteration will constitute dilution, and more leeway for alterations is appropriate in the context of satiric expression and humorous ads for noncompeting products. But some alterations have the potential to so lessen the selling power of a distinctive mark that they are appropriately proscribed by a dilution statute. Dilution of this sort is more likely to be found when the alterations are made by a competitor with both an incentive to diminish the favorable attributes of the mark and an ample opportunity to promote its products in ways that make no significant alteration.

We need not attempt to predict how New York will delineate the scope of its dilution statute in all of the various contexts in which an accurate depiction of a distinctive mark might be used, nor need we decide how variations of such a mark should be treated in different contexts. Some variations might well be de minimis, and the context in which even substantial variations occur may well have such meritorious purposes that any diminution in the identifying and selling power of the mark need not be condemned as dilution.

Wherever New York will ultimately draw the line, we can be reasonably confident that the MTD commercial challenged in this case crosses it. The commercial takes a static image of a graceful, full-size deer—symbolizing Deere's substance and strength—and portrays, in an animated version, a deer that appears smaller than a small dog and scampers away from the dog and a lawn tractor, looking over its shoulder in apparent fear. Alterations of that sort, accomplished for the sole purpose of promoting a competing product, are properly found to be within New York's concept of dilution because they risk the possibility that consumers will come to attribute unfavorable characteristics to a mark and ultimately associate the mark with inferior goods and services.

* * *

The order of the District Court granting a preliminary injunction as to activities within New York State is affirmed. * * *

Hormel Foods Corporation v. Jim Henson Productions, Inc.

United States Court of Appeals, Second Circuit, 1996
73 F.3d 497

■ VAN GRAAFEILAND, CIRCUIT JUDGE:

[The district court described the lawsuit as follows:

This lawsuit is sparked by the prospective appearance of a new Muppet who joins Kermit, Miss Piggy and others in the movie "Muppet Treasure Island," due to be released in about four months. The creators of the Muppets, Jim Henson Productions, Inc. ("Henson"), hope to provoke laughter by naming the new Muppet (an exotic, wild boar) "Spa'am"; they believe that the association between the exotic, wild boar and the tame, familiar luncheon meat, SPAM, will cause viewers to laugh. Hormel Foods Corporation ("Hormel") which manufactures SPAM, finds nothing humorous in the association, and fears that the use of the Spa'am character will cause a drop off in the consumption of SPAM, and a drop off in the consumption of SPAM tee-shirts and other SPAM-related merchandise. Although Henson has urged Hormel, effectively, to "lighten up," and to see the parody as a positive development for Hormel (especially in light of the fact that SPAM is regularly subjected to much more negative portrayals), Hormel insists on its right to a legal determination of whether Henson's use of the Spa'am character and name are lawful.

Hormel alleged trademark infringement, false advertising, and dilution. As to the infringement claim, the Second Circuit found: "the clarity of Henson's parodic intent, the widespread familiarity with Henson's Muppet parodies, and the strength of Hormel's mark, all weigh strongly against the likelihood of confusion * * *." Under the dilution claim, the court found that there was little likelihood that Henson's use would blur the association of the mark with Hormel's luncheon meat.]

Dilution may also occur by tarnishment. * * * Tarnishment can occur through a variety of uses. Some cases have found that a mark is tarnished when its likeness is placed in the context of sexual activity, obscenity, or illegal activity. However, tarnishment is not limited to seamy conduct. Hormel argues that the image of Spa'am, as a "grotesque," "untidy" wild boar will "inspire negative and unsavory associations with SPAM (R) luncheon meat." Both Hormel and Amicus Curiae rely heavily on our recent decision in *Deere* [Deere & Company v. MTD products, Inc., 41 F.3d 39 (2d Cir. 1994)] for the proposition that products that "pok[e] fun at widely recognized marks of non-competing products, risk diluting the selling power of the mark that is made fun of." Their reliance is misplaced.

In *Deere* we addressed the question "whether the use of an altered version of a distinctive trademark to identify a competitor's product and achieve a humorous effect can constitute trademark dilution." MTD produced a television commercial for its competing lawnmower tractor, altering the famous Deere trademark from a proud, majestic deer, to one that was cowardly and afraid * * * . We found a violation of the anti-dilution statute because "[a]lterations of that sort, accomplished for the sole purpose of promoting a competing product . . . risk the possibility that consumers will come to attribute unfavorable characteristics to a mark and ultimately associate the mark with inferior goods and services." This holding mirrors the rationale of the tarnishment doctrine. Thus, although the court below understood *Deere* to create a new category of dilution, we find that our decision in *Deere* is better understood as a recognition of a broad view of tarnishment, where that doctrine had been sometimes narrowly confined.

The sine qua non of tarnishment is a finding that plaintiff's mark will suffer negative associations through defendant's use. Hormel claims that linking its luncheon meat with a wild boar will adversely color consumers' impressions of SPAM. However, the district court found that Spa'am, a likeable, positive character, will not generate any negative associations. Moreover, contrary to Hormel's contentions, the district court also found no evidence that Spa'am is unhygienic or that his character places Hormel's mark in an unsavory context. Indeed, many of Henson's own plans involve placing the Spa'am likeness on food products. In addition, the court also noted that a simple humorous reference to the fact that SPAM is made from pork is unlikely to tarnish Hormel's mark. Absent any showing that

Henson's use will create negative associations with the SPAM mark, there was little likelihood of dilution.

Moreover, unlike *Deere*, Henson's merchandise will not be in direct competition with that of Hormel. This is an important, even if not determinative, factor. "Dilution of this sort is more likely to be found when the alterations are made by a competitor with both an incentive to diminish the favorable attributes of the mark and an ample opportunity to promote its products in ways that make no significant alteration." Here, Henson does not seek to ridicule SPAM in order to sell more of its competitive products; rather, the parody is part of the product itself. Without Spa'am, the joke is lost. Indeed, we were mindful of this problem in *Deere* when we noted that "[t]he line-drawing in this area becomes especially difficult when a mark is parodied for the dual purposes of making a satiric comment and selling a somewhat competing product." Thus, in *Deere* we did not proscribe any parody or humorous depiction of a mark. Overall, we took a cautious approach, stating that "we must be careful not to broaden section 368-d to prohibit all uses of a distinctive mark that the owner prefers not be made."

Therefore, in the instant case, where (1) there is no evidence that Henson's use will cause negative associations, (2) Henson is not a direct competitor, and (3) the parody inheres in the product, we find that there is no likelihood of dilution under a tarnishment theory.

L.L. Bean, Inc. v. Drake Publishers, Inc.

United States Court of Appeals, First Circuit, 1987.
811 F. 2d 26.

[The defendant published *High Society*, an adult erotic magazine. The October 1984 issue included a two-page article entitled "L.L. Beam's Back-To-School-Sex-Catalog" featuring pictures of nude models in sexually explicit positions using crudely described "products". The plaintiff, L.L. Bean, publishes a famous catalog of clothing and other products. The district court found the parody in *High Society* to violate the state dilution statute.]

* * * The Constitution is not offended when the anti-dilution statute is applied to prevent a defendant from using a trademark without permission in order to merchandise dissimilar products or services. Any residual effect on first amendment freedoms should be balanced against the need to fulfill the legitimate purpose of the anti-dilution statute. See Friedman v. Rogers, 440 U.S. 1, 15–16 (1979). The law of trademark dilution has developed to combat an unauthorized and harmful appropriation of a trademark by another for the purpose of identifying, manufacturing, merchandising or promoting dissimilar products or services. The harm occurs when a trademark's identity and integrity—its capacity to command respect in the market—is undermined due to its inappropriate and unauthorized use by other market actors. When presented with such circumstances, courts have found that trademark owners have suffered harm despite the fact that redressing such harm entailed some residual impact on the rights of expression of com-

mercial actors. See, e.g., Dallas Cowboys Cheerleaders v. Pussycat Cinema, Ltd., 604 F.2d 200 (plaintiff's mark damaged by unauthorized use in content and promotion of a pornographic film); Chemical Corp. of America v. Anheuser–Busch, Inc., 306 F.2d 433 (5th Cir.1962), cert. denied, 372 U.S. 965 (1963) (floor wax and insecticide maker's slogan, "Where there's life, there's bugs," harmed strength of defendant's slogan, "Where there's life, there's Bud."); Original Appalachian Artworks, Inc. v. Topps Chewing Gum, 642 F.Supp. 1031 (N.D.Ga.1986) (merchandiser of "Garbage Pail Kids" stickers and products injured owner of Cabbage Patch Kids mark); D.C. Comics, Inc. v. Unlimited Monkey Business, 598 F.Supp. 110 (N.D.Ga.1984) (holder of Superman and Wonder Woman trademarks damaged by unauthorized use of marks by singing telegram franchisor); General Electric Co. v. Alumpa Coal Co., 205 U.S.P.Q. (BNA) 1036 (D.Mass.1979) ("Genital Electric" monogram on underpants and T-shirts harmful to plaintiff's trademark); Gucci Shops, Inc. v. R.H. Macy & Co., 446 F.Supp. 838 (S.D.N.Y.1977) (defendant's diaper bag labeled "Gucchi Goo" held to injure Gucci's mark); Coca-Cola Co. v. Gemini Rising, Inc., 346 F.Supp. 1183 (E.D.N.Y.1972) (enjoining the merchandise of "Enjoy Cocaine" posters bearing logo similar to plaintiff's mark).

While the cases cited above might appear at first glance to be factually analogous to the instant one, they are distinguishable for two reasons. First, they all involved unauthorized commercial uses of another's trademark. Second, none of those cases involved a defendant using a plaintiff's trademark as a vehicle for an editorial or artistic parody. In contrast to the cases cited, the instant defendant used plaintiff's mark solely for noncommercial purposes. Appellant's parody constitutes an editorial or artistic, rather than a commercial, use of plaintiff's mark. The article was labeled as "humor" and "parody" in the magazine's table of contents section; it took up two pages in a one-hundred-page issue; neither the article nor appellant's trademark was featured on the front or back cover of the magazine. Drake did not use Bean's mark to identify or promote goods or services to consumers; it never intended to market the "products" displayed in the parody.

* * *

If the anti-dilution statute were construed as permitting a trademark owner to enjoin the use of his mark in a noncommercial context found to be negative or offensive, then a corporation could shield itself from criticism by forbidding the use of its name in commentaries critical of its conduct. The legitimate aim of the anti-dilution statute is to prohibit the unauthorized use of another's trademark in order to market incompatible products or services. The Constitution does not, however, permit the range of the anti-dilution statute to encompass the unauthorized use of a trademark in a noncommercial setting such as an editorial or artistic context.

NOTES

1. In *Deere* The district court enjoined MTD from using an animated or otherwise altered version of the deer trademark within the state of New

York. The Second Circuit affirmed stating that the district court had the power to grant a broader injunction but "particularly at this early stage in the litigation" and where the issue is one of "first impression" it was appropriate to limit relief to New York state. Would you permit an injunction to extend into a state without a dilution statute? One with a dilution statute that has a judicial interpretation precluding relief in this type of case? On remand, the parties agreed to permit a final decision to be rendered on the record of the preliminary injunction hearing. Deere & Co. v. MTD Products, Inc., 34 U.S.P.Q.2d 1706 (S.D.N.Y. 1995). The court found the defendant had violated the New York anti-dilution statute and made the preliminary injunction permanent. Finding that it had the authority to issue a nationwide injunction, the court refused to do so: "In making this decision, I am most persuaded by the fact that the injunction in this case is not based on common law unfair competition claims, which are more widely shared, but on New York's anti-dilution statute, which does not exist in at least half of the states, and which many states that did pass such legislation do not apply to competitors, and by the breadth of the injunction for which Deere seeks nationwide enforcement." The court had found that neither Illinois nor Ohio, where the parties had their principal place of business, would have upheld a dilution claim.

2. Does *Hormel* make clear that *Deere* is really a "tarnishment" case, in as much as the injury, from Deere's point of view, is the mockery of its deer logo? Can MTD run an advertisement where an announcer says: "Remember that little deer associated with the John Deere Company? When Yard-Man comes calling, that deer will scamper out of sight in fear?" Or an advertisement in which real deers are shown scampering away in fear on approach of the "Yard-Man"? Do you agree that *Hormel* is different because there the parties are not in direct competition? Aren't they competing in the merchandise (t-shirt, etc.) market?

3. Are you comfortable with the distinction between commercial and non-commercial parody proposed in *L.L. Bean*? Is the *Hormel* case a commercial or non-commercial case? Consider Mutual of Omaha Ins. Co. v. Novak, 775 F.2d 247 (8th Cir. 1985) where the court, without the benefit of a dilution statute, found a likelihood of confusion when the defendant marketed "Mutant of Omaha" t–Shirts, coffee mugs, and other products as part of an anti-nuclear war campaign. Mutual of Omaha sold similar items with its own logo to its agents to be used for incentives. The analysis in *Mutual* was rejected in Rogers v. Grimaldi, 875 F.2d 994 (2d Cir.1989). The defendant distributed a movie entitled "Ginger and Fred", a story about two fictional Italian performers who imitated the style of Ginger Rogers and Fred Astaire, two famous American dancers. Ginger Rogers brought suit arguing the title of the movie violated the Lanham Act and produced market surveys suggesting that the title misled consumers into believing Rogers was connected with the film. The court held for the defendant:

> We believe that in general the [Lanham] Act should be construed to apply to artistic works only where the public interest in avoiding consumer confusion outweighs the public interest in free expression. In the

context of allegedly misleading titles using a celebrity's name, that balance will normally not support application of the Act unless the title has no artistic relevance to the underlying work whatsoever, or, if it has some artistic relevance, unless the title explicitly misleads as to the source or the content of the work.

The Court then held that even if surveys were sufficient to prove likelihood of confusion, the risk of some confusion must be accepted to protect the interests in artistic expression.

4. Section 1125(c)(4) of the Lanham Act incorporates the commercial-noncommercial distinction adopted in *L.L. Bean*. The Restatement, Third, of Unfair Competition § 25, Comment *I*, at 272 (1995) draws a distinction between trademark and nontrademark use of another's mark as the line between protection under both confusion and dilution rationales and protected speech. Consider, Jews for Jesus v. Brodsky, 1998 WL 111676 (D.N.J. 1998). The plaintiff Jews for Jesus is an outreach ministry. The defendant is an Internet site developer critical of the plaintiff. Defendant establishes a website with the domain name "jewsforjesus.org". On the site the defendant publishes material critical of the plaintiff. There is also a hyperlink to a site for Outreach Judaism Organization which offers for sale tapes and books. However, defendant indicates on his site that he is not associated in anyway with Outreach Judaism. Is the defendant's use of the domain name a "commercial" use vulnerable to a claim of dilution under § 43(c)?

5. Trademark disparagement has been applied in circumstances not involving parody and without reference to a dilution statute. In Big O Tire Dealers, Inc. v. Goodyear Tire & Rubber Co., 408 F.Supp. 1219 (D.Colo.1976), *vacated on other grounds,* 561 F.2d 1365 (10th Cir.1977) Goodyear through a saturation advertising campaign of its own "Bigfoot" tire was able to consume the preexisting "Bigfoot" mark of plaintiff for tires. Consumers came to believe that plaintiff's use of the mark was an attempt to trade on the good will of Goodyear. The Tenth Circuit approved a cause of action for "trademark disparagement" which required proof of three elements: a false statement, malice, and special damages. The court awarded plaintiff substantial damages based on what plaintiff would need to counteract the defendant's advertising.

---

(4) Collateral Use

Champion Spark Plug Co. v. Sanders

Supreme Court of the United States, 1947.
331 U.S. 125, 67 S.Ct. 1136, 91 L.Ed. 1386.

■ MR. JUSTICE DOUGLAS delivered the opinion of the Court.

[Petitioner manufactures "Champion" spark plugs. Respondent reconditions and resells used spark plugs in boxes which retain the word "Champion" and the original letter and figure denoting style or type. Respondent also placed its legend on the box ("Perfect Process Renewed

Spark Plugs") and placed the word "renewed" on each plug. Finding trademark infringement and unfair competition the Court of Appeals denied an accounting but approved an injunction permitting continued use of the "Champion" mark but requiring the plugs to be repainted with the word "repaired" or "used" stamped on the plug and requiring the Respondent to clearly indicate on boxes that it was the source of these reconditioned plugs.]

We are dealing here with second-hand goods. The spark plugs, though used, are nevertheless Champion plugs and not those of another make. There is evidence to support what one would suspect, that a used spark plug which has been repaired or reconditioned does not measure up to the specifications of a new one. But the same would be true of a second-hand Ford or Chevrolet car. And we would not suppose that one could be enjoined from selling a car whose valves had been reground and whose piston rings had been replaced unless he removed the name Ford or Chevrolet. Prestonettes, Inc. v. Coty, 264 U.S. 359, was a case where toilet powders had as one of their ingredients a powder covered by a trade mark and where perfumes which were trade marked were rebottled and sold in smaller bottles. The Court sustained a decree denying an injunction where the prescribed labels told the truth. Mr. Justice Holmes stated, "A trade mark only gives the right to prohibit the use of it so far as to protect the owner's good will against the sale of another's product as his. * * * When the mark is used in a way that does not deceive the public we see no such sanctity in the word as to prevent its being used to sell the truth. It is not taboo." P. 368.

Cases may be imagined where the reconditioning or repair would be so extensive or so basic that it would be a misnomer to call the article by its original name, even though the words "used" or "repaired" were added. But no such practice is involved here. The repair or reconditioning of the plugs does not give them a new design. It is no more than a restoration, so far as possible, of their original condition. The type marks attached by the manufacturer are determined by the use to which the plug is to be put. But the thread size and size of the cylinder hole into which the plug is fitted are not affected by the reconditioning. The heat range also has relevance to the type marks. And there is evidence that the reconditioned plugs are inferior so far as heat range and other qualities are concerned. But inferiority is expected in most second-hand articles. Indeed, they generally cost the customer less. That is the case here. Inferiority is immaterial so long as the article is clearly and distinctively sold as repaired or reconditioned rather than as new. The result is, of course, that the second-hand dealer gets some advantage from the trade mark. But under the rule of Prestonettes, Inc. v. Coty, supra, that is wholly permissible so long as the manufacturer is not identified with the inferior qualities of the product resulting from wear and tear or the reconditioning by the dealer. Full disclosure gives the manufacturer all the protection to which he is entitled.

* * *

Affirmed.

NOTES

1. In Bulova Watch Co. v. Allerton Co., 328 F.2d 20 (7th Cir.1964) the defendant Allerton purchased Bulova watches from a third party, removed the Bulova movements, and transferred the movements into diamond decorated cases purchased from a watch case manufacturer. The movements contained the trademark "Bulova" on the dial after recasing. The Seventh Circuit agreed with the lower court that the recasing operation resulted in a "new construction" and was no longer a "Bulova" watch. Citing *Champion Spark Plug,* the court held that the defendant could make a proper collateral reference to the source of the watch movement if done in a way that did not deceive the public. Since it was impossible to make a full disclosure on the small dial of the watch, the court enjoined any use of the word "Bulova" on the recased watches. The court also required that any use of the word "Bulova" in advertising or on the catalogue pages indicate (1) that defendant takes plaintiff's movements and recases them, and (2) this is done independently of plaintiff.

2. May an automobile repair shop put the Volkswagen trademark in its yellow page advertisement and on the sign that hangs from the front of the shop to indicate that the repair shop repairs Volkswagen cars? May the shop indicate it "specializes in VW repair"? May the shop indicate it uses "genuine VW parts."?

PROBLEMS

1. Monte Carlo Shirt, Inc. contracted with Daewoo, a Korean shirt manufacturer, to produce 2400 dozen shirts to its specifications and with the Monte Carlo label. Monte Carlo rejected the shirts after they arrived in the United States because they were too late for Christmas sales. The American subsidiary of Daewoo purchased the rejected shirts and sold them with the Monte Carlo label to discount retailers. Monte Carlo's rejection of the goods is upheld. Can it also sue for trademark infringement? Would the answer be the same if the shirts had been rejected on the grounds they were defective?

2. Matrix manufacturers specialty hair-care products which are distributed through wholesalers contractually bound to resell only to licensed cosmetologists. Matrix intends for consumers prior to purchase to consult with cosmetologists in order to obtain the appropriate product for their hair and scalp condition. Matrix spends millions of dollars training cosmetologists for this purpose although it does not monitor sales to consumers to insure consultation occurs. Emporium, a high-volume, over-the-counter retail drug store obtained a large quantity of genuine Matrix products and offered them for sale directly to consumers under the Matrix trademark. Some of the bottles were labeled "Sold Only in Professional Salons". Is Emporium liable for trademark infringement or for misrepresentation under § 43(a) of the Lanham Act?

3. A French manufacturer produces "Java" brand face powder in France. A United States company purchases an assignment of exclusive rights in the "Java" mark for the United States market. A third party purchases authentic "Java" powder in France and imports it into the United States in competition with the domestic assignee. Should the United States company be entitled to prevent the importation of these authentic goods? Variation 2: Should it make any difference if the domestic company is a subsidiary of the French manufacturer and the domestic company registers the mark "Java" in its own name for the United States market?. Variation 3: Should it make any difference if the domestic company is the original owner of the "Java" mark and has licensed the French manufacturer to use the mark in France.

Problem 3 reflects some of the variants of what is known as parallel importation or "the gray market". The cases raise interesting trademark problems because the mark is used on authentic goods but in violation of privately arranged market allocations. Any confusion of source by consumers does not relate to the product purchased, and consumers may pay less for the product because discounters often rely on parallel imports as a major source of branded merchandise.

The leading trademark infringement case is A. Bourjois & Co. v. Katzel, 260 U.S. 689 (1923). Justice Holmes upheld an injunction in favor of the domestic company: "Ownership of the goods does not carry the right to sell them with a specific mark.... ['Java'] is the trademark of the plaintiff only in the United States and indicates in law, and, it is found, by public understanding, that the goods come from the plaintiff although not made by it." In all of the variations of the problem, if the domestic company can demonstrate the use of the mark in the United States reflects good will attributable to the domestic company and not to the foreign company, the parallel importation of gray market goods is a trademark infringement. See Osawa & Co. v. B & H Photo, 589 F.Supp. 1163 (S.D.N.Y.1984); Weil Ceramics & Glass, Inc. v. Dash, 618 F.Supp. 700 (D.N.J.1985). However, proof of a separate good will running to the domestic company may be very difficult.

After the Court of Appeals in *Bourjois* had ruled against the domestic company but before the Supreme Court reversed, Congress responded by adopting § 526 of the Tariff Act (now 15 U.S.C. § 1526) which provides: "It shall be unlawful to import into the United States any merchandise of foreign manufacture if such merchandise * * * bears a trademark owned by a citizen of * * * the United States * * *." See also, § 42 of the Lanham Act. This apparently all-inclusive prohibition had been narrowed by United States Customs Service regulations which permitted importation where the foreign manufacturer and the domestic trademark owner are "subject to common ownership or control" (variation 2) or where the domestic trademark owner authorizes the foreign manufacturer to use the mark (variation 3). This regulatory interpretation of the Tariff Act stood for over 50 years. However, in K Mart Corp. v. Cartier, Inc., 486 U.S. 281 (1988) a badly split Supreme Court upheld the regulations permitting importation where there is common ownership or control (variation 2)but invalidated the authorized use exception (variation 3).

4. Lever Brothers manufacturers "Shield" handsoap for the United States market. An affiliated company manufacturers "Shield" soap for the

British market. The soaps are separately formulated to respond to the different tastes of British and American consumers. A third party purchases British "Shield" soap in Britain and imports it into the United States for sale. Is this a trademark infringement?

Smith v. Chanel, Inc.

United States Court of Appeals, Ninth Circuit, 1968.
402 F.2d 562.

■ BROWNING, CIRCUIT JUDGE. Appellant R.G. Smith, doing business as Ta'Ron, Inc., advertised a fragrance called "Second Chance" as a duplicate of appellees' "Chanel No. 5," at a fraction of the latter's price. Appellees were granted a preliminary injunction prohibiting any reference to Chanel No. 5 in the promotion or sale of appellants' product. This appeal followed.

* * *

Appellees conceded below and concede here that appellants "have the right to copy, if they can, the unpatented formula of appellees' products" [citing *Sears* and *Compco*]. Moreover, for the purposes of these proceedings, appellees assume that "the products manufactured and advertised by [appellants] are *in fact* equivalents of those products manufactured by appellees." (Emphasis in original.) Finally, appellees disclaim any contention that the packaging or labeling of appellants' "Second Chance" is misleading or confusing.

I

The principal question presented on this record is whether one who has copied an unpatented product sold under a trademark may use the trademark in his advertising to identify the product he has copied. We hold that he may, and that such advertising may not be enjoined under either the Lanham Act, 15 U.S.C. § 1125(a) or the common law of unfair competition, so long as it does not contain misrepresentations or create a reasonable likelihood that purchasers will be confused as to the source, identity, or sponsorship of the advertiser's product.

* * *

The rule rests upon the traditionally accepted premise that the only legally relevant function of a trademark is to impart information as to the source or sponsorship of the product. Appellees argue that protection should also be extended to the trademark's commercially more important function of embodying consumer good will created through extensive, skillful, and costly advertising. The courts, however, have generally confined legal protection to the trademark's source identification function for reasons grounded in the public policy favoring a free, competitive economy.

* * *

A related consideration is also pertinent to the present case. Since appellees' perfume was unpatented, appellants had a right to copy it, as appellees concede. There was a strong public interest in their doing so, "[f]or imitation is the life blood of competition. It is the unimpeded availability of substantially equivalent units that permits the normal operation of supply and demand to yield the fair price society must pay for a given commodity." American Safety Table Co. v. Schreiber, 269 F.2d 255, 272 (2d Cir.1959). But this public benefit might be lost if appellants could not tell potential purchasers that appellants' product was the equivalent of appellees' product. "A competitor's chief weapon is his ability to represent his product as being equivalent and cheaper * * *." Alexander, Honesty and Competition, 39 So.Cal.L.Rev. 1, 4 (1966). The most effective way (and, where complex chemical compositions sold under trade names are involved, often the only practical way) in which this can be done is to identify the copied article by its trademark or trade name. To prohibit use of a competitor's trademark for the sole purpose of identifying the competitor's product would bar effective communication of claims of equivalence. Assuming the equivalence of "Second Chance" and "Chanel No. 5," the public interest would not be served by a rule of law which would preclude sellers of "Second Chance" from advising consumers of the equivalence and thus effectively deprive consumers of knowledge that an identical product was being offered at one third the price.

* * *

A large expenditure of money does not in itself create legally protectable rights. Appellees are not entitled to monopolize the public's desire for the unpatented product, even though they themselves created that desire at great effort and expense. As we have noted, the most effective way (and in some cases the only practical way) in which others may compete in satisfying the demand for the product is to produce it and tell the public they have done so, and if they could be barred from this effort appellees would have found a way to acquire a practical monopoly in the unpatented product to which they are not legally entitled.

* * *

NOTES

1. On remand, the trial court in the *Smith* case found that "Second Chance" did not duplicate "Chanel # 5" 100% and thus the advertising was in violation of § 43(a) of the Lanham Act even though no passing off was shown. Chanel, Inc. v. Smith, 178 U.S.P.Q. 630 (N.D.Cal.1973), affirmed 528 F.2d 284 (9th Cir.1976). And in Saxony Products v. Guerlain, Inc., 513 F.2d 716 (9th Cir.1975) where the defendant advertised its perfumes as "like" or "similar" to the plaintiff's, the court held that expert testimony and a smell test performed for the trial judge were sufficient to create a material fact on plaintiff's § 43(a) claim.

2. The clever copier can avoid proof of equivalency by not claiming it. In several perfume cases a "like/love" comparison is made, as in "If you like OBSESSION, you will love CONFESS" where "Obsession" is the well-known perfume and "Confess" is the cheaper substitute. Calvin Klein v.

Parfums de Coeur, 824 F.2d 665 (8th Cir. 1987). Is a "like/love" slogan a permissible use of a competitor's trademark? If you are troubled by it standing alone would you permit it with a disclaimer as in "If You Like OPIUM, a fragrance by Yves Saint Laurent, You'll Love OMNI, a fragrance by Deborah Int'l Beauty. Yves Saint Laurent and Opium are not related in any manner to Deborah Int'l Beauty and Omni"? Charles of the Ritz Group Ltd. v. Quality King Dist. Inc., 832 F.2d 1317 (2d Cir. 1987) (disclaimer not sufficient to cure confusion where type size of disclaimer and position on packaging reduced its impact).

3. Would a dilution statute alter the result of these cases?

PROBLEM

Tour 18 Ltd. operates a public golf course in Texas named "America's Greatest 18 Holes". Tour 18 has faithfully replicated some of the finest golf holes in the country including the 14th hole at Pebble Beach, the 3rd hole at Pinehurst, and the 18th hole at Sea Pines. The scorecards for Tour 18's course use the service marks of the golf courses from which the holes were copied as does some of the signs and advertising which claim that a particular hole is "like playing the 14th hole at Pebble Beach." Most written materials carry a disclaimer that the original golf courses are not affiliated with Tour 18 or endorse Tour 18's golf course. Pebble Beach, Pinehurst, and Sea Pines, the plaintiffs, sue for trademark infringement and dilution. What result?

New Kids on the Block v. News America Publishing, Inc.

United States Court of Appeals, Ninth Circuit, 1991
971 F.2d 302

■ KOZINSKI, CIRCUIT JUDGE.

The individual plaintiffs perform professionally as The New Kids on the Block, reputedly one of today's hottest musical acts. This case requires us to weigh their rights in that name against the rights of others to use it in identifying the New Kids as the subjects of public opinion polls.

* * *

The defendants, two newspapers of national circulation, conducted separate polls of their readers seeking an answer to a pressing question: Which one of the New Kids is the most popular? *USA Today*'s announcement contained a picture of the New Kids and asked, "Who's the best on the block?" The announcement listed a 900 number for voting, noted that "any USA Today profits from this phone line will go to charity," and closed with the following:

New Kids on the Block are pop's hottest group. Which of the five is your fave? Or are they a turn off? . . . Each call costs 50 cents. Results in Friday's Life section.

The *Star*'s announcement, under a picture of the New Kids, went to the heart of the matter: "Now which kid is the sexiest?" The announcement, which appeared in the middle of a page containing a story on a New Kids concert, also stated:

> Which of the New Kids on the Block would you most like to move next door? STAR wants to know which cool New Kid is the hottest with our readers.

Readers were directed to a 900 number to register their votes; each call cost 95 cents per minute.

Fearing that the two newspapers were undermining their hegemony over their fans, the New Kids filed a shotgun complaint in federal court raising no fewer than ten claims: (1) common law trademark infringement; (2) Lanham Act false advertising; (3) Lanham Act false designation of origin; (4) Lanham Act unfair competition; (5) state trade name infringement; (6) state false advertising; (7) state unfair competition; (8) commercial misappropriation; (9) common-law misappropriation; and (10) intentional interference with prospective economic advantage. The two papers raised the First Amendment as a defense, on the theory that the polls were part and parcel of their "news- gathering activities." The district court granted summary judgment for defendants.

* * *

Throughout the development of trademark law, the purpose of trademarks remained constant and limited: Identification of the manufacturer or sponsor of a good or the provider of a service. And the wrong protected against was traditionally equally limited: Preventing producers from free-riding on their rivals' marks. * * * The core protection of the Lanham Act remains faithful to this conception. * * *

* * *

With many well-known trademarks, such as Jell-O, Scotch tape and Kleenex, there are equally informative non-trademark words describing the products (gelatin, cellophane tape and facial tissue). But sometimes there is no descriptive substitute, and a problem closely related to genericity and descriptiveness is presented when many goods and services are effectively identifiable only by their trademarks. For example, one might refer to "the two-time world champions" or "the professional basketball team from Chicago," but it's far simpler (and more likely to be understood) to refer to the Chicago Bulls. In such cases, use of the trademark does not imply sponsorship or endorsement of the product because the mark is used only to describe the thing, rather than to identify its source.

Indeed, it is often virtually impossible to refer to a particular product for purposes of comparison, criticism, point of reference or any other such purpose without using the mark. For example, reference to a large automobile manufacturer based in Michigan would not differentiate among the Big Three; reference to a large Japanese manufacturer of home electronics would narrow the field to a dozen or more companies. Much useful social and commercial discourse would be all but impossible if speakers were under threat of an infringement lawsuit every time they made reference to a person, company or product by using its trademark.

* * *

* * * Indeed, we may generalize a class of cases where the use of the trademark does not attempt to capitalize on consumer confusion or to appropriate the cachet of one product for a different one. Such *nominative use* of a mark—where the only word reasonably available to describe a particular thing is pressed into service—lies outside the strictures of trademark law: Because it does not implicate the source- identification function that is the purpose of trademark, it does not constitute unfair competition; such use is fair because it does not imply sponsorship or endorsement by the trademark holder.

To be sure, this is not the classic fair use case where the defendant has used the plaintiff's mark to describe the defendant's *own* product. Here, the New Kids trademark is used to refer to the New Kids themselves. We therefore do not purport to alter the test applicable in the paradigmatic fair use case. If the defendant's use of the plaintiff's trademark refers to something other than the plaintiff's product, the traditional fair use inquiry will continue to govern. But, where the defendant uses a trademark to describe the plaintiff's product, rather than its own, we hold that a commercial user is entitled to a nominative fair use defense provided he meets the following three requirements: First, the product or service in question must be one not readily identifiable without use of the trademark; second, only so much of the mark or marks may be used as is reasonably necessary to identify the product or service; and third, the user must do nothing that would, in conjunction with the mark, suggest sponsorship or endorsement by the trademark holder.

B. The New Kids do not claim there was anything false or misleading about the newspapers' use of their mark. Rather, the first seven causes of action, while purporting to state different claims, all hinge on one key factual allegation: that the newspapers' use of the New Kids name in conducting the unauthorized polls somehow implied that the New Kids were sponsoring the polls. It is no more reasonably possible, however, to refer to the New Kids as an entity than it is to refer to the Chicago Bulls, Volkswagens or the Boston Marathon without using the trademark. Indeed, how could someone not conversant with the proper names of the individual New Kids talk about the group at all? While plaintiffs' trademark certainly deserves protection against copycats and those who falsely claim that the New Kids have endorsed or sponsored them, such protection does not extend to rendering newspaper articles, conversations, polls and comparative advertising impossible. The first nominative use requirement is therefore met.

Also met are the second and third requirements. Both *The Star* and *USA Today* reference the New Kids only to the extent necessary to identify them as the subject of the polls; they do not use the New Kids' distinctive logo or anything else that isn't needed to make the announcements intelligible to readers. Finally, nothing in the announcements suggests joint sponsorship or endorsement by the New Kids. The *USA Today* announcement implies quite the contrary by asking whether the New Kids might be "a turn off." *The Star*'s poll is more effusive but says nothing that expressly or by fair implication connotes endorsement or joint sponsorship on the part of the New Kids.

* * *

* * * While the New Kids have a limited property right in their name, that right does not entitle them to control their fans' use of their own money. Where, as here, the use does not imply sponsorship or endorsement, the fact that it is carried on for profit and in competition with the trademark holder's business is beside the point. Voting for their favorite New Kid may be, as plaintiffs point out, a way for fans to articulate their loyalty to the group, and this may diminish the resources available for products and services they sponsor. But the trademark laws do not give the New Kids the right to channel their fans' enthusiasm (and dollars) only into items licensed or authorized by them. The New Kids could not use the trademark laws to prevent the publication of an unauthorized group biography or to censor all parodies or satires which use their name. We fail to see a material difference between these examples and the use here.

Summary judgment was proper as to the first seven causes of action because they all hinge on a theory of implied endorsement; there was none here as the uses in question were purely nominative.

* * *

NOTES

1. Is Judge Kozinski's creation of the nominative fair use defense necessary to resolve this case? Isn't the third element of that defense, that the defendant does nothing that suggests sponsorship or endorsement, merely a restatement of the traditional trademark rule that there is no infringement if there is no likelihood of confusion? Does Judge Kozinski's formulation shift the burden on the issue of likelihood of confusion to the defendant?

2. The nominative fair use defense was rejected in Abdul-Jabbar v. General Motors Corp., 85 F.3d 407 (9th Cir. 1996) where Lew Alcindor's (now Kareem Abdul-Jabbar) record of winning the most valuable player award in the NCAA men's basketball tournament was referred to in a television advertisement for Oldsmobile. The court found a genuine issue of fact as to whether the use implied an endorsement by Abdul-Jabbar and distinguished *New Kids* because the "use of celebrity endorsements in television commercials is so well established by commercial custom that a jury might find an implied endorsement in General Motors' use of the celebrity's name in a commercial, which would not inhere in a newspaper poll."

3. A wide-spread practice in the over-the-counter drug and cosmetic industry is for larger retailers to market their own private labeled product side-by-side with the national branded product. Often the private labeled product mimics the trade dress, including container size and colors, of the better known national brand. The private labelers argue that the similarity of trade dress is not intended to confuse consumers but rather to inform consumers that the product is similar to and performs the same function as the national brand. Is this alone sufficient to overcome a claim of trademark infringement? What if, in addition, the private labeler adds to its label the phrase "Compare to [the national brand]"? In Conopco, Inc. v. May Department Stores Co., 46 F.3d 1556 (Fed. Cir. 1994) the court rejected a trademark infringement claim where the private label contained the "Compare to * * * " phrase and a black and white logo of the private labeler prominently displayed on the front of the package. The court observed: " * * * the marketing device employed by defendants in this case is neither new nor subtle. The cases have approved the general practice in a variety of settings, at least to the extent of not finding a violation of the Lanham Act absent a showing by the plaintiff that real consumers have real confusion or likelihood of it with regard to the origin of the products involved." The court discounted the testimony of one consumer who claimed to have been confused because her confusion arose "in part from her assumption * * * that national brand manufacturers secretly market private label brands. First, there is no evidence that this assumption is widely held by the relevant consumers * * *. Second, [where] the national brand is being sold side-by-side with the private label brand, the assumption is at best counter-intuitive—it assumes that a national brand manufacturer would embark on a scheme to deliberately erode its sales of the national brand."

PROBLEMS

1. Reconsider Problems 1 & 3 in Chapter 1 following INS v. AP. Do any of these situations represent trademark infringements? Would you support a state criminal statute that made it a crime for any person to use a trademark or logo "which would falsely state or imply that such person has permission or is legally authorized to use it?" Would such a statute prohibit unauthorized "linking" on the Internet? Would such a prohibition be constitutional?

2. The Rock and Roll Hall of Fame Foundation in Cleveland, Ohio, hired I.M. Pei, a world famous architect, to design a building to contain the Foundation's museum. The building, dramatic in its design, is constructed on the edge of Lake Erie. The Foundation registers the building design as its trademark. The museum sells posters featuring the building design. Charles Gentile, a professional photographer, begins selling a poster featuring one of his photographs of the building against a colorful sunset. In gold lettering in the border under the photograph are the words "Rock N'Roll Hall of Fame—Cleveland". Gentile's signature is in small print beneath the picture. Does the Foundation have any claim against Gentile?

3. National Football League Properties (League) has the exclusive right to license the names and logos of National Football League teams. The National Football League Players Association (Players) has the exclusive right to license the names and likenesses of National Football League players. Playoff Corporation obtains a license from Players to manufacture and sell trading cards with the names and likenesses of individual players. The players appear on the cards in their team uniforms which display the team names and logos. Playoff does not have a license from League. Can the League enjoin sale of the cards?

4. Beginning in the 1940s, the Illinois High School Association has used the term "March Madness" in association with its high school basketball tournament and licensed the use of the trademark on merchandise associated with the tournament. In 1982, CBS began broadcasting the NCAA college basketball tournament and in the course of a broadcast, Brent Musburger, the announcer, used the term "March Madness" to refer to the final championship games. The term caught on and was widely used by the media and the public to refer to the NCAA basketball tournament. In 1993 the NCAA began licensing the term for merchandise and Vantage begins making a "March Madness" CD-ROM game using the term. The Illinois Association sues Vantage. What result?

---

(5) Remedies

George Basch Co., Inc. v. Blue Coral, Inc.

United States Court of Appeals, Second Circuit, 1992
968 F.2d 1532, cert. denied 113 S.Ct. 510 (1992)

■ WALKER, CIRCUIT JUDGE:

[Both parties sell metal polishes. After Blue Coral failed to reach an agreement with Basch to distribute, NEVR-DULL, a Basch product, it obtained a similar product from another manufacturer and marketed it under the mark EVER BRITE with a trade dress similar to that of Basch. On its trade dress infringement claim, the district court denied damages because there was no evidence of consumer confusion or intent to deceive but awarded Basch Blue Coral's profits of $200,000.]

* * *

The rule in this circuit has been that an accounting for profits is normally available "only if the 'defendant is unjustly enriched, if the plaintiff sustained damages from the infringement, or if the accounting is necessary to deter a willful infringer from doing so again.'" Burndy Corp. v. Teledyne Industries, Inc., 748 F.2d 767, 772 (2d Cir.1984). Courts have interpreted the rule to describe three categorically distinct rationales.

* * *

Unjust Enrichment: * * *

Thus, a defendant who is liable in a trademark or trade dress infringement action may be deemed to hold its profits in constructive trust for the injured plaintiff. However, this results only "when the defendant's sales 'were attributable to its infringing use' of the plaintiff's" mark, *Burndy Corp.*, 748 F.2d at 772 and when the infringing use was at the plaintiff's expense. In other words, a defendant becomes accountable for its profits when the plaintiff can show that, were it not for defendant's infringement, the defendant's sales would otherwise have gone to the plaintiff.

At bottom, this is simply another way of formulating the element of consumer confusion required to justify a damage award under the Lanham Act. As such, it follows that a profits award, premised upon a theory of unjust enrichment, requires a showing of actual consumer confusion—or at least proof of deceptive intent so as to raise the rebuttable presumption of consumer confusion.

* * *

Where Plaintiff Sustains Damages: Historically, an award of defendant's profits has also served as a rough proxy measure of plaintiff's damages. Due to the inherent difficulty in isolating the causation behind diverted sales and injured reputation, damages from trademark or trade dress infringement are often hard to establish. * * *

Under this rule, profits from defendant's proven sales are awarded to the plaintiff unless the defendant can show "that the infringement had no relationship" to those earnings. Id. This shifts the burden of proving economic injury off the innocent party, and places the hardship of disproving economic gain onto the infringer. Of course, this "does not stand for the proposition that an accounting will be ordered merely because there has been an infringement." *Champion Plug Co.*, 331 U.S. at 131. Rather, in order to award profits there must first be "a basis for finding damage." Id.; *Mishawaka Mfg. Co.*, 316 U.S. at 206. While a plaintiff who seeks the defendant's profits may be relieved of certain evidentiary requirements otherwise carried by those trying to prove damages, a plaintiff must nevertheless establish its general right to damages before defendant's profits are recoverable.

Thus, under the "damage" theory of profits, a plaintiff typically has been required to show consumer confusion resulting from the infringement. Whether a plaintiff also had to show willfully deceptive conduct on the part of the defendant is not so clear. * * *

Deterrence: Finally, we have held that a court may award a defendant's profits solely upon a finding that the defendant fraudulently used the plaintiff's mark. The rationale underlying this holding is not compensatory in nature, but rather seeks to protect the public at large. By awarding the profits of a bad faith infringer to the rightful owner of a mark, we promote the secondary effect of deterring public fraud regarding the source and quality of consumer goods and services.

* * *

Although these three theories address slightly different concerns, they do share common ground. In varying degrees, a finding of defendant's intentional deceptiveness has always been an important consideration in determining whether an accounting was an appropriate remedy. In view of this, the American Law Institute has recently concluded that a finding of willful infringement is the necessary catalyst for the disgorgement of ill-gotten profits. *See Restatement* [(Third) of Unfair Competition, Tent. Draft No. 3, 1991], § 37(1)(a) ("One . . . is liable for the net profits earned on profitable transactions resulting from [the infringement], if, but only if, the actor engaged in conduct with the intention of causing confusion or deception ...").

We agree with the position set forth in § 37 of the *Restatement* and therefore hold that, under § 35(a) of the Lanham Act, a plaintiff must prove that an infringer acted with willful deception before the infringer's profits are recoverable by way of an accounting. Along with the *Restatement's* drafters, we believe that this requirement is necessary to avoid the conceivably draconian impact that a profits remedy might have in some cases. While damages directly measure the plaintiff's loss, defendant's profits measure the defendant's gain. Thus, an accounting may overcompensate for a plaintiff's actual injury and create a windfall judgment at the defendant's expense. See *Restatement*, § 37 at cmt. e. Of course, this is not to be confused with *plaintiff's* lost profits, which have been traditionally compensable as an element of plaintiff's damages.

So as to limit what may be an undue windfall to the plaintiff, and prevent the potentially inequitable treatment of an "innocent" or "good faith" infringer, most courts require proof of intentional misconduct before allowing a plaintiff to recover the defendant's profits. We underscore that in the absence of such a showing, a plaintiff is not foreclosed from receiving monetary relief. Upon proof of actual consumer confusion, a plaintiff may still obtain damages—which, in turn, may be inclusive of plaintiff's own lost profits.

* * *

Having stated that a finding of willful deceptiveness is necessary in order to warrant an accounting for profits, we note that it may not be sufficient. While under certain circumstances, the egregiousness of the fraud may, of its own, justify an accounting, generally, there are other factors to be considered. Among these are such familiar concerns as: (1) the degree of certainty that the defendant benefited from the unlawful conduct; (2) availability and adequacy of other remedies; (3) the role of a particular defendant in effectuating the infringement; (4) plaintiff's laches; and (5) plaintiff's unclean hands. *See generally Restatement*, § 37(2) at cmt. f & cases cited in the reporter's notes. The district court's discretion lies in assessing the relative importance of these factors and determining whether, on the whole, the equities weigh in favor of an accounting. As the Lanham Act dictates, every award is "subject to equitable principles" and should be determined "according to the circumstances of the case." 15 U.S.C. § 1117.

[The Court then reversed the district court's award of profits because there was no showing of sales diversion or bad faith.]

Sands, Taylor & Wood Co. v. The Quaker Oats Company

United States District Court, Northern District of Illinois, 1993
1993 WL 204092

[Sands, Taylor & Wood (Sands) is the successor in interest to the trademark "Thirst Aid" first used on soft drinks in 1921. In 1980 Pet, Inc., negotiated a nationwide license from Sands to use the mark on an isotonic beverage intended to compete with the popular "Gatorade", an isotonic beverage produced by Stokely, but after a five month test marketing and after capturing 25% of the test markets, Pet withdrew. In 1983 Stokely was acquired by Quaker Oats and shortly thereafter adopted the slogan "Gatorade is Thirst Aid for That Deep Down Body Thirst". Lawyers for Quaker concluded that the slogan was descriptive, that the use of "Thirst Aid" was not a use as a trademark, and that accordingly the slogan was a fair use and not an infringement. However, the district court granted summary judgment for Sands and awarded it 10 percent of Quaker's pre-tax profits on Gatorade. That award including prejudgment interest and attorneys fees was $42,629,399.09. Quaker appealed.

In *Sands I* (978 F.2d 947 (7th Cir. 1993), cert. denied 113 S.Ct. 1879 (1993) the Court of Appeals upheld the district court's holdings that Quaker's use of "Thirst Aid" was as a trademark and not a fair use and that there was a likelihood of reverse confusion. Judge Cudahy after finding the evidence of bad faith "thin" held:

> In such a case, an award of $24 million in profits is not "equitable"; rather, it is a windfall to the plaintiff. Quaker may have been unjustly enriched by using STW's mark without paying for it, but the award of profits bears no relationship to that enrichment. A reasonable royalty, perhaps related in some way to the fee STW was paid by Pet, would more accurately reflect both the extent of Quaker's unjust enrichment and the interest of STW that has been infringed. We therefore reverse the district court's award of profits and remand for a redetermination of damages. A generous approximation of the royalties Quaker would have had to pay STW for the use of the THIRST-AID mark had it recognized the validity of STW's claims seems to us an appropriate measure of damages, although perhaps not the only one. In any event, we can conceive of no rational measure of damages that would yield $24 million.

Judge Ripple agreed with Judge Cudahy that the profits award could not be sustained but doubted that a reasonable royalty measure would be sufficient. He, however, joined in the Cudahy opinion "to enable this issue to be decided by majority vote." Judge Fairchild would have affirmed the district court. The following opinion of Judge Marshall is on remand by the Court of Appeals.]

The Court of Appeals * * * has returned the case to me with instructions that I recalculate the award of damages using "a reasonable royalty as a baseline or starting point." Judge Cudahy suggests a "generous approximation." Judge Ripple "doubt[s] very much that damages measured by a 'reasonable royalty'—a speculative approximation itself— necessarily would suffice in this case." However, Judge Cudahy admonishes "no rational measure of damages . . . would yield $24 million." And Judge Ripple agrees that the original award of damages "is difficult to sustain." Thus the message appears to be: Be generous but not too generous, i.e., something less than $24 million.

* * *

The hypothetical determination of a reasonable royalty in a case such as this is a form of restitution designed to prevent unjust enrichment. * * * Determining a reasonable royalty is not a simple task. In Georgia-Pacific Corp. v. U.S. Plywood-Champion Papers, Inc., 318 F.Supp. 11 16 (S.D.N.Y.1970), modified and aff'd., 446 F.2d 295 (2d Cir.1971), cert. denied, 404 U.S. 870 (1971), the district court provided the following criteria for determining a reasonable royalty: (1) the royalty rates received in prior licenses by the licensor, (2) prior rates paid by the licensee, (3) the licensor's licensing policies, (4) the nature and scope of the infringer's infringing use, (5) the special value of the mark to the infringer, (6) the profitability of the infringer's use, (7) the lack of viable alternatives, (8) the opinion of expert witnesses, and (9) the amount that the licensor and licensee would have agreed upon in voluntary negotiations. These elements have received widespread acceptance and I apply them here. But the determination of a reasonable royalty remains a legal fiction, "created in an effort to 'compensate' when profits are not provable, a 'reasonable royalty' device conjures a 'willing' licensor and licensee, who like ghosts of Christmas Past are dimly seen as 'negotiating' a 'license.' There is, of course, no actual willingness on either side, and no license to do anything, the infringer being normally enjoined ... from further [use of the plaintiff's trademark]." Panduit Corp. v. Stahlin Bros. Fibre Works, Inc., [517 F.2d 1152 (2d Cir.1978)] at 1159.

So plaintiff sat at the hypothetical table with an incontestable registered mark of proven success in the isotonic beverage field while defendant was about to launch a new campaign in which THIRST-AID was its most attractive gambit. What royalty rate would a willing licensor and a willing licensee agree to? Plaintiff urges a running royalty of 1% of sales for the first year and .5% for each year thereafter. This rate is considerably less than plaintiff's witness Ralph Chapek's testimonial proposal of a $500,000 non-refundable fee, 2% of first year sales, 1.5% of second year sales, 1% of third through tenth year sales and .5% thereafter. Plaintiff's proposal is also less than its own 1% for King Arthur Flour, Chapek's Mrs. Fields/Sara Lee (5%), TGI Friday's/Stilwell Foods (24%), Ore/Ida (5%) and defendant's witnesses AAU (4–7%) and Baseball Hall of Fame/Admiral Awards (4–10%). And while plaintiff's proposal is greater than its license to Pet of .5% and .33%, plaintiff's bargaining position in 1984 was much stronger than it was in 1980 and defendant's need for THIRST-AID in 1984 was greater than Pet's in 1980.

For its part defendant says a flat fee of $100,000 would exceed the fair valuation of THIRST-AID in 1984. Certainly that is not a "generous approximation." Indeed, it does not comport with defendant's earlier assertion that plaintiff's Pet agreement "establishes a royalty rate," or its assertion in its brief on the nature of the hearing on remand that "the Seventh Circuit remanded the case only for a more precise calculation of a royalty-based profit disgorgement."

I find that plaintiff's proposal of 1%–5% of sales is reasonable and comports with the mandate of the Court of Appeals. In reaching this finding I have taken into account plaintiff's prior licenses, (defendant has declined to disclose its prior licenses), plaintiff's licensing policies, the nature and scope of defendant's infringing use (recounted in detail in my original decision and Judge Cudahy's opinion), the special value of THIRST-AID to defendant in 1984 (the huge increase in sales during infringement followed by a sharp decline after infringement ceased), the profitability of the defendant's infringement, the questionable attractiveness of defendant's alternatives, the expert opinions and defendant's persistent infringement in the face of the admonitions by its inside and outside counsel and my May 1985 ruling that it was infringing.

Applying this royalty rate to defendant's sales, less the $95 million in annual sales it enjoyed prior to its infringement, results in a royalty payment due plaintiff in the amount of $10,328,411 together with prejudgment interest (the award of which was affirmed by the Court of Appeals) in the amount of $5,431,413 for a total of $15,749,824.

Is this award adequate? Defendant knowingly and in bad faith infringed plaintiff's incontestable mark. Defendant knew of the mark. It knew of its registration. It knew it was incontestable. It knew that it had been used successfully by Pet. It was told immediately following its public use that it was infringing and would damage plaintiff's mark. It disregarded the advice of its outside trademark counsel to minimize the use of THIRST-AID in its advertising. It persisted for five years in its infringing use of plaintiff's THIRST-AID mark after I ruled in June, 1985 that its use was infringing. Will the imposition of a hypothetical licensing royalty deter predatory conduct such as defendant's? I doubt it. The royalty is nothing more than an approximation of what defendant would have paid plaintiff had defendant acted lawfully. "[An] infringer [has] nothing to lose, and everything to gain if [it] could count on paying only the normal, routine royalty, non-infringers might have paid ... [T]he infringer would be in a 'heads-I-win, tails-you-lose position.'" Panduit Corp. v. Stahlin Fibre Works, 575 F.2d 1152, 1158 (6th Cir.1978).

Plaintiff urges that I double or triple the royalty award. The Lanham Act provides for the trebling of damages in an appropriate case. * * *

* * *

After paying plaintiff a royalty of $10,328,411 defendant will realize a profit of $303,000,000 on its sales of GATORADE during the period of infringement. * * * Under the mandate in this case I "may take into account the possible need for deterrence, which may involve consideration of the amount of Quaker's profit." Indeed, Judge Ripple suggested a "substantial emphasis on deterrence."

I realize that the earlier award was large. Indeed, I am told by defendant it was the largest trademark award in history. But I know of no case in which an infringer has reaped the dollar benefits from infringement that defendant has here. To deter conduct such as defendant's, and in the exercise of my discretion under the Lanham Act, I double the amount of the hypothetical royalty to $20,656,822. However, prejudgment interest is applied only to the initial royalty award. Thus plaintiffs award of double royalty is $20,656,822 plus prejudgment interest of $5,431,413 for a total of $26,088,235.

NOTES

1. In Champion Spark Plug Co. v. Sanders, 331 U.S. 125 (1947) the Court held that where the likelihood of damage to the defendant is "slight" and there is no fraud or palming off shown, injunctive relief satisfies the "equities" of the case. This has become standard doctrine and injunctive relief is the ordinary remedy in trademark infringement cases. However, as the principal cases illustrate, monetary relief is available under certain circumstances. What is there about trademark infringement cases that makes the calculation of monetary damages so difficult?

2. If the defendant uses an infringing mark on goods that directly compete with the goods of the plaintiff, why isn't it logical to assume that confused customers who purchased from defendant would have, absent the confusion, purchased from the plaintiff? Doesn't this establish a justification for a profit award? And, if it does, should the plaintiff be required to show the number of confused customers? If the only confusion created by the infringement is confusion of sponsorship because the defendant's goods do not directly compete with plaintiff's, how could profits ever be justified? The leading case articulating the deterrence rationale for an award of profits is Maier Brewing Co. v. Fleischmann Distilling Corp., 390 F.2d 117 (9th Cir. 1968). Does the deterrence rationale require that the defendant willfully infringe?

3. Does the reasonable royalty calculation adopted in *Sands* provide a better market test of the value of the mark and the damages to the plaintiff associated with the infringement or does Judge Marshall's opinion make you uneasy about that remedy as well?

4. Why would Congress authorize judges to enhance the monetary remedies and at the same time require they be compensatory rather than punitive? In *Sands II,* Judge Marshall's revised $26+million dollar award was affirmed in part and remanded in part. Sands, Taylor & Wood v. The Quaker Oats Co., 34 F.3d 1340 (7th Cir. 1994). All three judges approved of the calculation of the reasonable royalty of $10 million but could not agree on the enhanced award thinking it may have been based on an "amorphous concern for deterrence" or that there may have been some double counting.

In Sands, Taylor & Wood Co. v. The Quaker Oats Co., 1995 WL 221871 (N.D. Ill. 1995), Judge Marshall, on remand, responded:

> The royalty which I awarded was 3.3% of defendant's profits during the period of infringement. In *Sands I* the court of appeals stated that my decision on remand could "involve consideration of the amount of Quaker's profits." 978 F.2d at 963 n. 19. Wouldn't Quaker, a profit-seeking person willing to violate federal law, pay 3.3 cents to make a dollar? Of course it would and did. Thus a base royalty would not make "the willful trademark infringement . . . sufficiently unprofitable." *Sands II* at 1348. The post-infringement royalty "becomes for the male-factor simply the cost of doing business." *Sands II* at 1351.

The enhancement is not a penalty. It reflects the inadequacy of the base royalty award in light of the "circumstances of the case," the extraordinary profits defendant realized as a consequence of its deliberate infringement. * * *

Furthermore, I assure the court of appeals that I did not "double-count" the factors which I used to determine the base royalty.

I can say no more.

5. *Corrective Advertising.* In West Des Moines State Bank v. Hawkeye Bancorporation, 722 F.2d 411 (8th Cir.1983) the Eighth Circuit applied a "corrective advertising" measure of damages based on Big O Tire Dealers, Inc. v. Goodyear Tire and Rubber Co., 561 F.2d 1365 (10th Cir.1977) which measures the plaintiff's damages as 75% of the amount of money spent by the infringer to bring the infringing mark to the public's attention. The theory is to reimburse the plaintiff for the costs of correcting the misperception of the public caused by the infringement. In Adray v. Adry-Mart, Inc., 68 F.3d 362 (9th Cir. 1995) the plaintiff sought to recover its prospective corrective advertising costs — the expenditures it would make in the future to correct the confusion created by the defendant's infringement. The district court refused, holding that prospective corrective advertising costs can only be recovered when plaintiff shows he was financially unable to conduct the advertising before trial. The Ninth Circuit reversed: "Prospective costs may be difficult to determine precisely and present a danger of overcompensation if they exceed the value of the mark; however, the burden of any uncertainty in the amount of damages should be borne by the wrongdoer and overcompensation can be avoided by appropriate limitation in the instruction." Do you see any reason why an award of prospective corrective advertising costs would not be appropriate in every infringement case?

6. In 1975 Congress amended the Lanham Act to specifically authorize the court to award attorneys fees to the prevailing party "in exceptional circumstances." Previously the Supreme Court had held the Act did not authorize such awards. Fleischmann Distilling Corp. v. Maier Brewing Co., 386 U.S. 714 (1967).

7. *Intentional Infringement: The Trademark Counterfeiting Act of 1984.* The penalties and damage provisions for some cases of intentional infringement were substantially enhanced by the Trademark Counterfeiting Act of 1984, P.L. 98–473 § 1501 et seq. The Act establishes substantial criminal penalties for anyone who "intentionally traffics * * * in goods or services and knowingly uses a counterfeit mark * * *." A "counterfeit mark" is defined as a "spurious mark" that is "identical or substantially indistinguishable" from a registered mark and which is used with goods and services in a way that is "likely to cause confusion, to cause mistake, or to deceive." The defendant need not know that the mark is registered but is entitled to any defenses applicable under the Lanham Act. 18 U.S.C. § 2320.

Perhaps more significantly, § 35(b) of the Lanham Act was added to strengthen the provisions for triple damages, triple profits, attorneys fees, and prejudgment interest in counterfeiting cases. See also § 35(c) which provides for statutory damages in counterfeit mark cases.

8. *Destruction of labels and goods.* Section 36 of the Lanham Act provides authority for the court to order the destruction of all labels and packages that are found to infringe a registered mark or are in violation of § 43(a). This section is a remedy available to the plaintiff after obtaining a judgment. Section 34(d) allows the pretrial seizure of "goods and counterfeit marks" in a civil action for trademark infringement involving a counterfeit mark.

9. *RICO.* Trademark owners may also find themselves able to take advantage of the Racketeer Influenced and Corrupt Organizations Act, 18 U.S.C. § 1961 et seq. (1982) which was originally enacted to attack organized crime but which has been interpreted to apply to a wide-range of business practices. The act requires a pattern of criminal activity but intentional trademark infringement may well involve mail fraud or other criminal charges that form the predicate offenses for a RICO violation. RICO provides triple damages and attorneys fees. See Cooley, RICO: Treble Damages and Attorneys Fees in Trademark Counterfeiting Actions, 73 Trademark Rep. 476 (1983).

---

(6) Contributory Infringement

Coca–Cola Co. v. Snow Crest Beverages, Inc.

United States District Court, D. Massachusetts, 1946.

64 F.Supp. 980, affirmed 162 F.2d 280, certiorari denied 332 U.S. 809, 68 S.Ct. 110, 92 L.Ed. 386.

■ WYZANSKI, DISTRICT JUDGE.

[Plaintiff is the owner of the trade-mark "Coca-Cola" and for many years spent millions of dollars advertising its soft drink. Defendant manufactures and sells "Polar Cola," a dark brown cola beverage similar to "Coca-Cola." Defendant convinced a distributor of liquor to run a promotion for bars whereby for every case of rum purchased the bar would receive 5 free cases of Polar Cola. A popular mixed drink at the time was a "Cuba Libre" made of rum and cola. The promotion was designed to get bartenders to use Polar Cola when customers ordered a "Cuba Libre." Polar Cola was cheaper than Coca-Cola. Thereafter plaintiff's investigators found several bars substituting Polar Cola when Coca-Cola was specifically requested. In addition to the findings discussed in the opinion below, the court found that defendants sales talk and advertising were designed to and did induce bars to use Polar Cola for orders not specifying a particular brand of cola but were not designed to encourage or suggest the substitution when Coca-Cola was requested.]

Upon these facts, the legal questions with respect to defendant's sales to bars reduce themselves to these:

(a) Was defendant under a duty not to sell its product to a bar for use by that bar in filling a customer's general order for a Cuba Libre or a rum (or whiskey) and cola?

(b) Before it had notice that some bars in filling a customer's specific order for a rum (or whiskey) and Coca-Cola used a substitute cola, was defendant under a duty to investigate possible passing off, or to take steps to safeguard against such passing off, or to eliminate or curtail sales of its product?

(c) After it had notice that some unnamed bars in filling a customer's order for a rum (or whiskey) and Coca-Cola used a substitute cola, was defendant under a duty to investigate such passing off, or to take steps to safeguard against such passing off, or to eliminate or curtail sales of its product?

The answer to the first question is simple. On the evidence in this case there is no basis for finding that plaintiff has any trademark upon or any special right to the names of "Cuba Libre" or "cola". So far as appears any one has a right to make or sell products under those names. Customers who ask for them are not asking for plaintiff's product. For them there cannot be confusion as to the source of the goods. In short, defendant was free to sell its own cola to a bar for use by the bar in filling a customer's general order for "Cuba Libre" or "rum (or whiskey) and cola."

In answering the second question these are the dominant facts. There is on this record a failure to prove that many bar customers ordinarily place specific orders for Coca-Cola, that a reasonable person in the bottling business would have known or that this defendant did know that a very large number of customers did make such specific orders or that a reasonable person in the bottling business would have known or that this defendant did know that upon receiving specific orders for Coca-Cola barkeepers would be more likely than the average man to substitute for Coca-Cola a cheaper product. So far as appears, the great majority of customers in a bar who order a drink mixed of rum or whiskey and cola do not specify the brand of the rum or the whiskey or the cola. The percentage who specify the type cola is much lower than the small percentage of drinkers who specify the type rum or whiskey they desire.

Even upon the view of the evidence most favorable to plaintiff, the testimony only shows that some customers do place specific orders for "rum (or whiskey) and Coca-Cola," that the defendant knew it, and that any man of common sense knows that in any line of business, including but not emphasizing the business of running bars and taverns, there are some unscrupulous persons who, when it is to their financial advantage to do so, will palm off on customers a different product from that ordered by the customer.

Upon these facts defendant was not under a duty to investigate possible passing off by bartenders, or to take steps to safeguard against such passing off, or to eliminate or curtail sales of its product.

It is, of course, defendant's duty to avoid intentionally inducing bars to market defendant's products as products of plaintiff. It is also defendant's duty to avoid knowingly aiding bars which purchase defendant's products from marketing those products in such a manner as to infringe plaintiff's trade-mark.

Under the principles just stated, it would have been a breach of duty if defendant's salesmen had induced bars to buy defendant's product for the stated or implied purpose of serving it when Coca-Cola was called for. It would also have been a breach of duty for defendant to have continued sales to bars without taking some precautionary measures if it had known or a normal bottler would have known that most bar customers specifically ordered Coca-Cola and that consequently a normal bottler would infer from defendant's large volume of sales that many bars which bought defendant's product were using defendant's product as a substitute in the case of specific orders of Coca-Cola and were not merely using it as an ordinary cola when a customer placed a general order for a "Cuba Libre" or a "rum (or whiskey) and cola." Likewise, it would have been a breach of duty if defendant had known that many bar customers specifically ordered Coca-Cola and had also known that some particular bars were in fact using defendant's product as a substitute in the case of specific orders for Coca-Cola.

But in the case at bar plaintiff seems to urge that defendant's obligation goes further. Plaintiff appears to contend that once a defendant has knowledge that some customers of bars specifically order "rum (or whiskey) and Coca-Cola," and that there are in all probability some rogues in the bar business as in other businesses, the defendant has a duty either (a) not to sell to any bar a cola until defendant first creates for that cola a special consumer demand, or (b) at least not to sell a cola to a bar before defendant has particularly cautioned the bar to be scrupulous against substitution. The law does not go that far. Before he can himself be held as a wrongdoer or contributory infringer one who supplies another with the instruments by which that other commits a tort, must be shown to have knowledge that the other will or can reasonably be expected to commit a tort with the supplied instrument. * * *

There is no broader legal principle that always makes the defendant his brother's or his customer's keeper. Where the defendant markets a product, defendant's accountability for his customer's wrongful use of that product turns on the issue whether a reasonable person in the defendant's position would realize either that he himself had created a situation which afforded a temptation to or an opportunity for wrong by l'homme moyen sensuel or was dealing with a customer whom he should know would be peculiarly likely to use the defendant's product wrongfully.

* * *

There remains the problem raised by the third question, that is, the duty of defendant after September 1944. In solving that problem the general principles applicable are not different from those reviewed in answering the second question. That is, plaintiff would have established a case against defendant if in the fall of 1944 or at any other time prior to November 14, 1944 when this suit was brought plaintiff had given defendant either (a) credible information that would have led a normal bottler in defendant's position to believe that so many bar customers specifically ordered "rum (or whiskey) and Coca-Cola" that in view of the volume of defendant's sales many bars must necessarily be passing off defendant's product as Coca-Cola, or (b) notice that particular named bars which defendant was continuing to supply were serving defendant's product when plaintiff's product was specifically ordered. But the evidence shows no such proffer of information that would persuade a reasonable man and no such notice by plaintiff. Plaintiff did not go beyond stating in a conversation of general scope that unnamed bars in unnamed quantities were serving defendant's product when plaintiff's was called for. * * *

Nothing herein intimates any opinion on the question whether defendant after having its attention drawn in the course of the trial of this case to testimony that particular bars have served defendant's product in response to customer's orders for plaintiff's product, is now under a duty to minimize or eliminate the risk that those or other bars will engage in a further confusion of defendant's goods with plaintiff's goods.

Decree dismissing complaint with costs.

Nike, Inc. v. Rubber Manufacturers Ass'n, Inc.

United States District Court, Southern District of New York, 1981.
509 F.Supp. 919.

[The case involves a counterclaim by Brooks, an athletic shoe manufacturer, against Nike, another manufacturer. Brooks' claim under 43(a) of the Lanham Act alleges that Nike paid several professional athletes to wear Nike shoes which all carry a "swoosh-stripe" emblem on the side and the word "NIKE" on the back. Some of these athletes, including Mike Schmidt, a star for the Philadelphia Phillies and voted the most valuable player in the major leagues, and Mark Moseley, place kicker for the Washington Redskins, wore shoes other than Nikes but doctored them to look like Nike shoes by adding a "swoosh-stripe" and the word "Nike." The athletes had contracted to wear only Nike shoes, but in some instances Nike shoes were not comfortable.]

Nike contends that it has not violated the provisions of the Lanham Act because the doctoring was done without its participation, knowledge or approval. The record indicates, however, that Nike knew of Schmidt's doctoring activity, since three of its employees observed Schmidt's doctored shoes. None of them informed Schmidt that this was a breach of his agreement. Indeed, their apparent acquiescence would indicate tacit approval.

Moreover, Nike's restrictive reading of Section 43(a) is not persuasive. In Stix Products, Inc. v. United Merchants & Manufacturers, Inc., 295 F.Supp. 479 (S.D.N.Y.1969), the court granted injunctive relief against those who knowingly played a significant role in the deception involved. * * *

* * *

At the hearing, vice-president Robert Woodell testified that Nike's corporate policy has been to oppose doctoring, and that this policy is reflected in language prohibiting such acts in the agreements signed by the players. However, it appears from the evidence that Nike has on occasion been less than vigilant in enforcing this policy. The existence of lucrative contracts between Nike and prominent players leads the players, as it did in the case of Schmidt, Boone and Unser, to doctor their shoes to look like Nike shoes if they find the Nike shoes uncomfortable and do not wish to wear them. Nike certainly knew of the likelihood of doctoring, just as it knew that by paying large sums of money to players it encouraged them to wear the Nike trademark on whatever shoes they wore. Therefore, Nike's contractual prohibition against doctoring does not shield it from liability.

NOTES

1. Assume that the defendant is presented credible evidence that a particular bar shows a pattern of substitution when Coca-Cola is requested. Should the court prohibit the defendant from selling to that bar? Should it matter that the substitution is unintentional?

2. Section 32(1)(b) of the Lanham Act, 15 U.S.C. § 1114(1)(b), states the controlling principles as applied to packagers, manufacturers, and reproducers. The important limitation is the requirement that no profits and damages can be recovered from such an infringer "unless the acts have been committed with knowledge that such imitation is intended to be used to cause confusion, or to cause mistake, or to deceive." Does the express limitation of remedy against innocent printers and publishers imply that all others who aid in a trademark infringement are subject to the full range of remedies under the Act? Is an advertising agency that prepares and a television station that broadcasts advertising for a product with an infringing label liable for damages caused the trademark owner?

PROBLEM

Plaintiff manufactures a prescription drug cyclandate under the brand name "Cyclospasmol" in distinctive red and blue capsules. Can the plaintiff prevent the defendant from selling the generic drug cyclandate in similar red and blue capsules? Are the following facts of any significance?

1. Plaintiff had enjoyed a 5 year monopoly on the production of cyclandate because it was the only manufacturer able to secure FDA approval for marketing.

2. Plaintiff had enjoyed an extended monopoly on the production of cyclandate because of a now expired patent.

3. Defendant advertises to pharmacists that its cyclandate is "comparable to Cyclospasmol."

4. Patients recognize the red and blue capsules as indicative of the drug prescribed by their physician.

5. A state statute permits pharmacists to fill a prescription with a generic substitute unless the prescribing physician specifies otherwise.

6. Customers rely on the color of capsules to assure they are taking the right medicine.

(7) Abandonment

Exxon Corp. v. Humble Exploration Co., Inc.

United States Court of Appeals, Fifth Circuit, 1983.
695 F.2d 96.

■ PATRICK E. HIGGINBOTHAM, CIRCUIT JUDGE.

[The Humble Oil & Refining Company began using the mark "Humble" on gasoline stations and automotive products in the early 1960's. In 1972 the company adopted the mark "Exxon" as a substitute, changed its corporate name to Exxon Company, U.S.A., and spent 12 million dollars advertising the mark and name change. However, the Board of Directors in 1972 passed a resolution calling for continued use of the "Humble" mark after the changeover and Exxon instituted a trademark maintenance program which involved limited sales using the "Humble" mark.

The appellant, the Humble Exploration Company was formed in 1974 and selected "Humble" as a mark because it was abandoned by Exxon. The company is actively involved in oil exploration. Exxon filed this suit to enjoin use of "Humble" by the appellant. Appellant raised the issue of abandonment.]

* * *

The district court framed the abandonment issue thus: "Is the limited use of a famous trademark solely for protective purposes a use sufficient to preclude abandonment under the common law and the Lanham Act?" It answered the question in the affirmative. Plaintiff-Appellee withdrew its Texas and common law claims in the district court, so the resolution of the abandonment issue must focus on the federal standards for abandonment set forth in the Lanham Act.

Under the Act,

A mark shall be deemed to be abandoned—

(a) When its use has been discontinued with intent not to resume use. Intent not to resume may be inferred from circumstances. Nonuse for two consecutive years shall be prima facie abandonment.

15 U.S.C. § 1127 (1982). The burden of proof is on the party claiming abandonment, but when a prima facie case of trademark abandonment exists because of nonuse of the mark for over two consecutive years, the owner of the mark has the burden to demonstrate that circumstances do not justify the inference of intent not to resume use. See Sterling Brewers, Inc. v. Schenley Industries, Inc., 441 F.2d 675, 679 (Cust. & Pat.App.1971).

Appellant argues that Exxon has not used the HUMBLE mark since its changeover program. Since that time, Exxon has (1) sold existing inventory of packaged products bearing the name "Humble Oil and Refining Company"; (2) made periodic sales of nominal amounts of Exxon gasoline, motor oil and grease in pails bearing the names HUMBLE and EXXON; (3) sold Exxon bulk gasoline and diesel fuel to selected customers, who received HUMBLE invoices, through three corporations organized for that purpose; and (4) sold 55–gallon drum products from the Baytown, Texas refinery, all bearing a stencil with the names HUMBLE and EXXON.

The existing inventory was depleted by mid–1974; the sale of 55 gallon drums began in 1977. Whether or not these sales are "uses" for the purposes of 15 U.S.C. § 1127, the period between those sales was longer than two years, and under the Lanham Act, "nonuse for two consecutive years is prima facie abandonment." 15 U.S.C. § 1127. During that period between sales of inventory and sales of 55–gallon drum products, Exxon can point to only two types of sales as possible uses. As earlier described, Exxon made limited sales of packaged products with both EXXON and HUMBLE on the labels to targeted customers in these amounts: $9.28 in 1973, $.0 in 1974, $140.12 in 1975 and $42.05 in 1976. Second, products in bulk form and not bearing a trade name or mark were sold to selected customers who received the explanation that they were receiving Exxon products. The only use of HUMBLE in connection with these sales was on the invoices sent to the customers. The issue, thus, is whether these two categories of arranged sales through the trademark protection program during that period constitute "use" sufficient to avoid prima facie abandonment.

* * *

In this case, the mark HUMBLE was used only on isolated products or selected invoices sent to selected customers. No sales were made that depended upon the HUMBLE mark for identification of source. To the contrary, purchasers were informed that the selected shipments would bear the HUMBLE name or be accompanied by an HUMBLE invoice but were the desired Exxon products. That is, the HUMBLE mark did not with these sales play the role of a mark. That casting, however, is central to the plot that the Lanham Act rests on the idea of registration of marks otherwise born of use rather than the creation of marks by the act of registration. That precept finds expression in the Lanham Act requirement that to maintain a mark in the absence of use there must be an intent to resume use. That expression is plain. The Act does not allow the preservation of a mark solely to prevent its use by others. Yet the trial court's reasoning allows precisely that warehousing so long as there is residual good will associated with the mark. Exxon makes the same argument here. While that may be good policy, we cannot square it with the language of the statute. In sum, these arranged sales in which the mark was not allowed to play its basic role of identifying source were not "use" in the sense of section 1127 of the Lanham Act.

* * *

[The district court had cited language in Lyon Metal Products, Inc. v. Lyon Inc., 134 U.S.P.Q. 31 (TTAB 1962) that there is a residual good will that remains after a mark is abandoned and that it might prevent another party from adopting the abandoned mark particularly given the likelihood of consumer confusion. The Court of Appeals viewed the statement as dicta and the case as not factually similar.]

* * *

This court recognizes that the good-will associated with the mark HUMBLE has immense value to Exxon. That fact, coupled with the efforts under the trademark maintenance program, could suggest Exxon's intent to resume use of the mark,[4] but the trial court did not make that finding. The court found that the trademark protection program evidenced "an intent not to relinquish HUMBLE" and "an intent not to abandon HUMBLE," but it did not specifically address Exxon's intent to resume use as required by section 1127 the Lanham Act. * * * There is a difference between intent not to abandon or relinquish and intent to resume use in that an owner may not wish to abandon its mark but may have no intent to resume its use. In factual contexts where there is no issue of a hoarding of a mark, the language "an intent to abandon or relinquish" may be used to express the Lanham Act requirement of an "intent not to resume use." For that reason, it is important that cases using the language of "intent to abandon" be carefully laid into their factual molds. * * * In the context of a challenge strictly under the Lanham Act to an alleged warehousing program, as the facts of this case present, the application of the statutory language is critical. That is, this court having found that the two types of uses under the trademark maintenance program were not sufficient uses to avoid prima facie proof of abandonment, the district court must specifically address Exxon's intent to resume use of the HUMBLE trademark. An "intent to resume" requires the trademark owner to have plans to resume commercial use of the mark. Stopping at an "intent not to abandon" tolerates an owner's protecting a mark with neither commercial use nor plans to resume commercial use. Such a license is not permitted by the Lanham Act.

III. EXXON'S CLAIM UNDER § 1125

Exxon argues here that even if the HUMBLE mark were abandoned, Exxon has the right to prevent a competitor from gaining an unfair advantage by using a "false designation of origin" or "a false representation" in interstate commerce in violation of section 43(a) of the Lanham Act, 15 U.S.C. § 1125(a). The district court found that appellant Humble Exploration's use of the trade name Humble constituted a misrepresentation of goods and services in commerce in violation of § 1125(a). That conclusion flows from its finding that Exxon had not abandoned the HUMBLE mark. This court having found that Exxon has discontinued use of the mark, abandonment of the mark is yet to be decided by the inquiry into intent to resume use. Whether the mark has been abandoned is in turn

---

4. In Sterling Brewers, Inc. v. Schenley Industries, Inc., 441 F.2d 675 (Cust. & Pat.App.1971), the court decided that the goodwill of a trademark for beer had not dissipated through eight years of nonuse. Significantly, the court found that "the continuous activity * * * directed to maintenance of the brewery during the period of non-use, coupled with the refusal to consider periodic efforts of appellant to negotiate purchase of the rights to the mark separately, demonstrates an intent to maintain conditions conducive to resumption of production under the mark on relatively short notice." Id. at 680.

precedent to Exxon's claim under § 1125. That is, to the extent that Exxon travels on a trademark infringement claim, § 1125(a) is to be read in a parallel fashion with §§ 1114 and 1115. While § 1125 has a broader reach than § 1114, and claims under it can be maintained by plaintiffs who are not owners of a trademark, when a claim is based on alleged ownership of a mark, the two sections must be applied in a parallel manner. Otherwise stated, the § 1125 claim rises or falls on the issue of abandonment for the reason that the only basis for the trial court's holding that § 1125 was violated was the use by appellant of the mark, a use not faulted if the mark has been abandoned. It would be incongruous to hold that Exxon had abandoned the mark, discontinued the mark with no intent to resume use, and thus that appellant had a right to use that mark because of Exxon's abandonment, and then to hold that appellant had engaged in false designation or representation of origin. Section 1125(a) "must still be read in the context of the statute in which it appears...." General Pool Corp. v. Hallmark Pool Corp., 259 F.Supp. 383, 386 (N.D.Ill.1966).

The judgment is reversed and the case is remanded for further proceedings consistent with this opinion. In doing so, we emphasize that we do not decide here whether the present record would support a finding that Exxon had sufficient intent to resume use of the Humble mark so as to avoid its loss, nor do we here address Exxon's rights under the common law to block any present use of the mark in a confusing manner. Finally, we leave to the trial court the decision whether additional evidence on the issue of intent to resume use ought to be heard.

Affirmed in part, reversed and remanded in part.

[On remand, the court held there was no abandonment. Exxon Corp. v. Humble Exploration Co., Inc., 592 F.Supp. 1226 (N.D.Tex.1984)].

NOTES

1. The doctrine of abandonment may arise in a number of situations. It serves as a defense to an infringement action. Abandonment may also play a significant feature in determining priority of competing marks where the current owner of a mark seeks to use the date of adoption of a prior user from whom he has purchased the mark in establishing an earlier priority. It may be argued in such cases that the prior user abandoned the mark and therefore the date of first use is the first use by the current owner. In cases where the Lanham Act preserves preexisting rights of common law trademarks against the exclusive claims of a federal registrant, the registrant often asserts that the prior user has abandoned the mark. But see Casual Corner Assoc., Inc. v. Casual Stores of Nevada, Inc., 493 F.2d 709 (9th Cir.1974) where the court held that the standards of proof relating to abandonment do not apply in determining whether a prior use has been "continuous" and thus preserved against a claim of incontestability by section 15 of the Lanham Act. The court found a one year period of non-use sufficient to defeat an assertion of "continuous" use in the absence of intent to abandon.

2. The definition of "abandonment" in § 45 provides two separate tests. The first, non-use with intent not to resume, is a traditional common law formulation. The second declares a mark abandoned if "any course of conduct of the owner, including acts of omission as well as commission, causes the mark to become the generic name for the goods or services * * * or otherwise to lose its significance as an indication of origin." For a detailed examination of the second definition see Wallpaper Manufacturers, Ltd. v. Crown Wallcovering Corp., 680 F.2d 755 (CCPA 1982). There the court recognizes that an expansive definition of abandonment would upset the attempt in §§ 14, 15 and 33 to provide for some security for trademark owners. In *Wallpaper* the junior user argued that since there was evidence that some consumers attributed the mark to him as well as the senior user, the mark was "abandoned" because it has lost its origin significance. The court, however, held that even where there was de facto evidence of consumer attribution to more than one source, to be abandoned the mark had to lose *all* significance for the prior user.

3. The defense of "abandonment" should be carefully distinguished from the defenses of "acquiescence" or "laches". "Acquiescence" arises where the plaintiff gives some measure of assurance, either express or implied, that he will not assert his trademark rights against a particular defendant. The defense of "laches" contemplates unreasonable delay by the plaintiff in asserting his rights with resultant prejudice to the defendant. Both defenses may only be asserted by those defendants directly affected by the plaintiff's acts or omissions; abandonment is a loss of trademark rights against the world.

4. In abandonment cases it may be important to define the scope of the abandonment in geographic or product market terms. In *Dawn Donut Co.*, supra pg. 336, the court held that a federal registrant is not considered to have abandoned his mark unless he has abandoned it on a nation-wide basis. See also, Sheila's Shine Products, Inc. v. Sheila Shine, Inc., 486 F.2d 114 (5th Cir.1973) where with regard to a common law mark, the issue of abandonment was evaluated on a state by state basis. "Since a state is an appropriate territory by which to define trade areas when two parties are competing over the right to use the same mark [citing United Drug Co. v. Theodore Rectanus Co., 248 U.S. 90 (1918)] we deem it consistent with general principles of trademark law to hold that a user may abandon a trademark in certain states without abandoning it in others." Id. at 124. Laches and acquiescence defenses are normally limited to the geographic market where the factual basis applies. Conan Properties, Inc. v. Conans Pizza, Inc., 752 F.2d 145 (5th Cir.1985).

PROBLEMS

1. CBS suspends use of the "Amos 'N' Andy" trademark for radio and television programs portraying black persons because of strong pressure from civil rights groups. The mark and tapes of past programs were occasionally licensed from 1964 through the 1980's for purposes of documentaries and copyrights on the programs were asserted and renewed.

CBS claims an intention to hold on to the marks for a time when public attitudes change. Can a third person use the mark to represent a new musical comedy he wants to create?

2. A trademark originally used on fishing lures in 1910 is now used exclusively on fishing poles. Does the owner's priority relate back to 1910? Would your answer change if instead of fishing poles the mark was switched to broom handles?

3. From 1952 through 1984 the National Football Team located in Baltimore was known as the "Baltimore Colts". In 1984 the team's owner moved the team to Indianapolis and it became the "Indianapolis Colts". In 1993, the Canadian Football League granted a franchise for a Baltimore team and wants to name the team the "Baltimore CFL Colts". Any problem?

4. The Brooklyn Dodger baseball team left Brooklyn in 1958 to become the Los Angeles Dodgers and the term "Brooklyn Dodgers" was not used except on infrequent occasions. Your client now wants to open a restaurant in Brooklyn and name it the "Brooklyn Dodger Sports Bar and Restaurant." Any problem?

---

(8) Assignment and Licensing

Pepsico, Inc. v. Grapette Co.

United States Court of Appeals, Eighth Circuit, 1969.
416 F.2d 285.

■ LAY, CIRCUIT JUDGE. PepsiCo, Inc., a holding company of several subsidiaries including Pepsi Cola Co., a national soft drink bottler, sought an injunction against Grapette-Aristocrat, Inc. and its holding company Grapette Co. (hereinafter referred collectively as Grapette) on the alleged infringement of its trademark "Pepsi." In 1965 Grapette purchased the mark "Peppy" and intended to bottle a soft "pepper" drink with that name. The district court found that the mark "Peppy" was confusingly similar to "Pepsi" and as such would constitute infringement under 15 U.S.C. § 1114. However, notwithstanding this finding of infringement, the court denied the plaintiff injunctive relief on the ground that it was guilty of laches. 288 F.Supp. at 937. PepsiCo., Inc., appeals. We reverse.

The evidence shows that Pepsi Cola Co. has bottled beverages duly registered under trademarks "Pepsi Cola," "Pepsi" and "Pep-Kola" for many years. See 15 U.S.C. § 1065. Grapette is a national bottler and distributor of soft drinks, concentrates and syrups. In 1965 it developed a formula for a new syrup to be used in a pepper type bottled beverage as opposed to a cola beverage. In searching for a name to market the new product, defendant discovered the 1926 registration of the mark "Peppy" by H. Fox and Co., a partnership. The mark had been renewed by Fox in 1946 and 1966. Sometime between 1932 and 1937 Fox began to use the mark "Peppy" in conjunction with a cola flavored syrup which was distributed on a local basis, confined mostly to the Eastern states of New York, New Jersey and Connecticut. The cola distribution was sold exclusively as syrup. Since

1958, Fox's syrup has been sold only to jobbers in 28 ounce consumer size bottles. Some ten to twelve years prior to this time it was sold also to the fountain trade as a syrup in gallon containers.

In 1965, Grapette Co. entered into an agreement with Fox Corp. in which the trademark "Peppy" was assigned to defendant for a consideration of $7,500. At this time Fox Corp. was in a Chapter 11 bankruptcy proceeding. Although Fox Corp. made a formal assignment of "good-will", it is conceded by defendant that none of Fox Corp.'s physical assets or plant were transferred with the trademark; no inventory, customer lists, formulas, etc. Upon acquisition of the "Peppy" mark, Grapette began arrangements to have this mark placed upon its new pepper flavored soft drink. Fox Corp. continued to sell its cola syrup under the mark "Fox Brand" as well as agreeing to act as a distributor of defendant's "Peppy." In 1965, plaintiff warned the defendant of possible litigation if it did not stop the use of its mark. On April 21, 1966, this action was begun.

Plaintiff contends (1) that the transfer of the trade-mark "Peppy" by Fox Corp. was invalid because it was an assignment in "gross" and that therefore, Grapette cannot stand in the shoes of its predecessor in order to assert the defense of laches; and (2) that the defense of laches is not supported by sufficient evidence.

It is not disputed that Grapette must stand in the place of Fox Corp. Without a valid assignment, Grapette's rights to the use of "Peppy" accrue only as of November 1965 and it could not assert the defense of laches. PepsiCo, Inc. asserts that the 1965 assignment of the trademark by Fox Corp. to Grapette was a legal nullity in that the trade-mark was transferred totally disconnected from any business or goodwill of the assignor. We must agree.

* * * [The court here set out Section 10 of the Lanham Act, 15 U.S.C. § 1060.]

The early common law rule that a trademark could not be assigned "in gross" was recognized in this circuit in Macmahan Pharmacal Co. v. Denver Chem. Mfg. Co., 113 F. 468 (8 Cir.1901) and in Carroll v. Duluth Superior Milling Co., 232 F. 675 (8 Cir.1916). This court in *Carroll* observed that a trademark could only be transferred "in connection with the assignment of the particular business in which it has been used, with its good will, and for continued use upon the same articles or class of articles." Id. at 680. We later explained "that there is no property in a trade-mark except as a right appurtenant to an established business or trade, when it becomes an element of good will." Atlas Beverage Co. v. Minneapolis Brewing Co., 113 F.2d 672, 674–675 (8 Cir.1940). The rule found derivation in Kidd v. Johnson, 100 U.S. 617 (1879). The necessity to assign more than the naked mark was premised upon the primary object of the trade-mark "to indicate by its meaning or association the *origin* of the article to which it is affixed." (Emphasis ours.) 100 U.S. at 620. * * *

Strict adherence to this rule has been vigorously criticized as impractical and legalistic. Schecter, The Rational Bases of Trademark Protection, 40 Harv.L.Rev. 813 (1926); Grismore, The Assignment of Trademarks and

Tradenames, 30 Mich.L.Rev. 489 (1932); Callman, Unfair Competition, Trademarks and Monopolies, § 78 (3d ed. 1969); Note, Trademark Protection Following Ineffective Assignment, 88 Pa.L.Rev. 863 (1940). According to these commentators, the continuum of the rule fails to comprehend the modern image of the trademark to the consuming public. Strict application of the rule undoubtedly fails to recognize the function of the trademark as representing as well (1) a guaranty of the product and (2) the inherent advertising value of the mark itself. Id.

Some recent cases have given recognition that in certain situations a naked assignment might be approved. Grapette emphasizes the case of Hy-Cross Hatchery, Inc. v. Osborne, 303 F.2d 947 (1962), as being controlling.

There the plaintiff sought cancellation of the trademark "Hy-Cross" solely on the basis that the assignee of the original registrant took nothing but the naked mark. The evidence showed that all the assignee received was the mark itself. Osborne, the assignor, did not continue in the same business of raising chickens. The court in discussing the issue of naked assignment stated the following:

> "Unlike the cases relied on, Osborne, so far as the record shows, was using the mark at the time he executed the assignment of it. He had a valid registration which he also assigned. With these two legal properties he also assigned, in the very words of the statute, 'that part of the goodwill of the business connected with the use of and symbolized by the mark * * *.' He was selling chicks which his advertising of record shows were designated as 'No. 111 HY–CROSS (Trade Mark) AMERICAN WHITES.' As part of his assignment, by assigning the goodwill, he gave up the right to sell 'HY–CROSS' chicks. This had been a part of his 'business.' By the assignment Welp, the assignee, acquired that right. The record shows that he began selling 'HY–CROSS Hatching Eggs' and chicks designated as 'HY–CROSS 501,' 'HY–CROSS 610,' and 'HY–CROSS 656.' Thus, what had once been Osborne's business in 'HY–CROSS' chicks became Welp's business. We do not see what legal difference it would have made if a crate of eggs had been included in the assignment, or a flock of chickens destined to be eaten.
>
> "As for the argument that the transfer should have been held illegal because Osborne sold one kind of chick and Welp sold another another [sic] under the mark, whereby the public would be deceived, we think the record does not support this. The type of chick appears to have been otherwise indicated than by the trademark, as by the numbers above quoted as well as by name. Osborne, moreover, was not under any obligation to the public not to change the breed of chicks he sold under the mark from time to time."

In the instant case we need not decide whether the strict common law rule must apply or whether the approach, as suggested by *Hy-Cross,* should prevail. Inherent in the rules involving the assignment of a trademark is the recognition of protection against consumer deception. Basic to this concept is the proposition that any assignment of a trademark and its goodwill (with or without tangibles or intangibles assigned) requires the mark itself be used by the assignee on a product having substantially the same characteristics. See e.g., Independent Baking Powder Co. v. Boorman, 175 F. 448 (C.C.D.N.J.1910) (alum baking powder is distinctive from phosphate baking powder); Atlas Beverage Co. v. Minneapolis Brewing Co., 113 F.2d 672 (8 Cir.1940) (whiskey is a different product than beer); H.H. Scott, Inc. v. Annapolis Electroacoustic Corp., 195 F.Supp. 208 (D.Md.1961) (audio reproduction equipment is distinctive from hi-fidelity consoles). Cf. W.T. Wagner's Sons Co. v. Orange Snap Co., 18 F.2d 554 (5 Cir.1927) (No infringement: gingerale is in a different class than fruit flavored soft drinks).

Historically, this requirement is founded in the early case of Filkins v. Blackman, 9 Fed.Cas. 50 (No. 4786) (C.C.D.Conn.1876), wherein the court observed:

> "If the assignee should make a different article, he would not derive, by purchase from Jonas Blackman, a right which a court of equity would enforce, to use the name which the inventor had given to his own article, because such a use of the name would deceive the public. The right to the use of a trade-mark cannot be so enjoyed by an assignee that he shall have the right to affix the mark to goods differing in character or species from the article to which it was originally attached." Id. at 52.

The philosophy of the rule is sound even though the pragmatic utility of it is sometimes difficult and confusing. Grapette urges that it intends to use the trademark "Peppy" on a product of the same general "classification" as Fox, its assignor. * * *

* * *

The ultimate concern in all cases is the welfare of the public. A case by case treatment of the problem as specific facts present themselves is desirable. * * *

Where a transferred trademark is to be used on a new and different product, any goodwill which the mark itself might represent cannot legally be assigned. "The trademark owner does not have the right to a particular word but to the use of the word as the symbol of particular goods." Callman, § 78.1(a) at 426. To hold otherwise would be to condone public deceit. The consumer might buy a product thinking it to be of one quality or having certain characteristics and could find it only too late to be another. To say that this would be remedied by the public soon losing faith in the product fails to give the consumer the protection it initially deserves.

It is here that Grapette's use of the mark "Peppy" meets terminal difficulty. Grapette's intended use of the mark is one to simply describe its new pepper beverage.[4] The evidence is clear that Grapette did not intend to adopt or exploit any "goodwill" from the name "Peppy" and Fox's long

---

4. Mr. Fooks, Chairman of the Board of Grapette, testified:

"We went into his [Mr. Fox's] office and I told him just frankly my situation, that I had this product ready for the market with no name and I thought his name was a very suitable name, and if it wasn't too valuable I would like to purchase it." Record at 176a–177a.

association and use of it *with a cola syrup*. When one considers that Grapette did not require any of the assets of Fox, did not acquire any formula or process by which the Fox syrup was made, cf. Mulhens & Kropff, Inc. v. Ferd Muelhens, Inc., 38 F.2d 287 (D.C.1929), rev'd 43 F.2d 937 (2 Cir.1930), mandate clarified 48 F.2d 206 (2 Cir.1931), and then changed the type of beverage altogether, the assignment on its face must be considered void. It seems fundamental that either the defendant did not acquire any "goodwill" as required by law or if it did, assuming as defendant argues the mark itself possesses "goodwill," by use of the mark on a totally different product, Grapette intended to deceive the public. Either ground is untenable to the validity of the assignment.

We hold that the assignment to Grapette of the trademark "Peppy" is void and that Grapette possesses no standing to raise the equitable defense of laches.

Judgment reversed and remanded for further relief to be determined by the district court.

BLACKMUN, CIRCUIT JUDGE (concurring).

I concur, but on the ground that Hy-Cross Hatchery, Inc. v. Osborne, 303 F.2d 947 (1962), the case relied upon by the district court here, is not, or should not be helpful authority for Grapette. *Hy-Cross* is a peculiar case factually in that, among other aspects, live baby chicks were the product of both assignor and assignee. The court did place some reliance on what it seemed to regard as a genuine transfer of goodwill, 303 F.2d at 950, and, accordingly, saw little legal significance in the absence of an assignment of tangible chicks themselves. See J.C. Hall Co. v. Hallmark Cards, Inc., 340 F.2d 960, 963, (1965), where the same court apparently relates the significance of *Hy-Cross* to the absence of a transfer of tangible assets.

But if, as Grapette urges, the Hy-Cross holding has greater import than its peculiar facts suggest for me, then I would regard it as aberrational to settled authority. I prefer to stay with the usual rule, long established I thought, that a trademark may not validly be assigned in gross. And product difference is only an aspect of this traditional rule. A naked assignment is all that Fox and Grapette attempted and effected. It is not enough.

J. Atkins Holdings Ltd. v. English Discounts, Inc.

United States District Court, Southern District of New York, 1990.
729 F.Supp. 945.

■ LEVAL, J.

[An English manufacturer, B & W–UK, owned the mark "B & W" for loudspeakers. Until 1987, Misobanke was the exclusive distributor of B & W trademarked goods in the United States pursuant to an agreement with B & W–UK. In April, 1987, Equity Investments, a Canadian company, purchased the exclusive distribution rights in the United States. This transaction was effected through an assignment by Misobanke of the distribution agreement with B & W–UK to Equity Investments and an assignment by Misobanke of its U.S. division, B & W–America, to Equity International, a company under common control with Equity Investments. Joseph Atkins, the President of Equity International, formed J. Atkins Holding, Ltd. ("Atkins"), a Massachusetts corporation and which in July, 1987, received an assignment of the United States registered trademark "B & W" from B & W–UK. This assignment agreement which purported to transfer the good-will of the business within the United States also required Atkins to license the mark to B & W–America and further provided that if the distributorship agreement were ever terminated so that B & W–America were no longer the exclusive distributor, ownership of the marks would revert to B & W–UK.

Atkins claims Sixth Avenue imported speakers bearing the B & W mark and sold them in the United States under the mark without authorization. Sixth Avenue contends that the assignment of the mark to Atkins was a transfer in gross because the business symbolized by the mark was in fact conducted by B & W–America.]

Defendant argues first that the assignment of the marks to Atkins pursuant to the Assignment Agreement was an invalid transfer in gross. It is well settled law that the transfer of a trademark or trade name without the attendant good-will of the business which it represents is an invalid "naked" or "in gross" transfer of rights. * * *

The rationale supporting this common-law rule is consumer protection. A trademark identifies the source and quality of the goods and services offered. For a company to purchase the rights to a well-known trademark to use it in a manner which is wholly unrelated to the business or products which made the trademark famous would confuse or deceive the consumer. * * *

Consonant with this purpose, courts have recognized exceptions to the general rule that trademarks cannot be assigned without the good-will of the accompanying business. For example, where there is "continuity of management," so that the assignee will continue to provide the same quality of service, a transfer without good-will is not subject to invalidation. [Marshak v. Green, 746 F.2d 927, 930 (2d Cir.1984)].

The facts in this case do not support the defendant's position. Sixth Avenue's argument seeks to substitute labels for commercial reality. To apply the rule forbidding "naked assignment" of a trademark in these circumstances would ignore the realities of the transaction. It is true that the assignment by B & W–UK to Atkins was technically "naked," if one looks only at that facet of the overall transaction. If, on the other hand, one looks at the overall facts, this is not an assignment that separates the trademark from the goods or services upon which its reputation is based. To the contrary, this was an assignment to a U.S. corporation for business convenience (and perhaps to qualify for a customs exclusion) which is designed to continue the employment of the trademarks in connection with the same goods on which their reputation is based—being the loudspeakers manufactured by B & W–UK.[4] Furthermore, B & W–America, the former distributor under B & W–UK's license to Misobanke, with its personnel essentially unchanged, but now related to Atkins, continues to exercise the license to distribute the trademarked goods.

Thus, the Atkins assignment is not a "naked assignment." It continues the association of the trademark with the very goods which created its reputation.[5] And under the "continuity of management" exception recognized in Marshak, a viable business continues to operate as licensee of the marks. The public continues to receive the same quality of goods and services which have always accompanied the B & W marks. The assignment to Atkins did not sever the relationship between the mark and the good-will which it had developed in the United States.

NOTES

1. What is the consequence in *Pepsico* of the court's decision invalidating the transfer? Who owns the mark? Can Grapette market a cola beverage under the mark "Peppy" pursuant to the assignment from Fox? Assuming Pepsi did not object to Grapette's use of "Peppy", what rights would Grapette have against a new entrant in the market who wanted to use the mark on a spicy tomato juice? If the assignment was invalid as an assignment in gross, does Fox or its successor still have rights in the mark? Could you argue that an ineffective assignment of a mark is an act of abandonment? If the mark is separated from the good will it represents, has it lost its significance as an indication of origin?

2. After *Pepsico* and *Atkins,* what seems to be the crucial factor in validating an assignment, the terms of the assignment or how the assignee uses the mark subsequent to the assignment? Consider the following:

a. A produces a soft drink under the mark SNAPPY for several years. Subsequently A sells the mark, the good will, the formula for the soft drink, and the manufacturing plant to B. B continues the business as before.

b. X produces a soft drink under the mark SNAPPY for several years. Subsequently X assigns the mark but not the good will, the formula, or the manufacturing plant. Y, however, is able to duplicate the exact formulation of the original SNAPPY soft drink and continues the business as before.

4. * * * As both B & W–UK and Joseph Atkins agreed to register the ownership of the B & W marks in Atkins' name, this court finds no reason why such a decision should be disturbed. Although it is not for the court to inquire into the matter, it appears that the decision not to conduct business actively through Atkins was made to avoid subjecting revenues to United States taxation. Atkins Dep. pp. 71–72.

5. The assignment of trademarks among related corporate entities is not uncommon. * * * Whether the reason is to avoid nationalization, or for tax or trademark purposes, the court does not "believe that an assignment motivated at least in part by sound business judgment should be set aside as a sham transaction." Money Store v. Harriscorp Finance, Inc., 689 F.2d 666, 678 (7th Cir.1982).

Would the result change in the first situation if *B* changed the formulation of SNAPPY? If you think this would make a difference, what would you do with an original trademark owner who changed the formulation of its trademarked product? Did the change to "New Coke" destroy the validity of the "Coke" mark?

3. A trademark can be a major asset of a firm. Does the assignment in gross rule permit the pledging of a trademark as security for a loan? Is the priority of the mark affected when the debtor agrees to assign the mark to the creditor in the event of a default? After default when the creditor enforces the agreement? If you were a creditor under what conditions would you accept a mark as collateral for a loan?

4. Section 10 of the Lanham Act codifies the prohibition against assignments in gross, requires assignments of registered marks to be in writing, and provides a recording system for assignments of registered marks. Applications to register based on an intent to use are not assignable "except to the successor to the business * * * to which the mark pertains if the business is ongoing and existing". But see, Article 21 of the GATT Trips agreement: " * * * the owner of a registered trademark shall have the right to assign his trademark with or without the transfer of the business to which the trademark belongs."

PROBLEM

"Globe" Dry Cleaners engaged in the dry cleaning business in Lincoln, Nebraska, for 30 years. In 1998 the business and the trademark are sold to a young couple with no previous experience in the dry cleaning business. May the young couple now advertise: "Globe Cleaners—30 years of dry cleaning experience".

Dawn Donut Co. v. Hart's Food Stores, Inc.

United States Court of Appeals, Second Circuit, 1959.
267 F.2d 358.

[The facts of this case are reproduced supra page 275].

■ LUMBARD, CIRCUIT JUDGE.

* * *

The final issue presented is raised by defendant's appeal from the dismissal of its counterclaim for cancellation of plaintiff's registration on the ground that the plaintiff failed to exercise the control required by the Lanham Act over the nature and quality of the goods sold by its licensees.

We are all agreed that the Lanham Act places an affirmative duty upon a licensor of a registered trademark to take reasonable measures to detect and prevent misleading uses of his mark by his licensees or suffer cancellation of his federal registration. The Act, 15 U.S.C. § 1064, provides that a trademark registration may be canceled because the trademark has been "abandoned." And "abandoned" is defined in 15 U.S.C. § 1127 to include any act or omission by the registrant which causes the trademark to lose its significance as an indication of origin.

Prior to the passage of the Lanham Act many courts took the position that the licensing of a trademark separately from the business in connection with which it had been used worked an abandonment. The theory of these cases was that:

> "A trade-mark is intended to identify the goods of the owner and to safeguard his good will. The designation if employed by a person other than the one whose business it serves to identify would be misleading. Consequently, 'a right to the use of a trade-mark or a trade-name cannot be transferred in gross.'" American Broadcasting Co. v. Wahl Co., supra, 121 F.2d at page 413.

Other courts were somewhat more liberal and held that a trademark could be licensed separately from the business in connection with which it had been used provided that the licensor retained control over the quality of the goods produced by the licensee. E.I. DuPont de Nemours & Co. v. Celanese Corporation of America, 1948, 167 F.2d 484; see also 3 A.L.R.2d 1226, 1277–1282 (1949) and cases there cited. But even in the DuPont case the court was careful to point out that naked licensing, viz. the grant of licenses without the retention of control, was invalid.

The Lanham Act clearly carries forward the view of these latter cases that controlled licensing does not work an abandonment of the licensor's registration, while a system of naked licensing does. 15 U.S.C. § 1055 provides:

> "Where a registered mark or a mark sought to be registered is or may be used legitimately by related companies, such use shall inure to the benefit of the registrant or applicant for registration, and such use shall not affect the validity of such mark or of its registration, provided such mark is not used in such manner as to deceive the public."

And 15 U.S.C. § 1127 defines "related company" to mean "any person who legitimately controls or is controlled by the registrant or applicant for registration in respect to the nature and quality of the goods or services in connection with which the mark is used."

Without the requirement of control, the right of a trademark owner to license his mark separately from the business in connection with which it has been used would create the danger that products bearing the same trademark might be of diverse qualities. If the licensor is not compelled to take some reasonable steps to prevent misuses of his trademark in the hands of others the public will be deprived of its most effective protection against misleading uses of a trademark. The public is hardly in a position to uncover deceptive uses of a trademark before they occur and will be at best slow to detect them after they happen. Thus, unless the licensor exercises supervision and control over the operations of its licensees the risk that the public will be unwittingly deceived will be increased and this is precisely what the Act is in part designed to prevent. Clearly the only effective way to protect the public where a trademark is used by licensees is to place on the licensor the affirmative duty of policing in a reasonable manner the activities of his licensees.

The critical question on these facts therefore is whether the plaintiff sufficiently policed and inspected its licensees' operations to guarantee the quality of the products they sold under its trademarks to the public. The trial court found that: "By reason of its contacts with its licensees, plaintiff exercised legitimate control over the nature and quality of the food products on which plaintiff's licensees used the trademark 'Dawn.' Plaintiff and its licensees are related companies within the meaning of Section 45 of the Trademark Act of 1946." It is the position of the majority of this court that the trial judge has the same leeway in determining what constitutes a reasonable degree of supervision and control over licensees under the facts and circumstances of the particular case as he has on other questions of fact; and particularly because it is the defendant who has the burden of proof on this issue they hold the lower court's finding not clearly erroneous.

I dissent from the conclusion of the majority that the district court's findings are not clearly erroneous because while it is true that the trial judge must be given some discretion in determining what constitutes reasonable supervision of licensees under the Lanham Act, it is also true that an appellate court ought not to accept the conclusions of the district court unless they are supported by findings of sufficient facts. It seems to me that the only findings of the district judge regarding supervision are in such general and conclusory terms as to be meaningless. In the absence of supporting findings or of undisputed evidence in the record indicating the kind of supervision and inspection the plaintiff actually made of its licensees, it is impossible for us to pass upon whether there was such supervision as to satisfy the statute. There was evidence before the district court in the matter of supervision, and more detailed findings thereon should have been made.

Plaintiff's licensees fall into two classes: (1) those bakers with whom it made written contracts providing that the baker purchase exclusively plaintiff's mixes and requiring him to adhere to plaintiff's directions in using the mixes; and (2) those bakers whom plaintiff permitted to sell at retail under the "Dawn" label doughnuts and other baked goods made from its mixes although there was no written agreement governing the quality of the food sold under the Dawn mark.

The contracts that plaintiff did conclude, although they provided that the purchaser use the mix as directed and without adulteration, failed to provide for any system of inspection and control. Without such a system plaintiff could not know whether these bakers were adhering to its standards in using the mix or indeed whether they were selling only products made from Dawn mixes under the trademark "Dawn."

The absence, however, of an express contract right to inspect and supervise a licensee's operations does not mean that the plaintiff's method of licensing failed to comply with the requirements of the Lanham Act. Plaintiff may in fact have exercised control in spite of the absence of any express grant by licensees of the right to inspect and supervise.

The question then, with respect to both plaintiff's contract and non-contract licensees, is whether the plaintiff in fact exercised sufficient control.

Here the only evidence in the record relating to the actual supervision of licensees by plaintiff consists of the testimony of two of plaintiff's local sales representatives that they regularly visited their particular customers and the further testimony of one of them, Jesse Cohn, the plaintiff's New York representative, that "in many cases" he did have an opportunity to inspect and observe the operations of his customers. The record does not indicate whether plaintiff's other sales representatives made any similar efforts to observe the operations of licensees.

Moreover, Cohn's testimony fails to make clear the nature of the inspection he made or how often he made one. His testimony indicates that his opportunity to observe a licensee's operations was limited to "those cases where I am able to get into the shop" and even casts some doubt on whether he actually had sufficient technical knowledge in the use of plaintiff's mix to make an adequate inspection of a licensee's operations.

* * *

Thus I do not believe that we can fairly determine on this record whether plaintiff subjected its licensees to periodic and thorough inspections by trained personnel or whether its policing consisted only of chance, cursory examinations of licensees' operations by technically untrained salesmen. The latter system of inspection hardly constitutes a sufficient program of supervision to satisfy the requirements of the Act.

* * *

NOTES

1. A defendant in a trademark infringement case often claims that the plaintiff has abandoned the mark by engaging in a naked license. Obviously if the licensee is unsupervised and produces goods of a different nature or quality than the licensor, the mark may lose its significance as a trademark and thus be abandoned. But abandonment is a question of fact and does not follow automatically from a naked license although a naked license may be some evidence of abandonment.

2. What level of control is necessary to protect a licensed trademark? Must a university that licenses the use of a likeness of its mascot maintain effective control over the quality of the products marketed with the likeness. Does a university have the expertise to so control the quality of the underlying products? Does the manufacturer of the soft drink "Coca–Cola" maintain quality control over "Coca–Cola" wearing apparel? It has been suggested that for these "merchandising marks" the quality control standards for valid licensing should be relaxed. See W. Borchard & R. Osman, Trademark Sublicensing and Quality Control, 70 Trademark Rep. 99 (1980); W. Keating, Promotional Trademark Licensing: A Concept Whose Time Has Come, 89 Dick.L.Rev. 363 (1985). The United States Trademark Association Trademark Review Commission decided "the public interest in avoiding deception in the licensing context was a very sensitive issue and that statutory relaxation of the quality control requirements was not appropriate." 77 Trademark Rep. at 448. See also the Restatement, Third, of Unfair Competition § 33, Comment *c*, at 340 (1995):

> The nature and extent of the control required under this Section is determined by the expectations that the licensee's use of the mark creates in consumers and the supervision that is reasonably necessary to insure that those expectations are not endangered. The expectations of consumers depend in part on the character of the licensee's use. If a licensee uses the trademark of a beer or soft drink manufacturer on clothing or glassware, for example, prospective purchasers may be unlikely to assume that the owner of the trademark had more than perfunctory involvement in the production or quality of the licensee's goods even if the manner of use clearly indicates sponsorship by the trademark owner. On the other hand, if the licensee's use is on goods similar or identical to those produced by the trademark owner, purchasers may be likely to assume that the goods are actually manufactured by the owner of the mark. Greater control by the licensor may then be necessary to safeguard the interests of consumers who may purchase the goods on the basis of the licensor's reputation for quality. If the use authorized by the trademark owner is not perceived by prospective purchasers as an indication of source or sponsorship but rather as a purely ornamental use, the designation as used by the licensee does not function as a trademark. The requirement of reasonable control over the nature and quality of the licensee's product is then inapplicable, and no rights accrue to the owner of the designation as a result of the licensee's use.

3. Prior to 1984 the United States Jaycees (USJ) prohibited women members and required their local "licensees" to do likewise. When some local chapters rebelled USJ sought to enjoin chapters admitting women from continuing to use the trademark "Jaycee". USJ argued it was exercising its responsibility to police the licensed mark. In United States Jaycees v. Philadelphia Jaycees, 639 F.2d 134 (3d Cir.1981) the court ruled in favor of USJ even after the Philadelphia chapter argued USJ had abandoned the mark because it did not enforce the provision against all licensees. "We conclude that, although the United States Jaycees did display a degree of tolerance toward some of its disobedient chapters in the use of its marks, such conduct did not constitute non-use and did not demonstrate an intent to abandon, nor did it cause its marks to lose their significance." However, in United States Jaycees v. Cedar Rapids Jaycees, 794 F.2d 379 (8th Cir.1986), USJ sought to enjoin a local chapter for its past admission of women even after USJ had subsequently changed its own policy in that regard. The court refused the injunction under the "principles of equity".

4. Trademark licensing may involve application of other regulatory regimes. The advent of franchising, based largely on the ability to license trademarks, resulted in substantial regulation to protect franchisees from fraudulent schemes. Similarly, the limitations on patent, copyright and trademark licensing occupies no small place in antitrust law. These regimes are outside the scope of this material.

CHAPTER 4

PREDATORY PRACTICES

———

A. Interference With Business Relations

(1) Refusals to Deal

In a competitive marketplace, actors are expected to make buying and selling decisions in their own best interest. This means that they must decide to deal with some and refuse to deal with other actors. Competition also assumes that traders will urge persons to deal with them and thereby induce them not to deal with other persons. Competition assumes some intentional attempts to injure others, at least by depriving them of sales.

At the same time, the power to withhold patronage may be used for purposes or objectives that are not permissible even in a competitive market. As *Tuttle v. Buck* suggests, there can be actions taken that look competitive but actually take on an anticompetitive cast. It should not be surprising that the common law had a difficult time working out the rules that segregated permissible from impermissible refusals to deal.

Initially the common law divided refusals to deal into mere individual refusals to deal, concerted refusals to deal, and inducing another to refuse to deal. These categories are carried forward in the antitrust laws because of the structure of the Sherman Act which in section 1 prohibits a "contract, combination, . . . or conspiracy" in restraint of trade. Section 1 contemplates concerted activity between two or more traders. Section 2, which deals with individual activity, prohibits monopolization or attempted monopolization and thus requires a substantial market effect.

Both at common law and under the antitrust laws, individual refusals to deal were protected in most instances but concerted refusals to deal (group boycotts) were more closely scrutinized. Inducing another to refuse to deal (secondary boycotts) evoked a more complex set of rules.

The common law doctrines were reflected in Restatement of Torts §§ 762–774 (1939). Section 762 permitted most individual refusals to deal as long as they were "not a breach of the actor's duty arising from the nature of his business or from a statute" or "not a means of illegally affecting competition." Section 765 prohibited concerted refusals to deal unless justified. Comment d to § 765 included the following: "When the purpose of a concerted refusal to deal is solely to satisfy spite or ill will, the refusal is not justified. But self-interest, particularly a purpose to advance the business interest of the actors, may be a justification even though the harm caused by the refusal is intended to be the means of advancing that interest." Sections 766–771 dealt with inducing a refusal to deal which served as forerunners to those provisions in the Restatement (Second) applicable to intentional interference with prospective advantage. These doctrines are considered later in this chapter.

Most refusal to deal cases in the marketplace are now governed by the Sherman Act. In an early opinion, Great Atlantic & Pacific Tea Co. v. Cream of Wheat Co., 227 Fed. 46 (2d Cir.1915), the court held that the Sherman Act did not alter the common law "right" of a trader to refuse business relations with any person. Four years later in United States v. Colgate & Co., 250 U.S. 300 (1919), Colgate announced suggested retail prices and refused to sell to any wholesaler or retailer who cut the price. The United States Supreme Court emphasized the unilateral nature of the refusal to deal and held the Sherman Act "does not restrict the long recognized right of trader or manufacturer engaged in an entirely private business, freely to exercise his own independent discretion as to parties with whom he will deal. And, of course, he may announce in advance the circumstances under which he will refuse to sell * * *."

Given the structure of the Sherman Act, the search in antitrust cases is for a "contract" or "conspiracy" in refusal to deal cases. *Colgate* continues to be cited as applicable to *individual* refusals to deal. The threshold of concerted action is reflected in United States v. Parke, Davis & Co., 362 U.S. 29 (1960) where Parke, Davis announced suggested minimum retail prices and a policy of refusing to deal with wholesalers and retailers who did not abide by the price structure. However, Parke, Davis also engaged in extensive activities to police and to persuade wholesalers to refuse to deal with price cutting retailers and this, the Court thought, went too far.

NOTE

The common law refusal to prohibit individual refusals to deal is the background for legislation that addresses practices in specific industries. For example, the termination of dealer franchise agreements in the automobile industry sparked passage of the Automobile Dealer Franchise Act, 15 U.S.C. §§ 1221–22, otherwise known as the Dealer's Day in Court Act. The act provides federal jurisdiction for a suit by a dealer against an automobile manufacturer for damages sustained "by reason of the failure of said automobile manufacturer * * * to act in good faith in performing or complying with any of the terms or provisions of the franchise, or in terminating, canceling, or not renewing the franchise with said dealer." "Good faith" means the duty to act in "a fair and equitable manner * * * so as to guarantee the one party freedom from coercion, intimidation, or threats of coercion or intimidation from the other party: *Provided,* That recommendation, endorsement, exposition, persuasion, urging or argument shall not be deemed to constitute a lack of good faith."

In several states the principle underlying the Automobile Dealer Franchise Act has been adopted for all franchise agreements. See, e.g.,

Conn.Gen.Stat.Ann. § 42–133 e–g (Supp.1997). And there are many other areas in which a person's common law right to refuse to engage in business with another person for any reason has been abrogated. See, e.g., Civil Rights Act of 1964, 42 U.S.C. § 2000a (1974) (preventing discrimination on the basis of race in public accommodations).

---

(2) Unfair Competition

Katz v. Kapper

District Court of Appeal, Second District, 1935.
7 Cal.App.2d 1, 44 P.2d 1060.

■ SHINN, JUSTICE PRO TEM.

* * *

Plaintiff and defendants were rival wholesale fish dealers in the city of Los Angeles. The defendants Kapper, Isenberg, Baker, and Simon comprised a single firm doing business under the name of "Central Market." The action is for damages alleged to have been sustained to plaintiff's business by reason of the acts of defendants, and for exemplary damages. The complaint alleges that plaintiff had a well-established wholesale fish business, the good will of which was valuable; that with the sole intention "to put the plaintiff out of business, ruin him, deprive him of his customers and custom, and to take away from him all of his business and trade, together with the good will, without any benefit to themselves," the defendants maliciously called meetings of the customers of plaintiff, threatened them that they would be driven out of business and ruined if they continued to purchase fish from plaintiff, but promised that if they purchased fish from defendants, they would be given substantial reductions in price, so that they could successfully compete with plaintiff and drive him out of business; that if said customers continued to buy from plaintiff, the defendants would open a retail store and would sell fish to the customers of plaintiff's customers at such low prices that plaintiff's customers would be driven out of business. It was further alleged that the defendants did open such a store, did widely advertise and sell fish at lower prices than either plaintiff or defendants could purchase the same, and at a loss to the defendants; that all of said acts were done for the purpose of driving plaintiff out of business; and that as a result thereof "a considerable number of said retailers and peddlers and customers ceased from doing business with plaintiff and made their purchases from these defendants to plaintiff's damage," etc.

To this complaint, defendants interposed a general and special demurrer, which was sustained by the court, and plaintiff declining to amend, judgment of dismissal was entered. The general demurrer presents the questions whether the purposes of the defendants were unlawful, and, if lawful, whether they were sought to be accomplished by unlawful means.

* * *

It very clearly appears from the allegations of the complaint that the primary purpose of the defendants was to acquire for themselves the business of plaintiff's customers, and that the detriment which would result to plaintiff's business from the accomplishment of defendants' purpose was incidental thereto. This view must be taken of the complaint, notwithstanding the allegation that the sole purpose was to drive plaintiff out of business. The defendants are not charged with making any effort to deprive plaintiff of his trade except by transferring the same to themselves. This is essentially business competition. The defendants did or threatened to do nothing other than to gain a business advantage proportionate to the losses sustained by plaintiff, and by the accomplishment of that end their purposes would have been satisfied. It cannot be said that the methods used by the defendants were unlawful. They threatened plaintiff's customers with the ruination of their businesses if they continued to trade with plaintiff, but a threat is not unlawful if it is to do a lawful thing.

* * *

The threats alleged in general terms are identified and particularized by the allegations that the defendants threatened to and did undersell the plaintiff and his customers at retail prices less than the wholesale prices at which the commodities could be purchased. These must be taken as the only acts of coercion either threatened or done, since no others are alleged. They were not unlawful nor were they committed in an unlawful manner. They related solely to the aims of the defendants to engage in business competition with plaintiff for the resulting business advantage to themselves. The fact that the methods used were ruthless, or unfair, in a moral sense, does not stamp them as illegal. It has never been regarded as the duty or province of the courts to regulate practices in the business world beyond the point of applying legal or equitable remedies in cases involving acts of oppression or deceit which are unlawful. Any extension of this jurisdiction must come through legislative action. In this case no questions of statutory law are involved. The alleged acts of defendants do not fall within the category of business methods recognized as unlawful, and hence they are not actionable. The demurrer to the complaint was properly sustained.

The judgment is affirmed.

NOTES

1. What restrictions, if any, would you place on the defendants in *Katz*? Would you be prepared to watch them drive the plaintiff out of business? Could you frame a rule that distinguishes a legitimate competitive price from a pricing policy that is sufficiently predatory to require legal intervention?

2. Is it unfair competition for a business to bribe the officers of a customer in order to retain or secure their patronage? If the customer is a foreign country and such bribes are, if not legal, at least commonplace? See Coffee, Beyond the Shut-Eyed Sentry: Toward a Theoretical View of Corporate Misconduct and an Effective Legal Response, 63 Va.L.Rev. 1099 (1977).

3. *Sales Below Cost.* Is it unfair competition to sell goods or services below cost? The desire to counteract loss leader selling, protect small independent merchants from the competition of large chain stores, and eliminate some of the agonies of intensely competitive markets led to promulgation of statutes directly prohibiting sales below cost or unreasonably low prices. These statutes, both on the state and federal levels, provide criminal penalties as well as injunctive relief. Some state statutes also authorize treble damage recoveries. Although the first state statute was passed early in the 1900's, the major push for legislation on the state level arose in the late 1930's. And Congress responded at the federal level with the passage of the Robinson-Patman Act in 1936. Section 3 of the Act reads in part as follows:

> It shall be lawful for any person engaged in commerce, in the course of such commerce * * * to sell, or contract to sell, goods at unreasonably low prices for the purpose of destroying competition or eliminating a competitor. Any person violating any of the provisions of this section shall, upon conviction thereof, be fined not more than $5,000 or imprisoned not more than one year, or both. 49 Stat. 1528, 15 U.S.C. § 13a.

At one time or another over thirty states enacted laws of general application prohibiting sales below cost and other states have passed such statutes for specific industries.

There is little uniformity in language among the state sales below cost legislation. Most contain (1) a prohibition against sales below cost where made with the intent to injure competitors or destroy competition; (2) a definition of cost; (3) exemptions for certain types of sales such as perishable commodities or sales to governmental agencies; (4) an exemption if the sale is made in good faith to meet the price of a competitor, and (5) provisions for both criminal penalties and injunctive relief.

The most difficult and most litigated issue under these statutes involves the definition of "cost". What is the seller's cost? Is it the price the seller paid for the goods or the price to be paid to restock the seller's inventory. What overhead expenses are included in the cost of goods?

Because criminal penalties are imposed by these statutes, the definition of cost has been challenged as constitutionally vague. A number of cases have upheld the statutory definitions of cost against such attacks by taking a broad view of how "cost" is to be determined. See State v. Langley, 53 Wyo. 332, 84 P.2d 767 (1938): "we must presume that the legislature did not intend to prescribe that the cost must be absolutely exact, and that it must be based upon the precise method of accounting which any one merchant might adopt, but meant, by 'cost', what business men generally mean, namely, the approximate cost arrived at by a reasonable rule. * * * In other words, all that a man is required to do under the statute is to act in good faith." In United States v. National Dairy Prod. Corp., 372 U.S. 29 (1963), the United States Supreme Court upheld the constitutionality of section 3 of the Robinson-Patman Act, which makes it a crime to sell goods at "unreasonably low prices for the purpose of destroying competition or eliminating a competitor." Early litigation made it clear that at least where criminal penalties were involved statutes prohibiting sales below cost would be unconstitutional unless they required some form of predatory intent. See e.g., Fairmont Creamery Co. v. State, 274 U.S. 1 (1927); State v. Fleming Co., 184 Kan. 674, 339 P.2d 12 (1959).

4. Sales below cost are part of what is recognized as "predatory pricing", a pricing strategy that lowers prices in an area to drive out competition with the expectation that losses sustained can be made up by higher prices once a monopoly position is established. The success of such a strategy depends on not only the ability to obtain some market power but also to sustain it long enough to recoup past losses with interest and to secure higher profits than would have resulted in the absence of the strategy. Some commentators are skeptical that such a strategy can be successful or is often attempted. R. Bork, The Antitrust Paradox 145 (1978); Easterbrook, Predatory Strategies and Counterstrategies, 48 U.Chi.L.Rev. 263 (1981). The Supreme Court apparently adopted this view in Matsushita Elec. Indus. Co. v. Zenith Radio, 475 U.S. 574 (1986). See also Areeda & Turner, Predatory Pricing and Related Practices Under Section 2 of the Sherman Act, 88 Harv.L.Rev. 697 (1975).

5. *Fair trade laws.* For many years many states authorized resale price maintenance agreements. These "fair trade" laws provided that a producer of branded goods could announce and enforce through a civil action a pricing policy which prevented any retailer from selling branded goods at a price less than that established by the producer. Those in favor of fair trade laws argued that the use by large chain stores of famous brand name merchandise as loss leaders was an appropriation of the goodwill attached to those brands for the benefit of the chainstore and, further, that the producers of branded merchandise suffered injury because small retailers would stop carrying merchandise used as loss leaders by larger stores. Opponents of "fair trade" laws argued that price manipulation by producers prevented price competition and injured consumers. Initially price maintenance agreements were in violation of the Sherman Act if they involved interstate commerce; in 1937, the Miller-Tydings amendment was adopted exempting such agreements from antitrust scrutiny if the agreement was authorized by state statute and the exemption was refined and broadened in 1952 by the McGuire Amendment to section 5 of the Federal Trade Commission Act. The validity of resale price maintenance agreements thus depended on state law. At one time or another, 45 states enacted fair trade legislation. However, in 1975 Congress repealed both Miller-Tydings and McGuire amendments and ended fair trade pricing. Consumer Goods Pricing Act of 1975, Pub.L. 94–145, 89 Stat. 801 (1975).

6. *Robinson-Patman Act.* The most elaborate and complex statute regulating price is the Robinson-Patman Act, 15 U.S.C. § 13, enacted in 1936 to strengthen the anti-trust laws and particularly the anti-discrimination provisions of § 2 of the Clayton Act. The Act is directed at discriminatory pricing. The heart of the statute is § 2(a). It is violated if there is (1) a difference in price between different purchasers of (2) commodities of (3) like grade and quality where (4) either of the purchases involved is in interstate commerce and (5) where the effect of such discrimination may be to substantially lessen competition. There are two important defenses to a violation of § 2(a): (1) that the differences in price were justified by differences in cost; and (2) that the favorable price was given in good faith to meet an equally low price of a competitor. Additional provisions prohibit sellers from providing promotional services to buyers on unequal terms and also prohibit buyers from inducing favorable treatment. The statute is very complex and beyond the scope of these materials. However, lawyers advising clients with regard to their pricing and promotional policies must consider the reach of Robinson-Patman.

———

(3) Interference with Contractual Relationships

Imperial Ice Co. v. Rossier

Supreme Court of California, 1941.
18 Cal.2d 33, 112 P.2d 631.

■ TRAYNOR, JUSTICE.

The California Consumers Company purchased from S.L. Coker an ice distributing business, inclusive of good will, located in territory comprising the city of Santa Monica and the former city of Sawtelle. In the purchase agreement Coker contracted as follows: "I do further agree in consideration of said purchase and in connection therewith, that I will not engage in the business of selling and or distributing ice, either directly or indirectly, in the above described territory so long as the purchasers, or anyone deriving title to the good will of said business from said purchasers, shall be engaged in a like business therein." Plaintiff, the Imperial Ice Company, acquired from the successor in interest of the California Consumers Company full title to this ice distributing business, including the right to enforce the covenant not to compete. Coker subsequently began selling in the same territory in violation of the contract ice supplied to him by a company owned by W. Rossier, J.A. Matheson, and Fred Matheson. Plaintiff thereupon brought this action in the superior court for an injunction to restrain Coker from violating the contract and to restrain Rossier and the Mathesons from inducing Coker to violate the contract. The complaint alleges that Rossier and the Mathesons induced Coker to violate his contract so that they might sell ice to him at a profit. The trial court sustained without leave to amend a demurrer to the complaint of the defendants Rossier and Matheson and gave judgment for those defendants. Plaintiff has appealed from the judgment on the sole ground that the complaint stated a cause of action against the defendants Rossier and the Mathesons for inducing the breach of contract.

The question thus presented to this court is under what circumstances may an action be maintained against a defendant who has induced a third party to violate a contract with the plaintiff.

It is universally recognized that an action will lie for inducing breach of contract by a resort to means in themselves unlawful such as libel, slander, fraud, physical violence, or threats of such action. Most jurisdictions also hold that an action will lie for inducing a breach of contract by the use of moral, social, or economic pressures, in themselves lawful, unless there is sufficient justification for such inducement. * * *

Such justification exists when a person induces a breach of contract to protect an interest which has greater social value than insuring the stability of the contract. Thus, a person is justified in inducing the breach of a contract the enforcement of which would be injurious to health, safety, or good morals. * * * The interest of labor in improving working conditions is of sufficient social importance to justify peaceful labor tactics otherwise lawful, though they have the effect of inducing breaches of contracts between employer and employee or employer and customer. * * * In numerous other situations, justification exists depending upon the importance of the interest protected. The presence or absence of ill-will, sometimes referred to as "malice", is immaterial, except as it indicates whether or not an interest is actually being protected. * * *

It is well established, however, that a person is not justified in inducing a breach of contract simply because he is in competition with one of the parties to the contract and seeks to further his own economic advantage at the expense of the other. Whatever interest society has in encouraging free and open competition by means not in themselves unlawful, contractual stability is generally accepted as of greater importance than competitive freedom. Competitive freedom, however, is of sufficient importance to justify one competitor in inducing a third party to forsake another competitor if no contractual relationship exists between the latter two. Katz v. Kapper, 7 Cal.App.2d 1, 44 P.2d 1060; * * * A person is likewise free to carry on his business, including reduction of prices, advertising, and solicitation in the usual lawful manner although some third party may be induced thereby to breach his contract with a competitor in favor of dealing with the advertiser. * * * Again, if two parties have separate contracts with a third, each may resort to any legitimate means at his disposal to secure performance of his contract even though the necessary result will be to cause a breach of the other contract. * * * A party may not, however, under the guise of competition actively and affirmatively induce the breach of a competitor's contract in order to secure an economic advantage over that competitor. The act of inducing the breach must be an intentional one. If the actor had no knowledge of the existence of the contractor his actions were not intended to induce a breach, he cannot be held liable though an actual breach results from his lawful and proper acts.

Rule

* * * The case of Katz v. Kapper, 7 Cal.App.2d 1, 44 P.2d 1060, relied upon by defendants, held only that a person by the use of lawful means could interfere with advantageous business relationships of a competitor by inducing customers to trade with him instead. The case did not involve a breach of contract * * *.

The complaint in the present case alleges that defendants actively induced Coker to violate his contract with plaintiffs so that they might sell ice to him.

The contract gave to plaintiff the right to sell ice in the stated territory free from the competition of Coker. The defendants, by virtue of their interest in the sale of ice in that territory, were in effect competing with plaintiff. By inducing Coker to violate his contract, as alleged in the complaint, they sought to further their own economic advantage at plaintiff's expense. Such conduct is not justified. Had defendants merely sold ice to Coker without actively inducing him to violate his contract, his distribution of the ice in the forbidden territory in violation of his contract would not then have rendered defendants liable. They may carry on their business of selling ice as usual without incurring liability for breaches of contract by their customers. It is necessary to prove that they intentionally and actively induced the breach. Since the complaint alleges that they did so and asks for an injunction on the grounds that damages would be inadequate, it states a cause of action, and the demurrer should therefore have been overruled.

The judgment is reversed.

Leigh Furniture & Carpet Co. v. Isom

Supreme Court of Utah, 1982.
657 P.2d 293.

[W.S. Leigh, owner of Leigh Furniture, entered into a contract to sell his furniture business to Richard Isom. Isom agreed to maintain inventory, cash, and accounts receivable at a level of at least $60,000 as security for the balance of the purchase price. The contract provided Isom with a ten-year lease of the first floor of the building in which the store was located and an option to buy the entire building once the $60,000 was paid. The price for exercising the option was to be determined by three appraisers appointed by the parties.

This controversy arose because Leigh became dissatisfied with the contract and expressed openly that he wanted to sell the building outright and could not because of Isom's lease. Leigh, his wife, and his bookkeeper, pursued a course of making life difficult for Isom. They visited him in his store, questioned him about his operations, made various demands and were abusive. At one point Leigh suggested Isom needed a partner and he should contact one Talbot. In fact Isom entered negotiations with one Hunter until Leigh told him he would never accept Hunter in the store.

The parties eventually entered into a supplemental agreement which provided that Isom would pay an additional $20,000 in cash toward the purchase price of the business and that Leigh would have the right to approve any person to whom Isom intended to convey any interest in the business. The agreement was also intended to resolve all disputes between the parties. It did not, however, and shortly thereafter Leigh filed two frivolous suits against Isom and the campaign of visits, demands, and disruption continued. Isom finally attempted to pay off the entire purchase price of the business, add Talbot as a partner, and exercise his option to purchase the building but Leigh refused to accept the money, approve Talbot, or appoint an appraiser.

Ultimately Leigh filed a suit against Isom seeking the balance of the purchase price and a repossession of the premises. Isom counterclaimed alleging intentional interference with contract and prospective advantage. Shortly after the suit was filed, Isom declared bankruptcy. Although he had been able to make a profit at some points during this affair, he claims the disruption and actions of Leigh made it impossible to continue. Leigh, being the secured creditor, reacquired the inventory and building through the bankruptcy proceedings. The jury found for Isom on the counterclaim and awarded him compensatory and punitive damages. Leigh appealed.]

■ OAKS, Justice:

II. INTERFERENCE WITH CONTRACT

Leigh Furniture first contends that Isom's recovery cannot be sustained as an interference with contract because the evidence showed no conduct which "intentionally and improperly interferes with the performance of a contract *** between another and a third person by inducing or otherwise causing the third person not to perform the contract." *Restatement (Second) of Torts* § 766 (1979). In this case, the only contract in evidence was the contract between Isom and the Leigh Corporation. It is settled that one party to a contract cannot be liable for the tort of interference with contract for inducing a breach by himself or the other contracting party. Isom having failed to prove a cause of action for intentional interference with contract, we cannot sustain the verdict on that theory.

However, the right of action for interference with a specific contract is but one instance, rather than the total class, of protections against wrongful interference with advantageous economic relations. We therefore proceed to consider whether the jury's verdict for Isom can be sustained on the basis of the related tort of interference with prospective economic relations.

* * *

III. INTERFERENCE WITH PROSPECTIVE ECONOMIC RELATIONS

A. History and Elements of the Tort

The tort of intentional interference with prospective economic relations reaches beyond protection of an interest in an existing contract and protects a party's interest in prospective relationships of economic advantage not yet reduced to a formal contract (and perhaps not expected to be).

* * *

The plethora of decided cases and abundant literature on the tort of intentional interference with prospective economic relations has been helpful in our consideration.[3] In summarizing the history of this tort, the Restatement (Second) of Torts, ch. 37, "Interference with Contract or

---

3. See, e.g., Estes, "Expanding Horizons in the Law of Torts—Tortious Interference," 23 Drake L.Rev. 341 (1974); Harper, "Interference with Contractual Relations," 47 Nw.U.L.Rev. 873 (1953); Perlman, "Interference with Contract and Other Economic Expectancies: A Clash of Tort and Contract Doctrine," 49 U.Chi.L.Rev. 61 (1982); Sayre, "Inducing Breach of Contract," 36 Harv.L.Rev. 663 (1922–23); "Developments in the Law— Competitive Torts," 77 Harv.L.Rev. 888 (1964); Note, "Tortious Interference with Contract: A Reassertion of Society's Interest in Commercial Stability and Contractual Integrity," 81 Colum.L.Rev. 1491 (1981); "Interference with Contract Relations." 41 Harv.L.Rev. 728 (1927–28); Annot., 9 A.L.R.2d 228 (1950); Annot., 5 A.L.R.4th 9 (1981); Annot., 6 A.L.R.4th 195 (1981).

Prospective Contractual Relation" (1979), observes that its elements are a curious blend of the principles of liability for intentional torts (in which the plaintiff proves a prima facie case of liability, subject to the defendant's proof of justification) and for negligent torts (in which the plaintiff must prove liability based on the interplay of various factors). The disagreement and confusion incident to this blend of intentional and negligent tort principles has produced two different approaches to the definition of this tort.

Influenced by the model of the intentional tort, many jurisdictions and the first *Restatement of Torts* define the tort of intentional interference with prospective economic relations as a prima facie tort, subject to proof of privilege as an affirmative defense. To recover, the plaintiff need only prove a prima facie case of liability, i.e., that the defendant intentionally interfered with his prospective economic relations and caused him injury. As with other intentional torts, the burden of going forward then shifts to the defendant to demonstrate as an affirmative defense that under the circumstances his conduct, otherwise culpable, was justified and therefore privileged. This is the approach assumed in several Utah decisions describing the related tort of interference with contract.

* * *

The problem with the prima facie-tort approach is that basing liability on a mere showing that defendant intentionally interfered with plaintiff's prospective economic relations makes actionable all sorts of contemporary examples of otherwise legitimate persuasion, such as efforts to persuade others not to eat certain foods, use certain substances, engage in certain activities, or deal with certain entities. The major issue in the controversy—justification for the defendant's conduct—is left to be resolved on the affirmative defense of privilege. In short, the prima facie approach to the tort of interference with prospective economic relations requires too little of the plaintiff.

Under the second approach, which is modeled after other negligent torts, the plaintiff must prove liability based on the interplay of various factors. The *Restatement (Second) of Torts* now defines an actionable interference with prospective economic relations as an interference that is both "intentional" and "improper." Id. at § 766B. Under this approach, the trier of fact must determine whether the defendant's interference was "improper" by balancing and counterbalancing seven factors, including the interferor's motive, the nature of his conduct and interests, and the nature of the interests with which he has interfered. Id. at § 767. In those jurisdictions which have followed the negligence model, the plaintiff bears the burden of proving that in view of all of these factors the defendant's interference was improper. This obviously imposes a very significant burden on the plaintiff and magnifies the difficulty of resolving some contested issues on the pleadings. So far as we have been able to discover, only four states have specifically adopted the *Restatement (Second)* definition of the elements of this tort, though others have apparently applied some portion of the Restatement formulation in their own definitions.

In short, there is no generally acknowledged or satisfactory majority position on the definition of the elements of the tort of intentional interference with prospective economic relations. * * *. We concur in the

Restatement (Second) 's rejection of the prima facie tort approach because it leaves too much uncertainty about the requirements for a recognized privilege and the defendant's burden of pleading and proving these and other matters. Id. But we also reject the *Restatement (Second)* 's definition of the tort because of its complexity. We seek a better alternative.

Oregon has outlined a middle ground by defining the tort of interference with prospective economic relations so as to require the plaintiff to allege and prove more than the prima facie tort, but not to negate all defenses of privilege. Privileges remain as affirmative defenses. This approach originated with Justice Linde's opinion in Top Service Body Shop, Inc. v. Allstate Insurance Co., 283 Or. 201, 582 P.2d 1365 (1978). After summarizing the history of this tort and specifically refusing to require a plaintiff to prove that the interference was "improper" under the balancing-of-factors approach specified in the *Restatement (Second),* the court defined the cause of action for "wrongful interference with economic relationships" as follows:

> Either the pursuit of an improper objective of harming plaintiff or the use of wrongful means that in fact cause injury to plaintiff's contractual or business relationships may give rise to a tort claim for those injuries * * *. In summary, such a claim is made out when interference resulting in injury to another is wrongful by some measure beyond the fact of the interference itself. Defendant's liability may arise from improper motives or from the use of improper means.

Top Service Body Shop, Inc., 283 Or. at 205, 209, 582 P.2d at 1368, 1371. A subsequent decision of that court restated and elaborated what the plaintiff must prove, as follows:

> In *Top Service* we decided that the defendant's improper intent, motive or purpose to interfere was a necessary element of the plaintiff's case, rather than a lack thereof being a matter of justification or privilege to be asserted as a defense by defendant. Thus, to be entitled to go to a jury, plaintiff must not only prove that defendant intentionally interfered with his business relationship but also that defendant had a duty of non-interference; i.e., that he interfered for an improper purpose rather than for a legitimate one, or that defendant used improper means which resulted in injury to plaintiff.

Straube v. Larson, 287 Or. 357, 361, 600 P.2d 371, 374 (1979).

We recognize a common-law cause of action for intentional interference with prospective economic relations, and adopt the Oregon definition of this tort. Under this definition, in order to recover damages, the plaintiff must prove (1) that the defendant intentionally interfered with the plaintiff's existing or potential economic relations, (2) for an improper purpose or by improper means, (3) causing injury to the plaintiff. Privilege is an affirmative defense, Searle v. Johnson, Utah, 646 P.2d 682 (1982), which does not become an issue unless "the acts charged would be tortious on the part of an unprivileged defendant." Top Service Body Shop, Inc., 283 Or. at 210, 582 P.2d at 1371.

* * *

C. Evidence of Intentional Interference and Causation

Reviewing the record, we conclude that there was sufficient evidence to sustain the jury's verdict against the Leigh Corporation for intentional interference with prospective economic relations that caused injury to Isom.

There was ample evidence that Isom had business relationships with various customers, suppliers, and potential business associates, and that Leigh, the former owner of the business, understood the value of those relationships. There was also substantial competent evidence that the Corporation, through Leigh, his wife, and his bookkeeper, intentionally interfered with and caused a termination of some of those relationships (actual or potential). Their frequent visits to Isom's store during business hours to confront him, question him, and make demands and inquiries regarding the manner in which he was conducting his business repeatedly interrupted sales activities, caused his customers to comment and complain, and more than once caused a customer to leave the store. Driving away an individual's existing or potential customers is the archetypical injury this cause of action was devised to remedy.

Other actions by which the Leigh Corporation imposed heavy demands on Isom's time and financial resources to the detriment of his ability to attract and retain customers and conduct the other activities of his business included: numerous letters of complaint, Leigh's demand for an audit of Isom's books and inventory during the busy holiday season, his continued threats to cancel the contract and sell the building and business to another buyer, his refusal to pay the contracted share of the heating bills or the cost of repairing the furnace and the store's broken window, his refusal of the tendered payment of the balance due under the contract, and his suit for repossession, termination, and injunction. Leigh's refusals also prevented Isom from consummating potentially advantageous business associations with Hunter, with Talbot, and finally with Applegate, all experienced retailers able to contribute expertise and additional capital to Isom's business.

Taken in isolation, each of the foregoing interferences with Isom's business might be justified as an overly zealous attempt to protect the Corporation's interests under its contract of sale. As such, none would establish the intentional interference element of this tort, though some might give rise to a cause of action for breach of specific provisions in the contract or of the duty of good faith performance which inheres in every contractual relation. Even in small groups, these acts might be explained as merely instances of aggressive or abrasive—though not illegal or tortious—tactics, excesses that occur in contractual and commercial relationships. But in total and in cumulative effect, as a course of action extending over a period of three and one-half years and culminating in the failure of Isom's business, the Leigh Corporation's acts cross the threshold beyond what is incidental and justifiable to what is tortious. The Corporation's acts provide sufficient evidence to establish two of the elements in the definition of this tort: an intentional interference with present or prospective economic relations that caused injury to the plaintiff.

D. Improper Purpose

The alternative of improper purpose (or motive, intent, or objective) will support a cause of action for intentional interference with prospective economic relations even where the defendant's means were proper. * * *

Because it requires that the improper purpose predominate, this alternative takes the long view of the defendant's conduct, allowing objectionable short-run purposes to be eclipsed by legitimate long-range economic motivation. Otherwise, much competitive commercial activity, such as a businessman's efforts to forestall a competitor in order to further his own long-range economic interests, could become tortious. In the rough and tumble of the marketplace, competitors inevitably damage one another in the struggle for personal advantage. The law offers no remedy for those damages—even if intentional—because they are an inevitable byproduct of competition. Problems inherent in proving motivation or purpose make it prudent for commercial conduct to be regulated for the most part by the improper means alternative, which typically requires only a showing of particular conduct.

The alternative of improper purpose will be satisfied where it can be shown that the actor's predominant purpose was to injure the plaintiff.

* * *

As noted earlier, there is substantial evidence that the Leigh Corporation deliberately injured Isom's economic relations. But that injury was not an end in itself. It was an intermediate step toward achieving the long-range financial goal of profitably reselling the building free of Isom's interest. Because that economic interest seems to have been controlling, we must conclude that the evidence in this case would not support a jury finding that the Corporation's predominant purpose was to injure or ruin Isom's business merely for the sake of injury alone.

* * *

E. Improper Means

The alternative requirement of improper means is satisfied where the means used to interfere with a party's economic relations are contrary to law, such as violations of statutes, regulations, or recognized common-law rules. Such acts are illegal or tortious in themselves and hence are clearly "improper" means of interference, unless those means consist of constitutionally protected activity, like the exercise of First Amendment rights. "Commonly included among improper means are violence, threats or other intimidation, deceit or misrepresentation, bribery, unfounded litigation, defamation, or disparaging falsehood." Top Service Body Shop, Inc., 582 P.2d at 1371 & n. 11. Means may also be improper or wrongful because they violate "an established standard of a trade or profession." Id. at 1371.

By forcing Isom to defend what appear to have been two groundless lawsuits, the Leigh Corporation was clearly employing an improper means of interference with Isom's business. Such use of civil litigation as a weapon to damage another's business, besides being an intolerable waste of judicial resources, may give rise to independent causes of action in tort for abuse of process and malicious prosecution.

The jury's verdict can therefore be sustained on the ground that the Leigh Corporation intentionally interfered with Isom's economic relations by improper means.

There is also another basis for affirming that verdict on the basis of improper means.

A deliberate breach of contract, even where employed to secure economic advantage, is not, by itself, an "improper means." Because the law remedies breaches of contract with damages calculated to give the aggrieved party the benefit of the bargain, there is no need for an additional remedy in tort (unless the defendant's conduct would constitute a tort independent of the contract).

Neither a deliberate breach of contract nor an immediate purpose to inflict injury which does not predominate over a legitimate economic end will, by itself, satisfy this element of the tort. However, they may do so in combination. This is so because contract damages provide an insufficient remedy for a breach prompted by an immediate purpose to injure, and that purpose does not enjoy the same legal immunity in the context of contract relations as it does in the competitive marketplace. As a result, a breach of contract committed for the immediate purpose of injuring the other contracting party is an improper means that will satisfy this element of the cause of action for intentional interference with economic relations.

Two cases illustrate how breach of contract (or lease), when done with a purpose to injure, satisfy this element of the tort. In both cases, the defendant committed a breach not just to obtain relief from its obligation under the contract or lease (for which contract damages would have made the plaintiff whole), but to achieve a larger advantage by injuring the plaintiff in a manner not compensable merely by contract damages. In both cases, the defendant ruined the plaintiff's business by its breach, and in both cases the plaintiff was given substantial damages for the tort of interference with prospective economic relations.

In Buxbom v. Smith, 23 Cal.2d 535, 145 P.2d 305 (1944), a retail grocery chain contracted with the plaintiff to publish and distribute a "shopping news." In order to do so, the plaintiff abandoned his printing customers and expanded his distribution organization. After becoming the plaintiff's sole customer and acquiring complete knowledge of his business, the retailer deliberately breached its contract in order to ruin the plaintiff's business by cutting off the work required to sustain it and then hired his employees. The California Supreme Court affirmed a verdict for the plaintiff, awarding damages for breach of contract and additional damages for "tortious interference with his business" in order to give him "complete recompense for his combined injuries * * *." Id. at 546, 145 P.2d at 310. The gravamen of the tort, the court explained, was the defendant's breaching its contract with plaintiff as a means of acquiring plaintiff's employees[.]

* * *

In Cherberg v. Peoples National Bank of Washington, 88 Wash.2d 595, 564 P.2d 1137 (1977), a lessor deliberately breached its duty to repair a structurally unsound wall on the leased premises in order to destroy the restaurant business of a lessee who had leased a portion of the premises. The lessor's purpose was to retake the entire building as soon as possible, demolish the structure, and erect a more profitable building. The jury gave a verdict of $42,000 against the lessor. Apart from the $3,100 damages for breach of the lease (economic losses from temporary closure of the restaurant business), this verdict represented a recovery of damages for inconvenience, discomfort, and mental anguish for "the tort of intentional interference with business expectancies." The Washington Supreme Court sustained the verdict in an opinion that squarely relies on the combination of improper means and improper purpose in defendant's deliberate breach for the purpose of injuring the plaintiff.

* * *

In the case at bar, the Leigh Corporation breached its contract in various ways.

It breached its implied duty to exercise all of its rights under the contract reasonably and in good faith.

* * * Leigh's unexplained refusal to approve Isom's prospective business partners without consideration of their merits indicates an absence of good faith and provides evidence that the Corporation's breach was intended to deprive Isom's business of additional capital and valuable expertise which (at least with regard to Talbot) Leigh himself had repeatedly urged Isom to acquire. Similar refusals to approve prospective subtenants under a contract clause in order to injure the tenant's business have been held to constitute tortious interference with economic relations. In addition, Leigh, his wife, and his bookkeeper continually interrupted sales activities with their visits, letters, threats, and demands, causing customers to comment and complain and sometimes to leave. Although the contract entitled the Corporation, as lessor and secured party, to reasonable supervision of Isom's business, the jury had sufficient evidence to conclude that this conduct constituted an unreasonable exercise of contract rights and/or was done in bad faith for the purpose of injuring Isom's business relations.

The Corporation also breached its contractual duty by refusing Isom's tender of the balance of the purchase price and by refusing to appoint an appraiser to establish a price for the sale of the entire building, thereby preventing Isom from exercising his purchase option. There is evidence of Leigh's purpose in the fact that he openly regretted his contract with Isom and frequently expressed his desire to "get Richard out" of the business and building. Furthermore, he continually contacted prospective buyers for the building, even approaching two of Isom's employees for this purpose.

All of the above provide substantial evidence from which the jury could have concluded that the Corporation breached its express and implied contractual duties for the purpose of ruining Isom's business and obtaining possession of the building in order to sell it more profitably elsewhere. By themselves, the Corporation's breaches would not satisfy the requirement of "improper means," but they could do so when coupled with the improper purpose of injuring Isom. In combination, a breach of contract and an intent to injure satisfy the improper means requirement for the cause of action for intentional interference with prospective economic relations.

* * *

Penna v. Toyota Motor Sales, U.S.A., Inc.

Supreme Court of California, 1995
45 Cal.Rptr.2d 436, 11 Cal.4th 376, 902 P.2d 740

■ ARABIAN, JUSTICE

[Toyota Motors required their American Lexus dealers to sign "no export" clauses preventing them from selling Lexus automobiles to individuals intending to export them back to Japan. Penna purchased several automobiles from a dealer for export but Toyota applied pressure by, among other things, publishing an "offenders list" and threatening to reduce or eliminate supplies of automobiles to offenders. Penna sued Toyota for interfering with its source of Lexus to export. The California Supreme Court reviewed the history of the interference tort and noted the disarray of the California cases.]

IV

In searching for a means to recast the elements of the economic relations tort and allocate the associated burdens of proof, we are guided by an overmastering concern articulated by high courts of other jurisdictions and legal commentators: The need to draw and enforce a sharpened distinction between claims for the tortious disruption of an existing contract and claims that a prospective contractual or economic relationship has been interfered with by the defendant. Many of the cases do in fact acknowledge a greater array of justificatory defenses against claims of interference with prospective relations. Still, in our view and that of several other courts and commentators, the notion that the two torts are analytically unitary and derive from a common principle sacrifices practical wisdom to theoretical insight, promoting the idea that the interests invaded are of nearly equal dignity. They are not.

The courts provide a damage remedy against third party conduct intended to disrupt an existing contract precisely because the exchange of promises resulting in such a formally cemented economic relationship is deemed worthy of protection from interference by a stranger to the agreement. Economic relationships short of contractual, however, should stand on a different legal footing as far as the potential for tort liability is reckoned. Because ours is a culture firmly wedded to the social rewards of commercial contests, the law usually takes care to draw lines of legal liability in a way that maximizes areas of competition free of legal penalties.

A doctrine that blurs the analytical line between interference with an existing business contract and interference with commercial relations less than contractual is one that invites both uncertainty in conduct and unpredictability of its legal effect. The notion that inducing the breach of an existing contract is simply a subevent of the "more inclusive" class of acts that interfere with economic relations, while perhaps theoretically unobjectionable, has been mischievous as a practical matter. Our courts should, in short, firmly distinguish the two kinds of business contexts, bringing a greater solicitude to those relationships that have ripened into agreements, while recognizing that relationships short of that subsist in a zone where the rewards and risks of competition are dominant.

Beyond that, we need not tread today. It is sufficient to dispose of the issue before us in this case by holding that a plaintiff seeking to recover for alleged interference with prospective economic relations has the burden of pleading and proving that the defendant's interference was wrongful "by some measure beyond the fact of the interference itself." (Top Service, supra, 582 P.2d at p. 1371.) It follows that the trial court did not commit error when it modified BAJI No. 7.82 to require the jury to find that defendant's interference was "wrongful." And because the instruction defining "wrongful conduct" given the jury by the trial court was offered by plaintiff himself, we have no occasion to review its sufficiency in this case. The question of whether additional refinements to the plaintiff's pleading and proof burdens merit adoption by California courts—questions embracing the precise scope of "wrongfulness," or whether a "disinterested malevolence," in Justice Holmes's words (American Bank & Trust Co. v. Federal Reserve Bank (1921) 256 U.S. 350, 358, 41 S.Ct. 499, 500, 65 L.Ed. 983) is an actionable interference in itself, or whether the underlying policy justification for the tort, the efficient allocation of social resources, justifies including as actionable conduct that is recognized as anticompetitive under established state and federal positive law (see, e.g., Perlman, Interference with Contract and Other Economic Expectancies; A Clash of Tort and Contract Doctrine, supra, 49 U.Chi.L.Rev. 61)—are matters that can await another day and a more appropriate case.

CONCLUSION

We hold that a plaintiff seeking to recover for an alleged interference with prospective contractual or economic relations must plead and prove as part of its case-in-chief that the defendant not only knowingly interfered with the plaintiff's expectancy, but engaged in conduct that was wrongful by some legal measure other than the fact of interference itself. The judgment of the Court of Appeal is reversed and the cause is remanded with directions to affirm the judgment of the trial court.

NOTES

1. The tort of interference with contractual relations was first formulated out of the controversy between Benjamin Lumley and Frederick Gye over the operatic talents of Johanna Wagner. Miss Wagner being under contract with

Mr. Lumley to sing at the Queen's Theatre, was offered more money by Mr. Gye to sing at the Covent Garden Theatre. Miss Wagner as part of her contract with Lumley engaged "herself not to use her talents at any other theatre, nor in any concert or reunion, public or private, without the written authorization of Mr. Lumley." Lumley first obtained an injunction to enforce the above quoted provision of the contract restraining Miss Wagner from singing for Gye. Lumley v. Wagner, 1 DeG., M. & G. 604 (1852). He then brought suit for damages against Gye for interfering with his contractual relations with Miss Wagner. Lumley v. Gye, 2 El. & Bl. 213, 95 Rev.Rep. 501 (Q.B. 1852). In awarding judgment for the plaintiff, Crompton, J. held: "I think that we are justified in applying the principle of the action for enticing away servants to a case where the defendant maliciously procures a party, who is under a valid contract to give her exclusive personal services to the plaintiff for a specified period, to refuse to give such services during the period for which she had so contracted, whereby the plaintiff was injured." Coleridge, J., dissenting, expressed the concern that "to draw a line between advice, persuasion, enticement and procurement is practically impossible in a court of justice; who shall say how much of a free agent's resolution flows from the interference of other minds, or the independent resolution of his own?"

2. Many of the interference with contract cases, like Lumley v. Gye, involve attempts by an actor to secure the employees of a competitor. These cases often illustrate the conflicting interests in stark contrast. The initial employer may expend substantial resources educating and training the employee and providing the employee with competitively advantageous information. By permitting a potential second employer to lure the employee away permits this second employer to profit from the investment of the first employer. If this is permitted it ultimately detracts from the incentives for employers to train their employees. At the same time, however, the employee has a substantial interest in marketing his services to the highest bidder. If the employee is unable to do so, it reduces the employee's incentives to become better trained. Society's interest in competition for goods and services is also involved.

How would you advise a businessman anxious to secure a key employee of his competitor to proceed under either of the principal cases? Judge Learned Hand in Triangle Film Corp. v. Artcraft Pictures Corp., 250 Fed. 981 (2d Cir. 1918) recognized the "right to offer better terms to another's employee, so long as the latter is free to leave." In a few cases courts have attached liability to attempts to systematically induce a substantial number of employees to leave one employer with the result that the first employer's business would be substantially disrupted. Wear-Ever Aluminum v. Townecraft Industries, 75 N.J.Super. 135, 182 A.2d 387 (Super.Ct. 1962) (violation for soliciting substantial part of sales team even though most were at-will employees).

3. Consider Hannigan v. Sears, Roebuck & Co., 410 F.2d 285 (7th Cir. 1969). Fabricated had signed a contract agreeing to produce outdoor metal lockers exclusively for Hannigan so when Fabricated began selling lockers to Sears, Hannigan was paid a royalty. Subsequently to reduce its costs in purchasing lockers, Sears put pressure on Fabricated to get out of its royalty agreement. Fabricated was economically dependent on Sears for sale of its lockers; Hannigan was dependent on Fabricated as its sole supply of lockers. Thus Sears successfully forced the two parties to alter their royalty agreement giving Hannigan substantially less royalty on lockers sold to Sears. The Seventh Circuit upheld a jury verdict against Sears for actual and punitive damages on the basis of intentional interference with the contract. Do you agree with the result? Does the case illustrate the problems Justice Oaks foresaw in *Leigh Furniture* if the tort were interpreted broadly?

4. *Privileged interferences.* Not all activity that results in an interference with another's contract is actionable. Consider Los Angeles Airways, Inc. v. Davis, 687 F.2d 321 (9th Cir.1982) where LAA claimed that interests owned by Howard Hughes orally agreed to purchase LAA but Davis, an attorney and business advisor to the Hughes interests, induced the companies to breach the agreement. LAA alleged that Davis's motives were twofold: (1) to force LAA into bankruptcy and thus permit its acquisition by Hughes at a "distress" price, and (2) to enhance Davis' position within the Hughes Organization. Observing that California law provided a privilege for inducing breach of contract by lawful means "in order to protect an interest that has greater social value than the mere stability of the particular contract in question" the court held Davis' actions privileged:

> We conclude that where, as here, an advisor is motivated in part by a desire to benefit his principal, his conduct in inducing a breach of contract should be privileged. The privilege is designed to further certain societal interests by fostering uninhibited advise by agents to their principals. The goal of the privilege is promoted by protecting advice that is motivated, even in part, by a good faith intent to benefit the principal's interest.

> We believe that advice by an agent to a principal is rarely, if ever, motivated purely by a desire to benefit only the principal. An agent naturally hopes that by providing beneficial advice to his principal, the agent will benefit indirectly by gaining the further trust and confidence of his principal. If the protection of the privilege were denied every time that an advisor acted with such mixed motive, the privilege would be greatly diminished and the societal interests it was designed to promote would be frustrated. 687 F.2d at 328.

The Restatement (Second) of Torts §§ 768–773 provides a number of privileges for inducing contractual breach that permit individuals with a legitimate personal interest to act to protect their interest or to give others honest advice.

5. *Competition as Privilege.* If a privilege is established when societal interests exceed the interest in contract compliance, shouldn't an act of contract interference be justified if a result of normal business competition? The Restatement (Second) of Torts § 768 provides that competition is *not* a justification for inducing breach of a contract but does justify interference with prospective relationships.

At least where there is a formal contract, is there any justification for inducing one of the parties to the contract to breach its provisions? An economic analysis of the purpose of contracts suggests that in many instances society gains from breached agreements because it permits resources to move to higher valued uses. Assume that *A* agrees to sell a widget to *B* with delivery in one week for $5000. Two days later *C* offers *A* $7500 if it will use its factory to make a gidget instead. *A* changes production breaching his agreement with *B*. However the factory is now producing more valuable goods and *B* will be made whole by the law of contracts that will give him the difference between the contract price ($5000) and whatever he must pay to buy a widget on the open market. Assume *B* can purchase a substitute widget for $5000, he is in the same position had the contract been performed and *A* and *C* have an additional $2500 gain to split between them. Shouldn't these types of breaches be encouraged? Should we make *C* liable under the doctrines of intentional interference with a contract if he knew about the initial agreement?

6. Interference with contract or prospective advantage cases involve determining what behavior on the part of the defendant constitutes an improper inducement and the extent to which the behavior of the defendant is privileged. These issues become intertwined in many cases. It may be useful to divide the cases into at least two classes. In the first class the defendant's behavior is independently tortious. Many of the cases decided under other rubrics such as misrepresentation, disparagement, predatory pricing, and use of force can be cast as "interference" cases. In the second class are those cases that involve no independent tortious behavior and involve conduct on the part of the defendant that at least can be arguably characterized as part of the competitive process. In this class of case, the intensity of the conflict of interests is more clearly seen. Consider whether and on what basis you would impose liability on the inducer in any of the following cases:

a. *A* supplies fishing reels to both *B* and *C* under annually renewable contractual arrangements. When *A* becomes financially troubled, *B* purchases one-sixth of the stock in *A* and makes *A* an interest free loan. As part of the transaction *A* agrees not to renew the contract with *C*. *C* sues *B*. See Fury Imports, Inc. v. Shakespeare Co., 554 F.2d 1376 (5th Cir.1977).

b. *A, B* and *C* are associates in a major New York law firm. They decide to form their own partnership and notify the firm's clients of their actions. The firm sues *A, B* and *C* for interfering with its relationships with its clients. See Adler, Barish, Daniels, Levin & Creskoff v. Epstein, 252 Pa.Super. 553, 382 A.2d 1226 (1977), reversed 482 Pa. 416, 393 A.2d 1175 (1978).

c. An automobile liability insurance company offers to settle with a plaintiff in a tort case contingent on the plaintiff breaching a contingent fee contract with his lawyer. See Herron v. State Farm Mutual Ins. Co., 56 Cal.2d 202, 14 Cal.Rptr. 294, 363 P.2d 310 (1961). And, a husband in a divorce action threatens "to refuse any and all reconciliation efforts" unless the wife discharges the plaintiff as her attorney. Abrams & Fox, Inc. v. Briney, 39 Cal.App.3d 604, 114 Cal.Rptr. 328 (1974).

d. A major bank owns an apartment house. *A*, a real estate broker, initiates conversations with the bank on behalf of *B*, a potential buyer, to determine if the bank is willing to sell. Finding the bank receptive, *A* submits a contract of sale to the bank containing a requirement that the bank pay *A* a real estate commission. The bank rejects the contract. Thereafter, *B* approaches the bank directly and they enter a contract for sale, a term of the contract requires *B* to indemnify the bank against any claim to commissions by *A*. *A* sues *B* for inducing a breach of a prospective relationship. Leonard Duckworth, Inc. v. Michael L. Field & Co., 516 F.2d 952 (5th Cir. 1975).

   e. *A* has a contract terminable at will with *B*. *B* has a contract terminable at will with *C*. *A* threatens to terminate his contract with *B* unless *B* terminates his contract with *C*. See Smith v. Ford Motor Co., 289 N.C. 71, 221 S.E.2d 282 (1976).

7. Would you allow the party to the contract to recover a tort measure of damages against the inducer even though that party would only be able to recover contractual damages against the breaching party? The courts are divided. Punitive damages have been awarded in some cases.

8. There has been much contemporary interest in the interference tort because, viewed broadly, it is basic to the law governing competitive practices. Compare Harvey Perlman, Interference with Contract and Other Economic Expectancies: A Clash of Tort and Contract Theory, 49 U.Chi.L.Rev. 61 (1982); Richard Epstein, Inducement of Breach of Contract as a Problem of Ostensible Ownership, 16 J.Leg.Stud. 1 (1987); Lillian BeVier, Reconsidering Inducement, 76 Va.L.Rev. 877 (1990); and Mark P. Gergen, Tortious Interference: How it Is Engulfing Commercial Law, Why this Is Not Entirely Bad, and a Prudential Response, 38 Ariz. L. Rev. 1175 (1996). See also, Rizzo, A Theory of Economic Loss in the Law of Torts, 11 J. Legal Stud. 281 (1982); Dobbs, Tortious Interference with Contractual Relationships, 34 Ark.L.Rev. 335 (1980); Note, Tortious Interference with Contractual Relations in the Nineteenth Century: The Transformation of Property, Contract, and Tort, 93 Harv.L.Rev. 1510 (1980); Note, An Analysis of the Formation of Property Rights Underlying Tortious Interference with Contracts and Other Economic Relations, 50 U.Chi.L.Rev. 1116 (1983).

B. Appropriation
(1) The Protection of Ideas
Kenneth J. Arrow, Economic Welfare and the Allocation of Resources for Invention*

in National Bureau of Economic Research, The Rate and Direction of Inventive Activity: Economic and Social Factors, at 609, 614–616 (1962)*

Information as a Commodity

Uncertainty usually creates a still more subtle problem in resource allocation; information becomes a commodity. Suppose that in one part of the economic system an observation has been made whose outcome, if known, would affect anyone's estimates of the probabilities of the different states of nature. Such observations arise out of research but they also arise in the daily course of economic life as a by-product of other economic activities. An entrepreneur will automatically acquire a knowledge of demand and production conditions in his field which is available to others only with special effort. Information will frequently have an economic value, in the sense that anyone possessing the information can make greater profits than would otherwise be the case.

It might be expected that information will be traded in, and of course to a considerable extent this is the case, as is illustrated by the numerous economic institutions for transmission of information, such as newspapers. But in many instances, the problem of an optimal allocation is sharply raised. The cost of transmitting a given body of information is frequently very low. If it were zero, then optimal allocation would obviously call for unlimited distribution of the information without cost. In fact, a given piece of information is by definition an indivisible commodity, and the classical problems of allocation in the presence of indivisibilities appear here. The owner of the information should not extract the economic value which is there, if optimal allocation is to be achieved; but he is a monopolist, to some small extent and will seek to take advantage of this fact.

In the absence of special legal protection, the owner cannot, however, simply sell information on the open market. Any one purchaser can destroy the monopoly, since he can reproduce the information at little or no cost. Thus the only effective monopoly would be the use of the information by the original possessor. This, however, will not only be socially inefficient, but also may not be of much use to the owner of the information either, since he may not be able to exploit it as effectively as others.

With suitable legal measures, information may become an appropriable commodity. Then the monopoly power can indeed be exerted. However, no amount of legal protection can make a thoroughly appropriable commodity of something so intangible as information. The very use of the information in any productive way is bound to reveal it, at least in part. Mobility of personnel among firms provides a way of spreading information. Legally imposed property rights can provide only a partial barrier, since there are obviously enormous difficulties in defining in any sharp way an item of information and differentiating it from other similar sounding items.

The demand for information also has uncomfortable properties. In the first place, the use of information is certainly subject to indivisibilities; the use of information about production possibilities, for example, need not depend on the rate of production. In the second place, there is a fundamental paradox in the determination of demand for information; its value for the purchaser is not known until he has the information, but then he has in effect acquired it without cost. Of course, if the seller can retain property rights in the use of the information, this would be no problem, but given incomplete appropriability, the potential buyer will base his decision to purchase information on less than optimal criteria. He may act, for example, on the average value of information in that class as revealed by past experience. If any particular item of information has differing values for different economic agents, this procedure will lead both to a nonoptimal purchase of information at any given price and also to a nonoptimal allocation of the information purchased.

It should be made clear that from the standpoint of efficiently distributing an existing stock of information, the difficulties of appropriation are an advantage, provided there are no costs of transmitting information, since then optimal allocation calls for free distribution. The chief point made here is the difficulty of creating a market for information if one should be desired for any reason.

It follows from the preceding discussion that costs of transmitting information create allocative difficulties which would be absent otherwise. Information should be transmitted at marginal cost, but then the demand difficulties raised above will exist. From the viewpoint of optimal allocation, the purchasing industry will be faced with the problems created by indivisibilities; and we still leave unsolved the problem of the purchaser's inability to judge in advance the value of the information he buys. There is a strong case for centralized decision making under these circumstances.

Reeves v. Alyeska Pipeline Service Company

Supreme Court of Alaska, 1996
926 P. 2d 1130

PER CURIAM.

I. INTRODUCTION

This case raises issues concerning the protection of ideas. It arises out of John Reeves' claims that in 1991 Alyeska Pipeline Service Company (Alyeska) appropriated his idea for a visitor center at a popular turnout overlooking the Trans-Alaska Pipeline. The superior court granted summary judgment to Alyeska. We reverse in part and remand for further proceedings.

II. FACTS AND PROCEEDINGS

In 1985 Alyeska created a visitor turnout at Mile 9 of the Steese Highway between Fox and Fairbanks. The turnout had informational signs and provided visitors a view of the Trans-Alaska Pipeline. Before Alyeska constructed the turnout, visitors gained access to the pipeline by a nearby road and trespassed on the Trans-Alaska Pipeline right-of-way.

John Reeves, owner of Gold Dredge No. 8, a tourist attraction outside Fairbanks and near the turnout, contacted Alyeska in January 1991 to discuss a tourism idea he had. He spoke with Keith Burke, Alyeska's Fairbanks Manager. After receiving Burke's assurance that the tourism idea was "between us," Reeves orally disclosed his idea to build a visitor center at the turnout. He proposed that Alyeska lease him the land and he build the center, sell Alyeska merchandise, and display a "pig"[2] and a cross-section of pipe.

---

2. A "pig" is a device which passes through the pipeline to clean interior pipe walls, survey interior pipe shape and detect corrosion.

Burke told him the idea "look[ed] good" and asked Reeves to submit a written proposal, which Reeves did two days later. The proposal explained Reeves' idea of operating a visitor center on land leased to him by Alyeska. The proposal included plans to provide small tours, display a "pig," pipe valve, and section of pipe, sell refreshments and pipeline memorabilia, and plant corn and cabbage.

After submitting the proposal, Reeves met with Burke once again. At this meeting Burke told Reeves the proposal looked good and was exactly what he wanted. In Reeves' words, Burke told him, "We're going to do this deal, and I'm going to have my Anchorage lawyers draw it." Reeves claimed he and Burke envisioned that the visitor center would be operating by the 1991 summer tourist season.

Reeves alleges that Alyeska agreed during this meeting (1) to grant access to the turnout for twenty years; (2) to allow Reeves to construct and operate an information center; and (3) to allow Reeves to sell merchandise and charge a $2.00 admission fee. Reeves stated that, in exchange, he agreed to pay Alyeska ten percent of gross receipts.

Over the next several months, Burke allegedly told Reeves that the deal was "looking good" and not to worry because it takes time for a large corporation to move. However, in spring 1991, Burke told Reeves that the visitor center was such a good idea that Alyeska was going to implement it without Reeves. By August 1991 Alyeska had installed a portable building at the turnout to serve as a visitor center; it built a permanent log cabin structure in 1992.

The members of the Alyeska Pipeline Club North (APCN) operated the visitor center and sold T-shirts, hats, and other items.[3] APCN does not charge admission. A section of pipeline and a "pig" are on display. APCN employees provide information and answer visitors' questions. Members of APCN had suggested in 1987 that Alyeska create a visitor center at the turnout. However, Alyeska had rejected the idea at that time. Before meeting with Reeves, Burke did not know that APCN's visitor center idea had been raised and rejected by Alyeska in 1987.

Approximately 100,000 people visited the visitor center each summer in 1992 and 1993. It grossed over $50,000 in sales each year. The net profit for 1993 was calculated to be $5,000–$15,000. APCN received all the profit.

Reeves filed suit in May 1993. By amended complaint, he alleged a variety of tort and contract claims. Judge Charles R. Pengilly granted Alyeska's motion for summary judgment on all claims; Reeves appeals. Reeves also appeals the superior court's denial of Reeves' motion to compel production of Burke's daily calendar.

* * *

---

3. Alyeska Pipeline Club North is a non-profit corporation run by Alyeska employees. It raises money to fund activities such as picnics and Christmas parties for Alyeska employees.

Reeves sued Alyeska on claims of breach of oral contract, promissory estoppel, breach of implied contract, quasi-contract (unjust enrichment and quantum meruit), breach of the covenant of good faith and fair dealing, breach of license and/or lease agreement, and various torts related to the contractual relationships alleged.

This case presents several questions of first impression concerning the protection of business ideas. Reeves claims that Alyeska contracted for both the disclosure and use of his idea. Alyeska maintains that Reeves' "idea" was not novel or original and that an Alyeska employee had proposed an identical idea in 1987. Therefore, Alyeska argues that most of Reeves' claims fail because his idea was not novel or original. Alyeska also argues that Reeves' claims are barred by the statute of frauds. Before reaching the merits of Reeves' claims we must first briefly discuss the law relating to the protection of ideas and the roles of novelty and originality.

A. Protection of Ideas

The law pertaining to the protection of ideas must reconcile the public's interest in access to new ideas with the perceived injustice of permitting some to exploit commercially the ideas of others. * * *

Creating a middle ground between no protection and the legal monopolies created by patent and copyright law, courts have protected ideas under a variety of contract and contract-like theories. These theories protect individuals who spend their time and energy developing ideas that may benefit others. It would be inequitable to prevent these individuals from obtaining legally enforceable compensation from those who voluntarily choose to benefit from the services of the "idea-person." * * *

We have not had occasion to address these theories in the context of the protection of ideas. In addressing each of Reeves' claims we must determine whether the special nature of ideas affects the application of traditional contract and contract-like claims. In making these determinations we are mindful of the competing policies of retaining the free exchange of ideas and compensating those who develop and market their ideas. On the one hand, protecting ideas by providing compensation to the author for their use or appropriation rewards the idea person and encourages the development of creative and intellectual ideas which will benefit humankind. On the other hand, protecting ideas also inevitably restricts their free use, potentially delaying or restricting the benefit any given idea might confer on society.

Reeves argues that requiring novelty and originality, as did the trial court, erroneously imports property theories into contract-based claims. He contends that so long as the parties bargained for the disclosure of the idea, the disclosure serves as consideration and the idea itself need not have the qualities of property. Alyeska argues that novelty and originality should be employed as limiting factors in idea cases because these cases are based on a theory of idea as intellectual property. Alyeska contends that in order to be protected, an idea must have "not been suggested to or known by the public at any prior time."

We find that the manner in which requirements such as novelty or originality are applied depends largely on which theory of recovery is pursued.

Thus, we will address the parties' arguments concerning novelty as they apply to each of Reeves' theories of recovery.

B. Express Contract Claims

Reeves argues that he and Alyeska entered into three different oral contracts: (1) a confidentiality or disclosure agreement by which Alyeska promised not to use Reeves' idea without his participation, if Reeves disclosed the idea; (2) a lease agreement by which Alyeska promised to lease the turnout to Reeves in exchange for a percentage of the center's profits; and (3) a memorialization agreement by which Alyeska promised to commit the agreement to writing.

* * *

1. The Disclosure Agreement

Reeves alleges that in exchange for the disclosure of his idea, Alyeska promised to keep the idea confidential and not to use the idea without entering into a contract with Reeves to implement the idea. Reeves' deposition testimony, when all inferences are taken in his favor, supports the existence of a disclosure agreement. * * *

We conclude that the statute of frauds does not apply to the alleged disclosure agreement. That alleged agreement was to be completed within one year. If Alyeska chose to implement the idea, it was to enter into a lease agreement with Reeves by the summer tourist season. Moreover, Reeves' disclosure to Alyeska constituted full performance of his side of the contract for disclosure. The statute of frauds consequently does not apply.

2. The Lease Agreement

Reeves claims he had an oral contract with Alyeska to lease the turnout for twenty years. Reeves concedes that this agreement falls within the scope of the statute of frauds because it was for a long-term lease that could not be performed within one year. * * *

[The Court rejects Reeves claims that the statute of frauds did not apply because the contract was fully performed and he relied on the oral promise. The idea was not disclosed in reliance on the lease agreement. The Court also found the Memorialization Agreement violated the statute of frauds.]

C. Implied-in-Fact Contract

Reeves has made out a prima facie case for an implied contract. We have held that an implied-in-fact contract, like an express contract, is based on the intentions of the parties.

There are three primary factual scenarios under which ideas may be submitted to another. The first involves an unsolicited submission that is involuntarily received. The idea is submitted without warning; it is transmitted before the recipient has taken any action which would indicate a promise to pay for the submission. Under this scenario, a contract will not be implied.

The second involves an unsolicited submission that is voluntarily received. In this situation, the idea person typically gives the recipient advance warning that an idea is to be disclosed; the recipient has an opportunity to stop the disclosure, but through inaction allows the idea to be disclosed. Under California law, if the recipient at the time of disclosure understands that the idea person expects to be paid for the disclosure of the idea, and does not attempt to stop the disclosure, inaction may be seen as consent to a contract.

This view has been criticized as unfairly placing a duty on the recipient to take active measures to stop the submission. The critics argue that inaction generally should not be considered an expression of consent to a contract.

We believe that a contract should not be implied under this scenario. An implied-in-fact contract is based on circumstances that demonstrate that the parties intended to form a contract but failed to articulate their promises. Only under exceptional circumstances would inaction demonstrate an intent to enter a contract.[14]

The third scenario involves a solicited submission. Here, a request by the recipient for disclosure of the idea usually implies a promise to pay for the idea if the recipient uses it.

Reeves argues that Alyeska solicited his idea. He alleges that Burke asked him what the idea was, and later requested a written proposal. He contends that the request and Alyeska's later use of the idea created an implied contract for payment. These allegations are sufficient to survive summary judgment. A reasonable fact-finder could determine that Burke's actions implied a promise to pay for the disclosure of Reeves' idea. A fact-finder could also determine that Reeves volunteered the idea before Burke took any affirmative action that would indicate an agreement to pay for the disclosure. These possible conclusions present genuine issues of material fact.

Relying largely on cases from New York, Alyeska argues that novelty and originality should be required in an implied-in-fact claim. Reeves responds that we should follow California's example and not require novelty as an essential element of this sort of claim.

Idea-based claims arise most frequently in the entertainment centers of New York and California, but New York requires novelty, whereas California does not. * * *

We prefer the California approach. An idea may be valuable to the recipient merely because of its timing or the manner in which it is presented. * * *

Implied-in-fact contracts are closely related to express contracts. Each requires the parties to form an intent to enter into a contract. It is ordinarily not the court's role to evaluate the adequacy of the consideration agreed upon by the parties. The bargain should be left in the hands of the parties. If parties voluntarily choose to bargain for an individual's services in disclosing or developing a non-novel or unoriginal idea, they have the power to

---

14. We recognize the possibility of a rare case in which inaction could express intent to form a contract. For example, a contract would be implied if the parties' history of dealings demonstrated that they had entered into similar contracts in the past, or if it were proven in a particular field or industry that a recipient's silence constitutes agreement to pay for an idea upon use.

do so. The *Desny* [Desny v. Wilder, 46 Cal.2d 715, 299 P.2d 257 (1956)] court analogized the services of a writer to the services of a doctor or lawyer and determined there was little difference; each may provide a product that is not novel or original. It held that it would not impose an additional requirement of novelty on the work. Although Reeves is not a writer, his ideas are entitled to no less protection than those of writers, doctors, or lawyers. Therefore, Reeves should be given the opportunity to prove the existence of an implied-in-fact contract for disclosure of his idea.

D. Promissory Estoppel

Reeves claims that the trial court erred in granting summary judgment to Alyeska on his promissory estoppel claim. He argues that there were genuine fact questions. Alyeska argues that Reeves presented no evidence of detrimental reliance.

Under Alaska law, a promissory estoppel claim has four requirements:

1) The action induced amounts to a substantial change of position;

2) it was either actually foreseen or reasonably foreseeable by the promisor;

3) an actual promise was made and itself induced the action or forbearance in reliance thereon; and

4) enforcement is necessary in the interest of justice.

Reeves contends that in reliance on promises made by Alyeska in context of separate disclosure, lease, and memorialization agreements, he took two actions that changed his position: he disclosed the idea, and he failed to hire an attorney to draft the contract. Although forbearance may sometimes be considered an action that changes one's position, Reeves' failure to hire an attorney did not amount to a substantial change of position. As noted above, even if Reeves had presented a written contract to Alyeska, no evidence permits an inference Alyeska would have executed it.

By disclosing his idea, however, Reeves substantially changed his position. Once he disclosed the idea, Reeves' ability to bargain for terms was significantly reduced. It was reasonably foreseeable that a promise of confidentiality and a promise to allow Reeves to participate in any use of the idea would induce disclosure. There was evidence permitting an inference Alyeska's alleged promises induced the disclosure. Consequently, genuine fact disputes exist regarding the first three requirements for promissory estoppel.

The fourth requirement, that enforcement is necessary in the interest of justice, presents fact questions that ordinarily should not be decided on summary judgment. * * *

E. Quasi-Contract Claim

Reeves argues that Alyeska was unjustly enriched because it solicited and received Reeves' services, ideas, and opinions without compensating Reeves. He argues that the trial court erred in granting summary judgment to Alyeska on his quasi-contract cause of action.

We have required the following three elements for a quasi-contract claim:

1) a benefit conferred upon the defendant by the plaintiff;

2) appreciation by the defendant of such benefit; and

3) acceptance and retention by the defendant of such benefit under such circumstances that it would be inequitable for him to retain it without paying the value thereof.

The trial court understood Reeves to be arguing that his idea was a property right that was stolen by Alyeska. Reeves, however, argues that "Alyeska took Reeves' concept, proposal and services without any payment to Reeves." Reeves' quasi-contract claims must be divided into two categories. His claim that Alyeska appropriated his idea for a visitor center is necessarily a property-based claim that seeks recovery for the value of the idea itself; Reeves seeks a recovery based on "his" idea. His claims that Alyeska benefitted from his proposal and services, however, do not necessarily rely on the visitor center idea being property; these claims are based on his services of disclosing and drafting the proposal. The property and non- property claims are treated differently.

An idea is usually not regarded as property because our concept of property implies something that can be owned and possessed to the exclusion of others. To protect an idea under a property theory requires that the idea possess property-like traits. Courts consider the elements of novelty or originality necessary for a claim of "ownership" in an idea or concept. These elements distinguish protectable ideas from ordinary ideas that are freely available for others to use. It is the element of originality or novelty that lends value to the idea itself.

If the idea is not distinguished in this manner, its use cannot satisfy the requirements of a quasi-contract claim. The idea, even if beneficial to the defendant, cannot be conferred if the plaintiff has no right of possession. With no right of possession, the idea cannot be said to have been conferred by the plaintiff. Despite Reeves' protestations, the idea of establishing a visitor center near the pipeline is neither original nor novel.

Nevertheless, not all of Reeves' quasi-contract claims require that his idea be considered property and consequently novel or original. Reeves argues that Alyeska was unjustly enriched "by Reeves' efforts on its behalf, not merely on the 'concept that [Reeves'] idea was intellectual property.' " Therefore, we must analyze whether the parties' transactions give rise to a quasi-contract.

The facts alleged by Reeves demonstrate that Burke specifically asked Reeves to draw up a proposal and that Alyeska was going to "do this deal." There is also evidence Reeves was familiar with the Fairbanks summer tourist industry and had special expertise in that area. These facts present a genuine issue of fact as to whether Alyeska benefited from Reeves' experience or his written plan. Thus, there is a question of fact whether Reeves' idea had value to Alyeska in its timing or in how it was presented, rather than in its novelty or originality. Reeves' endorsement of the idea, in combination with his experience in the Fairbanks tourism industry, may have also been valuable to Alyeska. The fact that Alyeska rejected a similar idea in 1987 may indicate that some feature of Reeves' plan or presentation caused

Alyeska to go forward with a visitor center. If Reeves' services unjustly enriched Alyeska, he should be compensated for the value of those services.

* * *

G. Reeves' Tort Claims

The trial court granted summary judgment to Alyeska on Reeves' tort claims of fraud and negligent misrepresentation because Reeves cited no evidence of detrimental reliance. Because Reeves presented evidence of detrimental reliance in regard to disclosing the idea, we remand the fraud and negligent misrepresentation claims which are based on a disclosure agreement. However, the trial court did not err in dismissing the tort claims that are dependent on the lease or memorialization agreements.

NOTES

1. The difficulty of transacting in ideas has become known as the "Arrow paradox" after Kenneth Arrow's article reproduced above. Which legal theory, contract or property, best serves to resolve the paradox?

2. Under the contract theory in *Reeves*, what is the consideration for Burke's express or implied promise to pay? Can the act of disclosure be the consideration if what is disclosed is not novel or useful? If Reeves has no property right in the idea disclosed? Can I agree to pay you if you will tell me the headline in tomorrow's paper? If you breach, what are the damages? Can Alyeska argue that Burke was not authorized to make an agreement with Reeves? If the agreement is only to disclose the idea, does that mean that Alyeska will have to pay even if they don't use the idea? Since Alyeska already knew about the idea, can Reeves ever prove that Alyeska used his idea rather than the original submission in 1987? What if Alyeska delays for another five years before constructing the visiting center?

3. What if Burke had said: "Disclose the idea and we'll pay you if we like it. If we don't, we'll return it." Can you return an idea?

4. The New York requirement that the idea be original and novel is illustrated in Murray v. National Broadcasting Co., 844 F.2d 988 (2d Cir. 1988). In 1980, Murray approached NBC and was invited to submit his idea for a new television series. One of his submissions was for a series entitled "Father's Day" which would star Bill Cosby and focus on family life in an African-American family. NBC rejected the idea. Four years later "The Cosby Show" began starring Bill Cosby and featuring episodes about everyday life in an upper middle-class African-American family. Murray sued. The court found Murray's idea to be neither novel or original:

> We recognize of course that even novel and original ideas to a greater or lesser extent combine elements that are themselves not novel. Originality does not exist in a vacuum. Nevertheless, where, as here, an idea consists in essence of nothing more than a variation on a basic theme—in this case, the family situation comedy—novelty cannot be found to exist. The addition to this basic theme of the portrayal of blacks in nonstereotypical roles does not alter our conclusion, especially

in view of the fact that Bill Cosby previously had expressed a desire to do a situation comedy about a black family and that, as the district court found, Cosby's entire career has been a reflection of the positive portrayal of blacks and the black family on television.

Compare *Murray* with Landsberg v. Scrabble Crossword Game Players, Inc., 802 F.2d 1193 (9th Cir. 1986). Landsberg disclosed the idea of a book on strategy for winning the Scrabble board game to Scrabble. They rejected it and then produced their own strategy book. The court regarded the issue under California law to be whether the disclosure came before or after the defendant knew that compensation was expected. The court upheld the lower court's findings that disclosure occurred after the defendant should have known that Landsberg expected compensation if his idea was used.

5. If in Landsberg it was also proved that Scrabble sufficiently copied the material submitted by Landsberg to constitute a copyright infringement, could Landsberg still recover under state contract law for use of the idea or would such a recovery be preempted by *Sears* and *Compco*? Can states adopt the property theory to confer protection on ideas after *Sears* and *Compco*?

PROBLEM

If a corporation requires anyone submitting an idea for consideration to accept in writing the following eight conditions is it adequately protected against additional liability? Are all the conditions necessary?

1. An idea must be submitted by its originator or his or her duly appointed attorney or agent.

2. An idea will be considered only on the understanding that its submission and the submission of any related material is not in confidence. No confidential or other unusual relationship may be established by or implied from the submission or our consideration of the idea or related material.

3. The corporation cannot and does not agree that the idea or any related material submitted will be kept a secret.

4. The corporation will give an idea only such consideration as it believes the idea merits, and no obligation is assumed other than to notify the submitter as to whether or not the company is interested in negotiating further for rights to the idea.

5. Receipt, or consideration of, or subsequent negotiation or offer with respect to any idea will be without prejudice to us. This includes, without limitation, our rights to contest the validity of any existing or future patent on the idea. Furthermore, and also without limitation, receipt or consideration of, or negotiation or offer on an idea, shall not be deemed an admission of the novelty or patentability of the idea, or of priority or originality on the part of the submitter or any other person.

6. We cannot consider any idea on condition that we shall return any material submitted.

7. If your idea is patented, and of interest to us, negotiations may be entered into. In the event that no agreement is concluded the submitter shall rely solely upon such rights as he may have under United States Patent Laws.

8. Where your idea is not patented, in the event the idea proves new, and the corporation uses it, the company agrees to pay and you agree to accept the sum of One Thousand Dollars ($1,000.00) for all rights to such idea. However, if any such unpatented idea shall later be covered by a patent, the foregoing provisions of this paragraph shall not apply to any rights under the patent, and the submitter shall thereafter rely solely upon such rights as he may have under United States Patent Laws.

See Sylvania Electric Prods., Inc. v. Brainerd, 166 U.S.P.Q. 387 (D.C.Mass.1970).

(2) Published and Unpublished Works
(a) Common Law Copyright

Prior to the revision of the Copyright Act in 1976, the doctrine of "common-law copyright" protected "unpublished" works. As a general proposition the author of a work had the right of first publication, and until exercised the common law protected the work from tortious misappropriations. Once the work was published, common law rights were divested and the author was forced to look to federal statutory copyright law for protection. Federal copyright protection commenced when a work was published with a proper notice of copyright attached. Section 2 of the 1909 Copyright Act specifically preserved state protection of unpublished works.

This deceptively simple allocation of power between state and federal law was considerably more complex in practice. First, section 12 of the 1909 Act gave authors of most types of works other than books an option to obtain statutory protection prior to publication by depositing a complete copy of the work with the copyright office. Second, there was no requirement that publication sufficient to *divest* common law rights be construed to mean the same thing as publication to *invest* statutory copyright. Indeed, it was unclear whether publication was to be defined by state or federal law. Third, the dividing line between a published and an unpublished work was unclear. Some kinds of works can be exploited without reproduction in copies—generally by display or performance. Should the display of a painting or the performance of a play be sufficient publication to divest common law rights?

The difficulties were considerably complicated by the invention, in White v. Kimmell, 94 F.Supp. 502 (S.D.Calif.1950), reversed on other grounds 193 F.2d 744 (9th Cir.1952), of the self-contradictory doctrine of limited publication—a publication, if sufficiently limited, is not a publication. The courts applied themselves with energy to the task of separating general from limited publications.

King v. Mister Maestro, Inc., 224 F.Supp. 101 (S.D.N.Y.1963) is illustrative. Martin Luther King distributed an advanced text of his "I Have A Dream" speech to the press. As part of the news coverage some newspapers printed all or excerpts from the speech. The New York Post offered reprints for sale to the public. The speech was also recorded on a newsreel from which records of the speech were made and sold to the public. Dr. King did not consent to either the sale of reprints or records, and sought an injunction prohibiting the unauthorized sale. The issue as framed by the court was whether there had been a general publication of the speech so as to place it in the public domain.

The word "general" with respect to publication in this sense is of greatest significance. There can be a limited publication, which is a communication of the work to others under circumstances showing no dedication of the work to the public. A general publication is one which shows a dedication to the public so as to lose copyright. The public exhibition of a painting without notice of copyright in a gallery the rules of which forbade copying is not a general publication. * * *

The public performance of a play is not a general publication. * * *

The public delivery of lectures on [the subject of] a memory system is not a general publication. * * *

The playing of a song in public is not a general publication of the work. * * *

The broadcast by radio of a script is not a general publication thereof. * * *

* * *

Defendants stress the delivery without copyright notice of an advance text of his speech and the distribution of it to the press. But within the concept of publication just examined, it is clear that this was a limited, as opposed to a general, publication. There is nothing to suggest that copies of the speech were ever offered to the public; the fact is clear that the "advance text" was given to the press only.

(b) The Copyright Revision of 1976

The general revision of the copyright law of 1976 became effective on January 1, 1978. The Act abandoned the concept of publication as the demarcation between state and federal law. Section 102 announced that federal copyright law "subsists" in original works "fixed in any tangible means of expression." Thus, for example, a manuscript or other written work is protected by federal copyright law from the instant it is fixed on paper. The filing of an application for registration or other acts by the author are not required as a precondition to protection. Thus, at least for those works that are within the subject matter capable of being copyrighted (§ 102), common law copyright is no longer relevant. Furthermore, § 301 preempts all "legal or equitable rights that are equivalent to any of the exclusive rights within the general scope of copyright * * *" derived from the common law or statutes of any state. The section applies to works created before or after January 1, 1978.

(c) Federal-State Conflicts

There are three separate interests embodied in a recording of a musical composition: the composer's, the performer's, and the recording company's.

Prior to October, 1971, the Copyright Act provided protection only to the composer's interest by authorizing the composer to copyright the sheet music. The Act provided no protection for the sound of a performance embodied in a record or other device from which it could be reproduced. This was partly the result of White-Smith Music Pub. Co. v. Apollo Co., 209 U.S. 1 (1908). That case held that a player piano roll was not a "copy" in the technical copyright sense, and hence not an infringement of copyrighted sheet music. The 1909 Act in § 101(e), 17 U.S.C.A. § 101(e), reversed the narrow holding of *Apollo,* providing that a recording infringes copyrighted sheet music.

However, the Act also provided that once a composer authorized the recording of his composition by one person, he was obliged to allow others to record the composition on payment of 2 cents a record. The Act did not provide protection for the performer or the recording company who were forced to look to common law for a remedy against appropriation. This set the stage for a creative duel between the state courts, sensitive to the apparent unjust enrichment by those who appropriated another's work, and the federal courts, led by Judge Learned Hand, who sought to preserve the supremacy of the federal copyright and patent systems and to limit economic monopolies over creative works. The major skirmishes are outlined below:

NOTES

1. In a famous trilogy, the Second Circuit and the state courts struggled with the protection of performances. In Waring v. WDAS Broadcasting Station, Inc., 327 Pa. 433, 194 A. 631 (1937), the Pennsylvania Supreme Court held that Fred Waring was entitled to an injunction preventing the broadcast by a radio station of a recording made by Waring's orchestra and sold with a label which read: "not licensed for radio broadcast." The court enforced the limitation on the label and cited *INS* as an independent ground for the decision. Three years later in RCA Mfg. Co. v. Whiteman, 114 F.2d 86 (2d Cir.1940), cert. denied 311 U.S. 712 (1940), Judge Hand, on facts similar to *Waring,* found for the defendant on the theory that sale of the records was a general publication of the performance and to allow state law protection would be "contrary to the whole policy of the Copyright Act and of the Constitution." Although *Whiteman* was decided after *Erie* there was little New York law in conflict with Hand's view. However in Metropolitan Opera Ass'n v. Wagner-Nichols Recorder Corp., 199 Misc. 786, 101 N.Y.S.2d 483 (1950), a case again involving facts similar to *Waring* and *Whiteman,* the state courts held as a matter of *state* law that the performances were not "general publications" divesting common-law rights. *INS* was also asserted as the law of New York. In Capitol Records, Inc. v. Mercury Records, 221 F.2d 657 (2d Cir.1955), another performance appropriation case, a majority, pursuant to its *Erie* obligations, applied the New York law of misappropriation modeled after *INS* to grant recovery to the plaintiff.

Judge Hand, however, was not to be so easily converted. In dissent, he argued that whether a work was "published" must be a question of federal not state law and once a work is published it can be freely copied unless protected by copyright. In language unquestionably the forerunner of *Sears* and *Compco*, Hand argued:

> [If the states are free to determine what constitutes publication] they could grant to an author a perpetual monopoly, although he exploited the "work" with all the freedom he would have enjoyed, had it been copyrighted. I cannot believe that the failure of Congress to include within the Act all that the Clause covers should give the states so wide a power. To do so would pro tanto defeat the overriding purpose of the Clause, which was to grant only for "limited Times" the untrammelled exploitation of an author's "Writings." Either he must be content with such circumscribed exploitation as does not constitute "publication," or he must eventually dedicate his "work" to the public. The situation is no different from that of patents, where such bilateral character of the grant is a commonplace. I would hold that the clause has that much effect ex proprio vigore; and that the states are not free to follow their own notions as to when an author's right shall be unlimited both in user and in duration. Such power of course they have as to "works" that are not "Writings"; but I submit that, once it is settled that a "work" is in that class, the Clause enforces upon the author the choice I have just mentioned; and, if so, it must follow that it is a federal question whether he has published the "work."

2. Federal supremacy was reasserted in *Sears* and *Compco*. Do these cases mandate that "publication" be defined by federal law? Could a state protect performances after *Sears* and *Compco*? In Capitol Records, Inc. v. Greatest Records, Inc., 43 Misc.2d 878, 252 N.Y.S.2d 553 (1964), decided after *Sears* and *Compco*, a temporary injunction was granted against a defendant who made "counterfeit" records of performances of "The Beatles" from Capitol's albums and marketed them at a retail price significantly lower than the Capitol album. *Sears* and *Compco* were distinguished on the basis that they dealt with acts of "imitation" and did not prevent state law protection against "unauthorized appropriation, reproduction or duplication of the actual performances. * * * Actually, what was here done was not the copying of some article or goods made and sold by another but rather *the appropriation* of the very product itself. * * *" Does *Bonito Boats* undermine the imitation-appropriation distinction?

3. Tape and record piracy became a national issue and many states enacted penal statutes prohibiting the activity. These statutes were generally upheld by lower courts. In spite of their successes in the lower courts, the record manufacturers continued to seek statutory copyright protection largely because the common law provided recovery only against the "pirate"—who is usually impossible to find and insolvent when found—while the copyright act provided potent remedies against distributors and retailers. When in 1971 the Copyright Revision Bill appeared hopelessly delayed in Congress, copyright protection was extended to sound recordings by Public Law 92–140, an amendment to the 1909 Act. The amendment was incorporated into the revision bill when it was adopted.

Goldstein v. California

Supreme Court of The United States, 1973.
412 U.S. 546, 93 S.Ct. 2303, 37 L.Ed.2d 163.

■ MR. CHIEF JUSTICE BURGER delivered the opinion of the Court.

[Petitioners were convicted of violating a California statute making it a crime to transfer sounds recorded on a phonograph record without the consent of the owner. Petitioners purchased a single tape or recording of a popular performance, make copies of the recording, and sell the copies to the public. Petitioners attack their convictions on the grounds that the California statute, § 653h, is in conflict with the patent and copyright clause of the United States Constitution.

The Court held that the 1971 amendments to the Copyright Act conferring copyright protection for the first time to sound recordings did not apply to this case. The Court then addressed the question whether states had relinquished to Congress the exclusive right to grant copyrights and patents.]

Although the Copyright Clause thus recognizes the potential benefits of a national system, it does not indicate that all writings are of national interest or that state legislation is, in all cases, unnecessary or precluded. The patents granted by the States in the 18th century show, to the contrary, a willingness on the part of the States to promote those portions of science and the arts which were of local importance. Whatever the diversity of people's backgrounds, origins, and interests, and whatever the variety of business and industry in the 13 Colonies, the range of diversity is obviously far greater today in a country of 210 million people in 50 States. In view of that enormous diversity, it is unlikely that all citizens in all parts of the country place the same importance on works relating to all subjects. Since the subject matter to which the Copyright Clause is addressed may thus be of purely local importance and not worthy of national attention or protection, we cannot discern such an unyielding national interest as to require an inference that state power to grant copyrights has been relinquished to *exclusive* federal control.

The question to which we next turn is whether, in actual operation, the exercise of the power to grant copyrights by some States will prejudice the interests of other States. As we have noted, a copyright granted by a particular State has effect only within its boundaries. If one State grants such protection, the interests of States which do not are not prejudiced since their citizens remain free to copy within their borders those works which may be protected elsewhere. The interests of a State which grants copyright protection may, however, be adversely affected by other States that do not; individuals who wish to purchase a copy of a work protected in their own State will be able to buy unauthorized copies in other States where no protection exists. However, this conflict is neither so inevitable nor so severe as to compel the conclusion, that state power has been relinquished to the exclusive jurisdiction of the Congress. Obviously when some States do not grant copyright protection—and most do not—that circumstance reduces the economic value of a state copyright, but it will hardly render the copyright worthless. The situation is no different from that which may arise in regard to other state monopolies, such as a state lottery, or a food concession in a limited enclosure like a state park; in each case, citizens may escape the effect of one State's monopoly by making purchases in another area or another State. Similarly, in the case of state copyrights, except as to individuals willing to travel across state lines in order to purchase records or other writings protected in their own State, each State's copyrights will still serve to induce new artistic creations within that State—the very objective of the grant of protection. We do not see here the type of prejudicial conflicts which would arise, for example, if each State exercised a sovereign power to impose imposts and tariffs; nor can we discern a need for uniformity such as that which may apply to the regulation of interstate shipments.

Similarly, it is difficult to see how the concurrent exercise of the power to grant copyrights by Congress and the States will necessarily and inevitably lead to difficulty. At any time Congress determines that a particular category of "writing" is worthy of national protection and the incidental expenses of federal administration, federal copyright protection may be authorized. Where the need for free and unrestricted distribution of a writing is thought to be required by the national interest, the Copyright Clause and the Commerce Clause would allow Congress to eschew all protection. In such cases, a conflict would develop if a State attempted to protect that which Congress intended to be free from restraint or to free that which Congress had protected. However, where Congress determines that neither federal protection nor freedom from restraint is required by the national interest, it is at liberty to stay its hand entirely. Since state protection would not then conflict with federal action, total relinquishment of the States' power to grant copyright protection cannot be inferred.

III

Our conclusion that California did not surrender its power to issue copyrights does not end the inquiry. We must proceed to determine whether the challenged state statute is void under the Supremacy Clause. * * *

By Art. I, § 8, cl. 8, of the Constitution, the States granted to Congress the power to protect the "Writings" of "Authors." These terms have not been construed in their narrow literal sense but, rather, with the reach necessary to reflect the broad scope of constitutional principles. While an "author" may be viewed as an individual who writes an original composition, the term, in its constitutional sense, has been construed to mean an "originator," "he to whom anything owes its origin." Burrow-Giles Lithographic Co. v. Sarony, 111 U.S. 53, 58 (1884). Similarly, although the word "writings" might be limited to script or printed material, it may be interpreted to include any physical rendering of the fruits of creative intellectual or aesthetic labor. Thus, recordings of artistic performances may be within the reach of Clause 8.

While the area in which Congress *may* act is broad, the enabling provision of Clause 8 does not require that Congress act in regard to all categories of materials which meet the constitutional definitions. Rather, whether any specific category of "Writings" is to be brought within the purview of the federal statutory scheme is left to the discretion of the Congress. The history of federal copyright statutes indicates that the congressional determination to consider specific classes of writings is dependent, not only on the character of the writing, but also on the commercial importance of the product to the national economy. As our technology has expanded the means available for creative activity and has provided economical means for reproducing manifestations of such activity, new areas of federal protection have been initiated.

* * *

Sears and *Compco,* on which petitioners rely, do not support their position. In those cases, the question was whether a State could, under principles of a state unfair competition law, preclude the copying of mechanical configurations which did not possess the qualities required for the granting of a federal design or mechanical patent. * * *

In regard to mechanical configurations, Congress had balanced the need to encourage innovation and originality of invention against the need to insure competition in the sale of identical or substantially identical products. The standards established for granting federal patent protection to machines thus indicated not only which articles in this particular category Congress wished to protect, but which configurations it wished to remain free. The application of state law in these cases to prevent the copying of articles which did not meet the requirements for federal protection disturbed the careful balance which Congress had drawn and thereby necessarily gave way under the Supremacy Clause of the Constitution. No comparable conflict between state law and federal law arises in the case of recordings of musical performances. In regard to this category of "Writings," Congress has drawn no balance; rather, it has left the area unattended, and no reason exists why the State should not be free to act.

IV

More than 50 years ago, Mr. Justice Brandeis observed in dissent in International News Service v. Associated Press:

> "The general rule of law is, that the noblest of human productions— knowledge, truths ascertained, conceptions, and ideas—become, after voluntary communication to others, free as the air to common use." 248 U.S. 215, 250 (1918).

But there is no fixed, immutable line to tell us which "human productions" are private property and which are so general as to become "free as the air." In earlier times, a performing artist's work was largely restricted to the stage; once performed, it remained "recorded" only in the memory of those who had seen or heard it. Today, we can record that performance in precise detail and reproduce it again and again with utmost fidelity. The California statutory scheme evidences a legislative policy to prohibit "tape piracy" and "record piracy," conduct that may adversely affect the continued production of new recordings, a large industry in California. Accordingly, the State has, by statute, given to recordings the attributes of property. No restraint has been placed on the use of an idea or concept; rather, petitioners and other individuals remain free to record the same compositions in precisely the same manner and with the same personnel as appeared on the original recording.

* * *

We conclude that the State of California has exercised a power which it retained under the Constitution, and that the challenged statute, as applied in this case, does not intrude into an area which Congress has, up to now, preempted. Until and unless Congress takes further action with respect to recordings fixed prior to February 15, 1972, the California statute may be enforced against acts of piracy such as those which occurred in the present case.

Affirmed.

Mr. Justice DOUGLAS, with whom Mr. Justice BRENNAN and Mr. Justice BLACKMUN concur, dissenting.

* * *

California's law promotes monopoly; the federal policy promotes monopoly only when a copyright is issued, and it fosters competition in all other instances. Moreover, federal law limits its monopoly to 28 years plus a like renewal period, while California extends her monopoly into perpetuity.

Cases like *Sears* were surcharged with "unfair competition" and the present one with "pirated recordings." But free access to products on the market is the consumer interest protected by the failure of Congress to extend patents or copyrights into various areas. * * *

I would reverse the judgment below.

Mr. Justice MARSHALL, with whom Mr. Justice BRENNAN and Mr. Justice BLACKMUN join, dissenting.

NOTES

1. Can you construct an outline of the permissible areas of state concern which is consistent with *Sears, Compco* and *Goldstein*? Can the states continue to protect ideas? Industrial designs?

2. Is the pejorative term "pirate" as applied in *Goldstein* equally applicable in the following situations:

(a) a law student tapes a professor's lecture, reduces it to written form and sells it to other students.

(b) a student borrows his friend's copy of a popular sound recording and tapes it for his personal use.

(c) a Justice of the United States Supreme Court borrows his colleague's copy of the Virginia Law Review and photocopies an article for use in writing an opinion.

(d) a cable television company carries a televised broadcast of a live sporting event.

3. Is there a "national policy" emanating from the "limited times" provision, that works be dedicated to the public? Is this policy compromised by *Goldstein*?

4. Are you as certain as Chief Justice Burger that there is more diversity in intellectual and aesthetic tastes now than there was 200 years ago?

5. Early cable television cases were based on assertions of state misappropriation law. In Intermountain Broadcasting & Television Corp. v. Idaho Microwave, Inc., 196 F.Supp. 315 (D.Idaho 1961) the court refused to apply *INS* in a suit by a Salt Lake City plaintiff whose television broadcasts were transmitted by a cable company to Twin Falls, Idaho, an area outside the plaintiff's broadcast area, on the theory that *INS* required competition between the parties. The same court, however, found in favor of a Twin Falls station who competed with the cable company and who had an exclusive contract with the networks on the theory that the cable's transmission of broadcasts originating in Salt Lake was a tortious interference with the contract rights of the plaintiff. Cable Vision, Inc. v. KUTV, Inc., 211 F.Supp. 47 (D.Idaho 1962). On appeal, the Ninth Circuit reversed based on the intervening decisions of *Sears* and *Compco.* Cable Vision, Inc. v. KUTV, Inc., 335 F.2d 348 (9th Cir.1964), cert. denied 379 U.S. 989 (1964). Thereafter, the United States Supreme Court held that the Federal Communications Commission had authority to regulate CATV at least where the regulations were "reasonably ancillary to the effective performance of the Commission's various responsibilities for the regulation of television broadcasting." United States v. Southwestern Cable Co., 392 U.S. 157 (1968).

6. In contrast to the CATV cases, there is precedent distinguishing between a "reproduction" and a "recreation". In Loeb v. Turner, 257 S.W.2d 800 (Tex.Civ.App.1953) a Dallas radio station assigned an agent to listen to the plaintiff's broadcast of a stock car race in Phoenix and to transmit the bare facts by long distance telephone to Dallas. In Dallas, the information was given to A.L. Turner "a talented and experienced announcer" who recreated a description of the race over the Dallas radio station as though he were present at the race. The court held that once the news was published by broadcast in Phoenix plaintiff was free to use it to recreate the description of the race. But see, National Exhibition Co. v. Fass, 143 N.Y.S.2d 767 (1955) where the defendant was enjoined and held to account for profits for listening to authorized broadcasts of the New York Giants games from the Polo Grounds and distributing the facts to radio stations for simultaneous "recreated radio broadcasts of the games." To what extent do these cases survive *Sears, Compco,* and *Goldstein*?

Copyright Act of 1976

17 U.S.C. § 301*

§ 301. Preemption with respect to other laws

(a) On and after January 1, 1978, all legal or equitable rights that are equivalent to any of the exclusive rights within the general scope of copy-

---

* In 1988 Congress amended § 301 by adding a new subsection (e) which reads: "(e) The scope of Federal preemption under this section is not affected by the adherence of the United States to the Berne Convention or the satisfaction of obligations of the United States thereunder." Pub.L. 100–568 (Oct. 31, 1988). See Chapter 5. for a discussion of U.S. adherence to Berne.

right as specified by section 106 in works of authorship that are fixed in a tangible medium of expression and come within the subject matter of copyright as specified by sections 102 and 103, whether created before or after that date and whether published or unpublished, are governed exclusively by this title. Thereafter, no person is entitled to any such right or equivalent right in any such work under the common law or statutes of any State.

(b) Nothing in this title annuls or limits any rights or remedies under the common law or statutes of any State with respect to—

(1) subject matter that does not come within the subject matter of copyright as specified by sections 102 and 103, including works of authorship not fixed in any tangible medium of expression; or

(2) any cause of action arising from undertakings commenced before January 1, 1978; or

(3) activities violating legal or equitable rights that are not equivalent to any of the exclusive rights within the general scope of copyright as specified by section 106.

(c) With respect to sound recordings fixed before February 15, 1972, any rights or remedies under the common law or statutes of any State shall not be annulled or limited by this title until February 15, 2047. The preemptive provisions of subsection (a) shall apply to any such rights and remedies pertaining to any cause of action arising from undertakings commenced on and after February 15, 2047. Notwithstanding the provisions of section 303, no sound recording fixed before February 15, 1972, shall be subject to copyright under this title before, on, or after February 15, 2047.

(d) Nothing in this title annuls or limits any rights or remedies under any other Federal statute.

Senate Bill S. 22, § 301
94th Cong., 2d Sess. (1976).

§ 301. Preemption with respect to other laws*

* * *

(b) Nothing in this title annuls or limits any rights or remedies under the common law or statutes of any State with respect to—

* * *

(3) activities violating legal or equitable rights that are not equivalent to any of the exclusive rights within the general scope of copyright as specified by section 106, including rights against misappropriation not equivalent to any of such exclusive rights, breaches of contract, breaches of trust, trespass, conversion, invasion of privacy, defamation, and deceptive trade practices such as passing off and false representation.

* * *

* The omitted subsections are identical to the section as finally enacted—ed.

House Comm. On the Judiciary, Copyright Law Revision
H.R.Rep. No. 94–1476, 94th Cong., 2d Sess. pg. 132 (1976).

[The following excerpt from the report relates to the version of § 301 contained in S. 22 above.]

The examples in clause (3), while not exhaustive, are intended to illustrate rights and remedies that are different in nature from the rights comprised in a copyright and that may continue to be protected under State common law or statute. The evolving common law rights of "privacy," "publicity," and trade secrets, and the general laws of defamation and fraud, would remain unaffected as long as the causes of action contain elements, such as an invasion of personal rights or a breach of trust or confidentiality, that are different in kind from copyright infringement. Nothing in the bill derogates from the rights of parties to contract with each other and to sue for breaches of contract; however, to the extent that the unfair competition concept known as "interference with contract relations" is merely the equivalent of copyright protection, it would be preempted.

The last example listed in clause (3)—"deceptive trade practices such as passing off and false representation"—represents an effort to distinguish between those causes of action known as "unfair competition" that the copyright statute is not intended to preempt and those that it is. Section 301 is not intended to preempt common law protection in cases involving activities such as false labeling, fraudulent representation, and passing off even where the subject matter involved comes within the scope of the copyright statute.

"Misappropriation" is not necessarily synonymous with copyright infringement, and thus a cause of action labeled as "misappropriation" is not preempted if it is in fact based neither on a right within the general scope of copyright as specified by section 106 nor on a right equivalent thereto. For example, state law should have the flexibility to afford a remedy (under traditional principles of equity) against a consistent pattern of unauthorized appropriation by a competitor of the facts (i.e., not the literary expression) constituting "hot" news, whether in the traditional mold of International News Service v. Associated Press, 248 U.S. 215 (1918), or in the newer form of data updates from scientific, business, or financial data bases. Likewise, a person having no trust or other relationship with the proprietor of a computerized data base should not be immunized from sanctions against electronically or cryptographically breaching the proprietor's security arrangements and accessing the proprietor's data. The unauthorized data access which should be remediable might also be achieved by the intentional interception of data transmissions by wire, microwave or laser transmissions, or by the common unintentional means of "crossed" telephone lines occasioned by errors in switching.

Debates on Copyright Law Revision
122 Cong. Rec. H. 10910 (Daily ed. Sept. 22, 1976).

[The following debate was on Mr. Seiberling's amendment, ultimately adopted, which removed the examples from § 301(b)(3). The views of the Department of Justice, referred to in the debate, were contained in a letter to Senator Hugh Scott from Assistant Attorney General Thomas Kauper and printed at 122 Cong.Rec. S. 2042 (daily ed. Feb. 19, 1976). The Department argued against including "misappropriation" in the list of examples because the doctrine was "highly anticompetitive" and its inclusion would "defeat the underlying purpose of the preemption section."]

MR. SEIBERLING. Mr. Chairman, my amendment is intended to save the "Federal preemption" of State law section, which is section 301 of the bill, from being inadvertently nullified because of the inclusion of certain examples in the exemptions from preemption.

This amendment would simply strike the examples listed in section 301(b)(3).

The amendment is strongly supported by the Justice Department, which believes that it would be a serious mistake to cite as an exemption from preemption the doctrine of "misappropriation." The doctrine was created by the Supreme Court in 1922, and it has generally been ignored by the Supreme Court itself and by the lower courts ever since.

Inclusion of a reference to the misappropriation doctrine in this bill, however, could easily be construed by the courts as authorizing the States to pass misappropriation laws. We should not approve such enabling legislation, because a misappropriation law could be so broad as to render the preemption section meaningless.

* * *

MR. RAILSBACK. Mr. Chairman, may I ask the gentleman from Ohio, for the purpose of clarifying the amendment that by striking the word "misappropriation," the gentleman in no way is attempting to change the existing state of the law, that is as it may exist in certain States that have recognized the right of recovery relating to "misappropriation"; is that correct?

MR. SEIBERLING. That is correct. All I am trying to do is prevent the citing of them as examples in a statute. We are, in effect, adopting a rather amorphous body of State law and codifying it, in effect. Rather I am trying to have this bill leave the State law alone and make it clear we are merely dealing with copyright laws, laws applicable to copyrights.

MR. RAILSBACK. Mr. Chairman, I personally have no objection to the gentleman's amendment in view of that clarification and I know of no objections from this side.

* * *

MR. KASTENMEIER. Mr. Chairman, I too have examined the gentleman's amendment and was familiar with the position of the Department of Justice. Unfortunately, the Justice Department did not make its position known to the committee until the last day of markup.

MR. SEIBERLING. I understand.

MR. KASTENMEIER. However, Mr. Chairman, I think that the amendment the gentleman is offering is consistent with the position of the Justice Department and accept it on this side as well.

MR. SEIBERLING. I thank the gentleman.

THE CHAIRMAN. The question is on the amendment offered by the gentleman from Ohio (Mr. SEIBERLING).

The amendment was agreed to.

The National Basketball Association v. Motorola, Inc.

United States Court of Appeals, Second Circuit, 1997.
105 F. 3d 841.

■ WINTER, CIRCUIT JUDGE:

[Motorola and Sports Team analysis and Tracking Systems (STATS) sold subscriptions to a pager service through which customers could receive real time scores and other data on National Basketball Association (NBA) games. Motorola hired reporters to watch games on TV or listen to them on the radio and feed information into a personal computer for receipt by subscribers on hand held pagers. Scores were updated every two to three minutes. STATS also maintained a website that provided more comprehensive and detailed real-time game information. The website was updated ever 15 seconds. The NBA sued Motorola and STATS under New York misappropriation law based on International News Service v. Associated Press (see Chapter 1).

The court first reviewed the *INS* case and the history of Federal Copyright law. Prior to 1976 copyright law did not protect live athletic events and it was unclear whether one could obtain a copyright on a recorded broadcast of a live event. The Copyright Act of 1976 provides for copyright for simultaneously recorded broadcasts of live performances but that protection does not extend to the underlying event.

The lower court granted the NBA an injunction prohibiting the STATS service, holding that since the underlying games were not within the subject matter protected by copyright, § 301 of the Copyright Act did not preempt a claim for misappropriation even though the broadcasts were protected. The lower court relied on a "partial preemption" analysis. The Court of Appeals rejected any "partial preemption" doctrine. It then faced the more general question of whether a state misappropriation doctrine could be applied to the facts of this case.]

Under the general scope requirement, Section 301 "preempts only those state law rights that 'may be abridged by an act which, in and of itself, would infringe one of the exclusive rights' provided by federal copyright law." Computer Assoc. Int'l, Inc. v. Altai, Inc., 982 F.2d 693, 716 (2d Cir.1992). However, certain forms of commercial misappropriation otherwise within the general scope requirement will survive preemption if an "extra-element" test is met. As stated in Altai:

> But if an "extra element" is "required instead of or in addition to the acts of reproduction, performance, distribution or display, in order to constitute a state-created cause of action, then the right does not lie 'within the general scope of copyright,' and there is no preemption."

We turn, therefore, to the question of the extent to which a "hot-news" misappropriation claim based on *INS* involves extra elements and is not the equivalent of exclusive rights under a copyright. Courts are generally agreed that some form of such a claim survives preemption. Financial Information, Inc. v. Moody's Investors Service, Inc., 808 F.2d 204, 208 (2d Cir.1986), ("*FII*"). This conclusion is based in part on the legislative history of the 1976 amendments. The House Report stated:

> "Misappropriation" is not necessarily synonymous with copyright infringement, and thus a cause of action labeled as "misappropriation" is not preempted if it is in fact based neither on a right within the general scope of copyright as specified by section 106 nor on a right equivalent thereto. For example, state law should have the flexibility to afford a remedy (under traditional principles of equity) against a consistent pattern of unauthorized appropriation by a competitor of the facts (i.e., not the literary expression) constituting "hot" news, whether in the traditional mold of International News Service v. Associated Press, 248 U.S. 215 (1918), or in the newer form of data updates from scientific, business, or financial data bases.

H.R. No. 94–1476 at 132, reprinted in 1976 U.S.C.C.A.N. at 5748 (footnote omitted), see also *FII*, 808 F.2d at 209 (" 'misappropriation' of 'hot' news, under International News Service, [is] a branch of the unfair competition doctrine not preempted by the Copyright Act according to the House Report" (citation omitted)). The crucial question, therefore, is the breadth of the "hot-news" claim that survives preemption.

In *INS*, the plaintiff AP and defendant INS were "wire services" that sold news items to client newspapers. AP brought suit to prevent INS from selling facts and information lifted from AP sources to INS-affiliated newspapers. One method by which INS was able to use AP's news was to lift facts from AP news bulletins. *INS*, 248 U.S. at 231. Another method was to sell facts taken from just-published east coast AP newspapers to west coast INS newspapers whose editions had yet to appear. Id. at 238. The Supreme Court held (prior to Erie R. Co. v. Tompkins, 304 U.S. 64, (1938)), that INS's use of AP's information was unlawful under federal common law. It characterized INS's conduct as

> amount[ing] to an unauthorized interference with the normal operation of complainant's legitimate business precisely at the point where the profit is to be reaped, in order to divert a material portion of the profit from those who have earned it to those who have not; with special advantage to defendant in the competition because of the fact that it is not burdened with any part of the expense of gathering the news.

INS, 248 U.S. at 240.

The theory of the New York misappropriation cases relied upon by the district court is considerably broader than that of *INS*. For example, the district court quoted at length from Metropolitan Opera Ass'n v. Wagner-Nichols Recorder Corp., 199 Misc. 786, 101 N.Y.S.2d 483 (N.Y.Sup.Ct.1950), aff'd, 279 A.D. 632, 107 N.Y.S.2d 795 (1st Dep't 1951). * * * However, we believe that Metropolitan Opera's broad misappropriation doctrine based on amorphous concepts such as "commercial immorality" or society's "ethics" is preempted. Such concepts are virtually synonymous for wrongful copying and are in no meaningful fashion distinguishable from infringement of a copyright. The broad misappropriation doctrine relied upon by the district court is, therefore, the equivalent of exclusive rights in copyright law.

* * *

In light of cases such as *FII* and *Altai* that emphasize the narrowness of state misappropriation claims that survive preemption, most of the broadcast cases relied upon by the NBA are simply not good law. Those cases were decided at a time when simultaneously-recorded broadcasts were not protected under the Copyright Act and when the state law claims they fashioned were not subject to federal preemption. For example, Metropolitan Opera, 101 N.Y.S.2d 483, involved the unauthorized copying, marketing, and sale of opera radio broadcasts. As another example, in Mutual Broadcasting System v. Muzak Corp., 177 Misc. 489, 30 N.Y.S.2d 419 (Sup.Ct.1941), the defendant simultaneously retransmitted the plaintiff's baseball radio broadcasts onto telephone lines. As discussed above, the 1976 amendments to the Copyright Act were specifically designed to afford copyright protection to simultaneously-recorded broadcasts, and *Metropolitan Opera* and *Muzak* could today be brought as copyright infringement cases. Moreover, we believe that they would have to be brought as copyright cases because the amendments affording broadcasts copyright protection also preempted the state law misappropriation claims under which they were decided.

* * *

In our view, the elements central to an *INS* claim are: (i) the plaintiff generates or collects information at some cost or expense; (ii) the value of the information is highly time-sensitive; (iii) the defendant's use of the information constitutes free-riding on the plaintiff's costly efforts to generate or collect it; (iv) the defendant's use of the information is in direct competition with a product or service offered by the plaintiff; (v) the ability of other parties to free-ride on the efforts of the plaintiff would so reduce the incentive to produce the product or service that its existence or quality would be substantially threatened. [8]

INS is not about ethics; it is about the protection of property rights in time-sensitive information so that the information will be made available to the public by profit seeking entrepreneurs. If services like AP were not

---

8. Some authorities have labeled this element as requiring direct competition between the defendant and the plaintiff in a primary market. "[I]n most of the small number of cases in which the misappropriation doctrine has been determinative, the defendant's appropriation, like that in INS, resulted in direct competition in the plaintiffs' primary market. Appeals to the misappropriation doctrine are almost always rejected when the appropriation does not intrude upon the plaintiff's primary market.", Restatement (Third) of Unfair Competition, § 38 cmt. c, at 412–13 * * *.

assured of property rights in the news they pay to collect, they would cease to collect it. The ability of their competitors to appropriate their product at only nominal cost and thereby to disseminate a competing product at a lower price would destroy the incentive to collect news in the first place. The newspaper-reading public would suffer because no one would have an incentive to collect "hot news."

We therefore find the extra elements—those in addition to the elements of copyright infringement—that allow a "hot news" claim to survive preemption are: (i) the time-sensitive value of factual information, (ii) the free-riding by a defendant, and (iii) the threat to the very existence of the product or service provided by the plaintiff.

2. The Legality of SportsTrax

We conclude that Motorola and STATS have not engaged in unlawful misappropriation under the "hot-news" test set out above. To be sure, some of the elements of a "hot-news" *INS* claim are met. The information transmitted to SportsTrax is not precisely contemporaneous, but it is nevertheless time-sensitive. Also, the NBA does provide, or will shortly do so, information like that available through SportsTrax. It now offers a service called "Gamestats" that provides official play-by-play game sheets and half-time and final box scores within each arena. It also provides such information to the media in each arena. In the future, the NBA plans to enhance Gamestats so that it will be networked between the various arenas and will support a pager product analogous to SportsTrax. SportsTrax will of course directly compete with an enhanced Gamestats.

However, there are critical elements missing in the NBA's attempt to assert a "hot-news" *INS*-type claim. As framed by the NBA, their claim compresses and confuses three different informational products. The first product is generating the information by playing the games; the second product is transmitting live, full descriptions of those games; and the third product is collecting and retransmitting strictly factual information about the games. The first and second products are the NBA's primary business: producing basketball games for live attendance and licensing copyrighted broadcasts of those games. The collection and retransmission of strictly factual material about the games is a different product: e.g., box-scores in newspapers, summaries of statistics on television sports news, and real-time facts to be transmitted to pagers. In our view, the NBA has failed to show any competitive effect whatsoever from SportsTrax on the first and second products and a lack of any free-riding by SportsTrax on the third.

With regard to the NBA's primary products—producing basketball games with live attendance and licensing copyrighted broadcasts of those games—there is no evidence that anyone regards SportsTrax or the AOL site as a substitute for attending NBA games or watching them on television. In fact, Motorola markets SportsTrax as being designed "for those times when you cannot be at the arena, watch the game on TV, or listen to the radio . . ."

The NBA argues that the pager market is also relevant to a "hot-news" *INS*-type claim and that SportsTrax's future competition with Gamestats satisfies any missing element. We agree that there is a separate market for the real-time transmission of factual information to pagers or similar devices, such as STATS's AOL site. However, we disagree that SportsTrax is in any sense free-riding off Gamestats.

An indispensable element of an *INS* "hot-news" claim is free riding by a defendant on a plaintiff's product, enabling the defendant to produce a directly competitive product for less money because it has lower costs. SportsTrax is not such a product. The use of pagers to transmit real-time information about NBA games requires: (i) the collecting of facts about the games; (ii) the transmission of these facts on a network; (iii) the assembling of them by the particular service; and (iv) the transmission of them to pagers or an on-line computer site. Appellants are in no way free- riding on Gamestats. Motorola and STATS expend their own resources to collect purely factual information generated in NBA games to transmit to SportsTrax pagers. They have their own network and assemble and transmit data themselves.

To be sure, if appellants in the future were to collect facts from an enhanced Gamestats pager to retransmit them to SportsTrax pagers, that would constitute free-riding and might well cause Gamestats to be unprofitable because it had to bear costs to collect facts that SportsTrax did not. If the appropriation of facts from one pager to another pager service were allowed, transmission of current information on NBA games to pagers or similar devices would be substantially deterred because any potential transmitter would know that the first entrant would quickly encounter a lower cost competitor free-riding on the originator's transmissions.

However, that is not the case in the instant matter. SportsTrax and Gamestats are each bearing their own costs of collecting factual information on NBA games, and, if one produces a product that is cheaper or otherwise superior to the other, that producer will prevail in the marketplace. This is obviously not the situation against which *INS* was intended to prevent: the potential lack of any such product or service because of the anticipation of free-riding.

For the foregoing reasons, the NBA has not shown any damage to any of its products based on free-riding by Motorola and STATS, and the NBA's misappropriation claim based on New York law is preempted.

[The Court denied the NBA's Cross-Appeal on the dismissal of all false advertising claims.]

NOTES

1. Does § 301 announce a preemption doctrine different from that in *Goldstein?* The standard formulation for § 301 preemption requires satisfaction of two conditions: (1) the subject matter for which state protection is sought must be within the subject matter of the copyright laws, and (2) the state law rights must be equivalent to the exclusive rights provided by the copyright law. Because most original works of authorship are within the copyright statute (at least once they are fixed in a tangible medium of expression) the preemption cases focus on the second condition, whether the state right is infringed by mere acts of copying (preemption) or whether the state law requires an "extra qualitative element". See Harper & Row, Publishers Inc. v. Nation Enterprises, 723 F.2d 195 (2d Cir.1983), *reversed on other grounds,* 471 U.S. 539 (1985). In *Harper* excerpts of President Ford's memoirs were published without permission. The court held that claims for conversion and tortious interference with contract were preempted because they were based on the sole act of publishing a copyrighted work. See also Ehat v. Tanner, 780 F.2d 876 (10th Cir.1985) (conversion action preempted; damages based on profits of defendant rather than fair market value is evidence that relief was granted for act of publication and not act of physical deprivation).

2. Does the "hot news" exception to preemption adopted in *Motorola* leave much room for state misappropriation law? Copyright law protects the manner of expression in a written work but not the facts contained in that work. In *INS*, INS appropriated the entire expression of the AP dispatches. The expression of these dispatches would be subject matter protected by copyright. Would rejection of "partial preemption" mean that the *INS* brand of misappropriation could not be applied to the facts of *INS*? Or does the "hot news" exception take precedence over the fact that the copyrightable material is being protected by state law? Is retaining the right of states to protect "hot news" defensible on the ground that it does not offend the "limited times" provision of the Patent and Copyright Clause of the Constitution?

3. When the Supreme Court reaffirmed *Sears* and *Compco* in *Bonito Boats* (see Chapter 1), it also reaffirmed *Goldstein.* Notwithstanding the concern in *Bonito* of state interference with the uniformity of federal protection, the Court recognized that state law could "promote originality and creativity in their own domains" where Congress has made no decision whether protection is warranted. The Court appears to accept the idea underlying § 301 that some expressions are not within the subject matter protected by copyright and thus states may continue to provide protection. With respect to "ideas," however, the Court seems to suggest the federal patent laws preempt the field. If designs were not specifically accorded patent protection, could the states grant protection?

4. Does § 301 preempt trade dress or other causes of action built on consumer confusion? Does it affect state trademark dilution statutes? In *Bonito Boats* the court goes to some length to preserve state unfair competition law protection for nonfunctional features where there was a potential for a likelihood of confusion. Application of the New York dilution statute to a bottle design used for the sale of perfume was held preempted in Escada AG v. The Limited, Inc., 810 F. Supp. 571 (S.D.N.Y. 1993):

> The Court [in *Bonito Boats*], however, did not prohibit all regulation of potentially patentable designs: it is permissible for states to require that goods be labeled, or that other precautionary steps, not directed to the copying or reproduction itself, be taken to prevent consumers from being misled as to the source of a product. Thus, a state may, without conflicting with patent law, protect trade secrets, and forbid industrial espionage. * * * In regulating unfair competition a state may also give

limited protection to a particular design to prevent consumer confusion. However, one cannot argue that the New York dilution statute serves that purpose in this case, for the statute does not require any showing of consumer confusion as to the source of goods or services. Under the statute, plaintiffs attempt to enjoin defendants from making, using or selling bottle designs which allegedly mimic the Escada bottle design. Such an application of the dilution statute is not limited to a specific goal outside the contemplation of the federal patent scheme.

Were the statute to be so applied, a would-be inventor in New York would not have to meet the rigorous standards for obtaining a patent and his right to exclude copiers would not be confined to a design patent's 14 year limit. 35 U.S.C. §§ 171, 173. When the subject matter is potentially patentable the state interest in protecting the manufacturer from dilution must yield to the national interest in uniform patent law.

5. The application of § 301 preemption requires a clear understanding of what subject matter is protected by the Federal Copyright Act and the elements of proof for copyright infringement. These issues are considered in Chapter 5.

---

(3) Trade Secrets
(a) Common Law Protection

Smith v. Snap-On Tools Corp.

United States Court of Appeals, Fifth Circuit, 1987.
833 F.2d 578.

■ ALVIN B. RUBIN, CIRCUIT JUDGE:

Basil Smith, a resident of Mississippi, made a ratchet by combining parts of two existing tools. Hoping to see his ratchet made available for sale, he brought it to the attention of Snap–On Tools, Inc., a corporation with its principal place of business in Wisconsin, by showing the ratchet to an independent dealer, then submitting a tool suggestion form to corporate headquarters. Snap–On began manufacturing and selling the ratchet without paying any part of the proceeds to Smith. Smith brought a diversity action against Snap–On, claiming that the ratchet was a trade secret, that he submitted the ratchet in confidence to Snap–On, that Snap–On misappropriated the trade secret, and that Snap–On was liable in damages to him for the misappropriation. The district court, applying Wisconsin law, held that Snap–On had misappropriated Smith's trade secret and awarded Smith damages in the amount of two and one-half percent of Snap–On's gross sales from the ratchet plus pre-judgment interest. Smith appealed the damage award, seeking to recover Snap–On's profits rather than a reasonable royalty. Snap–On cross-appealed * * *. Because the record does not support the finding that there was a confidential relationship between Smith and Snap–On, we reverse.

Wisconsin law prescribes two essential elements in a cause of action for misappropriation of trade secrets: an actual trade secret and a breach of confidence. The essence of the tort of trade secret misappropriation is the inequitable use of the secret. Even when a trade secret exists, a person who learns the secret legitimately, without any duty of confidentiality, is free to use it.

Wisconsin therefore follows trade secrets law as set out in § 757 of the Restatement of Torts. Under the Restatement, "[o]ne who discloses or uses another's trade secret, without a privilege to do so, is liable to the other if . . . his disclosure or use constitutes a breach of confidence reposed in him by the other in disclosing the secret to him." As the comment to this provision states, the proprietor of a trade secret may not unilaterally create a confidential relationship without the knowledge or consent of the party to whom he discloses the secret. No particular form of notice is necessary, however; the question is whether the recipient of the information knew or should have known that the disclosure was made in confidence.

* * *

Under certain circumstances, courts have found liability for misappropriation of trade secrets in cases involving implied confidentiality between an inventor and a manufacturer. When a manufacturer has actively solicited disclosure from an inventor, then made use of the disclosed material, the manufacturer may be liable for use or disclosure of the secret in the absence of any expressed understanding as to confidentiality. In this case, however, Smith disclosed the invention on his own initiative, without any prompting from Snap–On. Alternatively, courts have imposed liability when the disclosing inventor did not specifically request confidentiality from the manufacturer, but did make clear that the disclosure was intended as part of a course of negotiations aimed at creating a licensing agreement or entering into a similar business transaction. These cases are also distinguishable because Smith did not indicate that he wanted any pecuniary recompense for his suggestion. * * *

In February, 1978, more than two years after Smith showed the ratchet to Clark, Smith's lawyer sent a letter to the supervisor of Snap–On's Product Management Division in which he asked that Smith receive compensation. Reliance on confidentiality, however, must exist at the time the disclosure is made. An attempt to establish a special relationship long after an initial disclosure comes too late.

Because there was no confidential relationship between Smith and Snap–On, Snap–On violated no obligation to Smith by manufacturing the ratchet. We therefore REVERSE.

Phillip v. Frey

United States Court of Appeals, Fifth Circuit, 1994.
20 F. 3d 623.

■ REYNALDO G. GARZA, CIRCUIT JUDGE:

[Phillips owned and operated Ambusher, Inc., which manufactured single pole deer stands for use by hunters. The defendants approached Phillips about purchasing the business and Phillips mentioned a price of $140,000. To allow the defendants to evaluate the business, Phillips disclosed secret information regarding how the stands were manufactured. Shortly thereafter, defendants indicated they were having trouble arranging financing for the purchase and offered a lower price. Phillips refused. Seven months later defendants began marketing a similar deer stand.]

However, appellants deny that there was ever any confidential relationship established that would prevent them from using the information given to them. Appellants assert that the fact that a sale of Ambusher was contemplated does not create a per se confidential relationship between the parties.

* * *

* * * The proprietor of a trade secret may not unilaterally create a confidential relationship without the knowledge or consent of the party to whom he discloses the secret. However, no particular form of notice is needed; the question raised is whether the recipient of the information knew or should have known that the information was a trade secret and the disclosure was made in confidence.

The case before us is strikingly distinguishable [from *Smith v. Snap-On Tools Corp.*]. Even in *Snap-On* we implied that a manufacturer who has actively solicited disclosure from an inventor, and then used the disclosed material, would be liable for misappropriation of trade secrets even where the disclosure was made in the absence of any expressed understanding about confidentiality. Although Phillips never explicitly requested that the secret of his manufacturing process, which gave him a competitive advantage over competitors, be held in confidence, both parties mutually came to the negotiation table, and the disclosure was made within the course of negotiations for the sale of a business. The jury could validly accept such evidence that the defendants knew or should have known that the information was a trade secret and the disclosure was made in confidence.

Metallurgical Industries, Inc. v. Fourtek, Inc.

United States Court of Appeals, Fifth Circuit, 1986.
790 F.2d 1195.

[The alleged trade secrets relate to the reclamation of carbide from scrap metals. Metallurgical Industries (MI) began to consider a newly discovered "zinc recovery process" using a furnace. MI purchased such a furnace from Therm–O–Vac but it proved unsuccessful until MI added a number of modifications. Subsequently MI sought a second furnace and disclosed its own modifications to Consarc, another furnace manufacturer. Consarc was unwilling to manufacture the furnace so MI turned once again to Therm–O–Vac which produced a second furnace incorporating the modifications. Therm–O–Vac went bankrupt and its former employees formed the defendant, Fourtek, which produced for Smith International a recovery furnace incorporating MI's modifications. MI filed suit for misappropriation of trade secrets against Smith and the former Therm–O–Vac employees (Bielefeldt, Montesino, Boehm and Sarvadi) even though Smith had never put the furnace to commercial operation. The trial court granted the defendants' motions for directed verdict finding there were no trade secrets involved.]

■ GEE, Circuit Judge.

* * *

III. Defining a "Trade Secret"

We begin by reviewing the legal definition of a trade secret. Of course, to qualify as one, the subject matter involved must, in fact, be a secret; "[m]atters of general knowledge in an industry cannot be appropriated by one as his secret." Wissman v. Boucher, 150 Tex. 326, 240 S.W.2d 278, 280 (1951); * * *. Smith emphasizes the absence of any secret because the basic zinc recovery process has been publicized in the trade. Acknowledging the publicity of the zinc recovery process, however, we nevertheless conclude that Metallurgical's particular modification efforts can be as yet unknown to the industry. A general description of the zinc recovery process reveals nothing about the benefits unitary heating elements and vacuum pump filters can provide to that procedure. That the scientific principles involved are generally known does not necessarily refute Metallurgical's claim of trade secrets.

Metallurgical, furthermore, presented evidence to back up its claim. One of its main witnesses was Arnold Blum, a consultant very influential in the decisions to modify the furnaces. Blum testified as to his belief that Metallurgical's changes were unknown in the carbide reclamation industry. The evidence also shows Metallurgical's efforts to keep secret its modifications. Blum testified that he noted security measures taken to conceal the furnaces from all but authorized personnel. The furnaces were in areas hidden from public view, while signs warned all about restricted access. Company policy, moreover, required everyone authorized to see the furnace to sign a non-disclosure agreement. These measures constitute evidence probative of the existence of secrets. One's subjective belief of a secret's existence suggests that the secret exists. Security measures, after all, cost money; a manufacturer therefore presumably would not incur these costs if it believed its competitors already knew about the information involved. * * *

Smith argues, however, that Metallurgical's disclosure to other parties vitiated the secrecy required to obtain legal protection. As mentioned before, Metallurgical revealed its information to Consarc Corporation in 1978; it also disclosed information in 1980 to La Floridienne, its European licensee of carbide reclamation technology. Because both these disclosures occurred before Bielefeldt allegedly misappropriated the knowledge of modifications, others knew of the information when the Smith furnace was built. This being so, Smith argues, no trade secret in fact existed.

Although the law requires secrecy, it need not be absolute. Public revelation would, of course, dispel all secrecy, but the holder of a secret need not remain totally silent:

He may, without losing his protection, communicate it to employees involved in its use. He may likewise communicate it to others pledged to secrecy. . . . Nevertheless, a substantial element of secrecy must exist, so that except by the use of improper means, there would be difficulty in acquiring the information.

Restatement of Torts, § 757 Comment b (1939). We conclude that a holder may divulge his information to a limited extent without destroying its status as a trade secret. To hold otherwise would greatly limit the holder's ability to profit from his secret. If disclosure to others is made to further the holder's economic interests, it should, in appropriate circumstances, be considered a limited disclosure that does not destroy the requisite secrecy. The only question is whether we are dealing with a limited disclosure here.

Prior case law provides no guidance on what constitutes limited disclosure. Metallurgical cites Hyde Corp. v. Huffines, 158 Tex. 566, 314 S.W.2d 763, cert. denied, 358 U.S. 898 (1958), and Sikes v. McGraw Edison Co., 665 F.2d 731 (5th Cir.), cert. denied 458 U.S. 1108 (1982), in contending that subsequent disclosure of a trade secret does not free one from the constraint of a prior confidential disclosure. In both of these cases, however, publication of the trade secret by its holder followed an improper use by one in whom the holder had confided. This factual difference renders these cases inapposite.

Looking instead to the policy considerations involved, we glean two reasons why Metallurgical's disclosures to others are limited and therefore insufficient to extinguish the secrecy Metallurgical's other evidence has suggested. First, the disclosures were not public announcements; rather, Metallurgical divulged its information to only two businesses with whom it was dealing. This case thus differs from Luccous v. J.C. Kinley Co., 376 S.W.2d 336 (Tex.1964), in which the court concluded that the design of a device could not be a trade secret because it had been patented—and thus revealed to all the world—before any dealing between the parties. Second, the disclosures were made to further Metallurgical's economic interests. Disclosure to Consarc was made with the hope that Consarc could build the second furnace. A longstanding agreement gave La Floridienne the right, as a licensee, to the information in exchange for royalty payments. Metallurgical therefore revealed its discoveries as part of business transactions by which it expected to profit.

Metallurgical's case would have been stronger had it also presented evidence of confidential relationships with these two companies, but we are unwilling to regard this failure as conclusively disproving the limited nature of the disclosures. Smith correctly points out that Metallurgical bears the burden of showing the existence of confidential relationships. Contrary to Smith's assertion, however, confidentiality is not a requisite; it is only a factor to consider. Whether a disclosure is limited is an issue the resolution of which depends on weighing many facts. The inferences from those facts, construed favorably to Metallurgical, is that it wished only to profit from its secrets in its business dealings, not to reveal its secrets to the public. We therefore are unpersuaded by Smith's argument.

Existing law, however, emphasizes other requisites for legal recognition of a trade secret. In *Huffines*, 314 S.W.2d 763, a seminal case of trade secret law, Texas adopted the widely-recognized pronouncements of the American Law Institute's Restatement of the Law. The Texas Supreme Court quoted the Restatement's definition of a trade secret:

> A trade secret may consist of any formula, pattern, device or compilation of information which is used in one's business, and which gives him an opportunity to obtain an advantage over competitors who do not know it. It may be a chemical compound, a process of manufacturing, treating or preserving materials, a pattern for a machine or other device or a list of customers.

Id. at 776, *quoting* Restatement of Torts, § 757 Comment b (1939). From this the criterion of value to the holder of the alleged secret arises, a criterion we have noted before. * * *

Metallurgical met the burden of showing the value of its modifications. Lawrence Lorman, the company's vice president, testified that the zinc recovery process gave Metallurgical an advantage over its two competitors by aiding in the production of the highest quality reclaimed carbide powder. The quality of the powder, in fact, makes it an alternative to the more costly virgin carbide. Lorman testified that customers regarded Metallurgical's zinc reclaimed powder as a better product than that reclaimed by the cold-stream process used by others. This evidence clearly indicates that the modifications that led to the commercial operation of the zinc recovery furnace provided a clear advantage over the competition.

Another requisite is the cost of developing the secret device or process. * * * No question exists that Metallurgical expended much time, effort, and money to make the necessary changes. It clearly has met the burden of demonstrating the effort involved in making a complex manufacturing process work.

That the cost of devising the secret and the value the secret provides are criteria in the legal formulation of a trade secret shows the equitable underpinnings of this area of the law. It seems only fair that one should be able to keep and enjoy the fruits of his labor. If a businessman has worked hard, has used his imagination, and has taken bold steps to gain an advantage over his competitors, he should be able to profit from his efforts. Because a commercial advantage can vanish once the competition learns of it, the law should protect the businessman's efforts to keep his achievements secret. As is discussed below, this is an area of law in which simple fairness still plays a large role.

We do not say, however, that all these factors need exist in every case. Because each case must turn on its own facts, no standard formula for weighing the factors can be devised. Secrecy is always required, of course, but beyond that there are no universal requirements. In a future case, for example, should the defendant's breach of confidence be particularly egregious, the injured party might still seek redress in court despite the possibility that the subject matter was discovered at little or no cost or that the object of secrecy is not of great value to him. The definition of "trade secret" will therefore be determined by weighing all equitable considerations. It is easy to recognize the possibility of a trade secret here, however, because Metallurgical presented evidence of all three factors discussed above.

* * *

IV. Existence of a Confidential Relationship

Deciding whether a confidential relationship existed between Metallurgical and Bielefeldt must naturally precede an inquiry into his possible breach of Metallurgical's confidence. * * *

* * * Our review of the evidence on the existence of a confidential relationship is hampered to some degree by the district court's exclusion of several items of evidence. As we discuss below, the exclusions were improper; but regardless of the evidence excluded, the record contains testimony of Metallurgical's president, Ira Friedman, that he informed Bielefeldt of the confidentiality Metallurgical expected. Although these references are few, they would have sufficed to allow a reasonable jury to have believed that a confidential relationship existed between Metallurgical and Bielefeldt.

V. Obtaining Secrets From Another

At this point we must devote separate attention to Smith, which stands in a different light from Bielefeldt. It had no significant dealings with Metallurgical and apparently was not heavily involved in the design of the furnace it purchased. The question therefore becomes whether Smith as purchaser, and thus as beneficiary of Bielefeldt's alleged misappropriation, can also be held liable for it.

The law imposes liability not only on those who wrongfully misappropriate trade secrets by breach of confidence but also, in certain situations, on others who might benefit from the breach:

> One who discloses or uses another's trade secret, without a privilege to do so, is liable to the other if . . . (c) he learned the secret from a third person with notice of the facts that it was a secret and that the third person's disclosure of it was otherwise a breach of his duty to the other. . . .

* * *

> One has notice of facts under the rule stated in this Section when he knows of them or when he should know of them. . . . He should know of them if, from the information which he has, a reasonable man would infer the facts in question, or if, under the circumstances, a reasonable man would be put on inquiry and an inquiry pursued with reasonable intelligence and diligence would disclose the facts.

Restatement, § 757 & comment 1. Under this standard, we believe a reasonable jury could find that Smith should have inquired into the relationship between Bielefeldt and Metallurgical. Testimony shows that, during negotiations for the purchase of a furnace, Bielefeldt told Smith of his current involvement in then-pending litigation with Metallurgical regarding trade secrets in New Jersey. Smith learned that Metallurgical claimed ownership of the design and manufacturing processes of the zinc recovery furnace, a furnace which Smith wished Bielefeldt to build. Apparently satisfied by Bielefeldt's assertion of the meritlessness of Metallurgical's claims, Smith eventually gave him the go-ahead for construction of the furnace. There is no indication that it ever investigated the danger that Bielefeldt was wrongfully misappropriating the ideas of others. The evidence as it stood at the end of Metallurgical's presentation thus suggests that Smith knew of possible problems and did nothing but rely on Bielefeldt's dismissals. We think that this inattention to possible wrongdoing, unless refuted, amounts to a failure to reasonably inquire into the facts involved. Under § 757(c), Smith might therefore be held accountable, provided it used any trade secrets conveyed. This brings us to the next issue.

VI. Disclosure or Use of a Trade Secret

Wrongful misappropriation occurs if one "discloses or uses another's trade secret without a privilege to do so . . . ." Restatement, § 757. The district court directed verdict for appellees in part because it saw no evidence of Bielefeldt's actual use or disclosure of Metallurgical's secrets. In reviewing this conclusion, we keep in mind the rule of *Boeing Co. v. Shipman* [411 F.2d. 365 (5th Cir. 1969] by scouring the record for reasonable inferences favorable to Metallurgical. One fact jumps out from this review: in their original form, the furnaces delivered to Metallurgical differed from those that Smith purchased. The former furnaces lacked the key features needed to achieve commercial operation, while the latter possessed those features—features that Metallurgical had devised by extensive and expensive trial and error. Bielefeldt himself testified that he did not look to public sources of information in designing the Smith furnace; he instead claimed that he relied on his memory. That his earlier efforts lacked the features at issue suggests that his "memories" may well have been of working with Metallurgical. This issue is therefore an inappropriate ground for a directed verdict.

Smith's liability can arise, however, only if it in turn used the secrets gained from Bielefeldt. "Use," as it turns out, is not so easily defined. Smith claims that it never used any secrets gained because its inability to procure substantial quantities of scrap carbide prevented commercial operation of the furnace Fourtek provided. [University Computing Co. v. Lykes-Youngstown Corp., 504 F.2d. 518 (5th Cir. 1974)] guides us in determining commercial use. We must first recognize the unfortunate blurring of analyses in that case. The *Lykes–Youngstown* court's discussion of commercial use was in the context of inquiring whether damages might be available. It is preferable, of course, to divorce these concepts. Commercial use is an element of the tort as announced in § 757 of the Restatement; while the nature of the use may be relevant in determining the proper extent of damages, its existence must also be shown to establish wrongdoing in the first place. Despite this confusion, *Lykes–Youngstown* provides useful analysis.

Metallurgical looked to that case in arguing that the law provides a liberal definition of "commercial use." *Lykes–Youngstown* does indeed state a broad definition; "any misappropriation, followed by an exercise of control and dominion . . . must constitute a commercial use . . . ." 504 F.2d at 542. *Lykes–Youngstown* differs from our case, however, in one very important respect. It was a case in which "the trade secret itself was what was to be sold . . . ." Id. at 540. The court there explicitly contrasted a case like ours, "where the trade secret is used to improve manufacturing, and subsequently manufactured items were sold at a profit . . . ." Id. Although the court made this distinction in determining the proper method of computing damages, we think it also applies logically to developing a definition of "use." The discussion in *Lykes–Youngstown* following this distinction is therefore inapposite to our case, for which we instead employ the everyday meaning of the term. If Smith has not put the furnace into commercial operation to produce carbide powder it can then use, then no commercial use has occurred. Because Metallurgical failed to provide any evidence that Smith has so far benefitted from any misappropriation, directed verdict in Smith's favor was proper. Should it in future seek to profit from use or sale of the furnace, a new fact situation will be presented.

* * *

VIII. Remedies and Other Matters

We now come to the issue of remedies available to Metallurgical. The district court apparently found crucial Smith's inability to operate its furnace profitably. Because there was no commercial use, it concluded that damages were unavailable. We have already concluded that Smith did not "use" the alleged secrets Bielefeldt provided; to say that this circumstance precludes all remedies goes too far, however. The court failed to distinguish consideration of the individual appellees; Smith is out of the picture, but Bielefeldt remains. Should he be found liable on retrial, the appropriate damages should be based on the tenets of *Lykes–Youngstown*. We there adopted the concept of the "reasonable royalty." This does not mean a simple percentage of actual profits; instead, the trier of fact, should it find Bielefeldt liable, must determine "the actual value of what has been appropriated." 504 F.2d at 537, quoting Vitro Corp. v. Hall Chemical Co., 292 F.2d 678, 683 (6th Cir.1961). We later expounded this concept:

> [T]he proper measure is to calculate what the parties would have agreed to as a fair price for licensing the defendant to put the trade secret to the use the defendants intended at the time the misappropriation took place. In calculating what a fair licensing price would have been had the parties agreed, the trier of fact should consider such factors as the resulting and foreseeable changes in the parties' competitive posture; the prices past purchasers or licensees may have paid; the total value of the secret to the plaintiff, including the plaintiff's development cost and the importance of the secret to the plaintiff's business; the nature and extent of the use the defendant intended for the secret, and finally whatever other unique factors in the particular case might have been affected by the parties' agreement, such as the ready availability of alternative process.

Id. at 540. Estimation of damages, however, should not be based on sheer speculation. If too few facts exist to permit the trier of fact to calculate proper damages, then a reasonable remedy in law is unavailable. In that instance, a permanent injunction is a proper remedy for the breach of a confidential relationship. * * *

The district court's order is AFFIRMED in part, REVERSED in part, and the cause is REMANDED.

OMNITECH INTERNATIONAL INC. v. THE CLOROX CO., 11 F.3d 1316 (5th Cir.), cert. denied 513 U.S. 815 (1994). [Clorox entered into a confidential relationship with Omnitech that permitted Clorox to evaluate Omnitech's "Dr. X" line of insecticides as part of Clorox's interest in entering the insecticide business. While the evaluation was being conducted, American Cyanamid announced the public auction of its Shulton Division which marketed "Combat" insecticides. Clorox ultimately purchased Shulton and broke off negotiations with Omnitech. Omnitech sued for misappropriation of its trade secrets. The court, holding that a cause of action for misappropriation of trade secrets requires proof that the defendant either disclosed or used the trade secret, found for Clorox:]

At best, and as Omnitech conceded at oral argument, Omnitech claims that its trade secrets made Clorox "smarter" about the market in investigating the potential Combat purchase. Certainly "misappropriation" of a trade secret means more than simply using knowledge gained through a variety of experiences, including analyses of possible target companies, to evaluate a potential purchase. To hold otherwise would lead to one of two unacceptable results: (i) every time a company entered into preliminary negotiations for a possible purchase of another company's assets in which the acquiring company was given limited access to the target's trade secrets, the acquiring party would effectively be precluded from evaluating other potential targets; or (ii) the acquiring company would, as a practical matter, be forced to make a purchase decision without the benefit of examination of the target company's most important assets—its trade secrets.

NOTES

1. Trade secret law can be applied in different contexts such as where an unsolicited idea is disclosed (*Snap–On Tools*), an employee competes with his former employer (*Metallurgical*), information is disclosed during negotiations for the sale of a business (*Omnitech*), or where persons without any relationship to or contact with the owner of the information misappropriate its value (*Christopher, infra*). Should the context make a difference in fashioning the doctrinal content of trade secret law? Are the policies at stake in each of these contexts the same?

2. Does trade secret law solve the Arrow paradox?

3. *Subject matter protected.* Section 776 of the Restatement, cited in *Metallurgical*, defined a "trade secret" with some specificity. Section 1 of the

Uniform Trade Secrets Act appears to expand the definition: " 'Trade secret' means information, including a formula, pattern, compilation, program, device, method, technique or process, that: (1) derives independent economic value, actual or potential from not being generally known to, and not being readily ascertainable by proper means by, other persons who can obtain economic value from its disclosure or use, and (ii) is the subject of efforts that are reasonable under the circumstances to maintain its secrecy." The Restatement, Third, of Unfair Competition, § 39 (1995) expanded the definition to include all economically valuable information. See Comment *d*:

> The prior Restatement of this topic limited the subject matter of trade secret law to information capable of "continuous use in the operation of a business," thus excluding information relating to single events such as secret bids and impending business announcements or information whose secrecy is quickly destroyed by commercial exploitation. See Restatement of Torts § 757, Comment *b* (1939). Both the case law and the prior Restatement, however, offered protection against the improper acquisition of such short-term information under rules virtually identical to those applicable to trade secrets. See *id.* § 759, Comment *c*. The Restatement, Second, of Agency in § 396 similarly protects both trade secrets and "other similar confidential matters" from unauthorized use or disclosure following the termination of an agency relationship. The definition of "trade secret" adopted in the Uniform Trade Secrets Act does not include any requirement relating to the duration of the information's economic value. See Uniform Trade Secrets Act § 1(4) and the accompanying Comment. The definition adopted in this Section similarly contains no requirement that the information afford a continuous or long-term advantage.

How easy will it be to apply trade secret doctrine to such economically valuable information as knowledge that a particular activity is profitable or that a particular firm is excessively risk adverse, or that the CEO of a company has a weakness for Cuban cigars?

4. Are the idea submission cases just another example of application of the law of trade secrets? See Restatement, Third, of Unfair Competition § 39, Comment *h*.

5. *Customer Lists.* One of the more troubling issues arising from the employment context is whether customer lists are protected as trade secrets. Should an employee who learns the names and requirements of customers of his employer be entitled to use the information for a subsequent employer? The Restatement (Second) of Agency, § 396 (1958) proposed a test that prohibited a former employee from using or disclosing "written lists of names" although the agent "is entitled to use * * * names of the customers retained in his memory, if not acquired in violation of his duty as agent." The memory rule has been controversial. Compare, Developments—Competitive Torts, 77 Harv. L. Rev. 888, 956 (1964) ("This 'memory' rule in most cases seems to have little merit other than as an arbitrary rule of thumb.") with Blake, Employee Agreements Not to Compete, 73 Harv. L. Rev. 625, 656 (1960) ("The explanation seems to be that the 'memory' rule of thumb, in application, allows the former employee to solicit those customers whom he has played some personal role in obtaining or retaining for the former employer, giving him the benefit of a rather wide margin of doubt."). The Restatement (Third) of Unfair Competition §42, comment *j* (1995) draws no absolute rule but suggests that the manner of taking by the employee may be evidence of the value or secrecy of the list. For a modern view see Stampede Tool Warehouse, Inc. v. May, 272 Ill. App. 3d 580, 651 N.E.2d 209 (Ill.App. 1995):

In determining whether information is a trade secret, the focus of both the common law and the ITSA is on the secrecy of the information sought to be protected. The key to secrecy is the ease with which information can be readily duplicated without involving considerable time, effort or expense.

Under the ITSA [Illinois Trade Secret Act], there are two requirements to consider: (1) whether the customer list is sufficiently secret to derive economic value, actual or potential, from not being generally known to other persons who can obtain economic value from its disclosure or use; and (2) whether the customer list is the subject of efforts that are reasonable under the circumstances to maintain its secrecy or confidentiality.

Section 2(d)(2) of the ITSA is similar to the common law factors used in determining whether information is a trade secret, which include: (1) the extent to which the information is known outside the employer's business; (2) the extent to which it is known by employees and others involved in the business; (3) the extent of measures taken by the employer to guard the secrecy of the information; (4) the value of the information to the employer and his or her competitors; (5) the amount of effort or money expended by the employer in developing the information; and (6) the ease or difficulty with which the information could be properly acquired or duplicated by others.

Although an employee's general knowledge is not a trade secret, the general knowledge in this case is the method defendants used in finding prospective customers, not the actual customer information. When the information learned is confidential, as here, it can be a trade secret.

In this case, the record shows that the customer list is a trade secret. The customer list has been developed through the laborious method of prospecting, which requires a substantial amount of time, effort, and expense by Stampede. A list of jobbers is not readily available from any one public source. Instead, the salesmen obtain a list of end users through telephone books, catalogues, and other publicly available sources; then contact those people to get the names of jobbers, who are the potential customers. The salesmen then develop a relationship with those potential customers.

In addition, Stampede protects its customer list using reasonable efforts to maintain its secrecy and confidentiality. Its offices are locked, garbage is checked daily, special computer access codes are used, customer information is limited to persons on a need-to-know basis, hard copies of customer lists are kept locked in the office or in Kuhn's basement at home, salesmen's call books and customer cards are kept locked up and cannot be removed from the office, and security cameras are used. Moreover, both defendants signed employee confidentiality agreements that stated that the names of Stampede's customers could not be used or disclosed because they belonged to Stampede and were confidential. As a result, we conclude that Stampede's customer list is a trade secret that is protectable under the ITSA.

We must now consider whether defendants misappropriated the trade secret. * * *

Defendants assert that Stampede's customer list is not protectable because there was no physical taking of the list, but instead was committed to memory. Defendants contend that any general knowledge or information that they took with them when they left Stampede was not a misappropriation.

In response, Stampede asserts that actual misappropriation of the trade secret information was established because they intentionally copied or memorized the customer list. Stampede argues that the ITSA does not require a plaintiff to prove actual theft or conversion of physical documents embodying the trade secret information. We agree.

Although an employee may take general knowledge or information he or she has developed during their employment, he or she may not take any confidential information, including trade secrets. That taking does not have to be a physical taking by actually copying the names. A trade secret can be misappropriated by physical copying or by memorization.

There was substantial evidence that defendants misappropriated the customer list either through copying down names or through memorization. In fact, defendants admitted that they redeveloped their customer lists by remembering the names and locations of at least some of their Stampede customers. Using memorization to rebuild a trade secret does not transform that trade secret from confidential information into non-confidential information. The memorization is one method of misappropriation. Since the trial court's findings were not against the manifest weight of the evidence, we affirm the injunctions.

Can the list of customers on a delivery route be secret if one could acquire the list by following and openly observing the delivery truck?

6. *Novelty.* Should the information protected by trade secret law have to meet some standard of novelty or inventiveness? Early courts quickly rejected any idea that the strenuous standard of inventiveness of the patent laws should apply to trade secrets. See A.O. Smith Corp. v. Petroleum Iron Works Co., 73 F.2d 531 (6th Cir.1934). At the same time courts suggest that some modest novelty standard may be imposed. If the information is not novel can it be secret? Would you expect to see a company expend resources keeping an old or known idea secret?

7. The law in this area is synthesized in Kitch, The Law and Economics of Rights in Valuable Information, 9 J. Legal Stud. 683, 683–708

(1980). The business side of the issue is discussed in Stanley H. Lieberstein, Who Owns What Is In Your Head? (1979).

PROBLEMS: TRADE SECRETS AND EMPLOYEES

1. AMP, Incorporated, is the world's leading producer of electrical and electronic connection devices. Molex is a principle competitor of AMP's Components and Assemblies Division. James Fleishhacker, a graduate of the University of Minnesota and MIT began working for AMP in 1973. By 1982, he had worked his way up to manager of the Components and Assemblies Division. His duties included approving business programs, implementing strategic policies and plans, and developing personnel. His evaluations were exceptional and he was told he had the potential to continue to rise within the company. In 1982 Molex created a Director of Marketing position and an executive search firm directed them to Fleischhacker. In 1984 Fleischhacker accepted Molex's offer of employment. Fleischhacker brings to Molex his general skill and experience in the business as well as his particular knowledge relating to the customers, methods of operation and plans of AMP. AMP seeks your advice on what they can do to prohibit Fleischhacker from exploiting on Molex's behalf his training and knowledge all acquired at AMP's expense.

2. Evan Brown is a self-described "computer geek" who begins working for DSC Communications in 1987 and signs an employment agreement making all inventions discovered by Brown during the course of his employment the property of DSC. During the period he was employed by DSC, Brown conceptualized an algorithm that could convert old computer code into modern source code. He claims he thought of the idea while coming home from a long weekend. DSC now claims rights in the invention. Brown has not reduced the algorithm to writing but carries it around in his head. Does the idea belong to DSC? Can DSC force Brown to give it to them. How do you answer Brown's question: "Does the company own your thoughts 24 hours a day?"

NOTES: TRADE SECRETS AND EMPLOYEES

1. Problem 1 illustrates a common situation. Many employers make a substantial and costly investment in their employees. They provide training and experience and inevitably disclose valuable business information. The more valuable the employee becomes the more vulnerable he is to outside inducements but his increased value comes, at least in part, from the expenditures of his employer. What are the competing public policy issues that must be balanced in these circumstances?

2. The balance between an employer's interest in secrecy and an employee's interest in mobility is often drawn by the definition of what qualifies for trade secret protection. In AMP Inc. v. Fleischhacker, 823 F.2d 1199 (7th Cir.1987) the court affirmed a judgment for the employee:

. . . While an enforceable restrictive covenant may protect material, such as confidential information revealed to an employee during the course of his employment, which does not constitute a trade secret, an employer's protection absent a restrictive covenant is narrower and extends only to trade secrets or near-permanent customer relationships. * * *

Because Mr. Fleischhacker is not subject to any enforceable contractual restrictions, AMP was first required to establish the existence of genuine trade secrets in order for injunctive relief to be warranted. * * * It is generally recognized in Illinois that at the termination of employment, an employee may not take with him confidential, particularized plans or processes developed by his employer and disclosed to him while the employer-employee relationship existed, which are unknown to others in the industry and which give the employer an advantage over his competitors. On the other hand, an employee is free to take with him general skills and knowledge acquired during his tenure with his former employer. * * * Furthermore, while recognizing that a business must be afforded protection against the wrongful appropriation of confidential information by a prior employee who held a position of confidence and trust, the Illinois Supreme Court has emphasized that:

> the right of an individual to follow and pursue the particular occupation for which he is best trained is a most fundamental right. Our society is extremely mobile and our free economy is based upon competition. One who has worked in a particular field cannot be compelled to erase from his mind all of the general skills, knowledge and expertise acquired through his experience. These skills are valuable to such employee in the market place for his services. Restraints cannot be lightly placed upon his right to compete in the area of his greatest worth.

In other cases the balance is accomplished by examining the extent to which the employment relationship imposes an implied obligation of confidentiality.

3. It is clear that the employer-employee relationship is a confidential one although not all information about the employer's business learned by the employee is protected. One factor that may be important is whether the employer gave the employee the information or whether the employee developed it himself. A leading case is Wexler v. Greenberg, 399 Pa. 569, 160 A.2d 430 (1960) where Greenberg was originally hired by Buckingham Wax Company as a chemist whose duty was to reverse engineer and reproduce competing products for sale by Buckingham. Greenberg subsequently was hired by Brite and Brite began competing with Buckingham. The court held that Greenberg had an unqualified privilege to use his technical knowledge and skill acquired during his prior employment.

See also, Winston Research Corp. v. Minnesota Min. & Mfg. Co., 350 F.2d 134 (9th Cir.1965) where former employees of MMM produced a precision tape recorder that competed with the one they had helped develop while working for MMM:

Winston argues that information is protected from disclosure only if communicated to the employee by the employer who is seeking protection, and that the information involved in this case was not disclosed by Mincom to the employees subsequently hired by Winston, but rather was developed by these employees themselves, albeit while employed by Mincom.

We need not examine the soundness of the rule for which Winston contends, or its applicability to a case such as this in which a group of specialists engaged in related facets of a single development project change their employer. The rule is apparently based upon the notion that unless the first employer conveys the information to the employee, subsequent disclosure by the employee cannot be a breach of a duty of confidence owed that employer. Futurecraft Corp. v. Clary Corp., * * * 23 Cal.Rptr. 198. As the court in *Futurecraft* recognized, an obligation not to disclose may arise from circumstances other than communication in confidence by the employer. It may also rest upon an express or implied agreement. In the present case, an agreement not to disclose might be implied from Mincom's elaborate efforts to maintain the secrecy of its development program, and the employees' knowledge of these efforts and participation in them. In any event, Mincom and its employees entered into express written agreements binding the latter not to disclose confidential information, and these agreements did not exclude information which the employee himself contributed.

4. Does the following information help solve Problem 2? If an employee is hired specifically to invent or develop new ideas, the employer is entitled to any discoveries and may assert trade secret rights as well as requiring an assignment of any subsequent patents. If the employee is not hired specifically to invent, the employee is entitled to any discoveries resulting from the performance of duties for the employer. However, if the employee uses the employer's time and facilities in developing the invention, the employer is entitled to a nonexclusive license to use the invention even if the employee subsequently obtains a patent. And the Fifth Circuit has recently held this "shop right" applies even where the employer does not provide assistance to the employee in reducing the idea to practice if the employee initially consents to the employer putting the idea into commercial use. Wommack v. Durham Pecan Co., Inc., 715 F.2d 962 (5th Cir.1983). It has been held that the employer and employee can alter the above rules by contract. Restatement, Second Agency § 397 (1958).

Section 201 of the Copyright Act, 17 U.S.C. § 201, provides that copyright vests initially in the author of a work but that in the case of a "work made for hire" the employer is considered the author, and owns the copyright unless there is a written, signed agreement to the contrary. A "work made for hire" is defined in § 101 to include a work "prepared by an employee within the scope of his or her employment. * * * " The legislative history reflects rejection of a "shop right" provision that would have given the copyright to the employee subject to the employer's royalty free right to use the work. House Comm. on Judiciary, Copyright Law Revision, H.R.Rep. No. 94–1476,

94th Cong., 2d Sess. (1976). For further discussion of the work made for hire doctrine in copyright see Chapter 5.

Section 111 of the patent laws specifically requires that the application for a patent be made by the "inventor". If the employee is the "inventor" the application must be made in the employee's name although the employee may be forced to assign the patent to the employer. On the other hand where a supervisor conceives of the invention and the employee is merely a means through which the supervisor puts the conception into practice, the supervisor would be the "inventor". In these situations there may likewise be a presumption running in favor of the employer.

5. With the doctrines considered above, how does an employer recoup the costs of training skilled employees? If employees are entitled to receive training and then establish rival business establishments will this discourage "on the job training" programs by private enterprise? Can you recommend alternatives to the present law? Consider in passing the Statute of Apprentices, 5 Eliz. 1, Ch. 4 which provided for a seven-year apprenticeship at no wages with assurance at the end of the seventh year that the apprentice could freely ply the trade. Could contractual agreements solve many of these problems?

In a similar vein, do the common law doctrines outlined above which regulate employer-employee rights to inventions serve to stimulate technological advance? If employers and employees are free to bargain over the rights to inventions and wages, do the rules of trade secrets impact adversely on incentives to innovate? Does the "shop right" rule provide an appropriate default rule in the absence of an agreement?

E. I. DuPont DeNemours & Co., Inc. v Christopher

United States Court of Appeals, Fifth Circuit, 1970.
431 F.2d 1012
cert.denied 400 U.S. 1024,, reh. denied 401 U.S. 967.

■ GOLDBERG, CIRCUIT JUDGE.

[DuPont claimed as its trade secret a secret process for producing methanol. DuPont began constructing a methanol plant in Beaumont, Texas, to use the process. The Christophers, free lance photographers, were hired by a third party to fly over and take pictures of the partially completed plant. DuPont contends that because construction of the plant was not complete, parts of the secret process was exposed and the photographs would permit a skilled person to learn the process. The Christophers refused to disclose the name of the third party who had hired them so DuPont sued them for trade secret appropriation.]

This is a case of first impression, for the Texas courts have not faced this precise factual issue, and sitting as a diversity court we must sensitize our *Erie antennae* to divine what the Texas courts would do if such a situation were presented to them. The only question involved in this interlocutory appeal is whether DuPont has asserted a claim upon which relief can be granted. The Christophers argued both at trial and before this court that they committed no "actionable wrong" in photographing the DuPont facility and passing these photographs on to their client because they conducted all of their activities in public airspace, violated no government aviation standard, did not breach any confidential relation, and did not engage in any fraudulent or illegal conduct. In short, the Christophers argue that for an appropriation of trade secrets to be wrongful there must be a trespass, other illegal conduct, or breach of a confidential relationship. We disagree.

It is true, as the Christophers assert, that the previous trade secret cases have contained one or more of these elements. However, we do not think that the Texas courts would limit the trade secret protection exclusively to these elements. On the contrary, in Hyde Corporation v. Huffines, 1958, 158 Tex. 566, 314 S.W.2d 763, the Texas Supreme Court specifically adopted the rule found in the Restatement of Torts which provides:

> "One who discloses or uses another's trade secret, without a privilege to do so, is liable to the other if
>
> (a) he discovered the secret by improper means, or
>
> (b) his disclosure or use constitutes a breach of confidence reposed in him by the other in disclosing the secret to him * * *."
> Restatement of Torts § 757 (1939).

Thus, although the previous cases have dealt with a breach of confidential relationship, a trespass, or other illegal conduct, the rule is much broader than the cases heretofore encountered. Not limiting itself to specific wrongs, Texas adopted subsection (a) of the Restatement which recognizes a cause of action for the discovery of a trade secret by any "improper" means.

The defendants, however, read Furr's Inc. v. United Specialty Advertising Co., Tex.Civ.App.1960, 338 S.W.2d 762, writ ref'd n.r.e., as limiting the Texas rule to breach of a confidential relationship. * * * We do not read *Furr's* as limiting the trade secret protection to a breach of confidential relationship when the facts of the case do raise the issue of some other wrongful conduct on the part of one discovering the trade secrets of another. If breach of confidence were meant to encompass the entire panoply of commercial improprieties, subsection (a) of the Restatement would be either surplusage or persiflage, an interpretation abhorrent to the traditional precision of the Restatement. We therefore find meaning in subsection (a) and think that the Texas Supreme Court clearly indicated by its adoption that there is a cause of action for the discovery of a trade secret by any "improper means."

The question remaining, therefore, is whether aerial photography of plant construction is an improper means of obtaining another's trade secret. We conclude that it is and that the Texas courts would so hold. The Supreme Court of that state has declared that "the undoubted tendency of the law has been to recognize and enforce higher standards of commercial morality in the business world." Hyde Corporation v. Huffines, supra, 314 S.W.2d at 773. That court has quoted with approval articles indicating that the *proper* means of gaining possession of a competitor's secret process is "through inspection and analysis" of the product in order to create a duplicate. Later another Texas court explained:

> "The means by which the discovery is made may be obvious, and the experimentation leading from known factors to presently unknown results may be simple and lying in the public domain. But these facts do not destroy the value of the discovery and will not advantage a competitor who by unfair means obtains the knowledge *without paying the price expended by the discoverer*." Brown v. Fowler, Tex.Civ.App.1958, 316 S.W.2d 111, 114, writ ref'd n.r.e. (emphasis added).

We think, therefore, that the Texas rule is clear. One may use his competitor's secret process if he discovers the process by reverse engineering applied to the finished product; one may use a competitor's process if he discovers it by his own independent research; but one may not avoid these labors by taking the process from the discoverer without his permission at a time when he is taking reasonable precautions to maintain its secrecy. To obtain knowledge of a process without spending the time and money to discover it independently is *improper* unless the holder voluntarily discloses it or fails to take reasonable precautions to ensure its secrecy.

In the instant case the Christophers deliberately flew over the DuPont plant to get pictures of a process which DuPont had attempted to keep secret. The Christophers delivered their pictures to a third party who was certainly aware of the means by which they had been acquired and who may be planning to use the information contained therein to manufacture methanol by the DuPont process. The third party has a right to use this process only if he obtains this knowledge through his own research efforts, but thus far all information indicates that the third party has gained this knowledge solely by taking it from DuPont at a time when DuPont was making reasonable efforts to preserve its secrecy. In such a situation DuPont has a valid cause of action to prohibit the Christophers from improperly discovering its trade secret and to prohibit the undisclosed third party from using the improperly obtained information.

We note that this view is in perfect accord with the position taken by the authors of the Restatement. * * *

In taking this position we realize that industrial espionage of the sort here perpetrated has become a popular sport in some segments of our industrial community. However, our devotion to free wheeling industrial competition must not force us into accepting the law of the jungle as the standard of morality expected in our commercial relations. Our tolerance of the espionage game must cease when the protections required to prevent another's spying cost so much that the spirit of inventiveness is dampened. Commercial privacy must be protected from espionage which could not have been reasonably anticipated or prevented. We do not mean to imply, however, that everything not in plain view is within the protected vale, nor that all information obtained through every extra optical extension is forbidden. Indeed, for our industrial competition to remain healthy there must be breathing room for observing a competing industrialist. A competitor can and must shop his competition for pricing and examine his products for quality, components, and methods of manufacture. Perhaps ordinary fences and roofs must be built to shut out incursive eyes, but we need not require the discoverer of a trade secret to guard against the unanticipated, the undetectable, or the unpreventable methods of espionage now available.

In the instant case DuPont was in the midst of constructing a plant. Although after construction the finished plant would have protected much of the process from view, during the period of construction the trade secret was exposed to view from the air. To require DuPont to put a roof over the unfinished plant to guard its secret would impose an enormous expense to prevent nothing more than a school boy's trick. We introduce here no new or radical ethic since our ethos has never given moral sanction to piracy. The market place must not deviate far from our mores. We should not require a person or corporation to take unreasonable precautions to prevent another from doing that which he ought not do in the first place. Reasonable precautions against predatory eyes we may require, but an impenetrable fortress is an unreasonable requirement, and we are not disposed to burden industrial inventors with such a duty in order to protect the fruits of their efforts. "Improper" will always be a word of many nuances, determined by time, place, and circumstances. We therefore need not proclaim a catalogue of commercial improprieties. Clearly, however, one of its commandments does say "thou shall not appropriate a trade secret through deviousness under circumstances in which countervailing defenses are not reasonably available."

* * *

The decision of the trial court is affirmed and the case remanded to that court for proceedings on the merits.

Rockwell Graphic Systems, Inc. v. DEV Industries, Inc.

United States Court of Appeals, Seventh Circuit, 1991.
925 F.2d 174.

■ POSNER, CIRCUIT JUDGE.

[Rockwell manufactures printing presses and sells replacement parts which are often manufactured by outside vendors. Rockwell supplies these vendors with "piece part drawings" that indicate the dimensions and tolerances for making the parts. Parts cannot be successfully reverse engineered by examining the parts themselves because the parts do not disclose the method of manufacture or the tolerances required. Fleck and Peloso left responsible positions with Rockwell to work for DEV. When DEV began making parts for Rockwell presses, Rockwell filed suit and through pretrial discovery found DEV to be in possession of 100 of Rockwell's piece part drawings. DEV claimed it lawfully obtained the drawings from the outside vendors and that the drawings were not trade secrets because Rockwell did not take adequate precautions to keep them secret.]

On this, the critical, issue [whether Rockwell took adequate precautions to keep the drawing secret], the record shows the following. (Because summary judgment was granted to DEV, we must construe the facts as favorably to Rockwell as is reasonable to do.) Rockwell keeps all its engineering drawings, including both piece part and assembly drawings, in a vault. Access not only to the vault, but also to the building in which it is located, is limited to authorized employees who display identification. These are mainly engineers, of whom Rockwell employs 200. They are required to sign agreements not to disseminate the drawings, or disclose their contents, other than as authorized by the company. An authorized employee who needs a drawing must sign it out from the vault and return it when he has finished with it. But he is permitted to make copies, which he is to destroy when he no longer needs them in his work. The only outsiders allowed to see piece part drawings are the vendors (who are given copies, not originals). They too are required to sign confidentiality agreements, and in addition each drawing is stamped with a legend stating that it contains proprietary material. Vendors, like Rockwell's own engineers, are allowed to make copies for internal working purposes, and although the confidentiality agreement that they sign requires the vendor to return the drawing when the order has been filled, Rockwell does not enforce this requirement. The rationale for not enforcing it is that the vendor will need the drawing if Rockwell reorders the part. Rockwell even permits unsuccessful bidders for a piece part contract to keep the drawings, on the theory that the high bidder this round may be the low bidder the next. But it does consider the ethical standards of a machine shop before making it a vendor, and so far as appears no shop has ever abused the confidence reposed in it.

The mere fact that Rockwell gave piece part drawings to vendors—that is, disclosed its trade secrets to "a limited number of outsiders for a particular purpose"—did not forfeit trade secret protection. On the contrary, such disclosure, which is often necessary to the efficient exploitation of a trade secret, imposes a duty of confidentiality on the part of the person to whom the disclosure is made. But with 200 engineers checking out piece part drawings and making copies of them to work from, and numerous vendors receiving copies of piece part drawings and copying them, tens of thousands of copies of these drawings are floating around outside Rockwell's vault, and many of these outside the company altogether. Although the magistrate and the district judge based their conclusion that Rockwell had not made adequate efforts to maintain secrecy in part at least on the irrelevant fact that it took no measures at all to keep its assembly drawings secret, DEV in defending the judgment that it obtained in the district court argues that Rockwell failed to take adequate measures to keep even the piece part drawings secret. Not only did Rockwell not limit copying of those drawings or insist that copies be returned; it did not segregate the piece part drawings from the assembly drawings and institute more secure procedures for the former. So Rockwell could have done more to maintain the confidentiality of its piece part drawings than it did, and we must decide whether its failure to do more was so plain a breach of the obligation of a trade secret owner to make reasonable efforts to maintain secrecy as to justify the entry of summary judgment for the defendants.

The requirement of reasonable efforts has both evidentiary and remedial significance, and this regardless of which of the two different conceptions of trade secret protection prevails. (Both conceptions have footholds in Illinois law, as we shall see.) The first and more common merely gives a remedy to a firm deprived of a competitively valuable secret as the result of an independent legal wrong, which might be conversion or other trespass or the breach of an employment contract or of a confidentiality agreement. Under this approach, because the secret must be taken by improper means for the taking to give rise to liability the only significance of trade secrecy is that it allows the victim of wrongful appropriation to obtain damages based on the competitive value of the information taken. The second conception of trade secrecy, illustrated by E.I. duPont de Nemours & Co. v. Christopher, 431 F.2d 1012 (5th Cir.1970), is that "trade secret" picks out a class of socially valuable information that the law should protect even against nontrespassory or other lawful conduct—in *Christopher*, photographing a competitor's roofless plant from the air while not flying directly overhead and hence not trespassing or committing any other wrong independent of the appropriation of the trade secret itself.

Since, however, the opinion in *Christopher* describes the means used by the defendant as "improper," which is also the key to liability under the first, more conventional conception of trade secret protection, it is unclear how distinct the two conceptions really are. It is not as if *Christopher* proscribes all efforts to unmask a trade secret. It specifically mentions reverse engineering as a proper means of doing so. This difference in treatment is not explained, but it may rest on the twofold idea that reverse engineering involves the use of technical skills that we want to encourage, and that anyone should have the right to take apart and to study a product that he has bought.

It should be apparent that the two different conceptions of trade secret protection are better described as different emphases. The first emphasizes the desirability of deterring efforts that have as their sole purpose and effect the redistribution of wealth from one firm to another. The second emphasizes the desirability of encouraging inventive activity by protecting its fruits from efforts at appropriation that are, indeed, sterile wealth-redistributive—not productive—activities. The approaches differ, if at all, only in that the second does not limit the class of improper means to those that fit a preexisting pigeonhole in the law of tort or contract or fiduciary duty—and it is by no means clear that the first approach assumes a closed class of wrongful acts, either.

Under the first approach, at least if narrowly interpreted so that it does not merge with the second, the plaintiff must prove that the defendant obtained the plaintiff's trade secret by a wrongful act, illustrated here by the alleged acts of Fleck and Peloso in removing piece part drawings from Rockwell's premises without authorization, in violation of their employment contracts and confidentiality agreements, and using them in competition with Rockwell. Rockwell is unable to prove directly that the 100 piece part drawings it got from DEV in discovery were stolen by Fleck and Peloso or obtained by other improper means. But if it can show that the probability that DEV could have obtained them otherwise—that is, without engaging in wrongdoing—is slight, then it will have taken a giant step toward proving what it must prove in order to recover under the first theory of trade secret protection. The greater the precautions that Rockwell took to maintain the secrecy of the piece part drawings, the lower the probability that DEV obtained them properly and the higher the probability that it obtained them through a wrongful act; the owner had taken pains to prevent them from being obtained otherwise.

Under the second theory of trade secret protection, the owner's precautions still have evidentiary significance, but now primarily as evidence that the secret has real value. For the precise means by which the defendant acquired it is less important under the second theory, though not completely unimportant; remember that even the second theory allows the unmasking of a trade secret by *some* means, such as reverse engineering. If Rockwell expended only paltry resources on preventing its piece part drawings from falling into the hands of competitors such as DEV, why should the law, whose machinery is far from costless, bother to provide Rockwell with a remedy? The information contained in the drawings cannot have been worth much if Rockwell did not think it worthwhile to make serious efforts to keep the information secret.

The remedial significance of such efforts lies in the fact that if the plaintiff has allowed his trade secret to fall into the public domain, he would enjoy a windfall if permitted to recover damages merely because the defendant took the secret from him, rather than from the public domain as it could have done with impunity. It would be like punishing a person for stealing property that he believes is owned by another but that actually is abandoned property. If it were true, as apparently it is not, that Rockwell had given the piece part drawings at issue to customers, and it had done so without requiring the customers to hold them in confidence, DEV could have obtained the drawings from the customers without committing any wrong. The harm to Rockwell would have been the same as if DEV had stolen the drawings from it, but it would have had no remedy, having parted with its rights to the trade secret. This is true whether the trade secret is regarded as property protected only against wrongdoers or (the logical extreme of the second conception, although no case—not even *Christopher*—has yet embraced it and the patent statute might preempt it) as property protected against the world. In the first case, a defendant is perfectly entitled to obtain the property by lawful conduct if he can, and he can if the property is in the hands of persons who themselves committed no wrong to get it. In the second case the defendant is perfectly entitled to obtain the property if the plaintiff has abandoned it by giving it away without restrictions.

* * *

But only in an extreme case can what is a "reasonable" precaution be determined on a motion for summary judgment, because the answer depends on a balancing of costs and benefits that will vary from case to case and so require estimation and measurement by persons knowledgeable in the particular field of endeavor involved. On the one hand, the more the owner of the trade secret spends on preventing the secret from leaking out, the more he demonstrates that the secret has real value deserving of legal protection, that he really was hurt as a result of the misappropriation of it, and that there really was misappropriation. On the other hand, the more he spends, the higher his costs. The costs can be indirect as well as direct. The more Rockwell restricts access to its drawings, either by its engineers or by the vendors, the harder it will be for either group to do the work expected of it. Suppose Rockwell forbids *any* copying of its drawings. Then a team of engineers would have to share a single drawing, perhaps by passing it around or by working in the same room, huddled over the drawing. And how would a vendor be able to make a piece part—would Rockwell have to bring all that work in house? Such reconfigurations of patterns of work and production are far from costless; and therefore perfect security is not optimum security.

There are contested factual issues here, bearing in mind that what is reasonable is itself a fact for purposes of Rule 56 of the civil rules. Obviously Rockwell took some precautions, both physical (the vault security, the security guards—one of whom apprehended Peloso *in flagrante delicto*) and contractual, to maintain the confidentiality of its piece part drawings. Obviously it could have taken more precautions. But at a cost, and the question is whether the additional benefit in security would have exceeded that cost. We do not suggest that the question can be answered with the same precision with which it can be posed, but neither can we say that no reasonable jury could find that Rockwell had done enough and could then go on to infer misappropriation from a combination of the precautions Rockwell took and DEV's inability to establish the existence of a lawful source of the Rockwell piece part drawings in its possession.

This is an important case because trade secret protection is an important part of intellectual property, a form of property that is of growing importance to the competitiveness of American industry. Patent protection is at once costly and temporary, and therefore cannot be regarded as a perfect substitute. If trade secrets are protected only if their owners take extravagant, productivity-impairing measures to maintain their secrecy, the incentive to invest resources in discovering more efficient methods of production will be reduced, and with it the amount of invention. And given the importance of the case we must record our concern at the brevity of the district court's opinion granting summary judgment (one and a half printed pages). Brevity is the soul of wit, and all that, and the district judge did have the benefit of a magistrate's opinion; but it is vital that commercial litigation not appear to be treated as a stepchild in the federal courts. The future of the nation depends in no small part on the efficiency of industry, and the efficiency of industry depends in no small part on the protection of intellectual property.

The judgment is reversed and the case remanded to the district court for further proceedings consistent with this opinion (including reinstatement of the pendent counts).

NOTES

1. What if DuPont had installed the components of the secret process before the walls of the new plant had been constructed and the

Christophers had taken their photographs from an adjoining sidewalk? Would the result be different? What if a DuPont competitor had sent its chief engineer to walk along the sidewalk and view the process? See Restatement, Third, of Unfair Competition § 43, Illustration 3 (1995). What if the defendants had systematically rifled through DuPont's trash and discovered copies of the plans for the plant? Does Judge Posner provide a principle for determining when the acquisition of a trade secret is "improper"?

2. To what extent is the reasonableness of the precautions taken dictated by the assumption the trade secret owner makes about the likely level of investment by others in uncovering the secret? If DuPont knew of a customary practice by those in the methanol industry to take fly-over photographs, should it be required to complete the roof before installing the process? Or should the law of trade secrets prohibit all unauthorized appropriation and thus reduce the need for investment in security. Aren't all security investments wasteful?

3. Why is reverse engineering, but not fly-over photography, permissible? Professor Posner argues that authorizing aerial photography would not generate information but rather encourage the expenditure of resources to conceal the plant. Reverse engineering, on the other hand, will generate information, presumably because the only self-help available to the trade secret owner is to forego exploiting the product. Posner, The Right of Privacy, 12 Ga.L.Rev. 393, 410 (1978). But can a product be designed to make it more difficult to copy, like, for instance, a dollar bill?

4. In Chicago Lock Co. v. Fanberg, 676 F.2d 400 (9th Cir.1982), the Chicago Lock Company made a tubular lock which was particularly secure because its keys were difficult to duplicate. The Company maintained a file on all locks so that a customer could obtain a replacement key directly from the company. Owners of locks could also have a locksmith "pick" the lock and duplicate the key. When a locksmith "picks" a lock he will usually record the serial number and the tumbler combination so that if called again he does not have to repick the lock. Fanberg decided to publish to other locksmiths a compilation of the serial numbers and tumbler combinations for these tubular locks and solicited from other locksmiths their records as well as using his own. Chicago Lock, regarding this information as its trade secret sought to prevent publication of the compilation. Held: Defendant did not use unfair means or violate a confidential relationship. Improper means under the Restatement assumes a duty not to disclose and since the tumbler combinations were in all instances secured by reverse engineering no duty not to disclose can be implied. The court also rejected the argument that since the locksmith owed a duty of confidentiality to his customers (the lock owners) that violation of this duty was also a breach of a duty to the company.

5. Compare with *Christopher,* Dow Chemical Co. v. United States, 476 U.S. 227 (1986), where it was held that the Environmental Protection Agency's aerial inspection of a chemical plant to detect violations of the Clean Air Act did not violate the Fourth Amendment.

6. Whether information is secret or is reasonably ascertainable by others is a component of whether the defendant's conduct is "improper". In *DuPont*, the process was not reasonably ascertainable because of the extraordinary lengths necessary to discover the secret. The issue of reasonably ascertainable arises in another context. Assume that the defendant acquired a secret by means that were clearly improper, i.e., breach of confidence. Should the defendant be able to successfully argue that "I could have learned the secret by proper means and therefore its not a trade secret"? Consider the following variations:

(a) The defendant acquires the secret under a confidentiality agreement and subsequently the secret is published by the owner. Can the defendant use the secret after it's in the public domain?

(b) The defendant acquires the secret design for a product within the context of a confidential relationship. The product is sold on the open market and can be easily reverse engineered.

(c) The same facts as (b) except that the defendant proves the product could be reverse engineered only with a significant investment of time and effort.

7. Assume in *DuPont* that the "third party" who hired the Christophers was a national news magazine investigating a tip that the new process for making methanol represented considerable risks to the environment. Could DuPont assert its trade secret rights to enjoin publication of the photographs?

8. What if a trade secret is disclosed by mistake? The plaintiff company sells its old desk top computers to a used computer store. Plaintiff's employees forget to reformat one of the hard drives which contains a secret and valuable customer list. The purchaser of the computer finds the list and sells it to the defendant, one of plaintiff's competitors. Can plaintiff enjoy the defendant from using the information? Or consider the result where a company faxes a secret formula to the wrong number. What result if there is a legend on the fax cover sheet saying: "This material is confidential and constitutes a trade secret. If you receive this transmission by mistake, please return to the sender without reading it?"

Brunswick Corp. v. Outboard Marine Corp.

Supreme Court of Illinois, 1980.
79 Ill.2d 475, 38 Ill.Dec. 781, 404 N.E.2d 205.

* * * [Mercury and Outboard (OMC) compete in manufacturing and sale of outboard motors and in outboard motorboat racing. Mercury adapted a Bendix fuel-injection system for its outboard motors and had great success. Anderson, while an employee of Mercury, worked on the development and refinement of the system which was protected by Mercury as a trade secret. In January, 1975, a Mercury race driver named Van der Velden described the Mercury adaptation to officers of OMC. In December, 1976, Anderson left Mercury and began working for OMC. In May, 1977, Mercury learned that Anderson had ordered a Bendix-injection system and brought suit.]

■ RYAN, JUSTICE.

* * *

The trial court found the time required to successfully install a Bendix mechanical-fuel-injection system on an outboard engine for use in competitive boat racing would be, from conception to project completion, anywhere from 8 to 12 months. It also found that if OMC had tried to install a Bendix fuel-injection system on its racing engines, using the Van der Velden disclosures, it could have successfully completed the project by not later than November 30, 1976. In granting defendant's motion for summary judgment the trial court relied upon Northern Petrochemical Co. v. Tomlinson (7th Cir.1973), 484 F.2d 1057. In *Northern,* a diversity case governed by Illinois law, the Federal court interpreted ILG Industries, Inc. v. Scott (1971), 49 Ill.2d 88, 273 N.E.2d 393, and Schulenburg v. Signatrol, Inc. (1965), 33 Ill.2d 379, 212 N.E.2d 865, as holding that an abstention by a thief from the use of a trade secret, for a period in which it could have been developed lawfully, prevented the victim from enjoining the use at a later time. Thus, the trial court determined this action was barred.

The appellate court examined the *Northern* opinion and concluded that the Federal court of appeals misconstrued Illinois law. We do not find the holding in *Northern* to be helpful in this case. Also *ILG Industries* and *Schulenberg,* while helpful, are also not in point.

* * *

The judicial application of trade secret law has advanced two doctrinal bases for trade secret protection: (1) encouragement of invention and (2) maintenance of commercial morality. * * * Actually, a third element enters into the shaping of the remedy, that is, a public interest in having free competition in the sale and manufacture of goods not protected by a valid patent. * * *

In applying the three doctrinal bases to the facts of a case, one must consider that a permanent injunction, while punishing the wrongdoer, thereby promoting commercial morality, would, if the secret were lawfully discoverable, give to the plaintiff a windfall protection and would subvert the public interest in fostering competition and in allowing employees to make full use of their knowledge and ability. If no injunctive relief is granted, the faithless employee and wrongdoing competitor would be unpunished and would retain the benefit of a head start advantage over legitimate competitors. The innovator of the trade secret would also be afforded no protection. By enjoining the use of wrongfully acquired trade secrets for the approximate length of time it would require a legitimate competitor to develop a competitive product following a lawful disclosure of the information, the wrongdoer is deprived of any advantage from his wrongdoing, the developer of the trade secret is placed in the same position it would have occupied if the breach of confidence had not occurred, and the minimum restraint consistent with the other objectives would be placed upon competitors and the utilization of the competitors' and the employees' skills.

In our case there was no finding by the court that there was ever a lawful disclosure of the trade secret. The court found that it would take one year to reproduce this engine through the process of reverse engineering. This it considered to be the length of time that the defendant could be required to abstain from production. The court measured this period of time from the disclosure of the trade secret by Van der Velden and concluded that since the defendant had abstained from producing the engine longer than the time it would take to develop it, the plaintiff was not entitled to an injunction. However, the disclosure by Van der Velden is conceded to have been tortious. The plaintiff's racing engine is not sold to the general public, and the record does not indicate that there has been any lawful disclosure of the trade secret from which this information could be discovered through reverse engineering or otherwise. Furthermore, the 1-year period the trial court found as the time it would take to reproduce the trade secret comes from an affidavit of a vice-president of the company stating that it would take from 8 to 12 months at a minimum from conception to completion for a competitor to develop an engine using the Bendix fuel-injection system. This statement, however, appears to have been made in connection with the previous paragraph in the affidavit which referred to developing the system from photographs or sketches of the Mercury engine and through reverse engineering from such sketches or photographs. There appears to be no evidence in the record as to how long it would take to reproduce plaintiff's trade secret absent the tortious disclosure of the information. The facts actually involved in this case can be fully developed when the case is heard on its merits on retrial and the appropriate relief, if any, fashioned from the principles of trade secret law reviewed in this opinion.

We hold that the trial court erred in granting summary judgment in favor of the defendants. The judgment of the appellate court is therefore affirmed, and the cause is remanded to the circuit court of Lake County for further proceedings in accordance with this opinion.

Affirmed and remanded.

NOTES

1. *Northern Petrochemical,* cited in *Brunswick,* held that an injunction for trade secret appropriation could not extend beyond the date that the secret could have been acquired by lawful means. See also, Syntex Ophthalmics, Inc. v. Novicky, 745 F.2d 1423 (Fed.Cir.1984). Doesn't that make trade secret theft a winning proposition? If the theft is not detected, the thief clearly benefits, and there are many reasons to think that most trade secret thefts are not detected. See Kitch, The Law and Economics of Rights in Valuable Information, 9 J.Legal Stud. 683, 690–91 (1980). If the theft is detected, then the thief is no worse off and the monetary award is limited to his profits or the plaintiff's damages. Where the secret involved a more efficient process and the thief did not increase his market share, the plaintiff will have no damages. So the thief can turn over his profits and go right back to using the secret. Why isn't the permanent injunction, with its punitive element, appropriate in this situation?

Section 2 of the Uniform Trade Secrets Act provides that "the injunction shall be terminated when the trade secret has ceased to exist, but the injunction may be continued for an additional reasonable period of time in order to eliminate commercial advantage * * *." What does the "additional period" represent?

2. Some courts have suggested that *Sears* and *Compco* may require limiting injunctive relief in trade secret cases to the period of time necessary to put the plaintiff in the position he would have been in had the secret not been taken. See Hampton v. Blair Mfg. Co., 374 F.2d 969 (8th Cir.1967) reversing a perpetual injunction. Do you agree?

3. See Curtiss-Wright Corp. v. Edel-Brown Tool & Die Co., Inc., 407 N.E.2d 319 (Mass.1980) where the court approved a permanent injunction but noted that the defendant could in the future seek to have the injunction dissolved if there was a "substantial change of circumstances." The Uniform Trade Secrets Act § 2 (1979) also contemplates permanent injunctive relief subject to application for dissolution. But see Valco Cincinnati, Inc. v. N & D Machining Service, Inc., 24 Ohio St.3d 41, 492 N.E.2d 814 (1986) where a permanent injunction against an employee was affirmed because the particular actions of the employee were "so egregious and violative of the relationship of the parties involved * * * that the ultimate sanction of a permanent injunction * * * " was appropriate.

4. What is the appropriate measure for monetary relief in a trade secret case? Should the focus be on what the plaintiff has lost or what the defendant has gained? Courts have adopted both a damage and a restitution perspective, although it is generally held the plaintiff may not recover damages *and* the defendant's profits arising out of the use of the secret. The appropriate damage measure may depend on the particular facts of each case. Relevant factors will include whether the plaintiff or defendant commercially exploited the secret and whether the secrecy of the information was destroyed by defendant's use. Consider the following possibilities:

a. The secret involves a process which is not disclosed by sale of the product it produces. Plaintiff markets the product and defendant, by unlawful appropriation of the secret, is able to compete with plaintiff. Has plaintiff suffered any damage other than the loss of profits from sales plaintiff would have made but for defendant's competition? Is the measure of plaintiff's *damages* the profits of the defendant?

b. Assume the facts in "a" except that, in addition, the defendant's appropriation results in disclosure of the secret so that subsequently there are several innocent third party exploiters of the process.

c. Assume the facts in "a" except that the plaintiff does not exploit the process.

d. Assume the facts in "a" except that the defendant is unable to profit from the process.

5. *Reasonable royalty.* Situation "d" is the *Northern Petrochemical* case supra note 1. The Fifth Circuit in University Computing Co. v. Lykes-Youngstown Corp., 504 F.2d 518, 539 (5th Cir.1974) imposed a "reasonable royalty" rate, that is the royalty that a willing trade secret owner and a willing trade secret user would have agreed to for the use made of the secret by the defendant. In making this determination the lower court was directed to consider such factors as "the resulting and foreseeable changes in the parties' competitive posture; the prices past purchasers or licensees may have paid; the total value of the secret to the plaintiff, including the plaintiff's development costs and the importance of the secret to the plaintiff's business; the nature and extent of the use the defendant intended for the secret; and finally whatever other unique factors in the particular case which might have affected the parties' agreement, such as the ready availability of alternative processes." In *Lykes*, the defendant made no profits from the plaintiff's secret.

In all of these cases, in establishing a reasonable royalty can you establish the maximum figure the defendant would be willing to pay for the secret? The minimum figure the plaintiff would accept? If there is a bargaining range, who should be assumed to have had the best of the bargain? Is this "bargained for" price adequate to deter trade secret appropriation? See Vermont Microsystems, Inc. v. Autodesk, Inc., 45 U.S.P.Q.2d 2014 (2d Cir. 1998) where the Second Circuit reversed the lower court which had doubled the royalty rate to take into account the "cost of infringement". The Second Circuit found the phrase too vague to be meaningful and noted that a punitive deterrent award is not permissible under the Uniform Trade Secrets Act which authorizes damages for "actual loss".

6. Over what time period should damages in trade secret cases be measured?

7. Other remedies available in trade secret infringement cases include punitive damages, attorneys fees, surrender or destruction of plans or other fruits from the appropriation, and assignment of patents acquired by the defendant as a result of the appropriation. See Johnston, Remedies in Trade Secret Litigation, 72 Nw.U.L.Rev. 1004 (1978).

PepsiCo, Inc. v. Redmond

United States Court of Appeals, Seventh Circuit, 1995.
54 F.3d 1262.

■ FLAUM, CIRCUIT JUDGE.

[PepsiCo's "All Sport" and iced teas competed in the sports drink and new age drink markets with Quaker Oats' "Gatorade" and "Snapple" drinks. As a general manager of PepsiCo's Northern California unit (PCNA), Redmond learned of PepsiCo's operating and strategic plans, pricing architecture and innovations in its selling and delivery systems for 1995. Redmond had signed a confidentiality agreement that stated he: "would not disclose at any time, to anyone . . . or make use of, confidential information relating to the business of [PepsiCo] . . . obtained while in the employ of [PepsiCo], which shall not be generally known or available to the public or recognized as standard practices." On November 8, 1994, Redmond accepted an offer to become Vice-President of Field Operations for Quaker. On November 16, 1994, PepsiCo filed suit for an injunction to prevent him from disclosing confidential information and from assuming his new duties at Quaker, arguing that Redmond's use of information regarding PepsiCo's confidential plans was inevitable. The district court, on December 15, 1994, issued an order enjoining Redmond from working for Quaker through May, 1995.]

The question of threatened or inevitable misappropriation in this case lies at the heart of a basic tension in trade secret law. Trade secret law serves to protect "standards of commercial morality" and "encourage . . . invention and innovation" while maintaining "the public interest in having free and open competition in the manufacture and sale of unpatented goods." 2 Jager, [Trade Secrets Law] § IL.03 at IL–12. Yet that same law should not prevent workers from pursuing their livelihoods when they leave their current positions.

This tension is particularly exacerbated when a plaintiff sues to prevent not the actual misappropriation of trade secrets but the mere threat that it will occur. * * *

[The Illinois Trade Secret Act and prior cases] lead to the same conclusion: a plaintiff may prove a claim of trade secret misappropriation by demonstrating that defendant's new employment will inevitably lead him to rely on the plaintiff's trade secrets. * * *

PepsiCo presented substantial evidence at the preliminary injunction hearing that Redmond possessed extensive and intimate knowledge about PCNA's strategic goals for 1995 in sports drinks and new age drinks. The district court concluded on the basis of that presentation that unless Redmond possessed an uncanny ability to compartmentalize information, he would necessarily be making decisions about Gatorade and Snapple by relying on his knowledge of PCNA trade secrets. * * *

Admittedly, PepsiCo has not brought a traditional trade secret case, in which a former employee has knowledge of a special manufacturing process or customer list and can give a competitor an unfair advantage by transferring the technology or customers to that competitor. PepsiCo has not contended that Quaker has stolen the All Sport formula or its list of distributors. Rather PepsiCo has asserted that Redmond cannot help but rely on PCNA trade secrets as he helps plot Gatorade and Snapple's new course, and that these secrets will enable Quaker to achieve a substantial advantage by knowing exactly how PCNA will price, distribute, and market its sports drinks and new age drinks and being able to respond strategically. This type of trade secret problem may arise less often, but it nevertheless falls within the realm of trade secret protection under the present circumstances.

Quaker and Redmond assert that they have not and do not intend to use whatever confidential information Redmond has by virtue of his former employment. They point out that Redmond has already signed an agreement with Quaker not to disclose any trade secrets or confidential information gleaned from his earlier employment. They also note with regard to distribution systems that even if Quaker wanted to steal information about PCNA's distribution plans, they would be completely useless in attempting to integrate the Gatorade and Snapple beverage lines.

The defendants' arguments fall somewhat short of the mark. Again, the danger of misappropriation in the present case is not that Quaker threatens to use PCNA's secrets to create distribution systems or co-opt PCNA's advertising and marketing ideas. Rather, PepsiCo believes that Quaker, unfairly armed with knowledge of PCNA's plans, will be able to anticipate its distribution, packaging, pricing, and marketing moves. Redmond and Quaker even concede that Redmond might be faced with a decision that could be influenced by certain confidential information that he obtained while at PepsiCo. In other words, PepsiCo finds itself in the position of a coach, one of whose players has left, playbook in hand, to join the opposing team before the big game. Quaker and Redmond's protestations that their distribution systems and plans are entirely different from PCNA's are thus not really responsive.

* * *

For the foregoing reasons, we affirm the district court's order enjoining Redmond from assuming his responsibilities at Quaker through May, 1995, and preventing him forever from disclosing PCNA trade secrets and confidential information.

AFFIRMED.

NOTES

1. Does the nature of the trade secret make a difference as to whether the court should enjoin a person from accepting employment? If the concern is with a formula or some secret technology isn't it easier to determine subsequently whether the secret was actually used? How would you ever know whether Redmond used PepsiCo's secret plans? Injunctions requiring former employees to sit on the sidelines for a period of time seem to be increasing. See, DoubleClick, Inc. v. Henderson, 1997 WL 731413 (N.Y.Co. Ct. 1997); Lenzner and Shook, Whose Rolodex Is It, Anyway? Forbes, Feb. 23, 1998, at 100.

2. Consider Baxter International, Inc. v. Morris, 976 F.2d 1189 (8th Cir. 1992). Morris, a research scientist for Microscan, signed an employment agreement prohibiting him from working for a competitor for one year after terminating his employment with Microscan. He quit and began working for Vitek, Microscan's only competitor. Microscan sought an injunction to prohibit disclosure of any trade secret and to prohibit Morris from working for one year. The lower court enjoyed Morris from disclosing any trade secrets for one year but found the noncompetition agreement void and refused to enjoin his employment by Vitek. The Eighth Circuit affirmed, noting that there was evidence that Morris would not disclose trade secrets nor be asked by Vitek to do so. The one year limit on disclosure was based on the fact that the noncompetition agreement had only been for one year. With such a case, how would you fashion an employment contract for an employer concerned about disclosure of its trade secrets? Is there a difference between a noncompetition agreement and a nondisclosure agreement?

3. Does the *Pepsico* case raise the cost of hiring management employees?

NOTE: TRADE SECRET LAW RECONSIDERED

The law of trade secrets has been largely a creature of the common law. Even with the adoption of the Uniform Trade Secrets Act by a majority of states, trade secret doctrines have retained their common law character. Nonetheless there appears to be growing concern about protection of secret information as the economy becomes more dependent on technology. The ever shortening half-life of new ideas may enhance the gains from getting to the market first. This means keeping an invention secret may be more important than pursuing the time consuming process of applying for a patent. In an international context, there is growing concern that domestic secret commercial information will migrate to foreign countries. These factors have led to two significant additions to the arsenal of weapons against trade secret appropriation.

In the TRIPS agreement associated with the GATT negotiations, signatory countries are obliged to provide "effective protection" for "undisclosed information". The central provision in this regard is Section 7, Article 39(2) which reads as follows:

2. Natural and legal persons shall have the possibility of preventing information lawfully within their control from being disclosed to, acquired by, or used by others without their consent in a manner contrary to honest commercial practices so long as such information:
— is secret in the sense that it is not, as a body or in the precise configuration and assembly of its components, generally known among or readily accessible to persons within the circles that normally deal with the kind of information in question;
— has commercial value because it is secret; and
— has been subject to reasonable steps under the circumstances, by the person lawfully in control of the information, to keep it secret.

In 1996 Congress enacted the Economic Espionage Act of 1996, 18 U.S.C.A. § 1831 et. seq. The Act provides criminal penalties for "economic espionage" which in § 1831 relates to the appropriation of trade secrets to benefit a foreign government, instrumentality, or agent. However, § 1832 applies federal criminal penalties to all domestic trade secret appropriations. Section 1839 defines "trade secret" for purposes of these criminal penalties as follows:

(3) the term "trade secret" means all forms and types of financial, business, scientific, technical, economic, or engineering information, including patterns, plans, compilations, program devices, formulas, designs, prototypes, methods, techniques, processes, procedures, programs, or codes, whether tangible or intangible, and whether or how stored, compiled, or memorialized physically, electronically, graphically, photographically, or in writing if—

(A) the owner thereof has taken reasonable measures to keep such information secret; and

(B) the information derives independent economic value, actual or potential, from not being generally known to, and not being readily ascertainable through proper means by, the public.

What do these provisions do to the common law of trade secrets? Might there be some information that would be included under these definitions that might not be included under the common law definition of trade secret? Certainly, the least that can be said is that these provisions, particularly the federal criminal statute, sends a strong message that trade secret protection is very important and one might expect firms to be more willing to pursue civil remedies with the leverage of potential criminal actions. There had been earlier attempts to criminally prosecute the theft of information but such prosecutions were rare. See, Carpenter v. United States, 484 U.S. 19 (1987) (upholding conviction for mail fraud of Wall Street Journal reporter who used knowledge of future "Heard on the Street" columns to profit in the stock market). At the margin where the actual secrecy of information is in doubt, would you not expect employees to be much more reluctant to take the risk of disclosing or using information acquired from a former employer? Will employers be less willing to hire employees from a competitor? Does this significant enhancement in the penalities for trade secret appropriation run the risk of diminishing competition and undermining employee mobility?

(b) Trade Secrets and the Government

Courts have long held that the interest of a manufacturer to protect his trade secrets yields to a valid governmental interest in disclosure. Corn Products Refining Co. v. Eddy, 249 U.S. 427 (1919) (sustaining state labeling statute requiring a listing on the label of the percentage of each ingredient in a product against the argument that it deprived the manufacturer of property without due process). The owner may confront the potential for disclosure or use of its trade secrets by government in a number of different contexts. We only mention a few in passing here.

Discovery. Trade secrets are subject to discovery during litigation although Fed.R.Civil Proc. 26 authorizes federal courts to limit discovery of "trade secrets or confidential research, development, or commercial information" or to require disclosure in a specific way. It is common to have the court issue a protective order prohibiting individuals who see the material from disclosing it further.

Freedom of Information Act. The regulation of products by governmental agencies often requires the disclosure of trade secrets as part of the regulatory process. Regulation of safety, quality, or performance may require the disclosure of secret ingredients, formulas, or cost and pricing information. Agencies traditionally kept this information secret. However with passage of the Freedom of Information Act, 5 U.S.C. § 552, most information in the possession of federal agencies can be obtained by private citizens or disclosed voluntarily by the government. However, § 552(b)(4) exempts from mandatory disclosure "trade secrets and commercial or financial information obtained from a person and privileged or confidential." The definitions of "trade secret" and "commercial or financial information" in the exemption have created substantial litigation. See Public Citizen Health Research Group v. FDA, 704 F.2d 1280 (D.C.Cir.1983) (adopting narrower definition of trade secret than Restatement of Torts formulation; must be a secret that is used for making a commodity and is the end product of innovation or substantial effort); National

Parks & Conservation Ass'n v. Morton, 498 F.2d 765 (D.C.Cir.1974) (defining confidential financial information as information the disclosure of which would impair the Government's ability to obtain information voluntarily from firms or that would cause substantial competitive harm to the owner of the information).

Safety and Effectiveness Testing. To market a new drug the company must secure clearance from the Food and Drug Administration as to the safety and effectiveness of the drug. To market a new pesticide the company must obtain a registration from the Environmental Protection Agency relative to the safety of the product. In both cases (and others) the firm must conduct extensive and expensive testing to convince the agency of the safety and effectiveness of the product. Should the results of these tests be public information or regarded as trade secrets?

If Company *A* receives marketing clearance for its new drug ABC, should Company *X* be allowed to market drug XYZ if it proves that the two drugs are identical without conducting similar tests for safety and effectiveness? To protect the testing information as a trade secret is to require other companies to engage in duplicative and wasteful testing. To disclose the test results or to permit their use by subsequent firms is to provide a competitive advantage to those firms that "appropriate" the investment in testing of other firms.

There appears to be no single solution to this problem. The Federal Insecticide, Fungicide, and Rodenticide Act, 7 U.S.C. § 136 et seq. permits use of test results by subsequent parties but requires compensation to the original tester and provides for binding arbitration if the amount of compensation cannot be agreed upon. The act was upheld against various claims in Thomas v. Union Carbide Agricultural Products Co., 473 U.S. 568 (1985); Ruckelshaus v. Monsanto Co., 467 U.S. 986 (1984). See also the Drug Price Competition and Patent Term Restoration Act of 1984, 21 U.S.C. § 301, which permits the extension of the patent term for new drugs for up to five years to account for the delays in premarket clearance by the FDA but also permits, upon expiration of the patent, subsequent parties to obtain clearance for copies of the patented drug without the need for duplicate testing. See generally, McGarity & Shapiro, The Trade Secret Status of Health and Safety Testing Information: Reforming Agency Disclosure Policies, 93 Harv.L.Rev. 837 (1980); Kitch, The Patent System and the New Drug Application: An Evaluation of the Incentives for Private Investment in New Drug Research and Marketing, in Univ. of Chicago Center for Policy Study, Regulating New Drugs 81 (Landau ed. 1973).

G.S. Rasmussen & Associates, Inc. v. Kalitta Flying Service, Inc.

United States Court of Appeals, Ninth Circuit, 1992.
958 F.2d 896, cert. denied 113 S. Ct. 2927 (1993).

■ KOZINSKI, CIRCUIT JUDGE:

[Rasmussen developed modifications for a DC–8 cargo plane, conducted extensive safety tests as required by the FAA, and received from the FAA a

Supplemental Type Certificate (STC) permitting the plane as modified to fly. Kalitta acquired a Rasmussen plane, reverse engineered the modifications and incorporated the modifications in its own DC–8s. It applied for a certificate of airworthiness by using Rasmussen's STC number and a photocopy of Rasmussen's STC certificate. The FAA issued Kalitta a certificate based on the submission. Kalitta thus did not conduct safety tests. Rasmussen sued for conversion of its STC and for unjust enrichment.]

To the extent we can distill a principle on the basis of this somewhat amorphous body of [California] law, three criteria must be met before the law will recognize a property right: First, there must be an interest capable of precise definition; second, it must be capable of exclusive possession or control;[12] and third, the putative owner must have established a legitimate claim to exclusivity.[13] The interest Rasmussen asserts here easily meets these criteria.

The nature and extent of the rights afforded by an STC are capable of precise definition: It enables an airplane owner to obtain an airworthiness certificate for a particular design modification without the delay, burden and expense of proving to the FAA that a plane so modified will be safe. Federal law also limits the interest in a significant way: The rights created by an STC are only applicable to airplanes within the safety jurisdiction of the FAA—"civil aircraft in air commerce." Thus, Kalitta is free to make Rasmussen's modification on airplanes it flies entirely outside the United States.

Nor are there any conceptual or practical difficulties in restricting the right to the holder of the STC, or to someone who is a transferee or licensee. In fact, the federal regulations contemplate exactly that. Rasmussen's interest is thus precisely defined and capable of exclusive possession.

The final requirement—that Rasmussen have established a legitimate claim to exclusivity—is also amply met here. Rasmussen expended considerable time and effort in research and design; he conducted the appropriate tests and compiled the necessary data; he prepared an operations manual and lined up an instrument manufacturer; he convinced the FAA that the modification is safe; and he obtained a certificate which results in preferential rights in the issuance of airworthiness certificates by the FAA. Without Rasmussen's efforts, the STC Kalitta relied on simply would not exist. Rasmussen has the type of reasonable investment-backed expectations that give rise to a legitimate claim of exclusive control over the STC.

---

12. As the saying goes, some of the best things in life are free, and the reason may be that they cannot be reduced to possession: The air we breathe, scenic views, the night sky, the theory of relativity and the friendship of others cannot be reduced to possession and therefore cannot be the basis of property rights.

13. Opinions defining property for takings purposes often use the phrase "reasonable investment-backed expectations" to describe such claims. The phrase aptly describes the nature of the interest needed to establish property rights for purposes of California law. The degree of investment—monetary or otherwise—is relevant, especially when dealing with intangibles, in determining whether the purported owner has developed a stake in the thing sufficient to warrant invoking the protections of the law of property.

We therefore hold that Rasmussen has a property interest in his STC under California law, unless such an interest conflicts with federal law. We turn to that question now.

B. *Preemption*

[With respect to copyright preemption the court held: " * * * Were Rasmussen claiming an exclusive right to copy the manual, the drawings and plans or the STC itself, his claim would surely be preempted by the Copyright Act. * * * Rasmussen claims a much different interest, however: The right to use the STC as a basis for obtaining an airworthiness certificate for an airplane that is modified in a particular way. Rasmussen thus complains not about the actual copying of the documents, but of their use as a shortcut in obtaining a valuable government privilege—the right to modify an airplane in a particular way without going to the trouble and expense of proving that the modification meets FAA standards. * * * Federal copyright law governs only copying. Enforcement of Rasmussen's property right in his STC leaves Kalitta free to make as many copies of the certificate as it wishes; to the extent the manual supplement is not protected by the copyright laws, the same is true of it. That Kalitta is prevented from then using these copies to obtain an airworthiness certificate from the FAA does not interfere in any way with the operation of the copyright laws."

[Regarding patent preemption the court held: "* * * The Supreme Court has summarized its preemption approach as follows: 'States may not offer *patent-like protection* to intellectual creations which would otherwise remain unprotected as a matter of federal law.' *Bonito Boats,* 489 U.S. at 156, 109 S.Ct. at 980 (emphasis added). * * * The right involved here, however, is not 'patent-like' at all. Rasmussen claims no exclusive right to modify DC–8s as described in his STC. Kalitta or anyone else may perform the necessary studies and obtain an STC from the FAA—even if the modification so certified is identical to Rasmussen's. * * * Granting Rasmussen a property right in his STC will serve many of the same purposes of the patent laws, because it will promote innovation in the field of aeronautics. * * * There is no patent law preemption."]

C. *State-Law Claims*

1. The Pirated STC

In California, conversion has three elements: ownership or right to possession of property, wrongful disposition of the property right and damages. Our earlier discussion establishes the first element: Rasmussen has an ownership interest in the use of his STC, which is property under California law. The second requirement is also satisfied: Kalitta photocopied the certificate, presented it to the FAA, and thereby obtained a valuable benefit as a consequence of using Rasmussen's STC without authorization or permission. Rasmussen has also suffered damages by being denied a return on his investment as a condition for granting Kalitta the right to use his STC. Thus, under California law, Kalitta tortiously converted Rasmussen's STC when it used the STC to obtain airworthiness certification for the modified DC–8.

Rasmussen also alleges that Kalitta has been unjustly enriched. Under California law, a contract will be implied when one party has something which "in equity and good conscience" it ought not. Kalitta has materially benefited from the pirated STC: Its DC–8 can now carry substantially more cargo, and the parties agree that use as a cargo plane would be economically infeasible without the modification. Conversely, Kalitta has been spared the delay and expense it would have had to incur in obtaining its own STC. This benefit is due solely to Rasmussen's STC, for which Kalitta has paid nothing. Confronted with such facts, the California courts would imply a contract between Rasmussen and Kalitta. On remand, the district court shall fix its terms based on further evidence.

* * *

AFFIRMED in part, REVERSED in part and REMANDED for further proceedings consistent with this opinion.

NOTES

1. Does the *Rasmussen* decision provide a sensible solution to the problem of use of information collected solely for purposes of governmental regulation? Are the facts similar to *International News Service v. Associated Press*? Are any of Justice Brandeis's concerns expressed in his dissent in *INS* applicable here?

2. On remand how should the district court measure the damages? Under the claim for conversion, should it be the full fair market value of the STC or the value to Kalitta? Under the unjust enrichment claim, should the damages be the cost to Kalitta of independently testing the modifications?

3. Is there any social value in requiring Kalitta and others in its position to duplicate Rasmussen's tests?

4. In the absence of the regulatory framework, how would this situation be resolved? Assume Rasmussen develops a modification for DC–8s that is obvious upon inspection of a modified aircraft. Rasmussen advertises to the industry that it has undertaken extensive testing and has determined the modification to be safe. (If you were the owner of a DC–8, would you expect to see such testing before you adopted the modification?) Kalitta examines a modified aircraft to determine the nature of the modification and then incorporates the modification on its own aircraft, comforted by the knowledge that Rasmussen has tested the modification for safety. Would Kalitta face any liability?

5. *TRIPS Agreement.* Section 7, Article 39 (3) of the TRIPS agreement obligates the signatory countries as follows:

3. Members, when requiring, as a condition of approving the marketing of pharmaceutical or of agricultural chemical products which utilize new chemical entities, the submission of undisclosed test or other data, the origination of which involves a considerable effort, shall protect such data against unfair commercial use. In addition, Members shall protect such data against disclosure, except where necessary to

protect the public, or unless steps are taken to ensure that the data are protected against unfair commercial use.

Does this section lend support for the rule in *Kalitta* at least in cases involving pharmaceuticals or agricultural chemicals?

(c) The Statutory Alternative: Patent

The patent system often offers an alternative to the common law of trade secrets for protection of certain types of business information. This alternative protection is limited to a large degree by the requirements of subject matter and standard of invention found in the patent laws. The purpose of this section is to suggest some of the issues in a trade secret context which the owner of valuable information must face because of the existence of the patent laws.

Conmar Prod. Corp. v. Universal Slide Fastener Co.

United States Court of Appeals, Second Circuit, 1949.
172 F.2d 150.

[Plaintiff, Conmar Products, sued on three causes of action, the first two involving patent infringement and the third for inducing plaintiff's employees to divulge trade secrets. The plaintiff's patents involve improvements on the manufacturing of zippers. Zippers were originally protected under patents which at the time of this action had expired. The court held all of the claims in the plaintiff's patents invalid. The facts involving the third cause of action were these: One Voity worked for the plaintiff in a position that made him familiar with all the details of plaintiff's secrets. Voity, as did other of plaintiff's employees, signed a contract promising not to divulge anything which he might learn of plaintiff's methods. During the summer of 1939, Voity and others quit plaintiff and began working for defendant. While employed by defendant, Voity devised a machine embodying seven of the plaintiff's secrets. The lower court found and the court here affirmed that the defendant did not know that Voity had signed the secrecy agreement with plaintiff until November, 1940, after they had committed $40,000 for the machines. The court noted that plaintiff's active exploitation of patents for protection and a lack of custom in the art to require employee secrecy agreements would negate the inference that defendant should have known of the secrecy agreement.

Of the seven secrets alleged by plaintiff to be utilized in defendant's machine, six and part of the seventh were found in the disclosures of the two patents which the court here found, invalid. The other part of the seventh was disclosed in two patents issued in 1944–45.]

■ L. HAND, CHIEF JUDGE.

* * *

Courts have been accustomed to speak of trade secrets as "property," and at times to deal with them as if they were. That may be permissible and to some extent desirable, when the question is whether the wrongdoer has got access to them by some wrongful means, like breaking into a factory, or copying formulae or blue prints. When, however, the dispute turns, as it does here, upon whether the wrongdoer has acquired a secret from the employee who has himself acquired it lawfully, the wrong consists in inducing him to break his contract, or to be disloyal to a confidence reposed in him; and in either case it is a species of the tort—recognized now for over a century—of inducing an obligor to default upon an obligation. Since the specifications of the patents in suit disclosed the first six secrets and part of the seventh, that much of the secrets upon issue of the patents fell into the public demesne; and, prima facie, the defendants were free to use them. The Seventh Circuit, and apparently the Sixth as well, have, however, held that if before issue one has unlawfully obtained and used information which the specifications later disclose, he will not be free to continue to do so after issue; his wrong deprives him of the right which he would otherwise have had as a member of the public. We have twice refused to follow this doctrine; and we adhere to our decisions. Conceivably an employer might exact from his employees a contract not to disclose the information even after the patent issued. Of what possible value such a contract could be, we find it hard to conceive; but, if an employer did exact it, others would perhaps be obliged to turn to the specifications, if they would use the information. Be that as it may, we should not so construe any secrecy contract unless the intent were put in the most inescapable terms; and the plaintiff's contract had none such. In their absence we do not see why a wrongful inducement to divulge the disclosure before issue should deprive the wrongdoer of his right to avail himself of the patentee's dedication; for, as we have just said, the contract is to be construed as imposing secrecy only until issue. The doctrine must rest upon the theory that it is a proper penalty for the original wrong to deny the wrongdoer resort to the patent; and for that we can find no support in principle. Thus, any possible liability for exploiting whatever the patents in suit disclosed, ended with their issue. Since the earliest notice was on November 16, 1940, it is not necessary to resort to this reasoning as to the first six secrets and as to part of the seventh, because the two patents in suit issued before November 16, 1940; but the doctrine does become important as to the remaining part of the seventh secret.

It is almost, if not quite, impossible to learn what was that part of the seventh secret which did remain undisclosed after the issue of the Ulrich patent in suit; but for argument we will assume that the plaintiff proved that some parts did so remain. Whatever these were, they were all disclosed in two later patents to Ulrich: No. 2,338,884, issued January 11, 1944, and No. 2,370,380, issued February 27, 1945; and in any event the right to an injunction against exploiting any secrets whatever had therefore expired before the judgment was entered in November, 1947. All that could remain was the right to an accounting for profits or to a claim for damages between November 16, 1940, and the date of issue of these patents. We think, however, that the defendants had an excuse for exploiting that secret over that period, if they did so. As we have said, by November 16, 1940, they had invested $40,000 in the offending machine; that is, they had either paid or committed themselves to pay that much. The Restatement of Torts makes it an excuse for continued exploitation of a secret that at the time when one, who has theretofore been innocently exploiting it, first learns that he has induced the breach of an obligation, he has substantially changed his position. The opinions which support this are not very satisfactory; so far as we have found, in all but one or two it is doubtful whether what the judges say is more than dictum. However, they do all point the same way, for they assume that the situation is proper for the application of the doctrine that a bona fide purchaser takes free from a trust. The act of inducing the breach is the wrong, and the inducer's ignorance is an excuse only because one is not ordinarily held liable for consequences which one could not have anticipated. Although it is proper to prevent any continued use of the secret after the inducer has learned of the breach, the remedies must not invade the inducer's immunity over the period while he was ignorant. They may invade it, if the inducer has changed his position on the faith of his ignorance. We agree with the Comment of the Restatement that each case must stand on its facts; the answer depends upon weighing the loss to the inducer against the benefit to the obligee. In the case at bar we have no hesitation in deciding that issue in favor of the defendants. On November 16, 1940, when the defendants were first charged with any duty to desist, they had become free to exploit the major part of the secrets—the first six and an undetermined part of the seventh. Their duty at most extended no further than to change their machines and their methods, so as not to continue to exploit the still protected vestiges of the seventh; and even these would become free when the two other patents issued. Certainly, to compel them to make that change was seriously to invade the immunity they had enjoyed to that time; it would have compelled a disruption of their business and a redesigning of their machines. Opposed to this was a benefit to the plaintiff, the importance of which no one could even guess; for it must be measured by the advantage of suppressing only the use of the yet undisclosed part of the seventh secret, while the defendants remained free to use all the rest. The plaintiff had the burden of showing that the balance was in its favor, and we should be wholly unwarranted in deducing that conclusion from the maze of verbiage which wraps the issue.

The plaintiff finally argues that the defendants were liable because Voity was their agent, authorized to make the machines, and that while doing so, he knew of the contract and so supplied the missing factor in the liability and charged them as his principals. This reasoning would confine the excuse of ignorance to cases in which the inducer did not take the obligor into his own employ, and those are by far the greater number of cases in which he is aware of the obligation. For it will be seldom that one will innocently induce another's employees to disclose secrets of their employer's business, and yet not engage the employees in his own employ. That alone should be enough to condemn the reasoning practically. However, it is also wrong in theory. The fact that Voity knew of his own contract is immaterial; that knowledge might well have charged the defendants that he induced the breach of some other employee's obligation; but that he did not do. He did not induce himself to default in his own obligation. The transaction in which they ignorantly induced his breach was one in which Voity was the opposite party and did not represent them in any way. Having acquired the secrets innocently, they were entitled to exploit them till they learned that they had induced the breach of the contract.

Judgment affirmed.

NOTES

1. Does *Conmar* suggest the operation of the federal patent laws may have some preemptive effect on state trade secret law? What if a defendant acquires secret information by unfair means but could have acquired the same information from an issued patent subsequently held invalid. Can an injunction on the trade secret claim extend beyond the point the patent is declared invalid? Can an accounting be ordered for a time subsequent to the declaration of invalidity? See Schreyer v. Casco Prod. Corp. 190 F.2d 921 (2d Cir.1951) (accounting limited to period prior to declaration of invalidity, citing *Conmar*) and Franke v. Wiltschek, 209 F.2d 493 (2d Cir.1953) (permanent injunction upheld under New York law with no reference to *Conmar*).

2. What does the *Conmar* decision suggest is the philosophy of the patent laws regarding the disclosure of inventions?

3. The mere filing of the application for a patent is not regarded as a disclosure of the claims to the public. A.O. Smith Corp. v. Petroleum Iron Works Co., 73 F.2d 531 (6th Cir.1934). The Patent Office is required to keep applications confidential. 35 U.S.C. § 122. Consider 37 C.F.R. § 1.14(b) (1998) which provides that abandoned applications are not open to public inspection and will not be returned to applicant. An application is deemed abandoned if the applicant fails to prosecute his application within six months of receiving a rejection. 37 C.F.R. § 1.135 (1998). An applicant, on the other hand, may waive his rights to an enforceable patent by giving written consent to the Patent Office. 37 C.F.R. § 1.138 (1998). It has been held that the Freedom of Information Act does not require disclosure of abandoned applications. Sears v. Gottschalk, 502 F.2d 122 (4th Cir.1974), cert. denied 422 U.S. 1056 (1975). However the Patent Office was required to disclose 175 volumes of memorandum decisions involving abandoned and rejected patents after excising exempt material—quotations from the patent applications. Irons v. Gottschalk, 548 F.2d 992 (D.C.Cir.1976).

What are the arguments in favor of disclosure of abandoned patents? Is it not wasteful to have other inventors seeking patents for innovations already rejected? Should the patent office be able to rely on an abandoned patent to prove that another applicant is not the first inventor?

4. If the applicant fails to obtain a patent from the Patent Office and prosecutes an appeal into the courts, it has been held that the court has inherent authority to seal the record and order ex camera proceedings. In re Mosher, 199 U.S.P.Q. 82 (CCPA 1978).

5. Consider § 102 of the patent law. This section is designed to encourage timely applications for patents, and it has a direct bearing on the interrelationship of trade secret law and patent law. The various clauses of § 102 will be examined in Chapter 6.

In general, the patent law gives priority to the first to invent. However, the date of invention is presumed to be the date of application unless the applicant can show an earlier date. Both the date of invention and the date of application are significant to the implementation of § 102. Under § 102(b) an invention which has been "in public use or on sale" for more than one year prior to application for a patent may not be patented. And § 102(g) destroys the priority of a first inventor who suppresses or conceals his invention. Exploitation of an invention in reliance on trade secret doctrine has been held to constitute, in some circumstances, both a "public use" and a suppression or concealment of the invention. How do the provisions of § 102 relate to trade secret doctrines?

PROBLEM

A invents on January 1, 1970, and exploits his invention, relying on trade secret protection. *B* independently discovers the same innovation on January 1, 1975 and immediately applies for a patent. On July 1, 1975, *A* applies for a patent. Consider who is entitled to the patent. What are the rights of the respective parties after the patent issues?

(d) The Private Alternative: Contract

Reed, Roberts Associates, Inc. v. Strauman

Court of Appeals of New York, 1976.
40 N.Y.2d 303, 386 N.Y.S.2d 677, 353 N.E.2d 590.

[John Strauman was hired by Reed, Roberts, a firm supplying advice to employers on compliance with State unemployment laws. Strauman signed a restrictive covenant with his employer by which he agreed not to "directly or indirectly solicit any of your clients" or for a three year period engage in competition with Reed, Roberts within the geographical area of New York. Over a 10 year period, Strauman became a valuable employee with increased responsibility for the internal affairs of the company. He was not responsible for sales or obtaining new customers. After 11 years with Reed, Roberts, Strauman quit and formed his own company in direct competition with his former employer. This action was brought by Reed, Roberts to enforce the restrictive covenant.]

■ WACHTLER, JUDGE.

* * *

Generally negative covenants restricting competition are enforceable only to the extent that they satisfy the overriding requirement of reasonableness. Yet the formulation of reasonableness may vary with the context and type of restriction imposed. For example, where a business is sold, anticompetition covenants will be enforceable, if reasonable in time, scope and extent. These covenants are designed to protect the goodwill integral to the business from usurpation by the former owner while at the same time allowing an owner to profit from the goodwill which he may have spent years creating. * * * However, where an anticompetition covenant given by an employee to his employer is involved a stricter standard of reasonableness will be applied.

In this context a restrictive covenant will only be subject to specific enforcement to the extent that it is reasonable in time and area, necessary to protect the employer's legitimate interests, not harmful to the general public and not unreasonably burdensome to the employee * * *. Indeed, our economy is premised on the competition engendered by the uninhibited flow of services, talent and ideas. Therefore, no restrictions should fetter an employee's right to apply to his own best advantage the skills and knowledge acquired by the overall experience of his previous employment. This includes those techniques which are but "skillful variations of general processes known to the particular trade" (Restatement, Agency 2d, § 396, Comment b; see, also, Customer List—As Trade Secret-Factors, Ann., 28 A.L.R.3d 7).

Of course, the courts must also recognize the legitimate interest an employer has in safeguarding that which has made his business successful and to protect himself against deliberate surreptitious commercial piracy. Thus restrictive covenants will be enforceable to the extent necessary to prevent the disclosure or use of trade secrets or confidential customer information * * *.

In addition injunctive relief may be available where an employee's services are unique or extraordinary and the covenant is reasonable * * *. This latter principle has been interpreted to reach agreements between members of the learned professions (e.g., Karpinski v. Ingrasci, 28 N.Y.2d 45, 320 N.Y.S.2d 1, 268 N.E.2d 751).

With these principles in mind we consider first the issue of solicitation of customers in the case at bar. The courts below found, and Reed, Roberts does not dispute, that there were no trade secrets involved here. The thrust of Reed, Roberts' argument is that by virtue of Strauman's position in charge of internal administration he was privy to sensitive and confidential customer information which he should not be permitted to convert to his own use. The law enunciated in Leo Silfen, Inc. v. Cream, 29 N.Y.2d 387, 328 N.Y.S.2d 423, 278 N.E.2d 636 is dispositive. There, as here, the plaintiff failed to sustain its allegation that the defendant had pirated the actual customer list. Rather Silfen argued that in light of the funds expended to compile the list it would be unfair to allow the defendant to solicit the clients of his former employer. We held that where the employee engaged in no wrongful conduct and the names and addresses of potential customers were readily discoverable through public sources, an injunction would not lie. Similarly here there was no finding that Strauman acted wrongfully by either pilfering or memorizing the customer list * * *.

More important, by Reed, Roberts' own admission every company with employees is a prospective customer and the solicitation of customers was usually done through the use of nationally known publications such as Dun and Bradstreet's *Million Dollar Directory* where even the name of the person to contact regarding these services is readily available. It strains credulity to characterize this type of information as confidential. * * *

Apparently, the employer is more concerned about Strauman's knowledge of the intricacies of their business operation. However, absent any wrongdoing, we cannot agree that Strauman should be prohibited from utilizing his knowledge and talents in this area (see Restatement, Agency 2d, § 396, Comment *b*). A contrary holding would make those in charge of operations or specialists in certain aspects of an enterprise virtual hostages of their employers. Where the knowledge does not qualify for protection as a trade secret and there has been no conspiracy or breach of trust resulting in commercial piracy we see no reason to inhibit the employee's ability to realize his potential both professionally and financially by availing himself of opportunity. Therefore, despite Strauman's excellence or value to Reed, Roberts the trial court's finding that his services were not extraordinary or unique is controlling and properly resulted in a denial of the injunction against operating a competing business.

Eden Hannon & Co. v. Sumitomo Trust & Banking Co.

United States Court of Appeals for the Fourth Circuit, 1990.
914 F.2d 556.

■ RUSSELL, CIRCUIT JUDGE.

[The Hannon Co. advised institutional investors on how to fashion bids for purchase of Xerox lease portfolios. To provide this advice Hannon had to disclose to the investors its confidential methods and economic models. To protect itself, Hannon required investors to sign a "Nondisclosure and Noncircumvention" agreement that obligated the investor not to disclose any of Hannon's methods or to independently bid on Xerox portfolios for a three year period. Sumitomo signed the agreement, received Hannon's advice, but independently and successfully bid on a portfolio. The Fourth Circuit held the agreement valid and imposed a constructive trust on the profits from the portfolio on Hannon's behalf.]

The Noncircumvention and Nondisclosure Agreement (in the forthcoming discussion, we will call this a "noncircumvention agreement") is nearly identical in purpose to an employment agreement. Most importantly, an employment agreement enables an employer to expose his employees to the firm's trade secrets. Similarly, a noncircumvention agreement enables potential joint venturers to share confidential information regarding a possible deal. In both instances, the idea is to share trade secrets so that business can be conducted without losing control over the secrets. Often, the value of a firm is its special knowledge, and this knowledge may not be an idea protectible by patent or copyright. If that firm cannot protect that knowledge from immediate dissemination to competitors, it may not be able to reap the benefits from the time and money invested in building that knowledge. If firms are not permitted to construct a reasonable legal mechanism to protect that knowledge, then the incentive to engage in the building of such knowledge will be greatly reduced. Free riders will capture this information at little or no cost and produce a product cheaper than the firm which created the knowledge, because it will not have to carry the costs of creating that knowledge in its pricing. Faced with this free rider problem, this information may not be created, and thus everybody loses. To counteract that problem, an employer can demand that employees sign an employment agreement as a condition of their contract, and thus protect the confidential information. This means that if an employer takes in an employee and exposes that employee to trade secrets, the employer does not have to allow the employee to go across the street and set up shop once that employee has mastered the information. Although it was not explained in this detail, Virginia has recognized this interest in protecting confidential information.

These employment agreements (or in the present case, a noncircumvention agreement) are often necessary because it can be very difficult to prove the theft of a trade secret by a former employee. Often, the purpose of an employment agreement can be to prevent the dissemination of trade secrets, yet a mere ban on using trade secrets after the termination of employment would be difficult to enforce. Judge Lord explained the problem well in Greenberg v. Croydon Plastics Co., Inc., 378 F.Supp. 806, 814 (E.D.Pa.1974):

> Plaintiffs in trade secret cases, who must prove by a fair preponderance of the evidence disclosure to third parties and use of the trade secret by the third parties, are confronted with an extraordinarily difficult task. Misappropriation and misuse can rarely be proved by convincing direct evidence. In most cases plaintiffs must construct a web of perhaps ambiguous circumstantial evidence from which the trier of fact may draw inferences which convince him that it is more probable than not that what the plaintiffs allege happened did in fact take place. Against this often delicate construct of circumstantial evidence there frequently must be balanced defendants' witnesses who directly deny everything.

Actually, Judge Lord's description of the problem covers just the tip of the iceberg. There are several problems with trying to prevent former employees from illegally using the former employer's trade secrets, and these problems are caused by the status of the law regarding the misappropriation of trade secrets. First, as Judge Lord depicted so well, it is difficult to prove that the trade secret was actually used. Second, the former employee tends to get "one free bite" at the trade secret. Most courts will refuse to enjoin the disclosure or use of a trade secret until its illegal use is imminent or until it has already occurred. By that time, much of the damage may be done. Third, even if a clearly illegal use of the trade secret by a former employee can be shown, most courts will not enjoin that person from working for the competition on that basis. Instead, they will merely enjoin future disclosure of the trade secret. Yet, policing the former employee's compliance with that injunction will be difficult. Finally, even if the employee does not maliciously attempt to use his former employer's trade secrets in the new employer's workplace, avoiding this use can be difficult. It would be difficult for the employee to guard the trade secret of the former employer and be effective for the new employer.

In order to avoid these problems, many employers ask their employees to sign non-competition agreements. These agreements prevent an employee from working with the competition within a limited geographical range of the former employer and for a limited time. As seen above, Virginia courts will only enforce these agreements if they are reasonable. Yet, when they are valid, they make the guarding of a trade secret easier since they remove the opportunity for the former employee to pass on the trade secret to the competition, either malevolently or benevolently. This does not supplant the need for law protecting trade secrets. Non-competition agreements cannot prevent disclosure anywhere in the world and until the end of time, for they would be held unreasonable. Instead, a non-competition agreement will merely prevent the illegal use of a trade secret next door in the near future, where the use might do the most damage.

Warner-Lambert Pharm. Co. v. John J. Reynolds, Inc.

United States District Court, S.D. New York, 1959.
178 F.Supp. 655, aff'd on opinion below, 280 F.2d 197.

■ BRYAN, DISTRICT JUDGE.

[Plaintiff manufactured and sold an antiseptic liquid compound called "Listerine" under an exclusive license from the defendant, which is the successor in interest of the developer of the compound. The license agreement dates back to 1881 and contains a royalty payment by plaintiff to defendant based on the amount of Listerine manufactured and sold. Royalty payments at the time of the action amounted to about one and one-half million dollars per year. At the time of the original agreement, Listerine was a secret formula. Between the years 1881 and 1949, the formula became a matter of public knowledge and had been published in the United States Pharmacopia, the National Formulary and the Journal of the American Medical Association "and also as a result of proceedings brought against plaintiff's predecessor by the Federal Trade Commission." The plaintiff was not responsible for any of the publications. The plaintiff brings this action for a judgment declaring that it is no longer obligated to pay royalties because the formula is no longer secret. The court found that the unambiguous language of the agreement contemplated royalty payments as long as the plaintiff manufactured and sold "Listerine". The court rejected plaintiff's contention that this was a contract in "perpetuity" which the common law abhorred and should be interpreted as requiring royalties for a reasonable time—while the formula remained secret.]

There is nothing unreasonable or irrational about imposing such an obligation. It is entirely rational and sensible that the obligation to make payments should be based upon the business which flows from the formula conveyed. Whether or not the obligation continues is in the control of the plaintiff itself. For the plaintiff has the right to terminate its obligation to pay whenever in good faith it desires to cease the manufacture or sale of Listerine. * * * This would seem to end the matter.

However, plaintiff urges with vigor that the agreement must be differently construed because it involved the conveyance of a secret formula. The main thrust of its argument is that despite the language which the parties used the court must imply a limitation upon Lambert's obligation to pay measured by the length of time that the Listerine formula remained secret.

To sustain this theory plaintiff relies upon a number of cases involving the obligations of licensees of copyrights or patents to make continuing payments to the owner or licensor, and argues that these cases are controlling here.

It is quite plain that were it not for the patent and copyright features of such license agreements the term would be measured by use. * * *

There are other cases on which the plaintiff relies which hold that when a patent or copyright is held to be invalid before the expiration of the statutory term of the grant the obligation to pay royalties under a license terminates. This is but another aspect of the same principle. * * *

Paralleling the concept that the licensing of a patent or copyright contracts only for the statutory monopoly granted in such cases is the concept not so frequently expressed that public policy may require a termination of the obligation to pay when the patent or copyright term is ended. * * *

In the patent and copyright cases the parties are dealing with a fixed statutory term and the monopoly granted by that term. This monopoly, created by Congress, is designed to preserve exclusivity in the grantee during the statutory term and to release the patented or copyrighted material to the general public for general use thereafter. This is the public policy of the statutes in reference to which such contracts are made and it is against this background that the parties to patent and copyright license agreements contract.

Here, however, there is no such public policy. The parties are free to contract with respect to a secret formula or trade secret in any manner which they determine for their own best interests. A secret formula or trade secret may remain secret indefinitely. It may be discovered by someone else almost immediately after the agreement is entered into. Whoever discovers it for himself by legitimate means is entitled to its use.

But that does not mean that one who acquires a secret formula or a trade secret through a valid and binding contract is then enabled to escape from an obligation to which he bound himself simply because the secret is discovered by a third party or by the general public. I see no reason why the court should imply such a term or condition in a contract providing on its face that payment shall be co-extensive with use. To do so here would be to rewrite the contract for the parties without any indication that they intended such a result.

* * *

One who acquires a trade secret or secret formula takes it subject to the risk that there be a disclosure. The inventor makes no representation that the secret is non-discoverable. All the inventor does is to convey the knowledge of the formula or process which is unknown to the purchaser and which in so far as both parties then know is unknown to any one else. The terms upon which they contract with reference to this subject matter are purely up to them and are governed by what the contract they enter into provides.

If they desire the payments or royalties should continue only until the secret is disclosed to the public it is easy enough for them to say so. But there is no justification for implying such a provision if the parties do not include it in their contract, particularly where the language which they use by fair intendment provides otherwise.

* * *

If plaintiff wishes to avoid its obligations under the contract it is free to do so, and, indeed, the contract itself indicates how this may be done. The fact that neither the plaintiff nor its predecessors have done so, and that the plaintiff continues to manufacture and sell Listerine under the Lawrence formula with great success, indicates how valuable the rights under the contract are and how unjust it would be to permit it to have its cake and eat it too.

Thus, I hold that under the agreements in suit plaintiff is obligated to make the periodic payments called for by them as long as it continues to manufacture and sell the preparation described in them as Listerine.

* * *

Defendants' motions for summary judgment are in all respects granted. Judgment for defendants dismissing the second amended complaint will be entered accordingly.

It is so ordered.

NOTES

1. *Reed, Roberts* involved the activities of a former employee. Should the same requirement of reasonableness be applied to the seller of the good will of a business who after the sale solicits former customers for a competing firm? In Mohawk Maintenance Co., Inc. v. Kessler, 52 N.Y.2d 276, 419 N.E.2d 324 (1981) the New York Court of Appeals held that although an anticompetition agreement must be limited in duration and geographic scope, there is an independent tort duty implied from the circumstances not to solicit former customers after selling the "good will" of a business. This duty is not limited in duration! This unlimited duty applies only to sellers of good will and not to employees or contractors, Chevron U.S.A. Inc. v. Roxen Service, Inc., 813 F.2d 26 (2d Cir.1987). And the duty requires only a restraint on solicitation of former customers and not on subsequent transactions initiated by the customer. Hyde Park Products Corp. v. Maximilian Lerner Corp., 65 N.Y.2d 316, 491 N.Y.S.2d 302, 480 N.E.2d 1084 (1985).

2. In Ingersoll–Rand Co. v. Ciavatta, 216 N.J.Super. 667, 524 A.2d 866 (1987) the employee assigned to his employer all right, title, and interest in any invention or design that he conceived, developed, or perfected "within one year after termination of such employment if conceived as a result of and is attributable to work done during such employment and relates to [the employer's business]." Within one year of being terminated the employee invented a machine that competed with a machine of the employer. The trial judge found the employee's machine did not incorporate any trade secret or confidential information of the employer but did fit within the agreement. The trial judge ordered the employee to assign the patent to the employer. Held: Reversed. In the context of this case, as long as there are no trade secrets or confidential information used, the post-employment restraint fails to permit the employee to use his skill and training in subsequent employment and is thus unreasonable and unenforceable.

3. Why would a court be willing to enforce the contract in *Warner-Lambert* and not in the employment settings?

4. The plaintiff's predecessor in *Warner-Lambert* had first manufactured and sold the formula under the trademark "Listerine," thus acquiring the common law rights to the mark. If the defendant's successor in interest had first sold the formula under the name "Listerine" and then licensed the right to use the name, there would be no doubt about the outcome. Trademark rights are, given continued use, and, under the Lanham Act § 8(a), 15 U.S.C.A. § 1058(a), given reregistration every ten years, perpetual. If only the trademark were licensed, would the plaintiff remain free to manufacture and sell the formula under a different name? Would that be an important difference?

5. Is the effect of *Reed, Roberts* that restrictive covenants between employers and employees are useless? Does the case hold that an agreement is only enforceable if it reaches the same result that tort law would reach in the absence of the agreement? Does *Eden Hannon* cast further doubt on the efficacy of trade secret law? Is this inconsistent with *Warner-Lambert?* Judge Hand in *Conmar*, supra, suggested he would not interpret a contract for royalties on a secret to extend beyond the period of secrecy unless the terms of the contract were clear. Assume the parties clearly intended that result. Would you enforce it? Does *Eden Hannon* support enforcement of such agreements? Does the doctrine of *Sears* and *Compco* help answer these questions? Does the analysis in *Reed, Roberts* apply to a situation like *Warner-Lambert?*

6. For an excellent analysis of historical and current approaches to the problem of post-employment agreements see Blake, Employee Agreements Not to Compete, 73 Harv.L.Rev. 625 (1960).

The question of why courts are reluctant to enforce post-employment contractual restraints is discussed in Kitch, The Law and Economics of Rights in Valuable Information, 9 J.Leg.Stud. 683 (1980). The Blake article summarizes the two reasons traditionally given. First, that employees lack the sophistication and foresight necessary to bargain intelligently on their rights after the unexpected (at the time of bargaining) contingency of employment termination. Second, it is argued that post-employment contractual restraints are anti-competitive. Kitch argues that neither reason is very satisfactory.

The lack of capacity argument is unsatisfactory because the courts have permitted employees to freely bargain on far more difficult questions relating to post-employment pension rights and because the class of contracts approved and disapproved by the courts has no correspondence to the presence or absence of bargaining sophistication. Young baseball players, aspiring actors, and dairy route men have been held to their contracts while sophisticated executives like John Strauman in *Reed, Roberts* are allowed to avoid their contracts.

Second, there is nothing more anti-competitive about a post-employment contract than there is about any long term supply contract for an input to production. The contract does not keep an employee from moving to his highest valued use. It only means that some payment must be made to the employer to compensate him for the loss of his contract rights. Consider the frequency with which professional baseball players change teams in spite of the substantial restraints on post-employment choices which the law permits.

See also, Stewart Sterk, Restraints on Alienation of Human Capital, 79 Va. L. Rev. 383 (1993) arguing in favor of enforcement of restrictive covenants.

7. Is the "Arrow paradox" at work in the employer-employee relationship? One must assume that an employee gets something in return for signing a restrictive covenant, such as an increased wage or training and access to useful information that will increase the employee's future marketability. In situations where the employer wants the restrictive covenant to protect secret information, can the employee make an intelligent decision whether to sign the covenant before knowing what the information is? Does it matter whether the information to be provided by the employer to the employee is in the nature of general training applicable to the entire industry or whether the information is firm specific?

8. It is likely, is it not, that one important piece of information that John Strauman took from his employer in *Reed, Roberts* was the knowledge that the activity was profitable? Why is he entitled to exploit that information when he did not discover or develop the profitable opportunity?

PROBLEM

Assume that Microsoft sells its Windows 98 software in a shrink-wrapped box with a standard form license agreement inside the box. On the outside of the box there is a legend that informs the purchaser that by opening the shrink-wrap the purchaser agrees to be bound by the license agreement. A term of the license provides that the buyer may not sell or otherwise transfer the product to another person without Microsoft's consent. Would you enforce the agreement? If part of the computer program was secret? If the contract would have been negotiated rather than part of a standard form?

(e) Federal-State Conflicts

Sears, Roebuck & Co. v. Stiffel Co.

Supra, page 25

Compco Corp. v. Day-Brite Lighting Co.

Supra, page 28

Bonito Boats, Inc. v. Thunder Craft Boats

Supra, page 32

Brulotte v. Thys Co.

Supreme Court of the United States, 1964.
379 U.S. 29, 85 S.Ct. 176, 13 L.Ed.2d 99, rehearing denied 379 U.S. 985, 85 S.Ct. 638, 13 L.Ed.2d 579.

■ MR. JUSTICE DOUGLAS delivered the opinion of the Court.

Respondent, owner of various patents for hop-picking, sold a machine to each of the petitioners for a flat sum[1] and issued a license for its use. Under that license there is payable a minimum royalty of $500 for each hop-picking season or $3.33⅓ per 200 pounds of dried hops harvested by the machine, whichever is greater. The licenses by their terms may not be assigned nor may the machines be removed from Yakima County. The licenses issued to petitioners listed 12 patents relating to hop-picking machines; but only seven were incorporated into the machines sold to and licensed for use by petitioners. Of those seven all expired on or before 1957. But the licenses issued by respondent to them continued for terms beyond that date.

Petitioners refused to make royalty payments accruing both before and after the expiration of the patents. This suit followed. One defense was misuse of the patents through extension of the license agreements beyond the expiration date of the patents. The trial court rendered judgment for respondent and the Supreme Court of Washington affirmed. The case is here on a writ of certiorari.

We conclude that the judgment below must be reversed insofar as it allows royalties to be collected which accrued after the last of the patents incorporated into the machines had expired.

The Constitution by Art. I, § 8 authorizes Congress to secure "for limited times" to inventors "the exclusive right" to their discoveries. Congress exercised that power by 35 U.S.C.A. § 154 which *** [specifies a grant of seventeen years].

* * *

The Supreme Court of Washington held that in the present case the period during which royalties were required was only "a reasonable amount of time over which to spread the payments for the use of the patent." 62 Wash.2d, at 291, 382 P.2d, at 275. But there is intrinsic evidence that the

---

1. One petitioner paid $3,125 for "title" to a machine, the other petitioner, $3,300.

agreements were not designed with that limited view. As we have seen, the purchase price in each case was a flat sum, the annual payments not being part of the purchase price but royalties for use of the machine during that year. The royalty payments due for the post-expiration period are by their terms for use during that period, and are not deferred payments for use during the pre-expiration period. Nor is the case like the hypothetical ones put to us where non-patented articles are marketed at prices based on use. The machines in issue here were patented articles and the royalties exacted were the same for the post expiration period as they were for the period of the patent. That is peculiarly significant in this case in view of other provisions of the license agreements. The license agreements prevent assignment of the machines or their removal from Yakima County *after,* as well as before, the expiration of the patents.

Those restrictions are apt and pertinent to protection of the patent monopoly; and their applicability to the post-expiration period is a telltale sign that the licensor was using the licenses to project its monopoly beyond the patent period. They forcefully negate the suggestion that we have here a bare arrangement for a sale or a lease at an undetermined price, based on use. The sale or lease of *unpatented* machines on long-term payments based on a deferred purchase price or on use would present wholly different considerations. Those arrangements seldom rise to the level of a federal question. But patents are in the federal domain; and "whatever the legal device employed" * * * a projection of the patent monopoly after the patent expires is not enforceable. The present licenses draw no line between the term of the patent and the post-expiration period. The same provisions as respects both use and royalties are applicable to each. The contracts are, therefore, on their face a bald attempt to exact the same terms and conditions for the period after the patents have expired as they do for the monopoly period. We are, therefore, unable to conjecture what the bargaining position of the parties might have been and what resultant arrangement might have emerged had the provision for post-expiration royalties been divorced from the patent and nowise subject it to its leverage.

In light of those considerations, we conclude that a patentee's use of a royalty agreement that projects beyond the expiration date of the patent is unlawful *per se.* If that device were available to patentees, the free market visualized for the post-expiration period would be subject to monopoly influences that have no proper place there.

* * *

* * * We share the views of the Court of Appeals in Ar-Tik Systems, Inc. v. Dairy Queen, Inc., 302 F.2d 496, 510, that after expiration of the last of the patents incorporated in the machines "the grant of patent monopoly was spent" and that an attempt to project it into another term by continuation of the licensing agreement is unenforceable.

Reversed.

Mr. Justice HARLAN, dissenting.

The Court holds that the Thys Company unlawfully misused its patent monopoly by contracting with purchasers of its patented machines for royalty payments based on use beyond the patent term. I think that more discriminating analysis than the Court has seen fit to give this case produces a different result.

The patent laws prohibit post-expiration restrictions on the use of patented ideas; they have no bearing on use restrictions upon non-patented, tangible machines. We have before us a mixed case involving the sale of a tangible machine which incorporates an intangible, patented idea. My effort in what follows is to separate out these two notions, to show that there is no substantial restriction on the use of the Thys *idea,* and to demonstrate that what slight restriction there may be is less objectionable than other post-expiration use restrictions which are clearly acceptable.

I.

It surely cannot be questioned that Thys could have lawfully set a fixed price for its machine and extended credit terms beyond the patent period. It is equally unquestionable, I take it, that if Thys had had no patent or if its patent had expired, it could have sold its machines at a flexible, undetermined price based on use; for example, a phonograph record manufacturer could sell a recording of a song in the public domain to a juke-box owner for an undetermined consideration based on the number of times the record was played.

Conversely it should be equally clear that if Thys licensed another manufacturer to produce hop-picking machines incorporating any of the Thys patents, royalties could not be exacted beyond the patent term. Such royalties would restrict the manufacturer's exploitation of the *idea* after it falls into the public domain, and no such restriction should be valid. To give another example unconnected with a tangible machine, a song writer could charge a royalty every time his song—his idea—was sung for profit during the period of copyright. But once the song falls into the public domain each and every member of the public should be free to sing it.

In fact Thys sells both a machine and the use of an idea. The company should be free to restrict the use of its machine, as in the first two examples given above. It may not restrict the use of its patented idea once it has fallen into the public domain. Whether it has done so must be the point of inquiry.

Consider the situation as of the day the patent monopoly ends. Any manufacturer is completely free to produce Thys-type hop-pickers. The farmer who has previously purchased a Thys machine is free to buy and use any other kind of machine whether or not it incorporates the Thys idea, or make one himself if he is able. Of course, he is not entitled as against Thys to the *free* use of any Thys machine. The Court's opinion must therefore ultimately rest on the proposition that the purchasing farmer is restricted in using his particular machine, embodying as it does an application of the patented idea, by the fact that royalties are tied directly to use.

To test this proposition I again put a hypothetical. Assume that a Thys contract called for neither an initial flat-sum payment nor any annual minimum royalties; Thys' sole recompense for giving up ownership of its machine was a royalty payment extending beyond the patent term based on use, without any requirement either to use the machine or not to use a competitor's. A moment's thought reveals that, despite the clear restriction on use both before and after the expiration of the patent term, the arrangement would involve no misuse of patent leverage.[1] Unless the Court's opinion rests on technicalities of contract draftsmanship and not on the economic substance of the transaction, the distinction between the hypothetical and the actual case lies only in the cumulative investment consisting of the initial and minimum payments independent of use, which the purchaser obligated himself to make to Thys. I fail to see why this distinguishing feature should be critical. If anything the investment will encourage the purchaser to use his machine in order to amortize the machine's fixed cost over as large a production base as possible. Yet the gravamen of the majority opinion is restriction, not encouragement, of use.

II.

The essence of the majority opinion may lie in some notion that "patent leverage" being used by Thys to exact use payments extending beyond the patent term somehow allows Thys to extract more onerous payments from the farmers than would otherwise be obtainable. If this be the case, the Court must in some way distinguish long-term use payments from long-term installment payments of a flat-sum purchase price. For the danger which it seems to fear would appear to inhere equally in both, and as I read the Court's opinion, the latter type of arrangement is lawful despite the fact that failure to pay an installment under a conditional sales contract would permit the seller to recapture the machine, thus terminating—not merely restricting—the farmer's use of it. Furthermore, since the judgments against petitioners were based almost entirely on defaults in paying the $500 minimums and not on failures to pay for above-minimum use,[2] any such distinction of extended use payments and extended installments, even if accepted, would not justify eradicating all petitioners' obligations beyond the patent term, but only those based on use above the stated minimums; for the minimums by themselves, being payable whether or not a machine has been used, are precisely identical in substantive economic effect to flat installments.

In fact a distinction should not be accepted based on the assumption that Thys, which exploits its patents by selling its patented machines

---

1. Installment of a patented, coin-operated washing machine in the basement of an apartment building without charge except that the landlord and his tenants must deposit 25 cents for every use, should not constitute patent misuse.

2. Petitioner Charvet was indebted to Thys only to the extent of the minimums; petitioner Brulotte was in default approximately $4,500 of which $3,120 was attributable to minimums.

rather than licensing others to manufacture them, can use its patent leverage to exact more onerous payments from farmers by gearing price to use instead of charging a flat sum. Four possible situations must be considered. The purchasing farmer could overestimate, exactly estimate, underestimate, or have no firm estimate of his use requirements for a Thys machine. If he overestimates or exactly estimates, the farmer will be fully aware of what the machine will cost him in the long run, and it is unrealistic to suppose that in such circumstances he would be willing to pay more to have the machine on use than on straight terms. If the farmer underestimates, the thought may be that Thys will take advantage of him; but surely the farmer is in a better position than Thys or anyone else to estimate his own requirements and is hardly in need of the Court's protection in this respect. If the farmer has no fixed estimate of his use requirements he may have good business reasons entirely unconnected with "patent leverage" for wanting payments tied to use, and may indeed be willing to pay more in the long run to obtain such an arrangement. One final example should illustrate my point:

At the time when the Thys patent term still has a few years to run, a farmer who has been picking his hops by hand comes into the Thys retail outlet to inquire about the mechanical pickers. The salesman concludes his description of the advantages of the Thys machine with the price tag— $20,000. Value to the farmer depends completely on the use he will derive from the machine; he is willing to obligate himself on long credit terms to pay $10,000, but unless the machine can substantially outpick his old hand-picking methods, it is worth no more to him. He therefore offers to pay $2,000 down, $400 annually for 20 years, and an additional payment during the contract term for any production he can derive from the machine over and above the minimum amount he could pick by hand. Thys accepts, and by doing so, according to the majority, commits a *per se* misuse of its patent. I cannot believe that this is good law.[3]

III.

The possibility remains that the Court is basing its decision on the technical framing of the contract and would have treated the case differently if title had been declared to pass at the termination instead of the outset of the contract term, or if the use payments had been verbally disassociated from the patent licenses and described as a convenient means

---

3. The Court also adverts to the provisions in the license agreements prohibiting "assignment of the machines or their removal from Yakima County" (ante, p. 32) during the terms of the agreements. Such provisions, however, are surely appropriate to secure performance of what are in effect conditional sales agreements and they do not advance the argument for patent misuse.

Furthermore, it should not be overlooked that we are dealing here with a patent, not an antitrust, case, there being no basis in the record for concluding that Thys' arrangements with its licensees were such as to run afoul of the antitrust laws.

of spreading out payments for the machine. If indeed the impact of the opinion is that Thys must redraft its contracts to achieve the same economic results, the decision is not only wrong, but conspicuously ineffectual.

I would affirm.

NOTES

1. *Brulotte* was decided in the same year as *Sears* and *Compco*. Are they all based on the same basic philosophy? Could you reformulate the *Brulotte* opinion into one asserting federal preemption rather than patent misuse?

2. If Thys Co. can not extend royalty payments based on use beyond the expiration of the patents, can it exact royalty payments based on use *prior to* issuance of a patent? Would this unreasonably extend the patent monopoly? Would it make a difference if a patent application were pending? See Congoleum Industries, Inc. v. Armstrong Cork Co., 366 F.Supp. 220 (E.D.Pa.1973).

Lear, Inc. v. Adkins

Supreme Court of the United States, 1969.
395 U.S. 653, 89 S.Ct. 1902, 23 L.Ed.2d 610.

■ MR. JUSTICE HARLAN delivered the opinion of the Court.

[In 1952 Lear hired John Adkins to develop improvements in the gyroscope utilized in Lear's aircraft. The parties signed a "rudimentary one-page agreement" giving Adkins the property interest in all ideas or inventions in consideration for Adkins' agreement to license their use by Lear on a "mutually satisfactory royalty basis." Adkins' efforts bore fruit and in 1954 he applied for a patent on his gyroscope improvements. On September 15, 1955, after lengthy negotiations, Lear and Adkins signed a licensing agreement governing Lear's use of the improved gyroscope upon payment of specified royalties. The license agreement contained a clause giving Lear the right to terminate the agreement if the Patent Office refused to issue a patent or an issued patent was subsequently held invalid.

Lear began paying royalties. Adkins, however, had difficulty convincing the Patent Office of the novelty of his ideas. In 1957, Lear finally announced it would discontinue royalty payments on the belief that no patent would issue. In 1960, the Patent Office issued a patent to Adkins who immediately filed suit against Lear for royalties. Lear maintained that the patent was invalid because Adkins' inventions were anticipated by prior art. The California Supreme Court held that a licensee like Lear is estopped from asserting the invalidity of the licensed patent and accordingly approved an award for royalties owed pursuant to the agreement. In the part of the opinion omitted below, the United States Supreme Court reviews the history of the licensee estoppel doctrine, recognizes that several exceptions had been adopted, and concludes that the doctrine should be discarded in its entirety.

Recognizing that, on the one hand, "the law of contracts forbids a purchaser to repudiate his promises simply because he later becomes dissatisfied" and, on the other, that "federal law requires that all ideas in general circulation be dedicated to the common good unless they are protected by a valid patent [citing *Sears* and *Compco*]" the Court continues:]

III.

* * *

Surely the equities of the licensor do not weigh very heavily when they are balanced against the important public interest in permitting full and free competition in the use of ideas which are in reality a part of the public domain. Licensees may often be the only individuals with enough economic incentive to challenge the patentability of an inventor's discovery. If they are muzzled, the public may continually be required to pay tribute to would-be monopolists without need or justification. We think it plain that the technical requirements of contract doctrine must give way before the demands of the public interest in the typical situation involving the negotiation of a license after a patent has issued.

B.

The case before us, however, presents a far more complicated estoppel problem than the one which arises in the most common licensing context. The problem arises out of the fact that Lear obtained its license in 1955, more than four years before Adkins received his 1960 patent. Indeed, from the very outset of the relationship, Lear obtained special access to Adkins' ideas in return for its promise to pay satisfactory compensation.

Thus, during the lengthy period in which Adkins was attempting to obtain a patent, Lear gained an important benefit not generally obtained by the typical licensee. For until a patent issues, a potential licensee may not learn his licensor's ideas simply by requesting the information from the Patent Office. During the time the inventor is seeking patent protection, the governing federal statute requires the Patent Office to hold an inventor's patent application in confidence. If a potential licensee hopes to use the ideas contained in a secret patent application, he must deal with the inventor himself, unless the inventor chooses to publicize his ideas to the world at large. By promising to pay Adkins royalties from the very outset of their relationship, Lear gained immediate access to ideas which it may well not have learned until the Patent Office published the details of Adkins' invention in 1960. At the core of this case, then, is the difficult question whether federal patent policy bars a State from enforcing a contract regulating access to an unpatented secret idea.

Adkins takes an extreme position on this question. The inventor does not merely argue that since Lear obtained privileged access to his ideas *before 1960,* the company should be required to pay royalties accruing *before 1960* regardless of the validity of the patent which ultimately issued. He also argues that since Lear obtained special benefits before 1960, it should also pay royalties during the entire patent period (1960–1977), without regard to the validity of the Patent Office's grant. We cannot accept so broad an argument.

Adkins' position would permit inventors to negotiate all important licenses during the lengthy period while their applications were still pending at the Patent Office, thereby disabling entirely all those who have the strongest incentive to show that a patent is worthless. While the equities supporting Adkins' position are somewhat more appealing than those supporting the typical licensor, we cannot say that there is enough of a difference to justify such a substantial impairment of overriding federal policy.

Nor can we accept a second argument which may be advanced to support Adkins' claim to at least a portion of his post-patent royalties, regardless of the validity of the Patent Office grant. The terms of the 1955 agreement provide that royalties are to be paid until such time as the "patent * * * is held invalid," § 6, and the fact remains that the question of patent validity has not been finally determined in this case. Thus, it may be suggested that although Lear must be allowed to raise the question of patent validity in the present lawsuit, it must also be required to comply with its contract and continue to pay royalties until its claim is finally vindicated in the courts.

The parties' contract, however, is no more controlling on this issue than is the State's doctrine of estoppel, which is also rooted in contract principles. The decisive question is whether overriding federal policies would be significantly frustrated if licensees could be required to continue to pay royalties during the time they are challenging patent validity in the courts.

It seems to us that such a requirement would be inconsistent with the aims of federal patent policy. Enforcing this contractual provision would give the licensor an additional economic incentive to devise every conceivable dilatory tactic in an effort to postpone the day of final judicial reckoning. We can perceive no reason to encourage dilatory court tactics in this way. Moreover, the cost of prosecuting slow-moving trial proceedings and defending an inevitable appeal might well deter many licensees from attempting to prove patent invalidity in the courts. The deterrent effect would be particularly severe in the many scientific fields in which invention is proceeding at a rapid rate. In these areas, a patent may well become obsolete long before its 17-year term has expired. If a licensee has reason to believe that he will replace a patented idea with a new one in the near future, he will have little incentive to initiate lengthy court proceedings, unless he is freed from liability at least from the time he refuses to pay the contractual royalties. Lastly, enforcing this contractual provision would undermine the strong federal policy favoring the full and free use of ideas in the public domain. For all these reasons, we hold that Lear must be permitted to avoid the payment of all royalties accruing after Adkins' 1960 patent issued if Lear can prove patent invalidity.

C.

Adkins' claim to contractual royalties accruing before the 1960 patent issued is, however, a much more difficult one, since it squarely raises the question whether, and to what extent, the States may protect the owners of *unpatented* inventions who are willing to disclose their ideas to manufacturers only upon payment of royalties. The California Supreme Court did not address itself to this issue with precision, for it believed that the venerable doctrine of estoppel provided a sufficient answer to all of Lear's claims based upon federal patent law. Thus, we do not know whether the Supreme Court would have awarded Adkins recovery even on his pre-patent royalties if it had recognized that previously established estoppel doctrine could no longer be properly invoked with regard to royalties accruing during the 17-year patent period. Our decision today will, of course, require the state courts to reconsider the theoretical basis of their decisions enforcing the contractual rights of inventors and it is impossible to predict the extent to which this re-evaluation may revolutionize the law of any particular State in this regard. Consequently, we have concluded, after much consideration, that even though an important question of federal law underlies this phase of the controversy, we should not now attempt to define in even a limited way the extent, if any, to which the States may properly act to enforce the contractual rights of inventors of unpatented secret ideas. Given the difficulty and importance of this task, it should be undertaken only after the state courts have, after fully focused inquiry, determined the extent to which they will respect the contractual rights of such inventors in the future. Indeed, on remand, the California courts may well reconcile the competing demands of patent and contract law in a way which would not warrant further review in this Court.

IV.

We also find it inappropriate to pass at this time upon Lear's contention that Adkins' patent is invalid.

The judgment of the Supreme Court of California is vacated and the case is remanded to that court for further proceedings not inconsistent with this opinion.

It is so ordered.

Mr. Justice BLACK, with whom The CHIEF JUSTICE and Mr. Justice DOUGLAS join, concurring in part and dissenting in part.

I concur in the judgment and opinion of the Court, except for what is said in Part III, C, of the Court's opinion. What the Court does in this part of its opinion is to reserve for future decision the question whether the States have power to enforce contracts under which someone claiming to have a new discovery can obtain payment for disclosing it while his patent application is pending, even though the discovery is later held to be unpatentable. This reservation is, as I see it, directly in conflict with what this Court held to be the law in Sears, Roebuck v. Stiffel Co., 376 U.S. 225 (1964), and Compco Corp. v. Day-Brite Lighting, Inc., 376 U.S. 234 (1964). Brother Harlan concurred in the result in those cases, saying—contrary to what the Court held—"I see no reason why the State may not impose reasonable restrictions on the future 'copying' itself." Compco, supra, at 239. Consequently the Court is today joining in the kind of qualification that only Mr. Justice Harlan was willing to make at the time of our Stiffel and Compco decisions.

I still entertain the belief I expressed for the Court in Stiffel and Compco that no State has a right to authorize any kind of monopoly on what is claimed to be a new invention, except when a patent has been obtained from the Patent Office under the exacting standards of the patent laws. One who makes a discovery may, of course, keep it secret if he wishes, but private arrangements under which self-styled "inventors" do not keep their discoveries secret, but rather disclose them, in return for contractual payments, run counter to the plan of our patent laws, which tightly regulate the kind of inventions that may be protected and the manner in which they may be protected. The national policy expressed in the patent laws, favoring free competition and narrowly limiting monopoly, cannot be frustrated by private agreements among individuals, with or without the approval of the State.

Mr. Justice WHITE, concurring in part.

* * *

Although we have jurisdiction to review this state court judgment and to determine the licensee estoppel issue, it does not necessarily follow that we may or should deal with two other federal questions which come into focus once the licensee is free to challenge the patent. The first is whether the patent is valid. The second, which arises only if the patent is invalidated, is whether federal law forbids the collection of royalties which might otherwise be collectible under a contract rooted in state law. * * *

In the first place, we have no decision of the California Supreme Court affirming or denying, as a matter of federal law, that Adkins may not enforce his contract if his patent is held invalid. The California court held that the license agreement had not been terminated in accordance with its terms, that the doctrine of licensee estoppel prevented Lear from challenging the patent and that Lear was utilizing the teaching of Adkins' patent. There was thus no necessity or reason to consider whether the patent was invalid, or, if it was, whether either state or federal law prevented collection of the royalties reserved by the contract. * * *

There is no indication, however, that Lear, directly or by inference, urged in the California courts that if Adkins' patent were invalid, federal law overrode state contract law and precluded collection of the royalties which Lear had promised to pay. One of the defenses presented by Lear in its answer to Adkins' claim for royalties was that there had been a failure of consideration because of the absence of bargained-for patentability in Adkins' ideas. But failure of consideration is a state law question, and I find nothing in the record and nothing in this Court's opinion indicating that Lear at any time contended in the state courts that once Adkins' patent was invalidated, the royalty agreement was unenforceable as a matter of federal law.

Given Lear's failure below to "specially set up or claim" the federal bar to collection of royalties in the event Adkins' patent was invalidated, and without the California Supreme Court's "final judgment" on this issue, I doubt our jurisdiction to decide the issue. * * *

NOTES

1. Footnote 9 of the Court's opinion in Lear reads as follows:

9. Adkins also filed a second cause of action which contended that Lear had wrongfully appropriated a valuable trade secret and so was liable regardless of the validity of the inventor's contractual and quasi-contractual theories. The trial court, however, required Adkins' to choose between his contract and tort claims. Since the California Supreme Court completely vindicated the inventor's right to contractual royalties, it was not obliged to consider the propriety of this aspect of the trial judge's decision. Consequently, the tort claim is not before us at this time.

How do you evaluate Adkins' contention?

2. If, in the contract, Lear had expressly promised to pay royalties whether or not the patent was valid, would that have made any difference? Did § 6 of the agreement, providing that Lear could terminate if the patent was held invalid, have any role in the decision?

3. Suppose Adkins had entered into an agreement entitled "Agreement for compensation for services rendered to Lear, Inc. in connection with the successful development of improved vertical gyros" which provided that Adkins should be compensated for his services by royalties on the production of the devices described in the patent. Separately, Adkins executed an irrevocable, royalty free license of the patent to Lear, Inc. Would the compensation agreement be enforceable? Can Lear bring an action in the California courts to have his agreement reformed along these lines? Would section 6 be fatal to such an action?

4. *Lear* alone did not have much of an impact on patent licensing. The licensee often has a substantial interest in preserving the validity of the licensed patent since the licensee shares in the patent's market power. However, the resolution of some of the questions left open in *Lear* were of great concern to patent owners. If the patent is found invalid, could a licensee recover royalties already paid? If so, the licensee could exploit the license against third parties until near the end of the patent period and then contest the patent's validity recovering, if successful, his royalty payments. The situation became more interesting after the Court decided Blonder-Tongue Laboratories, Inc. v. University of Illinois Foundation, 402 U.S. 313 (1971).

The Court there held that once a patent owner has a full and fair chance to litigate the validity of his patent in one case and the patent is held invalid, the owner is estopped to assert the validity of the patent in subsequent litigation. However, a declaration of patent *validity* would not be binding on parties not involved in the earlier litigation. See Stevenson v. Sears, Roebuck & Co., 713 F.2d 705 (Fed.Cir. 1983). *Blonder-Tongue* provided additional incentive for a licensee to await the outcome of other litigation.

The leading case facing up to these difficulties is Troxel Mfg. Co. v. Schwinn Bicycle Co., 465 F.2d 1253 (6th Cir.1972) (*Troxel I*), and Troxel Mfg. Co. v. Schwinn Bicycle Co., 489 F.2d 968 (6th Cir.), cert. denied 416 U.S. 939 (1974) (*Troxel II*). Troxel was a licensee of a Schwinn patent. In unrelated litigation a California federal district court declared the patent invalid in January, 1969, and the Ninth Circuit affirmed on December 22, 1970. Troxel had stopped paying royalties in October, 1970. Troxel sued to recover all royalties paid under the invalid patent. Schwinn counterclaimed for royalties during the last quarter of 1970. In *Troxel I* the court held that *Lear* did not require or authorize the recovery of voluntarily paid royalties. In *Troxel II,* the court ordered Troxel to pay royalties through December 22, 1970. The *Troxel* cases were amplified in PPG Industries, Inc. v. Westwood Chemical, Inc., 530 F.2d 700 (6th Cir. 1976). There the court held the obligation to pay royalties ceases on the earliest of the following dates: (1) on the date some other party is successful in having the patent declared invalid; (2) the licensee stops paying royalties for the purpose of prompting an adjudication of validity (the mere refusal to pay without a further indication that the licensee contests the validity of the patent is insufficient); or (3) the licensee files a suit or counterclaim attacking the validity of the patent. See also Transitron Electronic Corp. v. Hughes Aircraft, 649 F.2d 871 (1st Cir. 1981) (licensee may recover back royalty payments if induced into the license by fraud).

5. The objective of the Court in *Lear* is to create an opportunity for licensees to challenge the validity of patents because, as the Court reasons, "Licensees may often be the only individuals with enough economic incentive to challenge the patentability of an inventor's discovery. If they are muzzled, the public may continually be required to pay tribute to would-be monopolists without need or justification." Is this true? The licensor and licensee are already in a close bargaining relationship. Once the *Lear* doctrine is clearly established, isn't it in both of their interests to simply renegotiate the license arrangement in light of the probabilities that the licensee could show the patent to be invalid? The licensee has no more interest than the licensor in creating a public, on-the-record determination that the patent is invalid. Thus isn't the only effect of the *Lear* decision to marginally reduce the value of all patents?

6. Does *Lear* suggest that an assignor of a patent may turn around and challenge its validity? Diamond Scientific Co. v. Ambico Inc., 848 F.2d 1220 (Fed.Cir. 1988) (No). What about a party to an agreement reached to settle litigation? See Hemstreet v. Spiegel Inc., 851 F.2d 348 (Fed.Cir. 1988) (No); Warner–Jenkinson Co. v. Allied Chemical Corp., 567 F.2d 184 (2d Cir. 1977) (Yes). A party to a consent decree? Wallace Clark & Co. Inc. v. Acheson Industries, Inc., 532 F.2d 846 (2d Cir. 1976) (No).

7. See generally, McCarthy. "Unmuzzling" The Patent Licensee: Chaos in the Wake of Lear v. Adkins, 45 Geo. Wash. L. Rev. 429 (1977), R. Dreyfuss, Dethroning *Lear*: Licensee Estoppel and the Incentive to Innovate, 72 Va. L. Rev. 677 (1986).

8. The mystery of Mr. Justice Harlan's dissent in *Brulotte* and the authorship of *Lear* becomes clear when one learns that he followed the practice of accepting as precedent binding on him decisions from which he dissented after the end of the term in which they were handed down. See Bourguignon, The Second Mr. Justice Harlan: His Principles of Judicial Decision Making, 1979 Sup. Ct. Rev. 251, 279–81. Indeed, his authorship of the *Lear* opinion enabled him to adopt a limited if somewhat illogical reading of *Brulotte*. Doesn't the logic of *Brulotte* require that once a court determines that a patent is invalid—and hence that it always has been invalid—that all royalties ever paid be returned?

9. Does § 294 of the Patent Act, providing for arbitration by agreement of patent disputes, partially overrule the *Lear* decision? Could parties agree in arbitration to pay royalties for an invalid patent? Consider Saturday Evening Post Co. v. Rumbleseat Press, Inc., 816 F.2d 1191 (7th Cir. 1987) holding arbitration and no contest clauses in a copyright licensing agreement valid.

Kewanee Oil Company v. Bicron Corporation

Supreme Court of the United States, 1974.
416 U.S. 470, 94 S.Ct. 1879, 40 L.Ed.2d 315.

■ MR. CHIEF JUSTICE BURGER delivered the opinion of the Court.

We granted certiorari to resolve a question on which there is a conflict in Courts of Appeals: whether state trade secret protection is pre-empted by operation of the federal patent law. * * *

[Petitioner, as a result of expenditures in excess of $1 million developed processes and techniques related to the production of synthetic crystals. Respondents were former employees of Petitioner who joined the Respondent, Bicron, a competitor of Petitioner. The trial court found that the Respondents had appropriated some 20 of Petitioner's trade secrets and pursuant to Ohio law enjoined them from disclosure or use of these secrets until they had been released to the public. The Court of Appeals agreed that the trial court's findings were not clearly erroneous but held that the Ohio law of trade secrets "could not grant monopoly protection to processes and manufacturing techniques that were appropriate subjects for consideration under 35 U.S.C. § 101 for a federal patent but which had been in commercial use for over one year and so were no longer eligible for patent protection under 35 U.S.C. § 102(b)".]

We hold that Ohio's law of trade secrets is not preempted by the patent laws of the United States, and, accordingly, we reverse.

[The Supreme Court reviewed the substance of the Ohio law of trade secrets which was derived from the Restatement of Torts. It then followed Goldstein v. California and held that Congress did not have exclusive power over "discoveries".]

IV

The question of whether the trade secret law of Ohio is void under the Supremacy Clause involves a consideration of whether that law "stands as an obstacle to the accomplishment and execution of the full purposes and objectives of Congress." Hines v. Davidowitz, 312 U.S. 52, 67 (1941). * * * The stated objective of the Constitution in granting the power to Congress to legislate in the area of intellectual property is to "promote the Progress of Science and useful Arts." The patent laws promote this progress by offering a right of exclusion for a limited period as an incentive for inventors to risk the often enormous costs in terms of time, research, and development. The productive effort thereby fostered will have a positive effect on society through the introduction of new products and processes of manufacture into the economy, and the emanations by way of increased employment and better lives for our citizens. In return for the right of exclusion—this "reward for inventions." Universal Oil Co. v. Globe Co., 322 U.S. 471, 484 (1944)—the patent laws impose upon the inventor a requirement of disclosure. To insure adequate and full disclosure so that upon the expiration of the 17-year period "the knowledge of the invention enures to the people, who are thus enabled without restriction to practice it and profit by its use." United States v. Dubilier Condenser Corp., 289 U.S. 178, 187 (1933), the patent laws require that the patent application shall include a full and clear description of the invention and "of the manner and process of making and using it" so that any person skilled in the art may make and use the invention. 35 U.S.C. § 112. When a patent is granted and the information contained in it is circulated to the general public and those especially skilled in the trade, such additions to the general store of knowledge are of such importance to the public weal that the Federal Government is willing to pay the high price of 17 years of exclusive use for its disclosure, which disclosure, it is assumed, will stimulate ideas and the eventual development of further significant advances on the art. The Court has also articulated another policy of the patent law: that which is in the public domain cannot be removed therefrom by action of the States.

> "[F]ederal laws require that all ideas in general circulation be dedicated to the common good unless they are protected by a valid patent." Lear, Inc. v. Adkins, supra, 395 U.S., at 668.

See also Goldstein v. California, supra, 412 U.S., at 570–571; Sears, Roebuck & Co. v. Stiffel Co., supra; Compco Corp. v. Day-Brite Lighting, Inc., 376 U.S. 234, 237–238 (1964); International News Service v. Associated Press, 248 U.S. 215, 250 (1918) (Brandeis, J., dissenting).

The maintenance of standards of commercial ethics and the encouragement of invention are the broadly stated policies behind trade secret law. "The necessity of good faith and honest, fair dealing, is the very life and spirit of the commercial world." National Tube Co. v. Eastern Tube Co., supra, 3 Ohio Cir.Ct.R., N.S. at 462. In A.O. Smith Corp. v. Petroleum Iron Works Co., supra, 73 F.2d, at 539, the Court emphasized that even though a discovery may not be patentable, that does not "destroy the value of the discovery to one who makes it, or advantage the competitor who by unfair means, or as the beneficiary of a broken faith, obtains the desired knowledge without himself paying the price in labor, money, or machines expended by the discoverer."

In Wexler v. Greenberg, 399 Pa. 569, 578–579, 160 A.2d 430 (1960), the Pennsylvania Supreme Court noted the importance of trade secret protection to the subsidization of research and development and to increased economic efficiency within large companies through the dispersion of responsibilities for creative developments.

Having now in mind the objectives of both the patent and trade secret law, we turn to an examination of the interaction of these systems of protection of intellectual property—one established by the Congress and the other by a State—to determine whether and under what circumstances the latter might constitute "too great an encroachment on the federal patent system to be tolerated." Sears, Roebuck & Co. v. Stiffel Co., supra, 376 U.S., at 232.

As we noted earlier, trade secret law protects items which would not be proper subjects for consideration for patent protection under 35 U.S.C. § 101. As in the case of the recordings in Goldstein v. California, Congress, with respect to nonpatentable subject matter, "has drawn no balance; rather, it has left the area unattended, and no reason exists why the State should not be free to act." Goldstein v. California, supra, 412 U.S., at 570 (footnote omitted).

Since no patent is available for a discovery, however useful, novel, and nonobvious, unless it falls within one of the express categories of patentable subject matter of 35 U.S.C. § 101, the holder of such a discovery would have no reason to apply for a patent whether trade secret protection existed or not. Abolition of trade secret protection would, therefore, not result in increased disclosure to the public of discoveries in the area of nonpatentable subject matter. Also, it is hard to see how the public would be benefited by disclosure of customer lists or advertising campaigns; in fact, keeping such items secret encourages businesses to initiate new and individualized plans of operation, and constructive competition results. This, in turn, leads to a greater variety of business methods than would otherwise be the case if privately developed marketing and other data were passed illicitly among firms involved in the same enterprise.

Congress has spoken in the area of those discoveries which fall within one of the categories of patentable subject matter of 35 U.S.C. § 101 and which are, therefore, of a nature that would be subject to consideration for a patent. Processes, machines, manufactures, compositions of matter and improvements thereof, which meet the tests of utility, novelty, and nonobviousness are entitled to be patented, but those which do not, are not. The question remains whether those items which are proper subjects for consideration for a patent may also have available the alternative protection accorded by trade secret law.

Certainly the patent policy of encouraging invention is not disturbed by the existence of another form of incentive to invention. In this respect the two systems are not and never would be in conflict. Similarly, the policy that matter once in the public domain must remain in the public domain is not incompatible with the existence of trade secret protection. By definition a trade secret has not been placed in the public domain.

The more difficult objective of the patent law to reconcile with trade secret law is that of disclosure, the *quid pro quo* of the right to exclude. We are helped in this stage of the analysis by Judge Henry Friendly's opinion in Painton & Company v. Bourns, Inc., 442 F.2d 216 (CA2 1971). There the Court of Appeals thought it useful, in determining whether inventors will refrain because of the existence of trade secret law from applying for patents thereby depriving the public from learning of the invention, to distinguish between three categories of trade secrets:

> "(1) the trade secret believed by its owner to constitute a validly patentable invention; (2) the trade secret known to its owner not to be so patentable; and (3) the trade secret whose valid patentability is considered dubious." Painton & Co. v. Bourns, Inc., 442 F.2d, at 224.

Trade secret protection in each of these categories would run against breaches of confidence—the employee and licensee situations—and theft and other forms of industrial espionage.

No policy reason for unpatentable ideas.

As to the trade secret known not to meet the standards of patentability, very little in the way of disclosure would be accomplished by abolishing trade secret protection. As with trade secrets of nonpatentable subject matter, the patent alternative would not reasonably be available to the inventor. "There can be no public interest in stimulating developers of such [unpatentable] knowhow to flood an overburdened Patent Office with applications for what they do not consider patentable." Ibid. The mere filing of applications doomed to be turned down by the Patent Office will bring forth no new public knowledge or enlightenment, since under federal statute and regulation patent applications and abandoned patent applications are held by the Patent Office in confidence and are not open to public inspection. 35 U.S.C. § 122; 37 CFR § 1.14(b).

Even as the extension of trade secret protection to patentable subject matter that the owner knows will not meet the standards of patentability will not conflict with the patent policy of disclosure, it will have a decidedly beneficial effect on society. Trade secret law will encourage invention in areas where patent law does not reach, and will prompt the independent innovator to proceed with the discovery and exploitation of his invention. Competition is fostered and the public is not deprived of the use of valuable, if not quite patentable, invention.

Even if trade secret protection against the faithless employee were abolished, inventive and exploitive effort in the area of patentable subject matter which did not meet the standards of patentability would continue, although at a reduced level. Alternatively with the effort that remained, however, would come an increase in the amount of self-help that innovative companies would employ. Knowledge would be widely dispersed among the employees of those still active in research. Security precautions necessarily would be increased, and salaries and fringe benefits of those few officers or employees who had to know the whole of the secret invention would be fixed in an amount thought sufficient to assure their loyalty. Smaller companies would be placed at a distinct economic disadvantage, since the costs of this kind of self-help could be great, and the cost to the public of the use of this invention would be increased. The innovative entrepreneur with limited resources would tend to confine his research efforts to himself and those few he felt he could trust without the ultimate assurance of legal protection against breaches of confidence. As a result, organized scientific and technological research could become fragmented, and society, as a whole would suffer.

Another problem that would arise if state trade secret protection were precluded is in the area of licensing others to exploit secret processes. The holder of a trade secret would not likely share his secret with a manufacturer who cannot be placed under binding legal obligation to pay a license fee or to protect the secret. The result would be to hoard rather than disseminate knowledge. Instead, then, of licensing others to use his invention and making the most efficient use of existing manufacturing and marketing structures within the industry, the trade secret holder would tend either to limit his utilization of the invention, thereby depriving the public of the maximum benefit of its use, or engage in the time-consuming and economically wasteful enterprise of constructing duplicative manufacturing and marketing mechanisms for the exploitation of the invention. The detrimental misallocation of resources and economic waste that would thus take place if trade secret protection were abolished with respect to employees or licensees cannot be justified by reference to any policy that the federal patent law seeks to advance.

Nothing in the patent law requires that States refrain from action to prevent industrial espionage. In addition to the increased costs for protection from burglary, wire-tapping, bribery and the other means used to misappropriate trade secrets, there is the inevitable cost to the basic decency of society when one firm steals from another. A most fundamental human right, that of privacy, is threatened when industrial espionage is condoned or is made profitable; the state interest in denying profit to such illegal ventures is unchallengeable.

The next category of patentable subject matter to deal with is the invention whose holder has a legitimate doubt as to its patentability. The risk of eventual patent invalidity by the courts and the costs associated with that risk may well impel some with a good-faith doubt as to patentability not to take the trouble to seek to obtain and defend patent protection for their discoveries, regardless of the existence of trade secret protection. Trade secret protection would assist those inventors in the more efficient exploitation of their discoveries and not conflict with the patent law. In most cases of genuine doubt as to patent validity the potential rewards of patent protection are so far superior to those accruing to holders of trade secrets, that the holders of such inventions will seek patent protection, ignoring the trade secret route. For those inventors "on the line" as to whether to seek patent protection, the abolition of trade secret protection might encourage some to apply for a patent who otherwise would not have done so. For some of those so encouraged, no patent will be granted and the result

> "will have been an unnecessary postponement in the divulging of the trade secret to persons willing to pay for it. If [the patent does issue], it may well be invalid, yet many will prefer to pay a modest royalty than to contest it, even though *Lear* allows them to accept a license and pursue the contest without paying royalties while the fight goes on. The result in such a case would be unjustified royalty payments from many who would prefer not to pay them rather than agreed fees from one or a few who are entirely willing to do so." Painton & Co. v. Bourns, Inc., supra, 442 F.2d, at 225.

The point is that those who might be encouraged to file for patents by the absence of trade secret law will include inventors possessing the chaff as well as the wheat. Some of the chaff—the nonpatentable discoveries—will be thrown out by the Patent Office, but in the meantime the society will have been deprived of use of those discoveries through trade secret-protected licensing. Some of the chaff may not be thrown out. This Court has noted the difference between the standards used by the Patent Office and the courts to determine patentability. In Lear, Inc. v. Adkins, supra, the Court thought that an invalid patent was so serious a threat to the free use of ideas already in the public domain that the Court permitted licensees of the patent holder to challenge the validity of the patent. Better had the invalid patent never issued. More of those patents would likely issue if trade secret law were abolished. Eliminating trade secret law for the doubtfully patentable invention is thus likely to have deleterious effects on society and patent policy which we cannot say are balanced out by the speculative gain which might result from the encouragement of some inventors with doubtfully patentable inventions which deserve patent protection to come forward and apply for patents. There is no conflict, then, between trade secret law and the patent law policy of disclosure, at least insofar as the first two categories of patentable subject matter are concerned.

The final category of patentable subject matter to deal with is the clearly patentable invention, i.e., that invention which the owner believes to meet the standards of patentability. It is here that the federal interest in disclosure is at its peak; these inventions, novel, useful and nonobvious, are "the things which are worth to the public the embarrassment of an exclusive patent." Graham v. John Deere Co., supra, 383 U.S., at 9 (quoting Thomas Jefferson). The interest of the public is that the bargain of 17 years of exclusive use in return for disclosure be accepted. If a State, through a system of protection, were to cause a substantial risk that holders of patentable inventions would not seek patents, but rather would rely on the state protection, we would be compelled to hold that such a system could not constitutionally continue to exist. In the case of trade secret law no reasonable risk of deterrence from patent application by those who can reasonably expect to be granted patents exists.

Trade secret law provides far weaker protection in many respects than the patent law. While trade secret law does not forbid the discovery of the trade secret by fair and honest means, e.g., independent creation and reverse engineering, patent law operates "against the world," forbidding any use of the invention for whatever purpose for a significant length of time. The holder of a trade secret also takes a substantial risk that the secret will be passed on to his competitors, by theft or by breach of a confidential relationship, in a manner not easily susceptible to discovery or proof. Where patent law acts as a barrier, trade secret law functions relatively as a sieve. The possibility that an inventor who believes his invention meets the standards of patentability will sit back, rely on trade secret law, and after one year of use forfeit any right to patent protection, 35 U.S.C. § 102(b), is remote indeed.

Nor does society face much risk that scientific or technological progress will be impeded from the rare inventor with a patentable invention who chooses trade secret protection over patent protection. The ripeness of time concept of invention, developed from the study of the many independent multiple discoveries in history, predicts that if a particular individual had not made a particular discovery others would have, and in probably a relatively short period of time. If something is to be discovered at all very likely it will be discovered by more than one person. R. Merton, Singletons and Multiples in Science (1961), The Sociology of Science (1973); J. Cole and S. Cole, Social Stratification in Science, 12–13, 229–230 (1973); Ogburn and Thomas, Are Inventions Inevitable?, 37 Political Science Quarterly, 83 (1922).[19] Even were an inventor to keep his discovery completely to himself, something that neither the patent nor trade secret laws forbid, there is a high probability that it will be soon independently developed. If the invention, though still a trade secret, is put into public use, the competition is alerted to the existence of the inventor's solution to the problem and may be encouraged to make an extra effort to independently find the solution thus known to be possible. The inventor faces pressures not only from private industry, but from the skilled scientists who work in our universities and our other great publicly supported centers of learning and research.

We conclude that the extension of trade secret protection to clearly patentable inventions does not conflict with the patent policy of disclosure. Perhaps because trade secret law does not produce any positive effects in the area of clearly patentable inventions, as opposed to the beneficial effects resulting from trade secret protection in the areas of the doubtfully patentable and the clearly unpatentable inventions, it has been suggested that partial pre-emption may be appropriate, and that courts should refuse to apply trade secret protection to inventions which the holder should have patented, and which would have been, thereby, disclosed.[20] However, since

19. See J. Watson, The Double Helix (1968). If Watson and Crick had not discovered the structure of DNA it is likely that Linus Pauling would have made the discovery soon. Other examples of multiple discovery are listed at length in the Ogburn and Thomas article.

20. See Note, Patent Preemption of Trade Secret Protection Meeting Judicial Standards of Patentability, 87 Harv.L.Rev. 807 (1974); Brief for the United States as *Amicus Curiae*, presenting the view within the Government favoring limited pre-emption (which view is not that of the United States which believes that patent law does not pre-empt state trade secret law).

there is no real possibility that trade secret law will conflict with the federal policy favoring disclosure of clearly patentable inventions partial preemption is inappropriate. Partial preemption, furthermore, could well create serious problems for state courts in the administration of trade secret law. As a preliminary matter in trade secret actions, state courts would be obliged to distinguish between what a reasonable inventor would and would not correctly consider to be clearly patentable, with the holder of the trade secret arguing that the invention was not patentable and the misappropriator of the trade secret arguing its undoubted novelty, utility and nonobviousness. Federal courts have a difficult enough time trying to determine whether an invention, narrowed by the patent application procedure and fixed in the specifications which describe the invention for which the patent has been granted, is patentable. Although state courts in some circumstances must join federal courts in judging whether an issued patent is valid, Lear, Inc. v. Adkins, supra, it would be undesirable to impose the almost impossible burden on state courts to determine the patentability—in fact and in the mind of a reasonable inventor—of a discovery which has not been patented and remains entirely uncircumscribed by expert analysis in the administrative process. Neither complete nor partial pre-emption of state trade secret law is justified.

* * *

Trade secret law and patent law have coexisted in this country for over one hundred years. Each has its particular role to play, and the operation of one does not take away from the need for the other. Trade secret law encourages the development and exploitation of those items of lesser or different invention than might be accorded protection under the patent laws, but which items still have an important part to play in the technological and scientific advancement of the Nation. Trade secret law promotes the sharing of knowledge, and the efficient operation of industry; it permits the individual inventor to reap the rewards of his labor by contracting with a company large enough to develop and exploit it. Congress, by its silence over these many years, has seen the wisdom of allowing the States to enforce trade secret protection. Until Congress takes affirmative action to the contrary, States should be free to grant protection to trade secrets.

Since we hold that Ohio trade secret law is not preempted by the federal patent law, the judgment of the Court of Appeals for the Sixth Circuit is reversed and the case is remanded to the Court of Appeals with directions to reinstate the judgment of the District Court.

It is so ordered.

Reversed and remanded for reinstatement of District Court judgment.

Mr. Justice POWELL took no part in the decision of this case.

Mr. Justice MARSHALL, concurring in the result.

Unlike the Court, I do not believe that the possibility that an inventor with a patentable invention will rely on state trade secret law rather than apply for a patent is "remote indeed." State trade secret law provides substantial protection to the inventor who intends to use or sell the invention himself rather than license it to others, protection which in its unlimited duration is clearly superior to the 17-year monopoly afforded by the patent laws. I have no doubt that the existence of trade secret protection provides in some instances a substantial disincentive to entrance into the patent system, and thus deprives society of the benefits of public disclosure of the invention which it is the policy of the patent laws to encourage. This case may well be such an instance.

But my view of sound policy in this area does not dispose of this case. Rather, the question presented in this case is whether Congress, in enacting the patent laws, intended merely to offer inventors a limited monopoly in exchange for disclosure of their invention, or instead to exert pressure on inventors to enter into this exchange by withdrawing any alternative possibility of legal protection for their inventions. I am persuaded that the former is the case. * * *

Mr. Justice DOUGLAS, with whom Mr. Justice BRENNAN concurs, dissenting.

NOTES

1. In a portion of the *Kewanee* opinion deleted above, Chief Justice Burger describes the Ohio law of trade secrets as prohibiting appropriation of another's secret information by:

"improper means which may include theft, wiretapping, or even aerial reconnaissance. A trade secret, however, does not offer protection against discovery by fair and honest means, such as by independent invention, accidental disclosure, or by so-called reverse engineering, that is by starting with the known product and working backward to divine the process which aided in its development or manufacturer."

Are states free to place their own interpretation on what is "improper means" as distinguished from "fair and honest means" or is that now a matter of federal law?

2. An unusually good opportunity to consider how the rule of *Kewanee* interacts with the rule of *Bonito Boats* occurred in Reingold v. Swiftships, Inc., 126 F.3d 645(5th Cir. 1997). Reingold leased a 90 foot female fiberglass boat mold to Swiftships under a contract in which Swiftships paid Reingold on the basis of use of the mold and agreed to return the mold to Reingold at the end of the lease. Swiftships made two holds from the mold for which Reingold was paid. It made another "thin test liner" for which it did not pay Reingold. The test liner would be the male plug derived from laying fiberglass into the female mold. The front 40 feet of this plug was used by Swiftships to make a female mold for a 110 foot hold. Reingold seeks compensation for this use, arguing that the 90 foot female mold was a trade secret and that Swiftships misappropriated that secret without compensation. Swiftships argued that under *Bonito Boats*, anyone could have used any of the 90 foot boats in existence to make a direct mold of the 90 foot hull and thus it was not precluded from using its own test liner. The Fifth Circuit held, however, that *Kewanee*, preserved state trade secret law, that the 90 foot mold was a trade secret, and that "protection will be accorded to a trade secret holder against disclosure or unauthorized use gained by improper means, even if others might have discovered the trade secret by legitimate means."

3. Do you accept the proposition that "the patent policy of encouraging invention is not disturbed by the existence of another form of incentive to invention." Could Congress reasonably conclude that there is too much incentive for innovative activity generally or in specific areas?

4. Does *Kewanee* affect the nature of the relief that can be granted by state courts for trade secret infringement? Are permanent injunctions prohibiting the use of infringing material permissible? Is an accounting for profits? See, Stern, A Reexamination of Preemption of State Trade Secret Law After Kewanee, 42 Geo.Wash.L.Rev. 927 (1974).

5. Should the fixation of a notice of copyright on a document preclude the assertion of trade secret rights? In Technicon Medical Information Systems Corp. v. Green Bay Packaging, Inc., 687 F.2d 1032 (7th Cir.1982), cert. denied 459 U.S. 1106 (1982) the Seventh Circuit held that under the 1909 Copyright Act the owner of copyrighted documents was not estopped from asserting that the publication of the documents was not a general publication but preserved trade secret rights. Does section 301 of the 1976 Act preempt trade secret protection? See Avco Corp. v. Precision Air Parts, Inc., 210 U.S.P.Q. 894 (M.D.Ala.1980), affirmed on other grounds 676 F.2d 494 (11th Cir.1982), cert. denied 459 U.S. 1037 (1982) and Warrington Associates, Inc. v. Real-Time Engineering Systems, Inc., 522 F.Supp. 367 (N.D.Ill.1981).

Aronson v. Quick Point Pencil Co.

Supreme Court of the United States, 1979.
440 U.S. 257, 99 S.Ct. 1096, 59 L.Ed.2d 296.

■ MR. CHIEF JUSTICE BURGER delivered the opinion of the Court.

We granted certiorari to consider whether federal patent law pre-empts state contract law so as to preclude enforcement of a contract to pay royalties to a patent applicant, on sales of articles embodying the putative invention, for so long as the contracting party sells them, if a patent is not granted.

(1)

In October 1955 the petitioner Mrs. Jane Aronson filed an application, Serial No. 542677, for a patent on a new form of keyholder. Although ingenious, the design was so simple that it readily could be copied unless it was protected by patent. In June 1956, while the patent application was pending Mrs. Aronson negotiated a contract with the respondent, Quick Point Pencil Company, for the manufacture and sale of the keyholder.

The contract was embodied in two documents. In the first, a letter from Quick Point to Mrs. Aronson, Quick Point agreed to pay Mrs. Aronson a royalty of 5% of the selling price in return for "the exclusive right to make and sell keyholders of the type shown in your application, Serial No. 542677." The letter further provided that the parties would consult one another concerning the steps to be taken "[i]n the event of any infringement."

The contract did not require Quick Point to manufacture the keyholder. Mrs. Aronson received a $750 advance on royalties and was entitled to rescind the exclusive license if Quick Point did not sell a million keyholders by the end of 1957. Quick Point retained the right to cancel the agreement whenever "the volume of sales does not meet our expectation." The duration of the agreement was not otherwise prescribed.

A contemporaneous document provided that if Mrs. Aronson's patent application was "not allowed within five (5) years, Quick Point Pencil Co. [would] pay two and one half percent (2½%) of sales * * * so long as you [Quick Point] continue to sell same."

In June 1961, when Mrs. Aronson had failed to obtain a patent on the keyholder within the five years specified in the agreement, Quick Point asserted its contractual right to reduce royalty payments to 2½% of sales. In September of that year the Board of Patent Appeals issued a final rejection of the application on the ground that the keyholder was not patentable, and Mrs. Aronson did not appeal. Quick Point continued to pay reduced royalties to her for 14 years thereafter.

The market was more receptive to the keyholder's novelty and utility than the Patent Office. By September 1975 Quick Point had made sales in excess of seven million dollars and paid Mrs. Aronson royalties totalling $203,963.84; sales were continuing to rise. However, while Quick Point was able to pre-empt the market in the earlier years and was long the only manufacturer of the Aronson keyholder, copies began to appear in the late 1960's. Quick Point's competitors, of course, were not required to pay royalties for their use of the design. Quick Point's share of the Aronson keyholder market has declined during the past decade.

(2)

In November 1975 Quick Point commenced an action in the United States District Court for a declaratory judgment, pursuant to 28 U.S.C. § 2201, that the royalty agreement was unenforceable. Quick Point asserted that state law which might otherwise make the contract enforceable was pre-empted by federal patent law. This is the only issue presented to us for decision.

Both parties moved for summary judgment on affidavits, exhibits, and stipulations of fact. The District Court concluded that the "language of the agreement is plain, clear and unequivocal and has no relation as to whether or not a patent is ever granted." Accordingly, it held that the agreement was valid, and that Quick Point was obliged to pay the agreed royalties pursuant to the contract for so long as it manufactured the keyholder.

The Court of Appeals reversed, one judge dissenting. It held that since the parties contracted with reference to a pending patent application, Mrs. Aronson was estopped from denying that patent law principles governed her contract with Quick Point. Although acknowledging that this Court has never decided the precise issue, the Court of Appeals held that our prior decisions regarding patent licenses compelled the conclusion that Quick Point's contract with Mrs. Aronson became unenforceable once she failed to obtain a patent. The court held that a continuing obligation to pay royalties would be contrary to "the strong federal policy favoring the full and free use of ideas in the public domain," Lear, Inc. v. Adkins, 395 U.S. 653, 674 (1969). The court also observed that if Mrs. Aronson actually had obtained a patent, Quick Point would have escaped its royalty obligations either if the patent were held to be invalid, or upon its expiration after 17 years, see Brulotte v. Thys Co., 379 U.S. 29 (1964). Accordingly, it concluded that a licensee should be relieved of royalty obligations when the licensor's efforts to obtain a contemplated patent prove unsuccessful.

(3)

On this record it is clear that the parties contracted with full awareness of both the pendency of a patent application and the possibility that a patent might not issue. The clause de-escalating the royalty by half in the event no patent issued within five years makes that crystal clear. Quick Point apparently placed a significant value on exploiting the basic novelty of the device, even if no patent issued; its success demonstrates that this judgment was well founded. Assuming, *arguendo,* that the initial letter and the commitment to pay a 5% royalty was subject to federal patent law, the provision relating to the 2½% royalty was explicitly independent of federal law. The cases and principles relied on by the Court of Appeals and Quick Point do not bear on a contract that does not rely on a patent, particularly where, as here, the contracting parties agreed expressly as to alternative obligations if no patent should issue.

Commercial agreements traditionally are the domain of state law. State law is not displaced merely because the contract relates to intellectual property which may or may not be patentable; the states are free to regulate the use of such intellectual property in any manner not inconsistent with federal law. Kewanee Oil Co. v. Bicron Corp., 416 U.S. 470, 479 (1974); see Goldstein v. California, 412 U.S. 546 (1973). In this as in other fields, the question of whether federal law pre-empts state law "involves a consideration of whether that law 'stands as an obstacle to the accomplishment and execution of the full purposes and objectives of Congress.' Hines v. Davidowitz, 312 U.S. 52, 67 (1941)." Kewanee Oil Co., supra. If it does not, state law governs.

In Kewanee Oil Co., supra, at 480–481, we reviewed the purposes of the federal patent system. First, patent law seeks to foster and reward invention; second, it promotes disclosure of inventions, to stimulate further innovation and to permit the public to practice the invention once the patent expires; third, the stringent requirements for patent protection seek to assure that ideas in the public domain remain there for the free use of the public.

Enforcement of Quick Point's agreement with Mrs. Aronson is not inconsistent with any of these aims. Permitting inventors to make enforceable agreements licensing the use of their inventions in return for royalties provides an additional incentive to invention. Similarly, encouraging Mrs. Aronson to make arrangements for the manufacture of her keyholder furthers the federal policy of disclosure of inventions; these simple devices display the novel idea which they embody wherever they are seen.

Quick Point argues that enforcement of such contracts conflicts with the federal policy against withdrawing ideas from the public domain and discourages recourse to the federal patent system by allowing states to extend "perpetual protection to articles too lacking in novelty to merit any patent at all under federal constitutional standards," Sears Roebuck & Co. v. Stiffel Co., 376 U.S. 225, 232 (1964).

We find no merit in this contention. Enforcement of the agreement does not withdraw any idea from the public domain. The design for the keyholder was not in the public domain before Quick Point obtained its license to manufacture it. See Kewanee Oil Co., supra, at 484. In negotiating the agreement, Mrs. Aronson disclosed the design in confidence. Had Quick Point tried to exploit the design in breach of that confidence, it would have risked legal liability. It is equally clear that the design entered the public domain as a result of the manufacture and sale of the keyholders under the contract.

Requiring Quick Point to bear the burden of royalties for the use of the design is no more inconsistent with federal patent law than any of the other costs involved in being the first to introduce a new product to the market, such as outlays for research and development and marketing and promotional expenses. For reasons which Quick Point's experience with the Aronson keyholder demonstrate, innovative entrepreneurs have usually found such costs to be well worth paying.

Finally, enforcement of this agreement does not discourage anyone from seeking a patent. Mrs. Aronson attempted to obtain a patent for over five years. It is quite true that had she succeeded, she would have received a 5% royalty only on keyholders sold during the 17-year life of the patent. Off-setting the limited terms of royalty payments, she would have received twice as much per dollar of Quick Point's sales, and both she and Quick Point could have licensed any others who produced the same keyholder. Which course would have produced the greater yield to the contracting parties is a matter of speculation; the parties resolved the uncertainties by their bargain.

(4)

No decision of this Court relating to patents justifies relieving Quick Point of its contract obligations. We have held that a state may not forbid the copying of an idea in the public domain which does not meet the requirements for federal patent protection. Compco Corp. v. Day-Brite Lighting, Inc., 376 U.S. 234 (1964); Sears Roebuck & Co. v. Stiffel Co., 376 U.S. 225 (1964). Enforcement of Quick Point's agreement, however, does not prevent anyone from copying the keyholder. It merely requires Quick Point to pay the consideration which it promised in return for the use of a novel device which enabled it to pre-empt the market.

In Lear, Inc. v. Adkins, 395 U.S. 653 (1969), we held that a person licensed to use a patent may challenge the validity of the patent, and that a licensee who establishes that the patent is invalid need not pay the royalties accrued under the licensing agreement subsequent to the issuance of the patent. Both holdings relied on the desirability of encouraging licensees to challenge the validity of patents, to further the strong federal policy that only inventions which meet the rigorous requirements of patentability shall be withdrawn from the public domain. Accordingly, neither the holding nor the rationale of *Lear* controls when no patent has issued, and no ideas have been withdrawn from public use.

Enforcement of the royalty agreement here is also consistent with the principles treated in Brulotte v. Thys Co., 379 U.S. 29 (1964). There, we held that the obligation to pay royalties in return for the use of a patented device may not extend beyond the life of the patent. The principle underlying that holding was simply that the monopoly granted *under a patent* cannot lawfully be used to "negotiate with the leverage of that monopoly." The Court emphasized that to "use that leverage to project those royalty payments beyond the life of the patent is analogous to an effort to enlarge the monopoly of a patent * * *." Id., at 33. Here the reduced royalty which is challenged, far from being negotiated "with the leverage" of a patent, rested on the contingency that no patent would issue within five years.

No doubt a pending patent application gives the applicant some additional bargaining power for purposes of negotiating a royalty agreement. The pending application allows the inventor to hold out the hope of an exclusive right to exploit the idea, as well as the threat that the other party will be prevented from using the idea for 17 years. However, the amount of leverage arising from a patent application depends on how likely the parties consider it to be that a valid patent will issue. Here, where no patent ever issued, the record is entirely clear that the parties assigned a substantial likelihood to that contingency, since they specifically provided for a reduced royalty in the event no patent issued within five years.

This case does not require us to draw the line between what constitutes abuse of a pending application and what does not. It is clear that whatever role the pending application played in the negotiation of the 5% royalty, it played no part in the contract to pay the 2½% royalty indefinitely.

Our holding in Kewanee Oil Co., supra, puts to rest the contention that federal law pre-empts and renders unenforceable the contract made by these parties. There we held that state law forbidding the misappropriation of trade secrets was not pre-empted by federal patent law. We observed:

"Certainly the patent policy of encouraging invention is not disturbed by the existence of another form of incentive to invention. In this respect the two systems [patent and trade secret law] are not and never would be in conflict." Id., at 484.

Enforcement of this royalty agreement is even less offensive to federal patent policies than state law protecting trade secrets. The most commonly accepted definition of trade secrets is restricted to confidential information which is not disclosed in the normal process of exploitation. See Restatement of Torts § 757, comment b (1939). Accordingly, the exploitation of trade secrets under state law may not satisfy the federal policy in favor of disclosure, whereas disclosure is inescapable in exploiting a device like the Aronson keyholder.

Enforcement of these contractual obligations, freely undertaken in arm's length negotiation and with no fixed reliance on a patent or a probable patent grant, will:

"encourage invention in areas where patent law does not reach, and will prompt the independent innovator to proceed with the discovery and exploitation of his invention. Competition is fostered and the public is not deprived of the use of valuable, if not quite patentable, invention." [Footnote omitted.] Id., at 485.

The device which is the subject of this contract ceased to have any secrecy as soon as it was first marketed, yet when the contract was negotiated the inventiveness and novelty were sufficiently apparent to induce an experienced novelty manufacturer to agree to pay for the opportunity to be first in the market. Federal patent law is not a barrier to such a contract.

Reversed.

Mr. Justice BLACKMUN, concurring in the result.

For me, the hard question is whether this case can meaningfully be distinguished from Brulotte v. Thys Co., 379 U.S. 29 (1964). There the Court held a patent licensor could not use the leverage of its patent to obtain a royalty contract that extended beyond the patent's 17-year term. Here Mrs. Aronson has used the leverage of her patent application to negotiate a royalty contract which continues to be binding even though the patent application was long ago denied.

The Court, * * * asserts that her leverage played "no part" with respect to the contingent agreement to pay a reduced royalty if no patent issued within five years. Yet it may well be that Quick Point agreed to that contingency in order to obtain its other rights that depended on the success of the patent application. The parties did not apportion consideration in the neat fashion the Court adopts.

In my view, the holding in *Brulotte* reflects hostility toward extension of a patent monopoly whose term is fixed by statute, 35 U.S.C. § 154. Such hostility has no place here. A patent application which is later denied temporarily discourages unlicensed imitators. Its benefits and hazards are of a different magnitude from those of a granted patent that prohibits all competition for 17 years. Nothing justifies estopping a patent application licensor from entering into a contract whose term does not end if the application fails. The Court points out, * * * that enforcement of this contract does not conflict with the objectives of the patent laws. The United States, as *amicus curiae,* maintains that patent application licensing of this sort is desirable because it encourages patent applications, promotes early disclosure, and allows parties to structure their bargains efficiently.

On this basis, I concur in the Court's holding that federal patent law does not pre-empt the enforcement of Mrs. Aronson's contract with Quick Point.

NOTES

1. In the 1989 decision in *Bonito Boats,* supra Chapter 1, the Supreme Court reaffirmed not only *Sears* and *Compco* but also *Lear, Kewanee,* and *Aronson.* After reiterating the analysis in *Kewanee* the Court observed:

> We have since reaffirmed the pragmatic approach which *Kewanee* takes to the pre-emption of state laws dealing with the protection of intellectual property. See, *Aronson* * * *. At the same time, we have consistently reiterated the teaching of *Sears* and *Compco* that ideas once placed before the public without the protection of a valid patent are subject to appropriation without significant restraint. Aronson * * *.

2. The opinion of the Eighth Circuit in *Quick Point* concluded:

> Aronson believed her invention was patentable and she submitted a patent application. Had a patent issued she would have had 17 years of exclusive rights to her invention before it became part of the public domain. She approached Quick Point with her idea and the parties entered into a contract anticipating that a patent would issue. If that had happened, under Brulotte v. Thys Co., supra, 379 U.S. at 32, Quick Point's liability for royalties would have ended after 17 years in spite of the contract. Furthermore, if a patent had issued and Quick Point had later questioned the patentability of the keyholder, under Lear, Inc. v. Adkins, supra, 395 U.S. at 674, it could have stopped making royalty payments and challenged the patent in court. If such a challenge were successful, Quick Point's liability for payments would have ended in spite of the contract. We do not believe the result should be different here. The principles discussed above strongly indicate that any other conclusion would violate public policy.

567 F.2d at 762 (8th Cir.1977). Do you think the Supreme Court adequately addressed this argument?

3. The combined effect of *Brulotte, Lear, Kewanee,* and *Aronson* is far from clear. *Brulotte* involved a patent license. *Lear* involved an agreement followed by the issuance of a patent. *Kewanee* did not involve patents. *Aronson* involved only the potential for a patent that subsequently failed to materialize. And *Aronson* involved a license agreement that adjusted the royalty rate depending on the validity of the patent. Several cases have attempted to determine to what extent contractual arrangements are enforceable where they contemplate a hybrid transfer of both patented or patentable ideas and trade secrets or "know-how":

(a) Pitney Bowes v. Mestre, 701 F.2d 1365 (11th Cir.1983). The parties signed a royalty agreement on machines for which patent applications were pending. The patents issued but the royalty agreement required payment beyond the patent period. The court held *Brulotte* applied and if the patent issues, all claims to royalties end at the patent's expiration.

(b) Boggild v. Kenner Products, 776 F.2d 1315 (6th Cir.1985). The parties entered into a royalty agreement prior to filing the patent application. The patent subsequently issued but the agreement required royalty payments beyond the patent period. The court held *Brulotte* applied because the parties entered the agreement with "clear expectations that a valid patent would issue." See also Meehan v. PPG Industries, Inc., 802 F.2d 881 (7th Cir.1986) following *Boggild* and holding royalty payments unenforceable after expiration of United States patent even though a Canadian patent still valid.

(c) Universal Gym Equipment Inc. v. ERWA Exercise Equipment Ltd., 827 F.2d 1542 (Fed.Cir.1987). The parties entered a distribution contract permitting defendant to distribute the plaintiff's exercise equipment. The contract specified that upon termination the defendant would not sell any equipment containing any of the features or designs of the plaintiff's equipment. After termination defendant manufactured and sold its own equipment. Plaintiff sued for both patent infringement and breach of contract claiming defendant's equipment had features similar to plaintiff's. The court held there was no patent infringement but defendant's equipment did contain similar features. The court upheld a damage award for breach of contract even though the similar features were not trade secrets, rejecting a *Sears* and *Compco* preemption defense. The Federal Circuit does not appear sympathetic to preemption. It had upheld a plug molding statute against preemption claims, a view rejected by the Supreme Court in *Bonito Boats,* supra Chapter 1. Could *Universal Gym* survive Supreme Court scrutiny?

4. Is the difference between the leverage of a patent and the leverage of a patent application a difference of kind or degree? Chief Justice Burger says that the leverage from an application depends on "how likely the parties consider it to be that a valid patent will issue." Isn't the leverage associated with a granted patent related to how likely it is that a court will enforce the patent? The Court leaves open the possibility that a patent applicant might abuse his patent application, perhaps a reference to the problem in *Brulotte*. Can you construct a situation where this might be true?

5. How would you decide a case in which a former employer seeks to enjoin a former employee from disclosing the employers trade secrets even though the secrets are already public? Would it make a difference if the employee had signed a non-disclosure agreement which extended beyond the disclosure of the secret?

6. Do the realities of private transactions prevent the enforcement of the licensing agreement from interfering with federal patent policies. If the licensee has agreed to pay a royalty which after disclosure of the secret makes it difficult for him to compete with others, will not the licensor have an incentive to reduce the royalty? Does the case change if, like *Brulotte,* the licensee agrees to a minimum royalty payment? Would any sensible licensee agree to such a provision?

ProCD, Inc v Zeidenberg

United States Court of Appeals, Seventh Circuit. 1996
86 F.3d 1447

■ EASTERBROOK, CIRCUIT JUDGE.

* * *

ProCD, the plaintiff, has compiled information from more than 3,000 telephone directories into a computer database. We may assume that this database cannot be copyrighted. [Feist Publications, Inc. v. Rural Telephone Service Co., 499 U.S. 340 (1991), considered in Chapter 5, held that an alphabetical listing of telephone numbers was not sufficiently "original" to qualify for copyright protection.] ProCD sells a version of the database, called SelectPhone (trademark), on CD-ROM discs. (CD-ROM means "compact disc—read only memory." The "shrinkwrap license" gets its name from the fact that retail software packages are covered in plastic or cellophane "shrinkwrap," and some vendors, though not ProCD, have written licenses that become effective as soon as the customer tears the wrapping from the package. Vendors prefer "end user license," but we use the more common term.) A proprietary method of compressing the data serves as effective encryption too. Customers decrypt and use the data with the aid of an application program that ProCD has written. This program, which is copyrighted, searches the database in response to users' criteria (such as "find all people named Tatum in Tennessee, plus all firms with 'Door Systems' in the corporate name"). The resulting lists (or, as ProCD prefers, "listings") can be read and manipulated by other software, such as word processing programs.

The database in SelectPhone (trademark) cost more than $10 million to compile and is expensive to keep current. It is much more valuable to some users than to others. The combination of names, addresses, and SIC codes enables manufacturers to compile lists of potential customers. Manufacturers and retailers pay high prices to specialized information intermediaries for such mailing lists; ProCD offers a potentially cheaper alternative. People with nothing to sell could use the database as a substitute for calling long distance information, or as a way to look up old friends who have moved to unknown towns, or just as an electronic substitute for the local phone book. ProCD decided to engage in price discrimination, selling its database to the general public for personal use at a low price (approximately $150 for the set of five discs) while selling information to the trade for a higher price. It has adopted some intermediate strategies too: access to the SelectPhone (trademark) database is available via the America Online service for the price America Online charges to its clients (approximately $3 per hour), but this service has been tailored to be useful only to the general public.

If ProCD had to recover all of its costs and make a profit by charging a single price—that is, if it could not charge more to commercial users than to the general public—it would have to raise the price substantially over $150. The ensuing reduction in sales would harm consumers who value the information at, say, $200. They get consumer surplus of $50 under the current arrangement but would cease to buy if the price rose substantially. If because of high elasticity of demand in the consumer segment of the market the only way to make a profit turned out to be a price attractive to commercial users alone, then all consumers would lose out—and so would the commercial clients, who would have to pay more for the listings because ProCD could not obtain any contribution toward costs from the consumer market.

To make price discrimination work, however, the seller must be able to control arbitrage. An air carrier sells tickets for less to vacationers than to business travelers, using advance purchase and Saturday-night-stay requirements to distinguish the categories. A producer of movies segments the market by time, releasing first to theaters, then to pay-per-view services, next to the videotape and laser disc market, and finally to cable and commercial tv. Vendors of computer software have a harder task. Anyone can walk into a retail store and buy a box. Customers do not wear tags saying "commercial user" or "consumer user." Anyway, even a commercial-user-detector at the door would not work, because a consumer could buy the software and resell to a commercial user. That arbitrage would break down the price discrimination and drive up the minimum price at which ProCD would sell to anyone.

Instead of tinkering with the product and letting users sort themselves—for example, furnishing current data at a high price that would be attractive only to commercial customers, and two-year-old data at a low price—ProCD turned to the institution of contract. Every box containing its consumer product declares that the software comes with restrictions stated in an enclosed license. This license, which is encoded on the CD-ROM disks as well as printed in the manual, and which appears on a user's screen every time the software runs, limits use of the application program and listings to non-commercial purposes.

Matthew Zeidenberg bought a consumer package of SelectPhone (trademark) in 1994 from a retail outlet in Madison, Wisconsin, but decided to ignore the license. He formed Silken Mountain Web Services, Inc., to resell the information in the SelectPhone (trademark) database. The corporation makes the database available on the Internet to anyone willing to pay its price—which, needless to say, is less than ProCD charges its commercial customers. Zeidenberg has purchased two additional SelectPhone (trademark) packages, each with an updated version of the database, and made the latest information available over the World Wide Web, for a price, through his corporation. ProCD filed this suit seeking an injunction against further dissemination that exceeds the rights specified in the licenses (identical in each of the three packages Zeidenberg purchased). The district court held the licenses ineffectual because their terms do not appear on the outside of the packages. The court added that the second and third licenses stand no different from the first, even though they are identical, because they might have been different, and a purchaser does not agree to—and cannot be bound by—terms that were secret at the time of purchase.

[The court first held that the shrink-wrap license was an enforceable contract under Article 2 of the Uniform Commercial Code if the buyer uses the software after having an opportunity to review the terms of the license, even if the buyer does not actually read the license.]

The district court held that, even if Wisconsin treats shrinkwrap licenses as contracts, § 301(a) of the Copyright Act, 17 U.S.C. § 301(a), prevents their enforcement. The relevant part of § 301(a) preempts any "legal or equitable rights [under state law] that are equivalent to any of the exclusive rights within the general scope of copyright as specified by section 106 in works of authorship that are fixed in a tangible medium of expression and come within the subject matter of copyright as specified by sections 102 and 103". ProCD's software and data are "fixed in a tangible medium of expression", and the district judge held that they are "within the subject matter of copyright". The latter conclusion is plainly right for the copyrighted application program, and the judge thought that the data likewise are "within the subject matter of copyright" even if, after *Feist*, they are not sufficiently original to be copyrighted. * * * One function of § 301(a) is to prevent states from giving special protection to works of authorship that Congress has decided should be in the public domain, which it can accomplish only if "subject matter of copyright" includes all works of a type covered by sections 102 and 103, even if federal law does not afford protection to them. Cf. Bonito Boats, Inc. v. Thunder Craft Boats, Inc., 489 U.S. 141 (1989) (same principle under patent laws).

But are rights created by contract "equivalent to any of the exclusive rights within the general scope of copyright"? Three courts of appeals have answered "no." National Car Rental System, Inc. v. Computer Associates International, Inc., 991 F.2d 426, 433 (8th Cir.1993); Taquino v. Teledyne Monarch Rubber, 893 F.2d 1488, 1501 (5th Cir.1990); Acorn Structures, Inc. v. Swantz, 846 F.2d 923, 926 (4th Cir.1988). The district court disagreed with these decisions, but we think them sound. Rights "equivalent to any of the exclusive rights within the general scope of copyright" are rights established by law—rights that restrict the options of persons who are strangers to the author. Copyright law forbids duplication, public performance, and so on, unless the person wishing to copy or perform the work gets permission; silence means a ban on copying. A copyright is a right against the world. Contracts, by contrast, generally affect only their parties; strangers may do as they please, so contracts do not create "exclusive rights." Someone who found a copy of

SelectPhone (trademark) on the street would not be affected by the shrinkwrap license—though the federal copyright laws of their own force would limit the finder's ability to copy or transmit the application program.

Think for a moment about trade secrets. One common trade secret is a customer list. After *Feist*, a simple alphabetical list of a firm's customers, with address and telephone numbers, could not be protected by copyright. Yet Kewanee Oil Co. v. Bicron Corp., 416 U.S. 470(1974), holds that contracts about trade secrets may be enforced—precisely because they do not affect strangers' ability to discover and use the information independently. If the amendment of § 301(a) in 1976 overruled *Kewanee* and abolished consensual protection of those trade secrets that cannot be copyrighted, no one has noticed—though abolition is a logical consequence of the district court's approach. Think, too, about everyday transactions in intellectual property. A customer visits a video store and rents a copy of Night of the Lepus. The customer's contract with the store limits use of the tape to home viewing and requires its return in two days. May the customer keep the tape, on the ground that § 301(a) makes the promise unenforceable?

A law student uses the LEXIS database, containing public-domain documents, under a contract limiting the results to educational endeavors; may the student resell his access to this database to a law firm from which LEXIS seeks to collect a much higher hourly rate? Suppose ProCD hires a firm to scour the nation for telephone directories, promising to pay $100 for each that ProCD does not already have. The firm locates 100 new directories, which it sends to ProCD with an invoice for $10,000. ProCD incorporates the directories into its database; does it have to pay the bill? Surely yes; Aronson v. Quick Point Pencil Co., 440 U.S. 257(1979), holds that promises to pay for intellectual property may be enforced even though federal law (in *Aronson*, the patent law) offers no protection against third-party uses of that property. But these illustrations are what our case is about. ProCD offers software and data for two prices: one for personal use, a higher price for commercial use. Zeidenberg wants to use the data without paying the seller's price; if the law student and Quick Point Pencil Co. could not do that, neither can Zeidenberg.

Although Congress possesses power to preempt even the enforcement of contracts about intellectual property * * * courts usually read preemption clauses to leave private contracts unaffected. * * * [Section 301] prevents states from substituting their own regulatory systems for those of the national government. Just as § 301(a) does not itself interfere with private transactions in intellectual property, so it does not prevent states from respecting those transactions. [We think it prudent to refrain from adopting a rule that anything with the label "contract" is necessarily outside the preemption clause: the variations and possibilities are too numerous to foresee. *National Car Rental* likewise recognizes the possibility that some applications of the law of contract could interfere with the attainment of national objectives and therefore come within the domain of § 301(a). But general enforcement of shrinkwrap licenses of the kind before us does not create such interference.

Aronson emphasized that enforcement of the contract between Aronson and Quick Point Pencil Company would not withdraw any information from the public domain. That is equally true of the contract between ProCD and Zeidenberg. Everyone remains free to copy and disseminate all 3,000 telephone books that have been incorporated into ProCD's database. Anyone can add SIC codes and zip codes. ProCD's rivals have done so. Enforcement of the shrinkwrap license may even make information more readily available, by reducing the price ProCD charges to consumer buyers. To the extent licenses facilitate distribution of object code while concealing the source code (the point of a clause forbidding disassembly), they serve the same procompetitive functions as does the law of trade secrets. Rockwell Graphic Systems, Inc. v. DEV Industries, Inc., 925 F.2d 174, 180 (7th Cir.1991). Licenses may have other benefits for consumers: many licenses permit users to make extra copies, to use the software on multiple computers, even to incorporate the software into the user's products. But whether a particular license is generous or restrictive, a simple two-party contract is not "equivalent to any of the exclusive rights within the general scope of copyright" and therefore may be enforced.

REVERSED AND REMANDED.

NOTES

1. Contracting for acquisition of software in the electronic age poses its own set of problems that are inadequately resolved by Article 2 of the Uniform Commercial Code which was designed to regulate sales of tangible goods. Accordingly the American Law Institute and the National Conference of Commissioners on Uniform State Laws are undertaking a project to promulgate Article 2B of the UCC to deal specifically with software contracts. Most recent drafts also cover "access contracts" — a contract permitting a user access to an electronic database such as Westlaw or Lexis. The structure of Article 2B is to authorize transactions which purport to transfer software pursuant to a "license" rather than as a "sale" and thus recognize the licensor's right to place limitations on the use of the product by the licensee.

In some instances, transactions in software appear to have elements of both sale and license. In *ProCD*, Zeidenberg purchased a package in a retail outlet. He received the tangible CD-ROM disk with a box and instructions, and he also received the intangible right to use the data base contained on the CD-ROM. In most such transactions, the common understanding of the buyer is that he "owns" that copy of the product even though there may or may not be some intellectual property interest in the contents of the copy. The transaction looks very similar to the purchase of a book from a bookstore. Title to the physical copy of the book is transferred to the buyer, but the copyright laws limit the buyer from making additional copies of its contents.

When tangible goods are sold outright, the common law ordinarily forbids the seller from imposing continuing obligations on the buyer with regard to the goods. For example, if Buyer purchases a television set Seller cannot prohibit Buyer from selling the set to someone else, or from moving the set to another location, or from allowing more than one person at a time to watch the set. Section 109 of the Copyright Act reflects this common law tradition by adopting the "first sale" doctrine which provides: " * * * the owner of a particular copy or phonograph lawfully made under this title, or any person authorized by such owner, is entitled, without the authority of the copyright owner, to sell or otherwise dispose of the possession of that copy or phonograph." Moreover, *Bonito Boats* would seem to permit Buyer to use the purchased object as a source from which to learn or imitate the design or other intellectual contribution of the object as long as that contribution is not protected by a copyright or patent.

Increasingly, software and other information products are sold by means of electronic access rather than as part of a transaction involving a tangible medium. Computer users are now able to download complete software packages from internet websites upon payment of a fee. And, users can access major newspapers from their websites or from a database such as Westlaw or Lexis. In these transactions, no tangible object passes from the seller to the buyer.

The proposed Article 2B addresses the fascinating issues of contract formation in an electronic age where the traditional notion of a "meeting of the minds" appears to be outdated. In most consumer transactions in software, the software is "sold" in a shrink-wrapped package, and the buyer is unable as a practical matter to review the terms of the transaction until after the price is paid. In electronic transactions the terms of the transactions are often posted on the computer screen and the buyer is asked to "Click Here" to accept the terms (click-wrapped products). And in many electronic transactions, the seller's computer and the buyer's computer are programmed to reach an agreement without the intervention of either the buyer or seller. These contract formation issues are beyond the scope of this book.

The extent to which parties to a contract may agree to expand the rights to intellectual property beyond those provided by the copyright and patent system are central to understanding the proposed Article 2B and to the future of intellectual property protection.

2. Judge Easterbrook in *ProCD* takes a strong freedom of contract approach to the issue of whether the copyright and patent statutes preempt contractual terms. He argues that copyright and patent deal with rights of intellectual property owners against the world whereas contractual rights only limit the activities of the parties to the contract. In the world of shrink-wrapped products containing standard form licenses, do you agree with his analysis? By way of example, he suggests that a third party finding a copy of the ProCD CD-ROM would not be "affected by the shrinkwrap license". Does this mean that the licensee can "abandon" the software and thus allow a third party to use it free of license restrictions? Does it mean that a person who steals the software has greater rights than a person who purchases it?

However, ProCD's product had the license and limitations of use embedded on the CD-ROM. If the third party was required to click on an "I agree to the license" icon before the program would operate, would that party be bound by its terms?

3. Is the decision as to whether a particular transaction is a license or a sale up to the parties? Does this mean that a computer software company, by adopting a standard form agreement structured as a "license" may impose any and all use restrictions on licensees? Consider whether a licensor could overcome by terms in a license some of the following provisions of the copyright act:

(a). Section 109 provides that the owner of a copy of a copyrighted work may freely transfer the copy. Can a license agreement forbid the licensee from selling his or her copy?

(b). Section 109(b)(1)(A) forbids the owner of a copy of a sound recording or computer program to dispose of the copy for direct or indirect commercial advantage by way of rental, lease, or lending. An exception to this prohibition applies to rental, lease or lending by a nonprofit library or nonprofit educational institution. Can a licensor adopt a standard form license agreement that would prohibit a nonprofit library from lending sound recordings or computer programs? Could the license agreement prohibit lending of a sound recording even if it were not for any commercial advantage?

(c). Can a license agreement forbid a use that is determined to be a "fair use" under § 107?

4. Could the owner of the appropriated boat hull in *Bonito Boats* solve its problem by transfering all of its boat hulls pursuant to a license that prohibited their use as a plug mold?

5. Is it useful to think of these "products" as two separate things: the tangible embodiment of the contents and the contents themselves? Judge Easterbrook uses the example of a rental videotape. But isn't his example focused on the tangible copy? The rental agreement requires the licensee to return the tape within 3 days. The copyright law protects against copying of the movie. Could Blockbuster impose a license term that prohibited a person renting a movie from watching it more than once?

6. If sellers of software can license their products and thereby limit downstream use of the product and its informational content, what about sellers of products that contain embedded computer software? Most automobiles have computer software embedded in the vehicle to operate some functional systems. Almost all computers are "sold" with software installed. Watches, television sets, and other electronic equipment also have embedded software. Can the sellers of these products limit the use of the products by declaring the transaction to be a license? If the licensing of the CD-ROM version of the telephone book allows the licensor to limit the use of the data contained on the CD-ROM, can the telephone company do the same for the data contained in the hard copy by distributing the phone book with a "license"?

(4) Publicity Rights

This section explores the extent to which a celebrity may prevent others from using his or her name, likeness, or personality without the celebrity's permission. The cases evolve under the tort of "invasion of the right of publicity" which is thought by some to be an aspect of the right of privacy. See Prosser, Privacy, 48 Calif.L.Rev. 383 (1960). In the first case to recognize a right of publicity by name, the plaintiff who held exclusive contracts to use certain baseball player's photographs on cards distributed with chewing gum successfully prevented a competing chewing gum manufacturer to use pictures of the same ballplayers. Haelan Laboratories, Inc. v. Topps Chewing Gum, Inc., 202 F.2d 866 (2d Cir.1953). Since then, cases applying the publicity right have protected the commercial value of the celebrity's creative efforts and provide an interesting review of concepts of misappropriation, trademark, and copyright preemption played against a background of first amendment concerns.

The Martin Luther King, Jr. Center for Social Change, Inc. v. American Heritage Products, Inc.

Supreme Court of Georgia, 1982.
250 Ga. 135, 296 S.E.2d 697.

■ HILL, PRESIDING JUSTICE.

These are certified questions regarding the "right of publicity". The certification comes from the United States Court of Appeals for the Eleventh Circuit. The facts upon which the questions arise are as follows:

The plaintiffs are the Martin Luther King, Jr. Center for Social Change (the Center), Coretta Scott King, as administratrix of Dr. King's estate, and Motown Record Corporation, the assignee of the rights to several of Dr. King's copyrighted speeches. Defendant James F. Bolen is the sole proprietor of a business known as B & S Sales, which manufactures and sells various plastic products as funeral accessories. Defendant James E. Bolen, the son of James F. Bolen, developed the concept of marketing a plastic bust of Dr. Martin Luther King, Jr., and formed a company, B & S Enterprises, to sell the busts, which would be manufactured by B & S Sales. B & S Enterprises was later incorporated under the name of American Heritage Products, Inc.

Although Bolen sought the endorsement and participation of the Martin Luther King, Jr. Center for Social Change, Inc., in the marketing of the bust, the Center refused Bolen's offer. Bolen pursued the idea, nevertheless, hiring an artist to prepare a mold and an agent to handle the promotion of the product. Defendant took out two half-page advertisements in the November and December 1980 issues of Ebony magazine, which purported to offer the bust as "an exclusive memorial" and "an opportunity to support the Martin Luther King, Jr., Center for Social Change." The advertisement stated that "a contribution from your order goes to the King Center for Social Change." Out of the $29.95 purchase price, defendant Bolen testified he set aside 3% or $.90, as a contribution to the Center. The advertisement also offered "free" with the purchase of the bust a booklet about the life of Dr. King entitled "A Tribute to Dr. Martin Luther King, Jr."

In addition to the two advertisements in Ebony, defendant published a brochure or pamphlet which was inserted in 80,000 copies of newspapers across the country. The brochure reiterated what was stated in the magazine advertisements, and also contained photographs of Dr. King and excerpts from his copyrighted speeches. The brochure promised that each "memorial" (bust) is accompanied by a Certificate of Appreciation "testifying that a contribution has been made to the Martin Luther King, Jr., Center for Social Change."

[Plaintiffs sought an injunction prohibiting the manufacture or sale of the busts by the defendants.]

In ruling on the third request for injunction, the court confronted the plaintiffs' claim that the manufacture and sale of the busts violated Dr. King's right of publicity which had passed to his heirs upon Dr. King's death. The defendants contended that no such right existed, and hence, an injunction should not issue. The district court concluded that it was not necessary to determine whether the "right of publicity" was devisable in Georgia because Dr. King did not commercially exploit this right during his lifetime. As found by the district court, the evidence of exploitation by Dr. King came from his sister's affidavit which stated that he had received "thousands of dollars in the form of honorariums from the use of his name, likeness, literary compositions, and speeches." The district court further found that "Dr. King apparently sold his copyrights in several speeches to Motown Records Corporation."

On plaintiffs' appeal of the partial denial of the preliminary injunction, the Eleventh Circuit Court of Appeals has certified the following questions:

(1) Is the "right of publicity" recognized in Georgia as a right distinct from the right of privacy?

(2) If the answer to question (1) is affirmative, does the "right to publicity" survive the death of its owner? Specifically, is the right inheritable and devisable?

(3) If the answer to question (2) is also affirmative, must the owner have commercially exploited the right before it can survive his death?

(4) Assuming the affirmative answers to questions (1), (2) and (3), what is the guideline to be followed in defining commercial exploitation and what are the evidentiary prerequisites to a showing of commercial exploitation?

As noted by the Eleventh Circuit, this case raises questions concerning the laws of Georgia as to which there are no controlling precedents directly on point. * * *

The right of publicity may be defined as a celebrity's right to the exclusive use of his or her name and likeness. The right is most often asserted by or on behalf of professional athletes, comedians, actors and actresses, and other entertainers. This case involves none of those occupations. As is known to all, from 1955 until he was assassinated on April 4, 1968, Dr. King, a Baptist minister by profession, was the foremost leader of the civil rights movement in the United States. He was awarded the Nobel Prize for Peace in 1964. Although not a public official, Dr. King was a public figure, and we deal in this opinion with public figures who are neither public officials nor entertainers. Within this framework, we turn to the questions posed.

1. Is the "right of publicity" recognized in Georgia as a right distinct from the right of privacy?

Georgia has long recognized the right of privacy. Following denial of the existence of the right of privacy in a controversial decision by the New York Court of Appeals in Roberson v. Rochester Folding-Box Co., 171 N.Y. 538, 64 N.E. 442 (1902), the Georgia Supreme Court became the first such court to recognize the right of privacy in Pavesich v. New England Life Ins. Co., 122 Ga. 190, 50 S.E. 68 (1905). See Prosser, Law of Torts, pp. 802–804 (1971).

In Pavesich v. New England Life Ins. Co., supra, the picture of an artist was used without his consent in a newspaper advertisement of the insurance company. Analyzing the right of privacy, this court held: "The publication of a picture of a person, without his consent, as a part of an advertisement, for the purpose of exploiting the publisher's business, is a violation of the right of privacy of the person whose picture is reproduced, and entitles him to recover without proof of special damage." 122 Ga. at 191(11), 50 S.E. at 68[11]. If the right to privacy had not been recognized, advertisers could use photographs of private citizens to promote sales and the professional modeling business would not be what it is today.

* * *

Recognizing the possibility of a conflict between the right of privacy and the freedoms of speech and press, this court said: "There is in the publication of one's picture for advertising purposes not the slightest semblance of an expression of an idea, a thought, or an opinion, within the meaning of the constitutional provision which guarantees to a person the right to publish his sentiments on any subject." 122 Ga. at 219, 50 S.E. at 80. The defendants in the case now before us make no claim under these freedoms and we find no violation thereof.

* * *

Finding that Pavesich, although an artist, was not recognized as a public figure, the court said: "It is not necessary in this case to hold, nor are we prepared to do so, that the mere fact that a man has become what is called a public character, either by aspiring to public office, or by holding public office, or by exercising a profession which places him before the public, or by engaging in a business which has necessarily a public nature, gives to every one the right to print and circulate his picture." 122 Ga. at 217–218, 50 S.E. at 79–80. Thus, although recognizing the right of privacy, the Pavesich court left open the question facing us involving the likeness of a public figure.

The "right of publicity" was first recognized in Haelan Laboratories, Inc. v. Topps Chewing Gum, Inc., 202 F.2d 866 (2d Cir.1953). There plaintiff had acquired by contract the exclusive right to use certain ball players' photographs in connection with the sales of plaintiff's chewing gum. An independent publishing company acquired similar rights from some of the same ball players. Defendant, a chewing gum manufacturer competing with plaintiff and knowing of plaintiff's contracts, acquired the contracts from the publishing company. As to these contracts the court found that the defendant had violated the ball players' "right of publicity" acquired by the plaintiff, saying (at 868):

"We think that, in addition to and independent of that right of privacy (which in New York derives from statute), a man has a right in the publicity value of his photograph, i.e., the right to grant the exclusive privilege of publishing his picture, and that such a grant may validly be made 'in gross,' i.e., without an accompanying transfer of a business or of anything else. Whether it be labeled a 'property' right is immaterial; for here, as often elsewhere, the tag 'property' simply symbolizes the fact that courts enforce a claim which has pecuniary worth.

"This right might be called a 'right of publicity.' For it is common knowledge that many prominent persons (especially actors and ballplayers), far from having their feelings bruised through public exposure of their likenesses, would feel sorely deprived if they no longer received money for authorizing advertisements, popularizing their countenances, displayed in newspapers, magazines, busses, trains and subways. This right of publicity would usually yield them no money unless it could be made the subject of an exclusive grant which barred any other advertiser from using their pictures."

* * *

The right of publicity was first recognized in Georgia by the Court of Appeals in Cabaniss v. Hipsley, 114 Ga.App. 367, 151 S.E.2d 496 (1966). There the court held that the plaintiff, an exotic dancer, could recover from the owner of the Atlanta Playboy Club for the unauthorized use of the dancer's misnamed photograph in an entertainment magazine advertising the Playboy Club. Although plaintiff had had her picture taken to promote her performances, she was not performing at the Playboy Club. The court used Dean William L. Prosser's four-pronged analysis of the right of privacy, saying:

". . . Dean Prosser has analyzed the many privacy cases in an article entitled 'Privacy,' published in 48 Calif.L.Rev. 383 (1960), and in reviewing the cases he suggests that the invasion of privacy is in reality a complex of four loosely related torts; that there are four distinct kinds of invasion of four different interests of plaintiff; that there are four disparate torts under a common name. These four torts may be described briefly as: (1) intrusion upon the plaintiff's seclusion or solitude, or into his private affairs; (2) public disclosure of embarrassing private facts about the plaintiff; (3) publicity which places the plaintiff in a false light in the public eye; (4) appropriation, for the defendant's advantage, of the plaintiff's name or likeness." 114 Ga.App. at 370, 151 S.E.2d at 499–500.

Finding no violation of the first three rights of privacy, the court found a violation of the fourth, saying (114 Ga.App. at 377, 151 S.E.2d 496):

> "Unlike intrusion, disclosure, or false light, appropriation does not require the invasion of something secret, secluded or private pertaining to plaintiff, nor does it involve falsity. It consists of the appropriation, for the defendant's benefit, use or advantage, of the plaintiff's name or likeness. . . . 'The interest protected [in the "appropriation" cases] is not so much a mental as a proprietary one, in the exclusive use of the plaintiff's name and likeness as an aspect of his identity.' Prosser, supra, at 406."

Although Ms. Hipsley was an entertainer (i.e., a public figure), the court found she was entitled to recover from the Playboy Club (but not from the magazine which published the Club's ad) for the unauthorized use of her photograph. However the court noted a difference in the damages recoverable in traditional right of privacy cases as opposed to right of publicity cases saying (114 Ga.App. at 378, 151 S.E.2d 496):

> "Recognizing, as we do, the fundamental distinction between causes of action involving injury to feelings, sensibilities or reputation and those involving an appropriation of rights in the nature of property rights for commercial exploitation, it must necessarily follow that there is a fundamental distinction between the two classes of cases in the measure of damages to be applied. In the former class (which we take to include the intrusion, disclosure, and false light aspects of the privacy tort), general damages are recoverable without proof of special damages. Pavesich v. New England Life Ins. Co., supra. In the latter class, the measure of damages is the value of the use of the appropriated publicity."

* * *

Thus, the courts in Georgia have recognized the rights of private citizens, Pavesich, supra, as well as entertainers, *Cabaniss* and *McQueen*, [McQueen v. Wilson, 117 Ga. App. 488, 161 S.E.2d 63 (1968)], supra, not to have their names and photographs used for the financial gain of the user without their consent, where such use is not authorized as an exercise of freedom of the press. We know of no reason why a public figure prominent in religion and civil rights should be entitled to less protection than an exotic dancer or a movie actress. Therefore, we hold that the appropriation of another's name and likeness, whether such likeness be a photograph or sculpture, without consent and for the financial gain of the appropriator is a tort in Georgia, whether the person whose name and likeness is used is a private citizen, entertainer, or as here a public figure who is not a public official.

In Pavesich, supra, 122 Ga. 190, 50 S.E. 68, this right not to have another appropriate one's photograph was denominated the right of privacy; in Cabaniss v. Hipsley, supra, 114 Ga.App. 367, 151 S.E.2d 496, it was the right of publicity. Mr. Pavesich was not a public figure; Ms. Hipsley was. We conclude that while private citizens have the right of privacy, public figures have a similar right of publicity, and that the measure of damages to a public figure for violation of his or her right of publicity is the value of the appropriation to the user. As thus understood the first certified question is answered in the affirmative.

2. Does the "right of publicity" survive the death of its owner (i.e., is the right inheritable and devisable)?

Although the Pavesich court expressly did not decide this question, the tenor of that opinion is that the right to privacy at least should be protectable after death.

The right of publicity is assignable during the life of the celebrity, for without this characteristic, full commercial exploitation of one's name and likeness is practically impossible. That is, without assignability the right of publicity could hardly be called a "right". Recognizing its assignability, most commentators have urged that the right of publicity must also be inheritable.

The courts that have considered the problem are not as unanimous. * * *

For the reasons which follow we hold that the right of publicity survives the death of its owner and is inheritable and devisable. Recognition of the right of publicity rewards and thereby encourages effort and creativity. If the right of publicity dies with the celebrity, the economic value of the right of publicity during life would be diminished because the celebrity's untimely death would seriously impair, if not destroy, the value of the right of continued commercial use. Conversely, those who would profit from the fame of a celebrity after his or her death for their own benefit and without authorization have failed to establish their claim that they should be the beneficiaries of the celebrity's death. Finally, the trend since the early common law has been to recognize survivability, notwithstanding the legal problems which may thereby arise. We therefore answer question 2 in the affirmative.

3. Must the owner of the right of publicity have commercially exploited that right before it can survive?

Exploitation is understood to mean commercial use by the celebrity other than the activity which made him or her famous, e.g., an inter vivos transfer of the right to the use of one's name and likeness.

[The court considered several cases including Hicks v. Casablanca Records, 464 F. Supp. 426 (S.D.N.Y. 1978) appearing to hold that unless the celebrity sold or otherwise commercially exploited his or her personality during life, the right was not descendible to heirs.]

The cases which have considered this issue, see above, involved entertainers. The net result of following them would be to say that celebrities and public figures have the right of publicity during their lifetimes (as others have the right of privacy), but only those who contract for bubble gum cards, posters and tee shirts have a descendible right of publicity upon their deaths. That we should single out for protection after death those entertainers and athletes who exploit their personae during life, and deny protection after death to those who enjoy public acclamation but did not exploit themselves during life, puts a premium on exploitation. Having found that there are valid reasons for recognizing the right of publicity during life, we find no reason to protect after death only those who took commercial advantage of their fame.

Perhaps this case more than others brings the point into focus. A well known minister may avoid exploiting his prominence during life because to do otherwise would impair his ministry. Should his election not to take commercial advantage of his position during life ipso facto result in permitting others to exploit his name and likeness after his death? In our view, a person who avoids exploitation during life is entitled to have his image protected against exploitation after death just as much if not more than a person who exploited his image during life.

Without doubt, Dr. King could have exploited his name and likeness during his lifetime. That this opportunity was not appealing to him does not mean that others have the right to use his name and likeness in ways he himself chose not to do. Nor does it strip his family and estate of the right to control, preserve and extend his status and memory and to prevent unauthorized exploitation thereof by others. Here, they seek to prevent the exploitation of his likeness in a manner they consider unflattering and unfitting. We cannot deny them this right merely because Dr. King chose not to exploit or commercialize himself during his lifetime.

Question 3 is answered in the negative, and therefore we need not answer question 4.

Certified questions 1 and 2 answered in the affirmative, question 3 answered in the negative, and question 4 not answered.

All the Justices concur, except WELTNER, J., who concurs specially.

WELTNER, Justice, concurring specially.

[Justice Weltner concurred arguing that rather than create a new right which has uncertain free speech implications, the court should have applied an unjust enrichment theory and awarded an accounting of the defendant's unjust gain.]

NOTES

1. What is the appropriate justification for legal protection of the right of publicity? Is this doctrine a modern successor to the misappropriation doctrine of *INS v. AP*? As Justice Weltner suggests, is this a form of unjust enrichment? Or is the doctrine designed to be a complement to the copyright and patent system by encouraging investment in celebrity status? Do you agree with the majority that the doctrine is needed to encourage effort and creativity? Should someone whose fame arises by accident be entitled to protection? Will a baseball player give less effort if the publicity right is not protected? Would professional sports teams have to pay their players more in salary if the players could not exploit their celebrity status?

2. Should the right of publicity expire on the death of the celebrity? Two leading cases that split on the issue are Factors Etc., Inc. v. Pro Arts, Inc., 579 F.2d 215 (2d Cir. 1978) (right is transferable at death; otherwise unrelated third parties would obtain a windfall), and Lugosi v. Universal Pictures, 25 Cal.3d 813, 603 P.2d 425 (1979) (4 to 3 decision against transferability at death). Does resolution of this issue depend on the basis for the right in the first instance? If the right is transferable at death, is there some limit on the duration of the right? Do you think the John Hancock Life Insurance Company needs the permission of the descendants of John Hancock? See West's Ann. Cal. Civ. Code § 990 for a statutory solution to the descendability problem that contains an intestacy distribution and a limitation on the right of 50 years from the death of the individual.

3. If the right of publicity is assignable during the life of the celebrity, doesn't it follow that the right should be transferable at death?

4. Does the right of publicity extend beyond the name and likeness of the celebrity? In Midler v. Ford Motor Co., 849 F.2d 460 (9th Cir. 1988) Ford Motor, after unsuccessfully seeking the services of Bette Midler for an advertising commercial, hired another person to imitate Midler's voice singing a famous Midler song. The court upheld a cause of action for appropriating the plaintiff's identity: "We need not and do not go so far as to hold that every imitation of a voice to advertise merchandise is actionable. We hold only that when a distinctive voice of a professional singer is widely known and is deliberately imitated in order to sell a product, the sellers have appropriated what is not theirs and have committed a tort in California." See, Motschenbacher v. R.J. Reynolds Tobacco Co., 498 F.2d 821 (9th Cir. 1974), where a photograph of a famous racing driver's racing car was used in a commercial for Winston cigarettes and even though the car had been modified it was still recognizable by some persons watching the commercial. The court held the defendants had appropriated the driver's identity. See also, Carson v. Here's Johnny Portable Toilets, Inc., 698 F.2d 831 (6th Cir. 1983) where the entertainer Johnny Carson successfully objected to the use of his famous introduction "Here's Johnny" on portable toilets.

5. The right of publicity is distinct from any trademark rights the celebrity may have in his or her name or likeness. See, Waits v. Frito-Lay, Inc., 978 F.2d 1093 (9th Cir. 1992), where the Ninth Circuit affirmed a jury award of $375,000 compensatory damages and $2 million punitive damages in favor of Tom Waits against Frito-Lay for broadcasting a radio commercial for its SalsoRio Doritos using an imitation of Waits' raspy singing voice. The court upheld a claim both for voice misappropriation under the common law right of publicity and a false endorsement claim under § 43(a) of the Lanham Act. A false endorsement claim assumes that consumers will believe that Waits endorsed Frito-Lay's products. Such a claim is certainly a false representation under the Lanham Act and is analogous to trademark infringement. What injury does Waits suffer if Frito-Lay adequately informs the public in the commercial that the voice is an imitation of Tom Waits? What about a commercial that begins with a person imitating Tom Waits singing and then continues: "This is a man imitating Tom Waits. You might like his performance. But don't accept imitations of SalsoRio Doritos"? How does such a commercial differ from one in which a man is shown eating from a bag of "TacoRight Corn Chips" and then a voice says, "This man is not smiling because he's eating the soggy chips. If you want crunch with your taste, eat Frito-Lay Corn Chips." Does the maker of TacoRight have a claim against Frito-Lay? Would the right of publicity prohibit all of these uses of Wait's voice and name, even if the imitation was made clear? And see, Allen v. National Video, Inc., 610 F.Supp. 612 (S.D.N.Y.1985) in which Woody Allen successfully enjoined the use of a "look-alike" actor in an advertisement for a national video rental chain under § 43(a) of the Lanham Act because of a likelihood of confusion even though he was unsuccessful under New York's limited publicity right.

6. What remedy is appropriate in these cases?

7. Some thirteen states have enacted statutes which establish a right of publicity. See, e.g., Cal. Civ. Code § 3344 for one of the more elaborate.

Zacchini v. Scripps–Howard Broadcasting Co.

Supreme Court of the United States, 1977.
433 U.S. 562, 97 S.Ct. 2849, 53 L.Ed.2d 965.

■ MR. JUSTICE WHITE delivered the opinion of the Court.

Petitioner, Hugo Zacchini, is an entertainer. He performs a "human cannonball" act in which he is shot from a cannon into a net some 200 feet away. Each performance occupies some 15 seconds. In August and September, 1972, petitioner was engaged to perform his act on a regular basis at the Geauga County Fair in Burton, Ohio. He performed in a fenced area, surrounded by grandstands, at the fair grounds. Members of the public attending the fair were not charged a separate admission fee to observe his act.

On August 30, a freelance reporter for Scripps-Howard Broadcasting Company, the operator of a television broadcasting station and respondent in this case, attended the fair. He carried a small movie camera. Petitioner noticed the reporter and asked him not to film the performance. The reporter did not do so on that day; but on the instructions of the producer of respondent's daily newscast, he returned the following day and videotaped the entire act. This film clip approximately 15 seconds in length, was shown on the 11 o'clock news program that night, together with favorable commentary.[1]

Petitioner then brought this action for damages, alleging that he is "engaged in the entertainment business," that the act he performs is one "invented by his father and * * * performed only by his family for the last fifty years," that respondent "showed and commercialized the film of his act

---

1. The script of the commentary accompanying the film clip read as follows:

"This * * * now * * * is the story of a *true spectator* sport * * * the sport of human cannonballing * * * in fact, the great *Zacchini* is about the only human cannonball around, these days * * * just happens that, *where* he is, is the Great Geauga County Fair, in Burton * * * and believe me, although it's not a *long* act, it's a thriller * * * and you really need to see it *in person* * * * to appreciate it. * * * " (Emphasis in original.) App. 12.

without his consent," and that such conduct was an "unlawful appropriation of plaintiff's professional property." * * *

[The trial court summarily granted respondent's motion for summary judgment. The Ohio Court of Appeals reversed finding the complaint stated a cause of action for conversion and for infringement of a common law copyright. The Supreme Court of Ohio reversed, holding that although the petitioner had a "right of publicity," the newscast was a matter of public interest and thus privileged.]

We granted certiorari to consider an issue unresolved by this Court: whether the First and Fourteenth Amendments immunized respondent from damages for its alleged infringement of petitioner's state law "right of publicity." Insofar as the Ohio Supreme Court held that the First and Fourteenth Amendments of the United States Constitution required judgment for respondent, we reverse the judgment of that court.

III

The Ohio Supreme Court held that respondent is constitutionally privileged to include in its newscasts matters of public interest that would otherwise be protected by the right of publicity, absent an intent to injure or to appropriate for some nonprivileged purpose. If under this standard respondent had merely reported that petitioner was performing at the fair and described or commented on his act, with or without showing his picture on television, we would have a very different case. But petitioner is not contending that his appearance at the fair and his performance could not be reported by the press as newsworthy items. His complaint is that respondent filmed his entire act and displayed that film on television for the public to see and enjoy. This, he claimed, was an appropriation of his professional property. The Ohio Supreme Court agreed that petitioner had "a right of publicity" that gave him "personal control over the commercial display and exploitation of his personality and the exercise of his talents." This right of "exclusive control over the publicity given to his performance" was said to be such a "valuable part of the benefit which may be attained by his talents and efforts" that it was entitled to legal protection. It was also observed, or at least expressly assumed, that petitioner had not abandoned his rights by performing under the circumstances present at the Geauga County Fair Grounds.

The Ohio Supreme Court nevertheless held that the challenged invasion was privileged, saying that the press "must be accorded broad latitude in its choice of how much it presents of each story or incident, and of the emphasis to be given to such presentation. No fixed standard which would bar the press from reporting or depicting either an entire occurrence or an entire discrete part of a public performance can be formulated which would not unduly restrict the 'breathing room' in reporting which freedom of the press requires." 47 Ohio St., at 235, 351 N.E.2d, at 461. Under this view, respondent was thus constitutionally free to film and display petitioner's entire act.

The Ohio Supreme Court relied heavily on Time, Inc. v. Hill, [385 U.S. 374 (1967)], but that case does not mandate a media privilege to televise a performer's entire act without his consent. Involved in Time, Inc. v. Hill was a claim under the New York "Right of Privacy" statute that Life Magazine, in the course of reviewing a new play, had connected the play with a long-past incident involving petitioner and his family and had falsely described their experience and conduct at that time. The complaint sought damages for humiliation and suffering flowing from these nondefamatory falsehoods that allegedly invaded Hill's privacy. The Court held, however, that the opening of a new play linked to an actual incident was a matter of public interest and that Hill could not recover without showing that the Life report was knowingly false or was published with reckless disregard for the truth—the same rigorous standard that had been applied in New York Times v. Sullivan, [376 U.S. 254 (1964)].

Time, Inc. v. Hill, which was hotly contested and decided by a divided court, involved an entirely different tort than the "right of publicity" recognized by the Ohio Supreme Court. As the opinion reveals in Time, Inc. v. Hill, the Court was steeped in the literature of privacy law and was aware of the developing distinctions and nuances in this branch of the law. The Court, for example, cited Prosser, Handbook of the Law of Torts (3d ed. 1964), and the same author's well-known article, Privacy, 48 Calif.L.Rev. 383 (1960), both of which divided privacy into four distinct branches. The Court was aware that it was adjudicating a "false light" privacy case involving a matter of public interest, not a case involving "intrusion," "appropriation" of a name or likeness for the purposes of trade, or "private details" about a non-newsworthy person or event. It is also abundantly clear that Time, Inc. v. Hill did not involve a performer, a person with a name having commercial value, or any claim to a "right of publicity." This discrete kind of "appropriation" case was plainly identified in the literature cited by the Court and had been adjudicated in the reported cases.

The differences between these two torts are important. First, the State's interests in providing a cause of action in each instance are different. "The interest protected" in permitting recovery for placing the plaintiff in a false light "is clearly that of reputation, with the same overtones of mental distress as in defamation." Prosser, supra, 48 Calif.L.Rev., at 400. By contrast, the State's interest in permitting a "right of publicity" is in protecting the proprietary interest of the individual in his act in part to encourage such entertainment.[10] As we later note, the State's interest is closely analogous to the goals of patent and copyright law, focusing on the right of the individual to reap the reward of his endeavors and having little to do

---

10. The Ohio Supreme Court expressed the view "that plaintiff's claim is one for invasion of the right of privacy by appropriation, and should be considered as such." 47 Ohio St., at 226, 351 N.E.2d, at 456. It should be noted, however, that the case before us is more limited than the broad category of law-suits that may arise under the heading of "appropriation." Petitioner does not merely assert that some general use, such as advertising, was made of his name or likeness; he relies on the much narrower claim that respondent televised an entire act that he ordinarily gets paid to perform.

with protecting feelings or reputation. Second, the two torts differ in the degree to which they intrude on dissemination of information to the public. In "false light" cases the only way to protect the interests involved is to attempt to minimize publication of the damaging matter, while in "right of publicity" cases the only question is who gets to do the publishing. An entertainer such as petitioner usually has no objection to the widespread publication of his act as long as he gets the commercial benefit of such publication. Indeed, in the present case petitioner did not seek to enjoin the broadcast of his act; he simply sought compensation for the broadcast in the form of damages.

* * *

* * * It is evident, and there is no claim here to the contrary, that petitioner's state-law right of publicity would not serve to prevent respondent from reporting the newsworthy facts about petitioner's act. Wherever the line in particular situations is to be drawn between media reports that are protected and those that are not, we are quite sure that the First and Fourteenth Amendments do not immunize the media when they broadcast a performer's entire act without his consent. The Constitution no more prevents a State from requiring respondent to compensate petitioner for broadcasting his act on television than it would privilege respondent to film and broadcast a copyrighted dramatic work without liability to the copyright owner. * * *

The broadcast of a film of petitioner's entire act poses a substantial threat to the economic value of that performance. As the Ohio court recognized, this act is the product of petitioner's own talents and energy, the end result of much time, effort and expense. Much of its economic value lies in the "right of exclusive control over the publicity given to his performance"; if the public can see the act for free on television, they will be less willing to pay to see it at the fair.[12] The effect of a public broadcast of the performance is similar to preventing petitioner from charging an admission fee. "The rationale for [protecting the right of publicity] is the straightforward one of preventing unjust enrichment by the theft of good will. No social purpose is served by having the defendant get for free some aspect of the plaintiff that would have market value and for which he would normally pay." Kalven, Privacy in Tort Law—Were Warren and Brandeis Wrong?, 31 Law and Contemporary Problems 326, 331 (1966). Moreover, the broadcast of petitioner's entire performance, unlike the unauthorized use of another's name for purposes of trade or the incidental use of a name or picture by the press, goes to the heart of petitioner's ability to earn a living as an entertainer. Thus in this case, Ohio has recognized what may be the strongest case for a "right of publicity"—involving not the appropriation of an entertainer's

---

12. It is possible, of course, that respondent's news broadcast increased the value of petitioner's performance by stimulating the public's interest in seeing the act live. In these circumstances, petitioner would not be able to prove damages and thus would not recover. But petitioner has alleged that the broadcast injured him to the extent of $25,000, and we think the State should be allowed to authorize compensation of this injury if proven.

reputation to enhance the attractiveness of a commercial product, but the appropriation of the very activity by which the entertainer acquired his reputation in the first place.

Of course, Ohio's decision to protect petitioner's right of publicity here rests on more than a desire to compensate the performer for the time and effort invested in his act; the protection provides an economic incentive for him to make the investment required to produce a performance of interest to the public. This same consideration underlies the patent and copyright laws long enforced by this Court. The Constitution does not prevent Ohio from making a similar choice here in deciding to protect the entertainer's incentive in order to encourage the production of this type of work. Cf. Goldstein v. California, 412 U.S. 546 (1973); Kewanee Oil Co. v. Bicron Corp., 416 U.S. 470 (1974).

There is no doubt that entertainment, as well as news, enjoys First Amendment protection. It is also true that entertainment itself can be important news. Time, Inc. v. Hill, supra. But it is important to note that neither the public nor respondent will be deprived of the benefit of petitioner's performance as long as his commercial stake in his act is appropriately recognized. Petitioner does not seek to enjoin the broadcast of his performance; he simply wants to be paid for it. Nor do we think that a state-law damages remedy against respondent would represent a species of liability without fault contrary to the letter or spirit of Gertz, supra. Respondent knew exactly that petitioner objected to televising his act, but nevertheless displayed the entire film.

We conclude that although the State of Ohio may as a matter of its own law privilege the press in the circumstances of this case, the First and Fourteenth Amendments do not require it to do so.

Reversed.

Mr. Justice POWELL, with whom Mr. Justice BRENNAN and Mr. Justice MARSHALL join, dissenting.

Disclaiming any attempt to do more than decide the narrow case before us, the Court reverses the decision of the Supreme Court of Ohio based on repeated incantation of a single formula: "a performer's entire act." * * * I doubt that this formula provides a standard clear enough even for resolution of this case. In any event, I am not persuaded that the Court's opinion is appropriately sensitive to the First Amendment values at stake, and I therefore dissent.

* * *

* * * When a film is used, as here, for a routine portion of a regular news program, I would hold that the First Amendment protects the station from a "right of publicity" or "appropriation" suit, absent a strong showing by the plaintiff that the news broadcast was a subterfuge or cover for private or commercial exploitation.

I emphasize that this is a "reappropriation" suit, rather than one of the other varieties of "right of privacy" tort suits identified by Dean Prosser in his classic article. Prosser, Privacy, 48 Calif.L.Rev. 383 (1960). In those other causes of action the competing interests are considerably different. The plaintiff generally seeks to avoid any sort of public exposure, and the existence of constitutional privilege is therefore less likely to turn on whether the publication occurred in a news broadcast or in some other fashion. In a suit like the one before us, however, the plaintiff does not complain about the fact of exposure to the public, but rather about its timing or manner. He welcomes some publicity, but seeks to retain control over means and manner as a way to maximize for himself the monetary benefits that flow from such publication. But having made the matter public—having chosen, in essence, to make it newsworthy—he cannot, consistently with the First Amendment, complain of routine news reportage. * * *

Since the film clip here was undeniably treated as news and since there is no claim that the use was subterfuge, respondent's actions were constitutionally privileged. I would affirm.

NOTES

1. What measure of damages would you adopt for cases like *Zacchini* ? Does the majority opinion place any first amendment limits on your range of choice? Isn't *Zacchini* really like the *DuPont* case [aerial photography]? Would it make any difference if the ticket to see Zacchini's act carried the legend "No Photographs".

2. Is the Ohio law of publicity preempted by § 301 of the Copyright Act? Does it matter that Zacchini's act was not fixed in a tangible medium of expression under § 102? Does Zacchini's act fit within one of the protectible categories mentioned in § 102? Is the right of publicity "equivalent" to a right in § 106? The Seventh Circuit struggled with these problems in Baltimore Orioles v. Major League Baseball Players, 805 F.2d 663 (7th Cir.1986) where major league baseball players argued they owned the broadcast rights to their performances during baseball games. As to the games that were videotaped, the court held the right of publicity was preempted by § 301. As to other games the court left open whether the employer owns the names, likenesses, and performances of employees within the scope of their employment. What do you think? See D. Shipley, Three Strikes and They're Out at the Old Ball Game: Preemption of Performers' Rights of Publicity Under the Copyright Act of 1976, 20 Ariz.St.L.J. 369 (1988).

3. Should the constitutional fault standard of the defamation and privacy cases apply to publicity cases? If a publisher publishes nude photographs he claims are of a particular celebrity and they turn out to be of someone else, should the celebrity be required to prove "actual malice". Does it matter whether the celebrity wants (a) an injunction against publication or (b) royalties? See Lerman v. Flynt Distributing Co., Inc., 745 F.2d 123 (2d Cir.1984). See also Tellado v. Time–Life Books, Inc., 643 F.Supp. 904 (D.N.J.1986) where the plaintiff objected to the use of his picture, taken during battle in Vietnam, as an advertisement for a series of picture books on the Vietnam war. The court held that a misappropriation claim was available for "predominantly commercial uses" of a person's likeness and such a cause of action would not violate the First Amendment.

4. Can you frame a response to the assertion that Scripps-Howard's activity in *Zacchini* is similar to broadcasting a copyrighted dramatic work as part of news coverage?

Cardtoons, L.C. v. Major League Baseball Players Association

United States Court of Appeals for the Tenth Circuit, 1996.
95 F.3d 959.

■ TACHA, CIRCUIT JUDGE.

Cardtoons formed in late 1992 to produce parody trading cards featuring caricatures of major league baseball players. Cardtoons contracted with a political cartoonist, a sports artist, and a sports author and journalist, who designed a set of 130 cards. The majority of the cards, 71, have caricatures of active major league baseball players on the front and humorous commentary about their careers on the back. The balance of the set is comprised of 20 "Big Bang Bucks" cards (cartoon drawings of currency with caricatures of the most highly paid players on the front, yearly salary statistics on the back), 10 "Spectra" cards (caricatures of active players on the front, nothing on the back), 10 retired player cards (caricatures of retired players on the front, humorous commentary about their careers on the back), 11 "Politics in Baseball" cards (cartoons featuring caricatures of political and sports figures on the front, humorous text on the back), 7 standing cards (caricatures of team logos on the front, humorous text on the back), and 1 checklist card. Except for the Spectra cards, the back of each card bears the Cardtoons logo and the following statement: "Cardtoons baseball is a parody and is NOT licensed by Major League Baseball Properties or Major League Baseball Players Association."

A person reasonably familiar with baseball can readily identify the players lampooned on the parody trading cards. The cards use similar names, recognizable caricatures, distinctive team colors, and commentary about individual players. For example, the card parodying San Francisco Giants' outfielder Barry Bonds calls him "Treasury Bonds," and features a recognizable caricature of Bonds, complete with earring, tipping a bat boy for a 24 carat gold "Fort Knoxville Slugger." * * *

* * *

MLBPA is the exclusive collective bargaining agent for all active major league baseball players, and operates a group licensing program in which it acts as the assignee of the individual publicity rights of all active players. Since 1966, MLBPA has entered into group licensing arrangements for a variety of products, such as candy bars, cookies, cereals, and, most importantly, baseball trading cards, which generate over seventy percent of its licensing revenue. MLBPA receives royalties from these sales and distributes the money to individual players.

[Cardtoons sought a declaratory judgment that it could distribute the cards. The district court submitted the matter to a magistrate who found Cardtoons had violated the right of publicity and was not protected by the First Amendment. The district court first adopted the magistrates opinion but subsequently vacated that decision and found for Cardtoons on the basis of an implied fair use exception to the Oklahoma right of publicity statute. The Tenth Circuit traced the development of the right of publicity in Oklahoma and held that the statutory cause of action did not have an exception for parody. The Court thus evaluated the First Amendment and found the trading cards to be fully protected speech, not commercial speech. The court then set out to balance the interests in free speech against the property interests of the ballplayers.]

C. Balancing Free Speech Rights with Property Rights

In resolving the tension between the First Amendment and publicity rights in this case, we find little guidance in cases involving parodies of other forms of intellectual property. Trademark and copyright, for example, have built-in mechanisms that serve to avoid First Amendment concerns of this kind. As discussed above, proof of trademark infringement under the Lanham Act requires proof of a likelihood of confusion, but, in the case of a good trademark parody, there is little likelihood of confusion, since the humor lies in the difference between the original and the parody. The Copyright Act of 1976 contains a similar mechanism, the fair use exception, which permits the use of copyrighted materials for purposes such as criticism and comment. Oklahoma's right of publicity statute, however, does not provide a similar accommodation for parody, and we must therefore confront the First Amendment issue directly.

* * *

This case instead requires us to directly balance the magnitude of the speech restriction against the asserted governmental interest in protecting the intellectual property right. We thus begin our analysis by examining the importance of Cardtoons' right to free expression and the consequences of limiting that right. We then weigh those consequences against the effect of infringing on MLBPA's right of publicity.

1. The Effect of Infringing Upon Cardtoons' Right to Free Speech

Cardtoons' interest in publishing its parody trading cards implicates some of the core concerns of the First Amendment. "Parodies and caricatures," noted Aldous Huxley, "are the most penetrating of criticisms." Point Counter Point, ch. 13 (1928); see [Hustler Magazine v. Falwell, 485 U.S. 46 at 53–55]. A parodist can, with deft and wit, readily expose the foolish and absurd in society. Parody is also a valuable form of self-expression that allows artists to shed light on earlier works and, at the same time, create new ones. Thus, parody, both as social criticism and a means of self-expression, is a vital commodity in the marketplace of ideas.

* * *

Because celebrities are an important part of our public vocabulary, a parody of a celebrity does not merely lampoon the celebrity, but exposes the weakness of the idea or value that the celebrity symbolizes in society. Cardtoons' trading cards, for example, comment on the state of major league baseball by turning images of our sports heroes into modern-day personifications of avarice. In order to effectively criticize society, parodists need access to images that mean something to people, and thus celebrity parodies are a valuable communicative resource. Restricting the use of celebrity identities restricts the communication of ideas.

Without First Amendment protection, Cardtoons' trading cards and their irreverent commentary on the national pastime cannot be freely distributed to the public. Instead, as required by Oklahoma law, the production and distribution of the cards would be subject to MLBPA's consent. The problem with this scheme, as the Supreme Court noted in the context of copyright parody, is that "the unlikelihood that creators of imaginative works will license critical reviews or lampoons of their own productions removes such uses from the very notion of a potential licensing market." The potential for suppression is even greater in the context of publicity rights because the product involved is the celebrity's own persona. Indeed, the director of licensing for MLBPA testified that MLBPA would never license a parody which poked fun at the players. Thus, elevating the right of publicity above the right to free expression would likely prevent distribution of the parody trading cards. This would not only allow MLBPA to censor criticism of its members, but would also have a chilling effect upon future celebrity parodies. Such a result is clearly undesirable, for "[t]he last thing we need, the last thing the First Amendment will tolerate, is a law that lets public figures keep people from mocking them." White, 989 F.2d at 1519 (Kozinski, J., dissenting).

2. The Effect of Infringing Upon MLBPA's Right of Publicity

We now turn to an evaluation of society's interest in protecting MLBPA's publicity right. The justifications offered for the right of publicity fall into two categories, economic and noneconomic. The right is thought to further economic goals such as stimulating athletic and artistic achievement, promoting the efficient allocation of resources, and protecting consumers. In addition, the right of publicity is said to protect various noneconomic interests, such as safeguarding natural rights, securing the fruits of celebrity labors, preventing unjust enrichment, and averting emotional harm. We examine the applicability of each of these justifications to the facts of this case.

The principal economic argument made in support of the right of publicity is that it provides an incentive for creativity and achievement. Under this view, publicity rights induce people to expend the time, effort, and resources to develop the talents prerequisite to public recognition. While those talents provide immediate benefit to those with commercially valuable identities, the products of their enterprise—such as movies, songs, and sporting events—ultimately benefit society as a whole. Thus, it is argued, society has an interest in a right of publicity that is closely analogous to its interest in other intellectual property protections such as copyright and patent law.

This incentives argument is certainly a compelling justification for other forms of intellectual property. Copyright law, for example, protects the primary, if not only, source of a writer's income, and thus provides a significant incentive for creativity and achievement. The incentive effect of publicity rights, however, has been overstated. Most sports and entertainment celebrities with commercially valuable identities engage in activities that themselves generate a significant amount of income; the commercial value of their identities is merely a by-product of their performance values. See Restatement (Third) of Unfair Competition § 46 cmt. c. Although no one pays to watch Cormac McCarthy write a novel, many people pay a lot of money to watch Demi Moore "act" and Michael Jordan play basketball. Thus, the analogy to the incentive effect of other intellectual property protections is strained because "[a]bolition of the right of publicity would leave entirely unimpaired a celebrity's ability to earn a living from the activities that have generated his commercially marketable fame." [Michael Madow, Private Ownership of Public Image: Popular Culture and Publicity Rights, 81 Cal. L. Rev. 127, 209 (1993)].

This distinction between the value of a person's identity and the value of his performance explains why Zacchini v. Scripps-Howard Broadcasting Corp., 433 U.S. 562, the Supreme Court's sole case involving a right of publicity claim, is a red herring. Hugo Zacchini, a performer in a human cannonball act, brought an action against a television station to recover damages he suffered when the station videotaped and broadcast his entire performance. The Supreme Court held that the First Amendment did not give the station the right to broadcast Zacchini's entire act in contravention of his state protected right of publicity. Id. at 574–75. Zacchini, however, complained of the appropriation of the economic value of his performance, not the economic value of his identity. The Court's incentive rationale is obviously more compelling in a right of performance case than in a more typical right of publicity case involving the appropriation of a celebrity's identity. See Restatement (Third) of Unfair Competition § 46 reporters' note cmt. c.

Moreover, the additional inducement for achievement produced by publicity rights are often inconsequential because most celebrities with valuable commercial identities are already handsomely compensated. * * * In addition, even in the absence of publicity rights, celebrities would still be able to reap financial reward from authorized appearances and endorsements. The extra income generated by licensing one's identity does not provide a necessary inducement to enter and achieve in the realm of sports and entertainment. Thus, while publicity rights may provide some incentive for creativity and achievement, the magnitude and importance of that incentive has been exaggerated.

The argument that publicity rights provide valuable incentives is even less compelling in the context of celebrity parodies. Since celebrities will seldom give permission for their identities to be parodied, granting them control over the parodic use of their identities would not directly provide them with any additional income. It would, instead, only allow them to shield themselves from ridicule and criticism. The only economic incentive gained by having control over the use of one's identity in parody is control over the potential effect the parody would have on the market for nonparodic use of one's identity. MLBPA claims, for example, that publication of the parody cards will decrease demand for traditional baseball cards because Cardtoons and other makers of parody trading cards would compete with manufacturers of licensed cards in the same limited trading card market. Parody, however, rarely acts as a market substitute for the original and there is no evidence in this record that convinces us otherwise. Even if there is some substitutive effect, and card collectors with limited resources decide to buy parody cards instead of traditional, licensed cards, the small amount of additional income generated by suppressing parody cards will have little, if any, effect on the incentive to become a major league baseball player.

The incentives argument would be even more tenuous, indeed perverse, if good-humored celebrities were to license use of their identities for parody. The right of publicity would then provide an incentive to engage in the socially undesirable behavior that might give rise to a reason to parody. Although part of any parody's market appeal depends upon the prominence of the celebrity, the critical element of the parody's value hinges on the accuracy of the caricature or criticism. Society does not have a significant interest in allowing a celebrity to protect the type of reputation that gives rise to parody.

We recognize that publicity rights do provide some incentive to achieve in the fields of sports and entertainment. However, the inducements generated by publicity rights are not nearly as important as those created by copyright and patent law, and the small incentive effect of publicity rights is reduced or eliminated in the context of celebrity parodies. In sum, it is unlikely that little leaguers will stop dreaming of the big leagues or major leaguers will start "dogging it" to first base if MLBPA is denied the right to control the use of its members' identities in parody.

The second economic justification for the right of publicity is that it promotes the efficient allocation of resources, a version of the familiar tragedy of the commons argument used to prove the superiority of private property over common property. See, e.g., Matthews v. Wozencraft, 15 F.3d 432, 437–38 (5th Cir.1994). Without the artificial scarcity created by publicity rights, identities would be commercially exploited until the marginal value of each use is zero. Id. "Creating artificial scarcity preserves the value to [the celebrity], to advertisers who contract for the use of his likeness, and in the end, to consumers, who receive information from the knowledge that he is being paid to endorse the product." Id. at 438. Giving people control of the commercial use of their identities, according to this analysis, maximizes the economic and informational value of those identities.

This efficiency argument is most persuasive in the context of advertising, where repeated use of a celebrity's likeness to sell products may eventually diminish its commercial value. The argument is not as persuasive, however, when applied to nonadvertising uses. It is not clear, for example, that the frequent appearance of a celebrity's likeness on t-shirts and coffee mugs will reduce its value; indeed, the value of the likeness may increase precisely because "everybody's got one." Madow, supra, at 222. Further, celebrities with control over the parodic use of their identities would not use the power to "ration the use of their names in order to maximize their value over time," Matthews, 15 F.3d at 438 n. 2. They would instead use that power to suppress criticism, and thus permanently remove a valuable source of information about their identity from the marketplace.

* * *

There are also several noneconomic reasons advanced for the right of publicity. First, some believe that publicity rights stem from some notion of natural rights. McCarthy, for example, argues that a natural rights rationale, resting more upon "visceral impulses of 'fairness'" than upon reasoned argument, "seems quite sufficient to provide a firm support for the existence of a Right of Publicity." McCarthy, supra, § 2.1[A]. McCarthy, however, offers little reason for this assertion, and blind appeals to first principles carry no weight in our balancing analysis.

The second noneconomic justification is that publicity rights allow celebrities to enjoy the fruits of their labors. See, e.g., Zacchini, 433 U.S. at 573; Uhlaender v. Henricksen, 316 F.Supp. 1277, 1282 (D.Minn.1970). According to this argument, "[a] celebrity must be considered to have invested his years of practice and competition in a public personality which eventually may reach marketable status." Uhlaender, 316 F.Supp. at 1282. People deserve the right to control and profit from the commercial value of their identities because, quite simply, they've earned it. Thus, in this view, the right of publicity is similar to the right of a commercial enterprise to profit from the goodwill it has built up in its name.

Celebrities, however, are often not fully responsible for their fame. Indeed, in the entertainment industry, a celebrity's fame may largely be the creation of the media or the audience.* * * Professional athletes may be more responsible for their celebrity status, however, because athletic success is fairly straightforwardly the result of an athlete's natural talent and dedication. Thus, baseball players may deserve to profit from the commercial value of their identities more than movie stars. Once again, however, the force of this justification is diminished in the case of parody, because there is little right to enjoy the fruits of socially undesirable behavior.

The third, related justification for publicity rights is the prevention of unjust enrichment. In this view, whether the commercial value of an identity is the result of a celebrity's hard work, media creation, or just pure dumb luck, no social purpose is served by allowing others to freely appropriate it. Cardtoons, however, is not merely hitching its wagon to a star. As in all celebrity parodies, Cardtoons added a significant creative component of its own to the celebrity identity and created an entirely new product. Indeed, allowing MLBPA to control or profit from the parody trading cards would actually sanction the theft of Cardtoons' creative enterprise.

A final justification offered for the right of publicity is that it prevents emotional injuries. For example, commercial misappropriation may greatly distress a celebrity who finds all commercial exploitation to be offensive. Even celebrities who crave public attention might find particular uses of their identities to be distressing. See, e.g., O'Brien v. Pabst Sales Co., 124 F.2d 167, 170 (5th Cir.1942) (professional football player, active in an organization devoted to discouraging alcohol use among young people, sued to stop the use of his image in a Pabst Blue Ribbon beer advertising calendar). The right of publicity allows celebrities to avoid the emotional distress caused by unwanted commercial use of their identities. Publicity rights, however, are meant to protect against the loss of financial gain, not mental anguish. Laws preventing unfair competition, such as the Lanham Act, and laws prohibiting the intentional infliction of emotional distress adequately cover that ground. Moreover, fame is a double-edged sword—the law cannot allow those who enjoy the public limelight to so easily avoid the ridicule and criticism that sometimes accompany public prominence.

Thus, the noneconomic justifications for the right of publicity are no more compelling than the economic arguments. Those justifications further break down in the context of parody, where the right to profit from one's persona is reduced to the power to suppress criticism. In sum, the effect of limiting MLBPA's right of publicity in this case is negligible.

IV. Conclusion

One of the primary goals of intellectual property law is to maximize creative expression. The law attempts to achieve this goal by striking a proper balance between the right of a creator to the fruits of his labor and the right of future creators to free expression. Underprotection of intellectual property reduces the incentive to create; overprotection creates a monopoly over the raw material of creative expression. The application of the Oklahoma publicity rights statute to Cardtoons' trading cards presents a classic case of overprotection. Little is to be gained, and much lost, by protecting MLBPA's right to control the use of its members' identities in parody trading cards. The justifications for the right of publicity are not nearly as compelling as those offered for other forms of intellectual property, and are particularly unpersuasive in the case of celebrity parodies. The cards, on the other hand, are an important form of entertainment and social commentary that deserve First Amendment protection. Accordingly, we AFFIRM.

NOTES

1. Can Cardtoons use real photographs of baseball players to advertise their trading cards without the player's consent?

2. The Restatement, Third, of Unfair Competition § 47 (1995) limits the protection of the right of publicity to those circumstances in which the defendant uses the plaintiff's identity "for purposes of trade" and goes on to state that "'for purposes of trade' does not ordinarily include the use of a person's identity in news reporting, commentary, entertainment, works of fiction or nonfiction, or in advertising that is incidental to such uses." Does this fail to restate the rule in *Zacchini*?

3. The First Amendment was asserted as justification for denying Cher relief against the unauthorized publication of an interview with her. Cher had given the interview to one magazine without securing contractual protection against use by others and ultimately the "Star" published part of the interview. The court held the First Amendment protected reports, commentaries, and interviews with public figures from claims of violation of the right of publicity. Cher v. Forum Int'l Ltd., 692 F.2d 634 (9th Cir.1982).

4. There is an expanding literature on the right of publicity. See generally, Goodenough, Go Fish: Evaluating the Restatement's Formulation of the Law of Publicity, 47 S.Car. L. Rev. 709 (1996); Rochelle Cooper Dreyfuss, We Are Symbols and Inhabit Symbols, So Should We Be Paying Rent? Deconstructing the Lanham Act and Rights of Publicity, 20 Colum.-VLA J.L. & Arts 123 (1996); Thomas McCarthy, The Human Personality as Commercial Property: The Right of Publicity, 19 Colum.-VLA J. L. & Arts 129 (1995); Mark Grady, A Positive Economic Theory of the Right of Publicity, 1 UCLA Ent. L. Rev. 97 (1994); Michael Madow, Private Ownership of Public Image: Popular Culture and Publicity Rights, 81 Calif. L. Rev. 127 (1993) Denicola, Institutional Publicity Rights: An Analysis of the Merchandising of Famous Trade Symbols, 62 N.C.L.Rev. 603 (1984), reprinted in 75 Trademark Rep. 41 (1985); Samuelson, Reviving *Zacchini*: Analyzing First Amendment Defenses in Right of Publicity and Copyright Cases, 57 Tulane L.Rev. 836 (1983). Publicity also has its own treatise: Thomas McCarthy, The Rights of Publicity and Privacy (1993).

White v. Samsung Electronics America, Inc.

United States Court of Appeals, Ninth Circuit, 1992.
971 F.2d 1395.

[Figure 1 on the next page is a picture of Vanna White as she appeared as hostess for the popular television show "Wheel of Fortune". Samsung Electronics ran a series of advertisements depicting a current item of popular culture with a Samsung electronic product but set in the twenty-first century, the idea being that the Samsung product would still be in use at that time. Figure 2 was used with an ad that read: "Longest-running game show. 2012 A.D." Vanna White did not give her consent to the ad and sued under the right of publicity.]

■ GOODWIN, SENIOR CIRCUIT JUDGE:

* * *

Although the defendants in these cases avoided the most obvious means of appropriating the plaintiffs' identities, each of their actions directly implicated the commercial interests which the right of publicity is designed to protect. * * * It is not important how the defendant has

Figure 1

Figure 2

appropriated the plaintiff's identity, but *whether* the defendant has done so. *Motschenbacher,* [Motschenbacher v. R.J. Reynolds Tobacco Co., 498 F.2d 821 (9th Cir. 1974)], *Midler* [Midler v. Ford Motor Co., 849 F.2d 460 (9th Cir. 1988)], and *Carson* [Carson v. Here's Johnny Portable Toilets, Inc., 698 F.2d 831 (6th Cir. 1983)], teach the impossibility of treating the right of publicity as guarding only against a laundry list of specific means of appropriating identity. A rule which says that the right of publicity can be infringed only through the use of nine different methods of appropriating identity merely challenges the clever advertising strategist to come up with the tenth.

* * *

Viewed separately, the individual aspects of the advertisement in the present case say little. Viewed together, they leave little doubt about the celebrity the ad is meant to depict. The female-shaped robot is wearing a long gown, blond wig, and large jewelry. Vanna White dresses exactly like this at times, but so do many other women. The robot is in the process of turning a block letter on a game-board. Vanna White dresses like this while turning letters on a game-board but perhaps similarly attired Scrabble-playing women do this as well. The robot is standing on what looks to be the Wheel of Fortune game show set. Vanna White dresses like this, turns letters, and does this on the Wheel of Fortune game show. She is the only one. Indeed, defendants themselves referred to their ad as the "Vanna White" ad. We are not surprised.

* * *

In defense, defendants cite a number of cases for the proposition that their robot ad constituted protected speech. Those cases involved parodies of advertisements run for the purpose of poking fun at Jerry Falwell and L.L. Bean, respectively. This case involves a true advertisement run for the purpose of selling Samsung VCRs. The ad's spoof of Vanna White and Wheel of Fortune is subservient and only tangentially related to the ad's primary message: "buy Samsung VCRs." Defendants' parody arguments are better addressed to non-commercial parodies.[3] The difference between a "parody" and a "knock-off" is the difference between fun and profit.

ALARCON, Circuit Judge, concurring in part, dissenting in part:

* * *

3. In warning of a first amendment chill to expressive conduct, the dissent reads this decision too broadly. This case concerns only the market which exists in our society for the exploitation of celebrity to sell products, and an attempt to take a free ride on a celebrity's celebrity value. Commercial advertising which relies on celebrity fame is different from other forms of expressive activity in two crucial ways. First, for celebrity exploitation advertising to be effective, the advertisement must evoke the celebrity's identity. The more effective the evocation, the better the advertisement. If, as Samsung claims, its ad was based on a "generic" game-show hostess and not on Vanna White, the ad would not have violated anyone's right of publicity, but it would also not have been as humorous or as effective. Second, even if some forms of expressive activity, such as parody, do rely on identity evocation, the first amendment hurdle will bar most right of publicity actions against those activities. In the case of commercial advertising, however, the first amendment hurdle is not so high. * * * Unless the first amendment bars all right of publicity actions—and it does not, see Zachini v. Scripps-Howard Broadcasting Co., 433 U.S. 562 (1977)—then it does not bar this case.

The only characteristic in the commercial advertisement that is not common to many female performers or celebrities is the imitation of the "Wheel of Fortune" set. This set is the only thing which might possibly lead a viewer to think of Vanna White. The Wheel of Fortune set, however, is not an attribute of Vanna White's identity. It is an identifying characteristic of a television game show, a prop with which Vanna White interacts in her role as the current hostess. To say that Vanna White may bring an action when another blond female performer or robot appears on such a set as a hostess will, I am sure, be a surprise to the owners of the show.

* * *

The effect of the majority's holding on expressive conduct is difficult to estimate. The majority's position seems to allow any famous person or entity to bring suit based on any commercial advertisement that depicts a character or role performed by the plaintiff. Under the majority's view of the law, Gene Autry could have brought an action for damages against all other singing cowboys. Clint Eastwood would be able to sue anyone who plays a tall, soft-spoken cowboy, unless, of course, Jimmy Stewart had not previously enjoined Clint Eastwood. Johnny Weismuller would have been able to sue each actor who played the role of Tarzan. Sylvester Stallone could sue actors who play blue-collar boxers. Chuck Norris could sue all karate experts who display their skills in motion pictures. Arnold Schwarzenegger could sue body builders who are compensated for appearing in public.

White v. Samsung Electronics America, Inc.

United States Court of Appeals, Ninth Circuit, 1993.
989 F.2d 1512, cert. denied 113 S.Ct. 2443 (1993).

The petition for rehearing is DENIED and the suggestion for rehearing en banc is REJECTED.

■ KOZINSKI, CIRCUIT JUDGE, with whom Circuit Judges O'SCANNLAIN and KLEINFELD join, dissenting from the order rejecting the suggestion for rehearing en banc.

I

Saddam Hussein wants to keep advertisers from using his picture in unflattering contexts.[1] Clint Eastwood doesn't want tabloids to write about him.[2] Rudolf Valentino's heirs want to control his film biography.[3]

---

1. See Eben Shapiro, *Rising Caution on Using Celebrity Images*, N.Y. Times, Nov. 4, 1992, at D20 (Iraqi diplomat objects on right of publicity grounds to ad containing Hussein's picture and caption "History has shown what happens when one source controls all the information").

2. Eastwood v. Superior Court, 149 Cal.App.3d 409, 198 Cal.Rptr. 342 (1983).

3. Guglielmi v. Spelling-Goldberg Prods., 25 Cal.3d 860, 160 Cal.Rptr. 352, 603 P.2d 454 (1979) (Rudolph Valentino); see also Maheu v. CBS, Inc., 201 Cal.App.3d 662, 668, 247 Cal.Rptr. 304 (1988) (aide to Howard Hughes).

The Girl Scouts don't want their image soiled by association with certain activities.[4] George Lucas wants to keep Strategic Defense Initiative fans from calling it "Star Wars."[5] Pepsico doesn't want singers to use the word "Pepsi" in their songs.[6] Guy Lombardo wants an exclusive property right to ads that show big bands playing on New Year's Eve.[7] Uri Geller thinks he should be paid for ads showing psychics bending metal through telekinesis.[8] Paul Prudhomme, that household name, thinks the same about ads featuring corpulent bearded chefs.[9] And scads of copyright holders see purple when their creations are made fun of.

Something very dangerous is going on here. Private property, including intellectual property, is essential to our way of life. It provides an incentive for investment and innovation; it stimulates the flourishing of our culture;

---

4. Girl Scouts v. Personality Posters Mfg., 304 F.Supp. 1228 (S.D.N.Y.1969) (poster of a pregnant girl in a Girl Scout uniform with the caption "Be Prepared").

5. Lucasfilm Ltd. v. High Frontier, 622 F.Supp. 931 (D.D.C.1985).

6. Pepsico Inc. claimed the lyrics and packaging of grunge rocker Tad Doyle's "Jack Pepsi" song were "offensive to [it] and [. . .] likely to offend [its] customers," in part because they "associate [Pepsico] and its Pepsi marks with intoxication and drunk driving." Deborah Russell, *Doyle Leaves Pepsi Thirsty for Compensation,* Billboard, June 15, 1991, at 43. Conversely, the Hell's Angels recently sued Marvel Comics to keep it from publishing a comic book called "Hell's Angel," starring a character of the same name. Marvel settled by paying $35,000 to charity and promising never to use the name "Hell's Angel" again in connection with any of its publications. Marvel, *Hell's Angels Settle Trademark Suit,* L.A. Daily J., Feb. 2, 1993, § II, at 1.

Trademarks are often reflected in the mirror of our popular culture. See Truman Capote, *Breakfast at Tiffany's* (1958); Kurt Vonnegut, Jr., *Breakfast of Champions* (1973); Tom Wolfe, *The Electric Kool-Aid Acid Test* (1968) (which, incidentally, includes a chapter on the Hell's Angels); Larry Niven, *Man of Steel, Woman of Kleenex,* in *All the Myriad Ways* (1971); *Looking for Mr. Goodbar* (1977); *The Coca-Cola Kid* (1985) (using Coca-Cola as a metaphor for American commercialism); *The Kentucky Fried Movie* (1977); *Harley Davidson and the Marlboro Man* (1991); *The Wonder Years* (ABC 1988-present) ("Wonder Years" was a slogan of Wonder Bread); Tim Rice & Andrew Lloyd Webber, *Joseph and the Amazing Technicolor Dream Coat* (musical). *Hear* Janis Joplin, *Mercedes Benz,* on *Pearl*

(CBS 1971); Paul Simon, *Kodachrome,* on *There Goes Rhymin' Simon* (Warner 1973); Leonard Cohen, *Chelsea Hotel,* on *The Best of Leonard Cohen* (CBS 1975); Bruce Springsteen, *Cadillac Ranch,* on *The River* (CBS 1980); Prince, *Little Red Corvette,* on *1999* (Warner 1982); dada, *Dizz Knee Land,* on *Puzzle* (IRS 1992) ("I just robbed a grocery store—I'm going to Disneyland / I just flipped off President George—I'm going to Disneyland"); Monty Python, *Spam,* on *The Final Rip Off* (Virgin 1988); Roy Clark, *Thank God and Greyhound [You're Gone],* on *Roy Clark's Greatest Hits Volume I* (MCA 1979); Mel Tillis, *Coca-Cola Cowboy,* on *The Very Best of* (MCA 1981) ("You're just a Coca-Cola cowboy / You've got an Eastwood smile and Robert Redford hair . . . "). *Dance to* Talking Heads, *Popular Favorites 1976-92: Sand in the Vaseline* (Sire 1992); Talking Heads, *Popsicle,* on id. Admire Andy Warhol, *Campbell's Soup Can.* Cf. REO Speedwagon, 38 Special, and Jello Biafra of the Dead Kennedys.

The creators of some of these works might have gotten permission from the trademark owners, though it's unlikely Kool-Aid relished being connected with LSD, Hershey with homicidal maniacs, Disney with armed robbers, or Coca-Cola with cultural imperialism. Certainly no free society can *demand* that artists get such permission.

7. Lombardo v. Doyle, Dane & Bernbach, Inc., 58 A.D.2d 620, 396 N.Y.S.2d 661 (1977).

8. Geller v. Fallon McElligott, No. 90-Civ-2839 (S.D.N.Y. July 22, 1991) (involving a Timex ad).

9. Prudhomme v. Procter & Gamble Co., 800 F.Supp. 390 (E.D.La. 1992).

it protects the moral entitlements of people to the fruits of their labors. But reducing too much to private property can be bad medicine. Private land, for instance, is far more useful if separated from other private land by public streets, roads and highways. Public parks, utility rights-of-way and sewers reduce the amount of land in private hands, but vastly enhance the value of the property that remains.

So too it is with intellectual property. Overprotecting intellectual property is as harmful as underprotecting it. Creativity is impossible without a rich public domain. Nothing today, likely nothing since we tamed fire, is genuinely new: Culture, like science and technology, grows by accretion, each new creator building on the works of those who came before. Overprotection stifles the very creative forces it's supposed to nurture.[11]

The panel's opinion is a classic case of overprotection. Concerned about what it sees as a wrong done to Vanna White, the panel majority erects a property right of remarkable and dangerous breadth: Under the majority's opinion, it's now a tort for advertisers to *remind* the public of a celebrity. Not to use a celebrity's name, voice, signature or likeness; not to imply the celebrity endorses a product; but simply to evoke the celebrity's image in the public's mind. This Orwellian notion withdraws far more from the public domain than prudence and common sense allow. It conflicts with the Copyright Act and the Copyright Clause. It raises serious First Amendment problems. It's bad law, and it deserves a long, hard second look.

* * *

The district judge quite reasonably held that, because Samsung didn't use White's name, likeness, voice or signature, it didn't violate her right of publicity. 971 F.2d at 1396–97. Not so, says the panel majority: The California right of publicity can't possibly be limited to name and likeness. If it were, the majority reasons, a "clever advertising strategist" could avoid using White's name or likeness but nevertheless remind people of her with impunity, "effectively eviscerat[ing]" her rights. To prevent this "evisceration," the panel majority holds that the right of publicity must extend beyond name and likeness, to any "appropri ation" of White's "identity"— anything that "evoke[s]" her personality. Id. at 1398–99.

III

But what does "evisceration" mean in intellectual property law? Intellectual property rights aren't like some constitutional rights, absolute guarantees protected against all kinds of interference, subtle as well as blatant. They cast no penumbras, emit no emanations: The very point of intellectual property laws is that they protect only against certain specific kinds of appropriation. I can't publish unauthorized copies of, say, *Presumed Innocent*; I can't make a movie out of it. But I'm perfectly free to write a

---

11. See Wendy J. Gordon, *A Property Right in Self Expression: Equality and Individualism in the Natural Law of* Intellectual Property, 102 Yale L.J. 1533, 1556–57 (1993).

book about an idealistic young prosecutor on trial for a crime he didn't commit.[14] So what if I got the idea from *Presumed Innocent*? So what if it reminds readers of the original? Have I "eviscerated" Scott Turow's intellectual property rights? Certainly not. All creators draw in part on the work of those who came before, referring to it, building on it, poking fun at it; we call this creativity, not piracy.

The majority isn't, in fact, preventing the "evisceration" of Vanna White's existing rights; it's creating a new and much broader property right, a right unknown in California law. It's replacing the existing balance between the interests of the celebrity and those of the public by a different balance, one substantially more favorable to the celebrity. Instead of having an exclusive right in her name, likeness, signature or voice, every famous person now has an exclusive right to *anything that reminds the viewer of her*. After all, that's all Samsung did: It used an inanimate object to remind people of White, to "evoke [her identity]."[17]

Consider how sweeping this new right is. What is it about the ad that makes people think of White? It's not the robot's wig, clothes or jewelry; there must be ten million blond women (many of them quasi-famous) who wear dresses and jewelry like White's. It's that the robot is posed near the "Wheel of Fortune" game board. Remove the game board from the ad, and no one would think of Vanna White. But once you include the game board, anybody standing beside it—a brunette woman, a man wearing women's clothes, a monkey in a wig and gown—would evoke White's image, precisely the way the robot did. It's the "Wheel of Fortune" set, not the robot's face or dress or jewelry that evokes White's image. The panel is giving White an exclusive right not in what she looks like or who she is, but in what she does for a living.[18]

This is entirely the wrong place to strike the balance. Intellectual property rights aren't free: They're imposed at the expense of future creators and of the public at large. Where would we be if Charles Lindbergh had an exclusive right in the concept of a heroic solo aviator? If Arthur Conan Doyle

14. It would be called "Burden of Going Forward with the Evidence," and the hero would ultimately be saved by his lawyer's adept use of Fed.R.Evid. 301.

17. Some viewers might have inferred White was endorsing the product, but that's a different story. The right of publicity isn't aimed at or limited to false endorsements, Eastwood v. Superior Court, 149 Cal.App.3d 409, 419–20, 198 Cal.Rptr. 342, 348 (1983); that's what the Lanham Act is for.

Note also that the majority's rule applies even to advertisements that unintentionally remind people of someone. California law is crystal clear that the common-law right of publicity may be violated even by unintentional appropriations. *Id.* at 417 n. 6, 198 Cal.Rptr. at 346 n. 6; Fairfield v. American

Photocopy Equipment Co., 138 Cal.App.2d 82, 87, 291 P.2d

18. Once the right of publicity is extended beyond specific physical characteristics, this will become a recurring problem: Outside name, likeness and voice, the things that most reliably remind the public of celebrities are the actions or roles they're famous for. A commercial with an astronaut setting foot on the moon would evoke the image of Neil Armstrong. Any masked man on horseback would remind people (over a certain age) of Clayton Moore. And any number of songs—"My Way," "Yellow Submarine," "Like a Virgin," "Beat It," "Michael, Row the Boat Ashore," to name only a few—instantly evoke an image of the person or group who made them famous, regardless of who is singing. * * *.

had gotten a copyright in the idea of the detective story, or Albert Einstein had patented the theory of relativity? If every author and celebrity had been given the right to keep people from mocking them or their work? Surely this would have made the world poorer, not richer, culturally as well as economically.[19]

This is why intellectual property law is full of careful balances between what's set aside for the owner and what's left in the public domain for the rest of us: The relatively short life of patents; the longer, but finite, life of copyrights; copyright's idea-expression dichotomy; the fair use doctrine; the prohibition on copyrighting facts; the compulsory license of television broadcasts and musical compositions; federal preemption of overbroad state intellectual property laws; the nominative use doctrine in trademark law; the right to make soundalike recordings. All of these diminish an intellectual property owner's rights. All let the public use something created by someone else. But all are necessary to maintain a free environment in which creative genius can flourish.

The intellectual property right created by the panel here has none of these essential limitations: No fair use exception; no right to parody; no idea-expression dichotomy. It impoverishes the public domain, to the detriment of future creators and the public at large. Instead of well-defined, limited characteristics such as name, likeness or voice, advertisers will now have to cope with vague claims of "appropriation of identity," claims often made by people with a wholly exaggerated sense of their own fame and significance. Future Vanna Whites might not get the chance to create their personae, because their employers may fear some celebrity will claim the persona is too similar to her own.[21] The public will be robbed of parodies of celebrities, and our culture will be deprived of the valuable safety valve that parody and mockery create.

Moreover, consider the moral dimension, about which the panel majority seems to have gotten so exercised. Saying Samsung "appropriated" something of White's begs the question: *Should* White have the exclusive right to something as broad and amorphous as her "identity"? Samsung's ad didn't simply copy White's schtick—like all parody, it created something new. True, Samsung did it to make money, but White does whatever she does to make money, too; the majority talks of "the difference between fun and profit," but

---

19. See generally Gordon, supra note 11; see also Michael Madow, *Private Ownership of Public Image: Popular Culture and Publicity Rights,* 81 Cal.L.Rev. 125, 201–03 (1993) (an excellent discussion).

21. If Christian Slater, star of "Heathers," "Pump up the Volume," "Kuffs," and "Untamed Heart"—an alleged Jack Nicholson clone—appears in a commercial, can Nicholson sue? Of 54 stories on LEXIS that talk about Christian Slater, 26 talk about Slater's alleged similarities to Nicholson. Apparently it's his nasal wisecracks and killer smiles, St. Petersburg Times, Jan. 10, 1992, at 13, his eyebrows, Ottawa Citizen, Jan. 10, 1992, at E2, his sneers, Boston Globe, July 26, 1991, at 37, his menacing presence, USA Today, June 26, 1991, at 1D, and his sing-song voice, Gannett News Service, Aug. 27, 1990 (or, some say, his insinuating drawl, L.A. Times, Aug. 22, 1990, at F5). That's a whole lot more than White and the robot had in common.

in the entertainment industry fun *is* profit. Why is Vanna White's right to exclusive for-profit use of her persona—a persona that might not even be her own creation, but that of a writer, director or producer—superior to Samsung's right to profit by creating its own inventions? Why should she have such absolute rights to control the conduct of others, unlimited by the idea-expression dichotomy or by the fair use doctrine?

* * *

IV

The panel, however, does more than misinterpret California law: By refusing to recognize a parody exception to the right of publicity, the panel directly contradicts the federal Copyright Act. Samsung didn't merely parody Vanna White. It parodied Vanna White appearing in "Wheel of Fortune," a copyrighted television show, and parodies of copyrighted works are governed by federal copyright law.

Copyright law specifically gives the world at large the right to make "fair use" parodies, parodies that don't borrow too much of the original. Federal copyright law also gives the copyright owner the exclusive right to create (or license the creation of) derivative works, which include parodies that borrow too much to qualify as "fair use."[24] When Mel Brooks, for instance, decided to parody *Star Wars*, he had two options: He could have stuck with his fair use rights under 17 U.S.C. § 107, or he could have gotten a license to make a derivative work under 17 U.S.C. § 106(b) from the holder of the *Star Wars* copyright. To be safe, he probably did the latter, but once he did, he was guaranteed a perfect right to make his movie.[25]

The majority's decision decimates this federal scheme. It's impossible to parody a movie or a TV show without at the same time "evok[ing]" the "identit[ies]" of the actors. You can't have a mock *Star Wars* without a mock Luke Skywalker, Han Solo and Princess Leia, which in turn means a mock Mark Hamill, Harrison Ford and Carrie Fisher. You can't have a mock Batman commercial without a mock Batman, which means someone emulating the mannerisms of Adam West or Michael Keaton. See Carlos v. Lozano, *West Loses Lawsuit over Batman TV Commercial*, L.A. Times, Jan. 18, 1990, at B3 (describing Adam West's right of publicity lawsuit over a commercial produced under license from DC Comics, owner of the Batman copyright). The public's right to make a fair use parody and the copyright owner's right to license a derivative work are useless if the parodist is held hostage by every actor whose "identity" he might need to "appropriate."

Our court is in a unique position here. State courts are unlikely to be particularly sensitive to federal preemption, which, after all, is a matter of

---

24. How much is too much is a hotly contested question, but one thing is clear: The right to make parodies belongs either to the public at large or to the copyright holder, not to someone who happens to appear in the copyrighted work.

25. See *Spaceballs* (1987). Compare *Madonna: Truth or Dare* (1991) with *Medusa: Dare to Be Truthful* (1991); *Loaded Weapon I* (1993) *with Lethal Weapon* (1987); *Young Frankenstein* (1974) *with Bride of Frankenstein* (1935).

first concern to the federal courts. The Supreme Court is unlikely to consider the issue because the right of publicity seems so much a matter of state law. That leaves us. It's our responsibility to keep the right of publicity from taking away federally granted rights, either from the public at large or from a copyright owner. We must make sure state law doesn't give the Vanna Whites and Adam Wests of the world a veto over fair use parodies of the shows in which they appear, or over copyright holders' exclusive right to license derivative works of those shows. In a case where the copyright owner isn't even a party—where no one has the interests of copyright owners at heart—the majority creates a rule that greatly diminishes the rights of copyright holders in this circuit.

V

The majority's decision also conflicts with the federal copyright system in another, more insidious way. Under the dormant Copyright Clause, state intellectual property laws can stand only so long as they don't "prejudice the interests of other States." Goldstein v. California, 412 U.S. 546, 558 (1973). A state law criminalizing record piracy, for instance, is permissible because citizens of other states would "remain free to copy within their borders those works which may be protected elsewhere." Id. But the right of publicity isn't geographically limited. A right of publicity created by one state applies to conduct everywhere, so long as it involves a celebrity domiciled in that state. If a Wyoming resident creates an ad that features a California domiciliary's name or likeness, he'll be subject to California right of publicity law even if he's careful to keep the ad from being shown in California.

The broader and more ill-defined one state's right of publicity, the more it interferes with the legitimate interests of other states. A limited right that applies to unauthorized use of name and likeness probably does not run afoul of the Copyright Clause, but the majority's protection of "identity" is quite another story. Under the majority's approach, any time anybody in the United States—even somebody who lives in a state with a very narrow right of publicity—creates an ad, he takes the risk that it might remind some segment of the public of somebody, perhaps somebody with only a local reputation, somebody the advertiser has never heard of. See note 17 *supra* (right of publicity is infringed by unintentional appropriations). So you made a commercial in Florida and one of the characters reminds Reno residents of their favorite local TV anchor (a California domiciliary)? Pay up.

This is an intolerable result, as it gives each state far too much control over artists in other states. No California statute, no California court has actually tried to reach this far. It is ironic that it is we who plant this kudzu in the fertile soil of our federal system.

VI

Finally, I can't see how giving White the power to keep others from evoking her image in the public's mind can be squared with the First Amendment. Where does White get this right to control our thoughts? The majority's creation goes way beyond the protection given a trademark or a copyrighted work, or a person's name or likeness. All those things control one particular way of expressing an idea, one way of referring to an object or a person. But not allowing *any* means of reminding people of someone? That's a speech restriction unparalleled in First Amendment law.

What's more, I doubt even a name-and-likeness-only right of publicity can stand without a parody exception. The First Amendment isn't just about religion or politics—it's also about protecting the free development of our national culture. Parody, humor, irreverence are all vital components of the marketplace of ideas. The last thing we need, the last thing the First Amendment will tolerate, is a law that lets public figures keep people from mocking them, or from "evok[ing]" their images in the mind of the public.[29]

The majority dismisses the First Amendment issue out of hand because Samsung's ad was commercial speech. So what? Commercial speech may be less protected by the First Amendment than noncommercial speech, but less protected means protected nonetheless. And there are very good reasons for this. Commercial speech has a profound effect on our culture and our attitudes. Neutral-seeming ads influence people's social and political attitudes, and themselves arouse political controversy. "Where's the Beef?" turned from an advertising catchphrase into the only really memorable thing about the 1984 presidential campaign. Four years later, Michael Dukakis called George Bush "the Joe Isuzu of American politics."

In our pop culture, where salesmanship must be entertaining and entertainment must sell, the line between the commercial and noncommercial has not merely blurred; it has disappeared. Is the Samsung parody any different from a parody on Saturday Night Live or in Spy Magazine? Both are equally profit-motivated. Both use a celebrity's identity to sell things— one to sell VCRs, the other to sell advertising. Both mock their subjects. Both try to make people laugh. Both add something, perhaps something worthwhile and memorable, perhaps not, to our culture. Both are things that the people being portrayed might dearly want to suppress.

Commercial speech is a significant, valuable part of our national discourse. The Supreme Court has recognized as much, and has insisted that lower courts carefully scrutinize commercial speech restrictions, but the panel totally fails to do this. The panel majority doesn't even purport to apply the *Central Hudson* test, which the Supreme Court devised specifically for determining whether a commercial speech restriction is valid. The majority doesn't ask, as *Central Hudson* requires, whether the speech restriction is justified by a substantial state interest. It doesn't ask whether the restriction directly advances the interest. It doesn't ask whether the

---

29. The majority's failure to recognize a parody exception to the right of publicity would apply equally to parodies of politicians as of actresses. Consider the case of Wok Fast, a Los Angeles Chinese food delivery service, which put up a billboard with a picture of then-L.A. Police Chief Daryl Gates and the text "When you can't leave the office. Or won't." (This was an allusion to Chief Gates's refusal to retire despite pressure from Mayor Tom Bradley.) Gates forced the restaurant to take the billboard down by threatening a right of publicity lawsuit. Leslie Berger, *He Did Leave the Office—And Now Sign Will Go, Too*, L.A. Times, July 31, 1992, at B2.

restriction is narrowly tailored to the interest. These are all things the Supreme Court told us—in no uncertain terms—we must consider; the majority opinion doesn't even mention them.

* * *

VII

For better or worse, we *are* the Court of Appeals for the Hollywood Circuit. Millions of people toil in the shadow of the law we make, and much of their livelihood is made possible by the existence of intellectual property rights. But much of their livelihood—and much of the vibrancy of our culture—also depends on the existence of other intangible rights: The right to draw ideas from a rich and varied public domain, and the right to mock, for profit as well as fun, the cultural icons of our time.

In the name of avoiding the "evisceration" of a celebrity's rights in her image, the majority diminishes the rights of copyright holders and the public at large. In the name of fostering creativity, the majority suppresses it. Vanna White and those like her have been given something they never had before, and they've been given it at our expense. I cannot agree.

NOTES

1. If there had been a voice over to the Samsung commercial in *White* that would have introduced the robot character as "Vanna White" would the case have fit more comfortably into the right of publicity? Do you think Judge Kosinski would have raised the constitutional concerns with the same intensity? In other words, is the concern with this case the question of whether Vanna White's identity was in fact appropriated or is it whether the law should protect her identity in this situation?

2. Do you agree with Judge Goodwin that a parody defense is limited to those cases where the defendant's use is not a use in advertising? The Restatement (Third) of Unfair Competition §§ 46–49 (1995) limits the reach of the publicity right by attaching liability only to uses of another's identity "for purposes of trade" and is not ordinarily applicable to "news reporting, commentary, entertainment, works of fiction or nonfiction, or in advertising that is incidental to such uses." How does this apply to *White*?

3. If the maker of a pole lamp has no protection against imitation, why should a television personality? If I can imitate a competitor's perfume and then advertise that my perfume smells the same, why can't I imitate Vanna White? On the other hand, should Vanna White have to endure a company exploiting her success by using her likeness to advertise their products without her permission? What implications are there in Judge Kosinski's observation that trademarks and personalities have become a part of our popular culture? Does this justify more or less protection? Consider in this regard, Wendt v. Host International Inc., 125 F.3d 806 (9th Cir. 1997). The actors who portrayed "Norm" and "Cliff" in the television series "Cheers" brought a publicity action against Host which operated bars in airports and placed robots in these bars bearing the likenesses of the television characters. The actors acknowledged that Paramount Studios owned the copyright in any creative element of the characters but argued that the robots imitated their personal likenesses. The Ninth Circuit denied Host a summary judgment holding there was an issue of material fact as to whether the robots looked enough like the actors to be an appropriation of their identities.

4. For an interesting extension of "name or likeness", see Cheatham v. Paisano Publications, Inc., 891 F. Supp. 381 (W.D. Ky. 1995) where the plaintiff claimed she created unique clothing designs which allowed a person's bottom to be displayed through fishnet fabric that replaced cut out portions of blue jeans. A picture of plaintiff wearing her creation was taken from behind (only from her waist to her thigh) and was used on defendant's T-shirts. The court overruled defendant's motion to dismiss arguing that if the clothing design were unique it would be possible to identify the plaintiff as the backside featured on the T-shirt.

PROBLEMS

1. George McFarland was the child actor who played "Spanky" in the "Our Gang" movies from the 1920's to the 1940's. The series was revived as a television series known as "Little Rascals". He became known as George "Spanky" McFarland and periodically sought to enforce his publicity rights in the character. In 1989, Joseph Miller opened a restaurant in New Jersey under the name "Spanky McFarland's". Should McFarland be able to enjoin use of the name by Miller? Would it make a difference if McFarland were dead?

2. As part of a divorce settlement John Riggins, a famous professional football player, gave his wife the former marital house. She, being a real estate agent and wanting to sell the house, produced a brochure for distribution to other real estate agents indicating that "John Riggins' Former Home" was for sale. Riggins sued his former wife and her real estate company under a Virginia statute prohibiting use of another's name for purposes of trade. Does Riggins have a claim under the statute or a common law right of publicity?

3. Joe Montana led the San Francisco 49'ers to four NFL championships between 1980 and 1990. The San Jose Mercury News, Inc., issued a special "Souvenir Section" devoted to the team. An artist's rendition of Montana graced the front page. Each page of the section was reproduced as a poster and sold to the general public. Does Montana have a claim for infringement of his right of publicity?

4. General Motors ran a television advertisement for Oldsmobile. A voice asks "How 'bout some trivia?" The voice then asks who holds the record for being the most outstanding player during the NCAA men's basketball tournament. The answer, "Lew Alcindor" appears on the screen. The voice then asks whether any car had made Consumer Digest's Best Buy list more than once followed by the answer, "Oldsmobile". There follows 7 seconds of Oldsmobile advertising. Does Alcindor, now Kareem Abdul-Jabbar, have a good claim against GM for infringement of his right of publicity?

5. Playgirl magazine published a portait of a nude black man seated in the corner of a boxing ring. The man was allegedly recognizeable as Muhammad Ali, the former heavyweight boxing champion. The picture was captioned "Mystery Man" and was accompanied by a verse referring to the man as "the Greatest". Does Muhammad Ali have a good claim for infringement of his right of publicity?

6. Lew Alcindor adopted a muslim name, Kareem Abdul-Jabbar, in 1971. Kareem was a star basketball player for UCLA in the 1970s and was admitted to the National Basketball Associations Hall of Fame. Sharmon Shah was born in 1974, underwent a religious affirmation of his Muslim faith in 1995, and changed his name to Karim Abdul-Jabbar. Karim starred for UCLA in football and went on to play for the Miami Dolphins of the National Football League. At UCLA and Miami, Karim selected to wear number 33, the same number worn by Kareem when he played basketball. Kareem sues Karim alleging that Kareem earns significant sums through endorsements and licensed products. Should Karim be obliged to change his name?

7. Bob Russen is the producer of The Big El Show which is a stage show modeled on an actual Elvis Presley stage show and includes an individual who impersonated Elvis Presley in his performance. The estate of the real Elvis Presley sues Russen to prevent the production. What result?

CHAPTER 5

COPYRIGHT

A copyright arises in an original work of authorship at the time the work is fixed in a tangible medium of expression. The moment the poet puts pen to paper, the copyright property right arises in her work. Not only does this property right arise under American law, but at the same time a copyright property right arises under the law of the more than 100 countries who are signatories of the Berne Convention, the key international agreement in copyright. No application or government action is required.

Authors, artists, musicians, computer programmers, and film makers, to name but a few of those for whom copyright is important, are often surprised to discover that they need not do anything to obtain a copyright. This feature of American law is relatively recent. Prior to 1989 it was necessary to affix a proper copyright notice with the name of the copyright owner and the date of publication on any published copy of the work. Many American copyrights were lost prior to 1989 because of the failure to affix the proper notice, particularly by non-American authors publishing outside the United States where a notice was not required under local law.

Although copyright notice is no longer required in order to preserve the copyright, a notice does cut off certain innocent infringer defenses in mitigation of damages (17 U.S.C. § 403(d)). The notice consists of (1) the symbol ©, or the word "Copyright", or the abbreviation "Copr."; (2) the year of the first publication of the work, and (3) the name of the owner of the copyright in the work (17 U.S.C. § 401(b)).

In order to bring a copyright infringement action (basically, an action for "trespass" on the copyright) for a work whose country of origin is the United States, it is necessary to register the copyright. This is done by filling out the form provided by the Register of Copyrights, an official in the Library of Congress, providing two copies (in most cases) of the copyrighted work, and paying the required fee of $20. Unless the Registrar determines that the work is not copyrightable, the Registrar issues a certificate of copyright registration. In any judicial proceeding a certificate issued within five years after the first publication of the work; constitutes "prima facie evidence of the validity of the copyright and of the facts stated in the certificate" (17 U.S.C. § 410(c)).

Because of the impact of copyright notice on damages and because of the prima facie evidence effect of a certificate of registration, it is prudent for someone claiming copyright in a work that may turn out to be valuable to affix a notice of copyright on any published copy and to register the copyright.

536

Copyright law is codified in Title 17. The core of Title 17 is a comprehensive recodification passed in 1976. There have been significant although marginal changes in the years since 1976, implemented through small modifications to numerous sections of the 1976 statute and the addition of a few new sections. Predecessor statutes date back to the first Congress. The text of Title 17 should be the first (and last) stopping place for the puzzled student of copyright. This statute will from here on be cited by section number alone.

The basic idea of copyright embedded in the 1976 statute is of copyright as a modified misappropriation right which enables authors of any type of work to capture most of the identifiable monetary gains which the work makes possible. It was the culmination of a long period of copyright development during which the subject matter of copyright expanded from maps, charts and books (the first Copyright Act of 1790) to include almost every conceivable kind of cultural creation and the term of copyright grew from 14 years to (in the 1976 Act) the life of the author plus 50 years.

From today's perspective the period leading up to the 1976 statute seems like an age of innocence. Copyright was viewed as a specialized subject, of concern only to authors, artists and their lawyers, whose admirable purpose was to enable relatively impecunious artists to obtain some return from their culturally laudable efforts. Viewed from this perspective, a statute whose objective was to ensure that authors and artists would have an effective cause of action against misappropriation by others was non-controversial.

Copyright is no longer innocent, and it is no longer uncontroversial. It is, however, more important. Copyrights constitute a significant portion of the assets controlled by media companies such as Time Warner or Disney. Copyrightable products such as movies, recorded music and software are an important U.S. export, whether measured by their cultural impact or their positive impact on the balance of payments. Issues about the scope of copyright are important to the future development of the Internet. Computer software, one of the most dynamic areas of the U.S. economy, is protected by copyright.

Copyright has become more controversial because new technologies have made it easier and easier to infringe the copyright. To take the example of the book, for many years the only way to make a copy of a book (other than copying by hand) was to laboriously set type, letter by letter. Then came Linotype machines. Then came offset printing. Then came copying machines. Today, it is possible for a person equipped with a personal computer and an Internet connection to copy a book-length document and transmit it to thousands of e-mail addresses around the world in a matter of minutes. Similarly, inexpensive audio and video recording devices are widely available. The decline in the costs of copying has meant that the law, and increasingly the law alone, is all that protects copyright owners from massive infringement. Congress has responded by strengthening the legal remedies, most notably by increasing the criminal penalties for copyright infringement. Because of the intangible nature of the copyright, and because a copyright can be infringed without harming the copyright owner's copy, copyright does not appear to have the same intuitive support that many people have for rights in tangible property.

Even before the 1976 statute, it was understood by well-informed and interested parties that copyright issues could be very important. The 1976 Copyright Act had a long legislative history, not because its basic misappropriation structure was controversial, but because of a host of detailed issues concerning such things as the ability of cable TV systems to provide off the air signals to their customers without paying royalties, the ability of movie producers to control the copyright in a movie made with the assistance of contract specialists, and the right of teachers to make copies of copyrighted works for classroom use. The first proposed revision bill was H.R. 11947 of the 88th Cong., introduced July 20, 1964, the product of the Registrar of Copyrights acting with help and input from copyright specialists. The legislative process lasted 12 years. Public Law 94–553 was signed by the President on October 19, 1976. The 12 years generated a voluminous legislative record. The most authoritative document is House Report 94–1476 on S. 22, of September 3, 1976, 1976 U.S.C.C.A.N. Vol. 5, p. 5659. That was the report of the Committee on the Judiciary to the House. The bill moved from the Committee to the House, conference and Presidential signature with only a few minor changes. This report is cited in these materials as House Report 94–1476. The legislative history is collected in A. Latman & J. Lightstone (eds.), The Kamenstein Legislative History Project: A Compendium and Analytic Index of Materials Leading to the Copyright Act of 1976, (6 vols. Fred Rothman, 1981–1985).

NOTES

1. Paul Goldstein, Copyright: Principles, Law and Practice (Boston: Little, Brown and Co., 2d ed. 1996) and Melville B. and David Nimmer, Nimmer on Copyright: A Treatise on the Law of Literature, Musical and Artistic Property, and the Protection of Ideas (New York: Matthew Bender, 1978) are the leading treatises. Both are regularly updated.

Prior to the introduction of the revision bill that subsequently became the 1976 Copyright Act, the Copyright Office commissioned a series of preparatory studies. They contain a wealth of information on American and foreign copyright law and are conveniently available in Copyright Society of the U.S.A., Studies on Copyright (Arthur Fisher Memorial Edition, 2 vols. 1963).

The economics of copyright protection is discussed in Arnold Plant, The Economic Aspects of Copyright in Books, 1 Economica 167 (new series 1934), reprinted in Arnold Plant, Selected Economic Essays and Addresses (1974); Hurt & Schuchman, The Economic Rationale of Copyright, 56 Am. Econ. Rev. 421 (1966); Stephen Breyer, The Uneasy Case for Copyright: A Study of Copyright in Books, Photocopies, and Computer Programs, 84 Harv. L. Rev. 281 (1970); Tyerman, The Economic Rationale for Copyright Protection for Published Books: A Reply to Professor Breyer, 18 U.C.L.A. Law Rev. 1100 (1971) and William Landes & Richard Posner, An Economic Analysis of Copyright Law, 18 J. of Legal Stud. 325 (1989).

A more recent assessment of copyright is Glynn S. Lunney, Jr., Reexamining Copyright's Incentive-Access Paradigm, 49 Vand. L. Rev. 483 (1996). Both copyright and patent are discussed and compared, with a focus on works or inventions that build on the past (as all do) in Mark Lemley, Economics of Improvement in Intellectual Property Law, 75 Tex. L. Rev. 989 (1997). A review of the arguments for and against copyright is to be found in Lloyd Weinreb, Copyright for Functional Expression, 111 Harvard L. Rev. 1149, 1211–1250 (1998).

Copyright has important effects on both culture and politics. The First Amendment protects the freedom to speak; copyright creates an incentive for the production of speech. These important aspects of copyright and their implications for various issues of copyright law are discussed in Neil Netanel, Copyright and A Democratic Civil Society, 106 Yale L. J. 283 (1996), which argues that "copyright's paramount objective is not allocative efficiency, but citizen participation in democratic self-rule." Id. At 386. "The copyright that the Founders envisioned would serve these objectives was a narrow, short-term right to make literal or near-literal copies of printed material. Today's copyright law bears only a scant resemblance to this original formulation." Ibid.

Paul Goldstein, Copyright's Highway: From Gutenberg to the Celestial Jukebox (New York: Hill and Wang, 1994), is a compact, lively and readable "behind the scenes" account of many of the issues and cases covered in this chapter.

An Overview of the Statute

The following discussion will be more helpful if you scan the related sections of the statute as you read it.

The statute begins with a comprehensive set of definitions in § 101 which apply throughout the statute. These definitions are often critical to a correct reading of the statute, and analysis of any section should always be undertaken with an eye to the question of whether it contains terms defined in § 101.

The statute has 11 chapters. The first, "Subject matter and Scope of Copyright" defines what works are, and what works are not, copyrightable and sets out the scope of the rights conferred by copyright. The key sections are 102, which sets out the general subject matter of copyright, and 106, which sets out the scope of the exclusive rights conferred upon the owner of works that are copyrighted. Section 106A, added by the Visual Artists Rights Act of 1990, confers rights of attribution and integrity on authors of works of visual art [a defined term]. Sections 103 to 105 are but amplifying footnotes to 102, and sections 107 through 120 (although very complex) are amplifying footnotes to 106. For the moment skip these sections, except for a brief glance at 107, which sets out the concept of "fair use," an important limit on the scope of copyright and a concept to which we devote considerable attention.

Chapter 2, "Copyright Ownership and Transfer," deals with the question of who initially owns the copyright in a work, establishes the way in which the right can be transferred, and sets up a recording system for transfers of the right.

Chapter 3, is incompletely entitled: "Duration of Copyright" because it also contains the important section 301 (which has already been addressed in this book in Chapter 4). The rest of the Chapter provides, in brief, that the term of a copyright is the life of the author plus fifty years, or in the case of a work made for hire [defined term], that the term of the copyright is 75 years (the employer that hires the employee who creates a work made for hire will usually be an institution, which cannot die). Seventy-five years was thought to be roughly equivalent, on average, to the remaining life expectancy of an author plus fifty years. (Should an old author set up a corporation and write for it in order to get the 75 year term?).

Chapter 4, "Copyright Notice, Deposit and Registration," deals with notice, registration and deposit. Prior to the U.S. adherence to the Berne Convention in 1989 (of which more shortly), notice was required in order to obtain copyright protection, and registration was required in order to bring a suit for infringement. Berne does not permit formalities as a condition of protection, so notice is no longer mandatory, registration before bringing a suit for infringement is required only of U.S. authors, and deposit is not a condition of copyright.

Registration for works originating in the United States is necessary in order to be able to bring a lawsuit enforcing copyright (§ 411) and deposit of works published in the United States is required (§ 407(a)), but there are monetary sanctions only if the Registrar makes a written demand and deposit is not made (§ 407(d)). (The deposit requirement has been an important source of the collection of the Library of Congress.) Registration and deposit creates a record of the origin and content of the work for which copyright is claimed and can simplify factual issues in subsequent infringement litigation.

A copyright owner may register his work at any time under § 408. Registration requires deposit (unless the work is exempt), payment of a fee, and submission of an application for copyright registration (§ 409).

Chapter 5 defines infringement (§ 501) and sets out the remedies for infringement of copyright. They are unusually sweeping. In addition to recovery of damages and lost profits (§ 504) and injunctions (§ 502), they include special statutory damages (§ 504(c)), impoundment and destruction of infringing works and the means for making further infringements (§ 503 in civil actions, § 509 in criminal actions), and the award of costs and attorney's fees (§ 505). In addition, infringement "willfully and for purposes of commercial advantage or private financial gain" or reproduction or distribution of an infringing copy or copies in a period of 180 days having a retail value in excess of $1000 is a crime (§ 506).

Chapter 6, § 601, (now expired) relates to a requirement of U.S. manufacture of certain copyrighted works, a protectionist provision dating from the nineteenth century designed to protect the U.S. printing industry. Sec. 602 makes importation into the United States of a copy (defined term) or phonorecord (defined term) of a copyrighted work an infringement, and

§ 603 gives the Post Office and the Customs Service authority to enforce this provision.

Chapter 7 establishes the Copyright Office within the Library of Congress, to be headed by the Registrar of Copyrights, and contains provisions relating to the operation of the office.

Chapter 8 creates procedures for the formation and proceedings of copyright arbitration royalty panels. The panels are convened to determine questions relating to certain compulsory royalty provisions in the statute.

Chapter 9 (omitted from the statutory supplement) provides a system of protection against copying of semiconductor chips.

Chapter 10 was added by the Audio Home Recording Act of 1992, P.L. 102–563 (1992). It was precipitated by the development of home digital recording technology, which would make it possible for a consumer to buy recording devices that had the capacity to make copies derived from copies without any degradation in their quality. The thought that the homes of America could be turned into little reproduction factories turning out millions of copies caused considerable apprehension in the recording industry. Chapter 10 requires that importers and manufacturers of digital audio recording devices and media pay a royalty of 2 percent on digital audio recording devices (capped at $8.00) and 3 percent on digital audio recording media, and that digital audio recording devices include a serial copy management system. The purpose of the serial copy management system is to prevent devices that can make copies of copies. The royalties are then distributed to the owners of musical copyrights (one-third) and to musicians (two-thirds).

An important section in Chapter 10 is 1008, which provides that no action can be brought under Title 17 "based on noncommercial use by a consumer of * * * a [recording] device or medium for making * * * musical recordings * * *"

Chapter 11 was added by § 512(a) of the Uruguay Round Agreements Act, P.L. 103–465 (1994). It provides that performers have the same remedies against unauthorized recordings of musical or audiovisual performances as the owners of the copyright have against infringers of copyright.

NOTES

1. The items exempted by the Registrar from deposit (where are we going to put all of these things?) are set out in 37 C.F.R. § 202.19(c). They include: architectural or engineering blueprints; mechanical drawings; anatomical models; greeting cards; picture postcards; stationery; lectures; sermons; speeches and addresses when published individually; literary dramatic and musical works published only as embodied in phonorecords (the record must be deposited); computer programs and automated data bases, published only in the form of machine readable copies such as magnetic tape or disks or punched cards; three-dimensional sculptural works and works published only on jewelry, dolls, toys, games, plaques, floor coverings, wallpaper, and textile or other fabrics; prints labels and advertising; and tests and answers to tests.

The Berne Convention and the GATT TRIPS

On March 1, 1989, the United States joined the Berne Convention for the Protection of Literary and Artistic Works. Thus ended more than a century of American isolation from the mainstream of world copyright law. The changes in American law made in order to conform to the requirements of the Berne Convention were made by the Berne Convention Implementation Act of 1988, P. L. 100–568, (1988).

In the nineteenth century, Europe was the center of the literary world and the authors of Great Britain the most important writers in the English language. The United States was a net importer of copyrighted works.

The United States declined to join the Berne Convention in 1886. Instead, the United States developed its own system of international copyright relationships beginning with the Chace Act of 1891, which provided that we would extend protection to foreign authors under our law when the foreign author's country did the same for our authors. But even this avenue of protection was limited by the requirement that the copies required to be deposited had to be actually printed in the United States. This latter provision evolved into the so-called manufacturing clause which survives in § 601 of the present act, but which has expired as of July 1, 1986. Apparently some portions of the printing industry whose business was based upon the printing of pirated foreign works feared that they would lose this business if the authors obtained copyright protection and sold in the United States works printed abroad. The manufacturing clause itself became a further obstacle to U.S. adherence to Berne. The manufacturing clause was subsequently extended to provide that all works distributed in or imported into the United States and protected by U.S. copyright had to be printed in the United States.

In the twentieth century the conditions that had made the case for adherence to Berne seem less than compelling to the United States changed. The United States itself became a major exporter of copyrighted works, with an interest in assuring protection for U.S. authors abroad. In the American period of hegemony after World War II, the United States took the lead in the formulation and widespread adoption of the Universal Copyright Convention (hereafter the "UCC"), based upon a system of national treatment of the nationals of all signatories—i.e., the author of any member country is entitled to the same treatment as a national of any member country gets in that country. Although this was also a basic principle of Berne, Berne went further in guaranteeing some minimum level of substantive protection free of any formalities. The UCC itself accepted the continuing preeminence of Berne by providing that where any two countries were signatories of both Berne and the UCC, the more demanding provisions of Berne should control. This meant that in reality the UCC was little more than a uniform system of bilateral relationships between the United States and the other countries of the world.

The UCC did, however, eliminate the operation of the manufacturing clause as applied to works of the authors of member countries. This meant that the only important, continuing function of the manufacturing clause was to prevent publishers of the works of American authors from making use of lower cost foreign printers. The American printing industry continued to fight for this protection.

Strong voices had advocated U.S. adherence to Berne from the beginning, and repeated efforts were made to move the U.S. in that direction. It had become clear by the 1970's that the U.S. incentives to join Berne were growing. The export of U.S. origin copyrighted works was becoming ever more important and the problem of foreign piracy was increasing. Berne and its affiliated organizations were the center of international copyright policy formulation and advancement. And it was difficult for the U.S. to deplore nonprotectionist policies of the underdeveloped countries who saw advantages to themselves in weak copyright protection (just as the U.S. had seen for itself in the nineteenth century) when the U.S. itself declined to join the dominant system of world copyright protection.

The first decisive move toward U.S. adherence to Berne came in the 1976 Copyright Revision Act. The act committed American copyright law to the concept of a broad scope of protected subject matter (§ 102), adopted the Berne Convention term of life plus 50 years, and placed an expiration date in the manufacturing clause. And for the first time the idea that an absence of notice upon publication would not destroy the underlying copyright was introduced.

After one more extension of the manufacturing clause at the behest of the printing industry and over the veto of President Reagan, the clause expired on July 1, 1986. The way was then open for U.S. adherence to Berne by eliminating mandatory formalities, and this the Berne Implementation Act accomplished.

The importance of U.S. international agreements in the copyright area was increased by the Agreement on Trade-Related Aspects of Intellectual Property Rights (known as the "TRIPS") of the General Agreement on Tariffs and Trade (known as the "GATT"). The U.S. acceptance of TRIPS, part of what was called the Uruguay negotiating round of the GATT, was implemented by the Uruguay Round Agreements Act, P.L. 103–465 (1994).

The provisions of the GATT TRIPS relating specifically to Copyright require that the signatories comply with the Berne Convention, except for the provision of Berne relating to moral rights, protect computer programs (Article 10.1), provide control over rental rights to owners of copyrights in computer programs and movies (Article 11), and attempt to limit "limitations or exceptions" (Article 13).

Since almost all of the signatories (including the United States) were already members of the Berne Convention, the commitment to comply with Berne might seem relatively trivial. However, the undertakings of the GATT (unlike the undertakings of the Berne Convention) are subject to enforcement proceedings. A member country that is of the view that another member is not actually complying with the GATT can institute a proceeding before the World Trade Organization seeking a determination of noncompliance, and if it succeeds, can then institute trade sanctions against the offending member. Under Berne, if a country signed the convention but did not actually comply, there was no remedy available to the other members.

In addition, the GATT TRIPS has requirements that member countries must also provide effective remedies for the rights created as a result of their obligations under the agreement. Part III, Articles 41 through 49, requires the members to provide effective enforcement remedies, and specifies what those remedies must be in considerable detail.

It was at the insistence of the United States that the subject of intellectual property was placed on the GATT trade agenda. The argument of the United States was that it is increasingly a supplier of knowledge-based goods and services to the world, and that the value of such goods and services can only be obtained through market transactions which occur within the framework of effective intellectual property laws. Thus other countries, particularly the underdeveloped countries, should accord to the United States a commitment to recognize and enforce intellectual property rights in exchange for the right of the underdeveloped countries to have the right of access to the markets of the developed world. The U.S. negotiating leverage was enhanced by the use of Special 301 proceedings in which the U.S. threatened various countries such as Brazil, Taiwan, Korea and China with loss of access to U.S. markets if they did not revise their intellectual property laws.

There is considerable historic irony in this role for the United States. Reflecting its own historic role as a developing country on the fringes of the more advanced European economies, the United States has traditionally been a non-participant in many of the major efforts to develop a coordinated system of effective intellectual property protection. Consider, for instance, its failure to join the Madrid Agreement on trademarks, and its long refusal to join the Berne Convention. The rhetoric of the U.S. initiative was that the agreements should require all signatories to come up to "our standard." But in fact, the U.S. standard was not the world "gold standard" for intellectual property protection. The European standard is. And once the U.S. sought allies for a uniform and effective commitment to intellectual property protection, it was inevitable that the emerging standard would be not a U.S. standard, but a European one. That means that various provisions of U.S. law may prove to be in violation of these agreements, and that other signatories can, if they wish, pursue remedies against the United States for these non-conforming provisions.

One non-conforming aspect of U.S. law addressed in the GATT negotiations was the fact that the U.S., prior to the effective date of the Berne Convention Implementation Act on March 1, 1989, had required a notice of copyright on published copies of a work. This requirement hit non-U.S. authors particularly hard since under their local practice (in conformity with Berne) they tended to be unaware of the notice requirement. An English language author whose publisher had an eye on the U.S. market might conform, but a non-English writer publishing only for the local market would probably be completely unaware of the U.S. notice requirement. For instance, the writer of a Spanish song published in 1965 probably published it without copyright notice, yet that song, thirty years later and well within the copyright term, might be of considerable value in the growing U.S. Hispanic market.

The U.S. agreed to provide a mechanism for the restoration of such copyrights. Section 514 of the Uruguay Round Agreements Act, P.L. 103–465 (1994) added new § 104A. Section 104A provides for restoration of the lost copyright when the owner files a notice of intent to enforce a restored copyright, and protection is provided for parties who have relied on the absence of copyright protection in the United States.

For general background, see Marshall Leaffer, Protecting United States Intellectual Property Abroad: Toward a New Multilateralism, 76 Iowa Law Rev. 273 (1991). For a discussion of TRIPS, see Monique Cordray, GATT v. WIPO, 76 J. Pat. & Trademark Off. Soc'y 121 (1994); Symposium: Intellectual Property Law in the International Marketplace: Papers by Rochelle Cooper Dreyfuss, Andreas F. Lowenfeld, Pamela Samuelson and Curtis A. Bradley; comments by J.H. Reichman, Judith H. Bello, Neil W. Netanel, Ralph S. Brown, Jane C. Ginsburg, Donald S. Chisum and Roger E. Schecter, 37 Va. J. Int'l L. 275–640 (1997); and the Symposium in 29 Vanderbilt Journal of Transnational Law 363–660 (1996).

NOTES

1. *Moral Rights.* Article 6bis of the Berne Convention requires that member states recognize, independently of the author's economic rights, that "the author shall have the right to claim authorship of the work and object to any distortion, mutilation or other modification of, or other derogatory action in relation to, the said work, which would be prejudicial to his honor or reputation." This concept of "moral rights" has been generally unknown in U.S. copyright law, but is well developed in some other member states, particularly France. A major issue in U.S. adherence to Berne was whether U.S. copyright law would be amended to protect these hitherto unknown non-economic rights.

The solution of the implementation act was to take the position that existing U.S. law does protect moral rights, not under the copyright statute, but under common law principles of unfair competition. The GATT TRIPS undertaking to comply with Berne exempts moral rights. See GATT TRIPS Article 9.

The United States in 1990, itself adopted a limited type of moral right for visual works in § 106A.

A. Copyrightable Subject Matter

(1) The Nature of the Material

Section 102 defines copyrightable subject matter. The first sentence, which contains no defined terms, sets out what appears to be a general principle of coverage. The second sentence offers eight categories of copyrightable works. Three are undefined: "musical works," "dramatic works," and "pantomimes and choreographic works." The other five are defined and it is important to consult the definitions.

The natural construction is that the list of eight merely illustrates by specific example the range of works included in the first sentence, a construction confirmed by House Report 94–1476 at 53.

Subsection (b) of 102 is stated in the form of a qualification of 102(a), but note that the things excluded from copyright by (b) are not explicitly included by (a). The House Report says of this section: "[It] * * * in no way enlarges or contracts the scope of copyright protection under the present law. Its purpose is to restate in the context of the new single Federal system of copyright, that the basic dichotomy between expression and idea remains unchanged." Id. at 57.

Baker v. Selden

Supreme Court of the United States, 1879.
101 U.S. (11 Otto) 99, 25 L.Ed. 841.

■ MR. JUSTICE BRADLEY delivered the opinion of the court.

Charles Selden, the testator of the complainant in this case, in the year 1859 took the requisite steps for obtaining the copyright of a book, entitled "Selden's Condensed Ledger, or Bookkeeping Simplified," the object of which was to exhibit and explain a peculiar system of bookkeeping. In 1860 and 1861, he took the copyright of several other books, containing additions to and improvements upon the said system. The bill of complaint was filed against the defendant, Baker, for an alleged infringement of these copyrights.

* * *

The book or series of books of which the complainant claims the copyright consists of an introductory essay explaining the system of bookkeeping referred to, to which are annexed certain forms or blanks, consisting of ruled lines, and headings, illustrating the system and showing how it is to be used and carried out in practice. This system effects the same results as bookkeeping by double entry; but, by a peculiar arrangement of columns and headings, presents the entire operation, of a day, a week, or a month, on a single page, or on two pages facing each other, in an account book. The defendant uses a similar plan so far as results are concerned; but makes a different arrangement of the columns, and uses different headings. If the complainant's testator had the exclusive right to the use of the system explained in his book it would be difficult to contend that the defendant does not infringe it, notwithstanding the difference in his form of arrangement; but if it be assumed that the system is open to public use, it seems to be equally difficult to contend that the books made and sold by the defendant are a violation of the copyright of the complainant's book considered merely as a book explanatory of the system. Where the truths of a science or the methods of an art are the common property of the whole world, any author has the right to express the one, or explain and use the other, in his own way. As an author, Selden explained the system in a particular way. It may be conceded that Baker makes and uses account books arranged on substantially the same system; but the proof fails to show that he has violated the copyright of Selden's book, regarding the latter merely as an explanatory work; or that he has infringed Selden's right in any way, unless the latter became entitled to an exclusive right in the system.

The evidence of the complainant is principally directed to the object of showing that Baker uses the same system as that which is explained and illustrated in Selden's books. It becomes important, therefore, to determine whether, in obtaining the copyright of his books, he secured the exclusive right to the use of the system or method of bookkeeping which the said books are intended to illustrate and explain. It is contended that he has secured such exclusive right, because no one can use the system without using substantially the same ruled lines and headings which he has appended to his books in illustration of it. * * *

It cannot be pretended, and indeed it is not seriously urged, that the ruled lines of the complainant's account book can be claimed under any special class of objects, other than books, named in the law of copyright existing in 1859. The law then in force was that of 1831, and specified only books, maps, charts, musical compositions, prints, and engravings. An account book, consisting of ruled lines and blank columns, cannot be called by any of these names unless by that of a book.

There is no doubt that a work on the subject of bookkeeping, though only explanatory of well-known systems, may be the subject of a copyright; but, then, it is claimed only as a book. Such a book may be explanatory either of old systems, or of an entirely new system; and, considered as a book, as the work of an author, conveying information on the subject of bookkeeping, and containing detailed explanations of the art, it may be a very valuable acquisition to the practical knowledge of the community. But there is a clear distinction between the book, as such, and the art which it is intended to illustrate. * * * The same distinction may be predicted of every other art as well as that of bookkeeping. A treatise on the composition and use of medicines, be they old or new; on the construction and use of ploughs, or watches, or churns; or on the mixture and application of colors for painting or dyeing; or on the mode of drawing lines to produce the effect of perspective,—would be the subject of copyright; but no one would contend that the copyright of the treatise would give the exclusive right to the art or manufacture described therein. * * * To give to the author of the book an exclusive property in the art described therein, when no examination of its novelty has ever been officially made, would be a surprise and a fraud upon the public. That is the province of letters-patent, not of copyright. The claim to an invention or discovery of an art or manufacture must be subjected to the examination of the Patent Office before an exclusive right therein can be obtained; and it can only be secured by a patent from the government.

The difference between the two things, letters-patent and copyright, may be illustrated by reference to the subject just enumerated. Take the case of medicines. Certain mixtures are found to be of great value in the healing art. If the discoverer writes and publishes a book on the subject (as regular physicians generally do), he gains no exclusive right to the manufacture and sale of the medicine; he gives that to the public. If he desires to acquire such exclusive right he must obtain a patent for the mixture as a new art, manufacture, or composition of matter. * * *

Of course, these observations are not intended to apply to ornamental designs, or pictorial illustrations addressed to the taste. Of these it may be said, that their form is their essence, and their object, the production of pleasure in their contemplation. This is their final end. They are as much the product of genius and the result of composition, as are the lines of the poet or the historian's periods. * * *

Recurring to the case before us, we observe that Charles Selden, by his books, explained and described a peculiar system of bookkeeping, and illustrated his method by means of ruled lines and blank columns, with proper headings on a page, or on successive pages. Now, whilst no one has a right to print or publish his book, or any material part thereof, as a book intended to convey instruction in the art, any person may practice and use the art itself which he has described and illustrated therein. The use of the art is a totally different thing from a publication of the book explaining it. The copyright of a book on bookkeeping cannot secure the exclusive right to make, sell, and use account books prepared upon the plan set forth in such book. Whether the art might or might not have been patented, is a question which is not before us. It was not patented, and is open and free to the use of the public. And, of course, in using the art, the ruled lines and headings of accounts must necessarily be used as incident to it.

The plausibility of the claim put forward by the complainant in this case arises from a confusion of ideas produced by the peculiar nature of the art described in the books which have been made the subject of copyright. In describing the art, the illustrations and diagrams employed happen to correspond more closely than usual with the actual work performed by the operator who uses the art. Those illustrations and diagrams consist of ruled lines and headings of accounts; and it is similar ruled lines and headings of accounts which, in the application of the art, the bookkeeper makes with his pen, or the stationer with his press; whilst in most other cases the diagrams and illustrations can only be represented in concrete forms of wood, metal, stone, or some other physical embodiment. But the principle is the same in all. The description of the art in a book, though entitled to the benefit of copyright, lays no foundation for an exclusive claim to the art itself. The object of the one is explanation; the object of the other is use. The former may be secured by copyright. The latter can only be secured, if it can be secured at all, by letters-patent.

* * *

The conclusion to which we have come is, that blank account books are not the subject of copyright; and that the mere copyright of Selden's book did not confer upon him the exclusive right to make and use account books, ruled and arranged as designated by him and described and illustrated in said book.

The decree of the Circuit Court must be reversed, and the cause remanded with instructions to dismiss the complainant's bill; and it is

So ordered.

Morrissey v. Proctor & Gamble Co.

United States Court of Appeals, First Circuit, 1967.
379 F.2d 675.

■ ALDRICH, CHIEF JUDGE.

This is an appeal from a summary judgment for the defendant. The plaintiff, Morrissey, is the copyright owner of a set of rules for a sales promotional contest of the "sweepstakes" type involving the social security numbers of the participants. Plaintiff alleges that the defendant, Proctor & Gamble Company, infringed, by copying, almost precisely, Rule 1. In its motion for summary judgment, based upon affidavits and depositions, defendant denies that plaintiff's Rule 1 is copyrightable material, and denies access. The district court held for the defendant on both grounds.

Taking the second ground first, the defendant offered affidavits or depositions of all of its allegedly pertinent employees, all of whom denied having seen plaintiff's rules. Although the plaintiff, by deposition, flatly testified that prior to the time the defendant conducted its contest he had mailed to the defendant his copyrighted rules with an offer to sell, the court ruled that the defendant had "proved" nonaccess, and stated that it was "satisfied that no material issue as to access * * * lurks * * * [in the record.]"

[The court held that in view of the "presumption arising from mailing" the facts were insufficiently clear to support summary judgment on the issue of access, relying on cases such as Arnstein v. Porter, 154 F.2d 464 (2d Cir. 1946). In a footnote, the court observed that "the [district] court did not discuss, nor need we, the additional fact that the almost exact following of plaintiff's wording and format in an area in which there is at least some room for maneuverability, might be found of itself to contradict defendant's denial of access."]

The second aspect of the case raises a more difficult question. Before discussing it we recite plaintiff's Rule 1, and defendant's Rule 1, the italicizing in the latter being ours to note the defendant's variations or changes.

"1. Entrants should print name, address and social security number on a boxtop, or a plain paper. Entries must be accompanied by * * * boxtop or by plain paper on which the name * * * is copied from any source. Official rules are explained on * * * packages or leaflets obtained from dealer. If you do not have a social security number you may use the name and number of any member of your immediate family living with you. Only the person named on the entry will be deemed an entrant and may qualify for prize.

"Use the correct social security number belonging to the person named on entry * * * wrong number will be disqualified."

(Plaintiff's Rule)

"1. Entrants should print name, address and Social Security number on a Tide boxtop, or on [a] plain paper. Entries must be accompanied by Tide boxtop (*any size*) or by plain paper on which the name 'Tide' is copied from any source. Official rules are *available* on Tide Sweepstakes packages, or *on leaflets at* Tide dealers, or *you can send a stamped, self-addressed, envelope* to: Tide 'Shopping Fling' Sweepstakes, P.O. Box 4459, Chicago 77, Illinois.

"If you do not have a Social Security number, you may use the name and number of any member of your immediate family living with you. Only the person named on the entry will be deemed an entrant and may qualify for a prize.

"Use the correct Social Security number, belonging to the person named on *the* entry–wrong numbers will be disqualified."

(Defendant's Rule)

The district court, following an earlier decision, Gaye v. Gillis, D.Mass., 1958, 167 F.Supp. 416, took the position that since the substance of the contest was not copyrightable, which is unquestionably correct, Baker v. Selden, 1879, 101 U.S. 99; * * * and the substance was relatively simple, it must follow that plaintiff's rule sprung directly from the substance and "contains no original creative authorship." 262 F.Supp. at 738. This does not follow. Copyright attaches to form of expression, and defendant's own proof, introduced to deluge the court on the issue of access, itself established that there was more than one way of expressing even this simple substance. Nor, in view of the almost precise similarity of the two rules, could defendant successfully invoke the principle of a stringent standard for showing infringement which some courts apply when the subject matter involved admits of little variation in form of expression. E.g., Dorsey v. Old Surety Life Ins. Co., 10 Cir., 1938, 98 F.2d 872, 874 ("a showing of appropriation in the exact form or substantially so."); Continental Casualty Co. v. Beardsley, 2 Cir., 1958, 253 F.2d 702, 705, cert. denied 358 U.S. 816, ("a stiff standard for proof of infringement.")

Nonetheless, we must hold for the defendant. When the uncopyrightable subject matter is very narrow, so that "the topic necessarily requires," Sampson & Murdock Co. v. Seaver-Radford Co., 1 Cir., 1905, 140 F. 539, 541; cf. Kaplan, An Unhurried View of Copyright, 64–65 (1967), if not only one form of expression, at best only a limited number, to permit copyrighting would mean that a party or parties, by copyrighting a mere handful of forms, could exhaust all possibilities of future use of the substance. In such circumstances it does not seem accurate to say that any particular form of expression comes from the subject matter. However, it is necessary to say that the subject matter would be appropriated by permitting the copyrighting of its expression. We cannot recognize copyright as a game of chess in which the public can be checkmated. Cf. Baker v. Selden, supra.

Upon examination the matters embraced in Rule 1 are so straightforward and simple that we find this limiting principle to be applicable. Furthermore, its operation need not await an attempt to copyright all possible forms. It cannot be only the last form of expression which is to be condemned, as completing defendant's exclusion from the substance. Rather, in these circumstances, we hold that copyright does not extend to the subject matter at all, and plaintiff cannot complain even if his particular expression was deliberately adopted.

Affirmed.

NOTES

1. In Consumers Union v. Hobart Mfg. Co., 189 F.Supp. 275 (S.D. N.Y. 1960), followed on summary judgment, 199 F.Supp. 860 (S.D.N.Y.1961), Consumers Union was denied a preliminary injunction against use by defendant of quotations from Consumers Reports in its sales literature directed to its distributors. The literature was designed to answer criticisms and emphasize favorable comments about defendant's KitchenAid dishwashers made in Consumers Reports. "In no instance did material which was copied into the [sales] Bulletin have any original literary form which would entitle it to copyright protection. Each item was a bald statement of fact which could hardly have been stated in any different fashion." 189 F.Supp. at 278. Plaintiff argued that it was injured because the use of its findings by manufacturers for sales purposes destroys the confidence of its subscribers in its integrity.

2. The effort to obtain protection for written systems and forms under the patent law, suggested in Baker v. Selden, has generally been unavailing due to a failure to satisfy the requirements of the patent statute. An exceptional case is Cincinnati Traction Co. v. Pope, 210 Fed. 443 (6th Cir. 1913), which upheld a patent on a particular type of transfer ticket. The form of the ticket made it possible to distinguish between transfers issued in the morning from those issued in the afternoon. This was done by means of a detachable coupon. When the coupon was detached, the hour indicated on the ticket was an A.M. hour. The court said:

> "[W]hile the case is perhaps near the border line, we think the device should be classed as an article to be used in a method of doing business and thus a 'manufacture' within the statute * * *. The device of the patent clearly involves structure. The claims themselves are * * * limited to such structure." 210 Fed. at 446.

In Berardini v. Tocci, 190 Fed. 329 (S.D.N.Y. 1911), the court held invalid a patent on a code system for transmitting instructions for disbursements of sums of money by cable without fear of mistakes arising out of errors in transmission. The court distinguished cases like *Cincinnati Traction Co.* on the ground that the patent was on the physical structure of the paper and the writing, while the patent involved in *Beradini* was for a "system of devising code messages." The patent, said the court, "is for an art only in the sense that one speaks of the art of painting, or the art of curving the thrown baseball. Such arts, however ingenious, difficult, or amusing, are not patentable within any statute of the United States."

In Wier v. Coe, 33 F.Supp. 142 (D.D.C. 1940), the court affirmed a patent office denial of an application for a patent on an improved system of musical notation. In the course of its opinion, the court said: "the claimed series of musically staffed sheets are merely printed matter for conveying intelligence. They do not involve physical structure and are not subject matter which may be protected under the patent laws." 83 F.Supp. at 143.

3. The distinction between a copy and a use lies at the heart of *Baker.* The distinction is more difficult to apply where the right of performance, as opposed to the right to copy is involved. If a dramatist obtains a copyright on a script which includes detailed instructions for the scenery to be used in the play, can he prevent another from incorporating scenery constructed in accordance with the directions in a different play? Consider the case of Daly v. Palmer, 6 F.Cas. 1132 (No. 3,552) (S.D.N.Y. 1868). Plaintiff's play had achieved great success, largely because of a "railroad scene" in which "one of the characters is represented as secured by another, and laid helpless upon the rails of a railroad track, in such manner, and with the presumed intent, that the railroad train, momentarily expected, shall run him down and kill him, and, just at the moment when such a fate seems inevitable, another of the characters contrives to reach the intended victim, and to drag him from the track as the train rushes in and passes over the spot." Defendant used a similar scene in his play, otherwise dissimilar. The court found infringement. Would this infringe the right of display? § 106(5).

Lotus Development Corp. v. Borland International, Inc.

United States Court of Appeals for the First Circuit, 1995.
49 F.3d 807, aff'd by an equally divided Court,
516 U.S. 233 (1996).

■ STAHL, CIRCUIT JUDGE.

This appeal requires us to decide whether a computer menu command hierarchy is copyrightable subject matter. In particular, we must decide whether, as the district court held, plaintiff-appellee Lotus Development Corporation's copyright in Lotus 1–2–3, a computer spreadsheet program, was infringed by defendant-appellant Borland International, Inc., when Borland copied the Lotus 1–2–3 menu command hierarchy into its Quattro and Quattro Pro computer spreadsheet programs. * * *

I.

BACKGROUND

Lotus 1–2–3 is a spreadsheet program that enables users to perform accounting functions electronically on a computer. Users manipulate and control the program via a series of menu commands, such as "Copy," "Print," and "Quit." Users choose commands either by highlighting them on the screen or by typing their first letter. In all, Lotus 1–2–3 has 469 commands arranged into more than 50 menus and submenus.

Lotus 1–2–3, like many computer programs, allows users to write what are called "macros." By writing a macro, a user can designate a series of command choices with a single macro keystroke. Then, to execute that series of commands in multiple parts of the spreadsheet, rather than typing the whole series each time, the user only needs to type the single pre-programmed macro keystroke, causing the program to recall and perform the designated series of commands automatically. Thus, Lotus 1–2–3 macros shorten the time needed to set up and operate the program.

Borland released its first Quattro program to the public in 1987, after Borland's engineers had labored over its development for nearly three years. Borland's objective was to develop a spreadsheet program far superior to existing programs, including Lotus 1–2–3. In Borland's words, "[f]rom the time of its initial release . . . Quattro included enormous innovations over competing spreadsheet products."

The district court found, and Borland does not now contest, that Borland included in its Quattro and Quattro Pro version 1.0 programs "a *virtually identical* copy of the entire 1–2–3 menu tree." * * * In so doing, Borland did not copy any of Lotus's underlying computer code; it copied only the words and structure of Lotus's menu command hierarchy. Borland included the Lotus menu command hierarchy in its programs to make them compatible with Lotus 1–2–3 so that spreadsheet users who were already familiar with Lotus 1–2–3 would be able to switch to the Borland programs without having to learn new commands or rewrite their Lotus macros.

In its Quattro and Quattro Pro version 1.0 programs, Borland achieved compatibility with Lotus 1–2–3 by offering its users an alternate user interface, the "Lotus Emulation Interface." By activating the Emulation Interface, Borland users would see the Lotus menu commands on their screens and could interact with Quattro or Quattro Pro as if using Lotus 1–2–3, albeit with a slightly different looking screen and with many Borland options not available on Lotus 1–2–3. In effect, Borland allowed users to choose how they wanted to communicate with Borland's spreadsheet programs: either by using menu commands designed by Borland, or by using the commands and command structure used in Lotus 1–2–3 augmented by Borland-added commands.

Lotus filed this action against Borland in the District of Massachusetts on July 2, 1990, four days after a district court held that the Lotus 1–2–3 "menu structure, taken as a whole—including the choice of command terms [and] the structure and order of those terms," was protected expression covered by Lotus's copyrights. Lotus Dev. Corp. v. Paperback Software Int'l, 740 F.Supp. 37, 68, 70 (D.Mass. 1990) ("Paperback"). Three days earlier, on the morning after the Paperback decision, Borland had filed a declaratory judgment action against Lotus in the Northern District of California, seeking a declaration of non-infringement. On September 10, 1990, the district court in California dismissed Borland's declaratory judgment action in favor of this action.

Lotus and Borland filed cross motions for summary judgment; the district court denied both motions on March 20, 1992, concluding that "neither party's motion is supported by the record." Borland I, 788 F.Supp. at 80. The district court invited the parties to file renewed summary judgment motions that would "focus their arguments more precisely" in light of rulings it had made in conjunction with its denial of their summary judgment motions. * * * Both parties filed renewed motions for summary judgment on April 24, 1992. In its motion, Borland contended that the Lotus 1–2–3 menus were not copyrightable as a matter of law and that no reasonable trier of fact could find that the similarity between its products and Lotus 1–2–3 was sufficient to sustain a determination of infringement. Lotus contended in its motion that Borland had copied Lotus 1–2–3's entire user interface and had thereby infringed Lotus's copyrights.

On July 31, 1992, the district court denied Borland's motion and granted Lotus's motion in part. The district court ruled that the Lotus menu command hierarchy was copyrightable expression because "[a] very satisfactory spreadsheet menu tree can be constructed using different commands and a different command structure from those of Lotus 1–2–3. In fact, Borland has constructed just such an alternate tree for use in Quattro Pro's native mode. Even if one holds the arrangement of menu commands constant, it is possible to generate literally millions of satisfactory menu trees by varying the menu commands employed." * * * The district court demonstrated this by offering alternate command words for the ten commands that appear in Lotus's main menu. For example, the district court stated that "[t]he 'Quit' command could be named 'Exit' without any other modifications," and that "[t]he 'Copy' command could be called 'Clone,' 'Ditto,' 'Duplicate,' 'Imitate,' 'Mimic,' 'Replicate,' and 'Reproduce,' among others." Because so many variations were possible, the district court concluded that the Lotus developers' choice and arrangement of command terms, reflected in the Lotus menu command hierarchy, constituted copyrightable expression.

In granting partial summary judgment to Lotus, the district court held that Borland had infringed Lotus's copyright in Lotus 1–2–3:

> [A]s a matter of law, Borland's Quattro products infringe the Lotus 1–2–3 copyright because of (1) the extent of copying of the "menu commands" and "menu structure" that is not *genuinely* disputed in this case, (2) the extent to which the copied elements of the "menu commands" and "menu structure" contain expressive aspects separable from the functions of the "menu commands" and "menu structure," and (3) the scope of those copied expressive aspects as an integral part of Lotus 1–2–3.

* * * The court nevertheless concluded that while the Quattro and Quattro Pro programs infringed Lotus's copyright, Borland had not copied the entire Lotus 1–2–3 user interface, as Lotus had contended. Accordingly, the court concluded that a jury trial was necessary to determine the scope of Borland's infringement, including whether Borland copied the long prompts of Lotus 1–2–3, whether the long prompts contained expressive elements, and to what extent, if any, functional constraints limited the number of possible ways that the Lotus menu command hierarchy could have been arranged at the time of its creation. * * *. Additionally, the district court granted Lotus summary judgment on Borland's affirmative defense of waiver, but not on its affirmative defenses of laches and estoppel. * * *

Immediately following the district court's summary judgment decision, Borland removed the Lotus Emulation Interface from its products. Thereafter, Borland's spreadsheet programs no longer displayed the Lotus 1–2–3 menus to Borland users, and as a result Borland users could no longer communicate with Borland's programs as if they were using a more sophisticated version of Lotus 1–2–3. Nonetheless, Borland's programs continued to be partially compatible with Lotus 1–2–3, for Borland retained what it called the "Key Reader" in its Quattro Pro programs. Once turned on, the Key Reader allowed Borland's programs to understand and perform some Lotus 1–2–3 macros. With the Key Reader on, the Borland programs used Quattro Pro menus for display, interaction, and macro execution, except when they encountered a slash ("/") key in a macro (the starting key for any Lotus 1–2–3 macro), in which case they interpreted the macro as having been written for Lotus 1–2–3. Accordingly, people who wrote or purchased macros to shorten the time needed to perform an operation in Lotus 1–2–3 could still use those macros in Borland's programs. The district court permitted Lotus to file a supplemental complaint alleging that the Key Reader infringed its copyright.

The parties agreed to try the remaining liability issues without a jury. The district court held two trials, the Phase I trial covering all remaining issues raised in the original complaint (relating to the Emulation Interface) and the Phase II trial covering all issues raised in the supplemental complaint (relating to the Key Reader). At the Phase I trial, there were no live witnesses, although considerable testimony was presented in the form of affidavits and deposition excerpts. The district court ruled upon evidentiary objections counsel interposed. At the Phase II trial, there were two live witnesses, each of whom demonstrated the programs for the district court.

After the close of the Phase I trial, the district court permitted Borland to amend its answer to include the affirmative defense of "fair use." Because Borland had presented all of the evidence supporting its fair-use defense during the Phase I trial, but Lotus had not presented any evidence on fair use (as the defense had not been raised before the conclusion of the Phase I trial), the district court considered Lotus's motion for judgment on partial findings of fact. See Fed. R. Civ. P. 52(c). The district court held that Borland had failed to show that its use of the Lotus 1–2–3 menu command hierarchy in its Emulation Interface was a fair use. * * *

In its Phase I-trial decision, the district court found that "each of the Borland emulation interfaces contains a virtually identical copy of the 1–2–3 menu tree and that the 1–2–3 menu tree is capable of a wide variety of expression." * * * The district court also rejected Borland's affirmative defenses of laches and estoppel. * * *

In its Phase II-trial decision, the district court found that Borland's Key Reader file included "a virtually identical copy of the Lotus menu tree structure, but represented in a different form and with first letters of menu command names in place of the full menu command names." * * * In other words, Borland's programs no longer included the Lotus command terms, but only their first letters. The district court held that "the Lotus menu structure, organization, and first letters of the command names . . . constitute part of the protectable expression found in [Lotus 1–2–3]." * * *Accordingly, the district court held that with its Key Reader, Borland had infringed Lotus's copyright. * * * The district court also rejected Borland's affirmative defenses of waiver, laches, estoppel, and fair use. * * * The district court then entered a permanent injunction against Borland * * * from which Borland appeals.

This appeal concerns only Borland's copying of the Lotus menu command hierarchy into its Quattro programs and Borland's affirmative defenses to such copying. Lotus has not cross-appealed; in other words, Lotus does not contend on appeal that the district court erred in finding that Borland had not copied other elements of Lotus 1–2–3, such as its screen displays.

II.

DISCUSSION

On appeal, Borland does not dispute that it factually copied the words and arrangement of the Lotus menu command hierarchy. Rather, Borland argues that it "lawfully copied the unprotectable menus of Lotus 1–2–3." Borland contends that the Lotus menu command hierarchy is not copyrightable because it is a system, method of operation, process, or procedure foreclosed from protection by 17 U.S.C. § 102(b). Borland also raises a number of affirmative defenses.

A. Copyright Infringement Generally

In this appeal, we are faced only with whether the Lotus menu command hierarchy is copyrightable subject matter in the first instance, for Borland concedes that Lotus has a valid copyright in Lotus 1–2–3 as a whole and admits to factually copying the Lotus menu command hierarchy. As a result, this appeal is in a very different posture from most copyright-infringement cases, for copyright infringement generally turns on whether the defendant has copied protected expression as a factual matter. Because of this different posture, most copyright-infringement cases provide only limited help to us in deciding this appeal. This is true even with respect to those copyright-infringement cases that deal with computers and computer software.

B. Matter of First Impression

Whether a computer menu command hierarchy constitutes copyrightable subject matter is a matter of first impression. * * * Thus we are navigating in uncharted waters.

Borland vigorously argues, however, that the Supreme Court charted our course more than 100 years ago when it decided Baker v. Selden, 101 U.S. 99 (1879).

The facts of *Baker v. Selden*, and even the arguments advanced by the parties in that case, are identical to those in this case. The only difference is that the "user interface" of Selden's system was implemented by pen and paper rather than by computer. To demonstrate that *Baker v. Selden* and this appeal both involve accounting systems, Borland even supplied this court with a video that, with special effects, shows Selden's paper forms "melting" into a computer screen and transforming into Lotus 1–2–3.

We do not think that *Baker v. Selden* is nearly as analogous to this appeal as Borland claims. Of course, Lotus 1–2–3 is a computer spreadsheet, and as such its grid of horizontal rows and vertical columns certainly resembles an accounting ledger or any other paper spreadsheet. Those grids, however, are not at issue in this appeal for, unlike Selden, Lotus does not claim to have a monopoly over its accounting system. Rather, this appeal involves Lotus's monopoly over the commands it uses to operate the computer. Accordingly, this appeal is not, as Borland contends, "identical" to Baker v. Selden.

C. * * *

D. The Lotus Menu Command Hierarchy: A "Method of Operation"

Borland argues that the Lotus menu command hierarchy is uncopyrightable because it is a system, method of operation, process, or procedure foreclosed from copyright protection by 17 U.S.C. § 102(b).

We think that "method of operation," as that term is used in § 102(b), refers to the means by which a person operates something, whether it be a car, a food processor, or a computer. Thus a text describing how to operate something would not extend copyright protection to the method of operation itself; other people would be free to employ that method and to describe it in their own words. Similarly, if a new method of operation is used rather than described, other people would still be free to employ or describe that method.

We hold that the Lotus menu command hierarchy is an uncopyrightable "method of operation." The Lotus menu command hierarchy provides the means by which users control and operate Lotus 1–2–3. If users wish to copy material, for example, they use the "Copy" command. If users wish to print material, they use the "Print" command. Users must use the command terms to tell the computer what to do. Without the menu command hierarchy, users would not be able to access and control, or indeed make use of, Lotus 1–2–3's functional capabilities.

The Lotus menu command hierarchy does not merely explain and present Lotus 1–2–3's functional capabilities to the user; it also serves as the method by which the program is operated and controlled. The Lotus menu command hierarchy is different from the Lotus long prompts, for the long prompts are not necessary to the operation of the program; users could operate Lotus 1–2–3 even if there were no long prompts. The Lotus menu command hierarchy is also different from the Lotus screen displays, for users need not "use" any expressive aspects of the screen displays in order to operate Lotus 1–2–3; because the way the screens look has little bearing on how users control the program, the screen displays are not part of Lotus 1–2–3's "method of operation." The Lotus menu command hierarchy is also different from the underlying computer code, because while code is necessary for the program to work, its precise formulation is not. In other words, to offer the same capabilities as Lotus 1–2–3, Borland did not have to copy Lotus's underlying code (and indeed it did not); to allow users to operate its programs in substantially the same way, however, Borland had to copy the Lotus menu command hierarchy. Thus the Lotus 1–2–3 code is not a uncopyrightable "method of operation."

The district court held that the Lotus menu command hierarchy, with its specific choice and arrangement of command terms, constituted an "expression" of the "idea" of operating a computer program with commands arranged hierarchically into menus and submenus. * * * Under the district court's reasoning, Lotus's decision to employ hierarchically arranged command terms to operate its program could not foreclose its competitors from also employing hierarchically arranged command terms to operate their programs, but it did foreclose them from employing the specific command terms and arrangement that Lotus had used. In effect, the district court limited Lotus 1–2–3's "method of operation" to an abstraction.

Accepting the district court's finding that the Lotus developers made some expressive choices in choosing and arranging the Lotus command terms, we nonetheless hold that that expression is not copyrightable because it is part of Lotus 1–2–3's "method of operation." We do not think that "methods of operation" are limited to abstractions; rather, they are the means by which a user operates something. If specific words are essential to operating something, then they are part of a "method of operation" and, as such, are unprotectable. This is so whether they must be highlighted, typed in, or even spoken, as computer programs no doubt will soon be controlled by spoken words.

The fact that Lotus developers could have designed the Lotus menu command hierarchy differently is immaterial to the question of whether it is a "method of operation." In other words, our initial inquiry is not whether the Lotus menu command hierarchy incorporates any expression. Rather, our initial inquiry is whether the Lotus menu command hierarchy is a "method of operation." Concluding, as we do, that users operate Lotus 1–2–3 by using the Lotus menu command hierarchy, and that the entire Lotus menu command hierarchy is essential to operating Lotus 1–2–3, we do not inquire further whether that method of operation could have been designed differently. The "expressive" choices of what to name the command terms and how to arrange them do not magically change the uncopyrightable menu command hierarchy into copyrightable subject matter.

Our holding that "methods of operation" are not limited to mere abstractions is bolstered by *Baker v. Selden*. In *Baker*, the Supreme Court explained that the teachings of science and the rules and methods of useful art have their final end in application and use; and this application and use are what the public derive from the publication of a book which teaches them. * * * The description of the art in a book, though entitled to the benefit of copyright, lays no foundation for an exclusive claim to the art itself. The object of the one is explanation; the object of the other is use. The former may be secured by copyright. The latter can only be secured, if it can be secured at all, by letters-patent. Baker v. Selden, 101 U.S. at 104–05. Lotus wrote its menu command hierarchy so that people could learn it and use it. Accordingly, it falls squarely within the prohibition on copyright protection established in *Baker v. Selden* and codified by Congress in § 102(b).

In many ways, the Lotus menu command hierarchy is like the buttons used to control, say, a video cassette recorder ("VCR"). A VCR is a machine that enables one to watch and record video tapes. Users operate VCRs by pressing a series of buttons that are typically labelled "Record, Play, Reverse, Fast Forward, Pause, Stop/Eject." That the buttons are arranged and labeled does not make them a "literary work," nor does it make them an "expression" of the abstract "method of operating" a VCR via a set of labeled buttons. Instead, the buttons are themselves the "method of operating" the VCR.

When a Lotus 1–2–3 user chooses a command, either by highlighting it on the screen or by typing its first letter, he or she effectively pushes a button. Highlighting the "Print" command on the screen, or typing the letter "P," is analogous to pressing a VCR button labeled "Play."

Just as one could not operate a buttonless VCR, it would be impossible to operate Lotus 1–2–3 without employing its menu command hierarchy. Thus the Lotus command terms are not equivalent to the labels on the VCR's buttons, but are instead equivalent to the buttons themselves. Unlike the labels on a VCR's buttons, which merely make operating a VCR easier by indicating the buttons' functions, the Lotus menu commands are essential to operating Lotus 1–2–3. Without the menu commands, there would be no way to "push" the Lotus buttons, as one could push unlabeled VCR buttons. While Lotus could probably have designed a user interface for which the command terms were mere labels, it did not do so here. Lotus 1–2–3 depends for its operation on use of the precise command terms that make up the Lotus menu command hierarchy.

One might argue that the buttons for operating a VCR are not analogous to the commands for operating a computer program because VCRs are not copyrightable, whereas computer programs are. VCRs may not be copyrighted because they do not fit within any of the § 102(a) categories of copyrightable works; the closest they come is "sculptural work." Sculptural works, however, are subject to a "useful-article" exception whereby "the design of a useful article . . . shall be considered a pictorial, graphic, or sculptural work only if, and only to the extent that, such design incorporates pictorial, graphic, or sculptural features that can be identified separately from, and are capable of existing independently of, the utilitarian aspects of the article." 17 U.S.C. § 101. A "useful article" is "an article having an intrinsic utilitarian function that is not merely to portray the appearance of the article or to convey information." Id. Whatever expression there may be in the arrangement of the parts of a VCR is not capable of existing separately from the VCR itself, so an ordinary VCR would not be copyrightable.

Computer programs, unlike VCRs, are copyrightable as "literary works." 17 U.S.C. § 102(a). Accordingly, one might argue, the "buttons" used to operate a computer program are not like the buttons used to operate a VCR, for they are not subject to a useful-article exception. The response, of course, is that the arrangement of buttons on a VCR would not be copyrightable even without a useful-article exception, because the buttons are an uncopyrightable "method of operation." Similarly, the "buttons" of a computer program are also an uncopyrightable "method of operation."

That the Lotus menu command hierarchy is a "method of operation" becomes clearer when one considers program compatibility. Under Lotus's theory, if a user uses several different programs, he or she must learn how to perform the same operation in a different way for each program used. For example, if the user wanted the computer to print material, then the user would have to learn not just one method of operating the computer such that it prints, but many different methods. We find this absurd. The fact that there may be many different ways to operate a computer program, or even many different ways to operate a computer program using a set of hierarchically arranged command terms, does not make the actual method of operation chosen copyrightable; it still functions as a method for operating the computer and as such is uncopyrightable.

Consider also that users employ the Lotus menu command hierarchy in writing macros. Under the district court's holding, if the user wrote a macro to shorten the time needed to perform a certain operation in Lotus 1–2–3, the user would be unable to use that macro to shorten the time needed to perform that same operation in another program. Rather, the user would have to rewrite his or her macro using that other program's menu command hierarchy. This is despite the fact that the macro is clearly the user's own work product. We think that forcing the user to cause the computer to perform the same operation in a different way ignores Congress's direction in § 102(b) that "methods of operation" are not copyrightable. That programs can offer users the ability to write macros in many different ways does not change the fact that, once written, the macro allows the user to perform an operation automatically. As the Lotus menu command hierarchy serves as the basis for Lotus 1–2–3 macros, the Lotus menu command hierarchy is a "method of operation."

* * *

We also note that in most contexts, there is no need to "build" upon other people's expression, for the ideas conveyed by that expression can be conveyed by someone else without copying the first author's expression. In the context of methods of operation, however, "building" requires the use of the precise method of operation already employed; otherwise, "building" would require dismantling, too. Original developers are not the only people entitled to build on the methods of operation they create; anyone can. Thus, Borland may build on the method of operation that Lotus designed and may use the Lotus menu command hierarchy in doing so.

Our holding that methods of operation are not limited to abstractions goes against Autoskill, [Inc. v. National Educational Support Systems, Inc.] 994 F.2d [1476] at 1495 n. 23 [10th Cir. 1993], in which the Tenth Circuit rejected the defendant's argument that the keying procedure used in a computer program was an uncopyrightable "procedure" or "method of operation" under § 102(b). The program at issue, which was designed to test and train students with reading deficiencies, id. at 1481, required students to select responses to the program's queries "by pressing the 1, 2, or 3 keys." Id. at 1495 n. 23. The Tenth Circuit held that, "for purposes of the preliminary injunction, . . . the record showed that [this] keying procedure reflected at least a minimal degree of creativity," as required by Feist [Publications, Inc. v. Rural Telephone Service Co., 499 U.S. 340 (1991), reproduced below] for copyright protection. Id. As an initial matter, we question whether a programmer's decision to have users select a response by pressing the 1, 2, or 3 keys is original. More importantly, however, we fail to see how "a student select[ing] a response by pressing the 1, 2, or 3 keys," id., can be anything but an unprotectable method of operation.

III.

CONCLUSION

Because we hold that the Lotus menu command hierarchy is uncopyrightable subject matter, we further hold that Borland did not infringe Lotus's copyright by copying it. Accordingly, we need not consider any of Borland's affirmative defenses. The judgment of the district court is Reversed.

■ BOUDIN, CIRCUIT JUDGE, concurring.

The importance of this case, and a slightly different emphasis in my view of the underlying problem, prompt me to add a few words to the majority's tightly focused discussion.

I.

Most of the law of copyright and the "tools" of analysis have developed in the context of literary works such as novels, plays, and films. In this milieu, the principal problem—simply stated, if difficult to resolve—is to stimulate creative expression without unduly limiting access by others to the broader themes and concepts deployed by the author. The middle of the spectrum presents close cases; but a "mistake" in providing too much protection involves a small cost: subsequent authors treating the same themes must take a few more steps away from the original expression.

The problem presented by computer programs is fundamentally different in one respect. The computer program is a means for causing something to happen; it has a mechanical utility, an instrumental role, in accomplishing the world's work. Granting protection, in other words, can have some of the consequences of patent protection in limiting other people's ability to perform a task in the most efficient manner. Utility does not bar copyright (dictionaries may be copyrighted), but it alters the calculus.

Of course, the argument for protection is undiminished, perhaps even enhanced, by utility: if we want more of an intellectual product, a temporary monopoly for the creator provides incentives for others to create other, different items in this class. But the "cost" side of the equation may be different where one places a very high value on public access to a useful innovation that may be the most efficient means of performing a given task. Thus, the argument for extending protection may be the same; but the stakes on the other side are much higher.

It is no accident that patent protection has preconditions that copyright protection does not—notably, the requirements of novelty and nonobviousness—and that patents are granted for a shorter period than copyrights. This problem of utility has sometimes manifested itself in copyright cases, such as Baker v. Selden, 101 U.S. 99 (1879), and been dealt with through various formulations that limit copyright or create limited rights to copy. But the case law and doctrine addressed to utility in copyright have been brief detours in the general march of copyright law.

Requests for the protection of computer menus present the concern with fencing off access to the commons in an acute form. A new menu may be a creative work, but over time its importance may come to reside more in the investment that has been made by users in learning the menu and in building their own mini-programs—macros—in reliance upon the menu. Better typewriter keyboard layouts may exist, but the familiar QWERTY keyboard dominates the market because that is what everyone has learned to use. See P. David, CLIO and the Economics of QWERTY, 75 Am. Econ. Rev. 332 (1985). The QWERTY keyboard is nothing other than a menu of letters.

Thus, to assume that computer programs are just one more new means of expression, like a filmed play, may be quite wrong. The "form"—the written source code or the menu structure depicted on the screen—look hauntingly like the familiar stuff of copyright; but the "substance" probably has more to do with problems presented in patent law or, as already noted, in those rare cases where copyright law has confronted industrially useful expressions. Applying copyright law to computer programs is like assembling a jigsaw puzzle whose pieces do not quite fit.

All of this would make no difference if Congress had squarely confronted the issue, and given explicit directions as to what should be done. The Copyright Act of 1976 took a different course. While Congress said that computer programs might be subject to copyright protection, it said this in very general terms; and, especially in § 102(b), Congress adopted a string of exclusions that if taken literally might easily seem to exclude most computer programs from protection. The only detailed prescriptions for computers involve narrow issues (like back-up copies) [in § 117] of no relevance here.

Of course, one could still read the statute as a congressional command that the familiar doctrines of copyright law be taken and applied to computer programs, in cookie cutter fashion, as if the programs were novels or play scripts. Some of the cases involving computer programs embody this approach. It seems to be mistaken on two different grounds: the tradition of copyright law, and the likely intent of Congress.

The broad-brush conception of copyright protection, the time limits, and the formalities have long been prescribed by statute. But the heart of copyright doctrine—what may be protected and with what limitations and exceptions—has been developed by the courts through experience with individual cases. B. Kaplan, An Unhurried View of Copyright 40 (1967). Occasionally Congress addresses a problem in detail. For the most part the interstitial development of copyright through the courts is our tradition.

Nothing in the language or legislative history of the 1976 Act, or at least nothing brought to our attention, suggests that Congress meant the courts to abandon this case-by-case approach. Indeed, by setting up § 102(b) as a counterpoint theme, Congress has arguably recognized the tension and left it for the courts to resolve through the development of case law. And case law development is adaptive: it allows new problems to be solved with help of earlier doctrine, but it does not preclude new doctrines to meet new situations.

* * *

[Judge Boudin then explored a number of possible approaches.] * * *. Thus, for me the question is not whether Borland should prevail but on what basis. Various avenues might be traveled, but the main choices are between holding that the menu is not protectable by copyright and devising a new doctrine that Borland's use is privileged. No solution is perfect and no intermediate appellate court can make the final choice.

* * *

NOTES

1. The Supreme Court granted certiorari, received briefs and heard oral argument, but then affirmed without opinion because the Court was equally divided. Mr. Justice Stevens did not participate in the case, leaving the Court with eight members.

2. Lloyd Weinreb, Copyright for Functional Expression, 111 Harvard L. Rev. 1149 (1998), is a long analysis of the issue in the Borland case. Weinreb concludes that the Copyright Act is Janus-faced. On the one hand, the statute clearly provides for the protection of computer programs. On the other hand, it leaves the resolution of the issue of what that means to general principles of copyright, and principles of copyright have dictated, not always consistently, that functional works, which computer programs are, are not copyrightable. Weinreb would resolve the tension by affording protection only against wholesale, literal copying of a program. "The least that a court must conclude, in order to give the statute any effect at all, is that the wholesale, literal copying of a program—a lazy copy—is infringement. Beyond such minimal protection, a court need not go. * * * In short, having acknowledged the legislative judgment and deferred to it so far as to protect programs against plain piracy, a court should not go further. Anything less than literal copying (itself a criterion that is not self-interpreting) should not constitute infringement, nor should literal or non-literal copying of any aspect of the program that is not part of the program code itself. On the latter basis, the decision of the court of appeals in Borland is correct." Id. at 1250.

3. The extension of the copyright statute to provide protection for computer programs was a by-product of the effort of the drafters of the 1976 copyright act to make the statute a more complete misappropriation scheme. A major change in the revision bill submitted in 1964 was in the definition of copy. Under the 1909 Act the term copy, as construed by the Supreme Court in White-Smith Music Publishing Co. v. Apollo Co., 209 U.S. 1 (1908), was that a copy was something which could be seen by the human eye to duplicate the copyrighted work. In that case the Court held that a player piano role was not a copy of sheet music. Under the principle of *Apollo* a record would not be a copy either. Congress amended the statute shortly after the decision to extend protection to recordings of sheet music under limitations specifically applicable to musical recordings. These basic limitations, somewhat revised, are still in the statute (§ 115).

The *Apollo* doctrine was much criticized, and to the drafters of the revision bill seemed unduly narrow. They also thought it odd that every time technology developed a new method of appropriating a work, that Congress would be called upon to pass (or not) new legislation. They successfully sought to redefine copy to cover the essence of what was the problem with copying without tying the definition to a particular technology. Their definition, which is the definition in the act today, was that "Copies" are "material objects, other than phonorecords, in which a work is fixed by any method now known or later developed, and from which the work can be perceived, reproduced, or otherwise communicated, either directly or with the aid of a machine or device" (§ 101). The focus of the definition shifted from the method of making the copy (sheet music, record, tape, piano roll) to the function of a copy, to its ability to reproduce or otherwise communicate the protected work.

Although the focus of the drafters was on drafting a "copyright act for the ages" that would precisely state the essence of the governing principles, this change in definition had important consequences for the protection of computer programs and thus for the computer industry. Some authors of computer programs were already claiming copyright on their programs as books. They would put notice on, and register and deposit with the copyright office, print outs of the source code written in a computer language. (Basic is perhaps the best known of computer languages. A computer programmer writes a program in the computer language. The words of the computer language are instructions to the computer. The source code is then either run directly in a computer with a program that can interpret the language, or is compiled into a digital code and the compiled version is then run directly in the computer.) They argued, with considerable merit, that these books, although not written in a spoken language, were written in a language that persons trained in the computer language could understand, and although they might not be very interesting to read (at least to someone who was not interested in the art of computer programming), they conveyed as much information as factual compilations.

The argument made sense, but it was unimportant, because even if a book written in a computer language source code was copyrightable, the compiled copy in the form of digital bits encoded on magnetic media would not be a copy under *Apollo*, and would not infringe the copyright. Thus a computer programmer could copyright the source code, but that would not give him the right to stop anyone from making copies of an electronic version of the program, useful in a computer.

The new definition of copy changed all of that, because the electronically encoded digital bits, indecipherable by the human eye, would be a copy. The computer industry was in conflict about whether this change would be good or bad. For one thing, the industry had had no experience with selling computer programs. Computers were then large machines that cost millions of dollars (although they had no more power than today's under $2,000 desktop machine). A user who bought or purchased a machine selected it in large part for the computer programs that could run on the machine. The computer programs were provided for "free", as part of the purchase price, and were written by the same firms that built the machines. They had a strong incentive to write programs for the machines because without programs the machines were useless. It was not until the advent of the personal computer with a standardized design at the end of the 1970's that the possibility of selling the machine (or hardware) separately from the program (or software) (just as consumers purchased record players separately from the records) became a potential commercial market of importance.

Needless to say, Congress was only confused by the issues. In 1974 it acted to get the issue out of its hair by creating a commission to study the issue and make recommendations. The issue thus defused, the act was passed leaving the existing law in place. This was done by providing in § 117 (not the present § 117) that as to computer programs the law previously in effect would remain in effect.

The Commission was called the National Commission on New Technological Uses of Copyrighted Works (CONTU). It reported in 1979. It recommended that computer programs should be protected by copyright, and that § 117 should be amended (with some limits) to provide for this. By then the issue had become uncontroversial for the industry. The age of the personal computer was dawning, there were doubts about the patentability of computer programs, and the copyright act was available. Congress amended § 117 to permit the protection of computer programs, with some limitations, and added a definition of a computer program to § 101. The age of copyright protection of computer programs was born.

After a few early cases involving blatant copying of entire computer programs which established that a program could indeed be protected by copyright, the litigation has focused on fleshing out the details of what parts of a program are protected, and what kinds of takings infringe. That process is still going on in the lower federal courts. The Supreme Court undertook to address these issues in *Lotus*, but produced only an equally divided court.

3. Mitel, Inc. v. Iqtel, Inc., 124 F.3d 1366 (10th Cir. 1997), involved a copyright dispute between two manufacturers of telephone call controllers. Mitel manufactured a successful line of telephone call controllers which were programmed by means of four digit codes. These codes were well known by service technicians in the industry. Iqtel introduced a competitive line of call controllers, and provided a conversion feature so that its controllers could be programmed with the same Mitel codes. Iqtel believed that if it did not offer the same codes there would be resistance by dealers to carrying its equipment since service technicians would have to learn a second set of codes. The Mitel codes were published in copyrighted equipment manuals.

Mitel sued Iqtel for copyright infringement. The Tenth Circuit held that there was no infringement, but declined to follow *Lotus* and declined to base its decision on §102(b). Instead, the Tenth Circuit held that the codes were not protected both because of lack of originality (of which more shortly) and as "scenes a faire." "We have extended this traditional copyright doctrine to exclude from protection against infringement those elements of a work that necessarily result from external factors inherent in the subject matter of the work. For computer-related applications, these external factors include hardware standards and mechanical specifications, software standards and compatibility requirements, computer manufacturer design standards, industry programming practices, and practices and demands of the industry being serviced." 124 F.3d 1375. Does this approach lead to different results than the *Lotus* approach?

4. There is an enormous literature on copyright protection of computer programs. *Symposium: Toward a Third Intellectual Property Paradigm*, 94 Colum. L. Rev. 2307 (1994), contains much useful material on the intellectual property protection of software.

Bleistein v. Donaldson Lithographing

Supreme Court of the United States, 1903.
188 U.S. 239, 23 S.Ct. 298, 47 L.Ed. 460.

■ MR. JUSTICE HOLMES delivered the opinion of the court.

This case comes here from the United States Circuit Court of Appeals for the Sixth Circuit by writ of error. * * * It is an action brought by the plaintiffs in error to recover the penalties prescribed for infringements of copyrights.

* * * The alleged infringements consisted in the copying in reduced form of three chromolithographs prepared by employees of the plaintiffs for advertisements of a circus owned by one Wallace. Each of the three contained a portrait of Wallace in the corner and lettering bearing some slight relation to the scheme of decoration, indicating the subject of the design and the fact that the reality was to be seen at the circus. One of the designs was of an ordinary ballet, one of a number of men and women, described as the Stirk family, performing on bicycles, and one of groups of men and women whitened to represent statues. The Circuit Court directed a verdict for the defendant on the ground that the chromolithographs were not within the protection of the copyright law, and this ruling was sustained by the Circuit Court of Appeals. Courier Lithographing Co. v. Donaldson Lithographing Co., 104 Fed.Rep. 993.

* * *

We shall do no more than mention the suggestion that painting and engraving unless for a mechanical end are not among the useful arts, the progress of which Congress is empowered by the Constitution to promote. The Constitution does not limit the useful to that which satisfies immediate bodily needs. Burrow-Giles Lithographic Co. v. Sarony, 111 U.S. 53. It is obvious also that the plaintiffs' case is not affected by the fact, if it be one, that the pictures represent actual groups—visible things. They seem from the testimony to have been composed from hints or description, not from sight of a performance. But even if they had been drawn from the life, that fact would not deprive them of protection. The opposite proposition would mean that a portrait by Velasquez or Whistler was common property because others might try their hand on the same face. Others are free to copy the original. They are not free to copy the copy. The copy is the personal reaction of an individual upon nature. Personality always contains something unique. It expresses its singularity even in handwriting, and a very modest grade of art has in it something irreducible, which is one man's alone. That something he may copyright unless there is a restriction in the words of the act.

* * *

These chromolithographs are "pictorial illustrations." The word "illustrations" does not mean that they must illustrate the text of a book, and that the etchings of Rembrandt or Muller's engraving of the Madonna di San Sisto could not be protected to-day if any man were able to produce them. Again, the act however construed, does not mean that ordinary posters are not good enough to be considered within its scope. * * * Certainly works are not the less connected with the fine arts because their pictorial quality attracts the crowd and therefore gives them a real use—if use means to increase trade and to help to make money. A picture is none the less a picture and none the less a subject of copyright that it is used for an advertisement. And if pictures may be used to advertise soap, or the theatre, or monthly magazines, as they are, they may be used to advertise a circus. Of course, the ballet is as legitimate a subject for illustration as any other. A rule cannot be laid down that would excommunicate the paintings of Degas.

Finally, the special adaptation of these pictures to the advertisement of the Wallace shows does not prevent a copyright. That may be a circumstance for the jury to consider in determining the extent of Mr. Wallace's rights, but it is not a bar. Moreover, on the evidence, such prints are used by less pretentious exhibitions when those for whom they were prepared have given them up.

It would be a dangerous undertaking for persons trained only to the law to constitute themselves final judges of the worth of pictorial illustrations, outside of the narrowest and most obvious limits. At the one extreme some works of genius would be sure to miss appreciation. Their very novelty would make them repulsive until the public had learned the new language in which their author spoke. It may be more than doubted, for instance, whether the etchings of Goya or the paintings of Manet would have been sure of protection when seen for the first time. At the other end, copyright would be denied to pictures which appealed to a public less educated than the judge. Yet if they command the interest of any public, they have a commercial value—it would be bold to say that they have not an aesthetic and educational value—and the taste of any public is not to be treated with contempt. It is an ultimate fact for the moment, whatever may be our hopes for a change. That these pictures had their worth and their success is sufficiently shown by the desire to reproduce them without regard to the plaintiffs' rights. * * *

We are of opinion that there was evidence that the plaintiffs have rights entitled to the protection of the law.

[Reversed.]

■ MR. JUSTICE HARLAN, with whom concurred MR. JUSTICE McKENNA, dissenting.

* * *

I entirely concur in the views [of the court below] and therefore dissent from the opinion and judgment of this court. The clause of the Constitution giving Congress power to promote the progress of science and useful arts, by securing for limited terms to authors and inventors the exclusive right to their respective works and discoveries, does not, as I think, embrace a mere advertisement of a circus. * * *

NOTE

Justice Holmes' ringing assertion that "It would be a dangerous undertaking for persons trained only to the law to constitute themselves final judges of the worth of pictorial illustrations, outside of the narrowest and most obvious limits" has exerted a strong influence on the development of copyright law. But is that really the issue? Why couldn't "artistic worth" be treated as a question of fact, and resolved through the testimony of experts, just as many other questions involving subjects beyond the scope of legal training are resolved?

The right of the author of a work of visual art to prevent the destruction of a work of "recognized stature" in new § 106A will require the courts to determine what is, and what is not, such a work.

Mazer v. Stein

Supreme Court of the United States, 1954.
347 U.S. 201, 74 S.Ct. 460, 98 L.Ed. 630,
rehearing denied 347 U.S. 949, 74 S.Ct. 637, 98 L.Ed. 1096.

■ MR. JUSTICE REED delivered the opinion of the Court.

This case involves the validity of copyrights obtained by respondents for statuettes of male and female dancing figures made of semi-vitreous china. The controversy centers around the fact that although copyrighted as "works of art," the statuettes were intended for use and used as bases for table lamps, with electric wiring, sockets and lamp shades attached.

Respondents are partners in the manufacture and sale of electric lamps. One of the respondents created original works of sculpture in the form of human figures by traditional clay-model technique. From this model, a production mold for casting copies was made. The resulting statuettes, without any lamp components added, were submitted by the respondents to the Copyright Office for registration as "works of art" or reproductions thereof under § 5(g) or § 5(h) of the copyright law, and certificates of registration issued. Sales (publication in accordance with the statute) as fully equipped lamps preceded the applications for copyright registration of the statuettes. * * * Thereafter, the statuettes were sold in quantity throughout the country both as lamp bases and as statuettes. The sales in lamp form accounted for all but an insignificant portion of respondents' sales.

Petitioners are partners and, like respondents, make and sell lamps. Without authorization, they copied the statuettes, embodied them in lamps and sold them.

* * *

Petitioners, charged by the present complaint with infringement of respondents' copyrights of reproductions of their works of art, seek here a reversal of the Court of Appeals decree upholding the copyrights. Petitioners in their petition for certiorari present a single question:

"Can statuettes be protected in the United States by copyright when the copyright applicant intended primarily to use the statuettes in the form of lamp bases to be made and sold in quantity and carried the intentions into effect? * * * * "

It is not the right to copyright an article that could have utility under §§ 5(g) and (h), * * * that petitioners oppose. Their brief accepts the copyrightability of the great carved golden saltcellar of Cellini but adds:

"If, however, Cellini designed and manufactured this item in quantity so that the general public could have salt cellars, then an entirely different conclusion would be reached. In such case, the salt cellar becomes an article of manufacture having utility in addition to its ornamental value and would therefore have to be protected by design patent."

It is publication as a lamp and registration as a statue to gain a monopoly in manufacture that they assert is such a misuse of copyright as to make the registration invalid.

* * *

The practice of the Copyright Office, under the 1870 and 1874 Acts and before the 1909 Act, was to allow registration "as works of the fine arts" of articles of the same character as those of respondents now under challenge.

Seven examples appear in the Government's brief *amicus curiae*.[22] * * * The *amicus* brief gives sixty examples selected at five-year intervals, 1912–1952, said to be typical of registrations of works of art possessing utilitarian aspects.[25] * * * So we have a contemporaneous and long-continued construction of the statutes by the agency charged to administer them that would allow the registration of such a statuette as is in question here.

* * *

The successive acts, the legislative history of the 1909 Act and the practice of the Copyright Office unite to show that "works of art" and "reproductions of works of art" are terms that were intended by Congress to include the authority to copyright these statuettes. * * *

The conclusion that the statues here in issue may be copyrighted goes far to solve the question whether their intended reproduction as lamp stands bars or invalidates their registration. This depends solely on statutory interpretation. Congress may after publication protect by copyright any writing of an author. Its statute creates the copyright. It did not exist at common law even though he had a property right in his unpublished work.

But petitioners assert that congressional enactment of the design patent laws should be interpreted as denying protection to artistic articles embodied or reproduced in manufactured articles. They say:

> "Fundamentally and historically, the Copyright Office is the repository of what each claimant considers to be a cultural treasure, whereas the Patent Office is the repository of what each applicant considers to be evidence of the advance in industrial and technological fields."

Their argument is that design patents require the critical examination given patents to protect the public against monopoly. Attention is called to Gorham Co. v. White, 14 Wall. 511, interpreting the design patent law of 1842, 5 Stat. 544, granting a patent to anyone who by "their own industry, genius, efforts, and expense, may have invented or produced any new and original design for a manufacture. . . . ." A pattern for flat silver was there upheld. The intermediate and present law differs little. "Whoever invents any new, original and ornamental design for an article of manufacture may obtain a patent therefor, . . . " subject generally to the provisions concerning patents for invention. § 171, 66 Stat. 805. As petitioner sees the effect of the design patent law:

> "If an industrial designer can not satisfy the novelty requirements of the design patent laws, then his design as used on articles of manufacture can be copied by anyone."

---

22. E.g., "A female figure bearing an urn in front partly supported by drapery around the head. The figure nude from the waist up and below this the form concealed by conventionalized skirt draperies which flow down and forward forming a tray at the base. Sides and back of skirt in fluted form. The whole being designed as a candlestick with match tray. The figure standing and bent forward from hips and waist."

25. E.g., "*Lighting fixture design.* By F.E. Guitini. [Bowl-shaped bracket embellished with figure of half-nude woman standing in bunch of flowers.] Copyright December 28, 1912. Registration number G 42645. Copyright claimant: Kathodion Bronze Works, New York."

Petitioner has furnished the Court a booklet of numerous design patents for statuettes, bases for table lamps and similar articles for manufacture, quite indistinguishable in type from the copyrighted statuettes here in issue. Petitioner urges that overlapping of patent and copyright legislation so as to give an author or inventor a choice between patents and copyrights should not be permitted. * * * [36]

As we have held the statuettes here involved copyrightable, we need not decide the question of their patentability. Though other courts have passed upon the issue as to whether allowance by the election of the author or patentee of one bars a grant of the other, we do not. We do hold that the patentability of the statuettes, fitted as lamps or unfitted, does not bar copyright as works of art. Neither the Copyright Statute nor any other says that because a thing is patentable it may not be copyrighted. We should not so hold.

Unlike a patent, a copyright gives no exclusive right to the art disclosed; protection is given only to the expression of the idea-not the idea itself. Thus, in Baker v. Selden, 101 U.S. 99, the Court held that a copyrighted book on a peculiar system of bookkeeping was not infringed by a similar book using a similar plan which achieved similar results where the alleged infringer made a different arrangement of the columns and used different headings. The distinction is illustrated in Fred Fisher, Inc. v. Dillingham, 298 F. 145, 151, when the court speaks of two men, each a perfectionist, independently making maps of the same territory. Though the maps are identical, each may obtain the exclusive right to make copies of his own particular map, and yet neither will infringe the other's copyright. Likewise a copyrighted directory is not infringed by a similar directory which is the product of independent work. The copyright protects originality rather than novelty or invention-conferring only "the sole right of multiplying copies." Absent copying there can be no infringement of copyright. Thus, respondents may not exclude others from using statuettes of human figures in table lamps; they may only prevent use of copies of their statuettes as such or as incorporated in some other article. Regulation § 202.8, supra, makes clear that artistic articles are protected in "form but not their mechanical or utilitarian aspects." See Stein v. Rosenthal, 103 F.Supp. 227, 231.

* * *

The economic philosophy behind the clause empowering Congress to grant patents and copyrights is the conviction that encouragement of individual effort by personal gain is the best way to advance public welfare through the talents of authors and inventors in "Science and useful Arts."

---

36. The English Copyright Act, 1911, § 22, 4 Halsbury's Statutes of England (2d ed.), p. 800, does not protect designs registrable under the Patents and Designs Act (now the Registered Designs Act, 1949, 17 Halsbury's Statutes of England (2d ed.)) unless such designs are not used or intended to be used as models or patterns to be multiplied by any industrial process. The Board of Trade has ruled that a design shall be deemed to be used as a model or pattern to be multiplied by industrial process within the meaning of § 22 when the design is reproduced or intended to be reproduced in more than fifty single articles. The Copyright (Industrial Designs) Rules, 1949, No. 2367, 1 Statutory Instruments 1949, p. 1453.

Sacrificial days devoted to such creative activities deserve rewards commensurate with the services rendered.

Affirmed.

* * *

House Report No. 94-1476
pp. 54-55.

In accordance with the Supreme Court's decision in Mazer v. Stein, 347 U.S. 201 (1954), works of "applied art" encompass all original pictorial, graphic, and sculptural works that are intended to be or have been embodied in useful articles, regardless of factors such as mass production, commercial exploitation, and the potential availability of design patent protection. The scope of exclusive rights in these works is given special treatment in section 113, to be discussed * * * [shortly].

The Committee has added language to the definition of "pictorial, graphic, and sculptural works" in an effort to make clearer the distinction between works of applied art protectable under the bill and industrial designs not subject to copyright protection. The declaration that "pictorial, graphic, and sculptural works" include "works of artistic craftsmanship insofar as their form but not their mechanical or utilitarian aspects are concerned" is classic language; it is drawn from Copyright Office regulations promulgated in the 1940's and expressly endorsed by the Supreme Court in the *Mazer* case.

The second part of the amendment states that "the design of a useful article * * * shall be considered a pictorial, graphic, or sculptural work only if, and only to the extent that, such design incorporates pictorial, graphic, or sculptural features that can be identified separately from, and are capable of existing independently of, the utilitarian aspects of the article." A "useful article" is defined as "an article having an intrinsic utilitarian function that is not merely to portray the appearance of the article or to convey information." This part of the amendment is an adaptation of language added to the Copyright Office Regulations in the mid-1950's in an effort to implement the Supreme Court's decision in the *Mazer* case.

In adopting this amendatory language, the Committee is seeking to draw as clear a line as possible between copyrightable works of applied art and uncopyrighted works of industrial design. A two-dimensional painting, drawing, or graphic work is still capable of being identified as such when it is printed on or applied to utilitarian articles such as textile fabrics, wallpaper, containers, and the like. The same is true when a statue or carving is used to embellish an industrial product or, as in the *Mazer* case, is incorporated into a product without losing its ability to exist independently as a work of art. On the other hand, although the shape of an industrial product may be aesthetically satisfying and valuable, the Committee's intention is not to offer it copyright protection under the bill. Unless the shape of an automobile, airplane, ladies' dress, food processor, television set, or any other industrial product contains some element that, physically or conceptually, can be identified as separable from the utilitarian aspects of that article, the design would not be copyrighted under the bill. The test of separability and independence from "the utilitarian aspects of the article" does not depend upon the nature of the design—that is, even if the appearance of an article is determined by esthetic (as opposed to functional) considerations, only elements, if any, which can be identified separately from the useful article as such are copyrightable. And, even if the three-dimensional design contains some such element (for example a carving on the back of a chair or a floral relief design on silver flatware), copyright protection would extend only to that element, and would not cover the over-all configuration of the utilitarian article as such.

A special situation is presented by architectural works. An architect's plans and drawings would, of course, be protected by copyright, but the extent to which that protection would extend to the structure depicted would depend on the circumstances. Purely nonfunctional or monumental structures would be subject to full copyright protection under the bill, and the same would be true of artistic sculpture or decorative ornamentation or embellishment added to a structure. On the other hand, where the only elements of shape in an architectural design are conceptually inseparable from the utilitarian aspects of the structure, copyright protection for the design would not be available.

The Committee has considered, but chosen to defer, the possibility of protecting the design of typefaces. A "typeface" can be defined as a set of letters, numbers, or other symbolic characters, whose forms are related by repeating design elements consistently applied in a notational system and are intended to be embodied in articles whose intrinsic utilitarian function is for use in composing text or other cognizable combinations of characters. The Committee does not regard the design of typeface, as thus defined, to be a copyrightable "pictorial, graphic, or sculptural work" within the meaning of this bill and the application of the dividing line in section 101.

NOTE

1. Robert C. Denicola, Applied Art and Industrial Design: A Suggested Approach to Copyright in Useful Articles, 67 Minn. L. Rev. 707 (1983), argues that the test for separating copyrightable from uncopyrightable commercial designs should focus on the design process rather than the physical object. His argument puts considerable weight upon the use of the term "conceptually" in the following sentence from the portion of the house report just quoted: "Unless the shape of an automobile, airplane, ladies' dress, food processor, television set, or any other industrial product contains some element that, physically or conceptually, can be identified as separable from the utilitarian aspects of that article, the design would not be copyrighted under the bill."

Denicola argues that the critical distinction between decorative art and industrial design is the role of functional considerations in the design process. If the design is dictated solely by aesthetic considerations, he argues, it should be copyrightable no matter what the style, even if it is sleek and modern. On the other hand, if the design has emerged out of the close relationship between form and function, it should not be copyrightable.

Denicola argues that a test of physical separability does not accurately reflect the case law because the courts have held many designs (such as fabric designs) copyrightable which cannot in fact be removed from the commercial product on which they exist.

2. Is an original type face or other symbol system eligible for copyright? Can a copy of a public domain work be protected against an exact reproduction by the use of an original, unusual type face or symbols? In Perris v. Hexamer, 99 U.S. 674 (1878), the court held that a map of Philadelphia did not infringe a map of New York even though it employed the same original, specialized system of symbols. The Court said: "The complainants have no more an exclusive right to use the form of the characters they employ to express their ideas upon the face of the map, than they have to use the form of type they select to print the key. Scarcely any map is published on which certain arbitrary signs, explained by a key printed at some convenient place for reference, are not used to designate objects of special interest, such as rivers, railroads, boundaries, cities, towns, etc.; and yet we think it has never been supposed that a simple copyright of the map gave the publisher an exclusive right to the use upon other maps of the particular signs and key which he saw fit to adopt for the purposes of his delineations. That, however, is what the complainants seek to accomplish in this case. The defendant has not copied their maps. All he has done at any time has been to use to some extent their system of arbitrary signs and their key." 99 U.S. 676.

In Eltra Corporation v. Ringer, 579 F.2d 294 (4th Cir. 1978), the plaintiff sought a writ of mandamus to compel the Registrar of Copyrights to register a typeface design which had been prepared by a well-known typeface designer for a fee of $11,000. Both the district court and the court of appeals held that a typeface design was not a work of art under the 1909 act.

Architectural Works

Article 2 of the Berne Convention provides that member states will protect works of architecture. A year after the Berne Convention Implementation Act, Congress adopted the Copyright Protection of Architectural Works Act, Title VIII of P.L. 101–650 §§ 701–706. This act amended § 102 to add architectural works to the list of protected works (thus taking them out of § 113), added a definition of architectural works to § 101, and added a new § 120.

The problem that the new § 120 addressed was that when an actual building (as opposed to plans and drawings) is protected, then anyone taking a picture of the building infringes the copyright in the building. For instance, if a building were built that occupied a prominent place in the skyline of a city, then no one could make or sell a picture of the skyline without the permission of the owner of the copyright in the building. Section 120(a) provides that the copyright in a building that has been constructed does not include the right to prevent the making of pictorial representations of the building.

There was also concern that alterations in the building might be considered an infringement of the exclusive right to make a derivative work. So §120(b) provides that notwithstanding § 106(2) (the section creating the derivative right) the owner of the copyrighted building could make alterations or tear it down without the permission of the owner of the architectural copyright.

Commercial Prints and Labels

Copyright protection has been accorded to commercial prints and labels by statute since 1874.

Copyright protection of commercial labels is attractive for two reasons. First, the plaintiff need only show copying, not consumer confusion. Where the copying is clear, this may make it easier to obtain a preliminary injunction, and in some cases it may even be possible to prevail on copyright where trademark would fail. See Kitchens of Sara Lee, Inc. v. Nifty Food Corp., 266 F.2d 541 (2d Cir. 1959), where plaintiff succeeded in copyright for the copying of pictures of cakes on its labels, but failed in unfair competition because of the absence of customer confusion. Secondly, copyright protection affords protection against use of the label in a non-trademark manner. This is particularly important where a company plans a continuing promotional campaign built around central symbols. Think, for instance, of the anguish at the Green Giant Co. if the Jolly Green Giant, a copyrighted figure to be sure, were made the subject of a cartoonist's satire, or worse, portrayed as the villain of the piece.

See generally, Pattishall, Protection of Labels Through Copyright Infringement and Unfair Competition Laws, 56 Trademark Rep. 408 (1966).

Commercial prints and labels are not specifically enumerated in § 102. The House Report states that "there is no intention whatever to narrow the scope of the subject matter now characterized in § 5(k) as 'prints or labels used for articles of merchandise.' However, since this terminology suggests the material object in which a work is embodied rather than the work itself, the bill does not mention this category separately." House Report No. 94–1476 at 54.

Designs

American law has historically provided little protection for commercial and industrial designs. Design statutes that would provide a form of limited protection with a shorter term than either copyright or patent have been repeatedly proposed to the Congress but have never passed. Their proponents argue that the lack of protection for applied design contributes to low aesthetic standards in an area of great importance, and that as a result American industrial design standards are lower than those of some other countries.

David Goldenberg, The Long and Winding Road: A History of the Fight Over Industrial Design Protection in the United States, 45 J. Copyright Soc'y U.S. 21 (1997), recounts the many failed efforts to persuade Congress to enact a general system of industrial design protection, including one effort made as part of the revision effort leading to the 1976 Copyright Act. He concludes:

> There is strong and consistent support for design protection, and while opponents have made valid claims of problems with design protection, it must be remembered that fabric manufacturers stated similar fears that there would be a monopoly on polka-dot patterns if textiles were protected. While textiles have been registrable under copyright for nearly fifty years, and all manufactured goods are registrable in many other countries without undue difficulties being created, the arguments of opponents often sound credible in theory and have so far proven strong enough to defeat any bill. It is said that Congress acts only when there is a crisis. The domestic consumer electronics industry has virtually been eliminated [outside of computers]. Foreign auto manufactures now represent 40% of the domestic new car market. Consumers say that is because foreign goods are simply "better made" or "better values." Yet we fail to make the connection between the lack of "better" American products and the lack of incentive to design better American products. It is the lack of this insight, not the lack of a crisis that holds back design protection."

Id. 62.

Absent a federal design statute, protection is available under copyright following *Mazer,* under the design patent statute, under the Lanham Act and under unfair competition doctrines. Article 25 of the GATT TRIPS provides that "Members shall provide for the protection of independently created industrial designs that are new or original." Whether or not current American law complies with this undertaking is an open question.

Under *Mazer* protection is regularly obtained on fabric designs, toys, jewelry and household decorative items, at least to judge by the active Second Circuit infringement docket in these areas.

Mazer would provide the basis for broad protection of industrial designs if the following stratagem were successful. Say, for instance, that you desired to obtain protection on a new design for a shoe. Take the shoe, glue it to a base, and title it: "Shoe in modern life." Register it as a statue and manufacture the shoe. Would a competitor who copied your shoe design infringe the copyright?

Does *Mazer* answer this question? How would Denicola answer this question?

Section 113(a) appears to answer this question in the affirmative. But it is limited by section 113(b). Protection "in a work that portrays a useful article as such" is to be no greater than existed under the 1909 law. House Report 94–1476 states:

Section 113 deals with the extent of copyright protection in "works of applied art." The section takes as its starting point the Supreme Court's decision in Mazer v. Stein, 347 U.S. 201 (1954), and the first sentence of subsection (a) restates the basic principle established by that decision. The rule of *Mazer*, as affirmed by the bill, is that copyright in a pictorial, graphic, or sculptural work will not be affected if the work is employed as the design of a useful article, and will afford protection to the copyright owner against the unauthorized reproduction of his work in useful as well as nonuseful articles. The terms "pictorial, graphic, and sculptural works" and "useful article" are defined in section 101, and these definitions are discussed above in connection with section 102.

The broad language of section 106(1) and of subsection (a) of section 113 raises questions as to the extent of copyright protection for a pictorial, graphic, or sculptural work that portrays, depicts, or represents an image of a useful article in such a way that the utilitarian nature of the article can be seen. To take the example usually cited, would copyright in a drawing or model of an automobile give the artist the exclusive right to make automobiles of the same design?

The 1961 Report of the Register of Copyrights stated, on the basis of judicial precedent, that "copyright in a pictorial, graphic, or sculptural work, portraying a useful article as such, does not extend to the manufacture of the useful article itself," and recommended specifically that "the distinctions drawn in this area by existing court decisions" not be altered by the statute. The Register's Supplementary Report, at page 48, cited a number of these decisions, and explained the insuperable difficulty of finding "any statutory formulation that would express the distinction satisfactorily." Section 113(b) reflects the Register's conclusion that "the real need is to make clear that there is no intention to change the present law with respect to the scope of protection in a work portraying a useful article as such." Id. at 105.

The design patent statute is a brief addition to the patent statute, 35 U.S.C. §§ 171–173. Protection is "subject to the conditions and requirements of this title" which includes the standard of non-obviousness required by section 35 U. S. C. § 103. In recent years the courts have been more likely to find design patents valid (along with all other patents) for reasons explained in the next chapter.

The *Sears* and *Compco* cases checked the development of state law as a source of design protection by analogy to unfair competition. The development of protection of product configurations under the Lanham Act, discussed in Chapter 3 in connection with the *Two Pesos* case, provides protection in some situations.

NOTE

1. Defining the line between copyright and industrial design, and finding a satisfactory approach to the protection of industrial design is a problem that has been difficult for other legal systems as well. The story of developments in numerous other systems, with careful parallels to issues faced in American law, is chronicled in an ambitious two-part study by Professor J.H. Reichman. J.H. Reichman, Design Protection in Domestic and Foreign Copyright Law: From the Berne Revision of 1948 to the Copyright Act of 1976, 1983 Duke L.J. 1143 (1983) and J.H. Reichman, Design Protection after the Copyright Act of 1976: A Comparative View of the Emerging Interim Models, 31 J. Copyright Soc'y. U.S. 267 (1984).

(2) Public Policy

Do any considerations of "public policy" limit the scope of copyrightable subject matter? The court in Mitchell Bros. Film Group v. Cinema Adult Theater, 604 F.2d 852 (5th Cir. 1979), thought not. The defendants argued that the plaintiff's film was not copyrightable because obscene and that the court should not enjoin infringement because the plaintiff had "unclean hands." (A technical equity doctrine which is a grounds for denying injunctive relief.) "Denying copyright protection to work adjudged obscene by the standards of one era would frequently result in lack of copyright protection (and thus lack of financial incentive to create) for works that later generations might consider to be not only non-obscene but even of great literary merit." 604 F.2d 857.

Practice Management Information Corp. v. The American Medical Ass'n, 121 F. 3d 516 (9th Cir. 1997) involved a copyright on numerical medical procedure codes that had been developed by the AMA. Some six thousand codes were developed and published in the AMA's Physician's Current Procedural Terminology ("the CPT"). The AMA had contracted with the U.S. Health Care Financing Administration (the "HCFA"), to permit the Agency to require the use of the CPT in a mandatory system for submitting claims for reimbursement under medical benefit programs. The plaintiff sought a declaratory judgment that it was free to use the government-mandated CPT to publish a competing guide without the consent of the AMA. The plaintiff argued that because the code was now part of the law, it was in the public domain because there is a public interest in open access to the law. The Court rejected the argument (although it held for the plaintiff on the ground that a term the contract with the HCFA which provided for the exclusive use of the CPT was misuse of the copyright).

Practice Management Information Corp. v. The American Medical Ass'n

United States Court of Appeals for the Ninth Circuit, 1997.
121 F. 3d 516, cert. den. 118 S.Ct. 339,
opinion amended 133 F.3d 1140 (1998),
pet. for cert. filed 66 USLW 3525 (1998).

* * *

Practice Management's argument that the CPT became law and entered the public domain when HCFA by regulation required its use rests ultimately upon Banks v. Manchester, 128 U.S. 244(1888), which held that judicial opinions are uncopyrightable. *Banks* in turn rests upon two grounds, neither of which would justify invalidation of the AMA's copyright.

The first ground for the *Banks* holding that judicial opinions are not subject to copyright is that the public owns the opinions because it pays the judges' salaries. Id. at 253. The second is that as a matter of public policy, "the whole work done by the judges constitutes the authentic exposition and interpretation of the law, which, binding every citizen, is free for publication to all. . . ." Id.

The first ground is clearly not applicable to the CPT. The copyright system was not significant in *Banks* because judges had no proprietary interest in their opinions. The copyright system is of central importance in this case because the AMA authored, owns, and maintains the CPT and claims a copyright in it.

The copyright system's goal of promoting the arts and sciences by granting temporary monopolies to copyrightholders was not at stake in *Banks* because judges' salaries provided adequate incentive to write opinions. In contrast, copyrightability of the CPT provides the economic incentive for the AMA to produce and maintain the CPT. "To vitiate copyright, in such circumstances, could, without adequate justification, prove destructive of the copyright interest, in encouraging creativity," a matter of particular significance in this context because of "the increasing trend toward state and federal adoptions of model codes." 1 Melville B. Nimmer & David Nimmer, Nimmer on Copyright § 5.06[C], at 5–92 (1996). As the AMA points out, invalidating its copyright on the ground that the CPT entered the public domain when HCFA required its use would expose copyrights on a wide range of privately authored model codes, standards, and reference works to invalidation. Non-profit organizations that develop these model codes and standards warn they will be unable to continue to do so if the codes and standards enter the public domain when adopted by a public agency.

The second consideration underlying *Banks*—the due process requirement of free access to the law—may be relevant but does not justify termination of the AMA's copyright. There is no evidence that anyone wishing to use the CPT has any difficulty obtaining access to it. See Texas v. West Publ'g Co., 882 F.2d 171, 177 (5th Cir. 1989). Practice Management is not a potential user denied access to the CPT, but a putative copier wishing to share in the AMA's statutory monopoly. Practice Management does not assert the AMA has restricted access to users or intends to do so in the future.

The AMA's right under the Copyright Act to limit or forgo publication of the CPT poses no realistic threat to public access. The AMA has no incentive to limit or forgo publication. If the AMA were to do so, HCFA would no doubt exercise its right to terminate its agreement with the AMA. Other remedies would also be available, including "fair use" and due process defenses for infringers, see 1 Nimmer & Nimmer, supra, § 5.06[C], at 5–92, and, perhaps most relevant, mandatory licensing at a reasonable royalty could be required in light of the great public injury that would result if adequate access to the CPT were denied.

The Supreme Court has not considered a case in which the author asserted a proprietary interest in material adopted by the government as law. However, the First and Second Circuits have declined to enjoin enforcement of private copyrights in these circumstances.

In Building Officials & Code Admin. v. Code Technology, Inc., 628 F.2d 730 (1st Cir. 1980), the district court preliminarily enjoined Code Technology, Inc. from copying a building code copyrighted by Building Officials & Code Administration ("BOCA"), a private, non-profit group, and adopted by the State. The First Circuit reversed. It recognized the problem posed by *Banks*, but nonetheless refrained from holding BOCA's copyright invalid:

> Groups such as BOCA serve an important public function; arguably they do a better job than could the state alone in seeing that complex yet essential regulations are drafted, kept up to date and made available. Since the rule denying copyright protection to judicial opinions and statutes grew out of a much different set of circumstances than do these technical regulatory codes, we think BOCA should at least be allowed to argue its position fully on the basis of an evidentiary record, into which testimony and materials shedding light on the policy issues discussed herein may be placed.

Id. at 736.

In CCC Info. Servs., Inc. v. Maclean Hunter Mkt. Reports, Inc., 44 F.3d 61 (2d Cir. 1994), the Second Circuit declined to invalidate the copyright on a privately prepared listing of automobile values that several states required insurance companies to use in calculating insurance awards:

> We are not prepared to hold that a state's reference to a copyrighted work as a legal standard for valuation results in loss of the copyright. While there are indeed policy considerations that support CCC's argument, they are opposed by countervailing considerations. For example, a rule that the adoption of such a reference by a state legislature or administrative body deprived the copyright owner of its property would raise very substantial problems under the Takings Clause of the Constitution. We note also that for generations, state education systems have assigned books under copyright to comply with a mandatory school curriculum. It scarcely extends CCC's argument to require that all such assigned books lose their copyright—as one cannot comply with the legal requirements without using the copyrighted works. Yet we think it unlikely courts would reach this conclusion. Although there is scant authority of CCC's argument, Nimmer's treatise opposes such a suggestion as antithetical to the interests sought to be advanced by the Copyright Act.

* * *

In Merritt Forbes & Co. v. Newman Investment Securities, Inc., 604 F.Supp. 943 (S.D.N.Y. 1985), the defendants argued that it is against public policy to permit a copyright in legal documents. The effect of copyright, they argued, would be to force competitors who wished to offer a product under the same contractual terms (relating, for instance, to a product warranty or, as in the case itself, to the terms of a bond offering) to change the language of the legal document although the purpose would be to create the same legal relationship. This would have two effects contrary to public policy. First, it would make it more difficult for purchasers to compare the offerings of competitors because they would have to "decode" the different legal language of the documents in order to decide whether there are significant differences. Second, it would undermine the usefulness of precedent since a decision construing the language of one document might or might not apply to a variant. The court held that there was no public policy doctrine limiting copyrightability, and said that these arguments would be relevant only to an argument that the claimed infringement was fair use under § 107. "The issue of whether or not bond underwriting documents are the proper subject for copyright protection has apparently never been addressed in this or any other jurisdiction. * * * [N]o court * * * [has] concluded that there is a public policy exemption for a particular classification of literary works which would otherwise be subject to copyright protection." 604 F.Supp. 949–951.

PROBLEM

Are the arguments in *Merritt Forbes & Co.* that copyright for legal documents will result in a needless cacophony of meaningless variants persuasive? Consider the fact that the leading operating systems for personal computers, MS–DOS (for Microsoft Disk Operating System), Windows 3.1, Windows 95, Windows 98, and Windows NT are copyrighted by the Microsoft Corporation. Yet the system is used on many different brands of personal computers, each maker of which has obtained a license from Microsoft. Does this example have any relevance to the case of legal forms?

(3) Originality

Section 102 requires a "work of authorship," echoing the Constitutional clause conferring upon Congress the power to enact the statute: "[t]o promote the Progress of Science and useful Arts, by securing for limited Times to Authors and Inventors the exclusive Right to their respective Writings and Discoveries." U.S. Const. art. I, § 8, cl. 8. Does the status of "authorship" require any originality, creativity or effort?

Feist Publications, Inc. v. Rural Telephone Service Co., Inc.

Supreme Court of the United States, 1991.
499 U.S. 340, 111 S.Ct. 1282, 112 L.Ed.2d 358.

■ JUSTICE O'CONNOR delivered the opinion of the Court.

This case requires us to clarify the extent of copyright protection available to telephone directory white pages.

I

Rural Telephone Service Company is a certified public utility that provides telephone service to several communities in northwest Kansas. It is subject to a state regulation that requires all telephone companies operating in Kansas to issue annually an updated telephone directory. Accordingly, as a condition of its monopoly franchise, Rural publishes a typical telephone directory, consisting of white pages and yellow pages. The white pages list in alphabetical order the names of Rural's subscribers, together with their towns and telephone numbers. The yellow pages list Rural's business subscribers alphabetically by category and feature classified advertisements of various sizes. Rural distributes its directory free of charge to its subscribers, but earns revenue by selling yellow pages advertisements.

Feist Publications, Inc., is a publishing company that specializes in area-wide telephone directories. Unlike a typical directory, which covers only a particular calling area, Feist's area-wide directories cover a much larger geographical range, reducing the need to call directory assistance or consult multiple directories. The Feist directory that is the subject of this litigation covers 11 different telephone service areas in 15 counties and contains 46,878 white pages listings—compared to Rural's approximately 7,700 listings. Like Rural's directory, Feist's is distributed free of charge and includes both white pages and yellow pages. Feist and Rural compete vigorously for yellow pages advertising.

As the sole provider of telephone service in its service area, Rural obtains subscriber information quite easily. Persons desiring telephone service must apply to Rural and provide their names and addresses; Rural then assigns them a telephone number. Feist is not a telephone company, let alone one with monopoly status, and therefore lacks independent access to any subscriber information. To obtain white pages listings for its area-wide directory, Feist approached each of the 11 telephone companies operating in northwest Kansas and offered to pay for the right to use its white pages listings.

Of the 11 telephone companies, only Rural refused to license its listings to Feist. Rural's refusal created a problem for Feist, as omitting these listings would have left a gaping hole in its area-wide directory, rendering it less attractive to potential yellow pages advertisers. In a decision subsequent to that which we review here, the District Court determined that this was precisely the reason Rural refused to license its listings. The refusal was motivated by an unlawful purpose "to extend its monopoly in telephone service to a monopoly in yellow pages advertising." Rural Telephone Service Co. v. Feist Publications, Inc., 787 F.Supp. 610, 622 (Kan. 1990).

Unable to license Rural's white pages listings, Feist used them without Rural's consent. Feist began by removing several thousand listings that fell outside the geographic range of its area-wide directory, then hired personnel to investigate the 4,935 that remained. These employees verified the data reported by Rural and sought to obtain additional information. As a result, a typical Feist listing includes the individual's street address, most of Rural's listings do not. Notwithstanding these additions, however, 1,309 of the 46,878 listings in Feist's 1983 directory were identical to listings in Rural's 1982–1983 white pages. App. 54 (¶ 15–16), 57. Four of these were fictitious listings that Rural had inserted into its directory to detect copying.

Rural sued for copyright infringement in the District Court for the District of Kansas taking the position that Feist, in compiling its own directory, could not use the information contained in Rural's white pages. Rural asserted that Feist's employees were obliged to travel door-to-door or conduct a telephone survey to discover the same information for themselves. Feist responded that such efforts were economically impractical and, in any event, unnecessary because the information copied was beyond the scope of copyright protection. The District Court granted summary judgment to Rural, explaining that "[c]ourts have consistently held that telephone directories are copyrightable" and citing a string of lower court decisions. 663 F.Supp. 214, 218 (1987). In an unpublished opinion, the Court of Appeals for the Tenth Circuit affirmed "for substantially the reasons given by the district court." App. to Pet. for Cert. 4a, judgt. order reported at 916 F.2d 718 (1990). We granted certiorari, 498 U.S. 808 (1990), to determine whether the copyright in Rural's directory protects the names, towns, and telephone numbers copied by Feist.

II

A

This case concerns the interaction of two well-established propositions. The first is that facts are not copyrightable; the other, that compilations of facts generally are. Each of these propositions possesses an impeccable pedigree. That there can be no valid copyright in facts is universally understood. The most fundamental axiom of copyright law is that "[n]o author may copyright his ideas or the facts he narrates." Harper & Row, Publishers, Inc. v. Nation Enterprises, 471 U.S. 539, 556 (1985). Rural wisely concedes this point, noting in its brief that "[f]acts and discoveries, of course, are not themselves subject to copyright protection." Brief for Respondent 24. At the same time, however, it is beyond dispute that compilations of facts are within the subject matter of copyright. Compilations were expressly mentioned in the Copyright Act of 1909, and again in the Copyright Act of 1976.

There is an undeniable tension between these two propositions. Many compilations consist of nothing but raw data—i.e. wholly factual information not accompanied by any original written expression. On what basis may one claim a copyright in such a work? Common sense tells us that 100 uncopyrightable facts do not magically change their status when gathered together in one place. Yet copyright law seems to contemplate that compilations that consist exclusively of facts are potentially within its scope.

The key to resolving the tension lies in understanding why facts are not copyrightable. The *sine qua non* of copyright is originality. To qualify for copyright protection, a work must be original to the author. See *Harper & Row,* supra, at 547–549. Original as the term is used in copyright, means only that the work was independently created by the author (as opposed to copied from other works), and that it possesses at least some minimal degree of creativity. 1 M. Nimmer & D. Nimmer, Copyright §§ 2.01[A], [B] (1990) (hereinafter Nimmer). To be sure, the requisite level of creativity is extremely low, even a slight amount will suffice. The vast majority of works make the grade quite easily, as they possess some creative spark, "no matter how crude, humble or obvious" it might be. Id. § 1.08[C][1]. Originality does not signify novelty, a work may be original even though it closely resembles other works so long as the similarity is fortuitous, not the result of copying. To illustrate, assume that two poets, each ignorant of the other, compose identical poems. Neither work is novel, yet both are original and, hence, copyrightable. See Sheldon v. Metro-Goldwyn Pictures Corp., 81 F.2d 49, 54 (CA2 1936).

Originality is a constitutional requirement. The source of Congress' power to enact copyright laws is Article I, § 8, cl. 8, of the Constitution, which authorizes Congress to "secur[e] for limited Times to Authors . . . the exclusive Right to their respective Writings." In two decisions from the late 19th Century—The Trade-Mark Cases, 100 U.S. 82 (1879); and Burrow-Giles Lithographic Co. v. Sarony, 111 U.S. 53 (1884)—this Court defined the crucial terms "authors" and "writings." In so doing, the Court made it unmistakably clear that these terms presuppose a degree of originality.

In *The Trade–Mark Cases,* the Court addressed the constitutional scope of "writings." For a particular work to be classified "under the head of writings of authors," the Court determined, "originality is required." 100 U.S., at 94. The Court explained that originality requires independent creation plus a modicum of creativity: "[W]hile the word *writings* may be liberally construed, as it has been, to include original designs for engraving, prints, &c., it is only such as are *original,* and are founded in the creative powers of the mind. The writings, which are to be protected are *the fruits of intellectual labor,* embodied in the form of books, prints, engravings, and the like." Ibid. (emphasis in original).

In *Burrow–Giles,* [a decision that held that the copyright on a photograph of Oscar Wilde was valid] the Court distilled the same requirement from the Constitution's use of the word "authors." The Court defined "author," in a constitutional sense, to mean "he to whom anything owes its origin; originator; maker." 111 U.S., at 58, 4 S.Ct., at 281 (internal quotations omitted). As in *The Trade–Mark Cases,* the Court emphasized the creative component of originality. It described copyright as being limited to "original intellectual conceptions of the author," ibid., and stressed the importance of requiring an author who accuses another of infringement to prove "the existence of those facts of originality, of intellectual production, of thought, and conception." Id., 111 U.S., at 59–60.

The originality requirement articulated in *The Trade–Mark Cases* and *Burrow–Giles* remains the touchstone of copyright protection today. See Goldstein v. California, 412 U.S. 546, 561–562 (1973). It is the very "premise of copyright law." Miller v. Universal City Studios, Inc., 650 F.2d 1365, 1368

(CA5 1981). Leading scholars agree on this point. As one pair of commentators succinctly puts it: "The originality requirement is *constitutionally mandated* for all works." Patterson & Joyce, Monopolizing the Law: The Scope of Copyright Protection for Law Reports and Statutory Compilations, 36 UCLA L. Rev. 719, 763, n. 155 (1989) (emphasis in original) (hereinafter Patterson & Joyce). Accord id., at 759–760, and n. 140. Nimmer § 1.06[A] ("originality is a statutory as well as a constitutional requirement"); id., § 1.08[C][1] ("a modicum of intellectual labor . . . clearly constitutes an essential constitutional element").

It is this bedrock principle of copyright that mandates the law's seemingly disparate treatment of facts and factual compilations. "No one may claim originality as to facts." Id., § 2.11[A], p. 2–157. This is because facts do not owe their origin to an act of authorship. The distinction is one between creation and discovery: the first person to find and report a particular fact has not created the fact he or she has merely discovered its existence. To borrow from *Burrow–Giles,* one who discovers a fact is not its "maker" or "originator." 111 U.S., at 58. "The discoverer merely finds and records." Nimmer § 2.03[E]. Census-takers, for example, do not "create" the population figures that emerge from their efforts; in a sense they copy these figures from the world around them. Denicola, Copyright in Collections of Facts: A Theory for the Protection of Nonfiction Literary Works, 81 Colum. L. Rev. 516, 525 (1981) (hereinafter Denicola). Census data therefore do not trigger copyright because these data are not "original" in the constitutional sense. Nimmer § 2.03[E]. The same is true of all facts—scientific, historical, biographical, and news of the day. "[T]hey may not be copyrighted and are part of the public domain available to every person." *Miller,* supra, at 1369.

Factual compilations, on the other hand, may possess the requisite originality. The compilation author typically chooses which facts to include, in what order to place them, and how to arrange the collected data so that they may be used effectively by readers. These choices as to selection and arrangement, so long as they are made independently by the compiler and entail a minimal degree of creativity, are sufficiently original that Congress may protect such compilations through the copyright laws. Nimmer §§ 2.11[D], 3.03; Denicola 523, n. 38. Thus, even a directory that contains absolutely no protectable written expression, only facts, meets the constitutional minimum for copyright protection if it features an original selection or arrangement. See *Harper & Row,* 471 U.S., at 547. Accord Nimmer § 3.03.

This protection is subject to an important limitation. The mere fact that a work is copyrighted does not mean that every element of the work may be protected. Originality remains the *sine qua non* of copyright, accordingly, copyright protection may extend only to those components of a work that are original to the author. Patterson & Joyce 800–802; Ginsburg, Creation and Commercial Value: Copyright Protection of Works of Information, 90 Colum. L. Rev. 1865, 1868, and n. 12 (1990) (hereinafter Ginsburg). Thus, if the compilation author clothes facts with an original collocation of words, he or she may be able to claim a copyright in this written expression. Others may copy the underlying facts from the publication, but not the precise words used to present them. In *Harper & Row*, for example, we explained that President Ford could not prevent others from copying bare historical facts from his autobiography, see 471 U.S., at 556–557, but that he could prevent others from copying his "subjective descriptions and portraits of public figures." Id., at 563. Where the compilation author adds no written expression but rather lets the facts speak for themselves, the expressive element is more elusive. The only conceivable expression is the manner in which the compiler has selected and arranged the facts. Thus, if the selection and arrangement are original, these elements of the work are eligible for copyright protection. See Patry, Copyright in Compilations of Facts (or Why the "White Pages" Are Not Copyrightable), 12 Com. & Law 37, 64 (Dec. 1990) (hereinafter Patry). No matter how original the format, however, the facts themselves do not become original through association. See Patterson & Joyce 776.

This inevitably means that the copyright in a factual compilation is thin. Notwithstanding a valid copyright, a subsequent compiler remains free to use the facts contained in another's publication to aid in preparing a competing work, so long as the competing work does not feature the same selection and arrangement. As one commentator explains it "[N]o matter how much original authorship the work displays, the facts and ideas it exposes are free for the taking. [T]he very same facts and ideas may be divorced from the context imposed by the author, and restated or reshuffled by second comers, even if the author was the first to discover the facts or to propose the ideas." Ginsburg 1868.

It may seem unfair that much of the fruit of the compiler's labor may be used by others without compensation. As Justice Brennan has correctly observed, however, this is not "some unforeseen byproduct of a statutory scheme." *Harper & Row*, 471 U.S., at 589 (dissenting opinion). It is, rather, "the essence of copyright," ibid., and a constitutional requirement. The primary objective of copyright is not to reward the labor of authors, but "[t]o promote the Progress of Science and useful Arts." Art. I, § 8, cl. 8. Accord Twentieth Century Music Corp. v. Aiken, 422 U.S. 151, 156 (1975). To this end, copyright assures authors the right to their original expression, but encourages others to build freely upon the ideas and information conveyed by a work. *Harper & Row*, supra, 471 U.S. at 556–557. This principle, known as the idea/expression or fact/expression dichotomy, applies to all works of authorship. As applied to a factual compilation, assuming the absence of original written expression, only the compiler's selection and arrangement may be protected; the raw facts may be copied at will. This result is neither unfair nor unfortunate. It is the means by which copyright advances the progress of science and art.

This Court has long recognized that the fact/expression dichotomy limits severely the scope of protection in fact-based works. More than a century ago, the Court observed: "The very object of publishing a book on science or the useful arts is to communicate to the world the useful knowledge which it contains. But this object would be frustrated if the knowledge could not be used without incurring the guilt of piracy of the book." Baker v. Selden, 101 U.S. 99, 103 (1880). We reiterated this point in *Harper & Row*.

"[N]o author may copyright facts or ideas. The copyright is limited to those aspects of the work—termed 'expression'—that display the stamp of the author's originality.

"[C]opyright does not prevent subsequent users from copying from a prior author's work those constituent elements that are not original—for example . . . facts, or materials in the public domain—as long as such use does not unfairly appropriate the author's original contributions." 471 U.S., at 547–548 (citation omitted).

This, then, resolves the doctrinal tension: Copyright treats facts and factual compilations in a wholly consistent manner. Facts, whether alone or as part of a compilation, are not original and therefore may not be copyrighted. A factual compilation is eligible for copyright if it features an original selection or arrangement of facts, but the copyright is limited to the particular selection or arrangement. In no event may copyright extend to the facts themselves.

B

As we have explained, originality is a constitutionally mandated prerequisite for copyright protection. The Court's decisions announcing this rule predate the Copyright Act of 1909, but ambiguous language in the 1909 Act caused some lower courts temporarily to lose sight of this requirement.

The 1909 Act embodied the originality requirement, but not as clearly as it might have. See Nimmer § 2.01. The subject matter of copyright was set out in § 3 and § 4 of the Act. Section 4 stated that copyright was available to "all the writings of an author." 35 Stat. 1076. By using the words "writings" and "author"—the same words used in Article I, § 8 of the Constitution and defined by the Court in *The Trade–Mark Cases* and *Burrow–Giles*—the statute necessarily incorporated the originality requirement articulated in the Court's decisions. It did so implicitly, however, thereby leaving room for error.

Section 3 was similarly ambiguous. It stated that the copyright in a work protected only "the copyrightable component parts of the work." It thus stated an important copyright principle, but failed to identify the specific characteristic—originality—that determined which component parts of a work were copyrightable and which were not.

Most courts construed the 1909 Act correctly, notwithstanding the less-than-perfect statutory language. They understood from this Court's decisions that there could be no copyright without originality. See Patterson & Joyce 760–761. As explained in the Nimmer treatise: "The 1909 Act neither defined originality, nor even expressly required that a work be 'original' in order to command protection. However, the courts uniformly inferred the requirement from the fact that copyright protection may only be claimed by 'authors'. . . . It was reasoned that since an author is 'the . . . creator, originator' it follows that a work is not the product of an author unless the work is original." Nimmer § 2.01 (footnotes omitted) (citing cases).

But some courts misunderstood the statute. See, e.g., Leon v. Pacific Telephone & Telegraph Co., 91 F.2d 484 (CA9 1937); Jeweler's Circular

Publishing Co. v. Keystone Publishing Co., 281 F. 83 (CA2 1922). These courts ignored § 3 and § 4, focusing their attention instead on § 5 of the Act. Section 5, however, was purely technical in nature: it provided that a person seeking to register a work should indicate on the application the type of work, and it listed 14 categories under which the work might fall. One of these categories was "[b]ooks, including composite and cyclopaedic works, directories, gazetteers, and other compilations." § 5(a). Section 5 did not purport to say that all compilations were automatically copyrightable. Indeed, it expressly disclaimed any such function, pointing out that "the subject-matter of copyright [i]s defined in section four." Nevertheless, the fact that factual compilations were mentioned specifically in § 5 led some courts to infer erroneously that directories and the like were copyrightable *per se,* "without any further or precise showing of original—personal—authorship." Ginsburg 1895.

Making matters worse, these courts developed a new theory to justify the protection of factual compilations. Known alternatively as "sweat of the brow" or "industrious collection," the underlying notion was that copyright was a reward for the hard work that went into compiling facts. The classic formulation of the doctrine appeared in Jeweler's Circular Publishing Co., 281 F., at 88:

> "The right to copyright a book upon which one has expended labor in its preparation does not depend upon whether the materials which he has collected consist or not of matters which are publici juris, or whether such materials show literary skill *or originality,* either in thought or in language, or anything more than industrious collection. The man who goes through the streets of a town and puts down the names of each of the inhabitants, with their occupations and their street number, acquires material of which he is the author" (emphasis added).

The "sweat of the brow" doctrine had numerous flaws, the most glaring being that it extended copyright protection in a compilation beyond selection and arrangement—the compiler's original contributions—to the facts themselves. Under the doctrine, the only defense to infringement was independent creation. A subsequent compiler was "not entitled to take one word of information previously published," but rather had to "independently wor[k] out the matter for himself, so as to arrive at the same result from the same common sources of information." Id., at 88–89 (internal quotations omitted). "Sweat of the brow" courts thereby eschewed the most fundamental axiom of copyright law—that no one may copyright facts or ideas. See Miller v. Universal City Studios, Inc., 650 F.2d at 1372 (criticizing "sweat of the brow" courts because "ensur[ing] that later writers obtain the facts independently . . . is precisely the scope of protection given . . . copyrighted matter, and the law is clear that facts are not entitled to such protection").

Decisions of this Court applying the 1909 Act make clear that the statute did not permit the "sweat of the brow" approach. The best example is International News Service v. Associated Press, 248 U.S. 215 (1918). In that decision, the Court stated unambiguously that the 1909 Act conferred copyright protection only on those elements of a work that were original to the author. International News Service had conceded taking news reported by Associated Press and publishing it in its own newspapers. Recognizing that § 5 of the Act specifically mentioned "[p]eriodicals, including newspapers," § 5(b), the Court acknowledged that news articles were copyrightable. Id., at 234. It flatly rejected, however, the notion that the copyright in an article extended to the factual information it contained. "[T]he news element—the information respecting current events contained in the literary production—is not the creation of the writer, but is a report of matters that ordinarily are *publici juris;* it is the history of the day." Ibid.*

Without a doubt, the "sweat of the brow" doctrine flouted basic copyright principles. Throughout history, copyright law has "recognize[d] a greater need to disseminate factual works than works of fiction or fantasy." *Harper & Row,* 471 U.S., at 563. Accord Gorman, Fact or Fancy: The Implications for Copyright, 29 J. Copyright Soc. 560, 563 (1982). But "sweat of the brow" courts took a contrary view; they handed out proprietary interests in facts and declared that authors are absolutely precluded from saving time and effort by relying upon the facts contained in prior works. In truth, "[i]t is just such wasted effort that the proscription against the copyright of ideas and facts, . . . [is] designed to prevent." Rosemont Enterprises, Inc. v. Random House, Inc., 366 F.2d 303, 310 (CA2 1966), cert. denied 385 U.S. 1009 (1967). "Protection for the fruits of such research . . . may in certain circumstances be available under a theory of unfair competition. But to accord copyright protection on this basis alone distorts basic copyright principles in that it creates a monopoly in public domain materials without the necessary justification of protecting and encouraging the creation of 'writings' by 'authors.' " Nimmer § 3.04, p. 3–23 (footnote omitted).

C

"Sweat of the brow" decisions did not escape the attention of the Copyright Office. When Congress decided to overhaul the copyright statute and asked the Copyright Office to study existing problems, see Mills Music, Inc. v. Snyder, 469 U.S. 153, 159 (1985), the Copyright Office promptly recommended that Congress clear up the confusion in the lower courts as to the basic standards of copyrightability. The Register of Copyrights explained in his first report to Congress that "originality" was a "basic requisit[e]" of copyright under the 1909 Act, but that "the absence of any reference to [originality] in the statute seems to have led to misconceptions as to what is copyrightable matter." Report of the Register of Copyrights on the General Revision of the U.S. Copyright Law, 87th Cong., 1st Sess., p. 9 (H. Judiciary Comm. Print 1961). The Register suggested making the originality requirement explicit. Ibid.

Congress took the Register's advice. In enacting the Copyright Act of 1976, Congress dropped the reference to "all the writings of an author" and replaced it with the phrase "original works of authorship." 17 U.S.C. § 102(a).

---

*. The Court ultimately rendered judgment for Associated Press on noncopyright grounds that are not relevant here. See 248 U.S., at 235, 241–242.

In making explicit the originality requirement, Congress announced that it was merely clarifying existing law: "The two fundamental criteria of copyright protection [are] originality and fixation in tangible form. . . . The phrase 'original works of authorship,' which is purposely left undefined, is intended to incorporate without change *the standard of originality established by the courts under the present [1909] copyright statute.*" H.R. Rep. No. 94–1476, p. 51 (1976) (emphasis added) (hereinafter H.R.Rep.); S. Rep. No. 94–473, p. 50 (1975), U.S. Code Cong. & Admin. News 1976, pp. 5659, 5664 (emphasis added) (hereinafter S. Rep.). This sentiment was echoed by the Copyright Office. "Our intention here is to maintain the *established standards* of originality . . . ." Supplementary Report of the Register of Copyrights on the General Revision of U.S. Copyright Law, 89th Cong., 1st Sess., Part 6, p. 3 (H. Judiciary Comm. Print 1965) (emphasis added).

To ensure that the mistakes of the "sweat of the brow" courts would not be repeated, Congress took additional measures. For example, § 3 of the 1909 Act had stated that copyright protected only the "copyrightable component parts" of a work, but had not identified originality as the basis for distinguishing those component parts that were copyrightable from those that were not. The 1976 Act deleted this section and replaced it with § 102(b), which identifies specifically those elements of a work for which copyright is not available: "In no case does copyright protection for an original work of authorship extend to any idea, procedure, process, system, method of operation, concept, principle, or discovery, regardless of the form in which it is described, explained, illustrated, or embodied in such work." Section 102(b) is universally understood to prohibit any copyright in facts. *Harper & Row,* supra, at 547, 556. Accord Nimmer § 2.03[E] (equating facts with "discoveries"). As with § 102(a), Congress emphasized that § 102(b) did not change the law, but merely clarified it. "Section 102(b) in no way enlarges or contracts the scope of copyright protection under the present law. Its purpose is to restate . . . that the basic dichotomy between expression and idea remains unchanged." H.R. Rep., at 57; S. Rep., at 54, U.S. Code Cong. & Admin. News 1976, p. 5670.

Congress took another step to minimize confusion by deleting the specific mention of "directories . . . and other compilations" in § 5 of the 1909 Act. As mentioned, this section had led some courts to conclude that directories were copyrightable *per se* and that every element of a directory was protected. In its place, Congress enacted two new provisions. First, to make clear that compilations were not copyrightable *per se,* Congress provided a definition of the term "compilation." Second, to make clear that the copyright in a compilation did not extend to the facts themselves, Congress enacted 17 U.S.C. § 103.

The definition of "compilation" is found in § 101 of the 1976 Act. It defines a "compilation" in the copyright sense as "a work formed by the collection and assembly of preexisting materials or of data *that* are selected, coordinated, or arranged *in such a way that* the resulting work as a whole constitutes an original work of authorship" (emphasis added).

The purpose of the statutory definition is to emphasize that collections of facts are not copyrightable *per se.* It conveys this message through its tripartite structure, as emphasized above by the italics. The statute identifies three distinct elements and requires each to be met for a work to qualify as a copyrightable compilation: (1) the collection and assembly of pre-existing material, facts, or data; (2) the selection, coordination, or arrangement of those materials; and (3) the creation, by virtue of the particular selection, coordination, or arrangement, of an "original" work of authorship. "[T]his tripartite conjunctive structure is self-evident, and should be assumed to 'accurately express the legislative purpose.'" Patry 51, quoting *Mills Music,* 469 U.S., at 164.

At first glance, the first requirement does not seem to tell us much. It merely describes what one normally thinks of as a compilation—a collection of pre-existing material, facts, or data. What makes it significant is that it is not the *sole* requirement. It is not enough for copyright purposes that an author collects and assembles facts. To satisfy the statutory definition, the work must get over two additional hurdles. In this way, the plain language indicates that not every collection of facts receives copyright protection. Otherwise, there would be a period after "data."

The third requirement is also illuminating. It emphasizes that a compilation, like any other work, is copyrightable only if it satisfies the originality requirement ("an *original* work of authorship"). Although § 102 states plainly that the originality requirement applies to all works, the point was emphasized with regard to compilations to ensure that courts would not repeat the mistake of the "sweat of the brow" courts by concluding that fact-based works are treated differently and measured by some other standard. As Congress explained it, the goal was to "make plain that the criteria of copyrightable subject matter stated in section 102 apply with full force to works . . . containing preexisting material." H.R. Rep., at 57; S. Rep., at 55, U.S. Code Cong. & Admin. News 1976, p. 5670.

The key to the statutory definition is the second requirement. It instructs courts that, in determining whether a fact-based work is an original work of authorship, they should focus on the manner in which the collected facts have been selected, coordinated, and arranged. This is a straight-forward application of the originality requirement. Facts are never original, so the compilation author can claim originality, if at all, only in the way the facts are presented. To that end, the statute dictates that the principal focus should be on whether the selection, coordination, and arrangement are sufficiently original to merit protection.

Not every selection, coordination, or arrangement will pass muster. This is plain from the statute. It states that, to merit protection, the facts must be selected, coordinated, or arranged "in such a way" as to render the work as a whole original. This implies that some "ways" will trigger copyright, but that others will not. See Patry 57, and n. 76. Otherwise, the phrase "in such a way" is meaningless and Congress should have defined "compilation" simply as "a work formed by the collection and assembly of preexisting materials or data that are selected, coordinated, or arranged." That Congress did not do so is dispositive. In accordance with "the established principle that a court should give effect, if possible, to every clause and word of a statute," Moskal v. United States, 498 U.S. 103, 109 (internal quotations omitted), we conclude that the statute envisions that there will be some fact-based works in which the selection, coordination, and arrangement are not sufficiently original to trigger copyright protection.

As discussed earlier, however, the originality requirement is not particularly stringent. A compiler may settle upon a selection or arrangement that others have used; novelty is not required. Originality requires only that the author make the selection or arrangement independently (*i.e.*, without copying that selection or arrangement from another work), and that it display some minimal level of creativity. Presumably, the vast majority of compilations will pass this test, but not all will. There remains a narrow category of works in which the creative spark is utterly lacking or so trivial as to be virtually nonexistent. See generally Bleistein v. Donaldson Lithographing Co., 188 U.S. 239, 251 (1903) (referring to "the narrowest and most obvious limits"). Such works are incapable of sustaining a valid copyright. Nimmer § 2.01[B].

Even if a work qualifies as a copyrightable compilation, it receives only limited protection. This is the point of § 103 of the Act. Section 103 explains that "[t]he subject matter of copyright . . . includes compilations," § 103(a), but that copyright protects only the author's original contributions—not the facts or information conveyed:

> "The copyright in a compilation . . . extends only to the material contributed by the author of such work, as distinguished from the preexisting material employed in the work, and does not imply any exclusive right in the preexisting material." § 103(b).

As § 103 makes clear, copyright is not a tool by which a compilation author may keep others from using the facts or data he or she has collected. "The most important point here is one that is commonly misunderstood today: copyright . . . has no effect one way or the other on the copyright or public domain status of the preexisting material." H.R. Rep., at 57; S. Rep., at 55, U.S. Code Cong. & Admin. News 1976, p. 5670. The 1909 Act did not require, as "sweat of the brow" courts mistakenly assumed, that each subsequent compiler must start from scratch and is precluded from relying on research undertaken by another. See, e.g., *Jeweler's Circular Publishing Co.,* 281 F., at 88–89. Rather, the facts contained in existing works may be freely copied because copyright protects only the elements that owe their origin to the compiler—the selection, coordination, and arrangement of facts.

In summary, the 1976 revisions to the Copyright Act leave no doubt that originality, not "sweat of the brow," is the touchstone of copyright protection in directories and other fact-based works. Nor is there any doubt that the same was true under the 1909 Act. The 1976 revisions were a direct response to the Copyright Office's concern that many lower courts had misconstrued this basic principle, and Congress emphasized repeatedly that the purpose of the revisions was to clarify, not change, existing law. The revisions explain with painstaking clarity that copyright requires originality, § 102(a); that facts are never original, § 102(b); that the copyright in a compilation does not extend to the facts it contains, § 103(b); and that a compilation is copyrightable only to the extent that it features an original selection, coordination, or arrangement, § 101.

The 1976 revisions have proven largely successful in steering courts in the right direction. A good example is Miller v. Universal City Studios, Inc., 650 F.2d, at 1369–1370: "A copyright in a directory . . . is properly viewed as resting on the originality of the selection and arrangement of the factual material, rather than on the industriousness of the efforts to develop the information. Copyright protection does not extend to the facts themselves, and the mere use of information contained in a directory without a substantial copying of the format does not constitute infringement" (citation omitted). Additionally, the Second Circuit, which almost 70 years ago issued the classic formulation of the "sweat of the brow" doctrine in *Jeweler's Circular Publishing Co.,* has now fully repudiated the reasoning of that decision. See, e.g., Financial Information, Inc. v. Moody's Investors Service, Inc., 808 F.2d 204, 207 (CA2 1986), cert. denied, 484 U.S. 820 (1987); Financial Information, Inc. v. Moody's Investors Service, Inc., 751 F.2d 501, 510 (CA2 1984) (Newman, J., concurring); Hoehling v. Universal City Studios, Inc., 618 F.2d 972, 979 (CA2 1980). Even those scholars who believe that "industrious collection" should be rewarded seem to recognize that this is beyond the scope of existing copyright law. See Denicola 516 ("the very vocabulary of copyright is ill suited to analyzing property rights in works of non-fiction"); id., at 520–521, 525; Ginsburg 1867, 1870.

III

There is no doubt that Feist took from the white pages of Rural's directory a substantial amount of factual information. At a minimum, Feist copied the names, towns, and telephone numbers of 1,309 of Rural's subscribers. Not all copying, however, is copyright infringement. To establish infringement, two elements must be proven: (1) ownership of a valid copyright, and (2) copying of constituent elements of the work that are original. See *Harper & Row,* 471 U.S., at 548. The first element is not at issue here; Feist appears to concede that Rural's directory, considered as a whole, is subject to a valid copyright because it contains some foreword text, as well as original material in its yellow pages advertisements. See Brief for Petitioner 18; Pet. for Cert. 9.

The question is whether Rural has proved the second element. In other words, did Feist, by taking 1,309 names, towns, and telephone numbers from Rural's white pages, copy anything that was "original" to Rural? Certainly, the raw data does not satisfy the originality requirement. Rural may have been the first to discover and report the names, towns, and telephone numbers of its subscribers, but this data does not " 'ow[e] its origin' " to Rural. *Burrow–Giles,* 111 U.S., at 58. Rather, these bits of information are uncopyrightable facts; they existed before Rural reported them and would have continued to exist if Rural had never published a telephone directory. The originality requirement "rule[s] out protecting . . . names, addresses, and telephone numbers of which the plaintiff by no stretch of the imagination could be called the author." Patterson & Joyce 776.

Rural essentially concedes the point by referring to the names, towns, and telephone numbers as "preexisting material." Brief for Respondent 17. Section 103(b) states explicitly that the copyright in a compilation does not extend to "the preexisting material employed in the work."

The question that remains is whether Rural selected, coordinated, or arranged these uncopyrightable facts in an original way. As mentioned, originality is not a stringent standard; it does not require that facts be presented in an innovative or surprising way. It is equally true, however, that the selection and arrangement of facts cannot be so mechanical or routine as to require no creativity whatsoever. The standard of originality is low, but it does exist. See Patterson & Joyce 760, n. 144 ("While this requirement is sometimes characterized as modest, or a low threshold, it is not without effect") (internal quotations omitted; citations omitted). As this Court has explained, the Constitution mandates some minimal degree of creativity, see The Trade-Mark Cases, 100 U.S., at 94; and an author who claims infringement must prove "the existence of . . . intellectual production, of thought, and conception." *Burrow–Giles,* supra, 111 U.S., at 59–60.

The selection, coordination, and arrangement of Rural's white pages do not satisfy the minimum constitutional standards for copyright protection. As mentioned at the outset, Rural's white pages are entirely typical. Persons desiring telephone service in Rural's service area fill out an application and Rural issues them a telephone number. In preparing its white pages, Rural simply takes the data provided by its subscribers and lists it alphabetically by surname. The end product is a garden-variety white pages directory, devoid of even the slightest trace of creativity.

Rural's selection of listings could not be more obvious: it publishes the most basic information—name, town, and telephone number—about each person who applies to it for telephone service. This is "selection" of a sort, but it lacks the modicum of creativity necessary to transform mere selection into copyrightable expression. Rural expended sufficient effort to make the white pages directory useful, but insufficient creativity to make it original.

We note in passing that the selection featured in Rural's white pages may also fail the originality requirement for another reason. Feist points out that Rural did not truly "select" to publish the names and telephone numbers of its subscribers; rather, it was required to do so by the Kansas Corporation Commission as part of its monopoly franchise. See 737 F.Supp., at 612. Accordingly, one could plausibly conclude that this selection was dictated by state law, not by Rural.

Nor can Rural claim originality in its coordination and arrangement of facts. The white pages do nothing more than list Rural's subscribers in alphabetical order. This arrangement may, technically speaking, owe its origin to Rural; no one disputes that Rural undertook the task of alphabetizing the names itself. But there is nothing remotely creative about arranging names alphabetically in a white pages directory. It is an age-old practice, firmly rooted in tradition and so commonplace that it has come to be expected as a matter of course. See Brief for Information Industry Association et al. as *Amici Curiae* 10 (alphabetical arrangement "is universally observed in directories published by local exchange telephone companies"). It is not only unoriginal, it is practically inevitable. This time-honored tradition does not possess the minimal creative spark required by the Copyright Act and the Constitution.

We conclude that the names, towns, and telephone numbers copied by Feist were not original to Rural and therefore were not protected by the copyright in Rural's combined white and yellow pages directory. As a constitutional matter, copyright protects only those constituent elements of a work that possess more than a *de minimis* quantum of creativity. Rural's white pages, limited to basic subscriber information and arranged alphabetically, fall short of the mark. As a statutory matter, 17 U.S.C. § 101 does not afford protection from copying to a collection of facts that are selected, coordinated, and arranged in a way that utterly lacks originality. Given that some works must fail, we cannot imagine a more likely candidate. Indeed, were we to hold that Rural's white pages pass muster, it is hard to believe that any collection of facts could fail.

Because Rural's white pages lack the requisite originality, Feist's use of the listings cannot constitute infringement. This decision should not be construed as demeaning Rural's efforts in compiling its directory, but rather as making clear that copyright rewards originality, not effort. As this Court noted more than a century ago, " 'great praise may be due to the plaintiffs for their industry and enterprise in publishing this paper, yet the law does not contemplate their being rewarded in this way.' " *Baker v. Selden,* 101 U.S., at 105.

The judgment of the Court of Appeals is

Reversed.

NOTES

1. Lloyd Weinreb has written of the *Feist* opinion that "The Court's references to the past and its reasoning in *Feist* have the ring of authenticity; but they are mostly made up. * * * More generally, the Court's statement that originality implicates creativity, albeit only 'a slight amount,' was not supported by anything in prior law, although the Court tried to suggest otherwise." Lloyd Weinreb, Copyright for Functional Expression, 111 Harv. L. Rev. 1149, 1196 (1998). The opinion is also criticized in Paul J. Heald, The Vices of Originality, 1991 Supreme Ct. Rev. 143.

Before *Feist*, the originality requirement was understood to be only a requirement that a work must have originated with an author, i.e. to be the work of the author claiming copyright and not the work of someone or something else. The issue in *Burrow-Giles* was whether because a photograph is produced by a camera it originates with the photographer or with the camera. The Court held the photographer, reasoning that the camera is simply a tool that the photographer uses. In the *Trademark cases,* the issue was whether the constitutionality of a federal statute relating to trademarks could be upheld as an exercise of Congressional power under the copyright and patent clause. The Court held that it could not on the ground that trademarks need not originate with an author, but must only be adopted and used.

2. In light of the fact that the statute requires that a protected work be original (§ 102), why did the Court consider it appropriate to reach and emphasize that the originality it was demanding is a Constitutional requirement? Is it because the Court understood that the accepted meaning of originality in the statute did not meet what in its view is the Constitutional requirement? Congress' different understanding of the requirement is documented in depth in Russ VerSteeg, Sparks in the Tinderbox: *Feist*, "Creativity," and the Legislative History of the 1976 Copyright Act, 56 Univ. of Pitt. L. Rev. 549 (1995).

3. Although the *Feist* opinion makes it clear that the originality requirement includes a requirement of some creativity, it did not clarify what that requirement is other than to observe that the requirement is "not particularly stringent." Is *Feist* an opinion about copyright in telephone white pages, or does it have broader implications? The problem for the lower courts has been to determine exactly what kinds of works are uncopyrightable because they lack sufficient creativity. See Key Publications, Inc. v. Chinatown Today Publishing Enters., Inc., 945 F.2d 509 (2d Cir. 1991) (selective yellow pages copyrightable); BellSouth Advertising & Publishing Corp. v. Donnelly Information Publishing, Inc., 999 F.2d 1436 (11th Cir. 1993) (en banc) (yellow pages not copyrightable); Warren Pub. v. Microdos Data Corp., 115 F. 3d 1509 (11th Cir. 1997) (directory of cable companies not copyrightable); and Transwestern Pub. v. Multimedia Marketing Assoc., 133 F. 3d 773 (10th Cir. 1998) (yellow pages not copyrightable); Entertainment Research Group, Inc. v. Genesis Creative Group, Inc., 122 F.3d 1211 (9th Cir. 1997), *cert. den.* 118 S.Ct. 1302 (1998) (walk-around, inflatable costumes approximately eight feet high of commercial cartoon characters such as the Pillsbury Doughboy or Cap'n Crunch lack sufficient originality).

West successfully sued Mead Data for copyright infringement when it proposed to introduce "star pagination" showing West Report page numbers into its LEXIS database service. West Publishing Co. v. Mead Data Central, Inc., 799 F.2d 1219 (8th Cir. 1986), decided prior to the *Feist* decision. The page numbers are a consequence of formatting and sequencing decisions in the course of assembling the reports. Do the page numbers embody enough originality under *Feist* to be copyrightable?

4. Because of the uncertainty thrown over copyrights in directories and other factual compilations such as databases by the *Feist* opinion, their publishers are seeking legislation in Congress, requiring customers to agree to contractual restrictions on their use of the information (see the *ProCD* opinion in Chapter 4) and asserting the *INS* appropriation cause of action. If a work is uncopyrightable under the *Feist* originality standard, does that mean that state law protection is not preempted because the work does not fall within the scope of the copyright statute? Or does it mean that state law cannot provide protection against copying because the copyright act incorporates a policy that the work should be freely copyable?

5. What is the role of the four fictional entries in the Rural telephone directory that Rural had inserted into its directory to detect copying? Since they were made up, they were surely creative. Didn't Feist infringe those entries by copying them? The trial court did not grant summary judgment on that ground, so it was not before the Supreme Court. Although infringement of four out of more than a thousand copied entries might sound unimportant, if it is copyright infringement it could give the copyright owner significant tactical advantage. If the work containing the four entries were infringing because of the entries, it might be necessary to destroy all the existing copies and start over with the design and production of the directory. Because of this possibility as well as the possibility that erroneous entries make it easy to prove copying, it has long been common for authors of factual works to introduce copying traps such as erroneous or arbitrary entries. (And in many cases, inadvertent errors copied by the defendant perform the same function.) For instance in Rockford Map Publishers, Inc. v. Directory Service Company of Colorado, Inc., 768 F.2d 145 (7th Cir. 1985), the plaintiff was a publisher of plat maps, compiled from land records, that showed the owners of the parcels on the map. The middle initials of the owners of a series of parcels were altered to spell out "ROCKFORD MAP INC." Does the introduction of a few such traps provide effective protection against a slavish appropriation of the factual work? Or would a Court simply say that this is a trivial amount of copying of no legal significance? Does effective protection of a factual work depend on how much erroneous information it contains?

6. And what of the copyrightability of photographs? The photograph held copyrightable in Burrow-Giles Lithographic Co. v. Sarony, 111 U.S. 53 (1884), cited by the Court, was a posed photograph of Oscar Wilde. The court below found that the photograph was the result of the photographer's "original mental conception, to which he gave visible form by posing the draperies, and other various accessories in said photograph, arranging the subject so as to present graceful outlines, arranging and disposing the light and shade, suggesting and evoking the desired expression, and from such disposition, arrangement, or representation, made entirely by plaintiff, he produced the picture in suit." The Court expressed no opinion on the copyrightability of the "ordinary production of a photograph."

But suppose a photographer simply lifts the camera and shoots. Indeed, suppose he shoots hundreds if not thousands of times, each shot faithfully recording the fact of the light pattern captured by the lens. And then one of those photographs turns out for some reason to be of value? Time, Inc. v. Bernard Geis Assoc., 293 F. Supp. 130 (S.D.N.Y. 1968), involved a movie of the assassination of President Kennedy taken by an amateur bystander with his home movie camera, who was photographing the passing procession. (For those who have followed the lore about the Kennedy assassination, this was the famous Zapruder movie which enabled analysts, by analyzing it frame by frame, to reach certain precise conclusions about the chain of events.) The court concluded that the movie was copyrightable, an easy decision to reach under the pre-*Feist* precedents.

Los Angeles New Service v. Reuters Television Int'l, 942 F. Supp. 1265 (C.D. Cal. 1996), involved video footage of the 1992 Los Angeles riots, including the Reginald Denny beating, which the plaintiff, a free-lance news gathering organization, had captured from its helicopter. The opinion, discussed below in connection with fair use, accepted (the issue appears to have been uncontested—the defendants were themselves news organizations) that the video tapes were copyrightable original works, and explicitly referred to the need to create an incentive for investments in a news-gathering organization that could capture such events. But isn't this simply the sweat of the brow theory?

B. Infringement

As the materials in the previous section illustrate, Congress has imposed few limits on copyrightable subject matter. To conclude that a work is copyrightable, however, says little about the scope of the protection actually conferred. In this section we turn to the issue of what uses of the copyrighted work infringe, i.e. what uses are in violation of the rights conferred by the statute?

Whether or not a work protected by copyright has been infringed depends on three questions.

1. Has one of the exclusive rights of the copyright owner been violated?

The copyright law does not give to the copyright owner the exclusive right to control all uses of his work. An infringer must have made some use which is within the scope of the exclusive rights conferred by § 106. To illustrate, you will be relieved to know that you are not infringing the copyright on this book by reading it. There is no exclusive right to read.

2. Is the use of the work of a type that infringes the copyright?

In brief, an infringement must have been taken from the copyrighted work and must constitute a taking of the protected elements of the work.

3. Is the use authorized by a provision of §§ 107 through 118?

The scope of the exclusive rights conferred by § 106 is limited by §§ 107 through 118. An example is the right of an owner of a copy to resell the copy under § 109(a). Another example is the doctrine of fair use, now codified in § 107. For example, if you write into your notes verbatim short passages from this book, you will have violated § 106(1) because you will have made a copy. But you will not have infringed because that is a classic example of "fair use."

(1) The Exclusive Rights

The exclusive rights of the copyright owner are set out in § 106. In order to understand how they work requires some effort, for the rights of the copyright owner are not intuitive. This section provides an introduction to these rights, but it does not contain enough material to permit you to master how the concepts actually work. Your understanding should improve as you study the cases in subsequent sections.

The reason that the rights are difficult to understand is that they have no spatial dimension. In contrast, the exclusive right of an owner of real or personal property can be understood in terms of the owner's exclusive right to exclude others from the three-dimensional space occupied by the property. Copyright has no existence in three-dimensional space. To take the example of the copyright in a book, the paradigmatic copyrightable subject matter, the physical book is not the subject of the copyright, it is only a copy of the copyrighted work. The copyright is that set of rights conferred on its owner in the copyrighted work, which must be fixed in a "tangible medium of expression" (§ 102) but which is not the tangible medium of expression. You might think of the six exclusive rights created by § 106 as existing in the fourth through tenth dimensions.

The first five exclusive rights, set out in the 1976 Act were explained in House Report 94–1476. The sixth exclusive right was added in 1995 in response to technological changes making digital transmission possible.

House Report No. 94–1476
Pages 61–65.

Section 106. Exclusive Rights in Copyrighted Works

General Scope of Copyright

The five fundamental rights that the bill gives to copyright owners—the exclusive rights of reproduction, adaptation, publication, performance, and display—are stated generally in section 106. These exclusive rights, which comprise the so-called "bundle of rights" that is a copyright, are cumulative and may overlap in some cases. * * *

The approach of the bill is to set forth the copyright owner's exclusive rights in broad terms in section 106, and then to provide various limitations, qualifications, or exemptions in the 12 sections that follow. Thus, everything in section 106 is made "subject to sections 107 through 118," and must be read in conjunction with those provisions. [Sections 119 to 121 were added in later amendments to the 1976 act.]

The exclusive rights accorded to a copyright owner under section 106 are "to do and to authorize" any of the activities specified in the five numbered clauses. Use of the phrase "to authorize" is intended to avoid any questions as to the liability of contributory infringers. For example, a person who lawfully acquires an authorized copy of a motion picture would be an infringer if he or she engages in the business of renting it to others for purposes of unauthorized public performance.

Rights of Reproduction, Adaptation, and Publication

The first three clauses of section 106, which cover all rights under a copyright except those of performance and display, extend to every kind of copyrighted work. The exclusive rights encompassed by these clauses, though closely related, are independent; they can generally be characterized as rights of copying, recording, adaptation, and publishing. A single act of infringement may violate all of these rights at once, as where a publisher reproduces, adapts, and sells copies of a person's copyrighted work as part of a publishing venture. Infringement takes place when any one of the rights is violated: where, for example, a printer reproduces copies without selling them or a retailer sells copies without having anything to do with their reproduction. The references to "copies or phonorecords," although in the plural, are intended here and throughout the bill to include the singular (1 U.S.C. § 1).

Reproduction.—Read together with the relevant definitions in section 101, the right "to reproduce the copyrighted work in copies or phonorecords" means the right to produce a material object in which the work is duplicated, transcribed, imitated, or simulated in a fixed form from which it can be "perceived, reproduced, or otherwise communicated, either directly or with the aid of a machine or device." As under the present law, a copyrighted work would be infringed by reproducing it in whole or in any substantial part, and by duplicating it exactly or by imitation or simulation. Wide departures or variations from the copyrighted works would still be an infringement as long as the author's "expression" rather than merely the author's "ideas" are taken. An exception to this general principle, applicable to the reproduction of copyrighted sound recordings, is specified in section 114.

"Reproduction" under clause (1) of section 106 is to be distinguished from "display" under clause (5). For a work to be "reproduced," its fixation in tangible form must be "sufficiently permanent or stable to permit it to be perceived, reproduced, or otherwise communicated for a period of more than transitory duration." Thus, the showing of images on a screen or tube would not be a violation of clause (1), although it might come within the scope of clause (5).

Preparation of Derivative Works.—The exclusive right to prepare derivative works, specified separately in clause (2) of section 106, overlaps the exclusive right of reproduction to some extent. It is broader than that right, however, in the sense that reproduction requires fixation in copies or phonorecords, whereas the preparation of a derivative work, such as a ballet, pantomime, or improvised performance, may be an infringement even though nothing is ever fixed in tangible form.

To be an infringement the "derivative work" must be "based upon the copyrighted work," and the definition in section 101 refers to "a translation, musical arrangement, dramatization, fictionalization, motion picture version, sound recording, art reproduction, abridgment, condensation, or any other form in which a work may be recast, transformed, or adapted." Thus, to constitute a violation of section 106(2), the infringing work must incorporate a portion of the copyrighted work in some form; for example, a detailed commentary on a work or a programmatic musical composition inspired by a novel would not normally constitute infringements under this clause.

* * *

Public Distribution.—Clause (3) of section 106 establishes the exclusive right of publication: The right "to distribute copies or phonorecords of the copyrighted work to the public by sale or other transfer of ownership, or by rental, lease, or lending." Under this provision the copyright owner would have the right to control the first public distribution of an authorized copy or phonorecord of his work, whether by sale, gift, loan, or some rental or lease arrangement. Likewise, any unauthorized public distribution of copies or phonorecords that were unlawfully made would be an infringement. As section 109 makes clear, however, the copyright owner's rights under section 106(3) cease with respect to a particular copy or phonorecord once he has parted with ownership of it.

Rights of Public Performance and Display

Performing Rights and the "For Profit" Limitation.—The right of public performance under section 106(4) extends to "literary, musical, dramatic, and choreographic works, pantomimes, and motion pictures and other audiovisual works and sound recordings" and, unlike the equivalent provisions now in effect, is not limited by any "for profit" requirement. The approach of the bill, as in many foreign laws, is first to state the public performance right in broad terms, and then to provide specific exemptions for educational and other nonprofit uses.

This approach is more reasonable than the outright exemption of the 1909 statute. The line between commercial and "nonprofit" organizations is increasingly difficult to draw. Many "non-profit" organizations are highly subsidized and capable of paying royalties, and the widespread public exploitation of copyrighted works by public broadcasters and other noncommercial organizations is likely to grow. In addition to these trends, it is worth noting that performances and displays are continuing to supplant markets for printed copies and that in the future a broad "not for profit" exemption could not only hurt authors but could dry up their incentive to write.

The exclusive right of public performance is expanded to include not only motion pictures, including works [such as] records on film, video tape, and video disks, but also audiovisual works such as filmstrips and sets of slides. This provision of section 106(4), which is consistent with the assimilation of motion pictures to audiovisual works throughout the bill, is also related to amendments of the definitions of "display" and "perform" discussed below. The important issue of performing rights in sound recordings is discussed in connection with section 114.

Right of Public Display.—Clause (5) of section 106 represents the first explicit statutory recognition in American copyright law of an exclusive right to show a copyrighted work, or an image of it, to the public. The existence or extent of this right under the present statute is uncertain and subject to challenge. The bill would give the owners of copyright in "literary, musical, dramatic, and choreographic works, pantomimes, and pictorial, graphic, or sculptural works", including the individual images of a motion picture or other audiovisual work, the exclusive right "to display the copyrighted work publicly."

Definitions

Under the definitions of "perform," "display," "publicly," and "transmit" in section 101, the concepts of public performance and public display cover not only the initial rendition or showing, but also any further act by which that rendition or showing is transmitted or communicated to the public. Thus, for example: a singer is performing when he or she sings a song; a broadcasting network is performing when it transmits his or her performance (whether simultaneously or from records); a local broadcaster is performing when it transmits the network broadcast; a cable television system is performing when it retransmits the broadcast to its subscribers; and any individual is performing whenever he or she plays a phonorecord embodying the performance or communicates the performance by turning on a receiving set. Although any act by which the initial performance or display is transmitted, repeated, or made to recur would itself be a "performance" or "display" under the bill, it would not be actionable as an infringement unless it were done "publicly," as defined in section 101. Certain other performances and displays, in addition to those that are "private," are exempted or given qualified copyright control under sections 107 through 118.

To "perform" a work, under the definition in section 101, includes reading a literary work aloud, singing or playing music, dancing a ballet or other choreographic work, and acting out a dramatic work or pantomime. A performance may be accomplished "either directly or by means of any device or process," including all kinds of equipment for reproducing or amplifying sounds or visual images, any sort of transmitting apparatus, any type of electronic retrieval system, and any other techniques and systems not yet in use or even invented.

The definition of "perform" in relation to "a motion picture or other audio visual work" is "to show its images in any sequence or to make the sounds accompanying it audible." The showing of portions of a motion picture, filmstrip, or slide set must therefore be sequential to constitute a "performance" rather than a "display", but no particular order need be maintained. The purely aural performance of a motion picture sound track, or of the sound portions of an audiovisual work, would constitute a performance of the "motion picture or other audiovisual work"; but, where some of the sounds have been reproduced separately on phonorecords, a performance from the phonorecord would not constitute performance of the motion picture or audiovisual work.

The corresponding definition of "display" covers any showing of a "copy" of the work, "either directly or by means of a film, slide, television image, or any other device or process." Since "copies" are defined as including the material object "in which the work is first fixed," the right of public display applies to original works of art as well as to reproductions of them. With respect to motion pictures and other audiovisual works, it is a "display" (rather than a "performance") to show their "individual images nonsequentially." In addition to the direct showings of a copy of a work, "display" would include the projection of an image on a screen or other surface by any method, the transmission of an image by electronic or other means, and the showing of an image on a cathode ray tube, or similar viewing apparatus connected with any sort of information storage and retrieval system.

Under clause (1) of the definition of "publicly" in section 101, a performance or display is "public" if it takes place "at a place open to the public or at any place where a substantial number of persons outside of a normal circle of a family and its social acquaintances is gathered." One of the principal purposes of the definition was to make clear that, contrary to the decision in Metro-Goldwyn-Mayer Distributing Corp. v. Wyatt, 21 C.O.Bull. 203 (D.Md. 1932), performances in "semipublic" places such as clubs, lodges, factories, summer camps, and schools are "public performances" subject to copyright control. The term "a family" in this context would include an individual living alone, so that a gathering confined to the individual's social acquaintances would normally be regarded as private. Routine meetings of businesses and governmental personnel would be excluded because they do not represent the gathering of a "substantial number of persons."

Clause (2) of the definition of "publicly" in section 101 makes clear that the concepts of public performance and public display include not only performances and displays that occur initially in a public place, but also acts that transmit or otherwise communicate a performance or display of the work to the public by means of any device or process. The definition of "transmit"—to communicate a performance or display "by any device or process whereby images or sound are received beyond the place from which they are sent"—is broad enough to include all conceivable forms and combinations of wired or wireless communications media, including but by no means limited to radio and television broadcasting as we know them. Each and every method by which the images or sounds comprising a performance or display are picked up and conveyed is a "transmission," and if the transmission reaches the public in * * * [any] form, the case comes within the scope of clauses (4) or (5) of section 106.

Under the bill, as under the present law, a performance made available by transmission to the public at large is "public" even though the recipients are not gathered in a single place, and even if there is no proof that any of the potential recipients was operating his receiving apparatus at the time of the transmission. The same principles apply whenever the potential recipients of the transmission represent a limited segment of the public, such as the occupants of hotel rooms or the subscribers of a cable television service. Clause (2) of the definition of "publicly" is applicable "whether the members of the public capable of receiving the performance or display receive it in the same place or in separate places and at the same time or at different times."

Limitations On the Exclusive Rights

The significance of the exclusive rights is affected in important ways by various limitations contained in sections 107 through 121. These materials provide only an introduction to the more important limitations. Some of them are quite narrow and relatively unimportant, other than to their beneficiaries. (For instance, performance of a nondramatic musical work by a . . . nonprofit agricultural or horticultural organization, in the course of an annual agricultural or horticultural fair or exhibition, § 110(6).) The basic structure of the statute is that § 106 states the exclusive rights which cumulatively amount to nearly a full misappropriation right, and the remaining sections limit those rights in some situations where the § 106 rights would have affected the existing practices of persons whose expectations had developed under pre-1976 law when their activities were not infringing.

You have already been introduced to some of these limitations. Section 117 permits the buyer of a computer program to load it into his computer, adapt it, and back it up without violating the exclusive rights to copy and make derivative works. Section 113(b) limits the scope of the rights that can be claimed over works embodied in useful articles to the rights recognized in the *Mazer* case. Section 120 limits the rights that can be claimed by the copyright owner in architectural works. The reason why some of the type of subject matter listed in § 102 are defined and others are not is that the defined types are those which have limited exclusive rights.

An important limitation on the exclusive right to distribute is in § 109. Section 109(a) provides that "Notwithstanding the provisions of section 106(3) [creating the exclusive right to distribute], the owner of a particular copy or phonorecord lawfully made under this title, or any person authorized by such owner is entitled, without the authority of the copyright owner, to sell or otherwise dispose of the possession of that copy or phonorecord." Without § 109, someone who purchased a book, recording or painting (which is not the same thing as purchasing the copyright) would not be able to resell it without the consent of the copyright owner.

Section 114 creates limitations on the exclusive rights conferred on the owner of a copyright in a sound recording, one of the types of copyrightable works enumerated in § 102. The authors of a sound recording are the persons who make the recording—the producer, the artists, etc. A sound recording copyright was created by Congress during the consideration of the 1976 Act, in 1971. The copyright in a sound recording is a different copyright than the copyright in music, whose author is the composer. Thus, for instance, if the Boston Symphony recorded Beethoven's Fifth Symphony prior to 1971 there was no copyright in their work because Beethoven's copyright has long since expired, and there was no new copyright in their particular performance, although it was fixed in a tangible medium of expression by the conductor, the orchestra and the recording engineers. That did not mean that the Boston Symphony would not get paid, only that it would be paid only as the result of the contract it had with the record company whose profits would come from selling copies of the record. Since there was no copyright, anyone could publicly perform the recording, and anyone could make a copy of the recording. However, prior to the 1970's the legal right to make a copy was no threat to the record companies because it was not possible to create copies of records of competitive quality. Technology has, of course, changed all of that.

The effort to create a sound recording copyright ran into objections from the broadcasters, who had been able to play records on the air by paying royalties only to the representatives of the composers of the music (when the copyright on the music had not expired) and the composers (who did not want additional competition for their royalty dollars). The broadcasters argued that they should not have to pay to play the recording on the air because air time helped sell records, from which the recording artists benefitted. So Congress chose to truncate the sound recording copyright, creating a right to prevent copying, but not creating a right to prevent a public performance (which was the exclusive right infringed by playing a record over the air). This was done in § 114, whose mechanics (in 1976, the section has since, as we shall see, been amended) are explained in the following extract from H.R. 94–1476.

House Report No. 94–1476
Page 106.

Section 114. Scope of Exclusive Rights in Sound Recordings

Subsection (a) of Section 114 specifies that the exclusive rights of the owner of copyright in a sound recording are limited to the rights to reproduce the sound recording in copies or phonorecords, to prepare derivative works based on the copyrighted sound recording, and to distribute copies or phonorecords of the sound recording to the public. Subsection (a) states explicitly that the owner's rights "do not include any right of performance under section 106(4)." The Committee considered at length the arguments in favor of establishing a limited performance right, in the form of a compulsory license, for copyrighted sound recordings, but concluded that the problem requires further study. * * *

Subsection (b) of section 114 makes clear that statutory protection for sound recordings extends only to the particular sounds of which the recording consists, and would not prevent a separate recording of another performance in which those sounds are imitated. Thus, infringement takes place whenever all or any substantial portion of the actual sounds that go to make up a copyrighted sound recording are reproduced in phonorecords by repressing [sic, probably reprocessing], transcribing, recapturing off the air, or any other method, or by reproducing them in the soundtrack or audio portion of a motion picture or other audiovisual work. Mere imitation of a recorded performance would not constitute a copyright infringement even where one performer deliberately sets out to simulate another's performance as exactly as possible.

Under section 114, the exclusive right of owner of copyright [sic] in a sound recording to prepare derivative works based on the copyrighted sound recording is recognized. However, in view of the expressed intention not to give exclusive rights against imitative or simulated performances and recordings, the Committee adopted an amendment to make clear the scope of rights under section 106(2) in this context. Section 114(b) provides that the "exclusive right of the owner of copyright in a sound recording under clause (2) of section 106 is limited to the right to prepare a derivative work in which the actual sounds fixed in the sound recording are rearranged, remixed, or otherwise altered in sequence or quality."

Another amendment deals with the use of copyrighted sound recordings "included in educational television and radio programs * * * distributed or transmitted by or through public broadcasting entities." This use of recordings is permissible without authorization from the owner of copyright in the sound recording, as long as "copies or phonorecords of said programs are not commercially distributed by or through public broadcasting entities to the general public."

The Digital Performance Right In Sound Recordings

The sixth exclusive right in § 106, providing for a digital performance right in sound recordings, was created in 1995. The reason for the creation of the right was changing technology. With the advent of digital transmission technology, high quality music broadcasts became possible. The music industry feared that such broadcasts would come to replace the sale of recordings themselves. Some envisage a "celestial jukebox" which will provide music in digital format to its customers on request. With such a service, customers would stop buying recordings altogether, and simply order up what they wanted when they wanted it. This technology has not yet been implemented, but precursors already exists. For instance, the DSS small dish satellite service offers some fifty channels of digital music. Although the customer cannot select particular works, the customer can select channels that play many different types of music. And it is now possible to download and play specific recordings from the Internet.

The Congressional response was not to change the existing arrangements for analog broadcasts. It was instead to create a separate digital performance right with coordinate but different limitations in § 114. This was done in the Digital Performance Right in Sound Recordings Act of 1995, P.L. 104–39 (1995). This act requires, for instance, that before an Internet site can offer to download a recording, it must have the permission of the owner of the copyright in the recording.

Derivative Works

Of the six exclusive rights, the one with the most expansive potential is clause (2), the exclusive right "to prepare derivative works based upon the copyrighted work." As the definition in § 101 makes clear, this was an effort to generalize the point that a "translation, musical arrangement, dramatization, fictionalization, motion picture version, sound recording, art reproduction, abridgement, or condensation" infringes the original work. The general principle is that a derivative work is any "form in which a work may be recast, transformed, or adapted." The following case deals with the scope of this exclusive right.

Lewis Galoob Toys, Inc. v. Nintendo of America, Inc.

United States Court of Appeals for the Ninth Circuit, 1992.
964 F.2d 965, certiorari denied 507 U.S. 985 (1993).

■ FARRIS, CIRCUIT JUDGE:

Nintendo of America appeals the district court's judgment following a bench trial (1) declaring that Lewis Galoob Toys' Game Genie does not violate any Nintendo copyrights and dissolving a temporary injunction and (2) denying Nintendo's request for a permanent injunction enjoining Galoob from marketing the Game Genie. Lewis Galoob Toys, Inc. v. Nintendo of America, Inc., 780 F. Supp. 1283 (N.D. Cal. 1991). * * * We affirm.

FACTS

The Nintendo Entertainment System is a home video game system marketed by Nintendo. To use the system, the player inserts a cartridge containing a video game that Nintendo produces or licenses others to produce. By pressing buttons and manipulating a control pad, the player controls one of the game's characters and progresses through the game. The games are protected as audiovisual works under 17 U.S.C. § 102(a)(6).

The Game Genie is a device manufactured by Galoob that allows the player to alter up to three features of a Nintendo game. For example, the Game Genie can increase the number of lives of the player's character, increase the speed at which the character moves, and allow the character to float above obstacles. The player controls the changes made by the Game Genie by entering codes provided by the Game Genie Programming Manual and Code Book. The player also can experiment with variations of these codes.

The Game Genie functions by blocking the value for a single data byte sent by the game cartridge to the central processing unit in the Nintendo Entertainment System and replacing it with a new value. If that value controls the character's strength, for example, then the character can be made invincible by increasing the value sufficiently. The Game Genie is inserted between a game cartridge and the Nintendo Entertainment System. The Game Genie does not alter the data that is stored in the game cartridge. Its effects are temporary.

DISCUSSION

1. Derivative work

The Copyright Act of 1976 confers upon copyright holders the exclusive right to prepare and authorize others to prepare derivative works based on their copyrighted works. See 17 U.S.C. § 106(2). * * *

A derivative work must incorporate a protected work in some concrete or permanent "form." The Copyright Act defines a derivative work as follows: A "derivative work" is a work based upon one or more preexisting works, such as a translation, musical arrangement, dramatization, fictionalization, motion picture version, sound recording, art reproduction, abridgment, condensation, or any other *form* in which a work may be recast, transformed, or adapted. A work consisting of editorial revisions, annotations, elaborations, or other modifications which, as a whole, represent an original work of authorship, is a "derivative work." 17 U.S.C. § 101 (emphasis added). The examples of derivative works provided by the Act all physically incorporate the underlying work or works. The Act's legislative history similarly indicates that "the infringing work must incorporate a portion of the copyrighted work in some form." 1976 U.S. Code Cong. & Admin. News 5659, 5675. See also Mirage Editions, Inc. v. Albuquerque A.R.T. Co., 856 F.2d 1341, 1343–44 (9th Cir. 1988) (discussing same), *cert. denied*, 489 U.S. 1018 (1989).

Our analysis is not controlled by the Copyright Act's definition of "fixed." The Act defines copies as "material objects, other than phonorecords, in which a work is *fixed* by any method." 17 U.S.C. § 101 (emphasis added). The Act's definition of "derivative work," in contrast, lacks any such reference to fixation. See id. Further, we have held in a copyright infringement action that "[i]t makes no difference that the derivation may not satisfy certain requirements for statutory copyright registration itself." Lone Ranger Television v. Program Radio Corp., 740 F.2d 718, 722 (9th Cir. 1984). See also Paul Goldstein, Derivative Rights and Derivative Works in Copyright, 30 J. Copyright Soc'y U.S.A. 209, 231 n. 75 (1983) ("the Act does not require that the derivative work be protectable for its preparation to infringe"). Cf. Kalem Co. v. Harper Bros., 222 U.S. 55, 61 (1911) (finding the movie "Ben Hur" infringed copyright in the book Ben Hur even though Copyright Act did not yet include movies as protectable works). A derivative work must be fixed to be protected under the Act, see 17 U.S.C. § 102(a), but not to infringe.

The argument that a derivative work must be fixed because "[a] 'derivative work' is a work," 17 U.S.C. § 101, and "[a] work is 'created' when it is fixed in a copy or phonorecord for the first time," id., relies on a misapplication of the Copyright Act's definition of "created": A work is 'created' when it is fixed in a copy or phonorecord for the first time; where a work is prepared over a period of time, the portion of it that has been fixed at any particular time constitutes the work as of that time, and where the work has been prepared in different versions, each version constitutes a separate work. Id. The definition clarifies the time at which a work is created. If the provision were a definition of "work," it would not use that term in such a casual manner. The Act does not contain a definition of "work." Rather, it contains specific definitions: "audiovisual works," "literary works," and "pictorial, graphic and sculptural works," for example. The definition of "derivative work" does not require fixation.

The district court's finding that no independent work is created, see Galoob, 780 F.Supp. at 1291, is supported by the record. The Game Genie merely enhances the audiovisual displays (or underlying data bytes) that originate in Nintendo game cartridges. The altered displays do not incorporate a portion of a copyrighted work in some concrete or permanent form. Nintendo argues that the Game Genie's displays are as fixed in the hardware and software used to create them as Nintendo's original displays. Nintendo's argument ignores the fact that the Game Genie cannot produce an audiovisual display; the underlying display must be produced by a Nintendo Entertainment System and game cartridge. Even if we were to rely on the Copyright Act's definition of "fixed," we would similarly conclude that the resulting display is not "embodied," see 17 U.S.C. § 101, in the Game Genie. It cannot be a derivative work.

Mirage Editions is illustrative. Albuquerque A.R.T. transferred artworks from a commemorative book to individual ceramic tiles. See *Mirage Editions*, 856 F.2d at 1342. We held that "[b]y borrowing and mounting the preexisting, copyrighted individual art images without the consent of the copyright proprietors . . . [Albuquerque A.R.T.] has prepared a derivative work and infringed the subject copyrights." Id. at 1343. The ceramic tiles physically incorporated the copyrighted works in a form that could be sold. Perhaps more importantly, sales of the tiles supplanted purchasers' demand for the underlying works. Our holding in *Mirage Editions* would have been much different if Albuquerque A.R.T. had distributed lenses that merely enabled users to view several artworks simultaneously.

Nintendo asserted at oral argument that the existence of a $150 million market for the Game Genie indicates that its audiovisual display must be fixed. We understand Nintendo's argument; consumers clearly would not purchase the Game Genie if its display was not "sufficiently permanent or stable to permit it to be perceived . . . for a period of more than transitory duration." 17 U.S.C. § 101. But, Nintendo's reliance on the Act's definition of "fixed" is misplaced. Nintendo's argument also proves too much; the existence of a market does not, and cannot, determine conclusively whether a work is an infringing derivative work. For example, although there is a market for kaleidoscopes, it does not necessarily follow that kaleidoscopes create unlawful derivative works when pointed at protected artwork. The same can be said of countless other products that enhance, but do not replace, copyrighted works.

Nintendo also argues that our analysis should focus exclusively on the audiovisual displays created by the Game Genie, *i.e.*, that we should compare the altered displays to Nintendo's original displays. Nintendo emphasizes that " '[a]udiovisual works' are works that consist of a series of related images . . . regardless of the nature of the material objects . . . in which the works are embodied." 17 U.S.C. § 101 (emphasis added). The Copyright Act's definition of "audiovisual works" is inapposite; the only question before us is whether the audiovisual displays created by the Game Genie are "derivative works." The Act does not similarly provide that a work can be a derivative work regardless of the nature of the material objects in which the work is embodied. A derivative work must incorporate a protected work in some concrete or permanent form. We cannot ignore the actual source of the Game Genie's display.

Nintendo relies heavily on Midway Mfg. Co. v. Arctic Int'l, Inc., 704 F.2d 1009 (7th Cir.), cert. denied, 464 U.S. 823 (1983). Midway can be distinguished. The defendant in Midway, Arctic International, marketed a computer chip that could be inserted in Galaxian video games to speed up the rate of play. The Seventh Circuit held that the speeded-up version of Galaxian was a derivative work. Id. at 1013–14. Arctic's chip substantially copied and replaced the chip that was originally distributed by Midway. Purchasers of Arctic's chip also benefited economically by offering the altered game for use by the general public. The Game Genie does not physically incorporate a portion of a copyrighted work, nor does it supplant demand for a component of that work. The court in Midway acknowledged that the Copyright Act's definition of "derivative work" "must be stretched to accommodate speeded-up video games." Id. at 1014. Stretching that definition further would chill innovation and fail to protect "society's competing interest in the free flow of ideas, information, and commerce." Sony Corp. of America v. Universal Studios, Inc., 464 U.S. 417, 429 (1984).

In holding that the audiovisual displays created by the Game Genie are not derivative works, we recognize that technology often advances by improvement rather than replacement. See Christian H. Nadan, Note, A Proposal to Recognize Component Works: How a Teddy Bears on the Competing Ends of Copyright Law, 78 Cal. L. Rev. 1633, 1635 (1990). Some time ago, for example, computer companies began marketing spell-checkers that operate within existing word processors by signaling the writer when a word is misspelled. These applications, as well as countless others, could not be produced and marketed if courts were to conclude that the word processor and spell-checker combination is a derivative work based on the word processor alone. The Game Genie is useless by itself, it can only enhance, and cannot duplicate or recaste, a Nintendo game's output. It does not contain or produce a Nintendo game's output in some concrete or permanent form, nor does it supplant demand for Nintendo game cartridges. Such innovations rarely will constitute infringing derivative works under the Copyright Act. See generally Nadan, *supra*, at 1667–72.

2. Fair use

[The court also affirmed the district court's conclusion that if the audiovisual displays created by the Game Genie are derivative works, they are fair use.]

* * *

AFFIRMED.

NOTES

1. Mirage Editions, Inc. v. Albuquerque A.R.T. Co., 856 F.2d 1341, 1343–44 (9th Cir.1988), *cert. denied*, 489 U.S. 1018 (1989), discussed in the principal case gives the concept of a derivative work a very broad meaning. In that case, the defendant separated artistic reproductions from a book, mounted them on ceramic tiles and then offered them for resale. Do you create a derivative work if you make notations in the margins of this casebook? The reason the derivative work issue was important in *Mirage Editions* is that the purchaser of a book gets the right to resell it under § 109, but does not get the right to create a derivative work. In the same way, the purchasers of the Nintendo Entertainment System have the right to use the machine, but they do not have the right to create a derivative work. If the sale of the Game Genie to owners of the Nintendo system facilitated their creation of an infringing derivative work, then Lewis Galoob Toys was contributing to their infringement by selling it.

The Seventh Circuit declined to follow *Mirage Editions* in Lee v. A.R.T. Co., 125 F.3d 580 (7th Cir. 1997) (involving mounting of note cards). The court said (Easterbrook, J.):

If mounting works is a "transformation," then changing a painting's frame or a photograph's mat equally produces a derivative work. Indeed, if Lee is right about the meaning of the definition's first sentence, then any alteration of a work, however slight, requires the author's permission. We asked at oral argument what would happen if a purchaser jotted a note on one of the note cards, or used it as a coaster for a drink, or cut it in half, or if a collector applied his seal (as is common in Japan); Lee's counsel replied that such changes prepare derivative works, but that as a practical matter artists would not file suit. A definition of derivative work that makes criminals [the court is exaggerating here, § 506 requires "commercial advantage or private financial gain"] out of art collectors and tourists is jarring despite Lee's gracious offer not to commence civil litigation.

Id. at 582.

There is also substantial authority for the proposition that a derivative work must involve sufficient originality under *Feist* to be independently copyrightable before it can be a derivative work, which would not seem to be the case for works "created" by removing them from a book and mounting them on tiles.

2. The Nintendo game cartridges are computer programs, embedded in a fixed, read only memory. The scope of the § 106(2) exclusive right to prepare derivative works is in the case of computer programs narrowed by § 117(1) which permits the owner of a computer program to make an adaptation "created as an essential step in the utilization of the computer program in conjunction with a machine." Does the fact that they are also audiovisual works make § 117(1) unavailable? Are not most computer programs also audiovisual works (because they produce screen displays and sounds), so such a reading would surprisingly narrow § 117(1), would it not? Of course, the owner who makes an adaptation under § 117(1) can only use the adaptation "in conjunction with a machine," he cannot sell it. But the argument can be made that the "Game Genie" is not the adaptation, the performance by the owner of the Nintendo machine using the Game Genie is the adaptation.

In Aymes v. Bonelli, 47 F.3d 23 (2d Cir. 1995), the court addressed the issue of whether and how much adaptation is permitted under §117(1). Aymes had written a program for Bonelli for use in his swimming pool business in 1980. Subsequently, Aymes hired other programmers to modify the program to adapt to new business needs and to enable the program to run on new computers. Aymes sued for infringement in 1985, and argued that these modifications were infringing derivative works. The court held that they were not infringing under § 117(1). The court said:

According to the Contu Report, copyright laws should reflect the fact that transactions involving computer programs are entered into with "full awareness that users will modify their copies to suit their own needs." Foresight Resources Corp. v. Pfortmiller, 719 F.Supp. 1006, 1009 (D. Kan. 1989) (quoting Contu Report). This right of adaption includes "the right to add features to the program that were not present at the time of rightful acquisition", id., and was intended to apply to modifications for internal use, as long as the adapted program is not distributed in an unauthorized manner. See id. at 1009–10; Apple Computer, Inc. v. Formula Int'l, Inc., 594 F.Supp. 617, 621 (C.D. Cal. 1984). The district court found that Island used the program for internal purposes only and did not distribute the program to its subsidiaries.

Nor does it appear that the modifications to the program were for any purpose other than Island's internal business needs. The original program made provisions for late charges, and Island did alter CSALIB to keep it current from year to year and to maintain the viability of the original software when Island upgraded its computer to accommodate successive generations of IBM systems. In this connection, the Contu Report also comments: "The conversion of a program from one higher-level language to another to facilitate use would fall within this right [of adaption], *as would the right to add features to the program that were not present at the time of rightful acquisition* . . . . Again, it is likely that many transactions involving copies of programs are entered into with *full awareness that users will modify their copies to suit their own needs*, and this should be reflected in the law. . . . Should proprietors feel strongly that they do not want rightful possessors of copies of their programs to prepare such adaptations, they could, of course, make such desires a contractual matter." Contu Report at 13–14 (emphasis added) quoted in, Foresight Resources, 719 F.Supp. at 1009.

Id. at 26–27.

PROBLEMS

1. Can the operators of a hotel make videotapes available to their guests for viewing in the guest rooms, conveniently equipped with a video cassette player? Assume that the tapes have been purchased at a video store where they were sold for home viewing. Would it make any difference if a separate fee was charged for the tape rental? Whether or not a big sign out front said: "Stop in and See our Movies"? Compare Columbia Pictures Indus. v. Professional Real Estate Investors, 228 U.S.P.Q. 743 (C.D. Cal. 1986).

2. Can nursing homes show videotapes (purchased or rented) to their residents? See CCH Copyright Law Rep. ¶ 20,600, Agreement on Showing Videotaped Movies in Nursing Homes, Aug. 3, 1990 (major firms in the movie business agreed to license Nursing Homes without charge to show videotaped movies to their residents.)

3. Can a photographer make and sell photographs of a performance of a copyrighted work of choreography (explicitly included as a copyrightable work under § 102(4)) without the permission of the owner of the copyright? What exclusive right would be violated? Would the photograph be a "derivative work?" Compare Horgan v. Macmillan, Inc., 789 F.2d 157 (2d Cir. 1986).

4. Are you now able to determine which state law doctrines are not "equivalent to any of the exclusive rights within the general scope of copyright" for purposes of § 301?

5. Most computer programs are sold with a licensing agreement in which the buyer "agrees" not to make copies of the program. Some are sold with built-in copy-protection schemes designed to make it difficult to copy the program. Other companies sold programs with names like "Nibble" that were designed to defeat the protection schemes and make copies of the protected programs. Does the seller of the copy-protected program have any cause of action (under either state or federal law) against the seller or user of the program designed to defeat the copy-protection scheme? Consider that § 117(2) provides that "it is not an infringement for the owner of a copy of a computer program to make or authorize the making of another copy or adaptation of that computer program provided * * * that such new copy or adaptation is for archival purposes only and that all archival copies are destroyed in the event that continued possession of the computer program should cease to be rightful." See Vault Corp. v. Quaid Software Ltd., 847 F.2d 255 (5th Cir. 1988).

(2) The Infringing Work

In order to infringe a work must

(1) have been taken (the verb "copied" is usually used but we shall use the term "taken" in order to clearly distinguish the technical copyright noun "copy") from the copyrighted work and not from some other source or from an independent imagination; and

(2) have taken those elements of the copyrighted work which are protected by the copyright.

Because a copyright owner is seldom in a position to actually prove that the alleged infringing work was in fact taken from his work, the courts shift the burden of persuasion to the alleged infringer to show that it was not taken upon proof

(1) that the source of the alleged infringing work had access to the plaintiff's work; and

(2) that the alleged infringing work is so similar to aspects of the copyrighted work not otherwise available to the source of the alleged infringing work that it is unlikely to have been created independently.

When the alleged infringing work is not a duplicate of the copyrighted work, a determination of whether protected elements have been taken requires a close analysis of the differences and similarities between the two works.

The statute does not codify the law of infringement.

Gaste v. Kaiserman

United States Court of Appeals, Second Circuit, 1988.
863 F.2d 1061.

■ JON O. NEWMAN, CIRCUIT JUDGE:

This appeal involves a copyright infringement action against the composer and publisher of the highly successful popular song "Feelings," brought by Louis Gaste, the composer of an obscure French song written nearly 17 years earlier. The appeal is from a judgment of the District Court for the Southern District of New York (William C. Conner, Judge), entered after a jury found defendants Morris Kaiserman and Fermata International Melodies, Inc. ("Fermata") liable for copyright infringement. The jury awarded damages of $268,000 against Fermata and $233,000 against Kaiserman. The District Court also issued a permanent injunction against further infringement. Judge Conner reduced the damages against Kaiserman to $135,140 after excluding profits attributable to foreign performances. Judge Conner denied defendants' motions for a judgment notwithstanding the verdict or a new trial.

Defendants appeal from Judge Conner's denial of a new trial or judgment notwithstanding the verdict on several grounds. They argue that: (1) * * * (2) plaintiff failed to prove copying [taking] as a matter of law; [and] (3) the District Court incorrectly instructed the jury on the issues of "access" and "striking similarity" * * *. For the reasons stated below, we reject appellants' arguments and affirm the judgment.

BACKGROUND

In 1956, plaintiff-appellee Gaste, a resident and citizen of France, composed the music to a song entitled "Pour Toi" as part of the score of a motion picture Le Feu aux Poudres, which was released in France that same year.[1] Gaste registered the sheet music for the song in the United States Copyright Office in 1957. Neither the movie nor the song, which was published and recorded separately in France, had great success. Worldwide revenues of "Pour Toi" have amounted to less than $15,000.

From France, the scene shifts to Brazil, nearly two decades later. In 1973, the then unheralded and relatively unknown Brazilian singer and composer Morris Kaiserman, known professionally as Morris Albert, composed and recorded the song "Feelings." "Feelings" became a smash hit internationally, winning "gold records" in a number of countries.

Gaste contended at trial that Kaiserman had gained access to Gaste's virtually unknown song through Enrique Lebendiger, the owner of Fermata, which was Kaiserman's publisher. Gaste's evidence, detailed below in the discussion of access, established that Fermata had had some dealings with Gaste's publishing company, Les Editions Louis Gaste, in the 1950s.

DISCUSSION

* * *

II. Copying [Taking]

Appellants next attack the jury's conclusion that they copied Gaste's work. Because copiers are rarely caught red-handed, copying has tradition-

---

1. Gaste did not compose the lyrics to "Pour Toi." His infringement suit involves only the music to the song.

ally been proven circumstantially by proof of access and substantial similarity. * * * Appellants argue that there was insufficient evidence for the jury to find access directly or to infer it from striking similarity.

A. Access. Kaiserman and Fermata argue that Gaste's proof of access was too remote and speculative to have sustained a reasonable finding of access.

The guiding principle in deciding whether to overturn a jury verdict for insufficiency of evidence is " 'whether the evidence is such that, without weighing the credibility of the witnesses or otherwise considering the weight of the evidence, there can be but one conclusion as to the verdict that reasonable men could have reached.' " Mattivi v. South African Marine Corp., 618 F.2d 163, 167 (2d Cir. 1980) (quoting Simblest v. Maynard, 427 F.2d 1, 4 (2d Cir. 1970)). In the context of copyright, it is well established that there must be evidence of a reasonable possibility of access. Access must be more than a bare possibility and may not be inferred through speculation or conjecture. See Ferguson v. National Broadcasting Co., 584 F.2d 111, 113 (5th Cir. 1978); 3 M. & D. Nimmer, [Nimmer on Copyright] § 13.02(A), at 13–12 [(1988)].

In this case, Gaste's principal theory of access was that Fermata's owner, Lebendiger, received a copy of "Pour Toi" in the 1950s, when Gaste was trying to market the song to subpublishers, and that Kaiserman obtained it from Lebendiger in 1973. Georges Henon, a former employee of Gaste who had been responsible for distributing materials to foreign subpublishers, testified that he gave a recording of "Pour Toi" to Lebendiger in France in the 1950s and that he sent copies of the sheet music and record to Lebendiger in Brazil.

Lebendiger testified that he never heard or saw copies of "Pour Toi" prior to the litigation. Defendants also presented several witnesses, including Kaiserman, in an effort to establish that Kaiserman composed "Feelings" in September 1973 and that he had had no contact with Lebendiger's publishing company before that date. The credibility of both this testimony and these witnesses' prior affidavits was significantly undercut, however, when Gaste introduced a contract between Kaiserman and Editora Augusta Ltd., a publishing company owned in part by Lebendiger; the contract was dated July 1, 1973, and Kaiserman's signature was notarized on July 11, 1973. The initial contract for "Feelings" was not signed until May 10, 1974.

Although Gaste's theory of access relies on a somewhat attenuated chain of events extending over a long period of time and distance, we cannot say as a matter of law that the jury could not reasonably conclude that Kaiserman had access to the song through Lebendiger. Access through third parties connected to both a plaintiff and a defendant may be sufficient to prove a defendant's access to a plaintiff's work. * * * The lapse of time between the original publication of "Pour Toi" and the alleged infringement and the distance between the locations of the two events may make copying less likely but not an unreasonable conclusion. Indeed, a copier may be more likely to plagiarize an obscure song from the distant past and a faraway land than a recent well-known hit.

Kaiserman and Gaste also challenge the District Court's instructions to the jury on the issue of access. Appellants asked for an instruction that would have told the jury it could not base its findings on mere speculation or conjecture. The District Judge declined to give such an instruction, saying he did not want the jurors to think they could not draw inferences from the evidence. Judge Conner did tell the jurors several times, however, that they could find access only if Kaiserman had a "reasonable opportunity" to see or hear "Pour Toi."

We find no error in Judge Conner's instruction. Requiring a finding of a "reasonable opportunity" for access adequately states the appropriate standard. It might have been helpful for the District Court to have added that, although the jurors could draw inferences from the evidence presented, they could not find access on the basis of mere conjecture or surmise. But we do not find that the omission of such a caution rendered the charge misleading or permitted the jury to apply an incorrect standard.

B. Striking Similarity. Appellants argue that the District Court incorrectly permitted the jury to find copying on the basis of "striking similarity." As with access, appellants again challenge both the District Court's instruction and the sufficiency of the evidence.

Judge Conner instructed the jury that if a copyrighted work and an allegedly infringing work are strikingly similar, "then access does not have to be proven."[3] Appellants, relying principally on Selle v. Gibb, 741 F.2d 896, 901 (7th Cir. 1984), argue that even where there is striking similarity, there must be at least some other evidence that would establish a "reasonable possibility" that the plaintiff's work was available to the alleged infringer.

In this Circuit, the test for proof of access in cases of striking similarity is less rigorous. In Arnstein v. Porter, 154 F.2d 464 (2d Cir. 1946), Judge Frank said, "In some cases, the similarities between the plaintiff's and defendant's work are so extensive and striking as, *without more,* both to justify an inference of copying and to prove improper appropriation." Id. at

---

3. The District Court's full instruction on striking similarity was as follows:

Now, there is one circumstance in which access does not have to be proven. If the two works, that is the copyrighted work and the allegedly infringing work, are what we call strikingly similar, then access does not have to be proven. By striking similarity what we mean is that the two songs are so much alike that the only reasonable explanation for such a great degree of similarity is that the later song was copied from the first. In other words, if they are so nearly alike that it is virtually inconceivable that the second was independently composed without knowledge of the first, then you may find that there was infringement without finding actual access. In other words, you are in effect presuming access from the fact of striking similarity. So

what you will have to decide is whether or not the songs are so much alike that it is virtually inconceivable that Feelings was independently composed without any derivation from Pour Toi. That issue as to whether the two works are strikingly similar in the sense that I have defined, in other words, so as to preclude any reasonable possibility of independent creation, is an issue which is to be determined by you on the basis of all of the evidence, including the expert testimony. Judge Conner also instructed the jury that independent creation of a copyrighted song was not infringement because there is no copying and that there is no infringement if the similarities between two songs are the result of the use of common musical sources or techniques.

468–69 (emphasis added); see also Ferguson v. National Broadcasting Co., supra, 584 F.2d at 113 ("If the two works are so strikingly similar as to preclude the possibility of independent creation, 'copying' may be proved without a showing of access."); 3 M. & D. Nimmer, supra, § 13.02(B), at 13–17 (criticizing the *Selle* requirement that there be a "reasonable possibility" of access—not just a "bare possibility"—even in cases of striking similarity).

Appellants contend that undue reliance on striking similarity to show access precludes protection for the author who independently creates a similar work. However, the jury is only permitted to infer access from striking similarity; it need not do so. Though striking similarity alone can raise an inference of copying, that inference must be reasonable in light of all the evidence. A plaintiff has not proved striking similarity sufficient to sustain a finding of copying if the evidence as a whole does not preclude any reasonable possibility of independent creation. See Arnstein v. Porter, supra, 154 F.2d at 468 ("If evidence of access is absent, the similarities must be so striking as to preclude the possibility that plaintiff and defendant independently arrived at the same result."); Ferguson v. National Broadcasting Co., supra, 584 F.2d at 113.

Thus, we find Judge Conner's instruction, taken as a whole, a correct statement of the law. Judge Conner said the issue was whether the plaintiff's proof "preclude[d] any reasonable possibility of independent creation" of the allegedly infringing work, and he instructed the jury to make its determination "on the basis of all of the evidence."

We also conclude that there was sufficient evidence to permit the jury to infer access based on striking similarity. Gaste's proof of striking similarity consisted of both aural renditions of the songs and expert testimony. Gaste's expert testified not merely to common musical phrases in the songs but said that "there is not one measure of 'Feelings' which . . . cannot be traced back to something which occurs in 'Pour Toi.'" He also pointed to a unique musical "fingerprint"—an "evaded resolution"[4]—that occurred in the same place in the two songs. The witness said that while modulation from a minor key to its relative major was very common, he had never seen this particular method of modulation in any other compositions.[5]

Appellants' expert criticized the analytical methods of Gaste's expert and disagreed with his conclusions. But these criticisms go to the weight of

---

4. As explained by Gaste's expert, in most compositions, a dominant seventh chord "resolves" or leads into the major or minor chord four tones up. Thus, a B seventh chord would resolve to E minor or major. But in 'Pour Toi' and 'Feelings,' this normal resolution is "evaded." The dominant seventh chord leads to a different key. In 'Pour Toi,' a B seventh chord resolves to C, in the key of G major. In 'Feelings,' an E dominant seventh chord, which would normally resolve to an A chord, resolves to C, again in the key of G major.

5. It is axiomatic that copyright protects only an author's expression, not his ideas. Drawing the line between ideas and expression, however, is not always easy, particularly in musical works. The "evaded resolution" described by Gaste's expert is arguably more a musical idea than expression. But the evaded resolution was identically placed in the two songs, and this sequencing of the technique could properly be considered expression.

the evidence, which, along with the credibility of the witnesses, was for the jury to determine.

In assessing this evidence, we are mindful of the limited number of notes and chords available to composers and the resulting fact that common themes frequently reappear in various compositions, especially in popular music. See Arnstein v. Edward B. Marks Music Corp., 82 F.2d 275, 277 (2d Cir. 1936). Thus, striking similarity between pieces of popular music must extend beyond themes that could have been derived from a common source or themes that are so trite as to be likely to reappear in many compositions. See Selle v. Gibb, supra, 741 F.2d at 905.

In their defense, Kaiserman and Fermata presented examples of prior art—by composers ranging from Bach and Schumann to Stan Kenton—to demonstrate that some of the similarities between "Feelings" and "Pour Toi" also appear in other works. But Gaste's expert analyzed these other works and testified that they were not substantially similar. In his opinion, similarity of themes in these works could not explain the extensive similarities between "Feelings" and "Pour Toi." He testified that he did not believe it would be possible to compose "Feelings" without copying from "Pour Toi." The dispute was properly left to the jury.

The judgment of the District Court is affirmed.

NOTE

One of the important differences between the patent and copyright systems is that the copyright system places no burden on the copyright holder to identify the elements of his work for which he claims protection. While 35 U.S.C. § 112 requires the patentee to make "one or more claims particularly pointing out and distinctly claiming the subject matter which the applicant regards as his invention," a copyright owner is protected against infringement of any part of his work that is protected. To illustrate, a person who publishes a book containing 2 original pages and 300 pages from the public domain is protected against infringement of the 2 pages even if inspection of the book would not have revealed which 2 pages were protected. In patent cases, the issue of the scope of patent rights is often raised by the question: is the claim valid? In copyright, the scope of copyright rights is raised by the question: is the work infringed?

The copyright statute departs narrowly from this approach in § 403, applying to works consisting preponderantly of works of the United States Government.

The failure of the copyright system to require the copyright owner to define the scope of his claimed rights is related to the difference between infringement under the two statutes. A patent is infringed by anyone who makes, uses or sells the claimed invention whether or not it was taken from the patentee. This draconian sweep requires procedural devices to narrow the scope of claimed rights. Copyright infringement, on the other hand, can (at least in theory) be avoided by not "taking."

Nichols v. Universal Pictures Corp.

United States Circuit Court of Appeals, Second Circuit, 1930.
45 F.2d 119, certiorari denied 282 U.S. 902
51 S.Ct. 216, 75 L.Ed. 795 (1931).

■ L. HAND, CIRCUIT JUDGE.

The plaintiff is the author of a play, "Abie's Irish Rose," which it may be assumed was properly copyrighted * * *. The defendant produced publicly a motion picture play, "The Cohens and The Kellys," which the plaintiff alleges was taken from it. As we think the defendant's play too unlike the plaintiff's to be an infringement, we may assume, arguendo, that in some details the defendant used the plaintiff's play, as will subsequently appear, though we do not so decide. It therefore becomes necessary to give an outline of the two plays.

"Abie's Irish Rose" presents a Jewish family living in prosperous circumstances in New York. The father, a widower, is in business as a merchant, in which his son and only child helps him. The boy has philandered with young women, who to his father's great disgust have always been Gentiles, for he is obsessed with a passion that his daughter-in-law shall be an orthodox Jewess. When the play opens the son, who has been courting a young Irish Catholic girl, has already married her secretly before a Protestant minister, and is concerned to soften the blow for his father, by securing a favorable impression of his bride, while concealing her faith and race. To accomplish this he introduces her to his father at his home as a Jewess, and lets it appear that he is interested in her, though he conceals the marriage. The girl somewhat reluctantly falls in with the plan; the father takes the bait, becomes infatuated with the girl, concludes that they must marry, and assumes that of course they will, if he so decides. He calls in a rabbi, and prepares for the wedding according to the Jewish rite.

Meanwhile the girl's father, also a widower, who lives in California, and is as intense in his own religious antagonism as the Jew, has been called to New York, supposing that his daughter is to marry an Irishman and a Catholic. Accompanied by a priest, he arrives at the house at the moment when the marriage is being celebrated, but too late to prevent it, and the two fathers, each infuriated by the proposed union of his child to a heretic, fall into unseemly and grotesque antics. The priest and the rabbi become friendly, exchange trite sentiments about religion, and agree that the match is good. Apparently out of abundant caution, the priest celebrates the marriage for a third time, while the girl's father is inveigled away. The second act closes with each father, still outraged, seeking to find some way by which the union, thus trebly insured, may be dissolved.

The last act takes place about a year later, the young couple having meanwhile been abjured by each father, and left to their own resources. They have had twins, a boy and a girl, but their fathers know no more than that a child has been born. At Christmas each, led by his craving to see his grandchild, goes separately to the young folks' home, where they encounter each other, each laden with gifts, one for a boy, the other for a girl. After some slapstick comedy, depending upon the insistence of each that he is right about the sex of the grandchild, they become reconciled when they learn the truth, and that each child is to bear the given name of a grandparent. The curtain falls as the fathers are exchanging amenities, and the Jew giving evidence of an abatement in the strictness of his orthodoxy.

"The Cohens and The Kellys" presents two families, Jewish and Irish, living side by side in the poorer quarters of New York in a state of perpetual enmity. The wives in both cases are still living, and share in the mutual animosity, as do two small sons, and even the respective dogs. The Jews have a daughter, the Irish a son; the Jewish father is in the clothing business; the Irishman is a policeman. The children are in love with each other, and secretly marry, apparently after the play opens. The Jew, being in great financial straits, learns from a lawyer that he has fallen heir to a large fortune from a great-aunt, and moves into a great house, fitted luxuriously. Here he and his family live in vulgar ostentation, and here the Irish boy seeks out his Jewish bride, and is chased away by the angry father. The Jew then abuses the Irishman over the telephone, and both become hysterically excited. The extremity of his feelings makes the Jew sick, so that he must go to Florida for a rest, just before which the daughter discloses her marriage to her mother.

On his return the Jew finds that his daughter has borne a child; at first he suspects the lawyer, but eventually learns the truth and is overcome with anger at such a low alliance. Meanwhile, the Irish family who have been forbidden to see the grandchild, go to the Jew's house, and after a violent scene between the two fathers in which the Jew disowns his daughter, who decides to go back with her husband, the Irishman takes her back with her baby to his own poor lodgings. The lawyer, who had hoped to marry the Jew's daughter, seeing his plan foiled, tells the Jew that his fortune really belongs to the Irishman, who was also related to the dead woman, but offers to conceal his knowledge, if the Jew will share the loot. This the Jew repudiates, and, leaving the astonished lawyer, walks through the rain to his enemy's house to surrender the property. He arrives in great dejection, tells the truth, and abjectly turns to leave. A reconciliation ensues, the Irishman agreeing to share with him equally. The Jew shows some interest in his grandchild, though this is at most a minor motive in the reconciliation, and the curtain falls while the two are in their cups, the Jew insisting that in the firm name for the business, which they are to carry on jointly, his name shall stand first.

It is of course essential to any protection of literary property, whether at common-law or under the statute, that the right cannot be limited literally to the text, else a plagiarist would escape by immaterial variations. That has never been the law, but, as soon as literal appropriation ceases to be the test, the whole matter is necessarily at large, so that, as was recently well said by a distinguished judge, the decisions cannot help much in a new case. Fendler v. Morosco, 253 N.Y. 281, 292, 171 N.E. 56. When plays are concerned, the plagiarist may excise a separate scene [Daly v. Webster, 56 F. 483 (C.C.A.2); Chappell v. Fields, 210 F. 864 (C.C.A.2); Chatterton v. Cave, L.R. 3 App.Cas.

483]; or he may appropriate part of the dialogue (Warne v. Seebohm, L.R. 39 Ch.D. 73). Then the question is whether the part so taken is "substantial," and therefore not a "fair use" of the copyrighted work; it is the same question as arises in the case of any other copyrighted work. Marks v. Feist, 290 F. 959 (C.C.A. 2); Emerson v. Davies, Fed.Cas.No. 4436, 3 Story, 768, 795–797. But when the plagiarist does not take out a block in situ, but an abstract of the whole, decision is more troublesome. Upon any work, and especially upon a play, a great number of patterns of increasing generality will fit equally well, as more and more of the incident is left out. The last may perhaps be no more than the most general statement of what the play is about, and at times might consist only of its title; but there is a point in this series of abstractions where they are no longer protected, since otherwise the playwright could prevent the use of his "ideas," to which, apart from their expression, his property is never extended. Holmes v. Hurst, 174 U.S. 82, 86; Guthrie v. Curlett, 36 F.(2d) 694 (C.C.A. 2). Nobody has ever been able to fix that boundary, and nobody ever can. In some cases the question has been treated as though it were analogous to lifting a portion out of the copyrighted work (Rees v. Melville, MacGillivray's Copyright Cases [1911–1916], 168); but the analogy is not a good one, because, though the skeleton is a part of the body, it pervades and supports the whole. In such cases we are rather concerned with the line between expression and what is expressed. As respects plays, the controversy chiefly centers upon the characters and sequence of incident, these being the substance.

We did not in Dymow v. Bolton, 11 F.(2d) 690, hold that a plagiarist was never liable for stealing a plot; that would have been flatly against our rulings in Dam v. Kirk La Shelle Co., 175 F. 902 and Stodart v. Mutual Film Co., 249 F. 513, affirming my decision in (D.C.) 249 F. 507; neither of which we meant to overrule. We found the plot of the second play was too different to infringe, because the most detailed pattern, common to both, eliminated so much from each that its content went into the public domain; and for this reason we said, "this mere subsection of a plot was not susceptible of copyright." But we do not doubt that two plays may correspond in plot closely enough for infringement. How far that correspondence must go is another matter. Nor need we hold that the same may not be true as to the characters, quite independently of the "plot" proper, though, as far as we know, such a case has never arisen. If Twelfth Night were copyrighted, it is quite possible that a second comer might so closely imitate Sir Toby Belch or Malvolio as to infringe, but it would not be enough that for one of his characters he cast a riotous knight who kept wassail to the discomfort of the household, or a vain and foppish steward who became amorous of his mistress. These would be no more than Shakespeare's "ideas" in the play, as little capable of monopoly as Einstein's Doctrine of Relativity, or Darwin's theory of the Origin of Species. It follows that the less developed the characters, the less they can be copyrighted; that is the penalty an author must bear for marking them too indistinctly.

In the two plays at bar we think both as to incident and character, the defendant took no more—assuming that it took anything at all—than the law allowed. The stories are quite different. One is of a religious zealot who insists upon his child's marrying no one outside his faith; opposed by another who is in this respect just like him, and is his foil. Their difference in race is merely an obbligato to the main theme, religion. They sink their differences through grand parental pride and affection. In the other, zealotry is wholly absent; religion does not even appear. It is true that the parents are hostile to each other in part because they differ in race; but the marriage of their son to a Jew does not apparently offend the Irish family at all, and it exacerbates the existing animosity of the Jew, principally because he has become rich, when he learns it. They are reconciled through the honesty of the Jew and the generosity of the Irishman; the grandchild has nothing whatever to do with it. The only matter common to the two is a quarrel between a Jewish and an Irish father, the marriage of their children, the birth of grandchildren and a reconciliation.

If the defendant took so much from the plaintiff, it may well have been because her amazing success seemed to prove that this was a subject of enduring popularity. Even so, granting that the plaintiff's play was wholly original, and assuming that novelty is not essential to a copyright, there is no monopoly in such a background. Though the plaintiff discovered the vein, she could not keep it to herself; so defined, the theme was too generalized an abstraction from what she wrote. It was only a part of her "ideas."

Nor does she fare better as to her characters. It is indeed scarcely credible that she should not have been aware of those stock figures, the low comedy Jew and Irishman. The defendant has not taken from her more than their prototypes have contained for many decades. If so, obviously so to generalize her copyright, would allow her to cover what was not original with her. But we need not hold this as matter of fact, much as we might be justified. Even though we take it that she devised her figures out of her brain de novo, still the defendant was within its rights.

There are but four characters common to both plays, the lovers and the fathers. The lovers are so faintly indicated as to be no more than stage properties. They are loving and fertile; that is really all that can be said of them, and anyone else is quite within his rights if he puts loving and fertile lovers in a play of his own, wherever he gets the cue. The plaintiff's Jew is quite unlike the defendant's. His obsession is his religion, on which depends such racial animosity as he has. He is affectionate, warm and patriarchal. None of these fit the defendant's Jew, who shows affection for his daughter only once, and who has none but the most superficial interest in his grandchild. He is tricky, ostentatious and vulgar, only by misfortune redeemed into honesty. Both are grotesque, extravagant and quarrelsome; both are fond of display; but these common qualities make up only a small part of their simple pictures, no more than any one might lift if he chose. The Irish fathers are even more unlike; the plaintiff's a mere symbol for religious fanaticism and patriarchal pride, scarcely a character at all. Neither quality appears in the defendant's, for while he goes to get his grandchild, it is rather out of a truculent determination not to be forbidden, than from pride in his progeny. For the rest he is only a grotesque hobbledehoy, used for low comedy of the most conventional sort, which any one might borrow, if he chanced not to know the exemplar.

The defendant argues that the case is controlled by my decision in Fisher v. Dillingham (D.C.) 298 F. 145. Neither my brothers nor I wish to throw doubt upon the doctrine of that case, but it is not applicable here. We assume that the plaintiff's play is altogether original, even to an extent that in fact it is hard to believe. We assume further that, so far as it has been anticipated by earlier plays of which she knew nothing, that fact is immaterial. Still, as we have already said, her copyright did not cover everything that might be drawn from her play; its content went to some extent into the public domain. We have to decide how much, and while we are as aware as any one that the line, wherever it is drawn, will seem arbitrary, that is no excuse for not drawing it; it is a question such as courts must answer in nearly all cases. Whatever may be the difficulties a priori, we have no question on which side of the line this case falls. A comedy based upon conflicts between Irish and Jews, into which the marriage of their children enters, is no more susceptible of copyright than the outline of Romeo and Juliet.

The plaintiff has prepared an elaborate analysis of the two plays, showing a "quadrangle" of the common characters, in which each is represented by the emotions which he discovers. She presents the resulting parallelism as proof of infringement, but the adjectives employed are so general as to be quite useless. Take for example the attribute of "love" ascribed to both Jews. The plaintiff has depicted her father as deeply attached to his son, who is his hope and joy; not so, the defendant, whose father's conduct is throughout not actuated by any affection for his daughter, and who is merely once overcome for the moment by her distress when he has violently dismissed her lover. "Anger" covers emotions aroused by quite different occasions in each case; so do "anxiety," "despondency" and "disgust." It is unnecessary to go through the catalogue for emotions are too much colored by their causes to be a test when used so broadly. This is not the proper approach to a solution; it must be more ingenuous, more like that of a spectator, who would rely upon the complex of his impressions of each character.

We cannot approve the length of the record, which was due chiefly to the use of expert witnesses. Argument is argument whether in the box or at the bar, and its proper place is the last. The testimony of an expert upon such issues, especially his cross-examination, greatly extends the trial and contributes nothing which cannot be better heard after the evidence is all submitted. It ought not to be allowed at all; and while its admission is not a ground for reversal, it cumbers the case and tends to confusion, for the more the court is led into the intricacies of dramatic craftsmanship, the less likely it is to stand upon the firmer, if more naive, ground of its considered impressions upon its own perusal. We hope that in this class of cases such evidence may in the future be entirely excluded, and the case confined to the actual issues; that is, whether the copyrighted work was original, and whether the defendant copied it, so far as the supposed infringement is identical.

* * *

Decree affirmed.

NOTES

1. *Nichols* was closely followed in Reyher v. Children's Television Workshop, 533 F.2d 87 (2d Cir. 1976). In that case the court found that the defendants did not infringe plaintiff's copyright on her children's book "My Mother Is The Most Beautiful Woman In The World" by publishing and selling the illustrated story "The Most Beautiful Woman in the World" in Sesame Street Magazine and elsewhere. Both works had a similar plot line involving a child separated from its homely mother who considers her the most beautiful woman in the world. The court found no infringement because of the differences in detail.

2. Learned Hand uses the term "fair use" to mean a taking that is not substantial enough to be infringing. The doctrine of fair use codified in § 107 and considered below is a different doctrine, which excuses a taking substantial enough to be an infringement. It reduces confusion to reserve the term "fair use" for the latter doctrine.

Sheldon v. Metro-Goldwyn Pictures Corp.

United States Circuit Court of Appeals, Second Circuit, 1936.
81 F.2d 49, certiorari denied 298 U.S. 669, 56 S.Ct. 835, 80 L.Ed. 1392.

■ L. HAND, CIRCUIT JUDGE.

The suit is to enjoin the performance of the picture play "Letty Lynton," as an infringement of the plaintiffs' copyrighted play, "Dishonored Lady." The plaintiffs' title is conceded, so too the validity of the copyright; the only issue is infringement. The defendants say that they did not use the play in any way to produce the picture; the plaintiffs discredit this denial because of the negotiations between the parties for the purchase of rights in the play, and because the similarities between the two are too specific and detailed to have resulted from chance. The judge thought that, so far as the defendants had used the play, they had taken only what the law allowed, that is, those general themes, motives, or ideas in which there could be no copyright. Therefore he dismissed the bill.

An understanding of the issue involves some description of what was in the public demesne, as well as of the play and the picture. In 1857 a Scotch girl, named Madeleine Smith, living in Glasgow, was brought to trial upon an indictment in three counts; two for attempts to poison her lover, a third for poisoning him. The jury acquitted her on the first count, and brought in a verdict of "Not Proven" on the second and third. The circumstances of the prosecution aroused much interest at the time not only in Scotland but in England; so much indeed that it became a cause célèbre, and that as late as 1927 the whole proceedings were published in book form. An outline of the story so published, which became the original of the play here in suit, is as follows: The Smiths were a respectable middle-class family, able to send their daughter to a "young ladies' boarding school"; they supposed her protected not only from any waywardness of her own, but from the wiles of seducers. In both they were mistaken, for when at the age of twenty-one she met a young Jerseyman of French blood, Emile L'Angelier, ten years older, and already the hero of many amorous adventures, she quickly succumbed and poured out her feelings in letters of the utmost ardor and indiscretion, and at times of a candor beyond the standards then, and even yet, permissible for well-nurtured young women. They wrote each other as though already married, he assuming to dictate her conduct and even her feelings; both expected to marry, she on any terms, he with the approval of her family. Nevertheless she soon tired of him and engaged herself to a man some twenty years older who was a better match, but for whom she had no more than a friendly complaisance. L'Angelier was not, however, to be fobbed off so easily; he threatened to expose her to her father by showing her letters. She at first tried to dissuade him by appeals to their tender memories, but finding this useless and thinking herself otherwise undone, she affected a return of her former passion and invited him to visit her again. Whether he did, was the turning point of the trial; the evidence, though it really left the issue in no doubt, was too indirect to satisfy the jury, perhaps in part because of her advocate's argument that to kill him only insured the discovery of her letters. It was shown that she had several times bought or tried to buy poison,—prussic acid and arsenic,—and that twice before his death L'Angelier became violently ill, the second time on the day after her purchase. He died of arsenical poison, which the prosecution charged that she had given him in a cup of chocolate. At her trial, Madeleine being incompetent as a witness, her advocate proved an alibi by the testimony of her younger sister that early on the night of the murder as laid in the indictment, she had gone to bed with Madeleine, who had slept with her throughout the night. As to one of the attempts her betrothed swore that she had been with him at the theatre.

This was the story which the plaintiffs used to build their play. As will appear they took from it but the merest skeleton, the acquittal of a wanton young woman, who to extricate herself from an amour that stood in the way of a respectable marriage, poisoned her lover. The incidents, the characters, the mis en scène, the sequence of events, were all changed; nobody disputes that the plaintiffs were entitled to their copyright. All that they took from the story they might probably have taken, had it even been copyrighted. Their heroine is named Madeleine Cary; she lives in New York, brought up in affluence, if not in luxury; she is intelligent, voluptuous, ardent and corrupt; but, though she has had a succession of amours, she is capable of genuine affection. Her lover and victim is an Argentinean, named Moreno, who makes his living as a dancer in night-clubs. Madeleine has met him once in Europe before the play opens, has danced with him, has excited his concupiscence; he presses presents upon her. The play opens in his rooms, he and his dancing partner who is also his mistress, are together; Madeleine on the telephone recalls herself to him and says she wishes to visit him, though it is already past midnight. He disposes of his mistress by a device which does not deceive her and receives Madeleine; at once he falls to wooing her, luring her among other devices by singing a Gaucho song. He finds her facile and the curtain falls in season.

The second act is in her home, and introduces her father, a bibulous dotard, who has shot his wife's lover in the long past; Laurence Brennan, a self-made man in the fifties, untutored, self-reliant and reliable, who has had with Madeleine a relation, half paternal, half-amorous since she grew up; and Denis Farnborough, a young British labor peer, a mannekin to delight the heart of well ordered young women. Madeleine loves him; he loves Madeleine; she will give him no chance to declare himself, remembering her mottled past and his supposedly immaculate standards. She confides to Brennan, who makes clear to her the imbecility of her self-denial; she accepts this enlightenment and engages herself to her high-minded paragon after confessing vaguely her evil life and being assured that to post-war generations all such lapses are peccadillo.

In the next act Moreno, who has got wind of the engagement, comes to her house. Disposing of Farnborough, who chances to be there, she admits Moreno, acknowledges that she is to marry Farnborough, and asks him to accept the situation as the normal outcome of their intrigue. He refuses to be cast off, high words pass, he threatens to expose their relations, she raves at him, until finally he knocks her down and commands her to go to his apartment that morning as before. After he leaves full of swagger, her eye lights on a bottle of strychnine which her father uses as a drug; her fingers slowly close upon it; the audience understands that she will kill Moreno. Farnborough is at the telephone; this apparently stiffens her resolve, showing her the heights she may reach by its execution.

The scene then shifts again to Moreno's apartment; his mistress must again be put out, most unwillingly for she is aware of the situation; Madeleine comes in; she pretends once more to feel warmly, she must wheedle him for he is out of sorts after the quarrel. Meanwhile she prepares to poison him by putting the strychnine in coffee, which she asks him to make ready. But in the course of these preparations during which he sings her again his Gaucho song, what with their proximity, and this and that, her animal ardors are once more aroused and drag her, unwillingly and protesting, from her purpose. The play must therefore wait for an hour or more until, relieved of her passion, she appears from his bedroom and while breakfasting puts the strychnine in his coffee. He soon discovers what has happened and tries to telephone for help. He does succeed in getting a few words through, but she tears away the wire and fills his dying ears with her hatred and disgust. She then carefully wipes away all traces of her finger prints and manages to get away while the door is being pounded in by those who have come at his call.

The next act is again at her home on the following evening. Things are going well with her and Farnborough and her father, when a district attorney comes in, a familiar of the household, now in stern mood; Moreno's mistress and a waiter have incriminated Madeleine, and a cross has been found in Moreno's pocket, which he superstitiously took off her neck the night before. The district attorney cross-questions her, during which Farnborough several times fatuously intervenes; she is driven from point to point almost to an avowal when as a desperate plunge she says she spent the night with

Brennan. Brennan is brought to the house and, catching the situation after a moment's delay, bears her out. This puts off the district attorney until seeing strychnine brought to relieve the father, his suspicions spring up again and he arrests Madeleine. The rest of the play is of no consequence here, except that it appears in the last scene that at the trial where she is acquitted, her father on the witness stand accounts for the absence of the bottle of strychnine which had been used to poison Moreno.

At about the time that this play was being written an English woman named Lowndes wrote a book called Letty Lynton, also founded on the story of Madeleine Smith. Letty Lynton lives in England; she is eighteen years old, beautiful, well-reared and intelligent, but wayward. She has had a more or less equivocal love affair with a young Scot, named McLean, who worked in her father's chemical factory, but has discarded him, apparently before their love-making had gone very far. Then she chances upon a young Swede—half English—named Ekebon, and their acquaintance quickly becomes a standardized amour, kept secret from her parents, especially her mother, who is an uncompromising moralist, and somewhat estranged from Letty anyway. She and her lover use an old barn as their place of assignation; it had been fitted up as a play house for Letty when she was a child. Like Madeleine Smith she had written her lover a series of indiscreet letters which he has kept, for though he is on pleasure bent Ekebon has a frugal mind, and means to marry his sweetheart and set himself up for life. They are betrothed and he keeps pressing her to declare it to her parents, which she means never to do. While he is away in Sweden Letty meets an unmarried peer considerably older than she, poor, but intelligent and charming; he falls in love with her and she accepts him, more because it is a good match than for any other reason, though she likes him well enough, and will make him suppose that she loves him.

Thereupon Ekebon reappears, learns of Letty's new betrothal, and threatens to disclose his own to her father, backing up his story with her letters. She must at once disown her peer and resume her engagement with him. His motive, like L'Angelier's, is ambition rather than love, though conquest is a flattery and Letty a charming morsel. His threats naturally throw Letty into dismay; she has come to loathe him and at any cost must get free, but she has no one to turn to. In her plight she thinks of her old suitor, McLean, and goes to the factory only to find him gone. He has taught her how to get access to poisons in his office and has told of their effect on human beings. At first she thinks of jumping out the window, and when she winces at that, of poisoning herself; that would be easier. So she selects arsenic which is less painful and goes away with it; it is only when she gets home that she thinks of poisoning Ekebon. Her mind is soon made up, however, and she makes an appointment with him at the barn; she has told her father, she writes, and Ekebon is to see him on Monday, but meanwhile on Sunday they will meet secretly once more. She has prepared to go on a week-end party and conceals her car near the barn. He comes; she welcomes him with a pretence of her former ardors, and tries to get back her letters. Unsuccessful in this she persuades him to drink a cup of chocolate into which she puts the arsenic. After carefully washing the pans and cups, she leaves with him, dropping him from her car near his home; he being still unaffected. On her way to her party she pretends to have broken down and by asking the help of a passing cyclist establishes an alibi. Ekebon dies at his home attended by his mistress; the letters are discovered and Letty is brought before the coroner's inquest and acquitted chiefly through the alibi, for things look very bad for her until the cyclist appears.

The defendants, who are engaged in producing speaking films on a very large scale in Hollywood, California, had seen the play and wished to get the rights. They found, however, an obstacle in an association of motion picture producers presided over by Mr. Will Hays, who thought the play obscene; not being able to overcome his objections, they returned the copy of the manu-script which they had had. That was in the spring of 1930, but in the autumn they induced the plaintiffs to get up a scenario, which they hoped might pass moral muster. Although this did not suit them after the plaintiffs prepared it, they must still have thought in the spring of 1931 that they could satisfy Mr. Hays, for they then procured an offer from the plaintiffs to sell their rights for $30,000. These negotiations also proved abortive because the play continued to be objectionable, and eventually they cried off on the bargain. Mrs. Lowndes' novel was suggested to Thalberg, one of the vice-presidents of the Metro-Goldwyn Company, in July, 1931, and again in the following November, and he bought the rights to it in December. At once he assigned the preparation of a play to Stromberg, who had read the novel in January, and thought it would make a suitable play for an actress named Crawford, just then not employed. Stromberg chose Meehan, Tuchock and Brown to help him, the first two with the scenario, the third with the dramatic production. All these four were examined by deposition; all denied that they had used the play in any way whatever; all agreed that they had based the picture on the story of Madeleine Smith and on the novel, "Letty Lynton." All had seen the play, and Tuchock had read the manuscript, as had Thalberg, but Stromberg, Meehan and Brown swore that they had not; Stromberg's denial being however worthless, for he had originally sworn the contrary in an affidavit. They all say that work began late in November or early in December, 1931, and the picture was finished by the end of March. To meet these denials, the plaintiffs appeal to the substantial identity between passages in the picture and those parts of the play which are original with them.

The picture opens in Montevideo where Letty Lynton is recovering from her fondness for Emile Renaul. She is rich, luxurious and fatherless, her father having been killed by his mistress's husband; her mother is seared, hard, selfish, unmotherly; and Letty has left home to escape her, wandering about in search of excitement. Apparently for the good part of a year she has been carrying on a love affair with Renaul; twice before she has tried to shake loose, has gone once to Rio where she lit another flame, but each time she has weakened and been drawn back. Though not fully declared as an amour, there can be no real question as to the character of her attachment. She at length determines really to break loose, but once again her senses are too much for her and it is indicated, if not declared, that she spends the night with Renaul. Though he is left a vague figure only indistinctly associated with South America somewhere or other, the part was cast for an actor with a marked foreign accent, and it is plain that he was meant to be understood, in origin anyway, as South American, like Moreno in the play. He is violent, possessive and sensual; his power over Letty lies in his strong animal attractions. However, she escapes in the morning while he is asleep, whether from his bed or not is perhaps uncertain; and with a wax figure in the form of a loyal maid—Letty in the novel had one—boards a steamer for New York. On board she meets Darrow, a young American, the son of a rich rubber manufacturer, who is coming back from a trip to Africa. They fall in love upon the faintest provocation and become betrothed before the ship docks, three weeks after she left Montevideo. At the pier she finds Renaul who has flown up to reclaim her. She must in some way keep her two suitors apart, and she manages to dismiss Darrow and then to escape Renaul by asking him to pay her customs duties, which he does. Arrived home her mother gives her a cold welcome and refuses to concern herself with the girl's betrothal. Renaul is announced; he has read of the betrothal in the papers and is furious. He tries again to stir her sensuality by the familiar gambit, but this time he fails; she slaps his face and declares that she hates him. He commands her to come to his apartment that evening; she begs him to part with her and let her have her life; he insists on renewing their affair. She threatens to call the police; he rejoins that if so her letters will be published and then he leaves. Desperate, she chances on a bottle of strychnine, which we are to suppose is an accoutrement of every affluent household, and seizes it; the implication is of intended suicide, not murder. Then she calls Darrow, tells him that she will not leave with him that night for his parents' place in the Adirondacks as they had planned; she renews to him the pledge of her love, without him she cannot live, an intimation to the audience of her purpose to kill herself.

That evening she goes to Renaul's apartment in a hotel armed with her strychnine bottle, for use on the spot; she finds him cooling champagne, but in bad temper. His caresses which he bestows plentifully enough, again stir her disgust not her passions, but he does not believe it and assumes that she will spend the night with him. Finding that he will not return the letters, she believes herself lost and empties the strychnine into a wine glass. Again he embraces her; she vilifies him; he knocks her down; she vilifies him again. Ignorant of the poison he grasps her glass, and she, perceiving it, lets him drink. He woos her again, this time with more apparent success, for she is terrified; he sings a Gaucho song to her, the same one that has been heard at Montevideo. The poison begins to work and, at length supposing that she has meant to murder him, he reaches for the telephone; she forestalls him, but she does not tear out the wire. As he slowly dies, she stands over him and vituperates him. A waiter enters; she steps behind a curtain; he leaves thinking Renaul drunk; she comes out, wipes off all traces of her fingerprints and goes out, leaving however her rubbers which Renaul had taken from her when she entered.

Next she and Darrow are found at his parents' in the Adirondacks; while there a detective appears, arrests Letty and takes her to New York; she is charged with the murder of Renaul; Darrow goes back to New York with her. The finish is at the district attorney's office; Letty and Darrow, Letty's mother, the wax serving maid are all there. The letters appear incriminating to an elderly rather benevolent district attorney; also the customs slip and the rubbers. Letty begins to break down; she admits that she went to Renaul's room, not to kill him but to get him to release her. Darrow sees that that story will not pass, and volunteers that she came to his room at a hotel and spent the night with him. Letty confirms this and mother, till then silent, backs up their story; she had traced them to the hotel and saw the lights go out, having ineffectually tried to dissuade them. The maid still further confirms them and the district attorney, not sorry to be discomfited, though unbelieving, discharges Letty.

We are to remember that it makes no difference how far the play was anticipated by works in the public demesne which the plaintiffs did not use. The defendants appear not to recognize this, for they have filled the record with earlier instances of the same dramatic incidents and devices, as though, like a patent, a copyrighted work must be not only original, but new. That is not however the law as is obvious in the case of maps or compendia, where later works will necessarily be anticipated. At times, in discussing how much of the substance of a play the copyright protects, courts have indeed used language which seems to give countenance to the notion that, if a plot were old, it could not be copyrighted. London v. Biograph Co. (C.C.A.) 231 F. 696; Eichel v. Marcin (D.C.) 241 F. 404. But we understand by this no more than that in its broader outline a plot is never copyrightable, for it is plain beyond peradventure that anticipation as such cannot invalidate a copyright. Borrowed the work must indeed not be, for a plagiarist is not himself pro tanto an "author"; but if by some magic a man who had never known it were to compose anew Keats's Ode on a Grecian Urn, he would be an "author," and, if he copyrighted it, others might not copy that poem, though they might of course copy Keats's. Bleistein v. Donaldson Lithographing Co., 188 U.S. 239, 249; Gerlach-Barklow Co. v. Morris & Bendien, Inc., 23 F.(2d) 159, 161 (C.C.A. 2); Weil, Copyright Law, p. 234. But though a copyright is for this reason less vulnerable than a patent, the owner's protection is more limited, for just as he is no less an "author" because others have preceded him, so another who follows him, is not a tort-feasor unless he pirates his work. Jewelers' Circular Publishing Co. v. Keystone Co., 281 F. 83, 92, 26 A.L.R. 571 (C.C.A. 2); General Drafting Co. v. Andrews, 37 F.(2d) 54, 56 (C.C.A. 2); Williams v. Smythe (C.C.) 110 F. 961; American, etc., Directory Co. v. Gehring Pub. Co. (D.C.) 4 F.(2d) 415; New Jersey, etc., Co. v. Barton Business Service (D.C.) 57 F.(2d) 353. If the copyrighted work is therefore original, the public demesne is important only on the issue of infringement; that is, so far as it may break the force of the inference to be drawn from likenesses between the work and the putative piracy. If the defendant has had access to other material which would have served him as well, his disclaimer becomes more plausible.

In the case at bar there are then two questions: First, whether the defendants actually used the play; second, if so, whether theirs was a "fair use." The judge did not make any finding upon the first question, as we said at the outset, because he thought the defendants were in any case justified;

in this following our decision in Nichols v. Universal Pictures Corporation, 45 F.(2d) 119. The plaintiffs challenge that opinion because we said that "copying" might at times be a "fair use"; but it is convenient to define such a use by saying that others may "copy" the "theme," or "ideas," or the like, of a work, though not its "expression." At any rate so long as it is clear what is meant, no harm is done. In the case at bar the distinction is not so important as usual, because so much of the play was borrowed from the story of Madeleine Smith, and the plaintiffs' originality is necessarily limited to the variants they introduced. Nevertheless, it is still true that their whole contribution may not be protected; for the defendants were entitled to use, not only all that had gone before, but even the plaintiffs' contribution itself, if they drew from it only the more general patterns; that is, if they kept clear of its "expression." We must therefore state in detail those similarities which seem to us to pass the limits of "fair use." Finally, in concluding as we do that the defendants used the play pro tanto, we need not charge their witnesses with perjury. With so many sources before them they might quite honestly forget what they took; nobody knows the origin of his inventions; memory and fancy merge even in adults. Yet unconscious plagiarism is actionable quite as much as deliberate. Buck v. Jewell-La Salle Realty Co., 283 U.S. 191, 198; Harold Lloyd Corporation v. Witwer, 65 F.(2d) 1, 16 (C.C.A. 9); Fred Fisher, Inc., v. Dillingham (D.C.) 298 F. 145.

The defendants took for their mis en scène the same city and the same social class; and they chose a South American villain. The heroines had indeed to be wanton, but Letty Lynton "tracked" Madeleine Cary more closely than that. She is overcome by passion in the first part of the picture and yields after announcing that she hates Renaul and has made up her mind to leave him. This is the same weakness as in the murder scene of the play, though transposed. Each heroine's waywardness is suggested as an inherited disposition; each has had an errant parent involved in scandal; one killed, the other becoming an outcast. Each is redeemed by a higher love. Madeleine Cary must not be misread; it is true that her lust overcomes her at the critical moment, but it does not extinguish her love for Farnborough; her body, not her soul, consents to her lapse. Moreover, her later avowal, which she knew would finally lose her her lover, is meant to show the basic rectitude of her nature. Though it does not need Darrow to cure Letty of her wanton ways, she too is redeemed by a nobler love. Neither Madeleine Smith, nor the Letty of the novel, were at all like that; they wished to shake off a clandestine intrigue to set themselves up in the world; their love as distinct from their lust, was pallid. So much for the similarity in character.

Coming to the parallelism of incident, the threat scene is carried out with almost exactly the same sequence of event and actuation; it has no prototype in either story or novel. Neither Ekebon nor L'Angelier went to his fatal interview to break up the new betrothal; he was beguiled by the pretence of a renewed affection. Moreno and Renaul each goes to his sweetheart's home to detach her from her new love; when he is there, she appeals to his better side, unsuccessfully; she abuses him, he returns the abuse and commands her to come to his rooms; she pretends to agree, expecting to finish with him one way or another. True, the assault is deferred in the picture from this scene to the next, but it is the same dramatic trick. Again, the poison in each case is found at home, and the girl talks with her betrothed just after the villain has left and again pledges him her faith. Surely the sequence of these details is pro tanto the very web of the authors' dramatic expression; and copying them is not "fair use."

The death scene follows the play even more closely; the girl goes to the villain's room as he directs; from the outset he is plainly to be poisoned while they are together. (The defendants deny that this is apparent in the picture, but we cannot agree. It would have been an impossible dénoument on the screen for the heroine, just plighted to the hero, to kill herself in desperation, because the villain has successfully enmeshed her in their mutual past; yet the poison is surely to be used on some one.) Moreno and Renaul each tries to arouse the girl by the memory of their former love, using among other aphrodisiacs the Gaucho song; each dies while she is there, incidentally of strychnine not arsenic. In extremis each makes for the telephone and is thwarted by the girl; as he dies, she pours upon him her rage and loathing. When he is dead, she follows the same ritual to eradicate all traces of her presence, but forgets telltale bits of property. Again these details in the same sequence embody more than the "ideas" of the play; they are its very raiment.

Finally in both play and picture in place of a trial, as in the story and the novel, there is substituted an examination by a district attorney; and this examination is again in parallel almost step by step. A parent is present; so is the lover; the girl yields progressively as the evidence accumulates; in the picture, the customs slip, the rubbers and the letters; in the play, the cross and the witnesses, brought in to confront her. She is at the breaking point when she is saved by substantially the same most unexpected alibi; a man declares that she has spent the night with him. That alibi there introduced is the turning point in each drama and alone prevents its ending in accordance with the classic canon of tragedy; i.e., fate as an inevitable consequence of past conduct, itself not evil enough to quench pity. It is the essence of the authors' expression, the very voice with which they speak.

We have often decided that a play may be pirated without using the dialogue. Daly v. Palmer, Fed. Cas. No. 3,552, 6 Blatch. 256; Daly v. Webster, 56 F. 483, 486, 487; Dam v. Kirke La Shelle Co., 175 F. 902, 907; Chappell & Co. v. Fields, 210 F. 864. Dymow v. Bolton, 11 F.(2d) 690; and Nichols v. Universal Pictures Corporation, supra, 45 F.(2d) 119, do not suggest otherwise. Were it not so, there could be no piracy of a pantomime, where there cannot be any dialogue; yet nobody would deny to pantomime the name of drama. Speech is only a small part of a dramatist's means of expression; he draws on all the arts and compounds his play from words and gestures and scenery and costume and from the very looks of the actors themselves. Again and again a play may lapse into pantomime at its most poignant and significant moments; a nod, a movement of the hand, a pause, may tell the audience more than words could tell. To be sure, not all this is always copyrighted, though there is no reason why it may not be, for those decisions do not forbid which hold that mere scenic tricks will not be protected. Serrana v. Jefferson (C.C.) 33 F. 347; Barnes v. Miner (C.C.) 122 F. 480; Bloom et al. v.

Nixon (C.C.) 125 F. 977. The play is the sequence of the confluents of all these means, bound together in an inseparable unity; it may often be most effectively pirated by leaving out the speech, for which a substitute can be found, which keeps the whole dramatic meaning. That as it appears to us is exactly what the defendants have done here; the dramatic significance of the scenes we have recited is the same, almost to the letter. True, much of the picture owes nothing to the play; some of it is plainly drawn from the novel; but that is entirely immaterial; it is enough that substantial parts were lifted; no plagiarist can excuse the wrong by showing how much of his work he did not pirate. We cannot avoid the conviction that, if the picture was not an infringement of the play, there can be none short of taking the dialogue.

The decree will be reversed and an injunction will go against the picture together with a decree for damages and an accounting. The plaintiffs will be awarded an attorney's fee in this court and in the court below, both to be fixed by the District Court upon the final decree.

Decree reversed.

NOTES

1. The analysis of the *Sheldon* opinion suggests that in some situations a character could be protected by copyright if the copying of the character's features and behavior were sufficiently detailed. In Warner Bros. v. American Broadcasting Companies, 654 F.2d 204 (2d Cir. 1981) (denial of preliminary injunction affirmed), 720 F.2d 231 (2d Cir. 1983) (summary judgment of no infringement affirmed), the owners of the copyright on Superman were unable to stop the ABC series "The Greatest American Hero" featuring the exploits of one Ralph Hinkley whose abilities and activities lightly spoofed the Superman story. Superman did once prevail against a comic book competitor in Detective Comics, Inc. v. Bruns Publications, Inc., 111 F.2d 432 (2d Cir. 1940), holding that the defendant's Wonderman infringed. In Selmon v. Hasbro Bradley, Inc., 669 F.Supp. 1267 (S.D.N.Y. 1987), the Whats were unable to stop the Wuzzles. The pun laden opinion is illustrated by ten pages of sketches of both Whats and Wuzzles. "The questions before us are really quite simple: 'Just what's a "What," what's the similarity between a "What" and a "Wuzzle," and "Wuzzle" we do about it?'"

2. The subject of legal protection of characters is carefully examined in Leslie A. Kurtz, The Independent Legal Lives of Fictional Characters, 1986 Wisc. L. Rev. 429 (1986).

Arnstein v. Porter

United States Circuit Court of Appeals, Second Circuit, 1946.
154 F.2d 464.

Action by Ira B. Arnstein against Cole Porter for infringement of copyrights, infringement of right to uncopyrighted musical compositions and wrongful use of the titles of others. From a judgment dismissing action on defendant's motion for summary judgment, the plaintiff appeals.

Modified in part; otherwise reversed and remanded.

Plaintiff, a citizen and resident of New York, brought this suit, charging infringement by defendant, a citizen and resident of New York, of plaintiff's copyrights to several musical compositions, infringement of his rights to other uncopyrighted musical compositions, and wrongful use of the titles of others. Plaintiff, when filing his complaint, demanded a jury trial. Plaintiff took the deposition of defendant, and defendant, the deposition of plaintiff. Defendant then moved for an order striking out plaintiff's jury demand, and for summary judgment. Attached to defendant's motion papers were the depositions, phonograph records of piano renditions of the plaintiff's compositions and defendant's alleged infringing compositions, and the court records of five previous copyright infringement suits brought by plaintiff in the court below against other persons, in which judgments had been entered, after trials, against plaintiff. Defendant also moved for dismissal of the action on the ground of "vexatiousness."

Plaintiff alleged that defendant's "Begin the Beguine" is a plagiarism from plaintiff's "The Lord Is My Shepherd" and "A Mother's Prayer." Plaintiff testified, on deposition, that "The Lord Is My Shepherd" had been published and about 2,000 copies sold, that "A Mother's Prayer" had been published, over a million copies having been sold. In his depositions, he gave no direct evidence that defendant saw or heard these compositions. He also alleged that defendant's "My Heart Belongs to Daddy" had been plagiarized from plaintiff's "A Mother's Prayer."

Plaintiff also alleged that defendant's "I Love You" is a plagiarism from plaintiff's composition "La Priere," stating in his deposition that the latter composition had been sold. He gave no direct proof that plaintiff knew of this composition.

He also alleged that defendant's song "Night and Day" is a plagiarism of plaintiff's song "I Love You Madly," which he testified had not been published but had once been publicly performed over the radio, copies having been sent to divers radio stations but none to defendant; a copy of this song, plaintiff testified, had been stolen from his room. He also alleged that "I Love You Madly" was in part plagiarized from "La Priere." He further alleged that defendant's "You'd Be So Nice To Come Home To" is plagiarized from plaintiff's "Sadness Overwhelms My Soul." He testified that this song had never been published or publicly performed but that copies had been sent to a movie producer and to several publishers. He also alleged that defendant's "Don't Fence Me In" is a plagiarism of plaintiff's song "A Modern Messiah" which has not been published or publicly performed; in his deposition he said that about a hundred copies had been sent to divers radio stations and band leaders but that he sent no copy to defendant. Plaintiff said that defendant "had stooges right along to follow me, watch me, and live in the same apartment with me," and that plaintiff's room had been ransacked on several occasions. Asked how he knew that defendant had anything to do with any of these "burglaries," plaintiff said, "I don't know that he had to do with it, but I only know that he could have." He also said " * * * many of my compositions had been published. No one had to break in to steal them. They were sung publicly."

Defendant in his deposition categorically denied that he had ever seen or heard any of plaintiff's compositions or had had any acquaintance with any persons said to have stolen any of them.

The prayer of plaintiff's original complaint asked "at least one million dollars out of the millions the defendant has earned and is earning out of all the plagiarism." In his amended complaint the prayer is "for judgment against the defendant in the sum of $1,000,000 as damages sustained by the plagiarism of all the compositions named in the complaint." Plaintiff, not a lawyer, appeared pro se below and on this appeal.

■ FRANK, CIRCUIT JUDGE. * * * The principal question on this appeal is whether the lower court, under Rule 56, properly deprived plaintiff of a trial of his copyright infringement action. * * * It is important to avoid confusing two separate elements essential to a plaintiff's case in such a suit: (a) that defendant copied from plaintiff's copyrighted work and (b) that the copying (assuming it to be proved) went so far as to constitute improper appropriation.

As to the first—copying—the evidence may consist (a) of defendant's admission that he copied or (b) of circumstantial evidence—usually evidence of access—from which the trier of the facts may reasonably infer copying. Of course, if there are no similarities, no amount of evidence of access will suffice to prove copying. If there is evidence of access and similarities exist, then the trier of the facts must determine whether the similarities are sufficient to prove copying. On this issue, analysis ("dissection") is relevant, and the testimony of experts may be received to aid the trier of the facts. If evidence of access is absent, the similarities must be so striking as to preclude the possibility that plaintiff and defendant independently arrived at the same result.

If copying is established, then only does there arise the second issue, that of illicit copying (unlawful appropriations). On that issue (as noted more in detail below) the test is the response of the ordinary lay hearer, accordingly, on that issue, "dissection" and expert testimony are irrelevant.

In some cases, the similarities between the plaintiff's and defendant's work are so extensive and striking as, without more, both to justify an inference of copying and to prove improper appropriation. But such double-purpose evidence is not required; that is, if copying is otherwise shown, proof of improper appropriation need not consist of similarities which, standing alone, would support an inference of copying.

Each of these two issues—copying and improper appropriation—is an issue of fact. If there is a trial, the conclusions on those issues of the trier of the facts—of the judge if he sat without a jury, or of the jury if there was a jury trial—bind this court on appeal, provided the evidence supports those findings, regardless of whether we would ourselves have reached the same conclusions. But a case could occur in which the similarities were so striking that we would reverse a finding of no access, despite weak evidence of access (or no evidence thereof other than the similarities); and similarly as to a finding of no illicit appropriation.

We turn first to the issue of copying. After listening to the compositions as played in the phonograph recordings submitted by defendant, we find similarities; but we hold that unquestionably, standing alone, they do not compel the conclusion, or permit the inference that defendant copied. The similarities, however, are sufficient so that, if there is enough evidence of access to permit the case to go to the jury, the jury may properly infer that the similarities did not result from coincidence.

Summary judgment was, then, proper if indubitably defendant did not have access to plaintiff's compositions. Plainly that presents an issue of fact. On that issue, the district judge who heard no oral testimony, had before him the depositions of plaintiff and defendant. The judge characterized plaintiff's story as "fantastic"; and, in the light of the references in his opinion to defendant's deposition, the judge obviously accepted defendant's denial of access and copying. Although part of plaintiff's testimony on deposition (as to "stooges" and the like) does seem "fantastic," yet plaintiff's credibility, even as to those improbabilities, should be left to the jury. If evidence is "of a kind that greatly taxes the credulity of the judge, he can say so, or if he totally disbelieves it, he may announce that fact, leaving the jury free to believe it or not." If, said Winslow, J., "evidence is to be always disbelieved because the story told seems remarkable or impossible, then a party whose rights depend on the proof of some facts out of the usual course of events will always be denied justice simply because his story is improbable." We should not overlook the shrewd proverbial admonition that sometimes truth is stranger than fiction.

But even if we were to disregard the improbable aspects of plaintiff's story, there remain parts by no means "fantastic." On the record now before us, more than a million copies of one of his compositions were sold; copies of others were sold in smaller quantities or distributed to radio stations or band leaders or publishers, or the pieces were publicly performed. If, after hearing both parties testify, the jury disbelieves defendant's denials, it can, from such facts, reasonably infer access. It follows that, as credibility is unavoidably involved a genuine issue of material fact presents itself. With credibility a vital factor, plaintiff is entitled to a trial where the jury can observe the witnesses while testifying. Plaintiff must not be deprived of the invaluable privilege of cross-examining the defendant—the "crucial test of credibility"—in the presence of the jury. Plaintiff, or a lawyer on his behalf, on such examination may elicit damaging admissions from defendant; more important, plaintiff may persuade the jury, observing defendant's manner when testifying, that defendant is unworthy of belief.

* * *

With all that in mind, we cannot now say—as we think we must say to sustain a summary judgment—that at the close of a trial the judge could properly direct a verdict.

* * * Assuming that adequate proof is made of copying, that is not enough; for there can be "permissible copying," copying which is not illicit.

Whether (if he copied) defendant unlawfully appropriated presents, too, an issue of fact. The proper criterion on that issue is not an analytic or other comparison of the respective musical compositions as they appear on paper or in the judgment of trained musicians.[19] The plaintiff's legally protected interest is not, as such, his reputation as a musician but his interest in the potential financial returns from his compositions which derive from the lay public's approbation of his efforts. The question, therefore, is whether defendant took from plaintiff's works so much of what is pleasing to the ears of lay listeners, who comprise the audience from whom such popular music is composed, that defendant wrongfully appropriated something which belongs to the plaintiff.

Surely, then, we have an issue of fact which a jury is peculiarly fitted to determine. Indeed, even if there were to be a trial before a judge, it would be desirable (although not necessary) for him to summon an advisory jury on this question.

We should not be taken as saying that a plagiarism case can never arise in which absence of similarities is so patent that a summary judgment for defendant would be correct. Thus suppose that Ravel's "Bolero" or Shostakovitch's "Fifth Symphony" were alleged to infringe "When Irish Eyes Are Smiling." But this is not such a case. For, after listening to the playing of the respective compositions, we are, at this time, unable to conclude that the likenesses are so trifling that, on the issue of misappropriation, a trial judge could legitimately direct a verdict for defendant.

At the trial, plaintiff may play, or cause to be played, the pieces in such manner that they may seem to a jury to be inexcusably alike, in terms of the way in which lay listeners of such music would be likely to react. The plaintiff may call witnesses whose testimony may aid the jury in reaching its conclusion as to the responses of such audiences. Expert testimony of musicians may also be received, but it will in no way be controlling on the issue of illicit copying, and should be utilized only to assist in determining the reactions of lay auditors. The impression made on the refined ears of musical experts or their views as to the musical excellence of plaintiff's or defendant's works are utterly immaterial on the issue of misappropriation; for the views of such persons are caviar to the general—and plaintiff's and defendant's compositions are not caviar.

In copyright infringement cases cited by defendant,[26] we have sustained judgments in favor of defendants based on findings of fact made by trial judges after trials, findings we held not to be "clearly erroneous." * * *

[R]eversed and remanded.

■ CLARK, CIRCUIT JUDGE (dissenting).

While the procedure followed below seems to me generally simple and appropriate, the defendant did make one fatal tactical error. In an endeavor to assist us, he caused to be prepared records of all the musical pieces here

---

19. Where plaintiff relies on similarities to prove copying (as distinguished from improper appropriation) paper comparisons and the opinions of experts may aid the court.

26. See, e.g., Arnstein v. Edward B. Marks Music Corporation, 2 Cir., 82 F.2d 275, 277; Arnstein v. Broadcast Music, Inc., 2 Cir., 137 F.2d 410, 412. * * *

involved, and presented these transcriptions through the medium of the affidavit of his pianist. Though he himself did not stress these records and properly met plaintiff's claims as to the written music with his own analysis, yet the tinny tintinnabulations of the music thus canned resounded through the United States Courthouse to the exclusion of all else, including the real issues in the case. Of course, sound is important in a case of this kind, but it is not so important as to falsify what the eye reports that the mind teaches. Otherwise plagiarism would be suggested by the mere drumming of repetitious sound from our usual popular music, as it issues from a piano, orchestra, or hurdy-gurdy—particularly when ears may be dulled by long usage, possibly artistic repugnance or boredom, or mere distance which causes all sounds to merge. And the judicial eardrum may be peculiarly insensitive after long years of listening to the "beat, beat, beat" (I find myself plagiarizing from defendant and thus in danger of my brothers' doom) of sound upon it, though perhaps no more so than the ordinary citizen juror—even if tone deafness is made a disqualification for jury service, as advocated.

* * *

NOTES

1. In Heim v. Universal Pictures Co., 154 F.2d 480 (2d Cir. 1946), decided five days later, the court affirmed a judgment of non-infringement in spite of proof of access and considerable similarity. Judge Frank said:

> In effect, [the trial judge] * * * found that plaintiff's method of dealing with the common trite note sequence did not possess enough originality, raising it above the level of banal, to preclude coincidence as an adequate explanation of the identity. We cannot say that the judge erred. Whether, had he reached a contrary conclusion, we would have affirmed, we do not consider. Id. at 488.

Judge Clark, concurring in the result, observed:

> Surely, if the *Arnstein* case teaches us anything, it must be that banality is no bar to a claim for plagiarism. That results at once so divergent and so musically astonishing as the decisions in these two cases can occur simultaneously I can attribute only to the novel conceptions of legal plagiarism first announced in the *Arnstein* case and now repeated here. By these the issue is no longer one of musical similarity or identity to justify the conclusion of copying—an issue to be decided with all the intelligence, musical as well as legal, we can bring to bear upon it—but is one first, of copying, to be decided more or less intelligently, and, second, of illicit copying, to be decided blindly on a mere cacophony of sounds. Just at which stage decision here has occurred, I am not sure. Id. at 491.

2. Is *Arnstein* to better understood as a case about summary judgment, not proof of infringement. As to summary judgment, it is clear that in the years since *Arnstein* the federal courts, including the Second Circuit, have become considerably more willing to grant motions for summary judgment.

In Denker v. Uhry, 820 F.Supp. 722, 729–30 (S.D. N.Y. 1992), *aff'd without opinion*, 996 F.2d 301 (2nd Cir. 1993), the court said the following of *Arnstein*:

Second, plaintiff cites *Arnstein* for the proposition that summary judgment on the issue of improper appropriation is inappropriate "if there is the slightest doubt as to the facts." 154 F.2d at 468. In *Arnstein* the Second Circuit reasoned that summary judgment in copyright actions should be avoided because juries are "peculiarly fitted to determine" the response of the lay public. Id. at 473.

The *Arnstein* court's conclusions regarding summary judgment, however, have been undermined by recent case law both on summary judgment in general and summary judgment in copyright actions in particular. The mere existence of disputed factual issues is no longer sufficient to defeat a motion for summary judgment. Knight v. United States Fire Ins. Co., 804 F.2d 9, 11–12 (2d Cir. 1986), *cert. denied*, 480 U.S. 932 (1987). Regardless of whether an issue is triable by jury, to avoid summary judgment the disputed issues of fact must be "material to the outcome of the litigation," id. 804 F.2d at 11, and must be backed by evidence that would allow "a rational trier of fact to find for the non-moving party." Matsushita Electric Indus. Co. v. Zenith Radio Corp., 475 U.S. 574 (1986).

In fact, the Second Circuit has repudiated Arnstein's "slightest doubt" standard, Beal v. Lindsay, 468 F.2d 287, 291 (2d Cir. 1972), and has held that summary judgment on the issue of improper appropriation is warranted if the "similarity involves only 'non-copyrightable elements of plaintiff's work,' or . . . no reasonable jury, properly instructed, could find that the two works are substantially similar." Warner Bros., Inc., 720 F.2d at 240 (quoting Hoehling, 618 F.2d at 977); Durham Industries, Inc. v. Tomy Corp., 630 F.2d 905, 918 (2d Cir. 1980).

3. Cases involving music seem to give the judges particular difficulty, or at least difficulty in verbally articulating the applicable standard, perhaps because the legal profession does not attract the musically trained or even talented. (Consider as well in this respect *Gaste v. Kaiserman*, above.) In Fred Fisher, Inc. v. Dillingham, 298 Fed. 145 (S.D.N.Y. 1924), Judge L. Hand held that Jerome Kern's "Kalua" had infringed the plaintiff's "Dardanella."

There is no similarity between the melodies of the two pieces in any part, but the supposed infringement is in the accompaniment of the chorus or refrain of 'Kalua,' which has in part an absolute identity with the accompaniment of the verse, though not the chorus, of 'Dardanella.' This accompaniment introduces the copyrighted song, and is known in music as an 'ostinato,' or constantly repeated figures, which produces the effect of a rolling underphrase for the melody, something like the beat of a drum or tomtom, except that it has a very simple melodic character of its own. It consists of only eight notes, written in two measures and repeated again and again, with no changes, except the variation of a musical fifth in the scale to accommodate itself harmonically to the changes in the melody. Precisely the same eight notes are in the accompaniment to the chorus or refrain of 'Kalua,' used also as an 'ostinato,' precisely as they are used in 'Dardanella,' giving the same effect, and designed, as the composer says, to indicate the booming of a surf upon the beach. 298 Fed. at 146.

Is *Fisher* consistent with the position that mere phrases, titles and slogans are not copyrightable?

4. The *Arnstein* case illustrates the fact that although in theory an infringing work must actually be taken from the copyrighted work, in practice copyright protection is somewhat greater. In the *Fisher* case, supra, Kern testified that he was not aware of any plagiarism. Although Hand was willing to believe him, he was unimpressed.

> Whether he unconsciously copied the figures, he cannot say, and does not try to. Everything registers somewhere in our memories, and no one can tell what may evoke it. On the whole, my belief is that, in composing the accompaniment to the refrain of 'Kalua,' Mr. Kern must have followed, probably unconsciously, what he had certainly often heard only a short time before. I cannot really see how else to account for a similarity, which amounts to identity. 298 Fed. at 147.

5. Judge Frank says: "On that issue [unlawful appropriation] * * * the test is the response of the ordinary lay hearer. * * * The question, therefore, is whether defendant took from plaintiff's works so much of what is pleasing to the ears of lay listeners, who comprise the audience from whom such popular music is composed, that defendant wrongfully appropriated something which belongs to the plaintiff." Is that statement consistent with Judge Hand's approach in *Nichols* and *Sheldon?* Do different standards apply to drama and music? If so, is that because they have different audiences? How does Judge Frank (or the jury) know when "so much of what is pleasing" is too much?

PROBLEMS

1. Is the standard for infringement of classical music the same as for popular music?

2. Should a judge who does not regularly listen to popular music disqualify himself as a trier of fact in a case involving infringement of such music? Can a juror be excluded for cause on such a ground? Cf. note 22 of the *Arnstein* opinion: "It would * * * be proper to exclude tone-deaf persons from the jury." 154 F.2d at 473.

Hoehling v. Universal City Studios, Inc.

United States Court of Appeals, Second Circuit, 1980.
618 F.2d 972.

■ IRVING R. KAUFMAN, CHIEF JUDGE.

A grant of copyright in a published work secures for its author a limited monopoly over the expression it contains. The copyright provides a financial incentive to those who would add to the corpus of existing knowledge by creating original works. Nevertheless, the protection afforded the copyright holder has never extended to history, be it documented fact or explanatory hypothesis. The rationale for this doctrine is that the cause of knowledge is best served when history is the common property of all, and each generation remains free to draw upon the discoveries and insights of the past. Accordingly, the scope of copyright in historical accounts is narrow indeed, embracing no more than the author's original expression of particular facts and theories already in the public domain. As the case before us illustrates, absent wholesale usurpation of another's expression, claims of copyright infringement where works of history are at issue are rarely successful.

I.

This litigation arises from three separate accounts of the triumphant introduction, last voyage, and tragic destruction of the Hindenburg, the colossal dirigible constructed in Germany during Hitler's reign. The zeppelin, the last and most sophisticated in a fleet of luxury airships, which punctually floated its wealthy passengers from the Third Reich to the United States, exploded into flames and disintegrated in 35 seconds as it hovered above the Lakehurst, New Jersey Naval Air Station at 7:25 p.m. on May 6, 1937. Thirty-six passengers and crew were killed but, fortunately, 52 persons survived. Official investigations conducted by both American and German authorities could ascertain no definitive cause of the disaster, but both suggested the plausibility of static electricity or St. Elmo's Fire, which could have ignited the highly explosive hydrogen that filled the airship. Throughout, the investigators refused to rule out the possibility of sabotage.

The destruction of the Hindenburg marked the concluding chapter in the chronicle of airship passenger service, for after the tragedy at Lakehurst, the Nazi regime permanently grounded the Graf Zeppelin I and discontinued its plan to construct an even larger dirigible, the Graf Zeppelin II.

The final pages of the airship's story marked the beginning of a series of journalistic, historical, and literary accounts devoted to the Hindenburg and its fate. Indeed, weeks of testimony by a plethora of witnesses before the official investigative panels provided fertile source material for would-be authors. Moreover, both the American and German Commissions issued official reports, detailing all that was then known of the tragedy. A number of newspaper and magazine articles had been written about the Hindenburg in 1936, its first year of trans-Atlantic service, and they, of course, multiplied many fold after the crash. In addition, two passengers—Margaret Mather and Gertrud Adelt—published separate and detailed accounts of the voyage, C.E. Rosendahl, commander of the Lakehurst Naval Air Station and a pioneer in airship travel himself, wrote a book titled *What About the Airship?*, in which he endorsed the theory that the Hindenburg was the victim of sabotage. In 1957, Nelson Gidding, who would return to the subject of the Hindenburg some 20 years later, wrote an unpublished "treatment" for a motion picture based on the deliberate destruction of the airship. In that year as well, John Toland published *Ships in the Sky* which, in its seventeenth chapter, chronicled the last flight of the Hindenburg. In 1962, Dale Titler released *Wings of Mystery*, in which he too devoted a chapter to the Hindenburg.[1]

---

1. Titler's account was published after the release of appellant's book. In an affidavit in this litigation, Titler states that he copied Hoehling's theory of sabotage. Hoehling, however, has never instituted a copyright action against Titler.

Appellant A.A. Hoehling published *Who Destroyed the Hindenburg?*, a full-length book based on his exhaustive research in 1962. Mr. Hoehling studied the investigative reports, consulted previously published articles and books, and conducted interviews with survivors of the crash as well as others who possessed information about the Hindenburg. His book is presented as a factual account, written in an objective, reportorial style.

The first half recounts the final crossing of the Hindenburg, from Sunday, May 2, when it left Frankfurt, to Thursday, May 6, when it exploded at Lakehurst. Hoehling describes the airship, its role as an instrument of propaganda in Nazi Germany, its passengers and crew, the danger of hydrogen, and the ominous threats received by German officials, warning that the Hindenburg would be destroyed. The second portion, headed *The Quest,* sets forth the progress of the official investigations, followed by an account of Hoehling's own research. In the final chapter, spanning eleven pages, Hoehling suggests that all proffered explanations of the explosion, save deliberate destruction, are unconvincing. He concludes that the most likely saboteur is one Eric Spehl, a "rigger" on the Hindenburg crew who was killed at Lakehurst.

According to Hoehling, Spehl had motive, expertise, and opportunity to plant an explosive device, constructed of dry-cell batteries and a flashbulb, in "Gas Cell 4," the location of the initial explosion. An amateur photographer with access to flashbulbs, Spehl could have destroyed the Hindenburg to please his ladyfriend, a suspected communist dedicated to exploding the myth of Nazi invincibility.

Ten years later appellee Michael MacDonald Mooney published his book, *The Hindenburg*. Mooney's endeavor might be characterized as more literary than historical in its attempt to weave a number of symbolic themes through the actual events surrounding the tragedy. His dominant theme contrasts the natural beauty of the month of May, when the disaster occurred, with the cold, deliberate progress of "technology." The May theme is expressed not simply by the season, but also by the character of Spehl, portrayed as a sensitive artisan with needle and thread. The Hindenburg, in contrast, is the symbol of technology, as are its German creators and the Reich itself. The destruction is depicted as the ultimate triumph of nature over technology, as Spehl plants the bomb that ignites the hydrogen. Developing this theme from the outset, Mooney begins with an extended review of man's efforts to defy nature through flight, focusing on the evolution of the zeppelin. This story culminates in the construction of the Hindenburg, and the Nazis' claims of its indestructibility. Mooney then traces the fateful voyage, advising the reader almost immediately of Spehl's scheme. The book concludes with the airship's explosion.

Mooney acknowledges, in this case, that he consulted Hoehling's book, and that he relied on it for some details. He asserts that he first discovered the "Spehl-as-saboteur" theory when he read Titler's *Wings of Mystery*. Indeed, Titler concludes that Spehl was the saboteur, for essentially the reasons stated by Hoehling. Mooney also claims to have studied the complete National Archives and New York Times files concerning the Hindenburg, as well as all previously published material. Moreover, he traveled to Germany, visited Spehl's birthplace, and conducted a number of interviews with survivors.

After Mooney prepared an outline of his anticipated book, his publisher succeeded in negotiations to sell the motion picture rights to appellee Universal City Studios. Universal then commissioned a screen story by writers Levinson and Link, best known for their television series, *Columbo,* in which a somewhat disheveled, but wise detective unravels artfully conceived murder mysteries. In their screen story, Levinson and Link created a Columbo-like character who endeavored to identify the saboteur on board the Hindenburg. Director Robert Wise, however, was not satisfied with this version, and called upon Nelson Gidding to write a final screenplay. Gidding, it will be recalled, had engaged in preliminary work on a film about the Hindenburg almost twenty years earlier.

The Gidding screenplay follows what is known in the motion picture industry as a "Grand Hotel" formula, developing a number of fictional characters and subplots involving them. This formula has become standard fare in so-called "disaster" movies, which have enjoyed a certain popularity in recent years. In the film, which was released in late 1975, a rigger named "Boerth," who has an anti-Nazi ladyfriend, plans to destroy the airship in an effort to embarrass the Reich. Nazi officials, vaguely aware of sabotage threats, station a Luftwaffe intelligence officer on the zeppelin, loosely resembling a Colonel Erdmann who was aboard the Hindenburg. This character is portrayed as a likeable fellow who soon discovers that Boerth is the saboteur. Boerth, however, convinces him that the Hindenburg should be destroyed and the two join forces, planning the explosion for several hours after the landing at Lakehurst, when no people would be on board. In Gidding's version, the airship is delayed by a storm, frantic efforts to defuse the bomb fail, and the Hindenburg is destroyed. The film's subplots involve other possible suspects, including a fictional countess who has had her estate expropriated by the Reich, two fictional confidence men wanted by New York City police, and an advertising executive rushing to close a business deal in America.

Upon learning of Universal's plans to release the film, Hoehling instituted this action against Universal for copyright infringement and common law unfair competition in the district court for the District of Columbia in October 1975. Judge Smith declined to issue an order restraining release of the film in December, and it was distributed throughout the nation.

In January 1976, Hoehling sought to amend his complaint to include Mooney as a defendant. The district court, however, decided that it lacked personal jurisdiction over Mooney. In June 1976, Hoehling again attempted to amend his complaint, this time to add Mooney's publishers as defendants. Judge Smith denied this motion as well, but granted Hoehling's request to transfer the litigation to the Southern District of New York, 28 U.S.C. § 1404(a), where Mooney himself was successfully included as a party. Judge Metzner, with the assistance of Magistrate Sinclair, supervised extensive discovery through most of 1978. After the completion of discovery, both Mooney and Universal moved for summary judgment, Fed.R.Civ.P. 56, which was granted on August 1, 1979.

II.

It is undisputed that Hoehling has a valid copyright in his book. To prove infringement, however, he must demonstrate that defendants "copied" his work and that they "improperly appropriated" his "expression." See Arnstein v. Porter, 154 F.2d 464, 468 (2d Cir. 1946). Ordinarily, wrongful appropriation is shown by proving a "substantial similarity" of *copyrightable* expression. See Nichols v. Universal Pictures Corp., 45 F.2d 119, 121 (2d Cir. 1930), *cert. denied,* 282 U.S. 902 (1931). Because substantial similarity is customarily an extremely close question of fact, see Arnstein, supra, 154 F.2d at 468, summary judgment has traditionally been frowned upon in copyright litigation, id. at 474. Nevertheless, while *Arnstein's* influence in other areas of the law has been diminished, see SEC v. Research Automation Corp., 585 F.2d 31 (2d Cir. 1978); 6 Moore's Federal Practice ¶ 56.17[14] (2d ed. 1976), a series of copyright cases in the Southern District of New York have granted defendants summary judgment when all alleged similarity related to *non*-copyrightable elements of the plaintiff's work, see, e.g., Alexander v. Haley, 460 F.Supp. 40 (S.D.N.Y. 1978); Musto v. Meyer, 434 F.Supp. 32 (S.D.N.Y.1977); Gardner v. Nizer, 391 F.Supp. 940 (S.D.N.Y. 1975); Fuld v. National Broadcasting Co., 390 F.Supp. 877 (S.D.N.Y.1975). These cases signal an important development in the law of copyright, permitting courts to put "a swift end to meritless litigation" and to avoid lengthy and costly trials. Quinn v. Syracuse Model Neighborhood Corp., 613 F.2d 438, 445 (2d Cir. 1980); accord, Donnelly v. Guion, 467 F.2d 290, 293 (2d Cir. 1972); American Manufacturers Mutual Insurance Co. v. American Broadcasting-Paramount Theatres, Inc., 388 F.2d 272, 278 (2d Cir. 1967). Drawing on these cases, Judge Metzner assumed both copying and substantial similarity, but concluded that all similarities pertained to various categories of non-copyrightable material. Accordingly, he granted appellees' motion for summary judgment. We affirm the judgment of the district court.

A

Hoehling's principal claim is that both Mooney and Universal copied the essential plot of his book—i.e., Eric Spehl, influenced by his girlfriend, sabotaged the Hindenburg by placing a crude bomb in Gas Cell 4. In their briefs, and at oral argument, appellees have labored to convince us that their plots are not substantially similar to Hoehling's. While Hoehling's Spehl destroys the airship to please his communist girlfriend, Mooney's character is motivated by an aversion to the technological age. Universal's Boerth, on the other hand, is a fervent anti-fascist who enlists the support of a Luftwaffe colonel who, in turn, unsuccessfully attempts to defuse the bomb at the eleventh hour.

Although this argument has potential merit when presented to a fact finder adjudicating the issue of substantial similarity, it is largely irrelevant to a motion for summary judgment where the issue of substantial similarity has been eliminated by the judge's affirmative assumption. Under

Rule 56(c), summary judgment is appropriate only when "there is no gen-uine issue as to any material fact." Accord, Heyman v. Commerce & Industry Insurance Co., 524 F.2d 1317 (2d Cir. 1975). Perhaps recognizing this, appellees further argue that Hoehling's plot is an "idea," and ideas are not copyrightable as a matter of law. See Sheldon v. Metro-Goldwyn Pictures Corp., 81 F.2d 49, 54 (2d Cir.), cert. denied, 298 U.S. 669 (1936).

Hoehling, however, correctly rejoins that while ideas themselves are not subject to copyright, his "expression" of *his* idea is copyrightable. Id. at 54. He relies on Learned Hand's opinion in *Sheldon,* supra, at 50, holding that *Letty Lynton* infringed *Dishonored Lady* by copying its story of a woman who poisons her lover, and Augustus Hand's analysis in Detective Comics, Inc. v. Bruns Publications, Inc., 111 F.2d 432 (2d Cir. 1940), con-cluding that the exploits of "Wonderman" infringed the copyright held by the creators of "Superman," the original indestructible man. Moreover, Hoehling asserts that, in both these cases, the line between "ideas" and "expression" is drawn, in the first instance, by the fact finder.

Sheldon and *Detective Comics,* however, dealt with works of fiction,[4] where the distinction between an idea and its expression is especially elu-sive. But, where, as here, the idea at issue is an interpretation of an histor-ical event, our cases hold that such interpretations are not copyrightable as a matter of law. In Rosemont Enterprises, Inc. v. Random House, Inc., 366 F.2d 303 (2d Cir. 1966), *cert. denied,* 385 U.S. 1009 (1967), we held that the defendant's biography of Howard Hughes did not infringe an earlier biog-raphy of the reclusive alleged billionaire. Although the plots of the two works were necessarily similar, there could be no infringement because of the "public benefit in encouraging the development of historical and bio-graphical works and their public distribution." Id. at 307; accord, Oxford Book Co. v. College Entrance Book Co., 98 F.2d 688 (2d Cir. 1938). To avoid a chilling effect on authors who contemplate tackling an historical issue or event, broad latitude must be granted to subsequent authors who make use of historical subject matter, including theories or plots. Learned Hand coun-seled in Myers v. Mail & Express Co., 36 C.O.Bull. 478, 479 (S.D.N.Y. 1919), "[t]here cannot be any such thing as copyright in the order of presentation of the facts, nor, indeed, in their selection."[5]

In the instant case, the hypothesis that Eric Spehl destroyed the Hindenburg is based entirely on the interpretation of historical facts, including Spehl's life, his girlfriend's anti-Nazi connections, the explosion's

---

4. In Sheldon, both works were loosely based on an actual murder committed by a young Scottish girl. Judge Hand, however, clearly dealt only with the fictional plots con-ceived by the respective authors. See Sheldon v. Metro-Goldwyn Pictures Corp., 81 F.2d 49, 54 (2d Cir.) cert. denied, 298 U.S. 669 (1936).

5. This circuit has permitted extensive reliance on prior works of history. See, e.g., Gardner v. Nizer, 391 F.Supp. 940 (S.D.N.Y. 1975) (the story of the Rosenberg trial not

copyrightable); Fuld v. National Broadcasting Co., 390 F.Supp. 877 (S.D. N.Y. 1975) ("Bugsy" Siegel's life story not copyrightable); Greenbie v. Noble, 151 F.Supp. 45 (S.D.N.Y. 1957) (the life of Anna Carroll, a member of Lincoln's cabinet, not copyrightable). The commenta-tors are in accord with this view. See, e.g. 1 Nimmer on Copyright § 2.11[A] (1979); Chafee, Reflections on the Law of Copyright: I, 45 Colum. L. Rev. 503, 511 (1945).

origin in Gas Cell 4, Spehl's duty station, discovery of a dry-cell battery among the wreckage, and rumors about Spehl's involvement dating from a 1938 Gestapo investigation. Such an historical interpretation, whether or not it originated with Mr. Hoehling, is not protected by his copyright and can be freely used by subsequent authors.

B

The same reasoning governs Hoehling's claim that a number of specific facts, ascertained through his personal research, were copied by appellees.[6] The cases in this circuit, however, make clear that factual information is in the public domain. See, e.g., Rosemont Enterprises, Inc., supra, 366 F.2d at 309; Oxford Book Co., supra, 98 F.2d at 691. Each appellee had the right to "avail himself of the facts contained" in Hoehling's book and to "use such information, whether correct or incorrect, in his own literary work." Greenbie v. Noble, 151 F.Supp. 45, 67 (S.D.N.Y. 1957). Accordingly, there is little consolation in relying on cases in other circuits holding that the fruits of original research are copyrightable. See, e.g., Toksvig v. Bruce Publications Corp., 181 F.2d 664, 667 (7th Cir. 1950); Miller v. Universal City Studios, Inc., 460 F.Supp. 984 (S.D.Fla. 1978). Indeed, this circuit has clearly repudiated *Toksvig* and its progeny. In Rosemont Enterprises, Inc., supra, 366 F.2d at 310, we refused to "subscribe to the view that an author is absolutely precluded from saving time and effort by referring to and relying upon prior published material. * * * It is just such wasted effort that the proscription against the copyright of ideas and facts * * * are designed to prevent." Accord, 1 Nimmer on Copyright § 2.11 (1979).

* * *

D

All of Hoehling's allegations of copying, therefore, encompass material that is non-copyrightable as a matter of law, rendering summary judgment entirely appropriate. We are aware, however, that in distinguishing between themes, facts, and *scenes a faire* on the one hand, and copyrightable expression on the other, courts may lose sight of the forest for the trees. By factoring out similarities based on non-copyrightable elements, a court runs the risk of overlooking wholesale usurpation of a prior author's expression. A

---

6. In detailed comparisons of his book with Mooney's work and Universal's motion picture, Hoehling isolates 266 and 75 alleged instances of copying, respectively. Judge Metzner correctly pointed out that many of these allegations are patently frivolous. The vast majority of the remainder deals with alleged copying of historical facts. It would serve no purpose to review Hoehling's specific allegations in detail in this opinion. The following ten examples, however, are illustrative: (1) Eric Spehl's age and birthplace; (2) Crew members had smuggled monkeys on board the Graf Zeppelin; (3) Germany's ambassador to the United States dismissed threats of sabotage; (4) A warning letter had been received from a Mrs. Rauch; (5) The Hindenburg's captain was constructing a new home in Zeppelinheim; (6) Eric Spehl was a photographer; (7) The airship flew over Boston; (8) The Hindenburg was "tail heavy" before landing; (9) A member of the ground crew had etched his name in the zeppelin's hull; and (10) The navigator set the Hindenburg's course by reference to various North Atlantic islands.

verbatim reproduction of another work, of course, even in the realm of non-fiction, is actionable as copyright infringement. See Wainwright Securities, Inc. v. Wall Street Transcript Corp., 558 F.2d 91 (2d Cir. 1977), cert. denied, 434 U.S. 1014 (1978). Thus, in granting or reviewing a grant of summary judgment for defendants, courts should assure themselves that the works before them are not virtually identical. In this case, it is clear that all three authors relate the story of the Hindenburg differently.

In works devoted to historical subjects, it is our view that a second author may make significant use of prior work, so long as he does not bodily appropriate the expression of another. Rosemont Enterprises, Inc., supra, 366 F.2d at 310. This principle is justified by the fundamental policy undergirding the copyright laws—the encouragement of contributions to recorded knowledge. The "financial reward guaranteed to the copyright holder is but an incident of this general objective, rather than an end in itself." Berlin v. E.C. Publications, Inc., 329 F.2d 541, 543–44 (2d Cir.), cert. denied, 379 U.S. 822 (1964). Knowledge is expanded as well by granting new authors of historical works a relatively free hand to build upon the work of their predecessors.[7]

III.

Finally, we affirm Judge Metzner's rejection of Hoehling's claims based on the common law of "unfair competition." Where, as here, historical facts, themes, and research have been deliberately exempted from the scope of copyright protection to vindicate the overriding goal of encouraging contributions to recorded knowledge, the states are pre-empted from removing such material from the public domain. See, e.g., Sears, Roebuck & Co. v. Stiffel Co., 376 U.S. 225 (1964); Compco Corp. v. Day-Brite Lighting, Inc., 376 U.S. 234 (1964). "To forbid copying" in this case, "would interfere with the federal policy * * * of allowing free access to copy whatever the federal patent and copyright laws leave in the public domain." Id. at 237.

The judgment of the district court is affirmed.

NOTE

The Fifth Circuit followed *Hoehling* and the other Second Circuit precedents in Miller v. Universal City Studios, 650 F.2d 1365 (5th Cir. 1981). Plaintiff was a reporter for the Miami Herald who had written in collaboration with the victim a book entitled "83 Hours Till Dawn," the story of the ordeal of the college-aged daughter of a wealthy Florida land developer who was abducted from an Atlanta motel room and buried alive in a plywood and fiberglass capsule from which she was rescued after five days. A Universal City Studios producer read the book and thought it good material for a television movie. When negotiations for purchase of the screen rights to "83 Hours Till Dawn" broke down, the studio proceeded with the project, instructing the

---

7. We note that publication of Mooney's book and release of the motion picture revived long dormant interest in the Hindenburg. As a result, Hoehling's book, which had been out of print for some time, was actually re-released after the film was featured in theaters across the country.

scriptwriter that no use was to be made of the book in preparing the script. The movie was completed and shown as the ABC Movie of the Week with the title "The Longest Night." Plaintiff sued for copyright infringement and won a jury verdict. The appellate court reversed because the instructions (and plaintiff's arguments) to the jury included the statement that "if an author, in writing a book concerning factual matters, engages in research on these matters, his research is copyrightable." 650 F.2d 1368.

The infringement cases studied so far have involved works of fiction, drama, history, music and graphic art, all close to the core of traditional copyright protection. In the past half century, however, there has been an expansion in the use of copyright to protect "works" which are more like commercial than artistic products—fabric designs, computer programs and data bases, promotional campaigns and symbols.

The *Mazer* doctrine has operated to bring to the courts many cases of infringement involving fabrics, dolls and other toys, and various novelties. Here the "ordinary observer" test is clearly the standard, and the "ordinary observer" is the person in the market for which the product is intended. For instance, in Peter Pan Fabrics, Inc. v. Martin Weiner Corp., 274 F.2d 487 (2d Cir. 1960), Judge Hand said that "In deciding that question [of how much similarity is too much] one should consider the uses for which the design is intended, especially the scrutiny that observers will give to it as used. In the case at bar we must try to estimate how far its overall appearance will determine its aesthetic appeal when the cloth is made into a garment." 274 F.2d at 489. This is in spite of the fact that the copyright act provides no protection for dress designs, only fabric designs. In Ideal Toy Corp. v. Sayco Doll Corp., 302 F.2d 623 (2d Cir. 1962), the court affirmed a preliminary injunction against defendant's "Chubby Toddler" doll. The district judge had found that a visual comparison between the copyrighted doll and the defendant's "establishes that the head of defendant's doll incorporates so many distinctive features and characteristics of the head of plaintiff's doll as to lead to the conclusion *prima facie* that defendant's doll head was copied." Judge Clark dissented, finding that it was not at all surprising that the heads of two dolls modeled on babies should have many distinctive features in common, and arguing that under the guise of affirming a finding of fact the court was creating an important commercial monopoly never intended by Congress.

An "ordinary observer in the market" test makes sense if one views the purpose of copyright in this area as one of conferring protection on the commercial designs involved. However, if one views the copyright protection as a secondary by-product of the protection afforded to the "work of art," then it would be logical to define the scope of the protection on the perspective of the art world rather than the market in which the fabric, toys and novelties are sold.

The standards for determining infringement of computer software is an area that has been the focus of extensive litigation since copyright protection was extended to computer programs in 1979.

Computer Associates International v. Altai

United States Court of Appeals for the Second Circuit, 1992.
982 F. 2d 693.

■ WALKER, CIRCUIT JUDGES.

* * *

* * * [T]his case deals with the challenging question of whether and to what extent the "non-literal" aspects of a computer program, that is, those aspects that are not reduced to written code, are protected by copyright. While a few other courts have already grappled with this issue, this case is one of first impression in this circuit. As we shall discuss, we find the results reached by other courts to be less than satisfactory. Drawing upon long-standing doctrines of copyright law, we take an approach that we think better addresses the practical difficulties embedded in these types of cases. In so doing, we have kept in mind the necessary balance between creative incentive and industrial competition.

This appeal comes to us from the United States District Court for the Eastern District of New York, the Honorable George C. Pratt, Circuit Judge, sitting by designation. By Memorandum and Order entered August 12, 1991, Judge Pratt found that defendant Altai, Inc.'s ("Altai"), OSCAR 3.4 computer program had infringed plaintiff Computer Associates' ("CA"), copyrighted computer program entitled CA-SCHEDULER. Accordingly, the district court awarded CA $364,444 in actual damages and apportioned profits. Altai has abandoned its appeal from this award. With respect to CA's second claim for copyright infringement, Judge Pratt found that Altai's OSCAR 3.5 program was not substantially similar to a portion of CA-SCHEDULER called ADAPTER, and thus denied relief. * * *

Because we are in full agreement with Judge Pratt's decision and in substantial agreement with his careful reasoning regarding CA's copyright infringement claim, we affirm the district court's judgment on that issue.

* * *

I. COMPUTER PROGRAM DESIGN

* * *

The first step in * * * [computer programming] is to identify a program's ultimate function or purpose. An example of such an ultimate purpose might be the creation and maintenance of a business ledger. Once this goal has been achieved, a programmer breaks down or "decomposes" the program's ultimate function into "simpler constituent problems or 'subtasks,'" Englund, [Note, Idea, Process, or Protected Expression?: Determining the Scope of Copyright Protection of the Structure of Computer Programs, 88 Mich. L. Rev. 866, 867–73 (1990)] at 870, which are also known as subroutines or modules. See Spivack, [Comment, Does Form Follow Function? The Idea/Expression Dichotomy In Copyright Protection of Computer Software, 35 U.C.L.A. L.

Rev. 723 (1988)] at 729. In the context of a business ledger program, a module or subroutine might be responsible for the task of updating a list of outstanding accounts receivable. Sometimes, depending upon the complexity of its task, a subroutine may be broken down further into sub-subroutines.

Having sufficiently decomposed the program's ultimate function into its component elements, a programmer will then arrange the subroutines or modules into what are known as organizational or flow charts. Flow charts map the interactions between modules that achieve the program's end goal. See Kretschmer, [Note, Copyright Protection For Software Architecture: Just Say No!, 1988 Colum. Bus. L. Rev. 823 (1988)] at 826.

In order to accomplish these intra-program interactions, a programmer must carefully design each module's parameter list. A parameter list, according to the expert appointed and fully credited by the district court, Dr. Randall Davis, is "the information sent to and received from a subroutine." See Report of Dr. Randall Davis, at 12. The term "parameter list" refers to the form in which information is passed between modules (e.g. for accounts receivable, the designated time frame and particular customer identifying number) and the information's actual content (e.g. 8/91–7/92; customer No. 3). Id. With respect to form, interacting modules must share similar parameter lists so that they are capable of exchanging information.

"The functions of the modules in a program together with each module's relationships to other modules constitute the 'structure' of the program." Englund, at 871. Additionally, the term structure may include the category of modules referred to as "macros." A macro is a single instruction that initiates a sequence of operations or module interactions within the program. Very often the user will accompany a macro with an instruction from the parameter list to refine the instruction (e.g. current total of accounts receivable (macro), but limited to those for 8/91 to 7/92 from customer No. 3 (parameters)).

In fashioning the structure, a programmer will normally attempt to maximize the program's speed, efficiency, as well as simplicity for user operation, while taking into consideration certain externalities such as the memory constraints of the computer upon which the program will be run. See id.; Kretschmer, at 826; Menell [Peter S. Menell, An Analysis of the Scope of Copyright Protection for Application Programs, 41 Stan. L. Rev. 1045, (1989)], at 1052. "This stage of program design often requires the most time and investment." Kretschmer, at 826.

Once each necessary module has been identified, designed, and its relationship to the other modules has been laid out conceptually, the resulting program structure must be embodied in a written language that the computer can read. This process is called "coding," and requires two steps. Whelan [Associates, Inc. v. Jaslow Dental Laboratory, Inc.,] 797 F.2d [1222] at 1230 [(3d Cir. 1986)]. First, the programmer must transpose the program's structural blue-print into a source code. This step has been described as "comparable to the novelist fleshing out the broad outline of his plot by crafting from words and sentences the paragraphs that convey the ideas." Kretschmer, at 826. The source code may be written in any one of several computer languages, such as COBAL, FORTRAN, BASIC, EDL, etc., depending upon the type of computer for which the program is intended. * * * Once the source code has been completed, the second step is to translate or "compile" it into object code. Object code is the binary language comprised of zeros and ones through which the computer directly receives its instructions. * * *

After the coding is finished, the programmer will run the program on the computer in order to find and correct any logical and syntactical errors. This is known as "debugging" and, once done, the program is complete. See Kretschmer, at 826–27.

II. FACTS

* * *

The subject of this litigation originates with one of CA's marketed programs entitled CA-SCHEDULER. CA-SCHEDULER is a job scheduling program designed for IBM mainframe computers. Its primary functions are straightforward: to create a schedule specifying when the computer should run various tasks, and then to control the computer as it executes the schedule. CA-SCHEDULER contains a sub-program entitled ADAPTER, also developed by CA. ADAPTER is not an independently marketed product of CA; it is a wholly integrated component of CA-SCHEDULER and has no capacity for independent use.

Nevertheless, ADAPTER plays an extremely important role. It is an "operating system compatibility component," which means, roughly speaking, it serves as a translator. An "operating system" is itself a program that manages the resources of the computer, allocating those resources to other programs as needed. The IBM System 370 family of computers, for which CA-SCHEDULER was created, is, depending upon the computer's size, designed to contain one of three operating systems: DOS/VSE, MVS, or CMS. As the district court noted, the general rule is that "a program written for one operating system, e.g., DOS/VSE, will not, without modification, run under another operating system such as MVS." Computer Assocs., 775 F.Supp. at 550. ADAPTER's function is to translate the language of a given program into the particular language that the computer's own operating system can understand.

The district court succinctly outlined the manner in which ADAPTER works within the context of the larger program. In order to enable CA-SCHEDULER to function on different operating systems, CA divided the CA-SCHEDULER into two components:

—a first component that contains only the task-specific portions of the program, independent of all operating system issues, and

—a second component that contains all the interconnections between the first component and the operating system.

In a program constructed in this way, whenever the first, task-specific, component needs to ask the operating system for some resource through a "system call", it calls the second component instead of calling the operating system directly. The second component serves as an "interface" or "compatibility component" between the task-specific portion of the program and the operating system. It receives the request from the first component and translates it into the appropriate system call that will be recognized by whatever operating system is installed on the computer, e.g., DOS/VSE, MVS, or CMS. Since the first, task-specific component calls the adapter component rather than the operating system, the first component need not be customized to use any specific operating system. The second, interface, component insures that all the system calls are performed properly for the particular operating system in use. Id. at 551. ADAPTER serves as the second, "common system interface" component referred to above.

A program like ADAPTER, which allows a computer user to change or use multiple operating systems while maintaining the same software, is highly desirable. It saves the user the costs, both in time and money, that otherwise would be expended in purchasing new programs, modifying existing systems to run them, and gaining familiarity with their operation. The benefits run both ways. The increased compatibility afforded by an ADAPTER-like component, and its resulting popularity among consumers, makes whatever software in which it is incorporated significantly more marketable.

Starting in 1982, Altai began marketing its own job scheduling program entitled ZEKE. The original version of ZEKE was designed for use in conjunction with a VSE operating system. By late 1983, in response to customer demand, Altai decided to rewrite ZEKE so that it could be run in conjunction with an MVS operating system.

At that time, James P. Williams ("Williams"), then an employee of Altai and now its President, approached Claude F. Arney, III ("Arney"), a computer programmer who worked for CA. Williams and Arney were longstanding friends, and had in fact been co-workers at CA for some time before Williams left CA to work for Altai's predecessor. Williams wanted to recruit Arney to assist Altai in designing an MVS version of ZEKE.

At the time he first spoke with Arney, Williams was aware of both the CA-SCHEDULER and ADAPTER programs. However, Williams was not involved in their development and had never seen the codes of either program. When he asked Arney to come work for Altai, Williams did not know that ADAPTER was a component of CA-SCHEDULER.

Arney, on the other hand, was intimately familiar with various aspects of ADAPTER. While working for CA, he helped improve the VSE version of ADAPTER, and was permitted to take home a copy of ADAPTER'S source code. This apparently developed into an irresistible habit, for when Arney left CA to work for Altai in January, 1984, he took with him copies of the source code for both the VSE and MVS versions of ADAPTER. He did this in knowing violation of the CA employee agreements that he had signed.

Once at Altai, Arney and Williams discussed design possibilities for adapting ZEKE to run on MVS operating systems. Williams, who had created the VSE version of ZEKE, thought that approximately 30% of his original program would have to be modified in order to accommodate MVS. Arney persuaded Williams that the best way to make the needed modifications was to introduce a "common system interface" component into ZEKE.

He did not tell Williams that his idea stemmed from his familiarity with ADAPTER. They decided to name this new component-program OSCAR.

Arney went to work creating OSCAR at Altai's offices using the ADAPTER source code. The district court accepted Williams' testimony that no one at Altai, with the exception of Arney, affirmatively knew that Arney had the ADAPTER code, or that he was using it to create OSCAR/VSE. However, during this time period, Williams' office was adjacent to Arney's. Williams testified that he and Arney "conversed quite frequently" while Arney was "investigating the source code of ZEKE" and that Arney was in his office "a number of times daily, asking questions." In three months, Arney successfully completed the OSCAR/VSE project. In an additional month he developed an OSCAR/MVS version. When the dust finally settled, Arney had copied approximately 30% of OSCAR's code from CA's ADAPTER program.

The first generation of OSCAR programs was known as OSCAR 3.4. From 1985 to August 1988, Altai used OSCAR 3.4 in its ZEKE product, as well as in programs entitled ZACK and ZEBB. In late July 1988, CA first learned that Altai may have appropriated parts of ADAPTER. After confirming its suspicions, * * * CA * * * brought this copyright and trade secret misappropriation action against Altai.

Apparently, it was upon receipt of the summons and complaint that Altai first learned that Arney had copied much of the OSCAR code from ADAPTER. After Arney confirmed to Williams that CA's accusations of copying were true, Williams immediately set out to survey the damage. Without ever looking at the ADAPTER code himself, Williams learned from Arney exactly which sections of code Arney had taken from ADAPTER.

Upon advice of counsel, Williams initiated OSCAR's rewrite. The project's goal was to save as much of OSCAR 3.4 as legitimately could be used, and to excise those portions which had been copied from ADAPTER. Arney was entirely excluded from the process, and his copy of the ADAPTER code was locked away. Williams put eight other programmers on the project, none of whom had been involved in any way in the development of OSCAR 3.4. Williams provided the programmers with a description of the ZEKE operating system services so that they could rewrite the appropriate code. The rewrite project took about six months to complete and was finished in mid-November 1989. The resulting program was entitled OSCAR 3.5.

From that point on, Altai shipped only OSCAR 3.5 to its new customers. Altai also shipped OSCAR 3.5 as a "free upgrade" to all customers that had previously purchased OSCAR 3.4. While Altai and Williams acted responsibly to correct Arney's literal copying of the ADAPTER program, copyright infringement had occurred.

* * *

DISCUSSION

* * *

* * * CA contends that the district court applied an erroneous method for determining whether there exists substantial similarity between

computer programs, and thus, erred in determining that OSCAR 3.5 did not infringe the copyrights held on the different versions of its CA-SCHEDULER program. CA asserts that the test applied by the district court failed to account sufficiently for a computer program's non-literal elements. * * *

I. COPYRIGHT INFRINGEMENT

* * *

For the purpose of analysis, the district court assumed that Altai had access to the ADAPTER code when creating OSCAR 3.5. See Computer Assocs., 775 F.Supp. at 558. Thus, in determining whether Altai had unlawfully copied protected aspects of CA's ADAPTER, the district court narrowed its focus of inquiry to ascertaining whether Altai's OSCAR 3.5 was substantially similar to ADAPTER. Because we approve Judge Pratt's conclusions regarding substantial similarity, our analysis will proceed along the same assumption.

* * *

A. Copyright Protection for the Non-literal Elements of Computer Programs

* * *

CA argues that, despite Altai's rewrite of the OSCAR code, the resulting program remained substantially similar to the structure of its ADAPTER program. As discussed above, a program's structure includes its non-literal components such as general flow charts as well as the more specific organization of inter-modular relationships, parameter lists, and macros. In addition to these aspects, CA contends that OSCAR 3.5 is also substantially similar to ADAPTER with respect to the list of services that both ADAPTER and OSCAR obtain from their respective operating systems. We must decide whether and to what extent these elements of computer programs are protected by copyright law.

* * *

1) Idea vs. Expression Dichotomy

It is a fundamental principle of copyright law that a copyright does not protect an idea, but only the expression of the idea. * * * [§ 102(b)] * * *.

* * *

The essentially utilitarian nature of a computer program further complicates the task of distilling its idea from its expression. See SAS Inst., [Inc. v. SGH Compter Sys., Inc.,] 605 F.Supp. [816] at 829 [M.D. Tenn. 1985]; cf. Englund, at 893. In order to describe both computational processes and abstract ideas, its content "combines creative and technical expression." See Spivack, at 755. The variations of expression found in purely creative compositions, as opposed to those contained in utilitarian works, are not directed towards practical application. For example, a narration of Humpty Dumpty's demise, which would clearly be a creative composition, does not serve the same ends as, say, a recipe for scrambled eggs—which is a more process oriented text. Thus, compared to aesthetic works, computer programs hover even more closely to the elusive boundary line described in § 102(b).

To the extent that an accounting text [such as that involved in *Baker v. Selden*] and a computer program are both "a set of statements or instructions . . . to bring about a certain result," 17 U.S.C. § 101, they are roughly analogous. In the former case, the processes are ultimately conducted by human agency; in the latter, by electronic means. In either case, as already stated, the processes themselves are not protectable. But the holding in *Baker* goes farther. The Court concluded that those aspects of a work, which "must necessarily be used as incident to" the idea, system or process that the work describes, are also not copyrightable. 101 U.S. at 104. Selden's ledger sheets, therefore, enjoyed no copyright protection because they were "necessary incidents to" the system of accounting that he described. Id. at 103. From this reasoning, we conclude that those elements of a computer program that are necessarily incidental to its function are similarly unprotectable.

While *Baker v. Selden* provides a sound analytical foundation, it offers scant guidance on how to separate idea or process from expression, and moreover, on how to further distinguish protectable expression from that expression which "must necessarily be used as incident to" the work's underlying concept. In the context of computer programs, the Third Circuit's noted decision in *Whelan* has, thus far, been the most thoughtful attempt to accomplish these ends.

The court in *Whelan* faced substantially the same problem as is presented by this case. There, the defendant was accused of making off with the non-literal structure of the plaintiff's copyrighted dental lab management program, and employing it to create its own competitive version. In assessing whether there had been an infringement, the court had to determine which aspects of the programs involved were ideas, and which were expression. In separating the two, the court settled upon the following conceptual approach:

> [T]he line between idea and expression may be drawn with reference to the end sought to be achieved by the work in question. In other words, the purpose or function of a utilitarian work would be the work's idea, and everything that is not necessary to that purpose or function would be part of the expression of the idea. . . . Where there are various means of achieving the desired purpose, then the particular means chosen is not necessary to the purpose; hence, there is expression, not idea.

797 F.2d at 1236 (citations omitted). The "idea" of the program at issue in *Whelan* was identified by the court as simply "the efficient management of a dental laboratory." Id. at n. 28.

So far, in the courts, the *Whelan* rule has received a mixed reception. While some decisions have adopted its reasoning, * * *, others have rejected it, * * *.

Whelan has fared even more poorly in the academic community, where its standard for distinguishing idea from expression has been widely criticized for being conceptually overbroad. * * * . The leading commentator in the field has stated that "[t]he crucial flaw in [*Whelan's*] reasoning is that it assumes that only one 'idea,' in copyright law terms, underlies any computer program, and that once a separable idea can be identified, everything else must be expression." 3 Nimmer § 13.03(F), at 13–62.34. This criticism focuses not upon the program's ultimate purpose but upon the reality of its structural design. As we have already noted, a computer program's ultimate function or purpose is the composite result of interacting subroutines. Since each subroutine is itself a program, and thus, may be said to have its own "idea," *Whelan's* general formulation that a program's overall purpose equates with the program's idea is descriptively inadequate.

* * *

2) Substantial Similarity Test for Computer Program Structure: Abstraction- Filtration-Comparison

We think that *Whelan's* approach to separating idea from expression in computer programs relies too heavily on metaphysical distinctions and does not place enough emphasis on practical considerations. * * *

As discussed herein, we think that district courts would be well-advised to undertake a three-step procedure, based on the abstractions test utilized by the district court, in order to determine whether the non-literal elements of two or more computer programs are substantially similar. This approach breaks no new ground; rather, it draws on such familiar copyright doctrines as merger, *scenes a faire*, and public domain. In taking this approach, however, we are cognizant that computer technology is a dynamic field which can quickly outpace judicial decisionmaking. Thus, in cases where the technology in question does not allow for a literal application of the procedure we outline below, our opinion should not be read to foreclose the district courts of our circuit from utilizing a modified version.

In ascertaining substantial similarity under this approach, a court would first break down the allegedly infringed program into its constituent structural parts. Then, by examining each of these parts for such things as incorporated ideas, expression that is necessarily incidental to those ideas, and elements that are taken from the public domain, a court would then be able to sift out all non-protectable material. Left with a kernel, or possible kernels, of creative expression after following this process of elimination, the court's last step would be to compare this material with the structure of an allegedly infringing program. The result of this comparison will determine whether the protectable elements of the programs at issue are substantially similar so as to warrant a finding of infringement. It will be helpful to elaborate a bit further.

Step One: Abstraction

As the district court appreciated * * * the theoretic framework for analyzing substantial similarity expounded by Learned Hand in the *Nichols* case is helpful in the present context. In *Nichols*, we enunciated what has now become known as the "abstractions" test for separating idea from expression * * *

* * *

As applied to computer programs, the abstractions test will comprise the first step in the examination for substantial similarity. Initially, in a manner that resembles reverse engineering on a theoretical plane, a court should dissect the allegedly copied program's structure and isolate each level of abstraction contained within it. This process begins with the code and ends with an articulation of the program's ultimate function. Along the way, it is necessary essentially to retrace and map each of the designer's steps—in the opposite order in which they were taken during the program's creation. * * *

As an anatomical guide to this procedure, the following description is helpful:

> At the lowest level of abstraction, a computer program may be thought of in its entirety as a set of individual instructions organized into a hierarchy of modules. At a higher level of abstraction, the instructions in the lowest- level modules may be replaced conceptually by the functions of those modules. At progressively higher levels of abstraction, the functions of higherlevel modules conceptually replace the implementations of those modules in terms of lower-level modules and instructions, until finally, one is left with nothing but the ultimate function of the program. . . . A program has structure at every level of abstraction at which it is viewed. At low levels of abstraction, a program's structure may be quite complex; at the highest level it is trivial. * * *

Step Two: Filtration

Once the program's abstraction levels have been discovered, the substantial similarity inquiry moves from the conceptual to the concrete. Professor Nimmer suggests, and we endorse, a "successive filtering method" for separating protectable expression from non-protectable material. See generally 3 Nimmer § 13.03[F]. This process entails examining the structural components at each level of abstraction to determine whether their particular inclusion at that level was "idea" or was dictated by considerations of efficiency, so as to be necessarily incidental to that idea; required by factors external to the program itself; or taken from the public domain and hence is nonprotectable expression. See also Kretschmer, at 844–45 (arguing that program features dictated by market externalities or efficiency concerns are unprotectable). The structure of any given program may reflect some, all, or none of these considerations. Each case requires its own fact specific investigation.

* * *

(a) Elements Dictated by Efficiency

The portion of *Baker v. Selden*, discussed earlier, which denies copyright protection to expression necessarily incidental to the idea being expressed, appears to be the cornerstone for what has developed into the doctrine of merger. * * *. The doctrine's underlying principle is that "[w]hen there is essentially only one way to express an idea, the idea and its expression are inseparable and copyright is no bar to copying that expression." Concrete Machinery Co. v. Classic Lawn Ornaments, Inc., 843 F.2d 600, 606 (1st Cir. 1988). Under these circumstances, the expression is said to have "merged" with the idea itself. In order not to confer a monopoly of the idea upon the copyright owner, such expression should not be protected. * * *

CONTU recognized the applicability of the merger doctrine to computer programs. In its report to Congress it stated that: [C]opyrighted language may be copied without infringing when there is but a limited number of ways to express a given idea. . . . In the computer context, this means that when specific instructions, even though previously copyrighted, are the only and essential means of accomplishing a given task, their later use by another will not amount to infringement. CONTU Report, at 20. While this statement directly concerns only the application of merger to program code, that is, the textual aspect of the program, it reasonably suggests that the doctrine fits comfortably within the general context of computer programs.

Furthermore, when one considers the fact that programmers generally strive to create programs "that meet the user's needs in the most efficient manner," Menell, at 1052, the applicability of the merger doctrine to computer programs becomes compelling. In the context of computer program design, the concept of efficiency is akin to deriving the most concise logical proof or formulating the most succinct mathematical computation. Thus, the more efficient a set of modules are, the more closely they approximate the idea or process embodied in that particular aspect of the program's structure.

While, hypothetically, there might be a myriad of ways in which a programmer may effectuate certain functions within a program,—i.e., express the idea embodied in a given subroutine—efficiency concerns may so narrow the practical range of choice as to make only one or two forms of expression workable options. See 3 Nimmer § 13.03[F][2], at 13–63; see also Whelan, 797 F.2d at 1243 n. 43 ("It is true that for certain tasks there are only a very limited number of file structures available, and in such cases the structures might not be copyrightable . . . ."). Of course, not all program structure is informed by efficiency concerns. See Menell, at 1052 (besides efficiency, simplicity related to user accommodation has become a programming priority). It follows that in order to determine whether the merger doctrine precludes copyright protection to an aspect of a program's structure that is so oriented, a court must inquire "whether the use of this particular set of modules is necessary efficiently to implement that part of the program's process" being implemented. Englund, at 902. If the answer is yes, then the expression represented by the programmer's choice of a specific module or group of modules has merged with their underlying idea and is unprotected. Id. at 902–03.

* * *

Efficiency is an industry-wide goal. Since, as we have already noted, there may be only a limited number of efficient implementations for any given program task, it is quite possible that multiple programmers, working independently, will design the identical method employed in the allegedly infringed work. Of course, if this is the case, there is no copyright infringement. * * *

Under these circumstances, the fact that two programs contain the same efficient structure may as likely lead to an inference of independent creation as it does to one of copying. See 3 Nimmer § 13.03[F][2], at 13–65; cf. *Herbert Rosenthal Jewelry Corp.* [v. Kalpakian], 446 F.2d [738] at 741 [9th Cir. 1971] (evidence of independent creation may stem from defendant's standing as a designer of previous similar works). Thus, since evidence of similarly efficient structure is not particularly probative of copying, it should be disregarded in the overall substantial similarity analysis. See 3 Nimmer § 13.03[F][2], at 13–65.

* * *

In Manufacturers Technologies, Inc. v. Cams, Inc., 706 F.Supp. 984, 995–99 (D. Conn. 1989), the infringement claims stemmed from various alleged program similarities "as indicated in their screen displays." Id. at 990. Stressing efficiency concerns in the context of a merger analysis, the court determined that the program's method of allowing the user to navigate within the screen displays was not protectable because, in part, "the process or manner of navigating internally on any specific screen displays . . . is limited in the number of ways it may be simply achieved to facilitate user comfort." Id. at 995.

The court also found that expression contained in various screen displays (in the form of alphabetical and numerical columns) was not the proper subject of copyright protection because it was "necessarily incident to the idea[s]" embodied in the displays. Id. at 996–97. Cf. Digital Communications, 659 F.Supp. at 460 (finding no merger and affording copyright protection to program's status screen display because "modes of expression chosen . . . are clearly not necessary to the idea of the status screen").

We agree with the approach taken in these decisions, and conclude that application of the merger doctrine in this setting is an effective way to eliminate non-protectable expression contained in computer programs.

(b) Elements Dictated By External Factors

We have stated that where "it is virtually impossible to write about a particular historical era or fictional theme without employing certain 'stock' or standard literary devices," such expression is not copyrightable. Hoehling v. Universal City Studios, Inc., 618 F.2d 972, 979 (2d Cir.), *cert. denied,* 449 U.S. 841 (1980). For example, the *Hoehling* case was an infringement suit stemming from several works on the Hindenberg disaster. There we concluded that similarities in representations of German beer halls, scenes depicting German greetings such as "Heil Hitler," or the singing of certain German songs would not lead to a finding of infringement because they were " 'indispensable, or at least standard, in the treatment of' " life in Nazi Germany. Id. (quoting Alexander v. Haley, 460 F.Supp. 40, 45 (S.D.N.Y. 1978)). This is known as the *scenes a faire* doctrine, and like "merger," it has its analogous application to computer programs. Cf. *Data East USA*, [Inc. v. Epyx, Inc.,] 862 F.2d [204,] at 208 [9th Cir. 1988] (applying *scenes a faire* to a home computer video game).

Professor Nimmer points out that "in many instances it is virtually impossible to write a program to perform particular functions in a specific computing environment without employing standard techniques."

3 Nimmer § 13.03[F][3], at 13–65. This is a result of the fact that a programmer's freedom of design choice is often circumscribed by extrinsic considerations such as (1) the mechanical specifications of the computer on which a particular program is intended to run; (2) compatibility requirements of other programs with which a program is designed to operate in conjunction; (3) computer manufacturers' design standards; (4) demands of the industry being serviced; and (5) widely accepted programming practices within the computer industry. Id. at 13–66–71.

Courts have already considered some of these factors in denying copyright protection to various elements of computer programs. In the *Plains Cotton* case, [Plains Cotton Co-op v. Goodpasture Computer Serv., Inc. 807 F.2d. 1256. (5th Cir. 1987)] the Fifth Circuit refused to reverse the district court's denial of a preliminary injunction against an alleged program infringer because, in part, "many of the similarities between the . . . programs [were] dictated by the externalities of the cotton market." 807 F.2d at 1262.

In *Manufacturers Technologies*, the district court noted that the program's method of screen navigation "is influenced by the type of hardware that the software is designed to be used on." 706 F.Supp. at 995. Because, in part, "the functioning of the hardware package impact[ed] and constrain[ed] the type of navigational tools used in plaintiff's screen displays," the court denied copyright protection to that aspect of the program. Id.; cf. Data East USA, 862 F.2d at 209 (reversing a district court's finding of audiovisual work infringement because, inter alia, "the use of the Commodore computer for a karate game intended for home consumption is subject to various constraints inherent in the use of that computer").

Finally, the district court in Q-Co Industries rested its holding on what, perhaps, most closely approximates a traditional *scenes a faire* rationale. There, the court denied copyright protection to four program modules employed in a teleprompter program. This decision was ultimately based upon the court's finding that "the same modules would be an inherent part of any prompting program." [Q-Co. Indus. v. Hoffman,] 625 F. Supp. [608] , at 616 [CS. D.N.Y. 1985].

Building upon this existing case law, we conclude that a court must also examine the structural content of an allegedly infringed program for elements that might have been dictated by external factors.

(c) Elements taken From the Public Domain

Closely related to the non-protectability of *scenes a faire*, is material found in the public domain. Such material is free for the taking and cannot be appropriated by a single author even though it is included in a copyrighted work. See E.F. Johnson Co. v. Uniden Corp. of America, 623 F.Supp. 1485, 1499 (D. Minn. 1985); see also Sheldon, 81 F.2d at 54. We see no reason to make an exception to this rule for elements of a computer program that have entered the public domain by virtue of freely accessible program exchanges and the like. See 3 Nimmer § 13.03[F][4]; see also Brown Bag Software [v. Symantec Corp.], 960 F.2d [1465] at 1473 [9th Cir. 1992] (affirming the district court's finding that " '[p]laintiffs may not claim copyright protection of an . . . expression that is, if not standard, then commonplace in the computer software industry.'"). Thus, a court must also filter out this material from the allegedly infringed program before it makes the final inquiry in its substantial similarity analysis.

Step Three: Comparison

The third and final step of the test for substantial similarity that we believe appropriate for non-literal program components entails a comparison. Once a court has sifted out all elements of the allegedly infringed program which are "ideas" or are dictated by efficiency or external factors, or taken from the public domain, there may remain a core of protectable expression. In terms of a work's copyright value, this is the golden nugget. See Brown Bag Software, 960 F.2d at 1475. At this point, the court's substantial similarity inquiry focuses on whether the defendant copied any aspect of this protected expression, as well as an assessment of the copied portion's relative importance with respect to the plaintiff's overall program. See 3 Nimmer § 13.03[F][5]; Data East USA, 862 F.2d at 208 ("To determine whether similarities result from unprotectable expression, analytic dissection of similarities may be performed. If . . . all similarities in expression arise from use of common ideas, then no substantial similarity can be found.").

3) Policy Considerations

We are satisfied that the three step approach we have just outlined not only comports with, but advances the constitutional policies underlying the Copyright Act. Since any method that tries to distinguish idea from expression ultimately impacts on the scope of copyright protection afforded to a particular type of work, "the line [it draws] must be a pragmatic one, which also keeps in consideration 'the preservation of the balance between competition and protection. . . .'" Apple Computer [, Inc. v. Franklin Computer Corp.], 714 F.2d at [1240] 1253 [(3rd Cir. 1983] (citation omitted).

CA and some amici argue against the type of approach that we have set forth on the grounds that it will be a disincentive for future computer program research and development. At bottom, they claim that if programmers are not guaranteed broad copyright protection for their work, they will not invest the extensive time, energy and funds required to design and improve program structures. While they have a point, their argument cannot carry the day. The interest of the copyright law is not in simply conferring a monopoly on industrious persons, but in advancing the public welfare through rewarding artistic creativity, in a manner that permits the free use and development of non-protectable ideas and processes.

* * *

Recently, the Supreme Court has emphatically reiterated that "[t]he primary objective of copyright is not to reward the labor of authors. . . ." Feist Publications, Inc. v. Rural Tel. Serv. Co., 499 U.S. 340, 349 (1991) (emphasis added). While the Feist decision deals primarily with the copyrightability of purely factual compilations, its underlying tenets apply to much of the work involved in computer programming. Feist put to rest the "sweat of the brow" doctrine in copyright law. 499 U.S. 359–60. The rationale of that doctrine "was that copyright was a reward for the hard work that went into compiling facts." 499 U.S. 352. The Court flatly rejected this justification for extending copyright protection, noting that it "eschewed the most fundamental axiom of copyright law—that no one may copyright facts or ideas." Id.

Feist teaches that substantial effort alone cannot confer copyright status on an otherwise uncopyrightable work. As we have discussed, despite the fact that significant labor and expense often goes into computer program flow-charting and debugging, that process does not always result in inherently protectable expression. Thus, *Feist* implicitly undercuts the *Whelan* rationale, "which allow[ed] copyright protection beyond the literal computer code . . . [in order to] provide the proper incentive for programmers by protecting their most valuable efforts. . . ." Whelan, 797 F.2d at 1237 (footnote omitted). We note that *Whelan* was decided prior to *Feist* when the "sweat of the brow" doctrine still had vitality. In view of the Supreme Court's recent holding, however, we must reject the legal basis of CA's disincentive argument.

Furthermore, we are unpersuaded that the test we approve today will lead to the dire consequences for the computer program industry that plaintiff and some amici predict. To the contrary, serious students of the industry have been highly critical of the sweeping scope of copyright protection engendered by the *Whelan* rule, in that it "enables first comers to 'lock up' basic programming techniques as implemented in programs to perform particular tasks." Menell, at 1087; see also Spivack, at 765 (*Whelan* "results in an inhibition of creation by virtue of the copyright owner's quasi-monopoly power").

To be frank, the exact contours of copyright protection for non-literal program structure are not completely clear. We trust that as future cases are decided, those limits will become better defined. Indeed, it may well be that the Copyright Act serves as a relatively weak barrier against public access to the theoretical interstices behind a program's source and object codes. This results from the hybrid nature of a computer program, which, while it is literary expression, is also a highly functional, utilitarian component in the larger process of computing.

Generally, we think that copyright registration—with its indiscriminating availability—is not ideally suited to deal with the highly dynamic technology of computer science. Thus far, many of the decisions in this area reflect the courts' attempt to fit the proverbial square peg in a round hole. The district court, see Computer Assocs., 775 F.Supp. at 560, and at least one commentator have suggested that patent registration, with its exacting up-front novelty and non-obviousness requirements, might be the more appropriate rubric of protection for intellectual property of this kind. See Randell M. Whitmeyer, Comment, A Plea for Due Processes: Defining the Proper Scope of Patent Protection for Computer Software, 85 Nw.U.L.Rev. 1103, 1123–25 (1991); see also Lotus Dev. Corp. v. Borland Int'l, Inc., 788 F.Supp. 78, 91 (D. Mass. 1992) (discussing the potentially supplemental relationship between patent and copyright protection in the context of computer programs). In any event, now that more than 12 years have passed since CONTU issued its final report, the resolution of this specific issue could benefit from further legislative investigation—perhaps a CONTU II.

In the meantime, Congress has made clear that computer programs are literary works entitled to copyright protection. Of course, we shall abide by these instructions, but in so doing we must not impair the overall integrity of copyright law. While incentive based arguments in favor of broad copyright protection are perhaps attractive from a pure policy perspective, see Lotus Dev. Corp., 740 F.Supp. at 58, ultimately, they have a corrosive effect on certain fundamental tenets of copyright doctrine. If the test we have outlined results in narrowing the scope of protection, as we expect it will, that result flows from applying, in accordance with Congressional intent, longstanding principles of copyright law to computer programs. Of course, our decision is also informed by our concern that these fundamental principles remain undistorted.

B. The District Court Decision

We turn now to our review of the district court's decision in this particular case. At the outset, we must address CA's claim that the district court erred by relying too heavily on the court appointed expert's "personal opinions on the factual and legal issues before the court."

1) Use of Expert Evidence in Determining Substantial Similarity Between Computer Programs

Pursuant to Fed.R.Evid. 706, and with the consent of both Altai and CA, Judge Pratt appointed and relied upon Dr. Randall Davis of the Massachusetts Institute of Technology as the court's own expert witness on the issue of substantial similarity. Dr. Davis submitted a comprehensive written report that analyzed the various aspects of the computer programs at issue and evaluated the parties' expert evidence. At trial, Dr. Davis was extensively cross-examined by both CA and Altai.

The well-established general rule in this circuit has been to limit the use of expert opinion in determining whether works at issue are substantially similar. As a threshold matter, expert testimony may be used to assist the fact finder in ascertaining whether the defendant had copied any part of the plaintiff's work. See Arnstein v. Porter, 154 F.2d 464, 468 (2d Cir. 1946). To this end, "the two works are to be compared in their entirety . . . [and] in making such comparison resort may properly be made to expert analysis. . . ." 3 Nimmer § 13.03[E][2], at 13–62.16.

However, once some amount of copying has been established, it remains solely for the trier of fact to determine whether the copying was "illicit," that is to say, whether the "defendant took from plaintiff's works so much of what is pleasing to [lay observers] who comprise the audience for whom such [works are] composed, that defendant wrongfully appropriated something which belongs to the plaintiff." Arnstein, 154 F.2d at 473. Since the test for illicit copying is based upon the response of ordinary lay observers, expert testimony is thus "irrelevant" and not permitted. Id. at 468, 473. We have subsequently described this method of inquiry as "merely an alternative way of formulating the issue of substantial similarity." Ideal Toy Corp. v. Fab-Lu Ltd. (Inc.), 360 F.2d 1021, 1023 n. 2 (2d Cir.1966).

Historically, *Arnstein's* ordinary observer standard had its roots in "an attempt to apply the 'reasonable person' doctrine as found in other areas of the law to copyright." 3 Nimmer § 13.03[E][2], at 13–62.10–11. That approach may well have served its purpose when the material under scrutiny was limited to art forms readily comprehensible and generally familiar to the average lay person. However, in considering the extension of the rule to the present case, we are reminded of Holmes' admonition that, "[t]he life of the law has not been logic: it has been experience." O.W. Holmes, Jr., THE COMMON LAW 1 (1881).

Thus, in deciding the limits to which expert opinion may be employed in ascertaining the substantial similarity of computer programs, we cannot disregard the highly complicated and technical subject matter at the heart of these claims. Rather, we recognize the reality that computer programs are likely to be somewhat impenetrable by lay observers—whether they be judges or juries—and, thus, seem to fall outside the category of works contemplated by those who engineered the *Arnstein* test. * * *

* * * [W]e leave it to the discretion of the district court to decide to what extent, if any, expert opinion, regarding the highly technical nature of computer programs, is warranted in a given case.

In this case, Dr. Davis' opinion was instrumental in dismantling the intricacies of computer science so that the court could formulate and apply an appropriate rule of law. While Dr. Davis' report and testimony undoubtedly shed valuable light on the subject matter of the litigation, Judge Pratt remained, in the final analysis, the trier of fact. The district court's use of the expert's assistance, in the context of this case, was entirely appropriate.

2) Evidentiary Analysis

The district court had to determine whether Altai's OSCAR 3.5 program was substantially similar to CA's ADAPTER. We note that Judge Pratt's method of analysis effectively served as a road map for our own, with one exception—Judge Pratt filtered out the non-copyrightable aspects of OSCAR 3.5 rather than those found in ADAPTER, the allegedly infringed program. We think that our approach—i.e., filtering out the unprotected aspects of an allegedly infringed program and then comparing the end product to the structure of the suspect program—is preferable, and therefore believe that district courts should proceed in this manner in future cases.

We opt for this strategy because, in some cases, the defendant's program structure might contain protectable expression and/or other elements that are not found in the plaintiff's program. Since it is extraneous to the allegedly copied work, this material would have no bearing on any potential substantial similarity between the two programs. Thus, its filtration would be wasteful and unnecessarily time consuming. Furthermore, by focusing the analysis on the infringing rather than on the infringed material, a court may mistakenly place too little emphasis on a quantitatively small misappropriation which is, in reality, a qualitatively vital aspect of the plaintiff's protectable expression.

The fact that the district court's analysis proceeded in the reverse order, however, had no material impact on the outcome of this case. Since Judge

Pratt determined that OSCAR effectively contained no protectable expression whatsoever, the most serious charge that can be levelled against him is that he was overly thorough in his examination.

The district court took the first step in the analysis set forth in this opinion when it separated the program by levels of abstraction. The district court stated: As applied to computer software programs, this abstractions test would progress in order of "increasing generality" from object code, to source code, to parameter lists, to services required, to general outline. In discussing the particular similarities, therefore, we shall focus on these levels. *Computer Assocs.*, 775 F.Supp. at 560. While the facts of a different case might require that a district court draw a more particularized blueprint of a program's overall structure, this description is a workable one for the case at hand.

Moving to the district court's evaluation of OSCAR 3.5's structural components, we agree with Judge Pratt's systematic exclusion of non-protectable expression. With respect to code, the district court observed that after the rewrite of OSCAR 3.4 to OSCAR 3.5, "there remained virtually no lines of code that were identical to ADAPTER." Id. at 561. Accordingly, the court found that the code "present[ed] no similarity at all." Id. at 562.

Next, Judge Pratt addressed the issue of similarity between the two programs' parameter lists and macros. He concluded that, viewing the conflicting evidence most favorably to CA, it demonstrated that "only a few of the lists and macros were similar to protected elements in ADAPTER; the others were either in the public domain or dictated by the functional demands of the program." Id. As discussed above, functional elements and elements taken from the public domain do not qualify for copyright protection. With respect to the few remaining parameter lists and macros, the district court could reasonably conclude that they did not warrant a finding of infringement given their relative contribution to the overall program. See Warner Bros., Inc. v. American Broadcasting Cos., Inc., 720 F.2d 231, 242 (2d Cir. 1983) (discussing de minimis exception which allows for literal copying of a small and usually insignificant portion of the plaintiff's work); 3 Nimmer § 13.03[F][5], at 13–74. In any event, the district court reasonably found that, for lack of persuasive evidence, CA failed to meet its burden of proof on whether the macros and parameter lists at issue were substantially similar. See *Computer Assocs.*, 775 F.Supp. at 562.

The district court also found that the overlap exhibited between the list of services required for both ADAPTER and OSCAR 3.5 was "determined by the demands of the operating system and of the applications program to which it [was] to be linked through ADAPTER or OSCAR. . . ." Id. In other words, this aspect of the program's structure was dictated by the nature of other programs with which it was designed to interact and, thus, is not protected by copyright.

Finally, in his infringement analysis, Judge Pratt accorded no weight to the similarities between the two programs' organizational charts, "because [the charts were] so simple and obvious to anyone exposed to the operation of the program[s]." Id. CA argues that the district court's action in this regard "is not consistent with copyright law"—that "obvious" expression is protected, and that the district court erroneously failed to realize this. However, to say that elements of a work are "obvious," in the manner in which the district court used the word, is to say that they "follow naturally from the work's theme rather than from the author's creativity." 3 Nimmer § 13.03 [F][3], at 13–65. This is but one formulation of the *scenes a faire* doctrine, which we have already endorsed as a means of weeding out unprotectable expression.

* * *

[The court affirmed the district court's judgment that OSCAR 3.5 did not infringe the copyright in CA-SCHEDULER.]

NOTES

1. Whelan Associates, Inc. v. Jaslow Dental Laboratory, Inc., 797 F.2d 1222 (3d Cir. 1986), discussed in the *Altai* opinion, involved a program for managing the records of a dental laboratory. The plaintiff had written the program in a computer language called EDL, which would run on IBM Series One computers. The defendant, who had become intimately familiar with the program as the principal in a dental lab supply firm that marketed the program, decided that the future market for such a program was a program that would run on the then new and much cheaper IBM personal computer. Those machines, however, would not run EDL. The uncontroverted evidence showed that the defendant simply converted the EDL source code to BASIC, a computer language that did run on the IBM personal computer. This was a challenging task, similar to translating an English language novel to French, but it was also clearly the creation of a derivative work and infringing. The Third Circuit, however, did not realize how easy the case was, and aware of the lack of case authority on what did and what did not infringe a computer program, wrote expansively on the subject.

Altai was, on its facts, a much more difficult case. The non-infringing program, OSCAR 3.5, in *Computer Associates* was written in a highly constraining technological environment. The task of the program was to interface between the application program (ZEKE) and the computer's operating system. In this environment, the structure of OSCAR will be determined by the design of the operating system and the way in which it requires other programs to communicate with it, and by the design of ZEKE, and the demands it makes on the operating system. The programmer simply needs to inventory the demands which ZEKE makes on the operating system, and develop routines that can translate the ZEKE demands into the form required by the operating system. This technological environment means that almost all of the content of both OSCAR and ADAPTER are functional, doesn't it? Therefore, infringement (absent the slavish copying present in OSCAR 3.4) is very unlikely.

2. Note how the opinion in *Computer* gets confused about whether the question is (1) whether there is sufficient similarity to support an inference of copying [taking], or (2) whether there is taking of the protectable elements of the copyrighted program.

OSCAR 3.5 was, according to the undisputed testimony summarized by the court, created through the use of what is called a "clean room" procedure.

The program was written by programmers who had not seen the code for ADAPTER. Instead, they were provided with information about the calls which ZEKE needed to make to the operating system, and information about the form in which the operating systems needed to have the calls passed to it (and of course, vice versa—how the operating system could pass information back to ZEKE and how ZEKE could receive the information). Provided with these basic, functional specifications, they then wrote a program to provide the necessary interface. Thus Altai could argue that there was no taking of any protected expression, and with no taking there is no infringement.

The court doesn't address the issue, which would seem to have provided a much easier ground for deciding the case. Is this because the court assumes that taking has been shown, perhaps because of the presumption derived from access and similarity? The Court assumes access, presumably because Altai's employee Claude F. Arney, III who wrote OSCAR 3.4 had access to the ADAPTER source code. But access plus similarity only shifts the burden of persuasion on the issue of taking. Thus Altai could have still won by showing the absence of taking, which it apparently did. Why doesn't the court address this argument? Is it because OSCAR 3.4 did infringe and therefore Altai faces an unusually demanding burden of persuasion to show that OSCAR 3.5 is "clean"? Is it because Arney, an employee of Altai, had the code, and therefore knowledge of the code is imputed to every employee of Altai? Or is the court so eager to write an opinion on the broader question that it overlooks the issue?

3. What advice would you have given if James P. Williams had shown up in your law office with the newly discovered problem that OSCAR 3.4 infringed ADAPTER? What options would you discuss with Williams? Would Altai have been in a stronger position if it had hired an outside, independent programming firm to write an interface between ZEKE and the operating system?

4. What is now called the "abstraction-filtration-comparison method" has swept the circuits. See, e.g., Kepner-Tregoe, Inc. v. Leadership Software Inc., 12 F.3d 527 (5th Cir. 1994); Brown Bag Software v. Symantec Corp., 960 F.2d 1465 (9th Cir. 1992); Autoskill, Inc. v. National Educational Support Systems, Inc., 994 F.2d 1476 (10th Cir. 1993) and Gates Rubber Co. v. Bando Chemical Indus., 9 F.3d 823 (10th Cir. 1993).

C. Fair Use

Prior to 1970 there were few fair use cases, and examples of takings thought to be clear examples of fair use fell into the following three categories.

1. Notes taken from a copyrighted work for the private use of the reader.

2. Quotations from a work used as part of a critical essay or response to the work and reasonably necessary to that purpose. In Consumers Union v. Hobart Mfg. Co., 189 F.Supp. 275 (S.D.N.Y. 1960), followed on summary judgment, 199 F.Supp. 860 (S.D.N.Y. 1961), the defendant had quoted criticisms of its KitchenAid dishwashers from Consumers Report in order to answer them. In the course of holding for the defendant on the ground of non-copyrightable subject matter the court observed: "[I]t must be admitted that one cannot, by copyrighting his unfavorable remarks about another, prevent that other from quoting those remarks and refuting them." 189 F.Supp. at 278.

3. Copyrighted material which is included incidentally in a documentary or commentary as part of the atmosphere without any special gain accruing to the user as a result of the inclusion. Karll v. Curtis Publishing Co., 39 F.Supp. 836 (E.D. Wisc. 1941), was a suit for infringement of the chorus of the official Green Bay Packer song "Go! You Packers Go!" which appeared in an article entitled "Little Town That Leads 'Em" appearing in the Saturday Evening Post. The article told of the history of the Packer organization and the strength of its community support, the song was quoted in passing. The court found fair use. And in Broadway Music Corp. v. F-R Publishing Corp., 31 F.Supp. 817 (S.D.N.Y. 1940), the court found that the New Yorker's use of twelve lines from the plaintiff's humorous song "Poor Pauline" in the course of a comment on the death of the actress Pauline White was fair use.

The frequency of reported litigation whose outcome involves the fair use concept has increased greatly since 1970. This is the result of three factors. First, the increased commercial value of copyrightable materials in a knowledge-based and entertainment-focused era. Second, the expansion of the subject matter of (§ 102) and exclusive rights conferred by (§ 106) copyright in the 1976 Act. And third, the development of inexpensive and widely available copying technologies.

Sony Corp. of America v. Universal City Studios, Inc.

Supreme Court of the United States, 1984.
464 U.S. 417, 104 S.Ct. 774, 78 L.Ed.2d 574.

■ JUSTICE STEVENS delivered the opinion of the Court.

Petitioners manufacture and sell home video tape recorders. Respondents own the copyrights on some of the television programs that are broadcast on the public airwaves. Some members of the general public use video tape recorders [in the opinion called "VTR's", but commonly known as "VCR's", for video cassette recorders] sold by petitioners to record some of these broadcasts, as well as a large number of other broadcasts. The question presented is whether the sale of petitioners' copying equipment to the general public violates any of the rights conferred upon respondents by the Copyright Act.

* * *

After a lengthy trial, the District Court denied respondents all the relief they sought and entered judgment for petitioners. 480 F.Supp. 429 (1979). The United States Court of Appeals for the Ninth Circuit reversed the District Court's judgment on respondent's copyright claim, holding petitioners liable for contributory infringement and ordering the District Court to fashion appropriate relief. 659 F.2d 963 (1981). We granted certiorari, 457 U.S. 1116 (1982); since we had not completed our study of the case last Term, we ordered reargument, 463 U.S. 1226 (1983).

We now reverse.

An explanation of our rejection of respondents' unprecedented attempt to impose copyright liability upon the distributors of copying equipment requires a * * * recitation of the findings of the District Court. In summary, those findings reveal that the average member of the public uses a VTR principally to record a program he cannot view as it is being televised and then to watch it once at a later time. This practice, known as "time-shifting," enlarges the television viewing audience. For that reason, a significant amount of television programming may be used in this manner without objection from the owners of the copyrights on the programs. For the same reason, even the two respondents in this case, who do assert objections to time-shifting in this litigation, were unable to prove that the practice has impaired the commercial value of their copyrights or has created any likelihood of future harm. Given these findings, there is no basis in the Copyright Act upon which respondents can hold petitioners liable for distributing VTR's to the general public. The Court of Appeals' holding that respondents are entitled to enjoin the distribution of VTR's, to collect royalties on the sale of such equipment, or to obtain other relief, if affirmed, would enlarge the scope of respondents' statutory monopolies to encompass control over an article of commerce that is not the subject of copyright protection. Such an expansion of the copyright privilege is beyond the limits of the grants authorized by Congress.

I

The two respondents in this action, Universal Studios, Inc. and Walt Disney Productions, produce and hold the copyrights on a substantial number of motion pictures and other audiovisual works. In the current marketplace, they can exploit their rights in these works in a number of ways: by authorizing theatrical exhibitions, by licensing limited showings on cable and network television, by selling syndication rights for repeated airings on local television stations, and by marketing programs on prerecorded videotapes or videodiscs. Some works are suitable for exploitation through all of these avenues, while the market for other works is more limited.

* * *

Several capabilities of the * * * [VTR] are noteworthy. The separate tuner in the Betamax enables it to record a broadcast off one station while the television set is tuned to another channel permitting the viewer, for example, to watch two simultaneous news broadcasts by watching one "live" and recording the other for later viewing. Tapes may be reused, and programs that have been recorded may be erased either before or after viewing. A timer in the Betamax can be used to activate and deactivate the equipment at predetermined times, enabling an intended viewer to record programs that are transmitted when he or she is not at home. Thus a person may watch a program at home in the evening even though it was broadcast while the viewer was at work during the afternoon. The Betamax is also equipped with a pause button and a fast-forward control. The pause button, when depressed, deactivates the recorder until it is released, thus enabling a viewer to omit a commercial advertisement from the recording, provided, of course, that the viewer is present when the program is recorded. The fast forward control enables the viewer of a previously recorded program to run the tape rapidly when a segment he or she does not desire to see is being played back on the television screen.

The respondents and Sony both conducted surveys of the way the Betamax machine was used by several hundred owners during a sample period in 1978. Although there were some differences in the surveys, they both showed that the primary use of the machine for most owners was "time-shifting,"—the practice of recording a program to view it once at a later time, and thereafter erasing it. Time-shifting enables viewers to see programs they otherwise would miss because they are not at home, are occupied with other tasks, or are viewing a program on another station at the time of a broadcast that they desire to watch. Both surveys also showed, however, that a substantial number of interviewees had accumulated libraries of tapes. Sony's survey indicated that over 80% of the interviewees watched at least as much regular television as they had before owning a Betamax. Respondents offered no evidence of decreased television viewing by Betamax owners.

Sony introduced considerable evidence describing television programs that could be copied without objection from any copyright holder, with special emphasis on sports, religious, and educational programming. For example, their survey indicated that 7.3% of all Betamax use is to record sports events, and representatives of professional baseball, football, basketball, and hockey testified that they had no objection to the recording of their televised events for home use.

Respondents offered opinion evidence concerning the future impact of the unrestricted sale of VTR's on the commercial value of their copyrights. The District Court found, however, that they had failed to prove any likelihood of future harm from the use of VTR's for time-shifting.

* * *

II

From its beginning, the law of copyright has developed in response to significant changes in technology.[11] Indeed, it was the invention of a new form of copying equipment—the printing press—that gave rise to the original need for copyright protection. Repeatedly, as new developments have occurred in this country, it has been the Congress that has fashioned the new rules that new technology made necessary. * * *

* * *

---

11. Thus, for example, the development and marketing of player pianos and perforated roles of music, see White-Smith Music Publishing Co. v. Apollo Co., 209 U.S. 1 (1908), preceded the enactment of the Copyright Act of 1909; innovations in copying techniques gave rise to the statutory exemption for library copying embodied in § 108 of the 1976 revision of the Copyright law; the development of the technology that made it possible to retransmit television programs by cable or by microwave systems, see Fortnightly Corp. v. United Artists, 392 U.S. 390 (1968), and Teleprompter Corp. v. CBS, 415 U.S. 394 (1974), prompted the enactment of the complex provisions set forth in 17 U.S.C. § 111(d)(2)(B) and § 111(d)(5) after years of detailed congressional study, see Eastern Microwave, Inc. v. Doubleday Sports, Inc., 691 F.2d 125, 129 (CA2 1982).

* * *

In a case like this, in which Congress has not plainly marked our course, we must be circumspect in construing the scope of rights created by a legislative enactment which never contemplated such a calculus of interests.

* * *

[The law] * * * has never accorded the copyright owner complete control over all possible uses of his work. Rather, the Copyright Act grants the copyright holder "exclusive" rights to use and to authorize the use of his work in five qualified ways, including reproduction of the copyrighted work in copies. § 106. * * *

* * *

The two respondents in this case do not seek relief against the Betamax users who have allegedly infringed their copyrights. Moreover, this is not a class action on behalf of all copyright owners who license their works for television broadcast, and respondents have no right to invoke whatever rights other copyright holders may have to bring infringement actions based on Betamax copying of their works. As was made clear by their own evidence, the copying of the respondents' programs represents a small portion of the total use of VTR's. It is, however, the taping of respondents own copyright programs that provides them with standing to charge Sony with contributory infringement. To prevail, they have the burden of proving that users of the Betamax have infringed their copyrights and that Sony should be held responsible for that infringement.

III

[In part III of the opinion the Court considered what the plaintiffs had to prove in order to hold that the defendants' sale of VTR's made them subject to remedies for the possible infringements of the purchasers. The Court concluded:] Accordingly, the sale of copying equipment, like the sale of other articles of commerce, does not constitute contributory infringement if the product is widely used for legitimate, unobjectionable purposes. Indeed, it need merely be capable of substantial non-infringing uses.

IV

[The Court then turned to the question of whether the Betamax is capable of significant noninfringing uses. It focused on two types of time-shifting (the record, relating to the period prior to 1978 when home video rentals were not widely available, showed that time-shifting was the principal consumer use): authorized and unauthorized time-shifting. The record revealed that owners of rights in sports, religious and educational programming had no objection to time-shifting. The Court made specific mention of] the testimony of Fred Rogers, president of the corporation that produces and owns the copyright on *Mr. Rogers' Neighborhood*. The program is carried by more public television stations than any other program. Its audience numbers over 3,000,000 families a day. He testified that he had absolutely no objection to home taping for noncommercial use and expressed the opinion that it is a real service to families to be able to record children's programs and to show them at appropriate times.

If there are millions of owners of VTR's who make copies of televised sports events, religious broadcasts, and educational programs such as *Mister Rogers' Neighborhood,* and if the proprietors of those programs welcome the practice, the business of supplying the equipment that makes such copying feasible should not be stifled simply because the equipment is used by some individuals to make unauthorized reproductions of respondents' works. The respondents do not represent a class composed of all copyright holders. Yet a finding of contributory infringement would inevitably frustrate the interests of broadcasters in reaching the portion of their audience that is available only through time-shifting.

B. *Unauthorized Time-Shifting*

Even unauthorized uses of a copyrighted work are not necessarily infringing. An unlicensed use of the copyright is not an infringement unless it conflicts with one of the specific exclusive rights conferred by the copyright statute. Twentieth Century Music Corp. v. Aiken, 422 U.S. 151, 154–155. Moreover, the definition of exclusive rights in § 106 of the present Act is prefaced by the words "subject to sections 107 through 118." Those sections describe a variety of uses of copyrighted material that "are not infringements of copyright notwithstanding the provisions of § 106." The most pertinent in this case is § 107, the legislative endorsement of the doctrine of "fair use."

That section identifies various factors that enable a Court to apply an "equitable rule of reason" analysis to particular claims of infringement. Although not conclusive, the first factor requires that "the commercial or nonprofit character of an activity" be weighed in any fair use decision. If the Betamax were used to make copies for a commercial or profit-making purpose, such use would presumptively be unfair. The contrary presumption is appropriate here, however, because the District Court's findings plainly establish that time-shifting for private home use must be characterized as a noncommercial, nonprofit activity. Moreover, when one considers the nature of a televised copyrighted audiovisual work, see 17 U.S.C. § 107(2), and that time-shifting merely enables a viewer to see such a work which he had been invited to witness in its entirety free of charge, the fact that the entire work is reproduced, see § 107(3), does not have its ordinary effect of militating against a finding of fair use.

This is not, however, the end of the inquiry because Congress has also directed us to consider "the effect of the use upon the potential market for or value of the copyrighted work." § 107(4). The purpose of copyright is to create incentives for creative effort. Even copying for noncommercial purposes may impair the copyright holder's ability to obtain the rewards that Congress intended him to have. But a use that has no demonstrable effect upon the potential market for, or the value of, the copyrighted work need not be prohibited in order to protect the author's incentive to create. The prohibition of such noncommercial uses would merely inhibit access to ideas without any countervailing benefit.

Thus, although every commercial use of copyrighted material is presumptively an unfair exploitation of the monopoly privilege that belongs to the owner of the copyright, noncommercial uses are a different matter. A challenge to a noncommercial use of a copyrighted work requires proof either that the particular use is harmful, or that if it should become widespread, it would adversely affect the potential market for the copyrighted work. Actual present harm need not be shown; such a requirement would leave the copyright holder with no defense against predictable damage. Nor is it necessary to show with certainty that future harm will result. What is necessary is a showing by a preponderance of the evidence that *some* meaningful likelihood of future harm exists. If the intended use is for commercial gain, that likelihood may be presumed. But if it is for a noncommercial purpose, the likelihood must be demonstrated.

In this case, respondents failed to carry their burden with regard to home time-shifting. The District Court described respondents' evidence as follows:

"Plaintiffs' experts admitted at several points in the trial that the time-shifting without librarying would result in 'not a great deal of harm.' Plaintiffs' greatest concern about time-shifting is with 'a point of important philosophy that transcends even commercial judgment.' They fear that with any Betamax usage, 'invisible boundaries' are passed: 'the copyright owner has lost control over his program.'" 480 F.Supp., at 467.

Later in its opinion, the District Court observed:

"Most of plaintiffs' predictions of harm hinge on speculation about audience viewing patterns and ratings, a measurement system which Sidney Sheinberg, MCA's president, calls a 'black art' because of the significant level of imprecision involved in the calculations."

There was no need for the District Court to say much about past harm. "Plaintiffs have admitted that no actual harm to their copyrights has occurred to date."

On the question of potential future harm from time-shifting, the District Court offered a more detailed analysis of the evidence. It rejected respondents' "fear that persons 'watching' the original telecast of a program will not be measured in the live audience and the ratings and revenues will decrease," by observing that current measurement technology allows the Betamax audience to be reflected. It rejected respondents' prediction "that live television or movie audiences will decrease as more people watch Betamax tapes as an alternative," with the observation that "[t]here is no factual basis for [the underlying] assumption." It rejected respondents' "fear that time-shifting will reduce audiences for telecast reruns," and concluded instead that "given current market practices, this should aid plaintiffs rather than harm them." And it declared that respondents' suggestion "that theater or film rental exhibition of a program will suffer because of time-shift recording of that program" "lacks merit."

* * *

The District Court's conclusions are buttressed by the fact that to the extent time-shifting expands public access to freely broadcast television programs, it yields societal benefits. * * *

When these factors are all weighed in the "equitable rule of reason" balance, we must conclude that this record amply supports the District Court's conclusion that home time-shifting is fair use. In light of the findings of the District Court regarding the state of the empirical data, it is clear that the Court of Appeals erred in holding that the statute as presently written bars such conduct.

* * *

The Betamax is * * * capable of substantial noninfringing uses. Sony's sale of such equipment to the general public does not constitute contributory infringement of respondent's copyrights.

V

One may search the Copyright Act in vain for any sign that the elected representatives of the millions of people who watch television every day have made it unlawful to copy a program for later viewing at home, or have enacted a flat prohibition against the sale of machines that make such copying possible.

It may well be that Congress will take a fresh look at this new technology, just as it so often has examined other innovations in the past. But it is not our job to apply laws that have not yet been written. Applying the copyright statute, as it now reads, to the facts as they have been developed in this case, the judgment of the Court of Appeals must be reversed.

It is so ordered.

[JUSTICES BLACKMUN, MARSHALL, POWELL, and REHNQUIST dissented.]

NOTES

1. The impact of time-shifting upon the demand for copyrighted program material is not clear. It is plausible that the effect of time-shifting is to make television viewing more convenient and accessible and thus to increase the viewing audience. Persons who are unable to view television during certain hours can record the program and view it at other times. Broadcast capacity during off hours such as the early morning can be used to broadcast programs which are taped by the viewer for viewing at another time. If time-shifting does increase the demand for programming in general (by lowering the costs of transmitting the program to some viewers), wouldn't it have been odd for the court to limit or bar the sale of VCR's at the behest of only a few copyright owners?

2. The statement in the *Sony* case that "every commercial use of copyrighted material is presumptively an unfair exploitation of the monopoly privilege that belongs to the owner of the copyright" has been modified by Campbell v. Acuff-Rose Music, Inc., 510 U.S. 569 (1994), below.

Audio Recording and Document Copying

The expansion of the scope of the rights conferred by copyright in § 106 (interacting with the definitions in § 101) played an important role in the *Sony* litigation. Prior to the new statute, a recording was not treated like a copy of a protected work because the concept of copy was limited to things which were visually similar to the original. White-Smith Music Publishing Co. v. Apollo Co., 209 U.S. 1 (1908) (perforated roll for player piano not an infringement of the copyright in the sheet music). Thus making a video tape was not a copying and not itself an infringement of the copyright on an underlying work. This was changed by the new definition of "Copies" in § 101: " 'Copies' are material objects * * * in which a work is fixed by any method * * * and from which the work can be perceived, reproduced, or otherwise communicated, either directly or with the aid of a machine or device." Video tapes fall within this definition.

Also important was the development of a relatively low cost and hence widely available copying technology for television programs. Similar devices had developed for audio recording (the sound tape recorder which had developed prior to the video recorder, now widely available in a standardized cassette form) and for copying the printed page (a technology now dominated by xerography), and their availability has raised similar fair use issues.

Audio Recording. The practices that had developed in relation to the audio tape recorder were relevant to the *Sony* litigation, for it is clear that the audio tape recorder is widely used to make copies of recorded music and broadcasts, and that these copies are (to use the argot of the *Sony* litigation) "libraried." No lawsuit has ever been filed to challenge this practice for personal, non-commercial use, perhaps because home recording was not a sufficiently good substitute for records to affect the market (the only people satisfied with cassette copies may be those who don't have the money to buy the record). Prior to the 1976 Act, the illegality of making personal audio recordings was less than clear. In a compromise at the time of the 1909 statute, adopted long before home recording was a possibility, much less a gleam in an engineer's eye, the statute provided that a recorded copy only entitled the owner of the copyright in the music (copyrighted in the form of transcribed sheet music) to collect a royalty fee, not to enjoin an infringement or pursue the other infringement remedies. So the personal use, home recorder could simply be viewed as someone from whom the owner of the copyright had not yet bothered to collect the few cents of compulsory royalty due. (Parenthetically, the compulsory royalty provisions live on in § 115, but restructured so that it is clear that they are not available to the casual, personal home recorder. For instance, a person claiming a compulsory license must have served notice of his intention to do so on the copyright owner.) Prior to 1976 the practice of home "librarying" of sound recordings developed in this legal setting (home video recording had just begun in 1976).

The issue came to a head in the early 1990's, with the development of digital audio technology. With digital technology it is possible to make copies which are as good as (indeed, the same as) the original. Home play back and recording machines using this technology were ready for introduction into the U.S. market. The music industry was concerned that these machines would have a significant negative impact on their market.

Congress responded with the Audio Home Recording Act of 1992, P.L. 106–563 (1992), which added a new Chapter 10 to Title 17, 17 U.S.C.

§§ 1001–1010. As previously explained, that act requires that importers and manufacturers of digital audio recording devices and media pay a royalty of 2 percent to be paid into a general fund to be shared by the owners of musical copyrights, and the statute also requires that digital audio recording devices include a serial copy management system (so that users of the machine can make a child copy, but not a grandchild copy).

Relevant to the issue here, 17 U.S.C. § 1008 provides that "No action may be brought under this title alleging infringement of copyright based on the manufacture, importation, or distribution of a digital audio recording device, a digital audio recording medium, an analog recording device, or an analog recording medium, [thus foreclosing a *Sony* type suit for audio recording devices] or based on the noncommercial use by a consumer of such a device or medium for making digital musical recordings or analog musical recordings."

Note that the form of § 1008 permitted Congress to authorize noncommercial use by a consumer without taking a position on whether or not the recording was otherwise infringement under the statute.

The developing ease of home recording led to the development of stores that would offer to rent sound recordings or computer programs for a few days, enough time for the customer to take them home and make a copy. The owner of a copy has traditionally enjoyed the right to lend or rent the copy. This right has, for instance, encouraged the development of lending libraries which can buy a book once and lend it out many times. However, when this practice became threatening, Congress amended § 109, first to prohibit the lending "for direct or indirect commercial advantage" of sound recordings, then of computer software. Record Rental Amendment of 1984, P.L. 98–450 (1984); Computer Software Rental Amendments Act of 1990, P.L. 101–650, Title VIII (1990). The rental prohibition does not extend to audiovisual works, both because of the substantial video rental industry, because few households have more than one VCR, and most customers watch a movie only once. Nonprofit libraries are permitted to lend computer programs. § 109(b)(2)(A). The GATT TRIPS contains provisions on this problem, Article 11 and Article 14.4.

Copying Machines. The use of copying machines to make copies of written works was the subject of the following decision.

American Geophysical Union v. Texaco Inc.

United States Court of Appeals for the Second Circuit, 1995.
60 F. 3d 913, certiorari dismissed 516 U.S. 1005,
116 S.Ct. 592, 133 L. Ed. 2d 486 (1995).

■ JON O. NEWMAN, CHIEF JUDGE:

This interlocutory appeal presents the issue of whether, under the particular circumstances of this case, the fair use defense to copyright infringement applies to the photocopying of articles in a scientific journal. This issue arises on the appeal of defendant Texaco Inc. from the July 23, 1992, order of the United States District Court for the Southern District of New

York (Pierre N. Leval, Judge) holding, after a limited-issue bench trial, that the photocopying of eight articles from the *Journal of Catalysis* for use by one of Texaco's researchers was not fair use. See American Geophysical Union v. Texaco Inc., 802 F.Supp. 1 (S.D.N.Y. 1992). Though not for precisely the same reasons, we agree with the District Court's conclusion that this particular copying was not fair use and therefore affirm.

BACKGROUND

The District Court Proceedings. Plaintiffs American Geophysical Union and 82 other publishers of scientific and technical journals (the "publishers") brought a class action claiming that Texaco's unauthorized photocopying of articles from their journals constituted copyright infringement. Among other defenses, Texaco claimed that its copying was fair use under section 107 of the Copyright Act, 17 U.S.C. § 107 (1988). Since it appeared likely that the litigation could be resolved once the fair use defense was adjudicated, the parties agreed that an initial trial should be limited to whether Texaco's copying was fair use, and further agreed that this issue would be submitted for decision on a written record.

Although Texaco employs 400 to 500 research scientists, of whom all or most presumably photocopy scientific journal articles to support their Texaco research, the parties stipulated—in order to spare the enormous expense of exploring the photocopying practices of each of them—that one scientist would be chosen at random as the representative of the entire group. The scientist chosen was Dr. Donald H. Chickering, II, a scientist at Texaco's research center in Beacon, New York, For consideration at trial, the publishers selected from Chickering's files photocopies of eight particular articles from the *Journal of Catalysis.*

In a comprehensive opinion, reported at 802 F.Supp. 1, the District Court considered the statutory fair use factors identified in section 107, weighed other equitable considerations, and held that Texaco's photocopying, as represented by Chickering's copying of these eight articles did not constitute fair use. The District Court certified its ruling for interlocutory appeal under 28 U.S.C. § 1292(b) (1988).

Essential Facts. Employing between 400 and 500 researchers nationwide, Texaco conducts considerable scientific research seeking to develop new products and technology primarily to improve its commercial performance in the petroleum industry. As part of its substantial expenditures in support of research activities at its Beacon facility, Texaco subscribes to many scientific and technical journals and maintains a sizable library with these materials. Among the periodicals that Texaco receives at its Beacon research facility is the *Journal of Catalysis* ("*Catalysis*"), a monthly publication produced by Academic Press, Inc., a major publisher of scholarly journals and one of the plaintiffs in this litigation. Texaco had initially purchased one subscription to *Catalysis* for its Beacon facility, and increased its total subscriptions to two in 1983. Since 1988, Texaco has maintained three subscriptions to *Catalysis.*

Each issue of *Catalysis* contains articles, notes, and letters (collectively "articles"), ranging in length from two to twenty pages. All of the articles are received by the journal's editors through unsolicited submission by various authors. Authors are informed that they must transfer the copyright in their writings to Academic Press if one of their articles is accepted for publication, and no form of money payment is ever provided to authors whose works are published. Academic Press typically owns the copyright for each individual article published in *Catalysis*, and every issue of the journal includes a general statement that no part of the publication is to be reproduced without permission from the copyright owner. The average monthly issue of *Catalysis* runs approximately 200 pages and comprises 20 to 25 articles.

Chickering, a chemical engineer at the Beacon research facility, has worked for Texaco since 1981 conducting research in the field of catalysis, which concerns changes in the rates of chemical reactions. To keep abreast of developments in his field, Chickering must review works published in various scientific and technical journals related to his area of research. Texaco assists in this endeavor by having its library circulate current issues of relevant journals to Chickering when he places his name on the appropriate routing list.

The copies of the eight articles from *Catalysis* found in Chickering's files that the parties have made the exclusive focus of the fair use trial were photocopied in their entirety by Chickering or by other Texaco employees at Chickering's request. Chickering apparently believed that the material and data found within these articles would facilitate his current or future professional research. The evidence developed at trial indicated that Chickering did not generally use the *Catalysis* articles in his research immediately upon copying, but placed the photocopied articles in his files to have them available for later reference as needed. Chickering became aware of six of the photocopied articles when the original issues of *Catalysis* containing the articles were circulated to him. He learned of the other two articles upon seeing a reference to them in another published article. As it turned out, Chickering did not have occasion to make use of five of the articles that were copied.

DISCUSSION

I. The Nature of the Dispute

The parties and many of the amici curiae have approached this case as if it concerns the broad issue of whether photocopying of scientific articles is fair use, or at least the only slightly more limited issue of whether photocopying of such articles is fair use when undertaken by a research scientist engaged in his own research. Such broad issues are not before us. Rather, we consider whether Texaco's photocopying by 400 or 500 scientists, as represented by Chickering's example, is fair use. This includes the question whether such institutional, systematic copying increases the number of copies available to scientists while avoiding the necessity of paying for license fees or for additional subscriptions. We do not deal with the question of copying by an individual, for personal use in research or otherwise (not for resale), recognizing that under the fair use doctrine or the de minimis doctrine, such a practice by an individual might well not constitute an infringement. In other words, our opinion does not decide the case that would arise if Chickering were a professor or an independent scientist engaged in copying and creating files for independent research, as opposed to being employed by an institution in the pursuit of his research on the institution's behalf.

Fair use is a doctrine the application of which always depends on consideration of the precise facts at hand, see Campbell v. Acuff-Rose Music, Inc., 510 U.S. 569, 577 (1994); Harper & Row, Publishers, Inc. v. Nation Enterprises, 471 U.S. 539, 549 (1985); Wright v. Warner Books, Inc., 953 F.2d 731, 740 (2d Cir. 1991); H.R. Rep. No. 1476, 94th Cong., 2d Sess. 65–66 (1976) ("no generally applicable definition [of fair use] is possible, and each case raising the question must be decided on its own facts"), and in this case the parties have helpfully circumscribed the scope of the issue to be decided by tendering for the District Court's decision the facts concerning the copying of eight particular articles. Our concern is whether the copying of these eight articles, as representative of the systematic copying that Texaco encouraged, was properly determined not to be fair use. Thus, the many background details stressed by each side are of only limited relevance in resolving this specific case.[1]

A. Fair Use and Photocopying

We consider initially the doctrine of fair use and its application to photocopying of documents. Seeking "to motivate the creative activity of authors . . . by the provision of a special reward," Sony Corporation of America v. Universal City Studios, Inc., 464 U.S. 417 (1984), copyright law grants certain exclusive rights in original works to authors, see 17 U.S.C. §§ 102(a), 106, 201(a). However, the fair use doctrine "tempers the protection of copyright by allowing . . . [the] use [of] a limited amount of copyrighted material under some circumstances." Twin Peaks Productions, Inc. v. Publications International, Ltd., 996 F.2d 1366, 1373 (2d Cir. 1993). Traditionally conceived as based on authors' implied consent to reasonable uses of their works, see Harper & Row, 471 U.S. at 549–50, or on an exception to authors' monopoly privileges needed in order to fulfill copyright's purpose to promote the arts and sciences, see *Campbell,* 510 U.S. 575, the fair use doctrine has a lengthy and rich common-law history, see William F. Patry, The Fair Use Privilege in Copyright Law 1–63 (1985) [hereinafter Patry, The Fair Use Privilege], and is now codified in section 107 of the Copyright Act, 17 U.S.C. § 107.

As with the development of other easy and accessible means of mechanical reproduction of documents, the invention and widespread availability of photocopying technology threatens to disrupt the delicate balances established

---

1. Texaco, for example, uses a significant portion of its initial brief to expound on photocopying activities in various industries. Similarly, a large part of the publishers' statement of facts is devoted to a broad discussion of Texaco's photocopying practices, the social importance of academic and scientific journals, and the economics of journal publication and photocopying. These and other details presented by the parties are discussed in the District Court's opinion, 802 F.Supp. at 4–9.

by the Copyright Act. See 3 Melville B. Nimmer & David Nimmer, Nimmer on Copyright § 13.05[E][1], at 13–225 to 13–226 (1994) [hereinafter Nimmer on Copyright] (noting that "unrestricted photocopying practices could largely undercut the entire law of copyright") * * * As a leading commentator astutely notes, the advent of modern photocopying technology creates a pressing need for the law "to strike an appropriate balance between the authors' interest in preserving the integrity of copyright, and the public's right to enjoy the benefits that photocopying technology offers." 3 Nimmer on Copyright § 13.05 [E][1], at 13–226.

Indeed, if the issue were open, we would seriously question whether the fair use analysis that has developed with respect to works of authorship alleged to use portions of copyrighted material is precisely applicable to copies produced by mechanical means. The traditional fair use analysis, now codified in section 107, developed in an effort to adjust the competing interests of authors—the author of the original copyrighted work and the author of the secondary work that "copies" a portion of the original work in the course of producing what is claimed to be a new work. Mechanical "copying" of an entire document, made readily feasible and economical by the advent of xerography, see SCM Corp. v. Xerox Corp., 463 F.Supp. 983, 991–94 (D.Conn. 1978), aff'd, 645 F.2d 1195 (2d Cir.1981), cert. denied, 455 U.S. 1016 (1982), is obviously an activity entirely different from creating a work of authorship. Whatever social utility copying of this sort achieves, it is not concerned with creative authorship.

Though we have been instructed to defer to Congress "when major technological innovations alter the market for copyrighted materials," Sony, 464 U.S. at 431, Congress has thus far provided scant guidance for resolving fair use issues involving photocopying, legislating specifically only as to library copying, see 17 U.S.C. § 108, and providing indirect advice concerning classroom copying. * * * However, we learn from the Supreme Court's consideration of copying achieved by use of a videotape recorder that mechanical copying is to be assessed for fair use purposes under the traditional mode of analysis, including the four statutory factors of section 107. See Sony, 464 U.S. at 447–56. We therefore are obliged to apply that analysis to the photocopying that occurred in this case.

B. The Precise Copyrights at Issue

We must first identify precisely the copyrighted works alleged to be infringed, since certain arguments made on appeal seem to focus on different works. The publishers typically hold two separate sets of copyrights in their journal publications. As a consequence of the publishers' requirement that authors transfer their copyrights when their articles are accepted for publication, the publishers usually possess the copyrights that subsist in each individual article appearing within their journals.[4] For various rea-

---

4. For various reasons, for example, because certain articles are the work of the United States Government (which makes copyright protection unavailable, see 17 U.S.C. § 105), the publishers do not always possess the copyrights for all articles within each journal.

sons, for example, because certain articles are the work of the United States Government (which makes copyright protection unavailable, see 17 U.S.C. § 105), the publishers do not always possess the copyrights for all articles within each journal. Moreover, to the extent that the compilation of a journal issue involves an original work of authorship, the publishers possess a distinct copyright in each journal issue as a collective work, * * *.

From the outset, this lawsuit concerned alleged infringement of the copyrights in individual journal articles, copyrights assigned by the authors to the publishers. More specifically, by virtue of the parties' stipulation, this case now concerns the copyrights in the eight articles from *Catalysis* found in Chickering's files, copyrights now owned by Academic Press. There are no allegations that raise questions concerning Academic Press's potential copyrights in whole issues or annual volumes of *Catalysis* as collective works.

C. Burdens of Proof and Standard of Review

Fair use serves as an affirmative defense to a claim of copyright infringement, and thus the party claiming that its secondary use of the original copyrighted work constitutes a fair use typically carries the burden of proof as to all issues in the dispute. See *Campbell*, 510 U.S. 590. Moreover, since fair use is a "mixed question of law and fact," Harper & Row, 471 U.S. at 560, we review the District Court's conclusions on this issue de novo, though we accept its subsidiary findings of fact unless clearly erroneous, see Twin Peaks, 996 F.2d at 1374.

II. The Enumerated Fair Use Factors of Section 107

Section 107 of the Copyright Act identifies four non-exclusive factors that a court is to consider when making its fair use assessment, see 17 U.S.C. § 107(1)–(4). The District Court concluded that three of the four statutory factors favor the publishers. As detailed below, our analysis of certain statutory factors differs somewhat from that of the District Court, though we are in agreement on the ultimate determination. Our differences stem primarily from the fact that, unlike the District Court, we have had the benefit of the Supreme Court's important decision in *Campbell*, decided after Judge Leval issued his opinion.

A. First Factor: Purpose and Character of Use

The first factor listed in section 107 is "the purpose and character of the use, including whether such use is of a commercial nature or is for nonprofit educational purposes." 17 U.S.C. § 107(1). Especially pertinent to an assessment of the first fair use factor are the precise circumstances under which copies of the eight *Catalysis* articles were made. After noticing six of these articles when the original copy of the journal issue containing each of them was circulated to him, Chickering had them photocopied, at least initially, for the same basic purpose that one would normally seek to obtain the original—to have it available on his shelf for ready reference if and when he needed to look at it. The library circulated one copy and invited all the researchers to make their own photocopies. It is a reasonable inference that the library staff wanted each journal issue moved around the building quickly and returned to the library so that it would be available for others to look at.

Making copies enabled all researchers who might one day be interested in examining the contents of an article in the issue to have the article readily available in their own offices. In Chickering's own words, the copies of the articles were made for "my personal convenience," since it is "far more convenient to have access in my office to a photocopy of an article than to have to go to the library each time I wanted to refer to it." Affidavit of Donald Chickering at 11 (submitted as direct trial testimony) [hereinafter Chickering testimony]. Significantly, Chickering did not even have occasion to use five of the photocopied articles at all, further revealing that the photocopies of the eight *Catalysis* articles were primarily made just for "future retrieval and reference." Id.

It is true that photocopying these articles also served other purposes. The most favorable for Texaco is the purpose of enabling Chickering, if the need should arise, to go into the lab with pieces of paper that (a) were not as bulky as the entire issue or a bound volume of a year's issues, and (b) presented no risk of damaging the original by exposure to chemicals. And these purposes might suffice to tilt the first fair use factor in favor of Texaco if these purposes were dominant. For example, if Chickering had asked the library to buy him a copy of the pertinent issue of *Catalysis* and had placed it on his shelf, and one day while reading it had noticed a chart, formula, or other material that he wanted to take right into the lab, it might be a fair use for him to make a photocopy, and use that copy in the lab (especially if he did not retain it and build up a mini-library of photocopied articles). This is the sort of "spontaneous" copying that is part of the test for permissible nonprofit classroom copying. See Agreement on Guidelines for Classroom Copying in Not-For-Profit Educational Institutions, quoted in Patry, The Fair Use Privilege, at 308.[5] But that is not what happened here as to the six items copied from the circulated issues.

As to the other two articles, the circumstances are not quite as clear, but they too appear more to serve the purpose of being additions to Chickering's office "library" than to be spontaneous copying of a critical page that he was reading on his way to the lab. One was copied apparently when he saw a reference to it in another article, which was in an issue circulated to him. The most likely inference is that he decided that he ought to have copies of both items—again for placement on his shelf for later use if the need arose. The last article was copied, according to his affidavit, when he saw a reference to it "elsewhere." Chickering testimony at 22. What is clear is that this item too

---

5. These guidelines were included in the legislative history of the 1976 revision of the Copyright Act, see H.R. Rep. No. 1476, 94th Cong., 2d Sess. 68–71 (1976), U.S. Code Cong. & Admin.News 1976, p. 5659 and were endorsed by the House Judiciary Committee as "a reasonable interpretation of the minimum standards of fair use." Id. at 72, U.S. Code Cong. & Admin. News 1976, at 5686. Though these guidelines are not considered necessarily binding on courts, see Marcus v. Rowley, 695 F.2d 1171, 1178 (9th Cir. 1983), they exist as a persuasive authority marking out certain minimum standards for educational fair uses, see Basic Books, Inc. v. Kinko's Graphics Corp., 758 F.Supp. 1522–36 (S.D.N.Y. 1991). See generally 3 Nimmer on Copyright § 13.05[E][3][a], at 13–226.1 to 13–226.2 (discussing nature and impact of guidelines); Patry, The Fair Use Privilege, at 307–09, 404–07 (same).

was simply placed "on the shelf." As he testified, "I kept a copy to refer to in case I became more involved in support effects research." Id.

The photocopying of these eight *Catalysis* articles may be characterized as "archival"—i.e., done for the primary purpose of providing numerous Texaco scientists (for whom Chickering served as an example) each with his or her own personal copy of each article without Texaco's having to purchase another original journal.[6] The photocopying "merely 'supersede[s] the objects' of the original creation," *Campbell*, 510 U.S. 579 (quoting Folsom v. Marsh, 9 F.Cas. 342, 348 (No. 4,901) (C.C.D. Mass. 1841)), and tilts the first fair use factor against Texaco. We do not mean to suggest that no instance of archival copying would be fair use, but the first factor tilts against Texaco in this case because the making of copies to be placed on the shelf in Chickering's office is part of a systematic process of encouraging employee researchers to copy articles so as to multiply available copies while avoiding payment.

Texaco criticizes three aspects of the District Court's analysis of the first factor. Relying largely on the Supreme Court's discussion of fair use in *Sony*, the District Court suggested that a secondary user will "win" this first factor by showing a "transformative (or productive) nonsuperseding use of the original, or [a] noncommercial use, generally for a socially beneficial or widely accepted purpose." 802 F.Supp. at 12. The District Court then concluded that Texaco's copying is "neither transformative nor noncommercial," id. at 13: not transformative because Texaco "simply makes mechanical photocopies of the entirety of relevant articles" and the "primary aspect" of Texaco's photocopying is to multiply copies, see id. at 13–15; and not noncommercial because, though it facilitates research, this research is conducted solely for commercial gain, see id. at 15–16.

Texaco asserts that the District Court mischaracterized the inquiry under the first factor and overlooked several relevant considerations. First, Texaco contends that the District Court inappropriately focussed on the character of the user rather than the nature of the use in labeling Texaco's copying as commercial. Texaco claims that its status as a for-profit corporation has no bearing on the fair use analysis, and that its use should be considered noncommercial since it photocopied articles in order to aid Chickering's research. Texaco emphasizes that "research" is explicitly listed in the preamble of section 107, a circumstance that Texaco contends should

---

6. In this regard, the District Court's conclusion that the "primary aspect" of Texaco's copying was to multiply copies is accurate, see 802 F.Supp. at 14–15, irrespective of the evidence (or lack of evidence) concerning the nature and scope of Texaco's photocopying activity for its entire population of scientists. Even if the photocopies of the *Catalysis* articles in Chickering's files were the only copies ever made by Texaco—which, as Texaco stresses, is all that the evidence developed below conclu-

sively showed—the primary objective in making these single copies was to provide Chickering with his own, additional, readily accessible copy of the original article. As the District Court noted, "[I]f Chickering were the subscriber and sole user of the subscription to *Catalysis*, and he made an extra copy of an article for use in the lab or for marking with scratch notes, the argument [for a transformative] fair use] might have considerable force." 802 F.Supp. at 14.

make its copying favored under the first factor and throughout the entire fair use analysis.[7]

Second, Texaco contends that the District Court put undue emphasis on whether its use was "transformative," especially since the Supreme Court appears to have rejected the view that a use must be transformative or productive to be a fair use. See *Sony*, 464 U.S. at 455 n. 40 ("The distinction between 'productive' and 'unproductive' uses may be helpful in calibrating the balance [of interests], but it cannot be wholly determinative."). Texaco asserts that the "transformative use" concept is valuable only to the extent that it focusses attention upon whether a second work unfairly competes with the original. Texaco states that in this case, where the photocopies it made were not sold or distributed in competition with the original, the nontransformative nature of its copying should not prevent a finding of fair use. Texaco also suggests that its use should be considered transformative: photocopying the article separated it from a bulky journal, made it more amenable to markings, and provided a document that could be readily replaced if damaged in a laboratory, all of which "transformed" the original article into a form that better served Chickering's research needs.

Finally, Texaco claims that it should prevail on the first factor because, as the District Court acknowledged, the type of photocopying it conducted is widespread and has long been considered reasonable and customary. Texaco stresses that some courts and commentators regard custom and common usage as integral to the fair use analysis. See, e.g., Williams & Wilkins Co. v. United States, 487 F.2d 1345, 1353–56 (Ct. Claims 1973), aff'd by equally divided Court, 420 U.S. 376 (1975); Lloyd L. Weinreb, Fair's Fair: A Comment on the Fair Use Doctrine, 103 Harv. L. Rev. 1137, 1140 (1990) [hereinafter Weinreb, Fair's Fair]. We consider these three lines of attack separately.

1. Commercial use. We generally agree with Texaco's contention that the District Court placed undue emphasis on the fact that Texaco is a for-profit corporation conducting research primarily for commercial gain. Since many, if not most, secondary users seek at least some measure of commercial gain from their use, unduly emphasizing the commercial motivation of a copier will lead to an overly restrictive view of fair use. See *Campbell*, 114 S.Ct. at 1174; see also Maxtone-Graham v. Burtchaell, 803 F.2d 1253, 1262 (2d Cir. 1986) (noting that if "commercial" nature of a secondary use is overemphasized in the analysis, "fair use would be virtually obliterated"), cert. denied, 481 U.S. 1059 (1987). See generally 3 Nimmer on Copyright § 13.05[A][1][c], at 13–162 to 13–163 (categorical rule against commercial uses unwarranted since this "would cause the fair use analysis to collapse in all but the exceptional case of nonprofit exploitation"). Though the Supreme Court had stated in *Sony* that every commercial use was "presumptively" unfair, see 464 U.S. at 451 that Court and lower courts have come to explain

---

7. Though Texaco claims that its copying is for "research" as that term is used in the preamble of section 107, this characterization might somewhat overstate the matter. Chickering has not used portions of articles from *Catalysis* in his own published piece of research, nor has he had to duplicate some portion of copyrighted material directly in the course of conducting an experiment or investigation. Rather, entire articles were copied as an intermediate step that might abet Chickering's research.

that the commercial nature of a secondary use simply "'tends to weigh against a finding of fair use.'" *Campbell,* 510 U.S. 584 (quoting Harper & Row, 471 U.S. at 562); accord Rogers v. Koons, 960 F.2d 301, 309 (2d Cir.), cert. denied, 113 S.Ct. 365 (1992); Sega Enterprises Limited v. Accolade, Inc., 977 F.2d 1510, 1522 (9th Cir. 1992); Maxtone-Graham, 803 F.2d at 1262.

Indeed, *Campbell* warns against "elevat[ing] . . . to a per se rule" *Sony's* language about a presumption against fair use arising from commercial use. 510 U.S. at 585. *Campbell* discards that language in favor of a more subtle, sophisticated approach, which recognizes that "the more transformative the new work, the less will be the significance of other factors, like commercialism, that may weigh against a finding of fair use." Id. at 579. The Court states that "the commercial or nonprofit educational purpose of a work is only one element of the first factor enquiry," id. at 584, and points out that "[i]f, indeed, commerciality carried presumptive force against a finding of fairness, the presumption would swallow nearly all of the illustrative uses listed in the preamble paragraph of § 107 . . . . Id."

We do not mean to suggest that the District Court overlooked these principles; in fact, the Court discussed them insightfully, see 802 F.Supp. at 12–13. Rather, our concern here is that the Court let the for-profit nature of Texaco's activity weigh against Texaco without differentiating between a direct commercial use and the more indirect relation to commercial activity that occurred here. Texaco was not gaining direct or immediate commercial advantage from the photocopying at issue in this case—i.e., Texaco's profits, revenues, and overall commercial performance were not tied to its making copies of eight *Catalysis* articles for Chickering. Cf. Basic Books, Inc. v. Kinko's Graphics Corp., 758 F.Supp. 1522 (S.D.N.Y. 1991) (revenues of reprographic business stemmed directly from selling unauthorized photocopies of copyrighted books). Rather, Texaco's photocopying served, at most, to facilitate Chickering's research, which in turn might have led to the development of new products and technology that could have improved Texaco's commercial performance. Texaco's photocopying is more appropriately labeled an "intermediate use." See Sega Enterprises, 977 F.2d at 1522–23 (labeling secondary use "intermediate" and finding first factor in favor of for-profit company, even though ultimate purpose of copying was to develop competing commercial product, because immediate purpose of copying computer code was to study idea contained within computer program).

We do not consider Texaco's status as a for-profit company irrelevant to the fair use analysis. Though Texaco properly contends that a court's focus should be on the use of the copyrighted material and not simply on the user, it is overly simplistic to suggest that the "purpose and character of the use" can be fully discerned without considering the nature and objectives of the user.[8]

---

8. See Patry, The Fair Use Privilege, at 416-17 (noting that the nature of person or entity engaging in use affects the character of the use); Report of the Register of Copyrights—Library Reproduction of Copyrighted Works (17 U.S.C. 108) 85 (1983) (explaining that though a scientist in a for-profit firm and a university student may engage in the same photocopying of scholarly articles to facilitate their research, "the copyright consequences are different: [the scientist's] copying is of a clearly commercial nature, and less likely to be fair use") quoted in Patry, The Fair Use Privilege, at 417 n. 307.

Ultimately, the somewhat cryptic suggestion in section 107(1) to consider whether the secondary use "is of a commercial nature or is for nonprofit educational purposes" connotes that a court should examine, among other factors, the value obtained by the secondary user from the use of the copyrighted material. See Rogers, 960 F.2d at 309 ("The first factor . . . asks whether the original was copied in good faith to benefit the public or primarily for the commercial interests of the infringer."); MCA, Inc. v. Wilson, 677 F.2d 180, 182 (2d Cir. 1981) (court is to consider "whether the alleged infringing use was primarily for public benefit or for private commercial gain"). The commercial/nonprofit dichotomy concerns the unfairness that arises when a secondary user makes unauthorized use of copyrighted material to capture significant revenues as a direct consequence of copying the original work. See Harper & Row, 471 U.S. at 562 ("The crux of the profit/nonprofit distinction is . . . whether the user stands to profit from exploitation of the copyrighted material without paying the customary price.").

Consistent with these principles, courts will not sustain a claimed defense of fair use when the secondary use can fairly be characterized as a form of "commercial exploitation," i.e., when the copier directly and exclusively acquires conspicuous financial rewards from its use of the copyrighted material. See Harper & Row, 471 U.S. at 562–63; Twin Peaks, 996 F.2d at 1375; Rogers, 960 F.2d at 309; Iowa State University Research Foundation, Inc. v. American Broadcasting Companies, Inc., 621 F.2d 57, 61 (2d Cir.1980); Meeropol v. Nizer, 560 F.2d 1061, 1069 (2d Cir. 1977) (examining whether use was "predominantly for commercial exploitation"), cert. denied, 434 U.S. 1013 (1978). Conversely, courts are more willing to find a secondary use fair when it produces a value that benefits the broader public interest. See Twin Peaks, 996 F.2d at 1375; Sega Enterprises, 977 F.2d at 1523; Rosemont Enterprises, Inc. v. Random House, Inc., 366 F.2d 303, 307–09 (2d Cir. 1966), cert. denied, 385 U.S. 1009 (1967). The greater the private economic rewards reaped by the secondary user (to the exclusion of broader public benefits), the more likely the first factor will favor the copyright holder and the less likely the use will be considered fair.

As noted before, in this particular case the link between Texaco's commercial gain and its copying is somewhat attenuated: the copying, at most, merely facilitated Chickering's research that might have led to the production of commercially valuable products. Thus, it would not be accurate to conclude that Texaco's copying of eight particular *Catalysis* articles amounted to "commercial exploitation," especially since the immediate goal of Texaco's copying was to facilitate Chickering's research in the sciences, an objective that might well serve a broader public purpose. See Twin Peaks, 996 F.2d at 1375; Sega Enterprises, 977 F.2d at 1522. Still, we need not ignore the for-profit nature of Texaco's enterprise, especially since we can confidently conclude that Texaco reaps at least some indirect economic advantage from its photocopying. As the publishers emphasize, Texaco's photocopying for Chickering could be regarded simply as another "factor of production" utilized in Texaco's efforts to develop profitable products. Conceptualized in this way, it is not obvious why it is fair for Texaco to avoid having to pay at least some price to copyright holders for the right to photocopy the original articles.

2. Transformative Use. The District Court properly emphasized that Texaco's photocopying was not "transformative." After the District Court issued its opinion, the Supreme Court explicitly ruled that the concept of a "transformative use" is central to a proper analysis under the first factor, see *Campbell,* 510 U.S. 578–83. The Court explained that though a "transformative use is not absolutely necessary for a finding of fair use, . . . the more transformative the new work, the less will be the significance of other factors, like commercialism, that may weigh against a finding of fair use." Id. at 579.

The "transformative use" concept is pertinent to a court's investigation under the first factor because it assesses the value generated by the secondary use and the means by which such value is generated. To the extent that the secondary use involves merely an untransformed duplication, the value generated by the secondary use is little or nothing more than the value that inheres in the original. Rather than making some contribution of new intellectual value and thereby fostering the advancement of the arts and sciences, an untransformed copy is likely to be used simply for the same intrinsic purpose as the original, thereby providing limited justification for a finding of fair use. See Weissmann v. Freeman, 868 F.2d 1313, 1324 (2d Cir.) (explaining that a use merely for the same "intrinsic purpose" as original "moves the balance of the calibration on the first factor against" secondary user and "seriously weakens a claimed fair use"), cert. denied, 493 U.S. 883 (1989).[9]

In contrast, to the extent that the secondary use "adds something new, with a further purpose or different character," the value generated goes beyond the value that inheres in the original and "the goal of copyright, to promote science and the arts, is generally furthered." *Campbell,* 510 U.S. at 579; see also Pierre N. Leval, Toward a Fair Use Standard, 103 Harv. L. Rev. 1105, 1111 (1990) [hereinafter Leval, Toward a Fair Use Standard]. It is therefore not surprising that the "preferred" uses illustrated in the preamble to section 107, such as criticism and comment, generally involve some transformative use of the original work. See 3 Nimmer on Copyright § 13.05[A][1][b], at 13–160.

Texaco suggests that its conversion of the individual *Catalysis* articles through photocopying into a form more easily used in a laboratory might constitute a transformative use. However, Texaco's photocopying merely transforms the material object embodying the intangible article that is the copyrighted original work. See 17 U.S.C. §§ 101, 102 (explaining that copyright protection in literary works subsists in the original work of authorship "regardless of the nature of the material objects . . . in which they are embodied"). Texaco's making of copies cannot properly be regarded as a transformative

---

9. See also Marcus v. Rowley, 695 F.2d at 1175 (emphasizing that "a finding that the alleged infringers copied the material to use it for the same intrinsic purpose for which the copyright owner intended it to be used is strong indicia of no fair use."). See generally Leon E. Seltzer, Exemptions and Fair Use in Copyright 24 (1978) (noting traditional limit on the applicability of fair use doctrine when reproduction of original work is done "in order to use it for its intrinsic purpose—to make what might be called the 'ordinary' use of it").

use of the copyrighted material. See Steven D. Smit, "Make a Copy for the File
. . .": Copyright Infringement by Attorneys, 46 Baylor L. Rev. 1, 15 & n. 58
(1994); see also Basic Books, 758 F.Supp. at 1530–31 (repackaging in anthology form of excerpts from copyrighted books not a transformative use).

Even though Texaco's photocopying is not technically a transformative
use of the copyrighted material, we should not overlook the significant independent value that can stem from conversion of original journal articles into
a format different from their normal appearance. See generally *Sony,* 464
U.S. at 454, 455 n. 40, (acknowledging possible benefits from copying that
might otherwise seem to serve "no productive purpose"); Weinreb, Fair's
Fair, at 1143 & n. 29 (discussing potential value from non- transformative
copying). As previously explained, Texaco's photocopying converts the individual *Catalysis* articles into a useful format. Before modern photocopying,
Chickering probably would have converted the original article into a more
serviceable form by taking notes, whether cursory or extended;[10] today he
can do so with a photocopying machine. Nevertheless, whatever independent value derives from the more usable format of the photocopy does not
mean that every instance of photocopying wins on the first factor. In this
case, the predominant archival purpose of the copying tips the first factor
against the copier, despite the benefit of a more usable format.

3. Reasonable and Customary Practice. Texaco contends that
Chickering's photocopying constitutes a use that has historically been considered "reasonable and customary." We agree with the District Court that
whatever validity this argument might have had before the advent of the
photocopying licensing arrangements discussed below in our consideration
of the fourth fair use factor, the argument today is insubstantial. As the
District Court observed, "To the extent the copying practice was 'reasonable'
in 1973 [when *Williams & Wilkins* was decided], it has ceased to be 'reasonable' as the reasons that justified it before [photocopying licensing] have
ceased to exist." 802 F.Supp. at 25.

In amplification of Texaco's arguments, our dissenting colleague makes
two further points about the first factor analysis that merit a response.
First, the dissent disputes our characterization of Chickering's use as
"archival" on the ground that such a use would occur in an institutional setting, whereas Chickering copied for his personal use. Second, the dissent
contends that Chickering's use is transformative because it is an important
step in the process of doing research. We think the proper response to these
observations emerges from considering how they would fare if the Texaco
library had sent around entire books, rather than issues of a journal.

---

10. In stating that a handwritten copy
would have been made, we do not mean to
imply that such copying would necessarily
have been a fair use. Despite the 1973 dictum
in *Williams & Wilkins* asserting that "it is
almost unanimously accepted that a scholar
can make a handwritten copy of an entire
copyrighted article for his own use . . . ," 487
F.2d at 1350, the current edition of the
Nimmer treatise reports that "[t]here is no
reported case on the question of whether a
single handwritten copy of all or substantially all of a book or other protected work
made for the copier's own private use is an
infringement or fair use." 3 Nimmer on
Copyright § 1305[E][4][a], at 13–229.

Clearly, Chickering (and all the other researchers at the Beacon facility) would be making archival use of the circulating books if they made photocopies of the books for their individual offices and thereby spared Texaco the expense of buying them all individual volumes. An individual copies for archival purposes even if the resulting archive remains in a private office. When a corporation invites such archival copying by circulating items likely to be worth copying (whether articles or entire books), any distinction between individual and institutional archiving loses all significance.

Moreover, the concept of a "transformative" use would be extended beyond recognition if it was applied to Chickering's copying simply because he acted in the course of doing research. The purposes illustrated by the categories listed in section 107 refer primarily to the work of authorship alleged to be a fair use, not to the activity in which the alleged infringer is engaged. Texaco cannot gain fair use insulation for Chickering's archival photocopying of articles (or books) simply because such copying is done by a company doing research. It would be equally extravagant for a newspaper to contend that because its business is "news reporting" it may line the shelves of its reporters with photocopies of books on journalism or that schools engaged in "teaching" may supply its faculty members with personal photocopies of books on educational techniques or substantive fields. Whatever benefit copying and reading such books might contribute to the process of "teaching" would not for that reason satisfy the test of a "teaching" purpose.

On balance, we agree with the District Court that the first factor favors the publishers, primarily because the dominant purpose of the use is systematic institutional policy of multiplying the available number of copies of pertinent copyrighted articles by circulating the journals among employed scientists for them to make copies, thereby serving the same purpose for which additional subscriptions are normally sold, or, as will be discussed, for which photocopying licenses may be obtained.

B. Second Factor: Nature of Copyrighted Work

The second statutory fair use factor is "the nature of the copyrighted work." 17 U.S.C. § 107(2). In assessing this factor, the District Court noted that the articles in *Catalysis* "are created for publication with the purpose and intention of benefiting from the protection of the copyright law," and that copyright protection "is vitally necessary to the dissemination of scientific articles of the sort that are at issue." 802 F.Supp. at 16. Nevertheless, the Court ultimately concluded that this factor favored Texaco because the photocopied articles were essentially factual in nature and the "'scope of fair use is greater with respect to factual than nonfactual works.'" Id. at 16–17 (quoting New Era Publications International, ApS v. Carol Publishing Group, 904 F.2d 152, 157 (2d Cir.), cert. denied, 498 U.S. 921 (1990)).

On appeal, the publishers stress the District Court's comments concerning the importance of broad copyright protection for journal publications in order to foster journal production. Further, citing *Harper & Row* for the proposition that the creativity of an original work weighs against finding fair use, see 471 U.S. at 563, the publishers also point out that "the journal articles are expressions of highly original, creative and imaginative thinking."

Though a significant measure of creativity was undoubtedly used in the creation of the eight articles copied from *Catalysis*, even a glance at their content immediately reveals the predominantly factual nature of these works.[11] Moreover, though we have previously recognized the importance of strong copyright protection to provide sufficient incentives for the creation of scientific works, see Weissmann, 868 F.2d at 1325, nearly every category of copyrightable works could plausibly assert that broad copyright protection was essential to the continued vitality of that category of works.

Ultimately, then, the manifestly factual character of the eight articles precludes us from considering the articles as "within the core of the copyright's protective purposes," *Campbell,* 510 U.S. 586; see also *Harper & Row,* 471 U.S. at 563 ("The law generally recognizes a greater need to disseminate factual works than works of fiction or fantasy."). Thus, in agreement with the District Court, we conclude that the second factor favors Texaco.

C. Third Factor: Amount and Substantiality of Portion Used

The third statutory fair use factor is "the amount and substantiality of the portion used in relation to the copyrighted work as a whole." 17 U.S.C. § 107(3). The District Court concluded that this factor clearly favors the publishers because Texaco copied the eight articles from *Catalysis* in their entirety.

Texaco makes various responses to the District Court's straightforward conclusion. First, Texaco claims that this factor is significant only as a means to determine whether a copy unfairly supersedes demand for the original and should be considered "largely irrelevant" where, as here, a copy is not sold or distributed. Second, Texaco claims that, rather than focus on Texaco's copying of entire articles, it is more appropriate to consider that Texaco copied only a very small portion of any particular issue or volume of *Catalysis*. Finally, Texaco cites *Sony* and *Williams & Wilkins* for the proposition that the copying of entire copyrighted works can still constitute fair use. See *Sony,* 464 U.S. at 449–50; *Williams & Wilkins,* 487 F.2d at 1353.

Texaco's suggestion that we consider that it copied only a small percentage of the total compendium of works encompassed within *Catalysis* is superficially intriguing, especially since *Catalysis* is traditionally marketed only as a periodical by issue or volume. However, as the District Court recognized, each of the eight articles in *Catalysis* was separately authored and constitutes a discrete "original work[ ] of authorship," 17 U.S.C. § 102. As we emphasized at the outset, each article enjoys independent copyright protection, which the authors transferred to Academic Press, and what the publishers claim has been infringed is the copyright that subsists in each individual article—not the distinct copyright that may subsist in each journal issue or volume by

---

11. Not only are the *Catalysis* articles essentially factual in nature, but the evidence suggests that Chickering was interested exclusively in the facts, ideas, concepts, or principles contained within the articles. Though scientists surely employ creativity and originality to develop ideas and obtain facts and thereafter to convey the ideas and facts in scholarly articles, it is primarily the ideas and facts themselves that are of value to other scientists in their research.

virtue of the publishers' original compilation of these articles. The only other appellate court to consider the propriety of photocopying articles from journals also recognized that each article constituted an entire work in the fair use analysis. See *Williams & Wilkins,* 487 F.2d at 1353.

Despite Texaco's claims that we consider its amount of copying "minuscule" in relation to the entirety of *Catalysis,* we conclude, as did the District Court, that Texaco has copied entire works. Though this conclusion does not preclude a finding of fair use, it militates against such a finding, see *Sony,* 464 U.S. at 449–50, and weights the third factor in favor of the publishers.

Finally, though we are sensitive to Texaco's claim that the third factor serves merely as a proxy for determining whether a secondary use significantly interferes with demand for the original—a concern echoed by some commentators, see William W. Fisher III, Reconstructing the Fair Use Doctrine, 101 Harv. L. Rev. 1661, 1678 (1988) [hereinafter Fisher, Reconstructing Fair Use]—we think this factor serves a further end that advances the fair use analysis. Specifically, by focussing on the amount and substantiality of the original work used by the secondary user, we gain insight into the purpose and character of the use as we consider whether the quantity of the material used was "reasonable in relation to the purpose of the copying." See *Campbell,* 510 U.S. 586. In this case, the fact that Texaco photocopied the eight *Catalysis* articles in their entirety weakens its assertion that the over-riding purpose and character of its use was to enable the immediate use of the article in the laboratory and strengthens our view that the predominant purpose and character of the use was to establish a personal library of pertinent articles for Chickering. Cf. id. at 1176 (intimating that extent of copying can provide insight into primary purpose of copying).

D. Fourth Factor: Effect Upon Potential Market or Value

The fourth statutory fair use factor is "the effect of the use upon the potential market for or value of the copyrighted work." 17 U.S.C. § 107(4). Assessing this factor, the District Court detailed the range of procedures Texaco could use to obtain authorized copies of the articles that it photocopied and found that "whatever combination of procedures Texaco used, the publishers' revenues would grow significantly." 802 F.Supp. at 19. The Court concluded that the publishers "powerfully demonstrated entitlement to prevail as to the fourth factor," since they had shown "a substantial harm to the value of their copyrights" as the consequence of Texaco's copying. See id. at 18–21.

Prior to *Campbell,* the Supreme Court had characterized the fourth factor as "the single most important element of fair use," Harper & Row, 471 U.S. at 566; accord 3 Nimmer on Copyright § 13.05[A][4], at 13–183. However, *Campbell's* discussion of the fourth factor conspicuously omits this phrasing. Apparently abandoning the idea that any factor enjoys primacy, *Campbell* instructs that "[a]ll [four factors] are to be explored, and the results weighed together, in light of the purposes of copyright." 510 U.S. 578.

In analyzing the fourth factor, it is important (1) to bear in mind the precise copyrighted works, namely the eight journal articles, and (2) to recognize the distinctive nature and history of "the potential market for or value of" these particular works.[12] Specifically, though there is a traditional market for, and hence a clearly defined value of, journal issues and volumes, in the form of per-issue purchases and journal subscriptions, there is neither a traditional market for, nor a clearly defined value of, individual journal articles. As a result, analysis of the fourth factor cannot proceed as simply as would have been the case if Texaco had copied a work that carries a stated or negotiated selling price in the market.

Like most authors, writers of journal articles do not directly seek to capture the potential financial rewards that stem from their copyrights by personally marketing copies of their writings. Rather, like other creators of literary works, the author of a journal article "commonly sells his rights to publishers who offer royalties in exchange for their services in producing and marketing the author's work." Harper & Row, 471 U.S. at 547. In the distinctive realm of academic and scientific articles, however, the only form of royalty paid by a publisher is often just the reward of being published, publication being a key to professional advancement and prestige for the author, see Weissmann, 868 F.2d at 1324 (noting that "in an academic setting, profit is ill-measured in dollars. Instead, what is valuable is recognition because it so often influences professional advancement and academic tenure."). The publishers in turn incur the costs and labor of producing and marketing authors' articles, driven by the prospect of capturing the economic value stemming from the copyrights in the original works, which the authors have transferred to them. Ultimately, the monopoly privileges conferred by copyright protection and the potential financial rewards therefrom are not directly serving to motivate authors to write individual articles; rather, they serve to motivate publishers to produce journals, which provide the conventional and often exclusive means for disseminating these individual articles. It is the prospect of such dissemination that contributes to the motivation of these authors.

Significantly, publishers have traditionally produced and marketed authors' individual articles only in a journal format, i.e., in periodical compilations of numerous articles. In other words, publishers have conventionally sought to capture the economic value from the "exclusive rights" to "reproduce" and "distribute copies" of the individual articles, see 17 U.S.C. § 106(1) & (3), solely by compiling many such articles together in a periodical journal and then charging a fee to subscribe. Publishers have not traditionally provided a simple or efficient means to obtain single copies of

---

12. We focus on the eight articles to emphasize the special characteristics of articles as distinguished from journal issues or bound volumes. In doing so, we recognize, as did the District Court, see 802 F.Supp. at 18 n. 15, that the fourth factor is concerned with the category of a defendant's conduct, not merely the specific instances of copying. See 3 Nimmer on Copyright § 13.05[A][4], at 13–183 to 13–184 ("[I]t is a mistake to view [the fourth] factor . . . as merely raising the question of the extent of damages to plaintiff caused by the particular activities of the defendant. This factor rather poses the issue of whether unrestricted and widespread conduct of the sort engaged in by the defendant . . . would result in a substantially adverse impact on the potential market for or value of the plaintiff's present work.") (emphasis added).

individual articles; reprints are usually available from publishers only in bulk quantities and with some delay.

This marketing pattern has various consequences for our analysis of the fourth factor. First, evidence concerning the effect that photocopying individual journal articles has on the traditional market for journal subscriptions is of somewhat less significance than if a market existed for the sale of individual copies of articles. Second, this distinctive arrangement raises novel questions concerning the significance of the publishers' establishment of an innovative licensing scheme for the photocopying of individual journal articles.

1. *Sales of Additional Journal Subscriptions, Back Issues, and Back Volumes.* Since we are concerned with the claim of fair use in copying the eight individual articles from *Catalysis*, the analysis under the fourth factor must focus on the effect of Texaco's photocopying upon the potential market for or value of these individual articles. Yet, in their respective discussions of the fourth statutory factor, the parties initially focus on the impact of Texaco's photocopying of individual journal articles upon the market for *Catalysis* journals through sales of *Catalysis* subscriptions, back issues, or back volumes.

As a general matter, examining the effect on the marketability of the composite work containing a particular individual copyrighted work serves as a useful means to gauge the impact of a secondary use "upon the potential market for or value of" that individual work, since the effect on the marketability of the composite work will frequently be directly relevant to the effect on the market for or value of that individual work.[13] Quite significantly, though, in the unique world of academic and scientific articles, the effect on the marketability of the composite work in which individual articles appear is not obviously related to the effect on the market for or value of the individual articles. Since (1) articles are submitted unsolicited to journals, (2) publishers do not make any payment to authors for the right to publish their articles or to acquire their copyrights, and (3) there is no evidence in the record suggesting that publishers seek to reprint particular articles in new composite works, we cannot readily conclude that evidence concerning the effect of Texaco's use on the marketability of journals provides an effective means to appraise the effect of Texaco's use on the market for or value of *individual journal articles*.

These considerations persuade us that evidence concerning the effect of Texaco's photocopying of individual articles within *Catalysis* on the traditional market for *Catalysis* subscriptions is of somewhat limited significance in determining and evaluating the effect of Texaco's photocopying "upon the

---

13. One reason that the effect on the marketability of the composite work is typically relevant is because the strength of the market for the composite work will influence the payment producers will be willing to give to the author of the individual work for permission to include that individual work. For example, if a secondary use of a copyrighted story adversely affects purchases of a collection of short stories in which this story appears, then other producers of short story collections will less likely seek to have, or will pay less to have, that story as part of their collections. In this way, the market for or value of the story has clearly been affected by the secondary use.

potential market for or value of" the individual articles. We do not mean to suggest that we believe the effect on the marketability of journal subscriptions is completely irrelevant to gauging the effect on the market for and value of individual articles. Were the publishers able to demonstrate that Texaco's type of photocopying, if widespread,[14] would impair the marketability of journals, then they might have a strong claim under the fourth factor. Likewise, were Texaco able to demonstrate that its type of photocopying, even if widespread, would have virtually no effect on the marketability of journals, then it might have a strong claim under this fourth factor.

On this record, however, the evidence is not resounding for either side. The District Court specifically found that, in the absence of photocopying, (1) "Texaco would not ordinarily fill the need now being supplied by photocopies through the purchase of back issues or back volumes . . . [or] by enormously enlarging the number of its subscriptions," but (2) Texaco still "would increase the number of subscriptions somewhat." 802 F.Supp. at 19.[15] This moderate conclusion concerning the actual effect on the marketability of journals, combined with the uncertain relationship between the market for journals and the market for and value of individual articles, leads us to conclude that the evidence concerning sales of additional journal subscriptions, back issues, and back volumes does not strongly support either side with regard to the fourth factor. Cf. *Sony,* 464 U.S. at 451–55 (rejecting various predictions of harm to value of copyrighted work based on speculation about possible consequences of secondary use). At best, the loss of a few journal subscriptions tips the fourth factor only slightly toward the publishers because evidence of such loss is weak evidence that the copied articles themselves have lost any value., 464 U.S. 449–50.

2. *Licensing Revenues and Fees.* The District Court, however, went beyond discussing the sales of additional journal subscriptions in holding

---

14. Properly applied, the fourth factor requires a court to consider "not only . . . particular actions of the alleged infringer, but also 'whether unrestricted and widespread conduct of the sort engaged in by the defendant . . . would result in a substantially adverse impact on the potential market' for the original." Campbell, 510 U.S. 590 (quoting 3 Nimmer on Copyright § 13.05 [A][4]). Accord Harper & Row, 471 U.S. at 568–69; Rogers, 960 F.2d at 312.

15. Texaco assails the conclusion that, without photocopying, it would increase subscriptions "somewhat" as an improper inference unsupported by the evidence. Though we accept Texaco's assertion that additional subscriptions provide an imperfect substitute for the copies of individual articles that scientists need and prefer, we cannot conclude that the District Court's factual finding that "Texaco would add at least a modest

number of subscriptions," 802 F.Supp. at 19, is clearly erroneous.

First, though Texaco claims that there is no reliable evidence suggesting that photocopying served to facilitate journal circulation, the evidence concerning Texaco's routing practices supports the District Court's inference that, without photocopying, Texaco will need a greater number of subscriptions to insure the prompt circulation of journals. Second, as discussed in connection with the first statutory factor, the dominant reason for, and value derived from, the copying of the eight particular *Catalysis* articles was to make them available on Chickering's shelf for ready reference when he needed to look at them. Thus, it is reasonable to conclude that Texaco would purchase at least a few additional subscriptions to serve this purpose, i.e., to provide certain researchers with personal copies of particular articles in their own offices.

that Texaco's photocopying affected the value of the publishers' copyrights. Specifically, the Court pointed out that, if Texaco's unauthorized photocopying was not permitted as fair use, the publishers' revenues would increase significantly since Texaco would (1) obtain articles from document delivery services (which pay royalties to publishers for the right to photocopy articles), (2) negotiate photocopying licenses directly with individual publishers, and/or (3) acquire some form of photocopying license from the Copyright Clearance Center Inc. ("CCC").[16] See 802 F.Supp. at 19. Texaco claims that the District Court's reasoning is faulty because, in determining that the value of the publishers' copyrights was affected, the Court assumed that the publishers were entitled to demand and receive licensing royalties and fees for photocopying. Yet, continues Texaco, whether the publishers can demand a fee for permission to make photocopies is the very question that the fair use trial is supposed to answer.

It is indisputable that, as a general matter, a copyright holder is entitled to demand a royalty for licensing others to use its copyrighted work, see 17 U.S.C. § 106 (copyright owner has exclusive right "to authorize" certain uses), and that the impact on potential licensing revenues is a proper subject for consideration in assessing the fourth factor, see, e.g., *Campbell*, 510 U.S. 592; Harper & Row, 471 U.S. at 568–69; Twin Peaks, 996 F.2d at 1377; DC Comics Inc. v. Reel Fantasy, Inc., 696 F.2d 24, 28 (2d Cir. 1982); United Telephone Co. of Missouri v. Johnson Publishing Co., Inc., 855 F.2d 604, 610 (8th Cir. 1988).

However, not every effect on potential licensing revenues enters the analysis under the fourth factor.[17] Specifically, courts have recognized limits on the concept of "potential licensing revenues" by considering only traditional, reasonable, or likely to be developed markets when examining and assessing a secondary use's "effect upon the potential market for or value of the

---

16. The CCC is a central clearing-house established in 1977 primarily by publishers to license photocopying. The CCC offers a variety of licensing schemes; fees can be paid on a per copy basis or through blanket license arrangements. Most publishers are registered with the CCC, but the participation of for-profit institutions that engage in photocopying has been limited, largely because of uncertainty concerning the legal questions at issue in this lawsuit. The CCC is fully described in the District Court's opinion. 802 F. Supp. at 7–9. A more extended discussion of the formation, development, and effectiveness of the CCC and its licensing schemes is contained in Stanley M. Besen & Sheila Nataraj Kirby, Compensating Creators of Intellectual Property: Collectives that Collect (1989).

17. As Texaco notes and others have recognized, a copyright holder can always assert some degree of adverse affect on its potential

licensing revenues as a consequence of the secondary use at issue simply because the copyright holder has not been paid a fee to permit that particular use. See Leval, Toward a Fair Use Standard, at 1124 ("By definition every fair use involves some loss of royalty revenue because the secondary user has not paid royalties."); Fisher, Reconstructing Fair Use, at 1671 (noting that in almost every case "there will be some material adverse impact on a 'potential market'" since the secondary user has not paid for the use). Thus, were a court automatically to conclude in every case that potential licensing revenues were impermissibly impaired simply because the secondary user did not pay a fee for the right to engage in the use, the fourth fair use factor would always favor the copyright holder. See Leval, Toward a Fair Use Standard, at 1125; Fisher, Reconstructing Fair Use, at 1672.

copyrighted work." See *Campbell,* 510 U.S. 592 ("The market for potential derivative uses includes only those that creators of original works would in general develop or license others to develop."); Harper & Row, 471 U.S. at 568, (fourth factor concerned with "use that supplants *any part* of the normal market for a copyrighted work") (emphasis added) (quoting S. Rep. No. 473, 94th Cong., 1st Sess. 65 (1975)); see also Mathieson v. Associated Press, 23 U.S.P.Q.2d 1685, 1690–91, (S.D.N.Y. 1992) (refusing to find fourth factor in favor of copyright holder because secondary use did not affect any aspect of the normal market for copyrighted work).

For example, the Supreme Court recently explained that because of the "unlikelihood that creators of imaginative works will license critical reviews or lampoons" of their works, "the law recognizes no derivative market for critical works," *Campbell,* 510 U.S. 592. Similarly, other courts have found that the fourth factor will favor the secondary user when the only possible adverse effect occasioned by the secondary use would be to a potential market or value that the copyright holder has not typically sought to, or reasonably been able to, obtain or capture. See Twin Peaks, 996 F.2d at 1377 (noting that fourth factor will favor secondary user when use "filled a market niche that the [copyright owner] simply had no interest in occupying"); Pacific and Southern Co. v. Duncan, 744 F.2d 1490, 1496 (11th Cir. 1984) cert. denied, 471 U.S. 1004 (1985) (noting that the fourth factor may not favor copyright owner when the secondary user "profits from an activity that the owner could not possibly take advantage of").[18]

Thus, Texaco is correct, at least as a general matter, when it contends that it is not always appropriate for a court to be swayed on the fourth factor by the effects on potential licensing revenues. Only an impact on potential licensing revenues for traditional, reasonable, or likely to be developed markets should be legally cognizable when evaluating a secondary use's "effect upon the potential market for or value of the copyrighted work."

Though the publishers still have not established a conventional market for the direct sale and distribution of individual articles, they have created, primarily through the CCC, a workable market for institutional users to obtain licenses for the right to produce their own copies of individual articles via photocopying. The District Court found that many major corporations now subscribe to the CCC systems for photocopying licenses. 802 F.Supp. at 25. Indeed, it appears from the pleadings, especially Texaco's

---

18. The Supreme Court's holding in *Sony* implicitly recognizes limits on the concept of "potential market for or value of the copyrighted work." Despite Justice Blackmun's dissenting view that the copying of television programs to enable private viewing at a more convenient time, i.e., "time-shifting," deprived copyright holders of the ability to exploit the "sizable market" of persons who "would be willing to pay some kind of royalty" for the "privilege of watching copyrighted work at their convenience," *Sony,* 464 U.S. at 485, the majority found that the copyright holders "failed to demonstrate that time-shifting would cause any likelihood of non-minimal harm to the potential market for, or the value of, their copyrighted works." Id. at 456. The Court thus implicitly ruled that the potential market in licensing royalties enunciated by Justice Blackmun should be considered too insubstantial to tilt the fourth fair use factor in favor of the copyright holder.

counterclaim, that Texaco itself has been paying royalties to the CCC. See Complaint ¶ 38; First Counterclaim ¶ 71. Since the Copyright Act explicitly provides that copyright holders have the "exclusive rights" to "reproduce" and "distribute copies" of their works, see 17 U.S.C. § 106(1) & (3), and since there currently exists a viable market for licensing these rights for individual journal articles, it is appropriate that potential licensing revenues for photocopying be considered in a fair use analysis.

Despite Texaco's claims to the contrary, it is not unsound to conclude that the right to seek payment for a particular use tends to become legally cognizable under the fourth fair use factor when the means for paying for such a use is made easier. This notion is not inherently troubling: it is sensible that a particular unauthorized use should be considered "more fair" when there is no ready market or means to pay for the use, while such an unauthorized use should be considered "less fair" when there is a ready market or means to pay for the use. The vice of circular reasoning arises only if the availability of payment is conclusive against fair use. Whatever the situation may have been previously, before the development of a market for institutional users to obtain licenses to photocopy articles, see *Williams & Wilkins,* 487 F.2d at 1357–59, it is now appropriate to consider the loss of licensing revenues in evaluating "the effect of the use upon the potential market for or value of" journal articles. It is especially appropriate to do so with respect to copying of articles from *Catalysis*, a publication as to which a photocopying license is now available. We do not decide how the fair use balance would be resolved if a photocopying license for *Catalysis* articles were not currently available.

In two ways, Congress has impliedly suggested that the law should recognize licensing fees for photocopying as part of the "potential market for or value of" journal articles. First, section 108 of the Copyright Act narrowly circumscribes the conditions under which libraries are permitted to make copies of copyrighted works. See 17 U.S.C. § 108. Though this section states that it does not in any way affect the right of fair use, see id. § 108(f)(4), the very fact that Congress restricted the rights of libraries to make copies implicitly suggests that Congress views journal publishers as possessing the right to restrict photocopying, or at least the right to demand a licensing royalty from nor.public institutions that engage in photocopying. Second, Congress apparently prompted the development of CCC by suggesting that an efficient mechanism be established to license photocopying, see S. Rep. No. 983, 93d Cong., 2d Sess. 122 (1974); S. Rep. No. 473, 94th Cong., 1st Sess. 70–71 (1975); H.R. Rep. No. 83, 90th Cong., 1st Sess. 33 (1968). It is difficult to understand why Congress would recommend establishing such a mechanism if it did not believe that fees for photocopying should be legally recognized as part of the potential market for journal articles.

Primarily because of lost licensing revenue, and to a minor extent because of lost subscription revenue, we agree with the District Court that "the publishers have demonstrated a substantial harm to the value of their copyrights through [Texaco's] copying," 802 F.Supp. at 21, and thus conclude that the fourth statutory factor favors the publishers.

E. Aggregate Assessment

We conclude that three of the four statutory factors, including the important first and fourth factors, favor the publishers. We recognize that the statutory factors provide a nonexclusive guide to analysis, see *Harper & Row,* 471 U.S. at 560, but to whatever extent more generalized equitable considerations are relevant, we are in agreement with the District Court's analysis of them. See 802 F.Supp. at 21–27. We therefore agree with the District Court's conclusion that Texaco's photocopying of eight particular articles from the *Journal of Catalysis* was not fair use.

Though we recognize the force of many observations made in Judge Jacobs's dissenting opinion, we are not dissuaded by his dire predictions that our ruling in this case "has ended fair-use photocopying with respect to a large population of journals," 60 F.3d at 938–39, or, to the extent that the transactional licensing scheme is used, "would seem to require that an intellectual property lawyer be posted at each copy machine," id. at 937–38. Our ruling does not consider photocopying for personal use by an individual. Our ruling is confined to the institutional, systematic, archival multiplication of copies revealed by the record—the precise copying that the parties stipulated should be the basis for the District Court's decision now on appeal and for which licenses are in fact available. And the claim that lawyers need to be stationed at copy machines is belied by the ease with which music royalties have been collected and distributed for performances at thousands of cabarets, without the attendance of intellectual property lawyers in any capacity other than as customers. If Texaco wants to continue the precise copying we hold not to be a fair use, it can either use the licensing schemes now existing or some variant of them, or, if all else fails, purchase one more subscription for each of its researchers who wish to keep issues of *Catalysis* on the office shelf.

The order of the District Court is affirmed.[19]

■ JACOBS, CIRCUIT JUDGE, dissenting:

The stipulated facts crisply present the fair use issues that govern the photocopying of entire journal articles for a scientist's own use, either in the laboratory or as part of a personal file assisting that scientist's particular inquiries. I agree with much in the majority's admirable review of the facts and the law. Specifically, I agree that, of the four nonexclusive considerations bearing on fair use enumerated in section 107, the second factor (the nature of the copyrighted work) tends to support a conclusion of fair use, and the third factor (the ratio of the copied portion to the whole copyrighted work) militates against it. I respectfully dissent, however, in respect of the

---

19. Though neither the limited trial nor this appeal requires consideration of the publishers' remedy if infringement is ultimately found, we note that the context of this dispute appears to make ill-advised an injunction, which, in any event, has not been sought. If the dispute is not now settled, this appears to be an appropriate case for exploration of the possibility of a court-imposed compulsory license. See *Campbell,* 510 U.S. 578; 3 Nimmer on Copyright § 13.05[E][4][e], at 13–241 to 13–242.

first and fourth factors. As to the first factor: the purpose and character of Dr. Chickering's use is integral to transformative and productive ends of scientific research. As to the fourth factor: the adverse effect of Dr. Chickering's use upon the potential market for the work, or upon its value, is illusory. For these reasons, and in light of certain equitable considerations and the overarching purpose of the copyright laws, I conclude that Dr. Chickering's photocopying of the *Catalysis* articles was fair use.

* * *

NOTES

1. *American Geophysical Union v. Texaco Inc.* was a test case whose objective was to encourage corporations to participate in the Copyright Clearance Center. Texaco, along with the other major oil companies, were members of the Center. (Note that Texaco was not licensed to copy only for purposes of the litigation.) As members they had an interest in encouraging other firms to join. And Texaco (and the other major oil companies) were unlikely to make an attractive proponent of fair use before a jury. The case was tried on a largely stipulated and limited record. The Second Circuit decided in favor of the publishers in 1994 with an opinion that broadly limited the scope of fair use. That opinion was published at 37 F.3d 881. Texaco then applied for certiorari, but while the petition was pending the parties settled the case with an agreement by Texaco to pay the Copyright Clearance Center a sum reputed to be in excess of "seven figures." After the tentative settlement but before the petition for certiorari was dismissed the opinion was amended in significant ways which narrowed its implications.

2. An earlier case is Williams & Wilkins Co. v. United States, 487 F.2d 1345 (1973), affirmed without opinion by an equally divided Court 420 U.S. 376 (1975). A private publisher of four specialized medical journals sued the United States government for copyright infringement based upon actions of the library of the National Institute of Health [known as the "NIH"] and the National Library of Medicine [the "NLM"].

The court described the activities of the library of the NIH as follows:

The NIH library subscribes to about 3,000 different journal titles, four of which are the journals in suit. The library subscribes to two copies of each of the journals involved. As a general rule, one copy stays in the library reading room and the other copy circulates among interested NIH personnel. Demand by NIH research workers for access to plaintiff's journals (as well as other journals to which the library subscribes) is usually not met by in-house subscription copies. Consequently, as an integral part of its operation, the library runs a photocopy service for the benefit of its research staff. On request, a researcher can obtain a photocopy of an article from any of the journals in the library's collection. Usually, researchers request photocopies of articles to assist them in their on-going projects; sometimes photocopies are requested simply for background reading. The library does not monitor the reason for requests or the use to which the photocopies are put. The photocopies are not returned to the library; and the record shows that, in most instances, researchers keep them in their private files for future reference.

The library's policy is that, as a rule, only a single copy of a journal article will be made per request and each request is limited to about 40 to 50 pages, though exceptions may be, and have been, made in the case of long articles, upon approval of the Assistant Chief of the library branch. Also, as a general rule, requests for photocopying are limited to only a single article from a journal issue. Exceptions to this rule are routinely made, so long as substantially less than an entire journal is photocopied, i.e., less than about half of the journal. Coworkers can, and frequently do, request single copies of the same article and such requests are honored.

Four regularly assigned employees operate the NIH photocopy equipment. The equipment consists of microfilm cameras and Xerox copying machines. In 1970, the library photocopy budget was $86,000 and the library filled 85,744 requests for photocopies of journal articles (including plaintiff's journals), constituting about 930,000 pages. On the average, a journal article is 10 pages long, so that, in 1970, the library made about 93,000 photocopies of articles. 487 F.2d 1347–48.

The court described the activities of the NLM as follows:

NLM, located on the Bethesda campus of NIH, was formerly the Armed Forces Medical Library. In 1956, Congress transferred the library from the Department of Defense to the Public Health Service (renaming it the National Library of Medicine), and declared its purpose to be " * * * to aid the dissemination and exchange of scientific and other information important to the progress of medicine and to the public health * * *." 42 U.S.C. § 275 (1970). NLM is a repository of much of the world's medical literature, in essence a "librarians' library." As part of its operation, NLM cooperates with other libraries and like research-and-education-oriented institutions (both public and private) in a so-called "interlibrary loan" program. Upon request, NLM will loan to such institutions, for a limited time, books and other materials in its collection. In the case of journals, the "loans" usually take the form of photocopies of journal articles which are supplied by NLM free of charge and on a no-return basis. NLM's "loan" policies are fashioned after the General Interlibrary Loan Code, which is a statement of self-imposed regulations to be followed by all libraries which cooperate in interlibrary loaning. The Code provides that each library, upon request for a loan of materials, shall decide whether to loan the original or provide a photoduplicate. The Code notes that photoduplication of copyrighted materials may raise copyright infringement problems, particularly with regard to "photographing *whole issues* of periodicals or books with *current copyrights,* or in making *multiple copies* of a publication." [Emphasis in original text.] NLM, therefore, will provide only one photocopy of a particular article, per request, and will not photocopy on any given request an entire journal issue. Each photocopy reproduced by NLM contains a statement in the margin, "This is a single photostatic copy made by the National Library of Medicine for purposes of study or research in lieu of lending the original."

In recent years NLM's stated policy has been not to fill requests for copies of articles from any of 104 journals which are included in a so-called "widely-available list." Rather, the requester is furnished a copy of the "widely-available list" and the names of the regional medical libraries which are presumed to have the journals listed. Exceptions are sometimes made to the policy, particularly if the requester has been unsuccessful in obtaining the journal elsewhere. The four journals involved in this suit are listed on the "widely-available list." A rejection on the basis of the "widely-available list" is made only if the article requested was published during the preceding 5 years, but requests from Government libraries are not refused on the basis of the "widely-available list."

Also, NLM's policy is not to honor an excessive number of requests from an individual or an institution. As a general rule, not more than 20 requests from an individual, or not more than 30 requests from an institution, within a month, will be honored. In 1968, NLM adopted the policy that no more than one article from a single journal issue, or three from a journal volume, would be copied. Prior to 1968, NLM had no express policy on copying limitations, but endeavored to prevent "excessive copying." Generally, requests for more than 50 pages of material will not be honored, though exceptions are sometimes made, particularly for Government institutions. Requests for more than one copy of a journal article are rejected, without exception. If NLM receives a request for more than one copy, a single copy will be furnished and the requester advised that it is NLM's policy to furnish only one copy.

In 1968, a representative year, NLM received about 127,000 requests for interlibrary loans. Requests were received, for the most part, from other libraries or Government agencies. However, about 12 percent of the requests came from private or commercial organizations, particularly drug companies. Some requests were for books, in which event the book itself was loaned. Most requests were for journals or journal articles; and about 120,000 of the requests were filled by photocopying single articles from journals, including plaintiff's journals. Usually, the library seeking an interlibrary loan from NLM did so at the request of one of its patrons. If the "loan" was made by photocopy, the photocopy was given to the patron who was free to dispose of it as he wished. NLM made no effort to find out the ultimate use to which the photocopies were put; and there is no evidence that borrowing libraries kept the "loan" photocopies in their permanent collections for use by other patrons. 487 F.2d 1348–49.

The Court of Claims held that these practices were fair use, concluding that the publisher had not shown concrete harm in the form of lost subscription income and that medicine and medical research would be injured by holding these practices infringing. How would a requirement that the libraries pay a royalty fee of some sort (or choose to buy more copies) be injurious to medicine? Is copyright in non-informational works produced to provide entertainment stronger than copyright in works that contain important and useful information?

The statute now addresses copying by libraries in § 108. Does § 108(d) codify the result in *Williams and Wilkins?*

The record in *Williams and Wilkins* was much more extensive than the record in *Texaco*, and is described in detail in Paul Goldstein, Copyright's Highway: From Gutenberg to the Celestial Jukebox (New York: Hill and Wang, 1994).

3. Princeton University Press v. Michigan Document Services, Inc., 99 F.3d 1381 (6th Cir. 1996) (en Banc), cert. den. 117 S.Ct. 1336 (1997), involved a copy service near the University of Michigan campus that provided course packs for use in courses. The course packs would contain readings selected by the Professors from various copyrighted books and would avoid the need for students to buy more of the books than they were going to read. The copies were made without the permission of the copyright owners. When sued for infringement, the defendant Michigan Document Services defended on the grounds of fair use. Such a system of massive copying, creating works that displaced the market for the copyrighted works and was carried on for profit, would seem unlikely to be considered fair use. The District Court so held, finding the infringement willful. A panel of the Sixth Circuit, however, reversed. 74 F.3d 1528. The panel was in turn reversed by the en banc court, which split 7 to 5. The surprising closeness of this result suggests that there may be more judicial concern about a copyright law which unduly constrains convenient use of copying machines than is apparent from the decisions so far.

4. The *Williams & Wilkins* decision is discussed at length in Wendy J. Gordon, Fair Use as Market Failure: A Structural and Economic Analysis of the *Betamax* Case and its Predecessors, 82 Colum. L. Rev. 1600 (1982). In the article Professor Gordon develops a general theory of the doctrine of fair use as a doctrine designed to prevent market failures that would otherwise arise from the copyright system. For instance an author might want to quote from a copyrighted work and the author of the copyrighted work might welcome the quotation (because of the attendant publicity for instance) but the cost of identifying the copyright owner and writing to get permission could easily exceed the benefit of using the quotation for the second author. If the quotation is fair use (and it is less costly to ascertain that it is fair use than it is to write for permission) then a quotation of benefit to all parties will be used. Or to illustrate in the context of the *Betamax* case (Professor Gordon is critical of the Ninth Circuit analysis of fair use, subsequently reversed by the Supreme Court), the owner of a program copyright might welcome home recording, and users might benefit from it, yet no such recording would take place because the cost of getting permission on a program by program basis would exceed the benefits of the recording. Id. at 1655. Professor Gordon applauds the court of claims in *Williams and Wilkins* for its cost-benefit approach, but is critical of its application in the particular situation. Id. at 1647–52. But why couldn't Mr. Rogers and other program owners who welcome recording grant consent for recording in a brief written message at the outset of their program and why couldn't journal publishers place an authorizing legend in their journals?

PROBLEMS

1. Suppose there had been a finding by the trial court in *Sony* that consumers use VCR's not only for time-shifting, but that when watching the recorded program they used the remote, fast-forward controls on the VCR to skip over the commercials? Different result? Doesn't the viewer's ability to avoid the commercials destroy the value of the program? Just how would the owners of the copyright enforce their rights, if they have them? Would an injunction enjoining the manufacture and sale of machines with remote fast-forward controls be appropriate?

2. Does it violate the copyright law to operate a used record store if it can be established that a large percentage of the customers resell the used record to the store a short time after they buy it?

3. Does a law firm that has copies made of copyrighted material such as case reports including headnotes and articles in academic journals to put into case files for easy retention and subsequent access infringe the copyright in those works? Is use by a law firm a commercial use? What about a judge, whose clerks do the same thing?

Harper & Row, Publishers, Inc. v. Nation Enterprises

Supreme Court of the United States, 1985.
471 U.S. 539, 105 S.Ct. 2218, 85 L.Ed.2d 588.

■ JUSTICE O'CONNOR delivered the opinion of the Court.

This case requires us to consider to what extent the "fair use" provision of the Copyright Revision Act of 1976 sanctions the unauthorized use of quotations from a public figure's unpublished manuscript. In March 1979, an undisclosed source provided The Nation magazine with the unpublished manuscript of "A Time to Heal: The Autobiography of Gerald R. Ford." Working directly from the purloined manuscript, an editor of The Nation produced a short piece entitled "The Ford Memoirs—Behind the Nixon Pardon." The piece was timed to "scoop" an article scheduled shortly to appear in Time magazine. Time had agreed to purchase the exclusive right to print prepublication excerpts from the copyright holders, Harper & Row Publishers, Inc. (hereinafter Harper & Row) and Reader's Digest Association, Inc. (hereinafter Reader's Digest). As a result of The Nation article, Time canceled its agreement. Petitioners brought a successful copyright action against The Nation. On appeal, the Second Circuit reversed the lower court's finding of infringement, holding that The Nation's act was sanctioned as a "fair use" of the copyrighted material. We granted certiorari, and we now reverse.

I

In February 1977, shortly after leaving the White House, former President Gerald R. Ford contracted with petitioners Harper & Row and The Reader's Digest, to publish his as yet unwritten memoirs. The memoirs were to contain "significant hitherto unpublished material" concerning the Watergate crisis, Mr. Ford's pardon of former President Nixon and "Mr. Ford's reflections on this period of history, and the morality and personalities involved." In addition to the right to publish the Ford memoirs in book form, the agreement gave petitioners the exclusive right to license prepublication excerpts, known in the trade as "first serial rights." Two years later, as the memoirs were nearing completion, petitioners negotiated a prepublication licensing agreement with Time, a weekly news magazine. Time agreed to pay $25,000, $12,500 in advance and an additional $12,500 at publication, in exchange for the right to excerpt 7,500 words from Mr. Ford's account of the Nixon pardon. The issue featuring the excerpts was timed to appear approximately one week before shipment of the full length book version to bookstores. Exclusivity was an important consideration; Harper & Row instituted procedures designed to maintain the confidentiality of the manuscript, and Time retained the right to renegotiate the second payment should the material appear in print prior to its release of the excerpts.

Two to three weeks before the Time article's scheduled release, an unidentified person secretly brought a copy of the Ford manuscript to Victor Navasky, editor of The Nation, a political commentary magazine. Mr. Navasky knew that his possession of the manuscript was not authorized and that the manuscript must be returned quickly to his "source" to avoid discovery. He hastily put together what he believed was "a real hot news story" composed of quotes, paraphrases and facts drawn exclusively from the manuscript. Mr. Navasky attempted no independent commentary, research or criticism, in part because of the need for speed if he was to "make news" by "publish[ing] in advance of publication of the Ford book." The 2,250 word article * * * appeared on April 3, 1979. As a result of The Nation's article, Time canceled its piece and refused to pay the remaining $12,500.

Petitioners brought suit in the District Court for the Southern District of New York, alleging conversion, tortious interference with contract and violations of the Copyright Act. After a 6-day bench trial, the District Judge found that "A Time to Heal" was protected by copyright at the time of The Nation publication and that respondents' use of the copyrighted material constituted an infringement under the Copyright Act * * *. The District Court rejected respondents' argument that The Nation's piece was a "fair use" sanctioned by § 107 of the Act. Though billed as "hot news," the article contained no new facts. The magazine had "published its article for profit," taking "the heart" of "a soon-to-be-published" work. This unauthorized use "caused the *Time* agreement to be aborted and thus diminished the value of the copyright." Although certain elements of the Ford memoir, such as historical facts and memoranda, were not *per se* copyrightable, the District Court held that it was "the totality of these facts and memoranda collected together with Ford's reflections that made them of value to The Nation,

[and] this * * * totality * * * is protected by the copyright laws." The court awarded actual damages of $12,500.

A divided panel of the Court of Appeals for the Second Circuit reversed. The majority recognized that Mr. Ford's verbatim "reflections" were original "expression" protected by copyright. But it held that the District Court had erred in assuming the "coupling [of these reflections] with uncopyrightable fact transformed that information into a copyrighted 'totality.' " 723 F.2d 195, 205 (CA2 1983). The majority noted that copyright attaches to expression, not facts or ideas. It concluded that, to avoid granting a copyright monopoly over the facts underlying history and news, " 'expression' [in such works must be confined] to its barest elements—the ordering and choice of the words themselves." Id., at 204. Thus similarities between the original and the challenged work traceable to the copying or paraphrasing of uncopyrightable material, such as historical facts, memoranda and other public documents, and quoted remarks of third parties, must be disregarded in evaluating whether the second author's use was fair or infringing.

> "When the uncopyrighted material is stripped away, the article in *The Nation* contains, at most, approximately 300 words that are copyrighted. These remaining paragraphs and scattered phrases are all verbatim quotations from the memoirs which had not appeared previously in other publications. They include a short segment of Ford's conversations with Henry Kissinger and several other individuals. Ford's impressionistic depictions of Nixon, ill with phlebitis after the resignation and pardon, and of Nixon's character, constitute the major portion of this material. It is these parts of the magazine piece on which [the court] must focus in [its] examination of the question whether there was a 'fair use' of copyrighted matter."

Examining the four factors enumerated in § 107, the majority found the purpose of the article was "news reporting," the original work was essentially factual in nature, the 300 words appropriated were insubstantial in relation to the 2,250 word piece, and the impact on the market for the original was minimal as "the evidence [did] not support a finding that it was the very limited use of expression *per se* which led to Time's decision not to print the excerpt." The Nation's borrowing of verbatim quotations merely "len[t] authenticity to this politically significant material * * * complementing the reporting of the facts." The Court of Appeals was especially influenced by the "politically significant" nature of the subject matter and its conviction that it is not "the purpose of the Copyright Act to impede that harvest of knowledge so necessary to a democratic state" or "chill the activities of the press by forbidding a circumscribed use of copyrighted words."

II

We agree with the Court of Appeals that copyright is intended to increase and not to impede the harvest of knowledge. But we believe the Second Circuit gave insufficient deference to the scheme established by the Copyright Act for fostering the original works that provide the seed and substance of this harvest. The rights conferred by copyright are designed to assure contributors to the store of knowledge a fair return for their labors. * * * As we noted last Term, "[this] limited grant is a means by which an important public purpose may be achieved. It is intended to motivate the creative activity of authors and inventors by the provision of a special reward, and to allow the public access to the products of their genius after the limited period of exclusive control has expired." Sony Corp. v. Universal City Studios, Inc., 464 U.S. 417, 429 (1984). "The monopoly created by copyright thus rewards the individual author in order to benefit the public." Id., at 477 (dissenting opinion). This principle applies equally to works of fiction and nonfiction. The book at issue here, for example, was two years in the making, and began with a contract giving the author's copyright to the publishers in exchange for their services in producing and marketing the work. In preparing the book, Mr. Ford drafted essays and word portraits of public figures and participated in hundreds of taped interviews that were later distilled to chronicle his personal viewpoint. It is evident that the monopoly granted by copyright actively served its intended purpose of inducing the creation of new material of potential historical value.

* * *

Creation of a nonfiction work, even a compilation of pure fact, entails originality. See, e.g., Schroeder v. William Morrow & Co., 566 F.2d 3 (CA7 1977) (copyright in gardening directory); cf. Burrow-Giles Lithographic Co. v. Sarony, 111 U.S. 53, 58 (1884) (originator of a photograph may claim copyright in his work). * * * [T]here is no dispute that the unpublished manuscript of "A Time to Heal," as a whole, was protected by § 106 from unauthorized reproduction. Nor do respondents dispute that verbatim copying of excerpts of the manuscript's original form of expression would constitute infringement unless excused as fair use. See 1 M. Nimmer, Nimmer on Copyright § 2.11[B], p. 2–159 (1984) (hereinafter Nimmer). Yet copyright does not prevent subsequent users from copying from a prior author's work those constituent elements that are not original—for example, quotations borrowed under the rubric of fair use from other copyrighted works, facts, or materials in the public domain—as long as such use does not unfairly appropriate the author's original contributions. Ibid.; A. Latman, Fair Use of Copyrighted Works (1958), reprinted as Study No. 14 in Copyright Law Revision Studies Nos. 14–16, Prepared for the Senate Committee on the Judiciary, 86th Cong., 2d Sess., 7 (1960) (hereinafter Latman). Perhaps the controversy between the lower courts in this case over copyrightability is more aptly styled a dispute over whether The Nation's appropriation of unoriginal and uncopyrightable elements encroached on the originality embodied in the work as a whole. Especially in the realm of factual narrative, the law is currently unsettled regarding the ways in which uncopyrightable elements combine with the author's original contributions to form protected expression. Compare Wainwright Securities Inc. v. Wall Street Transcript Corp., 558 F.2d 91 (CA2 1977) (protection accorded author's analysis, structuring of material and marshaling of facts), with Hoehling v. Universal City Studios, Inc., 618 F.2d 972 (CA2 1980) (limiting protection to ordering and choice of words). See, e.g., 1 Nimmer § 2.11[D], at 2–164–2–165.

We need not reach these issues, however, as The Nation has admitted to lifting verbatim quotes of the author's original language totalling between 300 and 400 words and constituting some 13% of The Nation article. In using generous verbatim excerpts of Mr. Ford's unpublished manuscript to lend authenticity to its account of the forthcoming memoirs, The Nation effectively arrogated to itself the right of first publication, an important marketable subsidiary right. For the reasons set forth below, we find that this use of the copyrighted manuscript, even stripped to the verbatim quotes conceded by The Nation to be copyrightable expression, was not a fair use within the meaning of the Copyright Act.

III

A

Fair use was traditionally defined as "a privilege in others than the owner of the copyright to use the copyrighted material in a reasonable manner without his consent." H. Ball, Law of Copyright and Literary Property 260 (1944) (hereinafter Ball). The statutory formulation of the defense of fair use in the Copyright Act of 1976 reflects the intent of Congress to codify the common-law doctrine. 3 Nimmer § 13.05. Section 107 requires a case-by-case determination whether a particular use is fair, and the statute notes four nonexclusive factors to be considered. This approach was "intended to restate the [pre-existing] judicial doctrine of fair use, not to change, narrow, or enlarge it in any way." H.R. Rep. No. 94–1476, p. 66 (1976) (hereinafter House Report), U.S.Code Cong. & Admin.News 1976, pp. 5659, 5680.

"[T]he author's consent to a reasonable use of his copyrighted works ha[d] always been implied by the courts as a necessary incident of the constitutional policy of promoting the progress of science and the useful arts, since a prohibition of such use would inhibit subsequent writers from attempting to improve upon prior works and thus * * * frustrate the very ends sought to be attained." Ball 260. Professor Latman, in a study of the doctrine of fair use commissioned by Congress for the revision effort, see Sony Corp. v. Universal City Studios, Inc., 464 U.S., at 462–463, n. 9 (dissenting opinion), summarized prior law as turning on the "importance of the material copied or performed from the point of view of the reasonable copyright owner. In other words, would the reasonable copyright owner have consented to the use?" Latman 15.[3]

As early as 1841, Justice Story, gave judicial recognition to the doctrine in a case that concerned the letters of another former President, George Washington.

---

3. Professor Nimmer notes, "[perhaps] no more precise guide can be stated than Joseph McDonald's clever paraphrase of the Golden Rule: 'Take not from others to such an extent and in such a manner that you would be resentful if they so took from you.'" 3 Nimmer § 13.05[A], at 13–66, quoting McDonald, Non-infringing Uses, 9 Bull. Copyright Soc. 466, 467 (1962). This "equi-table rule of reason," Sony Corp. v. Universal City Studios, Inc., 464 U.S., at 448, "permits courts to avoid rigid application of the copyright statute when, on occasion, it would stifle the very creativity which that law is designed to foster." Iowa State University Research Foundation, Inc. v. American Broadcasting Cos., 621 F.2d 57, 60 (CA2 1980). * * *

"[A] reviewer may fairly cite largely from the original work, if his design be really and truly to use the passages for the purposes of fair and reasonable criticism. On the other hand, it is as clear, that if he thus cites the most important parts of the work, with a view, not to criticise, but to supersede the use of the original work, and substitute the review for it, such a use will be deemed in law a piracy." Folsom v. Marsh, 9 F.Cas. 342, 344–345 (No. 4,901) (CC Mass.)

As Justice Story's hypothetical illustrates, the fair use doctrine has always precluded a use that "supersede[s] the use of the original." Ibid. Accord S. Rep. No. 94–473, p. 65 (1975) (hereinafter Senate Report).

Perhaps because the fair use doctrine was predicated on the author's implied consent to "reasonable and customary" use when he released his work for public consumption, fair use traditionally was not recognized as a defense to charges of copying from an author's as yet unpublished works. Under common-law copyright, "the property of the author * * * in his intellectual creation [was] absolute until he voluntarily part[ed] with the same." American Tobacco Co. v. Werckmeister, 207 U.S. 284, 299 (1907); 2 Nimmer § 8.23, at 8–273. This absolute rule, however, was tempered in practice by the equitable nature of the fair use doctrine. In a given case, factors such as implied consent through *de facto* publication on performance or dissemination of a work may tip the balance of equities in favor of prepublication use. * * * But it has never been seriously disputed that "the fact that the plaintiff's work is unpublished * * * is a factor tending to negate the defense of fair use." Ibid. Publication of an author's expression before he has authorized its dissemination seriously infringes the author's right to decide when and whether it will be made public, a factor not present in fair use of published works. Respondents contend, however, that Congress, in including first publication among the rights enumerated in § 106, which are expressly subject to fair use under § 107, intended that fair use would apply *in pari materia* to published and unpublished works. The Copyright Revision Act does not support this proposition.

The Copyright Revision Act of 1976 represents the culmination of a major legislative reexamination of copyright doctrine. Among its other innovations, it eliminated publication "as a dividing line between common law and statutory protection," House Report at 129, U.S. Code Cong. & Admin.News 1976, p. 5745, extending statutory protection to all works from the time of their creation. It also recognized for the first time a distinct statutory right of first publication, which had previously been an element of the common-law protections afforded unpublished works. The Report of the House Committee on the Judiciary confirms that "Clause (3) of section 106, establishes the exclusive right of publications. * * * Under this provision the copyright owner would have the right to control the first public distribution of an authorized copy * * * of his work." Id. at 62, U.S. Code Cong. & Admin. News 1976, p. 5675.

Though the right of first publication, like the other rights enumerated in § 106 is expressly made subject to the fair use provision of § 107, fair use analysis must always be tailored to the individual case. Id., at 65; 3 Nimmer

§ 13.05[A]. The nature of the interest at stake is highly relevant to whether a given use is fair. From the beginning, those entrusted with the task of revision recognized the "overbalancing reasons to preserve the common law protection of undisseminated works until the author or his successor chooses to disclose them." Copyright Law Revision, Report of the Register of Copyrights on the General Revision of the U.S. Copyright Law, 87th Cong., 1st Sess., 41 (Comm. Print 1961). The right of first publication implicates a threshold decision by the author whether and in what form to release his work. First publication is inherently different from other § 106 rights in that only one person can be the first publisher; as the contract with Time illustrates, the commercial value of the right lies primarily in exclusivity. Because the potential damage to the author from judicially enforced "sharing" of the first publication right with unauthorized users of his manuscript is substantial, the balance of equities in evaluating such a claim of fair use inevitably shifts.

The Senate Report confirms that Congress intended the unpublished nature of the work to figure prominently in fair use analysis. In discussing fair use of photocopied materials in the classroom the Committee Report states:

"A key, though not necessarily determinative, factor in fair use is whether or not the work is available to the potential user. If the work is 'out of print' and unavailable for purchase through normal channels, the user may have more justification for reproducing it. * * * The applicability of the fair use doctrine to unpublished works is narrowly limited since, although the work is unavailable, this is the result of a deliberate choice on the part of the copyright owner. Under ordinary circumstances, the copyright owner's 'right of first publication' would outweigh any needs of reproduction for classroom purposes." Senate Report, at 64.

Although the Committee selected photocopying of classroom materials to illustrate fair use, it emphasized that "the same general standards of fair use are applicable to all kinds of uses of copyrighted material." Id., at 65. We find unconvincing respondent's contention that the absence of the quoted passage from the House Report indicates an intent to abandon the traditional distinction between fair use of published and unpublished works. It appears instead that the fair use discussion of photocopying of classroom materials was omitted from the final report because educators and publishers in the interim had negotiated a set of guidelines that rendered the discussion obsolete. House Report, at 67. The House Report nevertheless incorporates the discussion by reference, citing to the Senate Report and stating that "The Committee has reviewed this discussion, and considers it still has value as an analysis of various aspects of the [fair use] problem." Ibid.

Even if the legislative history were entirely silent, we would be bound to conclude from Congress' characterization of § 107 as a "restatement" that its effect was to preserve existing law concerning fair use of unpublished works as of other types of protected works and not to "change, narrow, or enlarge it." Id., at 66. We conclude that the unpublished nature of a work is "[a] key, though not necessarily determinative, factor" tending to negate a defense of fair use. Senate Report, at 64. See 3 Nimmer § 13.05, at 13–62, n. 2; W. Patry, The Fair Use Privilege in Copyright Law 125 (1985) (hereinafter Patry).

We also find unpersuasive respondents' argument that fair use may be made of a soon-to-be-published manuscript on the ground that the author has demonstrated he has no interest in nonpublication. This argument assumes that the unpublished nature of copyrighted material is only relevant to letters or other confidential writings not intended for dissemination. It is true that common-law copyright was often enlisted in the service of personal privacy. See Brandeis & Warren, The Right to Privacy, 4 Harv. L. Rev. 193, 198–199 (1890). In its commercial guise, however, an author's right to choose when he will publish is no less deserving of protection. The period encompassing the work's initiation, its preparation, and its grooming for public dissemination is a crucial one for any literary endeavor. The Copyright Act, which accords the copyright owner the "right to control the first public distribution" of his work, House Report, at 62, echos the common law's concern that the author or copyright owner retain control throughout this critical stage. The obvious benefit to author and public alike of assuring authors the leisure to develop their ideas free from fear of expropriation outweighs any short term "news value" to be gained from premature publication of the author's expression. See Goldstein, Copyright and the First Amendment, 70 Colum. L. Rev. 983, 1004–1006 (1970) (The absolute protection the common law accorded to soon-to-be published works "[was] justified by [its] brevity and expedience"). The author's control of first public distribution implicates not only his personal interest in creative control but his property interest in exploitation of prepublication rights, which are valuable in themselves and serve as a valuable adjunct to publicity and marketing. * * * Under ordinary circumstances, the author's right to control the first public appearance of his undisseminated expression will outweigh a claim of fair use.

B

Respondents, however, contend that First Amendment values require a different rule under the circumstances of this case. The thrust of the decision below is that "[t]he scope of [fair use] is undoubtedly wider when the information conveyed relates to matters of high public concern." Consumers Union of the United States, Inc. v. General Signal Corp., 724 F.2d 1044, 1050 (CA2 1983) (construing Harper & Row Publishers, Inc. v. Nation Enterprises, 723 F.2d 195 (CA2 1983) (case below), as allowing advertiser to quote Consumer Reports), cert. denied, 469 U.S. 823 (1984). Respondents advance the substantial public import of the subject matter of the Ford memoirs as grounds for excusing a use that would ordinarily not pass muster as a fair use—the piracy of verbatim quotations for the purpose of "scooping" the authorized first serialization. Respondents explain their copying of Mr. Ford's expression as essential to reporting the news story it claims the book itself represents. In respondents' view, not only the facts contained in Mr. Ford's memoirs, but "the precise manner in which [he] expressed himself was as newsworthy as what he had to say." Brief for Respondents 38–39. Respondents argue that the public's interest in learning this news as fast as possible outweighs the right of the author to control its first publication.

The Second Circuit noted, correctly, that copyright's idea/expression dichotomy "strike[s] a definitional balance between the First Amendment and the Copyright Act by permitting free communication of facts while still protecting an author's expression." 723 F.2d, at 203. No author may copyright his ideas or the facts he narrates. 17 U.S.C. § 102(b). See, e.g., New York Times Co. v. United States, 403 U.S. 713, 726, n.* (1971) (Brennan, J., concurring) (Copyright laws are not restrictions on freedom of speech as copyright protects only form of expression and not the ideas expressed); 1 Nimmer § 1.10[B][2]. As this Court long ago observed: "[T]he news element—the information respecting current events contained in the literary production—is not the creation of the writer, but is a report of matters that ordinarily are *publici juris;* it is the history of the day." International News Service v. Associated Press, 248 U.S. 215, 234 (1918). But copyright assures those who write and publish factual narratives such as "A Time to Heal" that they may at least enjoy the right to market the original expression contained therein as just compensation for their investment. Cf. Zacchini v. Scripps-Howard Broadcasting Co., 433 U.S. 562, 575 (1977).

Respondents' theory, however, would expand fair use to effectively destroy any expectation of copyright protection in the work of a public figure. Absent such protection, there would be little incentive to create or profit in financing such memoirs and the public would be denied an important source of significant historical information. The promise of copyright would be an empty one if it could be avoided merely by dubbing the infringement a fair use "news report" of the book.

* * * 6

In our haste to disseminate news, it should not be forgotten that the Framers intended copyright itself to be the engine of free expression. By establishing a marketable right to the use of one's expression, copyright supplies the economic incentive to create and disseminate ideas. * * *

* * *

In view of the First Amendment protections already embodied in the Copyright Act's distinction between copyrightable expression and uncopyrightable facts and ideas, and the latitude for scholarship and comment traditionally afforded by fair use, we see no warrant for expanding the doctrine of fair use to create what amounts to a public figure exception to copyright. Whether verbatim copying from a public figure's manuscript in a given case is or is not fair must be judged according to the traditional equities of fair use.

---

6. It bears noting that Congress in the Copyright Act recognized a public interest warranting specific exemptions in a number of areas not within traditional fair use, see, e.g., 17 U.S.C. § 115 (compulsory license for records); § 105 (no copyright in government works). No such exemption limits copyright in personal narratives written by public servants after they leave government service.

IV

Fair use is a mixed question of law and fact. * * * Where the District Court has found facts sufficient to evaluate each of the statutory factors, an appellate court "need not remand for further factfinding * * * [but] may conclude as a matter of law that [the challenged use] do[es] not qualify as a fair use of the copyrighted work." * * * [quoting note 8 in Pacific and Southern Co. v. Duncan, 744 F.2d 1490 (11th Cir. 1984), infra.] Thus whether The Nation article constitutes fair use under § 107 must be reviewed in light of the principles discussed above. The factors enumerated in the section are not meant to be exclusive: "[S]ince the doctrine is an equitable rule of reason, no generally applicable definition is possible, and each case raising the question must be decided on its own facts." House Report, at 65, U.S. Code Cong. & Admin. News 1976, p. 5678. The four factors identified by Congress as especially relevant in determining whether the use was fair are: (1) the purpose and character of the use; (2) the nature of the copyrighted work; (3) the substantiality of the portion used in relation to the copyrighted work as a whole; (4) the effect on the potential market for or value of the copyrighted work. We address each one separately.

Purpose of the Use. The Second Circuit correctly identified news reporting as the general purpose of The Nation's use. News reporting is one of the examples enumerated in § 107 to "give some idea of the sort of activities the courts might regard as fair use under the circumstances." Senate Report, at 61. This listing was not intended to be exhaustive, see *id.;* § 101 (definition of "including" and "such as"), or to single out any particular use as presumptively a "fair" use. The drafters resisted pressures from special interest groups to create presumptive categories of fair use, but structured the provision as an affirmative defense requiring a case by case analysis. See H.R. Rep. No. 83, 90th Cong., 1st Sess., 37 (1967); Patry 477, n. 4. "[W]hether a use referred to in the first sentence of section 107 is a fair use in a particular case will depend upon the application of the determinative factors, including those mentioned in the second sentence." Senate Report, at 62. The fact that an article arguably is "news" and therefore a productive use is simply one factor in a fair use analysis.

* * *

The fact that a publication was commercial as opposed to non-profit is a separate factor that tends to weigh against a finding of fair use. "[E]very commercial use of copyrighted material is presumptively an unfair exploitation of the monopoly privilege that belongs to the owner of the copyright." Sony Corp. v. Universal City Studios, Inc., 464 U.S., at 451. In arguing that the purpose of news reporting is not purely commercial, The Nation misses the point entirely. The crux of the profit/nonprofit distinction is not whether the sole motive of the use is monetary gain but whether the user stands to profit from exploitation of the copyrighted material without paying the customary price.

In evaluating character and purpose we cannot ignore The Nation's stated purpose of scooping the forthcoming hardcover and Time abstracts.[7] The Nation's use had not merely the incidental effect but the *intended purpose* of supplanting the copyright holder's commercially valuable right of first publication. See Meredith Corp. v. Harper & Row Publishers, Inc., 378 F.Supp. 686, 690 (SDNY), (purpose of text was to compete with original), aff'd, 500 F.2d 1221 (CA2 1974). Also relevant to the "character" of the use is "the propriety of the defendant's conduct." 3 Nimmer § 13.05[A], at 13–72. "Fair use presupposes 'good faith' and 'fair dealing.'" Time Inc. v. Bernard Geis Associates, 293 F.Supp. 130, 146 (SDNY 1968), quoting Schulman, Fair Use and the Revision of the Copyright Act, 53 Iowa L. Rev. 832 (1968). The trial court found that The Nation knowingly exploited a purloined manuscript. Unlike the typical claim of fair use, The Nation cannot offer up even the fiction of consent as justification. Like its competitor newsweekly, it was free to bid for the right of abstracting excerpts from "A Time to Heal." Fair use "distinguishes between 'a true scholar and a chiseler who infringes a work for personal profit.'" Wainwright Securities Inc. v. Wall Street Transcript Corp., 558 F.2d, at 94, quoting from Hearings on Bills for the General Revision of the Copyright Law before the House Committee on the Judiciary, 89th Cong., 1st Sess., ser. 8, pt. 3, p. 1706 (1966) (Statement of John Schulman).

Nature of the Copyrighted Work. Second, the Act directs attention to the nature of the copyrighted work. "A Time to Heal" may be characterized as an unpublished historical narrative or autobiography. The law generally recognizes a greater need to disseminate factual works than works of fiction or fantasy. See Gorman, Fact or Fancy? The Implications for Copyright, 29 J. Copyright Soc. 560, 561 (1982).

> "[E]ven within the field of fact works, there are gradations as to the relative proportion of fact and fancy. One may move from sparsely embellished maps and directories to elegantly written biography. The extent to which one must permit expressive language to be copied, in order to assure dissemination of the underlying facts, will thus vary from case to case." Id., at 563.

Some of the briefer quotes from the memoir are arguably necessary adequately to convey the facts; for example, Mr. Ford's characterization of the White House tapes as the "smoking gun" is perhaps so integral to the idea expressed as to be inseparable from it. Cf. 1 Nimmer § 1.10[C]. But The Nation did not stop at isolated phrases and instead excerpted subjective descriptions and portraits of public figures whose power lies in the author's

---

7. The dissent excuses The Nation's unconsented use of an unpublished manuscript as "standard journalistic practice," taking judicial notice of New York Times articles regarding the memoirs of John Erlichman, John Dean's "Blind Ambition," and Bernstein & Woodward's "The Final Days" as proof of such practice. * * * Amici curiae sought to bring this alleged practice to the attention of the Court of Appeals for the Second Circuit, citing these same articles. The Court of Appeals, at Harper & Row's motion, struck these exhibits for failure of proof at trial, Record Doc. No. 19, thus they are not a proper subject for this Court's judicial notice.

individualized expression. Such use, focusing on the most expressive elements of the work, exceeds that necessary to disseminate the facts.

The fact that a work is unpublished is a critical element of its "nature." 3 Nimmer § 13.05[A]; Comment, 58 St. John's L. Rev., at 613. Our prior discussion establishes that the scope of fair use is narrower with respect to unpublished works. While even substantial quotations might qualify as fair use in a review of a published work or a news account of a speech that had been delivered to the public or disseminated to the press, see House Report, at 65, the author's right to control the first public appearance of his expression weighs against such use of the work before its release. The right of first publication encompasses not only the choice whether to publish at all, but also the choices when, where and in what form first to publish a work.

In the case of Mr. Ford's manuscript, the copyrightholders' interest in confidentiality is irrefutable; the copyrightholders had entered into a contractual undertaking to "keep the manuscript confidential" and required that all those to whom the manuscript was shown also "sign an agreement to keep the manuscript confidential." While the copyrightholders' contract with Time required Time to submit its proposed article seven days before publication, The Nation's clandestine publication afforded no such opportunity for creative or quality control. It was hastily patched together and contained "a number of inaccuracies." (testimony of Victor Navasky). A use that so clearly infringes the copyrightholder's interests in confidentiality and creative control is difficult to characterize as "fair."

Amount and Substantiality of the Portion Used. Next, the Act directs us to examine the amount and substantiality of the portion used in relation to the copyrighted work as a whole. In absolute terms, the words actually quoted were an insubstantial portion of "A Time to Heal." The district court, however, found that "[T]he Nation took what was essentially the heart of the book." We believe the Court of Appeals erred in overruling the district judge's evaluation of the qualitative nature of the taking. See, e.g., Roy Export Co. Establishment v. Columbia Broadcasting System, Inc., [503 F.Supp. 1137 (S.D.N.Y. 1980)] supra, at 1145 (taking of 55 seconds out of one hour and twenty-nine minute film deemed qualitatively substantial). A Time editor described the chapters on the pardon as "the most interesting and moving parts of the entire manuscript." The portions actually quoted were selected by Mr. Navasky as among the most powerful passages in those chapters. He testified that he used verbatim excerpts because simply reciting the information could not adequately convey the "absolute certainty with which [Ford] expressed himself," or show that "this comes from President Ford," or carry the "definitive quality" of the original. In short, he quoted these passages precisely because they qualitatively embodied Ford's distinctive expression.

As the statutory language indicates, a taking may not be excused merely because it is insubstantial with respect to the *infringing* work. As Judge Learned Hand cogently remarked, "[N]o plagiarist can excuse the wrong by showing how much of his work he did not pirate." Sheldon v. Metro-Goldwyn Pictures Corp., 81 F.2d 49, 56 (CA2), cert. denied, 298 U.S. 669 (1936). Conversely, the fact that a substantial portion of the infringing work was copied verbatim is evidence of the qualitative value of the copied material, both to the originator and to the plagiarist who seeks to profit from marketing someone else's copyrighted expression.

Stripped to the verbatim quotes, the direct takings from the unpublished manuscript constitute at least 13% of the infringing article. See Meeropol v. Nizer, 560 F.2d 1061, 1071 (CA2 1977) (copyrighted letters constituted less than 1% of infringing work but were prominently featured). The Nation article is structured around the quoted excerpts which serve as its dramatic focal points. * * * In view of the expressive value of the excerpts and their key role in the infringing work, we cannot agree with the Second Circuit that the "magazine took a meager, indeed an infinitesimal amount of Ford's original language."

Effect on the Market. Finally, the Act focuses on "the effect of the use upon the potential market for or value of the copyrighted work." This last factor is undoubtedly the single most important element of fair use.[9] See 3 Nimmer § 13.05[A], at 13–76, and cases cited therein. "Fair use, when properly applied, is limited to copying by others which does not materially impair the marketability of the work which is copied." 1 Nimmer § 1.10[D], at 1–87. The trial court found not merely a potential but an actual effect on the market. Time's cancellation of its projected serialization and its refusal to pay the $12,500 were the direct effect of the infringement. The Court of Appeals rejected this fact finding as clearly erroneous, noting that the record did not establish a causal relation between Time's nonperformance and respondents' unauthorized publication of Mr. Ford's *expression* as opposed to the facts taken from the memoirs. We disagree. Rarely will a case of copyright infringement present such clear cut evidence of actual damage. Petitioners assured Time that there would be no other authorized publication of *any* portion of the unpublished manuscript prior to April 23, 1979. *Any* publication of material from chapters 1 and 3 would permit Time to renegotiate its final payment. Time cited The Nation's article, which contained verbatim quotes from the unpublished manuscript, as a reason for its nonperformance. With respect to apportionment of profits flowing from a copyright infringement, this Court has held that an infringer who commingles infringing and noninfringing elements "must abide the consequences, unless he can make a separation of the profits so as to assure to the injured party all that justly belongs to him." Sheldon v. Metro-Goldwyn Pictures Corp., 309 U.S. 390, 406 (1940). Cf. 17 U.S.C. § 504(b) (the infringer is required to prove elements of profits attributable to other than the infringed work). Similarly, once a copyrightholder

---

9. Economists who have addressed the issue believe the fair use exception should come into play only in those situations in which the market fails or the price the copyright holder would ask is near zero. See, e.g., T. Brennan, Harper & Row v. The Nation, Copyrightability and Fair Use, Dept. of Justice Economic Policy Office Discussion Paper, 13-17 (1984); Gordon, Fair Use as Market Failure: A Structural and Economic Analysis of the *Betamax* Case and its Predecessors, 82 Colum. L. Rev. 1600, 1615 (1982). As the facts here demonstrate, there is a fully functioning market that encourages the creation and dissemination of memoirs of public figures. In the economists' view, permitting "fair use" to displace normal copyright channels disrupts the copyright market without a commensurate public benefit.

establishes with reasonable probability the existence of a causal connection between the infringement and a loss of revenue, the burden properly shifts to the infringer to show that this damage would have occurred had there been no taking of copyrighted expression. See 3 Nimmer § 14.02, pp. 14–7–14–8.1. Petitioners established a prima facie case of actual damage that respondent failed to rebut. The trial court properly awarded actual damages and accounting of profits. See 17 U.S.C. § 504(b).

More important, to negate fair use one need only show that if the challenged use "should become widespread, it would adversely affect the *potential* market for the copyrighted work." Sony Corp. v. Universal City Studios, Inc., 464 U.S., at 451 (emphasis added); id., at 484, and n. 36 (collecting cases) (dissenting opinion). This inquiry must take account not only of harm to the original but also of harm to the market for derivative works. "If the defendant's work adversely affects the value of any of the rights in the copyrighted work (in this case the adaptation [and serialization] right) the use is not fair." 3 Nimmer § 13.05[B], at 13–77–13–78 (footnote omitted).

It is undisputed that the factual material in the balance of The Nation's article, besides the verbatim quotes at issue here, was drawn exclusively from the chapters on the pardon. The excerpts were employed as featured episodes in a story about the Nixon pardon—precisely the use petitioners had licensed to Time. The borrowing of these verbatim quotes from the unpublished manuscript lent The Nation's piece a special air of authenticity—as Navasky expressed it, the reader would know it was Ford speaking and not The Nation. Thus it directly competed for a share of the market for prepublication excerpts. The Senate Report states:

"With certain special exceptions * * * a use that supplants any part of the normal market for a copyrighted work would ordinarily be considered an infringement." Senate Report, at 65.

Placed in a broader perspective, a fair use doctrine that permits extensive prepublication quotations from an unreleased manuscript without the copyright owner's consent poses substantial potential for damage to the marketability of first serialization rights in general. "Isolated instances of minor infringements, when multiplied many times, become in the aggregate a major inroad on copyright that must be prevented." Ibid.

V

The Court of Appeals erred in concluding that The Nation's use of the copyrighted material was excused by the public's interest in the subject matter. It erred, as well, in overlooking the unpublished nature of the work and the resulting impact on the potential market for first serial rights of permitting unauthorized prepublication excerpts under the rubric of fair use. Finally, in finding the taking "infinitesimal," the Court of Appeals accorded too little weight to the qualitative importance of the quoted passages of original expression. In sum, the traditional doctrine of fair use, as embodied in the Copyright Act, does not sanction the use made by The Nation of these copyrighted materials. Any copyright infringer may claim to benefit the public by increasing public access to the copyrighted work. But Congress has not designed, and we see no warrant for judicially imposing, a "compulsory license" permitting unfettered access to the unpublished copyrighted expression of public figures.

The Nation conceded that its verbatim copying of some 300 words of direct quotation from the Ford manuscript would constitute an infringement unless excused as a fair use. Because we find that The Nation's use of these verbatim excerpts from the unpublished manuscript was not a fair use, the judgment of the Court of Appeals is reversed and remanded for further proceedings consistent with this opinion.

It is so ordered.

[JUSTICES BRENNAN, WHITE and MARSHALL dissented.]

NOTES

1. Rosemont Enterprises v. Random House, 366 F.2d 303 (2d Cir. 1966), was an action by a shell corporation controlled by the secretive and reclusive (but always newsworthy and mysterious) millionaire Howard Hughes brought to stop the publication of a biography of Hughes. The biography, "Howard Hughes—a Biography by John Keats," was published in May 1966 and made use of some verbatim passages lifted from an article that appeared in *Look* magazine in 1954. In May, 1966 the plaintiff corporation purchased the copyright to the 1954 article and commenced an action for copyright infringement. The district court granted a preliminary injunction. The Court of Appeals reversed with an opinion that mingled the concepts of fair use and the equitable doctrine of "unclean hands," although the Court clearly stated that "The only issue presently before this court is: Was the preliminary injunction erroneously issued as a matter of law?" 366 F.2d 304. The court viewed the lawsuit as a stratagem designed to punish Random House for having undertaken to publish a book about Hughes by disrupting the production and promotion schedule while the offending passages were rewritten into paraphrase.

2. In Wainwright Securities Inc. v. Wall Street Transcript Corporation, 558 F.2d 91 (2d Cir. 1977), a brokerage house sued the publisher of a weekly newspaper concerned with economic, business and financial news, for publishing abstracts of its research reports for clients in its "Wall Street Roundup" column. The defendant argued fair use and pointed out that the *Wall Street Journal* does exactly the same thing in its "Heard on the Street" column. "The copying by the Transcript is easily distinguishable from the reporting of the Wainwright research reports by other publications. The *Wall Street Journal* articles referred to by appellants [also summarizing Wainwright reports], for example, were published a year apart. There apparently was no attempt to provide readers regularly with summaries of the Wainwright reports and there is no indication that the Wall Street Journal launched an advertising campaign portraying itself as a publisher of the same financial analyses available to large investors, but at a lower price. By contrast, the appellants' use of the Wainwright reports was blatantly self-serving, with obvious intent, if not the effect, of fulfilling the demand for the original work. * * * This was not legitimate coverage of a news event;

instead it was, and there is no other way to describe it, chiseling for personal profit." 558 F.2d 96–97. Held: not fair use.

Presumably the plaintiff objected to finding summaries of the essence of its research reports in the *Wall Street Transcript* each week, but didn't mind the publicity that came from an occasional mention in the much more widely read *Wall Street Journal*. If the plaintiff objected to the *Wall Street Journal's* summaries of its research reports, could the *Wall Street Journal* continue to summarize them when, in the judgment of its editorial staff, they constituted financial news?

3. In Meeropol v. Nizer, 560 F.2d 1061 (2d Cir. 1977), the defendant (a lawyer who has also enjoyed a successful writing career) had written an account of the events surrounding the espionage trial of Julius and Ethel Rosenberg entitled *The Implosion Conspiracy*. In the book there were reproduced substantial quotations from 28 letters written by the Rosenbergs. The plaintiffs were the sons of the Rosenbergs who had inherited the copyright in the letters (it has long been conventional doctrine that the copyright in a letter remains the property of the author-sender). The district court decided for the defendants on grounds of fair use. Reversed and remanded for further hearings on the purpose of the use and damages. *Rosemont* was distinguished on the ground that the taking there was less substantial, involved taking from a work about the subject, not by the subject, and was a bad faith action to suppress publication of the book.

4. Consumers Union of United States, Inc. v. General Signal Corp., 724 F.2d 1044 (2d Cir. 1983), rehearing denied 730 F.2d 47 (2d Cir. 1984), cert. denied 469 U.S. 823 (1985), was decided after the *Nation* case had been decided in the Second Circuit. Consumers Union, a non-profit corporation that publishes the widely-circulated magazine *Consumer Reports*, has long had the policy of prohibiting the use in product advertising of its product ratings and reports. Consumers Union had adopted this policy so that consumers can be confident that there is no relationship between Consumers Union and the manufacturers of products it recommends. In its July 1983 issue *Consumer Reports* evaluated lightweight vacuum cleaners and gave its highest, "check-rated" rating to the Regina Powerteam. The manufacturer of the product made use of the rating and a brief quotation in television advertisements, accompanied by the statement that "*Consumer Reports* is not affiliated with Regina and does not endorse Regina products or any other products." The district court granted a preliminary injunction. On appeal, reversed. The court of appeals concluded that the ad would have no negative effect on sales of the magazine issue reviewing light weight vacuum cleaners, and that Consumers Union's concern about its reputation for independence and integrity is not an interest protected by copyright.

If manufacturers are free to disseminate without payment favorable ratings from *Consumer Reports*, what is the effect on the consumer's incentive to buy the magazine?

5. In Maxtone-Graham v. Burtchaell, 803 F.2d 1253 (2d Cir. 1986), the plaintiff authored a book consisting of 17 anonymous interviews of women who had undergone unwanted pregnancies, some leading to adoption, others to abortion. The book was sympathetic to abortion. The defendant, a Catholic priest and professor of theology published a book of essays entitled *Rachel Weeping*. The title essay, critical of abortion, contained 37,000 words, of which 7,000 were quotations (with full attribution) from the plaintiff's book. The defendant requested permission to quote, but the permission was denied. The defendant justified the copying on the ground that "it [was] essential for the credibility of my essay that the words of abortion veterans themselves appear." He also felt that as a Catholic priest it would be impossible for him to conduct his own credible interviews and that his book would be perceived as fairer if he relied on interviews conducted by those sympathetic to the pro-choice position. The court held the copying fair use, relying heavily on the fact that the defendant's book did not injure the market for the plaintiff's book.

6. Prior to the 1976 revision act, copyright in unpublished works was provided by the states under the doctrine of "common law copyright." The 1976 act provided unitary federal protection for both published and unpublished works, and in § 301 preempted state common law copyright. Under common law copyright there was no precedent to suggest that one could copy unpublished works under the doctrine of fair use, and indeed much to suggest that the right to prevent copying was absolute on the ground that copying invaded the author's absolute and privacy-like right to control release of his own work. The 1976 revision act, by incorporating protection of unpublished works into its structure and expressly codifying the doctrine of fair use in § 107 without an exception for unpublished works, made it difficult to maintain any such absolute position. The Supreme Court's opinion in the *Nation* case, however, makes it clear that any claim of a right to copy unpublished works on grounds of fair use will be evaluated skeptically.

7. In Salinger v. Random House, Inc., 811 F.2d 90 (2d Cir.), rehrg. denied 818 F.2d 252, cert. denied 484 U.S. 890 (1987), the author of *Catcher in the Rye* sued to stop publication of a biography. The author of the biography, working without Salinger's assistance, had located in university libraries letters donated by recipients of letters from Salinger, and used them as a source of first-hand accounts of Salinger's life experiences. The sender of a letter, of course, continues to own the copyright. Following the *Nation* opinion, the Second Circuit rejected a claim of fair use, overruling Judge Leval of the district court. "To deny a biographer like Hamilton the opportunity to copy the expressive content of unpublished letters is not, as appellees contend, to interfere in any significant way with the process of enhancing public knowledge of history or contemporary events. The facts may be reported. * * * Public awareness of the expressive content of the letters will have to await either Salinger's decision to publish or the expiration of his copyright, save such special circumstances as might fall within the 'narrower' scope of fair use available for unpublished works. * * *" Of course, the same result would follow, even if the letters had been published, wouldn't it?

8. In New Era Publications International, ApS v. Henry Holt & Co. Inc., 873 F.2d 576 (2d Cir. 1989), a corporation holding copyrights from the Church of Scientology founded by one Ron Hubbard (who had bequeathed the copyrights to the church) sued to stop the publication of a highly critical biography of Hubbard called *The Bare Faced Messiah.* The biography contended that Hubbard was a fraud and religious charlatan. The suit alleged infringement of many of Hubbard's writings, including substantial copying from unpublished writings. Judge Leval, who was also the District Judge in the *Salinger* case, found that the copied passages were fair use. New Era Publications International, ApS v. Henry Holt & Co. Inc., 695 F.Supp. 1493 (S.D.N.Y. 1988). He found that verbatim quotation rather than paraphrase helped the biographer to make his point that Hubbard's very own words supported the biographer's view of the subject. "I conclude * * * that the very large majority of Miller's [the biographer] takings of Hubbard material display a powerful and compelling fair use purpose. These are not * * * talent of the subject to enliven and improve the secondary work. They are, rather, instances * * * where the critic exhibits chosen words of the subject to prove a critical point or to demonstrate a flaw in the subject's character." 695 F. Supp. 1507–08. In his analysis Judge Leval developed an interesting set of hypothetical examples to illustrate this point. See 695 F.Supp. at 1502. Judge Leval also concluded that since Hubbard was dead, he had no continuing privacy interest in the works, unlike Salinger.

The Second Circuit affirmed, but only on the grounds that laches barred an injunction. The majority opinion explicitly rejected Judge Leval's fair use analysis, placing heavy weight on the unpublished status of the copied works. Judge Leval's analysis was defended in an elaborate separate opinion by Judge Oakes, 873 F.2d at 585.

9. What are unpublished works for purposes of the restrictive scope of fair use of unpublished works suggested by the *Nation* case? Does unpublished for this purpose mean the same thing as unpublished (and hence protected by common law copyright) meant under the 1909 Act? (Note that this definition is carried forward in the definition of publication in § 101, and remains important for issues such as national origin under § 104, notice, and some aspects of the copyright term.) Or does it mean something else? The copyright definition of unpublished, particularly if we include as a gloss the concept of limited publication, includes many works that are publicly known and available. In the *Nation* case the manuscript had been stolen, and this improper method of acquisition clearly influenced the Court's attitude toward the defendant's copying. But that was not the situation in either *Salinger* or *New Era,* even though the Second Circuit thought it necessary to adopt the Supreme Court's attitude toward "unpublished" works.

In *Salinger* the letters had been obtained from university libraries, which had acquired them from recipients of the letters and made them available for research. Information contained in the letters was publicly available to researchers. It is true that the letters had not been published because sending a letter is not publication. But the sender does lose control of the substance of its content, if not of the copyright.

In *New Era* the biographer Miller learned of some documents by freedom of information requests to the federal government (for instance, Hubbard had written to the F.B.I. accusing his former wife of being a communist, and the letter was found in F.B.I. files) to which Hubbard had sent them. He apparently learned the content of others because the Church of Scientology permitted a dedicated member to undertake a biography of Hubbard. The member, one Armstrong, was given access to six filing cabinets of material, "only to become totally disillusioned with contradictory material on Hubbard's family background, naval and academic careers, fraudulent business background, tax evasion and evasion of the law." 873 F.2d at 585–86. The Church sued to get the documents back, and Miller learned of the documents from the lawsuit. Of this, Judge Leval said:

> Holt argues that many of these works were effectively published when they became part of the court record and were placed on public display during the conduct of a trial brought by the Church of Scientology in an effort to recover the documents from a member (Armstrong) who it claimed had taken them without authorization. Plaintiff disputes whether the court in fact placed the works on public display and also disputes whether such display would alter their unpublished status. Combining the fact that any public display in the course of the Armstrong litigation was over objection, with the small number of persons, at most, who saw the works, plaintiff has the better of the argument. If the bringing of a lawsuit to enforce a right necessarily resulted in its sacrifice, the right would be chimerical. 695 F.Supp. at 1500 n. 3.

This is too quick. There are procedures such as protective orders, closed proceedings, etc. that can be used to protect confidential material involved in litigation. If the biographer Miller had been subject to a protective order, he could not have used the material in violation of the order. But there is no suggestion that he was, in which case the materials were in fact part of a public record. Both *Salinger* and *New Era* involve conduct that is substantially different from that involved in *Nation*. Should the Second Circuit have considered the *Nation* case as controlling? It is easy to see why the Supreme Court found theft of the Ford manuscript "unfair." But is that true of the research methods involved in *Salinger* and *New Era*?

10. After *Nation* and the Second Circuit cases discussed in note 9, Congress considered at length and finally passed an amendment to § 107. The amendment added the final paragraph which provides: "The fact that a work is unpublished shall not itself bar a finding of fair use if such finding is made upon consideration of all the above factors." Pub.L. 102–492, Oct. 24, 1992, 106 Stat. 3145. What difference does the final paragraph make?

———

(1) Parody

Campbell aka Luke Skyywalker v. Acuff-Rose Music, Inc.

Supreme Court of the United States, 1994.
510 U.S. 569, 114 Sup. Ct. 1164, 127 L.Ed. 2d 500 (1994).

■ JUSTICE SOUTER delivered the opinion of the Court.

We are called upon to decide whether 2 Live Crew's commercial parody of Roy Orbison's song, "Oh, Pretty Woman," may be a fair use within the meaning of the Copyright Act of 1976, 17 U. S. C. § 107. Although the District Court granted summary judgment for 2 Live Crew, the Court of Appeals reversed, holding the defense of fair use barred by the song's commercial character and excessive borrowing. Because we hold that a parody's commercial character is only one element to be weighed in a fair use enquiry, and that insufficient consideration was given to the nature of parody in weighing the degree of copying, we reverse and remand.

I

In 1964, Roy Orbison and William Dees wrote a rock ballad called "Oh, Pretty Woman" and assigned their rights in it to respondent Acuff-Rose Music, Inc. See Appendix A, infra * * *. Acuff-Rose registered the song for copyright protection.

Petitioners Luther R. Campbell, Christopher Wongwon, Mark Ross, and David Hobbs, are collectively known as 2 Live Crew, a popular rap music group.[1] In 1989, Campbell wrote a song entitled "Pretty Woman," which he later described in an affidavit as intended, "through comical lyrics, to satirize the original work. . . ." App. to Pet. for Cert. 80a. On July 5, 1989, 2 Live Crew's manager informed Acuff-Rose that 2 Live Crew had written a parody of "Oh, Pretty Woman," that they would afford all credit for ownership and authorship of the original song to Acuff-Rose, Dees, and Orbison, and that they were willing to pay a fee for the use they wished to make of it. Enclosed with the letter were a copy of the lyrics and a recording of 2 Live Crew's song. See Appendix B, infra, * * *. Acuff-Rose's agent refused permission, stating that "I am aware of the success enjoyed by 'The 2 Live Crews', but I must inform you that we cannot permit the use of a parody of 'Oh, Pretty Woman.'" App. to Pet. for Cert. 85a. Nonetheless, in June or July 1989, 2 Live Crew released records, cassette tapes, and compact discs of "Pretty Woman" in a collection of songs entitled "As Clean As They Wanna Be." The albums and compact discs identify the authors of "Pretty Woman" as Orbison and Dees and its publisher as Acuff-Rose.

Almost a year later, after nearly a quarter of a million copies of the recording had been sold, Acuff-Rose sued 2 Live Crew and its record company, Luke Skyywalker Records, for copyright infringement. The District Court granted summary judgment for 2 Live Crew, reasoning that the commercial purpose of 2 Live Crew's song was no bar to fair use; that 2 Live Crew's version was a parody, which "quickly degenerates into a play on words, substituting predictable lyrics with shocking ones" to show "how bland and banal the Orbison song" is; that 2 Live Crew had taken no more than was necessary to "conjure up" the original in order to parody it; and that it was "extremely unlikely that 2 Live Crew's song could adversely affect the market for the original." 754 F. Supp. 1150, 1154–1155, 1157–1158

---

1. Rap has been defined as a "style of black American popular music consisting of improvised rhymes performed to a rhythmic accompaniment." The Norton/Grove Concise Encyclopedia of Music 613 (1988). 2 Live Crew plays "[b]ass music," a regional, hip-hop style of rap from the Liberty City area of Miami, Florida. Brief for Petitioners 34.

(M.D. Tenn. 1991). The District Court weighed these factors and held that 2 Live Crew's song made fair use of Orbison's original. Id., at 1158–1159.

The Court of Appeals for the Sixth Circuit reversed and remanded. 972 F. 2d 1429, 1439 (1992). Although it assumed for the purpose of its opinion that 2 Live Crew's song was a parody of the Orbison original, the Court of Appeals thought the District Court had put too little emphasis on the fact that "every commercial use . . . is presumptively . . . unfair," Sony Corp. of America v. Universal City Studios, Inc., 464 U. S. 417, 451 (1984), and it held that "the admittedly commercial nature" of the parody "requires the conclusion" that the first of four factors relevant under the statute weighs against a finding of fair use. 972 F. 2d, at 1435, 1437. Next, the Court of Appeals determined that, by "taking the heart of the original and making it the heart of a new work," 2 Live Crew had, qualitatively, taken too much. Id., at 1438. Finally, after noting that the effect on the potential market for the original (and the market for derivative works) is "undoubtedly the single most important element of fair use," Harper & Row, Publishers, Inc. v. Nation Enterprises, 471 U. S. 539, 566 (1985), the Court of Appeals faulted the District Court for "refus[ing] to indulge the presumption" that "harm for purposes of the fair use analysis has been established by the presumption attaching to commercial uses." 972 F. 2d, at 1438–1439. In sum, the court concluded that its "blatantly commercial purpose . . . prevents this parody from being a fair use." Id., at 1439.

We granted certiorari, 507 U. S. 1003 (1993), to determine whether 2 Live Crew's commercial parody could be a fair use.

II

It is uncontested here that 2 Live Crew's song would be an infringement of Acuff-Rose's rights in "Oh, Pretty Woman," under the Copyright Act of 1976, 17 U. S. C. § 106, but for a finding of fair use through parody.[4] From the infancy of copyright protection, some opportunity for fair use of copyrighted materials has been thought necessary to fulfill copyright's very purpose, "[t]o promote the Progress of Science and useful Arts. . . ." U. S. Const., Art. I, § 8, cl. 8. For as Justice Story explained, "[i]n truth, in literature, in science and in art, there are, and can be, few, if any, things, which in an abstract sense, are strictly new and original throughout. Every book in literature, science and art, borrows, and must necessarily borrow, and use much which was well known and used before." Emerson v. Davies, 8 F. Cas. 615, 619 (No. 4,436) (C.C.D. Mass. 1845). Similarly, Lord Ellenborough expressed the inherent tension in the need simultaneously to protect copyrighted material and to allow others to build upon it when he wrote, "while I shall think myself bound to secure every man in the enjoyment of his copyright, one must not put manacles upon science." Carey v. Kearsley, 4 Esp. 168, 170, 170 Eng. Rep. 679, 681 (K.B. 1803). In copyright

---

4. * * * 2 Live Crew concedes that it is not entitled to a compulsory license under § 115 because its arrangement changes "the basic melody or fundamental character" of the original. § 115(a)(2).

cases brought under the Statute of Anne of 1710, English courts held that in some instances "fair abridgements" would not infringe an author's rights, see W. Patry, The Fair Use Privilege in Copyright Law 6–17 (1985) (hereinafter Patry); Leval, Toward a Fair Use Standard, 103 Harv. L. Rev. 1105, 1105 (1990) (hereinafter Leval), and although the First Congress enacted our initial copyright statute, Act of May 31, 1790, 1 Stat. 124, without any explicit reference to "fair use," as it later came to be known, the doctrine was recognized by the American courts nonetheless.

* * *

Congress meant § 107 "to restate the present judicial doctrine of fair use, not to change, narrow, or enlarge it in any way" and intended that courts continue the common law tradition of fair use adjudication. H. R. Rep. No. 94–1476, p. 66 (1976) (hereinafter House Report); S. Rep. No. 94–473, p. 62 (1975) (hereinafter Senate Report). The fair use doctrine thus "permits [and requires] courts to avoid rigid application of the copyright statute when, on occasion, it would stifle the very creativity which that law is designed to foster." Stewart v. Abend, 495 U. S. 207, 236 (1990) (internal quotation marks and citation omitted).

The task is not to be simplified with bright-line rules, for the statute, like the doctrine it recognizes, calls for case-by-case analysis. *Harper & Row*, 471 U. S., at 560; *Sony*, 464 U. S., at 448, and n. 31; House Report, pp. 65–66; Senate Report, p. 62. The text employs the terms "including" and "such as" in the preamble paragraph to indicate the "illustrative and not limitative" function of the examples given, § 101; see *Harper & Row*, supra, at 561, which thus provide only general guidance about the sorts of copying that courts and Congress most commonly had found to be fair uses. Nor may the four statutory factors be treated in isolation, one from another. All are to be explored, and the results weighed together, in light of the purposes of copyright. See Leval 1110–1111; Patry & Perlmutter, Fair Use Misconstrued: Profit, Presumptions, and Parody, 11 Cardozo Arts & Ent. L. J. 667, 685–687 (1993) (hereinafter Patry & Perlmutter).[10]

---

10. Because the fair use enquiry often requires close questions of judgment as to the extent of permissible borrowing in cases involving parodies (or other critical works), courts may also wish to bear in mind that the goals of the copyright law, "to stimulate the creation and publication of edifying matter," Leval 1134, are not always best served by automatically granting injunctive relief when parodists are found to have gone beyond the bounds of fair use. See 17 U. S. C. § 502(a) (court "may . . . grant . . . injunctions on such terms as it may deem reasonable to prevent or restrain infringement") (emphasis added); Leval 1132 (while in the "vast majority of cases, [an injunctive] remedy is justified because most infringements are simple piracy," such cases are "worlds apart from many of those raising reasonable contentions of fair use" where "there may be a strong public interest in the publication of the secondary work [and] the copyright owner's interest may be adequately protected by an award of damages for whatever infringement is found"); Abend v. MCA, Inc., 863 F. 2d 1465, 1479 (CA9 1988) (finding "special circumstances" that would cause "great injustice" to defendants and "public injury" were injunction to issue), aff'd sub nom. Stewart v. Abend, 495 U. S. 207 (1990).

A

The first factor in a fair use enquiry is "the purpose and character of the use, including whether such use is of a commercial nature or is for nonprofit educational purposes." § 107(1). * * * The enquiry here may be guided by the examples given in the preamble to § 107, looking to whether the use is for criticism, or comment, or news reporting, and the like, see § 107. The central purpose of this investigation is to see, in Justice Story's words, whether the new work merely "supersede[s] the objects" of the original creation, Folsom v. Marsh, [9 F. Cas. 342, 348 (No. 4,901) (C.C.D. Mass. 1841)] * * * ; it asks, in other words, whether and to what extent the new work is "transformative." Leval 1111. Although such transformative use is not absolutely necessary for a finding of fair use, Sony, supra, at 455, n. 40,[11] the goal of copyright, to promote science and the arts, is generally furthered by the creation of transformative works. Such works thus lie at the heart of the fair use doctrine's guarantee of breathing space within the confines of copyright, see, e.g., Sony, supra, at 478–480 (Blackmun, J., dissenting), and the more transformative the new work, the less will be the significance of other factors, like commercialism, that may weigh against a finding of fair use.

This Court has only once before even considered whether parody may be fair use, and that time issued no opinion because of the Court's equal division. Benny v. Loew's Inc., 239 F.2d 532 (9th Cir. 1956), aff'd sub nom. Columbia Broadcasting System, Inc. v. Loew's Inc., 356 U.S. 43 (1958). Suffice it to say now that parody has an obvious claim to transformative value, as Acuff-Rose itself does not deny. Like less ostensibly humorous forms of criticism, it can provide social benefit, by shedding light on an earlier work, and, in the process, creating a new one. We thus line up with the courts that have held that parody, like other comment or criticism, may claim fair use under § 107. See, e.g., Fisher v. Dees, 794 F. 2d 432 (9th Cir. 1986) ("When Sonny Sniffs Glue," a parody of "When Sunny Gets Blue," is fair use); Elsmere Music, Inc. v. National Broadcasting Co., 482 F. Supp. 741 (S.D.N.Y.), aff'd, 623 F. 2d 252 (2nd Cir. 1980) ("I Love Sodom," a "Saturday Night Live" television parody of "I Love New York" is fair use); see also House Report, p. 65; Senate Report, p. 61 ("[U]se in a parody of some of the content of the work parodied" may be fair use).

The germ of parody lies in the definition of the Greek parodeia, quoted in Judge Nelson's Court of Appeals dissent, as "a song sung alongside another." 972 F. 2d, at 1440, quoting 7 Encyclopedia Britannica 768 (15th ed. 1975). Modern dictionaries accordingly describe a parody as a "literary or artistic work that imitates the characteristic style of an author or a work for comic effect or ridicule,"[12] or as a "composition in prose or verse in which the characteristic turns of thought and phrase in an author or class of

---

11. The obvious statutory exception to this focus on transformative uses is the straight reproduction of multiple copies for classroom distribution.

12. The American Heritage Dictionary 1317 (3d ed. 1992).

authors are imitated in such a way as to make them appear ridiculous."[13] For the purposes of copyright law, the nub of the definitions, and the heart of any parodist's claim to quote from existing material, is the use of some elements of a prior author's composition to create a new one that, at least in part, comments on that author's works. * * * If, on the contrary, the commentary has no critical bearing on the substance or style of the original composition, which the alleged infringer merely uses to get attention or to avoid the drudgery in working up something fresh, the claim to fairness in borrowing from another's work diminishes accordingly (if it does not vanish), and other factors, like the extent of its commerciality, loom larger.[14] Parody needs to mimic an original to make its point, and so has some claim to use the creation of its victim's (or collective victims') imagination, whereas satire can stand on its own two feet and so requires justification for the very act of borrowing.[15] * * *

The fact that parody can claim legitimacy for some appropriation does not, of course, tell either parodist or judge much about where to draw the line. Like a book review quoting the copyrighted material criticized, parody may or may not be fair use, and petitioner's suggestion that any parodic use is presumptively fair has no more justification in law or fact than the equally hopeful claim that any use for news reporting should be presumed fair, see Harper & Row, 471 U. S., at 561. The Act has no hint of an evidentiary preference for parodists over their victims, and no workable presumption for parody could take account of the fact that parody often shades into satire when society is lampooned through its creative artifacts, or that a work may contain both parodic and non-parodic elements. Accordingly, parody, like any other use, has to work its way through the relevant factors, and be judged case by case, in light of the ends of the copyright law.

Here, the District Court held, and the Court of Appeals assumed, that 2 Live Crew's "Pretty Woman" contains parody, commenting on and criticizing the original work, whatever it may have to say about society at large. As the District Court remarked, the words of 2 Live Crew's song copy the original's first line, but then "quickly degenerat[e] into a play on words, substituting predictable lyrics with shocking ones . . . [that] derisively demonstrat[e] how bland and banal the Orbison song seems to them." 754 F. Supp.,

---

13. 11 The Oxford English Dictionary 247 (2d ed. 1989).

14. A parody that more loosely targets an original than the parody presented here may still be sufficiently aimed at an original work to come within our analysis of parody. If a parody whose wide dissemination in the market runs the risk of serving as a substitute for the original or licensed derivatives (see infra, discussing factor four), it is more incumbent on one claiming fair use to establish the extent of transformation and the parody's critical relationship to the original. By contrast, when there is little or no risk of market substitution, whether because of the large extent of transformation of the earlier work, the new work's minimal distribution in the market, the small extent to which it borrows from an original, or other factors, taking parodic aim at an original is a less critical factor in the analysis, and looser forms of parody may be found to be fair use, as may satire with lesser justification for the borrowing than would otherwise be required.

15. Satire has been defined as a work "in which prevalent follies or vices are assailed with ridicule," 14 The Oxford English Dictionary 500 (2d ed. 1989), or are "attacked through irony, derision, or wit," The American Heritage Dictionary 1604 (3d ed. 1992).

at 1155 (footnote omitted). Judge Nelson, dissenting below, came to the same conclusion, that the 2 Live Crew song "was clearly intended to ridicule the white-bread original" and "reminds us that sexual congress with nameless streetwalkers is not necessarily the stuff of romance and is not necessarily without its consequences. The singers (there are several) have the same thing on their minds as did the lonely man with the nasal voice, but here there is no hint of wine and roses." 972 F. 2d, at 1442. Although the majority below had difficulty discerning any criticism of the original in 2 Live Crew's song, it assumed for purposes of its opinion that there was some. Id., at 1435–1436, and n. 8.

We have less difficulty in finding that critical element in 2 Live Crew's song than the Court of Appeals did, although having found it we will not take the further step of evaluating its quality. The threshold question when fair use is raised in defense of parody is whether a parodic character may reasonably be perceived.[16] Whether, going beyond that, parody is in good taste or bad does not and should not matter to fair use. As Justice Holmes explained, "[i]t would be a dangerous undertaking for persons trained only to the law to constitute themselves final judges of the worth of [a work], outside of the narrowest and most obvious limits. At the one extreme some works of genius would be sure to miss appreciation. Their very novelty would make them repulsive until the public had learned the new language in which their author spoke." Bleistein v. Donaldson Lithographing Co., 188 U. S. 239, 251 (1903) (circus posters have copyright protection); cf. Yankee Publishing Inc. v. News America Publishing, Inc., 809 F. Supp. 267, 280 (S.D.N.Y. 1992) (Leval, J.) ("First Amendment protections do not apply only to those who speak clearly, whose jokes are funny, and whose parodies succeed") (trademark case).

While we might not assign a high rank to the parodic element here, we think it fair to say that 2 Live Crew's song reasonably could be perceived as commenting on the original or criticizing it, to some degree. 2 Live Crew juxtaposes the romantic musings of a man whose fantasy comes true, with degrading taunts, a bawdy demand for sex, and a sigh of relief from paternal responsibility. The later words can be taken as a comment on the naivete of the original of an earlier day, as a rejection of its sentiment that ignores the ugliness of street life and the debasement that it signifies. It is this joinder of reference and ridicule that marks off the author's choice of parody from the other types of comment and criticism that traditionally have had a claim to fair use protection as transformative works.

The Court of Appeals, however, immediately cut short the enquiry into 2 Live Crew's fair use claim by confining its treatment of the first factor essentially to one relevant fact, the commercial nature of the use. The court then inflated the significance of this fact by applying a presumption ostensibly culled from *Sony*, that "every commercial use of copyrighted material

---

16. The only further judgment, indeed, that a court may pass on a work goes to an assessment of whether the parodic element is slight or great, and the copying small or extensive in relation to the parodic element, for a work with slight parodic element and extensive copying will be more likely to merely "supersede the objects" of the original. See infra, discussing factors three and four.

is presumptively . . . unfair. . . ." *Sony*, 464 U. S., at 451. In giving virtually dispositive weight to the commercial nature of the parody, the Court of Appeals erred.

The language of the statute makes clear that the commercial or non-profit educational purpose of a work is only one element of the first factor enquiry into its purpose and character. Section 107(1) uses the term "including" to begin the dependent clause referring to commercial use, and the main clause speaks of a broader investigation into "purpose and character." As we explained in *Harper & Row*, Congress resisted attempts to narrow the ambit of this traditional enquiry by adopting categories of presumptively fair use, and it urged courts to preserve the breadth of their traditionally ample view of the universe of relevant evidence. 471 U. S., at 561; House Report, p. 66. Accordingly, the mere fact that a use is educational and not for profit does not insulate it from a finding of infringement, any more than the commercial character of a use bars a finding of fairness. If, indeed, commerciality carried presumptive force against a finding of fairness, the presumption would swallow nearly all of the illustrative uses listed in the preamble paragraph of § 107, including news reporting, comment, criticism, teaching, scholarship, and research, since these activities "are generally conducted for profit in this country." *Harper & Row*, supra, at 592 (Brennan, J., dissenting). Congress could not have intended such a rule, which certainly is not inferable from the common-law cases, arising as they did from the world of letters in which Samuel Johnson could pronounce that "[n]o man but a blockhead ever wrote, except for money." 3 Boswell's Life of Johnson 19 (G. Hill ed. 1934).

Sony itself called for no hard evidentiary presumption. There, we emphasized the need for a "sensitive balancing of interests," 464 U. S., at 455, n. 40, noted that Congress had "eschewed a rigid, bright-line approach to fair use," id., at 449, n. 31, and stated that the commercial or nonprofit educational character of a work is "not conclusive," id., at 448–449, but rather a fact to be "weighed along with other[s] in fair use decisions." Id., at 449, n. 32 (quoting House Report, p. 66). The Court of Appeals's elevation of one sentence from *Sony* to a per se rule thus runs as much counter to *Sony* itself as to the long common-law tradition of fair use adjudication. Rather, as we explained in *Harper & Row*, *Sony* stands for the proposition that the "fact that a publication was commercial as opposed to nonprofit is a separate factor that tends to weigh against a finding of fair use." 471 U. S., at 562. But that is all, and the fact that even the force of that tendency will vary with the context is a further reason against elevating commerciality to hard presumptive significance. The use, for example, of a copyrighted work to advertise a product, even in a parody, will be entitled to less indulgence under the first factor of the fair use enquiry, than the sale of a parody for its own sake, let alone one performed a single time by students in school.

B

The second statutory factor, "the nature of the copyrighted work," § 107(2), draws on Justice Story's expression, the "value of the materials used." *Folsom v. Marsh*, 9 F. Cas., at 348. This factor calls for recognition that some works are closer to the core of intended copyright protection than others, with the consequence that fair use is more difficult to establish when the former works are copied. See, e.g., *Stewart v. Abend*, 495 U. S., at 237–238 (contrasting fictional short story with factual works); *Harper & Row*, 471 U. S., at 563–564 (contrasting soon-to-be-published memoir with published speech); *Sony*, 464 U. S., at 455, n. 40 (contrasting motion pictures with news broadcasts); *Feist*, 499 U. S., 348–351 (contrasting creative works with bare factual compilations); 3 M. Nimmer & D. Nimmer, Nimmer on Copyright § 13.05[A][2] (1993) (hereinafter Nimmer); Leval 1116. We agree with both the District Court and the Court of Appeals that the Orbison original's creative expression for public dissemination falls within the core of the copyright's protective purposes. 754 F. Supp., at 1155–1156; 972 F. 2d, at 1437. This fact, however, is not much help in this case, or ever likely to help much in separating the fair use sheep from the infringing goats in a parody case, since parodies almost invariably copy publicly known, expressive works.

C

The third factor asks whether "the amount and substantiality of the portion used in relation to the copyrighted work as a whole," § 107(3) (or, in Justice Story's words, "the quantity and value of the materials used," *Folsom v. Marsh*, supra, at 348) are reasonable in relation to the purpose of the copying. Here, attention turns to the persuasiveness of a parodist's justification for the particular copying done, and the enquiry will harken back to the first of the statutory factors, for, as in prior cases, we recognize that the extent of permissible copying varies with the purpose and character of the use. See *Sony*, 464 U. S., at 449–450 (reproduction of entire work "does not have its ordinary effect of militating against a finding of fair use" as to home videotaping of television programs); *Harper & Row*, 471 U. S., at 564 ("[E]ven substantial quotations might qualify as fair use in a review of a published work or a news account of a speech" but not in a scoop of a soon-to-be-published memoir). The facts bearing on this factor will also tend to address the fourth, by revealing the degree to which the parody may serve as a market substitute for the original or potentially licensed derivatives. See Leval 1123.

The District Court considered the song's parodic purpose in finding that 2 Live Crew had not helped themselves overmuch. 754 F. Supp., at 1156–1157. The Court of Appeals disagreed, stating that "[w]hile it may not be inappropriate to find that no more was taken than necessary, the copying was qualitatively substantial. . . . We conclude that taking the heart of the original and making it the heart of a new work was to purloin a substantial portion of the essence of the original." 972 F. 2d, at 1438.

The Court of Appeals is of course correct that this factor calls for thought not only about the quantity of the materials used, but about their quality and importance, too. In *Harper & Row*, for example, the Nation had taken only some 300 words out of President Ford's memoirs, but we signalled the significance of the quotations in finding them to amount to "the heart of the book," the part most likely to be newsworthy and important in licensing serialization. 471 U. S., at 564–566, 568 (internal quotation marks omitted). We also agree with the Court of Appeals that whether "a substantial portion of the infringing work was copied verbatim" from the copyrighted work is a relevant question, see id., at 565, for it may reveal a dearth of transformative character or purpose under the first factor, or a greater likelihood of market harm under the fourth; a work composed primarily of an original, particularly its heart, with little added or changed, is more likely to be a merely superseding use, fulfilling demand for the original.

Where we part company with the court below is in applying these guides to parody, and in particular to parody in the song before us. Parody presents a difficult case. Parody's humor, or in any event its comment, necessarily springs from recognizable allusion to its object through distorted imitation. Its art lies in the tension between a known original and its parodic twin. When parody takes aim at a particular original work, the parody must be able to "conjure up" at least enough of that original to make the object of its critical wit recognizable. See, e.g., Elsmere Music, 623 F. 2d, at 253, n. 1; Fisher v. Dees, 794 F. 2d, at 438–439. What makes for this recognition is quotation of the original's most distinctive or memorable features, which the parodist can be sure the audience will know. Once enough has been taken to assure identification, how much more is reasonable will depend, say, on the extent to which the song's overriding purpose and character is to parody the original or, in contrast, the likelihood that the parody may serve as a market substitute for the original. But using some characteristic features cannot be avoided.

We think the Court of Appeals was insufficiently appreciative of parody's need for the recognizable sight or sound when it ruled 2 Live Crew's use unreasonable as a matter of law. It is true, of course, that 2 Live Crew copied the characteristic opening bass riff (or musical phrase) of the original, and true that the words of the first line copy the Orbison lyrics. But if quotation of the opening riff and the first line may be said to go to the "heart" of the original, the heart is also what most readily conjures up the song for parody, and it is the heart at which parody takes aim. Copying does not become excessive in relation to parodic purpose merely because the portion taken was the original's heart. If 2 Live Crew had copied a significantly less memorable part of the original, it is difficult to see how its parodic character would have come through. See Fisher v. Dees, 794 F. 2d, at 439.

This is not, of course, to say that anyone who calls himself a parodist can skim the cream and get away scot free. In parody, as in news reporting, see Harper & Row, supra, context is everything, and the question of fairness asks what else the parodist did besides go to the heart of the original. It is significant that 2 Live Crew not only copied the first line of the original, but thereafter departed markedly from the Orbison lyrics for its own ends. 2 Live Crew not only copied the bass riff and repeated it,[19] but also produced oth-

---

19. This may serve to heighten the comic effect of the parody, as one witness stated, App. 32a, Affidavit of Oscar Brand; see also Elsmere Music, Inc. v. National Broadcasting Co., 482 F. Supp. 741, 747 (S.D.N.Y. 1980) (repetition of "I Love Sodom"), or serve to dazzle with the original's music, as Acuff-Rose now contends.

erwise distinctive sounds, interposing "scraper" noise, overlaying the music with solos in different keys, and altering the drum beat. See 754 F. Supp., at 1155. This is not a case, then, where "a substantial portion" of the parody itself is composed of a "verbatim" copying of the original. It is not, that is, a case where the parody is so insubstantial, as compared to the copying, that the third factor must be resolved as a matter of law against the parodists.

Suffice it to say here that, as to the lyrics, we think the Court of Appeals correctly suggested that "no more was taken than necessary," 972 F. 2d, at 1438, but just for that reason, we fail to see how the copying can be excessive in relation to its parodic purpose, even if the portion taken is the original's "heart." As to the music, we express no opinion whether repetition of the bass riff is excessive copying, and we remand to permit evaluation of the amount taken, in light of the song's parodic purpose and character, its transformative elements, and considerations of the potential for market substitution sketched more fully below.

D

The fourth fair use factor is "the effect of the use upon the potential market for or value of the copyrighted work." § 107(4). It requires courts to consider not only the extent of market harm caused by the particular actions of the alleged infringer, but also "whether unrestricted and widespread conduct of the sort engaged in by the defendant . . . would result in a substantially adverse impact on the potential market" for the original. Nimmer § 13.05[A] [4], p. 13–102.61 (footnote omitted); accord *Harper & Row*, 471 U. S., at 569; Senate Report, p. 65; Folsom v. Marsh, 9 F. Cas., at 349. The enquiry "must take account not only of harm to the original but also of harm to the market for derivative works." *Harper & Row, supra*, at 568.

Since fair use is an affirmative defense,[20] its proponent would have difficulty carrying the burden of demonstrating fair use without favorable evidence about relevant markets.[21] In moving for summary judgment, 2 Live Crew left themselves at just such a disadvantage when they failed to address the effect on the market for rap derivatives, and confined themselves to uncontroverted submissions that there was no likely effect on the market for the original. They did not, however, thereby subject themselves to the evidentiary presumption applied by the Court of Appeals. In assessing the likelihood of significant market harm, the Court of Appeals quoted from language in *Sony* that " '[i]f the intended use is for commercial gain, that likelihood may be presumed. But if it is for a noncommercial purpose, the likelihood must be demonstrated.'" 972 F. 2d, at 1438, quoting *Sony*, 464

---

20. Harper & Row, 471 U. S., at 561; H. R. Rep. No. 102-836, p. 3, n. 3 (1992).

21. Even favorable evidence, without more, is no guarantee of fairness. Judge Leval gives the example of the film producer's appropriation of a composer's previously unknown song that turns the song into a commercial success; the boon to the song does not make the film's simple copying fair. Leval 1124, n. 84. This factor, no less than the other three, may be addressed only through a "sensitive balancing of interests." Sony, 464 U. S., at 455, n. 40. Market harm is a matter of degree, and the importance of this factor will vary, not only with the amount of harm, but also with the relative strength of the showing on the other factors.

U. S., at 451. The court reasoned that because "the use of the copyrighted work is wholly commercial, . . . we presume a likelihood of future harm to Acuff-Rose exists." 972 F. 2d, at 1438. In so doing, the court resolved the fourth factor against 2 Live Crew, just as it had the first, by applying a presumption about the effect of commercial use, a presumption which as applied here we hold to be error.

No "presumption" or inference of market harm that might find support in *Sony* is applicable to a case involving something beyond mere duplication for commercial purposes. *Sony's* discussion of a presumption contrasts a context of verbatim copying of the original in its entirety for commercial purposes, with the non-commercial context of *Sony* itself (home copying of television programming). In the former circumstances, what Sony said simply makes common sense: when a commercial use amounts to mere duplication of the entirety of an original, it clearly "supersede[s] the objects," *Folsom v. Marsh*, 9 F. Cas., at 348, of the original and serves as a market replacement for it, making it likely that cognizable market harm to the original will occur. *Sony*, 464 U. S., at 451. But when, on the contrary, the second use is transformative, market substitution is at least less certain, and market harm may not be so readily inferred. Indeed, as to parody pure and simple, it is more likely that the new work will not affect the market for the original in a way cognizable under this factor, that is, by acting as a substitute for it ("supersed[ing] [its] objects"). See Leval 1125; Patry & Perlmutter 692, 697–698. This is so because the parody and the original usually serve different market functions. * * *

We do not, of course, suggest that a parody may not harm the market at all, but when a lethal parody, like a scathing theater review, kills demand for the original, it does not produce a harm cognizable under the Copyright Act. Because "parody may quite legitimately aim at garroting the original, destroying it commercially as well as artistically," B. Kaplan, An Unhurried View of Copyright 69 (1967), the role of the courts is to distinguish between "[b]iting criticism [that merely] suppresses demand [and] copyright infringement[, which] usurps it." *Fisher v. Dees*, 794 F. 2d, at 438.

This distinction between potentially remediable displacement and unremediable disparagement is reflected in the rule that there is no protectable derivative market for criticism. The market for potential derivative uses includes only those that creators of original works would in general develop or license others to develop. Yet the unlikelihood that creators of imaginative works will license critical reviews or lampoons of their own productions removes such uses from the very notion of a potential licensing market. "People ask . . . for criticism, but they only want praise." S. Maugham, Of Human Bondage 241 (Penguin ed. 1992). Thus, to the extent that the opinion below may be read to have considered harm to the market for parodies of "Oh, Pretty Woman," see 972 F. 2d, at 1439, the court erred. Accord, Fisher v. Dees, 794 F. 2d, at 437; Leval 1125; Patry & Perlmutter 688–691.[22]

---

22. We express no opinion as to the derivative markets for works using elements of an original as vehicles for satire or amusement, making no comment on the original or criticism of it.

In explaining why the law recognizes no derivative market for critical works, including parody, we have, of course, been speaking of the later work as if it had nothing but a critical aspect (i.e., "parody pure and simple," supra). But the later work may have a more complex character, with effects not only in the arena of criticism but also in protectable markets for derivative works, too. In that sort of case, the law looks beyond the criticism to the other elements of the work, as it does here. 2 Live Crew's song comprises not only parody but also rap music, and the derivative market for rap music is a proper focus of enquiry, see *Harper & Row*, 471 U. S., at 568; Nimmer § 13.05[B]. Evidence of substantial harm to it would weigh against a finding of fair use, because the licensing of derivatives is an important economic incentive to the creation of originals. * * * Of course, the only harm to derivatives that need concern us, as discussed above, is the harm of market substitution. The fact that a parody may impair the market for derivative uses by the very effectiveness of its critical commentary is no more relevant under copyright than the like threat to the original market.[24]

Although 2 Live Crew submitted uncontroverted affidavits on the question of market harm to the original, neither they, nor Acuff-Rose, introduced evidence or affidavits addressing the likely effect of 2 Live Crew's parodic rap song on the market for a non-parody, rap version of "Oh, Pretty Woman." And while Acuff-Rose would have us find evidence of a rap market in the very facts that 2 Live Crew recorded a rap parody of "Oh, Pretty Woman" and another rap group sought a license to record a rap derivative, there was no evidence that a potential rap market was harmed in any way by 2 Live Crew's parody, rap version. The fact that 2 Live Crew's parody sold as part of a collection of rap songs says very little about the parody's effect on a market for a rap version of the original, either of the music alone or of the music with its lyrics. The District Court essentially passed on this issue, observing that Acuff-Rose is free to record "whatever version of the original it desires," 754 F. Supp., at 1158; the Court of Appeals went the other way by erroneous presumption. Contrary to each treatment, it is impossible to deal with the fourth factor except by recognizing that a silent record on an important factor bearing on fair use disentitled the proponent of the defense, 2 Live Crew, to summary judgment. The evidentiary hole will doubtless be plugged on remand.

III

It was error for the Court of Appeals to conclude that the commercial nature of 2 Live Crew's parody of "Oh, Pretty Woman" rendered it presumptively unfair. No such evidentiary presumption is available to address either the first factor, the character and purpose of the use, or the fourth, market harm, in determining whether a transformative use, such as parody, is a fair one. The court also erred in holding that 2 Live Crew had necessarily copied

---

24. In some cases it may be difficult to determine whence the harm flows. In such cases, the other fair use factors may provide some indicia of the likely source of the harm. A work whose overriding purpose and character is parodic and whose borrowing is slight in relation to its parody will be far less likely to cause cognizable harm than a work with little parodic content and much copying.

excessively from the Orbison original, considering the parodic purpose of the use. We therefore reverse the judgment of the Court of Appeals and remand for further proceedings consistent with this opinion.

It is so ordered.

Appendix A

"Oh, Pretty Woman" by Roy Orbison and William Dees

Pretty Woman, walking down the street,
Pretty Woman, the kind I like to meet,
Pretty Woman, I don't believe you, you're not the truth,
No one could look as good as you
Mercy

Pretty Woman, won't you pardon me,
Pretty Woman, I couldn't help but see,
Pretty Woman, that you look lovely as can be
Are you lonely just like me?

Pretty Woman, stop a while,
Pretty Woman, talk a while,
Pretty Woman give your smile to me
Pretty woman, yeah, yeah, yeah
Pretty Woman, look my way,
Pretty Woman, say you'll stay with me
'Cause I need you, I'll treat you right
Come to me baby, Be mine tonight

Pretty Woman, don't walk on by,
Pretty Woman, don't make me cry,
Pretty Woman, don't walk away,
Hey, O. K.
If that's the way it must be, O. K.
I guess I'll go on home, it's late
There'll be tomorrow night, but wait!

What do I see
Is she walking back to me?
Yeah, she's walking back to me!
Oh, Pretty Woman.

Appendix B

"Pretty Woman" as Recorded by 2 Live Crew

Pretty woman walkin' down the street
Pretty woman girl you look so sweet
Pretty woman you bring me down to that knee
Pretty woman you make me wanna beg please
Oh, pretty woman

Big hairy woman you need to shave that stuff
Big hairy woman you know I bet it's tough
Big hairy woman all that hair it ain't legit
'Cause you look like 'Cousin It'

Big hairy woman

Bald headed woman girl your hair won't grow
Bald headed woman you got a teeny weeny afro
Bald headed woman you know your hair could look nice
Bald headed woman first you got to roll it with rice
Bald headed woman here, let me get this hunk of biz for ya
Ya know what I'm saying you look better than rice a roni
Oh bald headed woman

Big hairy woman come on in
And don't forget your bald headed friend
Hey pretty woman let the boys
Jump in

Two timin' woman girl you know you ain't right
Two timin' woman you's out with my boy last night
Two timin' woman that takes a load off my mind
Two timin' woman now I know the baby ain't mine
Oh, two timin' woman
Oh pretty woman

NOTES

1. The most important part of the *Acuff-Rose* opinion may prove to be footnote 10, which explicitly recognizes the possibility of a class of infringements for which no injunction will issue, thus creating the nucleus of what may become a compulsory licensing system for infringements which are close to, but not quite, fair use.

2. The Court accepted 2 Live Crew's concession that it was not entitled to a compulsory license because its parody changes "the basic melody or fundamental character" of the original. 17 U.S.C. § 115(a)(2). See note 4 of the opinion. House Report 94–1476, p. 109 says that "The second clause of subsection (a) is intended to recognize the practical need for a limited privilege to make arrangements of music being used under a compulsory license, but without allowing the music to be perverted, distorted, or travestied." Webster's Ninth New Collegiate Dictionary defines the verb to travesty as to parody. If Congress explicitly provided that a parody was not entitled to a compulsory license, isn't it a clear inference from the statute that a parody infringes?

3. Assume you were to represent one of the parties on remand. How would you formulate the instructions to the jury? What evidence would you present to the jury? If you were a member of the jury, would you find the instructions understandable?

4. Which party do you think is likely to win on remand?

5. Prior to the *Campbell* case, the Supreme Court had had one prior occasion to consider the problem of parody of a copyrighted work. Benny v. Loew's Inc., 239 F.2d 532 (9th Cir. 1956), aff'd without opinion by an equally divided Court, 356 U.S. 43 (1958), rehearing denied 356 U.S. 934. The *Benny* case involved Jack Benny's burlesque on his evening television show of the then popular movie "Gas Light," which starred Charles Boyer, Ingrid Bergman and Joseph Cotten. The Ninth Circuit analyzed the case as a standard infringement case, looking for taking of expression. The Ninth Circuit found infringement.

To the extent that the *Campbell* opinion indicates that there is an extra "thumb on the scales" for parody, it is a departure from the law of the Ninth Circuit *Benny* decision.

6. Berlin v. E.C. Publications, 329 F.2d 541 (2d Cir. 1964):

> Through depression and boom, war and peace, Tin Pan Alley has light-heartedly insisted that "the whole world laughs" with a laugher, and that "the best things in life are free." In an apparent departure from these delightful sentiments, the owners of the copyrights upon some twenty-five popular songs instituted this action against the publishers, employees and distributors of "Mad Magazine," alleging that Mad's publication of satiric parody lyrics to plaintiffs' songs infringed the copyrighted originals, despite Mad's failure to reproduce the music of plaintiffs' compositions in any form whatsoever. * * * The parodies were published as a "special bonus" to the Fourth Annual Edition of Mad, whose cover characterized its contents as "More Trash From Mad—A Sickening Collection of Humor and Satire From Past Issues," and almost prophetically carried this admonition for its readers: "For Solo or Group Participation (Followed by Arrest)." Defendants' efforts were billed as a collection of parody lyrics to 57 old standards which reflect the idiotic world we live in today. Divided into nine categories, ranging from "Songs of Space & The Atom" to "Songs of Sports," they were accompanied by the notation that they were to be "Sung to" or "Sung to the tune of" a well-known popular song—in twenty-five cases, the plaintiffs' copyrighted compositions. So that this musical direction might feasibly be obeyed, the parodies were written in the same meter as the original lyrics.

> The District Court observed that the theme and content of the parodies differed markedly from those of the originals. Thus, "The Last Time I Saw Paris," originally written as a nostalgic ballad which tenderly recalled pre-war France, became in defendants' hands "The First Time I Saw Maris," a caustic commentary upon the tendency of a baseball hero to become a television pitchman, more prone to tempt injury with the razor blade which he advertises than with the hazards of the game which he plays. Similarly, defendants transformed the plaintiffs' "A Pretty Girl Is Like a Melody", into "Louella Schwartz Describes Her Malady"; what was originally a tribute to feminine beauty became a burlesque of a feminine hypochondriac troubled with sleeplessness and a propensity to tell the world of her plight.

The court found no infringement. Is the doctrine of fair use necessary to reach such a result?

7. In Walt Disney Productions v. Air Pirates, 345 F.Supp. 108 (N.D.Cal. 1972), the defendant had parodied Mickey Mouse and other cartoon characters of Walt Disney. Defendant argued that it was necessary to copy the characters in order to parody them. The court found infringement, following *Benny.* Same result under *Campbell?*

8. The Fifth Circuit had no trouble affirming a preliminary injunction against infringement of a copyrighted poster of five members of the Dallas Cowboys cheerleaders. The infringing poster displayed five ex-members of the Dallas Cowboys cheerleaders with bare breasts. The court rejected the argument that the poster was parody and hence fair use. Dallas Cowboys Cheerleaders, Inc. v. Scoreboard Posters, Inc., 600 F.2d 1184 (5th Cir. 1979).

9. In Hustler Magazine, Inc. v. Moral Majority, Inc., 796 F.2d 1148 (9th Cir. 1986), *Hustler* magazine ran an ad which was a parody of Campari liquor advertisements. Campari advertisements consist of interviews with famous people about the first time they drank Campari, using double entendre to conflate the first drink of Campari and a first sexual experience. The parody ad featured the Rev. Jerry Falwell, a nationally famous fundamentalist minister, describing his "first time" as being incest with his mother in an outhouse. Falwell used copies of the ad in fund raising appeals (while also suing *Hustler* for libel) and Hustler sued Falwell for infringement. Falwell's use of the copies of the ad was held to be fair use.

10. Elsmere Music, Inc. v. National Broadcasting Co., Inc., 482 F.Supp. 741 (S.D.N.Y. 1980), affirmed 623 F.2d 252 (2d Cir. 1980), was an action for infringement of the promotional song "I Love New York." The song was parodied on Saturday Night Live as "I Love Sodom." Held: Fair use because the parody did not affect the value of the plaintiff's copyrighted song. But didn't the parody reduce the value of the song as a successful promotional device since viewers of the Saturday Night Live skit might be reminded of it every time they heard "I Love New York"? Note that the defendants in *Elsmere,* unlike the defendants in *Berlin,* supra note 6, sang the entire (albeit quite simple) melody of "I Love New York."

11. Suppose the *Nation* had combined its excerpts from the Ford memoirs with more extended and critical editorial material along the lines of "This is what Ford said he said or did, and isn't that ridiculous?" Would that have changed the outcome of the litigation? Can a copyright infringer find safety by combining infringement with controversial editorial material about the work infringed (just as magazines containing sexually explicit pictorials have found it helpful to add anti-establishment and anti-government articles)?

12. A factor to be considered but not enumerated in § 107 is the conduct of the defendant after the infringement has been detected, according to Iowa State Univ. Research Foundation, Inc. v. American Broadcasting Companies, 621 F.2d 57 (2d Cir. 1980). In that case students at Iowa State University had produced a 28 minute film entitled *Champion,* a short biography of fellow student and champion wrestler Dan Gable. ABC used several minutes of the film in connection with Gable's successful competition for a gold medal at the 1972 Olympics and in connection with Gable's appearance on an ABC program "Superstars." ABC unsuccessfully argued fair use. "We cannot ignore the fact, found by the district judge, that ABC copied *Champion* while purporting to assess its value for possible purchase, or that the network repeatedly denied that it had ever used the film. * * * ABC's conduct in the instant case is not irrelevant to the fairness of its use." 621 F.2d at 62. The district court awarded $15,250 in statutory damages and $17,500 in attorney's fees. 475 F.Supp. 78 (S.D.N.Y. 1979).

---

(2) Other Non-Competing Uses

Triangle Publications, Inc. v. Knight-Ridder Newspapers, Inc.

United States Court of Appeals, Fifth Circuit, 1980.
626 F.2d 1171.

■ JOHN R. BROWN, CIRCUIT JUDGE:

* * *

The plaintiff-appellant, Triangle Publications (Triangle), is the publisher of "TV Guide," a periodical containing television schedules and articles relating to television entertainment. The defendant-appellee, Knight-Ridder Newspapers (Knight-Ridder), publishes the Miami Herald Newspaper (the Herald). During the fall of 1977, Knight-Ridder began a campaign to promote a newly developed television booklet which was to be included as a supplement to the Sunday edition of the Herald. Like TV Guide, the booklet contains television schedules and articles related to that media. * * *

[T]he booklet was advertised in two thirty second television commercials. The first is based on the theme "Goldilocks and the Three Bears." It compares the size of the Herald's former television guide with the Herald's new supplement and with TV Guide, concluding that the former supplement is too large, that TV Guide is too small, but that the new supplement is just the right size for human beings.[3] While TV Guide is not mentioned by name, one of the actors in the commercial is shown briefly with a back-dated copy of TV Guide in hand. The cover of the TV Guide issue is clearly visible. The commercial was used for several weeks and was then discontinued. The second commercial is a monologue. After identifying TV Guide as the competing product, the announcer suggests that the Herald's supplement is a better value for the money because the purchaser gets the entire newspaper, not

---

3. This is the script of the commercial:

[Narrator]: "This is the story of Sidney Bear, Cindy Bear and Junior Bear. They all love to watch TV, but . . ."

[Middle Aged Man]: "This TV book is too small."

[Child]: "This TV book is too big."

[Middle Aged Woman]: "This TV section is just right."

[Narrator]: "It was the Sunday Herald's new TV book at no extra cost. The three bears loved the new . . . just-right size with its up-to-date and more complete listings. 'Til one day this little blonde kid—uh, but that's another story . . . . Something for everybody. Every day of the week." (Dots indicate pauses, not omitted material.)

merely a TV booklet.[4] During the course of his statement, the announcer holds up a backdated issue of TV Guide with the cover clearly visible. The announcer then puts down the TV Guide and holds up first a copy of the Herald's supplement and then a copy of the Sunday edition of the Herald. This commercial was being used at the time of the District Court's hearing and Knight-Ridder contemplated using it in the future.

The only conduct by the Herald being challenged here is the reproducing of TV Guide covers. The verbal reference to TV Guide made in the second commercial is not being attacked. Since each issue of TV Guide is individually copyrighted, and since magazine covers have in the past been afforded copyright protection, see, e.g., Conde Nast Publications, Inc. v. Vogue School of Fashion Modeling, Inc., 105 F.Supp. 325 (S.D.N.Y. 1952), Triangle claims that the Herald's showing of TV Guide covers violates § 106 of the new Copyright Act, 17 U.S.C. § 106. Triangle moved in the District Court for preliminary and permanent injunctions (and also sought damages). [The district court rejected the defendant's fair use defense, but nevertheless decided for the defendant on the ground that an injunction against infringement would violate free speech.]

* * *

In analyzing the fair use question, the District Court did not get beyond the first factor [of § 107]. The Court deemed it controlling that the use of the TV Guide covers by the Miami Herald was to obtain commercial advantage. The Court established what amounts to virtually a per se rule that commercial motive destroys the defense of fair use.

Clearly, § 107 makes commercial motive relevant to fair use analysis. But it is certainly not decisive. As the legislative history makes clear:

> This amendment is not intended to be interpreted as any sort of not-for-profit limitation on educational uses of copyrighted works. It is an express recognition that, as under the present law, the commercial and non-profit character of an activity, while not conclusive with respect to fair use, can and should be weighed along with other factors in fair use decisions.

House Report, at 66; U.S.Code Cong. & Admin.News, at 5679. See also Senate Report, at 62; 3 Nimmer on Copyright, § 13.05[A], at 13–52 (1978) (stating that commercial use does not necessarily negate fair use defense and citing string of cases to support proposition).

* * *

We believe that in viewing commercial motive as conclusive on the question of fair use, the District Court incorrectly applied § 107. Accordingly, its

---

4. This is the script of the commercial:

"This is TV Guide. When you buy it, that's all you get. No extras. This is The Miami Herald's TV Book. When you buy it, you get a few extras like more up-to-date listings, charts that let you see what's on at a glance. It even has extras on top of the extras. And the best part is, even if there's nothing good on TV . . . you can always sit back and read some of the extras. The Miami Herald."

(Dots indicate pauses, not omitted material.)

finding of no fair use defense is not subject to a clearly erroneous standard. Rather, we are more free to determine the question of fair use.

As § 107 makes clear, the first factor to consider in a fair use analysis is the purpose and character of the use. Here, Knight-Ridder used TV Guide covers for advertisements, and any commercial use tends to cut against a fair use defense. On the other hand, the precise characteristics of the commercial use in this case caution against too much weight being given to the fact that the use is commercial. Specifically, there was no attempt to palm off Triangle's product as that of the Herald's. Compare *Conde Nast Publications, Inc. v. Vogue School of Fashion Modeling, Inc.,* supra. Rather, the advertisement was a comparative advertisement done in a manner which is generally accepted in the advertising industry.[13]

The second factor specified in § 107 is the nature of the copyrighted work. One commentator has argued that because the copyrighted work—TV Guide—is itself commercial, the defense of fair use should more readily apply. See Wisconsin Note ["Copyright and the First Amendment—*Triangle Publications, Inc. v. Knight-Ridder Newspapers, Inc.,* 445 F.Supp. 875 (S.D. Fla. 1978), 1979 Wisc. L. Rev. 242], supra, at 261. However, other commentators have argued that "courts have tended to be most receptive to unauthorized use of educational, scientific, and historical works." Note, Copyright Infringement and the First Amendment, 79 Colum. L. Rev. 320, 326 n. 42 (hereafter referred to as Columbia Note) * * *. In our view, the fact that TV Guide is a commercial publication neither supports nor hurts Knight-Ridder's claim that a fair use defense is appropriate here.

The third factor to consider under § 107 is the amount and substantiality of the portion used in relation to the copyrighted work as a whole. Here,

---

13. As stated, the fact that the commercial use occurred in the course of a truthful comparative advertisement undercuts the significance of the commercial nature of the use. Congress emphasized that the doctrine of fair use must be flexible. House Report, at 66; U.S.Code Cong. & Admin. News, at 5680; Senate Report at 62. Today, the public interest in comparative advertising is well-recognized. As the Federal Trade Commission has stated:

The Commission has supported the use of brand comparisons where the bases of comparison are clearly identified. Comparative advertising, when truthful and nondeceptive, is a source of important information to consumers and assists them in making rational purchase decisions. Comparative advertising encourages product improvement and innovation, and can lead to lower prices in the marketplace. For these reasons, the Commission will continue to scrutinize carefully restraints upon its use.

16 C.F.R. § 14.15(c) (1980). One affidavit received as a part of the record cites several examples of comparative advertising, including many magazine ads reproducing covers of competing magazines. For example, the January 9, 1978 issue of Advertising Age contains an advertisement for Americana magazine with a display of covers of competing magazines. The December 1977 issue of Media Decisions contains an ad promoting Horizon magazine featuring pictures of covers of competing magazines. An advertisement in the July 8, 1977 issue of New Times promoting that magazine shows covers of Time and Newsweek, two newsweeklys with which New Times competes. Affidavit of Ken Keoughan, Director of Marketing Services, Beber, Silverstein & Partners, Inc. Thus, while the Miami Herald is clearly out to make a profit from its advertisements, there is certainly no palming off of Triangle's work. Rather, the Herald has used various covers of TV Guide for purposes of comparative advertisements.

Knight-Ridder did not copy what is the essence of TV Guide—the television schedules and articles. It simply reproduced covers of old TV Guide issues. We do not mean to trivialize the covers of TV Guide, but simply emphasize that this factor would have been entitled to more weight had, for example, some of the contents been used.

The fourth factor to analyze under § 107—the factor which is widely accepted to be the most important, is the effect of the use upon the potential market for, or the value of, the copyrighted work. We are simply unable to find any effect—other than possibly de minimus—on the commercial value of the copyright. To be sure, the Herald's advertisements may have had the effect of drawing customers away from TV Guide. But this results from the nature of advertising itself and in no way stems from the fact that TV Guide covers were used. Indeed, assuming that TV Guide covers offer positive artistic enjoyment, the reproduction of these covers in the Herald's ads may have shown why TV Guide is a better product than the Herald's guide and may have decreased the effectiveness of the ads. At no point has Triangle offered a cogent explanation of the logical link between the showing of TV Guide covers and the alleged harm to the copyright. We cannot see it. * * *

Applying the four factors specified in § 107—and giving heavy emphasis to the fourth factor—we conclude that the fair use defense applies in this case and that the District Court erred in holding that it did not. We simply cannot see how Triangle was harmed by the Herald's advertisements. Moreover, the public as well as the Herald benefits from comparative advertising, thus minimizing the importance of the fact that a commercial use was involved.

* * *

We affirm the decision of the District Court denying Triangle's motions for preliminary and permanent injunctions. * * *

Affirmed.

Pacific and Southern Co. v. Duncan

United States Court of Appeals, Eleventh Circuit, 1984.
744 F.2d 1490.

■ JOHNSON, CIRCUIT JUDGE:

[WXIA], a television station, charges that Carol Duncan, d/b/a TV News Clips, has infringed its copyright by videotaping its news broadcasts and selling the tapes to the subjects of the news reports. We hold that the appellant has violated the copyright laws because her activities do not constitute "fair use" of the material. We also conclude that the television station is entitled to a permanent injunction preventing the appellant from continuing to infringe its copyright. Accordingly, we affirm in part and reverse in part.

I. Facts

* * * WXIA-TV, a television station in Atlanta, Georgia * * * broadcasts four local news programs each day and places a notice of copyright at

the end of each newscast. A program consists of self-contained news stories originating outside the studio and linked together by live commentary from the anchor persons, along with weather reports and shorter news reports originating from the studio itself. WXIA records the entire program on videotape and audiotape. It retains a written transcript of the program for a year and the audiotape for an indefinite period of time; it also maintains videotape copies of all the news stories taped before broadcast and stories originating live from a location outside the studio. The station erases the videotape of the entire program after seven days, a practice that destroys any record of the visual element of segments of the show broadcast live from within the studio.

WXIA does not currently market videotape copies of its news stories. Nevertheless, some people ask the station for a chance to view a tape at the station or to purchase a copy for personal use. WXIA has always honored requests to view tapes and usually allows persons to buy the tapes they want.[1] The revenue from tape sales is a small portion of WXIA's total profits.

Carol Duncan operates a business known as TV News Clips, a commercial enterprise belonging to a nationwide association of news clipping organizations.[2] TV News Clips videotapes television news programs, identifies the persons and organizations covered by the news reports, and tries to sell them copies of the relevant portion of the newscast.[3] It does not seek the permission of WXIA or any other broadcaster before selling the tapes, nor does it place a notice of copyright on the tapes. A label on each tape does say, however, that it is "for personal use only not for rebroadcast." TV News Clips erases all tapes after one month.

This case began when TV News Clips sold a copy of a news feature to Floyd Junior College, the subject of a story aired by WXIA on March 11, 1981. WXIA obtained the tape purchased by Floyd Junior College, registered its copyright,[4] and brought this action to obtain damages for the infringement of its copyright and an injunction preventing unauthorized copying and sales of its news program. The district court found that the news feature was protected by the copyright laws and that TV News Clips had not made "fair use" of the material. It rejected the fair use defense without reaching the four factors listed in 17 U.S.C. § 107 (1977), because TV News Clips had not met its threshold burden of showing that its activity served a purpose such as "criticism, comment, news reporting, teaching * * * scholarship, or research," categories listed in the preamble to Section 107. Yet despite finding that TV News Clips had clearly violated WXIA's copyright, the district

---

1. The tapes cost one hundred dollars. WXIA will not sell tapes to political candidates because the sale could appear to be an endorsement or other show of support for the candidate. Out of a similar concern over favoritism, the station asks for a subpoena before selling a tape that will be used in litigation.

2. TV News Clips belongs to the International Association of Broadcast Monitors, an organization of 20 to 30 members. Ms. Duncan is a past president of the association.

3. The customers pay $65 for an initial purchase and $25 for subsequent purchases.

4. WXIA does not normally register the copyright for its news programs.

court denied the request for an injunction for three reasons. First, the sales did not seriously threaten WXIA's creativity, so an injunction would not significantly further the main objective of the copyright laws, fostering creativity. Second, the court feared that an injunction would threaten First Amendment values served by the increased public availability of the news made possible by TV News Clips. Finally, the court found that WXIA had abandoned its copyright on several portions of the newscasts; it declined to formulate a decree that would distinguish between the abandoned and unabandoned portions.

II. "Fair Use" Defense to Statutory Liability

The news feature broadcast by WXIA undoubtedly falls within the protection of the copyright laws. The editorial judgment used to present effectively the events covered by the broadcast made it an "original" work of authorship, and the feature became "fixed" in a tangible medium when it was recorded at the time of transmission.[5] Thus, it met the requirements of 17 U.S.C. § 102. The fact that the infringing tape is the only exact copy of the transmission still in existence does not nullify the copyright. The statute requires only that the original work be "fixed" for a period of "more than transitory duration," not for the entire term of the copyright. 17 U.S.C. §§ 101, 102.

* * *

TV News Clips argued in the district court that its use of the news broadcast was a fair use of the material because it served an important societal interest in full access to the news. The court rejected the fair use defense without considering the four statutory factors because TV News Clips did not copy and distribute the material for purposes such as the ones listed in the preamble. The district court reasoned that since TV News Clips' use was not "inherently productive or creative," like each of the preamble uses, analysis of the four factors was unnecessary.

We agree with TV News Clips that the district court should have considered the four factors set out in the statute. The statute uses mandatory language to the effect that in a fair use determination, the "factors to be considered *shall* include" (emphasis added) the four listed. The preamble merely illustrates the sorts of uses likely to qualify as fair uses under the four listed factors.

* * * The district court fashioned a per se rule that a use must be inherently productive or creative before it can be a fair use, but a doctrine meant to resolve unforeseen conflicts of values should not turn on such a narrow inquiry. The Supreme Court, in its recent fair use decision in Sony Corp. v. Universal City Studios, 464 U.S. 417 (1984), did not conduct any preliminary tests before analyzing the four statutory factors. It expressly refused to look to productivity alone in determining what constituted a fair use. Id. at n. 40. * * *

---

5. The feature in this case was prerecorded, but the final product broadcast by WXIA included a live introduction by the anchor person and graphics (stating the reporter's name and location) superimposed over the pretaped version.

Despite the district court's erroneous interpretation of the law, we need not remand this case for further factfinding. The district court resolved all the issues of fact necessary for us to conclude as a matter of law that TV News Clips' activities do not qualify as a fair use of the copyrighted work. See Triangle Publications, Inc. v. Knight-Ridder Newspapers, Inc., 626 F.2d 1171, 1175 (5th Cir. 1980) (analyzing usage under the four statutory factors where district court had made findings under an erroneous view of controlling legal principles).

The purpose and character of TV News Clips' use of WXIA's work heavily influences our decision in this case. TV News Clips copies and distributes the broadcast for unabashedly commercial reasons despite the fact that its customers buy the tapes for personal use. The district court characterized TV News Clips as a "full-fledged commercial operation." TV News Clips denies that its activities have a commercial purpose; instead, it says that its purpose is "private news reporting," meant to provide the public with a record of news reports. Of course, every commercial exchange of goods and services involves both the giving of the good or service and the taking of the purchase price. The fact that TV News Clips focuses on the giving rather than the taking cannot hide the fact that profit is its primary motive for making the exchange.

* * *

We also note that TV News Clips' use is neither productive nor creative in any way. It does not analyze the broadcast or improve it at all. Indeed, WXIA expressed concern over the technical inferiority of the tapes. TV News Clips only copies and sells. As the uses listed in the preamble to Section 107 indicate, fair uses are those that contribute in some way to the public welfare. * * *

The fourth fair use factor, the effect on the potential market for the work, is closely related to the first. By examining the effect of a use, a reviewing court can measure the success of the original purpose and single out those purposes that most directly threaten the incentives for creativity which the copyright tries to protect. Some commercial purposes, for example, might not threaten the incentives because the user profits from an activity that the owner could not possibly take advantage of. See Triangle Publications, Inc. v. Knight-Ridder Newspapers, Inc., supra. But in this case, TV News Clips uses the broadcasts for a purpose that WXIA might use for its own benefit. The fact that WXIA does not actively market copies of the news programs does not matter, for Section 107 looks to the "potential market" in analyzing the effects of an alleged infringement. Copyrights protect owners who immediately market a work no more stringently than owners who delay before entering the market. TV News Clips sells a significant number of copies that WXIA could itself sell if it so desired; therefore, TV News Clips competes with WXIA in a potential market and thereby injures the television station. This evidence is reinforced by a presumption established in *Sony* that a commercial use naturally produces harmful effects. 104 S.Ct. at 793. The actual harmful effect, along with the presumption, undermines any fair use defense.

The third factor directs our attention to the amount and substantiality of the portion used in relation to the copyrighted work as a whole. The Floyd Junior College story stands alone as a coherent narrative, and WXIA saves it as a distinct unit for future reference apart from the rest of the March 11 broadcast. The Register of Copyrights issued a certificate of copyright for the Floyd Junior College segment and for the entire broadcast. Moreover, the district court found that WXIA had properly registered the story and the whole broadcast.[9] We agree with the district court that the feature stands alone as a copyrighted work in this case.[10] Hence, TV News Clips copied an entire work. And even if the story could not stand independent of the entire newscast, we could not ignore the fact that TV News Clips tapes virtually all of the broadcast on a daily basis. By bringing a suit for injunctive relief as well as damages, WXIA is challenging the entire practice of copying and selling news stories, not just the sale of the Floyd Junior College story.[11] Because TV News Clips uses virtually all of a copyrighted work, the fair use defense drifts even further out of its reach.

Finally, the second factor calls on us to analyze the nature of the copyrighted work. This is the only factor that arguably works in favor of TV News Clips. The importance to society of the news could affect the definition of a fair use for a number of reasons.[12] But the courts should also take care not to discourage authors from addressing important topics for fear of losing their copyright protections. The necessarily limited impact of this second factor, along with the commercial and unproductive purpose of the use, the injury to the potential market, and the substantial amount of copying, leads us to conclude that TV News Clips has not made fair use of the protected work.

* * *

9. TV News Clips contends that the district court erred in its finding that WXIA had properly registered the Floyd Junior College story because WXIA had deposited, pursuant to 17 U.S.C. § 408(b) (1977), the copy made by News Clips. This invalidated the registration, it argues, because the copy was not fixed "under authority of the author." It is true that a work must be fixed under authority of the author in order for the protections of copyright to take effect. 17 U.S.C. § 101 (1977). But the tape that "fixes" a broadcast need not be the same tape that is deposited for registration.

10. This case differs from Triangle Publications, Inc. v. Knight-Ridder Newspapers, Inc., supra, where the court held that the cover of a magazine was not a copyrighted work apart from the whole magazine. There was no evidence in that case that the cover had been registered apart from the magazine or that they were stored or used separately.

11. In addition, we mention that a small portion of a work may be especially significant. The single story involving a particular

subject is by far the most significant portion of the newscast for that potential customer.

12. The Supreme Court has mentioned that use of a news program may give rise to a fair use defense more easily than use of a full-length motion picture. Sony, supra, 104 S.Ct. at 795, n. 40. The Court does not fully explain this distinction, but the context sugests that the large secondary market for motion picture copies makes fair use less appropriate in that context. As discussion of the fourth factor revealed, significant commercial harm is present in this case. Another court found that the great public interest in the contents of a book (the memoirs of Gerald Ford) called for application of the fair use doctrine. Harper & Row, Publishers, Inc. v. National Enterprises, 723 F.2d 195 (2d Cir. 1983). But the Harper & Row court also relied on other factors, particularly the fact that the alleged infringer used material from the book that was for the most part not copyrightable at all. Furthermore, the public interest in the average news story is far less than the interest in presidential memoirs.

[Part III of the opinion, rejecting defendant's First Amendment defense, is omitted.]

IV. Remedy

WXIA has proven that TV News Clips infringed its copyright. The district court found that TV News Clips had regularly copied the newscast and sold the tapes, and would continue to do so. Unless it can obtain an injunction, WXIA can only enforce its copyrights against TV News Clips by finding out which stories have been copied and sold, registering those stories, and bringing many different infringement actions against TV News Clips. Each infringement action would yield a rather small damage recovery. This is a classic case, then, of a past infringement and a substantial likelihood of future infringements which would normally entitle the copyright holder to a permanent injunction against the infringer pursuant to 17 U.S.C. § 502(a). The question is whether the district court abused its discretion in refusing to issue the injunction.[17] Because none of the three grounds relied upon by the court for denying injunctive relief are legally sufficient to support the decision, we hold that the court did abuse its discretion.

The court began its discussion by noting that an injunction would not greatly further the ends of the copyright laws, because the post-broadcast market is relatively unimportant to WXIA as a creative incentive. We agree but find that fact standing alone to be irrelevant. The disincentive to creativity caused by the infringement would be just as small if WXIA were to wait and bring infringement actions in the future. The weakness of WXIA's interest in stopping this infringement has no bearing on the choice between present injunctive relief and future damage relief unless some independent consideration weighs against the use of an injunction in this case.

The "modest" furtherance of First Amendment rights accomplished by TV News Clips, the second ground relied upon by the court, does not provide any such independent reason to disfavor an injunction. It is undoubtedly true that TV News Clips (like any copyright infringer) increases public access to the copyrighted work. But the First Amendment issue of public access was duly considered when resolving the liability issue. If the First

---

17. TV News Clips insists that WXIA is not legally entitled to an injunction, because it seeks an injunction against the infringement of works that have not been created (future newscasts) rather than an injunction applicable only to the March 11 program. The statute itself does not impose such a requirement, for it empowers district courts to issue injunctions "on such terms as it may deem reasonable to prevent or restrain infringement of a copyright." 17 U.S.C. § 502(a) (1977). The appellant bases its argument on the requirement that an author register a work before instituting an infringement action. 17 U.S.C. § 411 (1977). An injunction against the use of unregistered works would bypass this requirement.

The district court in this case had the power to issue such an injunction because the statute provides for injunctions to prevent infringement of "a copyright" (emphasis added), not necessarily the registered copyright that gave rise to the infringement action. The opposite result would be especially unjust in a case such as this one in which the registered work and the future works are so closely related, part of a series of original works created with predictable regularity and similar format and function. To refuse injunctive relief under these conditions would render meaningless the fact that registration is "not a condition of copyright protection." 17 U.S.C. § 408(a).

Amendment would not prevent WXIA from recovering for individual infringements in the future, it should not bar an injunction in the present. The scope of liability affects First Amendment interests, but the choice of the form of relief in this case does not.

Finally, the district court found injunctive relief inappropriate because WXIA regularly abandons the copyright on a portion of its program when it erases the videotape of the entire broadcast. Certainly the erasure shows that WXIA did not desire to distribute post-broadcast copies of parts of the program. Failure to distribute a work does not mean, however, that an owner intends to allow others to use the work, and it is questionable whether WXIA had such an intent. Destroying the only known copy of a work would seem to be the best way to assure that it will not be used by another. Still, we do not say that destruction of the only copy of a work can never establish intent to abandon. We defer to the trial court's factual finding that WXIA intended to abandon portions of its program.

Nevertheless, WXIA erased only a small portion of its broadcast. The entire audiotape still survives, along with many portions of the videotape. The district court, while recognizing this fact, declined to issue an injunction against the use of segments of the news program not erased by WXIA. It said that "the precise wording of an appropriately limited decree is unapparent." The fact that a court must make some difficult judgments should not prevent it from effectuating established legal rights. Moreover, the clear-cut test used by the district court to find an intent to abandon the copyright (destruction of the only copy) should make the formulation of the decree more manageable.

Thus, the trial court relied on irrelevant and insufficient grounds in its refusal to grant injunctive relief. It correctly found that TV News Clips had infringed the copyright of WXIA but abused its discretion by refusing to grant injunctive relief. Accordingly, the judgment is affirmed in part, reversed in part, and remanded for further proceedings consistent with this opinion.

NOTES

1. If TV News Clips had been engaged in fair use, what legal uses could the purchaser make of recordings purchased from TV News Clips?

2. Can anyone make and keep copies of copyrighted newscasts and other informational television programming? Such programs contain a wealth of information about contemporary society, and could be a valuable resource for future historians. If the television stations themselves do not go to the time and trouble to preserve them, does that mean they are lost forever? Section 108(a) appears to authorize any qualifying library or archive to make one copy of television broadcasts as long as the "reproduction or distribution is made without any purpose of direct or indirect commercial advantage." Section 108(f) permits "reproduction and distribution by lending of a limited number of copies and excerpts by a library or archives of an audiovisual news program [but no other type of program]."

Does limiting this activity to the noncommercial sector assure that there will be little of it? Is that a wise policy?

The American Television and Radio Archives Act, 5 U.S.C. § 170, authorizes the Librarian of Congress to establish an American Radio and Television Archive within the Library of Congress, to record newscasts off the air, and to distribute reproductions to libraries or archives which meet the requirements of § 108(a) "for use only in research and not for further reproduction or performance." Does that solve any problem?

3. The reliance by the district judge in *Pacific and Southern Co.* on the discretion of a court to refuse to issue an injunction has been an alternative theme in some fair use decisions. It was the principal ground of decision in Rosemont Enterprises v. Random House, 366 F.2d 303 (2d Cir. 1966), noted supra, where the court felt the injunction was sought not to further the purpose of the copyright laws (compensation for works of authorship) but to suppress information about Howard Hughes.

In [Judith Jacklin] Belushi v. [Bob] Woodward, 598 F.Supp. 36 (D.D.C. 1984), the defendant had written *Wired: The Short Life & Fast Times of John Belushi.* The book contained numerous photographs, including one entitled "John and Nena" which plaintiff claimed belonged to her and had been used without permission. One hundred and seventy-five thousand copies of the book had been printed, of which 145,000 had been distributed to bookstores. Plaintiff sought a preliminary injunction against distribution of the 30,000 copies remaining in the publisher's possession. "Defendants assert that if relief issues their carefully orchestrated and costly plans for selling and marketing the book will be disrupted, costing them a substantial amount in lost sales. Defendants emphasize that successful marketing of a book like *Wired* depends upon the coordination of advertising, serialization, author appearances, and reviews, and the release to the public of the book." Injunction denied. "The public interest clearly favors maintaining the integrity of the copyright laws. In this case, however, it appears that legal remedies would vindicate any rights that may have been impinged [through the award of damages]. Further, there is a competing public interest in this case: the promotion of free expression and robust debate. If this were a case in which relief would enjoin the distribution of an average commercial product, relief would not be so drastic." 598 F.Supp. 37.

How is the court to compute damages? What is the value of a single picture which was by itself probably not necessary for the book and which would have limited alternative commercial uses? Or will the amount of the recovery be determined in part by the success of the book, so that a remedy which undermines its effective promotion harms both parties? Suppose the plaintiff had refused to license the use of the photo at any price? Same result?

4. If the fact that the copyright owner does not itself exploit the copyright in the market being exploited by the defendant is a factor favoring fair use, what happens if the copyright owner subsequently decides to enter the defendant's market? Does the infringement then cease to be fair use? In National Business Lists, Inc. v. Dun & Bradstreet, Inc., 552 F.Supp. 89 (N.D. Ill. 1982), Dun & Bradstreet did not at first object when National Business Lists began using information from Dun & Bradstreet directories to create a computerized data base that enabled it to produce mailing lists with particular characteristics—for instance, businesses of a certain size, or in certain product markets, or located in certain places. After National Business had developed this business, Dun & Bradstreet decided to itself enter the field of providing specialized mailing lists using its own information. The court held that because of National Business List's reliance on Dun & Bradstreet's failure to object, that Dun & Bradstreet was estopped from using its copyright to stop the practice—even as to future editions of the Dun & Bradstreet Directories.

PROBLEMS

1. Can individuals who are interested in the TV news (or what the TV news is saying about them) make copies of newscasts on their own VCR's, and save them for review or a possible defamation suit?

2. If the answer to one is yes, can individuals hire a service like that of TV Clips to do the recording for them, with an advance understanding that a copy will be made available if the newscast is of interest to the subscribing client?

3. WXIA had the policy of not providing tapes to political candidates, see note 1 of the opinion. Could TV Clips provide its service to political candidates only?

Ringgold v. Black Entertainment Television, Inc.

United States Court of Appeals for the Second Circuit, 1997.
126 F.3d 70.

■ JON O. NEWMAN, CIRCUIT JUDGE:

This appeal primarily concerns the scope of copyright protection for a poster of an artistic work that was used as set decoration for a television program. Faith Ringgold appeals from the September 24, 1996, judgment of the District Court * * * dismissing, on motion for summary judgment, her copyright infringement suit against Black Entertainment Television, Inc. ("BET") and Home Box Office, Inc. ("HBO"). The District Court sustained defendants' defense of fair use. We conclude that summary judgment was not warranted, and we therefore reverse and remand for further consideration of plaintiff's claim.

BACKGROUND

1. *The copyrighted work.* Faith Ringgold is a successful contemporary artist who created, and owns the copyright in, a work of art entitled "Church Picnic Story Quilt" * * *. "Church Picnic" is an example of a new form of artistic expression that Ringgold has created. She calls the form a "story quilt design." These designs consist of a painting, a handwritten text, and quilting fabric, all three of which Ringgold unites to communicate parables. The painting is a silk screen on silk quilt. "Church Picnic" is an example of

this unusual art form, conveying aspects of the African-American experience in the early 1900's. The painting component of the work depicts a Sunday school picnic held by the Freedom Baptist Church in Atlanta, Georgia, in 1909. Above and below the painting are twelve numbered panels containing a text written in the idiomatic African-American dialect of the era.

The text relates the thoughts of a parishioner who attended the picnic and is waiting to tell her daughter about it when the daughter comes home. The parishioner's daughter is in love with the church pastor, but, as depicted in the painting, the pastor is in love with another woman, and he soon will ask that other woman to marry him. Because the young woman was born out-of-wedlock, the pastor's "high-brow" family is dismayed by the prospect of the imminent engagement. Surrounding the text and painting is a quilted border, consisting of multi-colored triangular shapes of fabric. The very edge of the work is finished with a thin red welt.

Although Ringgold has retained all rights in the copyright in "Church Picnic," the work itself is owned by the High Museum of Art * * * in Atlanta, Georgia. Since 1988 the High Museum has held a non-exclusive license to reproduce "Church Picnic" as a poster * * *, and to sell those reproductions. The "Church Picnic" poster sells for $20.00 a copy and was not produced as a limited edition. Thousands of copies of the poster have been sold since 1988. Although the license to reproduce poster copies of "Church Picnic" has terminated, copies of the poster remain available for sale.

Below the portion of the poster that displays "Church Picnic" are several identifying words. "High Museum of Art" appears in letters 1 1/4 inches high. Below these words is the phrase "Faith Ringgold, *Church Picnic Story Quilt*, 1988, gift of Don and Jill Childress" in letters 1/8 inch high. Below this line, in smaller type, appears "Courtesy Bernice Steinbaum Gallery, New York City. Poster 1988 High Museum of Art, Atlanta."

2. *The alleged infringing use.* HBO Independent Productions, a division of HBO, produced "ROC," a television "sitcom" series concerning a middle-class African-American family living in Baltimore. Some time prior to 1992, HBO Independent Productions produced an episode of ROC in which a "Church Picnic" poster, presumably sold by the High Museum, was used as part of the set decoration.

The title character of "ROC" lives with his wife, Eleanor, his adult brother, Joey, and his father. In the episode in question, Roc pressures Joey, a jazz trumpeter, into giving trumpet lessons to some children in the church congregation, so that Joey, a perpetually unemployed gambler, can earn money to repay a debt he owes to Roc. After the children have taken some lessons, the minister of the church suggests that they give a recital in the newly-remodeled church hall. A five-minute scene of the recital concludes the episode. The "Church Picnic" poster was used as a wall-hanging in the church hall.

As the church audience waits to hear the recital, Roc and Eleanor are standing in the background of the scene, next to the audience and slightly to the left of the poster. The minister is also standing in the background, slightly to the right of the poster. The children play very poorly, and it is evident to Roc and Eleanor that Joey has not taught them anything. The scene and the episode conclude with parents of some of the children thanking Joey for the lessons, each set of parents believing that their child played on key but was drowned out by the other children.

In the scene, at least a portion of the poster is shown a total of nine times. In some of those instances, the poster is at the center of the screen, although nothing in the dialogue, action, or camera work particularly calls the viewer's attention to the poster. The nine sequences in which a portion of the poster is visible range in duration from 1.86 to 4.16 seconds. The aggregate duration of all nine sequences is 26.75 seconds. We describe these sequences in more detail below.

The copy of the poster used in the episode was framed without the identifying wording that appears beneath the artwork. As framed, the poster includes a notice of copyright, but the type is too small to be discernible to a television viewer.

A broadcast television network first televised the episode in 1992, and in October 1994 BET aired the episode for the first time on cable television. In January 1995, Ringgold happened to watch the episode on BET (apparently a repeat showing), and at that time became aware of the defendants' use of the poster as part of the set decoration.

3. *District Court proceedings.* Ringgold sued the defendants, alleging infringement of her copyright in "Church Picnic Story Quilt," in violation of 17 U.S.C. § 106 (1994), because of the unauthorized use of the poster as part of the set decoration for the episode of "ROC." The complaint also alleged common law unfair competition and a violation of New York's statute protecting artistic authorship rights. See N.Y. Arts & Cult. Aff. Law § 14.03 (McKinney Supp. 1995).

Prior to discovery, the defendants moved for summary judgment, contending (i) that they were not liable for copyright infringement, because their use of the story quilt was either *de minimis* or a fair use, (ii) that the unfair competition claim was preempted by the Copyright Act, and (iii) that either (a) the plaintiff had not stated a claim under the Artists' Authorship Rights Law, or (b) the Court should decline to exercise supplemental jurisdiction over that state law claim. Ringgold cross-moved for a preliminary injunction to prevent further displays of her art in the sitcom episode.

The District Court denied the plaintiff's motion for a preliminary injunction, granted defendants' motion for summary judgment, and dismissed the complaint. Apparently accepting, or at least assuming, that the plaintiff had sufficiently alleged a claim of copyright infringement, Judge Martin rejected her infringement claim on the ground that undisputed facts established the defendants' fair use defense. He then dismissed her unfair competition claim on the ground of preemption, which she did not dispute, and declined to exercise supplemental jurisdiction over her remaining state law claim.

DISCUSSION

The Copyright Act grants certain exclusive rights to the owner of a copyright, see 17 U.S.C. § 106 (1994), including the right to make and distribute copies and derivative works based on the copyrighted work, and the right to display the copyrighted work publicly, id. § 106(1)–(3), (5). In the absence of defenses, these exclusive rights normally give a copyright owner the right to seek royalties from others who wish to use the copyrighted work. See American Geophysical Union v. Texaco, Inc., 60 F.3d 913, 929 (2d Cir. 1994, as amended, July 17, 1995) * * *; see also DC Comics, Inc. v. Reel Fantasy, Inc., 696 F.2d 24, 28 (2d Cir. 1982) (noting that one benefit of owning a copyright is the right to license its use for a fee). Ringgold contends that the defendants violated this licensing right by using the "Church Picnic" poster to decorate the set of their sitcom without her authorization.

The caselaw provides little illumination concerning claims that copyright in a visual work has been infringed by including it within another visual work. Compare Woods v. Universal City Studios, Inc., 920 F.Supp. 62 (S.D.N.Y. 1996) (film infringed architectural drawing), with Monster Communications, Inc. v. Turner Broadcasting System, Inc., 935 F.Supp. 490 (S.D.N.Y. 1996) (preliminary injunction denied to bar showing of film that included copyrighted film clips). The Nimmer treatise posits the problem of a motion picture in which an actor is reading a magazine of which the cover picture is observable, and acknowledges that "[t]he answer is by no means certain." See 4 Melville B. Nimmer & David Nimmer, Nimmer on Copyright § 13.05 [D][3], at 13–229 (1997) ("Nimmer"). The treatise observes, with uncharacteristic ambivalence, that a fair use defense might be supported on the ground that "the entire work does not supplant the function of the plaintiff's work," yet also points out that "ordinarily" the copying of a magazine cover into another medium "will constitute infringement, and not fair use." Id.

HBO and BET defend their use of the poster on two separate, though related grounds: (a) that their use of the poster was *de minimis*, and (b) that, as Judge Martin ruled, their use of the poster was a permissible "fair use," see 17 U.S.C. § 107.

The legal maxim "*de minimis non curat lex*" (sometimes rendered, "the law does not concern itself with trifles") insulates from liability those who cause insignificant violations of the rights of others. In the context of copyright law, the concept of *de minimis* has significance in three respects, which, though related, should be considered separately.

First, *de minimis* in the copyright context can mean what it means in most legal contexts: a technical violation of a right so trivial that the law will not impose legal consequences. Understandably, fact patterns are rarely litigated illustrating this use of the phrase, for, as Judge Leval has observed, such circumstances would usually involve "[q]uestions that never need to be answered." Pierre N. Leval, Nimmer Lecture: Fair Use Rescued, 44 U.C.L.A. L. Rev. 1449, 1457 (1997). He offers the example of a New Yorker cartoon put up on a refrigerator.[2] In Knickerbocker Toy Co. v. Azrak-Hamway International, Inc., 668 F.2d 699, 703 (2d Cir. 1982), we relied on

---

2. Presumably, Judge Leval has in mind the posting of a photocopy of the cartoon; photocopying the cartoon, if not insulated by the doctrine of *de minimis*, or subject to some recognized defense, might violate the copyright proprietor's right to reproduce a copy of the work, see 17 U.S.C. § 106(1), though if the original page of the magazine was posted, the work would not have been "display[ed] . . . publicly," id. § 106(5).

the *de minimis* doctrine to reject a toy manufacturer's claim based on a photograph of its product in an office copy of a display card of a competitor's product where the display card was never used. See id. at 702.

Second, *de minimis* can mean that copying has occurred to such a trivial extent as to fall below the quantitative threshold of substantial similarity, which is always a required element of actionable copying. * * *

In the pending case, there is no dispute about copying as a factual matter: the "Church Picnic" poster itself, not some poster that was similar in some respects to it, was displayed on the set of defendants' television program. What defendants dispute when they assert that their use of the poster was *de minimis* is whether the admitted copying occurred to an extent sufficient to constitute actionable copying, i.e., infringement. That requires "substantial similarity" in the sense of actionable copying, and it is that sense of the phrase to which the concept of *de minimis* is relevant.

* * *

Third, *de minimis* might be considered relevant to the defense of fair use. One of the statutory factors to be assessed in making the fair use determination is "the amount and substantiality of the portion used in relation to the copyrighted work as a whole," 17 U.S.C. § 107(3) (emphasis added). A defendant might contend, as the District Court concluded in this case, that the portion used was minimal and the use was so brief and indistinct as to tip the third fair use factor decisively against the plaintiff.[4]

Though the concept of *de minimis* is useful in insulating trivial types of copying from liability (the photocopied cartoon on the refrigerator) and in marking the quantitative threshold for actionable copying, see, e.g., Vault Corp. v. Quaid Software, Ltd., 847 F.2d 255, 267 (5th Cir. 1988) (30 characters out of 50 pages of source code held *de minimis*), the concept is an inappropriate one to be enlisted in fair use analysis. The third fair use factor concerns a quantitative continuum. Like all the fair use factors, it has no precise threshold below which the factor is accorded decisive significance. If the amount copied is very slight in relation to the work as a whole, the third factor might strongly favor the alleged infringer, but that will not always be the case. See, e.g., Iowa State University Research Foundation, Inc. v. American Broadcasting Companies, Inc., 621 F.2d 57, 59, 61–62 (2d Cir. 1980) (television program's copying of portions of copyrighted film, including an eight second segment). More important, the fair use defense involves a careful examination of many factors, often confronting courts with a perplexing task. If the allegedly infringing work makes such a quantitatively insubstantial use of the copyrighted work as to fall below the threshold required for actionable copying, it makes more sense to reject the claim on that basis and find

---

4. Whether a use of a copyrighted work that surpasses the *de minimis* threshold of "substantial similarity" for purposes of actionable copying can nevertheless be *de minimis* for purposes of the third fair use factor is an inquiry in the class of angelic terpsichore on heads of pins. Perhaps that is why the Supreme Court has quoted approvingly Professor Latman's reference to "the partial marriage between the doctrine of fair use and the legal maxim *de minimis non curat lex.*" See Sony Corp. of America v. Universal City Studios, Inc., 464 U.S. 417, 451 n. 34 (1984).

no infringement, rather than undertake an elaborate fair use analysis in order to uphold a defense.

* * *

Defendants contend that the nine instances in their television program in which portions of the poster were visible, individually and in the aggregate, were *de minimis*, in the sense that the quantity of copying (or at least the quantity of observable copying) was below the threshold of actionable copying. The parties appear to agree on the durational aspects of the copying. The segments of the program in which the poster was visible to any degree lasted between 1.86 and 4.16 seconds. The aggregate duration of all nine segments was 26.75 seconds.

The parties differ, at least in emphasis, as to the observability of what was copied. Our own inspection of a tape of the program reveals that some aspects of observability are not fairly in dispute. In the longest segment, between 4 and 5 seconds, nearly all of the poster, at least 80 percent, is visible. The camera is positioned to the right of about eight members of the audience seated on the left side of the center aisle (facing the stage), and the poster is on the wall immediately to the left of the end of the rows of two or three spectators. The minister stands to the right of the poster, partially obscuring the lower right quadrant, and a member of the audience stands to the left, partially obscuring the lower left quadrant. Roc and his wife stand farther to the left of the poster. The very top edge of the poster is not within the camera's "framing" of the scene. Since the camera focuses precisely on the members of the audience, the poster, hung to their left, is not in perfect focus, but it is so close to them that the poster is plainly observable, even though not in exact focus.[5] An observer can see that what is hung is some form of artwork, depicting a group of African-American adults and children with a pond in the background. The brevity of the segment and the lack of perfect focus preclude identification of the details of the work, but the two-dimensional aspect of the figures and the bold colors are seen in sufficient clarity to suggest a work somewhat in the style of Grandma Moses. Only the painting portion of the poster is observable; the text material and the bordering quilting cannot be discerned.

All the other segments are of lesser duration and/or contain smaller and less distinct portions of the poster.[6] However, their repetitive effect some-

---

5. The focus is such that the eight seated members of the audience who are visible and the four people standing along the wall to their left are all in clear focus. The poster is on the wall between two of these four people.

6. The segments are: (1) a long, wide-angle shot of the audience and a performer on the stage, with the full poster too indistinct for anything of significance to be discerned (between two and three seconds); (2) a full view of almost the entire poster, as observable as the segment described in the text, with the lower right and lower left portions partially obscured as Joey walks up the aisle (2 to 3 seconds); (3) a close-up view of the right half of the poster, with the lower right portion partially obscured by the minister, who is standing next to the poster and on whom the camera focuses (1 to 2 seconds); (4) the segment described in the text (4 to 5 seconds); (5) similar to segment (3) (3 to 4 seconds); (6) a view of the lower right quadrant, partially obscured by a person (3 to 4 seconds); (7) similar to segment (6) (3 to 4 seconds); (8) similar to segment (6) (2 to 3 seconds); (9) similar to segment (6) (1 to 2 seconds).

what reenforces the visual effect of the observable four-to-five-second segment just described.

A helpful analogy in determining whether the purpose and duration of the segments should be regarded as *de minimis* is the regulation issued by the Librarian of Congress providing for royalties to be paid by public broadcasting entities for the use of published pictorial and visual works. See 37 C.F.R. § 253.8 (1996) (implementing 17 U.S.C. § 118(b)). The Librarian appoints the Register of Copyrights, who serves as the director of the Copyright Office. See 17 U.S.C. § 701. The Librarian's regulation distinguishes between a "featured" and a "background" display, setting a higher royalty rate for the former. Id. § 253.8(b)(1)(i)(A), (B). Obviously the Librarian has concluded that use of a copyrighted visual work even as "background" in a television program normally requires payment of a license fee. Moreover, the Librarian has defined a "featured" display as "a full-screen or substantially full screen display for more than three seconds," id. § 253.8(b)(2), and a "background" display as "[a]ny display less than full-screen or substantially full-screen, or full-screen for three seconds or less," id. If defendants' program were to be shown on public television, plaintiff would appear to be entitled to a "background" license fee for a "less than full-screen" display.

From the standpoint of a quantitative assessment of the segments, the principal four-to-five-second segment in which almost all of the poster is clearly visible, albeit in less than perfect focus, reenforced by the briefer segments in which smaller portions are visible, all totaling 26 to 27 seconds, are not *de minimis* copying.

Defendants further contend that the segments showing any portion of the poster are *de minimis* from the standpoint of qualitative sufficiency and therefore not actionable copying because no protectable aspects of plaintiff's expression are discernible. In defendants' view, the television viewer sees no more than "some vague stylized [sic] painting that includes black people," Brief for Appellees at 18, and can discern none of Ringgold's particular expression of her subjects. That is about like saying that a videotape of the Mona Lisa shows only a painting of a woman with a wry smile. Indeed, it seems disingenuous for the defendant HBO, whose production staff evidently thought that the poster was well suited as a set decoration for the African-American church scene of a ROC episode, now to contend that no visually significant aspect of the poster is discernible. In some circumstances, a visual work, though selected by production staff for thematic relevance, or at least for its decorative value, might ultimately be filmed at such a distance and so out of focus that a typical program viewer would not discern any decorative effect that the work of art contributes to the set. But that is not this case. The painting component of the poster is recognizable as a painting, and with sufficient observable detail for the "average lay observer," see Rogers v. Koons, 960 F.2d 301, 307 (2d Cir. 1992) (internal quotation omitted), to discern African-Americans in Ringgold's colorful, virtually two-dimensional style. The *de minimis* threshold for actionable copying of protected expression has been crossed.

* * *

The District Court upheld the defendants' fair use defense after considering the four non-exclusive factors identified in 17 U.S.C. § 107. * * *. Concerning the first factor—purpose and character of the use—the Court acknowledged that defendants' use was commercial, but thought this circumstance was "undercut" by the fact that the defendants did not use the poster to encourage viewers to watch the ROC episode and did not try to "exploit" Ringgold's work. Ringgold v. Black Entertainment Television, No. 96 Civ. 0290, 1996 WL 535547, *3 (S.D.N.Y. Sept. 19, 1996). The Court acknowledged that the second factor—nature of the copyrighted work—favored Ringgold in view of the imaginative nature of her artwork.

The Court considered the third factor—amount and substantiality of the portion used in relation to the entire work—to favor the defendants because the segments of the program in which the poster is visible are brief, in some only a portion is seen, and in those showing nearly all the poster, it is not in exact focus.

The Court considered the fourth factor—effect of the use upon the potential market for the work—also to favor the defendants. Noting that the television episode cannot be considered a substitute for the poster, Judge Martin predicted "little likelihood" of any adverse impact on poster sales. Id., 1996 WL 535547 at *4. In addition, he observed that Ringgold did not claim that her ability to license the poster "has been negatively impacted by the defendants' use in the four years" since the episode was aired. Id. Concluding that defendants' use "had little or no effect on Ringgold's potential market for her work," id., he granted summary judgment in their favor, sustaining their fair use defense.

In reviewing the grant of summary judgment, we note preliminarily that the District Court gave no explicit consideration to whether the defendants' use was within any of the categories that the preamble to section 107 identifies as illustrative of a fair use, or even whether it was similar to such categories. Though the listed categories—criticism, comment, news reporting, teaching, scholarship, and research, see 17 U.S.C. § 107—have an "'illustrative and not limitative'" function, see Campbell v. Acuff-Rose Music, Inc., 510 U.S. 569, 577 (1994) (quoting 17 U.S.C. § 101), and the four factors should be considered even if a challenged use is not within any of these categories, see Pacific and Southern Co. v. Duncan, 744 F.2d 1490, 1495 (11th Cir.1984), the illustrative nature of the categories should not be ignored. As the Supreme Court's recent and significant fair use opinion in Campbell observes, "The enquiry [concerning the first fair use factor] may be guided by the examples given in the preamble to § 107, looking to whether the use is for criticism, or comment, or news reporting, and the like. . . ." Campbell, 510 U.S. at 578–79.

1. First factor. Considering the first fair use factor with the preamble illustrations as a "guide[ ]," id., we observe that the defendants' use of Ringgold's work to decorate the set for their television episode is not remotely similar to any of the listed categories. In no sense is the defen-

dants' use "'transformative,'" id. at 579 (quoting Pierre N. Leval, Toward a Fair Use Standard, 103 Harv. L. Rev. 1105, 1111 (1990)). In *Campbell*, Justice Souter explained a "transformative" use that would tip the first factor toward a defendant:

> The central purpose of this investigation is to see, in Justice Story's words, whether the new work merely "supersede[s] the objects" of the original creation, Folsom v. Marsh, [9 F. Cas. 342, 348 (C.C. Mass. 1841) (No. 4,901)]; accord, Harper & Row, [Publishers, Inc. v. Nation Enterprises], 471 U.S. [539, 562 (1985)] ("supplanting" the original), or instead adds something new, with a further purpose or different character, altering the first with new expression, meaning, or message. . . .

510 U.S. at 579.

The defendants have used Ringgold's work for precisely a central purpose for which it was created—to be decorative. Even if the thematic significance of the poster and its relevance to the ROC episode are not discernible, the decorative effect is plainly evident. Indeed, the poster is the only decorative artwork visible in the church hall scene. Nothing that the defendants have done with the poster "supplant[s]" the original or "adds something new." The defendants have used the poster to decorate their set to make it more attractive to television viewers precisely as a poster purchaser would use it to decorate a home.

In considering whether a visual work has been "supplant[ed]" by its use in a movie or a television program, care must be taken not to draw too close an analogy to copying of written works. When all or a substantial portion of text that contains protectable expression is included in another work, solely to convey the original text to the reader without adding any comment or criticism, the second work may be said to have supplanted the original because a reader of the second work has little reason to buy a copy of the original. Although some books and other writings are profitably reread, their basic market is the one- time reader. By contrast, visual works are created, and sold or licensed, usually for repetitive viewing. Thus, the fact that the episode of ROC does not supplant the need or desire of a television viewer to see and appreciate the poster (or the original) again and again does not mean that the defendants' use is of a "purpose and character" that favors fair use. Indeed, unauthorized displays of a visual work might often increase viewers' desire to see the work again. Nevertheless, where, as here, the purpose of the challenged use is, at a minimum, the same decorative purpose for which the poster is sold, the defendants' use has indeed "superseded the objects " of the original, see Folsom, 9 F. Cas. at 348 (emphasis added), and does not favor fair use. Of course, no one would buy a videotape of the ROC episode as a substitute for the poster, but the challenged use need not supplant the original itself, only, as Justice Story said, the "objects" of the original.

It is not difficult to imagine a television program that uses a copyrighted visual work for a purpose that heavily favors fair use. If a TV news program produced a feature on Faith Ringgold and included camera shots of her story quilts, the case for a fair use defense would be extremely strong.[11] The same would be true of a news feature on the High Museum that included a shot of "Church Picnic." See Italian Book Corp. v. American Broadcasting Cos., 458 F.Supp. 65 (S.D.N.Y. 1978) (fair use defense upheld for TV newscast of street festival that included copyrighted song). However, it must be recognized that visual works are created, in significant part, for their decorative value, and, just as members of the public expect to pay to obtain a painting or a poster to decorate their homes, producers of plays, films, and television programs should generally expect to pay a license fee when they conclude that a particular work of copyrighted art is an appropriate component of the decoration of a set.

The District Court's consideration of the first fair use factor was legally flawed in its failure to assess the decorative purpose for which defendants used the plaintiff's work. Instead, the Court tipped the first factor against the plaintiff because the presence of the poster was "incidental" to the scene and the defendants did not use the poster to encourage viewers to watch the ROC episode. The first point could be said of virtually all set decorations, thereby expanding fair use to permit wholesale appropriation of copyrighted art for movies and television. The second point uses a test that makes it far too easy for a defendant to invoke the fair use defense.[13]

2. *Second factor*. The District Court accepted the plaintiff's contention that the second fair use factor weighs in her favor because of the creative nature of her work.

3. *Third factor*. Though we have earlier noted that the *de minimis* concept is inappropriate for a fair use analysis, since a copying that is *de minimis* incurs no liability, without the need for an elaborate fair use inquiry, the third fair use factor obliges a court to consider the amount and substantiality of the portion used, whenever that portion crosses the *de minimis* threshold for actionable copying. The District Court properly considered the brevity of the intervals in which the poster was observable and the fact that in some segments only a portion of the poster and the nearly full view was not in precise focus. Our own viewing of the episode would incline us to weight the third factor less strongly toward the defendants than did Judge Martin, but we are not the fact-finders, and the fact-finding pertinent to each fair use factor, under proper legal standards, is for

---

11. We hesitate to say "conclusive" because even existing technological advances, much less those in the future, create extraordinary possibilities. For example, if the news program included a direct shot of an entire story quilt (whether original or poster reproduction), well lit and in clear focus, a viewer so inclined could tape the newscast at home, scan the tape, and with digital photographic technology, produce a full size copy of the original, thereby securing an attractive "poster"-like wall-hanging without paying the $20 poster fee. A news program that recom-

mended this technique would be a weak candidate for fair use.

13. To the extent that the defendants' good faith is relevant, see Rogers, 960 F.2d at 309, the fact-finder is entitled to consider that someone, likely a member of BET's production staff, cropped the poster before framing it so as to omit the legend identifying the poster with the High Museum. An available inference is that the production staff, if responsible, wanted the viewers to believe that the set was decorated with an original painting, rather than a poster reproduction.

the District Court, although the ultimate conclusion is a mixed question of law and fact, Harper & Row, 471 U.S. at 560, subject to *de novo* review, New Era Publications International, ApS v. Carol Publishing Group, 904 F.2d 152, 155 (2d Cir. 1990).

Even if the third factor favors the defendants, courts considering the fair use defense in the context of visual works copied or displayed in other visual works must be careful not to permit this factor too easily to tip the aggregate fair use assessment in favor of those whom the other three factors do not favor. Otherwise, a defendant who uses a creative work in a way that does not serve any of the purposes for which the fair use defense is normally invoked and that impairs the market for licensing the work will escape liability simply by claiming only a small infringement.

4. *Fourth factor.* The fourth fair use factor is "the effect of the use upon the potential market for or value of the copyrighted work." 17 U.S.C. § 107(4) (emphasis added). "It requires courts to consider not only the extent of market harm caused by the alleged infringer, but also 'whether unrestricted and widespread conduct of the sort engaged in by the defendant . . . would result in substantially adverse impact on the potential market for the original.'" *Campbell,* 510 U.S. at 590, (quoting Nimmer § 13.05 [A][4] (at 13–187 in 1997 edition)). Ringgold contends that there is a potential market for licensing her story quilts, Complaint ¶ 17, and stated in an affidavit that in 1995 she earned $31,500 from licensing her various artworks and that she is often asked to license her work for films and television. Affidavit of Faith Ringgold ¶¶ 13, 14. Specifically, she avers that in 1992 she was asked to license use of the "Church Picnic" poster by the producers of another TV sitcom and declined because of an inadequate price and inadequate artist's credit. Id. ¶ 15.

We have recognized the danger of circularity in considering whether the loss of potential licensing revenue should weight the fourth factor in favor of a plaintiff. See *American Geophysical,* at 929 n. 17, 931. Since the issue is whether the copying should be compensable, the failure to receive licensing revenue cannot be determinative in the plaintiff's favor. See id. at 931. We have endeavored to avoid the vice of circularity by considering "only traditional, reasonable, or likely to be developed markets" when considering a challenged use upon a potential market. See id. at 930; Nimmer § 13.05[A] [4], at 13–189. Ringgold's affidavit clearly raises a triable issue of fact concerning a market for licensing her work as set decoration. She is not alleging simply loss of the revenue she would have earned from a compensated copying; she is alleging an "exploitation of the copyrighted material without paying the customary price." See *Harper & Row,* 471 U.S. at 562 (emphasis added).[15]

The District Court's assessment of the fourth factor in favor of the defendants was legally flawed. The Court relied primarily on the fact that the ROC episode had little likelihood of adversely affecting poster sales and that Ringgold had not claimed that her ability to license the poster had been

---

15. The amicus curiae brief for the Artists Rights Society, Inc. and the Picasso Administration strongly indicates evidence of licensing of artistic works for film and television set decoration, evidence that plaintiff is entitled to present at trial.

"negatively impacted." 1996 WL 535547, at *4. The first consideration deserves little weight against a plaintiff alleging appropriation without payment of a customary licensing fee.[16] The second consideration confuses lack of one item of specific damages with lack of adverse impact on a potential market. See Nimmer § 13.05[A][4], at 13–187. Ringgold is not required to show a decline in the number of licensing requests for the "Church Picnic" poster since the ROC episode was aired. The fourth factor will favor her if she can show a "traditional, reasonable, or likely to be developed" market for licensing her work as set decoration. Certainly "unrestricted and widespread conduct of the sort engaged in by the defendant[s] . . . would result in substantially adverse impact on the potential market for [licensing of] the original." *Campbell,* 510 U.S. at 590 (internal quotation omitted). Particularly in view of what Ringgold has averred and is prepared to prove, the record on the fourth fair use factor is inadequate to permit summary judgment for the defendants. See id. at 593–94.

CONCLUSION

For all of these reasons, plaintiff's copyright infringement claim must be returned to the District Court to afford an opportunity for further development of the record and a sensitive aggregate assessment by the factfinder of the fair use factors in light of the applicable legal principles. Upon remand, the Court should give renewed consideration to plaintiff's claim under the New York Artists' Authorship Rights Act.[17] However, because Ringgold has not challenged the dismissal of her preempted unfair competition claim, we affirm the District Court's dismissal of that claim.

The judgment of the District Court is reversed, and the case is remanded.

---

16. Even if the unauthorized use of plaintiff's work in the televised program might increase poster sales, that would not preclude her entitlement to a licensing fee. See *DC Comics,* 696 F.2d at 28.

17. The New York Artists' Authorship Rights Act provides as follows:

1. [N]o person other than the artist or a person acting with the artist's consent shall knowingly display in a place accessible to the public or publish a work of fine art or limited edition multiple of not more than three hundred copies by that artist or a reproduction thereof in an altered, defaced, mutilated or modified form if the work is displayed, published or reproduced as being the work of the artist, or under circumstances under which it would reasonably be regarded as being the work of the artist, and damage to the artist's reputation is reasonably likely to result therefrom . . . .

2.(a) [T]he artist shall retain at all times the right to claim authorship, or, for just and valid reason, to disclaim authorship of such work. The right to claim authorship shall include the right of the artist to have his or her name appear on or in connection with such work as the artist.

. . . .

4.(a) An artist aggrieved under subdivision one or subdivision two of this section shall have a cause of action for legal and injunctive relief.

N.Y. Arts & Cult. Aff. Law § 14.03 (McKinney Supp. 1995). Ringgold claims that the defendants violated her statutory rights because they did not credit her as the creator of the story quilt. Though the defendants argued on various grounds that the statute does not apply to the facts alleged, the District Judge decided not to exercise supplemental jurisdiction over the claim. By our remand, we express no view as to the merits of this claim or of defendants' defenses

Educational, Archival and Non-Profit Use

Does the fact that infringement is undertaken in support of a particularly worthy or useful activity excuse the infringement? As a general matter, the answer is no. Sponsors of a charity benefit cannot make use of the popular songs of the day without paying a license fee simply because the fee will decrease the net amount raised. The owners of copyright are not singled out to provide subsidies to worthy causes through limitations on their rights. But the statute does not adhere strictly to this principle. Buried within sections 108 through 118 are sometimes economically substantial benefits for particular "good" organizations (usually nonprofit or governmental). They are briefly summarized below. No doubt a good deal of legal effort goes into construing the exact limits of these privileges as various groups maneuver to get within them.

Section 108 limits its privileges for libraries and archives to "reproduction or distribution * * * without any purpose of direct or indirect commercial advantage." The effect of this test is to limit these privileges for libraries maintained by for-profit, commercial organizations, or at least the House Report says that it is. See H.R. 94–1476, pp. 74–75.

Section 110 limits the exclusive rights of performance or display in a number of specific situations, many of which are defined in part by the character of the organization involved. Section 110(1) permits performance or display of works "by instructors or pupils in the course of face-to-face teaching activities of a nonprofit educational institution." Section 110(2) permits transmission of works into classrooms if "the performance or display is a regular part of the systematic instructional activities of a governmental body or a nonprofit educational institution." Section 110(3) permits performance or display in the course of religious services. Section 110(4) permits performance if there is no admission charge and the net proceeds "are used exclusively for educational, religious or charitable purposes," subject to the right of the copyright owner to object in advance. (There is no mechanism for ensuring that the copyright owner learns of the planned performance.) Section 110(6) confers limited protection on nonprofit agricultural or horticultural organizations in the course of annual fairs. Subsections (8) and (9) are designed to make specialized transmissions for the blind and deaf cheaper. Subsection (10) confers a special privilege upon nonprofit veterans' organizations or nonprofit fraternal organization where the net proceeds are for charitable purposes, with a more restrictive test applicable to college fraternities or sororities (lest every fraternity dance become an exempt occasion).

Section 111(4) confers a broad privilege of secondary transmission upon "a governmental body, or other nonprofit organization."

Section 114(b) protects public broadcasting entities who distribute educational television or radio programs from the copyright in the sound recording.

Section 118 confers upon public broadcasting stations the right to infringe copyrights, subject to the payment of royalties as determined by a copyright royalty arbitration panel.

Section 121 provides that it is not an infringement of copyright for an "authorized entity" "to reproduce or distribute copies or phonorecords of a previously published, nondramatic literary work if such copies or phonorecords are reproduced or distributed in specialized formats exclusively for use by blind or other persons with disabilities." The specialized formats include audio recordings, and an "authorized entity" is a "nonprofit organization or a governmental agency that has a primary mission to provide specialized services relating to training, education, or adaptive reading or information access needs of blind or other persons with disabilities." Section 121 was added by Public Law 104–197 (1996).

A major area of controversy during the consideration of the 1976 copyright act was the right of teachers to use copyrighted materials in the classroom. For instance a teacher might want to make copies of a poem for discussion in class, or to have the class perform a song in a school assembly. The wrath of the nation's teachers came down on the head of Congress when the National Education Association informed them that the new statute would make these practices infringement of copyright (failing to inform them that the existing statute already did. See Wihtol v. Crow, 309 F.2d 777 (8th Cir.1962), holding a music teacher liable for duplicating copies of his arrangement of a copyrighted song.) These concerns were addressed in guidelines, described as follows in House Report No. 94–1476.

House Report No. 94–1476
Pages 68–72.

Intention as to Classroom Reproduction

Although the works and uses to which the doctrine of fair use is applicable are as broad as the copyright law itself, most of the discussion of section 107 has centered around questions of classroom reproduction, particularly photocopying. The arguments on the question are summarized at pp. 30–31 of this Committee's 1967 report (H.R. Rep. No. 83, 90th Cong., 1st Sess.), and have not changed materially in the intervening years.

The Committee also adheres to its earlier conclusion, that "a specific exemption freeing certain reproductions of copyrighted works for educational and scholarly purposes from copyright control is not justified." At the same time the Committee recognizes, as it did in 1967, that there is a "need for greater certainty and protection for teachers." In an effort to meet this need the Committee has not only adopted further amendments to section 107, but has also amended section 504(c) to provide innocent teachers and other non-profit users of copyrighted material with broad insulation against unwarranted liability for infringement. * * *

In a joint letter to Chairman Kastenmeier, dated March 19, 1976, the representatives of the Ad Hoc Committee of Educational Institutions and Organizations on Copyright Law Revision, and of the Authors League of America, Inc., and the Association of American Publishers, Inc., stated:

You may remember that in our letter of March 8, 1976 we told you that the negotiating teams representing authors and publishers and the Ad Hoc Group had reached tentative agreement on guidelines to insert in the Committee Report covering educational copying from books and periodicals under Section 107 of H.R. 2223 and S. 22, and that as part of that tentative agreement each side would accept the amendments to Sections 107 and 504 which were adopted by your Subcommittee on March 3, 1976.

We are now happy to tell you that the agreement has been approved by the principals and we enclose a copy herewith. We had originally intended to translate the agreement into language suitable for inclusion in the legislative report dealing with Section 107, but we have since been advised by committee staff that this will not be necessary.

As stated above, the agreement refers only to copying from books and periodicals, and it is not intended to apply to musical or audiovisual works.

The full text of the agreement is as follows:

Agreement on Guidelines for Classroom Copying in Not For-Profit Educational Institutions

WITH RESPECT TO BOOKS AND PERIODICALS

The purpose of the following guidelines is to state the minimum standards of educational fair use under Section 107 of H.R. 2223. The parties agree that the conditions determining the extent of permissible copying for educational purposes may change in the future; that certain types of copying permitted under these guidelines may not be permissible in the future; and conversely that in the future other types of copying not permitted under these guidelines may be permissible under revised guidelines.

Moreover, the following statement of guidelines is not intended to limit the types of copying permitted under the standards of fair use under judicial decision and which are stated in Section 107 of the Copyright Revision Bill. There may be instances in which copying which does not fall within the guidelines stated below may nonetheless be permitted under the criteria of fair use.

GUIDELINES

I. *Single Copying for Teachers*

A single copy may be made of any of the following by or for a teacher at his or her individual request for his or her scholarly research or use in teaching or preparation to teach a class:

A. A chapter from a book;

B. An article from a periodical or newspaper;

C. A short story, short essay or short poem, whether or not from a collective work;

D. A chart, graph, diagram, drawing, cartoon or picture from a book, periodical, or newspaper.

II. *Multiple Copies for Classroom Use*

Multiple copies (not to exceed in any event more than one copy per pupil in a course) may be made by or for the teacher giving the course for classroom use or discussion; *provided that:*

A. The copying meets the tests of brevity and spontaneity as defined below; *and,*

B. Meets the cumulative effect test as defined below; *and,*

C. Each copy includes a notice of copyright.

Definitions

Brevity

(*i*) Poetry: (a) A complete poem if less than 250 words and if printed on not more than two pages or, (b) from a longer poem, an excerpt of not more than 250 words.

(*ii*) Prose: (a) Either a complete article, story or essay of less than 2,500 words, or (b) an excerpt from any prose work of not more than 1,000 words or 10% of the work, whichever is less, but in any event a minimum of 500 words.

[Each of the numerical limits stated in "i" and "ii" above may be expanded to permit the completion of an unfinished line of a poem or of an unfinished prose paragraph.]

(*iii*) Illustration: One chart, graph, diagram, drawing, cartoon or picture per book or per periodical issue.

(*iv*) "Special" works: Certain works in poetry, prose or in "poetry prose" which often combine language with illustrations and which are intended sometimes for children and at other times for a more general audience fall short of 2,500 words in their entirety. Paragraph "ii" above notwithstanding such "special works" may not be reproduced in their entirety; however, an excerpt comprising not more than two of the published pages of such special work and containing not more than 10% of the words found in the text thereof, may be reproduced.

Spontaneity

(*i*) The copying is at the instance and inspiration of the individual teacher, and

(*ii*) The inspiration and decision to use the work and the moment of its use for maximum teaching effectiveness are so close in time that it would be unreasonable to expect a timely reply to a request for permission.

Cumulative Effect

(*i*) The copying of the material is for only one course in the school in which the copies are made.

(*ii*) Not more than one short poem, article, story, essay or two excerpts may be copied from the same author, nor more than three from the same collective work or periodical volume during one class term.

(*iii*) There shall not be more than nine instances of such multiple copying for one course during one class term.

[The limitations stated in "ii" and "iii" above shall not apply to current news periodicals and newspapers and current news sections of other periodicals.]

III. *Prohibitions as to I and II Above*

Notwithstanding any of the above, the following shall be prohibited:

(A) Copying shall not be used to create or to replace or substitute for anthologies, compilations or collective works. Such replacement or substitution may occur whether copies of various works or excerpts therefrom are accumulated or reproduced and used separately.

(B) There shall be no copying of or from works intended to be "consumable" in the course of study or of teaching. These include workbooks, exercises, standardized tests and test booklets and answer sheets and like consumable material.

(C) Copying shall not:

(a) substitute for the purchase of books, publishers' reprints or periodicals;

(b) be directed by higher authority;

(c) be repeated with respect to the same item by the same teacher from term to term.

(D) No charge shall be made to the student beyond the actual cost of the photocopying.

Agreed March 19, 1976.

Ad Hoc Committee on Copyright Law Revision:

By SHELDON ELLIOTT STEINBACH.

Author-Publisher Group:

Authors League of America:

By IRWIN KARP, *Counsel.*

Association of American Publishers, Inc.:

By ALEXANDER C. HOFFMAN,

Chairman, Copyright Committee.

[The House Report then set out similar guidelines negotiated by interested organizations covering fair use of musical scores in an educational setting.]

* * *

The Committee appreciates and commends the efforts and the cooperative and reasonable spirit of the parties who achieved the agreed guidelines on books and periodicals and on music. Representatives of the American Association of University Professors and of the Association of American Law Schools have written to the Committee strongly criticizing the guidelines, particularly with respect to multiple copying, as being too restrictive with respect to classroom situations at the university and graduate level. However, the Committee notes that the Ad Hoc group did include representatives of higher education, that the stated "purpose of the * * * guidelines is to state the minimum and not the maximum standards of educational fair use" and that the agreement acknowledges "there may be instances in which copying which does not fall within the guidelines * * * may nonetheless be permitted under the criteria of fair use."

The Committee believes the guidelines are a reasonable interpretation of the minimum standards of fair use. Teachers [w]ill know that copying within the guidelines is fair use. Thus, the guidelines serve the purpose of fulfilling the need for greater certainty and protection for teachers. The Committee expresses the hope that if there are areas where standards other than these guidelines may be appropriate, the parties will continue their efforts to provide additional specific guidelines in the same spirit of good will and give and take that has marked the discussion of this subject in recent months.

* * *

Marcus v. Rowley

United States Court of Appeals for the Ninth Circuit, 1983.
695 F.2d 1171.

■ PFAELZER, DISTRICT JUDGE:

This is an appeal from a dismissal on the merits of a suit for copyright infringement brought by a public school teacher who is the owner of a registered copyright to a booklet on cake decorating. The defendant, also a public school teacher, incorporated a substantial portion of the copyrighted work into a booklet which she prepared for use in her classes. Both parties moved the district court for summary judgment. The district court denied both motions and dismissed the action on the merits on the ground that defendant's copying of plaintiff's material constituted fair use. We reverse.

From September 1972 to June 1974, plaintiff, Eloise Toby Marcus was employed by the defendant, San Diego Unified School District ("District") as a teacher of home economics. Plaintiff resigned from the District's employ in 1974 and taught adult education classes intermittently from 1975 to 1980. Shortly after leaving her teaching position with the District, she wrote a booklet entitled "Cake Decorating Made Easy".

* * *

Plaintiff sold all but six of the copies of her booklet for $2.00 each to the students in the adult education cake decorating classes which she taught. Plaintiff's profit was $1.00 on the sale of each booklet. Copies of plaintiff's booklet were never distributed to or sold by a bookstore or other outlet. Plaintiff never authorized anyone to copy or reproduce her booklet or any part of it.

Defendant, Shirley Rowley ("Rowley"), teaches food service career classes in the District. In the spring of 1975, she enrolled in one of plaintiff's cake decorating classes and purchased a copy of plaintiff's book. During the following summer, Rowley prepared a booklet entitled "Cake Decorating Learning Activity Package" ("LAP") for use in her food service career classes. The LAP consisted of twenty-four pages and was designed to be used by students who wished to study an optional section of her course devoted to cake decorating. Defendant had fifteen copies of the LAP made and put them in a file so that they would be available to her students. She used the LAP during the 1975, 1976 and 1977 school years. The trial court found that sixty of Rowley's two hundred twenty-five students elected to study cake decorating. The trial court further found that neither Rowley nor the District derived any profit from the LAP.

Rowley admits copying eleven of the twenty-four pages in her LAP from plaintiff's booklet. The eleven pages copied consisted of the supply list, icing recipes, three sheets dealing with color flow and mixing colors, four pages showing how to make and use a decorating bag, and two pages explaining how to make flowers and sugar molds. * * * Rowley did not give plaintiff credit for the eleven pages she copied, nor did she acknowledge plaintiff as the owner of a copyright with respect to those pages.

Plaintiff learned of Rowley's LAP in the summer of 1977 when a student in plaintiff's adult education class refused to purchase plaintiff's book. The student's son had obtained a copy of the LAP from Rowley's class. After examining Rowley's booklet, the student accused plaintiff of plagiarizing Rowley's work. Following these events, plaintiff made a claim of infringement against Rowley and the District. Both denied infringement and the plaintiff filed suit.

The parties filed cross-motions for summary judgment. The trial court denied both motions for summary judgment and dismissed the case on the merits. The ground for dismissal was that the defendant's copying of the plaintiff's material for nonprofit educational purposes constituted fair use.

* * *

The first factor to be considered in determining the applicability of the doctrine of fair use is the purpose and character of the use, and specifically whether the use is of a commercial nature or is for a nonprofit educational purpose. It is uncontroverted that Rowley's use of the LAP was for a nonprofit educational purpose and that the LAP was distributed to students at no charge. These facts necessarily weigh in Rowley's favor. Nevertheless, a finding of a nonprofit educational purpose does not automatically compel a finding of fair use.[5]

This court has often articulated the principle that a finding that the alleged infringers copied the material to use it for the same intrinsic purpose for which the copyright owner intended it to be used is strong indicia of no fair use. Jartech, Inc. v. Clancy, 666 F.2d 403 (1982); Universal City Studios, Inc. v. Sony Corp., 659 F.2d 963 at 969. See also Iowa State University v. American Broadcasting Cos., 621 F.2d 57 (the scope of fair use is constricted when the original and the copy serve the same function).

This same function test is addressed in the House of Representatives' 1967 Report, specifically in relation to classroom materials. The Report states that, with respect to the fair use doctrine, "[t]extbooks and other material prepared primarily for the school market would be less susceptible to reproduction for classroom use than material prepared for general public distribution." H.R.Rep. (1967) at 34.

In this case, both plaintiff's and defendant's booklets were prepared for the purpose of teaching cake decorating, a fact which weighs against a finding of fair use.[6]

Because fair use presupposes that the defendant has acted fairly and in good faith, the propriety of the defendant's conduct should also be weighed in analyzing the purpose and character of the use. See 3 Nimmer, supra § 13.05[A][1] at 13–61.

Here, there was no attempt by defendant to secure plaintiff's permission to copy the contents of her booklet or to credit plaintiff for the use of

---

5. In MacMillan v. King, 223 F. 862 (D. Mass. 1914), the district court was presented with the question of fair use in an educational setting. In that case, plaintiff, a teacher of economics at Harvard University, had written a textbook entitled "Principles of Economics" for use in university economics courses.

The defendant acted as a private tutor of a variety of subjects, including economics. Some of the defendant's students were using the plaintiff's textbook in their economics class and sought tutoring from the defendant in that course. In preparation for the tutoring sessions, defendant prepared a typewritten outline of the week's lessons. The outline was written to mirror the organization of plaintiff's textbook and often contained quotations from the textbook. None of the outlines were ever sold and the defendant claimed that the fee charged for the tutoring sessions was the same whether or not an outline was prepared for the session. The court found that plaintiff's copyright had been infringed due to "an appropriation [by the defendant] of the author's ideas

and language more extensive than the copyright law permits." Id. at 866. With respect to the argument that the copying was permissible because it was done in furtherance of educational pursuits, the court stated:

If the above conclusions are right, I am unable to believe that the defendant's use of the outlines is any the less infringement of the copyright because he is a teacher, because he uses them in teaching the contents of the book, because he might lecture upon the contents of the book without infringing, or because his pupils might have taken their own notes of his lectures without infringing.

Id. at 867.

6. Of course, this finding is not decisive on the issue of fair use. The fact that both works were used for the same intrinsic purpose carries less weight in a case such as this, because plainly the doctrine of fair use permits some copying of educational materials for classroom use. The critical issues here are the nature and the extent of defendant's copying.

her material even though Rowley's copying was for the most part verbatim.[8] Rowley's conduct in this respect weighs against a finding of fair use.

* * *

[Another] * * * factor to be considered is the amount and substantiality of the portion used in relation to the copyrighted work as a whole. * * *

With respect to this factor, this court has long maintained the view that wholesale copying of copyrighted material precludes application of the fair use doctrine. Benny v. Loew's, Inc., 239 F.2d 532 (9th Cir. 1956), aff'd by an equally divided Court sub nom. Columbia Broadcasting System v. Loew's, Inc., 356 U.S. 43 (1958). See also Walt Disney Productions v. Air Pirates, 581 F.2d 751 at 758, and Universal City Studios, Inc. v. Sony Corp., 659 F.2d 963 at 973. Other courts are in accord with this principle, and two courts have specifically addressed the issue in relation to copying for educational purposes.

Wihtol v. Crow, 309 F.2d 777 (8th Cir. 1962), involved alleged infringement by the defendant, a school teacher and church choir director, of a hymn entitled "My God and I". The defendant Crow incorporated plaintiff's original piano and solo voice composition into an arrangement for his choirs. He made forty-eight copies of his arrangement and had the piece performed on two occasions: once by the high school choir at the school chapel, and once in church on Sunday. The music was identified as "arranged Nelson E. Crow", but no reference was made to plaintiff as the original composer. The Eighth Circuit affirmed the trial court's finding that Crow had infringed plaintiff's copyright and in addressing the issue of whether Crow's copying constituted fair use, the court stated that "[w]hatever may be the breadth of the doctrine of 'fair use', it is not conceivable to us that the copying of all, or substantially all, of a copyrighted song can be held to be a 'fair use' merely because the infringer had no intent to infringe." Id. at 780.

The court in Encyclopaedia Britannica Educational Corp. v. Crooks, 447 F.Supp. 243 (W.D.N.Y. 1978), also considered the issue of fair use in the educational context. In that case, three corporations which produced educational motion picture films sued the Board of Cooperative Educational Services of Erie County ("BOCES") for videotaping several of plaintiffs' copyrighted films without permission. BOCES distributed the copied films to schools for delayed student viewing. Defendants' fair use defense was rejected on the ground that although defendants were involved in noncommercial copying to promote science and education, the taping of entire copyrighted films was too excessive for the fair use defense to apply. Id. at 251.[9] * * *

In this case, almost 50% of defendant's LAP was a verbatim copy of plaintiff's booklet and that 50% contained virtually all of the substance of

---

8. Attribution is, of course, but one factor. Moreover, acknowledgement of a source does not excuse infringement when the other factors listed in section 107 are present. * * *

9. Contra, Williams & Wilkins Co. v. United States, 487 F.2d 1345, 1352, 1354 (Ct. Cl. 1973), aff'd, 420 U.S. 376 (1975) (the existence of verbatim copying was not dispositive when the conduct encouraged scientific progress and did not cause plaintiff substantial monetary harm).

defendant's book. Defendant copied the explanations of how to make the decorating bag, how to mix colors, and how to make various decorations as well as the icing recipes. In fact, the only substantive pages of plaintiff's booklet which defendant did not put into her booklet were hints on how to ice a cake and an explanation of how to make leaves. Defendant argues that it was fair to copy plaintiff's booklet because the booklet contained only facts which were in the public domain. Even if it were true that plaintiff's book contained only facts, this argument fails because defendant engaged in virtually verbatim copying. Defendant's LAP could have been a photocopy of plaintiff's booklet but for the fact that defendant retyped plaintiff's material. This case presents a clear example of both substantial quantitative and qualitative copying.

* * *

The final factor to be considered with respect to the fair use defense is the effect which the allegedly infringing use had on the potential market for or value of the copyrighted work. The 1967 House Report points out that this factor is often seen as the most important criterion of fair use, but also warned that it "must almost always be judged in conjunction with the other three criteria." H.R. Rep. (1967) at 35. The Report explains that "a use which supplants any part of the normal market for a copyrighted work would ordinarily be considered an infringement." Id. Here, despite the fact that at least one of plaintiff's students refused to purchase her booklet as a result of defendant's copying, the trial court found that it was unable to conclude that the defendant's copying had any effect on the market for the plaintiff's booklet. Even assuming that the trial court's finding was not erroneous, and that that finding must be accepted and weighed in Rowley's favor, Sid & Marty Krofft Television Productions, Inc. v. McDonald's Corp., 562 F.2d 1157, 1166 (9th Cir. 1977), it does not alter our conclusion. The mere absence of measurable pecuniary damage does not require a finding of fair use. Universal City Studios, Inc. v. Sony Corp., 659 F.2d 963 at 974. Fair use is to be determined by a consideration of all of the evidence in the case. Mathews Conveyor Co. v. Palmer-Bee Co., 135 F.2d 73, 85 (6th Cir. 1943). Thus, despite the trial court's finding, we conclude that the factors analyzed weigh decisively in favor of the conclusion of no fair use. This conclusion is in harmony with the Congressional guidelines which, as a final point, also merit consideration with respect to the issue of fair use in an educational context.

* * *

The question of how much copying for classroom use is permissible was of such major concern to Congress that, although it did not include a section on the subject in the revised Act, it approved a set of guidelines with respect to it. The guidelines represent the Congressional Committees' view of what constitutes fair use under the traditional judicial doctrine developed in the case law. Conf.Rep. No. 1733, 94th Cong., 2d Sess. 70, reprinted in 1976 U.S.Cong. & Ad.News 5810, 5811. The guidelines were designed to give teachers direction as to the extent of permissible copying and to eliminate some of the doubt which had previously existed in this area of the copyright laws. The guidelines were intended to represent minimum standards of fair use. 3 Nimmer, supra,

§ 13.05[E][3] at 13–75. Thus, while they are not controlling on the court, they are instructive on the issue of fair use in the context of this case.

The guidelines relating to multiple copies for classroom use indicate that such copying is permissible if three tests are met. First, the copying must meet the test of "brevity" and "spontaniety." "Brevity" is defined, for prose, as "[e]ither a complete article, story or essay of less than 2,500 words, or an excerpt from any prose work of not more than 1,000 words or * * * 10% of the work, whichever is less * * *." H.R.Rep. (1976) at 68, U.S.Code Cong. & Admin.News 1976, p. 5682. Rowley's copying would not be permissible under either of these tests.

The guidelines also provide a separate definition of "brevity" for "special works." "Special works" are works "which often combine language with illustrations and which are intended sometimes for children and at other times for a more general audience." Id. at 69. Plaintiff's booklet arguably would fall into this category. The guidelines provide that, notwithstanding the guidelines for prose, " 'special works' may not be reproduced in their entirety; however, an excerpt comprising not more than two of the published pages of such special work and containing not more than 10% of the words found in the text thereof, may be reproduced." Id. Rowley's copying would not be permissible under this test.

Under the guidelines, "spontaneity" requires that "[t]he copying is at the instance and inspiration of the individual teacher, and * * * [t]he inspiration and decision to use the work and the moment of its use for maximum teaching effectiveness are so close in time that it would be unreasonable to expect a timely reply to a request for permission." Id. Defendant compiled her LAP during the summer of 1975 and first used it in her classes during the 1975–76 school year. She also used the LAP for the following two school years. Rowley's copying would not meet this requirement either.

The second test under the guidelines is that of "cumulative effect". Id. This test requires that the copied material be for only one course in the school. This aspect of the test would probably be met on these facts. The test also limits the number of pieces which may be copied from the same author and the number of times a teacher may make multiple copies for one course during one term. These latter two tests also appear to be met. The facts indicate that defendant copied only one piece of plaintiff's work. Defendant's conduct, therefore, would satisfy the second test under the guidelines.

The third test requires that each copy include a notice of copyright. As stated, defendant's LAP did not acknowledge plaintiff's authorship or copyright and therefore would not meet this test.

In conclusion, it appears that Rowley's copying would not qualify as fair use under the guidelines.

We conclude that the fair use doctrine does not apply to these facts as that doctrine has been articulated in the common law, in section 107 of the revised Copyright Act, or in the special guidelines approved by Congress for nonprofit educational institutions. Rowley's LAP work, which was used for the same purpose as plaintiff's booklet, was quantitatively and qualitatively a substantial copy of plaintiff's booklet with no credit given to plaintiff. Under these circumstances, neither the fact that the defendant used the plaintiff's booklet for nonprofit educational purposes nor the fact that plaintiff suffered no pecuniary damage as a result of Rowley's copying supports a finding of fair use.

The order of the district court is reversed, summary judgment is entered for the plaintiff, and the case is remanded for a determination of damages pursuant to the provisions of the Copyright Act.

Reversed and remanded.

NOTE

The opinion in Encyclopaedia Britannica Educational Corp. v. Crooks, 447 F.Supp. 243 (W.D.N.Y. 1978), cited in the *Marcus* case, rejected the fair use defense in the context of a motion for a preliminary injunction, which was granted. Final judgment against the defendants was entered in 1982. 542 F.Supp. 1156 (W.D.N.Y. 1982). The defendant in that case made recordings of off-the-air broadcasts of educational programs and permanently retained them for use by the area school systems. Under § 118(d)(3) the defendant (a government body) could make such recordings, but they have to be used within seven days and destroyed at the end of that period.

D. Ownership of Copyright

(1) Initial Ownership

"Copyright in a work protected under this title vests initially in the author or authors of the work." 17 U.S.C. § 201(a). Who, then is the "author"? The term is not further defined in the statute. However authorship is an idea central to the subject of copyrightable subject matter, because a work must be the work of an author to be copyrightable. 17 U.S.C. § 102(a). That law incorporates an expansive and undemanding test of authorship: finding almost any "work" copyrightable if it incorporates a minimal creative contribution.

It can be argued that the definition of author for purposes of assigning ownership should be more focused and demanding than the definition used for determining whether there is any element of copyrightable subject matter in a work. For purposes of identifying the owner of the copyright, the law of copyrightable subject matter suggests that works may have impracticably many authors. The writer of a novel is an author. But what about the book editor, the book publisher, or the book designer, each of whom make some contribution to the final "work"? What about the author's friends, from whom he may borrow ideas and suggestions? Are all these persons authors of the finished work, and is it necessary to trace the chain of title to all of them? And if a book, often the work of a single, identifiable writer, may present difficulties, what about works such as movies and television programs, which may involve the coordinated efforts of hundreds of people? The cases, without evidencing much thought about the problem, point in the direction of equating the minimal test of authorship used under § 102(b) with the test required to determine who owns the copyright under § 201.

These problems can all be dealt with by agreements that transfer any resulting copyright to the intended person or entity, and it is an important function of a lawyer to review the contracts in connection with a project leading to the production of copyrightable material to ensure that the property rights end up where the parties to the transaction intend them to be. The catch is that the intent of the parties alone will not control. A transfer of copyright must be in writing. An oral or implied term is not sufficient. "A transfer of copyright ownership * * * is not valid unless an instrument of conveyance, or a note or memorandum of the transfer, is in writing and signed by the owner of the rights conveyed or such owner's duly authorized agent." 17 U.S.C. § 204(a).

The ownership of the copyright is also important to buyers of copyrightable works. It is widely understood that the person who buys a copy of a book gets only the right to read, possess and resell the single copy purchased. But it is probably not so widely understood that a person who pays millions of dollars for an original painting or sculpture may be buying only the painting, not the right to prevent [or authorize] the reproduction and sale of copies of the painting. Or that a person who pays millions for a computer system (or for any of the many machines which include specialized computer sub-systems) containing extensive copyrighted software may not acquire the right to use all the features of the software. Just as a buyer may want to be assured of good title in the object, he or she may also want rights in relation to the copyright.

The complexity presented by the possibility of multiple authors of a work is ameliorated by the concept of works made for hire. "In the case of a work made for hire, the employer or other person for whom the work is prepared is considered the author * * * and, unless the parties have expressly agreed otherwise in a written instrument signed by them, owns all of the rights comprised in the copyright." 17 U.S.C. § 201(b). If all the persons who contribute to a work and thus are possible authors are employees of the same entity, then there is only one author, the employer, and there is no need for any further agreement about who owns the copyright.

As a general rule, the statute does not permit the parties to make a work into a "work made for hire" by agreement. A work made for hire is defined as "a work prepared by an employee within the scope of his or her employment," 17 U.S.C. § 101, "work made for hire" (1), and this is interpreted to mean a person who is in a common law employment relationship. Community for Creative Non-Violence v. Reid, 490 U.S. 730 (1989).

There is an exception to this rule for a curious list of works. "[A] work specially ordered or commissioned for use as a contribution to a collective work, as a part of a motion picture or other audiovisual work, as a translation, as a supplementary work, as a compilation, as an instructional text, as a test, as answer material for a test, or as an atlas." 17 U.S.C. § 101, "work made for hire" (2). In the case of these works, "if the parties expressly agree in a written instrument signed by them that the work shall be considered a work made for hire," then the work is a work made for hire. The reasons for this exception cannot be understood until we get to the subject of renewal and termination rights, but the exception makes it clear that unless a work falls within this list, the issue of whether or not a work is made for hire is not to be answered by what the parties in their agreements said it was.

The registration procedure under the statute can work to foreclose subsequent issues about authorship status. The application for registration must include "the name and nationality or domicile of the author or authors," 17 U.S.C. § 409. This information is contained in the certificate of registration, 17 U.S.C. § 410(a), and "[i]n any judicial proceedings the certificate of a registration * * * shall constitute prima facie evidence * * * of the facts stated in the certificate." 17 U.S.C. § 410(c). A claim of authorship status made long after a work has been published and registered by others is unlikely to fare well against this presumption.

If a work is "prepared by two or more authors with the intention that their contributions be merged into inseparable or interdependent parts of a unitary whole," 17 U.S.C. § 101, then the work is defined as a joint work, and the joint authors are co-owners of the copyright in the work. 17 U.S.C. § 201(a).

One purpose of the definition of joint works in the 1976 Act was to narrow the application of the concept to situations where there was a pre-existing plan to create a single work. For instance, if a lyricist and a composer collaborate in writing a song, they create a single joint work. However, if the composer first writes the music, and then a lyricist, hearing the tune, writes lyrics for it, each is an author of separate copyrightable works—the composer of the music and the lyricist of the lyrics.[1] This is not simply a difference of terminology. In the case of the joint work, each author as a co-owner has the right to perform or reproduce the song or authorize others to do so (although he or she must account for a share of the profits to the co-owner), while if there are two separate works no one— neither the authors nor any third party—can perform or reproduce the music and the lyrics without permission from both authors. In the joint work situation there is the possibility of multiple co-owners, each with the right to exploit all rights in the work in competition with the other co-owners. In the multiple copyrightable works situation, there is the possibility of overlapping rights, none of which can be exploited without the consent of all. Both the co-ownership and multiple separate rights situations can present difficulties in the absence of either a willingness of the multiple authors to cooperate or some binding agreement that assigns to some person or entity the ability to manage the exploitation of the work.

The difficulties that can arise for multiple authors in the absence of careful legal planning are illustrated by the facts of Community for Creative Non-Violence v. Reid, 490 U.S. 730 (1989). The Community for

---

1. This was the situation in Shapiro, Bernstein & Co. v. Jerry Vogel Music Co., 221 F.2d 569, on reh'g 223 F.2d 252 (2d Cir. 1955) (known as the "Twelfth Street Rag case"), which held that the resulting song was a joint work. The decision was much criticized, and the definition in the 1976 Act was intended to reverse the result of this case. Among other things, it meant that two authors who had never worked together became co-owners of a single work.

Creative Non-Violence (CCNV) was a nonprofit unincorporated association dedicated to eliminating homelessness in America, and Mitch Snyder was a member and trustee of CCNV. In the fall of 1985 CCNV decided to participate in the annual Christmastime Pageant of Peace in Washington, D.C., by sponsoring a display to dramatize the plight of the homeless.

Snyder and fellow CCNV members conceived of a display: a sculpture of a modern Nativity scene in which, in lieu of the traditional Holy Family, the two adult figures and the infant would appear as contemporary homeless people huddled on a streetside steam grate. The figures were to be life-sized, and the steam grate would be positioned atop a platform pedestal, or base within which special-effects equipment would be enclosed to emit simulated steam through the grate to swirl about the figures. They also settled upon a title for the work "Third World America"—and a legend for the pedestal: "and still there is no room at the inn."

The project thus conceived, Snyder undertook to locate a local artist to produce the sculpture. He found James Earl Reid, a professional sculptor. In the course of two telephone calls, Reid agreed to sculpt the three human figures in a non-durable synthetic material. CCNV agreed to obtain the steam grate and pedestal for the statue. Reid agreed to donate his services and charge $15,000 for materials.

Reid and CCNV members collaborated on details of the sculpture—the choice of models, their position in relation to the steam grate, the use of a shopping cart. The statue was completed by Reid, delivered to Washington and there joined with the steam grate and pedestal. CCNV paid Reid the $15,000. The display was apparently a success.

The parties then fell into a dispute over the ownership of the copyright in the statue, something they had never discussed. Snyder saw further fundraising possibilities for the sculpture, and began planning for a national tour. Reid, happy enough to donate his labor for the Christmas display, did not want to donate the copyright. He urged that the statue be cast in bronze or that a master mold be created from which multiple copies could be made. Perhaps Reid now foresaw that the statue might become famous. If CCNV had the copyright, he would be unable to make any further copies.

At this point the rights of the parties might seem easy enough to figure out. Since CCNV had purchased the statue, it owned the material object and was entitled to publicly display it, 17 U.S.C. § 109(c). Reid, the sculptor, was the author of a copyrightable work, and since there had been no transfer of the ownership of the copyright, he still owned the copyright, and could stop CCNV from making any copy of the work. For instance, CCNV would have the right to conduct a national tour of the sculpture in which it would be publicly displayed, but Reid could stop CCNV from selling souvenir copies of the statue.

CCNV sued Reid for a declaration that it owned the statue and the copyright. The District Court decided for CCNV on the ground that CCNV had commissioned the statue and that the intent of the parties was that CCNV should own it and the copyright. To reach this result, the court relied on cases under the 1909 Act which had held that commissioned works were works made for hire, and which had been followed in some circuits under the 1976 Act. On this point the Court of Appeals reversed, Community for Creative Non-Violence v. Reid, 846 F.2d 1485 (D.C. Cir. 1988), relying on the definition of works made for hire in § 101. The court of appeals was affirmed by the Supreme Court. Since Reid was not an employee of CCNV, but an independent contractor, the statue was not a work made for hire. Since Reid had not executed a writing transferring the copyright to CCNV, he still owned it. Reid's copyright troubles, however, were not over.

The Court of Appeals remanded the case to the District Court to consider whether the statue was a joint work, consisting of the pedestal, the steam grate, and the sculpted figures contributed by Reid. Not only did the Court of Appeals suggest that Reid and CCNV might be "joint authors," but raised the possibility that the cabinet maker who constructed the base and various persons who assisted Reid might also be joint authors, thus firmly embracing an approach to authorship under 17 U.S.C. § 201 which tracks the cases under 17 U.S.C. § 102 and opening wide the specter of multiple authorship problems in many situations. The court instructed the district court to determine if there were other parties who might be joint authors who should be joined in the action. The Supreme Court affirmed this aspect of the Court of Appeals decision in a single sentence, 490 U.S. at 753.

2. *Right of Termination and Renewal.* The ownership of copyright is complicated by the fact that the statute attempts to retain for the benefit of the author and his family an interest in roughly the last half of the copyright term. This objective adds considerable technical complexity to issues of ownership. The idea is implemented differently under the 1976 Act than it was under the 1909 Act. As to some works whose term extends across the effective date of the 1976 Act, the 1976 Act makes both the 1909 and the 1976 structures applicable. §§ 303, 304. These transition provisions will matter until 2005, but will not be further discussed here.

The basic problem which the statute attempts to address can be illustrated as follows. A young, unknown and struggling writer sells the copyright in a manuscript for a pittance. Years later, the manuscript turns out to be a famous and still popular book. The publisher gets rich, the writer (now, perhaps, old, infirm and penniless) gets nothing. There is no relief for the author, except for what under the 1909 act was a provision for a renewal term, and under the 1976 act is a provision for a termination right. Under these provisions, our penniless writer may get the copyright back, and can negotiate a new license reflecting the fame and success of the work.

The number of authors whose works retain commercial value long enough to make these provisions economically significant is very small. The appeal of the destitute but successful artist has nevertheless been thought by Congress to justify introducing substantial complexity into the statutory scheme.

Under the 1909 Act the copyright term of 56 years from publication consisted of two separate 28 year terms. (This two term structure actually goes back to the Statute of Anne, which in 1709 provided for two fourteen year terms.) The first term belonged to the author. The second term belonged to the author if he was then living, and if not to "the widow, widower, or children of the author," or if such author, widow, widower or children be not living, "then the author's executors, or in the absence of a will, his next of kin." 1909 Copyright Act § 24. The second term was obtained only if the eligible person made an application for renewal in the twenty-seventh year of the copyright. In the case of the many works for which no renewal was filed, they entered the public domain at the end of the twenty-eighth year.

The Supreme Court held that the author's contingent interest in the second term was fully assignable. Fred Fisher Music Co. v. M. Witmark & Sons, 318 U.S. 643 (1943) (involving the copyright for "When Irish Eyes are Smiling.") In the Court's view, the statute gave the author the ability not to assign the renewal term if he chose not to do so, but did not invalidate an otherwise valid assignment. So if publishers and others made it a standard provision of their contracts (which they did) that the author assigned both terms, then the publisher had both terms if the author was living in the twenty-seventh year. However, the author's assignment of his or her interest in the second term, would not include his wife's, or his children's, etc. Thus if the author had signed a contract which included the second term, but was still living in the twenty-seventh year, neither he or his family would get any benefit from the second term. If, however, he had died, and the statutory owner of the renewal term (most typically the widow or widower and children) filed for the renewal term, they could assert copyright free of any agreement signed by the author. This led to the rather odd result that the author would benefit from the renewal term only if dead.

The 1976 Act created a new scheme designed to protect the author in every case. "A provision of this sort is needed because of the unequal bargaining position of authors, resulting in part from the impossibility of determining a work's value until it has been exploited." H.R. Rep. No. 1476, p. 124. The term was made a single term, eliminating the need for a renewal application. But transfers made by the author were made subject to a termination right that can be exercised in every case by the author, or if the author is deceased, by the widow, widower, children and children of deceased children, in the five year period beginning at the end of the thirty-fifth year. If the author exercised the right to terminate, any prior "exclusive or nonexclusive grant of a transfer or license of copyright or of any right under a copyright, executed by the author on or after January 1, 1978, otherwise than by will," § 203(a), is set aside and "all rights under this title that were covered by the terminated grants revert to the author" or the persons owning the termination interest. § 203(b). Section 203 sets out the procedures for exercising the termination interest, which include an advance notice in writing which must be served not less than two or more than ten years before the date of the proposed termination. "Termination of the grant may be effected notwithstanding any agreement to the contrary, including an agreement to make a will or to make any future grant." § 203(a)(5).

One problem that had arisen under the renewal mechanism of the 1909 Act was the impact of the renewal term on derivative works. Suppose the author of a novel had granted movie rights. If the author of the novel was deceased in the twenty-seventh year, the renewal term would pass to the widow and children, who would be in a position to block any further showing of the movie. For an example of the problems that could arise, see G. Ricordi & Co. v. Paramount Pictures, 189 F.2d 469 (2d Cir. 1951), involving the ownership of the movie rights to the opera *Madam Butterfly* in light of the copyrights in the separately authored novel, play, and opera.

To ameliorate these problems, the statute provides an exception from the termination right for derivative works. Section 203(b) provides that "A derivative work prepared under authority of the grant before its termination may continue to be utilized under the terms of the grant after termination, but this privilege does not extend to the preparation after the termination of other derivative works based upon the copyrighted work covered by the terminated grant."

Although the termination provisions are conceived of as protecting authors, they have the fault of all paternal legislation: they actually reduce the author's rights. The author cannot give up the right of termination even if he or she wants to do so. The practical importance of the right of termination, however, is reduced by the fact that the right of termination begins thirty-five years after the date of the *grant*. This means that if the licensee gets a new grant every few years (perhaps in connection with promises to further promote or exploit the work) the time period starts over again.

3. *Works Made for Hire and Renewal and the Right of Termination.* Both the renewal term under the 1909 Act and the right of termination under the 1976 Act do not extend to a "work made for hire." Under the 1909 Act, works made for hire had a single 56 year term. Under the 1976 Act, there is no right of termination in works made for hire. The theory, if theory there be, is that an employer, the author of a work made for hire, would be sophisticated and not in need of the "protection" of a right of termination. Paul Goldstein, *Copyright: Principles, Law and Practice* (1996), § 4.10.1.3. The issue of whether a work is a work made for hire is important both for purposes of identifying who is the author for ownership purposes, but also for purposes of determining whether that author has any right to terminate.

It is the connection between works made for hire and the termination right that explains clause 2 of the definition of works made for hire in the 1976 act. "The right of termination would not apply to 'works made for hire,' which is one of the principal reasons the definition of that term assumed importance in the development of the bill." H.R. Rep. No. 1476, p. 125. The exception was not needed in order to affect the ownership of the copyright. The parties could provide for that equally well by requiring each possible "author" to assign the copyright in writing. Clause 2 permits "authors" of the enumerated types of works to contract out of the right of termination provisions by signing a written agreement that the work is a work made for hire.

The types of works covered by clause 2 have the following in common. (1) They are works of a type commonly involving creative input from a large number of people. (2) Many of the contributors will not be employees of the entity that funds the project, but rather will be specially commissioned to contribute. For instance, a textbook publisher may commission professors to contribute sections to the textbook, or to review and revise drafts, or a movie producer may hire composers, set and costume designers, and script writers to work on some aspect of the movie. (3) The works are produced by an organized industry that had the sophisticated representation necessary to participate in the long, technical process of copyright revision that unfolded in the Congress. The leading examples are the publishers of instructional materials ("an instructional text, as a test, as answer material for a test") and the movie industry ("as a part of a motion picture or other audiovisual work"). These industries feared the problems that would emerge if years after their creation of a copyrightable work all of the commissioned contributors could come forward and assert their termination rights.

NOTES

1. The concept of "work made for hire" is also important to the copyright term, because the term of a "work made for hire" is 75 years. Note that this is true even if the employer and statutory author are natural persons. Section 302(c).

2. Why are grants by will excluded from the termination right?

3. Even though the statute attempts to preserve the termination right for authors in the face of the demands of publishers and others to abandon the right, there is much that can be done to affect the right. Suppose for instance that the publisher of pulp novels who commissions writers to write for a set fee wants to make sure that there is no termination right. The publisher could, of course, hire the writers as employees, but might not want to do so because of tax withholding, labor regulation, and liability concerns. But suppose the publisher insists that it will only commission authors who first form their own wholly owned corporation and enter into an employment agreement with it providing that they are to be "President and staff novelist." The publisher then enters into an agreement not with the writer, but with the corporation. Doesn't this convert the commissioned novel into a "work made for hire"? Or will the courts examine the substance of the transaction to determine what it "really" was?

4. The position of the owner of a derivative work under the renewal rights provisions applicable to pre-1976 Act copyrights is illustrated by Stewart v. Abend, 495 U.S. 207 (1990), involving the right to show the Alfred Hitchcock movie "Rear Window." In 1942 Cornell Woolrich authored the story "It Had to Be Murder," which was published in Dime Detective Magazine. Woolrich retained all rights except the magazine publication rights. In 1945 he assigned the rights to make motion picture versions of six of his stories, including "It Had to Be Murder" and including both the first and renewal terms to a third party for $9,250.00. In 1953 actor Jimmy Stewart and director Alfred Hitchcock formed a production company which obtained these movie rights. "Rear Window" was the resulting picture. Woolrich died in 1968 without a widow or children, so under the renewal provisions of the 1909 Act the renewal right passed as directed in his will to a trust for the benefit of Columbia University. In 1969, Chase Manhattan Bank as trustee filed the

renewal application. The trust then assigned the renewal rights to Abend for $650 plus ten percent of all proceeds from exploitation of the story. Abend sued and won, and the Supreme Court granted certiorari to resolve a conflict with the Second Circuit in Rohauer v. Killiam Shows, Inc., 551 F.2d 484 (2d Cir. 1977), which held that the owner of the derivative work could continue to exploit it even in the face of objection from the owner of the renewal term, relying in part on the provisions of the 1976 Act relating to the post-termination exploitation of pre-existing derivative works. The Court affirmed the Ninth Circuit, rejected the interpretation of the Second, and held that Abend could enforce the renewal term against "Rear Window."[1]

The significance of *Abend* is reduced by the fact that the Ninth Circuit held that even though the copyright was valid, Abend could not obtain an injunction.

> The "Rear Window" film resulted from the collaborative efforts of many talented individuals other than Cornell Woolrich, the author of the underlying story. The success of the movie resulted in large part from factors completely unrelated to the underlying story, "It Had To Be Murder." It would cause a great injustice for the owners of the film if the court enjoined them from further exhibition of the movie. An injunction would also effectively foreclose defendants from enjoying legitimate profits derived from exploitation of the "new matter" comprising the derivative work. * * * We also note that an injunction could cause public injury by denying the public the opportunity to view a classic film for many years to come. 863 F.2d at 1479.

This aspect of the decision converted Abend's rights into a right only to receive damages, a kind of compulsory license, which might be quite favorable to the defendant depending on how the courts applied § 504 of the 1976 Act. The Supreme Court did not review this aspect of the Ninth Circuit decision. 495 U.S. 216.

(2) Transfer of Copyright

Section 204(a) is a statute of frauds for copyright transfers. It provides that a "transfer of copyright ownership, other than by operation of law, is not valid unless an instrument of conveyance, or a note or memorandum of the transfer, is in writing and signed by the owner of the rights conveyed * * * ." A "transfer of copyright ownership" is defined in § 101 as "an assignment, mortgage, exclusive license, or any other conveyance, alienation, or hypothecations of a copyright or of any of the exclusive rights comprised in a copyright, whether or not it is limited in time or place of effect, but not including a nonexclusive license."

---

1. Note that the enforcement of the renewal terms against the owners of the derivative work was particularly harsh in *Abend* because the author had died without a widow or children and under the 1909 Act renewal provisions the renewal right passed back to the executors, where it passed under the author's will. But the author had already agreed to give the owners of the derivative work rights in the renewal term. In *Rohauer* the renewal right had passed to a daughter. The Court considered *Abend* as if it were factually indistinguishable from *Rohauer*.

The Copyright Act also provides for a system of recording transfers in the Copyright Office (the equivalent of the recording office for transfers of land, in this case for copyrights), and provides that recording gives all persons constructive notice of the facts stated in the recorded document if (1) the document specifically identifies the work to which it relates so that after the document is indexed by the Registrar of Copyrights it would be revealed by a reasonable search under the title or registration number of the work, and (2) registration has been made for the work.

In re AEG Acquisition Corp.

United States Bankruptcy Appellate Panel, Ninth Circuit, 1993
161 B.R. 50, 30 Collier Bankr.Cas.2d 242, 24 Bankr.Ct.Dec. 1605

■ JONES, BANKRUPTCY JUDGE:

AEG Acquisition Corp. ("AEG") is a debtor under Chapter 11 of the Bankruptcy Code, 11 U.S.C. §§ 1101–1174, whose principal asset is a library of copyrights, distribution rights and licenses to more than 100 motion pictures. In 1987, Atlantic Entertainment Group, Inc. ("Atlantic"), AEG's predecessor, entered into three distribution agreements ("1987 Agreements") with Zenith Productions, Ltd. ("Zenith"). [Although these agreements are called distribution agreements, they apparently transferred ownership of the copyright in the films to AEG in exchange for the promise to pay $6 million.] The 1987 Agreements relate to three motion pictures entitled "Patty Hearst," "For Queen and Country," and "The Wolves of Willoughby Chase" ("Films"). Zenith delivered the Films to Atlantic in 1987, but Atlantic failed to pay guaranteed minimum advances totalling $6 million as provided for by the 1987 Agreements.

* * *

[AEG did not pay because it was in financial difficulty. After a long series of arrangements and negotiations, and new ownership of AEG, the parties finally entered into what they called a Restructuring Agreement. To secure AEG's performance under the Restructuring Agreement, which required the payment of the $6 million plus additional costs which had been incurred by Zenith, AEG gave Zenith a security interest in its rights in the films for amounts due under the Restructuring Agreement.

To perfect its security interest, Zenith filed financing statements in California, Indiana and New York under Article 9 of the Uniform Commercial Code, recorded a copyright mortgage for each of the Films with United States Copyright Office, and filed a certificate of copyright registration with respect to "Patty Hearst." Zenith did not file such a certificate with respect to the other two films because they were foreign works which Zenith believed were exempt from registration.

Shortly after the Restructuring Agreement, AEG entered bankruptcy. This decision is an appeal from the district court's decision in the bankruptcy case. The appeal involved a number of issues, but the only issue germane here is the enforceability of the security interest in the foreign films.]

The trial court determined that Zenith had failed to perfect its security interests in the foreign Films because the Films had not been registered with the United States Copyright Office. Zenith argues that the court erred because, under the Berne Convention for the Protection of Literary and Artistic Works (Paris Text 1971) ("Berne Convention"), registration is a prohibited formality.

Under United States law, recording a document in the Copyright Office gives all persons constructive notice of the information contained in the document only if the document identifies the work to which it relates and the work is registered. 17 U.S.C. § 205(c). The Berne Convention provides that authors of foreign works enjoy the same protections of any member country as do nationals of that country. Berne Convention, Art. 5(1). In addition, authors of Berne Convention works are entitled to copyright protections without complying with formalities. Berne Convention, Art. 5(2); AEG Acquisition, 127 B.R. at 42.

Zenith argues that requiring registration is a "formality" which may not be imposed on a Berne Convention work. Zenith points out that registration is not a prerequisite to the bringing of an infringement action for a Berne Convention work, while it is a prerequisite for a work not covered by the Berne Convention. 17 U.S.C. § 411. Zenith asserts that registration as a prerequisite to perfecting a security interest in a foreign film is a similarly prohibited formality.

As the trial court here noted, however, United States law provides no other exemptions for Berne Convention works. 127 B.R. at 42. Moreover, 17 U.S.C. § 205, which deals with recordation of transfers of copyrights, makes no distinction between foreign and domestic works. We therefore hold that Zenith's failure to register the two foreign Films before AEG filed bankruptcy defeats its attempt to perfect its security interest in the copyrights.

NOTES

1. Zenith filed financing statements in California, Indiana and New York because Article 9 of the Uniform Commercial Code defines copyrights (and trademarks and patents) as a general intangible (Uniform Commerical Code § 9–106), and provides that a security interest in a general intangible can be perfected by filing in the jurisidiction that is the debtor's place of business, or if the debtor has more than one, in the jurisdiciton of its chief executive office (U.C.C. § 9–103). Apparently, Zenith was unsure of the location of AEG's chief executive office, so to be safe it filed in California, Indiana and New York.

Zenith also filed the copyright mortgages in the Copyright Office in spite of Comment 1 to § 9–104 of the U.C.C. which states that "Although the Federal Copyright Act contains provisions permitting the mortgage of a copyright and for the recording of an assignment of a copyright * * * such a statute would not seem to contain sufficient provisions regulating the rights of the parties and third parties to exclude security interests in copyrights from the provisions of this Article."

The Bankruptcy Appellate Panel in *AEG* implicitly held that the U.C.C. filings were ineffective on the ground (1) that § 205 preempts Article 9 as to security interests in copyrights or (2) that under U.C.C. § 9–302(3)(a) a security interest in a copyright must be filed in the Copyright Office, or (3) that under U.C.C. § 9–104(a), § 205 displaces Article 9.

2. Both the Lanham Act (§ 10) and the Patent Act (§ 261) provide for the recording of assignments, but do not explicitly include security interests.

3. The solution for Zenith in the *AEG* case would have been to register the copyright for the foreign origin films in the copyright office, as well as filing under § 205.

The problems for computer software firms are more complex. Suppose a lender is considering loaning money to a computer software start up. The software product, which is the principal asset of the business and which appears promising, is protected by copyright. Can the lender obtain a good security interest in the copyright in the computer software? Assume, as seems likely, that the software is in an early form and is daily being debugged and improved by the company's programmers. Even if a version of the software has already been offered for sale, the company is probably working around the clock to improve it and to prepare the next version.

As to completed versions, the lender can obtain a security interest if the company registers the copyright on the software and the security interest is filed under § 205.

However, the security interest in the completed version will not create a security interest in the newer versions. Section 205 contains no provision extending its constructive notice to cover after-created works. If the borrower goes into bankruptcy the lender will have a good security interest in the old version, and the bankruptcy trustee will have the copyright in the most recently created version.

In In re Avalon Software Inc. 209 B.R. 517, 33 UCC Rep.Serv.2d 650 (Bankr. D. Az. 1997), the bankrupt was a computer software firm, the lender had taken a security interest in the unregistered software and attempted to perfect by filing in Arizona under the U.C.C. The bankruptcy court held that the security interest was not perfected.

4. For a somewhat dated but exhaustive review of procedures for obtaining security interests in trade secrets, trademarks, copyrights and patents see Robert S. Bramson, Intellectual Property as Collateral—Patents, Trade Secrets, Trademarks and Copyrights, 36 Bus. Law. 1567 (1981). See also Weinberg & Woodward, Easing Transfer and Security Interest Transactions in Intellectual Property: An Agenda for Reform, 79 Ky. L.J. 611 (1990). National Peregrine, Inc. v. Capitol Federal Savings & Loan, 116 B.R. 194 (Bankr. C.D. Cal. 1990) is an opinion on this subject by Kozinski, Circuit Judge, sitting as a District Court judge.

5. *The Significance of a Transfer of a Copy.* Under the common law it was understood that the sale of certain kinds of works implicitly included ownership in the copyright in the work. The purchaser of an original oil painting or an unpublished manuscript acquired both the object and the copyright.

(Unlike the purchaser, for instance, of a published book, who everyone understood, acquired only the single copy, not the right to the copyright.) The 1976 revision changed this law. House Report No. 94–1476, p. 124 says:

> The principle restated in section 202 is a fundamental and important one: that copyright ownership and ownership of a material object in which the copyrighted work is embodied are entirely separate things. Thus, transfer of a material object does not of itself carry any rights under the copyright, and this includes transfer of the copy or phonorecord—the original manuscript, the photographic negative, the unique painting or statue, the master tape recording, etc.—in which the work was first fixed. Conversely, transfer of a copyright does not necessarily require the conveyance of any material object.

> As a result of the interaction of this section and the provisions of section 204(a) and 301, the bill would change a common law doctrine exemplified by the decision in Pushman v. New York Graphic Society, Inc., 287 N.Y. 302, 39 N.E.2d 249 (1942). Under that doctrine, authors or artists are generally presumed to transfer common law literary property rights when they sell their manuscript or work of art, unless those rights are specifically reserved. This presumption would be reversed under the bill, since a specific written conveyance of rights would be required in order for a sale of any material object to carry with it a transfer of copyright.

The transfer of a copy does give the purchaser the right to make some uses of the copy free of further copyright restrictions. This doctrine of exhaustion is codified in § 109(a) which permits the purchaser of a copy to resell it, § 109(c) which permits the purchaser of a copy to display it, and § 117 which permits the purchaser of a copy of software to make copies necessary to use the software and to back it up. The purchaser of a copy is also permitted to do anything with the copy that is not infringing, for instance to read and observe it because these actions are not infringement under § 106.

Section 109(a) is a codification of Bobbs-Merrill Co. v. Straus, 210 U.S. 339 (1908), which held that a first sale exhausts the copyright, and that it cannot be enforced against a purchaser even if the seller attempts to retain copyright rights. In *Bobbs-Merrill* the publisher attempted to enforce resale price maintenance by putting a notice on the book licensing the copyright for resale only at a minimum resale price. There are similar decisions under the patent statute.

If, however, the copy is not sold then the copyright is not "exhausted." This is recognized in § 109(d). In recent years, sellers of computer software have attempted to take advantage of this provision by licensing rather than selling mass marketed software. The reasons why these "licenses" are likely to be held unenforceable by the courts are spelled out in David Rice, Licensing the Use of Computer Program Copies and the Copyright Act First Sale Doctrine, 30 Jurimetrics 157 (1990). But see ProCD, Inc. v. Zeidenberg, 86 F. 3d 1447 (7th Cir. 1996), in Chapter IV.

(3) Moral Rights

The owner of a copyright is in a position to maintain (or not) the integrity of the work. Adaptations, translations, abridgments and other modifications of the work can only be undertaken with the permission of the copyright owner. If he does not like the new version, he can refuse to authorize it. See Rochelle Cooper Dreyfuss, The Creative Employee and the Copyright Act of 1976, 54 U. Chi. L. Rev. 590 (1987) for numerous examples of how the author's continuing control over his or her own work can be an important aspect of the author's creativity.

These are important powers, but ones usually given up by the creator of the work. Authors customarily sign contracts with publishers which transfer the copyright to the publisher. Sculptors and painters sell their works, and that sale can include a transfer of the copyright.

Other legal systems, most notably the French, have long recognized a separate, non-transferable right called the "moral right" which remains with the author or creator of the work and enables him to invoke the aid of the courts in protecting the integrity of the work (which includes protection against alteration, mutilation or destruction) after the copyright has been transferred to others.

In the 1970's and 80's a version of this concept, applicable only to fine art, made its way into the statutory law of several states. See Edward J. Damich, The New York Artists' Authorship Rights Act: A Comparative Critique, 84 Colum. L. Rev. 1733 (1984), which describes and compares the French, California and New York law.

In 1990 the Copyright Statute was amended to provide such protection for works of visual art. The Visual Artists Rights Act of 1990 (VARA) added a new § 106A to the Copyright Act which created new rights of attribution and integrity. One consequence of this extension of federal law is that the state statutes on the same subject are now preempted, as is spelled out in a new § 301(f).

Section 106A gives the author of a work of visual art the right to claim authorship, to prevent false attributions of authorship, and to prevent the use of his or her name in the event of a distortion of the work. Most importantly the statute gives the author the right "(A) to prevent any intentional distortion, mutilation, or other modification of the work which would be prejudicial to his or her honor or reputation, and any intentional distortion, mutilation or modification of that work is a violation of that right, and (B) to prevent any destruction of a work of recognized stature, and any intentional or grossly negligent destruction of that work is a violation of that right." A definition of "work of visual art" is added to § 101. It is: "a painting, drawing, print, or sculpture, existing in a single copy, in a limited edition of 200 copies or fewer that are signed and consecutively numbered by the author, or, in the case of a sculpture, in multiple cast, carved or fabricated sculptures of two hundred or fewer that are consecutively numbered by the author and bear the signature or other identifying mark of the author," and a still photographic image subject to similar restrictions. Works made for hire are excluded.

The § 106A rights to attribution and integrity are the property of the author or authors and are non-transferable. However, they can be waived. § 106A(e).

There are special provisions relating to the removal or alteration of works of visual art incorporated in buildings, contained in § 113(d).

NOTE

The leading case construing VARA is Carter v. Helmsley-Spear, Inc., 71 F.3d 77 (2d Cir. 1995), cert. den. 517 U.S. 1208 (1996), reversing 861 F. Supp. 303 (S.D.N.Y. 1994). In that case three artists had been hired to design and install sculpture in the lobby of a high rise building in New York. The building owner decided to remove the sculpture, and the artists sued under VARA. The district court enjoined the building owner from removing, modifying or destroying the sculpture. The Court of Appeals reversed, finding that the artists were employees not independent contractors, that the work was a work for hire, and thus not within the definition of a work of visual art as defined in § 101. Although the building owner ultimately won in Helmsley-Spear, the case illustrates the importance of obtaining a waiver of VARA rights when an immoveable work of art is commissioned. And the purchaser of any covered work of art should be aware that VARA may make it difficult to avoid the obligation to permanently preserve the work of art, even if the purchaser tires of the work and there is no available resale market. Section 106A is discussed in Roberta Kwall, How Fine Art Fares Post VARA, 1 Marq. Intell. Prop. L. Rev. 1 (1997).

Gilliam v. American Broadcasting Companies, Inc.

United States Court of Appeals, Second Circuit, 1976.
538 F.2d 14.

■ LUMBARD, CIRCUIT JUDGE:

Plaintiffs, a group of British writers and performers known as "Monty Python,"[1] appeal from a denial by Judge Lasker in the Southern District of a preliminary injunction to restrain the American Broadcasting Company (ABC) from broadcasting edited versions of three separate programs originally written and performed by Monty Python for broadcast by the British Broadcasting Corporation (BBC). We agree with Judge Lasker that the appellants have demonstrated that the excising done for ABC impairs the integrity of the original work. We further find that the countervailing injuries that Judge Lasker found might have accrued to ABC as a result of an injunction at a prior date no longer exist. We therefore direct the issuance of a preliminary injunction by the district court.

---

1. Appellant Gilliam is an American citizen residing in England.

Since its formation in 1969, the Monty Python group has gained popularity primarily through its thirty-minute television programs created for BBC as part of a comedy series entitled "Monty Python's Flying Circus." In accordance with an agreement between Monty Python and BBC, the group writes and delivers to BBC scripts for use in the television series. This scriptwriters' agreement recites in great detail the procedure to be followed when any alterations are to be made in the script prior to recording of the program.[2] The essence of this section of the agreement is that, while BBC retains final authority to make changes, appellants or their representatives exercise optimum control over the scripts consistent with BBC's authority and only minor changes may be made without prior consultation with the writers. Nothing in the scriptwriters' agreement entitles BBC to alter a program once it has been recorded. The agreement further provides that, subject to the terms therein, the group retains all rights in the script.

Under the agreement, BBC may license the transmission of recordings of the television programs in any overseas territory. The series has been broadcast in this country primarily on non-commercial public broadcasting television stations, although several of the programs have been broadcast on commercial stations in Texas and Nevada. In each instance, the thirty-minute programs have been broadcast as originally recorded and broadcast in England in their entirety and without commercial interruption.

In October 1973, Time-Life Films acquired the right to distribute in the United States certain BBC television programs, including the Monty Python

---

2. The Agreement provides:

V. When script alterations are necessary it is the intention of the BBC to make every effort to inform and to reach agreement with the Writer. Whenever practicable any necessary alterations (other than minor alterations) shall be made by the Writer. Nevertheless the BBC shall at all times have the right to make (a) minor alterations and (b) such other alterations as in its opinion are necessary in order to avoid involving the BBC in legal action or bringing the BBC into disrepute. Any decision under (b) shall be made at a level not below that of Head of Department. It is however agreed that after a script has been accepted by the BBC alterations will not be made by the BBC under (b) above unless (i) the Writer, if available when the BBC requires the alterations to be made, has been asked to agree to them but is not willing to do so and (ii) the Writer has had, if he so requests and if the BBC agrees that time permits if rehearsals and recording are to pro-

ceed as planned, an opportunity to be represented by the Writers' Guild of Great Britain (or if he is not a member of the Guild by his agent) at a meeting with the BBC to be held within at most 48 hours of the request (excluding weekends). If in such circumstances there is no agreement about the alterations then the final decision shall rest with the BBC. Apart from the right to make alterations under (a) and (b) above the BBC shall not without the consent of the Writer or his agent (which consent shall not be unreasonably withheld) make any structural alterations as opposed to minor alterations to the script, provided that such consent shall not be necessary in any case where the Writer is for any reason not immediately available for consultation at the time which in the BBC's opinion is the deadline from the production point of view for such alterations to be made if rehearsals and recording are to proceed as planned.

series. Time-Life was permitted to edit the programs only "for insertion of commercials, applicable censorship or governmental * * * rules and regulations, and National Association of Broadcasters and time segment requirements." No similar clause was included in the scriptwriters' agreement between appellants and BBC. Prior to this time, ABC had sought to acquire the right to broadcast excerpts from various Monty Python programs in the spring of 1975, but the group rejected the proposal for such a disjoined format. Thereafter, in July 1975, ABC agreed with Time-Life to broadcast two ninety-minute specials each comprising three thirty-minute Monty Python programs that had not previously been shown in this country.

Correspondence between representatives of BBC and Monty Python reveals that these parties assumed that ABC would broadcast each of the Monty Python programs "in its entirety." On September 5, 1975, however, the group's British representative inquired of BBC how ABC planned to show the programs in their entirety if approximately 24 minutes of each 90 minute program were to be devoted to commercials. BBC replied on September 12, "we can only reassure you that ABC have decided to run the programmes 'back to back,' and that there is a firm undertaking not to segment them."

ABC broadcast the first of the specials on October 3, 1975. Appellants did not see a tape of the program until late November and were allegedly "appalled" at the discontinuity and "mutilation" that had resulted from the editing done by Time-Life for ABC. Twenty-four minutes of the original 90 minutes of recording had been omitted. Some of the editing had been done in order to make time for commercials; other material had been edited, according to ABC, because the original programs contained offensive or obscene matter.

In early December, Monty Python learned that ABC planned to broadcast the second special on December 26, 1975. The parties began negotiations concerning editing of that program and a delay of the broadcast until Monty Python could view it. These negotiations were futile, however, and on December 15 the group filed this action to enjoin the broadcast and for damages. Following an evidentiary hearing, Judge Lasker found that "the plaintiffs have established an impairment of the integrity of their work" which "caused the film or program * * * to lose its iconoclastic verve." According to Judge Lasker, "the damage that has been caused to the plaintiffs is irreparable by its nature." Nevertheless, the judge denied the motion for the preliminary injunction on the grounds that it was unclear who owned the copyright in the programs produced by BBC from the scripts written by Monty Python; that there was a question of whether Time-Life and BBC were indispensable parties to the litigation; that ABC would suffer significant financial loss if it were enjoined a week before the scheduled broadcast; and that Monty Python had displayed a "somewhat disturbing casualness" in their pursuance of the matter.

Judge Lasker granted Monty Python's request for more limited relief by requiring ABC to broadcast a disclaimer during the December 26 special to the effect that the group dissociated itself from the program because of the editing. A panel of this court, however, granted a stay of that order until this appeal could be heard and permitted ABC to broadcast, at the beginning of the special, only the legend that the program had been edited by ABC. We heard argument on April 13 and, at that time, enjoined ABC from any further broadcast of edited Monty Python programs pending the decision of the court.

We * * * reach the question whether there is a likelihood that appellants will succeed on the merits. In concluding that there is a likelihood of infringement here, we rely especially on the fact that the editing was substantial, i.e., approximately 27 per cent of the original program was omitted, and the editing contravened contractual provisions that limited the right to edit Monty Python material. * * *

Judge Lasker denied the preliminary injunction in part because he was unsure of the ownership of the copyright in the recorded program. Appellants first contend that the question of ownership is irrelevant because the recorded program was merely a derivative work taken from the script in which they hold the uncontested copyright. Thus, even if BBC owned the copyright in the recorded program, its use of that work would be limited by the license granted to BBC by Monty Python for use of the underlying script. We agree.

* * *

Since the copyright in the underlying script survives intact despite the incorporation of that work into a derivative work, one who uses the script, even with the permission of the proprietor of the derivative work, may infringe the underlying copyright. See Davis v. E. I. DuPont deNemours & Co., 240 F.Supp. 612 (S.D.N.Y. 1965) (defendants held to have infringed when they obtained permission to use a screenplay in preparing a television script but did not obtain permission of the author of the play upon which the screenplay was based).

If the proprietor of the derivative work is licensed by the proprietor of the copyright in the underlying work to vend or distribute the derivative work to third parties, those parties will, of course, suffer no liability for their use of the underlying work consistent with the license to the proprietor of the derivative work. Obviously, it was just this type of arrangement that was contemplated in this instance. The scriptwriters' agreement between Monty Python and BBC specifically permitted the latter to license the transmission of the recordings made by BBC to distributors such as Time-Life for broadcast in overseas territories.

One who obtains permission to use a copyrighted script in the production of a derivative work, however, may not exceed the specific purpose for which permission was granted. Most of the decisions that have reached this conclusion have dealt with the improper extension of the underlying work into media or time, i.e., duration of the license, not covered by the grant of permission to the derivative work proprietor. * * *

The rationale for finding infringement when a licensee exceeds time or media restrictions on his license—the need to allow the proprietor of the underlying copyright to control the method in which his work is presented to the public—applies equally to the situation in which a licensee makes an unauthorized use of the underlying work by publishing it in a truncated version. Whether intended to allow greater economic exploitation of the work, as in the media and time cases, or to ensure that the copyright proprietor retains a veto power over versions desired for the derivative work, the ability of the copyright holder to control his work remains paramount in our copyright law. We find, therefore, that unauthorized editing of the underlying work, if proven, would constitute an infringement of the copyright in that work similar to any other use of a work that exceeded the license granted by the proprietor of the copyright.

If the broadcast of an edited version of the Monty Python program infringed the group's copyright in the script, ABC may obtain no solace from the fact that editing was permitted in the agreements between BBC and Time-Life or Time-Life and ABC. BBC was not entitled to make unilateral changes in the script and was not specifically empowered to alter the recordings once made; Monty Python, moreover, had reserved to itself any rights not granted to BBC.

* * *

Our resolution of these technical arguments serves to reinforce our initial inclination that the copyright law should be used to recognize the important role of the artist in our society and the need to encourage production and dissemination of artistic works by providing adequate legal protection for one who submits his work to the public. See Mazer v. Stein, 347 U.S. 201 (1954). We therefore conclude that there is a substantial likelihood that, after a full trial, appellants will succeed in proving infringement of their copyright by ABC's broadcast of edited versions of Monty Python programs. In reaching this conclusion, however, we need not accept appellants' assertion that any editing whatsoever would constitute infringement. Courts have recognized that licensees are entitled to some small degree of latitude in arranging the licensed work for presentation to the public in a manner consistent with the licensee's style or standards. That privilege, however, does not extend to the degree of editing that occurred here especially in light of contractual provisions that limited the right to edit Monty Python material.

II

It also seems likely that appellants will succeed on the theory that, regardless of the right ABC had to broadcast an edited program, the cuts made constituted an actionable mutilation of Monty Python's work. This cause of action, which seeks redress for deformation of an artist's work, finds its roots in the continental concept of droit moral, or moral right, which may generally be summarized as including the right of the artist to have his work attributed to him in the form in which he created it. See 1 M. Nimmer, supra, at § 110.1.

American copyright law, as presently written, does not recognize moral rights or provide a cause of action for their violation, since the law seeks to vindicate the economic, rather than the personal, rights of authors. Nevertheless, the economic incentive for artistic and intellectual creation that serves as the foundation for American copyright law, Goldstein v. California, 412 U.S. 546 (1973); Mazer v. Stein, 347 U.S. 201 (1954), cannot be reconciled with the inability of artists to obtain relief for mutilation or misrepresentation of their work to the public on which the artists are financially dependent. Thus courts have long granted relief for misrepresentation of an artist's work by relying on theories outside the statutory law of copyright, such as contract law, Granz v. Harris, 198 F.2d 585 (2d Cir. 1952) (substantial cutting of original work constitutes misrepresentation), or the tort of unfair competition, Prouty v. National Broadcasting Co., 26 F.Supp. 265 (D. Mass. 1939). See Strauss, The Moral Right of the Author 128–138, in Studies on Copyright (1963). Although such decisions are clothed in terms of proprietary right in one's creation, they also properly vindicate the author's personal right to prevent the presentation of his work to the public in a distorted form. * * *

Here, the appellants claim that the editing done for ABC mutilated the original work and that consequently the broadcast of those programs as the creation of Monty Python violated the Lanham Act § 43(a), 15 U.S.C. § 1125(a). This statute, the federal counterpart to state unfair competition laws, has been invoked to prevent misrepresentations that may injure plaintiff's business or personal reputation, even where no registered trademark is concerned. * * * It is sufficient to violate the Act that a representation of a product, although technically true, creates a false impression of the product's origin. See Rich v. RCA Corp., 390 F.Supp. 530 (S.D.N.Y. 1975) (recent picture of plaintiff on cover of album containing songs recorded in distant past held to be a false representation that the songs were new); * * *. [A]n allegation that a defendant has presented to the public a [garbled], * * * distorted version of plaintiff's work seeks to redress the very rights sought to be protected by the Lanham Act, 15 U.S.C. § 1125(a), and should be recognized as stating a cause of action under that statute. * * *

During the hearing on the preliminary injunction, Judge Lasker viewed the edited version of the Monty Python program broadcast on December 26 and the original, unedited version. After hearing argument of this appeal, this panel also viewed and compared the two versions. We find that the truncated version at times omitted the climax of the skits to which appellants' rare brand of humor was leading and at other times deleted essential elements in the schematic development of a story line.[12] We therefore agree

---

12. A single example will illustrate the extent of distortion engendered by the editing. In one skit, an upper class English family is engaged in a discussion of the tonal quality of certain words as "woody" or "tinny." The father soon begins to suggest certain words with sexual connotations as either "woody" or "tinny," whereupon the mother fetches a bucket of water and pours it over his head. The skit continues from this point. The ABC edit eliminates this middle sequence so that the father is comfortably dressed at one moment and, in the next moment, is shown in a soaked condition without any explanation for the change in his appearance.

with Judge Lasker's conclusion that the edited version broadcast by ABC impaired the integrity of appellants' work and represented to the public as the product of appellants what was actually a mere caricature of their talents. We believe that a valid cause of action for such distortion exists and that therefore a preliminary injunction may issue to prevent repetition of the broadcast prior to final determination of the issues.[13]

For these reasons we direct that the district court issue the preliminary injunction sought by the appellants.

■ GURFEIN, CIRCUIT JUDGE (concurring):

I believe that this is the first case in which a federal appellate court has held that there may be a violation of Section 43(a) of the Lanham Act with respect to a common-law copyright. The Lanham Act is a trademark statute, not a copyright statute. Nevertheless, we must recognize that the language of Section 43(a) is broad. It speaks of the affixation or use of false designations of origin or false descriptions or representations, but proscribes such use "in connection with any goods or services." It is easy enough to incorporate trade names as well as trademarks into Section 43(a) and the statute specifically applies to common law trademarks, as well as registered trademarks. Lanham Act § 45, 15 U.S.C. § 1127.

In the present case, we are holding that the deletion of portions of the recorded tape constitutes a breach of contract, as well as an infringement of a common-law copyright of the original work. There is literally no need to discuss whether plaintiffs also have a claim for relief under the Lanham Act or for unfair competition under New York law. I agree with Judge Lumbard, however, that it may be an exercise of judicial economy to express our view on the Lanham Act claim, and I do not dissent therefrom. I simply wish to leave it open for the District Court to fashion the remedy.

The Copyright Act provides no recognition of the so-called *droit moral,* or moral right of authors. Nor are such rights recognized in the field of copyright law in the United States. See 1 Nimmer on Copyright, § 110.2 (1975 ed.). If a distortion or truncation in connection with a use constitutes an infringement of copyright, there is no need for an additional cause of action beyond copyright infringement. Id. at § 110.3. An obligation to mention the name of the author carries the implied duty, however, as a matter of contract, not to make such changes in the work as would render the credit line a false attribution of authorship, Granz v. Harris, 198 F.2d 585 (2 Cir. 1952).

---

13. Judge Gurfein's concurring opinion suggests that since the gravamen of a complaint under the Lanham Act is that the origin of goods has been falsely described, a legend disclaiming Monty Python's approval of the edited version would preclude violation of that Act. We are doubtful that a few words could erase the indelible impression that is made by a television broadcast, especially since the viewer has no means of comparing the truncated version with the complete work in order to determine for himself the talents of plaintiffs. Furthermore, a disclaimer such as the one originally suggested by Judge Lasker in the exigencies of an impending broadcast last December would go unnoticed by viewers who tuned into the broadcast a few minutes after it began.

We therefore conclude that Judge Gurfein's proposal that the district court could find some form of disclaimer would be sufficient might not provide appropriate relief.

So far as the Lanham Act is concerned, it is not a substitute for *droit moral* which authors in Europe enjoy. If the licensee may, by contract, distort the recorded work, the Lanham Act does not come into play. If the licensee has no such right by contract, there will be a violation in breach of contract. The Lanham Act can hardly apply literally when the credit line correctly states the work to be that of the plaintiffs which, indeed it is, so far as it goes. The vice complained of is that the truncated version is not what the plaintiffs wrote. But the Lanham Act does not deal with artistic integrity. It only goes to misdescription of origin and the like. * * *

The misdescription of origin can be dealt with, as Judge Lasker did below, by devising an appropriate legend to indicate that the plaintiffs had not approved the editing of the ABC version.[1] With such a legend, there is no conceivable violation of the Lanham Act. If plaintiffs complain that their artistic integrity is still compromised by the distorted version, their claim does not lie under the Lanham Act, which does not protect the copyrighted work itself but protects only against the misdescription or mislabelling.

* * *

NOTES

1. The *Gilliam* case is Exhibit 1 in support of the position that U.S. law meets the Berne Convention requirement that moral rights be protected.

2. Section 43(a) of the Lanham Act has also been successfully invoked by authors and artists claiming that they were not being given proper credit for their work. Smith v. Montoro, 648 F.2d 602 (9th Cir. 1981), involved an actor claiming that the film distributors had removed his name from the film credits and the advertising, and inserted another name. The court said this was "reverse passing off" actionable under § 43(a). In Dodd v. Fort Smith Special School Dist. No. 100, 666 F.Supp. 1278 (W.D. Ark. 1987), a junior high teacher and her students obtained a preliminary injunction enjoining the school district from publishing a book they had prepared without giving them authorship credit.

3. The case of an author who did not want credit was before the court in Follett v. Arbor House Publishing Co., 497 F.Supp. 304 (S.D.N.Y. 1980). There the author complained that the publisher was going to erroneously describe him as the author. The work was an account of a notorious bank robbery in Nice, France. Follett had translated the work into English from an account written by three French journalists. The work was first published in England, where Follett had pressed his publisher for authorship credit. But by the time the work was scheduled for publication in the United States, Follett had achieved great success here with *Eye of the Needle* and *Triple*. The American publisher of the translation wanted to capitalize on this success and Follett wanted to stop it, in part because of a forthcoming book with another publisher. The proposed description was: "by the author

---

1. I do not imply that the appropriate legend be shown only at the beginning of the broadcast. That is a matter for the District Court.

of TRIPLE and EYE OF THE NEEDLE KEN FOLLETT with Rene Louis Maurice." Rene Louis Maurice was a pseudonym used by the three French journalists. The court decreed that Follett and Maurice should be given equal credit.

4. Can the author of a letter to the editor keep control over the use made of the letter by claiming copyright? In Diamond v. Am-Law Publishing Corp., 745 F.2d 142 (2d Cir. 1984), the *American Lawyer* ran a story reporting that Diamond, a New York lawyer, had had a dispute over a $1,608.50 legal fee with a client, and that as a result of his persistent efforts to collect it the client had filed a grievance against him with the New York bar association. Diamond wrote to Stephen Brill, editor of the magazine, demanding a retraction and apology. Brill wrote to Diamond inviting him to write a letter for publication in the magazine stating that no grievance had been filed. Diamond wrote such a letter, criticizing the story and the reportorial work of the magazine. The letter stated "You are authorized to publish this letter but only in its entirety." Brill published the letter in edited form. Diamond sued for copyright infringement. Held: fair use. "[Section 107] expressly protects comments and news reporting, and Diamond's own demands for a retraction with regard to whether [the client] * * * had filed a grievance are more than enough to render the portion of the letter published newsworthy. A paraphrase of Diamond's version of the facts relating to the grievance would not have been a basis for an infringement action, and we fail to see why using his own words creates such liability." 745 F.2d 147. Does this holding survive the Supreme Court's *Nation* decision?

5. An issue related to the continuing rights of the author vis-a-vis the owner of the work is the right of the author to continue to make use of themes, ideas, and techniques incorporated in the (now transferred) copyrighted work. Artists and writers tend to work in similar or related styles or themes over a period of time. Think of the characters like Falstaff, who appears in several of Shakespeare's plays, or the practice of an author using a detective character like Sherlock Holmes through a series of books, or of Monet's water lilies. This is not surprising since it has probably taken considerable effort to find a successful approach, and the artist may even be able to enrich his work through subtle development and interplay among the various realizations of the idea. This is, like the other issues in this section, an issue that can be addressed at the time of the original transfer. But if the copyright has simply been transferred without further elaboration, what can the author or artist continue to use? The simple answer is, of course, that he can continue to use those elements of the work not protected by copyright. But some decisions suggest that the courts may be more receptive to the claim of an author or artist to use elements of his "own" work than they would be to a similar claim from a third-party.

In Warner Bros. Pictures, Inc. v. Columbia Broadcasting System, Inc., 216 F.2d 945 (9th Cir. 1954), Dashiell Hammett wrote a mystery-detective story entitled "The Maltese Falcon." The detective was named Sam Spade. Warner Brothers acquired the ownership of the copyright from Hammett and his publisher Knopf. Hammett used the characters from "The Maltese

Falcon" in later works, and Warner Bros. sued for infringement. The court construed the transfer of copyright to Warner Brothers as not including the right to use the characters in subsequent stories (although there was only one copyright, which the instrument made no effort to divide). "The conclusion that these rights are not within the granting instruments is strongly buttressed by the fact that historically and presently detective fiction writers have and do carry the leading characters with their names and individualisms from one story into succeeding stories. This was the practice of Edgar Allen Poe, Sir Arthur Conan Doyle, and others. * * * If the intention of the contracting parties had been to avoid this practice which was a very valuable one to the author, it is hardly reasonable that it would be left to a general clause following specific grants." 216 F.2d 945.

In Franklin Mint Corp. v. National Wildlife Art Exchange, Inc., 575 F.2d 62 (3d Cir. 1978), Gilbert, a nationally recognized wildlife artist, had painted a water color of cardinals entitled "Cardinals on Apple Blossom." Gilbert sold the painting to National Wildlife in exchange for a check bearing the notation "For Cardinal painting 20 X 24 including all rights—reproduction etc." National sold an edition of 300 prints of the painting. Gilbert later painted and sold to the Franklin Mint Corporation four water color bird life pictures, including one of cardinals with similarities to the National Wildlife painting. Franklin Mint made engravings of the four paintings, which were sold as a group. National Wildlife sued for infringement. In the course of affirming a finding of no infringement, the court observed that "There was also testimony on the tendency of some painters to return to certain basic themes time and time again. Winslow Homer's schoolboys, Monet's facade of Rouen Cathedral, and Bingham's flatboat characters were cited. Franklin Mint relied upon these examples of 'variations on a theme' as appropriate examples of the freedom which must be extended to artists to utilize basic subject matter more than once. National vigorously objects to the use of such a concept as being contrary to the theory of copyright. We do not find the phrase objectionable, however, because a 'variation' probably is not a copy and if a 'theme' is equated with an 'idea,' it may not be monopolized. We conceive of 'variations on a theme,' therefore, as another way of saying that an 'idea' may not be copyrighted and only its 'expressions may be protected'." 575 F.2d at 66.

6. French law provides the artist with the *droit de suite* or right to share in the sale price of a work after its initial sale. The right enables artists who sell their early works for low prices, but who later achieve success in the market, to share in the later appreciation in the value of the paintings. See generally, Monroe Price, Government Policy and Economic Security for Artists: The Case of the Droit de Suite, 77 Yale L.J. 1333 (1968). California has enacted a statute based upon the *droit de suite,* California Civil Code § 986. It provides that whenever a work of fine art is sold and the seller resides in California, or the sale takes place in California, the seller shall pay to the artist five percent of the amount of the sale. The statute was upheld against constitutional attack in Morseburg v. Balyon, 621 F.2d 972 (9th Cir. 1980). The statute is discussed in Stephen S. Ashley, Critical Comment on California's Droit de Suite, Civil Code Section 986, 29 Hast. L.J. 249 (1977) and Comment, The Droit de Suite Has Arrived: Can it Thrive in California as it Has in Calais?, 11 Creighton L. Rev. 529 (1977).

The statute was amended in 1982 to provide that the artist could assign this right to another entity (not the purchaser). This would make it possible to have an enforcement organization like ASCAP, described below, to monitor and enforce these rights. John E. McInerney III, California Resale Royalties Act: Private Sector Enforcement, 19 U. S.F. L. Rev. 1 (1984), discusses these amendments. The article concedes that "Apparent lack of effective means to collectively enforce the Act has made it virtually irrelevant." Id. at 2.

Can the California statute be avoided by directing the sale to an out-of-state (New York?) auction house?

If art work rises in value after the first sale, isn't that rise likely to be in part due to promotional efforts of the artist subsequent to the first sale? Doesn't the owner of an artist's work have an interest in giving the artist an incentive to promote the market for his work, including pieces already sold?

The *Morseburg* case was decided under the 1909 act. Different result under § 301? Note, The California Resale Royalties Act as a Test Case for Preemption, 81 Colum. L. Rev. 1315 (1981), concludes no preemption.

As part of the passage of VARA in 1990, Congress asked the Copyright Office to prepare a report on resale royalties. The report recommended against their adoption in the U.S. This conclusion is criticized in Michael B. Reddy, The Droit de Suite: Why American Fine Artists Should Have the Right to A Resale Royalty, 15 Loy. L.A. Ent. L.J. 509 (1995).

E. Copyright Enforcement

1. *The performing rights organizations.* Copyright law has led to the formation of an unusual kind of organization—the performing rights organization—which plays an important role in the enforcement of the performing rights. The principal organizations are ASCAP—the American Society of Composers, Authors and Publishers—and BMI—Broadcast Music, Inc.

ASCAP arose to provide a feasible system for the owners of musical copyrights to enforce their performance rights against broadcasters, theaters, bars, nightclubs and such. Musical performances (whether live or by playing a record) on every radio (and later TV) station, and at every theater, bar and night club in the land are infringements unless licensed, but it is hardly feasible for the copyright owner to go from bar to bar (or listen all night to the radio) until he finds an unauthorized performance of his song. Instead, the owner authorizes the society to license his work, and the society offers blanket licenses to enable the licensee to use all of the songs in the society's catalogue. If the society learns of a broadcaster or other establishment that has not obtained a license, it can listen to the station or send an investigator into the establishment. Given the size of the ASCAP catalogue, it will not be long before several unauthorized performances of ASCAP songs occur. A suit for infringement, complete with a claim for statutory damages and attorney's fees, follows shortly thereafter.

BMI is a non-profit corporation owned and operated by the broadcasters to compete with ASCAP. Both BMI and ASCAP obtain most of their revenues from the broadcasting industry.

The performing rights organizations have elaborate procedures for allocating the revenues they receive among the participating publishers and authors. These procedures depend upon sampling techniques to estimate the relative amount of time works are being played by licensees.

The Copyright Clearance Center or CCC, discussed in the second circuit *Texaco* decision above is modeled on ASCAP and BMI. It is designed to help publisher's collect copying royalties. One problem that the CCC faces, that ASCAP and BMI do not face, is that the infringements it polices do not occur in public spaces.

NOTES

1. ASCAP, as a combination of many of the music authors and publishers, has been the subject of numerous suits under the antitrust laws and operates under the terms of a consent decree entered in the Southern District of New York. The decree was first entered in 1941 and has been subject to many subsequent revisions. In Broadcast Music, Inc. v. Columbia Broadcasting System, Inc., 441 U.S. 1 (1979), the Supreme Court decided that the policy of both ASCAP and BMI of refusing to license on a work-by-work basis and offering only blanket licenses (licenses to use any song in the catalogue) was not a per se violation of the Sherman Act. CBS wanted the courts to force ASCAP and BMI to offer it licenses covering only the songs CBS wanted to use. The Court relied heavily on the right of members of ASCAP or licensors of BMI to separately and independently license their works if they wish to do so. This right is rarely if ever exercised, presumably because broadcasters find it too costly to deal with many separate authors and publishers.

2. *Copyright Arbitration Royalty Panels.* The panels are successors to the Copyright Royalty Tribunal, a permanent government agency created by the 1976 Act that was subsequently abolished and replaced by temporary panels. Their function is to fix compulsory royalty rates under §§ 111 (cable TV), 114 (nonexempt digital subscription transmissions), 115 (records and digital phonorecord deliveries), and 118 (public broadcasting), and to distribute the funds generated by the cable T.V. royalty, § 111(4). They are appointed on an issue by issue basis by the Librarian of Congress.

a. Cable TV. While the copyright act was pending in Congress the question arose in the courts as to whether a cable system which picked up a broadcast signal and transmitted it to subscribers was infringing the copyright. The Supreme Court held that it was not. Teleprompter Corp. v. Columbia Broadcasting System, 415 U.S. 394 (1974); Fortnightly Corp. v. United Artists Television, Inc., 392 U.S. 390 (1968). The cases turned on the Court's conclusion that the cable systems were not publicly performing the retransmitted works under the 1909 Act.

Meanwhile the issue was hotly contested in Congress in connection with the statutory revision effort. The broad protective sweep of § 106 threatened the immune status of the cable operators. In addition, the economic role of cable was increasing rapidly. Congress compromised between full copyright protection and no copyright protection by setting a compulsory royalty and gave the Copyright Royalty Tribunal (subsequently a copyright arbitration royalty panel) authority to readjust the royalty level.

b. Records. The 1909 Act, as almost an afterthought (records had just appeared) set a compulsory royalty of 2 cents per record. Sec. 1(e). By the 1970's long playing records and inflation had made the fee hopelessly obsolete. Congress raised the fee to 2 and three-fourths cents or half a cent a minute, whichever is greater, and gave the Copyright Royalty Tribunal (subsequently a copyright arbitration royalty panel) authority to revise it periodically.

c. Public broadcasting. Public broadcasting is provided a non-budget subsidy in § 118.

3. *Criminal Enforcement.* Criminal enforcement of the copyright laws has become important. Infringement of copyright has long been a federal crime. (Unlike infringement of a patent and until the enactment of the Trademark Counterfeiting Act of 1984, a trademark. Can you explain why?) But it was a rarely prosecuted crime until low-cost reproduction equipment made organized, large-scale sale of infringing records, tapes and movies big business. There are now numerous reported criminal prosecutions.

Dowling v. United States, 473 U.S. 207 (1985), involved a prosecution of three young men who had established a thriving business in the manufacture, promotion and sale of records of Elvis Presley performances, all made without copyright license. The records were not copies of commercially available records, but rather recordings made from unreleased performances such as movie sound tracks, broadcasts and so on, and of particular interest to Presley cultists. Conviction was obtained not only for criminal copyright infringement, but for interstate transportation of stolen property. Held: defendant did not engage in the interstate transportation of stolen property when he engaged in the interstate distribution of infringing records. The Court said:

> The broad consequences of the Government's theory, both in the field of copyright and in kindred fields of intellectual property law, provide a final and dispositive factor against reading § 2314 in the manner suggested. For example, in *Harper & Row,* supra, this Court very recently held that The Nation, a weekly magazine of political commentary, had infringed former President Ford's copyright in the unpublished manuscript of his memoirs by verbatim excerpting of some 300 words from the work. It rejected The Nation's argument that the excerpting constituted fair use. Presented with the facts of that case as a hypothetical at oral argument in the present litigation, the Government conceded that its theory of § 2314 would permit prosecution of the magazine if it transported copies of sufficient value across state lines. Tr. of Oral Arg. 35. Whatever the wisdom or propriety of The Nation's decision to publish the excerpts, we would pause, in the

absence of any explicit indication of congressional intention, to bring such conduct within the purview of a criminal statute making available serious penalties for the interstate transportation of goods "stolen, converted or taken by fraud."

Likewise, the field of copyright does not cabin the Government's theory, which would as easily encompass the law of patents and other forms of intellectual property. If "the intangible idea protected by the copyright is effectively made tangible by its embodiment upon the tapes," United States v. Gottesman, 724 F.2d 1517, 1520 (11th Cir. 1984), phonorecords, or films shipped in interstate commerce as to render those items stolen goods for purposes of § 2314, so too would the intangible idea protected by a patent be made tangible by its embodiment in an article manufactured in accord with patented specifications. Thus, as the Government as much as acknowledged at argument, Tr. of Oral Arg. 29, its view of the statute would readily permit its application to interstate shipments of patent-infringing goods. Despite its undoubted power to do so, however, Congress has not provided criminal penalties for distribution of goods infringing valid patents.[19] Thus, the rational supporting application of the statute under the circumstances of this case would equally justify its use in wide expanses of the law which Congress has evidenced no intention to enter by way of criminal sanction.[20] This factor militates strongly against the reading proffered by the Government, Cf. Williams v. United States, 458 U.S., at 287, 102 S.Ct., at 3093.

473 U.S., at 225–227.

David LaMacchia, a twenty-one year old student at the Massachusetts Institute of Technology set up a computer bulletin board on MIT's computer network and accessible from the Internet. He encouraged others to download copies of popular software applications and games to the bulletin board, and made them accessible to others for uploading. When the volume of world-wide Internet traffic attracted to his bulletin board was noticed by authorities, he was indicted for wire fraud, in violation of 18 U.S.C. § 1343. The district court dismissed the indictment, relying by analogy on Dowling

---

19. Congress instead had relied on provisions affording patent owners a civil cause of action. 35 U.S.C. §§ 281–294. Among the available remedies are treble damages for willful infringement.   § 284; see, e.g., American Safety Table Co. v. Schreiber, 415 F.2d 373, 378–379 (2d Cir. 1969), cert. denied 396 U.S. 1038 (1970). * * * The only criminal provision relating to patents is 18 U.S.C. § 497, which proscribes the forgery, counterfeiting, or false alteration of letters patent, or the uttering thereof. See also 35 U.S.C. § 292 ($500 penalty, one-half to go to person suing

and one-half to the United States, for false marking of patent status).

20. The Government's rationale would also apply to goods infringing trademark rights. Yet, despite having long and extensively legislated in this area, see federal Trademark Act of 1946 (Lanham Act), 15 U.S.C. § 1051 et seq., in the modern era Congress only recently has resorted to criminal sanctions to control trademark infringement.   See Trademark Counterfeiting Act of 1984, Pub.L. 98–473, ch. XV, 98 Stat. 2178. * * *

v. United States, 473 U.S. 207 (1985). United States v. LaMacchia, 871 F. Supp. 535 (1994).

LaMacchia could not be indicted under § 506 because he was running his bulletin board for fun, not "commercial advantage or private financial gain." Congress has now amended § 506 to include within criminal infringement willful infringement "by the reproduction or distribution, including by electronic means, during any 180-day period, of 1 or more copies or phonorecords of 1 or more copyrighted works, which have a total retail value of more than $1,000." §506(a)(2), P.L. 105–147 (1997).

CHAPTER 6

PATENTS

The patent statute (35 U.S.C. §§ 1-376, hereafter cited by Section number only) establishes nine major requirements for a valid patent. Five of the requirements are substantive, that is, they define what can be patented. Four are procedural, that is, they define the steps that must be taken to obtain a valid patent. The five substantive requirements are:

1. Patentable subject matter (§ 101);

2. Originality (§§ 101, 115);

3. Novelty (§§ 101, 102);

4. Utility (§ 101);

5. Non-obviousness (§ 103).

The four procedural requirements are:

1. An application filed with the patent office by the inventor or his representative (§§ 111, 115, 116, 117, 118);

2. within one year of the public use or publication of the invention (§ 102(b));

3. with a specification containing "a written description of the invention, and of the manner and process of making and using it, in such full, clear, concise, and exact terms as to enable any person skilled in the art to which it pertains * * * to make and use the same" (§§ 112, 113, 114), and concluding;

4. with one or more claims "pointing out and distinctly claiming the subject matter" which constitutes the invention, and no more (§ 112).

A patent is issued to an applicant only after the Patent and Trademark Office determines, based upon an examination of the application (§ 131), that it meets the statutory requirements (§ 151). If a patent owner subsequently wishes to enforce the patent, a suit for infringement is brought in a United States District Court. The District Courts have exclusive jurisdiction over infringement actions. 28 U.S.C. § 1338(a). The fact that the patent has already been reviewed and issued by the patent office does not prevent the defendant in an infringement action from proving that the patent does not meet the requirements of the statute, although an issued patent enjoys a presumption of validity (§ 282).

A valid patent confers upon its owner the exclusive right to make, use or sell the patented invention within the United States during the term of the patent, which is twenty years from the date of the application (§ 154) (except for design patents, which have a term of fourteen years from the date of the grant (§ 173)).

A patent is more difficult to obtain than a copyright, but confers more sweeping rights. In particular, there is no requirement that the infringer of a patent have copied from the patent (§ 271). Even if the infringer developed his own technology independently of any knowledge of the patent, he infringes if his technology falls within the claim of the patent. The burden is on the firm designing or purchasing a new product or using a new process to examine the record of issued patents in the patent office and determine whether or not any patents are infringed.

Appeals in patent cases from all of the district courts go to the United States Court of Appeals for the Federal Circuit, which is based in Washington but occasionally holds oral argument in other locations. The Federal Circuit has ruled that precedents of its predecessor courts (the Court of Claims and Court of Customs and Patent Appeals) announced prior to September 30, 1982 (the date of its creation), are binding precedent for it. South Corp. v. United States, 690 F.2d 1368 (Fed. Cir. 1982) (en banc). However, in patent cases on appeal from the district courts, issues in those cases other than patent law issues are to be governed by the law of the circuit in which the district court sits. Atari, Inc. v. JS & A Group, Inc., 747 F.2d 1422 (Fed. Cir. 1984).

Because the Federal Circuit hears all patent appeals, its opinions are, except for occasional Supreme Court decisions, the authoritative precedents on questions of patent law.

The Agreement on Trade Related Aspects of Intellectual Property of the General Agreement on Tariffs and Trade (the "GATT" "TRIPS") contains a section on patents, Articles 27 to 34. (For general background of the GATT TRIPS, see the discussion at the beginning of Chapter 5.) The U.S. was already a signatory of the Convention of Paris, the leading international agreement on patents, trademarks and unfair competition. The Convention of Paris was based almost entirely upon the principle of national treatment, i.e. each signatory undertook to treat applicants of other signatory states the same as it treats its own citizens. The only exception was a provision requiring member states to treat an application filed by a citizen of another member state as if it had been filed at the time of the home country application, as long as the application was filed within one year.

The GATT TRIPS contains provisions requiring that countries provide broad patent coverage. Two provisions in the GATT TRIPS required an immediate change in U.S. law. One was Article 33, which requires a patent term of twenty years from the filing date. The U.S. had previously had a term of seventeen years from the date of issue. Section 154(a)(2) was amended to conform to this requirement. The other was the provision of Article 27.1 which required that patent protection be available for inventions "without discrimination as to the place of invention." U.S. law had previously awarded priority to the first inventor in the United States, and did not count inventive activity outside the United States. Section 104 was amended to include inventive activity in a WIPO country (i.e. a country that is a signatory to the GATT). These amendments were made by the Uruguay Round Agreements Act, P.L 103–465 (1994).

NOTES

1. The patent and trademark office is financed by fees imposed on applicants for patents and trademarks. One advantage of this system is that it greatly reduces the incentive to obtain patents on inventions whose value is so low that it would be negative if the costs of administering the system are taken into account.

Congress has set many of the fees in § 41(a) and (b) and given the Commissioner the authority to set other fees so as to recover the costs of providing the service that is provided (§ 41(d)). The Commissioner also has authority to adjust the fees for inflation (§ 41(f)). The Commissioner is also instructed to reduce the fees by 50 percent for small businesses, independent inventors and nonprofit organizations (§ 41(h)(1)). In recent years the number of applications and issued patents has greatly increased, partly in response to the enhanced enforceability of U.S. patents. As a result, the office has been running a surplus. President Clinton has proposed to divert some of this surplus to the general U.S. budget.

Examples of some current fees (set out in 37 C.F.R. §§ 1.16–1.20) are: for a patent application, $790; for patent issue, $1,320; maintenance fee due three and one-half years after issue, $1,050; maintenance fee due seven and one-half years after issue, $2,100; maintenance fee due eleven years and six months after issue, $3,160.

2. Donald S. Chisum, Patents: A Treatise on the Law of Patentability, Validity and Infringement (New York: Matthew Bender, 1978, 5 vols., loose-leaf), is a useful resource, as is Peter D. Rosenberg, Patent Law Fundamentals (New York: Clark Boardman Co., Ltd., 1980, 3 vols., loose-leaf).

3. The economic effects of a patent system have been extensively analyzed. Fritz Machlup, An Economic Review of the Patent System, Study No. 15 of the Subcommittee on Patents, Trademarks and Copyrights of the Committee on the Judiciary, U.S. Senate, 85th Cong.2d Sess. (1958), is a comprehensive review of the literature up to 1958. Later contributions are Kenneth Arrow, Economic Welfare and the Allocation of Resources for Invention, in National Bureau of Economic Research, The Rate and Direction of Inventive Activity (Princeton: Princeton Univ. Press, 1962) at 617; Harold Demsetz, Information and Efficiency: Another Viewpoint, 12 J. of Law & Econ. 12 (1969); Edmund W. Kitch, The Nature and Function of the Patent System, 20 J. of Law & Econ. 265 (1977); Robert Merges and Richard Nelson, On the Complex Economics of Patent Scope, 90 Colum.L.Rev. 839 (1990); Kenneth W. Dam, The Economic Underpinnings of Patent Law, 23 J. Of Legal Studies 247 (1994).

An intriguing episode in world patent history was the failure of the Netherlands and Switzerland to provide patents during the nineteenth century. Their experience is described and analyzed in Eric Schiff, Industrialization Without National Patents (Princeton Univ. Press, 1971).

4. The right to obtain a patent is the right of the particular person (or persons, see § 116) who makes the invention (§ 111, with exceptions in §§ 117 and 118), even if the person has done the work on the invention while a full time research employee of a business. Such an employee is probably subject to an obligation to assign the patent to the employer if it is issued, and the employer probably handles the application and pays the expense of obtaining and enforcing the patent, but the application is pursued on behalf of the individual. This is in contrast to the copyright law, where a "work made for hire" [defined term] is treated as the work of the employer. 17 U.S.C. § 201(b).

A. Patentable Subject Matter

The statute provides that a patent may issue on "any new and useful process, machine, manufacture, or composition of matter, or any new and useful improvement thereof" (§ 101).

O'Reilly v. Morse

Supreme Court of the United States, 1853.
56 U.S. (15 How.) 62, 14 L.Ed. 601.

■ MR. CHIEF JUSTICE TANEY delivered the opinion of the court.

In proceeding to pronounce judgment in this case, the court is sensible, not only of its importance, but of the difficulties in some of the questions which it presents for decision. * * *

The appellants take three grounds of defense. In the first place they deny that Professor Morse, was the first and original inventor of the Electro-Magnetic Telegraphs described in his two reissued patents of 1848. Secondly, they insist that if he was the original inventor, the patents under which he claims have not been issued conformably to the acts of Congress, and do not confer on him the right to the exclusive use. And thirdly, if these two propositions are decided against them, they insist that the Telegraph of O'Reilly is substantially different from that of Professor Morse, and the use of it, therefore, no infringement of his rights. * * *

In relation to the first point (the originality of the invention), many witnesses have been examined on both sides.

It is obvious that, for some years before Professor Morse made his invention, scientific men in different parts of Europe were earnestly engaged in the same pursuit. Electro-magnetism itself was a recent discovery, and opened to them a new and unexplored field for their labors, and minds of a high order were engaged in developing its power and the purposes to which it might be applied.

Professor Henry, of the Smithsonian Institute, states in his testimony that, prior to the winter of 1819–20, an electro-magnetic telegraph—that is to say a telegraph operating by the combined influence of electricity and magnetism—was not possible; that the scientific principles on which it is founded were until then unknown; and that the first fact of electro-magnetism was discovered by Oersted, of Copenhagen, in that winter, and was widely published, and the account everywhere received with interest.

He also gives an account of the various discoveries, subsequently made from time to time, by different persons in different places, developing its properties and powers, and among them his own. He commenced his researches in 1828, and pursued them with ardor and success, from that time until the telegraph of Professor Morse was established and in actual operation. And it is due to him to say that no one has contributed more to enlarge the knowledge of electro-magnetism, and to lay the foundations of the great invention of which we are speaking, than the professor himself.

It is unnecessary, however, to give in detail the discoveries enumerated by him—either his own or those of others. But it appears from his testimony that very soon after the discovery made by Oersted, it was believed by men of science that this newly-discovered power might be used to communicate intelligence to distant places. And before the year 1823, Ampere of Paris, one of the most successful cultivators of physical science, proposed to the French Academy a plan for that purpose. But his project was never reduced to practice. And the discovery made by Barlow, of the Royal Military Academy of Woolwich, England, in 1825, that the galvanic current greatly diminished in power as the distance increased, put at rest, for a time, all attempts to construct an electro-magnetic telegraph. Subsequent discoveries, however, revived the hope; and in the year 1832, when Professor Morse appears to have devoted himself to the subject, the conviction was general among men of science everywhere that the object could, and sooner or later would, be accomplished.

The great difficulty in their way was the fact that the galvanic current, however strong in the beginning, became gradually weaker as it advanced on the wire; and was not strong enough to produce a mechanical effect, after a certain distance had been traversed. But, encouraged by the discoveries which were made from time to time, and strong in the belief that an electro-magnetic telegraph was practicable, many eminent and scientific men in Europe, as well as in this country, became deeply engaged in endeavoring to surmount what appeared to be the chief obstacle to its success. And in this state of things it ought not to be a matter of surprise that four different magnetic telegraphs, purporting to have overcome the difficulty, should be invented and made public so nearly at the same time that each has claimed a priority; and that a close and careful scrutiny of the facts in each case is necessary to decide between them. The inventions were so nearly simultaneous, that neither inventor can justly be accused of having derived any aid from the discoveries of the other.

* * *

We perceive no well-founded objection to the description which is given of the whole invention and its separate parts, nor to his right to a patent for the first seven inventions set forth in the specification of his claims. The difficulty arises on the eighth.

It is in the following words:

"Eighth. I do not propose to limit myself to the specific machinery or parts of machinery described in the foregoing specification and claims; the essence of my invention being the use of the motive power of the electric or galvanic current, which I call electromagnetism, however developed for marking or printing intelligible characters, signs, or letters, at any distances, being a new application of that power of which I claim to be the first inventor or discoverer."

It is impossible to misunderstand the extent of this claim. He claims the exclusive right to every improvement where the motive power is the electric or galvanic current, and the result is the marking or printing intelligible characters, signs, or letters at a distance.

If this claim can be maintained, it matters not by what process or machinery the result is accomplished. For aught that we now know some future inventor, in the onward march of science, may discover a mode of writing or printing at a distance by means of the electric or galvanic current, without using any part of the process or combination set forth in the plaintiff's specification. His invention may be less complicated—less liable to get out of order—less expensive in construction, and in its operation. But yet if it is covered by this patent the inventor could not use it, nor the public have the benefit of it without the permission of this patentee.

* * *

No one we suppose will maintain that Fulton could have taken out a patent for his invention of propelling vessels by steam, describing the process and machinery he used, and claimed under it the exclusive right to use the motive power of steam, however developed, for the purpose of propelling vessels. It can hardly be supposed that under such a patent he could have prevented the use of the improved machinery which science has since introduced; although the motive power is steam, and the result is the propulsion of vessels. * * *

Again, the use of steam as a motive power in printing presses is comparatively a modern discovery. Was the first inventor of a machine or process of this kind entitled to a patent, giving him the exclusive right to use steam as a motive power, however developed, for the purpose of marking or printing intelligible characters? Could he have prevented the use of any other press subsequently invented where steam was used? * * *

* * *

The leading case * * * is that of Neilson and others v. Harford and others in the English Court of Exchequer. It was elaborately argued and appears to have been carefully considered by the court. The case was this:

Neilson, in his specification, described his invention as one for the improved application of air to produce heat in fires, forges, and furnaces, where a blowing apparatus is required. And it was to be applied as follows: The blast or current of air produced by the blowing apparatus was to be passed from it into an air-vessel or receptacle made sufficiently strong to endure the blast; and through or from that vessel or receptacle by means of a tube, pipe, or aperture into the fire, the receptacle be kept artificially heated to a considerable temperature by heat externally applied. He then described in rather general terms the manner in which the receptacle might be constructed and heated, and the air conducted through it to the fire: stating that the form of the receptacle was not material, nor the manner of applying heat to it. * * * [T]he defendant among other defences insisted that a patent for throwing hot air into the furnace, instead of cold, and thereby increasing the intensity of the heat, was a patent for a principle, and that a principle was not patentable.

Baron Parke, who delivered the opinion of the court, said:

"It is very difficult to distinguish it from the specification of a patent for a principle, and this at first created in the minds of the court much difficulty; but after full consideration we think that the plaintiff does not merely claim a principle, but a machine, embodying a principle and a very valuable one. We think the case must be considered as if the principle being well known, the plaintiff had first invented a mode of applying it by a mechanical apparatus to furnaces, and his invention then consists in this: by interposing a receptacle for heated air between the blowing apparatus and the furnace. In this receptacle he directs the air to be heated by the application of heat externally to the receptacle, and thus he accomplishes the object of applying the blast, which was before cold air, in a heated state to the furnace."

We see nothing in this opinion differing in any degree from the familiar principles of law applicable to patent cases. Neilson claimed no particular mode of constructing the receptacle, or of heating it. He pointed out the manner in which it might be done; but admitted that it might also be done in a variety of ways; and at a higher or lower temperature; and that all of them would produce the effect in a greater or less degree, provided the air was heated by passing through a heated receptacle. And hence it seems that the court at first doubted, whether it was a patent for anything more than the discovery that hot air would promote the ignition of fuel better than cold. And if this had been the construction, the court, it appears, would have held his patent to be void; because the discovery of a principle in natural philosophy or physical science, is not patentable.

. But after much consideration, it was finally decided that this principle must be regarded as well known, and that the plaintiff had invented a mechanical mode of applying it to furnaces; and that his invention consisted in interposing a heated receptacle, between the blower and the furnace, and by this means heating the air after it left the blower, and before it was thrown into the fire. Whoever, therefore, used this method of throwing hot air into the furnace, used the process he had invented, and thereby infringed his patent, although the form of the receptacle or the mechanical arrangements for heating it, might be different from those described by the patentee. For whatever form was adopted for the receptacle, or whatever mechanical arrangements were made for heating it, the effect would be produced in a greater or less degree, if the heated receptacle was placed between the blower and the furnace, and the current of air passed through it.

Undoubtedly, the principle that hot air will promote the ignition of fuel better than cold, was embodied in this machine. But the patent was not supported because this principle was embodied in it. He would have been equally entitled to a patent, if he had invented an improvement in the mechanical arrangements of the blowing apparatus, or in the furnace, while a cold current of air was still used. But his patent was supported, because he had invented a mechanical apparatus, by which a current of hot air, instead of cold, could be thrown in. And this new method was protected by his patent. The interposition of a heated receptacle, in any form, was the novelty he invented.

* * *

This court has decided, that the specification required by this law is a part of the patent; and that the patent issues for the invention described in the specification.

Now whether the Telegraph is regarded as an art or machine, the manner and process of making or using it must be set forth in exact terms. The act of Congress makes no difference in this respect between an art and a machine. An improvement in the art of making bar iron or spinning cotton must be so described; and so must the art of printing by the motive power of steam. And in all of these cases it has always been held that the patent embraces nothing more than the improvement described and claimed as new, and that any one who afterwards discovered a method of accomplishing the same object, substantially and essentially differing from the one described, had a right to use it.

* * *

The provisions of the acts of Congress in relation to patents may be summed up in a few words.

Whoever discovers that a certain useful result will be produced, in any art, machine, manufacture, or composition of matter, by the use of certain means, is entitled to a patent for it; provided he specifies the means he uses in a manner so full and exact, that any one skilled in the science to which it appertains, can, by using the means he specifies, without any addition to, or subtraction from them, produce precisely the result he describes. And if this cannot be done by the means he describes, the patent is void. And if it can be done, then the patent confers on him the exclusive right to use the means he specifies to produce the result or effect he describes, and nothing more. And it makes no difference, in this respect, whether the effect is produced by chemical agency or combination; or by the application of discoveries or principles in natural philosophy known or unknown before his invention; or by machinery acting altogether upon mechanical principles. In either case he must describe the manner and process as above mentioned, and the end it accomplishes. And any one may lawfully accomplish the same end without infringing the patent, if he uses means substantially different from those described.

Indeed, if the eighth claim of the patentee can be maintained, there was no necessity for any specification, further than to say that he had discovered that, by using the motive power of electromagnetism, he could print intelligible characters at any distance. We presume it will be admitted on all hands, that no patent could have issued on such a specification. Yet this claim can derive no aid from the specification field. It is outside of it, and the patentee claims beyond it. And if it stands, it must stand simply on the ground that the broad terms above-mentioned were a sufficient description, and entitled him to a patent in terms equally broad. In our judgment the act of Congress cannot be so construed. * * * [The Court then held that although the eighth claim was illegal and void, the rest of the claims were good.] The only remaining question is, whether they or either of them have been infringed by the defendants.

* * *

It is a well-settled principle of law, that the mere change in the form of the machinery (unless a particular form is specified as the means by which the effect described is produced) or an alteration in some of its unessential parts; or in the use of known equivalent powers, not varying essentially the machine, or its mode of operation or organization, will not make the new machine a new invention. It may be an improvement upon the former; but that will not justify its use without the consent of the first patentee.

The Columbian (O'Reilly's) Telegraph does not profess to accomplish a new purpose, or produce a new result. Its object and effect is to communicate intelligence at a distance, at the end of the main line, and at the local circuits on its way. And this is done by means of signs or letters impressed on paper or other material. The object and purpose of the Telegraph is the same with that of Professor Morse.

Does he use the same means? Substantially, we think he does, both upon the main line and in the local circuits. He uses upon the main line the combination of two or more galvanic or electric circuits, with independent batteries for the purpose of obviating the diminished force of the galvanic current and in a manner varying very little in form from the invention of Professor Morse.

* * *

All of the efficient elements of the combination are retained, or their places supplied by well-known equivalents. Its organization is essentially the same.

Neither is the substitution of marks and signs, differing from those invented by Professor Morse, any defense to this action. His patent is not for the invention of a new alphabet; but for a combination of powers composed of tangible and intangible elements, described in his specification, by means of which marks or signs may be impressed upon paper at a distance, which can there be read and understood. And if any marks or signs or letters are impressed in that manner by means of a process substantially the same with his invention, or with any particular part of it covered by his patent, and those marks or signs can be read, and thus communicate intelligence, it is an infringement of his patent. The variation in the character of the marks would not protect it, if the marks could be read and understood.

* * *

The invasion of the plaintiff's rights, already stated, authorized the injunction granted by the Circuit Court, and so much of its decree must be affirmed. But, for the reasons hereinbefore assigned, the complainants are not entitled to costs, and that portion of the decree must be reversed, and a decree passed by this court, directing each party to pay his own costs, in this and in the Circuit Court.

Tilghman v. Proctor

Supreme Court of the United States, 1880.
102 U.S. (12 Otto) 707, 26 L.Ed. 279.

■ MR. JUSTICE BRADLEY delivered the opinion of the Court.

* * *

The patent in question relates to the treatment of fats and oils, and is for a process of separating their component parts so as to render them better adapted to the uses of the arts. It was discovered by Chevreul, an eminent French chemist, as early as 1813, that ordinary fat, tallow and oil are regular chemical compounds, consisting of a base which has been termed glycerine, and of different acids, termed generally fat acids, but specifically, stearic, margaric, and oleic acids. These acids, in combination severally with glycerine, form stearine, margarine, and oleine. They are found in different proportions in the various neutral fats and oils; stearine predominating in some, margarine in others, and oleine in others. When separated from their base (glycerine), they take up an equivalent of water, and are called free fat acids. In this state they are in a condition for being utilized in the arts. The stearic and margaric acids form a whitish, semi-transparent, hard substance, resembling spermaceti, which is manufactured into candles. They are separated from the oleic acid, which is a thin oily fluid, by hydrostatic or other powerful pressure; the oleine being used for manufacturing soap, and other purposes. The base, glycerine, when purified, has come to be quite a desirable article for many uses.

The complainant's patent is dated the third day of October, 1854, and relates back to the ninth day of January of that year, being the date of an English patent granted to the patentee for the same invention. It has but a single claim, the words of which are as follows: "Having now described the nature of my said invention, and the manner of performing the same, I hereby declare that I claim, as of my own invention, the manufacturing of fat acids and glycerine from fatty bodies by the action of water at a high temperature and pressure."

* * *

As having some bearing upon the proper construction of the patent in suit (which will presently be more particularly examined), it is proper to observe that Tilghman's actual invention, as demonstrated in his experiments made in 1853, before making any application for a patent, was not confined to the use of a coil of pipe in a heated chamber or furnace for effecting the process which he claims, but was frequently exhibited by using a simple digester, filled nearly full with a mixture of fat and water, and heated in a gas stove, or in a vertical position over a gas lamp; the mixture of fat with the water being kept up by a loose metallic rod or jumper, which thoroughly mixed the contents when the digester was shaken. * * *

An examination of the patent itself, which the preceding remarks will enable us better to understand, will show, we think, that it was intended to and does cover and secure to the patentee the general process which has been described, although only one particular method of applying and using it is pointed out.

The specification describes the invention as follows:—

"My invention consists of a process for producing free fat acids and solution of glycerine from those fatty and oily bodies of animal and vegetable origin which contain glycerine as their base. For this purpose, I subject these fatty or oily bodies to the action of water at a high temperature and pressure, so as to cause the elements of those bodies to combine with water, and thereby obtain at the same time free fat acids and solution of glycerine. I mix the fatty body to be operated upon with from a third to a half of its bulk of water, and the mixture may be placed in any convenient vessel in which it can be heated to the melting point of lead, until the operation is complete. The vessel must be closed and of great strength, so that the requisite amount of pressure may be applied to prevent the conversion of the water into steam.

"The process may be performed more rapidly and also continuously by causing the mixture of fatty matter and water to pass through a tube or continuous channel, heated to the temperature already mentioned; the requisite pressure for preventing the conversion of water into steam being applied during the process; and this I believe is the best mode of carrying my invention into effect. In the drawing hereunto annexed are shown figures of an apparatus for performing this process speedily and continuously, but which apparatus I do not intend to claim as any part of my invention."

The specification then goes on to describe, by the aid of the drawing referred to, the particular device mentioned. But it is evident, and indeed is expressly announced, that the process claimed does not have reference to this particular device, for the apparatus described was well known, being similar to that used for producing the hot-blast and for heating water for the purpose of warming houses. It consists of a coil of iron pipe, or other metallic tubing, erected in an oven or furnace, where it can be subjected to a high degree of heat; and through this pipe the mixture (of nearly equal parts of fat and water), made into an emulsion in a separate vessel by means of a rapidly vibrating piston, or dasher, is impelled by a force-pump in a nearly continuous current, with such regulated velocity as to subject it to the heat of the furnace for a proper length of time to produce the desired result; which time, when the furnace is heated to the temperature of 612 degrees Fahrenheit, is only about ten minutes. The fat and water are kept from separating by the vertical position of the tubes, as well as by the constant movement of the current; and are prevented from being converted into steam by weighting the exit valve by which the product is discharged into the receiving vessel, so that none of it can escape except as it is expelled by the pulsations produced by the working of the force-pump. Before arriving at the exit valve, the pipe is passed, in a second coil, through an exterior vessel filled with water, by which the temperature of the product is reduced. After the product is discharged into the receiving vessel, it is allowed to stand and cool until the glycerine settles to the bottom and separates itself from the fat acids. The latter are then subjected to washing and hydraulic pressure in the usual way.

After describing this apparatus it is added:—

"Although the decomposition of the neutral facts by water takes place with great quickness at the proper heat, yet I prefer that the pump should be worked at such a rate, in proportion to the length or capacity of the heating tubes, that the mixture, while flowing through them, should be maintained at the desired temperature for ten minutes before it passes into the refrigerator or cooling part of the apparatus."

It is evident that the passing of the mixture of fat and water through a heated coil of pipe standing in a furnace is only one of several ways in which the process may be applied. The patentee suggests it as what he conceived to be the best way, apparently because the result is produced with great rapidity and completeness. But other forms of apparatus, known and in public use at the time, can as well be employed without changing the process. A common digester, or boiler, can evidently be so used, provided proper means are employed to keep up the constant admixture of the water and fat, which is a *sine qua non* in the operation. Tilghman himself, as we have seen, often used such digesters in making his experiments before applying for his patent; and, in putting up machinery for his licensees after his patent was obtained, he did the same thing when the parties desired it. Yet surely the identity of the process was not changed by thus changing the form of apparatus. No great amount of invention was required to adapt different forms of well-known apparatus to the application of the process. The principal difficulty would be in providing an internal arrangement in the boiler, or digester, for successfully keeping up the intimate commixture of the fat and water. It is evident that this could be accomplished by means of revolving reels armed with buckets, or of a force-pump constantly transferring the heavy stratum of water from the bottom of the mass to the top, aided by horizontal diaphragms partially sectionizing the digester. These devices were resorted to by Tilghman and others when they used a boiler instead of a coil of pipe.

Whilst Tilghman in his patent recommends the high degree of heat named, he does not confine himself to that. It had been fully developed in his experiments, and was well known to him, that a lower degree of heat could be employed by taking longer time to perform the operation; and this would be necessary when boilers, or digesters, of considerable size were used instead of the coil of pipe, on account of the decreasing power of large vessels to resist the internal pressure. The specification, after describing the use of a metallic coil of pipe, proceeds to add:—

"The melting-point of lead has been mentioned as the proper heat to be used in this operation, because it has been found to give good results. But the change of fatty matters into fat acid and glycerine takes place with some materials (such as palm-oil) at or below the melting point of bismuth [510 degrees Fahrenheit]; yet the heat has been carried considerably above the melting-point of lead without any apparent injury, and the decomposing action of the water becomes more powerful as the heat is increased. By starting the apparatus at a low heat, and gradually increasing it, the temperature giving products most suitable to the intended application of the fatty body employed can easily be determined."

* * *

What did Tilghman discover? And what did he, in terms, claim by his patent? He discovered that fat can be dissolved into its constituent elements by the use of water alone under a high degree of heat and pressure; and he patented *the process* of "manufacturing fat acids and glycerine from fatty bodies by the action of water at a high temperature and pressure." Had the process been known and used before, and not been Tilghman's invention, he could not then have claimed anything more than the particular apparatus described in his patent; but being the inventor of the process, as we are satisfied was the fact, he was entitled to claim it in the manner he did.

That a patent can be granted for a process, there can be no doubt. The patent law is not confined to new machines and new compositions of matter, but extends to any new and useful art or manufacture. A manufacturing process is clearly an art, within the meaning of the law. Goodyear's patent was for a process, namely, the process of vulcanizing India-rubber by subjecting it to a high degree of heat when mixed with sulphur and a mineral salt. The apparatus for performing the process was not patented, and was not material. The patent pointed out how the process could be effected, and that was deemed sufficient. Neilson's patent was for the process of applying the hot-blast to furnaces by forcing the blast through a vessel or receptacle situated between the blowing apparatus and the furnace, and heated to a red heat; the form of the heated vessel being stated by the patent to be immaterial. These patents were sustained after the strictest scrutiny and against the strongest opposition.

* * *

It has been supposed that the decision in O'Reilly v. Morse was adverse to patents for mere processes. The mistake has undoubtedly arisen from confounding a patent for a process with a patent for a mere principle. We think that a careful examination of the judgment in that case will show that nothing adverse to patents for processes is contained in it. The eighth claim of Morse's patent was held to be invalid, because it was regarded by the court as being not for a process, but for a mere principle. It amounted to this, namely, a claim of the exclusive right to the use of electro-magnetism as a motive power for making intelligible marks at a distance; that is, a claim to the exclusive use of one of the powers of nature for a particular purpose. It was not a claim of any particular machinery, nor a claim of any particular process for utilizing the power; but a claim of the power itself,—a claim put forward on the ground that the patentee was the first to discover that it *could* be thus employed. This claim the court held could not be sustained.

* * *

The claim of the patent is not for a mere principle. The chemical principle or scientific fact upon which it is founded is, that the elements of neutral fat require to be severally united with an atomic equivalent of water in order to separate from each other and become free. This chemical fact was not discovered by Tilghman. He only claims to have invented a particular mode of bringing about the desired chemical union between the fatty elements and water. He does not claim every mode of accomplishing this result. He does not claim the lime-saponification process, nor the sulphuric-acid distillation process, and if, as contended, the result was accomplished by Dubrunfaut, Wilson, and Scharling, by means of steam distillation, he does not claim that process. He only claims the process of subjecting to a high degree of heat a mixture continually kept up, of nearly equal quantities of fat and water in a convenient vessel strong enough to resist the effort of the mixture to convert itself into steam. This is most certainly a process. It is clearly pointed out in the specification, and one particular mode of applying it and carrying it into effect is described in detail.

* * *

[The Court then held the patent valid and infringed.]

Application of Zoltan Tarczy-Hornoch

United States Court of Customs and Patent Appeals, 1968.
397 F.2d 856.

■ RICH, JUDGE. This appeal is from a decision of the Patent Office Board of Appeals affirming the examiner's rejection of claims 31–35 and 40 in appellant's application serial No. 23,739, filed April 21, 1960, entitled "Pulse Sorting Apparatus and Method." Claims 16–28, 29, 30 and 36–39 have been allowed.

The invention of the claims on appeal is a method for sorting or counting electrical pulses, effective in counting of such pulses of varying amplitudes even at extremely high repetition rates, i.e., at rates greater than 50,000,000 (50 megacycles per second). Appellant's method envisions the use of a multistage apparatus. The first stage counts every pulse within its capacity. Cancelling orders in the form of "inhibit" pulses are then sent to each of the succeeding stages to prevent another counting of those same pulses. Should the initial stage be unable to handle a pulse, no cancellation order is given the second stage. The pulse, then, is counted by the second stage. Thereupon, cancellation orders are sent to succeeding stages.

Claim 31 is illustrative:

31. In a method for sorting a plurality of input pulses by utilizing a plurality of serially connected stages adapted to accept pulses, causing each input pulse to be applied to each stage sequentially in time, generating an inhibit pulse in each stage which accepts an input pulse and applying the inhibit pulse to each succeeding stage in substantial coincidence with the input pulse so that the input pulse is canceled to thereby prevent registration of the same input pulse in a succeeding stage.

The examiner allowed appellant's apparatus claims. However, he rejected all the method claims on the ground that they merely defined the function of appellant's apparatus. * * *

The issue, therefore, is whether a process claim, otherwise patentable, should be rejected because the application, of which it is a part, discloses apparatus which will *inherently* carry out the recited steps. * * *

We have determined that our decisions requiring the rejection of such claims are justified neither by history nor policy. Today we overrule those decisions.

The expression "function of an apparatus" is our legacy of 19th century controversy over the patentability of processes. Early cases proscribed a kind of overweening claim in which the desirable result first effected by an invention was itself appropriated by the inventor. Two notorious examples will suffice.

Wyeth had obtained a patent for a machine for cutting ice into blocks of uniform size. His specification read: "It is claimed as new, to cut ice of a uniform size, by means of an apparatus worked by any other power than human. The invention of this art, as well as the particular method of the application of the principle, are claimed by * * * [Wyeth]." In an infringement suit, in 1840, Justice Story, sitting on circuit, held the claimed matter "unmaintainable" in point of law and a patent, granted for such, void as for an abstract principle and broader than the invention. "A claim broader than the actual invention of the patentee is, for that very reason, upon the principles of the common law, utterly void, and the patent is a nullity." Wyeth v. Stone, Fed.Cas.No.18,107, 1 Story 273, 285–286 (C.C.Mass.1840).

The first comprehensive review of process patents by the Supreme Court was occasioned some thirteen years later by Morse's attempt to enforce his telegraph patent. Chief Justice Taney wrote the opinion for the Court, which held several apparatus claims valid and infringed. O'Reilly v. Morse, 56 U.S. (15 How.) 62 (1854).

* * *

The [eighth] claim was, of course, held invalid because it did not correspond in scope to Morse's invention.

The [opinion in Morse] * * * apparently cast some doubt on the validity of claims for processes generally, whether mechanical or not. See Risdon Iron & Locomotive Works v. Medart, 158 U.S. 68, 75 (1894); Tilghman v. Proctor, 102 U.S. 707, 726 (1880); O'Reilly v. Morse, 56 U.S. (15 How.) 62 (1853) (Grier, J., dissenting). It shortly became clear, however, that the patentability of chemical processes at least had been unaffected. In Corning v. Burden, 56 U.S. (15 How.) 252 (1853), a case decided after *Morse* but during the same term, the issue was whether Burden's ambiguous claim was properly interpreted as for a process. The patent was ostensibly directed toward a machine for rolling puddle balls in the manufacture of iron. But the lower court had instructed the jury that the patent was for a new *method* of converting puddle balls to blooms "by continuous pressure and rotation * * * between converging surfaces." The Supreme Court held the claim limited to the machine, since, in the Court's mind, a contrary decision would call into question the validity of the claim. In an influential aside on the way to this conclusion, Justice Grier, for a unanimous Court, discussed the patentability of processes:

> A process, *eo nomine*, is not made the subject of a patent in our act of Congress. It is included under the general term "useful art." An art may require one or more processes or machines in order to produce a certain result or manufacture. The term machine includes every mechanical device or combination of mechanical powers and devices to perform some function and produce a certain effect or result. But where the result or effect is produced by chemical action, by the operation or application of some element or power of nature, or of one substance to another, such modes, methods, or operations, are called processes. A new process is usually the result of a discovery; a machine, of invention. The arts of tanning, dyeing, making water-proof cloth, vulcanizing India rubber, smelting ores, and numerous others are usually carried on by processes, as distinguished from machines. One may discover a new and useful improvement in the process of tanning, dyeing, & c., irrespective of any particular form of machinery or mechanical device. And another may invent a labor-saving machine by which this operation or process may be performed, and each may be entitled to his patent. As, for instance, A has discovered that by exposing India rubber to a certain degree of heat, in mixture or connection with certain metallic salts, he can produce a valuable product or manufacture; he is entitled to a patent for his discovery, as a process or improvement in the art, irrespective of any machine or mechanical device. B, on the contrary, may invent a new furnace or stove, or steam apparatus, by which this process may be carried on with much saving of labor, and expense of fuel; and he will be entitled to a patent for his machine, as an improvement in the art. Yet A could not have a patent for a machine, or B for a process; but each would have a patent for the means or method of producing a certain result, or effect, and not for the result or effect produced. It is for the discovery or invention of some practicable method or means of producing a beneficial result or effect, that a patent is granted, and not for the result or effect itself. It is when the term process is used to represent the means or method of producing a result that it is patentable, and it will include all methods or means which are not effected by mechanism or mechanical combinations.

> But the term process is often used in a more vague sense, in which it cannot be the subject of a patent. Thus we say that a board is under-

going the process of being planed, grain of being ground, iron of being hammered, or rolled. Here the term is used subjectively or passively as applied to the material operated on, and not to the method or mode of producing that operation, which is by mechanical means, or the use of a machine, as distinguished from a process.

In this use of the term it represents the function of a machine, or the effect produced by it on the material subjected to the action of the machine. But it is well settled that a man cannot have a patent for the function or abstract effect of a machine, but only for the machine which produces it.

The dictum is interesting for its reflection of the context in which the "function of a machine" objection to patentability was initially applied. It is clear that some processes were thought patentable and others not. It is also clear that "function of a machine" was symbolic of the latter. It is yet unclear, at this point in the development of the law, whether the dividing line marks a difference between means and result or chemistry and mechanics. In any event, the simple notion of undue breadth has been abandoned or, at least, considerably refined.

Several subsequent cases upheld process patents. Cochrane v. Deener, 94 U.S. 780 (1876); Tilghman v. Proctor, 102 U.S. 707 (1880). In the first of these a patent for a process of sifting flour was held valid and infringed. Justice Bradley wrote for the Court:

That a process may be patentable, irrespective of the particular form of the instrumentalities used, cannot be disputed. If one of the steps of a process be that a certain substance is to be reduced to a powder, it may not be at all material what instrument or machinery is used to effect that object, whether a hammer, a pestle and mortar, or a mill. Either may be pointed out; but if the patent is not confined to that particular tool or machine, the use of the others would be an infringement, the general process being the same. A process is a mode of treatment of certain materials to produce a given result. It is an act, or a series of acts, performed upon the subject-matter to be transformed and reduced to a different state or thing. If new and useful, it is just as patentable as is a piece of machinery. In the language of the patent law, it is an art. The machinery pointed out as suitable to perform the process may or may not be new or patentable; whilst the process itself may be altogether new, and produce an entirely new result. The process requires that certain things should be done with certain substances, and in a certain order; but the tools to be used in doing this may be of secondary consequence. [94 U.S. at 787–88]

This discussion as well as the validation itself of the flour-sifting process seemed to show that the connotation of the "function of a machine" rejection was not an objection to mechanical processes but rather to mere effects masquerading as processes.

Justice Bradley's language in Tilghman v. Proctor tended to reinforce this idea. In that case although the process in question was a chemical one, he again took up the patentability of processes in general and discussed, among other cases, O'Reilly v. Morse, supra, to show that Chief Justice Taney "fully acquiesced in the legality and validity of a patent for a process." The "true ground" of that decision, the opinion points out, was that Morse's eighth claim was directed to a principle, not a process, a claim to a power of nature itself by one who had only first employed that power.

In the Telephone Cases, 126 U.S. 1 (1888), the Court reiterated this theme in upholding the validity of Bell's fifth claim which read:

> 5. The method of, and apparatus for, transmitting vocal or other sounds telegraphically, as herein described, by causing electrical undulations, similar in form to the vibrations of the air accompanying the said vocal or other sounds, substantially as set forth.

It was urged that the decision in O'Reilly v. Morse required that this claim be held invalid. Chief Justice Waite, who wrote for the Court, replied that that case, on the contrary, required validation of the claim. Bell's claim, he observed, was for a method of using electricity, not for electricity "in its natural state."

The Court made it clear that as long as the claim *delineated a means and not a result,* the inventor would not be penalized for having invented the *only* means for effecting the result.

> It may be that electricity cannot be used at all for the transmission of speech, except in the way Bell has discovered, and that therefore, practically, his patent gives him its exclusive use for that purpose, but that does not make his claim one for the use of electricity distinct from the particular process with which it is connected in his patent. It will, if true, show more clearly the great importance of his discovery, but it will not invalidate his patent.

Only a few years later, however, the Court seemed to turn away from the means-result dichotomy. In Risdon Locomotive Works v. Medart, 158 U.S. 68 (1894), the validity of a patent for a process of manufacturing belt pulleys was an issue. The process involved the following steps: centering the pulley center or spider; grinding the ends of the arms of the spider concentrically with the axis of the pulley; boring the center; securing the rim to the spider; grinding the face of the rim concentrically with the axis of the pulley; and grinding or squaring the edges of the rim. The Court rightly observed that the process was "purely a mechanical one" and proceeded to declare it unpatentable. The Court's reasoning began with an analysis of the "great case" of O'Reilly v. Morse, supra, and asked whether Chief Justice Taney's comments on "processes involving chemical effects" were not too broad to be supported by subsequent cases. After a review of several of those cases, the Court concluded that the validity of process patents had, in fact, been upheld when the process was chemical or involved the use of one of the agencies of nature for a practical purpose. 158 U.S. at 77. See e.g., Telephone Cases, supra; New Process Fermentation Co. v. Maus, 122 U.S. 413 (1887).

The Court then cited Corning v. Burden, supra; Wyeth v. Stone, supra, and several fairly contemporaneous circuit court decisions for the proposition that it was "equally clear" that no valid patent could be obtained "for a process which involves nothing more than the operation of a piece of mechanism, or, in other words, for the function of a machine." The patent in issue was, of course, invalid since "it clearly falls within this category." * * *

This decision was understandably taken as proscribing patents for mechanical processes. * * * [The court then discussed extensively the subsequent, erratic history of the "function of a machine" doctrine in the Supreme Court, the lower courts, the patent office and the text writers.] * * *

Our present review of the major precedents has persuaded us that the decisions of the Supreme Court have not required the rejection of process claims merely because the process apparently could be carried out only with the disclosed apparatus. These rejections have been the product of decisions in the lower courts and especially in this court. We decide today that we will no longer follow those decisions.

In taking this step we are moved, to some extent, by the fact that the doctrine has been shown not to proceed from its purported well-springs. Even so, we would leave it undisturbed were it not the product of an essentially illogical distinction unwarranted by, and at odds with, the basic purposes of the patent system and productive of a range of undesirable results from the harshly inequitable to the silly.

* * *

* * * We feel that the basic rationale of the patent system demands the upholding of properly drawn claims for new, useful and unobvious processes, regardless of whether the inventor has invented one, two, or more machines to carry them out. Cf. Waxham v. Smith, supra.

* * *

[P]erpetuation of this doctrine only invites inequitable consequences. The essential difficulty is in the fact that, although at the time of the application only one apparatus may be known which is capable of carrying out the process, others may become available later. In which case, of course, the inventor may be cheated of his invention. It is peculiarly our responsibility to see that the decisional law does not require this kind of inequity.

In the *Telephone Cases,* supra, it was pointed out that Bell's invention, primarily a method, would have been lost to him had his process claim been held invalid since he had failed to claim the apparatus which later became commercially important. But the Court upheld the method claim: "Surely, a patent for such a discovery is not to be confined to the mere means he improvised to prove the reality of his conception." We think it clear that justice militates against so confining any process patent.

This case illustrates one of the peculiarities of the doctrine. Several method claims, generic to those rejected, have been allowed, simply because they admit of operation by two sets of apparatus. This would suggest that any two process claims, each unpatentable under the "function of the apparatus" theory could be merged into a patentable claim. We see no interest of the Patent System well served by such a practice.

Accordingly, the decision of the board is reversed.

NOTES

1. Prior to the 1952 revision, the patent statute provided:

> Any person who has invented or discovered any new and useful art, machine, manufacture, or composition of matter, or any new and useful improvements thereof, * * * may * * * obtain a patent therefor. 35 U.S.C. § 31 (1940); R.S. § 4886.

Does the explicit addition of "processes" in § 101 by Congress in 1952 have any bearing on the problem of the principal case?

2. Similar to the "function of an apparatus" doctrine is the rule that a patent cannot be obtained on a new use for an old product. Under this doctrine if A patents a chemical compound useful as an additive for a motor oil, B cannot later patent the compound as a cure for cancer. The compound, having already been disclosed to the art, is (subject to A's patent) available for any use. This doctrine was announced by Learned Hand in Old Town Ribbon & Carbon Co. v. Columbia Ribbon & Carbon Mfg. Co., 159 F.2d 379 (2d Cir. 1947). The patent in that case was on a device for making masters in a "gelatin pad" process of duplication. The same device had been disclosed in an earlier patent for use in a "spirit" process. The inventor had perceived the usefulness of the device in the "gelatin pad" process. In holding the patent invalid, Hand said:

> [T]here is no * * * reason for saying that Congress might not, if it chose, issue a patent for a new use of an old physical object, which is in fact closely akin to, if not identical with, an "art," like a process. There would be nothing unreasonable in so doing; substantially no "machine, manufacture or composition of matter" is ever new throughout; usually it is a combination of elements, all of which are severally old, and the invention consists in the mental act of fabricating the combination. Nevertheless, since 1793, unless a patent disclosed a "new and useful art," a new "machine," a new "manufacture," or a new "composition of matter," it has not been a valid patent. If it be merely for a new employment of some "machine, manufacture or composition of matter" already known, it makes not the slightest difference how beneficial to the public the new function may be, how long a search it may end, how many may have shared that search, or how high a reach of imaginative ingenuity the solution may have demanded. All the mental factors which determine invention may have been present to the highest degree, but it will not be patentable because it will not be within the terms of the statute. * * * It is scarcely necessary to add that the claims in suit are not for an "art" or "process."

159 F.2d at 382.

The force of Hand's opinion is somewhat weakened by the fact that the actual claims in suit, not set out in his opinion, were not limited to the use of the master in the gelatin process. See the opinion below, 66 F.Supp. 929, 930 (E.D.N.Y. 1946).

Does the inclusion of a "new use of a known process, machine, manufacture, composition of matter, or material" in the definition of process in § 100(b) of the 1952 Act change the result? Is the solution for the applicant to claim a new process rather than the old product?

Funk Bros. Seed Co. v. Kalo Inoculant Co.

Supreme Court of the United States, 1948.
333 U.S. 127, 68 S.Ct. 440, 92 L.Ed. 588.

■ MR. JUSTICE DOUGLAS delivered the opinion of the Court.

This is a patent infringement suit brought by respondent. The charge of infringement is limited to certain product claims[1] of Patent No. 2,200,532 issued to Bond on May 14, 1940. Petitioner filed a counterclaim asking for a declaratory judgment that the entire patent be adjudged invalid.[2] The District Court held the product claims invalid for want of invention and dismissed the complaint. It also dismissed the counterclaim. Both parties appealed. The Circuit Court of Appeals reversed, holding that the product claims were valid and infringed and that the counterclaim should not have been dismissed. 161 F.2d 981. The question of validity is the only question presented by this petition for certiorari.

Through some mysterious process leguminous plants are able to take nitrogen from the air and fix it in the plant for conversion to organic nitrogenous compounds. The ability of these plants to fix nitrogen from the air depends on the presence of bacteria of the genus Rhizobium which infect the roots of the plant and form nodules on them. These root-nodule bacteria of the genus Rhizobium fall into at least six species. No one species will infect the roots of all species of leguminous plants. But each will infect well-defined groups of those plants.[3] Each species of root-nodule bacteria is made up of distinct strains which vary in efficiency. Methods of selecting the strong

---

1. The product claims in suit are 1, 3, 4, 5, 6, 7, 8, 13, and 14. Claim 4 is illustrative of the invention which is challenged. It reads as follows:

"An inoculant for leguminous plants comprising a plurality of selected mutually non-inhibitive strains of different species of bacteria of the genus Rhizobium, said strains being unaffected by each other in respect to their ability to fix nitrogen in the leguminous plant for which they are specific."

2. The patent also contains process claims.

3. The six well-recognized species of bacteria and the corresponding groups (cross-inoculation groups) of leguminous plants are: Rhizobium trifolii—Red clover, crimson clover, mammoth clover, alsike clover; Rhizobium meliloti—Alfalfa, white or yellow sweet clovers; Rhizobium phaseoli—Garden beans; Rhizobium leguminosarum—Garden peas and vetch; Rhizobium lupini—Lupines; Rhizobium japonicum—Soy beans

strains and of producing a bacterial culture from them have long been known. The bacteria produced by the laboratory methods of culture are placed in a powder or liquid base and packaged for sale to and use by agriculturists in the inoculation of the seeds of leguminous plants. This also has long been well known.

It was the general practice, prior to the Bond patent, to manufacture and sell inoculants containing only one species of root-nodule bacteria. The inoculant could therefore be used successfully only in plants of the particular cross-inoculation group corresponding to this species. Thus if a farmer had crops of clover, alfalfa, and soy beans he would have to use three separate inoculants.[4] There had been a few mixed cultures for field legumes. But they had proved generally unsatisfactory because the different species of the Rhizobia bacteria produced an inhibitory effect on each other when mixed in a common base, with the result that their efficiency was reduced. Hence it had been assumed that the different species were mutually inhibitive. Bond discovered that there are strains of each species of root-nodule bacteria which do not exert a mutually inhibitive effect on each other. He also ascertained that those mutually non-inhibitive strains can, by certain methods of selection and testing, be isolated and used in mixed cultures. Thus he provided a mixed culture of Rhizobia capable of inoculating the seeds of plants belonging to several cross-inoculation groups. It is the product claims which disclose that mixed culture that the Circuit Court of Appeals has held valid.

We do not have presented the question whether the methods of selecting and testing the non-inhibitive strains are patentable. We have here only product claims. Bond does not create a state of inhibition or of non-inhibition in the bacteria. Their qualities are the work of nature. Those qualities are of course not patentable. For patents cannot issue for the discovery of the phenomena of nature. See Le Roy v. Tatham, 14 How. 156, 175. The qualities of these bacteria, like the heat of the sun, electricity, or the qualities of metals, are part of the storehouse of knowledge of all men. They are manifestations of laws of nature, free to all men and reserved exclusively to none. He who discovers a hitherto unknown phenomenon of nature has no claim to a monopoly of it which the law recognizes. If there is to be invention from such a discovery, it must come from the application of the law of nature to a new and useful end. See Telephone Cases, 126 U.S. 1, 532–533; De Forest Radio Co. v. General Electric Co., 283 U.S. 664, 684–685; Mackay Radio & Tel. Co. v. Radio Corp., 306 U.S. 86, 94; Cameron Septic Tank Co. v. Saratoga Springs, 159 F. 453, 462–463. The Circuit Court of Appeals thought that Bond did much more than discover a law of nature, since he made a new and different composition of non-inhibitive strains which contributed utility and economy to the manufacture and distribution of commercial inoculants. But we think that that aggregation of species fell short of invention within the meaning of the patent statutes.

4. See note 3, supra.

Discovery of the fact that certain strains of each species of these bacteria can be mixed without harmful effect to the properties of either is a discovery of their qualities of non-inhibition. It is no more than the discovery of some of the handiwork of nature and hence is not patentable. The aggregation of select strains of the several species into one product is an application of that newly-discovered natural principle. But however ingenious the discovery of that natural principle may have been, the application of it is hardly more than an advance in the packaging of the inoculants. Each of the species of root-nodule bacteria contained in the package infects the same group of leguminous plants which it always infected. No species acquires a different use. The combination of species produces no new bacteria, no change in the six species of bacteria, and no enlargement of the range of their utility. Each species has the same effect it always had. The bacteria perform in their natural way. Their use in combination does not improve in any way their natural functioning. They serve the ends nature originally provided and act quite independently of any effort of the patentee.

There is, of course, an advantage in the combination. The farmer need not buy six different packages for six different crops. He can buy one package and use it for any or all of his crops of leguminous plants. And, as respondent says, the packages of mixed inoculants also hold advantages for the dealers and manufacturers by reducing inventory problems and the like. But a product must be more than new and useful to be patented; it must also satisfy the requirements of invention or discovery. Cuno Engineering Corp. v. Automatic Devices Corp., 314 U.S. 84, 90, 91, and cases cited; 35 U.S.C. § 31, R.S. § 4886. The application of this newly-discovered natural principle to the problem of packaging of inoculants may well have been an important commercial advance. But once nature's secret of the non-inhibitive quality of certain strains of the species of Rhizobium was discovered, the state of the art made the production of a mixed inoculant a simple step. Even though it may have been the product of skill, it certainly was not the product of invention. There is no way in which we could call it such unless we borrowed invention from the discovery of the natural principle itself. That is to say, there is no invention here unless the discovery that certain strains of the several species of these bacteria are non-inhibitive and may thus be safely mixed is invention. But we cannot so hold without allowing a patent to issue on one of the ancient secrets of nature now disclosed. All that remains, therefore, are advantages of the mixed inoculants themselves. They are not enough.

Since we conclude that the product claims do not disclose an invention or discovery within the meaning of the patent statutes, we do not consider whether the other statutory requirements contained in 35 U.S.C. § 31, R.S. § 4886, are satisfied.

Reversed.

■ MR. JUSTICE FRANKFURTER, concurring.

My understanding of Bond's contribution is that prior to his attempts, packages of mixed cultures of inoculants presumably applicable to two or more different kinds of legumes had from time to time been prepared, but had met with indifferent success. The reasons for failure were not understood, but the authorities had concluded that in general pure culture inoculants were alone reliable because mixtures were ineffective due to the mutual inhibition of the combined strains of bacteria. Bond concluded that there might be special strains which lacked this mutual inhibition, or were at all events mutually compatible. Using techniques that had previously been developed to test efficiency in promoting nitrogen fixation of various bacterial strains, Bond tested such efficiency of various mixtures of strains. He confirmed his notion that some strains were mutually compatible by finding that mixtures of these compatible strains gave good nitrogen fixation in two or more different kinds of legumes, while other mixtures of certain other strains proved mutually incompatible.

If this is a correct analysis of Bond's endeavors, two different claims of originality are involved: (1) the idea that there are compatible strains, and (2) the experimental demonstration that there were in fact some compatible strains. Insofar as the court below concluded that the packaging of a particular mixture of compatible strains is an invention and as such patentable, I agree, provided not only that a new and useful property results from their combination, but also that the particular strains are identifiable and adequately identified. I do not find that Bond's combination of strains satisfies these requirements. The strains by which Bond secured compatibility are not identified and are identifiable only by their compatibility.

Unless I misconceive the record, Bond makes no claim that Funk Brothers used the same combination of strains that he had found mutually compatible. He appears to claim that since he was the originator of the idea that there might be mutually compatible strains and had practically demonstrated that some such strains exists, everyone else is forbidden to use a combination of strains whether they are or are not identical with the combinations that Bond selected and packaged together. It was this claim that, as I understand it, the District Court found not to be patentable, but which, if valid, had been infringed.

The Circuit Court of Appeals defined the claims to "cover a composite culture in which are included a plurality of species of bacteria belonging to the general Rhizobium genus, carried in a conventional base." 161 F.2d 981, 983. But the phrase "the claims cover a composite culture" might mean "a particular composite culture" or "any composite culture." The Circuit Court of Appeals seems to me to have proceeded on the assumption that only "a particular composite culture" was devised and patented by Bond, and then applies it to "any composite culture" arrived at by deletion of mutually inhibiting strains, but strains which may be quite different from Bond's composite culture.

The consequences of such a conclusion call for its rejection. Its acceptance would require, for instance in the field of alloys, that if one discovered a particular mixture of metals, which when alloyed had some particular desirable properties, he could patent not merely this particular mixture but the idea of alloying metals for this purpose, and thus exclude everyone else from contriving some other combination of metals which, when alloyed, had the same desirable properties. In patenting an alloy, I assume that both the qualities of the product and its specific composition would need to be specified. The strains that Bond put together in the product which he patented can be specified only by the properties of the mixture. The District Court, while praising Bond's achievement, found want of patentability. The Circuit Court of Appeals reversed the judgment of the District Court by use of an undistributed middle—that the claims cover a "composite culture"—in the syllogism whereby they found patentability.

It only confuses the issue, however, to introduce such terms as "the work of nature" and the "laws of nature." For these are vague and malleable terms infected with too much ambiguity and equivocation. Everything that happens may be deemed "the work of nature," and any patentable composite exemplifies in its properties "the laws of nature." Arguments drawn from such terms for ascertaining patentability could fairly be employed to challenge almost every patent. On the other hand, the suggestion that "if there is to be invention from such a discovery, it must come from the application of the law of nature to a new and useful end" may readily validate Bond's claim. Nor can it be contended that there was no invention because the composite has no new properties other than its ingredients in isolation. Bond's mixture does in fact have the new property of multi-service applicability. Multi-purpose tools, multivalent vaccines, vitamin complex composites, are examples of complexes whose sole new property is the conjunction of the properties of their components. Surely the Court does not mean unwittingly to pass on the patentability of such products by formulating criteria by which future issues of patentability may be prejudged. In finding Bond's patent invalid I have tried to avoid a formulation which, while it would in fact justify Bond's patent, would lay the basis for denying patentability to a large area within existing patent legislation.

NOTES

1. In Merck & Co. v. Olin Mathieson Chemical Corp., 253 F.2d 156 (4th Cir.1958), the court upheld a patent on a Vitamin B_{12} active composition which was a concentrate of Vitamin B_{12} obtained by extraction and purification from fermentation materials. The district court held the patent invalid on the ground that Vitamin B_{12} was a "product of nature." The court reversed:

A product of nature which is not a "new and useful * * * machine, manufacture, or composition of matter" is not patentable, for it is not within the statutory definition of those things which may be patented. Even though it be a new and useful composition of matter it still may be unpatentable if the subject matter as a whole was obvious within the meaning of § 103 (35 U.S.C. 103), or if other conditions of patentability are not satisfied.

In dealing with such considerations, unpatentable products have been frequently characterized as "products of nature." See Funk Brothers Seed Company v. Kalo Inoculant Company, 333 U.S. 127 * * *. But where the requirements of the Act are met, patents upon products of nature are granted and their validity sustained. * * *

To the extent that the product of nature defense has validity, as urged here, it is a contention that the patented compositions are not "new and useful * * * compositions of matter" within the meaning of § 101 of the Act. This defense may be separated into two doctrines, (1) that a patent may not be granted upon an old product though it be derived from a new source by a new and patentable process, and (2) that every step in the purification of a product is not a patentable advance, except, perhaps, as to the process, if the new product differs from the old "merely in degree, and not in kind."

In the first aspect of this defense, reliance is placed upon American Wood Paper Company v. Fibre Disintegrating Company, 90 U.S. 566, in which a patent upon cellulose produced from wood products was held invalid because cellulose derived from other sources was old and long had been used for paper making, and upon Cochrane v. Badische Anilin & Soda Fabrik, 111 U.S. 293, in which a patent upon synthetic alizarine was held invalid because alizarine, having the same chemical properties and uses, derived from the madder root, had long been known and used in dye-stuff.

It can hardly be doubted that, as was said in "The Wood-Paper Patent case," " * * * if one should discover a mode or contrive a process by which prussic acid could be obtained from a subject in which it is not now known to exist, he might have a patent for his process, but not for prussic acid." The fact that the product, itself, is not a "new and useful * * * machine, manufacture, or composition of matter," within the meaning of § 101, is fatal to the product claims. The facts here, however, are far from the premise of the principle. Until the patentees produced them, there were no such B_{12} active compositions. No one had produced even a comparable product. The active substance was unidentified and unknown. The new product, not just the method, had such advantageous characteristics as to replace the liver products. What was produced was, in no sense, an old product.

The second aspect of the defense is equally inapplicable to the facts. Each slight step in purification does not produce a new product. What is gained may be the old product, but with a greater degree of purity. Alpha alumina purified is still alpha alumina, In re Ridgway, 76 F.2d 602, and ultramarine from which flotable impurities have been removed is still ultramarine, In re Merz, 97 F.2d 599. The fact, however, that a new and useful product is the result of processes of extraction, concentration and purification of natural materials does not defeat its patentability. As was said in the aspirin case, Kuehmsted v. Farbenfabriken of Elberfeld Co., 7 Cir., 179 F. 701, 705:

"Hoffmann has produced a medicine indisputably beneficial to mankind—something new in a useful art, such as our patent policy was intended to promote. Kraut and his contemporaries, on the other hand, had produced only, at best, a chemical compound in an impure state. And it makes no difference, so far as patentability is concerned, that the medicine thus produced is lifted out of a mass that contained, chemically, the compound; for, though the difference between Hoffmann and Kraut be one of purification only—strictly marking the line, however where the one is therapeutically available and the others were therapeutically unavailable—patentability would follow. In the one case the mass is made to yield something to the useful arts; in the other case what is yielded is chiefly interesting as a fact in chemical learning."

* * * The patentees have given us for the first time a medicine which can be used successfully in the treatment of pernicious anemia, a medicine which avoids the dangers and disadvantages of the liver extracts, the only remedies available prior to this invention, a medicine subject to accurate standardization and which can be produced in large quantities and inexpensively, a medicine which is valuable for other purposes, as well as for the treatment of pernicious anemia. It did not exist in nature in the form in which the patentees produced it and was produced by them only after lengthy experiments. Nothing in the prior art either anticipated or suggested it.

The same patent was again upheld on a different record in Merck & Co. v. Chase Chemical Co., 273 F.Supp. 68 (D.N.J. 1967).

2. "Our reading of the Supreme Court's opinion in *Funk* leads us to conclude that the test of patentability of a natural phenomenon is as follows: Would an artisan, knowing the newly discovered natural phenomenon require more than ordinary skill to discover the process by which to apply that phenomenon as the patentee had done?" Armour Pharmaceutical Co. v. Richardson-Merrell, Inc., 396 F.2d 70, 74 (3d Cir. 1968). Is this test consistent with the holding in *Merck*? In *Armour Pharmaceutical* the court held invalid a patent on the use of an already known compound for use as an anti-inflammatory agent. The compound was to be taken orally in the form of a coated pill. The coating permitted the compound to pass through the acidic environment of the stomach and into the intestine, where it would be absorbed through the wall of the small intestine into the body. The critical discovery was the hitherto unknown fact that the compound would be absorbed by the lining of the small intestine—a fact discovered by experiments on rats. Once that fact was known, the preparation of a coated pill to deliver the compound to the small intestine required no new art. Is *Armour* distinguishable from *Merck* on the ground that extraction of Vitamin B_{12} was a difficult process requiring many years of experimentation before it was achieved, even though the fact that there was an "anti-pernicious anemia principle" later found to be Vitamin B_{12} had long been known?

3. Is a newly discovered plant patentable under 35 U.S.C. § 101? Is a plant a "composition of matter?" The assumption that a plant was not patentable led to a 1930 amendment to the patent act explicitly providing for plant patents. The provisions for plant patents are now contained in 35 U.S.C. §§ 161–64. Note the explicit exclusion of a "plant found in an uncultivated state" and the limitation of the patent owner's right to the right "to exclude others from asexually reproducing the plant or selling or using the plant so reproduced." What policy considerations led to these limitations on plant patents?

The House Report described the purpose of the amendment as follows:

> The purpose of the bill is to afford agriculture, so far as practicable, the same opportunity to participate in the benefits of the patent system as has been given industry, and thus assist in placing agriculture on a basis of economic equality with industry. The bill will remove the existing discrimination between plant developers and industrial inventors. To these ends the bill provides that any person who invents or discovers a new and distinct variety of plant shall be given by patent an exclusive right to propagate that plant by asexual reproduction; that is, by *grafting, budding, cuttings, layering, division, and the like, but not by seeds.* The bill does not provide for patents upon varieties of plants newly found by plant explorers or others, growing in an uncultivated or wild state.

> * * * To-day plant breeding and research is dependent, in large part, upon Government funds to Government experiment stations, or the limited endeavors of the amateur breeder. It is hoped that the bill will afford a sound basis for investing capital in plant breeding and consequently stimulate plant development through private funds,

> In addition, the breeder to-day must make excessive charges for specimens of the new variety disposed of by him at the start in order to avail himself of his only opportunity for financial reimbursement. Under the bill the breeder may give the public immediate advantage of the new varieties at a low price with the knowledge that the success of the variety will enable him to recompense himself through wide public distribution by him during the life of the patent. The farmers and general public that buy plants will be able promptly to obtain new improved plants at a more moderate cost.

In re Arzberger, 112 F.2d 834 (C.C.P.A. 1940), held that the plant patent statute did not extend to newly discovered bacteria even though a bacteria is scientifically a type of plant. "We think that Congress, in the use of the word 'plant,' was speaking 'in the common language of the people,' and did not use the word in its strict, scientific sense." 112 F.2d at 838.

4. The United States Plant Variety Protection Act, 84 Stat. 1542 (1970), 7 U.S.C. § 2321 et seq., is administered by the Agricultural Marketing Service of the U.S. Department of Agriculture. The statute is modelled in part on the patent statute, with numerous alterations to fit the plant context. It provides for protection of any novel variety of sexually reproduced plant other than fungi, bacteria, or first generation hybrids. Non-obviousness is not required. The term is 17 years.

5. Morton v. New York Eye Infirmary, 17 F. Cases 879 (No. 9,865) (C.C.S.D. N.Y. 1862), held a patent invalid on the discovery that ether when administered to an animal would make the animal insensitive to pain and enable a surgeon to operate. The discovery was an important and famous one, laying the basis for modern surgical techniques. The court said:

> [T]he specification presents nothing new except the effect produced by well-known agents, administered in well-known ways on well-known subjects. This new or additional effect [of rendering the patient insensitive to pain] is not produced by any new instrument by which the agent is administered nor by a different application of it to the body of the patient. It is simply produced by increasing the quantity of the vapor inhaled. And even this quantity is to be regulated by the discretion of the operator, and may vary with the susceptibilities of the patient to its influence. It is nothing more, in the eye of the law, than the application of a well-known agent, by well-known means, to a new or more perfect use, which is not sufficient to support a patent.

> * * * [T]he beneficient and imposing character of the discovery cannot change the legal principles upon which the law of patents is founded, nor abrogate the rules by which judicial construction must be governed. * * * No matter through what long, solitary vigils, or by what importunate efforts, the secret may have been wrung from the bosom of Nature, or to what useful purpose it may be applied. Something more is necessary. The new force or principle brought to light must be embodied and set to work, and can be patented only in connection or combination with the means by which, or the medium through which, it operates.

17 F. Cases 883–84. This decision, along with the "rule" of Cochrane v. Deener, 94 U.S. 780 (1877), that a process must work to transform or change the thing which is the subject of the process, has been repeatedly cited for the proposition that medical processes are not patentable.

In Ex parte Scherer, 103 U.S.P.Q. 107 (Pat.Off.Bd.App.1954), the Patent Office granted a patent on a method of injecting medications into the human body by means of a high pressure jet. The invention made it possible to give injections without the use of a needle. The Board appeared to distinguish the *Morton* case on the ground that the materials used there were old and well known whereas Scherer's apparatus was itself novel. A number of lower court decisions involving patents on various medical procedures and devices are discussed in Note, 23 Geo.Wash.L.Rev. 238 (1954).

6. Should the patent system exclude any technological advance from its coverage? Isn't the effect of including some technologies and excluding others to skew the incentive created by the patent system toward those fields that are covered? Is there any relationship between the scope of the patent laws and the fact that large government subsidies have been found necessary for agricultural and medical research?

7. Could Mr. Justice Frankfurter's concern about obtaining a unique description of the invention be solved by submitting a specimen of the composition to the PTO? Specimens can be provided in appropriate cases, but where the specimen is alive how is the PTO to care for it? This problem is now solved by the use of a third-party depository for microorganisms, presumably equipped to maintain the specimen. See U.S. Patent and Trademark Office, Manual of Patent Examining Procedure § 608.03 (6th Ed. 1995, Rev. 1997).

Diamond v. Chakrabarty

Supreme Court of the United States, 1980.
447 U.S. 303, 100 S.Ct. 2204, 65 L.Ed.2d 144.

■ MR. CHIEF JUSTICE BURGER delivered the opinion of the Court.

We granted certiorari to determine whether a live, human-made microorganism is patentable subject matter under 35 U.S.C. § 101.

I

In 1972, respondent Chakrabarty, a microbiologist, filed a patent application, assigned to the General Electric Company. The application asserted 36 claims related to Chakrabarty's invention of "a bacterium from the genus *Pseudomonas* containing therein at least two stable energy-generating plasmids, each of said plasmids providing a separate hydrocarbon degradative pathway."[1] This human-made, genetically engineered bacterium is capable of breaking down multiple components of crude oil. Because of this property, which is possessed by no naturally occurring bacteria, Chakrabarty's invention is believed to have significant value for the treatment of oil spills.[2]

Chakrabarty's patent claims were of three types: first, process claims for the method of producing the bacteria; second, claims for an inoculum comprised of a carrier material floating on water, such as straw, and the new bacteria; and third, claims to the bacteria themselves. The patent examiner allowed the claims falling into the first two categories, but

---

1. Plasmids are hereditary units physically separate from the chromosomes of the cell. In prior research Chakrabarty and an associate discovered that plasmids control the oil degradation abilities of certain bacteria. In particular, the two researchers discovered plasmids capable of degrading camphor and octane, two components of crude oil. In the work represented by the patent application at issue here, Chakrabarty discovered a process by which four different plasmids, capable of degrading four different oil components, could be transferred to and maintained stably in a single bacteria, which itself has no capacity for degrading oil.

2. At present, biological control of oil spills requires the use of a mixture of naturally occurring bacteria, each capable of degrading one component of the oil complex. In this way, oil is decomposed into simpler substances which can serve as food for aquatic life. However, for various reasons, only a portion of any such mixed culture survives to attack the oil spill. By breaking down multiple components of oil, Chakrabarty's micro-organism promises more efficient and rapid oil-spill control.

rejected claims for the bacteria. His decision rested on two grounds: (1) that micro-organisms are "products of nature," and (2) that as living things they are not patentable subject matter under 35 U.S.C. § 101.

Chakrabarty appealed the rejection of these claims to the Patent Office Board of Appeals, and the Board affirmed the Examiner on the second ground.[3] Relying on the legislative history of the 1930 Plant Patent Act, in which Congress extended patent protection to certain asexually reproduced plants, the Board concluded that § 101 was not intended to cover living things such as these laboratory created micro-organisms.

The Court of Customs and Patent Appeals, by a divided vote, reversed on the authority of its prior decision in *In re Bergy*, 563 F.2d 1031 (1978), which held that "the fact that microorganisms * * * are alive * * * [is] without legal significance" for purposes of the patent law.[4] Subsequently, we granted the Government's petition for certiorari in *Bergy,* vacated the judgment, and remanded the case "for further consideration in light of Parker v. Flook, 437 U.S. 584, 438 U.S. 902 (1978). The Court of Customs and Patent Appeals then vacated its judgment in *Chakrabarty* and consolidated the case with *Bergy* for reconsideration. After re-examining both cases in the light of our holding in *Flook,* that court, with one dissent, reaffirmed its earlier judgments. 596 F.2d 952 (1979).

The Government again sought certiorari, and we granted the writ as to both *Bergy* and *Chakrabarty.* 444 U.S. 924 (1979). Since then, *Bergy* has been dismissed as moot, 444 U.S. 1028 (1980), leaving only *Chakrabarty* for decision.

II

* * *

The question before us in this case is a narrow one of statutory interpretation requiring us to construe 35 U.S.C. § 101 * * *.

Specifically, we must determine whether respondent's microorganism constitutes a "manufacture" or "composition of matter" within the meaning of the statute.

* * *

[This case followed two decisions in which the Supreme Court had reversed Court of Customs and Patent Appeals decisions construing § 101 broadly. They were:

Gottschalk v. Benson, 409 U.S. 63 (1972). The Patent Office had rejected an application for a patent claiming a method of programming a general-purpose digital computer to convert code from binary-coded decimal

---

3. The Board concluded that the new bacteria were not "products of nature," because *Pseudomonas* bacteria containing two or more different energy-generating plasmids are not naturally occurring.

4. Bergy involved a patent application for a pure culture of the micro-organism *Streptomyces vellosus* found to be useful in the production of lincomycin, an antibiotic.

form into pure binary form. The Court of Customs and Patent Appeals had reversed, holding that the claim was for a useful process. The Supreme Court, in turn, reversed the Court of Customs and Patent Appeals and upheld the Patent Office position.

All information is stored in a computer in binary or "on-off" form. The information "on" or "off" can be treated as equivalent to 0 or 1, and 0 and 1 can be used together to represent all numbers in the form 0, 1, 10, 11, 100, 101, 111, and so on. These numbers can in turn be used in codes to represent letters or numbers. Binary-coded decimal form is a decimal number in which each position in the decimal number is represented by the appropriate binary number for the number in that position. This is a useful way for a computer to store numbers when they are to be displayed or printed in decimal form. The binary-coded decimal form, however, requires more machine memory than the pure binary form, so for purposes of storing the numbers or performing calculations it is useful to convert the numbers from binary-coded decimal form to pure binary form.

The claim of the patent was for a series of mechanical, computational steps which, when followed, converted a number from binary coded decimal form to pure binary form. The court read the claim as covering any use of the computational steps, whether performed with or without a computer. (The claim was limited to a "data processing method," which could have been read to limit the procedure to use in data processing, i.e., use on a machine, since we do not normally speak of penciled calculations as "data processing.")

There are passages in the opinion which suggest that the Court thought it was holding that all programs for digital computers are unpatentable subject matter. For instance: "If these programs are to be patentable, considerable problems are raised which only committees of Congress can manage, for broad powers of investigations are needed, including hearings which canvass the wide variety of views which those operating in this field entertain." 409 U.S. at 73.

But there were other passages that suggested that the Court was only holding that a claim on a formula, not limited to a particular use, was invalid. "Here the 'process' claim is so abstract and sweeping as to cover both known and unknown uses of the BCD to pure binary conversion. The end use may (1) vary from the operation of a train to verification of drivers' licenses to researching the law books for precedents and (2) be performed through any existing machinery or future-devised machinery or without any apparatus. * * * What we come down to in a nutshell is the following. It is conceded that one may not patent an idea. But in practical effect that would be the result if the formula for converting BCD numerals to pure binary numerals were patented in this case. The mathematical formula involved here has no substantial practical application except in connection with a digital computer, which means that if the judgment below is affirmed, the patent would wholly pre-empt the mathematical formula and in practical effect would be a patent on the algorithm itself." 409 U.S. at 68–73.

Gottschalk was followed by Parker v. Flook, 437 U.S. 584 (1978). The patent office rejected an application for a method for updating alarm limits.

The C.C.P.A. again reversed, and the Supreme Court again reversed the C.C.P.A.

As in *Gottschalk* the only novel element in the patent was a formula, in this case a formula which used a number to generate another number. But unlike *Gottschalk,* the claim was drafted to read only on the use of the formula in connection with the computation of process alarms limits in the catalytic chemical conversion of hydrocarbons. This claim, argued the applicant, did not "wholly preempt the mathematical formula."

The Court's opinion clearly held that a patent on a computer program was not patentable subject matter. "Difficult questions of policy concerning the kinds of programs that may be appropriate for patent protection and the form and duration of such protection can be answered by Congress on the basis of current empirical data not equally available to this tribunal." 437 U.S. at 595.]

III

* * *

Guided by * * * canons of construction, this Court has read the term "manufacture" in § 101 in accordance with its dictionary definition to mean "the production of articles for use from raw materials prepared by giving to these materials new forms, qualities, properties, or combinations, whether by hand labor or by machinery." American Fruit Growers, Inc. v. Brogdex Co., 283 U.S. 1, 11 (1931). Similarly, "composition of matter" has been construed consistent with its common usage to include "all compositions of two or more substances and . . . all composite articles, whether they be the results of chemical union, or of mechanical mixture, or whether they be gases, fluids, powders, or solids." Shell Dev. Co. v. Watson, 149 F.Supp. 279, 280 (D.C. 1957) (citing 1 A. Deller, Walker on Patents § 14, p. 55 (1st ed. 1937)). In choosing such expansive terms as "manufacture" and "composition of matter," modified by the comprehensive "any," Congress plainly contemplated that the patent laws would be given wide scope.

The relevant legislative history also supports a broad construction. The Patent Act of 1793, authored by Thomas Jefferson, defined statutory subject matter as "any new and useful art, machine, manufacture, or composition of matter, or any new or useful improvement [thereof]." Act of Feb. 21, 1793, ch. 11, § 1, 1 Stat. 318. The Act embodied Jefferson's philosophy that "ingenuity should receive a liberal encouragement." V Writings of Thomas Jefferson, at 75–76. See Graham v. John Deere Co., 383 U.S. 1, 7–10 (1966). Subsequent patent statutes in 1836, 1870, and 1874 employed this same broad language. In 1952, when the patent laws were recodified, Congress replaced the word "art" with "process," but otherwise left Jefferson's language intact. The Committee Reports accompanying the 1952 act inform us that Congress intended statutory subject matter to "include anything under the sun that is made by man." S. Rep. No. 1979, 82d Cong., 2d Sess., 5 (1952); H.R. Rep. No. 1923, 82d Cong., 2d Sess., 6 (1952).

This is not to suggest that § 101 has no limits or that it embraces every discovery. The laws of nature, physical phenomena, and abstract ideas have been held not patentable. See Parker v. Flook, 437 U.S. 584 (1978); Gottschalk v. Benson, 409 U.S. 63, 67 (1973); Funk Seed Co. v. Kalo Co., 333 U.S. 127, 130 (1948); O'Reilly v. Morse, 15 How. 62, 112–121 (1853); Le Roy v. Tatham, 14 How. 156, 175 (1852). Thus, a new mineral discovered in the earth or a new plant found in the wild is not patentable subject matter. Likewise, Einstein could not patent his celebrated law that $E=mc^2$ nor could Newton have patented the law of gravity. Such discoveries are "manifestations of * * * nature, free to all men and reserved exclusively to none." Funk, supra, 333 U.S., at 130.

Judged in this light, respondent's micro-organism plainly qualifies as patentable subject matter. His claim is not to a hitherto unknown natural phenomenon, but to a nonnaturally occurring manufacture or composition of matter—a product of human ingenuity "having a distinctive name, character [and] use." Hartranft v. Wiegmann, 121 U.S. 609, 615 (1887). The point is underscored dramatically by comparison of the invention here with that in *Funk*. There, the patentee had discovered that there existed in nature certain species of root-nodule bacteria which did not exert a mutually inhibitive effect on each other. He used that discovery to produce a mixed culture capable of inoculating the seeds of leguminous plants. Concluding that the patentee had discovered "only some of the handiwork of nature," the Court ruled the product nonpatentable:

> "Each of the species of root-nodule bacteria contained in the package infects the same group of leguminous plants which it always infected. No species acquires a different use. The combination of the six species produces no new bacteria, no change in the six bacteria, and no enlargement of the range of their utility. Each species has the same effect it always had. The bacteria perform in their natural way. Their use in combination does not improve in any way their natural functioning. They serve the same ends nature originally provided and act quite independently of any effort by the patentee." 333 U.S., at 131.

Here, by contrast, the patentee has produced a new bacterium with markedly different characteristics from any found in nature and one having the potential for significant utility. His discovery is not nature's handiwork, but his own; accordingly it is patentable subject matter under § 101.

IV

Two contrary arguments are advanced, neither of which we find persuasive.

(A)

The Government's first argument rests on the enactment of the 1930 Plant Patent Act, which afforded patent protection to certain asexually reproduced plants [35 U.S.C. § 161], and the 1970 Plant Variety Protection Act, which authorized patents for certain sexually reproduced plants but excluded bacteria from its protection [7 U.S.C. § 2402(a)]. In the Government's view, the passage of these Acts evidences congressional understanding that the terms "manufacture" or "composition of matter" do not include living things; if they did, the Government argues, neither Act would have been necessary.

We reject this argument. Prior to 1930, two factors were thought to remove plants from patent protection. The first was the belief that plants, even those artificially bred, were products of nature for purposes of the patent law. This position appears to have derived from the decision of the patent office in Ex parte Latimer, 1889 C.D. 123, in which a patent claim for fiber found in the needle of the *Pinus australis* was rejected. The Commissioner reasoned that a contrary result would permit "patents [to] be obtained upon the trees of the forests and the plants of the earth, which of course would be unreasonable and impossible." Id., at 126. The *Latimer* case, it seems, came to "se[t] forth the general stand taken in these matters" that plants were natural products not subject to patent protection. H. Thorne, Relation of Patent Law to Natural Products, 6 J.Pat.Off.Soc. 23, 24 (1923). The second obstacle to patent protection for plants was the fact that plants were thought not amenable to the "written description" requirement of the patent law. See 35 U.S.C. § 112. Because new plants may differ from old only in color or perfume, differentiation by written description was often impossible. See Hearings on H.R. 11372 before the House Committee on Patents, 71 Cong., 2d Sess. 4 (1930), p. 7 (memorandum of Patent Commissioner Robertson).

In enacting the Plant Patent Act, Congress addressed both of these concerns. It explained at length its belief that the work of the plant breeder "in aid of nature" was patentable invention. S.Rep. No. 315, 71st Cong., 2d Sess., 6–8 (1930); H.R.Rep. No. 1129, 71st Cong., 2d Sess., 7–9 (1930). And it relaxed the written description requirement in favor of "a description * * * as complete as is reasonably possible." 35 U.S.C. § 162. No Committee or Member of Congress, however, expressed the broader view, now urged by the Government, that the terms "manufacture" or "composition of matter" exclude living things. The sole support for that position in the legislative history of the 1930 Act is found in the conclusory statement of Secretary of Agriculture Hyde, in a letter to the Chairmen of the House and Senate Committees considering the 1930 Act, that "the patent laws * * * at the present time are understood to cover only inventions or discoveries in the field of inanimate nature." See S.Rep. No. 315, supra, at Appendix A; H.R.Rep. No. 1129, supra, at Appendix A. Secretary Hyde's opinion, however, is not entitled to controlling weight. His views were solicited on the administration of the new law and not on the scope of patentable subject matter—an area beyond his competence. Moreover, there is language in the House and Senate Committee reports suggesting that to the extent Congress considered the matter it found the Secretary's dichotomy unpersuasive. The reports observe:

> "There is a clear and logical distinction *between the discovery of a new variety of plant and of certain inanimate things*, such, for example, as a new and useful natural mineral. The mineral is created wholly by nature unassisted by man. * * * On the other hand, a plant discovery resulting from cultivation is unique, isolated, and is not repeated by nature, nor can it be reproduced by nature unaided by man. * * *" S.Rep. No. 315, supra, at 6; H.R.Rep. No. 1129, supra, at 7 (emphasis added).

Congress thus recognized that the relevant distinction was not between living and inanimate things, but between products of nature, whether living or not, and human-made inventions. Here, respondent's micro-organism is the result of human ingenuity and research. Hence, the passage of the Plant Patent Act affords the Government no support.

Nor does the passage of the 1970 Plant Variety Protection Act support the Government's position. As the Government acknowledges, sexually reproduced plants were not included under the 1930 Act because new varieties could not be reproduced true-to-type through seedlings. Brief for United States 27, n. 31. By 1970, however, it was generally recognized that true-to-type reproduction was possible and that plant patent protection was therefore appropriate. The 1970 Act extended that protection. There is nothing in its language or history to suggest that it was enacted because § 101 did not include living things.

In particular, we find nothing in the exclusion of bacteria from plant variety protection to support the Government's position. * * * The legislative history gives no reason for this exclusion. As the Court of Customs and Patent Appeals suggested, it may simply reflect congressional agreement with the result reached by that court in deciding In re Arzberger, 112 F.2d 834 (1940), which held that bacteria were not plants for the purposes of the 1930 Act. Or it may reflect the fact that prior to 1970 the Patent Office had issued patents for bacteria under § 101.[9] In any event, absent some clear indication that Congress "focused on [the] issues . . . directly related to the one presently before the Court," SEC v. Sloan, 436 U.S. 103, 120–121 (1978), there is no basis for reading into its actions an intent to modify the plain meaning of the words found in § 101. See TVA v. Hill, 437 U.S. 153, 189–193 (1978); United States v. Price, 361 U.S. 304, 313 (1960).

(B)

The Government's second argument is that micro-organisms cannot qualify as patentable subject matter until Congress expressly authorizes such protection. Its position rests on the fact that genetic technology was unforeseen when Congress enacted § 101. From this it is argued that resolution of the patentability of inventions such as respondent's should be left to Congress. The legislative process, the Government argues, is best equipped to weigh the competing economic, social, and scientific considerations involved, and to determine whether living organisms produced by genetic engineering should receive patent protection. In support of this position, the Government relies on our recent holding in Parker v. Flook, 437 U.S. 584 (1978), and the statement that the judiciary "must proceed cautiously when . . . asked to extend patent rights into areas wholly unforeseen by Congress." Id., at 596.

---

9. In 1873, the Patent Office granted Louis Pasteur a patent on "yeast, free from organic germs of disease, as an article of manufacture." And in 1967 and 1968, immediately prior to the passage of the Plant Variety Protection Act, that office granted two patents which, as the Government concedes, state claims for living micro-organisms.

It is, of course, correct that Congress, not the courts, must define the limits of patentability; but it is equally true that once Congress has spoken it is "the province and duty of the judicial department to say what the law is." Marbury v. Madison, 1 Cranch 137, 177 (1803). Congress has performed its constitutional role in defining patentable subject matter in § 101; we perform ours in construing the language Congress has employed. In so doing, our obligation is to take statutes as we find them, guided, if ambiguity appears, by the legislative history and statutory purpose. Here, we perceive no ambiguity. The subject matter provisions of the patent law have been cast in broad terms to fulfill the constitutional and statutory goal of promoting "the Progress of Science and the useful Arts" with all that means for the social and economic benefits envisioned by Jefferson. Broad general language is not necessarily ambiguous when congressional objectives require broad terms.

Nothing in *Flook* is to the contrary. That case applied our prior precedents to determine that a "claim for an improved method of calculation, even when tied to a specific end use, is unpatentable subject matter under § 101." 437 U.S., at 595, n. 18. The Court carefully scrutinized the claim at issue to determine whether it was precluded from patent protection under "the principles underlying the prohibition against patents for 'ideas' or phenomena of nature." Id., at 593. We have done that here. *Flook* did not announce a new principle that inventions in areas not contemplated by Congress when the patent laws were enacted are unpatentable *per se*.

To read that concept into *Flook* would frustrate the purposes of the patent law. This Court frequently has observed that a statute is not to be confined to the "particular application[s] * * * contemplated by the legislators." Barr v. United States, 324 U.S. 83, 90 (1945). This is especially true in the field of patent law. A rule that unanticipated inventions are without protection would conflict with the core concept of the patent law that anticipation undermines patentability. See Graham v. John Deere Co., 383 U.S., at 12–17. Mr. Justice Douglas reminded that the inventions most benefiting mankind are those that "push back the frontiers of chemistry, physics, and the like." A. & P. Tea Co. v. Supermarket Corp., 340 U.S. 147, 154 (1950) (concurring opinion). Congress employed broad general language in drafting § 101 precisely because such inventions are often unforeseeable.[10]

To buttress its argument, the Government, with the support of *amicus,* points to grave risks that may be generated by research endeavors such as respondent's. The briefs present a gruesome parade of horribles. Scientists, among them Nobel laureates, are quoted suggesting that genetic research may pose a serious threat to the human race, or, at the very least, that the dangers are far too substantial to permit such research to proceed apace at

---

10. Even an abbreviated list of patented inventions underscores the point: telegraph (Morse, No. 1647); telephone (Bell, No. 174,465); electric lamp (Edison, No. 223,898); airplane (the Wrights, No. 821,393); transistor (Bardeen & Brattain, No. 2,524,035); neutronic reactor (Fermi & Szilard, No. 2,708,656); laser (Schawlow & Townes, No. 2,929,922). See generally Revolutionary Ideas, Patents & Progress in America, Office of Patents (1976).

this time. We are told that genetic research and related technological developments may spread pollution and disease, that it may result in a loss of genetic diversity, and that its practice may tend to depreciate the value of human life. These arguments are forcefully, even passionately presented; they remind us that, at times, human ingenuity seems unable to control fully the forces it creates—that with Hamlet, it is sometimes better "to bear those ills we have than fly to others that we know not of."

It is argued that this Court should weigh these potential hazards in considering whether respondent's invention is patentable subject matter under § 101. We disagree. The grant or denial of patents on micro-organisms is not likely to put an end to genetic research or to its attendant risks. The large amount of research that has already occurred when no researcher had sure knowledge that patent protection would be available suggests that legislative or judicial fiat as to patentability will not deter the scientific mind from probing into the unknown any more than Canute could command the tides. Whether respondent's claims are patentable may determine whether research efforts are accelerated by the hope of reward or slowed by want of incentives, but that is all.

What is more important is that we are without competence to entertain these arguments—either to brush them aside as fantasies generated by fear of the unknown, or to act on them. The choice we are urged to make is a matter of high policy for resolution within the legislative process after the kind of investigation, examination, and study that legislative bodies can provide and courts cannot. That process involves the balancing of competing values and interests, which in our democratic system is the business of elected representatives. Whatever their validity, the contentions now pressed on us should be addressed to the political branches of the government, the Congress and the Executive, and not to the courts.

* * *

Accordingly, the judgment of the Court of Customs and Patent Appeals is affirmed.

Affirmed.

■ MR. JUSTICE BRENNAN, with whom MR. JUSTICE WHITE, MR. JUSTICE MARSHALL, and MR. JUSTICE POWELL join, dissenting.

* * *

* * * The sweeping language of the Patent Act of 1793, as re-enacted in 1952, is not the last pronouncement Congress had made in this area. In 1930 Congress enacted the Plant Patent Act affording patent protection to developers of certain asexually reproduced plants. In 1970 Congress enacted the Plant Variety Protection Act to extend protection to certain new plant varieties capable of sexual reproduction. Thus, we are not dealing—as the Court would have it—with the routine problem of "unanticipated inventions." * * * In these two Acts Congress has addressed the general problem of patenting animate inventions and has chosen carefully limited language granting protection to some kinds of discoveries, but specifically excluding others. These Acts strongly evidence a congressional limitation that excludes bacteria from patentability.

* * *

NOTES

1. If living micro-organisms can be patented, then why not any living thing? Pat. No. 4,736,866, assigned to Harvard University, claims a living mouse, particularly suitable for cancer research because it develops cancers not naturally occurring in mice. If a rodent, why not a mammal such as a cow which gives unusually good milk. And if a cow, why not a man, perhaps improved to exhibit more satisfactory social behavior? On April 21, 1987, the Commissioner issued a notice taking the position that all nonnaturally occurring nonhuman multicellular organisms, including animals, are patentable. 1077 Pat. & Trademark Off. Gazette 24. The position provoked hearings in Congress and attention in the press. For further analysis, see Robert P. Merges, Intellectual Property in Higher Life Forms: The Patent System and Controversial Technologies, 47 Md. L. Rev. 1051 (1988); Thomas T. Moga, Transgenic Animals as Intellectual Property (Or The Patented Mouse that Roared), 76 J. Pat. & Trademark Off. Soc'y 511 (1994).

The notice issued by the PTO on April 21, 1987, read as follows: "A decision by the Board of Patent Appeals and Interferences in Ex parte Allen, [2 U.S.P.Q.2d 1425] (P.T.O. Bd. Pat. App. & Int.), held that claimed polyploid oysters are nonnaturally occurring manufactures or compositions of matter within the meaning of 35 U.S.C. 101. The Board relied upon the opinion of the Supreme Court in Diamond v. Chakrabarty, 447 U.S. 303 (1980), as it had done in Ex parte Hibberd, 227 U.S.P.Q. 443 (P.T.O. Bd. Pat. App. & Int.), as controlling authority that Congress intended statutory subject matter to 'include anything under the sun that is made by man.' The Patent and Trademark Office now considers nonnaturally occurring non-human multicellular living organisms, including animals, to be patentable subject matter within the scope of 35 U.S.C. 101. The Board's decision does not affect the principle and practice that products found in nature will not be considered to be patentable subject matter under 35 U.S.C. 101 and/or 102. An article of manufacture or composition of matter occurring in nature will not be considered patentable unless given a new form, quality, properties or combination not present in the original article existing in nature in accordance with existing law. [Citations omitted]. A claim directed to or including within its scope a human being will not be considered to be patentable subject matter under 35 U.S.C. 101. The grant of a limited, but exclusive property right in a human being is prohibited by the Constitution. Accordingly, it is suggested that any claim directed to a non-plant multicellular organism which would include a human being within its scope include the limitation 'non-human' to avoid this ground of rejection. The use of a negative limitation to define the metes and bounds of the claimed subject matter is a permissible form of expression. In re Wakefield, 422 F.2d 897 (C.C.P.A. 1970). Accordingly, the Patent and Trademark Office is now examining claims directed to multicellular living organisms, including animals. To the extent that the claimed subject matter is directed to a non-human 'nonnaturally occurring manufacture or composition of matter—a product of human ingenuity' (Diamond v. Chakrabarty), such claims will not be rejected under 35 U.S.C. 101 as being directed to non-statutory subject matter."

The Harvard mouse patent was issued in 1988. No further animal patents issued until December 1992 when the PTO issued patents on three more mice: a virus-resistant mouse strain, a strain that fails to develop a functional immune system, and a strain whose males develop enlarged prostate glands. Two more mice and one rabbit patent have since issued. The reason that all but one of the patents are on mice is that experimenters have had poor success in introducing foreign genes into other animals.

2. *Chakrabarty* was one necessary component of the legal foundation behind the development of biotechnology start up companies, who could raise capital from venture capitalists based upon the research expertise of their principals and the assurance of the *Chakrabarty* decision that the fruits of their research would be patentable.

3. The theme of *Chakrabarty* that anything under the sun that is made by man is patentable appeared to answer previous doubts about the patentability of medical procedures. In 1992 Dr. Samuel L. Pallin received U.S. Patent No. 5,080,111 which related to a method for making self-sealing incisions in the episcleral of the eye. Dr. Pallin then sued another eye surgeon for practicing this procedure.

This lawsuit was ultimately settled on terms adverse to the plaintiff, but not before it had brought the issue of the patentability of medical procedures to the attention of the American Medical Association and other medical groups. They first sought an amendment to the patent act which would deny patentability to any medical procedure, but immediately encountered resistance from the pharmaceutical, medical device and biotechnology industries. A compromise was worked out with those industries which only addressed the issue of remedies, not patentability, and exempted the products of the objecting industries from its operation. The compromise was then attached by the Conference Committee to the Omnibus Consolidated Appropriations Act of 1997, P.L. 104–208 (1996), which added § 287(c) to the patent statute. That section exempts from the remedial sections of the statute "a medical practitioner's performance of a medical activity." The term "medical activity" is defined to mean "the performance of a medical or surgical procedure on a body, but shall not include (i) the use of a patented machine, manufacture, or composition of matter in violation of such patent, (ii) the practice of a patented use of a composition of matter in violation of such patent, or (iii) the practice of a process in violation of a biotechnology patent." For descriptions of this episode, and discussions of the AMA objections to the patenting of medical procedures, see Eric M. Lee, The Physician Immunity Statute, 79 J. Pat. & Trademark Off. Soc'y 701 (1997); Timothy J. Lithgow, Patent Infringement Immunity for Medical Practitioners and Related Health Care Entities, 37 Jurimetrics J. 251 (1997); Bradley J. Meier, The New Patent Infringement Liability

Exception for Medical Procedures, 23 J. Legis. 265 (1997); Silvy A. Miller, Should Patenting of Surgical Procedures and Other Medical Techniques by Physicians be Banned, 36 J.L. & Tech. 255 (1996).

Would it not be extremely difficult to enforce a patent on a medical procedure that can be carried out with standard instruments and facilities in a doctor's office or a hospital operating room?

4. Article 27 of the GATT TRIPS provides:

Article 27

Patentable Subject Matter

1. Subject to the provisions of paragraphs 2 and 3, patents shall be available for any inventions, whether products or processes, in all fields of technology, provided that they are new, involve an inventive step and are capable of industrial application. Subject to paragraph 4 of Article 65, paragraph 8 of Article 70 [paragraphs relating to transitional issues] and paragraph 3 of this Article, patents shall be available and patent rights enjoyable without discrimination as to the place of invention, the field of technology and whether products are imported or locally produced.

2. Members may exclude from patentability inventions, the prevention within their territory of the commercial exploitation of which is necessary to protect *ordre public* or morality, including to protect human, animal or plant life or health or to avoid serious prejudice to the environment, provided that such exclusion is not made merely because the exploitation is prohibited by their law.

3. Members may also exclude from patentability:

(a) diagnostic, therapeutic and surgical methods for the treatment of humans or animals;

(b) plants and animals other than micro-organisms, and essentially biological processes for the production of plants or animals other than non-biological and microbiological processes. However, Members shall provide for the protection of plant varieties either by patents or by an effective *sui generis* system or by any combination thereof. The provisions of this subparagraph shall be reviewed four years after the date of entry into force of the WTO Agreement.

Diamond v. Diehr

Supreme Court of the United States, 1981.
450 U.S. 175, 101 S.Ct. 1048, 67 L.Ed.2d 155.

■ MR. JUSTICE REHNQUIST delivered the opinion of the Court.

We granted certiorari to determine whether a process for curing synthetic rubber which includes in several of its steps the use of a mathematical formula and a programmed digital computer is patentable subject matter under 35 U.S.C. § 101.

I

The patent application at issue was filed by the respondents on August 6, 1975. The claimed invention is a process for molding raw, uncured synthetic rubber into cured precision products. The process uses a mold for precisely shaping the uncured material under heat and pressure and then curing the synthetic rubber in the mold so that the product will retain its shape and be functionally operative after the molding is completed.[1]

Respondents claim that their process ensures the production of molded articles which are properly cured. Achieving the perfect cure depends upon several factors including the thickness of the article to be molded, the temperature of the molding process, and the amount of time that the article is allowed to remain in the press. It is possible using well-known time, temperature, and cure relationships to calculate by means of the Arrhenius equation[2] when to open the press and remove the cured product. Nonetheless, according to the respondents, the industry has not been able to obtain uniformly accurate cures because the temperature of the molding press could not be precisely measured thus making it difficult to do the necessary computations to determine cure time.[3] Because the temperature *inside* the press has heretofore been viewed as an uncontrollable variable, the conventional industry practice has been to calculate the cure time as the shortest time in which all parts of the product will definitely be cured, assuming a reasonable amount of mold-opening time during loading and unloading. But the shortcoming of this practice is that operating with an uncontrollable variable inevitably led in some instances to overestimating the mold-opening time and overcuring the rubber, and in other instances to underestimating that time and undercuring the product.

Respondents characterize their contribution to the art to reside in the process of constantly measuring the actual temperature inside the mold. These temperature measurements are then automatically fed into a computer which repeatedly recalculates the cure time by use of the Arrhenius equation. When the recalculated time equals the actual time that has elapsed since the press was closed, the computer signals a device to open the press. According to the respondents, the continuous measuring of the

---

1. A "cure" is obtained by mixing curing agents into the uncured polymer in advance of molding and then applying heat over a period of time. If the synthetic rubber is cured for the right length of time at the right temperature, it becomes a useable product.

2. The equation is named after its discoverer Svante Arrhenius and has long been used to calculate the cure time, in rubber molding presses. The equation can be expressed as follows:

$$\ln v = CZ + x$$

wherein ln v is the natural logarithm of v, the total required cure time; C is the activation constant, a unique figure for each batch of each compound being molded, determined in

accordance with rheometer measurements of each batch; Z is the temperature in the mold; and x is a constant dependent on the geometry of the particular mold in the press. A rheometer is an instrument to measure flow of viscous substances.

3. During the time a press is open for loading, it will cool. The longer it is open, the cooler it becomes and the longer it takes to reheat the press to the desired temperature range. Thus, the time necessary to raise the mold temperature to curing temperature is an unpredictable variable. The respondents claim to have overcome this problem by continuously measuring the actual temperature in the closed press through the use of a thermocouple.

temperature inside the mold cavity, the feeding of this information to a digital computer which constantly recalculates the cure time, and the signaling by the computer to open the press, are all new in the art.

The patent examiner rejected the respondents' claims on the sole ground that they were drawn to nonstatutory subject matter under 35 U.S.C. § 101.[5] He determined that those steps in respondents' claims that

5. Respondents' application contained 11 different claims. Three examples are claims 1, 2, and 11 which provide:

"1. A method of operating a rubber-molding press for precision molded compounds with the aid of a digital computer, comprising:

"providing said computer with a data base for said press including at least,

"natural logarithm conversion data (1n),

"the activation energy constant (C) unique to each batch of said compound being molded, and

"a constant (x) dependent upon the geometry of the particular mold of the press,

"initiating an interval timer in said computer upon the closure of the press for monitoring the elapsed time of said closure,

"constantly determining the temperature (Z) of the mold at a location closely adjacent to the mold cavity in the press during molding,

"constantly providing the computer with the temperature (Z),

"repetitively calculating in the computer, at frequent intervals during each cure, the Arrhenius equation for reaction time during the cure, which is

"1n v=CZ + x

"where v is the total required cure time,

"repetitively comparing in the computer at said frequent intervals during the cure each said calculation of the total required cure time calculated with the Arrhenius equation and said elapsed time, and

"opening the press automatically when a said comparison indicates equivalence.

"2. The method of claim 1 including measuring the activation energy constant for the compound being molded in the press with a rheometer and automatically updating said data base within the computer in the event of changes in the compound being molded in said press as measured by said rheometer.

"11. A method of manufacturing precision molded articles from selected synthetic rubber compounds in an openable rubber molding press having at least one heated precision mold, comprising:

"(a) heating said mold to a temperature range approximating a pre-determined rubber curing temperature,

"(b) installing prepared unmolded synthetic rubber of a known compound in a molding cavity of a predetermined geometry as defined by said mold,

"(c) closing said press to mold said rubber to occupy said cavity in conformance with the contour of said mold and to cure said rubber by transfer of heat thereto from said mold,

"(d) initiating an interval timer upon the closure of said press for monitoring the elapsed time of said closure,

"(e) heating said mold during said closure to maintain the temperature thereof within said range approximating said rubber curing temperature,

"(f) constantly determining the temperature of said mold at a location closely adjacent said cavity thereof throughout closure of said press,

"(g) repetitively calculating at frequent periodic invervals throughout closure of said press the Arrhenius equation for reaction time of said rubber to determine total required cure time v as follows:

"1n v = CZ + x

"wherein c is an activation energy constant determined for said rubber being molded and cured in said press, z is the temperature of said mold at the time of each calculation of said Arrhenius equation, and x is a constant which is a function of said predetermined geometry of said mold,

"(h) for each repetition of calculation of said Arrhenius equation herein comparing the resultant calculated total required cure time with the monitored elapsed time measured by said interval timer,

"(i) opening said press when a said comparison of calculated total required cure time and monitored elapsed time indicates equivalence, and

"(j) removing from said mold the resultant precision molded and cured rubber article."

are carried out by a computer under control of a stored program constituted nonstatutory subject matter under this Court's decision in Gottschalk v. Benson, 409 U.S. 63 (1972). The remaining steps—installing rubber in the press and the subsequent closing of the press—were "conventional in nature and cannot be the basis of patentability." The examiner concluded that respondents' claims defined and sought protection of a computer program for operating a rubber molding press.

The Patent and Trademark Office Board of Appeals agreed with the examiner, but the Court of Customs and Patent Appeals reversed. The court noted that a claim drawn to subject matter otherwise statutory does not become nonstatutory because a computer is involved. The respondents' claims were not directed to a mathematical algorithm or an improved method of calculation but rather recited an improved process for molding rubber articles by solving a practical problem which had risen in the molding of rubber products.

The Government sought certiorari arguing that the decision of the Court of Customs and Patent Appeals was inconsistent with prior decisions of this Court. Because of the importance of the question presented, we granted the writ. 445 U.S. 926 (1980).

II

Last Term in Diamond v. Chakrabarty, 447 U.S. 303 (1980), this Court discussed the historical purposes of the patent laws and in particular 35 U.S. § 101. As in *Chakrabarty*, we must here construe 35 U.S.C. § 101:

* * *

The Patent Act of 1793 defined statutory subject matter as "any new and useful art, machine, manufacture or composition of matter, or any new or useful improvement [thereof]." Act of Feb. 21, 1793, ch. 11, § 1, 1 Stat. 318. Not until the patent laws were recodified in 1952 did Congress replace the word "art" with the word "process." It is that latter word which we confront today, and in order to determine its meaning we may not be unmindful of the Committee Reports accompanying the 1952 Act which inform us that Congress intended statutory subject matter to "include anything under the sun that is made by man." S.Rep. No. 1979, 82d Cong., 2d Sess., 5 (1952), H.R. Rep. No. 1923, 82d Cong., 2d Sess., 6 (1952), U.S. Code Cong. & Admin. News 1952, pp. 2394, 2399.

Although the term "process" was not added to 35 U.S.C. § 101 until 1952 a process has historically enjoyed patent protection because it was considered a form of "art" as that term was used in the 1793 Act. In defining the nature of a patentable process, the Court stated:

> "That a process may be patentable, irrespective of the particular form of the instrumentalities used, cannot be disputed. * * * A process is a mode of treatment of certain materials to produce a given result. It is an act, or a series of acts, performed upon the subject matter to be transformed and reduced to a different state or thing. If new and useful, it is just as patentable as is a piece of machinery. In the language

of the patent law, it is an art. The machinery pointed out as suitable to perform the process may or may not be new or patentable; whilst the process itself may be altogether new, and produce an entirely new result. The process requires that certain things should be done with certain substances, and in a certain order; but the tools to be used in doing this may be of secondary consequence." Cochrane v. Deener, 94 U.S. 780, 787–788 (1876).

Analysis of the eligibility of a claim of patent protection for a "process" did not change with the addition of that term to § 101. Recently, in Gottschalk v. Benson, 409 U.S. 63 (1972), we repeated the above definition recited in Cochrane v. Deener, adding "Transformation and reduction of an article 'to a different state or thing' is the clue to the patentability of a process claim that does not include particular machines." Id., at 70.

Analyzing respondents' claims according to the above statements from our cases, we think that a physical and chemical process for molding precision synthetic rubber products falls within the § 101 categories of possibly patentable subject matter. That respondents' claims involve the transformation of an article, in this case raw uncured synthetic rubber, into a different state or thing cannot be disputed. The respondents' claims describe in detail a step-by-step method for accomplishing such beginning with the loading of a mold with raw uncured rubber and ending with the eventual opening of the press at the conclusion of the cure. Industrial processes such as this are the type which have historically been eligible to receive the protection of our patent laws.

III

Our conclusion regarding respondents' claims is not altered by the fact that in several steps of the process a mathematical equation and a programmed digital computer are used. This Court has undoubtedly recognized limits to § 101 and every discovery is not embraced within the statutory terms. Excluded from such patent protection are laws of nature, physical phenomena and abstract ideas. See Parker v. Flook, 437 U.S. 584 (1978); Gottschalk v. Benson, 409 U.S. 63 (1973); Funk Bros. Seed Co. v. Kalo Co., 333 U.S. 127, 130 (1948). "An idea of itself is not patentable," Rubber-Tip Pencil Co. v. Howard, 20 Wall. 498, 507 (1874). "A principle, in the abstract, is a fundamental truth; an original cause; a motive; these cannot be patented, as no one can claim in either of them an exclusive right." Le Roy v. Tatham, 14 How. 156, 175 (1852).

* * *

Our recent holdings in Gottschalk v. Benson, supra, and Parker v. Flook, supra, both of which are computer-related, stand for no more than these long established principles. In *Benson,* we held unpatentable claims for an algorithm used to convert binary code decimal numbers to equivalent pure binary numbers. The sole practical application of the algorithm was in connection with the programming of a general purpose digital computer. We defined "algorithm" as a "procedure for solving a given type of mathematical problem," and we concluded that such an algorithm, or mathematical formula, is like a law of nature, which cannot be the subject of a patent.[9]

Parker v. Flook, supra, presented a similar situation. The claims were drawn to a method for computing an "alarm limit." An "alarm limit" is simply a number and the Court concluded that the application sought to protect a formula for computing this number. Using this formula, the updated alarm limit could be calculated if several other variables were known. The application, however, did not purport to explain how these other variables were to be determined,[10] nor did it purport "to contain any disclosure relating to the chemical processes at work, the monitoring of process variables, or the means of setting off an alarm system. All that is provided is a formula for computing an updated alarm limit." 437 U.S., at 586.

In contrast, the respondents here do not seek to patent a mathematical formula. Instead, they seek patent protection for a process of curing synthetic rubber. Their process admittedly employs a well known mathematical equation, but they do not seek to pre-empt the use of that equation. Rather, they seek only to foreclose from others the use of that equation in conjunction with all of the other steps in their claimed process. These include installing rubber in a press, closing the mold, constantly determining the temperature of the mold, constantly recalculating the appropriate cure time through the use of the formula and a digital computer, and automatically opening the press at the proper time. Obviously, one does not need a "computer" to cure natural or synthetic rubber, but if the computer use incorporated in the process patent significantly lessens the possibility of "overcuring" or "undercuring," the process as a whole does not thereby become unpatentable subject matter.

Our earlier opinions lend support to our present conclusion that a claim drawn to subject matter otherwise statutory does not become non-statutory simply because it uses a mathematical formula, computer program or digital computer. In Gottschalk v. Benson, supra, we noted "it is

9. The term "algorithm" is subject to a variety of definitions. The Government defines the term to mean:

"1. A fixed step-by-step procedure for accomplishing a given result; usually a simplified procedure for solving a complex problem, also a full statement of a finite number of steps. 2. A defined process or set of rules that leads [sic] and assures development of a desired output from a given input. A sequence of formulas and/or algebraic/logical steps to calculate or determine a given task; processing rules."

This definition is significantly broader than the definition this Court employed in Benson and Flook. Our previous decisions regarding the patentability of "algorithms" are necessarily limited to the more narrow definition employed by the Court and we do not pass judgment on whether processes falling outside the definition previously used by this Court, but within the definition offered by the Government, would be patentable subject matter.

10. As we explained in *Flook*, in order for an operator using the formula to calculate an updated alarm limit the operator would need to know the original alarm base, the appropriate margin of safety, the time interval that should elapse between each updating, the current temperature (or other process variable) and the appropriate weighing factor to be used to average the alarm base and the current temperature. 437 U.S. 584, 586. The patent application did not "explain how to select the approximate margin of safety, the weighing factor or any of the other variables." Ibid.

said that the decision precludes a patent for any program servicing a computer. We do not so hold." 409 U.S., at 71. Similarly, in Parker v. Flook, supra, we stated, "A process is not unpatentable simply because it contains a law of nature or a mathematical algorithm." 437 U.S., at 590. It is now common-place that an *application* of a law of nature or mathematical formula to a known structure or process may well be deserving of patent protection. See, e.g., Funk Bros. Seed Co. v. Kalo Co., 333 U.S. 127 (1948); Eibel Process Co. v. Minnesota & Ontario Paper Co., 261 U.S. 45 (1923); Cochrane v. Deener, 94 U.S. 780 (1876); O'Reilly v. Morse, 15 How. 62 (1853); and Le Roy v. Tatham, 14 How. 156 (1852). As Mr. Justice Stone explained four decades ago:

> "While a scientific truth, or the mathematical expression of it, is not a patentable invention, a novel and useful structure created with the aid of knowledge of scientific truth may be." Mackay Radio & Telegraph Co. v. Radio Corp. of America, 306 U.S. 86, 94 (1939).

We think this statement in *Mackay* takes us a long way toward the correct answer in this case. Arrhenius' equation is not patentable in isolation, but when a process for curing rubber is devised which incorporates in it a more efficient solution of the equation, that process is at the very least not barred at the threshold by § 101.

In determining the eligibility of respondents' claimed process for patent protection under § 101, their claims must be considered as a whole. It is inappropriate to dissect the claims into old and new elements and then to ignore the presence of the old elements in the analysis. This is particularly true in a process claim because a new combination of steps in a process may be patentable even though all the constituents of the combination were well known and in common use before the combination was made. The "novelty" of any element or steps in a process, or even of the process itself, is of no relevance in determining whether the subject matter of a claim falls within the § 101 categories of possibly patentable subject matter.[12]

It has been urged that novelty is an appropriate consideration under § 101. Presumably, this argument results from the language in § 101 referring to any "new and useful" process, machine, etc. Section 101, however, is a general statement of the type of subject matter that is eligible for patent protection "subject to the conditions and requirements of this title." Specific

---

12. It is argued that the procedure of dissecting a claim into old and new elements is mandated by our decision in *Flook* which noted that a mathematical algorithm must be assumed to be within the "prior art." It is from this language that the Government premises its argument that if everything other than the algorithm is determined to be old in the art, then the claim cannot recite statutory subject matter. The fallacy in this argument is that we did not hold in *Flook* that the mathematical algorithm could not be considered at all when making the § 101 determination. To accept the analysis proffered by the Government would, if carried to its extreme, make all inventions unpatentable because all inventions can be reduced to underlying principles of nature which, once known, make their implementation obvious. The analysis suggested by the Government would also undermine our earlier decisions regarding the criteria to consider in determining the eligibility of a process for patent protection. See, e.g., Gottschalk v. Benson, 409 U.S. 63 (1973); and Cochrane v. Deener, 94 U.S. 780 (1876).

conditions for patentability follow and § 102 covers in detail the conditions relating to novelty. The question therefore of whether a particular invention is novel is "fully apart from whether the invention falls into a category of statutory subject matter." In re Bergy, 596 F.2d 952, 961 (Cust. & Pat. App., 1979). See also Nickola v. Peterson, 580 F.2d 898 (CA6 1978). The legislative history of the 1952 Patent Act is in accord with this reasoning. The Senate Report provided:

> "Section 101 sets forth the subject matter than can be patented, 'subject to the conditions and requirement of this title.' The conditions under which a patent may be obtained follow, and *Section 102 covers the conditions relating to novelty*." S. Rep. No. 1979, 82d Cong., 2d Sess., 5 (1952), U.S. Code Cong. & Admin. News, 1952, p. 2399 (emphasis supplied).

It is later stated in the same report:

> "Section 102, in general, may be said to describe the statutory novelty required for patentability, and includes, in effect, the amplification and definition of 'new' in Section 101." Id., at 6, U.S. Code Cong. & Admin. News, 1952, p. 2399.

Finally, it is stated in the "Revision Notes":

> "The corresponding section of [the] existing statute is split into two sections, Section 101 relating to the subject matter for which patents may be obtained, and Section 102 defining statutory novelty and stating other conditions for patentability." Id., at 17, U.S.Code Cong. & Admin.News, 1952, p. 2409.

See also H.R.Rep. No. 1923, 82d Cong., 2d Sess. (1952), at 6, 7 and 17.

In this case, it may later be determined that the respondents' process is not deserving of patent protection because it fails to satisfy the statutory conditions of novelty under § 102 or nonobviousness under § 103. A rejection on either of these grounds does not affect the determination that respondents' claims recited subject matter which was eligible for patent protection under § 101.

IV

We have before us today only the question of whether respondents' claims fall within the § 101 categories of possibly patentable subject matter. We view respondents' claims as nothing more than a process for molding rubber products and not as an attempt to patent a mathematical formula. We recognize, of course, that when a claim recites a mathematical formula (or scientific principle or phenomenon of nature), an inquiry must be made into whether the claim is seeking patent protection for that formula in the abstract. A mathematical formula as such is not accorded the protection of our patent laws, Gottschalk v. Benson, supra, and this principle cannot be circumvented by attempting to limit the use of the formula to a particular technological environment. Parker v. Flook, supra. Similarly, insignificant post-solution activity will not transform an unpatentable principle into a patentable process. Ibid.[14] To hold otherwise would allow a competent draftsman to evade the recognized limitations on the type of subject matter eligible for patent protection. On the other hand, when a claim containing a mathematical formula implements or applies that formula in a structure or process which, when considered as a whole, is performing a function which the patent laws were designed to protect (e.g., transforming or reducing an article to a different state or thing), then the claim satisfies the requirements of § 101. Because we do not view respondents' claims as an attempt to patent a mathematical formula, but rather to be drawn to an industrial process for the molding of rubber products, we affirm the judgment of the Court of Customs and Patent Appeals.

* * *

NOTES

1. The Federal Circuit has not had an easy time delineating the distinction between a patentable process such as that in *Diehr* and an unpatentable algorithm such as that in *Gottschalk v. Benson*. Patent applicants are, of course, well-advised to focus the claims in their applications on the practical use of their invention and to down play the presence of any "alogrithm."

The Federal Circuit employs what it calls the *Freeman-Walter-Abele* test, named for three circuit precedents. "It is first determined whether a mathematical algorithm is recited directly or indirectly in the claim. If so, it is next determined whether the claimed invention as a whole is no more than the algorithm itself; that is, whether the claim is directed to a mathematical algorithm that is not applied to or limited by physical elements or

---

14. Arguably, the claims in *Flook* did more than present a mathematical formula. The claims also solved the calculation in order to produce a new number or "alarm limit" and then replaced the old number with the number newly produced. The claims covered all uses of the formula in processes "comprising the catalytic chemical conversion of hydrocarbons." There are numerous such processes in the petrochemical and oil refinery industries and the claims therefore covered a broad range of potential uses, 437 U.S., at 586. The claims, however, did not cover every conceivable application of the formula. We rejected in *Flook* the argument that because all possible uses of the mathematical formula were not pre-empted, the claim should be eligible for patent protection. Our reasoning in *Flook* is in no way inconsistent with our reasoning here. A mathematical formula does not suddenly become patentable subject matter simply by having the applicant acquiesce to limiting the reach of the patent for the formula to a particular technological use. A mathematical formula in the abstract is nonstatutory subject matter regardless of whether the patent is intended to cover all uses of the formula or only limited uses. Similarly, a mathematical formula does not become patentable subject matter merely by including in the claim for the formula token post-solution activity such as the type claimed in *Flook*. We were careful to note in *Flook* that the patent application did not purport to explain how the variables used in the formula were to be selected, nor did the application contain any disclosure relating to chemical processes at work or the means of setting off an alarm or adjusting the alarm unit. 437 U.S., at 586. All the application provided was a "formula for computing an updated alarm limit." 437 U.S., at 586.

process steps. Such claims are nonstatutory. However, when the mathematical algorithm is applied in one or more steps of an otherwise statutory process claim, or one or more elements of an otherwise statutory apparatus claim, the requirements of section 101 are met." Arrhythmia Research Technology, Inc. v. Corazonix Corp., 958 F.2d 1053, 1058 (Fed. Cir. 1992). In In re Warmerdam, 33 F.3d 1354, 1359 (Fed. Cir. 1994), Judge Plager remarked of the *Freeman-Walter-Abele* test that "The difficulty is that there is no clear agreement as to what is a 'mathematical algorithm', which makes rather dicey the determination of whether the claim as a whole is no more than that."

The PTO is issuing a significant number of software patents. In the 1990's they have proven to be of increasing practical importance. Although *Diehr* was decided in 1981, there were significant time lags as the PTO had to staff up its ability to examine software patents, and the industry had to learn how to structure and persuade the PTO to issue software patents.

An example of the current practical importance of software patents happened in 1994 when Stac Electronics won a jury verdict against Microsoft for $120,000,000 for infringement of its patent on a data compression system. Stac had developed and marketed a program, "Stacker," that would double the amount of storage space available on a hard disk. Microsoft decided to build a similar feature into Microsoft DOS 6.0, an upgrade for the popular operating system used on IBM-style personal computers. It first approached Stac for a license to use its software, but when negotiations broke down it developed its own system. The system was not a copy of Stacker, and hence not copyright infringement, but it employed some of the same techniques. The parties settled the litigation on June 21, 1994, agreeing to cross-license their disk compression technology and Microsoft agreeing to pay royalties of $1,000,0000 a month for 43 months and buy $39.9 million of non-voting convertible preferred Stac stock. 48 BNA Patent Trademark & Copyright Journal 193.

PROBLEMS

1. In the hours immediately after a heart attack the victim is particularly vulnerable to an acute type of heart arrhythmia known as ventricular tachycardia. This usually results in death. The onset of ventricular tachycardia can be prevented by the administration of drugs, but the drugs have dangerous side effects. Can a patent issue on a process of using standard data from an electrocardiogram, processing the data in a digital computer, and then using the resulting values to decide whether or not the patient is at risk for ventricular tachycardia?

2. Can electronic circuitry and the process employed by the circuitry for displaying a sharper picture on a television screen be patented, where the circuitry is implemented using standard components and methods, and where the essence of the process is described by the use of mathematical formulae specifying the changes made in the incoming picture signal?

3. Can a procedure for finding the shortest path between two points in light of various constraints, to be implemented on a digital computer, and capable of being used to analyze a wide variety of "short path" problems encountered in industry and computer science be patented?

4. Can a collision avoidance procedure to be programmed into mechanical robots and whose purpose is to efficiently process data obtained from robot sensors to determine whether or not a collision will occur be patented?

5. Would the answer to any of the above four problems be different under the standard of Article 27 of the GATT TRIPS?

Designs

The patent statute provides protection for "new, original and ornamental design for an article of manufacture." 35 U.S.C. § 171. The term of a design patent is fourteen years, 35 U.S.C. § 173. A design patent must meet all the requirements of the patent statute. Most importantly, this means a design patent must be non-obvious under 35 U.S.C. § 103, discussed infra.

A design patent has a single claim, which consists of drawings of the claimed ornamentation.

Although the provisions for a design patent are part of the patent statute, and a design patent is called a patent, it is important to understand that a design patent is practically the reverse a of regular patent. (Indeed, to make the distinction clearer, regular patents are called utility patents in contexts where it is useful to distinguish them from design patents.) A utility patent is awarded for an invention that has a useful function. A design patent is awarded only for an ornamental design. A design patent on a feature which primarily serves a utilitarian or functional purpose is invalid. It is possible to obtain a utility patent and a design patent on different aspects of the same product.

A design which has been copyrighted can also be the subject of a design patent. Application of Yardley, 493 F.2d 1389 (C.C.P.A.1974) (Copyright registration of Spiro Agnew watch does not bar design patent).

Article 25 of the GATT TRIPS provides that "Members shall provide for the protection of independently created industrial designs that are new or orginal." The duration of the protection required is ten years. Article 26 ¶ 3. Since the U.S. has no separate system providing protection for industrial designs (although such a system has been considered by Congress in the past, most notably in connection with the copyright revision bill), the only provisions in U.S. law that possibly comply with these requirements are the design patent sections of the patent statute.

Because a valid design patent must be non-obvious under § 103, rather than simply novel, it can be argued that U.S. law does not comply with the GATT TRIPS on this point. For many years observers were of the view that few, if any, design patents would be held valid by the U.S. courts under § 103. In recent years that has changed, and the Federal Circuit has held a number of design patents valid.

B. Utility

Brenner v. Manson

Supreme Court of the United States, 1966.
383 U.S. 519, 86 S.Ct. 1033, 16 L.Ed.2d 69.

■ MR. JUSTICE FORTAS delivered the opinion of the Court.

This case presents two questions of importance to the administration of the patent laws: First, whether this Court has certiorari jurisdiction, upon petition of the Commissioner of Patents, to review decisions of the Court of Customs and Patent Appeals; and second, whether the practical utility of the compound produced by a chemical process is an essential element in establishing a prima facie case for the patentability of the process. The facts are as follows:

In December 1957, Howard Ringold and George Rosenkranz applied for a patent on an allegedly novel process for making certain known steroids.[1] They claimed priority as of December 17, 1956, the date on which they had filed for a Mexican patent. United States Patent No. 2,908,693 issued late in 1959.

In January 1960, respondent Manson, a chemist engaged in steroid research, filed an application to patent precisely the same process described by Ringold and Rosenkranz. He asserted that it was he who had discovered the process, and that he had done so before December 17, 1956. Accordingly, he requested that an "interference" be declared in order to try out the issue of priority between his claim and that of Ringold and Rosenkranz.

A Patent Office examiner denied Manson's application, and the denial was affirmed by the Board of Appeals within the Patent Office. The ground for rejection was the failure "to disclose any utility for" the chemical compound produced by the process. Letter of Examiner, dated May 24, 1960. This omission was not cured, in the opinion of the Patent Office, by Manson's reference to an article in the November 1956 issue of the Journal of Organic Chemistry, 21 J.Org.Chem. 1333–1335, which revealed that steroids of a class which included the compound in question were undergoing screening for possible tumor-inhibiting effects in mice, and that a homologue[3] adjacent to Manson's steroid had proven effective in that role. Said

1. The applicants described the products of their process as "2-methyl dihydrotestosterone derivatives and esters thereof as well as 2-methyl dihydrotestosterone derivatives having a C-17 lower alkyl group. The products of the process of the present invention have a useful high anabolic-androgenic ratio and are especially valuable for treatment of those ailments where anabolic or antiestrogenic effect together with a lesser androgenic effect is desired."

3. "A homologous series is a family of chemically related compounds, the composition of which varies from member to member by CH_2(one atom of carbon and two atoms of hydrogen). * * * Chemists knowing the properties of one member of a series would in general know what to expect in adjacent members." * * *

the Board of Appeals, "It is our view that the statutory requirement of usefulness of a product cannot be presumed merely because it happens to be closely related to another compound which is known to be useful."

The Court of Customs and Patent Appeals (hereinafter CCPA) reversed, Chief Judge Worley dissenting. 52 C.C.P.A. (Pat.) 739, 745, 333 F.2d 234, 237–238. The court held that Manson was entitled to a declaration of interference since "where a claimed process produces a known product it is not necessary to show utility for the product," so long as the product "is not alleged to be detrimental to the public interest." Certiorari was granted, 380 U.S. 971, to resolve this running dispute over what constitutes "utility" in chemical process claims, as well as to answer the question concerning our certiorari jurisdiction. * * *

[The Court held that it had certiorari jurisdiction over the Court of Customs and Patent Appeals.]

Our starting point is the proposition, neither disputed nor disputable, that one may patent only that which is "useful."

* * *

As is so often the case, however, a simple, everyday word can be pregnant with ambiguity when applied to the facts of life. That this is so is demonstrated by the present conflict between the Patent Office and the CCPA over how the test is to be applied to a chemical process which yields an already known product whose utility—other than as a possible object of scientific inquiry—has not yet been evidenced.

* * *

It is not remarkable that differences arise as to how the test of usefulness is to be applied to chemical processes. Even if we knew precisely what Congress meant in 1790 when it devised the "new and useful" phraseology and in subsequent re-enactments of the test, we should have difficulty in applying it in the context of contemporary chemistry where research is as comprehensive as man's grasp and where little or nothing is wholly beyond the pale of "utility"—if that word is given its broadest reach.

Respondent does not—at least in the first instance—rest upon the extreme proposition, advanced by the court below, that a novel chemical process is patentable so long as it yields the intended product and so long as the product is not itself "detrimental." * * *

* * * [O]n the assumption that the process would be patentable were respondent to show that the steroid produced had a tumor-inhibiting effect in mice, we would not overrule the Patent Office finding that respondent has not made such a showing. The Patent Office held that, despite the reference to the adjacent homologue, respondent's papers did not disclose a sufficient likelihood that the steroid yielded by his process would have similar tumor-inhibiting characteristics. Indeed, respondent himself recognized that the presumption that adjacent homologues have the same utility has been challenged in the steroid field because of "a greater known unpredictability of compounds in that field." In these circumstances and in this

technical area, we would not overturn the finding of the Primary Examiner, affirmed by the Board of Appeals and not challenged by the CCPA.

The second and third points of respondent's argument present issues of much importance. Is a chemical process "useful" within the meaning of § 101 either (1) because it works—i.e., produces the intended product? or (2) because the compound yielded belongs to a class of compounds now the subject of serious scientific investigation? These contentions present the basic problem for our adjudication.

* * *

In support of his plea that we attenuate the requirement of "utility," respondent relies upon Justice Story's well-known statement that a "useful" invention is one "which may be applied to a beneficial use in society, in contradistinction to an invention injurious to the morals, health, or good order of society, or frivolous and insignificant"[20]—and upon the assertion that to do so would encourage inventors of new processes to publicize the event for the benefit of the entire scientific community, thus widening the search for uses and increasing the fund of scientific knowledge. Justice Story's language sheds little light on our subject. Narrowly read, it does no more than compel us to decide whether the invention in question is "frivolous and insignificant"—a query no easier of application than the one built into the statute. Read more broadly, so as to allow the patenting of any invention not positively harmful to society, it places such a special meaning on the word "useful" that we cannot accept it in the absence of evidence that Congress so intended. There are, after all, many things in this world which may not be considered "useful" but which, nevertheless, are totally without a capacity for harm.

It is true, of course, that one of the purposes of the patent system is to encourage dissemination of information concerning discoveries and inventions. And it may be that inability to patent a process to some extent discourages disclosure and leads to greater secrecy than would otherwise be the case. The inventor of the process, or the corporate organization by which he is employed, has some incentive to keep the invention secret while uses for the product are searched out. However, in light of the highly developed art of drafting patent claims so that they disclose as little useful information as possible—while broadening the scope of the claim as widely as possible—the argument based upon the virtue of disclosure must be warily evaluated. Moreover, the pressure for secrecy is easily exaggerated, for if the inventor of a process cannot himself ascertain a "use" for that which his process yields, he has every incentive to make his invention known to those able to do so. Finally, how likely is disclosure of a patented process to spur research by others into the uses to which the product may be put? To the extent that the patentee has power to enforce his patent, there is little incentive for others to undertake a search for uses.

20. Note on the Patent Laws, 3 Wheat. App. 13, 24. See also Justice Story's decisions on circuit in Lowell v. Lewis, 15 Fed. Cas. 1018 (No. 8568) (C.C.D. Mass.), and Bedford v. Hunt, 3 Fed. Cas. 37 (No. 1217) (C.C.D. Mass.).

Whatever weight is attached to the value of encouraging disclosure and of inhibiting secrecy, we believe a more compelling consideration is that a process patent in the chemical field, which has not been developed and pointed to the degree of specific utility, creates a monopoly of knowledge which should be granted only if clearly commanded by the statute. Until the process claim has been reduced to production of a product shown to be useful, the metes and bounds of that monopoly are not capable of precise delineation. It may engross a vast, unknown, and perhaps unknowable area. Such a patent may confer power to block off whole areas of scientific development, without compensating benefit to the public. The basic *quid pro quo* contemplated by the Constitution and the Congress for granting a patent monopoly is the benefit derived by the public from an invention with substantial utility. Unless and until a process is refined and developed to this point—where specific benefit exists in currently available form—there is insufficient justification for permitting an applicant to engross what may prove to be a broad field.

These arguments for and against the patentability of a process which either has no known use or is useful only in the sense that it may be an object of scientific research would apply equally to the patenting of the product produced by the process. Respondent appears to concede that with respect to a product, as opposed to a process, Congress has struck the balance on the side of nonpatentability unless "utility" is shown. Indeed, the decisions of the CCPA are in accord with the view that a product may not be patented absent a showing of utility greater than any adduced in the present case. We find absolutely no warrant for the proposition that although Congress intended that no patent be granted on a chemical compound whose sole "utility" consists of its potential role as an object of use-testing, a different set of rules was meant to apply to the process which yielded the unpatentable product. That proposition seems to us little more than an attempt to evade the impact of the rules which concededly govern patentability of the product itself.

This is not to say that we mean to disparage the importance of contributions to the fund of scientific information short of the invention of something "useful," or that we are blind to the prospect that what now seems without "use" may tomorrow command the grateful attention of the public. But a patent is not a hunting license. It is not a reward for the search, but compensation for its successful conclusion. "[A] patent system must be related to the world of commerce rather than to the realm of philosophy. * * * "

The judgment of the CCPA is

Reversed.

■ Mr. Justice Harlan, * * * dissenting in part.

* * *

Respondent has contended that a workable chemical process, which is both new and sufficiently nonobvious to satisfy the patent statute, is by its existence alone a contribution to chemistry and "useful" as the statute employs that term. Certainly this reading of "useful" in the statute is within the scope of the constitutional grant, which states only that "[t]o promote the Progress of Science and useful Arts," the exclusive right to "Writings and Discoveries" may be secured for limited times to those who produce them. Art. I, § 8. Yet the patent statute is somewhat differently worded and is on its face open both to respondent's construction and to the contrary reading given it by the Court. In the absence of legislative history on this issue, we are thrown back on policy and practice. Because I believe that the Court's policy arguments are not convincing and that past practice favors the respondent, I would reject the narrow definition of "useful" and uphold the judgment of the Court of Customs and Patent Appeals (hereafter CCPA).

The Court's opinion sets out about half a dozen reasons in support of its interpretation. Several of these arguments seem to me to have almost no force. For instance, it is suggested that "[u]ntil the process claim has been reduced to production of a product shown to be useful, the metes and bounds of that monopoly are not capable of precise delineation" * * * and "[i]t may engross a vast, unknown, and perhaps unknowable area" * * * I fail to see the relevance of these assertions; process claims are not disallowed because the products they produce may be of "vast" importance nor, in any event, does advance knowledge of a specific product use provide much safeguard on this score or fix "metes and bounds" precisely since a hundred more uses may be found after a patent is granted and greatly enhance its value.

The further argument that an established product use is part of "[t]he basic *quid pro quo*" * * * for the patent or is the requisite "successful conclusion" * * * of the inventor's search appears to beg the very question whether the process is "useful" simply because it facilitates further research into possible product uses. The same infirmity seems to inhere in the Court's argument that chemical products lacking immediate utility cannot be distinguished for present purposes from the processes which create them, that respondent appears to concede and the CCPA holds that the products are nonpatentable, and that therefore the processes are nonpatentable. Assuming that the two classes cannot be distinguished, a point not adequately considered in the briefs, and assuming further that the CCPA has firmly held such products nonpatentable, this permits us to conclude only that the CCPA is wrong either as to the products or as to the processes and affords no basis for deciding whether both or neither should be patentable absent a specific product use.

More to the point, I think, are the Court's remaining, prudential arguments against patentability: namely, that disclosure induced by allowing a patent is partly undercut by patent-application drafting techniques, that disclosure may occur without granting a patent, and that a patent will discourage others from inventing uses for the product. How far opaque drafting may lessen the public benefits resulting from the issuance of a patent is not shown by any evidence in this case but, more important, the argument operates against all patents and gives no reason for singling out the class involved here. The thought that these inventions may be more likely than most to be disclosed even if patents are not allowed may have more force;

but while empirical study of the industry might reveal that chemical researchers would behave in this fashion, the abstractly logical choice for them seems to me to maintain secrecy until a product use can be discovered. As to discouraging the search by others for product uses, there is no doubt this risk exists but the price paid for any patent is that research on other uses or improvements may be hampered because the original patentee will reap much of the reward. From the standpoint of the public interest the Constitution seems to have resolved that choice in favor of patentability.

What I find most troubling about the result reached by the Court is the impact it may have on chemical research. Chemistry is a highly interrelated field and a tangible benefit for society may be the outcome of a number of different discoveries, one discovery building upon the next. To encourage one chemist or research facility to invent and disseminate new processes and products may be vital to progress, although the product or process be without "utility" as the Court defines the term, because that discovery permits someone else to take a further but perhaps less difficult step leading to a commercially useful item. In my view, our awareness in this age of the importance of achieving and publicizing basic research should lead this Court to resolve uncertainties in its favor and uphold the respondent's position in this case.

This position is strengthened, I think, by what appears to have been the practice of the Patent Office during most of this century. While available proof is not conclusive, the commentators seem to be in agreement that until Application of Bremner, 37 C.C.P.A. (Pat.) 1032, 182 F.2d 216, in 1950, chemical patent applications were commonly granted although no resulting end use was stated or the statement was in extremely broad terms.[3] Taking this to be true, *Bremner* represented a deviation from established practice which the CCPA has now sought to remedy in part only to find that the Patent Office does not want to return to the beaten track. If usefulness was typically regarded as inherent during a long and prolific period of chemical research and development in this country, surely this is added reason why the Court's result should not be adopted until Congress expressly mandates it, presumably on the basis of empirical data which this Court does not possess.

Fully recognizing that there is ample room for disagreement on this problem when, as here, it is reviewed in the abstract, I believe the decision below should be affirmed.

---

3. See, e.g., the statement of a Patent Office Examiner-in-Chief: "Until recently it was also rather common to get patents on chemical compounds in cases where no use was indicated for the claimed compounds or in which a very broad indication or suggestion as to use was included in the application. [*Bremner* and another later ruling] * * * have put an end to this practice." Wolffe, Adequacy of Disclosure as Regards Specific Embodiment and Use of Invention, 41 J.Pat.Off.Soc. 61, 66 (1959). The Government's brief in this case is in accord: "[I]t was apparently assumed by the Patent Office [prior to 1950] * * * that chemical compounds were necessarily useful * * * and that specific inquiry beyond the success of the process was therefore unnecessary. * * * " Brief for the Commissioner, p. 25. * * *.

NOTES

1. Is United States Patent No. 2,908,693, mentioned in the second paragraph of the opinion, valid?

2. Mr. Justice Story's language, which the Court quotes in its opinion, was thought to have settled the question until the decision of the Supreme Court in *Manson.* He was not the only one to take the position that utility should mean only "not detrimental to the public interest." An editorial writer for the New York Times in 1871 set the argument out at length. "We see no warrant in sense or equity for these examiners sitting in judgment upon the prospective fate of the invention or its probabilities of utility, for these are matters which lie entirely between the patentee and the public. At all events, it seems a hardship to deny a patent on grounds which are merely hypothetical, particularly in instances where a failure of success with the public might lead to improvements which would be useful in the end. There are instances innumerable where our Patent Office has summarily, and even whimsically, denied applications made in good faith by men who had spent years upon schemes whose success *they,* at least, were willing to take the risk of. Such a course appears to us calculated to discourage, rather than foster, the inventive faculty, and to chill the enthusiasm which, if not useful, certainly is harmless. Any new invention is entitled to a patent, so long as the inventor is willing to pay the regulation fees. It is for the public to say whether the invention is practicable or useful, and that verdict is pretty sure to be a correct one." New York Times, p. 4, col. 5, Oct. 15, 1871.

3. Is it true, as Mr. Justice Fortas says, that a patent creates a "monopoly of knowledge?" Is it true, that "to the extent that the patentee has power to enforce his patent, there is little incentive for others to undertake a search for uses?" What is the probable effect of the *Manson* decision on research?

4. In Application of Bergel, 292 F.2d 955 (C.C.P.A.1961) the court reversed a decision of the Board of Appeals of the United States Patent Office affirming a rejection of an application on a chemical shown to have tumor inhibiting effects in rats. The Board of Appeals reasoned that "protection of rats, or mice, from the growth of cancer * * * is not in itself a sufficient usefulness within the purview of the patent statutes * * *," and went on to observe that "the elimination of rodents themselves would seem to be a more desirable objective." "The continued disease-free existence of rodents," said the Board, "is not a desirable objective." Id. at 957. In reversing, the Court of Customs and Patent Appeals said "our conclusion is influenced by a background of common knowledge that cancer is one of the dreadest of all diseases; that for years untold measures of time, talent, and treasure have been devoted to a search for means to prevent its spread and discover a cure; and that as of now those measures have been largely unsuccessful." Was this relevant? In light of *Manson,* was the decision in *Bergel* correct?

5. The utility requirement has been a convenient ground on which to reject applications such as those for perpetual motion machines, thus avoiding an argument as to whether or not the invention in fact works. Compare Puharich v. Brenner, 415 F.2d 979 (D.C.Cir.1969), affirming the patent office's denial of an application for a cage said to expand powers of extra sensory perception. The patent office had rejected on grounds of lack of utility and inoperability. Applicant refused to replicate his experiments which showed the cage worked on the ground that "it would be onerous to the point of practical impossibility to arrange a duplication." And in Application of Ferens, 417 F.2d 1072 (C.C.P.A.1969), the court affirmed a denial of a patent on a method of curing baldness in spite of affidavits from 21 persons that the method had worked on them.

One particularly persistent inventor obtained an order from the District Court requiring that his perpetual motion machine be tested by the government. See *In re Newman* 782 F.2d 971 (Fed. Cir. 1986). The tests, which the Government claimed cost $75,000, showed the device did not work.

6. Disputes over utility will seldom arise in an infringement suit since if the patent is worth infringing it must have some use. "We have no doubt that by copying and using the patented device the defendant has estopped itself from claiming want of utility in the sense of the patent statute." Nestle-Le Mur Co. v. Eugene, Ltd., 55 F.2d 854, 856 (6th Cir. 1932).

7. Mr. Justice Fortas assumed in *Manson* that an experimental use would infringe. But see Kaz Mfg. Co. v. Chesebrough-Pond's, Inc., 211 F.Supp. 815, 818 (S.D.N.Y.1962), affirmed 317 F.2d 679 (2d Cir. 1963):

> "The use of the patented machine for experiments for the sole purpose of gratifying a philosophical taste or curiosity or for instruction and amusement does not constitute an infringing use." Ruth v. Stearns Roger Manufacturing Co., 13 F.Supp. 697, 713 (D.C. Colo. 1935), reversed on other grounds, 87 F.2d 35 (10th Cir., 1936). Nor does construction of an infringing device purely for experimental purposes constitute an actionable infringement.

In Spray Refrigeration Co. v. Sea Spray Fishing, Inc., 322 F.2d 34 (9th Cir. 1963), the court agreed that a purely experimental use would not infringe, but held that use of a machine in regular commercial operations in order to determine whether or not it was satisfactory constituted infringement.

In Roche Products v. Bolar Pharmaceutical Co., 733 F.2d 858 (Fed.Cir. 1984), the plaintiff, a large, research-oriented pharmaceutical company, sought to enjoin Bolar, a manufacturer of generic drugs, from taking during the final year of a patent term the steps necessary to obtain regulatory approval for marketing a generic competitor from the Food and Drug Administration. A so-called "generic" drug is a copy of a successful branded drug, usually sold and promoted under its chemical or "generic" name on the basis of price. The generic competitor who is able to first introduce the drug after the patent expires has an advantage in establishing market share. Bolar imported a large quantity of the patented drug to form into "dosage form capsules, to obtain stability data, dissolution rates, bioequivalency studies, and blood serum studies" necessary for a marketing application to the F.D.A. Roche sued for infringement. The District Court denied relief on the ground that the use was experimental. The Federal Circuit reversed. "Bolar's intended 'experimental' use is solely for business reasons and not for amusement, to satisfy idle curiosity, or for strictly philosophical inquiry. * * * Bolar may intend to perform 'experiments,' but unlicensed experiments conducted with a view to the adaption of the patented invention to the experimentor's business is a violation of the rights of the patentee to exclude others from using his patented invention." 733 F.2d at 863.

8. When a new substance with a valuable use is found there are two contributions to the art, are there not? First, the discovery of the substance. And second, the discovery of the use. Should there not be two patents, one for the substance and one for the use? Can that be done in the medical area by making process claims? Are the therapeutic effects of a known substance a patentable process? Is it feasible to enforce such a claim? If such claims are not patentable, doesn't that skew drug research toward the discovery of the therapeutic properties possessed by new and hence patentable substances?

Time, April 20, 1970, p. 46 reported:

Last week * * * lithium carbonate was approved by the U.S. Food and Drug Administration for the treatment of mental patients in the overexcited mania phase of manic-depressive psychosis.

No less remarkable than the properties of the metal itself is the way its compound has won approval, primarily due to the work of Australian Psychiatrist John Frederick Joseph Cade. After 3½ years as a prisoner of war, Cade began to work in a mental hospital at Bundoora, near Melbourne, concentrating on possible biochemical differences between the manic and depressive phases of the same patient. Nothing was farther from his mind than lithium, which had been discredited as a hypnotic and again in 1949 as a substitute for table salt. "One can hardly imagine," says Cade, "a less propitious year," especially as the work was being done "by an unknown psychiatrist, in a small hospital, with no research training, primitive techniques and negligible equipment." Cade was led indirectly to lithium by inconclusive experiments with other substances. What he learned from his crude equipment and his guinea pigs was that lithium carbonate had a profound effect on the manic patient. He took it himself and suffered no harm. He gave it to a male patient, 51, who was "restless, dirty, destructive, who had been in a back ward for five years and bade fair to remain there the rest of his life." In three weeks the patient was better, and he soon went home and back to work. Lithium carbonate, Cade found, appeared to be of little or no value in the treatment of other psychotic states, notably schizophrenia, or in the depressive phase into which most manic patients usually subside.

Danish investigators extended Cade's findings: lithium-treated patients, after remission of their mania, did not become depressed as soon again or as often as those receiving other drugs. But lithium carbonate posed a problem for the drug industry. A common chemical, it could not be patented, so there could be little profit in its manufacture. Any schoolboy could buy it from a chemical supply house for his basement laboratory; the FDA insisted that only research psychiatrists could use it clinically, under rigid rules.

The following proposal was advanced by Paul H. Eggert, Uses, New Uses and Chemical Patents—A Proposal, 51 J. Pat. [& Trademark] Off. Soc'y 768, 784–87 (1969):

In reality, there are two, and only two, contributions in applied chemistry: discovery and disclosure of (1) how to make a compound and (2) how to put it to use. These basic contributions, for want of better terminology and to avoid confusion with established terms, will be designated a "howtomake" and a "howtouse." A howtomake is defined as a contribution to the useful arts comprising the discovery, reduction to practice, and disclosure of a *method* of synthesizing a given compound. A howtouse is defined as a contribution to the useful arts comprising the discovery, reduction to practice, and disclosure of a *method* of achieving a given result with a given compound.

A howtomake and a howtouse are independent contributions to the progress of the useful arts. A howtomake may exist without a substantial, corresponding howtouse, and vice versa. Since these contributions are distinct and nondependent, they should be rewarded independently. The public should reward each new howtomake and each new howtouse pertaining to a given compound if and when they are reduced to practice and disclosed. There should not be a reward covering any or all howtouses potentially discoverable in the future merely because one howtouse has been disclosed.

In what form should the public grant its reward? Traditionally it is done in the form of a patent. The patent grant would confer control over use of the *contribution* for a reasonable time.

The howtomake inventor should receive control over what he has contributed. If his contribution is truly beneficial, he will derive great economic benefit. If his contribution is valueless (although inventive), he will receive an appropriate economic reward, which may be nothing. In such a case, no harm will have been done, except perhaps a small economic waste. No unearned restriction of the field will result from patenting an unneeded howtomake.

The howtouse inventor should acquire control over what he has contributed. If his howtouse is a method of tanning leather, he should be granted control over *that* contribution. However, if a later inventor contributes an additional howtouse, perhaps as a cervicitis treatment, he, and not the earlier howtouse discoverer, should receive credit for that contribution. Or, if another inventor discloses an additional, nonobvious method of tanning leather with the specified compound, he should receive credit for that contribution. In this way no inventor will be granted control over more than he has contributed. A chemist will not virtually foreclose experimentation or reap the financial benefits of all future howtouses by virtue of his discovery of one.

Still unanswered is the question of what form control of the howtouse should take. Should the patentee be allowed to designate who, if anyone, will manufacture the metacresolsulfonic acid used to treat cervicitis, or should he be allowed only to designate who will treat cervicitis with compound? That is, should there be a free market in the compound which is the subject of the howtouse?

From an economic standpoint, it would seem more beneficial to the nation to permit control only at the user level. A free market in the compound would encourage competition within the chemical industry by allowing the existence of more than one source. Competition could induce lower prices and encourage the development of superior howtomakes for that chemical.

The following proposals would implement these policies:

1. Any method of producing a chemical (howtomake) should be patentable.

2. Any method of using a chemical (howtouse) should be patentable.

3. No chemical compound should be patentable.

("Patentable" is used here in the sense of "allowable subject matter for a patent." The other conditions of patentability, particularly nonobviousness, would still have to be met.)

Enactment would restore a balance between reward and contribution. No longer could an inventor profit, at the expense of the real contributor, from a use he never contemplated or disclosed. No longer would a chemist who finds an inventive use for a compound occurring in nature be denied a patent or restricted to one on the extraction process. No longer would an inventor of a long-sought, 'useless' molecule be denied a patent on his process. The first inventor would not be able to close the field to others by his securing a patent on the compound. Others could experiment and patent uncontemplated uses without fear of being blocked by a product patent. Vigorous competition in the sale of chemicals would be possible. One corporation could not control the availability of a chemical merely because it was the first to create it (unless it also held the sole process patent).

See Kitch, The Nature and Function of the Patent System, 20 J. of Law & Econ. 265 (1977), for an explanation of how a grant of all howtouse rights to the first inventor can enhance public welfare.

9. Although patents have played an important role in creating incentives for pharmaceutical research, and the advances resulting from privately-funded, patent-induced pharmaceutical research in the past fifty years have been remarkable, the relationship between patent law and drugs has been somewhat awkward. Patents are available for a new chemical substance showing some promise of utility, but a commercial product results only after years of investigation and testing have proven the existence of a safe and efficacious drug. In recent decades rising standards of investigational rigor, more stringent product liability law, and increased FDA regulatory requirements have made the process of bringing a new pharmaceutical product to market more costly and time consuming.

The FDA responded to this situation by creating an exclusive market position for the firm that first obtained regulatory approval for a drug. It did this by requiring the second firm that wanted to market a drug to complete the same clinical testing that was required of the first firm. The second firm was not permitted to simply copy the approved drug (already shown to be safe and efficacious by the first firm) and market it, but had to replicate the tests of the first firm. (It was such testing that Bolar Pharmaceutical wanted to complete prior to the expiration of the patent in Roche Products v. Bolar Pharmaceutical Co., 733 F.2d 858 (Fed. Cir. 1984), supra note 7). Since these tests were costly and the effect of the entry of the second firm would be to drive the price of the drug toward marginal cost (leaving little profit margin to contribute to recovery of the already-incurred testing costs), the effect of this requirement was to give the first firm a form of protection from competition which helped to overcome the disincentives for introducing new drugs created by the costs of complying with the FDA regulation and other factors. These practices of the FDA were not contemplated by the statute, which provided only for marketing approval of "a drug," and were successfully challenged in some courts.

Congress addressed the relationship between the Food and Drug Act, the incentives for development of new drugs, and the regulatory position of generic competitors in the Drug Price Competition and Patent Term Restoration Act of 1984, Pub.L. 98–417. Title I of the Act amended the Federal Food, Drug, and Cosmetic Act by adding a new 21 U.S.C. § 355(j) that permits the second firm to submit an "abbreviated new drug application" which asserts a right to approval based only on the fact that the same drug has already been approved, but permits such a new drug application to be granted only five years after the drug on which the application is based was approved. This gives the first firm a five year period of exclusive marketing rights under the regulation (apart from whatever exclusive rights are conferred by a patent).

Title II of the Act amended the Patent Statute by adding a new § 156 that permits extension of the patent term for the period that the marketing of the drug is delayed by the time required for regulatory approval. It also amended § 271 by adding a new § 271(e) which makes it possible for competitors to undertake FDA required testing prior to the expiration of the patent term. (Thus reversing the outcome of Roche Products v. Bolar Pharmaceutical Co., 733 F.2d 858 (Fed. Cir. 1984), supra note 7). (The student who looks at § 156 may also notice § 155, an earlier provision for extension of the patent term narrowly drafted to provide an extension for the artificial sweetener aspartame, marketed as Nutrasweet®.)

In Eli Lilly and Co. v. Medtronic, Inc., 496 U.S. 661 (1990), the Court held that § 271(e)(1) applies to a medical device.

10. What, under *Manson*, is a sufficient disclosure of utility? A disclosure that the substance smells? Lubricates? Can be converted to steam? Has a low boiling point? A high boiling point? Is a pretty color? Can be used to make another substance which can be used to make another substance which is known to be useful?

11. In spite of the fact that it has been generally assumed that utility need not be shown to obtain a patent, it was common in the 19th century to emphasize in advertising the fact that an article was patented. For instance the phrase "patent medicine" arises from the widespread sale of patented compounds as medical remedies of various degrees of efficacy.

Does the government by issuing a patent on an invention of little or no utility aid and abet consumer fraud? In Decker v. F.T.C., 176 F.2d 461 (D.C.Cir.1949), cert. den. 338 U.S. 878, the petitioners sought reversal of an F.T.C. cease and desist order enjoining them from making certain representations in relation to a device they sold under the name Vacudex. In their advertising the petitioners represented that Vacudex, when attached to the exhaust mechanism of automobiles, saved gasoline and oil; increased the power of the motor; caused it to give better performance; drew carbon, oil and moisture from the muffler; eliminated or reduced back pressure; reduced vibration of the motor; gave the motor greater acceleration, caused the motor to run more smoothly, and saved tires. The petitioners argued that their advertising representations were the same as the representations in the specifications of their patent on the Vacudex and argued that the cease and desist order was improper because it was in effect an attack on the patent, beyond the jurisdiction of the F.T.C. The Court rejected the argument, pointing out that the cease and desist order related only to the advertising, not the patent. One judge dissented, arguing that "if the utility of the invention as portrayed in the specification which is made a part of the Letters Patent cannot be advertised, then the invention, as a practical matter, cannot be sold."

C. Nonobviousness

Graham v. John Deere Co.

Supreme Court of the United States, 1966.
383 U.S. 1, 86 S.Ct. 684, 15 L.Ed.2d 545.

■ MR. JUSTICE CLARK delivered the opinion of the Court.

After a lapse of 15 years, the Court again focuses its attention on the patentability of inventions under the standard of Art. I, § 8, cl. 8, of the Constitution and under the conditions prescribed by the laws of the United States. Since our last expression on patent validity, A. & P. Tea Co. v. Supermarket Corp., 340 U.S. 147 (1950), the Congress has for the first time expressly added a third statutory dimension to the two requirements of novelty and utility that had been the sole statutory test since the Patent Act of 1793. This is the test of obviousness, i.e., whether "the subject matter sought to be patented and the prior art are such that the subject matter as a whole would have been obvious at the time the invention was made to a person having ordinary skill in the art to which said subject matter pertains. Patentability shall not be negatived by the manner in which the invention was made." § 103 of the Patent Act of 1952, 35 U.S.C. § 103 (1964 ed.).

The questions, involved in each of the companion cases before us, are what effect the 1952 Act had upon traditional statutory and judicial tests of patentability and what definitive tests are now required. We have concluded that the 1952 Act was intended to codify judicial precedents embracing the principle long ago announced by this Court in Hotchkiss v. Greenwood, 11 How. 248 (1851), and that, while the clear language of § 103 places emphasis on an inquiry into obviousness, the general level of innovation necessary to sustain patentability remains the same.

The Cases.

(a). No. 11, Graham v. John Deere Co., an infringement suit by petitioners, presents a conflict between two Circuits over the validity of a single patent on a "Clamp for vibrating Shank Plows." The invention, a combination of old mechanical elements, involves a device designed to absorb shock from plow shanks as they plow through rocky soil and thus to prevent damage to the plow. In 1955, the Fifth Circuit had held the patent valid under its rule that when a combination produces an "old result in a cheaper and otherwise more advantageous way," it is patentable. Jeoffroy Mfg., Inc. v. Graham, 219 F.2d 511, cert. denied 350 U.S. 826. In 1964, the Eighth Circuit held, in the case at bar, that there was no new result in the patented combination and that the patent was, therefore, not valid. 333 F.2d 529, reversing 216 F.Supp. 272. We granted certiorari, 379 U.S. 956. Although we have determined that neither Circuit applied the correct test, we conclude that the patent is invalid under § 103 and, therefore, we affirm the judgment of the Eighth Circuit.

(b). No. 37, Calmar, Inc. v. Cook Chemical Co., and No. 43, Colgate-Palmolive Co. v. Cook Chemical Co., both from the Eighth Circuit, were separate declaratory judgment actions, but were filed contemporaneously. Petitioner in *Calmar* is the manufacturer of a finger-operated sprayer with a "hold-down" cap of the type commonly seen on grocers' shelves inserted in bottles of insecticides and other liquids prior to shipment. Petitioner in *Colgate-Palmolive* is a purchaser of the sprayers and uses them in the distribution of its products. Each action sought a declaration of invalidity and noninfringement of a patent on similar sprayers issued to Cook Chemical as assignee of Baxter I. Scoggin, Jr., the inventor. By cross-action, Cook Chemical claimed infringement. The actions were consolidated for trial and the patent was sustained by the District Court. 220 F.Supp. 414. The Court of Appeals affirmed, 336 F.2d 110, and we granted certiorari, 380 U.S. 949. We reverse.

* * *

At the outset it must be remembered that the federal patent power stems from a specific constitutional provision which authorizes the Congress "To promote the Progress of * * * useful Arts, by securing for limited Times to * * * Inventors the exclusive Right to their * * * Discoveries." Art. I, § 8, cl. 8. The clause is both a grant of power and a limitation. This qualified authority, unlike the power often exercised in the sixteenth and seventeenth centuries by the English Crown, is limited to the promotion of advances in the "useful arts." It was written against the backdrop of the practices—eventually curtailed by the Statute of Monopolies—of the Crown in granting monopolies to court favorites in goods or businesses which had long before been enjoyed by the public. See Meinhardt, Inventions, Patents and Monopoly, pp. 30–35 (London, 1946). The Congress in the exercise of the patent power may not overreach the restraints imposed by the stated constitutional purpose. Nor may it enlarge the patent monopoly without regard to the innovation, advancement or social benefit gained thereby. Moreover, Congress may not authorize the issuance of patents whose effects are to remove existent knowledge from the public domain, or to restrict free access to materials already available. Innovation, advancement, and things which add to the sum of useful knowledge are inherent requisites in a patent system which by constitutional command must "promote the Progress of * * * useful Arts." This is the *standard* expressed in the Constitution and it may not be ignored. And it is in this light that patent validity "requires reference to a standard written into the Constitution." A. & P. Tea Co. v. Supermarket Corp., supra, at 154 (concurring opinion).

* * *

This Court formulated a general condition of patentability in 1851 in Hotchkiss v. Greenwood, 11 How. 248. The patent involved a mere substitution of materials—porcelain or clay for wood or metal in doorknobs—and the Court condemned it, holding:

> "[U]nless more ingenuity and skill * * * were required * * * than were possessed by an ordinary mechanic acquainted with the business, there was an absence of that degree of skill and ingenuity which constitute essential elements of every invention. In other words, the improvement is the work of the skilful mechanic, not that of the inventor." At p. 267.

Hotchkiss, by positing the condition that a patentable invention evidence more ingenuity and skill than that possessed by an ordinary mechanic acquainted with the business, merely distinguished between new and useful innovations that were capable of sustaining a patent and those that were not.

* * *

The language in the case, and in those which followed, gave birth to "invention" as a word of legal art signifying patentable inventions. Yet, as this Court has observed, "[t]he truth is the word ['invention'] cannot be defined in such manner as to afford any substantial aid in determining whether a particular device involves an exercise of the inventive faculty or not." McClain v. Ortmayer, 141 U.S. 419, 427 (1891); A. & P. Tea Co. v. Supermarket Corp., supra, at 151. Its use as a label brought about a large variety of opinions as to its meaning both in the Patent Office, in the courts, and at the bar. The *Hotchkiss* formulation, however, lies not in any label, but in its functional approach to questions of patentability. In practice, *Hotchkiss* has required a comparison between the subject matter of the patent, or patent application, and the background skill of the calling. It has been from this comparison that patentability was in each case determined.

The 1952 Patent Act.

The Act sets out the conditions of patentability in three sections. An analysis of the structure of these three sections indicates that patentability is dependent upon three explicit conditions: novelty and utility as articulated and defined in § 101 and § 102, and non-obviousness, the new statutory formulation, as set out in § 103. The first two sections, which trace closely the 1874 codification, express the "new and useful" tests which have always existed in the statutory scheme and, for our purposes here, need no clarification. The pivotal section around which the present controversy centers is § 103.

* * *

The section is cast in relatively unambiguous terms. Patentability is to depend, in addition to novelty and utility, upon the "non-obvious" nature of the "subject matter sought to be patented" to a person having ordinary skill in the pertinent art.

The first sentence of this section is strongly reminiscent of the language in *Hotchkiss*. Both formulations place emphasis on the pertinent art existing at the time the invention was made and both are implicitly tied to advances in that art. The major distinction is that Congress has emphasized "non-obviousness" as the operative test of the section, rather than the less definite "invention" language of *Hotchkiss* that Congress thought had led to "a large variety" of expressions in decisions and writings. In the title itself the Congress used the phrase "Conditions for patentability; *non-obvious subject matter*" (italics added), thus focusing upon "nonobviousness" rather than "invention." * * *

We believe that * * * [the] legislative history, as well as other sources, shows that the revision was not intended by Congress to change the general level of patentable invention. We conclude that the section was intended merely as a codification of judicial precedents embracing the *Hotchkiss* condition, with congressional directions that inquiries into the obviousness of the subject matter sought to be patented are a prerequisite to patentability.

Approached in this light, the § 103 additional condition, when followed realistically, will permit a more practical test of patentability. The emphasis on nonobviousness is one of inquiry, not quality, and, as such, comports with the constitutional strictures.

While the ultimate question of patent validity is one of law, A. & P. Tea Co. v. Supermarket Corp., supra, at 155, the § 103 condition, which is but one of three conditions, each of which must be satisfied, lends itself to several basic factual inquiries. Under § 103, the scope and content of the prior art are to be determined; differences between the prior art and the claims at issue are to be ascertained; and the level of ordinary skill in the pertinent art resolved. Against this background, the obviousness or nonobviousness of the subject matter is determined. Such secondary considerations as commercial success, long felt but unsolved needs, failure of others, etc., might be utilized to give light to the circumstances surrounding the origin of the subject matter sought to be patented. As indicia of obviousness or nonobviousness, these inquiries may have relevancy. See Note, Subtests of

"Nonobviousness": A Nontechnical Approach to Patent Validity, 112 U. Pa. L. Rev. 1169 (1964).

This is not to say, however, that there will not be difficulties in applying the nonobviousness test. What is obvious is not a question upon which there is likely to be uniformity of thought in every given factual context. The difficulties, however, are comparable to those encountered daily by the courts in such frames of reference as negligence and scienter, and should be amenable to a case-by-case development. We believe that strict observance of the requirements laid down here will result in that uniformity and definiteness which Congress called for in the 1952 Act.

While we have focused attention on the appropriate standard to be applied by the courts, it must be remembered that the primary responsibility for sifting out unpatentable material lies in the Patent Office. To await litigation is—for all practical purposes—to debilitate the patent system. We have observed a notorious difference between the standards applied by the Patent Office and by the courts. While many reasons can be adduced to explain the discrepancy, one may well be the free rein often exercised by Examiners in their use of the concept of "invention." In this connection we note that the Patent Office is confronted with a most difficult task. Almost 100,000 applications for patents are filed each year. Of these, about 50,000 are granted and the backlog now runs well over 200,000. 1965 Annual Report of the Commissioner of Patents 13–14. This is itself a compelling reason for the Commissioner to strictly adhere to the 1952 Act as interpreted here. This would, we believe, not only expedite disposition but bring about a closer concurrence between administrative and judicial precedent.

Although we conclude here that the inquiry which the Patent Office and the courts must make as to patentability must be beamed with greater intensity on the requirements of § 103, it bears repeating that we find no change in the general strictness with which the overall test is to be applied. We have been urged to find in § 103 a relaxed standard, supposedly a congressional reaction to the "increased standard" applied by this Court in its decisions over the last 20 or 30 years. The standard has remained invariable in this Court. Technology, however, has advanced—and with remarkable rapidity in the last 50 years. Moreover, the ambit of applicable art in given fields of science has widened by disciplines unheard of a half century ago. It is but an evenhanded application to require that those persons granted the benefit of a patent monopoly be charged with an awareness of these changed conditions. The same is true of the less technical, but still useful arts. He who seeks to build a better mousetrap today has a long path to tread before reaching the Patent Office.

We now turn to the application of the conditions found necessary for patentability to the cases involved here:

A. *The Patent in Issue in No. 11,* Graham v. John Deere Co.

This patent, No. 2,627,798 (hereinafter called the '798 patent) relates to a spring clamp which permits plow shanks to be pushed upward when they hit obstructions in the soil, and then springs the shanks back into normal position when the obstruction is passed over. The device, which we show diagrammatically in the accompanying sketches (Appendix, Fig. 1) [The Appendix Figures for this case are set out after the opinion], is fixed to the plow frame as a unit. The mechanism around which the controversy centers is basically a hinge. The top half of it, known as the upper plate (marked 1 in the sketches), is a heavy metal piece clamped to the plow frame (2) and is stationary relative to the plow frame. The lower half of the hinge, known as the hinge plate (3), is connected to the rear of the upper plate by a hinge pin (4) and rotates downward with respect to it. The shank (5), which is bolted to the forward end of the hinge plate (at 6), runs beneath the plate and parallel to it for about nine inches, passes through a stirrup (7), and then continues backward for several feet curving down toward the ground. The chisel (8), which does the actual plowing, is attached to the rear end of the shank. As the plow frame is pulled forward, the chisel rips through the soil, thereby plowing it. In the normal position, the hinge plate and the shank are kept tight against the upper plate by a spring (9), which is atop the upper plate. A rod (10) runs through the center of the spring, extending down through holes in both plates and the shank. Its upper end is bolted to the top of the spring while its lower end is hooked against the underside of the shank.

When the chisel hits a rock or other obstruction in the soil, the obstruction forces the chisel and the rear portion of the shank to move upward. The shank is pivoted (at 11) against the rear of the hinge plate and pries open the hinge against the closing tendency of the spring. (See sketch labeled "Open Position," Appendix, Fig. 1.) This closing tendency is caused by the fact that, as the hinge is opened, the connecting rod is pulled downward and the spring is compressed. When the obstruction is passed over, the upward force on the chisel disappears and the spring pulls the shank and hinge plate back into their original position. The lower, rear portion of the hinge plate is constructed in the form of a stirrup (7) which brackets the shank, passing around and beneath it. The shank fits loosely into the stirrup (permitting a slight up and down play). The stirrup is designed to prevent the shank from recoiling away from the hinge plate, and thus prevents excessive strain on the shank near its bolted connection. The stirrup also girds the shank, preventing it from fishtailing from side to side.

In practical use, a number of spring-hinge-shank combinations are clamped to a plow frame, forming a set of ground-working chisels capable of withstanding the shock of rocks and other obstructions in the soil without breaking the shanks.

Background of the Patent.

Chisel plows, as they are called, were developed for plowing in areas where the ground is relatively free from rocks or stones. Originally, the shanks were rigidly attached to the plow frames. When such plows were used in the rocky, glacial soils of some of the Northern States, they were found to have serious defects. As the chisels hit buried rocks, a vibratory motion was set up and tremendous forces were transmitted to the shank near its connection to the frame. The shanks would break. Graham, one of the petitioners, sought to meet that problem, and in 1950 obtained a patent,

U.S. No. 2,493,811 (hereinafter '811), on a spring clamp which solved some of the difficulties. Graham and his companies manufactured and sold the '811 clamps. In 1950, Graham modified the '811 structure and filed for a patent. That patent, the one in issue, was granted in 1953. This suit against competing plow manufacturers resulted from charges by petitioners that several of respondents' devices infringed the '798 patent.

The Prior Art.

Five prior patents indicating the state of the art were cited by the Patent Office in the prosecution of the '798 application. Four of these patents, 10 other United States patents and two prior-use spring-clamp arrangements not of record in the '798 file wrapper were relied upon by respondents as revealing the prior art. The District Court and the Court of Appeals found that the prior art "as a whole in one form or another contains all of the mechanical elements of the 798 Patent." One of the prior-use clamp devices not before the Patent Examiner—Glencoe—was found to have "all of the elements."

We confine our discussion to the prior patent of Graham, '811, and to the Glencoe clamp device, both among the references asserted by respondents. The Graham '811 and '798 patent devices are similar in all elements, save two: (1) the stirrup and the bolted connection of the shank to the hinge plate do not appear in '811; and (2) the position of the shank is reversed, being placed in patent '811 above the hinge plate, sandwiched between it and the upper plate. The shank is held in place by the spring rod which is hooked against the bottom of the hinge plate passing through a slot in the shank. Other differences are of no consequence to our examination. In practice the '811 patent arrangement permitted the shank to wobble or fishtail because it was not rigidly fixed to the hinge plate; moreover, as the hinge plate was below the shank, the latter caused wear on the upper plate, a member difficult to repair or replace.

Graham's '798 patent application contained 12 claims. All were rejected as not distinguished from the Graham '811 patent. The inverted position of the shank was specifically rejected as was the bolting of the shank to the hinge plate. The Patent Office examiner found these to be "matters of design well within the expected skill of the art and devoid of invention." Graham withdrew the original claims and substituted the two new ones which are substantially those in issue here. His contention was that wear was reduced in patent '798 between the shank and the heel or rear of the upper plate.[11] He also emphasized several new features, the relevant one

---

11. In '811, where the shank was above the hinge plate, an upward movement of the chisel forced the shank up against the underside of the rear of the upper plate. The upper plate thus provided the fulcrum about which the hinge was pried open. Because of this, as well as the location of the hinge pin, the shank rubbed against the heel of the upper plate causing wear both to the plate and to the shank. By relocating the hinge pin and by placing the hinge plate between the shank and the upper plate, as in '798, the rubbing was eliminated and the wear point was changed to the hinge plate, a member more easily removed or replaced for repair.

here being that the bolt used to connect the hinge plate and shank maintained the upper face of the shank in continuing and constant contact with the underface of the hinge plate.

Graham did not urge before the Patent Office the greater "flexing" qualities of the '798 patent arrangement which he so heavily relied on in the courts. The sole element in patent '798 which petitioners argue before us is the interchanging of the shank and hinge plate and the consequences flowing from this arrangement. The contention is that this arrangement—which petitioners claim is not disclosed in the prior art—permits the shank to flex under stress for its *entire* length. As we have sketched (see sketch, "Graham '798 Patent" in Appendix, Fig. 2), when the chisel hits an obstruction the resultant force (A) pushes the rear of the shank upward and the shank pivots against the rear of the hinge plate at (C). The natural tendency is for that portion of the shank between the pivot point and the bolted connection (i.e., between C and D) to bow downward and away from the hinge plate. The maximum distance (B) that the shank moves away from the plate is slight—for emphasis, greatly exaggerated in the sketches. This is so because of the strength of the shank and the short—nine inches or so—length of that portion of the shank between (C) and (D). On the contrary, in patent '811 (see sketch, "Graham '811 Patent" in Appendix, Fig. 2), the pivot point is the upper plate at point (c); and while the tendency for the shank to bow between points (c) and (d) is the same as in '798, the shank is restricted because of the underlying hinge plate and cannot flex as freely. In practical effect, the shank flexes only between points (a) and (c), and not along the entire length of the shank, as in '798. Petitioners say that this difference in flex, though small, effectively absorbs the tremendous forces of the shock of obstructions whereas prior art arrangements failed.

The Obviousness of the Differences.

We cannot agree with petitioners. We assume that the prior art does not disclose such an arrangement as petitioners claim in patent '798. Still we do not believe that the argument on which petitioners' contention is bottomed supports the validity of the patent. The tendency of the shank to flex is the same in all cases. If free-flexing, as petitioners now argue, is the crucial difference above the prior art, then it appears evident that the desired result would be obtainable by not boxing the shank within the confines of the hinge.[12] The only other effective place available in the arrangement was to attach it below the hinge plate and run it through a stirrup or bracket that would not disturb its flexing qualities. Certainly a person having ordinary skill in the prior art, given the fact that the flex in the shank could be utilized more effectively if allowed to run the entire length of the shank, would immediately see that the thing to do was what Graham did, i.e., invert the shank and the hinge plate.

---

12. Even petitioners' expert testified to that effect:

"Q. Given the same length of the forward portion of the clamp * * * you would anticipate that the magnitude of flex [in '798] would be precisely the same or substantially the same as in 811, wouldn't you?

"A. I would think so."

Petitioners' argument basing validity on the free-flex theory raised for the first time on appeal is reminiscent of Lincoln Engineering Co. v. Stewart-Warner Corp., 303 U.S. 545 (1938), where the Court called such an effort "an afterthought. No such function * * * is hinted at in the specifications of the patent. If this were so vital an element in the functioning of the apparatus it is strange that all mention of it was omitted." At p. 550. No "flexing" argument was raised in the Patent Office. Indeed, the trial judge specifically found that "flexing is not a claim of the patent in suit * * * " and would not permit interrogation as to flexing in the accused devices. Moreover, the clear testimony of petitioners' experts shows that the flexing advantages flowing from the '798 arrangement are not, in fact, a significant feature in the patent.[13]

We find no nonobvious facets in the '798 arrangement. The wear and repair claims were sufficient to overcome the patent examiner's original conclusions as to the validity of the patent. However, some of the prior art, notably Glencoe, was not before him. There the hinge plate is below the shank but, as the courts below found, all of the elements in the '798 patent are present in the Glencoe structure. Furthermore, even though the position of the shank and hinge plate appears reversed in Glencoe, the mechanical operation is identical. The shank there pivots about the underside of the stirrup, which in Glencoe is *above* the shank. In other words, the stirrup in Glencoe serves exactly the same function as the heel of the hinge plate in '798. The mere shifting of the wear point to the heel of the '798 hinge plate from the stirrup of Glencoe—itself a part of the hinge plate—presents no operative mechanical distinctions, much less nonobvious differences.

B. *The Patent in Issue in No. 37,* Calmar, Inc. v. Cook Chemical Co., *and in No. 43,* Colgate-Palmolive Co. v. Cook Chemical Co.

The single patent involved in these cases relates to a plastic finger sprayer with a "hold-down" lid used as a built-in dispenser for containers or bottles packaging liquid products, principally household insecticides. Only the first two of the four claims in the patent are involved here and we, therefore, limit our discussion to them. We do not set out those claims here since they are printed in 220 F.Supp., at 417–418.

In essence the device here combines a finger-operated pump sprayer, mounted in a container or bottle by means of a container cap, with a plastic overcap which screws over the top of and depresses the sprayer (see Appendix, Fig. 3). The pump sprayer passes through the container cap and

---

13. "Q. * * * Do you regard the small degree of flex in the forward end of the shank that lies between the pivot point and the point of spring attachment to be of any significance or any importance to the functioning of a device such as '798? A. Unless you are approaching the elastic limit, I think this flexing will reduce the maximum stress at the point of pivot there, where the maximum stress does occur. I think it will reduce that. I don't know how much.

"Q. Do you think it is a substantial factor, a factor of importance in the functioning of the structure? A. Not a great factor, no."

The same expert previously testified similarly in Jeoffroy Mfg. Inc. v. Graham, 219 F.2d 511.

extends down into the liquid in the container; the overcap fits over the pump sprayer and screws down on the outside of a collar mounting or retainer which is molded around the body of the sprayer. When the overcap is screwed down on this collar mounting a seal is formed by the engagement of a circular ridge or rib located above the threads on the collar mounting with a mating shoulder located inside the overcap above its threads.[15] The overcap, as it is screwed down, depresses the pump plunger rendering the pump inoperable and when the seal is effected, any liquid which might seep into the overcap through or around the pump is prevented from leaking out of the overcap. The overcap serves also to protect the sprayer head and prevent damage to it during shipment or merchandising. When the overcap is in place it does not reach the cap of the container or bottle and in no way engages it since a slight space is left between those two pieces.

The device, called a shipper-sprayer in the industry, is sold as an integrated unit with the overcap in place enabling the insecticide manufacturer to install it on the container or bottle of liquid in a single operation in an automated bottling process. The ultimate consumer simply unscrews and discards the overcap, the pump plunger springs up and the sprayer is ready for use.

The Background of the Patent.

For many years manufacturers engaged in the insecticide business had faced a serious problem in developing sprayers that could be integrated with the containers or bottles in which the insecticides were marketed. Originally, insecticides were applied through the use of tin sprayers, not supplied by the manufacturer. In 1947, Cook Chemical, an insecticide manufacturer, began to furnish its customers with plastic pump dispensers purchased from Calmar. The dispenser was an unpatented finger-operated device mounted in a perforated cardboard holder and hung over the neck of the bottle or container. It was necessary for the ultimate consumer to remove the cap of the container and insert and attach the sprayer to the latter for use.

Hanging the sprayer on the side of the container or bottle was both expensive and troublesome. Packaging for shipment had to be a hand operation, and breakage and pilferage as well as the loss of the sprayer during shipment and retail display often occurred. Cook Chemical urged Calmar to develop an integrated sprayer that could be mounted directly in a container or bottle during the automated filling process and that would not leak during shipment or retail handling. Calmar did develop some such devices but for various reasons they were not completely successful. The situation was aggravated in 1954 by the entry of Colgate-Palmolive into the insecticide trade with its product marketed in aerosol spray cans. These containers, which used compressed gas as a propellent to dispense the liquid, did not require pump sprayers.

During the same year Calmar was acquired by the Drackett Company. Cook Chemical became apprehensive of its source of supply for pump

---

15. Our discussion here relates to the overcap seal. The container itself is sealed in the customary way through the use of a container gasket located between the container and the container cap.

sprayers and decided to manufacture its own through a subsidiary, Bakan Plastics, Inc. Initially, it copied its design from the unpatented Calmar sprayer, but an officer of Cook Chemical, Scoggin, was assigned to develop a more efficient device. By 1956 Scoggin had perfected the shipper-sprayer in suit and a patent was granted in 1959 to Cook Chemical as his assignee. In the interim Cook Chemical began to use Scoggin's device and also marketed it to the trade. The device was well received and soon became widely used.

In the meanwhile, Calmar employed two engineers, Corsette and Cooprider, to perfect a shipper-sprayer and by 1958 it began to market its SS–40, a device very much similar to Scoggin's. When the Scoggin patent issued, Cook Chemical charged Calmar's SS–40 with infringement and this suit followed.

The Opinions of the District Court and the Court of Appeals.

At the outset it is well to point up that the parties have always disagreed as to the scope and definition of the invention claimed in the patent in suit. Cook Chemical contends that the invention encompasses a unique combination of admittedly old elements and that patentability is found in the result produced. Its expert testified that the invention was "the first commercially successful, inexpensive integrated shipping closure pump unit which permitted automated assembly with a container of household insecticide or similar liquids to produce a practical, ready-to-use package which could be shipped without external leakage and which was so organized that the pump unit with its hold-down cap could be itself assembled and sealed and then later assembled and sealed on the container without breaking the first seal." Cook Chemical stresses the long-felt need in the industry for such a device; the inability of others to produce it; and its commercial success—all of which, contends Cook, evidences the nonobvious nature of the device at the time it was developed. On the other hand, Calmar says that the differences between Scoggin's shipper-sprayer and the prior art relate only to the design of the overcap and that the differences are so inconsequential that the device as a whole would have been obvious at the time of its invention to a person having ordinary skill in the art.

Both courts accepted Cook Chemical's contentions. While the exact basis of the District Court's holding is uncertain, the court did find the subject matter of the patent new, useful and nonobvious. It concluded that Scoggin "had produced a sealed and protected sprayer unit which the manufacturer need only screw onto the top of its container in much the same fashion as a simple metal cap." 220 F.Supp., at 418. Its decision seems to be bottomed on the finding that the Scoggin sprayer solved the long-standing problem that had confronted the industry.[16] The Court of Appeals also found validity in the "novel 'marriage' of the sprayer with the insecticide container" which

---

16. "By the same reasoning, may it not also be said that if [the device] solved a long-sought need, it was likewise novel? If it meets the requirements of being new, novel and useful, it was the subject of invention, although it may have been a short step, nevertheless it was the last step that ended the journey. The last step is the one that wins and he who takes it when others could not, is entitled to patent protection." 220 F.Supp., at 421.

took years in discovery and in "the immediate commercial success" which it enjoyed. While finding that the individual elements of the invention were "not novel per se" the court found "nothing in the prior art suggesting Scoggin's unique combination of these old features * * * as would solve the * * * problems which for years beset the insecticide industry." It concluded that "the * * * [device] meets the exacting standard required for a combination of old elements to rise to the level of patentable invention by fulfilling the long-felt need with an economical, efficient, utilitarian apparatus which achieved novel results and immediate commercial success." 336 F.2d, at 114.

The Prior Art.

Only two of the five prior art patents cited by the Patent Office Examiner in the prosecution of Scoggin's application are necessary to our discussion, i.e., Lohse U.S. Patent No. 2,119,884 (1938) and Mellon U.S. Patent No. 2,586,687 (1952). Others are cited by Calmar that were not before the Examiner, but of these our purposes require discussion of only the Livingstone U.S. Patent No. 2,715,480 (1953). Simplified drawings of each of these patents are reproduced in the Appendix, Figs. 4–6 for comparison and description.

The Lohse patent (Fig. 4) is a shipper-sprayer designed to perform the same function as Scoggin's device. The differences, recognized by the District Court, are found in the overcap seal which in Lohse is formed by the skirt of the overcap engaging a washer or gasket which rests upon the upper surface of the container cap. The court emphasized that in Lohse "[t]here are no seals above the threads and below the sprayer head." 220 F.Supp., at 419.

The Mellon patent (Fig. 5), however, discloses the idea of effecting a seal above the threads of the overcap. Mellon's device, likewise a shipper-sprayer, differs from Scoggin's in that its overcap screws directly on the container, and a gasket, rather than a rib, is used to effect the seal.

Finally, Livingstone (Fig. 6) shows a seal above the threads accomplished without the use of a gasket or washer.[17] Although Livingstone's arrangement was designed to cover and protect pouring spouts, his sealing feature is strikingly similar to Scoggin's. Livingstone uses a tongue and groove technique in which the tongue located on the upper surface of the collar, fits into a groove on the inside of the overcap. Scoggin employed the rib and shoulder seal in the identical position and with less efficiency because the Livingstone technique is inherently a more stable structure, forming an interlock that withstands distortion of the overcap when subjected to rough handling. Indeed, Cook Chemical has now incorporated the Livingstone closure into its own shipper-sprayers as had Calmar in its SS–40.

The Invalidity of the Patent.

Let us first return to the fundamental disagreement between the parties. Cook Chemical, as we noted at the outset, urges that the invention

---

17. While the sealing feature was not specifically claimed in the Livingstone patent, it was disclosed in the drawings and specifications. Under long-settled law the feature became public property. Miller v. Brass Co., 104 U.S. 350, 352 (1882).

must be viewed as the overall combination, or—putting it in the language of the statute—that we must consider the subject matter sought to be patented taken as a whole. With this position, taken in the abstract, there is, of course, no quibble. But the history of the prosecution of the Scoggin application in the Patent Office reveals a substantial divergence in respondent's present position.

As originally submitted, the Scoggin application contained 15 claims which in very broad terms claimed the entire combination of spray pump and overcap. No mention of, or claim for, the sealing features was made. All 15 claims were rejected by the Examiner because (1) the applicant was vague and indefinite as to what the invention was, and (2) the claims were met by Lohse. Scoggin canceled these claims and submitted new ones. Upon a further series of rejections and new submissions, the Patent Office Examiner, after an office interview, at last relented. It is crystal clear that after the first rejection, Scoggin relied entirely upon the sealing arrangement as the exclusive patentable difference in his combination. It is likewise clear that it was on that feature that the Examiner allowed the claims. In fact, in a letter accompanying the final submission of claims, Scoggin, through his attorney, stated that "agreement was reached between the Honorable Examiner and applicant's attorney relative to *limitations* which must be in the claims in order to define novelty over the previously applied disclosure of Lohse when considered in view of the newly cited patents of Mellon and Darley, Jr." (Italics added.)

Moreover, those limitations were specifically spelled out as (1) the use of a rib seal and (2) an overcap whose lower edge did not contact the container cap. Mellon was distinguished, as was the Darley patent, infra, n. 18, on the basis that although it disclosed a hold-down cap with a seal located above the threads, it did not disclose a rib seal disposed in such position as to cause the lower peripheral edge of the overcap "to be maintained out of contacting relationship with [the container] cap * * * when * * * [the overcap] was screwed [on] tightly. * * * " Scoggin maintained that the "obvious modification" of Lohse in view of Mellon would be merely to place the Lohse gasket above the threads with the lower edge of the overcap remaining in tight contact with the container cap or neck of the container itself. In other words, the Scoggin invention was limited to the use of a rib—rather than a washer or gasket—and the existence of a slight space between the overcap and the container cap.

It is, of course, well settled that an invention is construed not only in the light of the claims, but also with reference to the file wrapper or prosecution history in the Patent Office. Hogg v. Emerson, 11 How. 587 (1850); Crawford v. Heysinger, 123 U.S. 589 (1887). Claims as allowed must be read and interpreted with reference to rejected ones and to the state of the prior art; and claims that have been narrowed in order to obtain the issuance of a patent by distinguishing the prior art cannot be sustained to cover that which was previously by limitation eliminated from the patent. Powers-Kennedy Co. v. Concrete Co., 282 U.S. 175, 185–186 (1930); Schriber Co. v. Cleveland Trust Co., 311 U.S. 211, 220–221 (1940).

Here, the patentee obtained his patent only by accepting the limitations imposed by the Examiner. The claims were carefully drafted to reflect these limitations and Cook Chemical is not now free to assert a broader view of Scoggin's invention. The subject matter as a whole reduces, then, to the distinguishing features clearly incorporated into the claims. We now turn to those features.

As to the space between the skirt of the overcap and the container cap, the District Court found:

> "Certainly without a space so described, there could be no inner seal within the cap, but such a space is not new or novel, but it is necessary to the formation of the seal within the hold-down cap.

> *"To me this language is descriptive of an element of the patent but not a part of the invention.* It is too simple, really, to require much discussion. In this device the hold-down cap was intended to perform two functions—to hold down the sprayer head and to form a solid tight seal between the shoulder and the collar below. In assembling the element it is necessary to provide this space in order to form the seal." 220 F.Supp., at 420. (Italics added.)

The court correctly viewed the significance of that feature. We are at a loss to explain the Examiner's allowance on the basis of such a distinction. Scoggin was able to convince the Examiner that Mellon's cap contacted the bottle neck while his did not. Although the drawings included in the Mellon application show that the cap might touch the neck of the bottle when fully screwed down, there is nothing—absolutely nothing—which indicates that the cap was designed at any time to *engage* the bottle neck. It is palpably evident that Mellon embodies a seal formed by a gasket compressed between the cap and the bottle neck. It follows that the cap in Mellon will not seal if it does not bear down on the gasket and this would be impractical, if not impossible, under the construction urged by Scoggin before the Examiner. Moreover, the space so strongly asserted by Cook Chemical appears quite plainly on the Livingstone device, a reference not cited by the Examiner.

The substitution of a rib built into a collar likewise presents no patentable difference above the prior art. It was fully disclosed and dedicated to the public in the Livingstone patent. Cook Chemical argues, however, that Livingstone is not in the *pertinent* prior art because it relates to liquid containers having pouring spouts rather than pump sprayers. Apart from the fact that respondent made no such objection to similar references cited by the Examiner,[18] so restricted a view of the applicable prior art is not justified. The problems confronting Scoggin and the insecticide industry

---

18. In addition to Livingstone and Mellon, the Examiner cited Slade, U.S. Patent No. 2,844,290 (hold-down cap for detergent cans having a pouring spout); Nilson, U.S. Patent No. 2,118,222 (combined cap and spout for liquid dispensing containers); Darley, Jr., U.S. Patent No. 1,447,712 (containers for toothpaste, cold creams and other semi-liquid substances).

were not insecticide problems; they were mechanical closure problems. Closure devices in such a closely related art as pouring spouts for liquid containers are at the very least pertinent references. See, II Walker on Patents § 260 (Deller ed. 1937).

Cook Chemical insists, however, that the development of a workable shipper-sprayer eluded Calmar, who had long and unsuccessfully sought to solve the problem. And, further, that the long-felt need in the industry for a device such as Scoggin's together with its wide commercial success supports its patentability. These legal inferences or subtests do focus attention on economic and motivational rather than technical issues and are, therefore, more susceptible of judicial treatment than are the highly technical facts often present in patent litigation. See Judge Learned Hand in Reiner v. I. Leon Co., 285 F.2d 501, 504 (1960). See also Note, Subtests of "Nonobviousness": A Nontechnical Approach to Patent Validity, 112 U.Pa.L.Rev. 1169 (1964). Such inquiries may lend a helping hand to the judiciary which, as Mr. Justice Frankfurter observed, is most ill-fitted to discharge the technological duties cast upon it by patent legislation. Marconi Wireless Co. v. United States, 320 U.S. 1, 60 (1943). They may also serve to "guard against slipping into use of hindsight," Monroe Auto Equipment Co. v. Heckethorn Mfg. & Sup. Co., 332 F.2d 406, 412 (1964), and to resist the temptation to read into the prior art the teachings of the invention in issue.

However, these factors do not, in the circumstances of this case, tip the scales of patentability. The Scoggin invention, as limited by the Patent Office and accepted by Scoggin, rests upon exceedingly small and quite nontechnical mechanical differences in a device which was old in the art. At the latest, those differences were rendered apparent in 1953 by the appearance of the Livingstone patent, and unsuccessful attempts to reach a solution to the problems confronting Scoggin made before that time became wholly irrelevant. It is also irrelevant that no one apparently chose to avail himself of knowledge stored in the Patent Office and readily available by the simple expedient of conducting a patent search—a prudent and nowadays common preliminary to well organized research. Mast, Foos & Co. v. Stover Mfg. Co., 177 U.S. 485 (1900). To us, the limited claims of the Scoggin patent are clearly evident from the prior art as it stood at the time of the invention.

We conclude that the claims in issue in the Scoggin patent must fall as not meeting the test of § 103, since the differences between them and the pertinent prior art would have been obvious to a person reasonably skilled in that art.

The judgment of the Court of Appeals in No. 11 is affirmed. The judgment of the Court of Appeals in Nos. 37 and 43 is reversed and the cases remanded to the District Court for disposition not inconsistent with this opinion.

It is so ordered.

* * *

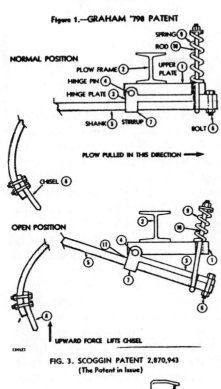

Figure 1.—GRAHAM '798 PATENT

NORMAL POSITION

SPRING ⑨
ROD ⑩
PLOW FRAME ②
UPPER PLATE ①
HINGE PIN ④
HINGE PLATE ③
SHANK ⑤   STIRRUP ⑦
BOLT ⑥

PLOW PULLED IN THIS DIRECTION ➡

CHISEL ⑧

OPEN POSITION

UPWARD FORCE LIFTS CHISEL

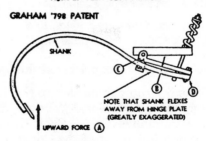

Figure 2.—FLEX COMPARISON

GRAHAM '798 PATENT

SHANK

NOTE THAT SHANK FLEXES AWAY FROM HINGE PLATE (GREATLY EXAGGERATED)

UPWARD FORCE Ⓐ

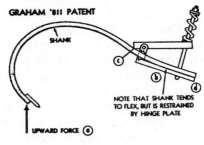

GRAHAM '811 PATENT

SHANK

NOTE THAT SHANK TENDS TO FLEX, BUT IS RESTRAINED BY HINGE PLATE

UPWARD FORCE Ⓑ

FIG. 3. SCOGGIN PATENT 2,870,943
(The Patent in Issue)

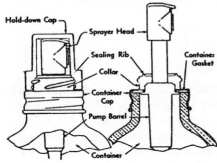

Hold-down Cap
Sprayer Head
Sealing Rib
Collar
Container Cap
Pump Barrel
Container Gasket
Container

FIG. 4. LOHSE PATENT 2,119,884
(Prior art 1938)

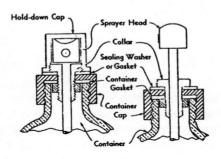

Hold-down Cap
Sprayer Head
Collar
Sealing Washer or Gasket
Container Gasket
Container Cap
Container

FIG. 5. MELLON PATENT 2,586,687
(Prior art 1952)

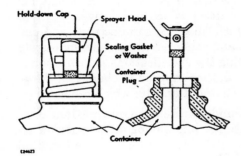

Hold-down Cap
Sprayer Head
Sealing Gasket or Washer
Container Plug
Container

FIG. 6. LIVINGSTONE PATENT 2,715,480
(Prior art 1953)

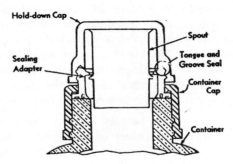

Hold-down Cap
Sealing Adapter
Spout
Tongue and Groove Seal
Container Cap
Container

United States v. Adams

Supreme Court of the United States, 1966.
383 U.S. 39, 86 S.Ct. 708, 15 L.Ed. 572.

■ MR. JUSTICE CLARK delivered the opinion of the Court.

This is a companion case to No. 11, Graham v. John Deere Co., decided this day along with Nos. 37 and 43, Calmar, Inc. v. Cook Chemical Co. and Colgate-Palmolive Co. v. Cook Chemical Co. The United States seeks review of a judgment of the Court of Claims, holding valid and infringed a patent on a wet battery issued to Adams. This suit under 28 U.S.C.A. § 1498 (1964 ed.) was brought by Adams and others holding an interest in the patent against the Government charging both infringement and breach of an implied contract to pay compensation for the use of the invention. The Government challenged the validity of the patent, denied that it had been infringed or that any contract for its use had ever existed. The Trial Commissioner held that the patent was valid and infringed in part but that no contract, express or implied, had been established. The Court of Claims adopted these findings, initially reaching only the patent questions, 165 Ct. Cl. 576, 330 F.2d 622, but subsequently, on respondents' motion to amend the judgment, deciding the contract claims as well. 165 Ct. Cl., at 598. The United States sought certiorari on the patent validity issue only. We granted the writ, along with the others, in order to settle the important issues of patentability presented by the four cases. 380 U.S. 949. We affirm.

* * *

The Patent in Issue and Its Background.

The patent under consideration, U.S. No. 2,322,210, was issued in 1943 upon an application filed in December 1941 by Adams. It relates to a non-rechargeable, as opposed to a storage, electrical battery. Stated simply, the battery comprises two electrodes—one made of magnesium, the other of cuprous chloride—which are placed in a container. The electrolyte, or battery fluid, used may be either plain or salt water.

The specifications of the patent state that the object of the invention is to provide constant voltage and current without the use of acids, conventionally employed in storage batteries, and without the generation of dangerous fumes. Another object is "to provide a battery which is relatively light in weight with respect to capacity" and which "may be manufactured and distributed to the trade in a dry condition and rendered serviceable by merely filling the container with water." Following the specifications, which also set out a specific embodiment of the invention, there appear 11 claims. Of these, principal reliance has been placed upon Claims 1 and 10, which read:

"1. A battery comprising a liquid container, a magnesium electropositive electrode inside the container and having an exterior terminal, a fused cuprous chloride electronegative electrode, and a terminal connected with said electronegative electrode."

"10. In a battery, the combination of a magnesium electropositive electrode, and an electronegative electrode comprising cuprous chloride fused with a carbon catalytic agent."

For several years prior to filing his application for the patent, Adams had worked in his home experimenting on the development of a wet battery. He found that when cuprous chloride and magnesium were used as electrodes in an electrolyte of either plain water or salt water an improved battery resulted.

The Adams invention was the first practical, water-activated, constant potential battery which could be fabricated and stored indefinitely without any fluid in its cells. It was activated within 30 minutes merely by adding water. Once activated, the battery continued to deliver electricity at a voltage which remained essentially constant regardless of the rate at which current was withdrawn. Furthermore, its capacity for generating current was exceptionally large in comparison to its size and weight. The battery was also quite efficient in that substantially its full capacity could be obtained over a wide range of currents. One disadvantage, however, was that once activated the battery could not be shut off; the chemical reactions in the battery continued even though current was not withdrawn. Nevertheless, these chemical reactions were highly exothermic, liberating large quantities of heat during operation. As a result, the battery performed with little effect on its voltage or current in very low temperatures. Relatively high temperatures would not damage the battery. Consequently, the battery was operable from 65% below zero Fahrenheit to 200% Fahrenheit. See findings at 330 F.2d, at 632.

Less than a month after filing for his patent, Adams brought his discovery to the attention of the Army and Navy. Arrangements were quickly made for demonstrations before the experts of the United States Army Signal Corps. The Signal Corps scientists who observed the demonstrations and who conducted further tests themselves did not believe the battery was workable. Almost a year later, in December 1942, Dr. George Vinal, an eminent government expert with the National Bureau of Standards, still expressed doubts. He felt that Adams was making "unusually large claims" for "high watt hour output per unit weight," and he found "far from convincing" the graphical data submitted by the inventor showing the battery's constant voltage and capacity characteristics. He recommended, "Until the inventor can present more convincing data about the performance of his [battery] cell, I see no reason to consider it further."

However, in November 1943, at the height of World War II, the Signal Corps concluded that the battery was feasible. The Government thereafter entered into contracts with various battery companies for its procurement. The battery was found adaptable to many uses. Indeed, by 1956 it was noted that "[t]here can be no doubt that the addition of water activated batteries to the family of power sources has brought about developments which would otherwise have been technically or economically impractical." See Tenth Annual Battery Research and Development Conference, Signal Corps Engineering Laboratories, Fort Monmouth, N.J., p. 25 (1956). Also, see Finding No. 24, 330 F.2d, at 632.

Surprisingly, the Government did not notify Adams of its changed views nor of the use to which it was putting his device, despite his repeated requests. In 1955, upon examination of a battery produced for the Government by the Burgess Company, he first learned of the Government's action. His request for compensation was denied in 1960, resulting in this suit.

The Prior Art.

The basic idea of chemical generation of electricity is, of course, quite old. Batteries trace back to the epic discovery by the Italian scientist Volta in 1795, who found that when two dissimilar metals are placed in an electrically conductive fluid an electromotive force is set up and electricity generated. Essentially, the basic elements of a chemical battery are a pair of electrodes of different electrochemical properties and an electrolyte which is either a liquid (in "wet" batteries) or a moist paste of various substances (in the so-called "dry-cell" batteries). Various material which may be employed as electrodes, various electrolyte possibilities and many combinations of these elements have been the object of considerable experiment for almost 175 years. See generally, Vinal, Primary Batteries (New York 1950).

At trial, the Government introduced in evidence 24 patents and treatises as representing the art as it stood in 1938, the time of the Adams invention.[2] Here, however, the Government has relied primarily upon only six of these references[3] which we may summarize as follows.

The Niaudet treatise describes the Marie Davy cell invented in 1860 and De La Rue's variations on it. The battery comprises a zinc anode and a silver chloride cathode. Although it seems to have been capable of working in an electrolyte of pure water, Niaudet says the battery was of "little interest" until De La Rue used a solution of ammonium chloride as an electrolyte. Niaudet also states that "[t]he capital advantage of this battery, as in all where zinc with sal ammoniac [ammonium chloride solution] is used, consists in the absence of any local or internal action as long as the electric circuit is open; in other words, this battery does not work upon itself." Hayes likewise discloses the De La Rue zinc-silver chloride cell, but with certain mechanical differences designed to restrict the battery from continuing to act upon itself.

The Wood patent is relied upon by the Government as teaching the substitution of magnesium, as in the Adams patent, for zinc. Wood's patent, issued in 1928, states: "It would seem that a relatively high voltage primary cell would be obtained by using * * * magnesium as the * * * [positive] electrode and I am aware that attempts have been made to develop such a cell. As far as I am aware, however, these have all been unsuccessful, and it has been generally accepted that magnesium could not be commercially

---

2. The references are listed in the opinion of the Court of Claims, 165 Ct. Cl., at 590, 330 F.2d, at 631.

3. Niaudet, Elementary Treatise on Electric Batteries (Fishback translation 1880); Hayes U.S. Patent No. 282,634 (1883); Wood U.S. Patent No. 1,696,873 (1928); Codd, Practical Primary Cells (London 1929); Wensky British Patent No. 49 of 1891; and Skrivanoff British Patent No. 4,341 (1880).

utilized as a primary cell electrode." Wood recognized that the difficulty with magnesium electrodes is their susceptibility to chemical corrosion by the action of acid or ammonium chloride electrolytes. Wood's solution to this problem was to use a "neutral electrolyte containing a strong soluble oxidizing agent adapted to reduce the rate of corrosion of the magnesium electrode on open circuit." There is no indication of its use with cuprous chloride, nor was there any indication that a magnesium battery could be water-activated.

The Codd treatise is also cited as authority for the substitution of magnesium. However, Codd simply lists magnesium in an electromotive series table, a tabulation of electrochemical substances in descending order of their relative electropositivity. He also refers to magnesium in an example designed to show that various substances are more electropositive than others, but the discussion involves a cell containing an acid which would destroy magnesium within minutes. In short, Codd indicates, by inference, only that magnesium is a theoretically desirable electrode by virtue of its highly electropositive character. He does not teach that magnesium could be combined in a water-activated battery or that a battery using magnesium would have the properties of the Adams device. Nor does he suggest, as the Government indicates, that cuprous chloride could be substituted for silver chloride. He merely refers to the cuprous *ion*—a generic term which includes an infinite number of copper compounds—and in no way suggests that cuprous chloride could be employed in a battery.

The Government then cites the Wensky patent which was issued in Great Britain in 1891. The patent relates to the use of cuprous chloride as a depolarizing agent. The specifications of his patent disclose a battery comprising zinc and copper electrodes, the cuprous chloride being added as a salt in an electrolyte solution containing zinc chloride as well. While Wensky recognized that cuprous chloride could be used in a constant-current cell, there is no indication that he taught a water-activated system or that magnesium could be incorporated in his battery.

Finally, the Skrivanoff patent depended upon by the Government relates to a battery designed to give intermittent, as opposed to continuous, service. While the patent claims magnesium as an electrode, it specifies that the electrolyte to be used in conjunction with it must be a solution of "alcoline, chloro-chromate, or a permanganate strengthened with sulphuric acid." The cathode was a copper or carbon electrode faced with a paste of "phosphoric acid, amorphous phosphorous, metallic copper in spangles, and cuprous chloride." This paste is to be mixed with hot sulfuric acid before applying to the electrode. The Government's expert testified in trial that he had no information as to whether the cathode, as placed in the battery, would, after having been mixed with the other chemicals prescribed, actually contain cuprous chloride. Furthermore, respondents' expert testified, without contradiction, that he had attempted to assemble a battery made in accordance with Skrivanoff's teachings, but was met first with a fire when he sought to make the cathode, and then with an explosion when he attempted to assemble the complete battery.

The Validity of the Patent.

The Government challenges the validity of the Adams patent on grounds of lack of novelty under 35 U.S.C.A. § 102(a) as well as obviousness under 35 U.S.C.A. § 103. As we have seen in Graham v. John Deere, Co., * * * novelty and nonobviousness—as well as utility—are separate tests of patentability and all must be satisfied in a valid patent.

The Government concludes that wet batteries comprising a zinc anode and silver chloride cathode are old in the art; and that the prior art shows that magnesium may be substituted for zinc and cuprous chloride for silver chloride. Hence, it argues that the "combination of magnesium and cuprous chloride in the Adams battery was not patentable because it represented either no change or an insignificant change as compared to prior battery designs." And, despite "the fact that, wholly unexpectedly, the battery showed certain valuable operating advantages over other batteries [these advantages] would certainly not justify a patent on the essentially old formula."

There are several basic errors in the Government's position. First, the fact that the Adams battery is water-activated sets his device apart from the prior art. It is true that Claims 1 and 10, supra, do not mention a water electrolyte, but, as we have noted, a stated object of the invention was to provide a battery rendered serviceable by the mere addition of water. While the claims of a patent limit the invention, and specifications cannot be utilized to expand the patent monopoly, Burns v. Meyer, 100 U.S. 671, 672 (1880); McCarty v. Lehigh Valley R. Co., 160 U.S. 110, 116 (1895), it is fundamental that claims are to be construed in the light of the specifications and both are to be read with a view to ascertaining the invention, Seymour v. Osborne, 11 Wall. 516, 547 (1871); Schriber-Schroth Co. v. Cleveland Trust Co., 311 U.S. 211 (1940); Schering Corp. v. Gilbert, 153 F.2d 428 (1946). Taken together with the stated object of disclosing a water-activated cell, the lack of reference to any electrolyte in Claims 1 and 10 indicates that water alone could be used. Furthermore, of the 11 claims in issue, three of the narrower ones include references to specific electrolyte solutions comprising water and certain salts. The obvious implication from the absence of any mention of an electrolyte—a necessary element in any battery—in the other eight claims reinforces this conclusion. It is evident that respondents' present reliance upon this feature was not the afterthought of an astute patent trial lawyer. In his first contact with the Government less than a month after the patent application was filed, Adams pointed out that "no acids, alkalines or any other liquid other than plain water is used in this cell. Water does not have to be distilled. * * * " Letter to Charles F. Kettering (January 7, 1942), R., pp. 415, 416. Also see his letter to the Department of Commerce (March 28, 1942), R., p. 422. The findings, approved and adopted by the Court of Claims, also fully support this conclusion.

Nor is Sinclair & Carroll Co. v. Interchemical Corp., 325 U.S. 327 (1945), apposite here. There the patentee had developed a rapidly drying printing ink. All that was needed to produce such an ink was a solvent which evaporated quickly upon heating. Knowing that the boiling point of a solvent is an indication of its rate of evaporation, the patentee merely made selections from a list of solvents and their boiling points. This was no more than "selecting the last piece to put into the last opening in a jig-saw puzzle." 325 U.S., at 335. Indeed, the Government's reliance upon *Sinclair & Carroll* points up the fallacy of the underlying premise of its case. The solvent in *Sinclair & Carroll* had no functional relation to the printing ink involved. It served only as an inert carrier. The choice of solvent was dictated by known, required properties. Here, however, the Adams battery is shown to embrace elements having an interdependent functional relationship. It begs the question, and overlooks the holding of the Commissioner and the Court of Claims, to state merely that magnesium and cuprous chloride were individually known battery components. If such a combination is novel, the issue is whether bringing them together as taught by Adams was obvious in the light of the prior art.

We believe that the Court of Claims was correct in concluding that the Adams battery is novel. Skrivanoff disclosed the use of magnesium in an electrolyte completely different from that used in Adams. As we have mentioned, it is even open to doubt whether cuprous chloride was a functional element in Skrivanoff. In view of the unchallenged testimony that the Skrivanoff formulation was both dangerous and inoperable, it seems anomalous to suggest that it is an anticipation of Adams. An inoperable invention or one which fails to achieve its intended result does not negative novelty. *Smith v. Snow,* 294 U.S. 1, 17 (1935). That in 1880 Skrivanoff may have been able to convince a foreign patent examiner to issue a patent on his device has little significance in the light of the foregoing.

Nor is the Government's contention that the electrodes of Adams were mere substitutions of pre-existing battery designs supported by the prior art. If the use of magnesium for zinc and cuprous chloride for silver chloride were merely equivalent substitutions, it would follow that the resulting device— Adams'— would have equivalent operating characteristics. But it does not. The court below found, and the Government apparently admits, that the Adams battery "wholly unexpectedly" has shown "certain valuable operating advantages over other batteries" while those from which it is claimed to have been copied were long ago discarded. Moreover, most of the batteries relied upon by the Government were of a completely different type designed to give intermittent power and characterized by an absence of internal action when not in use. Some provided current at voltages which declined fairly proportionately with time.[4] Others were so-called standard cells which, though producing a constant voltage, were of use principally for calibration or measurement purposes. Such cells cannot be used as sources of power.[5] For these reasons we find no equivalency.[6]

---

4. It is interesting to note in this connection that in testing the Adams cell the Signal Corps compared it with batteries of this type. The graphical results of the comparison are shown in respondents' brief, p. 51.

5. The standard text in the art states: "The best answer to the oft-repeated question: 'How much current can I draw from my standard cell?' is 'None.' " Vinal, Primary Batteries, p. 212 (New York 1950); see also Ruben U.S. Patent No. 1,920,151 (1933).

6. In their motion to dismiss the writ of certiorari as improvidently granted, respondents asserted that the Government was estopped to claim equivalency of cuprous chloride and silver chloride. We find no merit in this contention and, therefore, deny the motion.

We conclude the Adams battery was also nonobvious. As we have seen, the operating characteristics of the Adams battery have been shown to have been unexpected and to have far surpassed then-existing wet batteries. Despite the fact that each of the elements of the Adams battery was well known in the prior art, to combine them as did Adams required that a person reasonably skilled in the prior art must ignore that (1) batteries which continued to operate on an open circuit and which heated in normal use were not practical; and (2) water-activated batteries were successful only when combined with electrolytes detrimental to the use of magnesium. These long-accepted factors, when taken together, would, we believe, deter any investigation into such a combination as is used by Adams. This is not to say that one who merely finds new uses for old inventions by shutting his eyes to their prior disadvantages thereby discovers a patentable innovation. We do say, however, that known disadvantages in old devices which would naturally discourage the search for new inventions may be taken into account in determining obviousness.

Nor are these the only factors bearing on the question of obviousness. We have seen that at the time Adams perfected his invention noted experts expressed disbelief in it. Several of the same experts subsequently recognized the significance of the Adams invention, some even patenting improvements on the same system. Fischbach et al., U.S. Patent No. 2,636,060 (1953). Furthermore, in a crowded art replete with a century and a half of advancement, the Patent Office found not one reference to cite against the Adams application. Against the subsequently issued improvement patents to Fischbach, supra, and to Chubb, U.S. Reissue Patent No. 23,883 (1954), it found but three references prior to Adams—none of which are relied upon by the Government.

We conclude that the Adams patent is valid. The judgment of the Court of Claims is affirmed.

It is so ordered.

NOTES

1. *The history.* The history of the development of the invention requirement is assayed in depth in Kitch, Graham v. John Deere Co.: New Standards for Patents, 1966 Sup. Ct. Rev. 293, 303–327, 49 J.P.O.S. 237 (1967). The law has been confused. An important source of the confusion has been the statute itself which prior to 1954 provided in a single sentence:

> That any person or persons, having discovered or invented any new and useful art, machine, manufacture, or composition of matter, or any new and useful improvement on any art, machine, manufacture, or composition of matter, not known or used by others before his or their discovery or invention thereof, and not, at the time of his application for a patent, in public use or on sale, with his consent or allowance, as the inventor or discoverer; and shall desire to obtain an exclusive property therein, may make application, in writing, to the Commissioner of Patents * * *.

Patent Act of 1836 § 6, 5 Stat. 119.

(The language is from the 1836 Act, but the same basic wording structure was used from 1836 to 1952.) This language did not even require invention, since the applicant might merely have discovered something "new and useful." Simple novelty was, indeed, the test of patentability in the first decades of the nineteenth century. But this test was altogether unsatisfactory to the courts and they attempted to develop tests which would distinguish the really new from the simply different. These "novelty" tests were the central tests of invention during the nineteenth century. Because it is easier to say what is not new than what is, the tests tended to be put in negative form. The authoritative formulation of these tests was offered by Walker in his Text Book of the Patent Laws in 1883. He said:

§ 23. It has been shown that the word 'discovered,' in Section 4886 of the Revised Statutes, has the meaning of the word 'invented.' It follows that patents are grantable for things invented, and not for things otherwise produced. Novelty and utility must indeed characterize the subject of a patent, but they alone are not enough to make anything patentable; for the statute provides that things to be patented must be invented things, as well as new and useful things. The courts have therefore declared that not all improvement is invention, and entitled to protection as such, but that, to be thus entitled, a thing must be the produce of some exercise of the inventive faculties.

§ 24. The abstract rule stated in the last section is as certainly true as it is universally just, but its application to particular cases cannot be made without the guidance of more concrete propositions. The ideal line which separates things invented from things otherwise produced has never been completely defined nor described. There is no affirmative rule by which to determine the presence or absence of invention in every case. But there are several negative rules, each of which applies to a large class of cases, and all of which are entirely authoritative and sufficiently clear. To formulate those rules, and to state their qualifications and exceptions, and to review and explain the adjudged cases from which those rules, qualifications, and exceptions are deducible, is the scope of several sections which immediately follow.

§ 25. It is not invention to produce a device or process which any skillful mechanic or chemist would produce whenever required.

§ 26. But if a particular result was long desired and sometimes sought, but never attained, want of invention cannot be predicated of a device or process which first reached that result, on the ground that the simplicity of the means is so marked that many believe they could readily have produced it if required. * * *

§ 27. It is not invention to produce an article which differs from some older thing only in excellence of workmanship. * * *

§ 28. It is not invention to substitute superior for inferior materials, in making one or more or all of the parts of a thing. * * *

§ 29. The rule of the last section is not without exceptions. If the substitution involved a new mode of construction, or if it developed new uses and properties of the article made, it may amount to invention. * * *

§ 30. It is not invention to so enlarge and strengthen a machine that it will operate on larger materials than before. * * *

§ 31. It is not invention to change the degree of a thing, or of one feature of a thing. * * *

§ 32. Aggregation is not invention.

§ 33. The rule of the last section does not state nor imply that all the parts of a patentable combination must act at the same time. * * *

§ 34. It is not invention to duplicate one or more of the parts of a machine. * * *

§ 35. It is not invention to omit one or more of the parts of an existing thing, unless that omission causes a new mode of operation of the parts retained. * * *

§ 36. It is not invention to improve a known structure by substituting an equivalent for either of its parts. * * *

§ 37. It is not invention to combine old devices into a new article without producing any new mode of operation. * * *

§ 38. It is not invention to use an old thing or process for a new purpose. * * *

§ 39. The rule of the last section is an easy one to apply to a case to which it is relevant, if the thing or process covered by the patent in that case, is used for the new purpose, without being changed either in construction or mode of operation. That is, however, not always the fact, and where it is not the fact the rule is of but minor practical utility as a guide to a just conclusion. It does not apply to using any new thing for a new purpose; and in order to apply it to anything which differs somewhat from the most similar thing that preceded it, it is necessary first to determine whether that difference constitutes legal novelty; to determine whether the thing covered by the patent is really old. That question must be investigated by the aid of rules other than that of the last section, and when it is determined in the negative it will follow that the rule of that section does not apply to the case.

§ 40. Want of invention, if it really exists in a particular process or thing, can nearly always be detected by one or another of the foregoing rules. When a case arises to which neither of them applies, and relevant to which the mind remains in uncertainty, that uncertainty may be removed by means of the rule in Smith v. The Dental Vulcanite Co., namely: When the other facts in a case leave the question of invention in doubt, the fact that the device has gone into general use, and has displaced other devices which had previously been employed for analogous uses, is sufficient to turn the scale in favor of the existence of invention.

§ 41. To change the form of a machine or manufacture is sometimes invention, and sometimes it is not invention. Where a change of form is within the domain of mere construction, it is not invention, but where it involves a change of mode of operation, or a change of result, it is invention, unless it is held to be otherwise in pursuance of some rule other than any which relates to form.

§ 42. A question of invention is a question of fact and not of law; though it is to be determined by means of the rules of law set forth in this chapter.

§ 43. Every inventor or constructor is presumed by the law to have borrowed from another whatever he produces that was actually first invented and used by that other. It follows that such of the foregoing rules as involve an inquiry into the state of the art to which the thing or process in controversy pertains, may involve an inquiry into the date and the character of inventions which were in fact unknown to the patentee, when he produced that thing or that process.

These tests had two important difficulties. First, almost anything can be characterized as a new mode of use, a new result or a new effect. Second, many things that clearly could qualify under the tests were also, unfortunately, trivial. These deficiencies led the courts and the writers to formulate two additional tests. One test centered on the way in which the invention was made. It was most colorfully phrased as the "flash of genius" test. This test never did anything except add to the ambiguity surrounding the problem, and it was expressly eliminated from the law by the last sentence of § 103 in the 1952 Act. The second additional test was the test which, although formulated in many varying ways, and foreshadowed by Walker's § 25, became the non-obviousness test of § 103.

The courts, however, never thought of these three approaches as different but rather as all aspects of the law of invention. All too typical is the language of Mr. Justice Douglas in Cuno Eng'r Corp. v. Automatic Devices Corp., 314 U.S. 84, 91 (1941):

[T]he new device, however useful it may be, must reveal the flash of creative genius not merely the skill of the calling. * * * Tested by that principle Mead's device was not patentable. We cannot conclude that his skill in making this contribution reached the level of inventive genius. * * * A new application of an old device may not be patented if the "result claimed as new is the same in character as the original result. * * * *"

Section 103 should be interpreted to constitute a legislative choice of one of the three tests.

2. Under 35 U.S.C. § 282 a patent is presumed valid. This is an important assist to the holder of an issued patent, but some circuit courts had held that the presumption was weakened or disappeared where prior art was introduced in the infringement case that had not been considered by the patent examiner. Since this is often the case in infringement litigation, these holdings significantly weakened the effect of § 282. Perhaps the single most

significant consequence of the creation of the Federal Circuit for patent law is that the circuit follows CCPA precedents that held that the presumption of § 282 is never weakened.

Judge Rich explained the Federal Circuit view of § 282 in American Hoist & Derrick Co. v. Sowa & Sons, Inc., 725 F.2d 1350 (Fed. Cir. 1984), a decision that reversed a jury verdict of invalidity where the jury had been instructed (following the precedents of the circuit in which the district court sat) that "If * * * you find any of the prior art references which defendant has cited are more pertinent than the art utilized by the examiner * * * then that presumption of validity disappears." He explained:

> The two sentences of * * * § 282 * * * amount in substance to different statements of the same thing: the burden is on the attacker. And, as this court has been saying in other cases, that burden never shifts. The only question to be decided is whether the attacker is successful. When no prior art other than that which was considered by the PTO examiner is relied on by the attacker, he has the added burden of overcoming the deference that is due to a qualified government agency presumed to have properly done its job, which includes one or more examiners who are assumed to have some expertise in interpreting the references and to be familiar from their work with the level of skill in the art and whose duty it is to issue only valid patents. In some cases a PTO board of appeals may have approved the issuance of the patent.

> When an attacker, in sustaining the burden imposed by § 282, produced prior art or other evidence not considered in the PTO, there is, however, *no reason to defer* to the PTO so far as its effect on validity is concerned. Indeed, new prior art not before the PTO may so clearly invalidate a patent that the burden is fully sustained merely by proving its existence and applying the proper law; but that has no effect on the presumption or on who has the burden of proof. They are static and in reality different expressions of the same thing—a single hurdle to be cleared. Neither does the *standard* of proof change; it must be by clear and convincing evidence or its equivalent, by whatever form of words it may be expressed. What the production of new prior art or other invalidating evidence not before the PTO does is to eliminate, or at least reduce, the element of deference due the PTO, thereby partially, if not wholly, *discharging* the attacker's burden, but neither shifting nor lightening it or changing the standard of proof. When an attacker simply goes over the same ground travelled by the PTO, part of the burden is to show that the PTO was wrong in its decision to grant the patent. When new evidence touching validity of the patent not considered by the PTO is relied on, the tribunal considering it is not faced with having to *disagree* with the PTO or with *deferring* to its judgment or with taking its expertise into account. The evidence may, therefore, carry more weight and go further toward sustaining the attacker's unchanging burden.

> To summarize on this point, § 282 creates a presumption that a patent is valid and imposes the burden of proving invalidity on the attacker. That burden is constant and never changes and is to convince

the court of invalidity by clear evidence. Deference is due the Patent and Trademark Office decision to issue the patent with respect to evidence bearing on validity which it considered but no such deference is due with respect to evidence it did not consider. All evidence bearing on the validity issue, whether considered by the PTO or not, is to be taken into account by the tribunal in which validity is attacked.

725 F.2d 1359–1360.

3. *Design patents.* Design patents are subject to the requirements of § 103. The section has been difficult to apply to design patents because designs are often the result of inspiration rather than technological inquiry. The Federal Circuit's emphasis on the presumption of validity in § 282 has resulted in many more design patents being held valid. In Durling v. Spectrum Furniture Co., 101 F.3d 100, 103 (Fed. Cir. 1996), the court provided guidance on how the § 103 test is to be applied in the context of design patents.

In the design patent context, the ultimate inquiry under section 103 is whether the claimed design would have been obvious to a designer of ordinary skill who designs articles of the type involved. * * * More specifically, the inquiry is whether one of ordinary skill would have combined teachings of the prior art to create the same overall visual appearance as the claimed design. * * *

Before one can begin to combine prior art designs, however, one must find a single reference, "a something in existence, the design characteristics of which are basically the same as the claimed design." In re Rosen, 673 F.2d at 391, Once this primary reference is found, other references may be used to modify it to create a design that has the same overall visual appearance as the claimed design. See In re Harvey, 12 F.3d 1061, 1063 (Fed. Cir. 1993). These secondary references may only be used to modify the primary reference if they are "so related [to the primary reference] that the appearance of certain ornamental features in one would suggest the application of those features to the other." In re Borden, 90 F.3d at 1575.

4. The reliability of the examination process in the Patent and Trademark Office is in part a product of the procedures used. A patent application is a secret and ex-parte procedure in the patent office in which the applicant attempts to persuade the examiner to issue the patent and the examiner (who has many applications to review at one time) has the burden of determining whether the applicant's position is consistent with the statute and the nature of the prior art. The examiner has no assistance from outside interested parties or experts, although he does have the use of the patent office files and library, consultation with fellow examiners and patent office employees, and the expertise that comes from dealing with many related applications. One advantage of this approach is that it helps to simplify the application procedure. An inventor (who may be poorly funded, particularly before he can use the issued patent to raise venture capital) might find it difficult to overcome obstacles erected by potential competitors if a more open and adversarial procedure were used.

5. A procedure for reexamination is now codified in chapter 30 of Title 35 as the result of P.L. 96–517, Patent and Trademark Laws, December 12, 1980. This procedure enables a patent owner, after the commercial value of the invention has been established, and perhaps when litigation is in the offing, to request a reexamination of the patent by the PTO. A reexamination proceeds basically just like an original application. It can be used to obtain a patent office ruling on additional prior art and to reshape the claims in light of the patent owner's present understanding of that art.

An important procedural innovation in connection with reexaminations is provision for limited third party participation in the reexamination process. Under § 301 a third party can provide prior art to be included in the patent file. Under § 302 a third party can request a reexamination of a patent. And under § 304 the person requesting the reexamination can file a statement in writing replying to any statement filed by the patent owner.

A reexamination has now become a not uncommon aspect of patent infringement litigation. Either the patent owner, the defendant, or others who fear that the patent may be upheld, will consider it strategically advantageous to request a reexamination. In Gould v. Control Laser Corp., 705 F.2d 1340 (Fed. Cir. 1983), the PTO had decided to conduct a reexamination upon the request of a person other than the patent owner. The District Court stayed the infringement action until completion of the reexamination. The court dismissed the appeal for lack of jurisdiction, but in dictum quoted portions of the legislative history which imply that such stays should be routinely granted. As a result, a fresh examination of the patent office based upon a current review of the record and conducted with the knowledge that the patent is valuable and in dispute exists more often in patent cases. If the PTO does a good job of conducting these reexaminations, it is likely that the courts will increasingly defer to them. The Federal Circuit upheld the constitutionality of the reexamination procedure in Patlex Corp. v. Mossinghoff, 758 F.2d 594 (Fed. Cir. 1985).

6. The Court's favorable reference to the Note, Subtests of "Nonobviousness": A Nontechnical Approach to Patent Validity, 112 U. Pa. L. Rev. 1169 (1964), in *Graham* has given the tests importance in the lower courts, although it is impossible to determine from the opinions whether the judges rely on the tests in deciding the nonobviousness question or whether the tests are simply added to the opinions in support of decisions already made. The subtests discussed in the note are: (1) long-felt demand for the innovation which was only satisfied by the patentee's invention; (2) the commercial success of the invention in the marketplace; (3) acquiescence by competitors to the validity of the patent; (4) simultaneous solution of the problem solved by the patentee by others (tending to show no invention); (5) approval of the invention by technologists, scientific commentators, and university professors; (6) difficulty in obtaining a patent from the patent office (tending to show no invention). The note endorses all of these tests but the last one, with some cautionary qualifications.

These tests offer promise of a non-technical grounding for a nonobviousness determination, but they also lend themselves to misleading inferences. For instance, the patentee's innovation may have been made possible by some other technological advance, such as the development of a new material or testing procedure, which was not available to others who tried to satisfy the long felt demand. Commercial success may have been due to good timing, changes in consumer markets, or attractive packaging. Commercial acquiescence simply reflects the judgments of competitors that a license or non-infringement is cheaper than litigation. Simultaneous solution by others may simply show that the problem solved by the invention was widely regarded as important so that many able researchers were put to work on it. Approval by experts is ambiguous because usually not addressed to the technical patent question and constitutes a form of hearsay expert testimony. Difficulties in obtaining a patent from the patent office can result from many things, including an incompetent patent attorney.

Of all these tests, commercial success is the most troubling because it seems to create a presumption of validity whenever the patented innovation is commercially successful. Of course, if the patented innovation is not commercially successful, resolution of the patent question has little economic significance. The Supreme Court treated the commercial success test as not controlling in Anderson's-Black Rock, Inc. v. Pavement Salvage Co., 396 U.S. 57 (1969). In the course of holding a patent on a machine for laying bituminous concrete employing a radiant burner heater to achieve good bonding between strips invalid, the Court observed that "Use of the radiant burner in this important field marked a successful venture. But * * * more than that is needed for invention." 396 U.S. 63. The patented invention in the *Calmar* case was very successful, but the Supreme Court found the patent invalid, as the Eighth Circuit (which was reversed in *Calmar*) noted in General Mills, Inc. v. Pillsbury Co., 378 F.2d 666, 670 (8th Cir. 1967).

Cable Electric Products, Inc. v. Genmark, Inc., 770 F.2d 1015, 1027 (Fed. Cir. 1985): "[T]his court * * * has unequivocally stated that for commercial success of a product embodying a claimed invention to have true relevance to the issue of nonobviousness, that success must be shown to have in some way been due to the nature of the claimed invention, as opposed to other economic and commercial factors unrelated to the technical quality of the patented subject matter. Thus, a 'nexus is required between the merits of the claimed invention and the evidence offered, if the evidence is to be given substantial weight enroute to [a] conclusion on the obviousness issue.'"

7. Perhaps the most curious test, but one which appears not infrequently in the cases, is a test based upon the fact that the defendant's product is an exact copy of the plaintiff's. It is possible to reason that such exact copying shows that the patent owner has found the only way to accomplish the purpose of the patent. But if the patent is invalid, isn't the defendant entitled to copy? In Cable Electric Products, Inc. v. Genmark, Inc., 770 F.2d 1015, 1027–28 (Fed. Cir. 1985), the court said: "Access to, and analysis of, other products in the market is hardly rare, even in the design stages of competing devices * * * It is our conclusion that more than the mere fact of copying by an accused infringer is needed to make that action significant to a determination of the obviousness issue." In Vandenberg v. Dairy

Equipment Co., 740 F.2d 1560, 1567 (Fed. Cir. 1984), the court said that "The copying of an invention may constitute evidence that the invention is not an obvious one. * * * This would be particularly true where the copyist had itself attempted for a substantial length of time to design a similar device, and had failed."

8. The *Adams* case contains an example of highly persuasive evidence in support of a conclusion of nonobviousness: contemporary expert opinion that the invention was impossible. Given that evidence, what was the problem in *Adams?* Is there a problem in *Adams* not present in *Graham?* See Kitch, Graham v. John Deere Co.: New Standards for Patents, 1966 Sup. Ct. Rev. 293, 327–330, 49 J.P.O.S. 237, 277–81 (1967).

D. The Relevant Prior Art

Section 103 requires a determination of the content of the prior art. "Prior art" for purposes of § 103 is a technical term. It consists of two things. First, the body of knowledge known to a person skilled in the art. And second, certain enumerated documents and events which are constructively in the art whether or not actually known to those skilled in the art. This second category is closely related to the novelty, time bar and priority provisions of § 102. We will defer examination of it until we reach § 102. As an example of constructive prior art, any issued United States or foreign patent is in the prior art whether or not it is known to the contemporary practitioners of the art.

What types of technology are in the prior art? (This question is sometimes phrased as: what arts are "pertinent," or: what arts are "analogous.") The cases long reflected, usually unconsciously, two approaches to the question of the scope of the prior art. Sometimes they treated the prior art as the art of those who used the technology. Other times they treated the prior art as the art of those who were skilled in the art of solving the kind of technological problem to which the invention is addressed (which would include, in part, the knowledge of those who use the technology). This second approach is the approach that was followed by the C.C.P.A., and now by the Federal Circuit. The following two cases illustrate its application.

Application of Van Wanderham, 378 F.2d 981 (C.C.P.A. 1967). The application was for a system of providing a regular flow of extremely cold fuel such as liquid hydrogen to the pumps of a rocket engine. The problem was that the fuel would boil as it left the fuel tank and came in contact with warmer tubing and valves on its way to the pumps. The boiling introduced air into the fuel, causing the pumps to produce an uneven flow to the engine, with bad effects on the performance of the rocket (burp, burp). The solution for which a patent was claimed was to coat the inside of the tubing with a layer of thermal insulating material. The reference cited against the application was a report on the use of a coating by Japanese cutlery makers prior to quenching in order to obtain a perfect hardening of the metal. The cited reference reported that this process worked because the coating prevented the formation of a vapor film on the metal when it was first immersed, speeding up the rate of cooling. The patent office argued that this reference was prior art because the patent was directed to a problem of heat transfer, and one attempting to solve a problem of heat transfer would look to practices in metallurgy. The CCPA rejected the relevance of this reference. "[I]t does not seem to us that one seeking to eliminate pump cavitation problems *and* the problem of vapor in cryogenic liquid propellant flow system would turn to the cutlery art." 378 F.2d at 988.

Stratoflex, Inc. v. Aeroquip Corp., 713 F.2d 1530 (Fed. Cir. 1983). The patent was on tubing made of polytetrafluorethylene (or PTFE, trademarked by Du Pont as TEFLON) used in the aircraft and missile industry to convey pressurized fuel, lubricants, and other fluids. Tubing of PTFE had been in use since 1956, but after 1959, when hydrocarbon jet fuels were introduced, leaks developed. Engineers studied the matter and discovered that the leaks were caused by the arcing of electrostatic charges through the wall of the dielectric (nonconducting) PTFE. The patent claimed PTFE tubing lined with an inner layer of PTFE with sufficient carbon in it so that it is conductive. Such tubing is not subject to electrostatic buildup because the static charge is dissipated by the conductive layer. The trial court held the patent invalid, relying in part on prior art relating to rubber hoses. The patentee argued "that the scope of the relevant prior art excludes rubber hose because PTFE is a unique material, possessing properties that differ significantly from rubber, and that, because the claims are limited to PTFE, the rubber hose art could at most be peripherally relevant as background information." The Federal Circuit rejected this argument and affirmed. "The scope for the prior art has been defined as that 'reasonably pertinent to the particular problem with which the inventor was involved.' * * * The problem confronting * * * [the inventor] was preventing electrostatic buildup in PTFE tubing caused by hydrocarbon fuel flow while precluding leakage of fuel. None of the unique properties of PTFE would change the nature of that problem. Nor would anything of record indicate that one skilled in the art would not include the rubber hose art in his search for a solution to that problem." 713 F.2d at 1535.

In re Dillon

United States Court of Appeals for the Federal Circuit
(in banc), 1990.
919 F.2d 688.

■ LOURIE, CIRCUIT JUDGE.

Diane M. Dillon, assignor to Union Oil Company of California, appeals the November 25, 1987, decision of the Board of Patent Appeals and Interferences (Board) of the United States Patent and Trademark Office (PTO), Appeal No. 87–0944, rejecting claims 2–14, 16–22, and 24–37, all the remaining claims of patent application Serial No. 671,570 entitled "Hydrocarbon Fuel Composition." We affirm the rejection of all of the claims.[1]

The Invention

Dillon's patent application describes and claims her discovery that the inclusion of certain tetra-orthoester compounds in hydrocarbon fuel compositions will reduce the emission of solid particulates (i.e., soot) during combustion of the fuel. In this appeal Dillon asserts the patentability of claims to hydrocarbon fuel compositions containing these tetra-orthoesters, and to the method of reducing particulate emissions during combustion by combining these esters with the fuel before combustion.

Claim 2 is the broadest composition claim:

2. A composition comprising: a hydrocarbon fuel; and a sufficient amount of at least one orthoester so as to reduce the particulate emissions from the combustion of the hydrocarbon fuel, wherein the orthoester is of the formula:

$$R_3-O - \overset{\displaystyle O-R_7}{\underset{\displaystyle O-R_5}{\overset{|}{\underset{|}{C}}}} - O-R_6$$

wherein R_5, R_6, R_7, and R_8, are the same or different monovalent organic radical comprising 1 to about 20 carbon atoms.

The broadest method claim is claim 24:

24. A method of reducing the particulate emissions from the combustion of a hydrocarbon fuel comprising combusting a mixture of the hydrocarbon fuel and a sufficient amount of at least one orthoester so as to reduce the particulate emissions, wherein the orthoester is of the formula:

---

1. A panel of this court heard this appeal and reversed the Board on December 29, 1989. 892 F.2d 1554. The PTO petitioned for rehearing and suggested rehearing in banc on February 12, 1990. Rehearing in banc was ordered on May 21, 1990, and the judgment which was entered on December 29, 1989, was vacated, the accompanying opinion being withdrawn.

$$R_3 - O \underset{\underset{O - R_5}{|}}{\overset{\overset{O - R_7}{|}}{C}} - O - R_6$$

wherein R_5, R_6, R_7, and R_8, are the same or different monovalent organic radical comprising 1 to about 20 carbon atoms.

The other claims contain additional limitations and thus are narrower in scope.

The tetra-orthoesters are a known class of chemical compounds. It is undisputed that their combination with hydrocarbon fuel, for any purpose, is not shown in the prior art, and that their use to reduce particulate emissions from combustion of hydrocarbon fuel is not shown or suggested in the prior art.

The Rejection

The Board held all of the claims to be unpatentable on the ground of obviousness, 35 U.S.C. § 103, in view of certain primary and secondary references. As primary references the Board relied on two Sweeney U.S. patents, 4,390,417 ('417) and 4,395,267 ('267). Sweeney '417 describes hydrocarbon fuel compositions containing specified chemical compounds, viz., ketals, acetals, and tri-orthoesters,[2] used for "dewatering" the fuels, particularly diesel oil. Sweeney '267 describes three-component compositions of hydrocarbon fuels heavier than gasoline, immiscible alcohols, and tri-orthoesters, wherein the tri-orthoesters serve as cosolvents to prevent phase separation between fuel and alcohol. The Board explicitly found that the Sweeney patents do not teach the use of the tetra-orthoesters recited in appellant's claims.

The Board cited Elliott U.S. Patent 3,903,006 and certain other patents, including Howk U.S. Patent 2,840,613, as secondary references. Elliott describes tri-orthoesters and tetra-orthoesters for use as water scavengers in hydraulic (non-hydrocarbon) fluids. The Board stated that the Elliott reference shows equivalence between tetra-orthoesters and tri-orthoesters, and that "it is clear from the combined teachings of these references . . . that [Dillon's tetra-orthoesters] would operate to remove water from non-aqueous liquids by the same mechanism as the orthoesters of Sweeney."

The Board stated that there was a "reasonable expectation" that the tri- and tetra-orthoester fuel compositions would have similar properties, based on "close structural and chemical similarity" between the tri- and tetra-orthoesters and the fact that both the prior art and Dillon use these compounds as "fuel additives." The Commissioner argues on appeal that the

---

2. Tri-orthoesters have three -OR groups bonded to a central carbon atom, and the fourth carbon bond is to hydrogen or a hydrocarbon group (-R); they are represented as C(R)(OR). Tetra-orthoesters have four -OR groups bonded to a central carbon atom, and are represented as C(OR); see Dillon's claims, supra.

claimed compositions and method "would have been prima facie obvious from combined teachings of the references." On this reasoning, the Board held that unless Dillon showed some unexpected advantage or superiority of her claimed tetra-orthoester fuel compositions as compared with tri-orthoester fuel compositions, Dillon's new compositions as well as her claimed method of reducing particulate emissions are unpatentable for obviousness. It found that no such showing was made.

The Issue

The issue before this court is whether the Board erred in rejecting as obvious under 35 U.S.C. § 103 claims to Dillon's new compositions and to the new method of reducing particulate emissions, when the additives in the new compositions are structurally similar to additives in known compositions, having a different use, but the new method of reducing particulate emissions is neither taught nor suggested by the prior art.

The Broad Composition Claims

Claim 2, the broadest composition claim, comprises a hydrocarbon fuel and an amount of tetra-orthoester sufficient to reduce the particulate emissions from the combustion of the hydrocarbon fuel. The other composition claims contain various limitations including a minimum amount of emission reduction to be achieved (claim 3), percentages of ester in the fuel (claims 4, 5, 16, 20, 21), use of different esters (claims 6–10, 17–19), use of different fuels (claims 11–14, 22), and the requirement that the composition be essentially free of alcohol (claims 36, 37).

* * *

The Board found that the claims to compositions of a hydrocarbon fuel and a tetra-orthoester were prima facie obvious over Sweeney '417 and '267 in view of Elliott and Howk. We agree. Appellant argues that none of these references discloses or suggests the new use which she has discovered. That is, of course, true, but the composition claims are not limited to this new use; i.e., they are not physically or structurally distinguishable over the prior art compositions except with respect to the orthoester component. We believe that the PTO has established, through its combination of references, that there is a sufficiently close relationship between the tri-orthoesters and tetra-orthoesters (see the cited Elliott and Howk references) in the fuel oil art to create an expectation that hydrocarbon fuel compositions containing the tetra-esters would have similar properties, including water scavenging, to like compositions containing the tri-esters, and to provide the motivation to make such new compositions. Howk teaches use of both tri- and tetra-orthoesters in a similar type of chemical reaction. Elliott teaches their equivalence for a particular practical use.

* * *

Appellant cites In re Wright, 848 F.2d 1216, 1219 (Fed. Cir. 1988), for the proposition that a prima facie case of obviousness requires that the prior art suggest the claimed compositions' properties and the problem the applicant attempts to solve. The earlier panel opinion in this case, *In re Dillon*, 892 F.2d 1554 (now withdrawn), in fact stated "a *prima facie* case of obviousness is not deemed made unless both (1) the new compound or composition is structurally similar to the reference compound or composition and (2) there is some suggestion or expectation *in the prior art* that the new compound or composition will have the *same or a similar utility as that discovered by the applicant*." Id. at 1560 (emphasis added).

This court, in reconsidering this case in banc, reaffirms that structural similarity between claimed and prior art subject matter, proved by combining references or otherwise, where the prior art gives reason or motivation to make the claimed compositions, creates a *prima facie* case of obviousness, and that the burden (and opportunity) then falls on an applicant to rebut that *prima facie* case. Such rebuttal or argument can consist of a comparison of test data showing that the claimed compositions possess unexpectedly improved properties or properties that the prior art does not have (* * *), that the prior art is so deficient that there is no motivation to make what might otherwise appear to be obvious changes (* * *), or any other argument or presentation of evidence that is pertinent. There is no question that all evidence of the properties of the claimed compositions and the prior art must be considered in determining the ultimate question of patentability, but it is also clear that the discovery that a claimed composition possesses a property not disclosed for the prior art subject matter, does not by itself defeat a prima facie case. * * * Each situation must be considered on its own facts, but it is not necessary in order to establish a *prima facie* case of obviousness that both a structural similarity between a claimed and prior art compound (or a key component of a composition) be shown and that there be a suggestion in or expectation from *the prior art* that the claimed compound or composition will have the same or a similar utility *as one newly discovered by applicant*. To the extent that *Wright* suggests or holds to the contrary, it is hereby overruled. In particular, the statement that a *prima facie* obviousness rejection is not supported if no reference shows or suggests the newly-discovered properties and results of a claimed structure is not the law.[3]

Under the facts we have here, as described above, we have concluded that a *prima facie* case has been established. The art provided the motivation to make the claimed compositions in the expectation that they would have similar properties. Appellant had the opportunity to rebut the prima

---

3. The earlier, now-withdrawn *Dillon* opinion, this opinion, and the dissent cite and rely on cases involving claims to chemical compounds, whereas this case involves compositions. The reason for this reliance is that, in this case, the principal difference between the claimed and prior art compositions is the difference between chemical compounds, viz., tri-orthoesters and tetra-orthoesters. Cases dealing with chemical compounds are therefore directly analogous here and, in view of the history of this case and its in banc status, we will make much comment on these cases in this opinion. We do not, however, intend to imply that in all cases involving claimed compositions, structural obviousness between involved chemical compounds necessarily makes the claimed compositions prima facie obvious.

facie case. She did not present any showing of data to the effect that her compositions had properties not possessed by the prior art compositions or that they possessed them to an unexpectedly greater degree. She attempted to refute the significance of the teachings of the prior art references. She did not succeed and we do not believe the PTO was in error in its decision.

Appellant points out that none of the references relates to the problem she confronted, citing *In re Wright*, and that the combination of references is based on hindsight. It is clear, however, that appellant's claims have to be considered as she has drafted them, i.e., as compositions consisting of a fuel and a tetra-orthoester, and that Sweeney '417 and '267 describe the combination of a liquid fuel with a related compound, a tri-orthoester. While Sweeney does not suggest appellant's use, her composition claims are not limited to that use;[4] the claims merely recite compositions analogous to those in the Sweeney patents, and appellant has made no showing overcoming the *prima facie* presumption of similar properties for those analogous compositions. The mention in the appealed claims that the amount of orthoester must be sufficient to reduce particulate emissions is not a distinguishing limitation of the claims, unless that amount is different from the prior art and critical to the use of the claimed composition. * * *. That is not the case here. The amount of ester recited in the dependent claims can be from 0.05–49%, a very broad range; a preferred range is .05–9%, compared with a percentage in Sweeney '417 approximately equimolar to the amounts of water in the fuel which the ester is intended to remove (.01–5%).

Appellant attacks the Elliott patent as non-analogous art, being in the field of hydraulic fluids rather than fuel combustion. We agree with the PTO that the field of relevant prior art need not be drawn so narrowly. As this court stated in In re Deminski, 796 F.2d 436, 442 (Fed. Cir. 1986) (quoting In re Wood, 599 F.2d 1032, 1036 (CCPA 1979)):

> [t]he determination that a reference is from a nonanalogous art is therefore two-fold. First, we decide if the reference is within the field of the inventor's endeavor. If it is not, we proceed to determine whether the reference is reasonably pertinent to the particular problem with which the inventor was involved.

Following that test, one concerned with the field of fuel oils clearly is chargeable with knowledge of Sweeney '417, which discloses fuel compositions with tri-orthoesters for dewatering purposes, and chargeable with knowledge of other references to tri-orthoesters, including for use as dewatering agents for fluids, albeit other fluids. These references are "within the field of the inventor's endeavor." Moreover, the statement of equivalency between tri- and tetra-orthoesters in Elliott is not challenged. We therefore conclude that Elliott is not excludable from consideration as non-analogous art. It is evidence that

---

4. The dissent misinterprets this comment as indicating that claims to new compounds and compositions must contain a limitation to a specific use, and states that past cases have rejected this proposition. Our comment only points out that the composition claims on appeal are not structurally or physically distinguishable from the prior art compositions by virtue of the recitation of their newly-discovered use.

supports the Board's holding that the prior art makes the claimed compositions obvious, a conclusion that appellant did not overcome.

Appellant urges that the Board erred in not considering the unexpected results produced by her invention and in not considering the claimed invention as a whole. The Board found, on the other hand, that no showing was made of unexpected results for the claimed compositions compared with the compositions of Sweeney. We agree. Clearly, in determining patentability the Board was obligated to consider all the evidence of the properties of the claimed invention as a whole, compared with those of the prior art. However, after the PTO made a showing that the prior art compositions suggested the claimed compositions, the burden was on the applicant to overcome the presumption of obviousness that was created, and that was not done. For example, she produced no evidence that her compositions possessed properties not possessed by the prior art compositions. Nor did she show that the prior art compositions and use were so lacking in significance that there was no motivation for others to make obvious variants. There was no attempt to argue the relative importance of the claimed compositions compared with the prior art. * * *

Appellant's patent application in fact included data showing that the prior art compositions containing tri-orthoesters had equivalent activity in reducing particulate emissions (she apparently was once claiming such compositions with either tri-orthoesters or tetra-orthoesters). She asserts that the examiner used her own showing of equivalence against her in violation of the rule of In re Ruff, 256 F.2d 590, 596 (CCPA 1958). While we caution against such a practice, it is clear to us that references by the PTO to the comparative data in the patent application were not employed as evidence of equivalence between the tri- and tetra-orthoesters; the PTO was simply pointing out that the applicant did not or apparently could not make a showing of superiority for the claimed tetra-ester compositions over the prior art tri-ester compositions.

Other Claims

* * *

Regarding the method claims, the Commissioner urges affirmance, citing In re Durden, 763 F.2d 1406 (Fed. Cir. 1985), for the proposition that even "substitution of an unobvious starting material into an old process does not necessarily result in an unobvious process." The PTO has, as the Commissioner urges here, applied *Durden* regularly to claims to processes of making and processes of using, on the ground that the type of step involved in the claimed process is not novel.[5]

We make no judgment as to the patentability of claims that Dillon might have made and properly argued to a method directed to the novel aspects of her invention, except to question the lack of logic in a claim to a

---

5. See M.A. Litman, Obvious Process Rejections Under 35 USC 103, 71 JPTOS 775 (1989); H.C. Wegner, Much Ado About Durden, 71 JPTOS 785 (1989).

method of reducing particulate emissions by combusting. Suffice it to say that we do not regard *Durden* as authority to reject as obvious every method claim reading on an old *type of process*, such as mixing, reacting, reducing, etc. The materials used in a claimed process as well as the result obtained therefrom, must be considered along with the specific nature of the process, and the fact that new or old, obvious or nonobvious, materials are used or result from the process are only factors to be considered, rather than conclusive indicators of the obviousness or nonobviousness of a claimed process. When any applicant properly presents and argues suitable method claims, they should be examined in light of all these relevant factors, free from any presumed controlling effect of *Durden*. *Durden* did not hold that all methods involving old process steps are obvious; the court in that case concluded that the particularly claimed process was obvious; it refused to adopt an unvarying rule that the fact that nonobvious starting materials and nonobvious products are involved *ipso facto* makes the process nonobvious. Such an invariant rule always leading to the opposite conclusion is also not the law. Thus, we reject the Commissioner's argument that we affirm the rejection of the method claims under the precedent of *Durden*.

However, appellant did not argue in her brief the separate patentability of her method claims. The statement in her brief to the Board that "the invention 'as a whole' includes the property of the claimed compositions—which property is taken advantage of in the method claims" (Brief at 22, J.App. at 112) is not such a separate argument, since it implies more an added argument for the patentability of the composition claims than an argument that, even if the claimed compositions are found to have been obvious, the claimed methods were nonobvious for particularly stated reasons. Moreover, no such reasons were particularly stated by Dillon. We will therefore not analyze these claims separately and affirm the Board's rejection on that basis.

* * *

CONCLUSION

We affirm the Board's decision rejecting claims 2–14, 16–22, and 24–37.

In re Deuel

United States Court of Appeals for the Federal Circuit, 1995.
51 F.3d 1552.

■ Lourie, Circuit Judge.

Thomas F. Deuel, Yue-Sheng Li, Ned R. Siegel, and Peter G. Milner (collectively "Deuel") appeal from the November 30, 1993 decision of the U.S. Patent and Trademark Office Board of Patent Appeals and Interferences affirming the examiner's final rejection of claims 4–7 of application Serial No. 07/542,232, entitled "Heparin-Binding Growth Factor," as unpatentable on the ground of obviousness under 35 U.S.C. § 103 (1988). * * * Because the Board erred in concluding that Deuel's claims 5 and 7 directed to specific cDNA molecules would have been obvious in light of the applied references, and no other basis exists in the record to support the rejection with respect to claims 4 and 6 generically covering all possible DNA molecules coding for the disclosed proteins, we reverse.

BACKGROUND

The claimed invention relates to isolated and purified DNA and cDNA molecules encoding heparin-binding growth factors ("HBGFs").[1] HBGFs are proteins that stimulate mitogenic activity (cell division) and thus facilitate the repair or replacement of damaged or diseased tissue. DNA (deoxyribonucleic acid) is a generic term which encompasses an enormous number of complex macromolecules made up of nucleotide units. DNAs consist of four different nucleotides containing the nitrogenous bases adenine, guanine, cytosine, and thymine. A sequential grouping of three such nucleotides (a "codon") codes for one amino acid. A DNA's sequence of codons thus determines the sequence of amino acids assembled during protein synthesis. Since there are 64 possible codons, but only 20 natural amino acids, most amino acids are coded for by more than one codon. This is referred to as the "redundancy" or "degeneracy" of the genetic code.

DNA functions as a blueprint of an organism's genetic information. It is the major component of genes, which are located on chromosomes in the cell nucleus. Only a small part of chromosomal DNA encodes functional proteins.

Messenger ribonucleic acid ("mRNA") is a similar molecule that is made or transcribed from DNA as part of the process of protein synthesis. Complementary DNA ("cDNA") is a complementary copy ("clone") of mRNA, made in the laboratory by reverse transcription of mRNA. Like mRNA, cDNA contains only the protein-encoding regions of DNA. Thus, once a cDNA's nucleotide sequence is known, the amino acid sequence of the protein for which it codes may be predicted using the genetic code relationship between codons and amino acids. The reverse is not true, however, due to the degeneracy of the code. Many other DNAs may code for a particular protein. The functional relationships between DNA, mRNA, cDNA, and a protein may conveniently be expressed as follows:

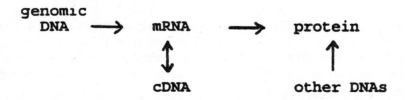

Collections ("libraries") of DNA and cDNA molecules derived from various species may be constructed in the laboratory or obtained from commercial

1. For a more extensive discussion of recombinant DNA technology, see In re O'Farrell, 853 F.2d 894, 895-99 (Fed. Cir. 1988); Amgen Inc. v. Chugai Pharmaceutical Co., 927 F.2d 1200 (Fed. Cir.), cert. denied, 502 U.S. 856 (1991).

sources. Complementary DNA libraries contain a mixture of cDNA clones reverse-transcribed from the mRNAs found in a specific tissue source. Complementary DNA libraries are tissue-specific because proteins and their corresponding mRNAs are only made ("expressed") in specific tissues, depending upon the protein. Genomic DNA ("gDNA") libraries, by contrast, theoretically contain all of a species' chromosomal DNA. The molecules present in cDNA and DNA libraries may be of unknown function and chemical structure, and the proteins which they encode may be unknown. However, one may attempt to retrieve molecules of interest from cDNA or gDNA libraries by screening such libraries with a gene probe, which is a synthetic radiolabelled nucleic acid sequence designed to bond ("hybridize") with a target complementary base sequence. Such "gene cloning" techniques thus exploit the fact that the bases in DNA always hybridize in complementary pairs: adenine bonds with thymine and guanine bonds with cytosine. A gene probe for potentially isolating DNA or cDNA encoding a protein may be designed once the protein's amino acid sequence, or a portion thereof, is known.

As disclosed in Deuel's patent application, Deuel isolated and purified HBGF from bovine uterine tissue, found that it exhibited mitogenic activity, and determined the first 25 amino acids of the protein's N-terminal sequence.[2] Deuel then isolated a cDNA molecule encoding bovine uterine HBGF by screening a bovine uterine cDNA library with an oligonucleotide probe designed using the experimentally determined N-terminal sequence of the HBGF. Deuel purified and sequenced the cDNA molecule, which was found to consist of a sequence of 1196 nucleotide base pairs. From the cDNA's nucleotide sequence, Deuel then predicted the complete amino acid sequence of bovine uterine HBGF disclosed in Deuel's application.

Deuel also isolated a cDNA molecule encoding human placental HBGF by screening a human placental cDNA library using the isolated bovine uterine cDNA clone as a probe. Deuel purified and sequenced the human placental cDNA clone, which was found to consist of a sequence of 961 nucleotide base pairs. From the nucleotide sequence of the cDNA molecule encoding human placental HBGF, Deuel predicted the complete amino acid sequence of human placental HBGF disclosed in Deuel's application. The predicted human placental and bovine uterine HBGFs each have 168 amino acids and calculated molecular weights of 18.9 kD. Of the 168 amino acids present in the two HBGFs discovered by Deuel, 163 are identical. Deuel's application does not describe the chemical structure of, or state how to isolate and purify, any DNA or cDNA molecule except the disclosed human placental and bovine uterine cDNAs, which are the subject of claims 5 and 7.

Claims 4–7 on appeal are all independent claims and read, in relevant part, as follows:

> 4. A purified and isolated DNA sequence consisting of a sequence encoding human heparin binding growth factor of 168 amino acids

---

2. Deuel determined that the N-terminal sequence of bovine uterus HBGF is Gly-Lys-Lys-Glu-Lys-Pro-Glu-Lys-Lys-Val-Lys—Lys- Ser-Asp-Cys—Gly-Glu-Trp-Gln-Trp-Ser-Val-Cys-Val-Pro.

having the following amino acid sequence: Met Gln Ala . . . [remainder of 168 amino acid sequence].

5. The purified and isolated cDNA of human heparin-binding growth factor having the following nucleotide sequence: GTCAAAG-GCA . . . [remainder of 961 nucleotide sequence].

6. A purified and isolated DNA sequence consisting of a sequence encoding bovine heparin binding growth factor of 168 amino acids having the following amino acid sequence: Met Gln Thr . . . [remainder of 168 amino acid sequence].

7. The purified and isolated cDNA of bovine heparin-binding growth factor having the following nucleotide sequence: GAGTGGA-GAG . . . [remainder of 1196 nucleotide sequence].

Claims 4 and 6 generically encompass all isolated/purified DNA sequences (natural and synthetic) encoding human and bovine HBGFs, despite the fact that Deuel's application does not describe the chemical structure of, or tell how to obtain, any DNA or cDNA except the two disclosed cDNA molecules. Because of the redundancy of the genetic code, claims 4 and 6 each encompass an enormous number of DNA molecules, including the isolated/purified chromosomal DNAs encoding the human and bovine proteins. Claims 5 and 7, on the other hand, are directed to the specifically disclosed cDNA molecules encoding human and bovine HBGFs, respectively.

During prosecution, the examiner rejected claims 4–7 under 35 U.S.C. § 103 as unpatentable over the combined teachings of Bohlen[3] and Maniatis.[4] The Bohlen reference discloses a group of protein growth factors designated as heparin-binding brain mitogens ("HBBMs") useful in treating burns and promoting the formation, maintenance, and repair of tissue, particularly neural tissue. Bohlen isolated three such HBBMs from human and bovine brain tissue. These proteins have respective molecular weights of 15 kD, 16 kD, and 18 kD. Bohlen determined the first 19 amino acids of the proteins' N-terminal sequences, which were found to be identical for human and bovine HBBMs.[5] Bohlen teaches that HBBMs are brain-specific, and suggests that the proteins may be homologous between species. The reference provides no teachings concerning DNA or cDNA coding for HBBMs.

Maniatis describes a method of isolating DNAs or cDNAs by screening a DNA or cDNA library with a gene probe. The reference outlines a general technique for cloning a gene; it does not describe how to isolate a particular

3. European Patent Application No. 0326075, naming Peter Bohlen as inventor, published August 2, 1989.

4. Maniatis et al., Molecular Cloning: A Laboratory Manual, "Screening Bacteriophage [lambda] Libraries for Specific DNA Sequences by Recombination in Escherichia coli," Cold Spring Harbor Laboratory, New York, 1982, pp. 353–361.

5. Bohlen's disclosed N-terminal sequence for human and bovine HBBMs is Gly-Lys-Lys-Glu-Lys-Pro-Glu-Lys-Lys-Val-Lys-Lys-Ser-Asp-Cys-Gly-Glu-Trp-Gln. This sequence matches the first 19 amino acids of Deuel's disclosed N-terminal sequence.

DNA or cDNA molecule. Maniatis does not discuss certain steps necessary to isolate a target cDNA, e.g., selecting a tissue-specific cDNA library containing a target cDNA and designing an oligonucleotide probe that will hybridize with the target cDNA.

The examiner asserted that, given Bohlen's disclosure of a heparin-binding protein and its N-terminal sequence and Maniatis's gene cloning method, it would have been prima facie obvious to one of ordinary skill in the art at the time of the invention to clone a gene for HBGF.[6] According to the examiner, Bohlen's published N-terminal sequence would have motivated a person of ordinary skill in the art to clone such a gene because cloning the gene would allow recombinant production of HBGF, a useful protein. The examiner reasoned that a person of ordinary skill in the art could have designed a gene probe based on Bohlen's disclosed N-terminal sequence, then screened a DNA library in accordance with Maniatis's gene cloning method to isolate a gene encoding an HBGF. The examiner did not distinguish between claims 4 and 6 generically directed to all DNA sequences encoding human and bovine HBGFs and claims 5 and 7 reciting particular cDNAs.

In reply, Deuel argued, inter alia, that Bohlen teaches away from the claimed cDNA molecules because Bohlen suggests that HBBMs are brain-specific and, thus, a person of ordinary skill in the art would not have tried to isolate corresponding cDNA clones from human placental and bovine uterine cDNA libraries. The examiner made the rejection final, however, asserting that [t]he starting materials are not relevant in this case, because it was well known in the art at the time the invention was made that proteins, especially the general class of heparin binding proteins, are highly homologous between species and tissue type. It would have been entirely obvious to attempt to isolate a known protein from different tissue types and even different species. No prior art was cited to support the proposition that it would have been obvious to screen human placental and bovine uterine cDNA libraries for the claimed cDNA clones. Presumably, the examiner was relying on Bohlen's suggestion that HBBMs may be homologous between species, although the examiner did not explain how homology between species suggests homology between tissue types.

The Board affirmed the examiner's final rejection. In its opening remarks, the Board noted that it is "constantly advised by the patent examiners, who are highly skilled in this art, that cloning procedures are routine in the art." According to the Board, "the examiners urge that when the sequence of a protein is placed into the public domain, the gene is also placed into the public domain because of the routine nature of cloning techniques." Addressing the rejection at issue, the Board determined that Bohlen's disclosure of the existence and isolation of HBBM, a functional protein, would also advise a person of ordinary skill in the art that a gene exists encoding

---

6. The examiner and the Board apparently used the term "gene" to refer both to natural (chromosomal) DNA and synthetic cDNA. We will use the several terms as appropriate.

HBBM. The Board found that a person of ordinary skill in the art would have been motivated to isolate such a gene because the protein has useful mitogenic properties, and isolating the gene for HBBM would permit large quantities of the protein to be produced for study and possible commercial use. Like the examiner, the Board asserted, without explanation, that HBBMs are the same as HBGFs and that the genes encoding these proteins are identical. The Board concluded that "the Bohlen reference would have suggested to those of ordinary skill in this art that they should make the gene, and the Maniatis reference would have taught a technique for 'making' the gene with a reasonable expectation of success." Responding to Deuel's argument that the claimed cDNA clones were isolated from human placental and bovine uterine cDNA libraries, whereas the combined teachings of Bohlen and Maniatis would only have suggested screening a brain tissue cDNA library, the Board stated that "the claims before us are directed to the product and not the method of isolation. Appellants have not shown that the claimed DNA was not present in and could not have been readily isolated from the brain tissue utilized by Bohlen." Deuel now appeals.[7]

DISCUSSION

Obviousness is a question of law, which we review de novo, though factual findings underlying the Board's obviousness determination are reviewed for clear error. * * *. The examiner bears the burden of establishing a prima facie case of obviousness. * * *. Only if this burden is met does the burden of coming forward with rebuttal argument or evidence shift to the applicant. * * *. When the references cited by the examiner fail to establish a prima facie case of obviousness, the rejection is improper and will be overturned. * * *.

On appeal, Deuel challenges the Board's determination that the applied references establish a prima facie case of obviousness. In response, the PTO maintains that the claimed invention would have been prima facie obvious over the combined teachings of Bohlen and Maniatis. Thus, the appeal raises the important question whether the combination of a prior art reference teaching a method of gene cloning, together with a reference disclosing a partial amino acid sequence of a protein, may render DNA and cDNA molecules encoding the protein prima facie obvious under § 103.

Deuel argues that the PTO failed to follow the proper legal standard in determining that the claimed cDNA molecules would have been prima facie obvious despite the lack of structurally similar compounds in the prior art. Deuel argues that the PTO has not cited a reference teaching cDNA molecules, but instead has improperly rejected the claims based on the alleged obviousness of a method of making the molecules. We agree.

---

7. Deuel is supported in its appeal by an amicus curiae brief submitted by the Biotechnology Industry Organization and the Bay Area Science Center. Amici urge that, contrary to controlling precedent, the PTO has unlawfully adopted a per se rule that a gene is prima facie obvious when at least part of the amino acid sequence of the protein encoded by the gene is known in the prior art.

Because Deuel claims new chemical entities in structural terms, a prima facie case of unpatentability requires that the teachings of the prior art suggest the claimed compounds to a person of ordinary skill in the art. Normally a prima facie case of obviousness is based upon structural similarity, i.e., an established structural relationship between a prior art compound and the claimed compound. Structural relationships may provide the requisite motivation or suggestion to modify known compounds to obtain new compounds. For example, a prior art compound may suggest its homologs because homologs often have similar properties and therefore chemists of ordinary skill would ordinarily contemplate making them to try to obtain compounds with improved properties. Similarly, a known compound may suggest its analogs or isomers, either geometric isomers (cis v. trans) or position isomers (e.g., ortho v. para).

In all of these cases, however, the prior art teaches a specific, structurally-definable compound and the question becomes whether the prior art would have suggested making the specific molecular modifications necessary to achieve the claimed invention. See In re Jones, 958 F.2d 347, 351 (Fed. Cir. 1992); In re Dillon, 919 F.2d 688, 692 (Fed. Cir. 1990) (en banc) ("structural similarity between claimed and prior art subject matter, . . . where the prior art gives reason or motivation to make the claimed compositions, creates a prima facie case of obviousness"), cert. denied, 500 U.S. 904 (1991); In re Grabiak, 769 F.2d 729, 731–32 (Fed. Cir. 1985) ("[I]n the case before us there must be adequate support in the prior art for the [prior art] ester/[claimed] thioester change in structure, in order to complete the PTO's prima facie case and shift the burden of going forward to the applicant."); In re Lalu, 747 F.2d 703, 705 (Fed. Cir. 1984) ("The prior art must provide one of ordinary skill in the art the motivation to make the proposed molecular modifications needed to arrive at the claimed compound.").

Here, the prior art does not disclose any relevant cDNA molecules, let alone close relatives of the specific, structurally-defined cDNA molecules of claims 5 and 7 that might render them obvious. Maniatis suggests an allegedly obvious process for trying to isolate cDNA molecules, but that, as we will indicate below, does not fill the gap regarding the subject matter of claims 5 and 7. Further, while the general idea of the claimed molecules, their function, and their general chemical nature may have been obvious from Bohlen's teachings, and the knowledge that some gene existed may have been clear, the precise cDNA molecules of claims 5 and 7 would not have been obvious over the Bohlen reference because Bohlen teaches proteins, not the claimed or closely related cDNA molecules. The redundancy of the genetic code precluded contemplation of or focus on the specific cDNA molecules of claims 5 and 7. Thus, one could not have conceived the subject matter of claims 5 and 7 based on the teachings in the cited prior art because, until the claimed molecules were actually isolated and purified, it would have been highly unlikely for one of ordinary skill in the art to contemplate what was ultimately obtained. What cannot be contemplated or conceived cannot be obvious.

The PTO's theory that one might have been motivated to try to do what Deuel in fact accomplished amounts to speculation and an impermissible hindsight reconstruction of the claimed invention. It also ignores the fact that claims 5 and 7 are limited to specific compounds, and any motivation that existed was a general one, to try to obtain a gene that was yet undefined and may have constituted many forms. A general motivation to search for some gene that exists does not necessarily make obvious a specifically-defined gene that is subsequently obtained as a result of that search. More is needed and it is not found here.

The genetic code relationship between proteins and nucleic acids does not overcome the deficiencies of the cited references. A prior art disclosure of the amino acid sequence of a protein does not necessarily render particular DNA molecules encoding the protein obvious because the redundancy of the genetic code permits one to hypothesize an enormous number of DNA sequences coding for the protein. No particular one of these DNAs can be obvious unless there is something in the prior art to lead to the particular DNA and indicate that it should be prepared. We recently held in In re Baird, 16 F.3d 380 (Fed.Cir.1994), that a broad genus does not necessarily render obvious each compound within its scope. Similarly, knowledge of a protein does not give one a conception of a particular DNA encoding it. Thus, a fortiori, Bohlen's disclosure of the N-terminal portion of a protein, which the PTO urges is the same as HBGF, would not have suggested the particular cDNA molecules defined by claims 5 and 7. This is so even though one skilled in the art knew that some DNA, albeit not in purified and isolated form, did exist. The compounds of claims 5 and 7 are specific compounds not suggested by the prior art. A different result might pertain, however, if there were prior art, e.g., a protein of sufficiently small size and simplicity, so that lacking redundancy, each possible DNA would be obvious over the protein. See In re Petering, 301 F.2d 676 (CCPA 1962) (prior art reference disclosing limited genus of 20 compounds rendered every species within the genus unpatentable). That is not the case here.

The PTO's focus on known methods for potentially isolating the claimed DNA molecules is also misplaced because the claims at issue define compounds, not methods. See In re Bell, 991 F.2d 781, 785 (Fed. Cir. 1993). In Bell, the PTO asserted a rejection based upon the combination of a primary reference disclosing a protein (and its complete amino acid sequence) with a secondary reference describing a general method of gene cloning. We reversed the rejection, holding in part that "[t]he PTO's focus on Bell's method is misplaced. Bell does not claim a method. Bell claims compositions, and the issue is the obviousness of the claimed compositions, not of the method by which they are made." Id.

We today reaffirm the principle, stated in Bell, that the existence of a general method of isolating cDNA or DNA molecules is essentially irrelevant to the question whether the specific molecules themselves would have been obvious, in the absence of other prior art that suggests the claimed DNAs. A prior art disclosure of a process reciting a particular compound or obvious variant thereof as a product of the process is, of course, another matter, raising issues of anticipation under 35 U.S.C. § 102 as well as obviousness under § 103. Moreover, where there is prior art that suggests a claimed compound, the existence, or lack thereof, of an enabling process for making that compound is surely a factor in any patentability determination. See In re Brown, 329 F.2d 1006 (CCPA 1964) (reversing rejection for lack of an enabling method of making the claimed compound). There must, however, still be prior art that suggests the claimed compound in order for a prima facie case of obviousness to be made out; as we have already indicated, that prior art was lacking here with respect to claims 5 and 7. Thus, even if, as the examiner stated, the existence of general cloning techniques, coupled with knowledge of a protein's structure, might have provided motivation to prepare a cDNA or made it obvious to prepare a cDNA, that does not necessarily make obvious a particular claimed cDNA. "Obvious to try" has long been held not to constitute obviousness. In re O'Farrell, 853 F.2d 894, 903 (Fed. Cir. 1988). A general incentive does not make obvious a particular result, nor does the existence of techniques by which those efforts can be carried out. Thus, Maniatis's teachings, even in combination with Bohlen, fail to suggest the claimed invention.

The PTO argues that a compound may be defined by its process of preparation and therefore that a conceived process for making or isolating it provides a definition for it and can render it obvious. It cites Amgen Inc. v. Chugai Pharmaceutical Co., 927 F.2d 1200 (Fed.Cir.), cert. denied, 502 U.S. 856 (1991), for that proposition. We disagree. The fact that one can conceive a general process in advance for preparing an undefined compound does not mean that a claimed specific compound was precisely envisioned and therefore obvious. A substance may indeed be defined by its process of preparation. That occurs, however, when it has already been prepared by that process and one therefore knows that the result of that process is the stated compound. The process is part of the definition of the compound. But that is not possible in advance, especially when the hypothetical process is only a general one. Thus, a conceived method of preparing some undefined DNA does not define it with the precision necessary to render it obvious over the protein it encodes. We did not state otherwise in Amgen. See Amgen, 927 F.2d at 1206–9 (isolated/purified human gene held nonobvious; no conception of gene without envisioning its precise identity despite conception of general process of preparation).

We conclude that, because the applied references do not teach or suggest the claimed cDNA molecules, the final rejection of claims 5 and 7 must be reversed. See also Bell, 991 F.2d at 784–85 (human DNA sequences encoding IGF proteins nonobvious over asserted combination of references showing gene cloning method and complete amino acid sequences of IGFs).

Claims 4 and 6 are of a different scope than claims 5 and 7. As is conceded by Deuel, they generically encompass all DNA sequences encoding human and bovine HBGFs. Written in such a result-oriented form, claims 4 and 6 are thus tantamount to the general idea of all genes encoding the protein, all solutions to the problem. Such an idea might have been obvious from the complete amino acid sequence of the protein, coupled with knowledge of the genetic code, because this information may have enabled a person of ordinary skill in the art to envision the idea of, and, perhaps with the aid of a computer, even identify all members of the claimed genus. The Bohlen reference, however, only discloses a partial amino acid sequence, and thus it appears that, based on the above analysis, the claimed genus would not have been obvious over this prior art disclosure. We will therefore also reverse the final rejection of claims 4 and 6 because neither the Board nor the patent examiner articulated any separate reasons for holding these claims unpatentable apart from the grounds discussed above.

One further matter requires comment. Because Deuel's patent application does not describe how to obtain any DNA except the disclosed cDNA molecules, claims 4 and 6 may be considered to be inadequately supported by the disclosure of the application. See generally Amgen Inc. v. Chugai Pharmaceutical Co., 927 F.2d 1200, 1212–14 (Fed. Cir.) (generic DNA sequence claims held invalid under 35 U.S.C. § 112, first paragraph), cert. denied, 502 U.S. 856 (1991); In re Fisher, 427 F.2d 833, 839 (CCPA 1970) (Section 112 "requires that the scope of the claims must bear a reasonable correlation to the scope of enablement provided by the specification to persons of ordinary skill in the art."). As this issue is not before us, however, we will not address whether claims 4 and 6 satisfy the enablement requirement of § 112, first paragraph, but will leave to the PTO the question whether any further rejection is appropriate.

* * * The Board's decision affirming the final rejection of claims 4–7 is reversed.

NOTE

Section 103(b) was added to section 103 by the Biotechnological Process Patents Act, P.L. 104–41 (1995). The act was passed in response to complaints from the biotechnology industry. One type of biotechnology innovation involves identifying the portion of human DNA that codes for a particular human protein, inserting that DNA into the gene of a bacteria, inserting that altered gene into the bacteria, and then using the modified bacteria to produce the protein. This can result in the production of the protein at lower cost and at a higher level of purity than has been possible by other methods. Insulin, for instance, important for diabetics, is now made this way. However, biotechnology companies found that the PTO was hesitant to issue a patent on the process, since it involved technology known to the biotechnolgy art, or to issue a patent on the final product, since it was the same as an already known and naturally occurring substance. This would leave the biotechnology innovator with only a patent on the host bacteria cell created by inserting the modfied gene. Such a patent would permit the patent holder to stop others from making the protein in the U.S. by this method, but it would not enable the patent holder to stop others from using the host cell in another country to produce the protein and then importing it into the United States. Section 103(b) provides that where the host cell is patentable, the process is also patentable. The patent on the process enables the patent owner to take advantage of the provisions of § 271(g) and exclude from the United States imports made with the use of the host cell.

Section 103(b) raises the question of whether it is a good idea for Congress to provide different rules of patent validity for different industries.

E. Section 102
(1) Introduction
Jamesbury Corp. v. Litton Industrial Products, Inc.

United States Court of Appeals, Federal Circuit, 1985.
756 F.2d 1556.

■ NIES, CIRCUIT JUDGE.

I.

Jamesbury Corp., the plaintiff below, charged Litton Industrial Products with infringing claims 7 and 8 of its U.S. Patent No. 2,945,666 to Freeman entitled "Ball Valve". Following a seven day jury trial, the jury returned a verdict for Litton, concluding, in answer to an interrogatory, that the asserted claims did not differ in any "significant particulars" from the prior art.[2] Under the court's instructions, this finding meant that the claims were invalid under 35 U.S.C. § 102(a) for lack of novelty. Jamesbury had timely objected to the jury charge on the issue of novelty and to the wording of the particular interrogatory under review, as well as to other instructions. No instructions were given with respect to obviousness of the claimed inventions, Litton having agreed that obviousness was not asserted as a ground for holding the claims invalid. Following entry of judgment, Jamesbury filed a motion under Fed.R.Civ.P. 50(b) for judgment notwithstanding the verdict, which was denied by the district court. In ruling on the motion, the district court stated:

> The jury returned a verdict for the defendant in this patent infringement suit. The plaintiff has moved for judgment notwithstanding the verdict. The plaintiff is seeking judgment on all disputed issues: the validity of the patent, infringement of the patent, the amount of damages, and the defenses of laches and estoppel.
>
> In its response to a special interrogatory, the jury made explicit its finding that the patent was invalid because of lack of novelty over the prior art. Thus the crucial issue to be resolved is whether the jury's finding of invalidity should be set aside. * * *

---

2. Jury interrogatory No. 1 reads as follows:

1. Does the ball valve construction shown and described in the Saunders British patent or any other prior art differ in any significant particulars from the ball valve defined by the express language of claims 7 and 8 of the Freeman patent? As to claim 7 Yes __ No X As to claim 8 Yes __ No X If you answer "No" as to both claim 7 and claim 8, do not answer any further questions. * * *

* * * The plaintiff alleges that the defendant has produced no evidence regarding the level of ordinary skill in the ball valve art. Although such proof is essential to support a finding of invalidity because of obviousness, see Environmental Designs v. Union Oil Co., 713 F.2d 693, 695 (Fed. Cir. 1983), the plaintiff has cited no authority requiring such proof to support a finding of invalidity because of lack of novelty over the prior art. On the issue of novelty, there was ample evidence to support the jury's verdict; there was certainly not an overwhelming amount of evidence in the plaintiff's favor that reasonable and fair minded men could not arrive at a verdict against it.

For the foregoing reasons, the motion for judgment n.o.v. is denied.

In this appeal, Jamesbury argues that because of erroneous and prejudicial error in the instructions to the jury, it is entitled at least to a new trial. Jamesbury further asserts that because lack of novelty was not established and other grounds asserted for holding the claims invalid, namely, obviousness and inequitable conduct, were withdrawn or waived, the court erred in its ruling on Jamesbury's motion JNOV. We agree and, therefore, reverse the holding of invalidity of claims 7 and 8. The case is remanded for resolution of other issues.

II.

* * *

A.

Jamesbury first attacks the following instruction which laid the foundation for the jury's deliberations:

[T]he public is a silent but nevertheless an important, an interested party in all patent litigation and it is entitled to protection against the monopolization of what is not lawfully patentable. In other words, it's not simply between Jamesbury and Litton. Other people are affected by it.

So I charge you that it is your duty to *subject the invention* defined in claims seven and eight of the Freeman patent *to careful scrutiny before endorsing Jamesbury's right to the patent monopoly* defined by such claims. [Emphasis added.]

Jamesbury argues that the effect of this instruction was to create a presumption of invalidity requiring Jamesbury to prove, beyond careful scrutiny, that it was entitled to maintain a monopoly, which, impliedly, was against the public interest. We agree that this instruction is legally erroneous and prejudicial.

The language that the jury must give "careful scrutiny" before "endorsing" the "patent monopoly" cannot be approved. While the language does not rise to the level of a presumption of invalidity, it does incorrectly suggest that the jury must affirmatively find the patent valid, which is never appropriate. * * *

Further, this court has disapproved of a challenger's characterization of a patentee by the term "monopolist", which is commonly regarded as pejorative. Union Carbide Corp. v. American Can Co., 724 F.2d 1567, 1574 n. 4 (Fed. Cir. 1984); Schenck v. Nortron Corp., 713 F.2d 782, 784 (Fed. Cir. 1983). In both of the cited cases, a bench trial was involved. Here, not only was Litton's counsel not admonished for so characterizing Jamesbury before the jury, a more serious impropriety than in a bench trial, but also the characterization found its way into the instructions. As stated in Connell v. Sears, Roebuck & Co., 722 F.2d 1542, 1548 (Fed. Cir. 1983), the characterization of a patent as a "monopoly" is misdirected:

> The phrase "patent monopoly" appears at various points. Under the statute, 35 U.S.C. § 261, a patent is a form of property right, and the right to exclude recognized in a patent is but the essence of the concept of property. Schenck v. Nortron Corp., 713 F.2d 782 (Fed. Cir. 1983).

Instructions which supplement the statutory body of law governing patent validity by interjecting language to the effect that the public must be "protected" against a "monopoly," a term found nowhere in the statute, are likely to be prejudicial and should be avoided.

B.

* * *

[The court held that the instructions on the burden of proof were in error.]

C.

Jamesbury's objections (also made to the district court) that the instructions and interrogatory No. 1, reproduced at note 2, supra, misstate the law respecting novelty were legitimate. The instruction * * * to the effect that the claims are invalid if the prior art Saunders patent discloses "substantially the same things" as claims 7 and 8, and Interrogatory No. 1 which speaks of the claims not differing in "significant particulars", are not legally correct.

The error in this interpretation of the statutory requirement of novelty is the same as that which was addressed in Connell, 722 F.2d at 1548:

> The opinion says anticipation may be shown by less than "complete anticipation" if one of ordinary skill may in reliance on the prior art "complete the work required for the invention", and that "it is sufficient for an anticipation 'if the general aspects are the same and the differences in minor matters is only such as would suggest itself to one of ordinary skill in the art.'" Those statements relate to obviousness, not anticipation. Anticipation requires the presence in a single prior art disclosure of all elements of a claimed invention arranged as in the claim. Soundscriber Corp. v. U.S., 360 F.2d 954, 960 (Ct. Claims 1966).

A prior art disclosure that "almost" meets that standard may render the claim invalid under § 103; it does not "anticipate."

Here, as well, anticipation is not shown by a prior art disclosure which is only "substantially the same" as the claimed invention.

Litton argues that elsewhere the district court amplified its interpretation by speaking of the prior art disclosing the claimed invention "in complete terms." However, that additional paragraph of instructions also speaks of "*substantially* the same subject matter * * * *in complete terms, thus enabling* a man skilled in the art to understand and practice the invention." We see no correction of the legal standard in the above statement.

III.

Because of the above legal errors, the verdict of invalidity for lack of novelty (i.e., anticipation) cannot stand.

* * *

IV.

Because the issues of infringement, laches and estoppel were not resolved at the conclusion of the trial, the case must be remanded for their disposition. * * *

* * *

CONCLUSION

For the foregoing reasons, the judgment is reversed and the case is remanded for disposition of all remaining issues other than the validity of claims 7 and 8 of Freeman Patent No. 2,945,666.

Reversed and remanded.

NOTES

1. The sharp distinction made by the Federal Circuit between anticipation under § 102 and obviousness under § 103 is consistent with the first sentence of § 103, which begins: "A patent may not be obtained though the invention is not *identically disclosed or described* as set forth in § 102 of this title * * *." Nevertheless, there was authority to the contrary in the other circuits. See, for instance, the opinion of Mr. Justice Stevens, then a circuit judge, in Frantz Manufacturing Co. v. Phenix Manufacturing Co., 457 F.2d 314 (7th Cir. 1972).

2. Although there is an important difference between anticipation under § 102 and obviousness under § 103, § 102 plays an important role in § 103 because § 102 has been held to inform the meaning of "prior art." The relationship between § 102 and § 103 is an issue that will recur in subsequent cases.

(2) "Known or Used"

Section 102(a) of Title 35 provides that "a person shall be entitled to a patent unless the invention was known or used by others in this country, or patented or described in a printed publication in this or a foreign country, before the invention thereof by the applicant for patent." It is less than satisfactory. If knowledge alone is sufficient to anticipate the invention, why does the statute proceed to enumerate use, a patent and a publication as things which also anticipate? Surely, knowledge encompasses and necessarily precedes use, a patent or a publication. Although the Supreme Court has not to this day resolved the matter, the answer of the best authorities—Judge Learned Hand again, as you might have guessed by now—is that "known" in § 102 means known in a manner accessible to the public. But the importation of "public" into § 102(a) is at odds with the explicit use of the term in § 102(b). But that is not only to simplify, but to jump ahead of the story. The extant Supreme Court precedent—most of it nineteenth century—does not provide a complete answer.

Gayler v. Wilder

Supreme Court of the United States, 1850.
51 U.S. (10 How.) 477, 13 L.Ed. 504.

■ MR. CHIEF JUSTICE TANEY delivered the opinion of the court.

* * *

The remaining question is upon the validity of the patent on which the suit was brought. [The patent was issued to one Fitzgerald for the invention of a fire-proof safe. The safe was made by constructing an inner and an outer safe of iron and then filling the space in between with plaster of paris. The circuit court (a trial court) held the patent valid.]

It appears that James Conner, who carried on the business of a stereotype founder in the city of New York, made a safe for his own use between the years 1829 and 1832, for the protection of his papers against fire; and continued to use it until 1838, when it passed into other hands. It was kept in his counting-room and known to the persons engaged in the foundry; and after it passed out of his hands, he used others of a different construction.

It does not appear what became of this safe afterwards. And there is nothing in the testimony from which it can be inferred that its mode of construction was known to the person into whose possession it fell, or that any value was attached to it as a place of security for papers against fire; or that it was ever used for that purpose.

Upon these facts the court instructed the jury, "that if Conner had not made his discovery public, but had used it simply for his own private purpose, and it had been finally forgotten or abandoned, such a discovery and use would be no obstacle to the taking out of a patent by Fitzgerald or those claiming under him, if he be an original, though not the first, inventor or discoverer."

The instruction assumes that the jury might find from the evidence that Conner's safe was substantially the same with that of Fitzgerald, and also prior in time. And if the fact was so, the question then was whether the patentee was "the original and first inventor or discoverer," within the meaning of the act of Congress.

* * *

[Where an inventor takes out an American patent on an invention which has been known or used in a foreign country] * * * the party who invents is not strictly speaking the first and original inventor. The law assumes that the improvement may have been known and used before his discovery. Yet his patent is valid if he discovered it by the efforts of his own genius, and believed himself to be the original inventor. * * * If the foreign invention had been printed or patented, it was already given to the world and open to the people of this country, as well as of others, upon reasonable inquiry. They would therefore derive no advantage from the invention here. It would confer no benefit upon the community, and the inventor therefore is not considered to be entitled to the reward. But if the foreign discovery is not patented, nor described in any printed publication, it might be known and used in remote places for ages, and the people of this country be unable to profit by it. The means of obtaining knowledge would not be within their reach; and, as far as their interest is concerned, it would be the same thing as if the improvement had never been discovered. It is the inventor here that brings it to them, and places it in their possession. And as he does this by the effort of his own genius, the law regards him as the first and original inventor, and protects his patent, although the improvement had in fact been invented before, and used by others.

So, too, as to the lost arts. It is well known that centuries ago discoveries were made in certain arts the fruits of which have come down to us, but the means by which the work was accomplished are at this day unknown. The knowledge has been lost for ages. Yet it would hardly be doubted, if any one now discovered an art thus lost, and it was a useful improvement, that, upon a fair construction of the act of Congress, he would be entitled to a patent. Yet he would not literally be the first and original inventor. But he would be the first to confer on the public the benefit of the invention. He would discover what is unknown, and communicate knowledge which the public had not the means of obtaining without his invention.

Upon the same principle and upon the same rule of construction, we think that Fitzgerald must be regarded as the first and original inventor of the safe in question. * * *

We do not understand the Circuit Court to have said that the omission of Conner to try the value of his safe by proper tests would deprive it of its priority; nor his omission to bring it into public use. He might have omitted both, and also abandoned its use, and been ignorant of the extent of its value; yet, if it was the same with Fitzgerald's, the latter would not upon such grounds be entitled to a patent, provided Conner's safe and its mode of construction were still in the memory of Conner before they were recalled by Fitzgerald's patent.

* * *

Upon the whole, therefore, we think there is no error in the opinion of the Circuit Court, and the judgment is therefore affirmed.

NOTES

1. The discussion in *Gayler* about non-U.S. inventions is outdated (after 1994), in light of the GATT TRIPS and the changes made to § 104, as to inventions made in WIPO member countries.

2. In Coffin v. Ogden, 85 U.S. (18 Wall.) 120 (1874), the court held a patent invalid due to prior construction of the invention by another. In dictum, the Court cast doubt upon the statement in *Gayler* that Conner need not have tried his safe:

> The case arose while the Patent Act of 1836 was in force, and must be decided under its provision. The sixth section of that act requires that to entitle the applicant to a patent, his invention or discovery must be one "not known or used by others before his invention or discovery thereof." The fifteenth section allowed a party sued for infringement to prove, among other defences, that the patentee "was not the original and first inventor of the thing patented, or of a substantial and material part thereof claimed to be new."
>
> The whole act is to be taken together and construed in the light of the context. The meaning of these sections must be sought in the import of their language, and in the object and policy of the legislature in enacting them. The invention or discovery relied upon as a defence, must have been complete, and capable of producing the result sought to be accomplished; and this must be shown by the defendant. The burden of proof rests upon him, and every reasonable doubt should be resolved against him. If the thing were embryotic or inchoate; if it rested in speculation or experiment; if the process pursued for its development had failed to reach the point of consummation, it cannot avail to defeat a patent founded upon a discovery or invention which was completed, while in the other case there was only progress, however near that progress may have approximated to the end in view. The law requires not conjecture, but certainty. If the question relate to a machine, the conception must have been clothed in substantial forms which demonstrate at once its practical efficacy and utility. The prior knowledge and use by a single person is sufficient. The number is immaterial. Until his work is done, the inventor has given nothing to the public. In Gayler v. Wilder the views of this court upon the subject were thus expressed: "We do not understand the Circuit Court to have said that the omission of Conner to try his safe by the proper tests would deprive it of its priority; nor his omission to bring it into public use. He might have omitted both, and also abandoned its use

and been ignorant of the extent of its value; yet if it was the same with Fitzgerald's, the latter would not, upon such grounds, be entitled to a patent; provided Conner's safe and its mode of construction were still in the memory of Conner before they were recalled by Fitzgerald's patent." Whether the proposition expressed by the proviso in the last sentence is a sound one, it is not necessary in this case to consider.

Id. at 124–25.

The law relating to reduction to practice, infra, is involved here. In summary, an invention is not reduced to practice, i.e. made, until it is proven operable. The relevance of this law arises from the argument that an invention cannot be known unless it has been made, that is, reduced to practice, since something that does not exist cannot be known. *Gayler* seemed to reject this argument, *Coffin* to accept it.

2. Judge Hand's statement was this: "To be patentable, an invention cannot have been 'known or used by others' in this country before the inventor 'invented or discovered' it. * * * Knowledge in this sense is to be distinguished from a public use or sale by the inventor himself for more than a year before he files his application, which is ipso facto an abandonment. * * * It is also true that another's experiment, imperfect and never perfected, will not serve either as an anticipation or as part of the prior art, for it has not served to enrich it. The patented invention does not become 'known' by such a use or sale, or by anything of which the art cannot take hold and make use as it stands. But the mere fact that an earlier 'machine' or 'manufacturer', sold or used, was an experiment does not prevent its becoming an anticipation or a part of the prior art, provided it was perfected and thereafter became publicly known. Whether it does become so depends upon how far it becomes a part of the stock of knowledge of the art in question." Picard v. United Aircraft Corp., 128 F.2d 632, 635 (2d Cir. 1942). As Supreme Court authority for this statement, Hand cited *Coffin* and one other nineteenth century case, both holding that a prior invention had been sufficiently developed to anticipate.

3. The most useful authorities on anticipating knowledge are those cases dealing with anticipating public uses, infra, because if a decision holds that a use did not anticipate, then it by implication holds that knowledge of that use did not anticipate.

Application of Borst

United States Court of Customs and Patent Appeals, 1965.
345 F.2d 851, certiorari denied 382 U.S. 973,
86 S.Ct. 537, 15 L.Ed.2d 465.

■ SMITH, JUDGE.

The invention for which appellant seeks a patent comprises means for safely and effectively controlling a relatively large neutron output by varying a small and easily controlled neutron input source. The application, serial No.

654,837, filed April 24, 1957, is aptly titled "Neutron Amplifier." Claim 27 is illustrative of appealed claims 27–33 and reads:

"27. A subcritical neutron amplifier having a controllable neutron source and, associated with said source in cascade, an input region of neutron moderator material in which neutrons of epithermal energy from the source are moderated to thermal energy levels, a sequent fuel region containing neutron fissionable material in mass concentration and geometric configuration adapted to augment the neutron flow by a subcritical reaction, and an output region comprising a thermal neutron barrier substantially opaque to thermal neutrons but transmissive to epithermal neutrons, whereby an amplified neutron output is subcritically produced." * * *

Appellant asserts that the claimed invention affords a revolutionary approach to the safety problem in the nuclear reactor art. As the amplifier is said to be inherently safe from divergent nuclear chain reaction, the intricate systems needed to monitor and control the operation of conventional neutron amplifiers to prevent an explosion are unnecessary.

The single reference relied upon by the Patent Office in rejecting the appealed claims is an Atomic Energy Commission document entitled "KAPL-M-RWS-1, A Stable Fission Pile with High Speed Control." The document is in the form of an unpublished memorandum authored by one Samsel, and will hereinafter be referred to as "Samsel." Samsel is dated February 14, 1947 and was classified as a secret document by the Commission until March 9, 1957, when it was declassified. In essence, Samsel sets forth and discusses the problems present in the control of a nuclear reactor, the concept of use of successive fuel stages to effect such control, and a description of the arrangement, composition and relative proportions of materials required to obtain the sought-for results. Samsel is prefaced by a statement that it was made to record an idea, and it nowhere indicates that the idea had been tested in an operating reactor.

The Patent Office does not invoke Samsel as a publication (which it apparently was not, at any pertinent date). Rather, the contention is that Samsel constitutes evidence of prior knowledge within the meaning of 35 U.S.C. § 102(a). * * *

In the case of In re Schlittler, 234 F.2d 882, this court was presented with the following situation: A manuscript containing an anticipatory disclosure of the appellants' claimed invention had been submitted to The Journal of the American Chemical Society and was later published. The date to which the appellants' application was entitled for purposes of constructive reduction to practice was earlier than the publication date of the Journal article, and therefore the Patent Office did not contend that the "printed publication" portion of section 102(a) was applicable. However, the manuscript bore a notation that it had been received by the publisher on a date prior to the effective filing date of the appellants' application. On the basis of this notation the Patent Office argued that the article constituted sufficient evidence of prior knowledge under section 102(a).

After an exhaustive review of the authorities, and of the legislative history of the Patent Act of 1952, this court rejected the contention of the Patent Office, and concluded that such a document was not proper evidence of prior knowledge. In reversing, the court stated (234 F.2d at 886):

> "In our opinion, one of the essential elements of the word 'known' as used in 35 U.S.C. § 102(a) is knowledge of an invention which has been completed by reduction to practice, actual or constructive, and is not satisfied by disclosure of a conception only."

And therefore, since the Journal article, "at best, could be evidence of nothing more than conception and disclosure of the invention," the

> " * * * placing of the Nystrom article in the hands of the publishers did not constitute either prima facie or conclusive evidence of knowledge or use by others in this country of the invention disclosed by the article, within the meaning of Title 35, § 102(a) of the United States Code, since the knowledge was of a conception only and not of a reduction to practice."

Another aspect of the court's discussion in Schlittler involved the well-established principle that "prior knowledge of a patented invention would not invalidate a claim of the patent unless such knowledge was available to the public." After reaffirming that principle, the court went on to state:

> "Obviously, in view of the above authorities, the mere placing of a manuscript in the hands of a publisher does not necessarily make it available to the public within the meaning of said authorities."

However, the court did not go on to determine whether the Journal article was in fact available to the public, since such determination was deemed unnecessary for disposition of the case, under the court's theory.

We shall consider first the public availability aspect of the Schlittler case. Although that portion of the Schlittler opinion is clearly dictum, we think it just as clearly represents the settled law. The knowledge contemplated by section 102(a) must be accessible to the public. * * *

In the instant case, Samsel was clearly not publicly available during the period it was under secrecy classification by the Atomic Energy Commission. We note that the date of declassification, however, was prior to appellant's filing date, and it is perhaps arguable that Samsel became accessible to the public upon declassification. But we do not find it necessary to decide that difficult question, for there is a statutory provision which is, we think, dispositive of the question of publicity. Section 155 of the Atomic Energy Act of 1954 (42 U.S.C. § 2185) provides:

> "In connection with applications for patents covered by this subchapter, the fact that the invention or discovery was known or used before shall be a bar to the patenting of such invention or discovery even though such prior knowledge or use was under secrecy within the atomic energy program of the United States."

We think the meaning and intent of this provision is so clear as to admit of no dispute: With respect to subject matter covered by the patent provisions of the Atomic Energy Act, prior knowledge or use under section 102(a) *need not* be accessible to the public. Therefore, Samsel is available as evidence of prior knowledge insofar as the requirement for publicity is concerned.

The remaining consideration regarding the status of Samsel as evidence of prior knowledge directly calls into question the correctness of the unequivocal holding in Schlittler that the knowledge must be of a reduction to practice, either actual or constructive. After much deliberation, we have concluded that such a requirement is illogical and anomalous, and to the extent Schlittler is inconsistent with the decision in this case, it is hereby expressly overruled.

The mere fact that a disclosure is contained in a patent or application and thus "constructively" reduced to practice, or that it is found in a printed publication, does not make the disclosure itself any more meaningful to those skilled in the art (and thus, ultimately, to the public). Rather, the criterion should be whether the disclosure is *sufficient to enable one skilled in the art to reduce the disclosed invention to practice.* In other words, the disclosure must be such as will give possession of the invention to the person of ordinary skill. Even the act of publication or the fiction of constructive reduction to practice will not suffice if the disclosure does not meet this standard. * * *

Where, as is true of Samsel, the disclosure constituting evidence of prior knowledge contains, in the words of the Board of Appeals, "a description of the invention fully commensurate with the present patent application," we hold that the disclosure need not be of an invention reduced to practice, either actually or constructively. We therefore affirm the rejection of claim 27.

* * *

NOTES

1. Your understanding of *Gayler, Borst* and subsequent cases will be facilitated if you ascertain the position of the court and answer to your own satisfaction each of the following five *separate* questions:

a. Was the patentee an original inventor? §§ 102(f), 115, 116.

b. Was the patentee the first inventor? §§ 102(a), 102(g), 104.

c. Even though the patentee was not the first inventor, did he acquire the rights of a first inventor due to acts of the true first inventor constituting abandonment? § 102(g).

d. Was the patent blocked by a time bar? § 102(b).

e. Was the invention obvious to one skilled in the art? § 103.

2. *Borst* is discussed in the Note, Novelty and Reduction to Practice: Patent Confusion, 75 Yale L. J. 1194 (1966). See also William C. Roch, Prior Knowledge Compared with Prior Invention as a Statutory Bar, 50 J. Pat. [& Trademark] Off. Soc'y 409 (1968).

3. The "unknown" anticipation. In Tilghman v. Proctor, 102 U.S. 707 (1880), supra, one of the arguments made against the patent was that it was anticipated by the occurrence of the same process in the course of the operation of Perkins' steam cylinder, Daneill's water barometer and Walther's process for purifying fats and oils preparatory to soapmaking. The Court conceded that in the course of these processes saponification did indeed occur, but dismissed them as anticipation. "If the acids were accidentally and unwittingly produced, whilst the operators were in pursuit of other and different results, without exciting attention and without its even being known what was done or how it had been done, it would be absurd to say that this was an anticipation of Tilghman's discovery." Id. at 711–712. To the same effect, see Davey Tree Expert Co. v. Easton, 283 Fed. 840 (S.D.N.Y. 1920). The limit of the principle is suggested by Vitamin Technologists, Inc. v. Wisconsin Alumni Research Foundation, 146 F.2d 941 (9th Cir. 1944). Patent on a process for producing vitamin D by exposing organic substances of dietary value to ultraviolet rays. The Court held those claims which encompassed irradiation by sunlight but not those claims limited to artificial sources of ultraviolet light invalid because of anticipation by "immemorial" agricultural processes:

> It is an undisputed fact that man in all historic time has used the process of cutting hays, whereby, by oozing from the cuts, is extracted their pro-vitamin containing sap, which is exposed to sun irradiation, and copra, thus so exposing the pro-vitamin-containing coconut oil so extracted from the meat of that fruit. Thereby the sun's ultra violet rays have created vitamin D in such "carbohydrates," "organic substances of dietary value," covered by claim 1 of the first patent. Such hays fed to animals and copra, the food of both man and animals, aids or cures rachitic conditions in both classes of mammals. We refuse to entertain the absurd proposition that because the farmer and copra grower did not know the photo chemical process involved in their immemorial practice, they may be enjoined as infringers.

> Assuming that Dr. Steenbock discovered, as he claims, that the sun's rays coming from millions of miles away could irradiate foods with vitamin D and that this was the reason, unknown to them, why farmers and coconut growers regarded their sun-cured hays and sun-dried copra were good foods, such a discovery does not entitle him to a patent on their processes.

> This court has held that it is a well established principle that if a process is disclosed in a prior art, a patent whose validity is attacked is anticipated even though the prior patent failed to state and the inventor did not know that his invention brought the process into operation. In Celite Corp. v. Dicalite Co., 9 Cir., 96 F.2d 242, 248, we stated:

>> ' * * * In answer to appellant's contention that the purpose of the North process was simply to remove organic matter and bleach the product, it is sufficient to state that, as the patented process in suit was disclosed by the North patent, it was anticipated by that process even though it be assumed that the North did not know, of the increased flow rate of the product produced. * * * '

* * * Under the cases, this discovery of the reason of a prior used process is not a patentable invention.

146 F.2d 948–49.

PROBLEMS

1. Suppose that vitamin B_{12}, the patent involved in Merck & Co. v. Olin Mathieson Chemical Corp., 253 F.2d 156 (4th Cir. 1958), supra, had always existed in a pure form in the livers of cats. Would the patent have then been invalid? Assume (1) that the existence of a substance in the liver of cats useful for treating pernicious anemia was known, or (2) that the existence of a substance with no known utility, only later found to be vitamin B_{12}, was known, or (3) that no one knew what was in cat liver. Is Acme Flexible Clasp Co. v. Cary Mfg. Co., 96 Fed. 344 (S.D.N.Y. 1899) relevant? Is it right? *Acme* held that staples used to construct a shipping box imported from China did not anticipate a patent on the same staple because they were covered by wrapping and therefore unknown to Americans.

2. The chemical maleic hydrazide (MH) was discovered in 1894. In 1947 employees of Uniroyal, Inc. discovered that when mixed with a wetting agent MH could inhibit the growth of certain plants without otherwise harming them. The discovery of this property was non-obvious. Mixing a chemical with a wetting agent is a standard procedure. Is a claim for MH mixed with a wetting agent valid? See Ansul Co. v. Uniroyal, Inc., 448 F.2d 872 (2d Cir. 1971).

Egbert v. Lippmann

Supreme Court of the United States, 1881.
104 U.S. (14 Otto) 333, 26 L.Ed. 755.

■ MR. JUSTICE WOODS delivered the opinion of the court.

This suit was brought for an alleged infringement of the complainant's reissued letters-patent, No. 5216, dated Jan. 7, 1873, for an improvement in corset-springs. * * *

We have * * * to consider whether the defence that the patented invention had, with the consent of the inventor, been publicly used for more than two years prior to his application for the original letters, is sustained by the testimony in the record.

The sixth, seventh, and fifteenth sections of the act of July 4, 1836, c. 357 (5 Stat. 117), as qualified by the seventh section of the act of March 3, 1839, c. 88 (id. 353), were in force at the date of his application. Their effect is to render letters-patent invalid if the invention which they cover was in public use, with the consent and allowance of the inventor, for more than two years prior to his application. Since the passage of the act of 1839 it has been strenuously contended that the public use of an invention for more than two years before such application, even without his consent and allowance, renders the letters-patent therefor void.

It is unnecessary in this case to decide this question, for the alleged use of the invention covered by the letters-patent to Barnes is conceded to have been with his express consent.

The evidence on which the defendants rely to establish a prior public use of the invention consists mainly of the testimony of the complainant.

She testifies that Barnes invented the improvement covered by his patent between January and May, 1855; that between the dates named the witness and her friend Miss Cugier were complaining of the breaking of their corset-steels. Barnes, who was present, and was an intimate friend of the witness, said he thought he could make her a pair that would not break. At their next interview he presented her with a pair of corset-steels which he himself had made. The witness wore these steels a long time. In 1858 Barnes made and presented to her another pair, which she also wore a long time. When the corsets in which these steels were used wore out, the witness ripped them open and took out the steels and put them in new corsets. This was done several times.

It is admitted, and, in fact, is asserted, by complainant, that these steels embodied the invention afterwards patented by Barnes and covered by the reissued letters-patent on which this suit is brought.

Joseph H. Sturgis, another witness for complainant, testifies that in 1863 Barnes spoke to him about two inventions made by himself, one of which was a corset-steel, and that he went to the house of Barnes to see them. Before this time, and after the transactions testified to by the complainant, Barnes and she had intermarried. Barnes said his wife had a pair of steels made according to his invention in the corsets which she was then wearing, and if she would take them off he would show them to witness. Mrs. Barnes went out, and returned with a pair of corsets and a pair of scissors, and ripped the corsets open and took out the steels. Barnes then explained to witness how they were made and used.

This is the evidence presented by the record, on which the defendants rely to establish the public use of the invention by the patentee's consent and allowance.

The question for our decision is, whether this testimony shows a public use within the meaning of the statute. * * *

* * * [S]ome inventions are by their very character only capable of being used where they cannot be seen or observed by the public eye. An invention may consist of a lever or spring, hidden in the running gear of a watch, or of a rachet, shaft, or cog-wheel covered from view in the recesses of a machine for spinning or weaving. Nevertheless, if its inventor sells a machine of which his invention forms a part, and allows it to be used without restriction of any kind, the use is a public one. So, on the other hand, a use necessarily open to public view, if made in good faith solely to test the qualities of the invention, and for the purpose of experiment, is not a public use within the meaning of the statute. Elizabeth v. Pavement Company, 97 U.S. 126; * * *.

Tested by these principles, we think the evidence of the complainant herself shows that for more than two years before the application for the original letters there was, by the consent and allowance of Barnes, a public use of the invention, covered by them. * * * He imposed no obligation of secrecy, nor any condition or restriction whatever. They were not presented for the purpose of experiment, nor to test their qualities. * * *

According to the testimony of the complainant, the invention was completed and put to use in 1855. The inventor slept on his rights for eleven years. * * * In the meantime, the invention had found its way into general, and almost universal use. * * *. It is fair to presume that having learned from this general use that there was some value in his invention, he attempted to resume, by an application for a patent, what by his acts he had clearly dedicated to the public. * * *

We are of opinion that the defence of two years' public use, by the consent and allowance of the inventor, before he made application for letters-patent, is satisfactorily established by the evidence.

Decree affirmed.

■ MR. JUSTICE MILLER dissenting.

* * * If the little steel spring inserted in a single pair of corsets and used by only one woman, covered by her outer-clothing, and in a position always withheld from public observation, is a public use of the piece of steel, I am at a loss to know the line between a private and a public use. * * *

NOTES

The statutory provisions relating to prior public use developed as follows.

1. Patent Act of 1793 § 1: "[W]hen any person * * * shall allege that he * * * [has] invented any new and useful art, machine, manufacture, or composition of matter, not known or used before the application * * * it shall * * * be lawful * * * [to issue letters-patent].

Patent Act of 1793 § 6: "[T]he defendant in such action [for infringement] shall be permitted to * * * prove * * * that the thing thus secured by patent was not originally discovered by the patentee, but had been in use, or had been described in some public work anterior to the supposed discovery of the patentee."

2. The contradiction between §§ 1 and 6 of the 1793 act came before the Court in Pennock v. Dialogue, 27 U.S. (2 Peters) 1 (1829). Patent for making pressure-tight joints in hose. The patent was applied for in 1818. Between 1811 and 1818 upward of 13,000 feet of hose were constructed and sold in the city of Philadelphia which followed the teaching of the patent, with the consent of the patentee. The court held the patent invalid, against the argument that section 6 of the act limited the defense of prior public use to uses prior to the date of invention. Mr. Justice Story said:

We think, then, the true meaning must be, not known or used by the public, before the application. And thus construed, there is much reason for the limitation thus imposed by the act. While one great object was, by holding out a reasonable reward to inventors, and giving them an exclusive right to their inventions for a limited period, to stimulate the efforts of genius; the main object was "to promote the progress of science and useful arts;" and this could be done best, by giving the public at large a right to make, construct, use and vend the thing invented, at as early a period as possible, having a due regard to the rights of the inventor. If an inventor should be permitted to hold back from the knowledge of the public the secrets of his invention; if he should, for a long period of years, retain the monopoly, and make and sell his invention publicly, and thus gather the whole profits of it, relying upon his superior skill and knowledge of the structure; and then, and then only, when the danger of competition should force him to secure the exclusive right, he should be allowed to take out a patent, and thus exclude the public from any further use than what should be derived under it, during his fourteen years; it would materially retard the progress of science and the useful arts, and give a premium to those who should be least prompt to communicate their discoveries.

Id. at 18.

The Court brushed aside § 6 by observing: "The sixth section certainly does not enumerate all the defenses which a party may make. * * * It gives the right to the first and true inventor, and to him only; if known or used, before his supposed discovery, he is not the first, although he may be a true inventor; and that is the case to which the clause looks. But it is not inconsistent with this doctrine, that although he is the first, as well as the true inventor, yet if he shall put it into public use, or sell it for public use, before he applies for a patent, that this should furnish another bar to his claim." Id. at 21–23.

3. Patent Act of 1836 § 6: "That any person * * * having discovered or invented any new and useful art, machine, manufacture, or composition of matter, * * * not known or used by others before his * * * invention thereof, and not, at the time of his application for a patent, in public use or on sale with his consent or allowance, as the inventor or discoverer * * * [may receive a patent therefor]."

4. Patent Act of 1839 § 7: "That every person or corporation who has, or shall have, purchased or constructed any newly invented machine, manufacture, or composition of matter, prior to the application by the inventor or discoverer for a patent, shall be held to possess the right to use, and vend to others to be used, the specific machine, manufacture, or composition of matter so made or purchased, without liability therefor to the inventor, or any other person interested in such invention; and no patent shall be held to be invalid, by reason of such purchase, sale, or use prior to the application for a patent as aforesaid, except on proof of abandonment of such invention to the public; or that such purchase, sale, or prior use has been for more than two years prior to such application for a patent."

5. In *Egbert* the Court apparently construed § 7 as applying to public uses with the consent of the applicant, creating a two year grace period both for uses by the applicant and by third parties. Is this what section 7 appears to do? Was the Court's construction influenced by the following statute?

Patent Act of 1870 § 24, Rev. Stat. § 4886: "That any person who has invented or discovered any new and useful art, machine, manufacture, or composition of matter * * * not known or used by others in this country, and not patented, or described in any printed publication in this or any foreign country, before his invention or discovery thereof, and not in public use or on sale for more than two years prior to his application, unless the same is proved to have been abandoned, may * * * obtain a patent therefor."

6. The statute remained essentially the same from 1870 until the codification of 1952, except that in 1897 the two-year time bar was extended to "not patented or described in any printed publication in this or any foreign country" and in 1939 the two year period was reduced to one year. 28 Stat. 692 (1897); 53 Stat. 1212 (1939).

Gillman v. Stern

United States Circuit Court of Appeals, Second Circuit, 1940.
114 F.2d 28, certiorari denied 311 U.S. 718,
61 S.Ct. 441, 85 L.Ed. 468.

■ L. HAND, CIRCUIT JUDGE.

Both the plaintiffs and the defendant appeal from the judgment in this action. The plaintiffs filed the usual complaint, asking an injunction for the infringement of Patent No.1,919,674, issued on July 25, 1933, to the Sterling Airbrush Co., assignee of Laszlo Wenczel, for a pneumatic "puffing machine." * * *

The patent was for a pneumatic machine for quilting; i.e., it blew thread or yarn "into pockets formed in the fabric to stuff the same to impart a raised or embossed design" * * *. It was made of a hollow needle through which the thread or yarn passed; the inner end of the needle being within a frame which contained an air-duct leading from a blower. When the blower was turned on, it blew the yarn through the needle and stuffed the pocket which the needle point had entered. Before passing into the needle the thread passed through a "tube, 40," one end of which telescoped within the inner end of the needle, but did not quite block the access of air from the blower, which passed around the end of the "tube," sucked the thread or yarn, as it emerged from the "tube," and carried it through the needle. In operation, after the yarn has once been started, the "tube" was somewhat withdrawn (being for that purpose mounted in a "threaded shank") in order to secure a stronger air-flow through the needle.

The art contained nothing of the kind before except Haas' machine, of which more later. It is true, it had been common practice in many arts to introduce an air blast around the outside of a hollow tube introduced into the entrance of a larger tube through which the air escaped, and by this means to suck material from the smaller, through the larger tube. The

Venturi carbureter is an example of this; the circle of swiftly moving air entering the larger tube creates a vacuum at the end of the smaller and sucks the gasoline forward to make the mixture. The first attack upon the patent is that it was merely for a new use of an old device. However, the only objection to patenting a new use is that the statute, § 31, Title 35, U.S. Code, 35 U.S.C.A. § 31, does not include "uses" among what can be patented, except so far as they are included within "arts"—i.e., processes. If, however, an old article must be physically changed, even slightly, to fit the new use, it becomes itself a new "machine" or "manufacture," and the statute is satisfied. In that case the only question open is whether the discovery of the new use demands enough original thought to be deemed an invention. Constitutionally only "discoveries" can be patented at all, and the ingenuity needed for the new conception, not the amount of physical readjustment, is the test of a valuable "discovery." * * * No machines on the Venturi principle would have served to quilt fabrics; they were sandblasters, sand engravers, vaporizers, grain conveyors, inspirators, air brushes, sprayers, separators, carbureters and the like. Most, if not all of them, were, moreover, of the true Venturi type; that is, they always worked by suction. As we have said, Wenczel's "puffer" did so too for as long as the end of the "tube, 40" was telescoped within the inner end of the needle; but not after it was withdrawn, as it had to be for "puffing." In that phase there was no suction at the end of the "tube," but probably some back-flow, though obviously not enough to counteract the increased air-flow through the needle. However, this modification of the old devices we need not count in holding that Wenczel made an invention; it was because he selected for an old need—quilting—a theretofore unused device that we think he showed more than ordinary insight, else it would have been made before.

However, upon the issue of invalidity the defendant relies less upon prior patents than upon the prior use by Haas. Haas at some time undoubtedly did invent a "puffing machine" designed to perform the same work as plaintiff's machine. Further, his first "puffer" was substantially the same as the plaintiff's; and, if it had been properly proved, it might be hard to support the patent. However, not only was there no evidence as to the date of it except the word of Haas and his wife—who knew incidentally nothing of its construction—but again and again, Haas spoke of it as an unsatisfactory temporary device which he had discarded before he began to do any business. It must certainly be considered an abandoned experiment and is therefore immaterial. Haas also testified that in the autumn of 1929 he invented another "puffer" * * * [the plaintiff's application was filed January 21, 1931] in general structure like the first, except that there was no means—as in Wenczel's machine—to vary the air pressure by changing the position of any member like the "tube, 40." The plaintiff insists that for this reason it cannot anticipate, and literally that is true; but possibly, if it could be deemed a part of the prior art, the step between it and Wenczel's disclosure would not justify a monopoly. Besides, claim one does not incorporate the "regulating valve," i.e., the "tube, 40." We need not, however, pass upon this question, or indeed whether the evidence of its date of production satisfied the exacting standard set by the Barbed Wire Patent Case, 143 U.S. 275, for it is clear that it was never in prior "public use," and that Haas was not a "first inventor." It was always kept as strictly secret as was possible, consistently with its exploitation. In general, everybody was carefully kept out of Haas' shop where the four machines were used. He testified that "no one was allowed to enter but my employees," girls he had had "for years"; and that he "had instructed my girls that if anybody should ask to get any kind of information simply tell them you don't know. In fact I have my shop door so arranged that it could only be opened from the inside." He also enjoined secrecy on his wife who testified "no one ever got into the place and no one ever saw the machine. He made everything himself." Indeed, as a condition upon even testifying in the case at bar Haas insisted, and the judge ordered, that the lawyers should be sworn to keep secret all he said about the construction of the "puffer," and that it should not be printed in the record, but typed and sealed for the inspection of the judges alone. It does not appear that the "girls" knew how the machines which they used were made, or how they operated. The only exception to this was a disclosure, such as it was, to two members of a firm going by the name of the Bona Fide Embroidery Co.— Custer and Kadison. In the same autumn of 1929 they and Haas testified that they had seen some of his quilting and were anxious to get the whole of his output. They went to his shop to satisfy themselves; Custer said that "it was very vital at that time that I should know the workings of the machine for my production of the proper designs." (By "workings" he could only have meant how it performed for he never learned its construction.) After this visit the two agreed that Haas should give them his whole production and that they should sell it; they even talked about taking out a patent, but did not have the necessary money. Thus, Haas kept his machine absolutely secret from the outside world except to secure selling agents for its product, and then it was only its performance, not its construction that even they learned. Moreover, Custer and Kadison had the same motive to suppress whatever information they got that Haas had, for without a patent the secret was all that protected their market.

Such a use is clearly not a "public" one, and such an inventor is not a "first inventor." In Gayler v. Wilder, 10 How. 477, 481, 497, the question was whether the condition—which has always been in the statute—that the patentee must be the "first and original inventor" was defeated by anyone who had earlier conceived the same invention, or only by one who had also in some way made public his results. A majority of the court held that only the second would defeat a patent on the ground that what had not in fact enriched the art, should not count; and the doctrine is now well fixed. Alexander Milburn Co. v. Davis-Bournonville Co., 270 U.S. 390. Just as a secret use is not a "public use," so a secret inventor is not a "first inventor." Acme Flexible Clasp Co. v. Cary Mfg. Co., C.C., 96 F. 344; * * * ; Peerless Roll Leaf Co. v. H. Griffin & Sons Co., 2 Cir., 29 F.2d 646. Haas' user was one where "the machine, process, and product were not well known to the employes in the plant," and where "efforts were made to conceal them from anyone who had a legitimate interest in understanding them," if by "legitimate interest" one means something more than curiosity or mischief. Electric Battery Co. v. Shimadzu, 307 U.S. 5, 20. * * *

We are to distinguish between a public user which does not inform the art (Hall v. Macneale, 107 U.S. 90, 97) and a secret user; some confusion has resulted from the failure to do so. It is true that in each case the fund of common knowledge is not enriched, and that might indeed have been good reason originally for throwing out each as anticipations. But when the statute made any "public use" fatal to a patent, and when thereafter the court held that it was equally fatal, whether or not the patentee had consented to it, there was no escape from holding—contrary to the underlying theory of the law—that it was irrelevant whether the use informed the public so that they could profit by it. Nevertheless, it was still true that secret uses were not public uses, whether or not public uses might on occasion have no public value. Perhaps it was originally open to argument that the statute merely meant to confine prior "public uses" to the prospective patentee and to be evidence of abandonment, and that "first inventor" meant to include anyone who first conceived the thing in tangible enough form to be persuasive. But, rightly or wrongly, the law did not develop so, and it is now too late to change. Hence the anomaly that, by secreting a machine one may keep it from becoming an anticipation, even though its public use would really have told nobody anything about it.

* * *

The judgment is reversed and the usual judgment will be entered for the plaintiffs on all claims. The counterclaim will of course be dismissed.

Metallizing Engineering Co. v. Kenyon Bearing & Auto Parts Co.

United States Circuit Court of Appeals, Second Circuit, 1946.
153 F.2d 516, certiorari denied 328 U.S. 840,
66 S.Ct. 1016, 90 L.Ed. 1615, rehearing denied 328 U.S. 881,
66 S.Ct. 1364, 90 L.Ed. 1648.

■ L. HAND, CIRCUIT JUDGE.

The defendants appeal from the usual decree holding valid and infringed all but three of the claims of a reissued patent, issued to the plaintiff's assignor, Meduna; the original patent issued on May 25, 1943, upon an application filed on August 6, 1942. The patent is for the process of "so conditioning a metal surface that the same is, as a rule, capable of bonding thereto applied spray metal to a higher degree than is normally procurable with hitherto known practices". It is primarily useful for building up the worn metal parts of a machine. The art had for many years done this by what the patent calls "spray metal," which means metal sprayed in molten form upon the surface which it is desired to build up. This process is called "metalizing," and it had been known for nearly thirty years before Meduna's invention; but about fifteen or twenty years ago it was found that, to secure a satisfactory bond between the "spray metal" and the surface, the surface must be roughened so that there would be fine undercut areas in it upon which the sprayed surface could take hold; and of course the surface must itself be clean. The art had developed two ways of producing such a surface; one, by sand-blasting, and the other, by a tool, so adjusted in a lathe as to tear tiny channels: "screw-threading." Meduna's invention was to prepare the surface by first depositing upon it a preliminary layer of metal by means of a process, disclosed in Patent No.1,327,267, issued to Brewster and Weisehan, on January 6, 1920. This process was practiced by what the art knew as the "McQuay-Norris" machine, which was "more particularly adapted and intended for use in the filling of cavities which may occur in castings or other metal objects". The "McQuay-Norris" device was operated by electric power, one terminal of the circuit being connected with the work, and the other being a fusable electrode, which melted at the temperature developed in the circuit, and deposited parts of itself at the places desired upon closing of the circuit by contact with the work. The process was described as follows: "The electrode is moved from spot to spot in the cavity and the foregoing operation repeated until the surface of the blow-hole is covered by a deposit of the metal by the electrode. It will thus be seen that the surface of the blow-hole is covered by a number of small particles of metal of the electrode, all of which particles are welded to the particular portion of the surface of the blow-hole with which the elctrode contacted." After this has been done, "a peening hammer is employed to peen the metal which has been introduced into the blow-hole, thus causing the metal to be compacted, and any inequalities of the surface of the metal reduced". Meduna did not peen the metal, indeed peening would have been entirely unfitted to his purpose, as it would have pressed together the undercut deposits which later serve to catch and hold the "spray metal." Moreover, his purpose was not to fill up "blow-holes," or fissures; but, as we have said, to prepare worn surfaces for rebuilding. However, he used the McQuay-Norris machine unchanged, prescribing a voltage of preferably not more than twenty volts—ordinarily between two and nine—and an amperage of between two hundred and three or four hundred. The surface was to be "repetitiously contacted and preferably repetitiously contact stroked with the electrode on successive areas, the stroking action depositing on these areas small amounts of electrode material firmly bonded thereto. Alternatively the electrode may be applied with a stippling action to the metal surface. While these procedures essentially involve breaking and making contact between the metal surface and the electrode, it is also possible, and sometimes advisable, to move the electrode relative to the base while maintaining resistant heating contact therebetween".

The only question which we find necessary to decide is as to Meduna's public use of the patented process more than one year before August 6, 1942. The district judge made findings about this, which are supported by the testimony and which we accept. They appear as findings 8, 9, 10, 11, 12 and 13 on pages 46 and 47 of volume 62 of the Federal Supplement; and we cannot improve upon his statement. The kernel of them is the following: "the inventor's main purpose in his use of the process prior to August 6, 1941, and especially in respect to all jobs for owners not known to him, was commercial, and * * * an experimental purpose in connection with such use was subordinate only." Upon this finding he concluded as matter of law that, since the use before the critical date—August 6, 1941—was not primarily for the purposes of experiment, the use was not excused for that reason. Smith & Griggs Manufacturing Co. v. Sprague, 123 U.S. 249, 256; Aerovox Corp. v. Polymet Manufacturing Corp., 2 Cir., 67 F.2d 860, 862. Moreover, he also concluded that the use was not public but secret, and for that reason that its predominantly commercial character did prevent it from invalidating the patent. For the last he relied upon our decisions in Peerless Roll Leaf Co. v. Griffin & Sons, 29 F.2d 646, and Gillman v. Stern, 114 F.2d 28. We think that his analysis of Peerless Roll Leaf Co. v. Griffin & Sons, was altogether correct, and that he had no alternative but to follow that decision; on the other hand, we now think that we were then wrong and that the decision must be overruled for reasons we shall state. Gillman v. Stern, supra, was, however, rightly decided.

Section one of the first and second Patent Acts, 1 Stat. 109 and 318, declared that the petition for a patent must state that the subject matter had not been "before known or used." Section six of the Act of 1836, 5 Stat. 117, changed this by providing in addition that the invention must not at the time of the application for a patent have been "in public use or on sale" with the inventor's "consent or allowance"; and § 7 of the Act of 1839, 5 Stat. 353, provided that "no patent shall be held to be invalid by reason of such purchase, sale, or use prior to the application for a patent * * * except on proof of abandonment of such invention to the public; or that such purchase, sale, or prior use has been for more than two years prior to such application * * *." Section 4886 of the Revised Statutes made it a condition upon patentability that the invention shall not have been "in public use or on sale for more than two years prior to his application," and that it shall not have been "proved to have been abandoned." This is in substance the same as the Act of 1839, and is precisely the same as § 31 of Title 35, U.S.C.A. except that the prior use is now limited to the United States, and to one year before the application. § 1, Chap. 391, 29 Stat. 692; § 1, Chap. 450, 53 Stat. 1212, 35 U.S.C.A. § 31. So far as we can find, the first case which dealt with the effect of prior use by the patentee was Pennock v. Dialogue, 2 Pet. 1, 4, in which the invention had been completed in 1811, and the patent granted in 1818 for a process of making hose by which the sections were joined together in such a way that the joints resisted pressure as well as the other parts. It did not appear that the joints in any way disclosed the process; but the patentee, between the discovery of the invention and the grant of the patent, had sold 13,000 feet of hose; and as to this the judge charged: "If the public, with the knowledge and tacit consent of the inventor, be permitted to use the invention, without opposition, it is a fraud on the public afterwards to take out a patent." The Supreme Court affirmed a judgment for the defendant, on the ground that the invention had been "known or used before the application." "If an inventor should be permitted to hold back from the knowledge of the public the secrets of his invention; if he should * * * make and sell his invention publicly, and thus gather the whole profits, * * * it would materially retard the progress of science and the useful arts" to allow him fourteen years of legal monopoly "when the danger of competition should force him to secure the exclusive right"

2 Pet. at page 19. In Shaw v. Cooper, 7 Pet. 292, the public use was not by the inventor, but he had neglected to prevent it after he had learned of it, and this defeated the patent. "Whatever may be the intention of the inventor, if he suffers his invention to go into public use, through any means whatsoever, without an immediate assertion of his right, he is not entitled to a patent." 7 Pet. at page 323. In Kendall v. Winsor, 21 How. 322, the inventor had kept the machine secret, but had sold the harness which it produced, so that the facts presented the same situation as here. Since the jury brought in a verdict for the defendant on the issue of abandonment, the case adds nothing except for the dicta on page 328 of 21 How.: "the inventor who designedly, and with the view of applying it indefinitely and exclusively for his own profit, withholds his invention from the public, comes not within the policy or objects of the Constitution or acts of Congress." In Egbert v. Lippmann, 104 U.S. 333, although the patent was for the product which was sold, nothing could be learned about it without taking it apart, yet it was a public use within the statute. In Hall v. Macneale, 107 U.S. 90, the situation was the same.

In the lower courts we may begin with the often cited decision in Macbeth-Evans Glass Co. v. General Electric Co., 6 Cir., 246 F. 695, which concerned a process patent for making illuminating glass. The patentee had kept the process as secret as possible, but for ten years had sold the glass, although this did not, so far as appears, disclose the process. The court held the patent invalid for two reasons, as we understand them: the first was that the delay either indicated an intention to abandon, or was of itself a forfeiture, because of the inconsistency of a practical monopoly by means of secrecy and of a later legal monopoly by means of a patent. So far, it was not an interpretation of "prior use" in the statute; but, beginning on page 702 of 246 F. 695 Judge Warrington seems to have been construing that phrase and to hold that the sales were such a use. In Allinson Manufacturing Co. v. Ideal Filter Co., 8 Cir., 21 F.2d 22, the patent was for a machine for purifying gasoline: the machine was kept secret, but the gasoline had been sold for a period of six years before the application was filed. As in Macbeth-Evans Glass Co. v. General Electric Co., supra, 6 Cir., 246 F. 695, the court apparently invalidated the patent on two grounds: one was that the inventor had abandoned the right to a patent, or had forfeited it by his long delay. We are disposed however to read the latter part—pages 27 and 28 of 21 F.2d—as holding that the sale of gasoline was a "prior use" of the machine, notwithstanding its concealment. Certainly, the following quotation from Pitts v. Hall, Fed.Cas.No.11,192, 2 Blatchf. 229, was not otherwise apposite; a patentee "is not allowed to derive any benefit from the sale or use of his machine, without forfeiting his right, except within two years prior to the time he makes his application." On the other hand in Stresau v. Ipsen, 77 F.2d 937, 22 C.C.P.A. (Patents) 1352, the Court of Customs and Patent Appeals did indeed decide that a process claim might be valid when the inventor had kept the process secret but had sold the product.

Coming now to our own decisions (the opinions in all of which I wrote), the first was Grasselli Chemical Co. v. National Aniline & Chemical Co., 2 Cir., 26 F.2d 305, in which the patent was for a process which had been kept secret, but the product had been sold upon the market for more than two years. We held that, although the process could not have been discovered from the product, the sales constituted a "prior use," relying upon Egbert v. Lippmann, supra, 104 U.S. 333, and Hall v. Macneale, supra, 107 U.S. 90. There was nothing in this inconsistent with what we are now holding. But in Peerles Roll Leaf Co. v. Griffin & Sons, supra, 2 Cir., 29 F.2d 646, where the patent was for a machine, which had been kept secret, but whose output had been freely sold on the market, we sustained the patent on the ground that "the sale of the product was irrelevant, since no knowledge could possibly be acquired of the machine in that way. In this respect the machine differs from a process * * * or from any other invention necessarily contained in a product" 29 F.2d at page 649. So far as we can now find, there is nothing to support this distinction in the authorities, and we shall try to show that we misapprehended the theory on which the prior use by an inventor forfeits his right to a patent. In Aerovox Corp. v. Polymet Manufacturing Corp., supra, 2 Cir., 67 F.2d 860, the patent was also for a process, the use of which we held not to have been experimental, though not secret. Thus our decision sustaining the patent was right; but apparently we were by implication reverting to the doctrine of the Peerless case when we added that it was doubtful whether the process could be detected from the product, although we cited only Hall v. Macneale, supra, 107 U.S. 90, and Grasselli Chemical Co. v. National Aniline Co., supra (2 Cir., 26 F.2d 305). In Gillman v. Stern, supra, 2 Cir., 114 F.2d 28, it was not the inventor, but a third person who used the machine secretly and sold the product openly, and there was therefore no question either of abandonment or forfeiture by the inventor. The only issue was whether a prior use which did not disclose the invention to the art was within the statute; and it is well settled that it is not. As in the case of any other anticipation, the issue of invention must then be determined by how much the inventor has contributed any new information to the art. Gayler v. Wilder, 10 How. 477, 496, 497; Tilghman v. Proctor, 102 U.S. 707, 711; * * *.

From the foregoing it appears that in Peerless Roll Leaf Co. v. Griffin & Sons, supra, 2 Cir., 29 F.2d 646, we confused two separate doctrines: (1) The effect upon his right to a patent of the inventor's competitive exploitation of his machine or of his process; (2) the contribution which a prior use by another person makes to the art. Both do indeed come within the phrase, "prior use"; but the first is a defence for quite different reasons from the second. It had its origin—at least in this country—in the passage we have quoted from Pennock v. Dialogue, supra, 2 Pet. 1, 7 L.Ed. 327; i.e., that it is a condition upon an inventor's right to a patent that he shall not exploit his discovery competitively after it is ready for patenting; he must content himself with either secrecy, or legal monopoly. It is true that for the limited period of two years he was allowed to do so, possibly in order to give him time to prepare an application; and even that has been recently cut down by half. But if he goes beyond that period of probation, he forfeits his right regardless of how little the public may have learned about the invention; just as he can forfeit it by too long concealment, even without exploiting the invention at all. Woodbridge v. United States, 263 U.S. 50; Macbeth-Evans Glass Co. v. General Electric Co., supra, 6 Cir., 246 F. 695. Such a forfeiture has nothing to do with abandonment, which presupposes a deliberate, though not necessarily an express, surrender of any right to a patent. Although the evidence of both may at times overlap, each comes from a quite different legal source: one, from the fact that by renouncing the right the inventor irrevocably surrenders it; the other, from the fiat of Congress that it is part of the consideration for a patent that the public shall as soon as possible begin to enjoy the disclosure.

It is indeed true that an inventor may continue for more than a year to practice his invention for his private purposes or his own enjoyment and later patent it. But that is, properly considered, not an exception to the doctrine, for he is not then making use of his secret to gain a competitive advantage over others; he does not thereby extend the period of his monopoly. Besides, as we have seen, even that privilege has its limits, for he may conceal it so long that he will lose his right to a patent even though he does not use it at all. With that question we have not however any concern here.

Judgment reversed; complaint dismissed.

NOTE

W. L. Gore & Associates, Inc. v. Garlock, Inc., 721 F.2d 1540 (Fed. Cir. 1983), involves the patent on a permeable but waterproof material made from polytetrafluorethylene (PTFE, trademarked by Du Pont as TEFLON) by rapid stretching. One of the products made by this process is widely marketed under the trademark GORETEX.

The District Court had held the patent invalid under § 102(b) because of a third-party practice of the invention. The Federal Circuit reversed, following *Metallizing Engineering* with no discussion of the statutory language. The third party had used a machine whose nature and operation it had promised to keep secret from all but its employees. The defendant argued that since the machine was not hidden from employees and was shown to some Du Pont employees, § 102(b) invalidated the patent. The court rejected the defense because the employees had signed confidentiality agreements and there was no evidence that the Du Pont employees could have learned anything about the particular process used to make the claimed product.

Evans Cooling Systems v. General Motors Corp.

United States Court of Appeals, Federal Circuit, 1997.
125 F.3d 1448.

■ MICHEL, CIRCUIT JUDGE.

Evans Cooling Systems, Inc. and Patent Enforcement Fund, Inc. (collectively, "Evans") appeal the September 30, 1996 order of the United States District Court for the District of Connecticut granting summary judgment to General Motors Corporation ("GM") of invalidity based on the "on sale" bar under 35 U.S.C. § 102(b). * * * Because there were no materially disputed questions of fact regarding whether the patented invention was offered for sale more than one year prior to the critical date and because we decline to create an exception to the on sale bar for those instances in which a third party misappropriates the invention and later places the invention on sale or causes an innocent third party to place the invention on sale, we affirm.

BACKGROUND

United States Patent Number 5,255,636 ("the '636 patent") issued on October 26, 1993 and claims an aqueous reverse flow cooling system for internal combustion engines. An understanding of the technology is not necessary to this appeal and we therefore do not discuss it. John Evans, the named inventor, admits he conceived the patented invention in 1984 and reduced it to practice in 1986. Mr. Evans did not file a patent application, however, until July 1, 1992.

In early 1994, Evans filed the present lawsuit alleging that GM infringed the '636 patent by the manufacture and sale of cars having GM's "LT1" and "L99" engines. GM counterclaimed for a declaration of invalidity and non-infringement. GM asserted that the '636 patent was invalid because GM and its independent dealers had placed the patented invention on sale prior to the critical date with the introduction of its 1992 Corvette. Specifically, GM sent an "Order Guide" for the 1992 Corvette to its independent dealers in late April or early May, 1991 to be used for ordering the vehicle described in the Order Guide. At about the same time, GM sent its dealers a supplemental brochure that provided additional ordering information for the 1992 Corvette, specifically stating that the car had reverse flow engine cooling. A representative of GM testified that it expected the dealers would start ordering the vehicles as soon as the Order Guide was sent to them. A sales representative at a GM dealership also testified that it was the dealership's common practice to order new cars and enter into agreements to sell new cars shortly after receiving the Guide. GM produced computer records documenting over 2000 orders placed by dealers around the country for the 1992 Corvette before the critical date. The orders, over 300 of which were placed on behalf of specific retail customers, were placed through a computer network and GM transmitted an acknowledgment back to the dealer after receiving the order. As a specific example, GM introduced evidence regarding a retail customer named Aram Najarian who visited a Corvette dealer in West Bloomfield, Michigan, in June, 1991. Mr. Najarian entered into a contract with a GM dealer on June 13, 1991 in which GM agreed to sell and Mr. Najarian agreed to buy a Corvette with an LT1 engine. Although a firm price was not established at that time, Mr. Najarian was informed that the price would be up to $2000 higher than the 1991 model and he placed a deposit on the car at that time. The order was transmitted to GM, and GM sent back an acknowledgment on June 14, 1991.

Evans asserted before the trial court that GM should not be allowed to invalidate the '636 patent because GM, in fact, stole the invention from Evans. Specifically, GM allegedly requested that Evans demonstrate its aqueous reverse flow cooling system at GM's test facility in the spring of

1989, and Evans alleges that GM stole the invention during this demonstration.

The district court granted summary judgment in favor of GM on September 30, 1996, because the record established that GM and its dealers placed the 1992 Corvette with the LT1 engine on sale prior to the critical date. The district court relied on the facts that Mr. Najarian entered into a contract with a GM dealer, the dealer agreed to sell and Mr. Najarian agreed to buy a 1992 Corvette, and Mr. Najarian paid a deposit and the dealer transmitted the order to GM. The court also noted that even an offer to sell will raise the on sale bar and that this transaction went beyond mere indefinite discussions about a possible sale. Turning to the policies underlying the on sale bar, the district court noted that John Evans claimed he reduced the invention to practice in 1986 but failed to file an application for some six years.

DISCUSSION

* * *

Evans * * * argue[s] that summary judgment was inappropriate because GM did not meet its burden of proving by clear and convincing evidence that the engine of the 1992 Corvette anticipated the claims of the '636 patent. Although GM conceded infringement for purposes of the summary judgment motion, it denied infringement in its answer and stated in sworn answers to interrogatories that the claims of the '636 patent were not infringed because the LT1 engine lacked certain elements of the claims. Evans argues, therefore, that GM has necessarily admitted, or at least created a genuine issue of material fact, that the engine of the 1992 Corvette does not anticipate any of the asserted claims.

We do not agree. This is not the typical case where the patentee has placed some device on sale prior to the critical date and the accused infringer must demonstrate that this device actually embodied or rendered obvious the patented invention. Here, the entire basis of the lawsuit is Evans'—the patentee's—contention that the LT1 engine—the device that was put on sale—contains a cooling system that infringes. GM denied that the LT1 engine infringed the '636 patent but, by conceding infringement for purposes of the summary judgment motion and its on sale defense, properly pled in the alternative. * * * Although GM bore the burden of proving that the LT1 engine embodied the patented invention or rendered it obvious for purposes of the summary judgment motion, this burden is met by Evans' allegation, forming the sole basis for the complaint, that the LT1 engine infringes. Indeed, even on appeal, Evans states in its brief, directed only to the on sale issue, that "GM uses an aqueous reverse flow cooling system in its LT1 engine."

Evans also argues, in effect, that there was no "sale" or offer for sale of the LT1 engine. Evans argues that, based on the totality of the circumstances, a reasonable jury could conclude that "the Najarian 'order' was an advance, non-binding order, cancelable by either party, that was not finalized until after July 1, 1991" and that it was void to the extent that it was an offer for sale. We have often stated that the totality of the circumstances and the policies underlying the bar must be considered in determining whether a definite offer for sale triggering section 102(b) has been made. See, e.g., Envirotech Corp. v. Westech Eng'g Inc., 904 F.2d 1571 (Fed. Cir. 1990). However, where there is a specific and definite offer for sale of a successfully tested device, such as that evidenced by a completed contract for sale, that embodies every limitation of the later patented invention as claimed prior to the critical date and that sale is clearly for commercial purposes, the analysis need not go any further. It is not that the totality of the circumstances test is not to be applied in such a case, but that there are then no circumstances, short of fraud or duress, that could turn such an offer into something other than a barring event.

Even if we were otherwise to consider the totality of the circumstances, Evans' relevant arguments on this point are easily discarded. Evans argues that Mr. Najarian's order is ineffective as a sale because it stated that "[a]ny provisions of this order prohibited by Michigan or Federal law shall be ineffective to the extent of such prohibition" and the Federal Fuel Economy Regulations and the Clean Air Act prohibited any offer for sale as of this date because GM had not yet received fuel economy labels or a Certificate of Conformity from the EPA. Even assuming this to be the case, the mere fact that the offer for sale was illegal or ineffective does not remove it from the purview of the section 102(b) bar. Jack Cauley Chevrolet thought it was offering to sell a 1992 Corvette to Mr. Najarian and Mr. Najarian thought he was agreeing to buy such a car. Moreover, there is no evidence that Mr. Najarian did not receive the car or that the offer was actually invalidated. Likewise, neither the fact that the price was not firm nor that the color had not been chosen avoids the section 102(b) bar. Mr. Najarian was given an estimated price range and it is not uncommon for car buyers to change their minds about the desired color. Similarly, the fact that the contract was cancelable or changeable under certain circumstances does not mean that it does not evidence a definite offer for sale. Finally, even if the independent dealership violated internal procedures by offering the 1992 Corvette for sale prior to the model announcement date GM had set, this does not make the offer for sale any less an offer.

Thus, we hold that the order entered into by Mr. Najarian and Jack Cauley Chevrolet on June 13, 1991—nearly a month prior to the critical date—evidences an effective offer for sale that invalidates the '636 patent. Although GM also argues that the '636 patent is invalid because GM placed the reverse flow cooling system in its engines on sale when it sent the Order Guide and supplemental information brochure to its dealers across the country in late April or early May of 1991, we do not reach or decide that issue here. See Intel Corp. v. International Trade Comm'n, 946 F.2d 821, 829 (Fed. Cir. 1991) ("A single sale or offer to sell is enough to bar patentability.").

II.

Although our analysis would normally be complete once we had concluded there was an invalidating offer for sale, Evans urges this court to create a new exception to the on sale bar. Specifically, Evans asks us to rule that an otherwise invalidating offer for sale does not invalidate a patent "where a third party surreptitiously steals an invention while it is a trade secret and then, unbeknownst to the inventor, allegedly puts the invention on sale [more than one year] before the inventor files a patent application covering the stolen invention."

Evans cites three Supreme Court cases and asserts that they state that prior use of an invention by one who misappropriates the invention cannot invalidate a patent. See Pennock v. Dialogue, 27 U.S. (2 Pet.) 1, 19–20 (1829) ("[i]f before his application for a patent his invention should be pirated by another, or used without his consent; it can scarcely be supposed, that the legislature had within its contemplation such knowledge or use. . . . The use here referred to has always been understood to be a public use, and not a private or surreptitious use in fraud of the inventor."); Shaw v. Cooper, 32 U.S. (7 Pet.) 292, 319–20 (1833) ("But there may be cases, in which a knowledge of the invention may be surreptitiously obtained, and communicated to the public, that do not affect the right of the inventor. . . . If the right were asserted by him who fraudulently obtained it, perhaps no lapse of time could give it validity."); Kendall v. Winsor, 62 U.S. (21 How.) 322 (1859) (affording immunity from suit to prior third party users of a patented invention but refusing to extend such immunity to those who received knowledge of the patented invention through fraud). Evans argues that these Supreme Court cases have never been expressly overruled and, in fact, the one time the Court of Customs and Patent Appeals addressed the issue it expressly left it open, stating:

> We do not find it here necessary to decide whether a fraudulent use of an invention for more than two years [then the bar period] prior to an application for a patent therefor bars the issue of the patent upon such application. . . . It may be that . . . said Minerals Separation should have been held to be estopped to bring a public use proceeding. But even so, as to this we express no opinion. . . .

In re Martin, 74 F.2d 951, 955–56 (CCPA 1935).

We, however, do not find any of these cases dispositive of the issue presented by this case. In *Pennock*, the Supreme Court actually invalidated the patents in suit under the public use bar, and in that case the use had been with the permission of the patentee, thereby rendering any statements regarding piracy mere dicta. Likewise, the statements relied on by Evans in *Shaw* are dicta, as there too the patent was invalidated because the innocent public had come to know and use the invention, although there was some evidence that the invention had first become known to the public by fraudulent means. The statutory on sale bar wasn't even in issue in *Kendall*. Rather, the issue was whether the defendant had the right to continue to use the invention after the patent issued. See also Eastman v. City of N.Y., 134 F. 844, 852–55 (2d Cir. 1904) (discussing whether "fraudulent, surreptitious, or piratical" use of an invention could raise the public use bar and rejecting statements in above Supreme Court cases as dicta).

We note as well that the one other court that has addressed this precise issue has rejected arguments similar to Evans' arguments. See Lorenz v.

Colgate-Palmolive-Peet Co., 167 F.2d 423 (3d Cir. 1948). There, the court addressed the following question: "Was it the intention of Congress that public use by one who employs a process in breach of a fiduciary relationship, who tortiously appropriates it or who pirates it, should bar the inventor from the fruits of his monopoly?" 167 F.2d at 426. Lorenz had disclosed his invention to Colgate. Although Colgate told Lorenz the idea was rejected, it later made substantial commercial use of Lorenz's invention and then sought to invalidate Lorenz's patent based on this use. Id. at 424–25, 167 F.2d 423. After reviewing the Supreme Court and other relevant case law, the court rejected an exception to the statutory bar, stating:

> The prior-public-use proviso . . . contains no qualification or exception which limits the nature of the public use. We think that Congress intended that if an inventor does not protect his discovery by an application for a patent within the period prescribed by the Act, and an intervening public use arises from any source whatsoever, the inventor must be barred from a patent or from the fruits of his monopoly, if a patent has issued to him. There is not a single word in the statute which would tend to put an inventor, whose disclosures have been pirated, in any different position from one who has permitted the use of his process. . . . [I]solated instances of injustice may result if the law be strictly applied, but the inventor's remedy is sure. He is master of the situation and by prompt action [in filing a patent application] can protect himself fully and render the defense of prior public use impossible.

Id. at 429–30 (footnote omitted). Although this decision is not binding on this court, it is persuasive.

Even if we were to create an exception to the on sale bar such that third parties accused of misappropriating an invention could not invalidate a patent based upon sales by the guilty third party, GM correctly asserts that *Martin* squarely holds that activities of third parties uninvolved in the alleged misappropriation raise the statutory bar, even if those activities are instigated by the one who allegedly misappropriated the invention. In *Martin,* Martin's employer stole Martin's invention and filed an application on it and disclosed it to a third party. 74 F.2d at 952–53. After learning of his employer's activities, Martin filed his own application. After an interference was declared, the employer argued Martin's application was barred based on the activities of the third party. Martin conceded his invention had been in public use, but argued that the bar should not apply because the third party's use was "instigated by [his] employer and was a surreptitious and fraudulent public use against him" Id. at 953. After reviewing the Supreme Court and other relevant case law, the Court of Customs and Patent Appeals noted it had "been unable to find any authoritative decisions upon the question of whether a fraudulent public use of an invention . . . prior to the filing of an application . . . , or such public use of an invention instigated by fraud, bars the issuance of a patent. . . ." Id. at 955. Although the Court of Customs and Patent Appeals did not address that precise issue, the Court of Customs and Patent Appeals did hold that allowance of the application was barred because the third party's public use had been innocent, even though it had obtained the technology from the employer. Id.

As discussed below, this holding is dispositive here because, although Evans has charged GM with misappropriation, it has never contended that the independent dealers had any participation in or knowledge of the alleged theft; nor is there any indication that Mr. Najarian had such knowledge. Thus, the independent dealers are innocent users who put the invention on sale by placing orders for innocent retail customers like Najarian.

While such a result may not seem fair, Evans is not without recourse if GM in fact misappropriated his invention. Evans would have an appropriate remedy in state court for misappropriation of a trade secret. We note as well that the facts Evans alleges in support of its misappropriation claim demonstrate that Evans knew GM stole the invention at the very time it was allegedly stolen because during the demonstration GM employees allegedly told Mr. Evans they intended to steal the invention and a sealed room was unsealed during the night between the tests. Evans' patent rights would have nevertheless been protected if Mr. Evans had filed a patent application no more than one year from the date of the demonstration. This he did not do; instead Mr. Evans waited for more than two years after the demonstration and some six years after it was reduced to practice.

CONCLUSION

The '636 patent is invalid due to the pre-critical date contract entered into between the independent GM dealership and Mr. Najarian whereby the dealership offered to sell and Mr. Najarian agreed to buy a 1992 Corvette containing the LT1 engine. Even if GM misappropriated the idea behind the LT1 engine cooling system from Mr. Evans, the invention was nevertheless on sale and we decline to create the suggested new exception to the 102(b) bar which has no basis in the language of the statute. The trial court's decision is therefore affirmed.

NOTE

The § 102(b) time bar can be activated by an offer to sell. The offer, however, must be for the subject matter of the patent. Envirotech Corp. v. Westech Eng'r Inc., 904 F.2d 1571 (Fed. Cir. 1990), cited by the court in *Evans Cooling*, involved a patent on a ballasted digester cover for use in wastewater treatment plants. Envirotech submitted a bid on May 8, 1980 to supply digester covers for a plant in Madison, Wisconsin. The patent application was filed on May 29, 1981. Envirotech had planned to supply covers conforming to the patented invention when it made the bid, and for that reason the district court entered judgment that the patent was invalid. However, the Federal Circuit reversed on the ground that the May 8, 1980 bid was made in accordance with the bid specifications, which did not incorporate the patented invention. The fact that Envirotech hoped at a later time to persuade the general contractor to accept the new cover design was not the same as offering the invention for sale at the time of the bid.

Cali v. Eastern Airlines, Inc.

United States Court of Appeals, Second Circuit, 1971.
442 F.2d 65.

■ KAUFMAN, CIRCUIT JUDGE.

Cali, plaintiff and appellant in this patent infringement action, is a mechanic employed by one of the pioneers in the airlines industry, Pan American World Airways (Pan Am). The kernel of the patented invention which is the subject of this suit was contained in an idea which Cali submitted to Pan Am on a standard form soliciting employees' suggestions in December 1962. Although of course Eastern Airlines, Inc., the appellee and alleged infringer, seeks to minimize its value, Cali's proposal apparently resulted in the correction of a persistent defect in the design of the JT-4 jet engine, then used in Pan Am's Boeing 707 and Douglas DC-8 aircraft before the introduction of the fan jet. Cali's "suggestion-box" solution had eluded the industry's professional engineers.

The sole question raised on this appeal is whether the trial court properly concluded on the basis of the pleadings, affidavits, and depositions before it, that no material fact remained to be tried, thus justifying the grant of Eastern's motion for summary judgment. Judge Dooling, whose opinion is reported at 318 F.Supp. 474, decided that Cali's "invention was * * * in public use" and not used primarily for experimental purposes "more than one year prior to the date" Cali filed his application for a patent and hence the patent was invalid, 35 U.S.C.A. § 102(b). Accordingly, the action was dismissed. While Eastern may yet ultimately prevail on the question of prior use or on other defenses raised below which are not before us on this appeal, we disagree with the district court that the relevant factual issues have been resolved with such clarity at this stage in the litigation as to justify summary judgment.

I.

Cali applied for his patent on September 1, 1964. The key date for purposes of the "public use" bar of Section 102(b) is thus September 1, 1963. As will appear in more detail, the central question before us involves the nature and purposes of the uses to which Pan Am put Cali's invention prior to that date. Before we evaluate those uses, the contours of Cali's concept must first be sketched.

Cali's patent relates to the design of the front or low pressure compression section of the "axial-flow" compressor, the type of compressor used on the JT-4, manufactured by Pratt & Whitney Aircraft Division of United Aircraft Corporation (Pratt & Whitney). This front end section includes several cylindrical stages, consisting of alternating fanlike rotor sections sandwiched between stationary "stator" sections. Successive rotors blow air back against the blades (or vanes) of the stators (or shrouds), which in turn guide the air inward through the tapering compressor chamber to an outlet section called the fairing. The last, or seventh, stator on the JT-4 was designed by Pratt & Whitney so that it connected loosely to the fairing by means of lugs and slats. The loose interconnection permitted the "floating" fairing to vibrate against the seventh stator assembly, causing abrasive wear of the stator lugs and fairing.

As a mechanic employed by Pan Am since 1957, Cali became familiar with the usual practice of periodically repairing worn stators and fairings. This was done by first rebuilding the worn surfaces by welding them and then machining the rebuilt surfaces to their proper dimensions. Cali's suggestion, submitted to his supervisor in December 1962, proposed as an alternative to this practice "to permanently weld the fairing to the 7th stage vane and shroud" and thus by rigidly interconnecting them to eliminate the abrasive wear and hence the need for periodic repairs. Although this solution was "simplicity itself once it was conceived and expressed," as Judge Dooling characterized it, "introducing rigidity may have been powerfully counterindicated by engine building lore," 318 F.Supp. at 475, primarily because of the danger of damage from stresses that might accumulate in the two vibrating assemblies.

While precise temporal relationships are unclear in many respects from this record, at approximately the time that Cali's suggestion was being evaluated, Pan Am engineers devised a variant application of the basic rigid-connection idea suggested by Cali's proposed weld technique. By this alternative method, the vibrating parts would be connected by means of long bolts or tie-rods. The tie-rod technique is conceded by both parties to be within the teaching of Cali's patent, whose critical language describes the two vibrating parts as being "rigidly connected" or secured. The primary advantage of the tie-rod variant appears to have been to permit easier assembly and servicing of the engine.

Both parties agree that Cali's suggestion initiated a period of indefinite length during which Pan Am, in the words of Eastern's brief, evaluated the rigid-connection concept at least with the object "of finding out whether the idea was worth using." Specifically, Judge Dooling identified three foci of "problems and hesitations that preceded Pan Am's unrestricted use of the invention." Thus, Pan Am was concerned with the relative merits of the weld and tie-rod methods. Second, as indicated above, the weld method caused difficulty in assembling the compressor (the solution finally hit upon for this problem, the details of which are irrelevant here, is included in Cali's patent). Third, the court referred to certain "consequential effect," such as cracking of the welded assembly which may have caused Pan Am for a time to doubt the efficacy of Cali's approach. 318 F.Supp. at 475–76.

Certain essential details of this period prior to Pan Am's unreserved acceptance of Cali's concept, are not in dispute. Thus, by a telegram dated January 4, 1963, Pratt & Whitney authorized use of the tie rod on a "trial basis." Similarly, on February 8, 1963, Pratt & Whitney wired Pan Am that it had "no objection" to use of the weld "on token number of engines based on your assertion that no assembly difficulty will be encountered." Pursuant to this authorization,[1] Pan Am subsequently installed and used engines incorporating the tie rod technique on one engine and incorporating the weld approach on at least three other engines. In each instance, the engines were installed and used on commercial aircraft in the normal course of Pan Am's business.

II.

The district court viewed each of these commercial uses as a "public use" within the meaning of Section 102(b), and this conclusion can hardly be challenged. That an invention or process employed in the regular conduct of a business is a "public use" for this purpose is a proposition settled long ago and never disturbed. * * * This settled concept of "public use" is "extraordinarily broad," Watson v. Allen, 254 F.2d 342, 345 (D.C. Cir. 1958) (Burger, Circuit Judge). It is a matter of legal indifference that the "public" use may be necessarily concealed from public awareness by the structure of the design or the manner of its use, Hall v. Macneale, 107 U.S. 90 (1882); Egbert v. Lippmann [104 U.S. 333 (1881)]; Metallizing Engineering Co. v. Kenyon Bearing & Auto Parts Co., 153 F.2d 516 (2d Cir. 1946), cert. denied 328 U.S. 840 (1946). Public use by a third party, with or without the knowledge or consent of the patentee, will generally defeat the patent as readily as public use by the inventor himself. * * *

We have previously explained the purposes of this sometimes harsh standard as intended "to require the inventor to see to it that he filed his application within [the statutory period] from the completion of his invention, so as to cut off all question of the defeat of his patent by a use or sale of it by others more than [the statutory period] prior to his application" and as designed to avoid the "perplexing questions which must frequently arise when the intent of the user and the bona fides of the use are questions to be determined. * * * " Eastman v. Mayor, etc., City of New York, 134 F. 844, 854 (2d Cir. 1904). See Walker on Patents 700 (2d Ed. 1964). It is thus clear beyond cavil that Pan Am's use of Cali's invention in commercial aircraft prior to September 1, 1963, would defeat Cali's patent, were the uses not included within the "experimental use" exception to the prior use bar which we shall discuss below.

On the other hand, although the parties have not dwelt on the matter, it is necessary to add that the present record would not appear to support a holding that Cali's action in submitting his suggestion to Pan Am constituted a "public use" regardless of the manner of Pan Am's subsequent exploitation of his idea. Cali did not conceal his invention from the public while using it to his commercial advantage more than a year before his

---

1. The tentative nature of the initial uses of Cali's idea at this early stage is indicated by two internal memoranda that passed between a Pan Am engineer, Frederick D. Curtin, and Pan Am's Inspection Department in February, 1963. These memoranda refer to an impending "trial installation" of the tie rod and "a service test" of the weld method. The tie rod was expressly forbidden for use "on any other engines until the results of the service testing were known."

application, thus extending the period of his monopoly beyond that protected by the patent laws. To prevent such an abuse and evasion of the patent laws seems to have been accepted by courts as an important purpose of the "public use" bar, see Watson v. Allen, supra, 254 F.2d at 346; Koehring v. National Auto Tool Co., 362 F.2d 100, 103 (7th Cir. 1966); Metallizing Engineering Co. v. Kenyon Bearing & Auto Parts Co., supra, 153 F.2d at 520, but one which has little importance in the circumstances of this case. Cali does not appear to stand in the position of an inventor who sells his patented device in the ordinary course of his business, for a predominantly commercial purpose, and without restriction or control over the uses to be made of the invention by the buyer. In such a case, the *buyer's* acts and purposes become irrelevant since the inventor's sale of the device is itself sufficient to defeat the patent. See Tool Research & Engineering Corp. v. Honcor Corp., 367 F.2d 449 (9th Cir. 1966), cert. denied 387 U.S. 919 (1967).

Eastern does stress the absence of any indication in this record that Cali attempted to control or in any way limit Pan Am's use of his idea. Similarly, the district court observed that Cali "put no restrictions on Pan Am's use" nor did he or *could* he "control the time * * * extent and nature of [Pan Am's] use" of his conception. 318 F.Supp. at 478. But the absence of any control by Cali, or any attempt to impose control, should not be elevated to the status of a per se test under the circumstances disclosed here and in the posture in which we receive this case. Cali lacked the means to develop his idea on his own resources beyond the bare conception of it. See Ry. Register Manuf. Co. v. Broadway & 7th Ave. Ry., 22 F. 655 (2d Cir. 1884); Harmon v. Struthers, 57 F. 637 (W.D.Pa. 1893). Nor was Cali, as an employee of Pan Am, in any position to dictate or even propose the terms of Pan Am's entirely gratuitous application of his concept. See General Electric Co. v. Continental Fibre Co., 256 F. 660, 663 (2d Cir. 1919). No purpose consonant with the scheme of the patent laws would be served were the statutory "public use" period to run in every case from the time that an employee communicated a raw idea to his superiors for evaluation and exploitation in their unfettered discretion. Indeed, such a doctrine might stifle inventiveness. See Note, The Public Use Bar to Patentability: Two New Approaches to the Experimental Use Exception, 52 Minn.L.Rev. 851, 855–56 (1968).

We do not imply that an inventor in Cali's situation might sell an idea to his employer and thereafter manifest no interest in the development, success, or failure of his invention, and yet take advantage of his employer's trial or experimental period. Such inaction and indifference would indicate that the inventor's intent was commercial—to secure the reward for the submission of the submitted concept, whatever its value—and not experimental, and would therefore constitute a "public" and nonexperimental use within the meaning of Section 102(b). Cali's acceptance of a financial reward for his idea, however, *after it was examined, tried, and ultimately adopted by Pan Am,* is consistent with a purpose to follow the idea through to its ultimate perfection and fate. Moreover, we do not see the purposes of the patent laws enhanced were the public use period to run from the date of submission, assuming Cali at that time and thereafter continued to maintain an interest in the progress of his suggestion, merely because Cali's inventiveness and thereafter his interest in the invention may have been whetted by the possibility of a financial reward should the concept prove useful to Pan Am.

Eastern does not now contend that Cali ever abandoned his idea to Pan Am in the sense suggested by the preceding paragraph. In any event, the evidence that Cali remained interested in the progress of his idea until and beyond the time it was unreservedly accepted by Pan Am is more than sufficient for purposes of our review of a grant of summary judgment. Accordingly, the determinative question becomes the nature and purpose of Pan Am's use of Cali's idea, as the parties and district court apparently seemed to agree.

III.

We turn to the issue principally briefed and argued, viz., whether Pan Am's public use of Cali's invention prior to September 1, 1963 falls within the judicially created exception to the "public use" bar for uses which are shown by "full, unequivocal, and convincing" proof, Smith & Griggs Manuf. Co., 123 U.S. 249, 264 (1888) to have been primarily intended as experimental rather than commercial. Aerovox Corp. v. Polymet Mfg. Corp., 67 F.2d 860 (2d Cir. 1933). Specifically, the question is whether this factual issue was resolved by the papers before the district court with sufficient clarity to permit an award of summary judgment.

At the threshold, we differ with the district court's interpretation of the scope of the "experimental use" exception. Judge Dooling appears to have believed that even Pan Am's "first use" of the tie rod and weld was not predominantly experimental even assuming that the primary purpose of the use was to determine whether Cali's idea should be adopted or rejected. Apparently the district court assumed that a use may not be "experimental" if the purpose is to see if the idea in question has any value at all, rather than to explore ways of improving the invention or "to determine or guide the direction of *modification of an emergent* inventive concept." 318 F.Supp. at 477 (emphasis added). The district court appears to have equated "experimental" with "developmental." Id.

This conception of the scope of the experimental use exception apparently underlay the whole of the district court's decision. We find it unduly restrictive. We see no good purpose in attempting to distinguish sharply between experimentation with an eye to going "back to the drawing board" for modification and rethinking in the event of initial failure on the one hand and experimentation directed more toward discovering whether a novel invention should be adopted and marketed or discarded in its entirety. Indeed, we have previously said as much in Aerovox Corp. v. Polymet Mfg. Corp., 67 F.2d 860, 862 (2d Cir. 1933) where we "assumed" that an inventor may experiment with an idea "not only to put it into definitive form, but to see whether his ideas are worth exploiting."

The leading case defining the reach of the experimental use exception, Elizabeth v. Pavement Co., 97 U.S. 126 (1877), involved experimentation to test the *durability* of the inventor's new kind of pavement. There was no indication that the inventor put the pavement to the test of six years' public wear to determine what improvements he might make, rather than simply to discover whether the idea was worth pursuing. Indeed, the Court's decision in favor of the patentee was premised on the assumption that the aim of the test might be "to bring his invention to perfection *or* to ascertain whether it [would] answer the purpose intended." 97 U.S. at 137 (emphasis added). Either sort of experimental use—if indeed any such sorting is tenable—would bring the invention within the experimental use exception because "it is the interest of the public, as well as [of the inventor] that the invention should be perfect *and* properly tested. * * * " Id. (Emphasis added.)

IV.

The crucial date therefore becomes that when Pan Am first publicly used Cali's concept with a predominantly commercial intent, rather than with the primary purpose of determining whether or in what form the idea should be put into general use.

In sum, we find that the record discloses a genuine issue of fact as to whether Pan Am publicly used Cali's invention prior to September 1, 1963, for predominantly non-experimental purposes.

Reversed.

NOTES

1. In re Smith, 714 F.2d 1127 (Fed. Cir. 1983). The court affirmed a PTO rejection of an application on a powdered carpet-treating composition, marketed as CARPET FRESH, on the basis of a § 102(b) public use. The product is sprinkled onto a carpet prior to vacuuming and is said to impart deodorizing, antistatic and antisoil characteristics to the carpet. More than a year prior to the application the applicant's company, Airwick, had conducted a consumer test of the product in St. Louis, using 76 customers. The test was conducted by first showing a video presentation introducing the product, and the consumers were then questioned about the pricing of the product, the believability of the claims made for the product, and their purchase intent. The consumers were then given samples of the product, without any express restrictions, to use in their own homes. After two weeks they were questioned further about their experience with the product. The applicant argued the use was experimental. "Contrary to appellants' contention that the St. Louis test was needed to obtain scientific data on their invention's operation and usefulness, such data could have been easily obtained in their own facilities. The operability and other properties of the claimed invention could have been verified without the assistance of 'typical housewives' (consumers). Instead, there was a more dominant purpose behind the St. Louis test, viz. to determine whether potential consumers would buy the product and how much they would pay for it-commercial exploitation." 714 F.2d at 1135. Would this test not have invalidated the patent if the 76 consumers had first been asked to sign confidentiality agreements?

2. Preemption Devices, Inc. v. Minnesota Mining & Mfg. Co., 732 F.2d 903 (Fed. Cir. 1984), affirming 559 F.Supp. 1250 (E.D. Pa. 1983), was an action for infringement of a patent on a device to enable emergency vehicles to control traffic lights, marketed under the trademark OPTICOM. The device involved the installation of a pulsed, high-intensity light on the emergency vehicle and a receiver-controller device at the traffic lights. As the emergency vehicle proceeds down the street it can send the light signal to the controller, which turns the traffic signal green in the direction of the oncoming vehicle. The infringer argued that the installation and demonstration of prototypes of the invention in two California cities and an application for a trademark registration on OPTICOM more than a year prior to the patent application invalidated the patent. The installed equipment was not sold, and was monitored by the inventor for the purpose of testing the performance of the equipment under actual use conditions and design changes were made in light of the experience. 559 F.Supp. at 1255–56. The patent owner successfully argued that the prototype installations were experimental. Of the trademark application, the Federal Circuit said: "We find particularly unconvincing * * * [the] argument based on the declaration filed in connection with the application to register the trademark OPTICOM, stating the date of first use and first use in commerce [more than one year prior to the patent application]. Those statements were not made with respect to the use of the invention but the use of the mark. The description of goods in the registration is very general and defines no particular apparatus." 732 F.2d 906.

3. A case very much like *Elizabeth v. Pavement Co.* is Manville Sales Corp. v. Paramount Systems, 917 F.2d 544 (Fed. Cir. 1990). The invention involved an outdoor lighting fixture for use at a highway rest stop in Wyoming. A previous light fixture had failed due to the rugged winter weather in Wyoming. The light fixture was installed at the site under express conditions of confidentiality, and ownership retained by the patent owner. The court held that the use was experimental.

4. Almost all cases that have applied the experimental use exception have been cases of experimental use by the inventor himself or others under his control. Indeed, it has been stated that the experimental use exception does not apply to public uses by third parties. Magnetics, Inc. v. Arnold Engineering Co., 438 F.2d 72, 74 (7th Cir. 1971). Should an experimental, non-secret use by a third party prior to the applicant's invention anticipate? Does it? Lyon v. Bausch & Lomb Optical Co., 224 F.2d 530, 534 (2d Cir. 1955) (Hand, J.), is helpful.

5. The ambiguities of public use and the draconian nature of the one year time bar make it important for an attorney, the minute he is consulted, to ascertain what steps his client has taken and will take to develop and exploit the invention. See Robert A. Choate, "On Sale"—Review and Circumspection, 47 J. Pat. Off. Soc'y 906 (1965). Even a present contract for the future sale of a product not yet manufactured can activate the time bar. Barmag Barmer Maschinenfabrik AG v. Murata Machinery, Ltd., 731 F.2d 831 (Fed. Cir. 1984). In UMC Electronics Co. v. United States, 816 F.2d 647

(Fed. Cir. 1987), cert. denied 484 U.S. 1025 (1988), the court held that an invention could be on sale at a time when it had not yet been completed or "reduced to practice." These holdings were followed in Pfaff v. Wells Electronics, Inc., 124 F.3d 1429 (Fed. Cir. 1997). The Supreme Court granted certiorari in that case. 118 S.Ct. 1183 (Mar 09, 1998).

---

(3) Patents

Alexander Milburn Co. v. Davis-Bournonville Co.

Supreme Court of the United States, 1926.
270 U.S. 390, 46 S.Ct. 324, 70 L.Ed. 651.

■ MR. JUSTICE HOLMES delivered the opinion of the Court.

This is a suit for the infringement of the plaintiff's patent for an improvement in welding and cutting apparatus alleged to have been the invention of one Whitford. The suit embraced other matters but this is the only one material here. The defense is that Whitford was not the first inventor of the thing patented, and the answer gives notice that to prove the invalidity of the patent evidence will be offered that one Clifford invented the thing, his patent being referred to and identified. The application for the plaintiff's patent was filed on March 4, 1911, and the patent was issued June 4, 1912. There was no evidence carrying Whitford's invention further back. Clifford's application was filed on January 31, 1911, before Whitford's, and his patent was issued on February 6, 1912. It is not disputed that this application gave a complete and adequate description of the thing patented to Whitford, but it did not claim it. The District Court gave the plaintiff a decree, holding that, while Clifford might have added this claim to his application, yet as he did not, he was not a prior inventor, 297 Fed.Rep. 846. The decree was affirmed by the Circuit Court of Appeals. 1 Fed. (2d) 227. There is a conflict between this decision and those of other Circuit Courts of Appeals, especially the sixth. Lemley v. Dobson-Evans Co., 243 Fed. 391. Naceskid Service Chain Co. v. Perdue, 1 Fed. (2d) 924. Therefore a writ of certiorari was granted by this Court. 266 U.S. 596.

The patent law authorizes a person who has invented an improvement like the present, "not known or used by others in this country, before his invention," &c., to obtain a patent for it. Rev.Sts. § 4886, amended, March 3, 1897, c. 391, § 1, 29 Stat. 692. Among the defences to a suit for infringement the fourth specified by the statute is that the patentee "was not the original and first inventor or discoverer of any material and substantial part of the thing patented." Rev. Sts. § 4920, amended, March 3, 1897, c. 391, § 2, 29 Stat. 692. Taking these words in their natural sense as they would be read by the common man, obviously one is not the first inventor if, as was the case here, somebody else has made a complete and adequate description of the thing claimed before the earliest moment to which the alleged inventor can carry his invention back. But the words cannot be taken quite so simply. In view of the gain to the public that the patent laws mean to secure we assume for purposes of decision that it would have been no bar to Whitford's patent if Clifford had written out his prior description and kept it in his portfolio uncommunicated to anyone. More than that, since the decision in the case of The Cornplanter Patent, 23 Wall. 181, it is said, at all events for many years, the Patent Office has made no search among abandoned patent applications, and by the words of the statute a previous foreign invention does not invalidate a patent granted here if it has not been patented or described in a printed publication. Rev.Sts. § 4923. See Westinghouse Machine Co. v. General Electric Co., 207 Fed. 75. These analogies prevailed in the minds of the Courts below.

On the other hand, publication in a periodical is a bar. This as it seems to us is more than an arbitrary enactment, and illustrates, as does the rule concerning previous public use, the principle that, subject to the exceptions mentioned, one really must be the first inventor in order to be entitled to a patent. Coffin v. Ogden, 18 Wall. 120. We understand the Circuit Court of Appeals to admit that if Whitford had not applied for his patent until after the issue to Clifford, the disclosure by the latter would have had the same effect as the publication of the same words in a periodical, although not made the basis of a claim. 1 Fed. (2d) 233. The invention is made public property as much in the one case as in the other. But if this be true, as we think that it is, it seems to us that a sound distinction cannot be taken between that case and a patent applied for before but not granted until after a second patent is sought. The delays of the patent office ought not to cut down the effect of what has been done. The description shows that Whitford was not the first inventor. Clifford had done all that he could do to make his description public. He had taken steps that would make it public as soon as the Patent Office did its work, although, of course, amendments might be required of him before the end could be reached. We see no reason in the words or policy of the law for allowing Whitford to profit by the delay and make himself out to be the first inventor when he was not so in fact, when Clifford had shown knowledge inconsistent with the allowance of Whitford's claim, [Webster] Loom Co. v. Higgins, 105 U.S. 580, and when otherwise the publication of his patent would abandon the thing described to the public unless it already was old. McClain v. Ortmayer, 141 U.S. 419, 424. Underwood v. Gerber, 149 U.S. 224, 230.

The question is not whether Clifford showed himself by the description to be the first inventor. By putting it in that form it is comparatively easy to take the next step and say that he is not an inventor in the sense of the statute unless he makes a claim. The question is whether Clifford's disclosure made it impossible for Whitford to claim the invention at a later date. The disclosure would have had the same effect as at present if Clifford had added to his description a statement that he did not claim the thing described because he abandoned it or because he believed it to be old. It is not necessary to show who did invent the thing in order to show that Whitford did not.

It is said that without a claim the thing described is not reduced to practice. But this seems to us to rest on a false theory helped out by the fiction that by a claim it is reduced to practice. A new application and a claim may be based on the original description within two years, and the original priority established notwithstanding intervening claims. Chapman v. Wintroath, 252 U.S. 126, 137. A description that would bar a patent if printed in a periodical or in an issued patent is equally effective in an application so far as reduction to practice goes.

As to the analogies relied upon below, the disregard of abandoned patent applications, however explained, cannot be taken to establish a principle beyond the rule as actually applied. As an empirical rule it no doubt is convenient if not necessary to the Patent Office, and we are not disposed to disturb it, although we infer that originally the practice of the Office was different. The policy of the statute as to foreign inventions obviously stands on its own footing and cannot be applied to domestic affairs. The fundamental rule we repeat is that the patentee must be the first inventor. The qualifications in aid of a wish to encourage improvements or to avoid laborious investigations do not prevent the rule from applying here.

Decree reversed.

Hazeltine Research, Inc. v. Brenner

Supreme Court of the United States, 1965.
382 U.S. 252, 86 S.Ct. 335, 15 L.Ed.2d 304, rehearing denied 382 U.S. 1000, 86 S.Ct. 527, 15 L.Ed.2d 489.

■ MR. JUSTICE BLACK delivered the opinion of the Court.

The sole question presented here is whether an application for patent pending in the Patent Office at the time a second application is filed constitutes part of the "prior art" as that term is used in 35 U.S.C. § 103 * * * .

The question arose in this way. On December 23, 1957, petitioner Robert Regis filed an application for a patent on a new and useful improvement on a microwave switch. On June 24, 1959, the Patent Examiner denied Regis' application on the ground that the invention was not one which was new or unobvious in light of the prior art and thus did not meet the standards set forth in § 103. The Examiner said that the invention was unpatentable because of the joint effect of the disclosures made by patents previously issued, one to Carlson (No. 2,491,644) and one to Wallace (No. 2,822,526). The Carlson patent had been issued on December 20, 1949, over eight years prior to Regis' application, and that patent is admittedly a part of the prior art insofar as Regis' invention is concerned. The Wallace patent, however, was pending in the Patent Office when the Regis application was filed. The Wallace application had been pending since March 24, 1954, nearly three years and nine months before Regis filed his application and the Wallace patent was issued on February 4, 1958, 43 days after Regis filed his application.[1]

---

1. It is not disputed that Regis' alleged invention, as well as his application, was made after Wallace's application was filed. There is, therefore, no question of priority of invention before us.

After the Patent Examiner refused to issue the patent, Regis appealed to the Patent Office Board of Appeals on the ground that the Wallace patent could not be properly considered a part of the prior art because it had been a "co-pending patent" and its disclosures were secret and not known to the public. The Board of Appeals rejected this argument and affirmed the decision of the Patent Examiner. Regis and Hazeltine, which had an interest as assignee, then instituted the present action in the District Court pursuant to 35 U.S.C. § 145 to compel the Commissioner to issue the patent. The District Court agreed with the Patent Office that the co-pending Wallace application was a part of the prior art and directed that the complaint be dismissed. 226 F.Supp. 459. On appeal the Court of Appeals affirmed per curiam. 340 F.2d 786. We granted certiorari to decide the question of whether a co-pending application is included in the prior art, as that term is used in 35 U.S.C. § 103. 380 U.S. 960.

Petitioners' primary contention is that the term "prior art," as used in § 103, really means only art previously publicly known. In support of this position they refer to a statement in the legislative history which indicates that prior art means "what was known before as described in section 102."[2] They contend that the use of the word "known" indicates that Congress intended prior art to include only inventions or discoveries which were already publicly known at the time an invention was made.

If petitioners are correct in their interpretation of "prior art," then the Wallace invention, which was not publicly known at the time the Regis application was filed, would not be prior art with regard to Regis' invention. This is true because at the time Regis filed his application the Wallace invention, although pending in the Patent Office, had never been made public and the Patent Office was forbidden by statute from disclosing to the public, except in special circumstances, anything contained in the application.[3]

The Commissioner, relying chiefly on Alexander Milburn Co. v. Davis-Bournonville Co., 270 U.S. 390, contends that when a patent is issued, the disclosures contained in the patent become a part of the prior art as of the time the application was filed, not, as petitioners contend, at the time the patent is issued. In that case a patent was held invalid because, at the time it was applied for, there was already pending an application which completely and adequately described the invention. In holding that the issuance of a patent based on the first application barred the valid issuance of a patent based on the second application, Mr. Justice Holmes, speaking for the Court, said, "The delays of the patent office ought not to cut down the effect of what has been done. * * * [The first applicant] had taken steps that would make it public as soon as the Patent Office did its work, although, of course, amendments might be required of him before the end

---

2. H.R.Rep.No.1923, 82d Cong., 2d Sess., p. 7 (1952).

3. 35 U.S.C. § 122 states: "Applications for patents shall be kept in confidence by the Patent Office and no information concerning the same given without authority of the applicant or owner unless necessary to carry out the provisions of any Act of Congress or in such special circumstances as may be determined by the Commissioner."

could be reached. We see no reason in the words or policy of the law for allowing [the second applicant] to profit by the delay. * * * " At p. 401.

In its revision of the patent laws in 1952, Congress showed its approval of the holding in *Milburn* by adopting 35 U.S.C. § 102(e) which provides that a person shall be entitled to a patent unless "(e) the invention was described in a patent granted on an application for patent by another filed in the United States before the invention thereof by the applicant for patent." Petitioners suggest, however, that the question in this case is not answered by mere reference to § 102(e), because in *Milburn,* which gave rise to that section, the copending applications described the same identical invention. But here the Regis invention is not precisely the same as that contained in the Wallace patent, but is only made obvious by the Wallace patent in light of the Carlson patent. We agree with the Commissioner that this distinction is without significance here. While we think petitioners' argument with regard to § 102(e) is interesting, it provides no reason to depart from the plain holding and reasoning in the *Milburn* case. The basic reasoning upon which the Court decided the *Milburn* case applies equally well here. When Wallace filed his application, he had done what he could to add his disclosures to the prior art. The rest was up to the Patent Office. Had the Patent Office acted faster, had it issued Wallace's patent two months earlier, there would have been no question here. As Justice Holmes said in *Milburn,* "The delays of the patent office ought not to cut down the effect of what has been done." P. 401.

To adopt the result contended for by petitioners would create an area where patents are awarded for unpatentable advances in the art. We see no reason to read into § 103 a restricted definition of "prior art" which would lower standards of patentability to such an extent that there might exist two patents where the Congress has plainly directed that there should be only one.

Affirmed.

F. Section 102 References as Prior Art

Application of Foster

United States Court of Customs and Patent Appeals, 1965.
343 F.2d 980, certiorari denied 383 U.S. 966, 86 S.Ct. 1270, 16 L.Ed.2d 307, rehearing denied 384 U.S. 934, 86 S.Ct. 1441, 16 L.Ed.2d 535.

■ ALMOND, JUDGE.

This is an appeal from the decision of the Board of Appeals affirming the rejection of the claims in appellant's patent application.

The invention relates to elastomeric synthetic polymers said to combine the desirable properties of natural Hevea rubber and the presently employed synthetic rubbers. These properties are described in the specification:

"Hevea natural rubber is characterized by excellent tack, especially after milling; thus being ideal for tire building operations. Hevea produces vulcanizates having excellent resilience and low hysteresis properties, high tensile, strength, and good flexibility at low temperatures. Gum vulcanizates formed from Hevea also possess high tensile strength. Hevea natural rubber is characterized by a crystallinity of at least about 40% and displays a crystalline X-ray diffraction pattern when stretched.

"Heretofore, the synthetic rubbers, in comparison with Hevea rubber, have exhibited low tack and no crystalline properties while their vulcanizates have been characterized by undesirably low tensile strengths and resilience, and undesirably high hysteresis. The synthetic rubbers, particularly the butadiene/styrene copolymer (GR-S), have been greatly superior to natural rubber in resisting crack initiation in service but have been markedly inferior to Hevea in resisting crack and cut growth. The undesirably high hysteresis of the synthetic rubber polymers has prevented their use in any substantial quantity in the production of such articles as the large tires employed on trucks, buses, and large off-the-road vehicles."

Infrared analysis of Hevea rubber has shown that the polymer consists of about 97.8% *cis*-1,4-structure. That is, the units of the rubber molecules are connected to each other in 1,4-addition to produce a linear chain with the spatial arrangement of the units in what is called the *cis*, as opposed to the *trans*, stereospecific configuration.

In contrast, the specification notes that "The butadiene portion of a typical GRS emulsion copolymer contains about 64% *trans*-1,4-structure, 18% *cis*-1,4-structure and 18% 1,2-structure."

By increasing the amount of *cis*-1,4-structure butadiene, the properties of the synthetic rubber are greatly improved.

* * *

The examiner and the Board of Appeals rejected all of the claims on the basis of the Binder reference. The record indicates that Binder, an employee of appellant's assignee, wrote an article in the magazine "Industrial and Engineering Chemistry." The article reports analyses of the microstructures of polybutadiene homopolymers and copolymers with styrene. The portions particularly relied upon by the Patent Office are:

1. Table V which lists polymer "39–1" as having 22.7% *cis*-1,4; 60.0% *trans*-1,4; and 17.3% 1,2 enstructures of butadiene. It is noted that the catalyst employed was a peroxide.

2. Conclusion: "The results of the analyses reported here show that while the amount of *cis*-1,4 addition increases with increasing temperature of polymerization, a polybutadiene containing 100% *cis*-1,4 or *trans*-1,4 addition cannot be made at any practical temperature."

It also should be noted that the Binder report at the outset states: "During the past 2 years, a large number of polybutadienes and butadiene-styrene copolymers have been prepared in these laboratories, in which various changes were made in the recipes with the object, mainly, of increasing the amount of *cis*-1,4 addition."

* * *

It is assumed by both parties—and it is unquestionably true—that when a reference fully discloses in every detail the subject matter of a claim, the statutory basis of a rejection on that reference is 35 U.S.C.A. § 102(a) if the reference date is before the applicant's *date of invention*, thereby establishing want of novelty, and section 102(b) if the reference date is more than one year prior to the actual United States *filing date*, thereby establishing a so-called "statutory bar," more accurately, a one-year time-bar which results in loss of right to a patent, regardless of when the invention was made. In either of these situations, it is often said that the invention is "anticipated" by the reference and the reference is termed an "anticipation."

Proofs submitted in this case under Patent Office Rule 131 with respect to a reference not before us (because it was overcome thereby) have established that the applicant's invention date was prior to December 26, 1952. The Binder reference is the August 1954 issue of a periodical. It is seen, therefore, that it is subsequent to the date of invention but more than one year prior to the filing date, which was August 21, 1956. * * * Since the date of invention is earlier than the reference date, section 102(a) is necessarily inapplicable because the printed publication was not "before the invention thereof by the applicant" and there is statutory novelty. This leaves paragraph (b) of section 102 as the only paragraph of that section having possible relevancy.

* * *

Because of the importance of the question to the law of patents, we have deemed it desirable to reconsider what is the statutory basis of this "unpatentable over" or obviousness type of rejection * * * under the circumstance that *the reference or references have effective dates more than one year prior to the filing date of the applicant.* More specifically, we have reconsidered the result again urged on us here, as allegedly authorized by section 103, that a reference having a date more than a year prior to the filing date may be disposed of by showing an invention date prior to the reference date, contrary to the express provision in Patent Office Rule 131.[8]

Sections 101, 102 and 103, generally speaking, deal with two different matters: (1) the factors to be considered in determining whether a

---

8. *"131. Affidavit of prior invention to overcome cited patent or publication.* (a) When any claim of an application is rejected on reference to a domestic patent which substantially shows or describes but does not claim the rejected invention, or on reference to a foreign patent or to a printed publication, and the applicant shall make oath to facts showing a completion of the invention in this country before the filing date of the application on which the domestic patent issued, or before the date of the foreign patent, or before the date of the printed publication, then the patent or publication cited shall not bar the grant of a patent to the applicant, *unless the* date of such patent or printed publication be more than one year prior to the date on which the application was filed in this country." [Emphasis ours.]

The italicized clause at the end of the foregoing paragraph or its equivalent has been present in the rule and its predecessor Rule 75 since January 1, 1898, when the rule was amended to include:

" * * * unless the date of such patent or printed publication is more than two years prior to the date on which application was filed in this country."

patentable invention has been *made*, i.e., novelty, utility, unobviousness, and the categories of patentable subject matter; and (2) "loss of right to patent" as stated in the heading of section 102, even though an otherwise patentable invention has been made. On the subject of loss of right, appellant's brief contains a helpful review of the development of the statutory law since 1793. It says:

"In 1897 the patent laws were amended to make the * * * two-year bar period apply to all public uses, publications and patents *regardless of the source* from which they emanated. The change was a consequence, primarily, of greatly improved communications within the country which had rendered inventors easily able to acquire knowledge of the public acts of others within their own fields. It was reasoned that any inventor who *delayed in filing* a patent application for more than two years after a public disclosure of the invention would obtain *an undeserved reward in derogation of the rights of the public* if he were granted a patent.

"In 1939, in recognition of further improvements in communications, Congress reduced the two-year bar period to one year. * * *

"That 1939 Act was carried over unchanged in the 1952 recodification of the patent laws as 35 U.S.C. § 102(b).

* * *

"Manifestly, Section 102(b) from its earliest beginnings has been and was intended to be directed toward the encouragement of *diligence* in the filing of patent applications and the protection of the public from monopolies on subject matter which had already been fully disclosed to it."

These statements are in accord with our understanding of the history and purposes of section 102(b). It presents a sort of statute of limitations, formerly two years, now one year, within which an inventor, even though he has made a patentable invention, must act on penalty of loss of his right to patent. What starts the period running is clearly the availability of the invention *to the public* through the categories of disclosure enumerated in 102(b), which include "a printed publication" anywhere describing the invention. There appears to be no dispute about the operation of this statute in "complete anticipation" situations but *the contention seems to be that 102(b) has no applicability where the invention is not completely disclosed in a single patent or publication*, that is to say where the rejection involves the addition to the disclosure of the reference of the ordinary skill of the art or the disclosure of another reference which indicates what those of ordinary skill in the art are presumed to know, *and to have known for more than a year before the application was filed.* Upon a complete reexamination of this matter, we are convinced that the contention is contrary to the policy consideration which motivated the enactment by Congress of a statutory bar. On logic and principle we think this contention is unsound, and we also believe it is contrary to the patent law as it has actually existed since at least 1898.

* * *

As to dealing with the express language of 102(b), for example, "described in a printed publication," technically, we see no reason to so read the words of the statute as to preclude the use of more than one reference; nor do we find in the context anything to show that "a printed publication" cannot include two or more printed publications.[9] * * *

As to what the law has been, more particularly what it was prior to 1953, when the new patent act and its section 103 became effective, there is a paucity of direct precedents on the precise problem. We think there is a reason for this. Under the old law (R.S. § 4886, where 102(b) finds its origin) patents were refused or invalidated on references dated more than a year before the filing date because the invention was anticipated or, if they were not, then *because there was no "invention,"* the latter rejection being based either on (a) a single nonanticipatory reference plus the skill of the art *or (b) on a plurality of references.* There was no need to seek out the precise statutory basis because it was R.S. § 4886 in any event, read in the light of the Supreme Court's interpretation of the law that there must always be "invention." This issue was determined on the disclosures of the references relied on and if they had dates more than one year before the filing date, it was assumed they could be relied on to establish a "statutory bar." There was an express prohibition in Rule 131 and in its predecessor Rule 75 against antedating a reference having a date more than a year prior to the filing date and there was no basis on which to contest it. The accepted state of law is exemplified by the following sentences in McCrady's Patent Office Practice, 4th ed. (1959), Sec. 127, p. 176:

> "Prior art specified by 35 U.S.C. § 102, which has an effective date more than one year prior to the effective filing date of an application, constitutes a bar under the language of that statute. Until 1940 the period was two years.

* * *

> "Procedurally, the significance of the statutory bar lies in the fact that it cannot be antedated by evidence of applicant's earlier invention, as by affidavits under Rule 131, or by evidence presented in an infringement suit."

Our decision in Palmquist [Application of Palmquist, 319 F.2d 547] appears to have been the first to hold otherwise.

* * *

It would seem that the practical operation of the prior law was that references having effective dates more than a year before applicant's filing

---

9. The construction of section 102(b) is subject to the provision of 1 U.S.C. § 1 which provides in pertinent part:

"In determining the meaning of any Act of Congress, unless the context indicates otherwise—words importing the singular include and apply to several persons, parties, or things; * * *."

date were always considered to be effective as references, regardless of the applicant's date of invention, and that rejections were then predicated thereon for "lack of invention" without making the distinction which we now seem to see as implicit in sections 102 and 103, "anticipation" or no novelty situations under 102 and "obviousness" situations under 103. But on further reflection, we now feel bound to point out that of equal importance is the question of *loss of right* predicated on a one-year *time-bar* which, it seems clear to us, has never been limited to "anticipation" situations, involving only a single reference, but has included as well "no invention" (now "obviousness") situations. It follows that where the time bar is involved, *the actual date of invention becomes irrelevant* and that it is not in accordance with either the letter or the principle of the law, or its past interpretation over a very long period, to permit an applicant to dispose of a reference having a date more than one year prior to his filing date by proving his actual date of invention.

Such a result was permitted by our decision in Palmquist and to the extent that it permitted a reference, having a publication date more than one year prior to the United States filing date to which the applicant was entitled, to be disposed of by proof of a date of invention earlier than the date of the reference, that decision is hereby overruled.

* * *

Since we must reject Foster's contention that he can dispose entirely of Binder by showing an earlier invention date, it becomes necessary for us to consider whether there was a loss of right to a patent, i.e., whether the invention became obvious to the public at the time of the Binder publication. Appellant has fully argued this issue in his briefs.

* * *

[The Court found that the invention became obvious at the time of the Binder publication.]

We, accordingly, reverse the decision of the Board of Appeals with regard to claims 22, 23, 25, 26, 28, 34 and 35. The rejection of claims 12, 13, 17, 18, 29, 30, 33, 36, 39 and 40 having been affirmed because the appellant has lost his right to these claims, the decision is modified.

Modified.

NOTES

1. The casenote on *Palmquist* (the decision overruled in *Foster*) at 32 Geo. Wash. L. Rev. 656 concludes as follows:

> An interpretation of § 103 which will encompass the one-year statutory bar clearly is possible in view of legislative and case history. The phrase "at the time the invention was made" apparently was inserted to establish a fictional consideration of an invention before it was disclosed to the Patent Office. However, the fiction does not stop

there; the artificial period "at the time the invention was made" is coupled with a second fiction, "the prior art." The "prior art" as used in § 103 was intended to encompass the type of prior art set forth in § 102. The "prior art" has been interpreted to include copending applications which were not public knowledge "at the time the invention was made," but of which the inventor is fictionally apprised. Furthermore, an applicant's own public use more than a year before his filing date and references uncovered in an interference are considered prior art. Even under § 103, prior art published more than a year before applicant's filing date is entitled to greater weight than recent prior art.

Further, events subsequent to invention may bar an applicant's opportunity to obtain a patent, as when his invention becomes obvious to those skilled in the art through his or another's disclosure. This bar arises from lack of diligence in filing a patent application, and the public reliance upon the knowledge obtained relative to the invention. The "prior art" therefore may include all public knowledge subsequent to invention limited only by a period of grace one year prior to the filing of a patent application. This interpretation of the statutory one-year bar as applicable equally to §§ 102(b) and 103 appears preferable to the creation of a basic distinction between the two sections.

The policy which requires a prospective patentee to contribute to the state of the art and proceed diligently does not distinguish between an invention placed in the public domain fully disclosed in a reference and one obvious to those skilled in the art. Indeed, the distinction between a complete anticipation and a difference merely obvious to those skilled in the art might approach the trivial. There appears to be no sound reason to cast the former as a statutory bar capable of cutting off an applicant's rights while allowing the latter, regardless of its date, to be removed as a reference by affidavit.

Id. at 662–63.

2. Section 102(b) requires a printed publication. In In re Bayer, 568 F.2d 1357 (C.C.P.A. 1978), the question was whether the inventor's master's thesis became a printed publication as of the date it was deposited with the University library or the date on which it was catalogued and made accessible on the library shelves. The court held that it was the date the thesis became available to the public.

3. *Hazeltine* held that the items described in § 102(e) are prior art. *Foster* held that the items described in § 102(b) are prior art. That left the question whether "an invention * * * made by another * * * who has not abandoned, suppressed, or concealed it" (§ 102(g)) is prior art. In Application of Bass, 474 F.2d 1276 (C.C.P.A. 1973), the court said that it is. The *Bass* construction had the advantage of statutory symmetry—all subsections in § 102 dealing with novelty were treated as defining a form of prior art for purposes of § 103. But the implication of that reading was that secret inventions of others unknown to the "art" and unknown to the inventor were nevertheless prior art. The court retreated from that implication of *Bass* by suggesting in

In re Clemens, 622 F.2d 1029, 1039–40 (C.C.P.A. 1980), that *Bass* did not operate where the inventor did not know of the work of others. That took care of the secret inventions of others, but created a difficult problem in the management of laboratories. If co-researchers working on related problems communicated with each other about their work, then there was the danger that their work would become prior art, each to the other. Thus a large industrial laboratory with a sophisticated staff doing work at a level far above that of the "art" in general might find that none of the work of its employees was patentable because as to an invention by any one employee, the inventions of all the other employees would be prior art. See Kimberly-Clark Corp. v. Johnson & Johnson, 745 F.2d 1437 (Fed. Cir. 1984), where the prior art considered in connection with a Kimberly-Clark patent on a sanitary napkin structure was work by other technicians employed by Kimberly-Clark. That problem could be solved under *Clemens* by forbidding the employees to tell each other about their work, but then the gains from sharing information within the laboratory would be lost and the employer might find itself paying separate research teams each to rediscover what other of its employees already knew. In *Kimberly-Clark* the court rejected the notion that knowledge of the invention was required under § 102(g), since the section doesn't mention it. 745 F.2d 1445. Then, in dictum, it suggested disaffection with *Bass*. "[T]he use of * * * secret art—as § 103 'prior art'—except as required by § 102(e), is not favored for reasons of public policy." 745 F.2d 1446. The Court, however, followed both *Bass* and *Kimberly-Clark* in E.I. DuPont de Nemours & Co. v. Phillips Petroleum Co., 849 F.2d 1430 (Fed. Cir. 1988).

The problems created by this doctrine for research management led Congress to add the last sentence of present § 103 in the Patent Law Amendments of 1984, P.L. 98–622: "Subject matter developed by another person, which qualifies as prior art only under subsection (f) or (g) of section 102 of this title, shall not preclude patentability under this section where the subject matter and the claimed invention were, at the time the invention was made, owned by the same person or subject to an obligation of assignment to the same person." The impact of this amendment was considered by the Federal Circuit in the following case.

Oddzon Products, Inc. v. Just Toys, Inc.

United States Court of Appeals for the Federal Circuit, 1997.
122 F.3d 1396.

■ LOURIE, CIRCUIT JUDGE.

* * *

OddzOn is a toy and sporting goods company that sells the popular "Vortex" tossing ball, a foam football-shaped ball with a tail and fin structure. The Vortex ball is OddzOn's commercial embodiment of its design patent, U.S. Patent D 346,001, which issued on April 12, 1994. Figure 1 of the patent is shown below:

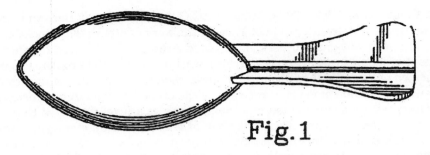

Fig. 1

Just Toys, Inc., another toy and sporting goods company, sells a competing line of "Ultra Pass" balls. Two versions of the allegedly infringing Ultra Pass balls are shown below:

OddzOn sued Just Toys for design patent infringement, trade dress infringement, and state-law unfair competition, asserting that the Ultra Pass line of tossing balls was likely to be confused with OddzOn's Vortex ball, and that the Ultra Pass packaging was likely to be confused with the Vortex packaging. Just Toys denied infringement and asserted that the patent was invalid. On cross-motions for summary judgment, the district court held that the patent was not shown to be invalid and was not infringed. The court also held that Just Toys did not infringe OddzOn's trade dress.

The district court determined that two confidential designs that had been disclosed to the inventor qualified as subject matter encompassed within the meaning of 35 U.S.C. § 102(f) (1994) and concluded that these designs could be combined with other prior art designs for purposes of a challenge to the validity of the patent under 35 U.S.C. § 103 (1994). Nonetheless, the district court held that the patented design would not have been obvious in light of the prior art, including the two confidential designs. The court construed the single claim of the patent as being directed to the design for:

> a ball shaped like a football, with a slender, straight tailshaft projecting from the rear of the football. In addition, the '001 Patent design has three fins symmetrically arranged around the tailshaft, each of which has a gentle curve up and outward which creates a fin with a larger surface area at the end furthest from the ball. The fins flare outwardly

along the entire length of the tailshaft, with the front end of the fin extending slightly up along the side of the football so that the fins seemingly protrude from the inside of the football.

After construing the claim, the court held that the patented design was not dictated solely by function and thus that it was not invalid on that ground. It also held that OddzOn failed to present sufficient evidence to allow a reasonable jury to find infringement. The district court considered OddzOn's proffered consumer survey evidence of similarity, but held that it was not probative on the question whether the accused balls were substantially similar to the patented design in terms of its protectable features, i.e., its ornamental features. The district court concluded that the survey evidence demonstrated nothing more than that any ball with a tail and fins, regardless of its ornamental features, would appear to be similar to the patented design.

The court found that OddzOn's proffered testimony from an expert was also not probative of any similarity between the ornamental features of the accused balls and the patented design. It noted that the bases for the expert's conclusion of similarity were unclear and that the legal standards applied to reach that conclusion were not apparent. The court excluded evidence of "actual confusion," stating that there was no basis to determine that the mistaken return of twenty-one of the accused balls to OddzOn would not have been typical in the industry absent "confusion." Furthermore, it stated that there was no way of determining whether the ornamental features caused the "confusion."

The district court also held that the accused balls and their packaging did not violate OddzOn's protectable trade dress rights. Holding that OddzOn's evidence was not probative of consumer confusion regarding the source of the accused balls, the court granted Just Toys' motion for summary judgment. Because the court found no likelihood of confusion, it did not reach the issues of inherent distinctiveness or secondary meaning. Finally, determining that California's unfair competition law is "substantially congruent" to trademark infringement law, the question being whether there is a likelihood of confusion with regard to source, the court ruled that OddzOn's state-law claim must fall with its federal trade dress claims. OddzOn appeals and Just Toys cross-appeals the grant of the respective summary judgment motions.

* * *

A. The Prior Art Status of § 102(f) Subject Matter

The district court ruled that two confidential ball designs (the "disclosures") which "inspired" the inventor of the OddzOn design were prior art for purposes of determining obviousness under § 103. The district court noted that this court had recently declined to rule definitively on the relationship between § 102(f) and § 103, see Lamb-Weston, Inc. v. McCain Foods, Ltd., 78 F.3d 540, 544 (Fed. Cir. 1996), but relied on the fact that the United States Patent and Trademark Office (PTO) interprets prior art under § 103 as including disclosures encompassed within § 102(f). OddzOn challenges the court's determination that subject matter encompassed within § 102(f) is prior art for purposes of an obviousness inquiry under § 103. OddzOn asserts that because these disclosures are not known to the public, they do not possess the usual hallmark of prior art, which is that they provide actual or constructive public knowledge. OddzOn argues that while the two disclosures constitute patent-defeating subject matter under 35 U.S.C. § 102(f), they cannot be combined with "real" prior art to defeat patentability under a combination of § 102(f) and § 103.

The prior art status under § 103 of subject matter derived by an applicant for patent within the meaning of § 102(f) has never expressly been decided by this court. We now take the opportunity to settle the persistent question whether § 102(f) is a prior art provision for purposes of § 103. As will be discussed, although there is a basis to suggest that § 102(f) should not be considered as a prior art provision, we hold that a fair reading of § 103, as amended in 1984, leads to the conclusion that § 102(f) is a prior art provision for purposes of § 103.

Section 102(f) provides that a person shall be entitled to a patent unless "he did not himself invent the subject matter sought to be patented." This is a derivation provision, which provides that one may not obtain a patent on that which is obtained from someone else whose possession of the subject matter is inherently "prior." It does not pertain only to public knowledge, but also applies to private communications between the inventor and another which may never become public. Subsections (a), (b), (e), and (g), on the other hand, are clearly prior art provisions. They relate to knowledge manifested by acts that are essentially public. Subsections (a) and (b) relate to public knowledge or use, or prior patents and printed publications; subsection (e) relates to prior filed applications for patents of others which have become public by grant; and subsection (g) relates to prior inventions of others that are either public or will likely become public in the sense that they have not been abandoned, suppressed, or concealed. Subsections (c) and (d) are loss-of-right provisions. Section 102(c) precludes the obtaining of a patent by inventors who have abandoned their invention. Section 102(d) causes an inventor to lose the right to a patent by delaying the filing of a patent application too long after having filed a corresponding patent application in a foreign country. Subsections (c) and (d) are therefore not prior art provisions.

In In re Bass, 474 F.2d 1276, 1290 (CCPA 1973), the principal opinion of the Court of Customs and Patent Appeals held that a prior invention of another that was not abandoned, suppressed, or concealed (102(g) prior art) could be combined with other prior art to support rejection of a claim for obviousness under § 103. The principal opinion noted that the provisions of § 102 deal with two types of issues, those of novelty and loss-of-right. It explained: "Three of [the subsections,] (a), (e), and (g), deal with events prior to applicant's invention date and the other, (b), with events more than one year prior to the U.S. application date. These are the 'prior art' subsections." Id. (emphasis in original). The principal opinion added, in dictum (§ 102(f) not being at issue), that "[o]f course, (c), (d), and (f) have no relation to § 103 and no relevancy to what is 'prior art' under § 103." Id. There is substantial logic to that conclusion. After all, the other prior art provisions all relate to subject matter that is, or eventually becomes, public. Even the "secret prior art" of § 102(e) is ultimately public in the form of an issued patent before it attains prior art status.

Thus, the patent laws have not generally recognized as prior art that which is not accessible to the public. It has been a basic principle of patent law, subject to minor exceptions, that prior art is:

> technology already available to the public. It is available, in legal theory at least, when it is described in the world's accessible literature, including patents, or has been publicly known or in . . . public use or on sale "in this country." That is the real meaning of "prior art" in legal theory—it is knowledge that is available, including what would be obvious from it, at a given time, to a person of ordinary skill in the art.

Kimberly-Clark Corp. v. Johnson & Johnson, 745 F.2d 1437, 1453 (Fed. Cir. 1984) (citations omitted).

Moreover, as between an earlier inventor who has not given the public the benefit of the invention, e.g., because the invention has been abandoned without public disclosure, suppressed, or concealed, and a subsequent inventor who obtains a patent, the policy of the law is for the subsequent inventor to prevail. See W.L. Gore & Assocs., Inc. v. Garlock, Inc., 721 F.2d 1540, 1550 (Fed. Cir. 1983) ("Early public disclosure is a linchpin of the patent system. As between a prior inventor [who does not disclose] and a later inventor who promptly files a patent application . . . , the law favors the latter."). Likewise, when the possessor of secret art (art that has been abandoned, suppressed, or concealed) that predates the critical date is faced with a later-filed patent, the later-filed patent should not be invalidated in the face of this "prior" art, which has not been made available to the public. Thus, prior, but non-public, inventors yield to later inventors who utilize the patent system.

However, a change occurred in the law after *Bass* was decided. At the time *Bass* was decided, § 103 read as follows:

> A patent may not be obtained though the invention is not identically disclosed or described as set forth in section 102 of this title, if the differences between the subject matter sought to be patented and the prior art are such that the subject matter as a whole would have been obvious at the time the invention was made to a person having ordinary skill in the art to which said subject matter pertains. Patentability shall not be negatived by the manner in which the invention was made.

35 U.S.C. § 103. The prior art being referred to in that provision arguably included only public prior art defined in subsections 102(a), (b), (e), and (g).

In 1984, Congress amended § 103, adding the following paragraph:

> Subject matter developed by another person, which qualifies as prior art only under subsection (f) or (g) of section 102 of this title, shall not

preclude patentability under this section where the subject matter and
the claimed invention were, at the time the invention was made, owned
by the same person or subject to an obligation of assignment to the same
person.

35 U.S.C. § 103 (now § 103(c)) (emphasis added). It is historically very clear
that this provision was intended to avoid the invalidation of patents under
§ 103 on the basis of the work of fellow employees engaged in team research.
See Section-by-Section Analysis: Patent Law Amendments Act of 1984, 130
Cong. Rec. 28069, 28071 (Oct. 1, 1984), reprinted in 1984 U.S.C.C.A.N. 5827,
5833 (stating that the amendment, which encourages communication among
members of research teams, was a response to Bass and In re Clemens, 622
F.2d 1029 (CCPA 1980), in which "an earlier invention which is not public
may be treated under Section 102(g), and possibly under 102(f), as prior
art"). There was no clearly apparent purpose in Congress's inclusion of
§ 102(f) in the amendment other than an attempt to ameliorate the problems
of patenting the results of team research. However, the language appears in
the statute; it was enacted by Congress. We must give effect to it.

The statutory language provides a clear statement that subject matter
that qualifies as prior art under subsection (f) or (g) cannot be combined with
other prior art to render a claimed invention obvious and hence unpatentable
when the relevant prior art is commonly owned with the claimed invention at
the time the invention was made. While the statute does not expressly state
in so many words that § 102(f) creates a type of prior art for purposes of § 103,
nonetheless that conclusion is inescapable; the language that states that
§ 102(f) subject matter is not prior art under limited circumstances clearly
implies that it is prior art otherwise. That is what Congress wrote into law in
1984 and that is the way we must read the statute.

This result is not illogical. It means that an invention, A', that is obvious in view of subject matter A, derived from another, is also unpatentable.
The obvious invention, A', may not be unpatentable to the inventor of A, and
it may not be unpatentable to a third party who did not receive the disclosure of A, but it is unpatentable to the party who did receive the disclosure.

The PTO's regulations also adopt this interpretation of the statute.
37 C.F.R. § 1.106(d) (1996) ("Subject matter which is developed by another
person which qualifies as prior art only under 35 U.S.C. § 102(f) or (g) may
be used as prior art under 35 U.S.C. § 103."). Although the PTO's interpretation of this statute is not conclusive, we agree with the district court that
it is a reasonable interpretation of the statute.

It is sometimes more important that a close question be settled one way
or another than which way it is settled. We settle the issue here (subject of
course to any later intervention by Congress or review by the Supreme
Court), and do so in a manner that best comports with the voice of Congress.
Thus, while there is a basis for an opposite conclusion, principally based on
the fact that § 102(f) does not refer to public activity, as do the other provisions that clearly define prior art, nonetheless we cannot escape the import
of the 1984 amendment. We therefore hold that subject matter derived from
another not only is itself unpatentable to the party who derived it under

§ 102(f), but, when combined with other prior art, may make a resulting obvious invention unpatentable to that party under a combination of §§ 102(f) and 103. Accordingly, the district court did not err by considering the two design disclosures known to the inventor to be prior art under the combination of §§ 102(f) and 103.

In addition to arguing that the district court properly considered § 102(f) to be a prior art provision for purposes of § 103, Just Toys argues that the two confidential disclosures known to the inventor, but not disclosed to the PTO, were "material to patentability" and hence should have been disclosed. Just Toys therefore asks this court to remand the case so that the district court can hear its mooted motion for summary judgment on the issue of inequitable conduct. We decline to do so. In light of the ambiguous nature of the statute and the unclear development of the case law regarding the prior art status of § 102(f) subject matter until this point, we hold as a matter of law that OddzOn could not have acted with deceptive intent when it failed to disclose this information to the PTO.

B. Non-Obviousness Under § 103

Just Toys cross-appeals from the district court's conclusion that Just Toys failed to establish obviousness of the design by clear and convincing evidence. Just Toys argues that both of the disclosed § 102(f) designs constitute primary "references" because they "show all of the basic design elements shown in the '001 patent: a football with a tailshaft and fins." This argument is unpersuasive.

Pursuant to 35 U.S.C. § 171 (1994), one may obtain a design patent for "any new, original, and ornamental design for an article of manufacture." The design must also be non-obvious. Id. ("The provisions for this title relating to patents for inventions shall apply to patents for designs, except as otherwise provided."); In re Borden, 90 F.3d 1570, 1574 (Fed. Cir. 1996). We agree with the district court that none of the cited designs, including the two confidential disclosures, render the patented design obvious, either individually or in combination. According to familiar law, a design patent only protects the ornamental aspects of the design. Because the presence of a tailshaft and fins has been shown to be necessary to have a ball with similar aerodynamic stability to OddzOn's commercial embodiment, such general features are functional and thus not protectable as such. Invalidating prior art must show or render obvious the ornamental features of a patented design. The existence of prior art simply showing a ball with a tailshaft and fins, without more, is not sufficient to render the patented design obvious. Just Toys does not dispute the fact that the fins of the confidential disclosures lack the ornamental features of the patented design. They do not appear to protrude from the ball while gently flaring outwardly. Because none of the prior art cited by Just Toys exhibits ornamental characteristics that are the same as or similar to OddzOn's design, we conclude that the district court did not err in holding that the cited references would not have rendered the patented design obvious.

* * *

[The court also affirmed the district court's finding of non-infringement. Although there was evidence that consumers confused the two balls, there was no evidence that this confusion was caused by the similarity of the ornamental features protected by the design patent, and because of differences in the ornamental features the court concluded there was no infringement.]

The district court did not err in granting Just Toys' motion for summary judgment on OddzOn's design patent claim and on its trade dress and state-law unfair competition claims. Furthermore, the district court did not err in granting OddzOn's motion for summary judgment that Just Toys failed to establish invalidity of the '001 patent. * * * Accordingly, the district court's judgment is affirmed.

G. First Inventor

Title 35 § 102(g) provides that "[a] person shall be entitled to a patent unless before the applicant's invention thereof the invention was made in this country by another who had not abandoned, suppressed, or concealed it." Questions of priority most frequently arise in the context of interference proceedings under 35 U.S.C. § 135. In an interference proceeding the Patent Office determines which of two or more applicants claiming the same invention is entitled to the patent. But questions of priority are equally important in infringement cases, for proof that the patentee was not the first inventor invalidates the patent.

Historically, the prior invention must be prior invention in the United States. This basic principle is still codified in 35 U.S.C. § 104(a), but it has been rapidly eroding. For instance in O'Reilly v. Morse, 56 U.S. (15 How.) 62 (1853), the Court disregarded proof of prior inventions by several Europeans partly on the ground that they were foreign inventions. Other aspects of the *Morse* opinion appear *supra*.

In 1990 the Inventions in Outer Space Act added a new § 105 to Title 35 that provides in essence that outer space on U.S. space vehicles is part of the United States "for purposes of this title". P.L. 101–580 (1990).

The Uruguay Round Agreements Act, Pub. L. 103–465, Dec. 8, 1994, amended 35 U.S.C. § 104 to include inventive activity occurring in a WTO member country. Other countries complained that the U.S. rule awarding priority only to first inventors in the United States discriminated against non-U.S. inventors. Article 27 ¶ 1 of the GATT TRIPS provides in part that "patents shall be available and patent rights enjoyable without discrimination as to the place of invention * * * ."

Other countries award priority to the first applicant to file, which is a simpler rule to administer.

The "hornbook" rule of priority in the United States can be stated with relative ease:

> The first inventor is (a) the person who first conceived of the invention and who from the time of the entry into the "field" of any other person claiming to be the first inventor was diligent in his efforts

to reduce his invention to practice or, if no such person exists, (b) the person who first reduced the invention to practice.

Definition of reduction to practice: An invention can be reduced to practice either by actually making it and demonstrating its operability or by filing a patent application which claims the invention and adequately discloses under 35 U.S.C. § 112 how to make and practice it.

Reduction to practice by filing is called constructive reduction to practice.

(1) Interference Practice

Interferences in the Patent Office are decided by the Board of Patent Appeals and Interferences 37 C.F.R. § 1.614. An interference can arise in two ways. First, an examiner who becomes aware of two applications covering the same subject matter can suggest a common claim to each of the applicants under Rule 1–605(a), 37 C.F.R. § 1.605(a). The applicants must both adopt the suggested claim if they desire the interference, and if they do not adopt the claim they are taken to have disclaimed the invention covered by the suggested claim. Second, an applicant who becomes aware of an issued patent (or in rare instances a pending application) covering the same subject matter as his application can copy claims from the issued patent. 37 C.F.R. §§ 1.604, 1.607.

The Patent Office policy is that:

If doubts exist as to whether there is an interference, an interference should not be declared.

U.S. Patent and Trademark Office, Manual of Patent Examining Procedure § 2301.01(f) (6th ed. 1995, rev. 1997).

(2) Reduction to Practice

In Sydeman v. Thoma, 32 App.D.C. 362 (1909), the court said:

Decisions involving this often-litigated question of actual reduction to practice may be divided into three general classes. The first class includes devices so simple and of such obvious efficacy that the complete construction of one of a size and form intended for and capable of practical use is held sufficient without test in actual use. Mason v. Hepburn, 13 App.D.C. 86, 89. * * * The second class consists of those where a machine embodying every essential element of the invention, having been tested and its practical utility for the intended purpose demonstrated to reasonable satisfaction, has been held to have been reduced to practice notwithstanding it may not be a mechanically perfect machine. In other words, it is sufficient reduction to practice, although a more desirable commercial result may be obtained by some simple and obvious mechanical improvement, or by substituting another well-known material for the one used in the original construction, as, for example, metal for wood, cast metal for sheet metal, and the like. * * * The third class includes those where the machine is of such a character that the particular use for which it is intended must be given special consideration, and requires satisfactory operation in the actual execution of the object.

In cases falling within the second and third classes described, long delay in putting the machine in actual use for the intended purpose has always been regarded as a potent circumstance in determining whether the test was successful, or only an abandoned experiment.

Scott v. Finney

United States Court of Appeals for the Federal Circuit, 1994.
34 F.3d 1058.

■ RADER, CIRCUIT JUDGE.

The Board of Patent Appeals and Interferences awarded priority in Interference No. 102,429 to the senior party, Dr. Roy P. Finney. The Board held that the junior party, Dr. F. Brantley Scott and John H. Burton, did not show a reduction to practice before Dr. Finney's date of invention. Because the Board imposed an overly strict requirement for testing to show reduction to practice, this court reverses and remands.

BACKGROUND

This interference involves Dr. Finney's United States Patent No. 4,791,917, which was accorded the benefit of its May 15, 1980 parent application, and the Scott and Burton application, Serial No. 07/241,826, which was accorded the benefit of its parent application Serial No. 06/264,202, filed May 15, 1981. Although the Scott and Burton application claims a joint invention of both applicants, Dr. Scott is the sole inventor of the subject matter in interference No. 102,429.

The invention is a penile implant for men unable to obtain or maintain an erection. The prosthetic device is a self-contained unit that permits the patient to simulate an erection. The implant contains two reservoirs connected through a valve. The invention operates by shifting the inflating liquid between the two reservoirs. When the penis is flaccid, the invention maintains inflating liquid in a reservoir at the base of the penis. A simulated erection occurs when the liquid shifts through the valve into the elongated reservoir implanted in the forward section of the penis.

Prior art devices fell into two categories: flexible rods and inflatable devices. Flexible rods had the disadvantage of making the penis permanently erect. The prior inflatable devices relied on fluid from a source and pump external to the body to inflate tubes implanted in the penis. These devices also had several disadvantages.

The Interference Count at issue states: An implantable penile prosthesis for implanting completely within a patient's penis comprising at least one elongated member having a flexible distal forward section for implantation within the pendulous penis, said forward section being constructed to rigidize upon being filled with pressuring fluid; a proximal, rearward section adapted to be implanted within the root end of the penis, said rearward section containing a fluid reservoir chamber, externally operable pump means in said member for transferring fluid under pressure to said flexible distal forward section of said member for achieving an erection; and valve means positioned within said member which open when said pump is operated so that fluid is forced from said pump through said valve means into said flexible distal forward section of said chamber.

The parties to this interference had contested related subject matter in an earlier interference, No. 101,149. The count of 101,149 was a species of the generic count in this interference. Dr. Scott won that earlier interference.

In this interference, No. 102,429, Dr. Finney's application has an earlier filing date than Scott's application. Dr. Scott still has, however, an earlier conception date. Dr. Scott did not present evidence of diligence after conception of his invention. See, e.g., Griffith v. Kanamaru, 816 F.2d 624, 626 (Fed. Cir. 1987). Rather, Dr. Scott opted to show an actual reduction to practice before Dr. Finney's date of invention.

Before the Board, Dr. Scott's primary evidence of actual reduction to practice was a videotape. The videotape showed an operation where the surgeon inserted Dr. Scott's prototype device into the penis of an anesthetized patient. The videotape showed the surgeon manipulating the implanted device. Several times the device simulated an erection when the surgeon manipulated the valve. Several times the fluid filled the forward reservoir. Several times the surgeon returned the penis to a flaccid condition by draining the fluid back into the rear reservoir. The Board found: It is uncontested that the penile implant used in the in-and-out procedure did rigidify the penis by pressurization of the rear chamber and did produce an erection. After the device was actuated to form the erection, the valve mechanism was manipulated to allow the device to become flaccid. . . . Board opinion at 8–9.

Although not part of the count, the parties agree that the invention envisions implantation of two devices—one on either side of the penis. In the videotaped demonstration, the surgeon implanted only a single prosthesis into the patient. Although using only a single prosthesis, the videotape showed a penis with enough rigidity to produce an erection. After manipulating the implanted device through the skin to simulate having and losing an erection, the surgeon removed Dr. Scott's prototype and inserted a prior art external pump mechanism.

Dr. Scott supplied other evidence as well. He presented evidence of testing for leakage, disclosed that the fabrication material was common in implanted devices, and supplied the testimony of Dr. Drogo K. Montague, an expert in the field. Dr. Montague personally handled the device at issue and viewed the videotape. He testified that the video showed, even with only a single tube, sufficient rigidity for intercourse.

In opposition, Dr. Finney testified personally about the difficulty of determining sufficient rigidity for intercourse on the basis of insertion in an anesthetized patient. Both Drs. Finney and Montague agreed that insertion of two tubes would greatly enhance rigidity.

The Board discerned insufficient evidence to show reduction to practice. Specifically, the Board determined that Dr. Scott had not shown utility, i.e., that the device would successfully operate under actual use conditions for a reasonable length of time. Thus, the Board required "testing of an implantable medical device under actual use conditions or testing under conditions that closely simulate actual use conditions for an appropriate period of time." Board opinion at 8.

Because Dr. Scott had not tested his device in actual intercourse or in similar conditions to intercourse for a proper period of time, the Board determined that Dr. Scott had not reduced his invention to practice. The Board awarded the count to Dr. Finney. This appeal followed.

DISCUSSION

* * *

The Scott and Burton application was copending with that of Dr. Finney. Consequently, as the junior party in this interference, Dr. Scott had the burden to show prior invention by a preponderance of evidence. * * * To show prior invention, the junior party must show reduction to practice of the invention before the senior party, or, if the junior party reduced to practice later, conception before the senior party followed by reasonable diligence in reducing it to practice. * * *

To show reduction to practice, the junior party must demonstrate that the invention is "suitable for its intended purpose." * * * When testing is necessary to show proof of actual reduction to practice, the embodiment relied upon as evidence of priority must actually work for its intended purpose. * * *. Because Dr. Scott relied on such testing, this court must examine the quality and quantity of testing asserted to show a reduction to practice.

* * *

All cases deciding the sufficiency of testing to show reduction to practice share a common theme. In each case, the court examined the record to discern whether the testing in fact demonstrated a solution to the problem intended to be solved by the invention. See, e.g., Farrand Optical Co. v. United States, 325 F.2d 328, 333 (2d Cir. 1963) ("The essential inquiry here is whether the advance in the art represented by the invention . . . was embodied in a *workable device* that demonstrated that it could do what it was claimed to be capable of doing.") (emphasis added). In tests showing the invention's solution of a problem, the courts have not required commercial perfection nor absolute replication of the circumstances of the invention's ultimate use. Rather, they have instead adopted a common sense assessment. This common sense approach prescribes more scrupulous testing under circumstances approaching actual use conditions when the problem includes many uncertainties. On the other hand, when the problem to be solved does not present myriad variables, common sense similarly permits little or no testing to show the soundness of the principles of operation of the invention.

In the prosthetic implants field, polyurethane materials and inflatable penile prostheses were old in the art. They were tested extensively. Only the insertion and hydraulics of a manipulable valve separating two implanted reservoirs were new. Thus, Dr. Scott had the burden to show that his novel valve and dual reservoir system would simulate an erection for sexual intercourse when manipulated through the skin. Consequently, the problem presented to Dr. Scott, when viewed from the vantage point of earlier proven aspects of penile implant technology, was relatively uncomplicated.

In the videotape presentation, Dr. Scott demonstrated sufficiently the workability of his invention to solve the problems of a wholly internal penile implant. The videotaped operation showed both rigidity for intercourse and operability of the valve to inflate and deflate the device through the skin. The use of materials previously shown to work in prosthetic implants over a reasonable period of time also showed the durability of the invention for its intended purpose. In sum, Dr. Scott showed sufficient testing to establish a reasonable expectation that his invention would work under normal conditions for its intended purpose, beyond a probability of failure.

The Board erred by setting the reduction to practice standard too high. The Board erroneously suggested that a showing of reduction to practice requires human testing in actual use circumstances for a period of time. See Engelhardt v. Judd, 369 F.2d 408, 410–11 (CCPA 1966) (human testing of antihistamine and antiserotonin unnecessary in light of tests on laboratory animals). Reduction to practice, however, does not require actual use, but only a reasonable showing that the invention will work to overcome the problem it addresses. The videotape showed the rigidity and manipulability of the valve through the skin necessary for actual use. Experts testified to the invention's suitability for actual use. In the context of this art and this problem, Dr. Scott made that reasonable showing.

The Board rejected these proofs because the device was not actually used during intercourse. In this instance of a solution to a relatively simple problem, the Board required more testing than necessary to show that the device would work for its intended purpose. Even accepting the Board's conclusion that the intended purpose is to facilitate normal sexual intercourse, prior art prosthetic devices had fully tested the workability of most features of Dr. Scott's invention. Dr. Scott used the same tested and workable materials and designs of prior art implants. Only the hydraulics of a fully self-contained internal prosthesis remained to be tested for workability. Dr. Scott adequately showed the workability of these features.

Testing for the full safety and effectiveness of a prosthetic device is more properly left to the Food and Drug Administration (FDA). Title 35 does not demand that such human testing occur within the confines of Patent and Trademark Office (PTO) proceedings. * * *

The Board's holding that Dr. Scott did not reduce his invention to practice before the May 15, 1980 filing date of Dr. Finney is reversed. Dr. Finney asserted that Dr. Scott abandoned, suppressed, or concealed the invention embodied by the count within the meaning of 35 U.S.C. § 102(g) (1988). The Board did not reach this issue in light of its holding that no reduction to practice occurred. Because the Board has not considered this issue, this court remands for a determination of whether Dr. Scott abandoned, suppressed, or concealed the invention within the meaning of 35 U.S.C. § 102(g).

NOTES

1. Note that the specification in the principal case did not claim that the invention would achieve successful intercourse, only an erection. The terms of the patent are important in determining when a claim has been reduced to practice. For an example see Land v. Regan, 342 F.2d 92 (C.C.P.A. 1965), involving a claim on a method for making copies. In that case reduction to practice was shown when poor quality copies were made successfully. Although the poor quality copies would have no commercial use, the claim only claimed a process for making copies, not commercially competitive copies. By drafting a patent so that it centers on those features of the invention achieved by the applicant at an early date, the patent attorney can give his client an advantage in a priority dispute. The advantage of choosing the most favorable ground will usually accrue to a senior party in an interference because most interferences occur when the junior party copies the senior party's claim and adds it to his application.

2. When is a claim for a new compound reduced to practice? When the compound is made? When a use for the compound is discovered? The C.C.P.A. has regularly held that the reduction to practice is not achieved until the use is discovered. See, e.g., Archer v. Papa, 265 F.2d 954 (C.C.P.A. 1959). This conclusion is, of course, reinforced by Brenner v. Manson, 383 U.S. 519 (1966), supra.

3. The *Brenner* case itself arose out of the refusal of the Patent Office to declare an interference, a fact little noted in the opinion of the Court. The reason for the refusal was that since Manson alleged no utility he could not show prior reduction to practice. See 333 F.2d at 235. The CCPA reversed on the ground that the successful practice of a process to make a useless compound was reduction to practice of the process. Application of Manson, 333 F.2d 234 (C.C.P.A. 1964). The distinction between a patent on a useless product and a patent to make a useless product, ridiculed by the Court in Brenner v. Manson, is difficult to support under 35 U.S.C. § 101. But it might be supported by the requirements of 35 U.S.C. § 112. An application, in order to be a constructive reduction to practice, must comply with the requirements of § 112. One of these is that the application disclose "how to use" the claimed invention. One can use a process to make a useless product, but one cannot use a useless product since, by definition, there is no use.

4. Estee Lauder Inc. v. L'Oreal, S.A., 129 F.3d 588 (Fed. Cir. 1997), involved an interference over a patent on a new formulation for sun-tan lotion. The junior party attempted to prove earlier reduction to practice by showing that it had sent the formulation out for biological testing with an independent testing firm. The tests had been completed at the relevant time and showed that the new formulation had desireable properties, but the test results were not reported to the junior party until after the senior party's filing date. "[W]e are left to answer a single question of law: where testing is required to establish utility, must there be some recognition of successful testing prior to the critical date for an invention to be reduced to practice, or is it only necessary that the testing be completed before the critical date and ultimately prove successful, regardless of when that success is appreciated or recognized? We hold that the law requires the former." 129 F.3d 593.

PROBLEMS

1. A claim is for stops on gates of hydraulic turbines placed so as not to interfere with the normal opening and closing of the gates but so as to prevent the movement of the gates into the turbine blades if the controls on the gates fail. A turbine embodying the invention was constructed and the stops were tested in the shop by manually swinging the gates from open to closed position very violently. The forces involved in the manual testing were substantially less than those that would be experienced under operating conditions upon failure of the controls. The controls on the turbine have never failed in operation and thus the stops have never been brought into play. The stops were engineered to withstand very large forces, but the forces that would be experienced upon failure of the controls cannot be calculated with assured accuracy. Was the claim reduced to practice (1) when the turbine was built, (2) when the gates were swung in the shop, (3) when the turbine was installed, (4) when the patent application was filed? See White v. Syvertsen, 46 F.2d 364 (C.C.P.A. 1931). See also Elmore v. Schmitt, 278 F.2d 510 (C.C.P.A. 1960) ("Bench" tests of binary counter held: not reduction to practice where it was not proven that the bench tests reproduced conditions that would be encountered in any practical use of the invention.).

2. Can an applicant for a patent on a compound overcome a publication prior to his filing date which discloses the structure of the compound but no utility for the compound by showing only that he had discovered the structure of the compound prior to the publication? See Application of Moore, 444 F.2d 572 (C.C.P.A. 1971).

(3) Burden of Proof

The application of the priority rules involves factual questions of considerable difficulty which must often be decided on the basis of the testimony of an interested party. Thus the burden of proof rules are of particular importance. In an interference the party first to file is called the senior party, the other party the junior party. If the junior party filed before the issuance of the senior party's patent, then the junior party must prove priority by a preponderance of the evidence. If the junior party filed after the issuance of a patent to the senior party then the junior party must prove priority beyond a reasonable doubt. The Patent Office will not award priority to a junior party on the basis of the junior applicant's uncorroborated testimony. For a striking application of that principle see Bainbridge v. Walton, 104 F.2d 808 (C.C.P.A. 1939).

Note that any application filed more than one year after the issuance of the senior patent is blocked by the time bar, 35 U.S.C. § 102(b). Furthermore, any claim filed more than one year after the issuance of a patent claiming the same subject matter is barred by 35 U.S.C. § 135(b), even if the claim is a proper amendment to a pending application entitled to an earlier filing date.

The applicable burden of proof on the issue of anticipation in an infringement proceeding is not clear because the Supreme Court has not faced the issue. The best available statement is Cardozo's:

> A patent regularly issued, and even more obviously a patent issued after a hearing of all the rival claimants, is presumed to be valid until the presumption has been overcome by convincing evidence of error. The force of that presumption has found varying expression in this and other courts. Sometimes it is said that in a suit for infringement, when the defense is a prior invention, "the burden of proof to make good this defense" is "upon the party setting it up," and "every reasonable doubt should be resolved against him." * * *

> Again it is said that "the presumption of the validity of the patent is such that the defense of invention by another must be established by the clearest proof—perhaps beyond reasonable doubt." * * * The context suggests that in these and like phrases the courts were not defining a standard in terms of scientific accuracy or literal precision, but were offering counsel and suggestion to guide the course of judgment. Through all the verbal variances, however, there runs this common core of thought and truth, that one otherwise an infringer who assails the validity of a patent fair upon its face bears a heavy burden of persuasion, and fails unless his evidence has more than a dubious preponderance.

Radio Corp. of America v. Radio Engineering Laboratories, Inc., 293 U.S. 1, 7–8 (1934).

PROBLEMS

1. X and Y are involved in an interference. They settle their differences and file a copy of their agreement as required by 35 U.S.C. § 135(c). Under the terms of the settlement X concedes that Y's patent is valid. In a suit for infringement by Y against A, a third party, can A defend on the ground that the patent is invalid because X was in fact the first inventor? In a suit for infringement by Y against X, can X defend on that ground?

2. Y is issued a patent by the Patent and Trademark Office. There is no interference. In an action for infringement the defendant proves by "clear and convincing" evidence that he invented the invention two months before *Y's* application date. What is the burden of proof on *Y* if he wishes to rebut the defense by proving that his actual date of invention was one year prior to the application date? Compare Karr v. Botkins Grain & Feed Co., 329 F.Supp. 411, 413 (S.D.Ohio 1970), United Shoe Machinery Corp. v. Brooklyn Wood Heel Corp., 77 F.2d 263, 264 (2d Cir.1935) (Hand, L., J.), Thayer v. Hart, 20 Fed. 693 (S.D.N.Y.1884) ("beyond a reasonable doubt") with Webster Loom Co. v. Higgins, 29 Fed. Cases 563, 567 (S.D.N.Y.1879) ("The burden of proof rests upon the defendants, to show, beyond any fair doubt, the prior knowledge and use set up; but, where they have sustained that burden by showing such knowledge and use prior to the patent, the burden of showing the still prior invention claimed, by at least a fair balance of proof, must rest upon the plaintiff."). Can Learned Hand be wrong?

---

(4) Conception and Diligence

Burroughs Wellcome Co. v. Barr Laboratories, Inc.

United States Court of Appeals for the Federal Circuit, 1994.
40 F.3d 1223, certiorari denied 516 U.S. 1071 (1996).

■ MAYER, CIRCUIT JUDGE.

Barr Laboratories, Inc., * * * appeal[s] the order of the United States District Court for the Eastern District of North Carolina, Burroughs Wellcome Co. v. Barr Lab., Inc., 828 F.Supp. 1208 (E.D.N.C. 1993), granting the motion of Burroughs Wellcome Co. for judgment as a matter of law that six United States patents were not invalid and were infringed. We affirm in part, vacate in part, and remand.

BACKGROUND

Burroughs Wellcome Co. is the owner of six United States patents that cover various preparations of 3'-azidothymidine (AZT) and methods for using that drug in the treatment of persons infected with the human immunodeficiency virus (HIV). Each of these patents names the same five inventors—Janet Rideout, David Barry, Sandra Lehrman, Martha St. Clair, and Phillip Furman (Burroughs Wellcome inventors)—all of whom were employed by Burroughs Wellcome at the time the inventions were alleged to have been conceived. The defendants-appellants concede that all five are properly named as inventors on the patents.

Burroughs Wellcome's patents arise from the same parent application filed on September 17, 1985. Five of the patents relate to the use of AZT to treat patients infected with HIV or who have acquired immunodeficiency syndrome (AIDS). The other patent, the '750 patent, covers a method of using AZT to increase the T-lymphocyte count of persons infected with HIV.

In the early 1980s, scientists began to see patients with symptoms of an unknown disease of the immune system, now known as AIDS. The disease attacks and destroys certain white blood cells known as CD4 T-lymphocytes or T-cells, which form an important component of the body's immune system. The level of destruction eventually becomes so great that the immune system is no longer able to mount an effective response to infections that pose little threat to a healthy person.

In mid-1984, scientists discovered that AIDS was caused by a retrovirus, known as HTLV III or, more commonly today, HIV. After the identification of HIV, Burroughs Wellcome began to search for a cure, screening compounds for antiretroviral activity using two murine (or mouse) retroviruses, the Friend leukemia virus and the Harvey sarcoma virus.

At about this time, scientists at the National Institutes of Health (NIH), led by Samuel Broder, were looking for effective AIDS therapies as well. Unlike Burroughs Wellcome, Broder and his colleagues used live HIV, and were able to develop a test that could demonstrate a compound's effectiveness against HIV in humans using a unique line of T-cell clones (the ATH8 cell line). The NIH scientists began to seek compounds from private pharmaceutical companies for screening in their cell line. After Burroughs Wellcome contacted Broder in the fall of 1984, he agreed to accept compounds from Burroughs Wellcome under code for testing against live HIV.

Burroughs Wellcome's Rideout selected AZT and a number of other compounds for testing in the murine screens on October 29, 1984. The tests, performed at Burroughs Wellcome facilities by St. Clair, showed that AZT had significant activity against both murine retroviruses at low concentrations. In light of these positive results, the Burroughs Wellcome inventors met on December 5, 1984, to discuss patenting the use of AZT in the treatment of AIDS. Burroughs Wellcome's patent committee thereafter recommended that the company prepare a patent application for future filing. By February 6, 1985, the company had prepared a draft application for filing in the United Kingdom. The draft disclosed using AZT to treat patients infected with HIV, and set out various pharmaceutical formulations of the compound in an effective dosage range to treat HIV infection.

Two days earlier, on February 4, 1985, Burroughs Wellcome had sent a sample of AZT, identified only as Compound S, to Broder at NIH. In an accompanying letter, Lehrman told Broder of the results of the murine retrovirus tests and asked that he screen the compound for activity against HIV in the ATH8 cell line. Another NIH scientist, Hiroaka Mitsuya, performed the test in mid-February 1985, and found that Compound S was active against HIV. Broder informed Lehrman of the results by telephone on February 20, 1985. Burroughs Wellcome filed its patent application in the United Kingdom on March 16, 1985.

After Burroughs Wellcome learned that AZT was active against HIV, it began the process of obtaining Food and Drug Administration (FDA) approval for AZT as an AIDS therapy. As a part of the clinical trials leading to FDA approval, Broder and another NIH scientist, Robert Yarchoan, conducted a Phase I human patient study which showed that treatment with AZT could result in an increase in the patient's T-cell count. Broder reported this result to Lehrman on July 23, 1985. In 1987, the FDA approved AZT for marketing by Burroughs Wellcome; Burroughs Wellcome markets the drug for treatment of HIV infection under the trademark Retrovir.

On March 19, 1991, Barr Laboratories, Inc. (Barr) sought FDA approval to manufacture and market a generic version of AZT by filing an Abbreviated New Drug Application (ANDA) pursuant to 21 U.S.C. § 355(j) (1988). As part of the process, Barr certified to the FDA that Burroughs Wellcome's patents were invalid or were not infringed by the product described in its ANDA. After Barr informed Burroughs Wellcome of its action, Burroughs Wellcome commenced this case for patent infringement against Barr on May 14, 1991, alleging technical infringement of its patents under 35 U.S.C. § 271(e)(2)(A) (1988).

Barr filed a counterclaim under 35 U.S.C. § 256 (1988) seeking correction of the patents to list Broder and Mitsuya as coinventors. Barr admitted that its AZT product would infringe the patents, but contended that it did not because Barr had obtained a license to manufacture and sell AZT from the government, which should be deemed the owner of the interest of coinventors Broder and Mitsuya in the AZT patents. Burroughs Wellcome denied that Broder and Mitsuya were coinventors and also responded that the assertion of any rights of Broder, Mitsuya, or the government in the patents was barred by laches, estoppel, and waiver.

* * *

After more than three weeks of trial, while Burroughs Wellcome was still in the process of presenting its case, the district court granted Burroughs Wellcome's motion for judgment as a matter of law against all of the defendants, concluding that the Burroughs Wellcome inventors had conceived of the subject matter of the inventions at some time before February 6, 1985, without the assistance of Broder, Mitsuya, or Yarchoan. The court rejected the arguments of Barr * * * that [it] * * * should be allowed to present evidence that the Burroughs Wellcome inventors had no reasonable belief that the inventions would actually work—that AZT was in fact active against HIV—until they were told the results of the NIH testing.

The court also rejected * * * [the] argument that the Burroughs Wellcome inventors had not conceived the invention of the '750 patent—the use of AZT to increase a patient's T-cell count—before July 23, 1985, when Broder reported the results of the NIH patient study to Lehrman. The court concluded that the increase in T-cell count was an obvious phenomenon known to the inventors that would result from administration of AZT. And the district court denied Barr's renewed motion for partial summary judgment on Burroughs Wellcome's equitable defenses to its counterclaim for correction of the patents under section 256.

DISCUSSION

The arguments of Barr * * * are directed to when the inventors conceived the invention. Burroughs Wellcome says it was before they learned the results of the NIH tests; Barr * * * say[s] that confirmation of the inventions' operability, which came from the NIH tests, was an essential part of the inventive process. If Burroughs Wellcome is right, then the patents name the proper inventors, they are not invalid, and the appellants are liable for infringement. If Barr * * * [is] correct, then Broder, Mitsuya, and Yarchoan should have been named as joint inventors and the resolution of Burroughs Wellcome's infringement suits is premature.

* * *

Conception is the touchstone of inventorship, the completion of the mental part of invention. * * *. It is "the formation in the mind of the inventor, of a definite and permanent idea of the complete and operative invention, as it is hereafter to be applied in practice." Hybritech Inc. v. Monoclonal Antibodies, Inc., 802 F.2d 1367, 1376 (Fed. Cir. 1986) (citation omitted). Conception is complete only when the idea is so clearly defined in the inventor's mind that only ordinary skill would be necessary to reduce the invention to practice, without extensive research or experimentation. * * * Because it is a mental act, courts require corroborating evidence of a contemporaneous disclosure that would enable one skilled in the art to make the invention. * * *

Thus, the test for conception is whether the inventor had an idea that was definite and permanent enough that one skilled in the art could understand the invention; the inventor must prove his conception by corroborating evidence, preferably by showing a contemporaneous disclosure. An idea is definite and permanent when the inventor has a specific, settled idea, a particular solution to the problem at hand, not just a general goal or research plan he hopes to pursue. * * * The conception analysis necessarily turns on the inventor's ability to describe his invention with particularity. Until he can do so, he cannot prove possession of the complete mental picture of the invention. These rules ensure that patent rights attach only when an idea is so far developed that the inventor can point to a definite, particular invention.

But an inventor need not know that his invention will work for conception to be complete. * * * He need only show that he had the idea; the discovery that an invention actually works is part of its reduction to practice. * * *

Barr * * * suggest[s] that the inventor's definite and permanent idea must include a reasonable expectation that the invention will work for its intended purpose. They argue that this expectation is of paramount importance when the invention deals with uncertain or experimental disciplines, where the inventor cannot reasonably believe an idea will be operable until some result supports that conclusion. Without some experimental confirmation, they suggest, the inventor has only a hope or an expectation, and has not yet conceived the invention in sufficiently definite and permanent form. But this is not the law. An inventor's belief that his invention will work or his reasons for choosing a particular approach are irrelevant to conception. * * *

* * *

It is undoubtedly true that "[i]n some instances, an inventor is unable to establish a conception until he has reduced the invention to practice through a successful experiment." Amgen[, Inc. v. Chugai Pharmaceutical Co., 927 F.2d [1200] at 1206 [(Fed. Cir. 1993)]; Alpert v. Slatin, 305 F.2d 891, 894 (CCPA 1962) (no conception "where results at each step do not follow as anticipated, but are achieved empirically by what amounts to trial and error"). But in such cases, it is not merely because the field is unpredictable; the alleged conception fails because * * * it is incomplete. Then the event of reduction to practice in effect provides the only evidence to corroborate conception of the invention.

Under these circumstances, the reduction to practice can be the most definitive corroboration of conception, for where the idea is in constant flux, it is not definite and permanent. A conception is not complete if the subsequent course of experimentation, especially experimental failures, reveals uncertainty that so undermines the specificity of the inventor's idea that it is not yet a definite and permanent reflection of the complete invention as it will be used in practice. See Amgen, 927 F.2d at 1207 (no conception until reduction to practice where others tried and failed to clone gene using suggested strategy); Rey-Bellet v. Engelhardt, 493 F.2d 1380, 1387 (CCPA 1974) (focusing on nature of subsequent research as indicator that inventors encountered no perplexing intricate difficulties). It is this factual uncertainty, not the general uncertainty surrounding experimental sciences, that bears on the problem of conception.

* * *

We emphasize that we do not hold that a person is precluded from being a joint inventor simply because his contribution to a collaborative effort is experimental. Instead, the qualitative contribution of each collaborator is the key—each inventor must contribute to the joint arrival at a definite and permanent idea of the invention as it will be used in practice.

Nor do we suggest that a bare idea is all that conception requires. The idea must be definite and permanent in the sense that it involves a specific approach to the particular problem at hand. It must also be sufficiently precise that a skilled artisan could carry out the invention without undue experimentation. And, of course, the alleged conception must be supported by corroborating evidence. On the facts before us, it is apparent that the district court correctly ruled against Barr * * * as to five of the patents, but that the court's judgment as to the sixth, the '750 patent, was premature.

The '232, '838, '130, '208, and '538 patents encompass compositions and methods of using AZT to treat AIDS. The Burroughs Wellcome inventors claim conception of these inventions prior to the NIH experiments, based on the draft British patent application. That document is not itself a conception, for conception occurs in the inventors' minds, not on paper. The draft simply corroborates the claim that they had formulated a definite and permanent idea of the inventions by the time it was prepared.

The Burroughs Wellcome inventors set out with the general goal of finding a method to treat AIDS, but by the time Broder confirmed that AZT was active against HIV, they had more than a general hope or expectation. They had thought of the particular antiviral agent with which they intended to address the problem, and had formulated the idea of the inventions to the point that they could express it clearly in the form of a draft patent application, which Barr * * * concede[s] would teach one skilled in the art to practice the inventions. The draft expressly discloses the intended use of AZT to treat AIDS. It sets out the compound's structure, which, along with at least one method of preparation, was already well known. The draft also discloses in detail both how to prepare a pharmaceutical formulation of AZT and how to use it to treat a patient infected with HIV. The listed dosages, dose forms, and routes of administration conform to those eventually approved by the FDA. The draft shows that the idea was clearly defined in the inventors' minds; all that remained was to reduce it to practice—to confirm its operability and bring it to market. See Haskell v. Colebourne, 671 F.2d 1362, 1365–66 (CCPA 1982) (enabling draft patent application sufficient to corroborate conception).

An examination of the events that followed the preparation of Burroughs Wellcome's draft confirms the soundness of the conception. Broder and Mitsuya received from Burroughs Wellcome a group of compounds, known to Broder and Mitsuya only by code names, selected for testing by the Burroughs Wellcome inventors. They then tested those compounds for activity against HIV in their patented cell line. The test results revealed for the first time that one of the compounds, later revealed to be AZT, was exceptionally active against the virus.

Here, though, the testing was brief, simply confirming the operability of what the draft application disclosed. True, the science surrounding HIV and AIDS was unpredictable and highly experimental at the time the Burroughs Wellcome scientists made the inventions. But what matters for conception is whether the inventors had a definite and permanent idea of the operative inventions. In this case, no prolonged period of extensive research, experiment, and modification followed the alleged conception. By all accounts, what followed was simply the normal course of clinical trials that mark the path of any drug to the marketplace.

That is not to say, however, that the NIH scientists merely acted as a "pair of hands" for the Burroughs Wellcome inventors. Broder and Mitsuya exercised considerable skill in conducting the tests, using their patented cell line to model the responses of human cells infected with HIV. Lehrman did suggest initial concentrations to Broder, but she hardly controlled the conduct of the testing, which necessarily involved interpretation of results for which Broder and Mitsuya, and very few others, were uniquely qualified. But because the testing confirmed the operability of the inventions, it showed that the Burroughs Wellcome inventors had a definite and permanent idea of the inventions. It was part of the reduction to practice and inured to the benefit of Burroughs Wellcome.

Barr * * * allege[s] error in the district court's refusal to hear their evidence of the poor predictive value of the murine retrovirus screens for activity against HIV. Regardless of the predictive value of the murine tests, however, the record shows that soon after those tests, the inventors determined, for whatever reason, to use AZT as a treatment for AIDS, and they prepared a draft patent application that specifically set out the inventions, including an enabling disclosure. Obviously, enablement and conception are distinct issues, and one need not necessarily meet the enablement standard of 35 U.S.C. § 112 to prove conception. See Fiers [v. Revel], 984 F.2d [1164] at 1169 [(Fed. Cir. 1993)]. But the enabling disclosure does suffice in this case to confirm that the inventors had concluded the mental part of the inventive process—that they had arrived at the final, definite idea of their inventions, leaving only the task of reduction to practice to bring the inventions to fruition.

The question is not whether Burroughs Wellcome reasonably believed that the inventions would work for their intended purpose, the focus of the evidence offered by Barr * * *, but whether the inventors had formed the idea of their use for that purpose in sufficiently final form that only the exercise of ordinary skill remained to reduce it to practice. See MacMillan v. Moffett, 432 F.2d at 1239 (Inventor's "reasons or lack of reasons for including U-5008 are not relevant to the question of conception. The important thing is that he did think in definite terms of the method claimed."). Whether or not Burroughs Wellcome believed the inventions would in fact work based on the mouse screens is irrelevant.

We do not know precisely when the inventors conceived their inventions, but the record shows that they had done so by the time they prepared the draft patent application that thoroughly and particularly set out the inventions as they would later be used. The district court correctly ruled that on this record, the NIH scientists were not joint inventors of these inventions.

The '750 patent is another question. It claims "[a] method of increasing the number of T-lymphocytes in a human infected with the [HIV] virus comprising administering to said human an effective amount of" AZT. * * * [It is] argue[d] that there is no evidence, under any test of inventorship, that the Burroughs Wellcome inventors conceived of this invention until after the Phase I patient study conducted by Broder and Yarchoan revealed that AZT could lead to increased levels of T-cells in AIDS patients.

* * * [T]he record is devoid of any statement that the inventors thought AZT could raise a patient's T-cell levels, but evidence need not always expressly show possession of the invention to corroborate conception. The district court held that the record supported conception as a matter of law, concluding that "an increase in T-lymphocyte count was an 'obvious,' natural phenomenon known to the [Burroughs Wellcome] inventors that would result from the inhibition of a retrovirus." Burroughs Wellcome Co. v. Barr Lab., Inc., 828 F.Supp. at 1213. Burroughs Wellcome argues that this conclusion was proper because increased T-cell count is simply an obvious property or use of the greater discovery at issue here, the treatment of HIV infection with AZT. Because an increase in T-lymphocytes follows inevitably from treatment of AIDS patients with AZT, Burroughs Wellcome says, Broder and Yarchoan merely observed that the method

invented by the Burroughs Wellcome inventors had qualities that the inventors failed to perceive. Burroughs Wellcome says this is not an inventive contribution to the claims of any of the AZT patents.

But even though all six patents arise from the same parent application and are subject to terminal disclaimers to avoid rejection for obviousness-type double patenting, each patent claims a different invention.[8] See In re Longi, 759 F.2d 887, 892 (Fed. Cir. 1985) (inventor can get only one patent for any single invention). It is true that the Patent Office determined that the method of the '750 patent would have been obvious to those skilled in the art in light of the inventions claimed in the other patents. That is, however, irrelevant to the question whether the Burroughs Wellcome inventors had conceived of the invention before they learned the results of the Phase I trials. For conception, we look not to whether one skilled in the art could have thought of the invention, but whether the alleged inventors actually had in their minds the required definite and permanent idea. Cf. Bosies v. Benedict, 27 F.3d 539, 543 (Fed. Cir. 1994) (testimony of noninventor as to noninventor's understanding of inventor's written formula insufficient to prove conception). The record does not now support resolution of this question as a matter of law.

The alleged conception is supported by testimony of Burroughs Wellcome's experts, Burroughs Wellcome's draft Phase I protocol, and the same draft patent application that corroborates conception of the other five inventions. The experts testified that those skilled in the art at the time expected increased immune function to accompany inhibition of HIV. The draft patent application discloses that HIV preferentially destroys T-cells, that AIDS is associated with progressive depletion of T-cells, and that AZT is an effective treatment for HIV infection. Finally, the draft protocol directs the administrators of the Phase I study to monitor patients' T-lymphocyte count. This evidence supports an inference that the Burroughs Wellcome inventors did have the necessary definite and permanent idea, for, given the virus' effect on T-lymphocytes, it seems logical to conclude that stopping the virus might reverse the process of T-cell destruction and restore the body's immune system to a pre-infection state. If this were the only evidence in the record, the court's judgment would be sustained.

But * * * evidence [was offered] suggesting that one skilled in the art would not have expected T-cell count to rise. On deposition, Broder testified that prior to the first patient study, "no one knew whether there was such a thing as recovery" of T-cells, based on the NIH's experience with suramin, a drug that entered clinical trials before AZT. Although suramin showed some activity against HIV, inhibition of the retrovirus apparently was not accompanied by increases in T-cell count or restoration of immune functions. Of course, there might be any number of other explanations for the

8. We must assume for the purposes of this case that the '750 patent is drawn to an invention different from each of the other five patents. The parties do not ask us to decide whether claims drawn to an effect or mechanism of action of AZT—its ability to raise T-cell count—reach the same invention as (that is, are inherent in) claims drawn to use of the drug to treat HIV infection or AIDS, and we express no opinion on that. * * *

results of the suramin trials; but they might suggest that although those skilled in the art recognized the significance of T-lymphocyte levels in HIV infection and AIDS, they might have expected inhibition of the virus simply to halt the continuing destruction of T-cells, not to increase T-cell count and restore immune function. This could support an inference that the inventors themselves did not conceive the invention prior to the Phase I study.

* * * [It is] also contend[ed] that Burroughs Wellcome prepared its Phase I protocol in collaboration with Broder and the NIH, possibly from a draft protocol prepared by Broder and Yarchoan pursuant to their study of suramin. These contentions are relevant to the conception inquiry for they tend to undermine the corroborative value of the draft protocol, and might even support joint inventorship based on that draft. See Coleman v. Dines, 754 F.2d [353] at 360 [(Fed. Cir. 1985)], (document's co-author cannot be considered sole inventor of invention disclosed in document without further proof). Because under Rule 50(a) all inferences must be taken against the moving party, the court's ruling on the '750 patent was inappropriate, and we vacate the judgment to that extent and remand for further proceedings.

CONCLUSION

Accordingly, the judgment of the United States District Court for the Eastern District of North Carolina is affirmed in part, vacated in part, and remanded.

Griffith v. Kanamaru

United States Court of Appeals, Federal Circuit, 1987.
816 F.2d 624.

■ NICHOLS, SENIOR CIRCUIT JUDGE.

Owen W. Griffith (Griffith) appeals the decision of the Board of Patent Appeals and Interferences (board) * * * that Griffith failed to establish a prima facie case that he is entitled to an award of priority against the filing date of Tsuneo Kanamaru, et al. (Kanamaru) for a patent on aminocarnitine compounds. We affirm.

BACKGROUND

This patent interference case involves the application of Griffith, an Associate Professor in the Department of Biochemistry at Cornell University Medical College, for a patent on an aminocarnitine compound, useful in the treatment of diabetes, and a patent issued for the same invention to Kanamaru, an employee of Takeda Chemical Industries. The inventors assigned their rights to the inventions to the Cornell Research Foundation, Inc. (Cornell) and to Takeda Chemical Industries respectively.

The technology established by this invention is not at issue in this appeal and is therefore not described further.

Griffith had established conception by June 30, 1981, and reduction to practice on January 11, 1984. Kanamaru filed for a United States patent on November 17, 1982. The board found, however, that Griffith failed to establish reasonable diligence for a prima facie case of prior invention and issued an order to show cause under 37 C.F.R. § 1.617 as to why summary judgment should not be issued.

The board considered the additional evidence submitted by Griffith pursuant to the show cause order and decided that Griffith failed to establish a prima facie case for priority against Kanamaru's filing date. This result was based on the board's conclusion that Griffith's explanation for inactivity between June 15, 1983, and September 13, 1983, failed to provide a legally sufficient excuse to satisfy the "reasonable diligence" requirement of 35 U.S.C. § 102(g). Griffith appeals on the issue of reasonable diligence.

ANALYSIS

I

This is a case of first impression and presents the novel circumstances of a university suggesting that it is reasonable for the public to wait for disclosure until the most satisfactory funding arrangements are made. The applicable law is the "reasonable diligence" standard contained in 35 U.S.C. § 102(g). * * *

Griffith must establish a prima facie case of reasonable diligence, as well as dates of conception and reduction to practice, to avoid summary judgment on the issue of priority. 37 C.F.R. § 1.617(a). As a preliminary matter we note that, although the board focused on the June 1983 to September 1983 lapse in work, and Griffith's reasons for this lapse, Griffith is burdened with establishing a prima facie case of reasonable diligence from immediately before Kanamaru's filing date of November 17, 1982, until Griffith's reduction to practice on January 11, 1984. 35 U.S.C. § 102(g); 37 C.F.R. § 1.617(a).

On appeal, Griffith presents two grounds intended to justify his inactivity on the aminocarnitine project between June 15, 1983, and September 13, 1983. The first is that, notwithstanding Cornell University's extraordinary endowment, it is reasonable, and as a policy matter desirable, for Cornell to require Griffith and other research scientists to obtain funding from outside the university. The second reason Griffith presents is that he reasonably waited for Ms. Debora Jenkins to matriculate in the Fall of 1983 to assist with the project. He had promised her she should have that task which she needed to qualify for her degree. We reject these arguments and conclude that Griffith has failed to establish grounds to excuse his inactivity prior to reduction to practice.

II

The reasonable diligence standard balances the interest in rewarding and encouraging invention with the public's interest in the earliest possible disclosure of innovation. * * * Griffith must account for the entire period from just before Kanamaru's filing date until his reduction to practice. * * * As one of our predecessor courts has noted:

> Public policy favors the early disclosure of inventions. This underlies the requirement for "reasonable diligence" in reducing an invention to practice, not unlike the requirement that, to avoid a holding of suppression or concealment, there be no unreasonable delay in filing an application once there has been a reduction to practice.

Naber v. Cricchi, 567 F.2d 382, 385 n. 5 (CCPA 1977), cert. denied, 439 U.S. 826 (1978) (citation omitted).

The board in this case was, but not properly, asked to pass judgment on the reasonableness of Cornell's policy regarding outside funding of research. The correct inquiry is rather whether it is reasonable for Cornell to require the public to wait for the innovation, given the well settled policy in favor of early disclosure. As the board notes, Chief Judge Markey has called early public disclosure the "linchpin of the patent system." Horwath v. Lee, 564 F.2d 948, 950 (CCPA 1977). A review of caselaw on excuses for inactivity in reduction to practice reveals a common thread that courts may consider the reasonable everyday problems and limitations encountered by an inventor. See, e.g., Bey v. Kollonitsch, 806 F.2d 1024 (Fed. Cir. 1986) (delay in filing excused where attorney worked on a group of related applications and other applications contributed substantially to the preparation of Bey's application); Reed v. Tornqvist, 436 F.2d 501 (CCPA 1971) (concluding it is not unreasonable for inventor to delay completing a patent application until after returning from a three week vacation in Sweden, extended by illness of inventor's father); Keizer v. Bradley, 270 F.2d 396 (CCPA 1959) (delay excused where inventor, after producing a component for a color television, delayed filing to produce an appropriate receiver for testing the component); Courson v. O'Connor, 227 F. 890, 894 (7th Cir. 1915) ("exercise of reasonable diligence * * * does not require an inventor to devote his entire time thereto, or to abandon his ordinary means of livelihood"); De Wallace v. Scott, 15 App.D.C. 157 (1899) (where applicant made bona fide attempts to perfect his invention, applicant's poor health, responsibility to feed his family, and daily job demands excused his delay in reducing his invention to practice); Texas Co. v. Globe Oil & Refining Co., 112 F.Supp. 455 (N.D. Ill. 1953) (delay in filing application excused because of confusion relating to war).

Griffith argues that the admitted inactivity of three months between June 15, 1983, and September 13, 1983, which he attributes to Cornell's "reasonable" policy requiring outside funding and to Griffith's "reasonable" decision to delay until a graduate student arrived, falls within legal precedent excusing inactivity in the diligence context. We disagree. We first note that, in regard to waiting for a graduate student, Griffith does not even suggest that he faced a genuine shortage of personnel. He does not suggest that Ms. Jenkins was the only person capable of carrying on with the aminocarnitine experiment. We can see no application of precedent to suggest that the convenience of the timing of the semester schedule justifies a three-month delay for the purpose of reasonable diligence. Neither do we believe that this excuse, absent even a suggestion by Griffith that Jenkins was uniquely qualified to do his research, is reasonable.

Griffith's second contention that it was reasonable for Cornell to require outside funding, therefore causing a delay in order to apply for such funds, is also insufficient to excuse his inactivity. The crux of Griffith's argument is that outside funding is desirable as a form of peer review, or monitoring of the worthiness of a given project. He also suggests that, as a policy matter, universities should not be treated as businesses, which ultimately would detract from scholarly inquiry. Griffith states that these considerations, if accepted as valid, would fit within the scope of the caselaw excusing inactivity for "reasonable" delays in reduction to practice and filing.

These contentions on delay do not fit within the texture and scope of the precedent cited by the parties or discussed in this opinion. Griffith argues this case is controlled by the outcome of Litchfield v. Eigen, 535 F.2d 72 (CCPA 1976). We disagree. In Litchfield, Judge Rich held that the inventors failed to establish due diligence because of their inactivity between April 1964 and September 1965. The court based this conclusion on the finding that the inventors possessed the capacity to test the invention and chose instead to test other compounds. Judge Rich did not reach the issue of the alleged budgetary limitations imposed by the sponsor and stated that the inventors failed to show any evidence of such financial limitations and that, therefore, the court could not consider this contention.

Griffith's excuses sound more in the nature of commercial development, not accepted as an excuse for delay, than the "hardship" cases most commonly found and discussed supra. Delays in reduction to practice caused by an inventor's efforts to refine an invention to the most marketable and profitable form have not been accepted as sufficient excuses for inactivity. D. Chisum, Patents § 10.07(2) at 10–122 & n. 4 (1986) (citations omitted). Griffith's case is analogous to that in Seeberger v. Dodge, 24 App.D.C. 476 (1905). In that case, the inventor was the first to conceive of an improvement in an escalator and was attempting to show diligence. The court noted:

> The testimony shows that he (Seeberger) was a man of means, and might have constructed an escalator had he undertaken to do so. Instead of this, his constant effort was to organize corporations, or to interest capital in other ways, for the purpose of engaging in the general manufacture of escalators.

Id. at 484–85.

The court held this unacceptable:

> One having the first complete conception of an invention cannot hold the field against all comers by diligent efforts, merely, to organize and procure sufficient capital to engage in the manufacture of his device or mechanism for commercial purposes. This is a different thing from diligence in actual reduction to practice.

Id. at 485 (citation omitted).

The comparison we draw is that Cornell University, like Seeberger, has made a clear decision against funding Griffith's project in order to avoid the risks and distractions, albeit different in each case, that would result from directly financing these inventions. Griffith has placed in the record, and relies on, an able article by President Bok of Harvard, Business and the Academy, *Harvard Magazine,* May-June 1981, 31. Bok is explaining the policy issues respecting academic funding of scientific research, for the benefit of Harvard's alumni who must, of course, make up by their contributions the University's annual deficit. While much academic research could produce a profit, pursuit of such profit may be business inappropriate for a university though it would be right and proper for a commercial organization. For example, it might produce conflicts between the roles of scientists as inventors and developers against their roles as members of the university faculty. However large the university's endowment may be, it may be better to enlist private funding and let this source of funds develop the commercial utilization of any invention as perhaps, the beneficial owner. If there is a patent, the source of funds may end up [as] assignee of the patent. It seems also implicit in this policy choice that faculty members may not be allowed single-minded pursuit of reduction to practice whenever they conceive some idea of value, and at times the rights of other inventors may obtain a priority that a single-minded pursuit would have averted. Bok says diligent reduction to practice, to satisfy the patent laws, may interfere with a faculty member's other duties. Bok is asking the approval of his alumni, not of the courts. The management of great universities is one thing, at least, the courts have not taken over and do not deem themselves qualified to undertake. Bok does not ask that the patent laws or other intellectual property law be skewed or slanted to enable the university to have its cake and eat it too, *i.e.,* to act in a noncommercial manner and yet preserve the pecuniary rewards of commercial exploitation for itself.

If, as we are asked to assume, Cornell also follows the policy Bok has so well articulated, it seems evident that Cornell has consciously chosen to assume the risk that priority in the invention might be lost to an outside inventor, yet, having chosen a noncommercial policy, it asks us to save it the property that would have inured to it if it had acted in single-minded pursuit of gain.

III

The board in this case considered primarily Griffith's contention that the Cornell policy was reasonable and therefore acceptable to excuse his delay in reduction to practice. Although we agree with the board's conclusion, it is appropriate to go further and consider other circumstances as they apply to the reasonable diligence analysis of 35 U.S.C. § 102(g). The record reveals that from the relevant period of November 17, 1982 (Kanamaru's filing date), to September 13, 1983 (when Griffith renewed his efforts towards reduction to practice), Griffith interrupted and often put aside the aminocarnitine project to work on other experiments. Between June 1982 and June 1983 Griffith admits that, at the request of the chairman of his department, he was primarily engaged in an unrelated research project on mitochondrial glutathione metabolism. Griffith also put aside the aminocarnitine experiment to work on a grant proposal on an unrelated project. Griffith's statement in the record that his unrelated grant application, if granted, might "support" a future grant request directed to the aminocarnitine project does not overcome the conclusion that he preferred one project over another and was not "continuously" or "reasonably" diligent. Griffith made only minimal efforts to secure funding directly for the aminocarnitine project.

The conclusion we reach from the record is that the aminocarnitine project was second and often third priority in laboratory research as well as the solicitation of funds. We agree that Griffith failed to establish a prima facie case of reasonable diligence or a legally sufficient excuse for inactivity to establish priority over Kanamaru.

CONCLUSION

Griffith has failed to establish a *prima facie* case of "reasonable diligence" to establish grounds for the award of priority as against Kanamaru's filing date.

Affirmed.

NOTES

1. Gould v. Schawlow, 363 F.2d 908 (C.C.P.A. 1966), involved an interference on a patent claim for a laser, a device for generating coherent beams of light that has become important in such applications as the compact disc player, which uses a laser beam to read digital information encoded on the disc, or for optical communications, which use a laser beam transmitted down an optical waveguide fiber. The senior applicants, Schawlow and Townes, with an application date of July 30, 1958, were an employee of Bell Telephone Laboratories and a consultant to the Laboratories who was also a Professor of Physics at Columbia University. The junior applicant, Gould, was a graduate student at Columbia who had conceived of the laser and made a notebook sketch of its key elements in November of 1957, prior to the Bell Telephone filing date. Gould lost, both on the ground that his notebook sketch was not a sufficiently clear conception and that he was not diligent. Gould's arguments that as a graduate student and later as a technical employee he was not in a position to reduce his invention to practice were rejected. The court pointed out that Gould could simply have filed for a patent without actually constructing the device, and thus obtained a constructive reduction to practice. Gould nevertheless persisted, and obtained some laser patents. See Patlex Corp. Inc. [the assignee of the Gould laser patents] v. Mossinghoff, 585 F.Supp. 713 (E.D. Pa. 1983); Gould v. Control Laser Corp., 866 F.2d 1391 (Fed. Cir. 1989). For the technological background see Bela A. Lengyel, Evolution of Masers and Lasers, 34 Am. J. Physics 903 (1966).

2. Rebecca S. Eisenberg, Proprietary Rights and the Norms of Science in Biotechnology Research, 97 Yale L. J. 177 (1987), considers the relationship between the patent system and the norms of basic scientific research.

3. Because it is impossible to foresee situations in which proof of conception, reasonable diligence and reduction to practice may be needed, the priority rules create incentives for some form of regular record-keeping in research laboratories. One common practice is to have each researcher keep a diary in which he records the results of each days work, and to have the entries witnessed and dated by another person.

Paulik v. Rizkalla

United States Court of Appeals, Federal Circuit, 1985.
760 F.2d 1270.

■ PAULINE NEWMAN, CIRCUIT JUDGE.

This appeal is from the decision of the United States Patent and Trademark Office Board of Patent Interferences (Board), awarding priority of invention to the senior party Nabil Rizkalla and Charles N. Winnick (Rizkalla), on the ground that the junior party and de facto first inventors Frank E. Paulik and Robert G. Schultz (Paulik) had suppressed or concealed the invention within the meaning of 35 U.S.C. § 102(g). We vacate this decision and remand to the Board.

I.

Rizkalla's patent application has the effective filing date of March 10, 1975, its parent application. Paulik's patent application was filed on June 30, 1975. The interference count is for a catalytic process for producing alkylidene diesters such as ethylidene diacetate, which is useful to prepare vinyl acetate and acetic acid. Paulik presented deposition testimony and exhibits in support of his claim to priority; Rizkalla chose to rely solely on his filing date.

The Board held and Rizkalla does not dispute that Paulik reduced the invention of the count to practice in November 1970 and again in April 1971. On about November 20, 1970 Paulik submitted a "Preliminary Disclosure of Invention" to the Patent Department of his assignee, the Monsanto Company. The disclosure was assigned a priority designation of "B", which Paulik states meant that the case would "be taken up in the ordinary course for review and filing."

Despite occasional prodding from the inventors, and periodic review by the patent staff and by company management, this disclosure had a lower priority than other patent work. Evidence of the demands of other projects on related technology was offered to justify the patent staff's delay in acting on this invention, along with evidence that the inventors and assignee continued to be interested in the technology and that the invention disclosure was retained in active status.

In January or February of 1975 the assignee's patent solicitor started to work toward the filing of the patent application; drafts of the application were prepared, and additional laboratory experiments were requested by the patent solicitor and were duly carried out by an inventor. The evidentiary sufficiency of these activities was challenged by Rizkalla, but the Board made no findings thereon, on the basis that these activities were not pertinent to the determination of priority. The Board held that "even if Paulik demonstrated continuous activity from prior to the Rizkalla effective filing date to his filing date * * * such would have no bearing on the question of priority in this case", and cited 35 U.S.C. § 102(g) as authority for the statement that "[w]hile diligence during the above noted period may be relied upon by one alleging prior conception and subsequent reduction to practice, it is of no significance in the case of the party who is not the last to reduce to practice". The Board thus denied Paulik the opportunity to antedate Rizkalla, for the reason that Paulik was not only the first to conceive but he was also the first to reduce to practice.

The Board then held that Paulik's four-year delay from reduction to practice to his filing date was prima facie suppression or concealment under the first clause of section 102(g), that since Paulik had reduced the invention to practice in 1971 and 1972 he was barred by the second clause of § 102(g) from proving reasonable diligence leading to his 1975 filing, and that in any event the intervening activities were insufficient to excuse the delay. The Board refused to consider Paulik's evidence of renewed patent-related activity.

II.

The Board's decision converted the case law's estoppel against reliance on Paulik's early work for priority purposes, into a forfeiture encompassing Paulik's later work, even if the later work commenced before the earliest activity of Rizkalla. According to this decision, once the inference of suppression or concealment is established, this inference cannot be overcome by the junior party to an interference. There is no statutory or judicial precedent that requires this result, and there is sound reason to reject it.

United States patent law embraces the principle that the patent right is granted to the first inventor rather than the first to file a patent application.[2] The law does not inquire as to the fits and starts by which an invention is made. The historic jurisprudence from which 35 U.S.C. § 102(g) flowed reminds us that "the mere lapse of time" will not prevent the inventor from receiving a patent. Mason v. Hepburn, 13 App.D.C. 86, 91, 1898 C.D. 510, 513 (1898). The sole exception to this principle resides in § 102(g) and the exigencies of the priority contest.

---

2. As observed by the Industrial Research Institute, a first-to-invent system "respects the value of the individual in American tradition and avoids inequities which can result from a 'race to the Patent Office'". Final Report of the Advisory Committee on Industrial Innovation, U.S. Dept. of Commerce, Sept. 1979, p. 174.

There is no impediment in the law to holding that a long period of inactivity need not be a fatal forfeiture, if the first inventor resumes work on the invention before the second inventor enters the field. We deem this result to be a fairer implementation of national patent policy, while in full accord with the letter and spirit of section 102(g).

The Board misapplied the rule that the first inventor does not have to show activity following reduction to practice to mean that the first inventor will not be allowed to show such activity. Such a showing may serve either of two purposes: to rebut an inference of abandonment, suppression, or concealment; or as evidence of renewed activity with respect to the invention. Otherwise, if an inventor were to set an invention aside for "too long" and later resume work and diligently develop and seek to patent it, according to the Board he would always be worse off than if he never did the early work, even as against a much later entrant.

Such a restrictive rule would merely add to the burden of those charged with the nation's technological growth. Invention is not a neat process. The value of early work may not be recognized or, for many reasons, it may not become practically useful, until months or years later. Following the Board's decision, any "too long" delay would constitute a forfeiture fatal in a priority contest, even if terminated by extensive and productive work done long before the newcomer entered the field.

We do not suggest that the first inventor should be entitled to rely for priority purposes on his early reduction to practice if the intervening inactivity lasts "too long," as that principle has evolved in a century of judicial analysis. Precedent did not deal with the facts at bar. There is no authority that would estop Paulik from relying on his resumed activities in order to pre-date Rizkalla's earliest date. We hold that such resumed activity must be considered as evidence of priority of invention. Should Paulik demonstrate that he had renewed activity on the invention and that he proceeded diligently to filing his patent application, starting before the earliest date to which Rizkalla is entitled—all in accordance with established principles of interference practice—we hold that Paulik is not prejudiced by the fact that he had reduced the invention to practice some years earlier.

III.

This appeal presents a question not previously treated by this court or, indeed, in the historical jurisprudence on suppression or concealment. We take this opportunity to clarify an apparent misperception of certain opinions of our predecessor court which the Board has cited in support of its holding.

There is over a hundred years of judicial precedent on the issue of suppression or concealment due to prolonged delay in filing. From the earliest decisions, a distinction has been drawn between deliberate suppression or concealment of an invention, and the legal inference of suppression or concealment based on "too long" a delay in filing the patent application. Both types of situations were considered by the courts before the 1952 Patent Act, and both are encompassed in 35 U.S.C. § 102(g). The result is consistent over this entire period—loss of the first inventor's priority as against an intervening second inventor—and has consistently been based on equitable principles and public policy as applied to the facts of each case.

The earliest decisions dealt primarily with deliberate concealment. In 1858, the Supreme Court in Kendall v. Winsor, 62 U.S. (21 How.) 322, 328 (1858) held that an inventor who "designedly, and with the view of applying it indefinitely and exclusively for his own profit, withholds his invention from the public" impedes "the progress of science and the useful arts".

In Mason v. Hepburn, supra, the classical case on inferred as contrasted with deliberate suppression or concealment, Hepburn was granted a patent in September 1894. Spurred by this news Mason filed his patent application in December 1894. In an interference, Mason demonstrated that he had built a working model in 1887 but showed no activity during the seven years thereafter. The court held that although Mason may have negligently rather than willfully concealed his invention, the "indifference, supineness, or willful act" of a first inventor is the basis for "the equity" that favors the second inventor when that person made and disclosed the invention during the prolonged inactivity of the first inventor. 13 App.D.C. at 96.

* * *

The legislative history of section 102(g) makes clear that its purpose was not to change the law. As described in H.R.Rep. No. 1923, 82d Cong., 2d Sess. 17–18 (1951), section 102(g) "retains the present rules of [the case] law governing the determination of priority of invention". The pre-1952 cases all dealt with situations whereby a later inventor made the same invention during a period of either prolonged inactivity or deliberate concealment by the first inventor, after knowledge of which (usually, but not always, by the issuance of a patent to the second inventor) the first inventor was "spurred" into asserting patent rights, unsuccessfully.

The decisions after the 1952 Act followed a similar pattern, as the courts considered whether to extinguish a first inventor's priority under § 102(g). The cases show either intentional concealment or an unduly long delay after the first inventor's reduction to practice. Some cases excused the delay, and some did not. A few examples will illustrate the application of the statute.

In Gallagher v. Smith, 206 F.2d 939 (CCPA 1953), a seven-year delay (from 1938 to 1945) was excused in the absence of evidence of actual concealment or suppression, as against a later applicant who had a reduction to practice in 1943. Note that the applicant who had delayed was nonetheless the first to file. In Schnick v. Fenn, 277 F.2d 935 (CCPA 1960), a lapse of nineteen months was excused absent intentional concealment or suppression and in view of the mitigating circumstances of uncertain market demand for the invention. In Woofter v. Carlson, 367 F.2d 436 (CCPA 1966), an eight-year delay after Carlson's reduction to practice was not excused, on evidence that Woofter's entry during this period had spurred Carlson into filing. The court found that there was deliberate concealment, and held that "[u]nder these circumstances, [Carlson] has forfeited its right to a patent". 367 F.2d at 448.

In Brokaw v. Vogel, 429 F.2d 476 (CCPA 1970), Vogel filed a patent application in 1963, having reduced the invention to practice in 1957. Brokaw filed in 1959. The court observed that Vogel remained inactive until he learned of Brokaw's issued patent, and that "there is nothing to show that any step was ever taken by Vogel during that time to make the invention available to the public and nothing tending to excuse Vogel's inaction." 429 F.2d at 480. In Palmer v. Dudzik, 481 F.2d 1377 (CCPA 1973), a first inventor's willful concealment of his invention, which continued until news of the junior party's independent invention spurred him to action, required "forfeiture" of his right to the patent in favor of the later inventor, even though in this case the first inventor got to the Patent Office first.

Young v. Dworkin, 489 F.2d 1277 (CCPA 1974), held that a 27-month delay amounted to suppression. Young had refrained from filing a patent application until he had acquired the machines to practice his invention commercially. Focusing on the character of Young's activity between his reduction to practice and filing date, the court found that during Young's prolonged period of inactivity Dworkin conceived the invention and filed his patent application. In concurrence, Judge Rich observed that "it is not the time elapsed that is the controlling factor but the total conduct of the first inventor," adding "[i]t may also be a relative matter, taking into account what the later inventor is doing too." 489 F.2d at 1285.

In Peeler v. Miller, 535 F.2d 647 (CCPA 1976), relied on by the Board, Miller was inactive during the four-year period following his reduction to practice, and the proffered excuse (that work of higher priority was done in other areas) was found inadequate. As noted by the Board, there are many similarities with the case at bar. The difference, however, is significant: Peeler had entered the field and filed his patent application while Miller remained dormant; Rizkalla entered the field, according to the record before us, after Paulik had renewed activity on the invention.

In Horwath v. Lee, 564 F.2d 948 (CCPA 1977), the court found an equitable estoppel based on Horwath's "suppression or concealment" of the invention for 66 months. Horwath filed in December 1971, and traced his invention back to an invention disclosure drawn up in April 1967 for which research had begun in November 1965. Attempting to account for the delay between the invention disclosure and his patent application, Horwath presented evidence of research to perfect his invention in 1971, well after Lee had filed in 1969. The court found Horwath's excuse inadequate. The same distinction exists as in other cases: the second inventor filed while the first inventor slept.

In Shindelar v. Holdeman, 628 F.2d 1337, (CCPA 1980), cert. denied, 451 U.S. 984 (1981), also relied on by the Board, there was a delay of two years and five months between reduction to practice and filing. This was held to be too long as against the second inventor who was the first (by two days) to file a patent application. The court held that the filing delay, attributed solely to the attorney's workload, "raised an inference of suppression * * * which has not been rebutted". 628 F.2d at 1341. The opinion is silent on the question of renewed work by the first inventor before the second inventor entered the field. Although the Board appeared to consider this case controlling as applied to Paulik, we do not see this case as controlling a situation which was not before it. The *Shindelar* court's closing words are: "We reiterate that each case involving the issue of suppression or concealment must be considered on its own particular set of facts." 628 F.2d at 1343.

IV.

The decisions applying section 102(g) balanced the law and policy favoring the first person to make an invention, against equitable considerations when more than one person had made the same invention: in each case where the court deprived the de facto first inventor of the right to the patent, the second inventor had entered the field during a period of either inactivity or deliberate concealment by the first inventor. Often the first inventor had been spurred to file a patent application by news of the second inventor's activities. Although "spurring" is not necessary to a finding of suppression or concealment, see Young v. Dworkin, 489 F.2d at 1281 and citations therein, the courts' frequent references to spurring indicate their concern with this equitable factor.

Some decisions used the word "forfeiture" to describe the first inventor's loss of priority; but none interpreted section 102(g) as requiring an absolute forfeiture rather than requiring a balance of equities. In *Brokaw v. Vogel,* for example, the court said "the *Mason v. Hepburn* principle is not a forfeiture in the true sense; rather it is a rule according to which the patent right goes to the most deserving. Realistically, it is a forfeiture by the de facto first inventor of the right to rely on his earlier reduction to practice." 429 F.2d at 480. In *Young v. Dworkin* Judge Rich wrote "I cannot agree with the board that the question in this case is whether Young 'forfeited his *right to a patent*'. But for Dworkin's conflicting claim, Young forfeited nothing and would get a patent. All he *forfeited* * * * was the right to rely on his prior actual reduction to practice in a priority dispute."

In no case where the first inventor had waited "too long" did he end his period of inactivity before the second inventor appeared. We affirm the longstanding rule that too long a delay may bar the first inventor from reliance on an early reduction to practice in a priority contest. But we hold that the first inventor will not be barred from relying on later, resumed activity antedating an opponent's entry into the field, merely because the work done before the delay occurred was sufficient to amount to a reduction to practice.

This result furthers the basic purpose of the patent system. The exclusive right, constitutionally derived, was for the national purpose of advancing the useful arts—the process today called technological innovation. As implemented by the patent statute, the grant of the right to exclude carries the obligation to disclose the workings of the invention, thereby adding to the store of knowledge without diminishing the patent-supported incentive to innovate.

But the obligation to disclose is not the principal reason for a patent system; indeed, it is a rare invention that cannot be deciphered more readily from its commercial embodiment than from the printed patent. The reason for the patent system is to encourage innovation and its fruits: new jobs and new industries, new consumer goods and trade benefits. We must keep this purpose in plain view as we consider the consequences of interpretations of the patent law such as in the Board's decision.

A foreseeable consequence of the Board's ruling is to discourage inventors and their supporters from working on projects that had been "too long" set aside, because of the impossibility of relying, in a priority contest, on either their original work or their renewed work. This curious result is neither fair nor in the public interest. We do not see that the public interest is served by placing so severe a sanction on failure to file premature patent applications on immature inventions of unknown value. In reversing the Board's decision we do not hold that such inventions are necessarily entitled to the benefits of their earliest dates in a priority contest; we hold only that they are not barred from entitlement to their dates of renewed activity.

* * *

Having established the principle that Paulik, although not entitled to rely on his early work, is entitled to rely on his renewed activity, we vacate the decision of the Board and, in the interest of justice, remand to the PTO for new interference proceedings in accordance with this principle.

Vacated and remanded.

* * *

NOTES

1. There are reasons to apply for a patent other than to obtain an enforceable patent. Because a patent application is a constructive reduction to practice, an application can serve to defend against patent claims of others on the same technology. Thus a firm might decide to apply for a patent even though it has no desire to enforce patent rights. Section 157, added by the Patent Law Amendments of 1984, P.L 98–622, now authorizes the PTO to publish a "statutory invention registration" which is not examined but has all the attributes of a patent, except that it does not confer any rights against infringement.

2. For an invention registration to work, it must properly disclose and claim the technology. Once this much work has been done, why shouldn't a firm let the patent office go ahead and examine the application? The PTO charges $920 for publication of a registration prior to action by the Examiner and $1,840 after action by the Examiner, 37 C.F.R. §§ 1.17(n), 1.17(o).

3. Can a person who has lost his right to obtain a patent either because of the § 102(b) time bar or because of § 102(g) abandonment enforce trade secret rights on the same subject matter under Kewanee v. Bicron, supra Chapter 4?

I. Specification and Claims

Drafting a patent is one of the most challenging tasks a lawyer can face. He must draft to satisfy the requirements of 35 U.S.C. § 112. They are three:

1. There must be a written description of the invention, and of the manner and process of making and using it, in such full, clear concise, and exact terms as to enable any person skilled in the art to which it pertains to make and use the same.

2. The patent must set forth the best mode contemplated by the inventor for carrying out his invention. Although no time is specifically designated, this is presumably the mode contemplated at the time of application.

3. The patent must conclude with one or more claims particularly pointing out and distinctly claiming the subject matter which constitutes the invention. (The statute says "which the applicant regards as his invention," but it has always been held that the claim must cover the invention in fact, no matter what the good faith belief of the applicant.)

The first requirement is a considerable challenge to the art of clear and effective descriptive writing. If you don't think that is difficult, write a description of the physical structure of this book. A good patent description should convey to the reader a sense of full disclosure rather than evasive obfuscation. See generally, Arthur M. Smith, The Art of Writing Readable Patents (P.L.I. 1958), which draws upon such authorities as U.S. Department of Health, Education and Welfare Training Manual No. 7, Getting Your Ideas Across Through Writing (U. S. Government Printing Office 1950), for the point that a good patent is a well written patent. The legal requirement of adequate description is not especially difficult to satisfy. Indeed, the same decisions which accord to the person skilled in the art considerable powers under § 103 would seem by implication to uphold highly technical descriptions under section 112. The custom is to err on the side of caution, writing the description so that it can be understood not only by one skilled in the art but by any person with a general technical background. This tends to make patent descriptions long and detailed and may even in some cases make them more difficult to understand. Alfred P. Orenzo, Insufficient Disclosure, Obviousness, and the Reasonable Man, 49 J. Pat. [& Trademark] Off. Soc'y 387 (1967), criticizes this practice. But with the ultimate decision in the hands of a lay judge and a legal penalty for underdisclosure but not for overdisclosure, it takes considerable courage, if not foolishness, to depart from the practice.

The second requirement requires close coordination between the drafting patent attorney and the inventor and his company, if any. For instance if a patent attorney were to obtain information on the best mode from the client, spend three months preparing the application, and submit it while the client was busy finding an improved best mode, the patent could turn out to be invalid.

Glaxo Inc. v. Novopharm Ltd.

United States Court of Appeals for the Federal Circuit, 1995.
52 F.3d 1043, certiorari denied 116 S.Ct. 516 (1995).

■ RICH, CIRCUIT JUDGE.

Novopharm Ltd. (Novopharm) appeals the judgment of the United States District Court for the Eastern District of North Carolina, Glaxo, Inc. v. Novopharm Ltd., 830 F.Supp. 871 (E.D.N.C. 1993), that United States Patent No. 4,521,431 was not invalid and was infringed, and enjoining Novopharm from the commercial manufacture or sale of the patented crystalline form of ranitidine hydrochloride. We affirm.

BACKGROUND

Glaxo Inc. and Glaxo Group Ltd. (collectively Glaxo) are the owner and exclusive United States licensee, respectively, of United States Patent No. 4,521,431 ('431 patent). The '431 patent claims a specific crystalline form of the compound ranitidine hydrochloride, designated as "Form 2," which Glaxo markets as an antiulcer medication under the brand name Zantac.[3] The '431 patent issued on June 4, 1985.

In 1976, Glaxo chemists investigating potential antiulcer medications synthesized an aminoalkyl furan derivative, later named ranitidine, which proved to be a potent histamine blocker, inhibiting the secretion of stomach acid. Later that year, Glaxo filed an application for a patent on ranitidine in the United Kingdom. It followed with an application for a United States patent, which issued as No. 4,128,658 ('658 patent) on December 5, 1978. The '658 patent claims a number of structurally similar compounds, including ranitidine and its hydrochloride salt. It discloses one method for preparing ranitidine hydrochloride, set forth in the '658 patent as Example 32.[4]

Glaxo prepared large quantities of ranitidine hydrochloride between 1977 and 1980 for use in toxicology and clinical studies. Instead of using the process of Example 32, however, Glaxo's chemists prepared this material using a similar process that they labelled Process 3A. They later developed a more efficient method that they called Process 3B. Until April 15, 1980,

---

3. Claims 1 and 2 of the '431 patent, in issue here, read: 1. Form 2 ranitidine hydrochloride characterised by an infra-red spectrum as a mull in mineral oil showing the following main peaks: [list of peaks] 2. Form 2 ranitidine hydrochloride according to claim 1 further characterised by the following x-ray powder diffraction pattern expressed in terms of "d" spacings and relative intensities (1) (s = strong, m = medium, w = weak, v = very, d = diffuse) and obtained by the Debye Scherrer method in a 114.6 mm diameter camera by exposure for 12 hours to CoK suba radiation

and for 3 hours to CuK suba radiation: [table] The '431 patent also claims various pharmaceutical compositions and methods of using Form 2 ranitidine hydrochloride. These claims are not at issue in this case.

4. Developed by Glaxo's David Collin in June 1977, that method involves dissolving ranitidine in industrial methylated spirit containing dissolved hydrogen chloride gas. Ethyl acetate is added to the solution, and ranitidine hydrochloride precipitates from solution as a crystalline solid characterized by a melting point of 133–134 degrees C.

both Process 3A and Process 3B yielded ranitidine hydrochloride identical in all respects to that originally produced using the Example 32 procedure.

On that date, however, Glaxo's Derek Crookes used Process 3B to prepare crystalline ranitidine hydrochloride that was visibly different from all previous batches of the salt. The difference was confirmed by infra-red (IR) spectroscopy and x-ray powder diffraction, which revealed that the new product was a crystalline form, or polymorph, of ranitidine hydrochloride that differed from the previously known form. Glaxo began to refer to this new polymorph as Form 2 ranitidine hydrochloride (designating the old polymorph as Form 1).

Because Form 2 had better filtration and drying properties, making it better suited for commercial applications, Glaxo decided to proceed with commercialization of Form 2 rather than Form 1. Form 2 was hampered by poor flow properties, however, which made the material difficult to measure and dispense in its pure form. Accordingly, Glaxo scientists developed a novel azeotroping process[5] to granulate the Form 2 salt, which made it much easier to make into pharmaceutical compositions. This process was the subject of a British patent application that Glaxo eventually abandoned without disclosing the process to the public.

Glaxo filed a patent application covering Form 2 ranitidine hydrochloride in the United Kingdom on October 1, 1980. It filed a United States application thereon the next year, which eventually issued as the '431 patent in suit. When George Graham Brereton, Glaxo's patent officer initially charged with pursuing the United States application, learned of the azeotropic granulation process and Glaxo's desire to keep that process secret, he recommended that Glaxo not claim pharmaceutical compositions of the Form 2 salt for fear of violating the best mode requirement. Brereton apparently believed that disclosure of the azeotroping process would be necessary because it was the best way to make the Form 2 salt for use in preparing pharmaceutical compositions. He later moved to another position at Glaxo. The U.S. application was eventually amended to include pharmaceutical composition claims, but Glaxo did not amend the specification to disclose the azeotroping process.

On August 9, 1991, Novopharm Ltd. filed an Abbreviated New Drug Application (ANDA) with the Food and Drug Administration (FDA), seeking FDA approval to manufacture and sell a generic version of Form 2 ranitidine hydrochloride beginning December 5, 1995, the expiration date of the '658 patent, well before the expiration date of the '431 patent in 2002. Glaxo filed this suit for patent infringement on November 13, 1991, alleging technical

---

5. Azeotroping is a technique for separating a chemical mixture, the components of which would otherwise be difficult to separate because of the similarity of their boiling points. An additional substance is added to the mixture, selected for its ability to interact with a component of the original mixture to form an azeotrope—a mixture of substances "the composition of which does not change upon distillation." See McGraw-Hill Dic- TIONARY OF SCIENTIFIC AND TECHNICAL TERMS 162 (4th ed. 1989). If the proper substance is selected, the resulting azeotrope will have a boiling point that differs substantially from the desired component of the original mixture. The desired component can then be successfully separated from the azeotrope by distillation. See HAWLEY'S CONDENSED CHEMICAL DICTIONARY 109 (11th ed. 1987).

infringement of claims 1 and 2 of the '431 patent by the ANDA filing as provided in 35 U.S.C. § 271(e)(2) (1988). Novopharm admitted infringement of the claims, but contended that the '431 patent was invalid because it was anticipated by the disclosure of the '658 patent.

Novopharm later amended its answer to add the defense of inequitable conduct arising from alleged false and misleading affidavits provided to the U.S. Patent and Trademark Office (PTO) during prosecution of the applications from which the '431 patent issued. Finally, on June 21, 1993, Novopharm sought summary judgment based on a third defense, Glaxo's alleged failure to disclose the best mode of practicing the claimed invention. The trial court denied the motion, and the case was tried to the court beginning on August 9, 1993.

On the question of anticipation, the court found that Novopharm had not carried its burden of proving by clear and convincing evidence that practice of Example 32 of the '658 patent always produced Form 2 ranitidine hydrochloride, so that Form 2 was not inherently disclosed by Example 32. As for inequitable conduct, the court agreed with Novopharm that the affidavits presented to the examiner were misleading and material, but it found that Novopharm had failed to prove any deceptive intent. The court also concluded that there was no violation of the best mode requirement because Novopharm had not proved that Crookes, the inventor, knew of the best mode, the statute and this court's precedent providing that knowledge by the inventor himself is required. Accordingly, the court held that the '431 patent was not invalid, was enforceable and infringed, and ordered that Novopharm refrain from commercial manufacture or sale of Form 2 ranitidine hydrochloride before the '431 patent expires. Novopharm appeals.

DISCUSSION

I. Example 32, anticipation

[The court affirmed the district court's finding of no anticipation.]

* * *

II. Inequitable Conduct

[The court affirmed the district court's finding that Glaxo did not intend to deceive when it made misrepresentations to the patent office.]

* * *

III. Best Mode

Novopharm next asserts that Glaxo failed to disclose the best mode of practicing the invention, that is, the azeotroping process it uses to formulate the claimed Form 2 ranitidine hydrochloride into pharmaceutical compositions. The best mode defense arose little more than two months before trial just after Glaxo produced documents based on which Novopharm filed a motion for summary judgment of invalidity for failure to disclose the best mode. Less than a week before trial, the district court denied Novopharm's motion stating that "the court cannot hold as a matter of law that Dr. Crookes knew that the azeotroping process was the best mode of manufacturing ranitidine hydrochloride, and summary judgment must therefore be denied." Glaxo, Inc. v. Novopharm Ltd., 830 F.Supp. 869, 871 (E.D.N.C. 1993). The district court further stated that it reserved for trial "ruling on the question of whether and to what extent the knowledge of other Glaxo employees and agents may be imputed to Dr. Crookes for purposes of finding a best mode analysis [sic, violation]." Id.

At trial, Novopharm produced evidence that officials at Glaxo knew of the azeotroping process and considered it to be the best mode of making Form 2 ranitidine hydrochloride into a pharmaceutical composition. Novopharm argued in district court, as it does here, that the knowledge of the azeotroping process by Glaxo officials should be imputed to inventor Crookes for purposes of finding a best mode violation.

The trial court found Novopharm's argument to have some "intuitive appeal" since Glaxo "has enjoyed the monopoly the issued patent provides." Glaxo, 830 F.Supp. 871, 881–82 (E.D.N.C. 1993). Indeed, the trial court stated that if it were to impute the knowledge of others to the inventor of the '431 patent, "then clearly the court would be required to find a best mode violation." Id. at 882. The trial court concluded, however, that the statute, 35 U.S.C. § 112, first paragraph, and this court's holding in Texas Instruments, Inc. v. United States International Trade Commission, 871 F.2d 1054 (Fed. Cir. 1989) do not permit using imputed knowledge in a best mode analysis. The district court concluded that Novopharm "as a matter of law . . . failed to show the '431 patent should be invalidated based on a best mode violation." Id. at 882. On appeal, Novopharm asserts that the district court erred as a matter of law in holding that a best mode defense cannot be found in the absence of proof that the inventor knew of that mode.

The statutory provision at issue sets forth that:

The specification . . . shall set forth the best mode contemplated by the inventor of carrying out his invention.

35 U.S.C. § 112, first paragraph (1988).

The statutory language could not be clearer. The best mode of carrying out an invention, indeed if there is one, to be disclosed is that "contemplated by the inventor." That the best mode "belongs" to the inventor finds consistent support in previous statutory language as well.[6] Additionally, the commentary on

6. The 1793 Act stated: "in the case of any machine [the inventor] shall fully explain the principle, and the several modes in which he has contemplated the application of that principle or character, by which it may be distinguished from other inventions." Act of Feb. 21, 1793, ch. 11, § 3, 1 Stat. 318. The 1836 Act stated: "in case of any machine, [the inventor] shall fully explain the principle, and the sev-

eral modes in which he has contemplated the application of the principle or character by which it may be distinguished from other inventions." Act of July 4, 1836, ch. 357, § 6, 5 Stat. 117. The Act of 1870 changed the 'several modes' provision of the previous Acts to the present-day 'best mode.' Act of July 7, 1870, ch. 230, § 26, 16 Stat. 198.

the 1952 Patent Act states with respect to the best mode provision that "[t]his requirement, it should be noted, is not absolute, since it only requires disclosure of the best mode contemplated by the inventor, presumably at the time of filing the application." P.J. Federico, Commentary on the New Patent Act, 35 U.S.C.A. 1, 25 (1954).

In arguing that Glaxo did not comply with the best mode requirement of § 112, first paragraph, Novopharm relies on Amgen, Inc. v. Chugai Pharmaceutical Co., 927 F.2d 1200 (Fed. Cir.), cert. denied, 502 U.S. 856 (1991), for the proposition that the best mode requirement lies at the heart of the statutory quid pro quo of the patent system. This is true enough. However, *Amgen*, consistent with the statute, speaks of the best mode requirement in terms of the best mode contemplated by the inventor. Amgen, 927 F.2d at 1210 ("Our case law has interpreted the best mode requirement to mean that there must be no concealment of a mode *known by the inventor* to be better than that which is disclosed.") (emphasis added). In fact, as we have previously stated, the sole purpose of the best mode requirement "is to restrain *inventors* from applying for patents while at the same time concealing from the public preferred embodiments of their inventions which *they* have in fact conceived." Chemcast Corp. v. Arco Indus. Corp., 913 F.2d 923, 926 (Fed. Cir. 1990) (emphasis added) (quoting In re Gay, 309 F.2d 769, 772 (CCPA 1962)); * * *

The best mode inquiry focuses on the inventor's state of mind at the time he filed his application, raising a subjective factual question. Chemcast, 913 F.2d at 926. The specificity of disclosure required to comply with the best mode requirement must be determined by the knowledge of facts within the possession of the inventor at the time of filing the application. Spectra-Physics, Inc. v. Coherent, Inc., 827 F.2d 1524, 1535 (Fed. Cir.), cert. denied, 484 U.S. 954 (1987).

That the best mode inquiry is grounded in knowledge of the inventor is even more evident upon contrasting the best mode requirement of § 112 with the enablement requirement of that section. Chemcast, 913 F.2d at 926. "Enablement looks to placing the subject matter of the claims generally in the possession of the public." Spectra-Physics, 827 F.2d at 1532. Best mode looks to whether specific instrumentalities and techniques have been developed by the inventor and known to him at the time of filing as the best way of carrying out the invention. Id.; Chemcast, 913 F.2d at 927–28. The enablement requirement, thus, looks to the objective knowledge of one of ordinary skill in the art, while the best mode inquiry is a subjective, factual one, looking to the state of the mind of the inventor. Indeed, recently this court in addressing whether an applicant's best mode had to be updated upon filing a continuation application affirmed that the best mode requirement "focuses on what the *inventor* knows." Transco Prods. Inc. v. Performance Contracting, Inc., 38 F.3d 551, 558 (Fed. Cir. 1994) (emphasis added), cert. denied, 115 S.Ct. 1102 (1995).

Based on the clear wording of the statute and our case law, the trial court properly rejected Novopharm's "imputed knowledge" best mode defense. As the trial court correctly noted, we held in Texas Instruments that there was no violation of the best mode requirement of § 112 by reason of knowledge of the purported best mode on the part of T.I. employees, other than the inventor, in the manufacturing group when the inventor did not know of or conceal this best mode. Texas Instruments, 871 F.2d at 1061.

There is simply no evidence in the record before us, indeed Novopharm points to none, that the inventor of the '431 patent knew of and concealed the azeotroping process when his application was filed. Inventor Crookes in a declaration in opposition to Novopharm's best mode summary judgment motion stated "I did not know of any azeotroping of ranitidine hydrochloride, or of its benefits, prior to commencement of this litigation. I did not—indeed, could not—consider the azeotrope process a 'best mode' of making ranitidine hydrochloride tablets at the time of filing any patent application." Crookes indicated that he worked in a different department than those who developed the azeotroping process.

As the district court observed, the record does indicate, however, that others at Glaxo knew of the azeotroping process and knew that this process would be used commercially to produce pharmaceutical forms of the claimed product.[7] The record also indicates that these individuals as well as their English patent agent were concerned that failure to disclose the azeotroping process may present a best mode problem. However, in neither instance did Glaxo nor its patent agent appropriately consider that inventor Crookes knew nothing of the azeotroping process. That Glaxo thought it may have a best mode problem either because of its incorrect or incomplete consideration of U.S. patent law does not make it so.

Novopharm maintains that Glaxo intentionally isolated Crookes from knowledge of the azeotroping process leaving "it to others to commercialize and reduce the invention to practice." Thus, Novopharm fears that Glaxo purposefully prevented the inventor from gaining knowledge of the most advantageous application for his invention, the azeotroping process, so that that process could be maintained as a trade secret. That fear does not equate with a best mode violation.

In this case, Crookes was unconcerned with the commercialization of the claimed compound. It is undisputed that Crookes invented a compound and was not involved in whatever processes were to be used to commercially produce it. Therefore, whether Glaxo deliberately walled off the inventor is irrelevant to the issue of failure of his application to disclose the best mode known to him.

In arguing that Crookes was screened from knowledge, Novopharm relies on testimony of Glaxo's in-house patent agent that Crookes was not consulted "at any time" during the preparation of the application that matured into the '431 patent. This however, completely ignores the requirement that patents are applied for "in the name of the actual inventor or

---

7. The claims at issue are not directed to a pharmaceutical compound. Therefore, there may be a question whether the azeotroping process is indeed the best mode of carrying out the claimed invention. See Chemcast, 913 F.2d at 927. In view of our decision, however, it is not necessary for us to reach this issue.

inventors" according to 37 C.F.R. § 1.41(a) (1983). The inventor(s) must submit an oath or declaration attesting that they have "reviewed and understand the contents of the specification" and believe "the named inventor or inventors to be the original and first inventor or inventors of the subject matter which is claimed and for which a patent is sought." 37 C.F.R. § 1.63(b)(1), (2) (1992); see also 37 C.F.R. § 1.51(a)(2) (1992). * * * Novopharm has not alleged that these requirements were violated.

It is therefore presumed that Crookes, the inventor and applicant, must have reviewed the specification and signed the required declaration before the application was filed. Without more, Novopharm is simply wrong when it alleges that Crookes had nothing to do with determining what needed to be disclosed in his patent application.

Novopharm additionally contends that looking solely to the inventor's knowledge in a best mode analysis "makes a mockery of the best mode requirement, and fosters a 'head in the sand' mentality for corporate applicants."

However, the practical reality is that inventors in most every corporate scenario cannot know all of the technology in which their employers are engaged. Therefore, whether intentionally or not, inventors will be effectively isolated from research no matter how relevant it is to the field in which they are working. Separating scenarios in which employers unintentionally isolate inventors from relevant research from instances in which employers deliberately set out to screen inventors from research, and finding a best mode violation in the latter case, would ignore the very words of § 112, first paragraph, and the case law as it has developed, which consistently has analyzed the best mode requirement in terms of knowledge of and concealment by the inventor. Congress was aware of the differences between inventors and assignees, see 35 U.S.C. §§ 100(d) and 152, and it specifically limited the best mode required to that contemplated by the inventor. We have no authority to extend the requirement beyond the limits set by Congress.

The dissent argues that imputing knowledge of others than the inventor to the inventor for purposes of considering what was "contemplated by the inventor" in a best mode analysis "may be necessary under appropriate circumstances, to protect the public's 'paramount interest in seeing that patent monopolies spring from backgrounds free from fraud or other inequitable conduct.'" The dissent contends that such knowledge can be imputed to the inventor under principles of agency law stating that, "[a]n agent's acts and knowledge can be imputed to the principal when necessary to protect the interests of others, so long as the acts or knowledge in question fall within the scope of the agent's authority," citing Restatement (Second) of Agency, § 261.

The Restatement defines agency as "the fiduciary relation which results from the manifestation of consent by one person to another that the other shall act on his behalf and subject to his control, and consent, by the other so to act." Restatement (Second) of Agency, § 1.

The flaw in the dissent's analysis is that a patent attorney does not enter into an agency relationship with the inventor for purposes of what is disclosed in the inventor's patent application. Simply, the inventor never authorizes his patent attorney to "act on his behalf" with respect to disclosing the invention. Or, in the terms used by the dissent, the scope of the patent attorney's authority does not include inventing, i.e., either supplementing or supplanting the inventor's knowledge of his own invention. Rather, the information disclosed in the inventor's patent application must be that which is actually known to him. The statute requires that he submit an oath to this effect. See 35 U.S.C. § 115 (1988).

An agency relationship may exist during prosecution before the PTO where the patent attorney is acting on the inventor's behalf. See 37 C.F.R. 1.56(a) (1992). An agency relationship does not exist, however, with respect to what an inventor must disclose in order to obtain a patent on his invention, which includes, of course, any best mode under § 112. Therefore, in addition to being inconsistent with § 112, as explained above, because an agency relationship does not exist for purposes of what is disclosed in a patent application, it would be improper to impute a patent attorney's knowledge of a best mode to the inventor for purposes of finding a best mode violation.

In any case, the dissent's application of general agency principles to the analysis of best mode disclosure under § 112 is an entirely new idea and is not existing law.

The trial court here correctly noted that this court has "found that the absence of a showing of *actual knowledge by the inventor* was dispositive of the defendant's best mode argument" and held that the law "does not permit using imputed knowledge" in a best mode defense. Glaxo, 830 F.Supp. at 881–82 (emphasis added). The district court therefore correctly rejected the best mode defense.

IV. Conclusion

Accordingly, the judgment of the United States District Court for the Eastern District of North Carolina is affirmed.

■ MAYER, CIRCUIT JUDGE, dissenting.

With this case, the court blesses corporate shell games resulting from organizational gerrymandering and willful ignorance by which one can secure the monopoly of a patent while hiding the best mode of practicing the invention the law expects to be made public in return for its protection. Because I believe this is a perverse interpretation of the law, I dissent.

* * *

The problem is that Glaxo's version of best mode, which the court now adopts, would allow, if not encourage, employers to isolate their employee/inventors from research directed to finding the most advantageous applications for their inventions, knowledge that the inventors would probably have had but for the employer's efforts to keep the work secret. As a result, inventors may have only limited perspective on the real value of their inventions, and can accordingly share only this limited perspective with the public. All the while, the employer/assignee will have a view of the big picture, fully aware, through its other employees, of superior modes of practicing the invention. But the assignee will be under no obligation to disclose those modes to the public. This deliberate subversion of the statutory disclosure would deprive the public of the benefits of the best mode of practicing the invention. There is no reason why this court should condone such abuse of the public trust.

I would hold that if there truly was such a pattern of deliberate concealment of information that would otherwise have been known to the inventor, the knowledge of those who sought to conceal that information and who now attempt to enforce the patent may be imputed to the inventor. The district court can refuse to enforce the patent and should be given the opportunity to do so with a correct understanding of its powers.

NOTES

1. McDougall, The Courts Are Telling Us: "Your Client's Best Mode Must Be Disclosed," 59 J. Pat [& Trademark] Off. Soc'y 321 (1977), reports that he could find no case prior to 1965 holding a patent invalid for failure to disclose the best mode. Since then there have been a number of cases. See, e.g., Spectra-Physics, Inc. v. Coherent, Inc., 827 F.2d 1524 (Fed. Cir. 1987).

2. Because the priority and time bar rules create incentives to apply for a patent before the invention has been commercialized, and because any commercial product will usually have to involve many patents, the best mode requirement does not enable a competitor to simply read the patents and go into business. By the time the patent expires some twenty years later, the best mode disclosure will be obsolete. What then, is the function of the best mode requirement? See Kitch, the Nature and Function of the Patent System, 20 J. of Law & Econ. 265, 287–88 (1977).

3. Wahl Instruments, Inc. v. Acvious, Inc., 950 F.2d 1575 (Fed. Cir. 1991), involved a patent on an egg-timer device made with plastic and thermochromic paint or ink. A thermochromic material is a material that changes color at a certain temperature. The patented device could be placed in the fluid being heated and would change color when the desired amount of heat had been applied. At the time of the application the inventor was involved in developing precise manufacturing techniques for commercial production, but he did not disclose the techniques in the patent. The district court entered summary judgment against the patent owner for failure to disclose his best mode. The Federal Circuit reversed on the ground that the undisclosed manufacturing procedures were simply routine manufacturing decisions involving techniques known to those with skill in the relevant arts. The court said:

A description of particular materials or sources or of a particular method or technique selected for manufacture may or may not be required as part of a best mode disclosure respecting a device. * * * Thus, the particulars of making a prototype or even a commercial embodiment do not necessarily equate with the "best mode" of "carrying out" an invention. Indeed, the inventor's manufacturing materials or sources or techniques used to make a device may vary from wholly irrelevant to critical. For example, if the inventor develops or knows of a particular method of making which substantially improves the operation or effectiveness of his invention, failure to disclose such peripheral development may well lead to invalidation. * * * . On the other hand, an inventor is not required to supply "production" specifications. * * * Under our case law, there is no mechanical rule that a best mode violation occurs because the inventor failed to disclose particular manufacturing procedures beyond the information sufficient for enablement. One must look at the scope of the invention, the skill in the art, the evidence as to the inventor's belief, and all of the circumstances in order to evaluate whether the inventor's failure to disclose particulars of manufacture gives rise to an inference that he concealed information which one of ordinary skill in the art would not know. * * *

950 F.2d 1579–80.

Amgen, Inc. v. Chugai Pharmaceutical Co., Ltd.

United States Court of Appeals for the Federal Circuit, 1991.
927 F. 2d 1200, certiorari denied 502 U.S. 856 (1991).

[This case involved Amgen's effort to enforce its patent on Erythropoietin (EPO), a protein which stimulates the production of red blood cells. It is used to treat anemias or other blood disorders characterized by low bone marrow production of red blood cells. The drug has been particularly useful for cancer or AIDS patients suffering from low red blood cell production as a result of other therapies. It has also been very profitable. The Amgen patent disclosed a method of producing EPO through use of biotechnology. One of the arguments of the defendants was that Amgen's disclosure of the best mode was inadequate because Amgen had not placed a sample of a key substance used in the process on deposit where competitors could obtain a sample.]

* * *

C. Best Mode

Defendants argue that the district court erred in failing to hold the '008 patent invalid under 35 U.S.C. § 112, asserting that Lin failed to disclose the best mammalian host cells known to him as of November 30, 1984, the date he filed his fourth patent application.

The district court found that the "best mode" of practicing the claimed invention was by use of a specific genetically-heterogeneous strain of Chinese hamster ovary (CHO) cells, which produced EPO at a rate greater than that of other cells. It further found that this strain was disclosed in Example 10 and that Lin knew of no better mode. GI argues that Lin's best mode was not adequately disclosed in Example 10 because one skilled in the art could not duplicate Lin's best mode without his having first deposited a sample of the specific cells in a public depository. The issue before us therefore is whether the district court erred in concluding that Example 10 of the '008 patent satisfied the best mode requirement as to the invention of the challenged claims and that a deposit of the preferred CHO cells was not necessary.

* * *

35 U.S.C. § 112 provides in relevant part: The specification shall contain a written description of the invention, and of the manner and process of making and using it, in such full, clear, concise, and exact terms as to enable any person skilled in the art to which it pertains, or with which it is most nearly connected, to make and use the same, and shall set forth *the best mode contemplated by the inventor of carrying out his invention*. (Emphasis added).

This court has recently discussed the best mode requirement, pointing out that its analysis has two components. Chemcast Corp. v. Arco Indus. Corp., 913 F.2d 923, 927 (Fed. Cir. 1990). The first is a subjective one, asking whether, at the time the inventor filed his patent application, he contemplated a best mode of practicing his invention. If he did, the second inquiry is whether his disclosure is adequate to enable one skilled in the art to practice the best mode or, in other words, whether the best mode has been concealed from the public. The best mode requirement thus is intended to ensure that a patent applicant plays "fair and square" with the patent system. It is a requirement that the quid pro quo of the patent grant be satisfied. One must not receive the right to exclude others unless at the time of filing he has provided an adequate disclosure of the best mode known to him of carrying out his invention. Our case law has interpreted the best mode requirement to mean that there must be no concealment of a mode known by the inventor to be better than that which is disclosed. Hybritech Inc. v. Monoclonal Antibodies, Inc., 802 F.2d 1367, 1384–85 (Fed. Cir. 1986), cert. denied, 480 U.S. 947 (1987). Section 282 imposes on those attempting to prove invalidity the burden of proof. We agree that the district court did not err in finding that defendants have not met their burden of proving a best mode violation.

As noted above, the district court found that the best mode of making the CHO cells was set forth in Example 10. As the district court stated, while it was not clear which of two possible strains Lin considered to be the best, the cell strain subjected to 1000 nanomolar MTX (methotrexate) or that subjected to 100 nanomolar MTX, the best mode was disclosed because both were disclosed.[6] Defendants argue that this disclosure is not enough, that a deposit of the cells was required.

Defendants contend that "[i]n the field of living materials such as microorganisms and cell cultures," we should require a biological deposit so that the public has access to exactly the best mode contemplated by the inventor. This presents us with a question of first impression concerning the

6. In its opinion, the district court stated that "the best way to express EPO was from mammalian cells . . . and that a cell line derived from 11 possible clones from the CHO B11 3,.1 cell strain was to be used for Amgen's master working cell bank, which was expected to be started on November 26, 1984." 13 USPQ2d at 1772. At another point, the court stated that Amgen "did disclose the best mode in Example 10 of the invention, when it described the production rates of the 100 nanomolar-amplified cells (the B11 3,.1 cell strain) and one micromolar-treated cells." Id.

best mode requirement for patents involving novel genetically-engineered biological subject matter.

For many years, it has been customary for patent applicants to place microorganism samples in a public depository when such a sample is necessary to carry out a claimed invention. This practice arose out of the development of antibiotics, when microorganisms obtained from soil samples uniquely synthesized antibiotics which could not be readily prepared chemically or otherwise. In re Argoudelis, 434 F.2d 1390 (CCPA 1970). Such a deposit has been considered adequate to satisfy the enablement requirement of 35 U.S.C. § 112, when a written description alone would not place the invention in the hands of the public and physical possession of a unique biological material is required. See, e.g., In re Wands, 858 F.2d 731, 735–36 (Fed. Cir. 1988) ("Where an invention depends on the use of living materials . . . it may be impossible to enable the public to make the invention (i.e., to obtain these living materials) solely by means of written disclosure."); In re Lundak, 773 F.2d 1216, 1220 (Fed. Cir. 1985) ("When an invention relates to a new biological material, the material may not be reproducible even when detailed procedures and a complete taxonomic description are included in the specification."); see generally Hampar, Patenting of Recombinant DNA Technology: The Deposit Requirement, 67 J. Pat. & Trademark Off. Soc'y 569, 607 (1985) ("The deposit requirement is a nonstatutory mechanism for ensuring compliance with the 'enabling' provision under 35 U.S.C. § 112.").

The district court found that the claims at issue require the use of biological materials that were capable of being prepared in the laboratory from readily available biological cells, using the description in Example 10. The court also found that there were no starting materials that were not publicly available, that were not described, or that required undue experimentation for their preparation in order to carry out the best mode. The court noted that Lin testified that the isolation of the preferred strain was a "routine limited dilution cloning procedure" well known in the art. Dr. Simonsen, GI's own expert, testified that the disclosed procedures were "standard" and that: with the vectors and the sequences shown in Example 10, I have no doubt that someone eventually could reproduce—well, could generate cell lines [sic, strains] making some level of EPO, and they could be better, they could be worse in terms of EPO production. The district court relied on this testimony, and, upon review, we agree with its determination. The testimony accurately reflects that the invention, as it relates to the best mode host cells, could be practiced by one skilled in the art following Example 10. Thus, the best mode was disclosed and it was adequately enabled.

These materials are therefore not analogous to the biological cells obtained from unique soil samples. When a biological sample required for the practice of an invention is obtained from nature, the invention may be incapable of being practiced without access to that organism. Hence the deposit is required in that case. On the other hand, when, as is the case here, the organism is created by insertion of genetic material into a cell obtained from generally available sources, then all that is required is a description of the best mode and an adequate description of the means of carrying out the invention, not deposit of the cells. If the cells can be prepared without undue experimentation from known materials, based on the description in the patent specification, a deposit is not required. See Feldman v. Aunstrup, 517 F.2d 1351, 1354 (CCPA 1975) ("No problem exists when the microorganisms used are known and readily available to the public."), cert. denied, 424 U.S. 912 (1976). Since the court found that that is the case here, we therefore hold that there is no failure to comply with the best mode requirement for lack of a deposit of the CHO cells, when the best mode of preparing the cells has been disclosed and the best mode cells have been enabled, i.e., they can be prepared by one skilled in the art from known materials using the description in the specification.

Defendants also contend that the examiner's rejection of the application that matured into the '008 patent for failure to make a publicly accessible biological deposit supports its argument. U.S. Patent Application Serial No. 675,298, Prosecution History at 179 (First Rejection July 3, 1986). However, that rejection was withdrawn after an oral interview and a written argument that the invention did not require a deposit. Id. at 208.

We also note that the PTO has recently prescribed guidelines concerning the deposit of biological materials. See 37 C.F.R. § 1.802(b) (1990) (biological material need not be deposited "if it is known and readily available to the public or can be made or isolated without undue experimentation"). The PTO, in response to a question as to whether the deposit requirement is applicable to the best mode requirement, as distinct from enablement, said: The best mode requirement is a safeguard against the possible selfish desire on the part of some people to obtain patent protection without making a full disclosure. The requirement does not permit an inventor to disclose only what is known to be the second-best embodiment, retaining the best. . . . The fundamental issue that should be addressed is whether there was evidence to show that the quality of an applicant's best mode disclosure is so poor as to effectively result in concealment. In re Sherwood, 615 [613] F.2d 809, (CCPA 1980). If a deposit is the only way to comply with the best mode requirement then the deposit must be made. 52 Fed.Reg. 34080, 34086 (Sept. 8, 1987).

We see no inconsistency between the district court's decision, which we affirm here, and these guidelines.

Defendants also assert that the record shows that scientists were unable to duplicate Lin's genetically-heterogeneous best mode cell strain. However, we have long held that the issue is whether the disclosure is "adequate," not that an exact duplication is necessary. Indeed, the district court stated that [t]he testimony is clear that no scientist could ever duplicate exactly the best mode used by Amgen, but that those of ordinary skill in the art could produce mammalian host cell strains or lines with similar levels of production identified in Example 10. 13 USPQ2d at 1774. What is required is an adequate disclosure of the best mode, not a guarantee that every aspect of the specification be precisely and universally reproducible.

* * *

The third requirement of § 112, that the patent must conclude with one or more claims particularly pointing out and distinctly claiming the subject matter which constitutes the invention, is challenging. The claim must point out and define those elements of the thing described which constitute the invention—in the legal sense. The elements claimed must be patentable; but a claim that extends beyond patentable elements is invalid. The drafter must tread the line between the claim which is so narrow as to destroy the commercial value of the patent and the claim that is so broad as to be invalid. This he must do at a time when the commercial significance of the invention is probably not fully appreciated by his client and without the benefit of the exhaustive searches that will be conducted if the patent proves valuable and is challenged in litigation. Furthermore, he must draft the claim so as to satisfy the immediate demands of the patent office while at the same time keeping an eye on the unknown court that may someday try an infringement case.

The difficulty of drafting claims is ameliorated by provision for multiple claims. These can be used as a form of alternative pleading, enabling the drafter to prepare for different eventualities. The statute puts no limit on this practice, providing simply for "one or more" claims. There are, however, extra fees for more than 3 claims.

The drafter can take some solace from the fact that should he fail to successfully negotiate the maze there is a provision for reissue of a patent that "through error without any deceptive intention," is "deemed wholly or partly inoperative or invalid, by reason of the patentee claiming more or less than he had a right to claim in the patent." 35 U.S.C. §§ 251, 252. The reissued patent cannot claim matter not disclosed in the original application.

The patent specification is not under the statute required to disclose the features that make the invention non-obvious. Nevertheless, patent specifications frequently describe the prior art and the advantages afforded by the invention. In part this simplifies the problem of describing the invention. And in part it may be thought that it gives the patent a stronger "aura" of validity. The practice is a risky one because a subsequent infringement court may hold the applicant bound to the theories of non-obviousness disclosed by the specification. This is wrong, but the courts are disconcerted by the thought that an applicant can make a patentable invention without ever understanding why his invention was non-obvious. See Robert A. Choate, Invention and Unobviousness—"Afterthoughts"—Reliance on Features and Advantages Undisclosed at Original Filing, 49 J.Pat.Off.Soc'y. 619 (1967).

Halliburton Oil Well Cementing Co. v. Walker

Supreme Court of the United States, 1946.
329 U.S. 1, 67 S.Ct. 6, 91 L.Ed. 3.

■ MR. JUSTICE BLACK delivered the opinion of the Court.

* * *

[Action for infringement of a patent on a device for measuring the depth of oil wells. Because of the machinery in and around the wells and the fact that some wells did not go straight down, it was impractical to measure their depth by simply lowering a line. It was important to know the depth of the well in order to properly place the pump in the well. The oil industry had made use of a sound echo device to measure the depth by measuring the elapsed time between a sound and its echo. But this method was inaccurate because sound in the wells did not travel at the uniform surface speed of 1100 feet per second. Walker, the inventor, undertook to search for a method which would more accurately indicate the sound and pressure wave velocity in each well. Walker was familiar with the structure of oil wells. The oil flow pipe in a well, known as a tubing string, is jointed and where these joints occur there are collars or shoulders. There are also one or more relatively prominent projections on the oil flow pipe known as tubing catchers. In wells where the distance to the tubing catcher is known, Walker observed that the distance to the fluid surface could be measured by a simple time-distance proportion formula.[4] For those wells in which the distance to the tubing catcher was unknown, Walker also suggested another idea. The sections of tubing pipe used in a given oil well are generally of equal length. Therefore the shoulders in a given well ordinarily are at equal intervals from each other. But the section length and therefore the interval may vary from well to well. Walker concluded that he could measure the unknown distance to the tubing catcher if he could observe and record the shoulder echo waves. Thus multiplication of the number of shoulders observed by the known length of a pipe section would produce the distance to the tubing catcher. With this distance, he could solve the distance to the fluid surface by the same proportion formula used when the distance to the tubing catcher was a matter of record. The Lehr and Wyatt instrument could record all these echo waves. But the potential usefulness of the echoes from the shoulders and the tubing catcher which their machine recorded had not occurred to Lehr and Wyatt and consequently they had made no effort better to observe and record them. Walker's contribution which he claims to be invention was in effect to add to Lehr and Wyatt's apparatus a well-known device which would make the regularly appearing shoulder echo waves more prominent on the graph and easier to count.

The device added was a mechanical acoustical resonator. This was a short pipe which would receive wave impulses at the mouth of the well. Walker's testimony was, and his specifications state, that by making the length of this tubal resonator one-third the length of the tubing joints, the resonator would serve as a tuner, adjusted to the frequency of the shoulder echo waves. It would simultaneously amplify these echo waves and eliminate

---

4. The known distance from well top to the tubing catcher is to the unknown distance from well top to the fluid surface as the time an echo requires to travel from the tubing catcher is to the time required for an echo to travel from the fluid surface.

Walker's patent emphasizes that his invention solves the velocity of sound waves in wells of various pressures in which sound did not travel at open-air or a uniform speed. Mathematically, of course, his determination of the distance by proportions determines the distance to the fluid surface directly without necessarily considering velocity in feet per second as a factor.

unwanted echoes from other obstructions thus producing a clearer picture of the shoulder echo waves. His specifications show, attached to the tubal resonator, a coupler, the manipulation of which would adjust the length of the tube to one-third of the interval between shoulders in a particular well. His specifications and drawings also show the physical structure of a complete apparatus, designed to inject pressure impulses into a well, and to receive, note, record and time the impulse waves.

The District Court held the claims here in suit valid upon its finding that Walker's "apparatus differs from and is an improvement over the prior art in the incorporation in such apparatus of a tuned acoustical means which performs the function of a sound filter * * * " The Circuit Court of Appeals affirmed this holding, stating that the trial court had found "that the only part of this patent constituting invention over the prior art is the 'tuned acoustical means which performs the functions of a sound filter.'"

For our purpose in passing upon the sufficiency of the claims against prohibited indefiniteness we can accept without ratifying the findings of the lower court that the addition of "a tuned acoustical means" performing the "function of a sound filter" brought about a new patentable combination, even though it advanced only a narrow step beyond Lehr and Wyatt's old combination.[5] We must, however, determine whether, as petitioner charges, the claims here held valid run afoul of Rev.Stat. 4888 because they do not describe the invention but use "conveniently functional language at the exact point of novelty." General Electric Co. v. Wabash Appliance Corp., supra, at 371.

* * *

A claim typical of all of those held valid only describes the resonator and its relation with the rest of the apparatus as "means associated with said pressure responsive device for tuning said receiving means to the frequency of echoes from the tubing collars of said tubing sections to clearly distinguish the echoes from said couplings from each other."[7] The language of the claim thus describes this most crucial element in the "new" combination in terms of what it will do rather than in terms of its own physical characteristics or

---

5. See Hailes v. Van Wormer, 20 Wall. 353; Knapp v. Morss, 150 U.S. 221, 227–28; Textile Machine Works v. Louis Hirsch Textile Machines, Inc., 302 U.S. 490; Lincoln Engineering Co. v. Stewart-Warner Corp., 303 U.S. 545, 549–50.

7. Both parties have used Claim 1 as a typical example for purposes of argument throughout the litigation. Other claims need not be set out. Claim 1 is as follows:

"In an apparatus for determining the location of an obstruction in a well having therein a string of assembled tubing sections interconnected with each other by coupling collars, means communicating with said well for creating a pressure impulse in said well, echo receiving means including a pressure responsive device exposed to said well for receiving pressure impulses from the well and for measuring the lapse of time between the creation of the impulse and the arrival at said receiving means of the echo from said obstruction, and means associated with said pressure responsive device for tuning said receiving means to the frequency of echoes from the tubing collars of said tubing sections to clearly distinguish the echoes from said couplings from each other."

its arrangement in the new combination apparatus. We have held that a claim with such a description of a product is invalid as a violation of Rev.Stat. 4888. Holland Furniture Co. v. Perkins Glue Co., 277 U.S. 245, 256–57; General Electric Co. v. Wabash Appliance Corp., supra. We understand that the Circuit Court of Appeals held that the same rigid standards of description required for product claims is not required for a combination patent embodying old elements only. We have a different view.

* * *

Patents on machines which join old and well-known devices with the declared object of achieving new results, or patents which add an old element to improve a pre-existing combination, easily lend themselves to abuse. And to prevent extension of a patent's scope beyond what was actually invented, courts have viewed claims to combinations and improvements or additions to them with very close scrutiny. * * *

This patent and the infringement proceedings brought under it illustrate the hazards of carving out an exception to the sweeping demand Congress made in [the statute] * * *. Neither in the specification, the drawing, nor in the claims here under consideration, was there any indication that the patentee contemplated any specific structural alternative for the acoustical resonator or for the resonator's relationship to the other parts of the machine. Petitioner was working in a field crowded almost, if not completely, to the point of exhaustion. In 1920, Tucker, in Patent No. 1,351,356, had shown a tuned acoustical resonator in a sound detecting device which measured distances. Lehr and Wyatt had provided for amplification of their waves. Sufficient amplification and exaggeration of *all* the different waves which Lehr and Wyatt recorded on their machine would have made it easy to distinguish the tubing catcher and regular shoulder waves from all others. For, even without this amplification, the echo waves from tubing collars could by proper magnification have been recorded and accurately counted, had Lehr and Wyatt recognized their importance in computing the velocity. Cf. General Electric Co. v. Jewel Incandescent Lamp Co., 326 U.S. 242.

Under these circumstances the broadness, ambiguity, and overhanging threat of the functional claim of Walker become apparent. What he claimed in the court below and what he claims here is that his patent bars anyone from using in an oil well any device heretofore or hereafter invented which combined with the Lehr and Wyatt machine performs the function of clearly and distinctly catching and recording echoes from tubing joints with regularity. Just how many different devices there are of various kinds and characters which would serve to emphasize these echoes, we do not know. The Halliburton device, alleged to infringe, employs an electric filter for this purpose. In this age of technological development there may be many other devices beyond our present information or indeed our imagination which will perform that function and yet fit these claims. And unless frightened from the course of experimentation by broad functional claims like these, inventive genius may evolve many more devices to accomplish the same purpose. See United Carbon Co. v. Binney & Smith Co., 317 U.S. 228, 236;

Burr v. Duryee, 1 Wall. 531, 568; O'Reilly v. Morse, 15 How. 62, 112–13. Yet if Walker's blanket claims be valid, no device to clarify echo waves, now known or hereafter invented, whether the device be an actual equivalent of Walker's ingredient or not, could be used in a combination such as this, during the life of Walker's patent.

Had Walker accurately described the machine he claims to have invented, he would have had no such broad rights to bar the use of all devices now or hereafter known which could accent waves. For had he accurately described the resonator together with the Lehr and Wyatt apparatus, and sued for infringement, charging the use of something else used in combination to accent the waves, the alleged infringer could have prevailed if the substituted device (1) performed a substantially different function; (2) was not known at the date of Walker's patent as a proper substitute for the resonator; or (3) had been actually invented after the date of the patent. Fuller v. Yentzer, supra, at 296–97; Gill v. Wells, supra, at 29. Certainly, if we are to be consistent with Rev.Stat. 4888, [predecessor to § 112] a patentee cannot obtain greater coverage by failing to describe his invention than by describing it as the statute commands.

* * *

Reversed.

NOTES

1. General Electric Co. v. Wabash Corp., 304 U.S. 364 (1938), relied on in *Halliburton,* involved a patent on an improved tungsten filament for light bulbs. Tungsten filaments were subject to "offsetting" and "sagging" which reduced their useful life by causing premature burn outs. By use of an alkaline silicate the inventor was able to make a tungsten filament with larger, coarser grains which would not sag or offset in use. The claim in suit read:

> A filament for electric incandescent lamps or other devices, composed substantially of tungsten and made up mainly of a number of comparatively large grains of such size and contour as to prevent substantial sagging and offsetting during a normal or commercially useful life for such a lamp or other device.

The Court held the claim defective. "The claim uses indeterminate adjectives which describe the function of the grains to the exclusion of any structural definition, and thus falls within the condemnation of the doctrine that a patentee may not broaden his product claims by describing the product in terms of function. Claim 25 vividly illustrates the vice of a description in terms of function. 'As a description of the invention it is insufficient and if allowed would extend the monopoly beyond the invention.' " The Court of Appeals had held that "in view of the difficulty, if not impossibility, of describing adequately a number of microscopic and heterogeneous shapes of crystals, it may be that * * * [the inventor] made the best disclosure possible, * * * ." The Court answered, "It may be doubted whether one who discovers or invents a product he knows to be new will ever find it impossible to describe some aspect of its novelty."

The patent in the *Wabash* case also contained process claims on the method for making the filament, but the plaintiff sued only on the product claims. At the trial below the defendant refused to reveal the method by which it made its filaments. 17 F.Supp. at 904. The district court, however, found that the defendant's filament was identical to the plaintiff's filament. Id. at 906.

2. Could the patentee in the principal case have claimed a process for measuring the depth of oil wells? O'Reilly v. Morse, 56 U.S. 62 (1853), supra, and Tilghman v. Proctor, 102 U.S. 707 (1880), supra, are pertinent here. Should the *O'Reilly* case have ever been read for anything other than the proposition that a claim broader than the applicant's invention is invalid?

3. The third paragraph of § 112 states:

> An element in a claim for a combination may be expressed as a means or step for performing a specified function without the recital of structure, material, or acts in support thereof, and such claim shall be construed to cover the corresponding structure, material, or acts described in the specification and equivalents thereof.

P.J. Federico, Commentary on the New Patent Act (printed in front of the first volume of 35 U.S.C. in 1954) 25–26 (1954), explains:

> The last paragraph of § 112 relating to so-called functional claims is new. It provides that an element of a claim for a combination (and a combination may be not only a combination of mechanical elements, but also a combination of substances in a composition claim, or steps in a process claim) may be expressed as a means or step for performing a specified function, without the recital of structure, material or acts in support thereof. It is unquestionable that some measure of greater liberality in the use of functional expressions in combination claims is authorized than had been permitted by some court decisions, and that decisions such as that in Halliburton Oil Well Cementing Co. v. Walker, 329 U.S. 1 (1946), are modified or rendered obsolete, but the exact limits of the enlargement remain to be determined. The language specifies "an" element, which means 'any' element, and by this language, as well as by application of the general rule that the singular includes the plural, it follows that more than one of the elements of a combination claim may be expressed as different "means" plus statements of function. The language does not go so far as to permit a so-called single means claim, that is a claim which recites merely one means plus a statement of function and nothing else. Attempts to evade this by adding purely nominal elements to such a claim will undoubtedly be condemned. The paragraph ends by stating that such a claim shall be construed to cover the corresponding structure, material, or acts described in the specification and equivalents thereof. This relates primarily to the construction of such claims for the purpose of determining when the claim is infringed (note the use of the word "cover"), and would not appear to have much, if any, applicability in determining the patentability of such claims over the prior art, that is, the Patent Office is not authorized to allow a claim which 'reads on' the prior art.

Does the third paragraph of § 112 by implication invalidate functional claims for all inventions other than those for combinations? What, for purposes of the paragraph, is a combination? See Application of Barr, 444 F.2d 588 (C.C.P.A. 1971).

4. Generally speaking, the longer a claim is the less it will cover. Each additional item included in the claim will be an item whose absence will keep something from being within the terms of the claim.

5. The claim of a design patent is of the form "a design as shown in the diagram." A design infringes if a comparison of the defendant's design with the patented design shows that the defendant's design is substantially similar in appearance to the patented design considered as a whole.

In Oddzon Products, Inc. v. Just Toys, Inc., 122 F.3d 1396 (Fed. Cir. 1997), supra, the Federal Circuit affirmed a judgment of non-infringement. The plaintiff had shown that some consumers confused the defendant's product with the plaintiff's, and experts testified to the overall similarity of the products. However, the court said this evidence was insufficient because it did not show the similarity of the ornamental features protected by the design patent.

J. Scope of Patent Rights

A patent confers the right to exclude others from making, using or selling the patented invention (see 35 U.S.C. § 271). The patented invention is that which is covered by the claims of the patent, that portion of the specification that points out and distinctly claims the subject matter (see 35 U.S.C. § 112).

The owner of a patent does not acquire by virtue of the ownership of the patent the right to practice the invention if doing so would otherwise be illegal. For instance, if practice of an invention would violate laws regulating pollution or involve the possession of an illegal substance, the patent offers no protection against such laws.

An illustration of this point is that an invention within the claims of one patent can also be within the claims of another patent and thus infringe the other patent. This may come about if the claim is for an improvement to the invention of the other patent. In this situation, the owner of the patent whose invention falls within the other patent cannot practice it without the consent of the owner of that other patent. In this situation, the other patent is said to "block" the patent. Indeed, if one patent contains a broad but commercially impracticable claim while the second contains a commercially viable implementation of the first, it may be impossible for either patent owner to market a successful product without the consent of the other.

An understanding of the scope of the right to exclude conferred by a particular claim is important to understanding the practical significance of the patent, and each step of the drafting and application process must be informed by an understanding of the practical value of the rights that particular claims will confer.

Infringement is defined in 35 U.S.C. § 271. Subsection (a) provides that "whoever makes, uses or sells any patented invention within the United States during the term of the patent therefor, infringes the patent."

A person infringes when he makes, uses or sells something that falls within the scope of the claims of the patent. The claims of the patent are like the boundary descriptions in a deed to real estate: they demarcate the subject matter as to which the owner of the patent has a right to exclude.

(1) Make, Use or Sell

Not every use of a patent infringes, even uses of benefit to the user. For instance, examination and study of a patent is not infringement, even if the information obtained enables a person to make a successful non-infringing product. In Van Kannell Revolving Door Co. v. Revolving Door & Fixture Co., 293 Fed. 261 (S.D.N.Y. 1920), the defendant had bid on a revolving door job whose bid specifications specified a door within the claims of the plaintiff's patent. After winning the bid, the defendant persuaded the customer that an equivalent but non-infringing design would be suitable, and completed the job. The patent owner sued claiming that submitting a bid that fell within the terms of the patent was infringement. Judge Learned Hand ruled that it was not.

> The defendant under these circumstances neither made, sold, nor used the patented door. Now a patent confers an exclusive right upon the patentee, limited in those terms. He may prevent anyone from making, selling, or using a structure embodying the invention, but the monopoly goes no further than that. It restrains everyone from the conduct so described, and it does not restrain him from anything else. If, therefore, anyone says to a possible customer of a patentee, "I will make the article myself; don't buy of the patentee," while he may be doing the patentee a wrong, and while equity will forbid his carrying out his promise, the promise itself is not part of the conduct which the patent forbids; it is not a "subtraction" from the monopoly. If it injures the plaintiff, though never performed, perhaps it is a wrong, like a slander upon his title; but certainly it is not an infringement of the patent. Luten v. Town of Lee (D.C.) 206 Fed. 904. And while equity forbids the carrying out of the promise, equity does not thereby adjudge the promise to be a wrong, but only evidence of a proximate wrong; i.e., infringement. To procure an adjudication that the promise is a wrong, and its accompanying injunction, the plaintiff must rest his case, not upon any subtraction from the monopoly, but upon an injury analogous to injuries arising from similar conduct which affects the value of any kind of property.

On the other hand, use and use alone of an invention infringes. Thus in Aro Mg. Co. v. Convertible Top Co., 377 U.S. 476 (1964), the Court held that owners of Ford automobiles with convertible top designs that infringed the plaintiff's patent infringed that patent simply by owning and driving their cars. "Not only does [§ 271(a)] * * * explicitly regard an unauthorized user of a patented invention as an infringer, but it has often and clearly been held that unauthorized use, without more, constitutes infringement." 377 U.S. 476, 483.

Since there is no requirement that an infringer have any knowledge or even any reason to know that a patent is being infringed, it is possible to engage in extensive patent infringement without being aware that it is occurring. For instance if a firm itself designs and introduces a new product, it will be liable for infringement if any feature of that product infringes a valid patent. The only protection for the firm would be to pay for a patent search making use of the patents available in the patent office to determine whether or not any patents in force contain claims which encompass the product. Not only is such a search a demanding (and thus likely to be costly) professional task, but it may be technically impossible, since not all presently in-force patents can always be located in the patent office at any one time.

Where a product is purchased from another, the buyer can protect itself by obtaining a warranty of non-infringement. Section 2–312(3) of the Uniform Commercial Code provides:

> Unless otherwise agreed a seller who is a merchant regularly dealing in goods of the kind warrants that the goods shall be delivered free of the rightful claims of any third person by way of infringement or the like but a buyer who furnishes specifications to the seller must hold the seller harmless against any such claim which arises out of compliance with the specifications.

If the product turns out to be infringing, the buyer is subject to a suit for infringement, but can bring an action over against the seller for the amount of damages resulting from the infringement. Of course, if the seller becomes insolvent, the warranty may provide little or no protection.

Roche Products, Inc. v. Bolar Pharmaceutical Co.

United States Court of Appeals, Federal Circuit, 1984.
733 F.2d 858.

■ NICHOLS, SENIOR CIRCUIT JUDGE.

This is an appeal from a judgment entered on October 14, 1983, in which the United States District Court * * * for the Eastern District of New York held United States Patent No. 3,299,053 not infringed and denied relief. We reverse and remand.

I

At stake in this case is the length of time a pharmaceutical company which has a patent on the active ingredient in a drug can have exclusive access to the American market for that drug. Plaintiff-appellant Roche Products, Inc. (Roche), a large research-oriented pharmaceutical company, wanted the United States district court to enjoin Bolar Pharmaceutical Co., Inc. (Bolar), a manufacturer of generic drugs, from taking, during the life of a patent, the statutory and regulatory steps necessary to market, after the patent expired, a drug equivalent to a patented brand name drug. Roche argued that the use of a patented drug for federally mandated premarketing tests is a use in violation of the patent laws.

Roche was the assignee of the rights in U.S. Patent No. 3,299,053 (the '053 patent), which expired on January 17, 1984. The '053 patent, which was issued on January 17, 1967, is entitled "Novel 1 and/or 4-substituted alkyl 5-aromatic-3H-1, 4-benzodiazepines and benzodiazepine-2-ones." One of the chemical compounds claimed in the '053 patent is flurazepam hydrochloride (flurazepam hcl), the active ingredient in Roche's successful brand name prescription sleeping pill "Dalmane."

In early 1983, Bolar became interested in marketing, after the '053 patent expired, a generic drug equivalent to Dalmane. Because a generic drug's commercial success is related to how quickly it is brought on the market after a patent expires, and because approval for an equivalent of an established drug can take more than 2 years, Bolar, not waiting for the '053 patent to expire, immediately began its effort to obtain federal approval to market its generic version of Dalmane. In mid-1983, Bolar obtained from a foreign manufacturer 5 kilograms of flurazepam hcl to form into "dosage form capsules, to obtain stability data, dissolution rates, bioequivalency studies, and blood serum studies" necessary for a New Drug Application to the United States Food and Drug Administration (FDA).

* * *

The [district] court held that Bolar's use of the patented compound for federally mandated testing was not infringement of the patent in suit because Bolar's use was *de minimis* and experimental. * * *

II

The district court correctly recognized that the issue in this case is narrow: does the limited use of a patented drug for testing and investigation strictly related to FDA drug approval requirements during the last 6 months of the term of the patent constitute a use which, unless licensed, the patent statute makes actionable? The district court held that it does not. This was an error of law.

III

A

When Congress enacted the current revision of the Patent Laws of the United States, the Patent Act of 1952 * * * a statutory definition of patent infringement existed for the first time since section 5 of the Patent Act of 1793 was repealed in 1836. Title 35 U.S.C. § 271(a) * * * .

It is beyond argument that performance of only one of the three enumerated activities is patent infringement. It is well-established, in particular, that the use of a patented invention, without either manufacture or sale, is actionable. See Aro Manufacturing Co. v. Convertible Top Replacement Co., 377 U.S. 476, 484 (1964); * * * . Thus, the patentee does not need to have any evidence of damage or lost sales to bring an infringement action.

Section 271(a) prohibits, on its face, any and all uses of a patented invention. Of course, as Judge Learned Hand observed in Cabell v. Markham, 148 F.2d 737, 739 (2d Cir.), aff'd, 326 U.S. 404 (1945):

"[I]t is true that the words used, even in their literal sense, are the primary, and ordinarily the most reliable, source of interpreting the meaning of any writing: be it a statute, a contract, or anything else. But it is one of the surest indexes of a mature and developed jurisprudence not to make a fortress out of the dictionary; but to remember that statutes always have some purpose or object to accomplish, whose sympathetic and imaginative discovery is the surest guide to their meaning."

Because Congress has never defined use, its meaning has become a matter of judicial interpretation. Although few cases discuss the question of whether a particular use constitutes an infringing use of a patented invention, they nevertheless convincingly lead to the conclusion that the word "use" in section 271(a) has never been taken to its utmost possible scope. See, e.g., Pitcairn v. United States, 547 F.2d 1106 (Ct. Cl. 1976), cert. denied, 434 U.S. 1051 (1978) (experimental use may be a defense to infringement); United States v. Univis Lens Co., 316 U.S. 241 (1942) ("An incident to the purchase of any article, whether patented or unpatented, is the right to use and sell it, * * *." Id. at 249); General Electric Co. v. United States, 572 F.2d 745 (1978) ("[I]t can be properly assumed that as part of the bargain the seller of a device incorporating a patented combination * * * authorizes the buyer to continue to use the device so long as the latter can and does use the elements he purchased from the patentee or licensor." Id. at 784–85).

Bolar argues that its intended use of flurazepam hcl is excepted from the use prohibition. It claims two grounds for exception: the first ground is based on a liberal interpretation of the traditional experimental use exception; the second ground is that public policy favors generic drugs and thus mandates the creation of a new exception in order to allow FDA required drug testing. We discuss these arguments seriatim.

B

The so-called experimental use defense to liability for infringement generally is recognized as originating in an opinion written by Supreme Court Justice Story while on circuit in Massachusetts. In Whittemore v. Cutter, 29 Fed.Cas. 1120, 1121, (C.C. D. Mass. 1813) (No. 17,600), Justice Story sought to justify a trial judge's instruction to a jury that an infringer must have an intent to use a patented invention for profit, stating:

"[I]t could never have been the intention of the legislature to punish a man who constructed such a machine merely for philosophical experiments, or for the purpose of ascertaining the sufficiency of the machine to produce its described effects."

Despite skepticism, see, e.g., Byam v. Bullard, 4 Fed.Cas. 934 (C.C. D. Mass. 1852) (No. 2,262) (opinion by Justice Curtis), Justice Story's seminal statement evolved until, by 1861, the law was "well-settled that an experiment with a patented article for the sole purpose of gratifying a philosophical taste, or curiosity, or for mere amusement is not an infringement of the rights of the patentee." Peppenhausen v. Falke, 19 Fed.Cas. 1048, 1049 (C.C.S.D. N.Y. 1861) (No. 11,279). (For a detailed history and analysis of the experimental use exception, see Bee, Experimental Use as an Act of Patent

Infringement, 39 J.Pat.Off.Soc'y 357 (1957).) Professor Robinson firmly entrenched the experimental use exception into the patent law when he wrote his famous treatise, W. Robinson, The Law of Patents for Useful Inventions § 898 (1890):

"§ 898. No Act an Infringement unless it Affects the Pecuniary Interests of the Owner of the Patented Invention.

"[T]he interest to be promoted by the wrongful employment of the invention must be hostile to the interest of the patentee. The interest of the patentee is represented by the emoluments which he does or might receive from the practice of the invention by himself or others. These, though not always taking the shape of money, are of a pecuniary character, and their value is capable of estimation like other property. Hence acts of infringement must attack the right of the patentee to these emoluments, and either turn them aside into other channels or prevent them from accruing in favor of any one. An unauthorized sale of the invention is always such an act. But the manufacture or the use of the invention may be intended only for other purposes, and produce no pecuniary result. *Thus where it is made or used as an experiment, whether for the gratification of scientific tastes, or for curiosity, or for amusement, the interests of the patentee are not antagonized, the sole effect being of an intellectual character in the promotion of the employer's knowledge or the relaxation afforded to his mind.* But if the products of the experiment are sold, or used for the convenience of the experimentor, or if the experiments are conducted with a view to the adaptation of the invention to the experimentor's business, the acts of making or of use are violations of the rights of the inventor and infringements of his patent. In reference to such employments of a patented invention the law is diligent to protect the patentee, and even experimental uses will be sometimes enjoined though no injury may have resulted admitting of positive redress." [Emphasis supplied, footnotes omitted.]

The Court of Claims, whose precedents bind us, on several occasions has considered the defense of experimental use. * * * [cites]. Bolar concedes, as it must, that its intended use of flurazepam hcl does not fall within the "traditional limits" of the experimental use exception as established in these cases or those of other circuits. Its concession here is fatal. Despite Bolar's argument that its tests are "true scientific inquiries" to which a literal interpretation of the experimental use exception logically should extend, we hold the experimental use exception to be truly narrow, and we will not expand it under the present circumstances. Bolar's argument that the experimental use rule deserves a broad construction is not justified.

Pitcairn, the most persuasive of the Court of Claims cases concerning the experimental use defense, sets forth the law which must control the disposition of this case: "[t]ests, demonstrations, and experiments * * * [which] are in keeping with the legitimate business of the * * * [alleged infringer]" are infringements for which "[e]xperimental use is not a defense." 547 F.2d at 1125–1126. We have carefully reviewed each of the other Court of Claims cases, and although they contain some loose language on which Bolar relies, they are unpersuasive. * * *

Bolar's intended "experimental" use is solely for business reasons and not for amusement, to satisfy idle curiosity, or for strictly philosophical inquiry. Bolar's intended use of flurazepam hcl to derive FDA required test data is thus an infringement of the '053 patent. Bolar may intend to perform "experiments," but unlicensed experiments conducted with a view to the adaption of the patented invention to the experimentor's business is a violation of the rights of the patentee to exclude others from using his patented invention. It is obvious here that it is a misnomer to call the intended use *de minimis*. It is no trifle in its economic effect on the parties even if the quantity used is small. It is no dilettante affair such as Justice Story envisioned. We cannot construe the experimental use rule so broadly as to allow a violation of the patent laws in the guise of "scientific inquiry," when that inquiry has definite, cognizable, and not insubstantial commercial purposes.

* * *

The decision of the district court holding the '053 patent not infringed is reversed. The case is remanded with instructions to fashion an appropriate remedy.

NOTE

Congress rejected the *Bolar* result as applied to drugs by adding § 271(e) as part of the Drug Price Competition and Patent Term Restoration Act of 1984, P.L. 98–417. Under that statute, owners of patented drugs got the opportunity to extend the patent term to compensate for delays caused by the regulatory review of the Food and Drug Administration, while their potential "generic" competitors got the right to initiate regulatory testing and approval procedures prior to the expiration of the patent term. The interrelationship of the F.D.A. regulation and patent incentives was first analyzed in E.W. Kitch, "The Patent System and the New Drug Application: An Evaluation of the Incentives for Private Investment in New Drug Research and Marketing," in Landau (ed.), *Regulating New Drugs* (University of Chicago Center for Policy Study, 1973).

---

(2) Within the United States

Deepsouth Packing Co. v. Laitram Corp.

Supreme Court of the United States, 1972.
406 U.S. 518, 92 S.Ct. 1700, 32 L.Ed.2d 273.

■ MR. JUSTICE WHITE delivered the opinion of the Court.

The United States District Court for the Eastern District of Louisiana has written:

"Shrimp, whether boiled, broiled, barbecued or fried, are a gustatory delight, but they did not evolve to satisfy man's palate. Like other crustaceans, they wear their skeletons outside their bodies in order to shield their savory pink and white flesh against predators, including man. They also carry their intestines, commonly called veins, in bags (or sand bags) that run the length of their bodies. For shrimp to be edible, it is necessary to remove their shells. In addition, if the vein is removed, shrimp become more pleasing to the fastidious as well as more palatable."

Such "gustatory" observations are rare even in those piscatorially favored federal courts blissfully situated on the Nation's Gulf Coast, but they are properly recited in this case. Petitioner and respondent both hold patents on machines that devein shrimp more cheaply and efficiently than competing machinery or hand labor can do the job. Extensive litigation below has established that respondent, the Laitram Corp., has the superior claim and that the distribution and use of petitioner Deepsouth's machinery in this country should be enjoined to prevent infringement of Laitram's patents. * * * We granted certiorari * * * to consider a related question: Is Deepsouth, barred from the American market by Laitram's patents, also foreclosed by the patent laws from exporting its deveiners, in less than fully assembled form, for use abroad?

I

A rudimentary understanding of the patents in dispute is a prerequisite to comprehending the legal issue presented. The District Court determined that the Laitram Corp. held two valid patents for machinery used in the process of deveining shrimp. One, granted in 1954, accorded Laitram rights over a "slitter" which exposed the veins of shrimp by using water pressure and gravity to force the shrimp down an inclined trough studded with razor blades. As the shrimp descend through the trough their backs are slit by the blades or other knife-like objects arranged in a zig-zag pattern. The second patent, granted in 1958, covers a "tumbler, 'a device to mechanically remove substantially all veins from shrimp whose backs have previously been slit,' " * * * by the machines described in the 1954 patent. This invention uses streams of water to carry slit shrimp into and then out of a revolving drum fabricated from commercial sheet metal. As shrimp pass through the drum the hooked "lips" of the punched metal, "projecting at an acute angle from the supporting member and having a smooth rounded free edge for engaging beneath the vein of a shrimp and for wedging the vein between the lip and the supporting member," * * * engage the veins and remove them.

Both the slitter and the tumbler are combination patents; that is,

"[n]one of the parts referred to are new, and none are claimed as new; nor is any portion of the combination less than the whole claimed as new, or stated to produce any given result. The end in view is proposed to be accomplished by the union of all, arranged and combined together in the manner described. And this combination, composed of all the parts mentioned in the specification, and arranged with reference to each other, and to other parts of the (machine) in the manner therein described, is stated to be the improvement, and is the thing patented." Prouty v. Ruggles, 16 Pet. 336, 341, 10 L.Ed. 985 (1842).

The slitter's elements as recited in Laitram's patent claim were: an inclined trough, a "knife" (actually, knives) positioned in the trough, and a means (water sprayed from jets) to move the shrimp down the trough. The tumbler's elements include a "lip," a "support member," and a "means" (water thrust from jets). As is usual in combination patents, none of the elements in either of these patents were themselves patentable at the time of the patent, nor are they now. The means in both inventions, moving water, was and is, of course, commonplace. (It is not suggested that Deepsouth infringed Laitram's patents by its use of water jets.) The cutting instruments and inclined troughs used in slitters were and are commodities available for general use. The structure of the lip and support member in the tumbler were hardly novel: Laitram concedes that the inventors merely adapted punched metal sheets ordered from a commercial catalog in order to perfect their invention. The patents were warranted not by the novelty of their elements but by the novelty of the combination they represented. Invention was recognized because Laitram's assignors combined ordinary elements in an extraordinary way—a novel union of old means was designed to achieve new ends. Thus, for both inventions "the whole in some way exceed(ed) the sum of its parts." Great A. & P. Tea Co. v. Supermarket Equipment Corp., 340 U.S. 147, 152 (1950).

II

The lower court's decision that Laitram held valid combination patents entitled the corporation to the privileges bestowed by 35 U.S.C. § 154, the keystone provision of the patent code. "(F)or the term of seventeen years" from the date of the patent, Laitram had "the right to exclude others from making, using, or selling the invention throughout the United States * * *." The § 154 right in turn provides the basis for affording the patentee an injunction against direct, induced, and contributory infringement, 35 U.S.C. § 283, or an award of damages when such infringement has already occurred, 35 U.S.C. § 284. Infringement is defined by 35 U.S.C. § 271 * * *.

As a result of these provisions the judgment of Laitram's patent superiority forecloses Deepsouth and its customers from any future use (other than a use approved by Laitram or occurring after the Laitram patent has expired) of its deveiners "throughout the United States." The patent provisions taken in conjunction with the judgment below also entitle Laitram to the injunction it has received prohibiting Deepsouth from continuing to "make" or, once made, to "sell" deveiners "throughout the United States." Further, Laitram may recover damages for any past unauthorized use, sale, or making "throughout the United States." This much is not disputed.

But Deepsouth argues that it is not liable for every type of past sale and that a portion of its future business is salvageable. Section 154 and related provisions obviously are intended to grant a patentee a monopoly only over the United States market; they are not intended to grant a patentee the bonus of a favored position as a flagship company free of American competition in international commerce. Deepsouth, itself barred from using its deveining machines, or from inducing others to use them "throughout the United States," barred also from making and selling the machines in the United States, seeks to make the parts of deveining machines, to sell them to foreign buyers, and to have the buyers assemble the parts and use the machines abroad. Accordingly, Deepsouth seeks judicial approval, expressed through a modification or interpretation of the injunction against it, for continuing its practice of shipping deveining equipment to foreign customers in three separate boxes, each containing only parts of the 1¾-ton machines, yet the whole assemblable in less than one hour. The company contends that by this means both the "making" and the "use" of the machines occur abroad and Laitram's lawful monopoly over the making and use of the machines throughout the United States is not infringed.

Laitram counters that this course of conduct is based upon a hyper-technical reading of the patent code that, if tolerated, will deprive it of its right to the fruits of the inventive genius of its assignors. "The right to make can scarcely be made plainer by definition . . . ," Bauer v. O'Donnell, 229 U.S. 1, 10 (1913). Deepsouth in all respects save final assembly of the parts "makes" the invention. It does so with the intent of having the foreign user effect the combination without Laitram's permission. Deepsouth sells these components as though they were the machines themselves; the act of assembly is regarded, indeed advertised, as of no importance.

The District Court, faced with this dispute, noted that three prior circuit courts had considered the meaning of "making" in this context and that all three had resolved the question favorably to Deepsouth's position. * * * The District Court held that its injunction should not be read as prohibiting export of the elements of a combination patent even when those elements could and predictably would be combined to form the whole.

> "It may be urged that . . . [this] result is not logical . . . But it is founded on twin notions that underlie the patent laws. One is that a combination patent protects only the combination. The other is that monopolies—even those conferred by patents—are not viewed with favor. These are logic enough." * * *

The Court of Appeals for the Fifth Circuit reversed, thus departing from the established rules of the Second, Third, and Seventh Circuits. In the Fifth Circuit panel's opinion, those courts that previously considered the question "worked themselves into * * * a conceptual box" by adopting "an artificial, technical construction" of the patent laws, a construction, more-over, which in the opinion of the panel, "[subverted] the Constitutional scheme of promoting 'the Progress of Science and useful Arts'" by allowing an intrusion on a patentee's rights, * * * , citing U.S. Const., Art. I, § 8.

III

We disagree with the Court of Appeals for the Fifth Circuit. Under the common law the inventor had no right to exclude others from making and using his invention. If Laitram has a right to suppress Deepsouth's export trade it must be derived from its patent grant, and thus from the patent statute. We find that 35 U.S.C. § 271, the provision of the patent laws on which Laitram relies, does not support its claim.

Certainly if Deepsouth's conduct were intended to lead to use of patented deveiners inside the United States its production and sales activity would be subject to injunction as an induced or contributory infringement. But it is established that there can be no contributory infringement without the fact or intention of a direct infringement. * * *

The statute makes it clear that it is not an infringement to make or use a patented product outside of the United States. 35 U.S.C. § 271. * * * Thus, in order to secure the injunction it seeks, Laitram must show a § 271(a) direct infringement by Deepsouth in the United States, that is, that Deepsouth "makes," "uses," or "sells" the patented product within the bounds of this country.

Laitram does not suggest that Deepsouth "uses" the machines. Its argument that Deepsouth sells the machines—based primarily on Deepsouth's sales rhetoric and related indicia such as price—cannot carry the day unless it can be shown that Deepsouth is selling the "patented invention." The sales question thus resolves itself into the question of manufacture: did Deepsouth "make" (and then sell) something cognizable under the patent law as the patented invention, or did it "make" (and then sell) something that fell short of infringement?

The Court of Appeals, believing that the word "makes" should be accorded "a construction in keeping with the ordinary meaning of that term," * * * held against Deepsouth on the theory that "makes" "means what it ordinarily connotes—the substantial manufacture of the constituent parts of the machine." * * * Passing the question of whether this definition more closely corresponds to the ordinary meaning of the term than that offered by Judge Swan in *Andrea* [Radio Corp. of America v. Andrea, 79 F.2d 626 (CA2 Cir. 1935)] 35 years earlier (something is made when it reaches the state of final "operable" assembly), we find the Fifth Circuit's definition unacceptable because it collides head on with a line of decisions so firmly embedded in our patent law as to be unassailable absent a congressional recasting of the statute.

We cannot endorse the view that the "substantial manufacture of the constituent parts of [a] machine" constitutes direct infringement when we have so often held that a combination patent protects only against the operable assembly of the whole and not the manufacture of its parts. "For as we pointed out in Mercoid v. Mid-Continent Investment Co. [320 U.S. 661] a patent on a combination is a patent on the assembled or functioning whole, not on the separate parts." Mercoid Corp. v. Minneapolis-Honeywell Regulator Co., 320 U.S. 680, 684 (1944).

It was this basic tenet of the patent system that led Judge Swan to hold in the leading case, Radio Corp. of America v. Andrea, 79 F.2d 626 (CA2 1935), that unassembled export of the elements of an invention did not infringe the patent.

"[The] relationship is the essence of the patent.

". . . No wrong is done the patentee until the combination is formed. His monopoly does not cover the manufacture of sale of separate elements capable of being, but never actually, associated to form the invention. Only when such association is made is there a direct infringement of his monopoly, and not even then if it is done outside the territory for which the monopoly was granted." Id., at 628.

* * *

We reaffirm this conclusion today.

Reversed and remanded.

NOTES

1. Congress rejected the result in *Laitram*. See 35 U.S.C. § 271(f), added by Public Law 98–622 § 101 (1984).

2. Doesn't Congress' rejection of *Laitram* favor foreign producers over U.S. producers? A foreign firm can still manufacture and ship the machine without infringing the U.S. patent (assuming that there is no applicable foreign patent) but a U.S. firm cannot. But if there is foreign competition, wouldn't we expect the U.S. patent owner to price its machines for export so as to meet that competition?

3. The limitation of infringement to acts performed within the United States is particularly important in the area of process claims. If one holds a patent claiming a product then any importation of that product into the United States will infringe. But the practice of a process patent outside the United States and importation of the resulting unpatented product into the United States does not infringe under § 271(a). This would be true even if the product could only be made through the use of the patented process. In 1988 Congress added § 271(g) which makes it an infringement of a U.S. patent to import into, or sell or use in, the United States a product manufactured by means of a process which if practiced in the United States would be patent infringement. P.L. 100–418 § 9003 (1988). Note the limitations on § 271(g). What considerations justify them?

4. Article 28.1(b) of the GATT TRIPS provides: "where the subject matter of a patent is a process, [the patent owner shall have the exclusive right] to prevent third parties not having the owner's consent from the act of using the process, and from the acts of: using, offering for sale, selling, or importing for these purposes at least the product obtained directly by that process."

---

(3) Within the Term of the Patent

Paper Converting Machine Co. v. Magna-Graphics Corp.

United States Court of Appeals, Federal Circuit, 1984.
745 F.2d 11.

■ NICHOLS, SENIOR CIRCUIT JUDGE.

This appeal is from a judgment of the United States District Court for the Eastern District of Wisconsin * * * entered on December 1, 1983, and awarding plaintiff Paper Converting Machine Company (Paper Converting) $893,064 as compensation for defendant Magna-Graphics Corporation's (Magna-Graphics) willful infringement of United States Patent No. Re. 28,353. We *affirm-in-part and vacate-in-part.*

I

Although the technology involved here is complex, the end product is one familiar to most Americans. The patented invention relates to a machine used to manufacture rolls of densely wound ("hard-wound") industrial toilet tissue and paper toweling. The machine, commonly known as an automatic rewinder, unwinds a paper web continuously under high tension at speeds up to 2,000 feet per minute from a large-diameter paper roll—known as the parent roll or bedroll—and simultaneously rewinds it onto paperboard cores to form individual consumer products.

Before the advent of automatic rewinders, toilet tissue and paper towel producers used "stop-start" rewinders. With these machines, the entire rewinding operation had to cease after a retail-sized "log" was finished so that a worker could place a new mandrel (the shaft for carrying the paperboard core) in the path of the paper web. In an effort to increase production, automatic rewinders were introduced in the early 1950's. These machines automatically moved a new mandrel into the path of the paper web while the machine was still winding the paper web onto another mandrel, and could operate at a steady pace at speeds up to about 1,200 feet per minute.

In 1962, Nystrand, Bradley, and Spencer invented the first successful "sequential" automatic rewinder, a machine which not only overcame previous speed limitations, but also could handle two-ply tissue. This rewinder simultaneously cut the paper web and impaled it on pins against the parent roll. Then, after a new mandrel was automatically moved into place, a "pusher" would move the paper web away from the parent roll and against a glue-covered paperboard core to begin winding a new paper log.

On April 20, 1965, United States Patent No. 3,179,348 (the '348 patent) issued, giving to Paper Converting (to whom rights in the invention had been assigned) patent protection for machines incorporating the sequential rewinding approach. On September 1, 1972, Paper Converting applied to have the claims of the '348 patent narrowed by reissue, and on March 4, 1975, United States Patent No. Re. 28,353 (the '353 patent) issued on this application. The '353 patent, like the original '348 patent on which it is based, received an expiration date of April 20, 1982. Claim 1 of the '353 patent defines the improvement in the web-winding apparatus as an improvement comprising:

> "(C) means for transversely severing said web to provide a free leading edge on said web for approaching a mandrel on which said web is to be wound in said path, and
>
> "(D) pin means extensibly mounted on said roll for maintaining a web portion spaced from said edge in contact with said roll, and pusher means extensibly mounted on said roll to urge said maintained web portion against an adjacent mandrel."

Paper Converting achieved widespread commercial success with its patented automatic rewinder. Although there are not many domestic producers of toilet tissue and paper toweling, Paper Converting has sold more than 500 machines embodying the invention.

In 1979, Paper Converting brought the present action against Magna-Graphics for infringement of the '353 patent. After a trial concerning only issues of liability, the district court held the '353 patent valid and found it willfully infringed * * *. It awarded treble damages, finding that Magna-Graphics had acted without the advice of counsel as to the change it made in its machines to avoid infringement. The Seventh Circuit affirmed * * *. The parties commendably raise no issues here which the Seventh Circuit has already decided as to Magna-Graphics' liability.

When the district court held the accounting for damages (after the Seventh Circuit had affirmed it on the liability portion of the case), it found that Magna-Graphics had made two sales of infringing rewinders and associated equipment: one to the Fort Howard Paper Company (Fort Howard) under circumstances to be described, and one to the Scott Paper Company (Scott). The court awarded to Paper Converting $112,163 for Magna-Graphics' sale to Scott, and $145,583 for Magna-Graphics' sale to Fort Howard. The court then trebled these damages, and added $119,826 as prejudgment interest on the untrebled award. This appeal is from the judgment awarding damages.

II

* * * Magna-Graphics contends that the district court erred in finding the sale, substantial manufacture, and delivery of the Fort Howard rewinder to be an infringement * * *.

III

A

Magna-Graphics first argues that it should bear no liability whatsoever for its manufacture, sale, or delivery of the Fort Howard rewinder because that machine was never *completed* during the life of the '353 patent. We disagree.

In early 1980 Fort Howard became interested in purchasing a new high-speed rewinder line. Both Paper Converting and Magna-Graphics offered bids. Because Magna–Graphics offered to provide an entire rewinder line for about 10 percent less than did Paper Converting, it won the contract. Delivery would have been before the '353 patent expired. Magna-Graphics began to build the contracted for machinery, but before it completed the rewinder, on February 26, 1981, the federal district court in Wisconsin determined that a similar Magna-Graphics' rewinder built for and sold to Scott infringed the '353 patent. The court enjoined Magna-Graphics from any future infringing activity.

Because at the time of the federal injunction the rewinder intended for Fort Howard was only 80 percent complete, Magna-Graphics sought a legal way to fulfill its contract with Fort Howard rather than abandon its machine. First, Magna-Graphics tried to change the construction of the rewinder so as to avoid infringement. It submitted to Paper Converting's counsel three drawings illustrating three proposed changes, and asked for an opinion as to whether the changes would avoid infringement. Paper Converting's counsel replied, however, that until a fully built and operating machine could be viewed, no opinion could be given. Magna-Graphics, believing such a course of action unfeasible because of the large risks in designing, engineering, and building a machine without knowing whether it would be considered an infringement, instead negotiated with Fort Howard to delay the final assembly and delivery of an otherwise infringing rewinder until after the '353 patent expired in April 1982.

Magna-Graphics thereafter continued to construct the Fort Howard machine, all the while staying in close consultation with its counsel. After finishing substantially all of the machine, Magna-Graphics tested it to ensure that its moving parts would function as intended at a rate of 1,600 feet of paper per minute. Although Magna-Graphics normally *fully* tested machines at its plant before shipment, to avoid infringement in this instance, Magna-Graphics ran its tests in two stages over a period of several weeks in July and August of 1981.

To understand Magna-Graphics' testing procedure, it is necessary to understand the automatic transfer operation of the patented machine. First, from within a 72-inch long "cutoff" roll, a 72–inch blade ejects to sever the continuous web of paper which is wound around the bedroll. Then, pins attached to the bedroll hold the severed edge of the web while pushers, also attached to the bedroll, transfer the edge of the web towards the mandrel (the roll on which the paperboard core is mounted).

In the first stage of its test, Magna-Graphics checked the bedroll to determine whether the pushers actuated properly. It installed on the bedroll two pusher pads instead of the thirty pads normally used in an operating machine. It greased the pads and operated the bedroll to determine whether the pads, when unlatched, would contact the core on the mandrel. (Magna-Graphics greased the pads so as to provide a visual indication that they had touched the core.) During this stage of tests, no cutoff blades or pins were installed.

In the second stage of the test, Magna-Graphics checked the cutoff roll to determine whether the cutting blade actuated as intended. It tested the knife actuating mechanism by installing into the cutoff roll a short 4-inch section of cutter blade rather than the 72-inch blade normally used. After taping a 4-inch wide piece of paper to the outer surface of the cutoff roll, Magna-Graphics operated the cutoff roll to determine whether the latch mechanism would eject the blade to cut the paper. During this phase of the testing, no pins or pusher pads were installed. At no time during the tests were the pins, pushers, and blade installed and operated together.

To further its scheme to avoid patent infringement, Magna-Graphics negotiated special shipment and assembly details with Fort Howard. Under the advice of counsel, Fort Howard and Magna-Graphics agreed that the rewinder's cutoff and transfer mechanism would not be finally assembled until April 22, 1982, two days after the expiration of the '353 patent. With this agreement in hand, Magna-Graphics shipped the basic rewinder machine to Fort Howard on September 17, 1981, and separately shipped the cutoff roll and bedroll on October 23, 1981. The rewinder machine was not assembled or installed at the Fort Howard plant until April 26, 1982.

B

With this case we are once again confronted with a situation which tests the temporal limits of the American patent grant. See Roche Products, Inc. v. Bolar Pharmaceutical Co., 733 F.2d 858 (Fed. Cir. 1984). We must decide here the extent to which a competitor of a patentee can *manufacture* and test during the life of a patent a machine intended solely for post-patent use. Magna-Graphics asserts that no law prohibits it from soliciting orders for, *substantially* manufacturing, testing, or even delivering machinery which, if *completely* assembled during the patent term, would infringe. We notice, but Magna-Graphics adds that it is totally irrelevant, that Paper Converting has lost, during the term of its patent, a contract for the patented machine which it would have received but for the competitor's acts.

Clearly, any federal right which Paper Converting has to suppress Magna-Graphics' patent-term activities, or to receive damages for those activities, must be derived from its patent grant, and thus from the patent statutes. "Care should be taken not to extend by judicial construction the rights and privileges which it was the purpose of Congress to bestow." Bauer v. O'Donnell, 229 U.S. 1, 10 (1913). * * *

Here, the dispositive issue is whether Magna-Graphics engaged in the making, use, or sale of something which the law recognizes as embodying an invention protected by a patent. Magna-Graphics relies on Deepsouth Packing Co. v. Laitram Corp., 406 U.S. 518 (1972). * * *

Magna-Graphics' effort to apply *Deepsouth* as precedential runs into the obvious difficulty that the element of extraterritoriality is absent here, yet it obviously was of paramount importance to the *Deepsouth* Court. We must be cautious in extending five to four decisions by analogy * * *. The analysis of *where* infringement occurs is applicable, Magna-Graphics says, to determining *when* an infringement occurs, whether before or after a patent expires. We have not found any case that has so held, and are not cited to any. It does not at all necessarily follow, for the *Deepsouth* analysis is made to avert a result, extraterritoriality, that would not occur whatever analysis was made in the instant case.

Although in *Deepsouth* the Court at times used broad language in reaching its decision, it is clear that *Deepsouth* was intended to be narrowly construed as applicable only to the issue of the extraterritorial effect of the American patent law. The Court so implied not only in *Deepsouth* ("[A]t stake here is the right of American companies to compete with an American patent holder *in foreign markets. Our patent system makes no claim to extraterritorial effect,* * * * " 406 U.S. at 531 (emphasis added)), but in a subsequent decision as well ("The question under consideration [in

Deepsouth] was whether a patent is infringed when unpatented elements are assembled into the combination *outside the United States."* Dawson Chemical Co. v. Rohm & Haas Co., 448 U.S. 176, 216 (1980) (emphasis added)). Moreover, in Decca Limited v. United States, 544 F.2d 1070 (Ct. Cl. 1976), the Court of Claims considered the worldwide system of electronic navigation aids called "Omega," which employs as a means of fixing the locations of ships and planes "master" and "slave" transmission stations, and receivers making computer printouts on board the ships and planes to be guided. The government relied on *Deepsouth* to establish that the involved patent, if enforced against it, would be given an extraterritorial application. The Court of Claims held that the application was not extraterritorial and therefore *Deepsouth* was not implicated. The Court of Claims viewed *Deepsouth* as simply and wholly a decision against extraterritorial application of United States patent laws. Id. at 1072–74.

While there is thus a horror of giving extraterritorial effect to United States patent protection, there is no corresponding horror of a valid United States patent giving economic benefits not cut off entirely on patent expiration. Thus, we hold that the expansive language used in *Deepsouth* is not controlling in the present case. The facts in *Deepsouth* are not the facts here. Because no other precedent controls our decision here, however, we nevertheless look to *Deepsouth* and elsewhere for guidance on the issue of whether what Magna-Graphics did is an infringement of the '353 patent.

A further examination of the *Deepsouth* opinion reveals that the Court stated what was for it a most unusual reliance on a precedent established in an inferior court, the case being Radio Corporation of America v. Andrea, 79 F.2d 626 (2d Cir. 1935). The reason for this was the eminently logical one that when in 1952 the Congress recodified the patent law, and specifically § 271, the most relevant precedent was *Andrea* as to the legal effect of exporting, unassembled, components that if exported assembled would infringe a "combination patent." Presumably the Congress accepted and enacted Judge Swan's interpretation in *Andrea,* absent any relevant pronouncement by our highest court.

Judge Swan's opinion on the appeal from a preliminary injunction is, indeed, a rather dramatic application of the view of the law he announced. The patents related to radio receiving sets. The alleged infringer, Andrea, exported them complete except for vacuum tubes exported *in the same package,* but not in their sockets. All the buyer had to do to have a patented set was, therefore, to put the tube in the socket designed to receive it. Swan's opinion does not mention any horror of extraterritoriality. Rather, the analysis is that the sale in this condition, even to domestic users, is not a direct infringement, but is only a contributory infringement. Thus, the practical impact of the Swan opinion, but not its reasoning, is limited to export sales, where contributory infringement is not logically applicable. Swan notes, however, as possible direct infringement evidence, that the alleged infringer put the tubes in their sockets to test them, and the sets generally, and then disassembled for export, and the reversal leaves it open to the trial court to look into this.

The trial court thereafter made further findings and entered its final judgment (then called its decree) and the case came up again, same name, 90 F.2d 612 (2d Cir. 1937). Where previously the panel had consisted of only Swan and the subsequently ill-famed Manton, this time Circuit Judge Chase was added and Manton authored the opinion. The matter of testing was now clarified, and it was also now clear to the panel:

"The purchaser to connect the tube needs only insert it in the socket. No adjustment is required; no screw or nut need be tightened. Where the elements of an invention are thus sold in substantially unified and combined form, infringement may not be avoided by a separation or division of parts which leaves to the purchaser a simple task of integration. Otherwise a patentee would be denied adequate protection." (Id. at 613.)

The court further noted that in part the sets were fully assembled for testing in the United States and that the sales of the completed though partly disassembled sets were made in the United States. The main problem dealt with in the second *Andrea* opinion was what "implied license" the infringer acquired when it bought the tubes separately.

Swan dissented, saying the holding that the sale of the disassembled parts in this country was an infringement overruled the decision in 79 F.2d 626. This history was, of course, not overlooked in the Supreme Court * * *.

What are we to make of all this? It does seem as if the concept of an "operable assembly" put forward by Justice White in his majority opinion is probably something short of a full and complete assembly; thus, if the infringer makes an "operable assembly" of the components of the patented invention, sufficient for testing, it need not be the same thing as the complete and entire invention. The other thing is, if the infringer has tested his embodiment of the invention sufficiently to satisfy him, this may be a "use," because as held in *Roche Products, Inc.,* "use" includes use for the purpose of testing. Apparently, this was also a factor in the second *Andrea* decision, though given the confusing way Manton put his opinion together, it is hard to be sure. Swan also may be right that Manton is simply overruling the interlocutory 79 F.2d 626 decision. If so, apparently the Supreme Court majority liked the first holding better. That is, the part quoted above of the second decision is not law. But there is no apparent difference between Swan and the rest of the second panel as to the legal effect of testing and sale.

In any case, we would not be justified in thinking Justice White and the Supreme Court majority intended to hold, or to be understood as holding, that the second *Andrea* decision in 90 F.2d 612, was not before Congress just as much as the first *Andrea* decision in 79 F.2d 626, or was not just as much to be considered in interpreting § 271, as reenacted in 1952.

* * *

It is undisputed that Magna-Graphics intended to finesse Paper Converting out of the sale of a machine on which Paper Converting held a valid patent during the life of that patent. Given the amount of testing performed here, coupled with the sale and delivery during the patent-term of a "completed" machine (completed by being ready for assembly and with no useful noninfringing purpose), we are not persuaded that the district court committed clear error in finding that the Magna-Graphics' machine infringed the '353 patent.

To reach a contrary result would emasculate the congressional intent to prevent the making of a patented item during the patent's full term of 17 years. If without fear of liability a competitor can assemble a patented item past the point of testing, the last year of the patent becomes worthless whenever it deals with a long lead-time article. Nothing would prohibit the unscrupulous competitor from aggressively marketing its own product and constructing it to all but the final screws and bolts, as Magna-Graphics did here. We rejected any reduction to the patent-term in *Roche;* we cannot allow the inconsistency in the patent law which would exist if we permitted it here. Magna-Graphics built and tested a patented machine, albeit in a less than preferred fashion. Because an "operable assembly" of components was tested, this case is distinguishable from Interdent Corp. v. United States, 531 F.2d 547, 552 (Ct. Cl. 1976) (omission of a claimed element from the patented combination avoids infringement) and Decca Ltd. v. United States, 640 F.2d 1156, 1168 (Ct. Cl. 1980) (infringement does not occur until the combination has been constructed and available for use). Where, as here, significant, unpatented assemblies of elements are tested during the patent term, enabling the infringer to deliver the patented combination in parts to the buyer, without testing the entire combination together as was the infringer's usual practice, testing the assemblies can be held to be in essence testing the patented combination and, hence, infringement.

That the machine was not operated in its optimum mode is inconsequential: imperfect practice of an invention does not avoid infringement. We affirm the district court's finding that "[d]uring the testing of the Fort Howard machine in July and August 1981, Magna-Graphics completed an operable assembly of the infringing rewinder."

* * *

The judgment of the district court awarding damages and prejudgment interest for Paper Converting's lost profits on two automatic rewinder lines is affirmed. The trebling of damages on the Fort Howard machine is vacated, and remanded for a determination of willfulness.

■ NIES, CIRCUIT JUDGE, dissenting-in-part.

I dissent from the majority's holding that Magna-Graphics' activities in connection with the Fort Howard machine constitute direct infringement of any claim of Paper Converting's patent. The majority's conclusion necessitates giving a meaning to "patented invention" contrary to the definition set forth by the Supreme Court in Deepsouth Packing Co. v. Laitram Corp., 406 U.S. 518 (1972).

I do not see in *Deepsouth* that the Supreme Court's only concern was the extraterritorial operation of our patent laws. The activities of Deepsouth under attack were all performed in the United States and were found not to result in direct or contributory infringement of the patent. That the activities of final assembly occurred abroad merely precluded a holding that Deepsouth's activities constituted contributory infringement. Contributory infringement cannot arise without a direct infringement. Mercoid Corp. v. Mid-Continent Investment Co., 320 U.S. 661, 677 (1944). The situation in *Deepsouth* is exactly comparable to the one at hand. That the activities of final assembly occurred after the patent expired precludes holding Magna-Graphics to be a contributory infringer, there being no direct infringement by another to which the charge can be appended.

Thus, we are back to the dispositive direct infringement issue in *Deepsouth,* which is the same as the issue here. What is the meaning of "patented invention" in 35 U.S.C. § 271(a)? The alleged infringer, in each case, made and sold something, but was it the "patented invention"?

* * *

Nothing in Justice White's opinion in *Deepsouth* indicates that the concept of an operable assembly is "probably something short of a full and complete assembly," as the majority states. The Court had before it the Fifth Circuit opinion which had analyzed just such less-than-full-assembly situations. Repeatedly, the Court emphasized that the "patented invention" means that all of its claimed elements must be united.

Thus, if the claimed invention comprises the elements A, B, C and D, it is only the combination in its entirety that is protected. The making of the lesser combination A, B and D falls short of direct infringement, even though the missing element C is also supplied by the alleged infringer.

* * *

Indeed, the *Deepsouth* decision is not without redeeming virtue. This is one of the few areas of patent law where a bright line can be, and has been, drawn. That consideration in itself has merit. A competitor should be able to look to the patent claims and know whether his activity infringes or not. Here, the majority provides no guidance to industry or the district courts. One cannot tell from the opinion whether testing and sales activity must also accompany substantial assembly, as it appears to hold, or whether simply substantially making the device preparatory to selling after the patent expires would be sufficient. Given the disjunctive language of the statute, no basis appears for "summing up" partial making with the testing of partial assemblies and with sales made by the alleged infringer. Those activities do not, in some nebulous way, supply the missing physical elements of the "patented invention."

* * *

NOTE

In Joy Technologies v. Flakt Inc., 6 F.3d 770 (Fed. Cir. 1993), the district court enjoined the defendant from entering into any contracts for the sale of a machine to be used to practice a patented process prior to the end of the term on the process patent. The Federal Circuit reversed, distinguishing Magna-Graphics as follows:

> *Paper Converting Machine* is easily distinguishable from the present case. In *Paper Converting Machine*, * * * we stated:
>
> > "It is undisputed that [the defendant] intended to finesse [the patentee] out of the sale of a machine on which [the patentee] held a valid patent during the life of that patent."
>
> While a method claim had been asserted along with the apparatus claims, the method claim was not discussed nor found infringed by the Fort Howard devices. The analysis focused solely on the patented machine, not on the process implemented by the machine.
>
> In the present case, the patent contains only method claims, which, as discussed above, are directly infringed only when the method is practiced. Joy is basically seeking to convert its method claims into apparatus claims. The facts of *Paper Converting Machine* do not support the injunction in the present case.

(4) Contributory Infringement

The courts have long recognized that someone who does not himself infringe may be liable because of actions which significantly contribute to the infringement of another. This doctrine has already been discussed in the *Laitram* decision, *supra*, when the court made the point that the purchasers who fully assembled and used the machine abroad would not be infringing, and thus providing them with the instruments to infringe was not contributory infringement. The doctrine is analogous to the general doctrine that one who aids or abets the commission of a tort will be liable as a tortfeasor.

Contributory infringement is codified in 35 U.S.C. § 271(b).

Dawson Chemical Co. v. Rohm and Haas Co.

Supreme Court of the United States, 1980.
448 U.S. 176, 100 S.Ct. 2601, 65 L.Ed.2d 696.

■ MR. JUSTICE BLACKMUN delivered the opinion of the Court.

This case presents an important question of statutory interpretation arising under the patent laws. The issue before us is whether the owner of a patent on a chemical process is guilty of patent misuse, and therefore is barred from seeking relief against contributory infringement of its patent rights, if it exploits the patent only in conjunction with the sale of an unpatented article that constitutes a material part of the invention and is not suited for commercial use outside the scope of the patent claims. The answer will determine whether respondent, the owner of a process patent on a chemical herbicide, may maintain an action for contributory infringement against other manufacturers of the chemical used in the process. To resolve this issue, we must construe the various provisions of 35 U.S.C. § 271, which Congress enacted in

1952 to codify certain aspects of the doctrines of contributory infringement and patent misuse that previously had been developed by the judiciary.

I

The doctrines of contributory infringement and patent misuse have long and interrelated histories. The idea that a patentee should be able to obtain relief against those whose acts facilitate infringement by others has been part of our law since Wallace v. Holmes, 29 F.Cas. 74 (No. 17,100) (CC Conn. 1871). The idea that a patentee should be denied relief against infringers if he has attempted illegally to extend the scope of his patent monopoly is of somewhat more recent origin, but it goes back at least as far as Motion Picture Patents Co. v. Universal Film Mfg. Co., 243 U.S. 502. The two concepts, contributory infringement and patent misuse, often are juxtaposed, because both concern the relationship between a patented invention and unpatented articles or elements that are needed for the invention to be practiced.

Both doctrines originally were developed by the courts. But in its 1952 codification of the patent laws Congress endeavored, at least in part, to substitute statutory precepts for the general judicial rules that had governed prior to that time. Its efforts find expression in 35 U.S.C. § 271 * * *.

Of particular import to the present controversy are subsections (c) and (d) [of § 271]. The former defines conduct that constitutes contributory infringement; the latter specifies conduct of the patentee that is not to be deemed misuse.

A

The catalyst for this litigation is a chemical compound known to scientists as "3,4-dichloropropionanilide" and referred to in the chemical industry as "propanil." In the late 1950's, it was discovered that this compound had properties that made it useful as a selective, "post-emergence" herbicide particularly well suited for the cultivation of rice. If applied in the proper quantities, propanil kills weeds normally found in rice crops without adversely affecting the crops themselves. It thus permits spraying of general areas where the crops are already growing, and eliminates the necessity for hand weeding or flooding of the rice fields. Propanil is one of several herbicides that are commercially available for use in rice cultivation.

Efforts to obtain patent rights to propanil or its use as a herbicide have been continuous since the herbicidal qualities of the chemical first came to light. The initial contender for a patent monopoly for this chemical compound was the Monsanto Company. In 1957, Monsanto filed the first of three successive applications for a patent on propanil itself. After lengthy proceedings in the United States Patent Office, a patent, No. 3,382,280, finally was issued in 1968. It was declared invalid, however, when Monsanto sought to enforce it by suing Rohm and Haas Company (Rohm & Haas), a competing manufacturer, for direct infringement. * * * The District Court held that propanil had been implicitly revealed in prior art dating as far back as 1902, even though its use as a herbicide had been discovered only recently. * * *

Monsanto subsequently dedicated the patent to the public, and it is not a party to the present suit.

Invalidation of the Monsanto patent cleared the way for Rohm & Haas, respondent here, to obtain a patent on the method or process for applying propanil. This is the patent on which the present lawsuit is founded. Rohm & Haas' efforts to obtain a propanil patent began in 1958. These efforts finally bore fruit when, on June 11, 1974, the United States Patent Office issued Patent No. 3,816,092 (the Wilson patent) to Harold F. Wilson and Dougal H. McRay. The patent contains several claims covering a method for applying propanil to inhibit the growth of undesirable plants in areas containing established crops.[2] Rohm & Haas has been the sole owner of the patent since its issuance.

Petitioners, too, are chemical manufacturers. They have manufactured and sold propanil for application to rice crops since before Rohm & Haas received its patent. They market the chemical in containers on which are printed directions for application in accordance with the method claimed in the Wilson patent. Petitioners did not cease manufacture and sale of propanil after that patent issued, despite knowledge that farmers purchasing their products would infringe on the patented method by applying the propanil to their crops. Accordingly, Rohm & Haas filed this suit, in the United States District Court for the Southern District of Texas, seeking injunctive relief against petitioners on the ground that their manufacture and sale of propanil interfered with its patent rights.

The complaint alleged not only that petitioners contributed to infringement by farmers who purchased and used petitioners' propanil, but also that they actually induced such infringement by instructing farmers how to apply the herbicide. See 35 U.S.C. §§ 271(b) and (c). Petitioners responded to the suit by requesting licenses to practice the patented method. When Rohm & Haas refused to grant such licenses, however, petitioners raised a defense of patent misuse and counterclaimed for alleged antitrust violations by respondent. The parties entered into a stipulation of facts, and petitioners moved for partial summary judgment. They argued that Rohm & Haas has misused its patent by conveying the right to practice the patented method only to purchasers of its own propanil.

The District Court granted summary judgment for petitioners. * * * It agreed that Rohm & Haas was barred from obtaining relief against infringers of its patent because it had attempted illegally to extend its patent monopoly. The District Court recognized that 35 U.S.C. § 271(d)

---

2. The Wilson patent contains several claims relevant to this proceeding. Of these the following are illustrative: 1. "A method for selectively inhibiting growth of undesirable plants in an area containing growing undesirable plants in an established crop, which comprises applying to said area 3,4-dichloropropionanilide at a rate of application which inhibits growth of said undesirable plants and which does not adversely affect the growth of said established crop." 2. "The method according to claim 1 wherein the 3,4-dichloropropionanilide is applied in a composition comprising 3,4-dichloropropionanilide and an inert diluent therefor at a rate of between 0.5 and 6 pounds of 3,4-dichloropropionanilide per acre."

specifies certain conduct which is not to be deemed patent misuse. The court ruled, however, that "[t]he language of § 271(d) simply does not encompass the totality of (Rohm & Haas') conduct in this case." * * * It held that respondent's refusal to grant licenses, other than the "implied" licenses conferred by operation of law upon purchasers of its propanil, constituted an attempt by means of a "tying" arrangement to effect a monopoly over an unpatented component of the process. The District Court concluded that this conduct would be deemed patent misuse under the judicial decisions that preceded § 271(d), and it held that "[n]either the legislative history nor the language of § 271 indicates that this rule has been modified." * * *

The United States Court of Appeals for the Fifth Circuit reversed. * * * It emphasized the fact that propanil, in the terminology of the patent law, is a "nonstaple" article, that is, one that has no commercial use except in connection with respondent's patented invention. After a thorough review of the judicial developments preceding enactment of § 271, and a detailed examination of the legislative history of that provision, the court concluded that the legislation restored to the patentee protection against contributory infringement that decisions of this Court theretofore had undermined. To secure that result, Congress found it necessary to cut back on the doctrine of patent misuse. The Court of Appeals determined that, by specifying in § 271(d) conduct that is not to be deemed misuse, "Congress *did* clearly provide for a patentee's right to exclude others and reserve to itself, if it chooses, the right to sell nonstaples used substantially only in its invention." 599 F.2d, at 704 (emphasis in original). Since Rohm & Haas' conduct was designed to accomplish only what the statute contemplated, the court ruled that petitioners' misuse defense was of no avail.

We granted certiorari to forestall a possible conflict in the lower courts and to resolve an issue of prime importance in the administration of the patent law.

B

For present purposes certain material facts are not in dispute. First, the validity of the Wilson patent is not in question at this stage in the litigation. We therefore must assume that respondent is the lawful owner of the sole and exclusive right to use, or to license others to use, propanil as a herbicide on rice fields in accordance with the methods claimed in the Wilson patent. Second, petitioners do not dispute that their manufacture and sale of propanil together with instructions for use as a herbicide constitute contributory infringement of the Rohm & Haas patent. * * * Accordingly, they admit that propanil constitutes "a material part of [respondent's] invention," that it is "especially made or especially adapted for use in an infringement of [the] patent," and that it is "not a staple article or commodity of commerce suitable for substantial noninfringing use," all within the language of 35 U.S.C. § 271(c).[6] They also concede that they have produced and sold

---

6. We follow the practice of the Court of Appeals and the parties by using the term "nonstaple" throughout this opinion to refer to a component as defined in 35 U.S.C. § 271(c), the unlicensed sale of which would constitute contributory infringement. A "staple" component is one that does not fit this definition. We recognize that the terms "staple" and "nonstaple" have not always been defined precisely in this fashion.

propanil with knowledge that it would be used in a manner infringing on respondent's patent rights. To put the same matter in slightly different terms, as the litigation now stands, petitioners admit commission of a tort and raise as their only defense to liability the contention that respondent, by engaging in patent misuse, comes into court with unclean hands.

As a result of these concessions, our chief focus of inquiry must be the scope of the doctrine of patent misuse in light of the limitations placed upon that doctrine by § 271(d). On this subject, as well, our task is guided by certain stipulations and concessions. The parties agree that Rohm & Haas makes and sells propanil; that it has refused to license petitioners or any others to do the same; that it has not granted express licenses either to retailers or to end users of the product; and that farmers who buy propanil from Rohm & Haas may use it, without fear of being sued for direct infringement, by virtue of an "implied license" they obtain when Rohm & Haas relinquishes its monopoly by selling the propanil. * * * The parties further agree that §§ 271(d)(1) and (3) permit respondent both to sell propanil itself and to sue others who sell the same product without a license, and that under § 271(d)(2) it would be free to demand royalties from others for the sale of propanil if it chose to do so.

The parties disagree over whether respondent has engaged in any additional conduct that amounts to patent misuse. Petitioners assert that there has been misuse because respondent has "tied" the sale of patent rights to the purchase of propanil, an unpatented and indeed unpatentable article, and because it has refused to grant licenses to other producers of the chemical compound. They argue that § 271(d) does not permit any sort of tying arrangement, and that resort to such a practice excludes respondent from the category of patentees "otherwise entitled to relief" within the meaning of § 271(d). Rohm & Haas, understandably, vigorously resists this characterization of its conduct. It argues that its acts have been only those that § 271(d), by express mandate, excepts from characterization as patent misuse. It further asserts that if this conduct results in an extension of the patent right to a control over an unpatented commodity, in this instance the extension has been given express statutory sanction.

II

* * *

As we have noted, the doctrine of contributory infringement had its genesis in an era of simpler and less subtle technology. Its basic elements are perhaps best explained with a classic example drawn from that era. In Wallace v. Holmes, 29 F.Cas. 74 (No. 17,100) (CC Conn.1871), the patentee had invented a new burner for an oil lamp. In compliance with the technical rules of patent claiming, this invention was patented in a combination that also included the standard fuel reservoir, wick tube, and chimney necessary for a properly functioning lamp. After the patent issued, a competitor began to market a rival product including the novel burner but not the chimney. * * * Under the sometimes scholastic law of patents, this conduct did not amount to direct infringement, because the competitor had not replicated every single element of the patentee's claimed combination. Cf., e.g., Prouty v. Ruggles, 16 Pet. 336, 341, 10 L.Ed. 985 (1842). Yet the court held that there had been "palpable interference" with the patentee's legal rights, because purchasers would be certain to complete the combination, and hence the infringement, by adding the glass chimney. 29 F.Cas., at 80. The court permitted the patentee to enforce his rights against the competitor who brought about the infringement, rather than requiring the patentee to undertake the almost insuperable task of finding and suing all the innocent purchasers who technically were responsible for completing the infringement. Ibid. * * *

The Wallace case demonstrates, in a readily comprehensible setting, the reason for the contributory infringement doctrine. It exists to protect patent rights from subversion by those who, without directly infringing the patent themselves, engage in acts designed to facilitate infringement by others. This protection is of particular importance in situations, like the oil lamp case itself, where enforcement against direct infringers would be difficult, and where the technicalities of patent law make it relatively easy to profit from another's invention without risking a charge of direct infringement. * * *

Although the propriety of the decision in *Wallace v. Holmes* seldom has been challenged, the contributory infringement doctrine it spawned has not always enjoyed full adherence in other contexts. The difficulty that the doctrine has encountered stems not so much from rejection of its core concept as from a desire to delimit its outer contours. In time, concern for potential anticompetitive tendencies inherent in actions for contributory infringement led to retrenchment on the doctrine. The judicial history of contributory infringement thus may be said to be marked by a period of ascendancy, in which the doctrine was expanded to the point where it became subject to abuse, followed by a somewhat longer period of decline, in which the concept of patent misuse was developed as an increasingly stringent antidote to the perceived excesses of the earlier period.

The doctrine of contributory infringement was first addressed by this Court in Morgan Envelope Co. v. Albany Paper Co., 152 U.S. 425 (1894). That case was a suit by a manufacturer of a patented device for dispensing toilet paper against a supplier of paper rolls that fit the patented invention. The Court accepted the contributory infringement doctrine in theory but held that it could not be invoked against a supplier of perishable commodities used in a patented invention. The Court observed that a contrary outcome would give the patentee "the benefit of a patent" on ordinary articles of commerce, a result that it determined to be unjustified on the facts of that case. * * *

Despite this wary reception, contributory infringement actions continued to flourish in the lower courts. Eventually the doctrine gained more wholehearted acceptance here. In Leeds & Catlin Co. v. Victor Talking Machine Co., 213 U.S. 325 (1909), the Court upheld an injunction against contributory infringement by a manufacturer of phonograph discs specially designed for use in a patented disc-and-stylus combination. Although the disc itself was not patented, the Court noted that it was essential to the functioning of the patented combination, and that its method of interaction with the stylus was what "mark(ed) the advance upon the prior art." Id., at 330. It also stressed that the disc was capable of use only in the patented combination, there being no other commercially available stylus with which it would operate. The Court distinguished the result in Morgan Envelope on the broad grounds that "[n]ot one of the determining factors there stated exists in the case at bar," and it held that the attempt to link the two cases "is not only to confound essential distinctions made by the patent laws, but essential differences between entirely different things." 213 U.S., at 335.

The contributory infringement doctrine achieved its high-water mark with the decision in Henry v. A.B. Dick Co., 224 U.S. 1 (1912). In that case a divided Court extended contributory infringement principles to permit a conditional licensing arrangement whereby a manufacturer of a patented printing machine could require purchasers to obtain all supplies used in connection with the invention, including such staple items as paper and ink, exclusively from the patentee. The Court reasoned that the market for these supplies was created by the invention, and that sale of a license to use the patented product, like sale of other species of property, could be limited by whatever conditions the property owner wished to impose. Id., at 31–32. The *A.B. Dick* decision and its progeny in the lower courts led to a vast expansion in conditional licensing of patented goods and processes used to control markets for staple and nonstaple goods alike.

This was followed by what may be characterized through the lens of hindsight as an inevitable judicial reaction. In Motion Picture Patents Co. v. Universal Film Mfg. Co., 243 U.S. 502 (1917), the Court signalled a new trend that was to continue for years thereafter.[10] The owner of a patent on projection equipment attempted to prevent competitors from selling film for use in the patented equipment by attaching to the projectors it sold a notice purporting to condition use of the machine on exclusive use of its film. The film previously had been patented but that patent had expired. The Court addressed the broad issue whether a patentee possessed the right to condition sale of a patented machine on the purchase of articles "which are no part of the patented machine, and which are not patented." Id., at 508. Relying upon the rule that the scope of a patent "must be limited to the invention described in the claims," id., at 511, the Court held that the attempted restriction on use of unpatented supplies was improper:

> "Such a restriction is invalid because such a film is obviously not any part of the invention of the patent in suit; because it is an attempt, without statutory warrant, to continue the patent monopoly in this particular character of film after it has expired, and because to enforce it would be to create a monopoly in the manufacture and use of moving

---

10. In addition to this judicial reaction, there was legislative reaction as well. In 1914, partly in response to the decision in Henry v. A.B. Dick Co., 224 U.S. 1 (1912), Congress enacted § 3 of the Clayton Act, 38 Stat. 731, 15 U.S.C. § 14. See International Business Machines Corp. v. United States, 298 U.S. 131, 137-138 (1936).

picture films, wholly outside of the patent in suit and of the patent law as we have interpreted it." Id., at 518.

By this reasoning, the Court focused on the conduct of the patentee, not that of the alleged infringer. It noted that as a result of lower court decisions, conditional licensing arrangements had greatly increased, indeed, to the point where they threatened to become "perfect instrument[s] of favoritism and oppression." Id., at 515. The Court warned that approval of the licensing scheme under consideration would enable the patentee to "ruin anyone unfortunate enough to be dependent upon its confessedly important improvements for the doing of business." Ibid. This ruling was directly in conflict with Henry v. A.B. Dick Co., supra, and the Court expressly observed that that decision "must be regarded as overruled." 243 U.S., at 518.

The broad ramifications of the Motion Picture case apparently were not immediately comprehended, and in a series of decisions over the next three decades litigants tested its limits. In Carbice Corp. v. American Patents Corp., 283 U.S. 27 (1931), the Court denied relief to a patentee who, through its sole licensee, authorized use of a patented design for a refrigeration package only to purchasers from the licensee of solid carbon dioxide ("dry ice"), a refrigerant that the licensee manufactured. The refrigerant was a well-known and widely used staple article of commerce, and the patent in question claimed neither a machine for making it nor a process for using it. Id., at 29. The Court held that the patent holder and its licensee were attempting to exclude competitors in the refrigerant business from a portion of the market, and that this conduct constituted patent misuse. * * *

Although none of these decisions purported to cut back on the doctrine of contributory infringement itself, they were generally perceived as having that effect, and how far the developing doctrine of patent misuse might extend was a topic of some speculation among members of the patent bar. The Court's decisions had not yet addressed the status of contributory infringement or patent misuse with respect to nonstaple goods, and some courts and commentators apparently took the view that control of nonstaple items capable only of infringing use might not bar patent protection against contributory infringement. This view soon received a serious, if not fatal, blow from the Court's controversial decisions in Mercoid Corp. v. Mid-Continent Investment Co., 320 U.S. 661 (1944) (Mercoid I), and Mercoid Corp. v. Minneapolis-Honeywell Regulator Co., 320 U.S. 680 (1944) (Mercoid II). In these cases, the Court definitely held that any attempt to control the market for unpatented goods would constitute patent misuse, even if those goods had no use outside a patented invention. Because these cases served as the point of departure for congressional legislation, they merit more than passing citation.

Both cases involved a single patent that claimed a combination of elements for a furnace heating system. Mid-Continent was the owner of the patent, and Honeywell was its licensee. Although neither company made or installed the furnace system, Honeywell manufactured and sold stoker switches especially made for and essential to the system's operation. The right to build and use the system was granted to purchasers of the stoker switches, and royalties owed the patentee were calculated on the number of stoker switches sold. Mercoid manufactured and marketed a competing stoker switch that was designed to be used only in the patented combination. Mercoid had been offered a sublicense by the licensee but had refused to take one. It was sued for contributory infringement by both the patentee and the licensee, and it raised patent misuse as a defense.

In *Mercoid I* the Court barred the patentee from obtaining relief because it deemed the licensing arrangement with Honeywell to be an unlawful attempt to extend the patent monopoly. The opinion for the Court painted with a very broad brush. Prior patent misuse decisions had involved attempts "to secure a partial monopoly in supplies consumed . . . or unpatented materials employed" in connection with the practice of the invention. None, however, had involved an integral component necessary to the functioning of the patented system. 320 U.S., at 665. The Court refused, however, to infer any "difference in principle" from this distinction in fact. Ibid. Instead, it stated an expansive rule that apparently admitted no exception:

> "The necessities or convenience of the patentee do not justify any use of the monopoly of the patent to create another monopoly. The fact that the patentee has the power to refuse a license does not enable him to enlarge the monopoly of the patent by the expedient of attaching conditions to its use. . . . The method by which the monopoly is sought to be extended is immaterial. . . . When the patentee ties something else to his invention, he acts only by virtue of his right as the owner of property to make contracts concerning it and not otherwise. He then is subject to all the limitations upon that right which the general law imposes upon such contracts. The contract is not saved by anything in the patent laws because it relates to the invention. If it were, the mere act of the patentee could make the distinctive claim of the patent attach to something which does not possess the quality of invention. Then the patent would be diverted from its statutory purpose and become a ready instrument for economic control in domains where the anti-trust acts or other laws not the patent statutes define the public policy." Id., at 666.

The Court recognized that its reasoning directly conflicted with *Leeds & Catlin Co. v. Victor Talking Machine Co.*, supra, and it registered disapproval, if not outright rejection, of that case. 320 U.S., at 668. It also recognized that "[t]he result of this decision, together with those which have preceded it, is to limit substantially the doctrine of contributory infringement." Id., at 669. The Court commented, rather cryptically, that it would not "stop to consider" what "residuum" of the contributory infringement doctrine "may be left." Ibid.

* * *

What emerges from this review of judicial development is a fairly complicated picture, in which the rights and obligations of patentees as against contributory infringers have varied over time. We need not decide how respondent would have fared against a charge of patent misuse at any particular point prior to the enactment of 35 U.S.C. § 271. Nevertheless, certain inferences that are pertinent to the present inquiry may be drawn from these historical developments.

First, we agree with the Court of Appeals that the concepts of contributory infringement and patent misuse "rest on antithetical underpinnings." 599 F.2d at 697. The traditional remedy against contributory infringement is the injunction. And an inevitable concomitant of the right to enjoin another from contributory infringement is the capacity to suppress competition in an unpatented article of commerce. See, e.g., Thomson-Houston Electric Co. v. Kelsey Electric R. Specialty Co., 72 F. 1016, 1018–1019 (CC Conn. 1896). Proponents of contributory infringement defend this result on the grounds that it is necessary for the protection of the patent right, and that the market for the unpatented article flows from the patentee's invention. They also observe that in many instances the article is "unpatented" only because of the technical rules of patent claiming, which require the placement of an invention in its context. Yet suppression of competition in unpatented goods is precisely what the opponents of patent misuse decry. If both the patent misuse and contributory infringement doctrines are to coexist, then, each must have some separate sphere of operation with which the other does not interfere.

Second, we find that the majority of cases in which the patent misuse doctrine was developed involved undoing the damage thought to have been done by *A.B. Dick*. The desire to extend patent protection to control of staple articles of commerce died slowly, and the ghost of the expansive contributory infringement era continued to haunt the courts. As a result, among the historical precedents in this Court, only the *Leeds & Catlin* and *Mercoid* cases bear significant factual similarity to the present controversy. Those cases involved questions of control over unpatented articles that were essential to the patented inventions, and that were unsuited for any commercial noninfringing use. In this case, we face similar questions in connection with a chemical, propanil, the herbicidal properties of which are essential to the advance on prior art disclosed by respondent's patented process. Like the record disc in *Leeds & Catlin* or the stoker switch in the *Mercoid* cases, and unlike the dry ice in *Carbice* * * *, propanil is a nonstaple commodity which has no use except through practice of the patented method. Accordingly, had the present case arisen prior to *Mercoid*, we believe it fair to say that it would have fallen close to the wavering line between legitimate protection against contributory infringement and illegitimate patent misuse.

III

The *Mercoid* decisions left in their wake some consternation among patent lawyers and a degree of confusion in the lower courts. Although some courts treated the *Mercoid* pronouncements as limited in effect to the specific kind of licensing arrangement at issue in those cases, others took a much more expansive view of the decision. Among the latter group, some courts held that even the filing of an action for contributory infringement, by threatening to deter competition in unpatented materials, could supply evidence of patent misuse. See, e.g., Stroco Products, Inc. v. Mullenbach,

67 USPQ 168, 170 (SD Cal. 1944). This state of affairs made it difficult for patent lawyers to advise their clients on questions of contributory infringement and to render secure opinions on the validity of proposed licensing arrangements. Certain segments of the patent bar eventually decided to ask Congress for corrective legislation that would restore some scope to the contributory infringement doctrine. With great perseverance, they advanced their proposal in three successive Congresses before it eventually was enacted in 1952 as 35 U.S.C. § 271.

The critical inquiry in this case is how the enactment of § 271 affected the doctrines of contributory infringement and patent misuse. Viewed against the backdrop of judicial precedent, we believe that the language and structure of the statute lend significant support to Rhom & Haas' contention that, because § 271(d) immunizes its conduct from the charge of patent misuse, it should not be barred from seeking relief. The approach that Congress took toward the codification of contributory infringement and patent misuse reveals a compromise between those two doctrines and their competing policies that permits patentees to exercise control over nonstaple articles used in their inventions.

Section 271(c) identifies the basic dividing line between contributory infringement and patent misuse. It adopts a restrictive definition of contributory infringement that distinguishes between staple and nonstaple articles of commerce. It also defines the class of nonstaple items narrowly. In essence, this provision places materials like the dry ice of the *Carbice* case outside the scope of the contributory infringement doctrine. As a result, it is no longer necessary to resort to the doctrine of patent misuse in order to deny patentees control over staple goods used in their inventions.

The limitations on contributory infringement written into § 271(c) are counterbalanced by limitations on patent misuse in § 271(d). Three species of conduct by patentees are expressly excluded from characterization as misuse. First, the patentee may "deriv[e] revenue" from acts that "would constitute contributory infringement" if "performed by another without his consent." This provision clearly signifies that a patentee may make and sell nonstaple goods used in connection with his invention. Second, the patentee may "licens[e] or authoriz[e] another to perform acts" which without such authorization would constitute contributory infringement. This provision's use in the disjunctive of the term "authoriz[e]" suggests that more than explicit licensing agreements is contemplated. Finally, the patentee may "enforce his patent rights against . . . contributory infringement." This provision plainly means that the patentee may bring suit without fear that his doing so will be regarded as an unlawful attempt to suppress competition. The statute explicitly states that a patentee may do "one or more" of these permitted acts, and it does not state that he must do any of them.

In our view, the provisions of § 271(d) effectively confer upon the patentee, as a lawful adjunct of his patent rights, a limited power to exclude others from competition in nonstaple goods. A patentee may sell a nonstaple article himself while enjoining others from marketing that same good without his

authorization. By doing so, he is able to eliminate competitors and thereby
to control the market for that product. Moreover, his power to demand royalties from others for the privilege of selling the nonstaple item itself implies
that the patentee may control the market for the nonstaple good; otherwise,
his "right" to sell licenses for the marketing of the nonstaple good would be
meaningless, since no one would be willing to pay him for a superfluous
authorization. * * *

Rohm & Haas' conduct is not dissimilar in either nature or effect from
the conduct that is thus clearly embraced within § 271(d). It sells propanil;
it authorizes others to use propanil; and it sues contributory infringers.
These are all protected activities. Rohm & Haas does not license others to
sell propanil, but nothing on the face of the statute requires it to do so. To be
sure, the sum effect of Rohm & Haas' actions is to suppress competition in
the market for an unpatented commodity. But as we have observed, in this
its conduct is no different from that which the statute expressly protects.

The one aspect of Rohm & Haas' behavior that is not expressly covered
by § 271(d) is its linkage of two protected activities—sale of propanil and
authorization to practice the patented process—together in a single transaction. Petitioners vigorously argue that this linkage, which they characterize pejoratively as "tying," supplies the otherwise missing element of
misuse. They fail, however, to identify any way in which this "tying" of two
expressly protected activities results in any extension of control over
unpatented materials beyond what § 271(d) already allows. Nevertheless,
the language of § 271(d) does not explicitly resolve the question when linkage of this variety becomes patent misuse. In order to judge whether this
method of exploiting the patent lies within or without the protection
afforded by § 271(d), we must turn to the legislative history.

B

Petitioners argue that the legislative materials indicate at most a modest purpose for § 271. Relying mainly on the Committee Reports that accompanied the "Act to Revise and Codify the Patent Laws" (1952 Act), 66 Stat.
792, of which § 271 was a part, petitioners assert that the principal purpose
of Congress was to "clarify" the law of contributory infringement as it had
been developed by the courts, rather than to effect any significant substantive change. They note that the 1952 Act undertook the major task of codifying all the patent laws in a single title, and they argue that substantive
changes from recodifications are not lightly to be inferred. * * * They further argue that, whatever the impact of § 271 in other respects, there is not
the kind of "clear and certain signal from Congress" that should be required
for an extension of patent privileges. See Deepsouth Packing Co. v. Laitram
Corp., 406 U.S. 518, 531 (1972). We disagree with petitioners' assessment. In
our view, the relevant legislative materials abundantly demonstrate an
intent both to change the law and to expand significantly the ability of
patentees to protect their rights against contributory infringement.

The 1952 Act was approved with virtually no floor debate. Only one
exchange is relevant to the present inquiry. In response to a question

whether the Act would effect any substantive changes, Senator McCarran, a spokesman for the legislation, commented that the Act "codif(ies) the patent laws." 98 Cong.Rec. 9323 (1952). He also submitted a statement, which explained that, although the general purpose of the Act was to clarify existing law, it also included several changes taken "[i]n view of decisions of the Supreme Court and others." Ibid. Perhaps because of the magnitude of the recodification effort, the Committee Reports accompanying the 1952 Act also gave relatively cursory attention to its features. Nevertheless, they did identify § 271 as one of the "major changes or innovations in the title." H.R.Rep. No. 1923, 82d Cong., 2d Sess., 5 (1952). In explaining the provisions of § 271, the Reports stated that they were intended "to codify in statutory form the principles of contributory infringement and at the same time (to) eliminate . . . doubt and confusion" that had resulted from "decisions of the courts in recent years." Id., at 9. The Reports also commented that §§ 271(b), (c), and (d) "have as their main purpose clarification and stabilization." Ibid.

These materials sufficiently demonstrate that the 1952 Act did include significant substantive changes, and that § 271 was one of them.

The principal sources for edification concerning the meaning and scope of § 271, however, are the extensive hearings that were held on the legislative proposals that led up to the final enactment. * * *

[The Court undertook an extended review of the legislative history, which it found consistent with the view that § 271 did effect a significant change in the law] * * *.

There is one factual difference between this case and *Mercoid:* the licensee in the *Mercoid* cases had offered a sublicense to the alleged contributory infringer, which offer had been refused. *Mercoid II,* 320 U.S., at 683. Seizing upon this difference, petitioners argue that respondent's unwillingness to offer similar licenses to its would-be competitors in the manufacture of propanil legally distinguishes this case and sets it outside § 271(d). To this argument, there are at least three responses. First, as we have noted, § 271(d) permits such licensing but does not require it. Accordingly, petitioners' suggestion would import into the statute a requirement that simply is not there. Second, petitioners have failed to adduce any evidence from the legislative history that the offering of a license to the alleged contributory infringer was a critical factor in inducing Congress to retreat from the result of the *Mercoid* decisions. Indeed, the *Leeds & Catlin* decision, which did not involve such an offer to license, was placed before Congress as an example of the kind of contributory infringement action the statute would allow. Third, petitioners' argument runs contrary to the long-settled view that the essence of a patent grant is the right to exclude others from profiting by the patented invention. 35 U.S.C. § 154 * * *. If petitioners' argument were accepted, it would force patentees either to grant licenses or to forfeit their statutory protection against contributory infringement. Compulsory licensing is a rarity in our patent system, and we decline to manufacture such a requirement out of § 271(d).

IV

Petitioners argue, finally, that the interpretation of § 271(d) which we have adopted is foreclosed by decisions of this Court following the passage of the 1952 Act. They assert that in subsequent cases the Court has continued to rely upon the *Mercoid* decisions, and that it has effectively construed § 271(d) to codify the result of those decisions, rather than to return the doctrine of patent misuse to some earlier stage of development. We disagree.

* * *

The only two decisions that touch at all closely upon the issues of statutory construction presented here are Aro Mfg. Co. v. Convertible Top Co., 365 U.S. 336 (1961) (*Aro I*), and Aro Mfg. Co. v. Convertible Top Co., 377 U.S. 476 (1964) (*Aro II*). These decisions emerged from a single case involving an action for contributory infringement based on the manufacture and sale of a specially cut fabric designed for use in a patented automobile convertible top combination. In neither case, however, did the Court directly address the question of § 271(d)'s effect on the law of patent misuse.

The controlling issue in *Aro I* was whether there had been any direct infringement of the patent. The Court held that purchasers of the specially cut fabric used it for "repair" rather than "reconstruction" of the patented combination; accordingly, under the patent law they were not guilty of infringement. 365 U.S., at 340, 346. Since there was no direct infringement by the purchasers, the Court held that there could be no contributory infringement by the manufacturer of the replacement tops. This conclusion rested in part on a holding that § 271(c) "made no change in the fundamental precept that there can be no contributory infringement in the absence of a direct infringement." Id., at 341. It in no way conflicts with our decision.

* * *

Aro II is a complicated decision in which the Court mustered different majorities in support of various aspects of its opinion. See 377 U.S., at 488, n. 8. After remand from *Aro I,* it became clear that the Court's decision in that case had not eliminated all possible grounds for a charge of contributory infringement. Certain convertible top combinations had been sold without valid license from the patentee. Because use of these tops involved direct infringement of the patent, there remained a question whether fabric supplied for their repair might constitute contributory infringement notwithstanding the Court's earlier decision.

Aro II decided several questions of statutory interpretation under § 271. First, it held that repair of an unlicensed combination was direct infringement under the law preceding enactment of § 271, and that the statute did not effect any change in this regard. 377 U.S., at 484. * * *

Second, the Court held that supplying replacement fabrics specially cut for use in the infringing repair constituted contributory infringement under § 271(c). The Court held that the specially cut fabrics, when installed in infringing equipment, qualified as nonstaple items within the language of § 271(c), and that supply of similar materials for infringing repair had been treated as contributory infringement under the judicial law that § 271(c) was designed to codify. 377 U.S., at 485–488. It also held that § 271(c) requires a showing that an alleged contributory infringer knew that the combination for which his component was especially designed was both patented and infringing. 377 U.S., at 488–491. We regard these holdings as fully consistent with our understanding of § 271(c). In any event, since petitioners have conceded contributory infringement for the purposes of this decision, the scope of that subsection is not directly before us.

Third, the Court held that the alleged contributory infringer could not avoid liability by reliance on the doctrine of the *Mercoid* decisions. Although those decisions had cast contributory infringement into some doubt, the Court held that § 271 was enacted "for the express purpose . . . of overruling any blanket invalidation of the (contributory infringement) doctrine that could be found in the *Mercoid* opinions." 377 U.S., at 492. Although our review of the legislative history finds a broader intent, it is not out of harmony with *Aro II*'s analysis. The Court explicitly noted that a defense of patent misuse had not been pressed. Id., at 491. Accordingly, its discussion of legislative history was limited to those materials supporting the observation, sufficient for purposes of the case, that any direct attack on the contributory infringement doctrine in its entirety would be contrary to the manifest purpose of § 271(c). Since the Court in *Aro II* was not faced with a patent misuse defense, it had no occasion to consider other evidence in the hearings relating to the scope of § 271(d).

* * *

Perhaps the quintessential difference between the *Aro* decisions and the present case is the difference between the primary-use market for a chemical process and the replacement market out of which the Aro litigation arose. The repair-reconstruction distinction and its legal consequences are determinative in the latter context, but are not controlling here. Instead, the staple-nonstaple distinction, which *Aro I* found irrelevant to the characterization of replacements, supplies the controlling benchmark. This distinction ensures that the patentee's right to prevent others from contributorily infringing his patent affects only the market for the invention itself. Because of this significant difference in legal context, we believe our interpretation of § 271(d) does not conflict with these decisions.

V

Since our present task is one of statutory construction, questions of public policy cannot be determinative of the outcome unless specific policy choices fairly can be attributed to Congress itself. In this instance, as we have already stated, Congress chose a compromise between competing policy interests. The policy of free competition runs deep in our law. It underlies both the doctrine of patent misuse and the general principle that the boundary of a patent monopoly is to be limited by the literal scope of the patent claims. But the policy of stimulating invention that underlies the entire patent system runs no less deep. And the doctrine of contributory infringement, which has been called "an expression both of law and morals,"

Mercoid I, 320 U.S., at 677 (Frankfurter J., dissenting), can be of crucial importance in ensuring that the endeavors and investments of the inventor do not go unrewarded.

It is perhaps, noteworthy that holders of "new use" patents on chemical processes were among those designated to Congress as intended beneficiaries of the protection against contributory infringement that § 271 was designed to restore. * * * We have been informed that the characteristics of practical chemical research are such that this form of patent protection is particularly important to inventors in that field. The number of chemicals either known to scientists or disclosed by existing research is vast. It grows constantly, as those engaging in "pure" research publish their discoveries.[23] The number of these chemicals that have known uses of commercial or social value, in contrast, is small. Development of new uses for existing chemicals is thus a major component of practical chemical research. It is extraordinarily expensive.[24] It may take years of unsuccessful testing before a chemical having a desired property is identified, and it may take several years of further testing before a proper and safe method for using that chemical is developed.[25]

Under the construction of § 271(d) that petitioners advance, the rewards available to those willing to undergo the time, expense, and interim frustration of such practical research would provide at best a dubious incentive. Others could await the results of the testing and then jump on the profit bandwagon by demanding licenses to sell the unpatented, nonstaple chemical used in the newly developed process. Refusal to accede to such a demand, if accompanied by any attempt to profit from the invention through sale of the unpatented chemical, would risk forfeiture of any patent protection whatsoever on a finding of patent misuse. As a result, noninventors would be almost assured of an opportunity to share in the spoils, even though they had contributed nothing to the discovery. The incentive to await the discoveries of others might well prove sweeter than the incentive to take the initiative oneself.

---

23. As of March 1980, the Chemical Registry System maintained by the American Chemical Society listed in excess of 4,848,000 known chemical compounds. The list grows at a rate of about 350,000 per year. The Society estimates that the list comprises between 50% and 60% of all compounds that ever have been prepared. * * *

24. For example, the average cost of developing one new pharmaceutical drug has been estimated to run as high as $54 million. Hansen, The Pharmaceutical Development Process: Estimates of Development Costs and Times and the Effects of Proposed Regulatory Changes, in Issues in Pharmaceutical Economics 151, 180 (R. Chien ed. 1979).

25. See Wardell, The History of Drug Discovery, Development, and Regulation, in Issues in Pharmaceutical Economics 1, 8–10 (R. Chien ed. 1979) (describing modern techniques and testing requirements for development of pharmaceuticals). Although testing of chemicals destined for pharmaceutical use may be the most extensive, testing for environmental effects of chemicals used in industrial or agricultural settings also can be both expensive and prolonged. See A. Wechsler, J. Harrison, & J. Neumeyer, Evaluation of the Possible Impact of Pesticide Legislation on Research and Development Activities of Pesticide Manufacturers 18–52 (Environmental Protection Agency, Office of Pesticide Programs, pub. no. 540/9–75–018, 1975). See generally A. Baines, F. Bradbury, & C. Suckling, Research in the Chemical Industry 82–163 (1969).

Whether such a regime would prove workable, as petitioners urge, or would lead to dire consequences, as respondent and several amici insist, we need not predict. Nor do we need to determine whether the principles of free competition could justify such a result. Congress' enactment of § 271(d) resolved these issues in favor of a broader scope of patent protection. In accord with our understanding of that statute, we hold that Rohm & Haas has not engaged in patent misuse, either by its method of selling propanil, or by its refusal to license others to sell that commodity. The judgment of the Court of Appeals is therefore affirmed.

It is so ordered.

MR. JUSTICE WHITE, with whom MR. JUSTICE BRENNAN, MR. JUSTICE MARSHALL, and MR. JUSTICE STEVENS joined, dissented.

* * *

NOTES

1. The doctrine of patent misuse is closely related to the cases that have held that certain patent licensing practices can constitute unreasonable restraints of trade in violation of the antitrust laws. It is clear that any licensing practice that is an antitrust violation is also misuse. It is probably also true that any licensing practice that is patent misuse is at the least almost an antitrust violation. Because the doctrine of patent misuse is so closely related to antitrust law, it is not further examined here. The topic of antitrust constraints on patent licensing is left for the antitrust course, although it should be noted that any lawyer who handles a patent or technology licensing transaction must be sensitive to the antitrust doctrines.

Remember that *Brulotte v. Thys Co.,* in the preemption section of Chapter 4, was decided as a patent misuse case.

2. As a matter of antitrust theory, contractual restrictions in relation to patents should be analyzed like any other contractual provision made in relation to a property right. However, patents have attracted special skepticism in antitrust cases because the judges have tended to view patents as monopolies. The *reductio ad absurbum* of course would be the idea that simply enforcing a patent is a violation of the antitrust laws, a position to which the Court came perilously close in *Mercoid* itself. In any case, the antitrust issues have had the practical consequence that many patent infringement complaints are met with an antitrust counterclaim, a move that greatly increases the costs of licensing and enforcing patents. Ironically, one safe way to proceed has always been to license the patent to no one, thus restricting its availability.

Antitrust hostility to patents has begun to recede in recent years. Section 271(d) enacted in 1952 appears to have been a precursor of a less hostile attitude, although one should note that as late as 1980 only five members of the Supreme Court were willing to venture the conclusion that § 271(d) means what it said. Congress has since used § 271(d) as a vehicle to further protect patents from antitrust hostility. See §§ 272(d)(4) and (5), added by P.L. 100–703, Nov. 19, 1988.

The view that patents are monopolies, although instinctively appealing, has been challenged by one of the present authors. See Edmund W. Kitch, Patents: Monopolies or Property Rights?, 8 Research in Law and Economics 31 (1986). There is a vast literature on patents and antitrust which can be accessed through any of the antitrust treatises. Ward S. Bowman, Jr., Patent and Antitrust Law: A Legal and Economic Appraisal (Chicago and London: Univ. of Chicago Press, 1973), is among the most thoughtful extended examinations of the subject.

(5) Construction of the Claims

The scope of the patent is determined by the claims. These function like a boundary description in a real estate deed. They tell the world (and the courts) what is and what is not within a patent. The more elements that a claim contains the smaller its scope since only a product or process that has all of the elements required by the claim will infringe.

The problem of construing claims can be analogized to the problem of construing language in any document, whether a contract or a statute. When the language in question is not sufficently clear to provide an answer to the question before the court, the court may look to the surrounding context (which in the case of patents would be the rest of the patent document, and the technological and industrial contexts) and the history of the language itself (which in the case of patents would be the history of the prosecution of the patent application in the patent office).

In Markman v. Westview Instruments, Inc., 517 U.S. 370 (1996), the Supreme Court held that issues of claim construction are issues of law, to be decided by the judge not the jury. In a jury trial, the judge formulates instructions to the jury explaining what the claims of the patent mean.

Warner-Jenkinson Co. v. Hilton Davis Chemical Co.

Supreme Court of the United States, 1997.
520 U.S. 17, 117 S. Ct. 1040, 137 L.Ed.2d 146.

■ JUSTICE THOMAS delivered the opinion of the Court.

Nearly 50 years ago, this Court in Graver Tank & Mfg. Co. v. Linde Air Products Co., 339 U.S. 605 (1950), set out the modern contours of what is known in patent law as the "doctrine of equivalents." Under this doctrine, a product or process that does not literally infringe upon the express terms of a patent claim may nonetheless be found to infringe if there is "equivalence" between the elements of the accused product or process and the claimed elements of the patented invention. Id., at 609. Petitioner, which was found to have infringed upon respondent's patent under the doctrine of equivalents, invites us to speak the death of that doctrine. We decline that invitation. The significant disagreement within the Court of Appeals for the Federal

Circuit concerning the application of *Graver Tank* suggests, however, that the doctrine is not free from confusion. We therefore will endeavor to clarify the proper scope of the doctrine.

I

The essential facts of this case are few. Petitioner Warner-Jenkinson Co. and respondent Hilton Davis Chemical Co. manufacture dyes. Impurities in those dyes must be removed. Hilton Davis holds United States Patent No. 4,560,746 ('746 patent), which discloses an improved purification process involving "ultrafiltration." The '746 process filters impure dye through a porous membrane at certain pressures and pH levels,[26] resulting in a high purity dye product.

The '746 patent issued in 1985. As relevant to this case, the patent claims as its invention an improvement in the ultrafiltration process as follows:

"In a process for the purification of a dye . . . the improvement which comprises: subjecting an aqueous solution . . . to ultrafiltration through a membrane having a nominal pore diameter of 5–15 Angstroms under a hydrostatic pressure of approximately 200 to 400 p.s.i.g., *at a pH from approximately 6.0 to 9.0,* to thereby cause separation of said impurities from said dye. . . ." App. 36–37 (emphasis added).

The inventors added the phrase "at a pH from approximately 6.0 to 9.0" during patent prosecution. At a minimum, this phrase was added to distinguish a previous patent (the "Booth" patent) that disclosed an ultrafiltration process operating at a pH above 9.0. The parties disagree as to why the low-end pH limit of 6.0 was included as part of the claim.[27]

In 1986, Warner-Jenkinson developed an ultrafiltration process that operated with membrane pore diameters assumed to be 5–15 Angstroms, at pressures of 200 to nearly 500 p.s.i.g., and at a pH of 5.0. Warner-Jenkinson did not learn of the '746 patent until after it had begun commercial use of its ultrafiltration process. Hilton Davis eventually learned of Warner-Jenkinson's use of ultrafiltration and, in 1991, sued Warner-Jenkinson for patent infringement.

---

26. The pH, or power (exponent) of Hydrogen, of a solution is a measure of its acidity or alkalinity. A pH of 7.0 is neutral; a pH below 7.0 is acidic; and a pH above 7.0 is alkaline. Although measurement of pH is on a logarithmic scale, with each whole number difference representing a ten-fold difference in acidity, the practical significance of any such difference will often depend on the context. Pure water, for example, has a neutral pH of 7.0, whereas carbonated water has an acidic pH of 3.0, and concentrated hydrochloric acid has a pH approaching 0.0. On the other end of the scale, milk of magnesia has a pH of 10.0, whereas household ammonia has a pH of 11.9. 21 Encyclopedia Americana 844 (Int'l ed. 1990).

27. Petitioner contends that the lower limit was added because below a pH of 6.0 the patented process created "foaming" problems in the plant and because the process was not shown to work below that pH level. Brief for Petitioner 4, n. 5, 37, n. 28. Respondent counters that the process was successfully tested to pH levels as low as 2.2 with no effect on the process because of foaming, but offers no particular explanation as to why the lower level of 6.0 pH was selected. Brief for Respondent 34, n. 34.

As trial approached, Hilton Davis conceded that there was no literal infringement, and relied solely on the doctrine of equivalents. Over Warner-Jenkinson's objection that the doctrine of equivalents was an equitable doctrine to be applied by the court, the issue of equivalence was included among those sent to the jury. The jury found that the '746 patent was not invalid and that Warner-Jenkinson infringed upon the patent under the doctrine of equivalents. The jury also found, however, that Warner-Jenkinson had not intentionally infringed, and therefore awarded only 20% of the damages sought by Hilton Davis. The District Court denied Warner-Jenkinson's post-trial motions, and entered a permanent injunction prohibiting Warner-Jenkinson from practicing ultrafiltration below 500 p.s.i.g. and below 9.01 pH. A fractured en banc Court of Appeals for the Federal Circuit affirmed. 62 F.3d 1512 (C.A. Fed. 1995).

The majority below held that the doctrine of equivalents continues to exist and that its touchstone is whether substantial differences exist between the accused process and the patented process. Id., at 1521–1522. The court also held that the question of equivalence is for the jury to decide and that the jury in this case had substantial evidence from which it could conclude that the Warner-Jenkinson process was not substantially different from the ultrafiltration process disclosed in the '746 patent. Id., at 1525.

There were three separate dissents, commanding a total of 5 of 12 judges. Four of the five dissenting judges viewed the doctrine of equivalents as allowing an improper expansion of claim scope, contrary to this Court's numerous holdings that it is the claim that defines the invention and gives notice to the public of the limits of the patent monopoly. Id., at 1537–1538 (Plager, J., dissenting). The fifth dissenter, the late Judge Nies, was able to reconcile the prohibition against enlarging the scope of claims and the doctrine of equivalents by applying the doctrine to each element of a claim, rather than to the accused product or process "overall." Id., at 1574 (Nies, J., dissenting). As she explained it, "[t]he 'scope' is not enlarged if courts do not go beyond the substitution of equivalent elements." Ibid. All of the dissenters, however, would have found that a much narrowed doctrine of equivalents may be applied in whole or in part by the court. Id., at 1540–1542 (Plager, J., dissenting); id., at 1579 (Nies, J., dissenting).

We granted certiorari, 116 S.Ct. 1014 (1996), and now reverse and remand.

II

In *Graver Tank* we considered the application of the doctrine of equivalents to an accused chemical composition for use in welding that differed from the patented welding material by the substitution of one chemical element. 339 U.S., at 610. The substituted element did not fall within the literal terms of the patent claim, but the Court nonetheless found that the "question which thus emerges is whether the substitution [of one element for the other] . . . is a change of such substance as to make the doctrine of equivalents inapplicable; or conversely, whether under the circumstances the change was so insubstantial that the trial court's invocation of the doctrine of equivalents was justified." Ibid. The Court also described some of the considerations that go into applying the doctrine of equivalents:

"What constitutes equivalency must be determined against the context of the patent, the prior art, and the particular circumstances of the case. Equivalence, in the patent law, is not the prisoner of a formula and is not an absolute to be considered in a vacuum. It does not require complete identity for every purpose and in every respect. In determining equivalents, things equal to the same thing may not be equal to each other and, by the same token, things for most purposes different may sometimes be equivalents. Consideration must be given to the purpose for which an ingredient is used in a patent, the qualities it has when combined with the other ingredients, and the function which it is intended to perform. An important factor is whether persons reasonably skilled in the art would have known of the interchangeability of an ingredient not contained in the patent with one that was." Id., at 609.

Considering those factors, the Court viewed the difference between the chemical element claimed in the patent and the substitute element to be "colorable only," and concluded that the trial court's judgment of infringement under the doctrine of equivalents was proper. Id., at 612.

A

Petitioner's primary argument in this Court is that the doctrine of equivalents, as set out in *Graver Tank* in 1950, did not survive the 1952 revision of the Patent Act, 35 U.S.C. § 100 et seq., because it is inconsistent with several aspects of that Act. In particular, petitioner argues: (1) the doctrine of equivalents is inconsistent with the statutory requirement that a patentee specifically "claim" the invention covered by a patent, 35 U.S.C. § 112; (2) the doctrine circumvents the patent reissue process—designed to correct mistakes in drafting or the like—and avoids the express limitations on that process, 35 U.S.C. §§ 251–252; (3) the doctrine is inconsistent with the primacy of the Patent and Trademark Office (PTO) in setting the scope of a patent through the patent prosecution process; and (4) the doctrine was implicitly rejected as a general matter by Congress' specific and limited inclusion of the doctrine in one section regarding "means" claiming, 35 U.S.C. § 112, ¶ 6. All but one of these arguments were made in *Graver Tank* in the context of the 1870 Patent Act, and failed to command a majority.

The 1952 Patent Act is not materially different from the 1870 Act with regard to claiming, reissue, and the role of the PTO. Compare, e.g., 35 U.S.C. § 112 ("The specification shall conclude with one or more claims particularly pointing out and distinctly claiming the subject matter which the applicant regards as his invention") with The Consolidated Patent Act of 1870, ch. 230, § 26, 16 Stat. 198, 201 (the applicant "shall particularly point out and distinctly claim the part, improvement, or combination which he claims as his invention or discovery"). Such minor differences as exist between those provisions in the 1870 and the 1952 Acts have no bearing on the result reached in *Graver Tank,* and thus provide no basis for our overruling it. In the context of infringement, we have already held that pre-1952 precedent survived the passage of the 1952 Act. See Aro Mfg. Co. v.

Convertible Top Replacement Co., 365 U.S. 336, 342 (1961) (new section defining infringement "left intact the entire body of case law on direct infringement"). We see no reason to reach a different result here.

Petitioner's fourth argument for an implied congressional negation of the doctrine of equivalents turns on the reference to "equivalents" in the "means" claiming provision of the 1952 Act. Section 112, ¶ 6, a provision not contained in the 1870 Act, states:

> "An element in a claim for a combination may be expressed as a means or step for performing a specified function without the recital of structure, material, or acts in support thereof, and such claim shall be construed to cover the corresponding structure, material, or acts described in the specification and *equivalents* thereof." (Emphasis added.)

Thus, under this new provision, an applicant can describe an element of his invention by the result accomplished or the function served, rather than describing the item or element to be used (e.g., "a means of connecting Part A to Part B," rather than "a two-penny nail"). Congress enacted § 112, ¶ 6 in response to Halliburton Oil Well Cementing Co. v. Walker, which rejected claims that "do not describe the invention but use 'conveniently functional language at the exact point of novelty,'" 329 U.S. 1, 8 (1946) (citation omitted). See In re Donaldson Co., 16 F.3d 1189, 1194 (C.A. Fed. 1994) (Congress enacted predecessor of § 112, ¶ 6 in response to *Halliburton*); In re Fuetterer, 319 F.2d 259, 264, n. 11 (1963) (same); see also, 2 D. Chisum, Patents § 8.04[2], at 63–64 (1996) (discussing 1954 commentary of then-Chief Patent Examiner P.J. Federico). Section 112, ¶ 6 now expressly allows so-called "means" claims, with the proviso that application of the broad literal language of such claims must be limited to only those means that are "equivalent" to the actual means shown in the patent specification. This is an application of the doctrine of equivalents in a restrictive role, narrowing the application of broad literal claim elements. We recognized this type of role for the doctrine of equivalents in Graver Tank itself. 339 U.S., at 608–609. The added provision, however, is silent on the doctrine of equivalents as applied where there is no literal infringement.

Because § 112, ¶ 6 was enacted as a targeted cure to a specific problem, and because the reference in that provision to "equivalents" appears to be no more than a prophylactic against potential side effects of that cure, such limited congressional action should not be overread for negative implications. Congress in 1952 could easily have responded to *Graver Tank* as it did to the *Halliburton* decision. But it did not. Absent something more compelling than the dubious negative inference offered by petitioner, the lengthy history of the doctrine of equivalents strongly supports adherence to our refusal in *Graver Tank* to find that the Patent Act conflicts with that doctrine. Congress can legislate the doctrine of equivalents out of existence any time it chooses. The various policy arguments now made by both sides are thus best addressed to Congress, not this Court.

B

We do, however, share the concern of the dissenters below that the doctrine of equivalents, as it has come to be applied since *Graver Tank*, has taken on a life of its own, unbounded by the patent claims. There can be no denying that the doctrine of equivalents, when applied broadly, conflicts with the definitional and public-notice functions of the statutory claiming requirement. Judge Nies identified one means of avoiding this conflict:

"[A] distinction can be drawn that is not too esoteric between substitution of an equivalent for a component in an invention and enlarging the metes and bounds of the invention beyond what is claimed.

. . . .

"Where a claim to an invention is expressed as a combination of elements, as here, 'equivalents' in the sobriquet 'Doctrine of Equivalents' refers to the equivalency of an element or part of the invention with one that is substituted in the accused product or process.

. . . .

"This view that the accused device or process must be more than 'equivalent' overall reconciles the Supreme Court's position on infringement by equivalents with its concurrent statements that 'the courts have no right to enlarge a patent beyond the scope of its claims as allowed by the Patent Office.' [Citations omitted.] The 'scope' is not enlarged if courts do not go beyond the substitution of equivalent elements." 62 F.3d, at 1573–1574 (Nies, J., dissenting) (emphasis in original).

We concur with this apt reconciliation of our two lines of precedent. Each element contained in a patent claim is deemed material to defining the scope of the patented invention, and thus the doctrine of equivalents must be applied to individual elements of the claim, not to the invention as a whole. It is important to ensure that the application of the doctrine, even as to an individual element, is not allowed such broad play as to effectively eliminate that element in its entirety. So long as the doctrine of equivalents does not encroach beyond the limits just described, or beyond related limits to be discussed infra, * * * we are confident that the doctrine will not vitiate the central functions of the patent claims themselves.

III

Understandably reluctant to assume this Court would overrule *Graver Tank,* petitioner has offered alternative arguments in favor of a more restricted doctrine of equivalents than it feels was applied in this case. We address each in turn.

A

Petitioner first argues that *Graver Tank* never purported to supersede a well-established limit on non-literal infringement, known variously as "prosecution history estoppel" and "file wrapper estoppel." See Bayer Aktiengesellschaft v. Duphar Int'l Research B.V., 738 F.2d 1237, 1238 (C.A. Fed. 1984). According to petitioner, any surrender of subject matter during patent prosecution, regardless of the reason for such surrender, precludes recapturing any part of that subject matter, even if it is equivalent to the matter expressly claimed. Because, during patent prosecution, respondent limited the pH element of its claim to pH levels between 6.0 and 9.0, petitioner would have those limits form bright lines beyond which no equivalents may be claimed. Any inquiry into the reasons for a surrender, petitioner claims, would undermine the public's right to clear notice of the scope of the patent as embodied in the patent file.

We can readily agree with petitioner that *Graver Tank* did not dispose of prosecution history estoppel as a legal limitation on the doctrine of equivalents. But petitioner reaches too far in arguing that the reason for an amendment during patent prosecution is irrelevant to any subsequent estoppel. In each of our cases cited by petitioner and by the dissent below, prosecution history estoppel was tied to amendments made to avoid the prior art, or otherwise to address a specific concern—such as obviousness—that arguably would have rendered the claimed subject matter unpatentable. Thus, in Exhibit Supply Co. v. Ace Patents Corp., Chief Justice Stone distinguished inclusion of a limiting phrase in an original patent claim from the "very different" situation in which "the applicant, in order to meet objections in the Patent Office, *based on references to the prior art*, adopted the phrase as a substitute for the broader one" previously used. 315 U.S. 126, 136 (1942) (emphasis added). Similarly, in Keystone Driller Co. v. Northwest Engineering Corp., 294 U.S. 42 (1935), estoppel was applied where the initial claims were "rejected on the prior art," id., at 48, n. 6, and where the allegedly infringing equivalent element was outside of the revised claims and within the prior art that formed the basis for the rejection of the earlier claims, id., at 48.

It is telling that in each case this Court probed the reasoning behind the Patent Office's insistence upon a change in the claims. In each instance, a change was demanded because the claim as otherwise written was viewed as not describing a patentable invention at all—typically because what it described was encompassed within the prior art. But, as the United States informs us, there are a variety of other reasons why the PTO may request a change in claim language. Brief for United States as Amicus Curiae 22–23 (counsel for the PTO also appearing on the brief). And if the PTO has been requesting changes in claim language without the intent to limit equivalents or, indeed, with the expectation that language it required would in many cases allow for a range of equivalents, we should be extremely reluctant to upset the basic assumptions of the PTO without substantial reason for doing so. Our prior cases have consistently applied prosecution history estoppel only where claims have been amended for a limited set of reasons, and we see no substantial cause for requiring a more rigid rule invoking an estoppel regardless of the reasons for a change.[6]

---

6. That petitioner's rule might provide a brighter line for determining whether a patentee is estopped under certain circumstances is not a sufficient reason for adopting such a rule. This is especially true where, as here, the PTO may have relied upon a flexible rule of estoppel when deciding whether to ask for a change in the first place. To change so substantially the rules of the game now could very well subvert the various balances the PTO sought to strike when issuing the numerous patents which have not yet expired and which would be affected by our decision.

In this case, the patent examiner objected to the patent claim due to a perceived overlap with the Booth patent, which revealed an ultrafiltration process operating at a pH above 9.0. In response to this objection, the phrase "at a pH from approximately 6.0 to 9.0" was added to the claim. While it is undisputed that the upper limit of 9.0 was added in order to distinguish the Booth patent, the reason for adding the lower limit of 6.0 is unclear. The lower limit certainly did not serve to distinguish the Booth patent, which said nothing about pH levels below 6.0. Thus, while a lower limit of 6.0, by its mere inclusion, became a material element of the claim, that did not necessarily preclude the application of the doctrine of equivalents as to that element. See Hubbell v. United States, 179 U.S. 77, 82 (1900) ("'[A]ll [specified elements] must be regarded as material,'" though it remains an open "'question whether an omitted part is supplied by an equivalent device or instrumentality'" (citation omitted)). Where the reason for the change was not related to avoiding the prior art, the change may introduce a new element, but it does not necessarily preclude infringement by equivalents of that element.[7]

We are left with the problem, however, of what to do in a case like the one at bar, where the record seems not to reveal the reason for including the lower pH limit of 6.0. In our view, holding that certain reasons for a claim amendment may avoid the application of prosecution history estoppel is not tantamount to holding that the absence of a reason for an amendment may similarly avoid such an estoppel. Mindful that claims do indeed serve both a definitional and a notice function, we think the better rule is to place the burden on the patent-holder to establish the reason for an amendment required during patent prosecution. The court then would decide whether that reason is sufficient to overcome prosecution history estoppel as a bar to application of the doctrine of equivalents to the element added by that amendment. Where no explanation is established, however, the court should presume that the PTO had a substantial reason related to patentability for including the limiting element added by amendment. In those circumstances, prosecution history estoppel would bar the application of the doctrine equivalents as to that element. The presumption we have described, one subject to rebuttal if an appropriate reason for a required amendment is established, gives proper deference to the role of claims in defining an invention and providing public notice, and to the primacy of the PTO in ensuring that the claims allowed cover only subject matter that is properly patentable in a proffered patent application. Applied in this fashion, prosecution history estoppel places reasonable limits on the doctrine of equivalents, and further insulates the doctrine from any feared conflict with the Patent Act.

---

7. We do not suggest that, where a change is made to overcome an objection based on the prior art, a court is free to review the correctness of that objection when deciding whether to apply prosecution history estoppel. As petitioner rightly notes, such concerns are properly addressed on direct appeal from the denial of a patent, and will not be revisited in an infringement action. Smith v. Magic City Kennel Club, Inc., supra, 282 U.S. at 789–790. What is permissible for a court to explore is the reason (right or wrong) for the objection and the manner in which the amendment addressed and avoided the objection.

Because respondent has not proffered in this Court a reason for the addition of a lower pH limit, it is impossible to tell whether the reason for that addition could properly avoid an estoppel. Whether a reason in fact exists, but simply was not adequately developed, we cannot say. On remand, the Federal Circuit can consider whether reasons for that portion of the amendment were offered or not and whether further opportunity to establish such reasons would be proper.

B

Petitioner next argues that even if *Graver Tank* remains good law, the case held only that the absence of substantial differences was a necessary element for infringement under the doctrine of equivalents, not that it was sufficient for such a result. Brief for Petitioner 32. Relying on *Graver Tank's* references to the problem of an "unscrupulous copyist" and "piracy," 339 U.S., at 607, petitioner would require judicial exploration of the equities of a case before allowing application of the doctrine of equivalents. To be sure, *Graver Tank* refers to the prevention of copying and piracy when describing the benefits of the doctrine of equivalents. That the doctrine produces such benefits, however, does not mean that its application is limited only to cases where those particular benefits are obtained.

Elsewhere in *Graver Tank* the doctrine is described in more neutral terms. And the history of the doctrine as relied upon by *Graver Tank* reflects a basis for the doctrine not so limited as petitioner would have it. In Winans v. Denmead, 15 How. 330, 343, 14 L.Ed. 717 (1854), we described the doctrine of equivalents as growing out of a legally implied term in each patent claim that "the claim extends to the thing patented, however its form or proportions may be varied." Under that view, application of the doctrine of equivalents involves determining whether a particular accused product or process infringes upon the patent claim, where the claim takes the form— half express, half implied—of "X and its equivalents."

Union Paper-Bag Machine Co. v. Murphy, 97 U.S. 120, 125 (1878), on which *Graver Tank* also relied, offers a similarly intent-neutral view of the doctrine of equivalents:

"[T]he substantial equivalent of a thing, in the sense of the patent law, is the same as the thing itself; so that if two devices do the same work in substantially the same way, and accomplish substantially the same result, they are the same, even though they differ in name, form, or shape."

If the essential predicate of the doctrine of equivalents is the notion of identity between a patented invention and its equivalent, there is no basis for treating an infringing equivalent any differently than a device that infringes the express terms of the patent. Application of the doctrine of equivalents, therefore, is akin to determining literal infringement, and neither requires proof of intent.

Petitioner also points to *Graver Tank's* seeming reliance on the absence of independent experimentation by the alleged infringer as supporting an equitable defense to the doctrine of equivalents. The Federal Circuit explained this factor by suggesting that an alleged infringer's behavior, be it copying, designing around a patent, or independent experimentation, indirectly reflects the substantiality of the differences between the patented invention and the accused device or process. According to the Federal Circuit, a person aiming to copy or aiming to avoid a patent is imagined to be at least marginally skilled at copying or avoidance, and thus intentional copying raises an inference—rebuttable by proof of independent development—of having only insubstantial differences, and intentionally designing around a patent claim raises an inference of substantial differences. This explanation leaves much to be desired. At a minimum, one wonders how ever to distinguish between the intentional copyist making minor changes to lower the risk of legal action, and the incremental innovator designing around the claims, yet seeking to capture as much as is permissible of the patented advance.

But another explanation is available that does not require a divergence from generally objective principles of patent infringement. In both instances in *Graver Tank* where we referred to independent research or experiments, we were discussing the known interchangeability between the chemical compound claimed in the patent and the compound substituted by the alleged infringer. The need for independent experimentation thus could reflect knowledge—or lack thereof—of interchangeability possessed by one presumably skilled in the art. The known interchangeability of substitutes for an element of a patent is one of the express objective factors noted by *Graver Tank* as bearing upon whether the accused device is substantially the same as the patented invention. Independent experimentation by the alleged infringer would not always reflect upon the objective question whether a person skilled in the art would have known of the interchangeability between two elements, but in many cases it would likely be probative of such knowledge.

Although *Graver Tank* certainly leaves room for petitioner's suggested inclusion of intent-based elements in the doctrine of equivalents, we do not read it as requiring them. The better view, and the one consistent with *Graver Tank's* predecessors and the objective approach to infringement, is that intent plays no role in the application of the doctrine of equivalents.

C

Finally, petitioner proposes that in order to minimize conflict with the notice function of patent claims, the doctrine of equivalents should be limited to equivalents that are disclosed within the patent itself. A milder version of this argument, which found favor with the dissenters below, is that the doctrine should be limited to equivalents that were known at the time the patent was issued, and should not extend to after-arising equivalents.

As we have noted, supra, * * * with regard to the objective nature of the doctrine, a skilled practitioner's knowledge of the interchangeability between claimed and accused elements is not relevant for its own sake, but rather for what it tells the fact-finder about the similarities or differences between those elements. Much as the perspective of the hypothetical "reasonable person" gives content to concepts such as "negligent" behavior, the perspective of a skilled practitioner provides content to, and limits on, the concept of "equivalence." Insofar as the question under the doctrine of equivalents is whether an accused element is equivalent to a claimed element, the proper time for evaluating equivalency—and thus knowledge of interchangeability between elements—is at the time of infringement, not at the time the patent was issued. And rejecting the milder version of petitioner's argument necessarily rejects the more severe proposition that equivalents must not only be known, but must also be actually disclosed in the patent in order for such equivalents to infringe upon the patent.

IV

The various opinions below, respondents, and amici devote considerable attention to whether application of the doctrine of equivalents is a task for the judge or for the jury. However, despite petitioner's argument below that the doctrine should be applied by the judge, in this Court petitioner makes only passing reference to this issue. See Brief for Petitioner 22, n. 15 ("If this Court were to hold in Markman v. Westview Instruments, Inc., No. 95–26, 1996 WL 12585 (argued Jan. 8, 1996), that judges rather than juries are to construe patent claims, so as to provide a uniform definition of the scope of the legally protected monopoly, it would seem at cross-purposes to say that juries may nonetheless expand the claims by resort to a broad notion of 'equivalents'"); Reply Brief for Petitioner 20 (whether judge or jury should apply the doctrine of equivalents depends on how the Court views the nature of the inquiry under the doctrine of equivalents).

Petitioner's comments go more to the alleged inconsistency between the doctrine of equivalents and the claiming requirement than to the role of the jury in applying the doctrine as properly understood. Because resolution of whether, or how much of, the application of the doctrine of equivalents can be resolved by the court is not necessary for us to answer the question presented, we decline to take it up. The Federal Circuit held that it was for the jury to decide whether the accused process was equivalent to the claimed process. There was ample support in our prior cases for that holding. See, e.g., Union Paper-Bag Machine Co. v. Murphy, 97 U.S., at 125 ("in determining the question of infringement, the court or jury, as the case may be, . . . are to look at the machines or their several devices or elements in the light of what they do, or what office or function they perform, and how they perform it, and to find that one thing is substantially the same as another, if it performs substantially the same function in substantially the same way to obtain the same result"); Winans v. Denmead, 15 How., at 344 ("[It] is a question for the jury" whether the accused device was "the same in kind, and effected by the employment of [the patentee's] mode of operation in substance"). Nothing in our recent *Markman* decision necessitates a different result than that reached by the Federal Circuit. Indeed, *Markman* cites with considerable favor, when discussing the role of judge and jury, the seminal *Winans* decision. Markman v. Westview Instruments, Inc., 116 S.Ct. 1384, 1392–1393 (1996). Whether, if the issue were squarely presented to us, we would reach a different conclusion than did the Federal Circuit is not a question we need decide today.[8]

V

All that remains is to address the debate regarding the linguistic framework under which "equivalence" is determined. Both the parties and the Federal Circuit spend considerable time arguing whether the so-called "triple identity" test—focusing on the function served by a particular claim element, the way that element serves that function, and the result thus obtained by that element—is a suitable method for determining equivalence, or whether an "insubstantial differences" approach is better. There seems to be substantial agreement that, while the triple identity test may be suitable for analyzing mechanical devices, it often provides a poor framework for analyzing other products or processes. On the other hand, the insubstantial differences test offers little additional guidance as to what might render any given difference "insubstantial."

In our view, the particular linguistic framework used is less important than whether the test is probative of the essential inquiry: Does the accused product or process contain elements identical or equivalent to each claimed element of the patented invention? Different linguistic frameworks may be more suitable to different cases, depending on their particular facts. A focus on individual elements and a special vigilance against allowing the concept of equivalence to eliminate completely any such elements should reduce considerably the imprecision of whatever language is used. An analysis of the role played by each element in the context of the specific patent claim will thus inform the inquiry as to whether a substitute element matches the function, way, and result of the claimed element, or whether the substitute element plays a role substantially different from the claimed element. With these limiting principles as a backdrop, we see no purpose in going further and micromanaging the Federal Circuit's particular word-choice for analyzing equivalence. We expect that the Federal Circuit will refine the formulation of the test for equivalence in the orderly course of case-by-case determinations,

---

8. With regard to the concern over unreviewability due to black-box jury verdicts, we offer only guidance, not a specific mandate. Where the evidence is such that no reasonable jury could determine two elements to be equivalent, district courts are obliged to grant partial or complete summary judgment. See Fed. Rule Civ. Proc. 56; Celotex Corp. v. Catrett, 477 U.S. 317, 322–323 (1986). If there has been a reluctance to do so by some courts due to unfamiliarity with the subject matter, we are confident that the Federal Circuit can remedy the problem. Of course, the various legal limitations on the application of the doctrine of equivalents are to be determined by the court, either on a pretrial motion for partial summary judgment or on a motion for judgment as a matter of law at the close of the evidence and after the jury verdict. Fed. Rule Civ. Proc. 56; Fed. Rule Civ. Proc. 50. Thus, under the particular facts of a case, if prosecution history estoppel would apply or if a theory of equivalence would entirely vitiate a particular claim element, partial or complete judgment should be rendered by the court, as there would be no further material issue for the jury to resolve. Finally, in cases that reach the jury, a special verdict and/or interrogatories on each claim element could be very useful in facilitating review, uniformity, and possibly postverdict judgments as a matter of law. See Fed. Rule Civ. Proc. 49; Fed. Rule Civ. Proc. 50. We leave it to the Federal Circuit how best to implement procedural improvements to promote certainty, consistency, and reviewability to this area of the law.

and we leave such refinement to that court's sound judgment in this area of its special expertise.

VI

Today we adhere to the doctrine of equivalents. The determination of equivalence should be applied as an objective inquiry on an element-by-element basis. Prosecution history estoppel continues to be available as a defense to infringement, but if the patent-holder demonstrates that an amendment required during prosecution had a purpose unrelated to patentability, a court must consider that purpose in order to decide whether an estoppel is precluded. Where the patentholder is unable to establish such a purpose, a court should presume that the purpose behind the required amendment is such that prosecution history estoppel would apply. Because the Court of Appeals for the Federal Circuit did not consider all of the requirements as described by us today, particularly as related to prosecution history estoppel and the preservation of some meaning for each element in a claim, we reverse and remand for further proceedings consistent with this opinion.

It is so ordered.

■ JUSTICE GINSBURG, with whom JUSTICE KENNEDY joins, concurring.

I join the opinion of the Court and write separately to add a cautionary note on the rebuttable presumption the Court announces regarding prosecution history estoppel. I address in particular the application of the presumption in this case and others in which patent prosecution has already been completed. The new presumption, if applied woodenly, might in some instances unfairly discount the expectations of a patentee who had no notice at the time of patent prosecution that such a presumption would apply. Such a patentee would have had little incentive to insist that the reasons for all modifications be memorialized in the file wrapper as they were made. Years after the fact, the patentee may find it difficult to establish an evidentiary basis that would overcome the new presumption. The Court's opinion is sensitive to this problem, noting that "the PTO may have relied upon a flexible rule of estoppel when deciding whether to ask for a change" during patent prosecution. Ante, at 1050, n. 6.

Because respondent has not presented to this Court any explanation for the addition of the lower pH limit, I concur in the decision to remand the matter to the Federal Circuit. On remand, that court can determine—bearing in mind the prior absence of clear rules of the game—whether suitable reasons for including the lower pH limit were earlier offered or, if not, whether they can now be established.

NOTE

Mr. Justice Jackson's opinion in *Graver Tank* observed that the doctrine of equivalents may be applied against, as well as for, the patentee. This was a reference to decisions which find that a literal infringement is *not* infringement because the infringing device is really quite different. This is called "the reverse doctrine of equivalents."

The reverse doctrine of equivalents was applied in Scripps Clinic & Research Foundation v. Genentech, Inc., 927 F.2d 1565 (Fed. Cir. 1991). Scripps owned a patent on the product human blood Factor VIII:C, necessary for clotting, obtained through purification. Genentech wished to make the same product through the use of recombinant DNA technology. The Scripps patents contained claims, obtained in a reissue proceeding, covering Factor VIII:C. Genentech argued that its Factor VIII:C did not infringe under the reverse doctrine of equivalents. The trial court entered summary judgment of infringement. The court reversed and remanded to the trial court for further fact finding on issues such as whether there are any differences between the two products and the differences in the technologies. "Application of the doctrine requires that facts specific to the accused device be determined and weighted against the equitable scope of the claims, which in turn is determined in light of the specification, the prosecution history, and the prior art." 927 F.2d 1581.

PROBLEMS

1. Corning pioneered the development of optical waveguide fibers, which are used in modern telecommunications to guide light beams generated by lasers over long distances. Corning received a patent on an optical waveguide fiber made from silica (a chemical found in sand which is used to make glass) in which the fiber consisted of a core combined with a dopant that raised the refractive index and a cladding which was undoped. The difference in the refractive index between the core and the cladding creates a reflective surface at the boundary between the core and the cladding which guides the light down the fiber. A Japanese company developed an optical waveguide fiber in which the cladding was doped to lower the refractive index of the cladding, creating the same effect. Does the Japanese fiber infringe the Corning patent?

2. A patent issues on a fruit sorting machine, which sorts fruit by size and color. The machine has a scale and an optical sensor. It is hard-wired so that it opens and closes gates that route the fruit along the appropriate channel depending on its measured size and color. Defendant develops a device that performs the same functions, but instead of using hard-wired circuitry, the readings from the scale and the optical sensor are sent to a general-purpose digital computer, which then determines the appropriate gates to open or close. Does the defendant's device infringe the patent?

----

(6) Absent Exhaustion of the Right

Keeler v. Standard Folding-Bed Co.

Supreme Court of the United States, 1895.
157 U.S. 659, 15 S.Ct. 738, 39 L.Ed. 848.

■ MR. JUSTICE SHIRAS delivered the opinion of the court.

* * * [The defendant purchased a carload of wardrobe bedsteads in the state of Michigan, brought them to Boston and are engaged in reselling

them there. The wardrobe bedsteads were of a design covered by a patent. The plaintiff is the exclusive licensee of the patent for the state of Massachusetts. The firm that sold the bedsteads to the defendant is the exclusive licensee of the patent for the state of Michigan. The plaintiff sued defendant for infringement, and prevailed in the circuit court below.]

Where the patentee has not parted, by assignment, with any of his original rights, but chooses himself to make and vend a patented article of manufacture, it is obvious that a purchaser can use the article in any part of the United States, and, unless restrained by contract with the patentee, can sell or dispose of the same. It has passed outside of the monopoly, and is no longer under the peculiar protection granted to patented rights. As was said by Mr. Justice Clifford in Goodyear v. Rubber Co., 1 Cliff. 348, Fed. Cas. No. 5,557: "Having manufactured the material and sold it for a satisfactory compensation, whether as material or in the form of a manufactured article, the patentee, so far as that product of his invention is concerned, has enjoyed all the rights secured to him by his letters patent, and the manufactured article and the material of which it is composed go to the purchaser for a valuable consideration, discharged of all the rights of the patentee previously attached to it or impressed upon it by the act of congress under which the patent was granted."

Suppose, however, the patentee has exercised his statutory right of assigning by conveying to another an exclusive right under the patent to a specified part of the United States. What are the rights of a purchaser of patented articles from the patentee himself within the territory reserved to him? Does he thereby obtain an absolute property in the article, so that he can use and vend it in all parts of the United States, or, if he take the article into the assigned territory, must he again pay for the privilege of using and selling it? If, as is often the case, the patentee has divided the territory of the United States into 20 or more "specified parts," must a person who has bought and paid for the patented article in one part, from the vender having an exclusive right to make and vend therein, on removing from one part of the country to another, pay to the local assignee for the privilege of using and selling his property, or else be subjected to an action for damages as a wrongdoer? And is there any solid distinction to be made, in such a case, between the right to use and the right to sell? Can the owner of the patented article hold and deal with it the same as in case of any other description of property belonging to him, and, on his death, does it pass, with the rest of his personal estate, to his legal representatives, and thus, as a part of the assets to be administered, become liable to be sold?

These are questions which, although already in effect answered by this court in more cases than one, are now to be considered in the state of facts disclosed in this record.

* * *

* * * [In] Adams v. Burke, 17 Wall. 453 * * * Lockhart and Seelye owned, by assignment, all the right, title, and interest which the patentees had in a certain patented coffin lid, in a circular district of a diameter of 10 miles, whereof the city of Boston was the center. Adams, also by assignment, was the

owner of all other rights under the patent. Burke, an undertaker, carried on his business at Natick, and within the territory covered by the patent as owned by Adams. To a bill for an infringement, filed by Adams in the circuit court of the United States for the district of Massachusetts, Burke pleaded that the patented coffins used by him in his business were purchased by him from Lockhart and Seelye, and were sold to him without condition or restriction.

The validity of this plea was sustained by the circuit court, and its decree dismissing the bill was affirmed by this court.

Mr. Justice Miller, in giving the opinion of the court, said: "In the essential nature of things, when the patentee, or the person having his right, sells a machine or instrument whose sole value is in its use, he receives in consideration for its use, and he parts with the right to restrict that use. The article, in the language of the court, passes without the limit of the monopoly; that is to say, the patentee or his assignee having in the act of sale received all the royalty or consideration which he claims for the use of his invention in that particular machine or instrument, it is open to the use of the purchaser without further restriction on account of the monopoly of the patentee. * * * A careful examination of the plea satisfies us that the defendant, who, as an undertaker, purchased each of these coffins, and used it in burying the body which he was employed to bury, acquired the right to this use of it, freed from any claim of the patentee, though purchased within the ten-mile circle and used without it."

It is obvious that necessarily the use made by Burke of these coffins involved a sale in every case. He did not put them to his personal use, unless we are permitted to suppose that he was himself buried in each one of the coffins. He bought the coffins for the purpose of selling them to others, and the legal significance of the decision upholding his defense is that a person who buys patented articles from a person who has a right to sell, though within a restricted territory, has a right to use and sell such articles in all and any part of the United States; that, when the royalty had once been paid to a party entitled to receive it, the patented article then becomes the absolute, unrestricted property of the purchaser, with the right to sell it as an essential incident of such ownership.

That this was the meaning of this decision not only appears from the language used, and from the necessary legal effect of the conclusion reached as between the parties, but from the dissenting opinion of Justice Bradley, whose reasoning went wholly upon the assumption that such was its meaning.

Boesch v. Graff, 133 U.S. 698, is cited by the defendant in error. But it is not out of line with the previous cases. The exact question presented was whether a dealer residing in the United States could purchase in another country articles patented there from a person authorized there to sell them, and import them to and sell them in the United States without the license or consent of the owners of the United States patent, and the court held that the sale of articles in the United States under a United States patent cannot be controlled by foreign laws. In this case neither the patentee nor any assignee had ever received any royalty or given any license to use the patented article in any part of the United States.

* * *

This brief history of the cases shows that in Wilson v. Rousseau, 4 How. 688, and cases following it, it was held that as between the owner of a patent, on the one side, and a purchaser of an article made under the patent, on the other, the payment of a royalty once, or, what is the same thing, the purchase of the article from one authorized by the patentee to sell it, emancipates such article from any further subjection to the patent throughout the entire life of the patent, even if the latter should be by law subsequently extended beyond the term existing at the time of the sale, and that, in respect of the time of enjoyment, by those decisions the right of the purchaser, his assigns or legal representatives, is clearly established to be entirely free from any further claim of the patentee or any assignee; that in Adams v. Burke, 17 Wall. 453, it was held that as respects the place of enjoyment, and as between the purchaser of patented articles in one specified part of the territory and the assignee of the patent of another part, the right once legitimately acquired to hold, use, and sell will protect such purchaser from any further subjection to the monopoly; that in Hobbie v. Jennison, 149 U.S. 355, it was held that, as between assignees of different parts of the territory, it is competent for one to sell the patented articles to persons who intend, with the knowledge of the vender, to take them for use into the territory of the other.

Upon the doctrine of these cases, we think it follows that one who buys patented articles of manufacture from one authorized to sell them becomes possessed of an absolute property in such articles, unrestricted in time or place. Whether a patentee may protect himself and his assignees by special contracts brought home to the purchasers is not a question before us, and upon which we express no opinion. It is, however, obvious that such a question would arise as a question of contract, and not as one under the inherent meaning and effect of the patent laws.

The conclusion reached does not deprive a patentee of his just rights, because no article can be unfettered from the claim of his monopoly without paying its tribute. The inconvenience and annoyance to the public that an opposite conclusion would occasion are too obvious to require illustration.

* * *

The decree of the court below is reversed, and the cause remanded, with directions to dismiss the bill.

Reversed.

NOTES

1. The issue addressed in *Keeler* is an issue of patent law. After an authorized first sale, the patent owner or his successors in interest cannot sue the purchaser for infringement, even if the sale was conditional. But the fact that the patent owner cannot sue the purchaser for infringement is separate from the question of whether he could sue the first seller both for breach of the licensing contract and for infringement itself, as well as sue a purchaser who knew of the license restriction for inducing a breach of contract.

2. A system of exclusive distribution territories can be created by contract. A licensee who had promised not to make sales outside a licensed territory and who did so would be violating the contract and subject to an action for breach of contract. Thus a company might be licensed to manufacture a product and to sell it to persons who are purchasing for their own use and who are resident in the state, and breach of the agreement might be enjoinable on the ground that the damages flowing from a breach would be difficult to prove and hence an inadequate remedy. Exclusive distribution arrangements such as these have frequently been challenged as unreasonable restraints of trade under the antitrust laws. In United States v. Arnold, Schwinn & Co., 388 U.S. 365 (1967), the Court held that a system of exclusive distribution territories created by a manufacturer through clauses in its dealer agreements was a *per se* violation of the Sherman antitrust act. *Schwinn* was overruled in Continental T.V., Inc. v. GTE Sylvania Inc., 433 U.S. 36 (1977), which held that such restraints were to be analyzed under a "rule of reason." Under the rule of reason, arrangements which serve legitimate commercial objectives of the contracting parties generally will be upheld. Although neither case involved a patented product, the same rule would seem to apply to distribution contracts for a patented as for an unpatented product.

In United States v. Studiengesellschaft Kohle, 670 F.2d 1122 (D.C. Cir. 1981), the court followed *Continental T.V.* in using a rule of reason analysis to test the legality under the antitrust laws of restrictions in a license to practice a process patent which restricted the licensee to producing for its own use. The restrictions were upheld.

3. The owner of a patented machine acquired from the patentee or a licensee is entitled to use the machine, and that includes the right to make regular and necessary repairs. The owner, cannot, however, engage in a reconstruction, building a new machine from components obtained from the old one. The distinction between the permissible repair and the prohibited reconstruction is an issue in many reported cases. For instance in *Aro I* (Aro Mfg. Co. v. Convertible Top Co., 365 U.S. 336 (1961)), discussed in the *Dawson* opinion, supra, the issue was whether replacing a worn out convertible top was a repair or a reconstruction of a patented combination claim on the fabric top and associated structure. The Court held that it was a repair. An example of a decision finding a reconstruction is Monroe Auto Equip. Co. v. Precision Rebuilders, Inc., 229 F.Supp. 347 (D. Kan. 1964), which held that it was reconstruction to rebuild worn out shock absorbers.

Met-Coil Systems Corp. v. Korners Unlimited, Inc.

United States Court of Appeals, Federal Circuit, 1986.
803 F.2d 684.

■ NIES, CIRCUIT JUDGE.

The determinative issue in this appeal is whether a patent owner's unrestricted sale of a machine useful only in practicing the claimed [process] inventions presumptively carries with it an implied license under the patent [to use components purchased from others required to practice the patented process]. The United States District Court for the Western District of Pennsylvania decided that legal issue in the affirmative. We affirm.

I.

Met-Coil Systems Corp. is the assignee of U.S. Patent No. 4,466,641, which claims an apparatus and method for connecting sections of metal ducts of the kind used in heating and air conditioning systems. Under the claimed inventions, the ends of the metal duct sections are bent to form integral flanges, specially shaped corner pieces are snapped in place, and the sections are bolted together. Met-Coil makes and sells roll-forming machines that its customers use to bend integral flanges in the ends of metal ducts so as to practice the claimed inventions. Met-Coil also sells the specially shaped corner pieces for use with the integral flanges. Korners Unlimited, Inc. makes corner pieces for use with Met-Coil's integral flanges and sells them to purchasers of Met-Coil's machines. Met-Coil sued Korners for inducing infringement of claims 1–12, 14–25 of its patent. Korners moved for summary judgment.

The basis of Korners' motion for summary judgment was that Met-Coil, by selling the roll-forming machine, granted an implied license under the patent to its customers. Because of that license, Korners contended, Met-Coil's customers cannot infringe the claims of the patent and, thus, Korners can neither induce infringement nor contributorily infringe. Met-Coil, on the other hand, contended that its sales of the machines do not confer an implied license under the patent upon its customers.

II.

The district court recognized that "[t]he integral flanges are an essential part of Met-Coil's patented duct connecting system" and that the "flanges have no use other than in the practice of the duct connecting system." Applying the holding of United States v. Univis Lens Co., 316 U.S. 241 (1942), to those facts, the court held that purchasers of Met-Coil's machines enjoyed an implied license under the patent.

In *Univis,* the patent covered multifocal eyeglass lenses, and the patent owner sold blank eyeglass lenses to its licensees. The Court held that the sale of the blanks carried a license to complete the lenses:

"But in any case it is plain that where the sale of the blank is by the patentee or his licensee—here the Lens Company—to a finisher, the only use to which it could be put and the only object of the sale is to enable the latter to grind and polish it for use as a lens by the prospective wearer. An incident to the purchase of any article, whether patented or unpatented, is the right to use and sell it, and upon familiar principles the authorized sale of an article which is capable of use only in practicing the patent is a relinquishment of the patent monopoly with respect to the article sold. Leitch Mfg. Co. v. Barber Co., 302 U.S. 458, 460–61 (1938); B.B. Chemical Co. v. Ellis, 314 U.S. 495 (1942). Sale of a lens blank by the patentee or by his licensee is thus in itself both a complete transfer of ownership of the blank, which is within the protection of the patent law, and a license to practice the final stage of the patent procedure.

". . . (W)here one has sold an uncompleted article which, because it embodies essential features of his patented invention, is within the protection of his patented invention, and has destined the article to be finished by the purchaser in conformity to the patent, he has sold his invention so far as it is or may be embodied in that particular article. The reward he has demanded and received is for the article and the invention which it embodies and which his vendee is to practice upon it."

316 U.S. at 249–51. The trial court recognized that Univis was factually distinct from the instant case, but found the distinction to be of no effect:

"It should be noted, however, that unlike Univis . . . , the practice of the final stage of Met-Coil's patented system requires not just "finishing" the element sold, i.e. forming the integral flanges, but also the purchase of an additional element of the patented system, i.e. the corner pieces. Met-Coil cites no authority which suggests that this difference takes the present case out of the rule of Univis.

Met-Coil appealed the district court's judgment of noninfringement to this court.

III.

On appeal, Met-Coil urges that the district court erred in relying on *Univis*. To support that proposition, Met-Coil cites Bandag, Inc. v. Al Bolser's Tire Stores, Inc., 750 F.2d 903 (Fed. Cir. 1984). In that case, the owner of a patent claiming a method for retreading tires sued a retreader who had purchased retreading equipment from a former licensee of the patent owner. This court set out two requirements for the grant of an implied license by virtue of a sale of nonpatented equipment used to practice a patented invention. First, the equipment involved must have no noninfringing uses. Id. at 924. In *Bandag,* the retreading equipment had noninfringing uses, so no license could be implied. To the contrary, Met-Coil's machines have no noninfringing use. Second, the circumstances of the sale must "plainly indicate that the grant of a license should be inferred." Id. at 925, quoting Hunt v. Armour & Co., 185 F.2d 722, 729 (7th Cir. 1950). The circumstances of the sale in *Bandag,* purchase of the equipment from the former licensee of the patent owner, did not plainly indicate that the grant of a license should be inferred.

Met-Coil contends that this case does not meet the two-part test set out in *Bandag,* that is, although the machines sold have no noninfringing use, the circumstances do not plainly indicate that the grant of a license should be inferred. In this connection Met-Coil introduced certain written notices to customers with respect to the purchase of corner pieces from unlicensed sources.[4] Met-Coil relies on cases holding that no implied license arises where the original sale was accompanied by an express notice negating the

---

4. Met-Coil's subsidiary Iowa Precision Industries, Inc. sent a letter to owners of Lockformer machines and distributors of Iowa Precision's corner pieces, notifying them that "as long as you are a customer of ours, you are automatically licensed to use the (claimed invention) insofar as your use involves forming rolls and corners purchased from us but not from other unauthorized sources."

grant of an implied license. Radio Corp. of America v. Andrea, 90 F.2d 612, 615 (2d Cir. 1937); General Electric Co. v. Continental Lamp Works, Inc., 280 F. 846, 851 (2d Cir. 1922). Those cases, however, are inapposite. Met-Coil does not assert that its customers were notified at the time of the sale of the machine. Rather, the customers were notified after they purchased the machine. The subsequent notices are not a part of the circumstances at the time of the sale, when the implied license would have arisen. After the fact notices are of no use in ascertaining the intent of Met-Coil and its customers at the time of the sales. * * *

Met-Coil urges that, even though it has not shown that the sales were accompanied by an express disclaimer of license, Korners has not met its burden of proof. As the alleged infringer, Korners has the burden of showing the establishment of an implied license. *Bandag*, 750 F.2d at 924. We agree with the district court that Korners met that burden. A patent owner's unrestricted sales of a machine useful only in performing the claimed process and producing the claimed product "plainly indicate that the grant of a license should be inferred." Korners established a prima facie case, thereby shifting the burden of going forward to Met-Coil. Met-Coil offered nothing to carry its burden. Absent any circumstances tending to show the contrary, we see no error in the district court's holding that Met-Coil's customers enjoyed an implied license under the patent.[5]

The sole disputed issue decided by the trial court, the existence of an implied license, is a question of law. See *Bandag*, 750 F.2d at 926 ("the conclusion of the district court that an implied license of the Carver patent was extended to Bolser"); AMP, Inc. v. United States, 389 F.2d 448, 451 n. 3 (Ct. Cl. 1968) ("the legal issue of implied license"). The parties raised no genuine issue of material fact. Because of our affirmance of the district court's holding that Met-Coil's customers enjoyed an implied license to practice the inventions claimed in Met-Coil's patent, there can be no direct infringement under the facts of this case. Absent direct infringement of the patent claims, there can be neither contributory infringement, Porter v. Farmers Supply Service, Inc., 790 F.2d 882, 884 (Fed. Cir. 1986), nor inducement of infringement, Stukenborg v. Teledyne, Inc., 441 F.2d 1069, 1072 (9th Cir. 1971). Therefore, Korners was entitled to summary judgment of noninfringement as a matter of law. Accordingly, we affirm the judgment of the district court.

Affirmed.

———

5. Because our review is limited to the case before us, we emphasize that this case does not involve sales accompanied by a notice expressly precluding the grant of a license under the patent. Nor do we express any opinion on the legality of requiring the combined purchase of a machine and corner pieces. Moreover, our affirmance of the district court's holding that Met-Coil's customers enjoy an implied license prevents us from reaching the arguments raised by Met-Coil as to why Korners' sales are infringing.

General Talking Pictures Corp. v. Western Electric Co.

Supreme Court of the United States, 1938.
305 U.S. 124, 59 S.Ct. 116, 83 L.Ed. 81.

■ MR. JUSTICE BRANDEIS delivered the opinion of the Court.

In this case, we affirmed on May 2, 1938 (304 U.S. 175), the judgment of the Circuit Court of Appeals (2 Cir., 91 F.2d 922), which held that petitioner had infringed certain patents relating to vacuum tube amplifiers. On May 31st, we granted a rehearing, upon the following questions which had been presented by the petition for certiorari.

1. Can the owner of a patent, by means thereof, restrict the use made of a device manufactured under the patent, after the device has passed into the hands of a purchaser in the ordinary channels of trade, and full consideration paid therefor?

2. Can a patent owner, merely by a "license notice" attached to a device made under the patent, and sold in the ordinary channels of trade, place an enforceable restriction on the purchaser thereof as to the use to which the purchaser may put the device?

Upon further hearing we are of opinion that neither question should be answered. For we find that, while the devices embody the inventions of the patents in suit, they were not manufactured or sold "under the patent[s]" and did not "pass into the hands of a purchaser in the ordinary channels of trade."

These are the relevant facts. Amplifiers embodying the invention here involved are useful in several distinct fields. Among these is (a) the commercial field of sound recording and reproducing, which embraces talking picture equipment for theatres, and (b) the private or home field, which embraces radio broadcast reception, radio amateur reception and radio experimental reception. For the commercial field exclusive licenses had been granted by the patent pool to Western Electric Company and Electrical Research Products, Inc. For the private or home field the patent pool granted non-exclusive licenses to about fifty manufacturers. Among these was American Transformer Company. It was licensed

> "solely and only to the extent and for the uses hereinafter specified and defined * * * to manufacture * * *, and to sell * * * only for radio amateur reception, radio experimental reception and radio broadcast reception * * * licensed apparatus so manufactured by the Licensee. * * * "

The license provided further:

> "Nothing herein contained shall be regarded as conferring upon the Licensee either expressly or by estoppel, implication or otherwise, a license to manufacture or sell, any apparatus except such as may be manufactured by the Licensee in accordance with the express provision of this Agreement."

Transformer Company, knowing that it had not been licensed to manufacture or to sell amplifiers for use in theatres as part of talking picture equipment, made for that commercial use the amplifiers in controversy and sold them to Pictures Corporation for that commercial use. Pictures Corporation ordered the amplifiers and purchased them knowing that Transformer Company had not been licensed to make or sell them for such use in theatres. Any use beyond the valid terms of a license is, of course, an infringement of a patent. Robinson on Patents, § 916. If where a patented invention is applicable to different uses, the owner of the patent may legally restrict a licensee to a particular field and exclude him from others, Transformer Company was guilty of an infringement when it made the amplifiers for, and sold them to, Pictures Corporation. And as Pictures Corporation ordered, purchased and leased them knowing the facts, it also was an infringer.

The question of law requiring decision is whether the restriction in the license is to be given effect. That a restrictive license is legal seems clear. Mitchell v. Hawley, 16 Wall. 544, 21 L.Ed. 322. As was said in United States v. General Electric Co., 272 U.S. 476, 489, the patentee may grant a license "upon any condition the performance of which is reasonably within the reward which the patentee by the grant of the patent is entitled to secure." The restriction here imposed is of that character. The practice of granting licenses for a restricted use is an old one, see Providence Rubber Company v. Goodyear, 9 Wall. 788, 799, 800, 19 L.Ed. 566; Gamewall Fire-Alarm Telegraph Co. v. Brooklyn, C.C., 14 F. 255. So far as appears, its legality has never been questioned. The parties stipulated that

> "it is common practice where a patented invention is applicable to different uses, to grant written licenses to manufacture under United States Letters Patents restricted to one or more of the several fields of use permitting the exclusive or non-exclusive use of the invention by the licensee in one field and excluding it in another field."

As the restriction was legal and the amplifiers were made and sold outside the scope of the license, the effect is precisely the same as if no license whatsoever had been granted to Transformer Company. And as Pictures Corporation knew the facts, it is in no better position than if it had manufactured the amplifiers itself without a license. It is liable because it has used the invention without license to do so.

We have consequently no occasion to consider what the rights of the parties would have been if the amplifier had been manufactured "under the patent" and "had passed into the hands of a purchaser in the ordinary channels of trade." Nor have we occasion to consider the effect of a "licensee's notice" which purports to restrict the use of articles lawfully sold.

Affirmed.

NOTES

1. Why did the sale of the amplifiers by the Transformer Company not "exhaust" the patent right so that the purchaser Talking Pictures Corporation was entitled to use them in any manner it wished? It is true

that Pictures Corporation knew of the restriction, and thus might be liable for inducing Transformer Company to breach its contract with Western Electric, but the case involves only an action for patent infringement. In spite of the tension between *Talking Pictures* and *Keeler*, *Talking Pictures* continues to be regarded as good law in the lower courts.

2. One way to eliminate the tension is to read *Keeler* as resting only on a construction of an implied license, a result subject to change by a supervening explicit agreement with different terms. Note that the Federal Circuit in *Met–Coil* implies that an explicit contractual restriction might have been effective to change the result in that case. But such a construction is not consistent with the facts of *Keeler*, is it?

3. Does the notion that the patent owner is entitled to only one reward before the patent right is exhausted make any sense? Can a patent owner lease instead of sell machines, and set a lease royalty rate based on the duration of the lease or the number of times the machine is used? The answer is yes. But why isn't each lease payment beyond the first more than "one" reward? Isn't the answer that the scope of the reward turns on what the payer of the reward has bargained for?

4. Isn't the common sense concern of *Keeler* a concern about the position of innocent purchasers in a world where goods were frequently sold with limited licenses? But couldn't this problem be resolved by implying an unlimited license unless the purchaser has reasonable notice of a limited license? Would it be adequate notice to place a plate upon the machine or folding bed carrying the following legend: "Only the immediate purchaser from the original manufacturer or its licensees is licensed to use this [bed, machine, etc.]. Others may purchase licenses to use by writing to: [*here insert name and address of patentee*]." Would you buy something subject to such a restriction?

* * *

K. Protection of Inventors
Roberts v. Sears, Roebuck and Co.

United States Court of Appeals, Seventh Circuit, 1978.
573 F.2d 976.

■ SPRECHER, CIRCUIT JUDGE.

The major issues in this case are whether the district court properly declined to decide the validity of plaintiff's patent in a suit for fraud, breach of a confidential relationship and negligent misrepresentation in defendant's procurement of an assignment of plaintiff's patent rights and whether the district court properly concluded that plaintiff had elected his legal remedies and, therefore, was barred from seeking his equitable remedies of rescission and restitution.

I

This case involves the efforts of one of this nation's largest retail companies, Sears, Roebuck & Co. (Sears), to acquire through deceit the monetary benefits of an invention of a new type of socket wrench created by one of its sales clerks during his off-duty hours. That sales clerk, Peter M. Roberts (Plaintiff), initiated the unfortunate events that led to this appeal in 1963, when at the age of 18 he began work on a ratchet or socket wrench that would permit the easy removal of the sockets from the wrench. He, in fact, designed and constructed a prototype tool with a quick-release feature in it that succeeded in permitting its user to change sockets with one hand. Based on that prototype, plaintiff filed an application for a United States patent. In addition, since he was in the employ of Sears, a company that sold over a million wrenches per year, and since he had only a high school education and no business experience, he decided to show his invention to the manager of the Sears store in Gardner, Massachusetts where he worked. Plaintiff was persuaded to submit formally his invention as a suggestion to Sears. In May 1964, the prototype, along with a completed suggestion form, was sent to Sears' main office in Chicago, Illinois. Plaintiff, thereafter, left Sears' employ when his parents moved to Tennessee.

It was from this point on that Sears' conduct became the basis for the jury's determination that Sears appropriated the value of the plaintiff's invention by fraudulent means. Plaintiff's evidence proved that Sears took steps to ascertain the utility of the invention and that based on the information it acquired, Sears became convinced that the invention was in fact valuable. Sears had two sets of tests run on plaintiff's wrench by its custom manufacturer of wrenches, Moore Drop Forging Co. (Moore). The first test was conducted in July 1964, and it proved that the wrench operated normally and that the quick-release feature did not substantially weaken the structure of the wrench. The second test, conducted in May 1965, showed that actual mechanics liked the quick-release feature. Moore reported the results of these tests to Sears.

Based presumably on these tests, and the expert opinion of its senior tool buyer, Arthur Griesbaum, Sears in March 1965, had Moore design a fine-tooth wrench with the quick-release feature built into it. In addition, at about the same time, Sears put in motion plans to incorporate the quick-release feature into then-existing wrench models that constituted 74.27 percent of all the wrenches Sears sold. Thus, by early 1965, it was clear to Sears that this invention was very useful and probably would be quite profitable.

Sears also received reports from Moore regarding the manufacturing cost of plaintiff's quick-release feature. In the initial prototype built by Moore, the cost was 44 cents per unit. By June of 1965, Sears had received a report indicating that the cost could be reduced to 20 cents per unit. Thus, early in 1965, Sears learned that the feature was relatively inexpensive to manufacture.

Sears also took pains to ascertain the patentability of the quick-release feature. In April 1965, it received outside patent counsel's advice that there was "some basis for limited patentability" (defendant's Exhibit 9). It had previously learned in February 1965 from plaintiff's lawyer, Charles Fay, that he believed the invention was patentable based on a limited search. In addition, Sears was informed in early May 1965, by plaintiff's lawyer that a patent had been issued to plaintiff.[1]

With all of this information either available or soon to be available, Sears contacted plaintiff in January 1965, and began negotiations regarding the purchase of rights to use plaintiff's invention. During these negotiations, conducted with plaintiff's attorney, Sears' lawyer, Leonard Schram, made various representations to plaintiff that serve as the essential basis for plaintiff's complaint. In April 1965, in a letter seeking merely a license, Schram first told plaintiff that the invention was not new and that the claims in any patent that would be permitted would be "quite limited" (plaintiff's Exhibit 34). Second, Schram told plaintiff that the cost of the quick-release feature would be 40–50 cents. Third, he told plaintiff the feature would sell only to the extent it would be promoted and thus $10,000 was all that the feature was worth. Finally, and perhaps most ironically, Schram wrote to plaintiff that "[o]nce we have paid off the royalty expense, then we would probably take the amount previously allocated to said expense and use it for promotional expenses *if we desire to maintain sales on the item.*" (Emphasis added).

Based on this letter, plaintiff entered into the agreement on July 29, 1965, which provided for a two cent royalty per unit up to a maximum of $10,000 to be paid in return for a complete *assignment* of all of plaintiff's rights. In fact, for no extra charge, plaintiff's attorney gave Sears all of plaintiff's foreign patent rights. A provision was included in the contract regarding what would happen if Sears failed to sell 50,000 wrenches in a given year, thus reinforcing the impression that the wrenches might not sell very well. Also, a provision was inserted dealing with the contingency that a patent might not be issued, notwithstanding that Sears already knew, and plaintiff did not, that the patent had been granted.

By July, Sears knew that it planned to sell several hundred thousand wrenches with a cost per item increase of only 20 cents, that a patent had issued and that this product in all likelihood would have tremendous appeal with mechanics. Nonetheless, it entered into this agreement both having failed to disclose vital information about the product's appeal and structural utility and having made representations to plaintiff that were either false at the time they were made or became false without disclosure prior to the time of the signing of the contract.

Within days after the signing of the contract, Sears was manufacturing 44,000 of plaintiff's wrenches per week—all with plaintiff's patent number prominently stamped on them—and within three months, Sears was mar-

---

1. We might note here that Mr. Fay contacted Sears before informing plaintiff that a patent had issued. In addition, it was shown that Sears had contacted Mr. Fay during the period of these negotiations about doing some work for it and that he, in fact, did perform a couple of routine matters for Sears, thus raising some doubt about the independence of his advice to plaintiff.

keting them as a tremendous breakthrough. Within *nine months,* Sears had sold over 500,000 wrenches and paid plaintiff his maximum royalty thereby acquiring all of plaintiff's rights. Between 1965 and 1975, Sears sold in excess of 19 million wrenches, many at a premium of one to two dollars profit because no competition was able to market a comparable product for several years. To say the least, plaintiff's invention has been a commercial success.

Plaintiff, a Tennessee resident, filed suit against Sears, an Illinois Corporation, in federal district court in December 1969, based on diversity jurisdiction, seeking alternatively return of the patent and restitution or damages for fraud, breach of a confidential relationship and negligent misrepresentation. A jury trial was held from December 20, 1976, until January 18, 1977. During the trial, plaintiff basically proved the facts as presented above. Sears argued that it did not misrepresent any facts to plaintiff, that he had a lawyer and thus there was no confidential relationship and that the success of the wrenches was a function of advertising and the unforeseeable boom in do-it-yourself repairs, and thus Sears did not misrepresent the salability of plaintiff's wrenches. The jury was instructed on each of the three counts in plaintiff's complaint and told that it could award plaintiff profits for Counts I and II and could consider a reasonable royalty as a remedy for Count III. The jury apparently believed the plaintiff's evidence because it found Sears guilty on all three counts and entered judgment for one million dollars on each count, but the award was not cumulative.

Both parties filed post-trial motions. Sears filed for judgment NOV and plaintiff sought rescission of the contract and restitution. The district court denied both motions holding as to Sears' motion that the jury verdict was in accordance with the evidence and that the damages award was reasonable and holding as to plaintiff's motion that when he permitted the case to go to the jury he had elected his legal remedy and could not later also seek his equitable relief. Plaintiff appealed seeking equitable relief and Sears cross-appealed the one million dollar judgment against it. Since Sears' cross-appeal raises basic issues of liability, we will deal with it first. We will subsequently consider plaintiff's appeal on the issues of the appropriate remedy.

II

Sears' primary argument in its cross-appeal is that the district court erred in not determining conclusively the validity of plaintiff's patent as a precondition to trying plaintiff's claims for fraud, breach of a confidential relationship and misrepresentation. Relying on Lear, Inc. v. Adkins, 395 U.S. 653 (1969), Sears contends that if the district court had concluded that the patent was invalid, then plaintiff could not have been injured by any fraud Sears may have committed since it paid $10,000 for a "worthless" invention.

Sears' analysis, however, misconceives the Supreme Court's holding in *Lear.* There the Court held that a patent licensee was not estopped to contest the validity of the licensor's patent, and, in fact, was not required to pay the contractually-provided royalties for the license on the invalid patent during the pendency of the litigation. Contrary to Sears' implication, the *Lear* Court did not hold that the potentially invalid patent was worthless and thus the royalties offered in exchange for the right to use that patent would be unjustified. Instead, the Court explicitly recognized that there was significant economic value in the rights to an unchallenged patent. 395 U.S. at 669. In this regard the Court stated that "the existence of an unchallenged patent may deter others from attempting to compete with the licensee," thereby creating a monopoly in fact if not in law. Id.

Other courts have also acknowledged that significant economic value attaches to the rights to an uncontested patent. The Supreme Court recognized this recently in an opinion by Chief Justice Burger: "[E]ven though a discovery may not be patentable that does not 'destroy the value of the discovery * * *.'" Kewanee Oil Co. v. Bicron Corp., 416 U.S. 470, 482 (1974). Similarly, this court has held that "[w]hile there are paradoxical aspects of allowing recovery to arise from illegal interference with the sale of something which ultimately was proven to have no sales value, it cannot be said that there was no such value during the period of the presumptive validity of the patent." Moraine Products v. ICI America, Inc., 538 F.2d 134, 149 (7th Cir. 1976).

The facts of this case, by themselves, make abundantly clear both that Sears believed that the uncontested patent had significant economic value as a deterrent to competitors and that the patent, in fact, did serve to deter competitors. Sears had the patent number stamped on all of its wrenches with plaintiff's quick-release feature, which presumably was done for the purpose of scaring off competitors. Also, Sears' competitors did not enter this lucrative market for several years after it became clear that this product had genuine sales appeal, which can only be explained by the existence of the patent.

It is at least somewhat disingenuous for Sears to argue before this court that plaintiff's patent was valueless when it made every effort in its marketing to exploit the economic value of the uncontested patent, received the benefits of a factual monopoly for several years because of that uncontested patent and to this day has refused to return the patent rights to plaintiff in return for the $10,000 originally paid to acquire these "valueless" rights. We, therefore, have little difficulty finding that Sears' deception caused plaintiff to be injured in fact.

The issue remains whether the public interest, recognized in *Lear*, in having patent validity challenged is of such significance that we should extend *Lear* to cover this case. The *Lear* Court held that a licensee should be permitted to contest the validity of a licensor's patent because "[l]icensees may often be the only individuals with enough economic incentive to challenge the patentability of an inventor's discovery." 395 U.S. at 670. Thus, the Court feared that if licensees "are muzzled, the public may continually be required to pay tribute to would-be monopolists without need or justification." Id.

We believe that the reasoning in *Lear* does not extend to this case for two reasons. First, we deal here with a complete assignment of plaintiff's patent rights to Sears. * * * Thus, the primary evil that the Court in *Lear* sought to end—that the public might have to pay tribute to a "would-be monopolist"—is completely irrelevant to this case. Plaintiff has no legal basis for exacting any "tribute" until the patent rights are returned to him. At that point in time, the patent's validity can be tested either in an infringement suit or after plaintiff enters into a licensing agreement. The public's interest would not be injured by our decision to bar Sears from contesting this patent at this time.

Second, and perhaps even more fundamentally, the Court's analysis in *Lear* initiated with an assessment of "the spirit of contract law, which seeks to balance the claims of promisor and promisee in accord with the requirements of *good faith.*" 395 U.S. at 670 (emphasis added). Only after the Court satisfied itself that the equities were balanced on each side did it proceed to a consideration of the needs of patent law and the public interest. Sears' actions in this matter have violated completely the basic assumption in *Lear* that there was good faith in the dealings between the parties. There is no balance of equities between Sears and plaintiff in their contractual relations. For this court to employ the public interest in patent law to sanction Sears' conduct is unjustifiable. Certainly nothing in patent law requires this court to permit fraud to go unremedied. Cf. Kewanee Oil Co. v. Bicron Corp., 416 U.S. 470, 487 (1974) (nothing in patent law discourages states from preventing industrial espionage). We, therefore, hold that the district court properly concluded that *Lear, Inc. v. Adkins,* is no bar to plaintiff's recovery.

* * *

IV

Sears' final argument in its cross-appeal is that plaintiff failed to prove the existence of a confidential relationship between himself and Sears. In assessing that argument, we recognize at the outset that there are no hard and fast rules for determining whether a confidential relationship exists. See G. Bogert, The Law of Trusts and Trustees § 482 (2d ed. 1960). The trier of fact must examine all of the circumstances surrounding the relationship between the parties and determine whether "one person reposes trust and confidence in another who thereby gains a resulting influence and superiority over the first." Kester v. Crilly, 405 Ill. 425, 91 N.E.2d 419, 423 (1950).

Various factors have been recognized judicially as being of particular relevance to that inquiry. Among them are disparity of age, education and business experience between the parties. Melish v. Vogel, 35 Ill.App.3d 125, 343 N.E.2d 17, 26 (1975). Additional factors are the existence of an employment relationship and the exchange of confidential information from one party to the other. See Yamins v. Zeitz, 322 Mass. 268, 76 N.E.2d 769, 772 (1948). All five of those factors are present in this case. In addition, one of Sears' witnesses admitted that the company expected plaintiff to "believe" and to "rely" on various representations that Sears made to him (Tr. at 1981). Obviously, this question is best left to the trier of fact, and this court under any circumstances would hesitate to disturb the jury's findings. That hesitation is especially strong here where so many factors suggest that a confidential relationship in fact existed.

Sears argues, however, that there are two factors involved here that eliminate any possible confidential relationship. They are that plaintiff never proved that Sears had knowledge of the confidential relationship upon which plaintiff was relying and that plaintiff retained counsel to guide him, and therefore, did not rely on Sears. We find neither factor sufficient to justify overturning the jury's verdict on this issue.

* * *

V

Plaintiff, in his appeal, seeks review of the district court's decision that he elected his legal remedies by taking the case to the jury, and therefore, is barred from pursuing his equitable remedies of rescission and restitution. Plaintiff argues that the district court, as a court of equity, should have accepted the jury's liability determination, but should have disregarded its damages verdict and instead should have granted rescission and restitution.

* * *

The general rule as to when an election is necessary is that " 'a certain state of facts relied on as the basis of a certain remedy is inconsistent with, and repugnant to, another certain state of facts relied on as the basis of another remedy.' " Prudential Oil Corp. v. Phillips Petroleum Co., 418 F.Supp. 254, 257 (S.D.N.Y. 1975). Here, the jury was instructed that plaintiff could receive profits for Counts I and II, fraud and breach of a confidential relationship. Apparently dissatisfied with the size of the jury verdict, plaintiff sought in a post-trial motion to have the court reconsider the evidence and award relief based on essentially the same standard the jury used. To have granted plaintiff's request would have been completely unfair to Sears. It might have been better for the court to require the plaintiff to elect his remedy expressly prior to instructing the jury, but plaintiff did not object to the court's procedure, and therefore, must have been satisfied to let the jury determine the appropriate award. Having let the case go to the jury, without getting the issue clarified, plaintiff should not be heard to complain about the outcome of that procedure.

With regard to an election between the profits awarded by the jury and return of the patent based on rescission, however, we see no basis for invoking the election of remedies doctrine. Based on the jury instruction, plaintiff will receive one million dollars as the measure of *past* profits earned by Sears up to the time of trial. That award, however, is not inconsistent with return of the patent so that plaintiff can receive the *future* benefits of the patent that Sears fraudulently acquired. There will be neither a double recovery nor a factual inconsistency between these remedies. See Prudential Oil Corp., supra at 257; G. Bogert, The Law of Trusts and Trustees § 946 (2d ed. 1962). Therefore, we conclude that going to the jury under a past profits instruction did not bar plaintiff from seeking rescission and thereby possibly recovering his patent. Whether rescission is appropriate, however, is an issue that should be decided in the first instance by the district court.

For the reasons stated above, we affirm the district court's judgment against Sears on all three counts in plaintiff's complaint and the court's decision not to alter plaintiff's monetary award, but reverse the court's determination that it lacked the power to award rescission and remand to the district court for a determination of whether rescission is appropriate under the facts of this case.

Affirmed in part; reversed in part; and remanded.

NOTES

1. Is the patent on the Roberts' socket wrench valid? If it is not valid, just what did Sears obtain from Roberts? As part of the relief in the litigation, Sears reassigned the patent to Roberts. Roberts then sued Sears for infringement for the period after the reassignment. The District Court held the patent valid, but the Seventh Circuit reversed. A panel held the patent invalid, 697 F.2d 796 (7th Cir. 1983), but the court granted rehearing *en banc* and reversed, 723 F.2d 1324 (7th Cir. 1983). The en banc court held that the instructions to the jury, which permitted it to decide the ultimate question of patent validity, were improper, and remanded the case for retrial.

2. Robert L. Gullette, State Legislation Governing Ownership Rights In Inventions Under Employee Invention Agreements, 62 J. Pat. [& Trademark] Off. Soc'y 721 (1980), reports on statutes passed in a few states that limit the ability of employers by contract to require employees to assign to them rights in inventions made on their own time and without the use of the employer's facilities.

3. An independent inventor faces many problems before he can expect to benefit from his invention. The inventor will not infrequently lack the resources to develop and market it, may be wildly overoptimistic about its prospects, and may lack the cash to pay for expert advice. In recent years some firms have appeared that promoted themselves as invention developers but who in fact profited only from fees charged to hopeful inventors. See Paul Shemin, Idea Promotor Control: The Time Has Come, 60 J. Pat. [& Trademark] Off. Soc'y 261 (1978); Robert J. Thomas, Invention Development Services and Inventors: Recent Inroads on Caveat Inventor, 60 J. Pat. [& Trademark] Off. Soc'y 355 (1978). The F.T.C. has proceeded against some of these firms and some states have passed statutes regulating their disclosures to prospective clients and providing additional remedies in the event of fraud or deception.

INDEX

References are to pages.

1087